One-Stop Internet Resources

Log on to
tarvol1.glencoe.com

ONLINE STUDY TOOLS

- Chapter Overviews
- Interactive Tutor
- Self-Check Quizzes
- E-Flashcards

ONLINE RESEARCH

- Student Web Activities
- Web Resources
- Current Events
- State Resources
- Beyond the Textbook Features

ONLINE STUDENT EDITION

- Complete Interactive Student Edition
- Textbook Updates

FOR TEACHERS

- Teacher Forum
- Web Activity Lesson Plans
- Literature Connections

Honoring America

For Americans, the flag has always had a special meaning. It is a symbol of our nation's freedom and democracy.

Flag Etiquette

Over the years, Americans have developed rules and customs concerning the use and display of the flag. One of the most important things every American should remember is to treat the flag with respect.

- The flag should be raised and lowered by hand and displayed only from sunrise to sunset. On special occasions, the flag may be displayed at night, but it should be illuminated.

- The flag may be displayed on all days, weather permitting, particularly on national and state holidays and on historic and special occasions.

- No flag may be flown above the American flag or to the right of it at the same height.

- The flag should never touch the ground or floor beneath it.

- The flag may be flown at half-staff by order of the president, usually to mourn the death of a public official.

- The flag may be flown upside down only to signal distress.

- The flag should never be carried flat or horizontally, but always carried aloft and free.

- When the flag becomes old and tattered, it should be destroyed by burning. According to an approved custom, the Union (stars on blue field) is first cut from the flag; then the two pieces, which no longer form a flag, are burned.

★ ★ ★ ★ ★ ★ ★ ★

The American's Creed

I believe in the United States of America as a Government of the people, by the people, for the people, whose just powers are derived from the consent of the governed; a democracy in a republic; a sovereign Nation of many sovereign States; a perfect union, one and inseparable; established upon those principles of freedom, equality, justice, and humanity for which American patriots sacrificed their lives and fortunes.

I therefore believe it is my duty to my Country to love it; to support its Constitution; to obey its laws; to respect its flag, and to defend it against all enemies.

The Pledge of Allegiance

I pledge allegiance to the Flag of the United States of America and to the Republic for which it stands, one Nation under God, indivisible, with liberty and justice for all.

The American Republic
To 1877

Joyce Appleby, Ph.D.

Alan Brinkley, Ph.D.

Albert S. Broussard, Ph.D.

James M. McPherson, Ph.D.

Donald A. Ritchie, Ph.D.

NATIONAL GEOGRAPHIC

McGraw Hill Glencoe

New York, New York   Columbus, Ohio   Chicago, Illinois   Peoria, Illinois   Woodland Hills, California

Authors

Joyce Appleby, Ph.D. is Professor of History at UCLA. Dr. Appleby's published works include *Inheriting the Revolution: The First Generation of Americans; Capitalism and a New Social Order: The Jeffersonian Vision of the 1790s;* and *Ideology and Economic Thought in Seventeenth-Century England,* which won the Berkshire Prize. She served as president of both the Organization of American Historians and the American Historical Association, and chaired the Council of the Institute of Early American History and Culture at Williamsburg. Dr. Appleby has been elected to the American Philosophical Society and the American Academy of Arts and Sciences, and is a Corresponding Fellow of the British Academy.

Alan Brinkley, Ph.D. is Allan Nevins Professor of American History at Columbia University. His published works include *Voices of Protest: Huey Long, Father Coughlin, and the Great Depression,* which won the 1983 National Book Award; *The End of Reform: New Deal Liberalism in Recession and War; The Unfinished Nation: A Concise History of the American People;* and *Liberalism and its Discontents.* He received the Levenson Memorial Teaching Prize at Harvard University.

Albert S. Broussard, Ph.D. is Professor of History and Graduate Coordinator at Texas A&M University. Before joining the Texas A&M faculty, Dr. Broussard was Assistant Professor of History and Director of the African American Studies Program at Southern Methodist University. Among his publications are the books *Black San Francisco: The Struggle for Racial Equality in the West, 1900–1954* and *African American Odyssey: The Stewarts, 1853–1963.* Dr. Broussard has also served as president of the Oral History Association.

James M. McPherson, Ph.D. is George Henry Davis Professor of American History at Princeton University. Dr. McPherson is the author of 11 books about the Civil War era. These include *Battle Cry of Freedom: The Civil War Era,* for which he won the Pulitzer Prize in 1989, and *For Cause and Comrades: Why Men Fought in the Civil War,* for which he won the 1998 Lincoln Prize. He is a member of many professional historical associations, including the the Civil War Preservation Trust.

Donald A. Ritchie, Ph.D. is Associate Historian of the United States Senate Historical Office. Dr. Ritchie received his doctorate in American history from the University of Maryland after service in the U.S. Marine Corps. He has taught American history at various levels, from high school to university. He edits the Historical Series of the Senate Foreign Relations Committee and is the author of several books, including *Doing Oral History; The Oxford Guide to the United States Government;* and *Press Gallery: Congress and the Washington Correspondents,* which received the Organization of American Historians Richard W. Leopold Prize. Dr. Ritchie has served as president of the Oral History Association and as a council member of the American Historical Association.

The National Geographic Society, founded in 1888 for the increase and diffusion of geographic knowledge, is the world's largest nonprofit scientific and educational organization. Since its earliest days, the Society has used sophisticated communication technologies, from color photography to holography, to convey knowledge to a worldwide membership. The School Publishing Division supports the Society's mission by developing innovative educational programs—ranging from traditional print materials to multimedia programs including CD-ROMs, videodiscs, and software. "National Geographic Geography & History," featured in each unit of this textbook, was designed and developed by the National Geographic Society's School Publishing Division.

About the Cover The background images on the cover show immigrants bound for the United States. The smaller images, from left to right, are: Native American of the Southwest, Abigail Adams, statue of Thomas Jefferson, pioneers traveling west, and Civil War soldier.

The McGraw·Hill Companies

Send all inquiries to:
Glencoe/McGraw-Hill, 8787 Orion Place, Columbus, Ohio 43240–4027

ISBN 0-07-860983-6 (Student Edition) ISBN 0-07-860984-4 (Teacher Wraparound Edition)
Printed in the United States of America.
027/043 08 07 06 05

Academic Consultants

Richard G. Boehm, Ph.D.
Professor of Geography
Southwest Texas State University
San Marcos, Texas

Margo J. Byerly, Ph.D.
Assistant Professor of Social
    Studies Methods
Ball State University
Muncie, Indiana

Maureen D. Danner
Project CRISS
National Training Consultant
Kalispell, MT

Frank de Varona
Visiting Associate Professor
Department of Curriculum and
    Instruction
Florida International University
Miami, Florida

FOLDABLES **Dinah Zike**
Educational Consultant
Dinah–Might Activities, Inc.
San Antonio, Texas

William E. Nelson, Jr., Ph.D.
Research Professor of Black Studies and
    Professor of Political Science
The Ohio State University
Columbus, Ohio

Bernard Reich, Ph.D.
Professor of Political Science and
    International Affairs
George Washington University
Washington, D.C.

Carol Santa, Ph.D.
CRISS Project Developer
Kalispell, MT

Elmer Whitcraft
Project CRISS Master Trainer
Kalispell, MT

Teacher Reviewers

Barbara P. Barge
Teacher
Woodlake Hills Middle School
San Antonio, Texas

John R. Doyle
Director, Division of Social Sciences
Dade County Public Schools
Miami, Florida

David J. Engstrom
American History Teacher
Discovery Junior High School
Fargo, North Dakota

Bette Gilmore
Campus Instructional Specialist
Killeen Independent School District
Killeen, Texas

Harry J. Hancock
Social Studies Teacher
Theodore Roosevelt Middle School
Kenner, Louisiana

Mary Lynn Johnson
Program Director for Social Studies
Spring Independent School District
Houston, Texas

Tony Murillo
Teacher
Socorro Middle School
El Paso, Texas

Ronald A. Murphy
Classroom Teacher
Grand Prairie High School
Grand Prairie, Texas

Elysa E. Toler Robinson, Ed.D.
Program Supervisor
Detroit Public Schools
Detroit, Michigan

Kay R. Selah
Social Studies Teacher
Landmark Middle School
Jacksonville, Florida

Deborah N. Smith
Social Studies Teacher
New Albany Middle School
New Albany, Ohio

Larry John Smith
United States History Teacher
Mt. Savage School
Mt. Savage, Maryland

Melissa Taylor
Teacher
Twin Creeks Middle School
Spring, Texas

Renée Marie Trufant
Social Studies and Communications
    Skills Teacher
Brevard Middle School
Brevard, North Carolina

Sonya Lou Weaver
Social Studies Teacher
Greencastle-Antrim Middle School
Greencastle, Pennsylvania

Glenda Gail Williams
Classroom Teacher
Webb Middle School
Garland, Texas

Carol Davenport Wood
Social Studies Teacher
Lusher Extension
New Orleans, Louisiana

Contents

UNIT 1

Different Worlds Meet   12
Beginnings to 1625

UNIT 2

Colonial Settlement   66
1587–1770

UNIT 3

Creating a Nation   128
1763–1791

Contents

Two ViewPoints

More About...

TECHNOLOGY & History

Linking Past & Present

What If...

You Decide

TIME NOTEBOOK

Why It Matters

Causes and Effects

Features

Primary Source Quotes

A variety of quotations and excerpts throughout the text express the thoughts, feelings, and life experiences of people, past and present.

Abigail Adams

Primary Source Quotes

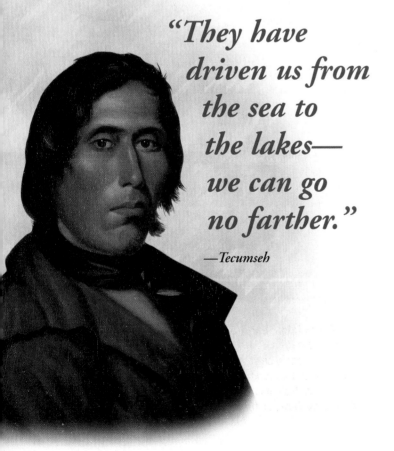

"They have driven us from the sea to the lakes— we can go no farther."

—*Tecumseh*

Primary Source Quotes

Frederick Douglass

Charts & Graphs

NATIONAL GEOGRAPHIC Maps

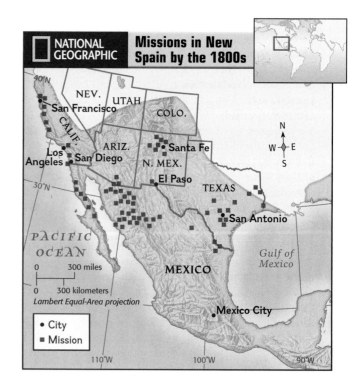

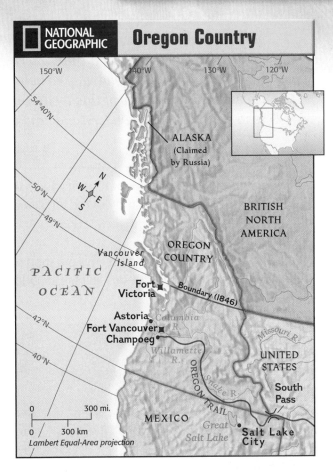

Previewing Your Textbook

Your textbook has been organized to help you learn about the significant events and people that make up American history. Before you start reading, though, here is a road map to help you understand what you will encounter in the pages of this textbook. Follow this road map before you read so that you can understand how this textbook works.

Units

Your textbook is divided into 7 units. Each unit begins with two pages of information to help you begin your study of the topics.

WHY IT MATTERS

Each unit begins with *Why It Matters.* This is a short summary about what you will study in the unit and the important topics in the unit.

QUOTATION

A short quotation gives a glimpse of the idea of a key figure from the era.

UNIT

1

Different Worlds Meet

Beginnings to 1625

Why It Matters

As you study Unit 1, you will learn that the first immigrants came to the Americas long before written history. From their descendants evolved a rich variety of cultures. The following resources offer more information about this period.

Primary Sources Library

See pages 592–593 for primary source readings to accompany Unit 1.

Use the *American History Primary Source Document Library* **CD-ROM** to find additional primary sources about Native American life.

Astrolabe, early astronomical instrument

Monument Valley

"*I found very many islands peopled....*"

— Christopher Columbus, 1493

PRIMARY SOURCE LIBRARY

This tells you where to find the *Primary Sources Library* readings that accompany the unit.

VISUALS

A photograph or painting shows you what life was like during the time period.

Chapters

Each unit in *The American Republic to 1877* is made up of chapters. Each chapter starts by providing you with background information to help you get the most out of the chapter.

CHAPTER TITLE
The chapter title tells you the main topic you will be reading about.

WHY IT MATTERS
Why It Matters tells you why events you will study are important.

THE IMPACT TODAY
The Impact Today explains how these events changed the way we live today.

CHAPTER 1

The **First Americans**

Prehistory to 1492

Why It Matters
Thousands of years ago small groups of hunters crossed a bridge of land that connected Siberia and Alaska. Eventually, they spread throughout North and South America.

The Impact Today
These first people, called Native Americans, influenced later cultures. Native Americans are part of the modern world, yet many of them also preserve the ways of life, customs, and traditions developed by their ancestors centuries ago.

The American Republic to 1877 Video The chapter 1 video, "Before Columbus," examines the diverse cultures of North America before Europeans arrived, focusing on the Anasazi.

City in the Sky Inca workers built the city of Machu Picchu high in the Andes mountain ranges.

FOLDABLES
Study Organizer

Categorizing Study Foldable Group information into categories to make sense of what you are learning. Make this foldable to learn about the first Americans.

Step 1 Fold one sheet of paper in half from top to bottom.

Step 2 Fold in half again, from side to side.

Step 3 Unfold the paper once. Cut up the fold of the top flap only.

This cut will make two tabs.

Step 4 Turn the paper vertically and sketch the continents of North and Central and South America on the front tabs.

Reading and Writing As you read the chapter, write under the flaps of your foldable what you learn about the Native American people living in these regions.

c. 28,000 B.C.
• Asian hunters enter North America

c. 1500 B.C.
• Rise of Olmec in Mexico

c. A.D. 700
• Maya empire reaches peak

c. A.D. 1130
• Drought strikes Anasazi communities

c. A.D. 1300
• Hohokam civilization begins to decline

A.D. 1325
• Aztec establish Tenochtitlán

c. A.D. 1400
• Inca empire begins to expand

The Americas

Prehistory   900   1100   1300   1500

World

c. 10,000 B.C.
• Last Ice Age ends

c. A.D. 33
• Jesus Christ is crucified

A.D. 610
• Muhammad preaches Islam in Makkah

A.D. 1095
• The Crusades begin

A.D. 1215
• England's King John signs Magna Carta

A.D. 1295
• Italian traveler Marco Polo returns from China

A.D. 1312
• Mansa Musa begins rule of West African kingdom of Mali

A.D. 1368
• Ming dynasty begins in China

HISTORY Online
Chapter Overview
Visit tarvol1.glencoe.com and click on **Chapter 1— Chapter Overviews** to preview chapter information.

14   CHAPTER 1   The First Americans

CHAPTER 1   The First Americans   15

TIME LINE
The time line shows you when and where events happened during the period of time covered in the chapter.

VISUALS
A photograph or painting shows how people of the time lived.

WEB SITE
History Online directs you to the Internet where you can find more information, activities, and quizzes.

Previewing Your Textbook

Sections

A section is a division, or part, of the chapter. The first page of the section, the section opener, helps you set a purpose for reading.

READING STRATEGY

Completing the *Reading Strategy* activity will help you organize the information as you read the section.

READ TO LEARN

Keep the *Read to Learn* statements in mind as you read the section.

SECTION THEMES

Your textbook organizes the events of your nation's past and present around themes. You can read about the themes on pages xx–xxi.

MAIN IDEA

The *Main Idea* of this section is introduced here. Below it, are important terms you will encounter as you read the section.

TIME LINE

The time line identifies important events you will study in the section.

AN AMERICAN STORY

Think of *An American Story* as a moment in time. It introduces you to an important event that you will read about.

SECTION 1 **Early Peoples**

Guide to Reading

Main Idea
The first Americans spread throughout North, Central, and South America.

Key Terms
archaeology, artifact, Ice Age, nomad, migration, maize, carbon dating, culture

Reading Strategy
Determining Cause and Effect As you read Section 1, re-create the diagram below and explain why the first Americans came to the continent and the consequences of their arrival.

Migration to the Americas	
Causes	Effects

Read to Learn
- how the first people arrived in the Americas.
- which discovery changed the lives of the early Native Americans.

Section Theme
Geography and History The Ice Age made it possible for hunters to migrate to the Americas.

Preview of Events

♦30,000 B.C.	♦10,000 B.C.	♦5000 B.C.	♦1000 B.C.
c. 28,000 B.C. Asian hunters enter North America	**c. 10,000 B.C.** Last Ice Age ends	**c. 7000 B.C.** Farming develops in Mexico	**c. 3000 B.C.** Early villages established in Mexico

---

AN American Story

Arrowhead, hand-chipped stone

No one knows for sure how the first people arrived in America. They may have crossed a land bridge that many scientists think connected Asia and North America thousands of years ago. They may have come by boat from Asia or Europe. Why they came is also a mystery. Possibly they followed mammoths or other game animals or were hunting seals and whales along the coast. Over time these people settled in America, becoming the first "native Americans."

The Journey From Asia

These first Americans arrived thousands of years ago. As food supplies improved, the population of the Americas increased. By A.D. 1500, millions of Native Americans, belonging to more than 2,000 different groups, lived on the two continents of North America and South America.

When Europeans arrived in the Americas in the late 1400s, they found Native Americans living there. The Europeans wondered where these peoples had come from and how they happened to settle in the Americas. Some believed the Native Americans had come from Atlantis, an island that was supposed to have sunk beneath the waves of the Atlantic Ocean.

16   CHAPTER 1   The First Americans

Previewing Your Textbook

Reading Roadmap

You will get more out of your textbook if you recognize the different elements that help you to understand what you read.

MAPS

Easy-to-read maps provide a link between geography and history. Questions test your understanding of the map's information.

READING CHECKS

This *Reading Check* helps you check yourself. Did you understand the main ideas?

OUTLINE

Think of the headings as forming an outline. The blue titles are the main heading. The red titles that follow are the subsections.

VOCABULARY

The terms in blue are the key terms. The definition is also included here.

SECTION ASSESSMENT

The *Section Assessment* is the last item in every section. Completing the assessment can help evaluate how well you understand.

PHOTOGRAPHS

Photographs show you important people, places, and events of the time.

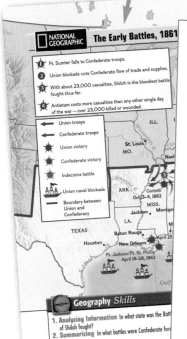

NATIONAL GEOGRAPHIC — **The Early Battles, 1861**

- ★ Ft. Sumter falls to Confederate troops.
- ② Union blockade cuts Confederate flow of trade and supplies.
- With about 23,000 casualties, Shiloh is the bloodiest battle fought thus far.
- Antietam costs more casualties than any other single day of the war — over 23,000 killed or wounded.

Legend:
- → Union troops
- → Confederate troops
- ★ Union victory
- ★ Confederate victory
- ★ Indecisive battle
- Union naval blockade
- Boundary between Union and Confederacy

ILL. St. Louis MO. Nash. Arkansas ARK. Corinth Oct 3–4, 1862 MISS. Jackson Montgom. LA. TEXAS Baton Rouge April 25 Houston New Orleans Ft. Jackson/Ft. St. Philip April 18–28, 1862 Gulf

Geography Skills

1. **Analyzing Information** In what state was the Batt[le] of Shiloh fought?
2. **Summarizing** In what battles were Confederate forc[es] victorious?

McClellan thoroughly reorganized and [trained] the Army of the Potomac. However, whe[n faced] with the prospect of battle, McClellan [grew cau]tious and worried that his troops w[ere not] ready. He hesitated to fight because o[f reports] that overestimated the size of the Rebe[l army.] Finally, in March 1862, the Army of the [Potomac] was ready for action. Its goal was to [capture] Richmond, the Confederate capital.

470 CHAPTER 16 The Civil War

the lavish mansions shown in fictional accounts of the Old South. Most white Southerners fit into one of four categories: yeomen, tenant farmers, the rural poor, or plantation owners.

Small Farmers and the Rural Poor

The farmers who did not have sl[aves—] yeomen—made up the largest group of whites in the South. Most yeomen owned land. Although they lived throughout the region, they were most numerous in the Upper South and in the hilly rural areas of the Deep South, where the land was unsuited to large plantations.

A yeoman's farm usually ranged from 50 to 200 acres. Yeomen grew crops both for their own use and to sell, and they often traded their produce to local merchants and workers for goods and services.

Most Southern whites did not live in elegant mansions or on large plantations. They lived in far simpler homes, though the structure of their homes changed over time. In the early 1800s many lived in cottages built of wood and plaster with thatched roofs. Later many lived in one-story frame houses or log cabins.

Not all Southern whites owned land. Some rented land, or worked as tenant farmers, on landlords' estates. Others—the rural poor—lived in crude cabins in wooded areas where they could clear a few trees, plant some corn, and keep a hog or a cow. They also fished and hunted for food.

The poor people of the rural South were stubbornly independent. They refused to take any job that resembled the work of enslaved people. Although looked down on by other whites, the rural poor were proud of being self-sufficient.

Reading Check **Identifying** What group made up the largest number of whites in the South?

Plantations

A large plantation might cover several thousand acres. Well-to-do plantation owners usually lived in comfortable but not luxurious farmhouses. They measured their wealth partly by the number of enslaved people they controlled and partly by such possessions as homes, furnishings, and clothing. A small group of plantation owners—about 4 percent—held 20 or more slaves in 1860. The large majority of slaveholders held fewer than 10 enslaved workers.

A few free African Americans possessed slaves. The Metoyer family of Louisiana owned thousands of acres of land and more than 400 slaves. Most often, these slaveholders were free African Americans who purchased their own family members in order to free them.

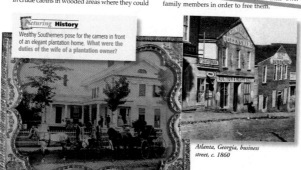

Picturing History
Wealthy Southerners pose for the camera in front of an elegant plantation home. What were the duties of the wife of a plantation owner?

Atlanta, Georgia, business street, c. 1860

SECTION 4 ASSESSMENT

Checking for Understanding

1. **Key Terms** Write a sentence in which you correctly use each of the following terms: mercantilism, Columbian Exchange, Northwest Passage, coureur de bois
2. **Reviewing Facts** What were English, French, and Dutch explorers searching for while charting the coast of North America?

Reviewing Themes

3. **Global Connections** How did French goals in the Americas differ from the goals of other European nations?

Critical Thinking

4. **Identifying Central Issues** How did the economic theory of mercantilism influence the exploration and settlement of North America by Europeans?
5. **Determining Cause and Effect** Re-create the diagram below and explain how the Columbian Exchange affected both sides of the Atlantic Ocean.

Columbian Exchange	
Effects on the Americas	Effects on Europe

Analyzing Visuals

6. **Geography Skills** Review the map, *French Explorers, 1535–1682,* on page 61. Which of the French explorers traveled farthest south? Along what river did Marquette and Joliet travel?

Interdisciplinary Activity

Persuasive Writing Write a letter to one of the explorers who searched for a Northwest Passage. In the letter, explain why it is important for your nation to find a Northwest Passage.

62 CHAPTER 2 Exploring the Americas

xvii

Previewing Your Textbook

Special Features

A variety of special features will help you as you study *The American Republic to 1877*.

PEOPLE IN HISTORY

People In History tells you the story of individuals that influenced American history.

SKILLBUILDERS

Skillbuilders teach valuable skills that will be useful throughout the book.

TWO VIEWPOINTS

Two Viewpoints compares the opposing viewpoints of two historic figures on a particular issue.

AMERICA'S LITERATURE

America's Literature analyzes excerpts from famous pieces of American fiction and describes its historical lessons.

People In History

Benjamin Franklin 1706–1790

Ben Franklin learned the printer's trade as a young man. By the time he was 23, he owned his own newspaper in Philadelphia. Soon afterward he began publishing *Poor Richard's Almanack*, a calendar filled with advice, philosophy, and wise say-

a man healthy, wealthy, and wise."

Franklin was deeply interested in science. He invented the lightning rod, bifocal eyeglasses, and the Franklin stove for heating. Energetic and open-minded, Franklin served in the Pennsylvania Assembly for many years. He founded a hos-

America's first lending library, and an academy of higher learning that later became the University of Pennsylvania.

Franklin's greatest services to his fellow Americans would come during the 1770s. As a statesman and patriot, Franklin would help guide the colonies toward

Social Studies SKILLBUILDER

Understanding the Parts of a Map

Why Learn This Skill?

Maps can direct you down the street or around the world. There are as many different kinds of maps as there are uses for them. Being able to read a map begins with learning about its parts.

NATIONAL GEOGRAPHIC

TWO VIEWPOINTS

Union or Secession?

President Abraham Lincoln and Jefferson Davis, president of the Confederacy, were inaugurated just several weeks apart. These excerpts from their Inaugural Addresses will help you understand differing points of view about secession from the United States in 1861.

Abraham Lincoln's Inaugural Address, March 4, 1861

Abraham Lincoln

One section of our country believes slavery is *right* and ought to be extended, while the other believes it is *wrong* and ought not to be extended. This is the only substantial dispute . . . .

Physically speaking, we can not separate. We can not remove our respective sections from each other nor build an impassable wall between them. A husband and wife may be divorced and go out of the presence and beyond the reach of each other; but the different parts of our country can not do this. . . .

In *your* hands, my dissatisfied fellow countrymen, and not in *mine*, is the momentous issue of civil war.

Jefferson Davis's Inaugural Address, February 18, 1861

As a necessity, not a choice, we have resorted to the remedy of separation, and henceforth our energies must be directed to the conduct of our own affairs, and the [continuation] of the Confederacy which we have formed. If a just perception of mutual interest shall permit us peaceably to pursue our separate political career, my most earnest desire will have been fulfilled. But if this be denied to us . . . [we will be forced] to appeal to arms. . . .

Jefferson Davis

Learning From History

1. According to Lincoln, what was the only substantial disagreement between the North and the South?
2. What did Lincoln compare the United States to?
3. Did Lincoln and Davis say anything in their inaugural addresses that was similar?

450   CHAPTER 15   Road to Civil War

Douglas for ported pop ern Democ slavery—no inridge of the *Dred S* from both had form Union Part Tennessee. tion on sla

Lincoln N

The Rep ham Li designed quarters, left undis that it sh territories however, would er

Lincoln

With coln wor toral v received ular vo any oth second

The tional even a Southe Northe the Sor states. Misso seven

In e had o for L howev to lea

✓ Reading Check **Examining** caused the split in the Democratic Party in 1860?

America's LITERATURE

Esther Forbes (1891–1967)

Esther Forbes wrote a number of books; among them is the prize-winning biography *Paul Revere and the World He Lived In*. As she researched Paul Revere's life, Forbes learned that many young apprentices played a role in the American Revolution. *Johnny Tremain*, a fictional work, tells the story of such an apprentice.

READ TO DISCOVER

In this passage from *Johnny Tremain*, 14-year-old Johnny and his friend Rab have disguised themselves as Mohawks. They join the crowd at Griffin's Wharf in Boston Harbor, where three English ships carrying tea are docked and are unable to leave or unload their cargo.

READER'S DICTIONARY

boatswain: officer on a ship
warped: roped
jargon: strange language
hold: place where cargo is stored on a ship
winch: machine for hauling

Johnny Tremain

There was a **boatswain's** whistle, and in silence one group boarded the *Dartmouth*. The *Eleanor* and the *Beaver* had to be **warped** in to the wharf. Johnny was close to Mr. Revere's heels. He heard him calling for the captain, promising him, in the **jargon** everyone talked that night, that not one thing should be damaged on the ship except only the tea, but the captain and all his crew had best stay in the cabin until the work was over.

Captain Hall shrugged and did as he was told, leaving his cabin boy to hand over the keys to the **hold**. The boy was grinning with pleasure. The "tea party" was not unexpected. . . .

The **winches** rattled and the heavy chests began to appear—one hundred and fifty of them. As some men worked in the hold, others broke open the chests and flung the tea into the harbor. But one thing made them unexpected difficulty. The tea inside the chests was wrapped in heavy canvas. The axes went through the wood easily enough—the canvas made endless trouble. Johnny had never worked so hard in his life.

Then Mr. Revere called the captain to come up and inspect. The tea was utterly gone, but Captain Hall agreed that beyond that there had not been the slightest damage.

It was close upon dawn when the work on all three ships was done. And yet the great, silent audience on the wharf, men, women, and children, had not gone home. As the three groups came off the ships, they formed in fours along the wharf, their axes on their shoulders. Then a hurrah went up and a fife began to play.

Paul Revere

Excerpt from *Johnny Tremain* by Esther Forbes. Copyright © 1943 by Esther Forbes Hoskins, © renewed 1971 by Esther Forbes M. Erskine, Jr., Executor of the Estate of Esther Forbes Hoskins. Reprinted by permission of Houghton Mifflin Co. All rights reserved.

ANALYZING LITERATURE

1. **Recall and Interpret** Why was the "tea party" expected?
2. **Evaluate and Connect** What does the conduct of the "tea party" participants suggest about the protest? Explain your answer.

Interdisciplinary Activity

Expository Writing Write a one-page paper about how you think you would react in Johnny's situation.

140

Jefferson Davis, a senator from ... their president.

They we

Scavenger Hunt

The American Republic to 1877 contains a wealth of information. The trick is to know where to look to access all the information in the book. If you run through this scavenger hunt exercise with your teachers or parents, you will see how the textbook is organized, and how to get the most out of your reading and study time. Let's get started!

1. How many chapters and how many units are in the book?

2. What time period does Unit 2 cover?

3. How many chapters are there in Unit 3? What is this unit about?

4. What is the title of Chapter 14, Section 3?

5. On what page of Chapter 4 can you find the *Foldables* Activity? What does the Activity help you do?

6. What is the skill you practice when you do the Chapter 8 Skillbuilder?

7. There are 3 Web sites in Chapter 5. The first previews the chapter and the second summarizes it. What does the third one do?

8. You want to quickly find all the maps in the book on the Civil War? Where do you look?

9. Most sections of a chapter open with an excerpt from a primary source—a document or other testimony dating from the period. Where else can you find extended primary sources in the textbook?

10. Where can you learn the definition of a physical map, a political map, and a special-purpose map?

How Do I Study History?

As you read *The American Republic to 1877*, you will be given help in sorting out all the information you encounter. This textbook organizes the events of your nation's past and present around 10 themes. A theme is a concept, or main idea that happens again and again throughout history. By recognizing these themes, you will better understand events of the past and how they affect you today.

Themes in *The American Republic to 1877*

Culture and Traditions
Being aware of cultural differences helps us understand ourselves and others. People from around the world for generations have sung of the "land of the Pilgrims' pride, land where our fathers died" even though their ancestors arrived on these shores long after these events occurred.

Continuity and Change
Recognizing our historic roots helps us understand why things are the way they are today. This theme includes political, social, religious, and economic changes that have influenced the way Americans think and act.

Geography and History
Understanding geography helps us understand how humans interact with their environment. The United States succeeded in part because of its rich natural resources and its vast open spaces. In many regions, the people changed the natural landscape to fulfill their wants and needs.

Individual Action

Responsible individuals have often stepped forward to help lead the nation. America's strong family values helped create such individuals. These values spring in part from earlier times when the home was the center of many activities, including work, education, and daily worship.

Groups and Institutions

Identifying how political and social groups and institutions work helps us work together. From the beginning, Americans formed groups and institutions to act in support of their economic, political, and religious beliefs.

Government and Democracy

Understanding the workings of government helps us become good citizens. Abraham Lincoln explained the meaning of democracy as "government of the people, by the people, for the people." Democracy, at its best, is "among" the people.

Science and Technology

Americans have always been quick to adopt innovations. The nation was settled and built by people who blended their old ways with new ways. Americans' lives are deeply influenced by technology, the use of science and machines. Perhaps no machine has so shaped modern life as the automobile. Understanding the roles of science and technology helps us see their impact on our society and the roles they will play in the future.

Economic Factors

The free enterprise economy of the United States is consistent with the nation's history of rights and freedoms. Freedom of choice in economic decisions supports other freedoms. Understanding the concept of free enterprise is basic to studying American history.

Global Connections

The world seems smaller than it did only 50 years ago. Modern transportation and communication have brought people around the globe closer together. As a result, countries today are more dependent on one another. As citizens of the United States and members of the global community, we have a responsibility to keep informed about developments in other nations and the world. Being aware of global interdependence helps us make decisions and deal with the difficult issues we will encounter.

Civic Rights and Responsibilities

For a democratic system to survive, its citizens must take an active role in government. The foundation of democracy is the right of every person to take part in government and to voice one's views on issues. An appreciation for the struggle to preserve these freedoms is vital to the understanding of democracy.

Using the Themes

You will find Section Themes at the beginning of every section of your text. You are asked questions that help you put it all together to better understand how ideas and themes are connected across time—and to see why history is important to you today.

Reading Skills Handbook

READING TO LEARN

This handbook focuses on skills and strategies that can help you understand the words you read. The strategies you use to understand whole texts depend on the kind of text you are reading. In other words, you don't read a textbook the way you read a novel. You read a textbook mainly for information; you read a novel mainly for fun. To get the most out of your reading, you need to choose the right strategy to fit the reason you're reading.

USE THIS HANDBOOK TO HELP YOU LEARN

- **how to identify new words and build your vocabulary**
- **how to adjust the way you read to fit your reason for reading**
- **how to use specific reading strategies to better understand what you read**
- **how to use critical thinking strategies to think more deeply about what you read**

You will also learn about

- **text structures**
- **reading for research**

Identifying Words and Building Vocabulary

What do you do when you come across a word you do not know as you read? Do you skip over the word and keep reading? If you are reading for fun or entertainment, you might. But if you are reading for information, an unfamiliar word may get in the way of your understanding. When that happens, try the following strategies to figure out how to say the word and what the word means.

Reading Unfamiliar Words

Sounding out the word One way to figure out how to say a new word is to sound it out, syllable by syllable. Look carefully at the word's beginning, middle, and ending. Inside the word, do you see a word you already know how to pronounce? What vowels are in the syllables? Use the following tips when sounding out new words.

- **Roots and base words** The main part of a word is called its root. When the root is a complete word, it may be called the base word. When you come across a new word, check whether you recognize its root or base word. It can help you pronounce the word and figure out the word's meaning.

ASK YOURSELF

- What letters make up the beginning sound or beginning syllable of the word?

  Example: In the word *coagulate, co* rhymes with *so.*

- What sounds do the letters in the middle part of the word make?

  Example: In the word *coagulate,* the syllable *ag* has the same sound as the *ag* in *bag,* and the syllable *u* is pronounced like the letter *u.*

- What letters make up the ending sound or syllable?

  Example: In the word *coagulate, late* is a familiar word you already know how to pronounce.

- Now try pronouncing the whole word:

  co ag u late.

- **Prefixes** A prefix is a word part that can be added to the beginning of a root or base word. For example, the prefix *pre-* means "before," so *prehistory* means "before history." Prefixes can change, or even reverse, the meaning of a word. For example, *un-* means "not," so *unconstitutional* means "not constitutional."

- **Suffixes** A suffix is a word part that can be added to the end of a root or base word to change the word's meaning. Adding a suffix to a word can also change that word from one part of speech to another. For example, the word *joy,* which is a noun, becomes an adjective when the suffix *-ful* (meaning "full of") is added. *Joyful* means "full of joy."

Determining a Word's Meaning

Using syntax Like all languages, the English language has rules and patterns for the way words are arranged in sentences. The way a sentence is organized is called the **syntax** of the sentence. If English is your first language, you have known this pattern since you started talking in sentences. If you're learning English now, you may find the syntax is different from the patterns you know in your first language.

In a simple sentence in English, someone or something (the *subject*) does something (the *predicate* or *verb*) to or with another person or thing (the *object*): The *soldiers attacked* the *enemy*.

Sometimes adjectives, adverbs, and phrases are added to add details to the sentence: *The courageous young* soldiers *fearlessly* attacked the *well-entrenched* enemy *shortly after dawn*.

CHECK IT OUT

Knowing about syntax can help you figure out the meaning of an unfamiliar word. Just look at how syntax can help you figure out the following nonsense sentence.

The blizzy kwarkles sminched the flerky fleans.

Your experience with English syntax tells you that the action word, or verb, in this sentence is *sminched*. Who did the *sminching?* The *kwarkles*. What kind of kwarkles were they? *Blizzy*. Whom did they *sminch?* The fleans. What kind of fleans were they? *Flerky*. Even though you don't know the meaning of the words in the nonsense sentence, you can make some sense of the entire sentence by studying its syntax.

Using context clues You can often figure out the meaning of an unfamiliar word by looking at its context, the words and sentences that surround it. To learn new words as you read, follow these steps for using context clues.

1. Look before and after the unfamiliar word for:
   • a definition or a synonym, another word that means the same as the unfamiliar word.
   • a general topic associated with the word.
   • a clue to what the word is similar to or different from.
   • an action or a description that has something to do with the word.
2. Connect what you already know with what the author has written.
3. Predict a possible meaning.
4. Use the meaning in the sentence.
5. Try again if your guess does not make sense.

Using reference materials Dictionaries and other reference sources can help you learn new words. Check out these reference sources:

• A **dictionary** gives the pronunciation and the meaning or meanings of words. Some dictionaries also give other forms of words, their parts of speech, and synonyms. You might also find the historical background of a word, such as its Greek, Latin, or Anglo-Saxon origins.

• A **glossary** is a word list that appears at the end—or Appendix—of a book or other written work and includes only words that are in that work. Like dictionaries, glossaries have the pronunciation and definitions of words.

• A **thesaurus** lists groups of words that have the same, or almost the same, meaning. Words with similar meanings are called *synonyms.* Seeing the synonyms of words can help you build your vocabulary.

Recognizing Word Meanings Across Subjects

Have you ever learned a new word in one class and then noticed it in your reading for other subjects? The word probably will not mean exactly the same thing in each class. But you can use what you know about the word's meaning to help you understand what it means in a different subject area.

CHECK IT OUT

Look at the following example from three subjects:

Social studies: One major **product** manufactured in the South is cotton cloth.

Math: After you multiply those two numbers, explain how you arrived at the **product.**

Science: One **product** of photosynthesis is oxygen.

Reading for a Reason

Why are you reading that paperback mystery? What do you hope to get from your geography textbook? And are you going to read either of these books in the same way that you read a restaurant menu? The point is, you read for different reasons. The reason you are reading something helps you decide on the reading strategies you use with a text. In other words, how you read will depend on **why** you're reading.

Knowing Your Reason for Reading

In school and in life, you will have many reasons for reading, and those reasons will lead you to a wide range of materials. For example,

- **to learn and understand new information,** you might read news magazines, textbooks, news on the Internet, books about your favorite pastime, encyclopedia articles, primary and secondary sources for a school report, instructions on how to use a calling card, or directions for a standardized test.

- **to find specific information,** you might look at the sports section for the score of last night's game, a notice on where to register for a field trip, weather reports, bank statements, or television listings.

- **to be entertained,** you might read your favorite magazine, e-mails or letters from friends, the Sunday comics, or even novels, short stories, plays, or poems!

Adjusting How Fast You Read

How quickly or how carefully you should read a text depends on your purpose for reading it. Because there are many reasons and ways to read, think about your purpose and choose a strategy that works best. Try out these strategies:

- **Scanning** means quickly running your eyes over the material, looking for *key words or phrases* that point to the information you're looking for. Scan when you need to find a particular piece or type of information. For example, you might scan a newspaper for movie show times.

- **Skimming** means quickly reading a piece of writing *to find its main idea* or to *get a general overview* of it. For example, you might skim the sports section of the daily newspaper to find out how your favorite teams are doing. Or you might skim a chapter in your textbook to prepare for a test.

- **Careful reading** involves *reading slowly and paying attention* with a purpose in mind. Read carefully when you're learning new concepts, following complicated directions, or preparing to explain information to someone else.

Understanding What You Read

Reading without understanding is like trying to drive a car on an empty gas tank. Fortunately, there are techniques you can use to help you concentrate on and understand what you read. Skilled readers adopt a number of strategies before, during, and after reading to make sure they understand what they read.

Previewing

If you were making a preview for a movie, you would want to let your audience know what the movie is like. When you preview a piece of writing, you are trying to get an idea about that piece of writing. If you know what to expect before reading, you will have an easier time understanding ideas and relationships. Follow these steps to preview your reading assignments.

DO IT!

1. Look at the title and any illustrations that are included.
2. Read the headings, subheadings, and anything in bold letters.
3. Skim over the passage to see how it is organized. Is it divided into many parts?

Is it a long poem or short story? Don't forget to look at the graphics—pictures, maps, or diagrams.

4. Set a purpose for your reading. Are you reading to learn something new? Are you reading to find specific information?

Using What You Know

Believe it or not, you already know quite a bit about what you are going to read. You bring knowledge and personal experience to a selection. Drawing on your own background is called *activating prior knowledge*, and it can help you create meaning in what you read. Ask yourself, *What do I already know about this topic?*

Predicting

You do not need any special knowledge to make *predictions* when you read. The predictions do not even have to be accurate. Take educated guesses before and during your reading about what might happen in the story or article you are reading.

Visualizing

Creating pictures in your mind as you read—called *visualizing*—is a powerful aid to understanding. As you read, set up a movie theater in your imagination. Picture the setting—city streets, the desert, or the surface of the moon. If you can visualize what you read, selections will be more vivid, and you will recall them better later on.

Identifying Sequence

When you discover the logical order of events or ideas, you are identifying *sequence.* Do you need to understand step-by-step directions? Are you reading a persuasive speech with the reasons listed in order of importance? Look for clues and signal words that will help you find the way information is organized.

Determining the Main Idea

When you look for the *main idea* of a selection, you look for the most important idea. The examples, reasons, and details that further explain the main idea are called *supporting details.* Some main ideas are clearly stated within a passage—often in the first sentence of a paragraph, or sometimes in the last sentence of a passage. Other times, an author does not directly state the main idea but provides details that help readers figure out what the main idea is.

ASK YOURSELF

- **What is each sentence about?**
- **Is there one sentence that tells about the whole passage or that is more important than any of the other sentences?**
- **What main idea do the supporting details point out?**

Questioning

Keep up a conversation with yourself as you read by *asking questions* about the text. Ask about the importance of the information you are reading. Ask how one event relates to another. Ask yourself if you understand what you just read. As you answer your questions, you are making sure that you understand what is going on.

Clarifying

Clear up, or *clarify,* confusing or difficult passages as you read. When you realize you do not understand something, try these techniques to help you clarify the ideas.
- *Reread* the confusing parts slowly and carefully.
- *Look up* unfamiliar words.
- Simply *"talk out"* the part to yourself.
Reread the passage. The second time is often easier and more informative.

Reviewing

You probably *review* in school what you learned the day before so the ideas are firm in your mind. Reviewing when you read does the same thing. Take time now and then to pause and review what you have read. Think about the main ideas and reorganize them for yourself so you can recall them later. Filling in study aids such as graphic organizers, notes, or outlines can help you review.

Monitoring Your Comprehension

As you read, check your understanding by using the following strategies.

- **Summarize** what you read by pausing from time to time and telling yourself the main ideas of what you have just read. Answer the questions *Who? What?*

Where? When? Why? and *How?* Summarizing tests your comprehension by encouraging you to clarify key points in your own words.

- **Paraphrase** Sometimes you read something that you "sort of" understand, but not quite. Use paraphrasing as a test to see whether you really got the point. *Paraphrasing* is retelling something in your own words. So shut the book and try putting what you have just read into your own words. If you cannot explain it clearly, you should probably have another look at the text.

Thinking About Your Reading

Sometimes it is important to think more deeply about what you have read so you can get the most out of what the author says. These critical thinking skills will help you go beyond what the words say and get at the important messages of your reading.

Interpreting

When you listen to your best friend talk, you do not just hear the words he or she says. You also watch your friend, listen to the tone of voice, and use what you already know about that person to put meaning to the words. In doing so, you are interpreting what your friend says. Readers do the same thing when they interpret as they read. *Interpreting* is asking yourself, *What is the writer really saying here?* and then using what you know about the world to help answer that question.

Inferring

You may not realize it, but you infer, or make inferences, every day. Here is an example: You run to the bus stop a little later than usual. There is no one there. "I have missed the bus," you say to yourself. You may be wrong, but that is the way our minds work. You look at the evidence (you are late; no one is there) and come to a conclusion (you have missed the bus).

When you read, you go though exactly the same process because writers don't always directly state what they want you to understand. By providing clues and interesting details, they suggest certain information. Whenever you combine those clues with your own background and knowledge, you are making an inference.

An *inference* involves using your thinking and experience to come up with an idea based on what an author implies or suggests. In reading, you *infer* when you use context clues and your own knowledge to figure out the author's meaning.

Drawing Conclusions

Skillful readers are always *drawing conclusions,* or figuring out much more than an author says directly. The process is like a detective solving a mystery. You combine information and evidence that the author provides to come up with a statement about the topic. Drawing conclusions helps you find connections between ideas and events and gives you a better understanding of what you are reading.

Analyzing

Analyzing, or looking at separate parts of something to understand the entire piece, is a way to think critically about written work.

- In analyzing persuasive *nonfiction,* you might look at the writer's reasons to see if they actually support the main point of the argument.

- In analyzing *informational text,* you might look at how the ideas are organized to see what is most important.

Distinguishing Fact From Opinion

Distinguishing between fact and opinion is one of the most important reading skills you can learn. A *fact* is a statement that can be proved with supporting information. An *opinion,* on the other hand, is what a writer believes, on the basis of his or her personal viewpoint. Writers can support their opinions with facts, but an opinion is something that cannot be proved.

FOR EXAMPLE

Look at the following examples of fact and opinion.

Fact: George III was the British king during the American Revolution.

Opinion: King George III was an evil despot.

You could prove that George III was king during that period. It's a fact. However, not everyone might see that King George III was a despot. That's someone's opinion.

As you examine information, always ask yourself, "Is this a fact or an opinion?" Don't think that opinions are always bad. Very often they are just what you want. You read editorials and essays for their authors' opinions. Reviews of books, movies, plays, and CDs can help you decide whether to spend your time and money on something. It's when opinions are based on faulty reasoning or prejudice or when they are stated as facts that they become troublesome.

Evaluating

When you form an opinion or make a judgment about something you are reading, you are *evaluating.* If you are reading informational texts or something on the Internet, it is important to evaluate how qualified the author is to be writing about the topic and how reliable the information is that is presented. Ask yourself whether the author seems biased, whether the information is one-sided, and whether the argument presented is logical.

Synthesizing

When you *synthesize,* you combine ideas (maybe even from different sources) to come up with something new. It may be a new understanding of an important idea or a new way of combining and presenting information. For example, you might read a manual on coaching soccer, combine that information with your own experiences playing soccer, and come up with a winning plan for coaching your sister's team this spring.

Understanding Text Structure

Good writers do not just put together sentences and paragraphs in any order. They structure each piece of their writing in a specific way for a specific purpose. That pattern of organization is called *text structure.* When you know the text structure of a selection, you will find it easier to locate and recall an author's ideas. Here are four ways that writers organize text.

Comparison and Contrast

Comparison-and-contrast structure shows the similarities and differences between people, things, and ideas. Maybe you have overheard someone at school say something like "He is better at throwing the football, but I can run faster than he can." This student is using comparison-and-contrast structure. When writers use comparison-and-contrast structure, often they want to show you *how things that seem alike are different, or how things that seem different are alike.*

- **Signal words and phrases:** *similarly, on the one hand, on the other hand, in contrast to, but, however*

Cause and Effect

Just about everything that happens in life is the cause or the effect of some other event or action. Sometimes what happens is pretty minor: You do not look when you are pouring milk *(cause);* you spill milk on the table *(effect).* Sometimes it is a little more serious: You do not look at your math book before the big test *(cause);* you mess up on the test *(effect).*

Writers use cause-and-effect structure to explore the reasons for something happening and to examine the results of previous events. This structure helps answer the question that everybody is always asking: *Why?* A historian might tell us why an empire rose and fell. Cause-and-effect structure is all about explaining things.

- **Signal words and phrases:** *so, because, as a result, therefore, for the following reasons*

Problem and Solution

How did scientists overcome the difficulty of getting a person to the moon? How will I brush my teeth when I have forgotten my toothpaste? These questions may be very different in importance, but they have one thing in common: Each identifies a problem and asks how to solve it. *Problems* and *solutions* are part of what makes life interesting. Problems and solutions also occur in fiction and nonfiction writing.

- **Signal words and phrases:** *how, help, problem, obstruction, difficulty, need, attempt, have to, must*

Sequence

Take a look at three common forms of sequencing, *the order in which thoughts are arranged.*

- **Chronological order** refers to the order in which events take place. First you wake up; next you have breakfast; then you go to school. Those events don't make much sense in any other order.

    Signal words: *first, next, then, later,* and *finally.*

- **Spatial order** tells you the order in which to look at objects. For example, take a look at this description of an ice cream sundae: *At the bottom of the dish are two scoops of vanilla. The scoops are covered with fudge and topped with whipped cream and a cherry.* Your eyes follow the sundae from the bottom to the top. Spatial order is important in descriptive writing because it helps you as a reader to see an image the way the author does.

Signal words: *above, below, behind,* and *next to.*

- **Order of importance** is going from most important to least important or the other way around. For example, a typical news article has a most-to-least-important structure.

  Signal words: *principal, central, important,* and *fundamental.*

CHECK IT OUT

- **Tables of contents** Look at the table of contents first to see whether a resource offers information you need.
- **Indexes** An index is an alphabetical listing of significant topics covered in a book. It is found in the back of a book.
- **Headings and subheadings** Headings often tell you what information is going to follow in the text you're reading. Subheadings allow you to narrow your search for information even further.
- **Graphic features** Photos, diagrams, maps, charts, graphs, and other graphic features can communicate large amounts of information at a glance.

Reading for Research

An important part of doing research is knowing how to get information from a wide variety of sources. The following skills will help you when you have a research assignment for a class or when you want information about a topic outside of school.

Reading Text Features

Researching a topic is not only about asking questions; it is about finding answers. Textbooks, references, magazines, and other sources provide a variety of text features to help you find those answers quickly and efficiently.

Organizing Information

When researching a topic, you have to make sense of that information, organize it, and put it all together in ways that will help you explain it to someone else. Here are some ways of doing just that.

- **Record** information from your research and keep track of your resources on note cards.

- **Interpret graphic aids** carefully. These could include charts, graphs, maps and photographs.

- **Summarize** information before you write it on a note card. That way you will have the main ideas in your own words.

- **Outline** ideas so you can see how subtopics and supporting information will fit under the main ideas.

- **Make a table or graph** to compare items or categories of information.

REFERENCE ATLAS

ATLAS KEY

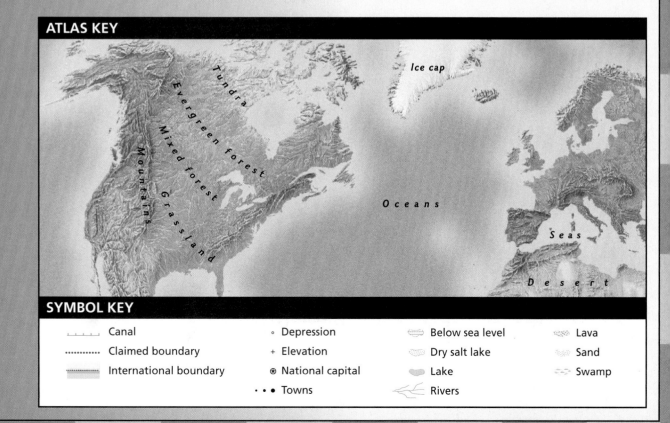

Tundra

Ice cap

Evergreen forest

Mixed forest

Mountains

Grassland

Oceans

Seas

Desert

SYMBOL KEY

⌐⌐⌐⌐ Canal	∘ Depression	⟷ Below sea level	Lava
.... Claimed boundary	+ Elevation	Dry salt lake	Sand
Internationalboundary	⊛ National capital	Lake	Swamp
	• • ● Towns	Rivers	

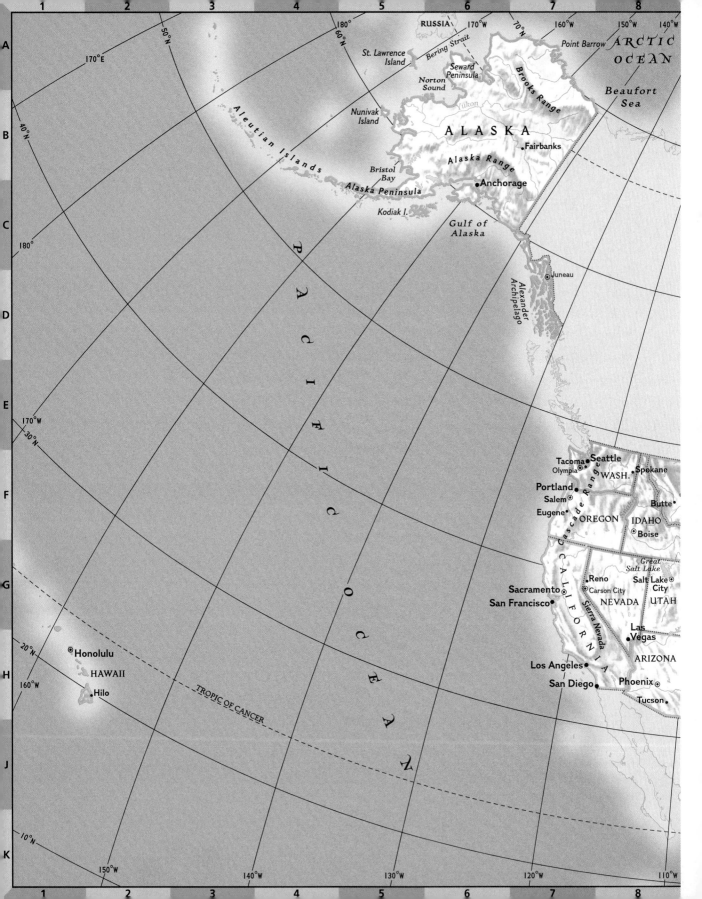

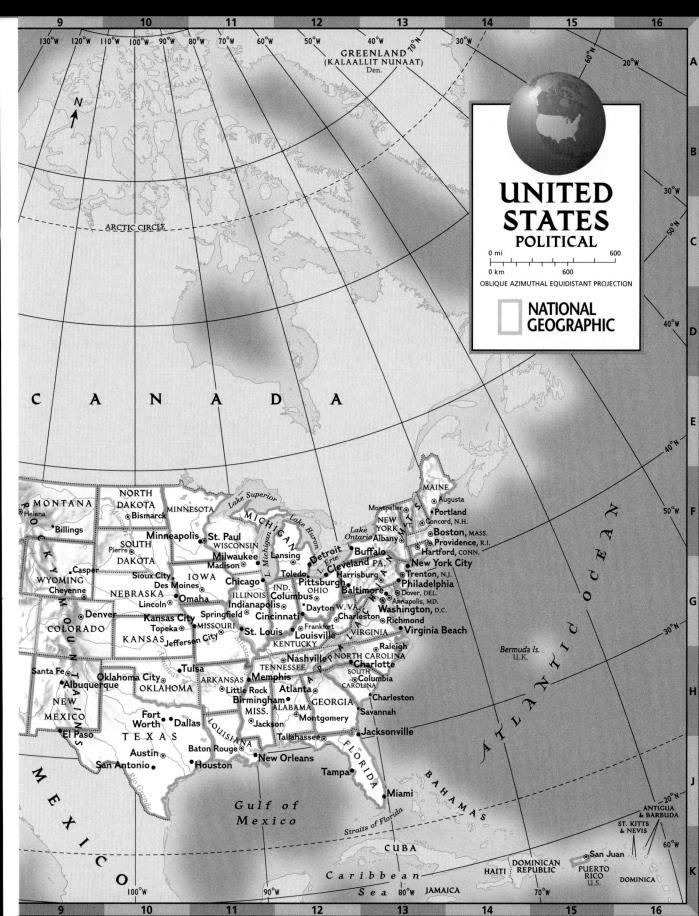

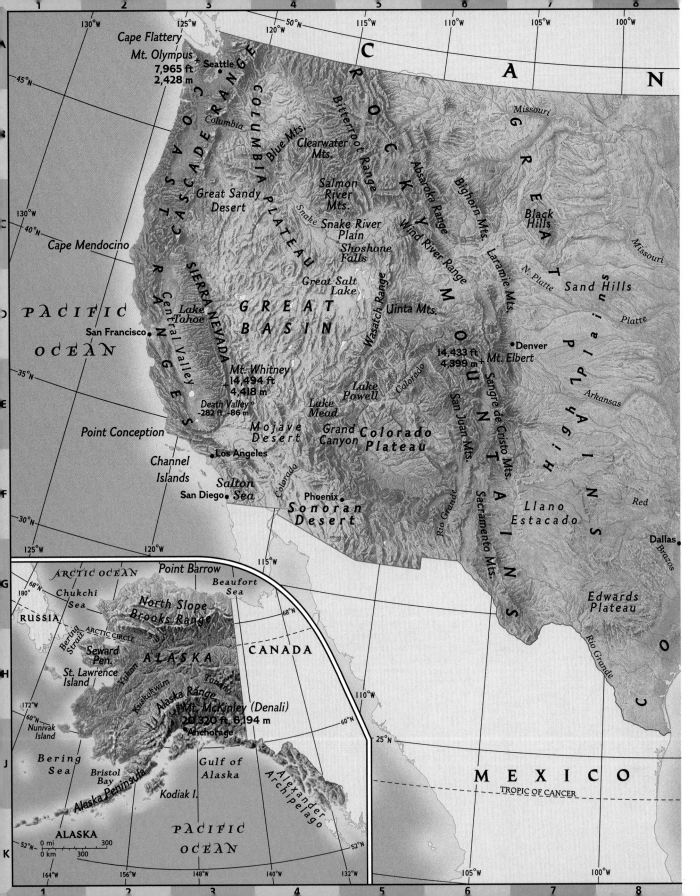

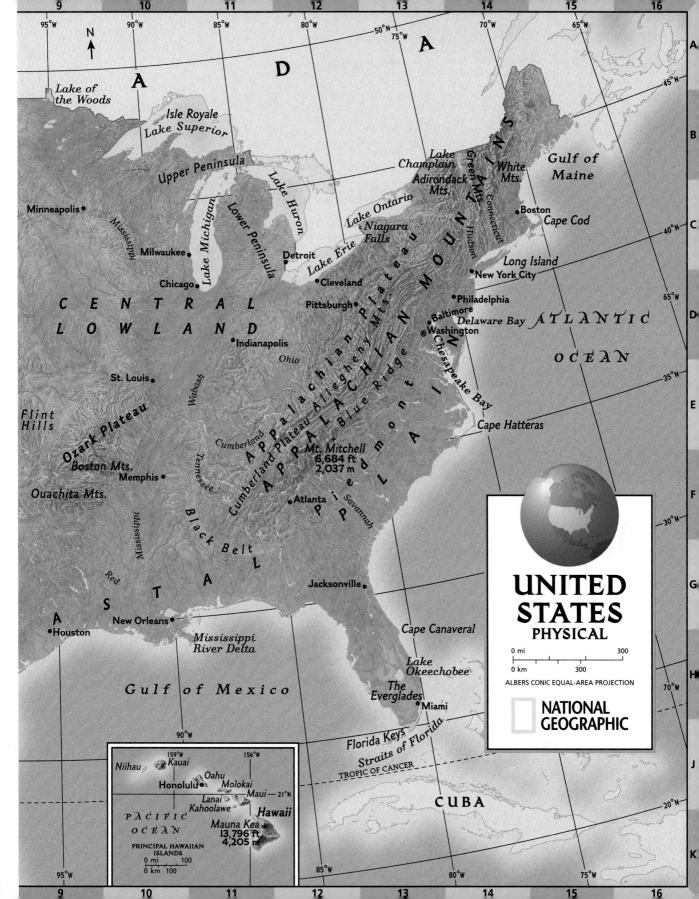

N

CANADA

Lake of the Woods

Isle Royale
Lake Superior
Upper Peninsula

Minneapolis

Lake Michigan
Lower Peninsula
Lake Huron

Milwaukee

Chicago

CENTRAL
LOWLAND

St. Louis

Flint
Hills

Ozark Plateau

Boston Mts.
Memphis

Ouachita Mts.

Mississippi

Detroit
Lake Erie
Cleveland

Pittsburgh

Indianapolis

Ohio

Wabash

Tennessee

Black Belt

Red

Lake Champlain
Adirondack Mts.

Green Mts.
White Mts.
Gulf of Maine

Connecticut

Boston
Cape Cod

Lake Ontario
Niagara Falls

Hudson

APPALACHIAN MOUNTAINS

Appalachian Plateau
Allegheny Mts.
Cumberland Plateau
Cumberland
Blue Ridge

Mt. Mitchell
6,684 ft
2,037 m

Atlanta

Savannah

Long Island
New York City

Philadelphia
Baltimore
Washington
Delaware Bay
Chesapeake Bay

Piedmont

ATLANTIC

OCEAN

Cape Hatteras

COASTAL

Houston

New Orleans

Mississippi
River Delta

Gulf of Mexico

Jacksonville

PLAIN

Cape Canaveral

Lake
Okeechobee

The
Everglades

Miami

Florida Keys
Straits of Florida
TROPIC OF CANCER

CUBA

UNITED STATES PHYSICAL

0 mi   300

0 km   300

ALBERS CONIC EQUAL-AREA PROJECTION

NATIONAL GEOGRAPHIC

Inset map (Hawaii)

159°W
Niihau
Kauai

Oahu
Honolulu
Molokai
Maui — 21°N

Lanai
Kahoolawe

Hawaii

Mauna Kea
13,796 ft
4,205 m

156°W

PACIFIC OCEAN

PRINCIPAL HAWAIIAN ISLANDS

0 mi   100
0 km   100

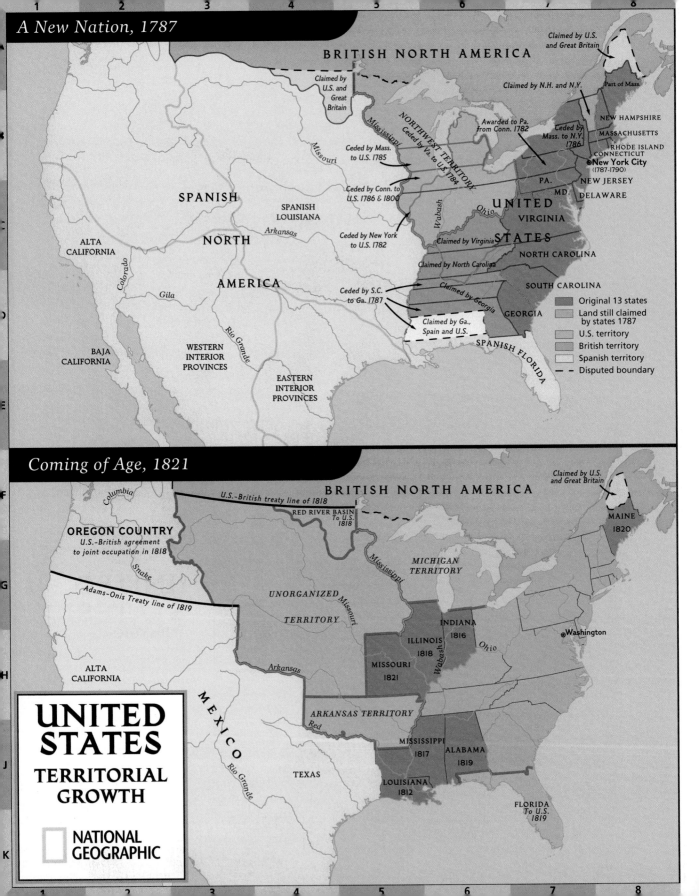

A New Nation, 1787

BRITISH NORTH AMERICA

Claimed by U.S. and Great Britain

Claimed by U.S. and Great Britain

Claimed by N.H. and N.Y.

Part of Mass.

Missouri

NORTHWEST TERRITORY
Ceded by Va. to U.S. 1784

Awarded to Pa. from Conn. 1782

Ceded by Mass. to N.Y. 1786

NEW HAMPSHIRE

MASSACHUSETTS

Ceded by Mass. to U.S. 1785

RHODE ISLAND

CONNECTICUT

New York City
(1787-1790)

SPANISH

SPANISH
LOUISIANA

Arkansas

Ceded by Conn. to U.S. 1786 & 1800

Ceded by New York to U.S. 1782

PA.

MD.

NEW JERSEY

DELAWARE

NORTH

Wabash

Ohio

UNITED

VIRGINIA

STATES

Claimed by Virginia

NORTH CAROLINA

AMERICA

Claimed by North Carolina

ALTA
CALIFORNIA

Colorado

Gila

SOUTH CAROLINA

Ceded by S.C. to Ga. 1787

Claimed by Georgia

GEORGIA

BAJA
CALIFORNIA

Rio Grande

WESTERN
INTERIOR
PROVINCES

Claimed by Ga., Spain and U.S.

SPANISH FLORIDA

EASTERN
INTERIOR
PROVINCES

Original 13 states

Land still claimed by states 1787

U.S. territory

British territory

Spanish territory

Disputed boundary

Coming of Age, 1821

Columbia

U.S.-British treaty line of 1818

BRITISH NORTH AMERICA

Claimed by U.S. and Great Britain

RED RIVER BASIN
To U.S. 1818

MAINE
1820

OREGON COUNTRY
U.S.-British agreement to joint occupation in 1818

Snake

Mississippi

MICHIGAN
TERRITORY

Adams-Onis Treaty line of 1819

UNORGANIZED

Missouri

TERRITORY

INDIANA
1816

ALTA
CALIFORNIA

Arkansas

ILLINOIS
1818

MISSOURI
1821

Ohio

Wabash

Washington

M E X I C O

ARKANSAS TERRITORY

Red

MISSISSIPPI
1817

ALABAMA
1819

Rio Grande

TEXAS

LOUISIANA
1812

FLORIDA
To U.S.
1819

UNITED STATES
TERRITORIAL GROWTH

**NATIONAL
GEOGRAPHIC**

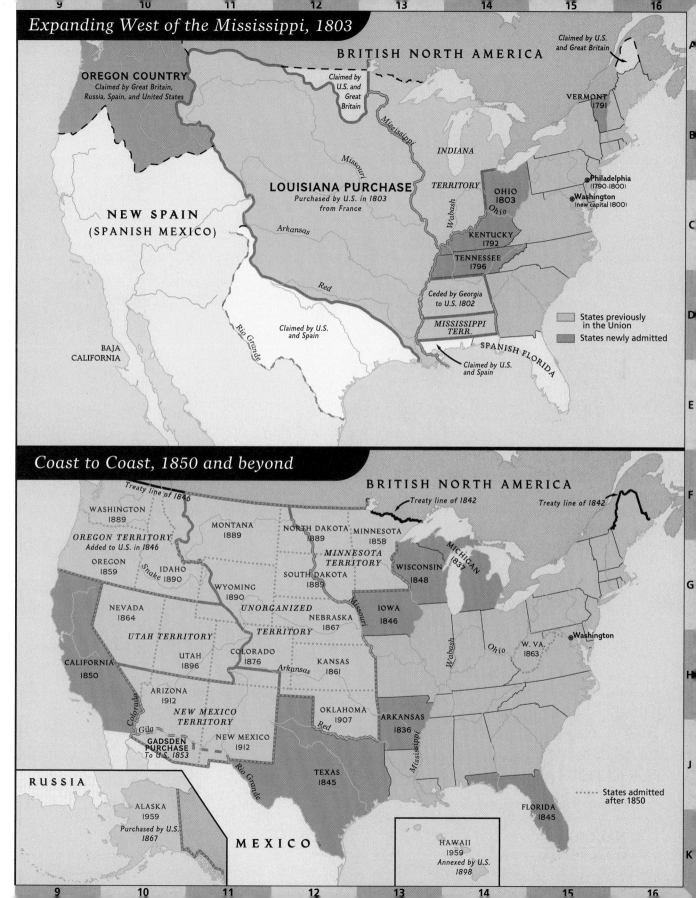

Expanding West of the Mississippi, 1803

BRITISH NORTH AMERICA

Claimed by U.S. and Great Britain

OREGON COUNTRY
Claimed by Great Britain, Russia, Spain, and United States

Claimed by U.S. and Great Britain

Mississippi

INDIANA TERRITORY

Missouri

VERMONT 1791

●Philadelphia (1790–1800)

●Washington (new capital 1800)

LOUISIANA PURCHASE
Purchased by U.S. in 1803 from France

OHIO 1803
Ohio

NEW SPAIN (SPANISH MEXICO)

Arkansas

KENTUCKY 1792

TENNESSEE 1796

Wabash

Red

Ceded by Georgia to U.S. 1802

Rio Grande

Claimed by U.S. and Spain

MISSISSIPPI TERR.

☐ States previously in the Union
☐ States newly admitted

BAJA CALIFORNIA

Claimed by U.S. and Spain

SPANISH FLORIDA

Claimed by U.S. and Spain

Coast to Coast, 1850 and beyond

BRITISH NORTH AMERICA

Treaty line of 1846

Treaty line of 1842

Treaty line of 1842

WASHINGTON 1889

OREGON TERRITORY
Added to U.S. in 1846

MONTANA 1889

NORTH DAKOTA 1889

MINNESOTA 1858

MINNESOTA TERRITORY

MICHIGAN 1837

OREGON 1859

Snake

IDAHO 1890

WYOMING 1890

SOUTH DAKOTA 1889

Missouri

WISCONSIN 1848

NEVADA 1864

UTAH TERRITORY

UTAH 1896

UNORGANIZED TERRITORY

NEBRASKA 1867

IOWA 1846

●Washington

W. VA. 1863

Wabash

Ohio

CALIFORNIA 1850

COLORADO 1876

Arkansas

KANSAS 1861

ARIZONA 1912

Colorado

Gila

NEW MEXICO TERRITORY

OKLAHOMA 1907

ARKANSAS 1836

NEW MEXICO 1912

GADSDEN PURCHASE
To U.S. 1853

Red

Mississippi

Rio Grande

TEXAS 1845

RUSSIA

ALASKA 1959
Purchased by U.S. 1867

MEXICO

FLORIDA 1845

HAWAII 1959
Annexed by U.S. 1898

······ States admitted after 1850

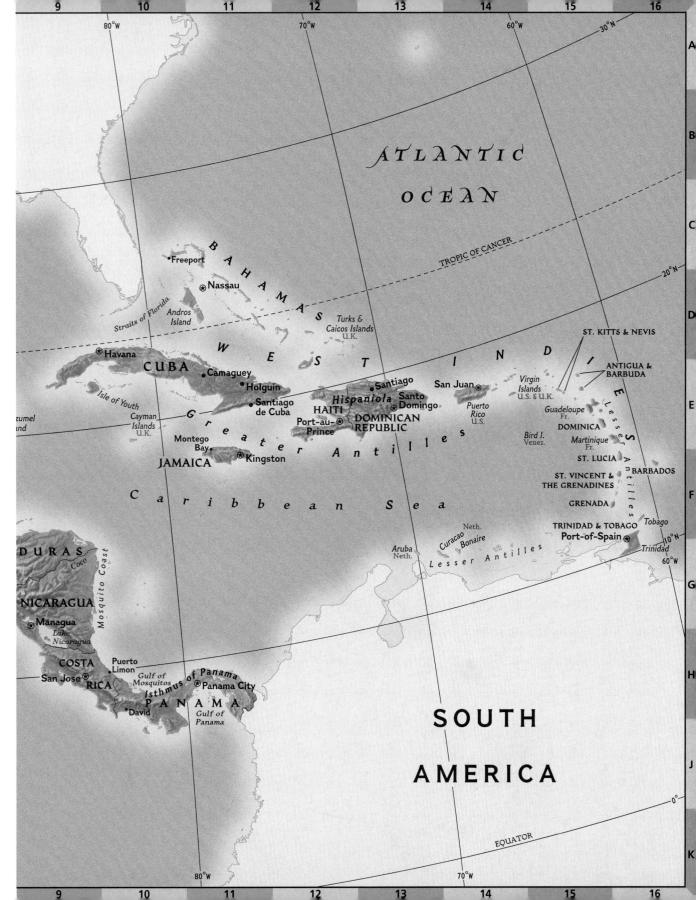

ATLANTIC

OCEAN

TROPIC OF CANCER

20°N

•Freeport

B A H A M A S

⊛ Nassau

W   E   S   T   I   N   D   I   E   S

Straits of Florida

Andros
Island

Turks &
Caicos Islands
U.K.

ST. KITTS & NEVIS

⊛ Havana

CUBA

•Camaguey

Santiago   San Juan ⊛

Virgin
Islands
U.S. & U.K.

ANTIGUA &
BARBUDA

Cozumel
Island

Isle of Youth

•Holguin

G   •Santiago
                        de Cuba

Hispaniola
HAITI   Santo
              Domingo
Port-au-   DOMINICAN
Prince   REPUBLIC

Puerto
Rico
U.S.

Guadeloupe
Fr.

Lesser

DOMINICA

Cayman
Islands
U.K.

Bird I.
Venez.

Martinique
Fr.

Antilles

Montego
Bay•

r   e   a   t   e   r   A   n   t   i   l   l   e   s

ST. LUCIA

BARBADOS

JAMAICA

⊛ Kingston

ST. VINCENT &
THE GRENADINES

C   a   r   i   b   b   e   a   n   S   e   a

GRENADA

Neth.
Curacao Bonaire

Tobago

TRINIDAD & TOBAGO
Port-of-Spain ⊛

Aruba
Neth.

Lesser Antilles

Trinidad

10°N
60°W

DURAS

Coco

Mosquito Coast

NICARAGUA

⊛ Managua
Lake
Nicaragua

SOUTH

COSTA

Puerto
Limon

Gulf of
Mosquitos

Isthmus of Panama

San Jose ⊛
RICA

⊛ Panama City

AMERICA

P   A   N   A   M   A

•David

Gulf of
Panama

EQUATOR

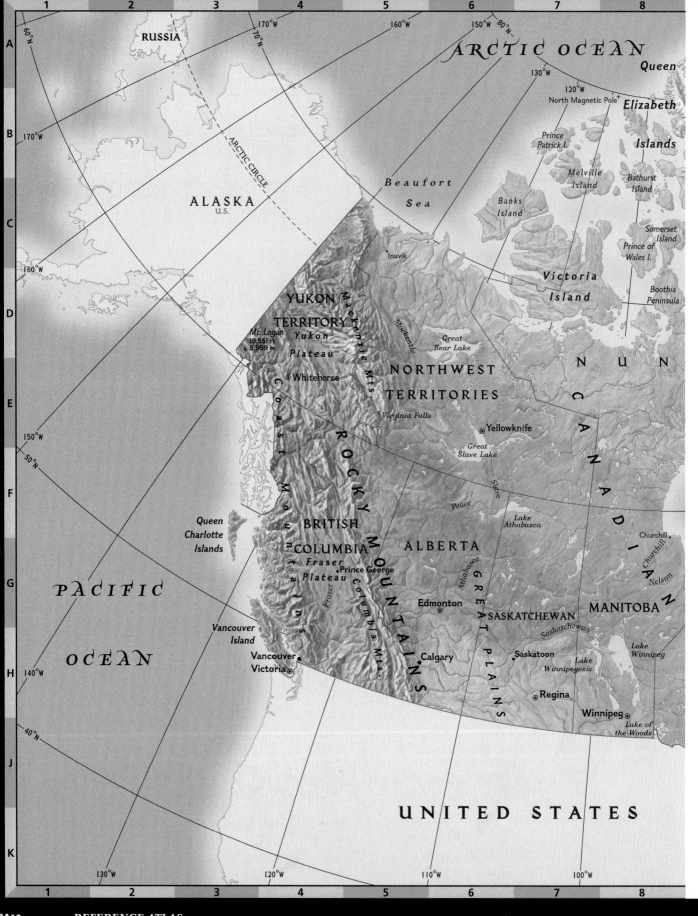

ARCTIC OCEAN

Queen

80 N

North Magnetic Pole

Elizabeth

Islands

RUSSIA

170°W

70°N

160°W

150°W

130°W

120°W

60°N

170°W

ARCTIC CIRCLE

ALASKA
U.S.

Beaufort Sea

Prince
Patrick I.

Melville
Island

Bathurst
Island

Banks
Island

Somerset
Island

Prince of
Wales I.

160°W

· Inuvik

*Victoria
Island*

Boothia
Peninsula

YUKON

TERRITORY

Mt. Logan
19,551 ft
5,959 m

*Yukon
Plateau*

Mackenzie Mts.

Mackenzie

Great
Bear Lake

N U N

NORTHWEST

TERRITORIES

© Whitehorse

Virginia Falls

Yellowknife

Great
Slave Lake

C
A
N
A
D
I
A
N

150°W

50 N

ROCKY MOUNTAINS

Slave

Peace

Queen
Charlotte
Islands

BRITISH

COLUMBIA

*Fraser
Plateau*

Prince George

Fraser

Columbia Mts.

ALBERTA

Athabasca

Lake
Athabasca

Churchill

Churchill

G R E A T   P L A I N S

Nelson

MANITOBA

PACIFIC

Edmonton ⊙

SASKATCHEWAN

Saskatchewan

Lake
Winnipeg

Vancouver
Island

Calgary ·

Saskatoon ·

Lake
Winnipegosis

140°W

OCEAN

Vancouver ·
Victoria ⊙

Regina ⊙

Winnipeg ⊙

Lake of
the Woods

40 N

UNITED   STATES

130°W

120°W

110°W

100°W

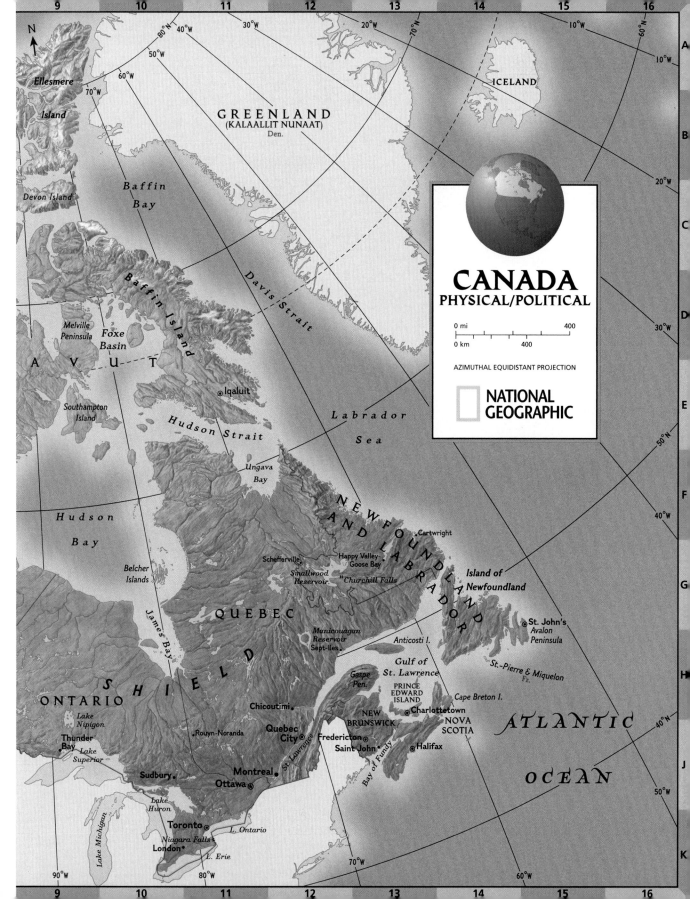

CANADA
PHYSICAL/POLITICAL

0 mi   400

0 km   400

AZIMUTHAL EQUIDISTANT PROJECTION

NATIONAL GEOGRAPHIC

N

Ellesmere Island

Devon Island

GREENLAND
(KALAALLIT NUNAAT)
Den.

ICELAND

Baffin Bay

Davis Strait

Melville Peninsula

Foxe Basin

Baffin Island

N U N A V U T

Southampton Island

⊙ Iqaluit

Hudson Strait

Labrador Sea

Ungava Bay

NEWFOUNDLAND AND LABRADOR

Hudson Bay

.Cartwright

Belcher Islands

Schefferville. Happy Valley-Goose Bay

Smallwood Reservoir "Churchill Falls

Island of Newfoundland

James Bay

QUEBEC

Manicouagan Reservoir
Sept-Iles.

⊙ St. John's
Avalon Peninsula

Anticosti I.

St.-Pierre & Miquelon
Fr.

S H I E L D

Gulf of St. Lawrence

ONTARIO

Lake Nipigon

Gaspe Pen.

PRINCE EDWARD ISLAND

Cape Breton I.

A T L A N T I C

Chicoutimi.

⊙ Charlottetown

Thunder Bay.

Rouyn-Noranda.

Quebec City ⊙

NEW BRUNSWICK

NOVA SCOTIA

Lake Superior

Fredericton.

Sudbury.

Montreal.

St. Lawrence

Saint John.

⊙ Halifax

O C E A N

Ottawa ⊙

Bay of Fundy

Lake Huron

Lake Michigan

Toronto ⊙

L. Ontario

Niagara Falls.

London.

L. Erie

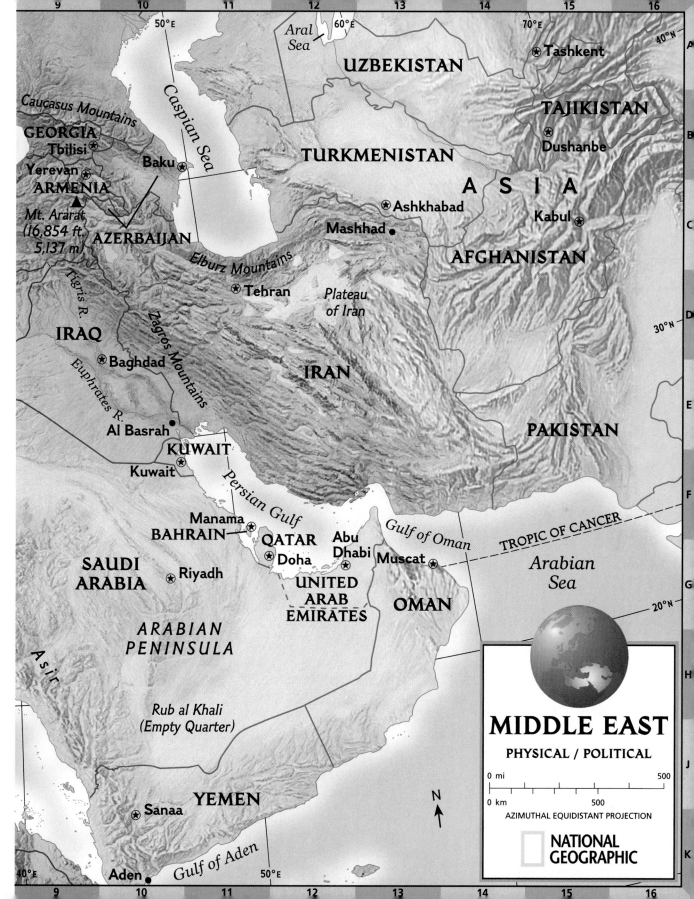

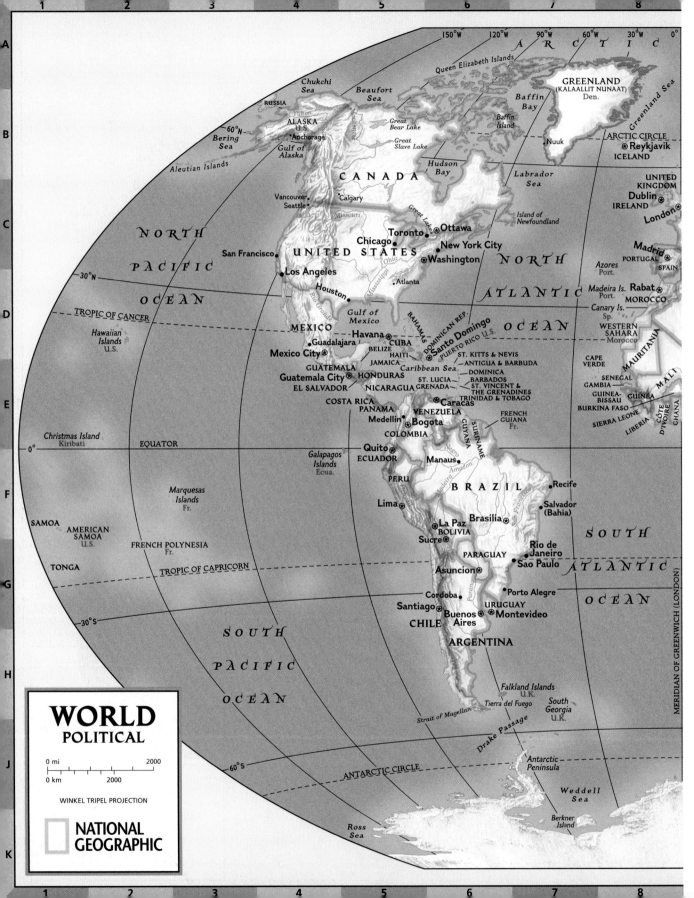

WORLD POLITICAL

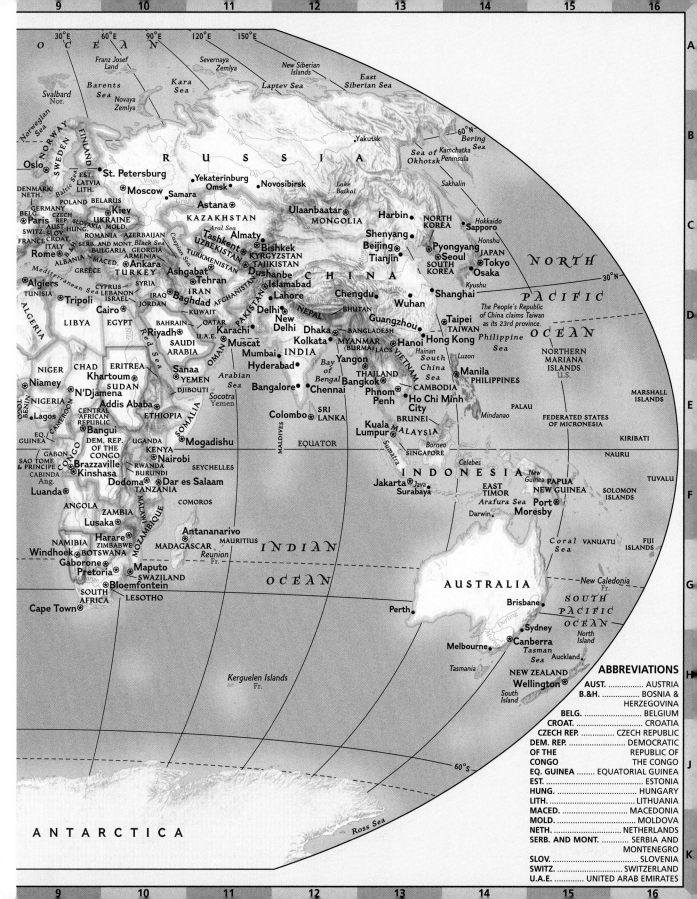

United States Facts

Washington, D.C.
Population: 572,059
Land area: 61 sq. mi.

U.S. Territories

Puerto Rico
Population: 3,808,610
Land area: 3,425 sq. mi.

Guam
Population: 155,000 (est.)
Land area: 210 sq. mi.

U.S. Virgin Islands
Population: 121,000 (est.)
Land area: 134 sq. mi.

American Samoa
Population: 65,000 (est.)
Land area: 77 sq. mi.

The states are listed in the order they were admitted to the Union.

Population figures are based on U.S. Bureau of the Census for 2000. House of Representatives figures are from the Clerk of the House of Representatives. States are not drawn to scale.

---

1 Delaware
Year Admitted: 1787
Population: 783,600
Land area: 1,955 sq. mi.
Representatives: 1
★ Dover

2 Pennsylvania
Year Admitted: 1787
Population: 12,281,054
Land area: 44,820 sq. mi.
Representatives: 19
Harrisburg ★

3 New Jersey
Year Admitted: 1787
Population: 8,414,350
Land area: 7,419 sq. mi.
Representatives: 13
Trenton ★

9 New Hampshire
Year Admitted: 1788
Population: 1,235,786
Land area: 8,969 sq. mi.
Representatives: 2
Concord ★

10 Virginia
Year Admitted: 1788
Population: 7,078,515
Land area: 39,598 sq. mi.
Representatives: 11
Richmond ★

11 New York
Year Admitted: 1788
Population: 18,976,457
Land area: 47,224 sq. mi.
Representatives: 29
★ Albany

17 Ohio
Year Admitted: 1803
Population: 11,353,140
Land area: 40,953 sq. mi.
Representatives: 18
★ Columbus

18 Louisiana
Year Admitted: 1812
Population: 4,468,976
Land area: 43,566 sq. mi.
Representatives: 7
★ Baton Rouge

19 Indiana
Year Admitted: 1816
Population: 6,080,485
Land area: 35,870 sq. mi.
Representatives: 9
Indianapolis ★

25 Arkansas
Year Admitted: 1836
Population: 2,673,400
Land area: 52,075 sq. mi.
Representatives: 4
Little Rock ★

26 Michigan
Year Admitted: 1837
Population: 9,938,444
Land area: 56,809 sq. mi.
Representatives: 15
Lansing ★

27 Florida
Year Admitted: 1845
Population: 15,982,378
Land area: 53,997 sq. mi.
Representatives: 25
★ Tallahassee

33 Oregon
Year Admitted: 1859
Population: 3,421,399
Land area: 96,003 sq. mi.
Representatives: 5
★ Salem

34 Kansas
Year Admitted: 1861
Population: 2,688,418
Land area: 81,823 sq. mi.
Representatives: 4
Topeka ★

35 West Virginia
Year Admitted: 1863
Population: 1,808,344
Land area: 24,087 sq. mi.
Representatives: 3
★ Charleston

36 Nevada
Year Admitted: 1864
Population: 1,998,257
Land area: 109,806 sq. mi.
Representatives: 3
★ Carson City

42 Washington
Year Admitted: 1889
Population: 5,894,121
Land area: 66,582 sq. mi.
Representatives: 9
★ Olympia

43 Idaho
Year Admitted: 1890
Population: 1,293,953
Land area: 82,751 sq. mi.
Representatives: 2
★ Boise

44 Wyoming
Year Admitted: 1890
Population: 493,782
Land area: 97,105 sq. mi.
Representatives: 1
Cheyenne ★

45 Utah
Year Admitted: 1896
Population: 2,233,169
Land area: 82,168 sq. mi.
Representatives: 3
★ Salt Lake City

4 Georgia
Year Admitted: 1788
Population: 8,186,453
Land area: 57,919 sq. mi.
Representatives: 13
★ Atlanta

5 Connecticut
Year Admitted: 1788
Population: 3,405,565
Land area: 4,845 sq. mi.
Representatives: 5
★ Hartford

6 Massachusetts
Year Admitted: 1788
Population: 6,349,097
Land area: 7,838 sq. mi.
Representatives: 10
Boston ★

7 Maryland
Year Admitted: 1788
Population: 5,296,486
Land area: 9,775 sq. mi.
Representatives: 8
Annapolis ★

8 South Carolina
Year Admitted: 1788
Population: 4,012,012
Land area: 30,111 sq. mi.
Representatives: 6
Columbia ★

12 North Carolina
Year Admitted: 1789
Population: 8,049,313
Land area: 48,718 sq. mi.
Representatives: 13
★ Raleigh

13 Rhode Island
Year Admitted: 1790
Population: 1,048,319
Land area: 1,045 sq. mi.
Representatives: 2
★ Providence

14 Vermont
Year Admitted: 1791
Population: 608,827
Land area: 9,249 sq. mi.
Representatives: 1
★ Montpelier

15 Kentucky
Year Admitted: 1792
Population: 4,041,769
Land area: 39,732 sq. mi.
Representatives: 6
Frankfort ★

16 Tennessee
Year Admitted: 1796
Population: 5,689,283
Land area: 41,220 sq. mi.
Representatives: 9
★ Nashville

20 Mississippi
Year Admitted: 1817
Population: 2,844,658
Land area: 46,914 sq. mi.
Representatives: 4
★ Jackson

21 Illinois
Year Admitted: 1818
Population: 12,419,293
Land area: 55,593 sq. mi.
Representatives: 19
★ Springfield

22 Alabama
Year Admitted: 1819
Population: 4,447,100
Land area: 50,750 sq. mi.
Representatives: 7
Montgomery ★

23 Maine
Year Admitted: 1820
Population: 1,274,923
Land area: 30,865 sq. mi.
Representatives: 2
★ Augusta

24 Missouri
Year Admitted: 1821
Population: 5,595,211
Land area: 68,898 sq. mi.
Representatives: 9
Jefferson City ★

28 Texas
Year Admitted: 1845
Population: 20,851,820
Land area: 261,914 sq. mi.
Representatives: 32
Austin ★

29 Iowa
Year Admitted: 1846
Population: 2,926,324
Land area: 55,875 sq. mi.
Representatives: 5
Des Moines ★

30 Wisconsin
Year Admitted: 1848
Population: 5,363,675
Land area: 54,314 sq. mi.
Representatives: 8
Madison ★

31 California
Year Admitted: 1850
Population: 33,871,648
Land area: 155,973 sq. mi.
Representatives: 53
★ Sacramento

32 Minnesota
Year Admitted: 1858
Population: 4,919,479
Land area: 79,617 sq. mi.
Representatives: 8
Saint Paul ★

37 Nebraska
Year Admitted: 1867
Population: 1,711,263
Land area: 76,878 sq. mi.
Representatives: 3
Lincoln ★

38 Colorado
Year Admitted: 1876
Population: 4,301,261
Land area: 103,730 sq. mi.
Representatives: 7
Denver ★

39 North Dakota
Year Admitted: 1889
Population: 642,200
Land area: 68,994 sq. mi.
Representatives: 1
Bismarck ★

40 South Dakota
Year Admitted: 1889
Population: 754,844
Land area: 75,898 sq. mi.
Representatives: 1
Pierre ★

41 Montana
Year Admitted: 1889
Population: 902,195
Land area: 145,556 sq. mi.
Representatives: 1
★ Helena

46 Oklahoma
Year Admitted: 1907
Population: 3,450,654
Land area: 68,679 sq. mi.
Representatives: 5
Oklahoma City ★

47 New Mexico
Year Admitted: 1912
Population: 1,819,046
Land area: 121,365 sq. mi.
Representatives: 3
★ Santa Fe

48 Arizona
Year Admitted: 1912
Population: 5,130,632
Land area: 113,642 sq. mi.
Representatives: 8
Phoenix ★

49 Alaska
Year Admitted: 1959
Population: 626,932
Land area: 570,374 sq. mi.
Representatives: 1
Juneau ★

50 Hawaii
Year Admitted: 1959
Population: 1,211,537
Land area: 6,423 sq. mi.
Representatives: 2
Honolulu ★

Geography Handbook

Acadia National ▶
Park, Maine

▲ Monument
Valley, Arizona

The Tongass National Forest in ▶
Southeastern Alaska, covering
nearly 17 million acres, is the
single largest national
forest in America.

What Is Geography?

The story of the United States begins with geography—the study of the earth in all of its variety. Geography describes the earth's land, water, and plant and animal life. It is the study of places and the complex relationships between people and their environments.

Geography of the United States

The United States is a land of startling physical differences. It is also a nation of diverse groups of people. A study of geography can help explain how the United States acquired its diversity.

The United States—with a total land area of 3,537,441 square miles (9,161,930 sq. km)—is the world's fourth-largest country in size.

The 50 States

Most of the United States—48 of the 50 states—spans the entire middle part of North America. This group of states touches three major bodies of water—the Atlantic Ocean, the Gulf of Mexico, and the Pacific Ocean. Two states—Alaska and Hawaii—lie apart from the 48 states.

Our Nation's Growth

Within the borders of the United States stretch a variety of landscapes—dense forests, hot deserts, rolling grasslands, and snow-capped mountains. Because of its large size and diverse regions, the United States throughout its history offered many opportunities. Over the centuries people from Europe, Africa, Asia, and other parts of the Americas have journeyed here. Today more than 281 million people make their homes in the United States.

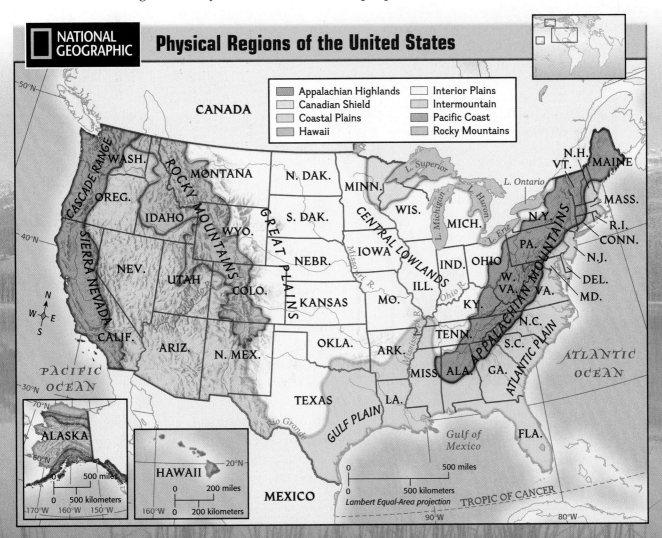

NATIONAL GEOGRAPHIC

Physical Regions of the United States

- Appalachian Highlands
- Canadian Shield
- Coastal Plains
- Hawaii
- Interior Plains
- Intermountain
- Pacific Coast
- Rocky Mountains

I Study Geography?

To understand how our world is connected, some geographers have broken down the study of geography into five themes. The **Five Themes of Geography** are (1) location, (2) place, (3) human/environment interaction, (4) movement, and (5) regions. You will see these themes highlighted in the Geography Skills accompanying the maps of *The American Republic to 1877.*

Six Essential Elements

Recently, geographers have begun to look at geography in a different way. They break down the study of geography into **Six Essential Elements,** which are explained below. Being aware of these elements will help you sort out what you are learning about geography.

Element 2

Places and Regions

Place has a special meaning in geography. It means more than where a place is. It also describes what a place is like. These features may be physical characteristics such as landforms, climate, and plant or animal life. They may also be human characteristics, including language and way of life.

To help organize their study, geographers often group places or areas into regions. **Regions** are united by one or more common characteristics.

Element 1

The World in Spatial Terms

Geographers first take a look at where a place is located. **Location** serves as a starting point by asking "Where is it?" Knowing the location of places helps you develop an awareness of the world around you.

Element 3

Physical Systems

When studying places and regions, geographers analyze how **physical systems**—such as hurricanes, volcanoes, and glaciers—shape the earth's surface. They also look at communities of plants and animals that depend upon one another and their surroundings for survival.

Human Systems

Geographers also examine human systems, or how people have shaped our world. They look at how boundary lines are determined and analyze why people settle in certain places and not in others. A key theme in geography is the continual **movement** of people, ideas, and goods.

Element 5

Environment and Society

"How does the relationship between people and their natural surroundings influence the way people live?" This is one of the questions that the theme of **human/ environment interaction** answers. This theme also shows how people use the environment and how their actions affect the environment.

Element 6

The Uses of Geography

Knowledge of geography helps people understand the relationships among people, places, and environments over time. Understanding geography, and knowing how to use the tools and technology available to study it, prepares you for life in our modern society.

I Use Maps?

Maps of many different kinds are used in *The American Republic to 1877* to help you see the connection between geography and the history of our nation.

Different Kinds of Maps

Physical Maps

A physical map shows the physical features of an area, such as its mountains and rivers. Physical maps use color and shadings to show **relief**—how flat or rugged the land surface is. Colors also may be used to show **elevation**—the height of an area above sea level.

Political Maps

Political maps generally show political, or human-made, divisions of countries or regions. The political map on pages RA2–RA3, for example, shows boundaries between the states that comprise the United States.

Special-Purpose Maps

Besides showing political or physical features, some maps have a special purpose. Human activities such as exploration routes, territorial expansion, or battle sites appear on special-purpose maps, also called **thematic maps.** The maps on pages RA6–RA7, for example, show territorial growth of the United States.

Latitude and Longitude

Maps have lines of latitude and longitude that form a grid. Lines of latitude circle the earth, either north or south of the Equator (0° latitude). Lines of longitude stretch from the North Pole to the South Pole, either east or west of the Prime Meridian (0° longitude). The distance between the lines is measured in degrees (°). Every place on the earth has a unique position or "address" on this grid.

Knowing this address makes it easier for you to locate cities and other places on a map. For example, the map on page RA5 shows you that the address of New Orleans is 30°N latitude, 90°W longitude.

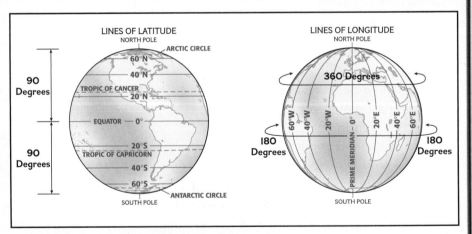

Parts of Maps

Map Key The map key explains the lines, symbols, and colors used on a map. For example, the map on this page shows the various climate regions of the United States. The key shows what climates the different colors represent. Map keys also may show structures created by people. Cities are usually symbolized by a solid circle (•). A star within a circle represents capitals (⊛). On this map, you can see the capital of Texas and the cities of New Orleans, Los Angeles, and Chicago.

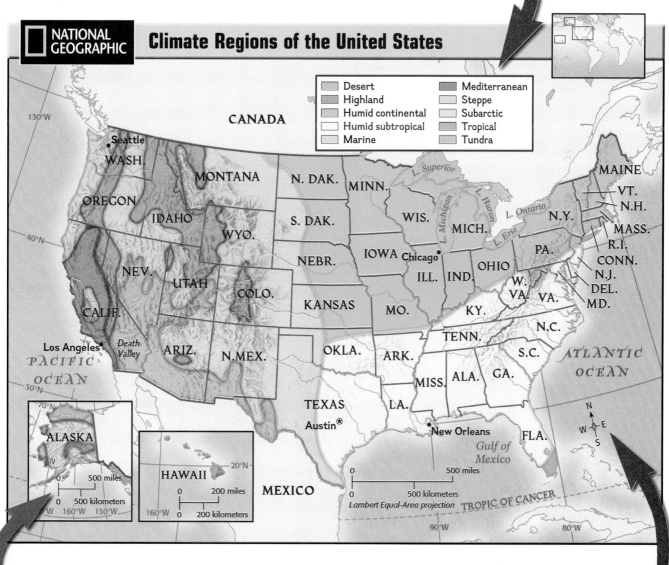

NATIONAL GEOGRAPHIC

Climate Regions of the United States

Key:
- Desert
- Highland
- Humid continental
- Humid subtropical
- Marine
- Mediterranean
- Steppe
- Subarctic
- Tropical
- Tundra

CANADA

130°W — Seattle, WASH., OREGON, IDAHO, MONTANA, WYO., NEV., UTAH, CALIF., Los Angeles, Death Valley, ARIZ., N.MEX.

PACIFIC OCEAN

ALASKA — 0 500 miles / 0 500 kilometers — W, 160°W, 150°W, 70°N

HAWAII — 0 200 miles / 0 200 kilometers — 160°W, 20°N

MEXICO

N. DAK., S. DAK., NEBR., KANSAS, OKLA., TEXAS, Austin⊛

MINN., WIS., IOWA, Chicago, ILL., IND., MO., ARK., MISS., LA., New Orleans

L. Superior, L. Michigan, L. Huron, MICH., OHIO, KY., TENN., ALA., GA.

L. Ontario, L. Erie, N.Y., PA., W. VA., VA., N.C., S.C.

MAINE, VT., N.H., MASS., R.I., CONN., N.J., DEL., MD.

ATLANTIC OCEAN

FLA., Gulf of Mexico

0 500 miles / 0 500 kilometers
Lambert Equal-Area projection — TROPIC OF CANCER

90°W, 80°W

N, W, E, S

Scale A measuring line, often called a **scale bar,** helps you determine distance on the map. The map scale tells you what distance on the earth is represented by the measurement on the scale bar.

Compass Rose An important first step in reading any map is to find the direction marker. A map has a symbol that tells you where the **cardinal directions**—north, south, east, and west—are positioned.

How Does Geography Influence History?

Geographic factors—landforms, waterways, natural resources—have shaped America's history. Here are some examples of geography's influences in history that are highlighted in *The American Republic to 1877.*

Unit 2 Colonial Settlement Beginning in the 1500s, Europeans came to North America seeking land, riches, and freedom. Groups from Spain, France, Great Britain, and other countries established colonies. The British colonies along the Atlantic coast were hemmed in by the Appalachian Mountains—the first physical barrier to the West.

Unit 1 Different Worlds Meet As settlement spread, Native Americans created distinctive civilizations appropriate to their climates and resources. For example, Native Americans in the Great Plains depended on herds of buffalo for food, clothing, shelter, and tools.

Unit 3 Creating a Nation The hardships of the land shaped the colonial settlers' cultural identities. The colonists were isolated from much of the world and became more independent. Eventually they broke away from Great Britain and won their independence.

Unit 4 The New Republic When the United States was established, many doubted that the young government could control people over such great distances. New rivers, roads, and canals helped to open up the country. At the same time an Industrial Revolution had begun in New England.

Unit 5 The Growing Nation Through wars, treaties, and purchases, the United States gained control of the lands west of the Mississippi River. Settlers were drawn to Western territories by opportunities. Native Americans were forced onto reservations. Railroads enabled people to overcome geographic barriers.

Unit 6 Civil War and Reconstruction Demand for cotton by the textile industry increased the demand for labor provided by enslaved African Americans. In 1861 regional differences and a dispute over slavery sparked the Civil War between the North and South.

Unit 7 Modern America Emerges In the late 1800s and early 1900s, the United States became an urban industrial nation and took the leading role in international affairs. Americans entered the twenty-first century as a free nation committed to the truths expressed in the Declaration of Independence.

Geographic Dictionary

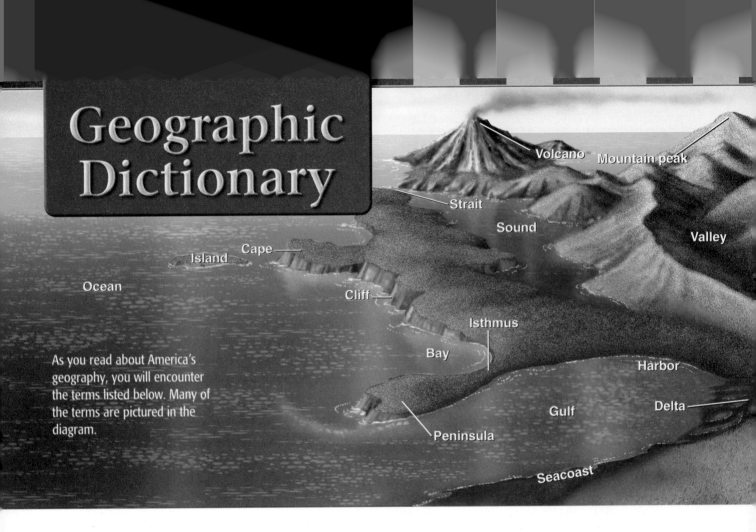

As you read about America's geography, you will encounter the terms listed below. Many of the terms are pictured in the diagram.

Labels on diagram: Volcano, Mountain peak, Strait, Sound, Valley, Cape, Island, Ocean, Cliff, Isthmus, Bay, Harbor, Gulf, Delta, Peninsula, Seacoast

absolute location exact location of a place on the earth described by global coordinates

basin area of land drained by a given river and its branches; area of land surrounded by lands of higher elevations

bay part of a large body of water that extends into a shoreline, generally smaller than a gulf

canyon deep and narrow valley with steep walls

cape point of land that extends into a river, lake, or ocean

channel wide strait or waterway between two land-masses that lie close to each other; deep part of a river or other waterway

cliff steep, high wall of rock, earth, or ice

continent one of the seven large landmasses on the earth

cultural feature characteristic that humans have created in a place, such as language, religion, housing, and settlement pattern

delta flat, low-lying land built up from soil carried downstream by a river and deposited at its mouth

divide stretch of high land that separates river systems

downstream direction in which a river or stream flows from its source to its mouth

elevation height of land above sea level

Equator imaginary line that runs around the earth halfway between the North and South Poles; used as the starting point to measure degrees of north and south latitude

glacier large, thick body of slowly moving ice

gulf part of a large body of water that extends into a shoreline, generally larger and more deeply indented than a bay

harbor a sheltered place along a shoreline where ships can anchor safely

highland elevated land area such as a hill, mountain, or plateau

hill elevated land with sloping sides and rounded summit; generally smaller than a mountain

island land area, smaller than a continent, completely surrounded by water

isthmus narrow stretch of land connecting two larger land areas

lake a sizable inland body of water

latitude distance north or south of the Equator, measured in degrees

longitude distance east or west of the Prime Meridian, measured in degrees

lowland land, usually level, at a low elevation

map drawing of the earth shown on a flat surface

meridian one of many lines on the global grid running from the North Pole to the South Pole; used to measure degrees of longitude

mesa broad, flat-topped landform with steep sides; smaller than a plateau

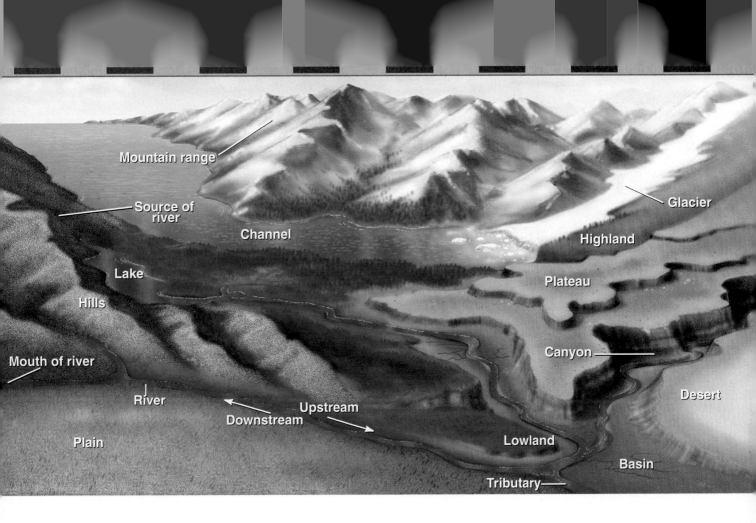

mountain land with steep sides that rises sharply (1,000 feet or more) from surrounding land; generally larger and more rugged than a hill

mountain peak pointed top of a mountain

mountain range a series of connected mountains

mouth (of a river) place where a stream or river flows into a larger body of water

ocean one of the four major bodies of salt water that surround the continents

ocean current stream of either cold or warm water that moves in a definite direction through an ocean

parallel one of many lines on the global grid that circle the earth north or south of the Equator; used to measure degrees of latitude

peninsula body of land jutting into a lake or ocean, surrounded on three sides by water

physical feature characteristic of a place occurring naturally, such as a landform, body of water, climate pattern, or resource

plain area of level land, usually a low elevation and often covered with grasses

plateau area of flat or rolling land at a high elevation, about 300–3,000 feet high

Prime Meridian line of the global grid running from the North Pole to the South Pole through Greenwich, England; starting point for measuring degrees of east and west longitude

relief changes in elevation over a given area of land

river large natural stream of water that runs through the land

sea large body of water completely or partly surrounded by land

seacoast land lying next to a sea or ocean

sea level position on land level with surface of nearby ocean or sea

sound body of water between a coastline and one or more islands off the coast

source (of a river) place where a river or stream begins, often in highlands

strait narrow stretch of water joining two larger bodies of water

tributary small river or stream that flows into a large river or stream; a branch of the river

upstream direction opposite the flow of a river; toward the source of a river or stream

valley area of low land between hills or mountains

volcano mountain created as liquid rock or ash erupts from inside the earth

Reading for Information

Think about your textbook as a tool that helps you learn more about the world around you. It is an example of nonfiction writing—it describes real-life events, people, ideas, and places. Here is a menu of reading strategies that will help you become a better textbook reader. As you come to passages in your textbook that you don't understand, refer to these reading strategies for help.

✓ Before You Read

Set a purpose
- Why are you reading the textbook?
- How does the subject relate to your life?
- How might you be able to use what you learn in your own life?

Preview
- Read the chapter title to find what the topic will be.
- Read the subtitles to see what you will learn about the topic.
- Skim the photos, charts, graphs, or maps. How do they support the topic?
- Look for vocabulary words that are bold-faced. How are they defined?

Draw From Your Own Background
- What have you read or heard concerning new information on the topic?
- How is the new information different from what you already know?
- How will the information that you already know help you understand the new information?

Question

- What is the main idea?
- How do the photos, charts, graphs, and maps support the main idea?

Connect

- Think about people, places, and events in your own life. Are there any similarities with those in your textbook?
- Can you relate the textbook information to other areas of your life?

Predict

- Predict events or outcomes by using clues and information that you already know.
- Change your predictions as you read and gather new information.

Visualize

- Pay careful attention to details and descriptions.
- Create graphic organizers to show relationships that you find in the information.

Look For Clues As You Read

Comparison and Contrast Sentences

- Look for clue words and phrases that signal comparison, such as *similarly, just as, both, in common, also,* and *too.*
- Look for clue words and phrases that signal contrast, such as *on the other hand, in contrast to, however, different, instead of, rather than, but,* and *unlike.*

Cause-and-Effect Sentences

- Look for clue words and phrases such as *because, as a result, therefore, that is why, since, so, for this reason,* and *consequently.*

Chronological Sentences

- Look for clue words and phrases such as *after, before, first, next, last, during, finally, earlier, later, since,* and *then.*

✓ After You Read

Summarize

- Describe the main idea and how the details support it.
- Use your own words to explain what you have read.

Assess

- What was the main idea?
- Did the text clearly support the main idea?
- Did you learn anything new from the material?
- Can you use this new information in other school subjects or at home?
- What other sources could you use to find more information about the topic?

1 Different Worlds Meet

Beginnings to 1625

Why It Matters

As you study Unit 1, you will learn
that the first immigrants came to the
Americas long before written history.
From their descendants evolved a rich
variety of cultures. The following
resources offer more information
about this period.

Astrolabe, early
astronomical instrument

Primary Sources Library

See pages 592–593 for primary source
readings to accompany Unit 1.
 Use the **American History
Primary Source Document Library
CD-ROM** to find additional primary
sources about Native American life.

Monument Valley

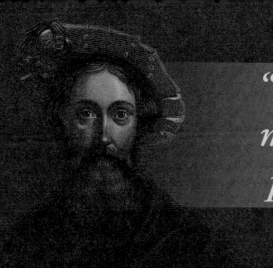

"*I found very many islands peopled....*"

—*Christopher Columbus, 1493*

The First Americans

Prehistory to 1492

Why It Matters

Thousands of years ago small groups of hunters crossed a bridge of land that connected Siberia and Alaska. Eventually, they spread throughout North and South America.

The Impact Today

These first people, called Native Americans, influenced later cultures. Native Americans are part of the modern world, yet many of them also preserve the ways of life, customs, and traditions developed by their ancestors centuries ago.

The American Republic to 1877 *Video* *The chapter 1 video, "Before Columbus," examines the diverse cultures of North America before Europeans arrived, focusing on the Anasazi.*

The Americas

Prehistory

C. 28,000 B.C.
• Asian hunters enter North America

C. 1500 B.C.
• Rise of Olmec in Mexico

C. A.D. 700
• Maya empire reaches peak

C. A.D. 1130
• Drought strikes Anasazi communities

900

1100

World

C. 10,000 B.C.
• Last Ice Age ends

C. A.D. 33
• Jesus Christ is crucified

A.D. 613
• Muhammad preaches Islam in Makkah

A.D. 1095
• The Crusades begin

City in the Sky   Inca workers built the city of Machu Picchu high in the Andes mountain ranges.

FOLDABLES™
Study Organizer

Categorizing Study Foldable Group information into categories to make sense of what you are learning. Make this foldable to learn about the first Americans.

Step 1 Fold one sheet of paper in half from top to bottom.

Step 2 Fold in half again, from side to side.

Step 3 Unfold the paper once. Cut up the fold of the top flap only.

This cut will make two tabs.

Step 4 Turn the paper vertically and sketch the continents of North and Central and South America on the front tabs.

Native Americans
North America
Central and South America

Reading and Writing As you read the chapter, write under the flaps of your foldable what you learn about the Native American people living in these regions.

C. A.D. **1300**
• Hohokam civilization begins to decline

A.D. **1325**
• Aztec establish Tenochtitlán

C. A.D. **1400**
• Inca empire begins to expand

HISTORY
Online

Chapter Overview
Visit tarvol1.glencoe.com and click on **Chapter 1— Chapter Overviews** to preview chapter information.

1300   1500

A.D. **1368**
• Ming dynasty begins in China

A.D. **1215**
• England's King John signs Magna Carta

A.D. **1295**
• Italian traveler Marco Polo returns from China

A.D. **1312**
• Mansa Musa begins rule of West African kingdom of Mali

Early Peoples

Guide to Reading

Main Idea
The first Americans spread throughout North, Central, and South America.

Key Terms
archaeology, artifact, Ice Age, nomad, migration, maize, carbon dating, culture

Reading Strategy
Determining Cause and Effect As you read Section 1, re-create the diagram below and explain why the first Americans came to the continent and the consequences of their arrival.

Migration to the Americas	
Causes	Effects

Read to Learn
- how the first people arrived in the Americas.
- which discovery changed the lives of the early Native Americans.

Section Theme
Geography and History The Ice Age made it possible for hunters to migrate to the Americas.

Preview of Events

♦30,000 B.C.	♦10,000 B.C.	♦5000 B.C.	♦1000 B.C.

c. 28,000 B.C.
Asian hunters enter North America

c. 10,000 B.C.
Last Ice Age ends

c. 7000 B.C.
Farming develops in Mexico

c. 3000 B.C.
Early villages established in Mexico

★★★★★★★★★
AN
American Story

No one knows for sure how the first people arrived in America. They may have crossed a land bridge that many scientists think connected Asia and North America thousands of years ago. They may have come by boat from Asia or Europe. Why they came is also a mystery. Possibly they followed mammoths or other game animals or were hunting seals and whales along the coast. Over time these people settled in America, becoming the first "native Americans."

Arrowhead, hand-chipped stone

The Journey From Asia

These first Americans arrived thousands of years ago. As food supplies improved, the population of the Americas increased. By A.D. 1500, millions of Native Americans, belonging to more than 2,000 different groups, lived on the two continents of North America and South America.

When Europeans arrived in the Americas in the late 1400s, they found Native Americans living there. The Europeans wondered where these peoples had come from and how they happened to settle in the Americas. Some believed the Native Americans had come from Atlantis, an island that was supposed to have sunk beneath the waves of the Atlantic Ocean.

Modern scientists are still trying to determine how the first people came to North and South America. The story of the first Americans is still being pieced together by experts in archaeology, the study of ancient peoples. Archaeologists learn about the past from artifacts, things left behind by early people, such as stone tools, weapons, baskets, and carvings. Their discoveries show that many early peoples may have come across a land that later sank into the sea. It was not the mythical Atlantis, however, but a strip of land called **Beringia** that once joined Asia and the Americas.

Crossing the Land Bridge

During its long history, the earth has passed through several Ice Ages. These are periods of very cold temperatures when part of the earth was covered with large ice sheets. Much of the water from the oceans was frozen into these sheets, or glaciers. For that reason the sea levels were much lower than they are today.

The most recent Ice Age began 100,000 years ago and ended about 12,000 years ago. During this period many scientists think the lower sea level exposed a wide strip of land between Asia and North America. This land bridge would have run from **Siberia** in northeastern Asia to present-day **Alaska,** the westernmost part of the Americas. The land bridge, Beringia, now lies under the **Bering Strait.**

One popular scientific theory states that the first Americans were people from Asia who crossed over Beringia during the last Ice Age. These early peoples reached the Americas thousands of years ago.

In Search of Hunting Grounds

The early Americans were nomads, people who moved from place to place. They gathered wild grains and fruits but depended on hunting for much of their food. While traveling in search of animals to hunt, they crossed Beringia into what is now Alaska and Canada.

The crossing of the land bridge was a migration, a movement of a large number of people into a new homeland. It did not happen in a single journey. As the centuries passed, many groups of people traveled from Asia either on foot across the land bridge or in boats. From the north, the migrants gradually moved into new territory. They spread out across the Americas, going as far east as the Atlantic Ocean and as far south as the tip of South America.

Hunting for Food

Native American legends tell of giant beasts that roamed the earth in ancient times. When the first Americans arrived from Asia, they did indeed find huge mammals. There was the saber-toothed tiger, the woolly mammoth, and the mastodon. The mammoth and mastodon resembled modern elephants in size and shape but had shaggy fur and long tusks.

The early Americans were skilled at hunting these beasts. The hunters shaped pieces of stone and bone to make tools for chopping and scraping. They chipped rocks into extremely sharp points and fastened them on poles to make spears. Bands of hunters armed with these spears stalked herds of bison, mastodons, or

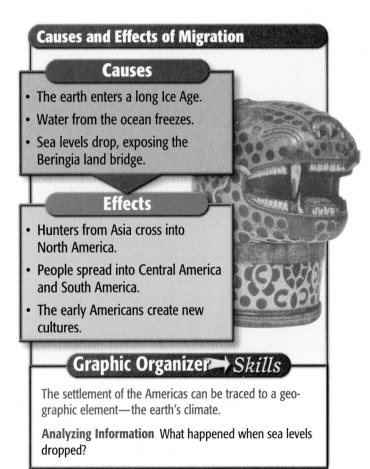

Causes and Effects of Migration

Causes
- The earth enters a long Ice Age.
- Water from the ocean freezes.
- Sea levels drop, exposing the Beringia land bridge.

Effects
- Hunters from Asia cross into North America.
- People spread into Central America and South America.
- The early Americans create new cultures.

Graphic Organizer → Skills

The settlement of the Americas can be traced to a geographic element—the earth's climate.

Analyzing Information What happened when sea levels dropped?

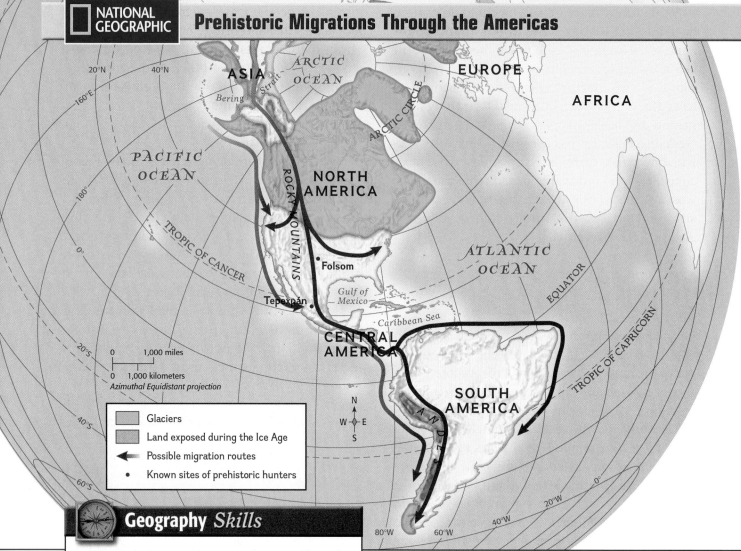

Prehistoric Migrations Through the Americas

Glaciers

Land exposed during the Ice Age

Possible migration routes

• Known sites of prehistoric hunters

0   1,000 miles

0   1,000 kilometers
Azimuthal Equidistant projection

Geography *Skills*

Over thousands of years, prehistoric people migrated from other lands to the Americas.
1. **Movement** Along what major mountain ranges did the migration routes flow?
2. **Interpreting Information** How was it possible for prehistoric people to cross the Bering Strait?

---

mammoths and then charged at the animals, hurling their weapons.

A single mammoth provided tons of meat, enough to feed a group of people for months. The hunters and their families used every part of the animal. They made the skin into clothing, carved the bones into weapons and tools, and may have used the long ribs to build shelters.

About 15,000 years ago the earth's temperatures began to rise. The Ice Age was drawing to an end. As the great glaciers melted, the oceans rose, and Beringia was submerged again. The

Americas were cut off from Asia. At the same time, the hunters of America faced a new challenge. The mammoths and other large animals began to die out, either from being overhunted or because of changes in the environment. The early Americans had to find other sources of food.

Reading Check **Describing** How did early American nomads hunt for food?

Settling Down

As the large animals disappeared, the early Americans found new sources of food. They hunted smaller game, such as deer, birds, and rodents. Those who lived along rivers or near the seacoast learned to catch fish with nets and traps. They continued to gather wild berries and grains.

Planting Seeds

About 9,000 years ago, people living in present-day **Mexico** made a discovery that would shape the lives of Native Americans for thousands of years. They learned to plant and raise an early form of corn called maize. Their harvests of maize provided a steady, reliable source of food. No longer did they have to move from place to place in order to find food.

Early Americans in Mexico also experimented with other kinds of seeds. They planted pumpkins, beans, and squashes. They soon began producing more than enough food to feed themselves. The population grew along with the growing food supply.

Early Communities

With rising numbers of people and a dependable supply of food, early Americans in Mexico started to form stationary communities. Scientists have found traces of early villages that date from about 5,000 years ago. Scientists use a method called carbon dating to find out how old an artifact is. By measuring the amount of radioactive carbon that remains in something that was once alive—such as a bone or a piece of wood—they can tell approximately how long ago it lived. Carbon dating is imprecise and can only give a rough estimate of an artifact's age.

Sometime after the early settlements in Mexico, people began farming in what is now the southwestern United States. Not all the early peoples in the Americas farmed, however. Some remained nomadic hunters, and others relied on fishing or trading instead of agriculture.

The Growth of Cultures

Farming allowed people to spend time on activities other than finding food. Knowing that they would harvest an abundant supply of grains and vegetables, the people of ancient Mexico began to improve their lives in other ways. They built permanent shelters of clay, brick, stone, or wood. They made pottery and cloth and decorated these goods with dyes made from roots and herbs. They also began to develop more complex forms of government.

Agriculture changed the lives of these early people and led to a new culture, or way of life. Rather than move from place to place in search of food, the people who farmed were able to settle down. They formed communities and developed common customs, beliefs, and ways of protecting themselves. Over time, the many different groups of people living in the Americas developed their own cultures.

Reading Check **Summarizing** What did farming mean for nomadic people?

SECTION 1 ASSESSMENT

Checking for Understanding

1. **Key Terms** Use each of the following terms in a complete sentence that will help explain its meaning: archaeology, artifact, Ice Age, migration, culture.
2. **Reviewing Facts** Why did the first people come to the Americas?

Reviewing Themes

3. **Geography and History** How did an Ice Age make it possible for Asian hunters to migrate to the Americas?

Critical Thinking

4. **Determining Cause and Effect** How do you think the first Americans discovered that they could grow their own plants?
5. **Organizing Information** Re-create the diagram below and explain how early Native Americans depended on their environment and natural resources.

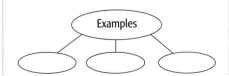

Analyzing Visuals

6. **Geography Skills** Study the map on page 18. In which direction did the travelers migrate across the Bering Strait?

Interdisciplinary Activity

Geography Create a version of the map on page 18. Your version can be larger, if needed. Label all land masses and bodies of water. Illustrate the map to tell the story of how the first Americans migrated to North America.

New Ways to the New World

An old Virginia sandpit may change our views of the earliest Americans

IT HAS BEEN CALLED THE GREATEST STORY OF IMMIGRATION TO THE Americas. At the end of the last Ice Age, brave women and men from Siberia walked across the Bering Sea land bridge. This is a piece of land that once connected the Asian continent with North America. Within 500 years, their descendants had settled most of the hemisphere, from the Arctic Circle to the tip of South America. But it seems they may not have been first.

Cactus Hill

Well known archaeologist **JOSEPH McAVOY** and his team reported that they have located an ancient campsite that is about 18,000 years old. The place, known as Cactus Hill, is about 45 miles south of Richmond, Virginia (see map).

Scientists now believe the site may actually be thousands of years older than the land-bridge site. If that's true, then people were living in North America much earlier than once believed. "If the dates hold up, and I think they will," says archaeologist Dennis Stanford, "this is probably some of the oldest material in North America, if not the entire New World."

For decades, experts thought that 11,200-year-old stone spear points from a site in Clovis, New Mexico, were the earliest evidence of settlement in the hemisphere. But since the 1970s, older sites have been discovered on both sides of the North American continent. The most important finding has been a 17,000-year-old rock shelter in Meadowcroft, Pennsylvania.

More Proof

Now Cactus Hill presents still more proof that humans settled in North America earlier than anyone had thought. McAvoy's team has unearthed a variety of stone tools, probably used for hunting and butchering animals. The team also found burned bones of mud turtles, white-tailed deer, and other mammals, and bits of charcoal left over from hunters cooking the animals.

High-tech instruments were used to figure out how old the bones and objects are. The Meadowcroft rock shelter's chief archaeologist, James Adovasio, says: "This is another indication that people were running around North America earlier than 13,000 years ago."

McAvoy and wife, Lynn, working on what may be one of the oldest campsites in the Americas

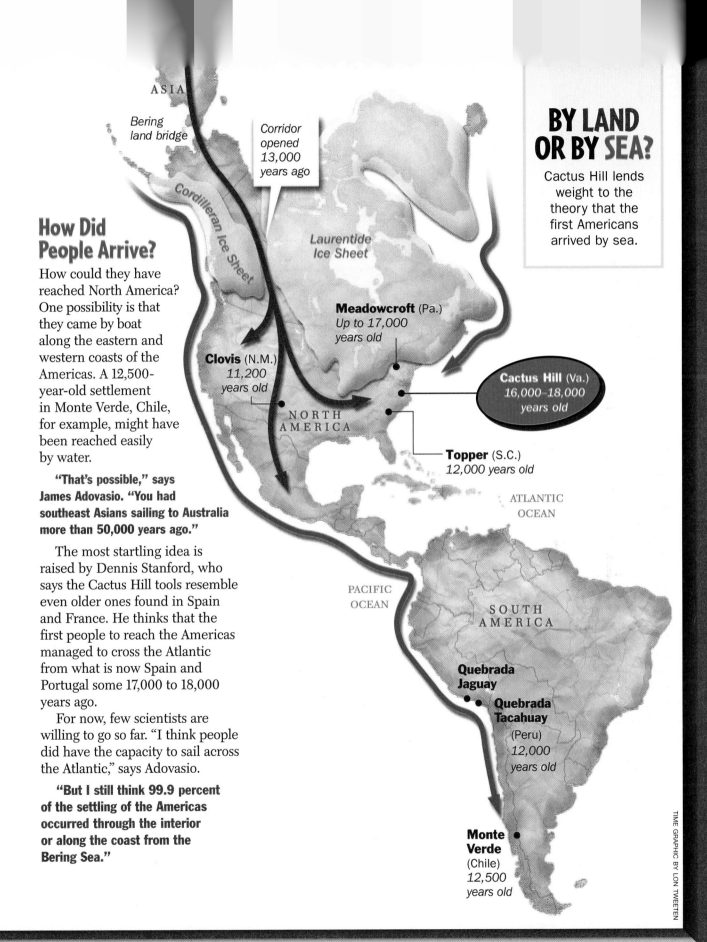

Bering land bridge

Corridor opened 13,000 years ago

Cordilleran Ice Sheet

Laurentide Ice Sheet

BY LAND OR BY SEA?

Cactus Hill lends weight to the theory that the first Americans arrived by sea.

How Did People Arrive?

How could they have reached North America? One possibility is that they came by boat along the eastern and western coasts of the Americas. A 12,500-year-old settlement in Monte Verde, Chile, for example, might have been reached easily by water.

"That's possible," says James Adovasio. "You had southeast Asians sailing to Australia more than 50,000 years ago."

The most startling idea is raised by Dennis Stanford, who says the Cactus Hill tools resemble even older ones found in Spain and France. He thinks that the first people to reach the Americas managed to cross the Atlantic from what is now Spain and Portugal some 17,000 to 18,000 years ago.

For now, few scientists are willing to go so far. "I think people did have the capacity to sail across the Atlantic," says Adovasio.

"But I still think 99.9 percent of the settling of the Americas occurred through the interior or along the coast from the Bering Sea."

Meadowcroft (Pa.)
Up to 17,000 years old

Clovis (N.M.)
11,200 years old

NORTH AMERICA

Cactus Hill (Va.)
16,000–18,000 years old

Topper (S.C.)
12,000 years old

ATLANTIC OCEAN

PACIFIC OCEAN

SOUTH AMERICA

Quebrada Jaguay

Quebrada Tacahuay
(Peru)
12,000 years old

Monte Verde
(Chile)
12,500 years old

TIME GRAPHIC BY LON TWEETEN

Cities and Empires

Preview of Events

| 1500 B.C. | B.C./A.D. | A.D. 1200 | A.D. 1400 |

C. 1500 B.C.
Rise of the Olmec in Mexico

C. A.D. 700
Maya civilization at its height in Central America

C. A.D. 1325
Aztec establish Tenochtitlán in Mexico

C. A.D. 1400
Inca Empire begins to expand

Artifact, c. A.D. 900

★★★★★★★★★★★
AN
American Story

Rumors of a lost city led American historian Hiram Bingham to the mountains of Peru in 1911. Bingham followed a steep mountain trail, pulling himself along by grabbing vines. After many hours of climbing, he reached a clearing. Suddenly he saw acres of huge, crumbling walls and pillars of white stone covered with vines and moss. "It fairly took my breath away," wrote Bingham. He knew that these temples and monuments were the remains of a very advanced people.

Early American Civilizations

Bingham had discovered the ruins of an early Inca city, Machu Picchu (MAH•choo PEE•choo). It is a small city—Machu Picchu covers only about five square miles (13 sq. km)—but it is an extraordinary place. Its structures, carved from the gray granite of the mountaintop, are wonders of design and craftsmanship and equal the achievements of the civilizations of Europe, Asia, and Africa.

Long before the arrival of Europeans in the early 1500s, several great civilizations, or highly developed societies, arose in present-day Mexico and in

Central and South America. These civilizations built enormous cities in thick jungles and on mountaintops that were hard to reach. They also developed complex systems for writing, counting, and tracking time.

Among the largest and most advanced of these early civilizations were the **Olmec,** the **Maya,** the **Aztec,** and the **Inca.** Each civilization spread out over hundreds of miles, included millions of people, and thrived for centuries.

The Olmec flourished between 1500 B.C. and 300 B.C. along the Gulf Coast of what are now Mexico, Guatemala, and Honduras. Olmec farmers produced enough food to sustain cities containing thousands of people. Olmec workers sculpted large stone monuments and built stone pavements and drainage systems. Their civilization strongly influenced their neighbors.

Reading Check **Identifying** What are civilizations?

The Maya

The Maya built their civilization in the steamy rain forests of present-day **Mexico, Guatemala, Honduras,** and **Belize.** They planted maize, beans, sweet potatoes, and other vegetables. They also pulled enormous stones from the earth to build monuments and pyramids that still stand today. Much of this labor was performed by enslaved people, usually prisoners of war.

Mayan Cities

By A.D. 300 the Maya had built many large cities. Each city had at least one stone pyramid. Some pyramids reached about 200 feet (60 m)—the height of a 20-story building. Steps ran up the pyramid sides to a temple on top. The largest Mayan city, **Tikal,** in present-day Guatemala, was surrounded by five pyramids.

The temples on top of the pyramids were religious and governmental centers. Wearing gold jewelry and detailed headdresses, the priests in the temples performed rituals dedicated to the Mayan gods. On special days, the city's people attended religious festivals.

The Maya believed the gods controlled everything that happened on earth. Because only priests knew the gods' wishes, the priests held great power in Mayan society and made most of the important decisions. The civilization of the Maya was a theocracy, a society ruled by religious leaders.

To keep accurate records for their religious festivals, the Maya became skilled astronomers. The Mayan priests believed that the gods were

America's *Architecture*

In Tikal and other cities, the Maya built huge pyramids where people could gather for ceremonies honoring the deities. A model of a Mayan city is shown (top left). **How were the Maya governed?**

visible in the stars, sun, and moon. They used their knowledge of the sun and stars to predict eclipses and to develop a 365-day calendar. Their desire to measure time increased their knowledge of mathematics. The Maya also developed a form of writing called **hieroglyphics.** Hieroglyphics use symbols or pictures to represent things, ideas, and sounds.

$ Economics
Transport and Trade

The Maya did not have wheeled vehicles or horses, so everything they transported overland was carried on human backs. Mayan traders traveled on a network of roads that had been carved out of the jungle. Farmers brought maize and vegetables to outdoor markets in the cities. They exchanged their crops for cotton cloth, pottery, deer meat, and salt.

Mayan traders also transported goods by water. Mayan canoes traveled up and down Mexico's east coast. The canoes carried jade statues, turquoise jewelry, cacao beans for making chocolate, and other goods to traders throughout a large area.

Decline of a Civilization

Around A.D. 900 the Maya civilization in the lowlands began to decline. By A.D. 1100 the great cities were almost ghost towns. The jungle crept back across the plazas, roads, and fields. No one knows what caused the decline. Perhaps slaves and farmers revolted against their Mayan masters. Perhaps the soil became too exhausted by erosion and fire to produce enough food for the people. The Maya civilization collapsed, but descendants of the Maya still live in parts of Mexico and Central America.

✓ Reading Check **Explaining** What is a theocracy?

The Aztec

Centuries after the fall of the Maya, a group of hunters called the Aztec wandered through central Mexico, searching for a permanent home. In 1325 they came upon an island in Lake Texcoco, today part of Mexico City. There the

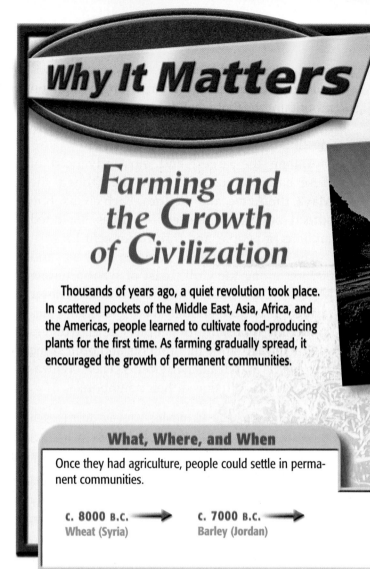

Why It Matters

Farming and the Growth of Civilization

Thousands of years ago, a quiet revolution took place. In scattered pockets of the Middle East, Asia, Africa, and the Americas, people learned to cultivate food-producing plants for the first time. As farming gradually spread, it encouraged the growth of permanent communities.

What, Where, and When

Once they had agriculture, people could settle in permanent communities.

c. 8000 B.C. ➡️
Wheat (Syria)

c. 7000 B.C. ➡️
Barley (Jordan)

Aztec saw a sign: an eagle sitting on a cactus, with a snake in its beak. That meant this island was to be their home.

Tenochtitlán

On this island emerged **Tenochtitlán** (tay•NAWCH•teet•LAHN), one of the greatest cities in the Americas. Its construction was a miracle of engineering and human labor. Directed by priests and nobles, workers toiled day and night. They pulled soil from the bottom of the lake to make causeways, or bridges of earth, linking the island and the shore. They filled parts of the lake with earth so they could grow crops.

In time the Aztec capital expanded to the mainland around the lake. At its height Tenochtitlán was the largest city in the Americas, and one of the largest in the world. Tenochtitlán also served as a center of trade, attracting thousands of merchants to its outdoor marketplaces.

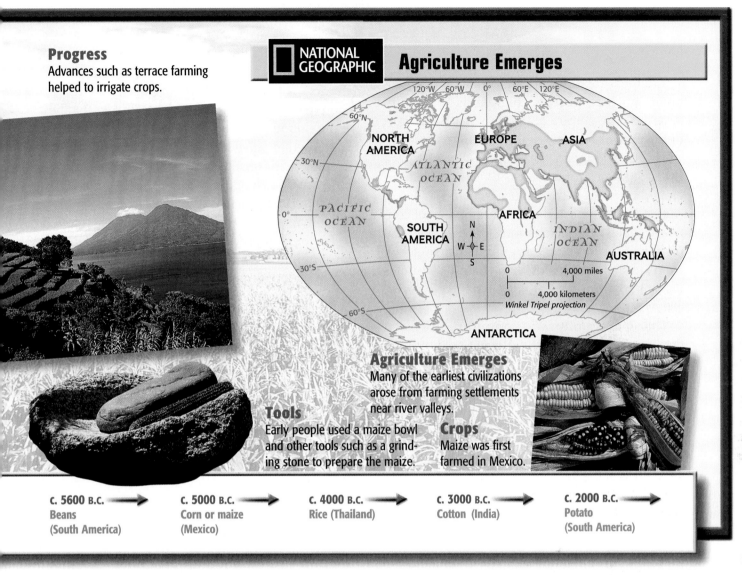

Progress
Advances such as terrace farming helped to irrigate crops.

NATIONAL GEOGRAPHIC | **Agriculture Emerges**

Agriculture Emerges
Many of the earliest civilizations arose from farming settlements near river valleys.

Tools
Early people used a maize bowl and other tools such as a grinding stone to prepare the maize.

Crops
Maize was first farmed in Mexico.

c. 5600 B.C. ➡	c. 5000 B.C. ➡	c. 4000 B.C. ➡	c. 3000 B.C. ➡	c. 2000 B.C. ➡
Beans (South America)	Corn or maize (Mexico)	Rice (Thailand)	Cotton (India)	Potato (South America)

War and Religion

The Aztec civilization grew into a military empire. In the 1400s the Aztec army marched through central and southern Mexico, conquering nearly all rival communities. Aztec warriors took everything they could carry from their victims, including maize, cotton cloth, copper, and weapons. Conquered people were forced to work as slaves in Aztec cities and villages.

Like the Maya, the Aztec organized their society around their religion. The Aztec believed that human sacrifices were necessary to keep the gods pleased and to ensure abundant harvests. Thousands of prisoners of war were sacrificed.

A Great City Remembered

The first Europeans to see the Aztec capital were awed by its splendor. In 1519, 550 Spanish soldiers entered Tenochtitlán, led by Hernán Cortés. He wrote:

❝There are forty towers at least, all of stout construction and very lofty. . . . The workmanship both in wood and stone could not be bettered anywhere.❞

Bernal Díaz del Castillo, one of the soldiers, marveled at the

❝great stone towers and temples and buildings that rose straight up out of the water.❞

Tenochtitlán, he explained, was a city of water, and many of the streets were waterways for canoes. Some of the Spanish soldiers thought that Tenochtitlán was more magnificent than Rome and the other great European capitals of the time.

✓**Reading Check** **Making Generalizations** Why was the Aztec city of Tenochtitlán a great city?

The Inca

Another great American civilization developed in the western highlands of South America. The empire of the Inca was the largest of the early American civilizations.

The Inca founded their capital city of **Cuzco** (KOOS•koh) around A.D. 1200. In 1438 an emperor named Pachacuti (PAH•chah•KOO•tee) came to the throne and began a campaign of conquest against the neighboring peoples. He and his son, Topa Inca, built an empire that stretched from north to south for more than 3,000 miles (4,800 km), from present-day Colombia to northern Argentina and Chile.

The Incan army was powerful. All men between 25 and 50 years old could be drafted to serve in the army for up to five years. Their weapons included clubs, spears, and spiked copper balls on ropes. Using slings of woven cloth, Incan soldiers could throw stones 30 yards (27 m).

Life in the Empire

At its height, the Inca Empire had a population of more than nine million, including many conquered peoples. To control this large empire, the Inca built at least 10,000 miles (16,000 km) of stone-paved roads that ran over mountains, across deserts, and through jungles. Rope bridges, made from grass, crossed canyons and rivers.

Runners carrying messages to and from the emperor linked remote outposts of the empire to Cuzco. The Inca language, Quechua (KEH•chuh•wuh), became the official language for the entire empire. Although the Inca did not have a system of writing, they developed a system of record keeping with string called *quipus* (KEE•poos). Using various lengths and colors of string, knotted in special patterns, the *quipus* carried information about resources such as grain supplies.

Although mountainous land is not well suited for farming, the Inca devised ways to produce a steady supply of food. They cut terraces, or broad platforms, into steep slopes so they could plant crops. They built stone walls on the terraces to hold the soil and plants in place. Incan farmers grew maize, squash, tomatoes, peanuts, chili peppers, melons, cotton, and potatoes.

All Inca land belonged to the emperor, who was believed to be a descendant of the sun god. Because the Inca thought that the sun god enjoyed displays of gold, they made magnificent gold jewelry and temple ornaments. The Inca also built special cities devoted to religious ceremonies. One of these cities was Machu Picchu, the mountaintop site described in "An American Story" on page 22.

✓ **Reading Check** **Explaining** How did the Inca farm steep slopes?

SECTION 2 ASSESSMENT

Checking for Understanding

1. **Key Terms** Using standard grammar, write a short paragraph in which you use all of the following terms: civilization, theocracy, hieroglyphics, terrace.
2. **Reviewing Facts** Why did the Aztec choose the location of Tenochtitlán as their permanent home?

Reviewing Themes

3. **Culture and Traditions** Why did priests hold great power in Mayan society?

Critical Thinking

4. **Making Inferences** How does trade help to enrich a civilization? Provide examples in your answer.
5. **Analyzing Information** Re-create the diagram below and give three reasons the Maya, Aztec, and Inca are considered advanced civilizations.

Advanced Civilizations

Analyzing Visuals

6. **Picturing History** Study the photograph of the pyramid on page 23. Why do you think the Maya built such large pyramids?

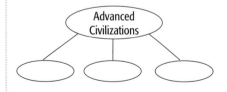

Interdisciplinary Activity

Art Compile illustrations of some of the accomplishments of the Maya, Aztec, and Inca in the areas of communication, science, and math. Use your own drawings or use photographs from newspapers and magazines.

Understanding the Parts of a Map

Why Learn This Skill?

Maps can direct you down the street or around the world. There are as many different kinds of maps as there are uses for them. Being able to read a map begins with learning about its parts.

Learning the Skill

Maps usually include a key, a compass rose, and a scale bar. The map key explains the meaning of special colors, symbols, and lines used on the map.

After reading the map key, look for the compass rose. It is the direction marker that shows the cardinal directions of north, south, east, and west.

A measuring line, often called a scale bar, helps you estimate distance on a map. The map's scale tells you what distance on the earth is represented by the measurement on the scale bar. For example, 1 inch (2.54 cm) on the map may represent 100 miles (160.9 km) on the earth.

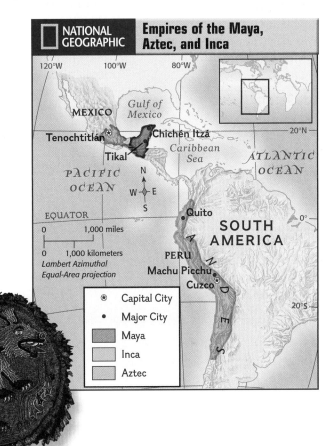

NATIONAL GEOGRAPHIC — **Empires of the Maya, Aztec, and Inca**

⊛	Capital City
•	Major City
	Maya
	Inca
	Aztec

Lambert Azimuthal Equal-Area projection

Practicing the Skill

The map on this page shows where the ancient Maya, Aztec, and Inca built their empires in North America and South America. Look at the parts of this map, then answer the questions that follow.

❶ What information is given in the key?

❷ What color shows the Inca Empire?

❸ What direction would you travel to go from Tenochtitlán to Chichén Itzá?

❹ About how many miles long was the Inca Empire?

❺ What was the capital of the Aztec Empire?

Applying the Skill

Drawing a Map Picture a mental image of your house or room. Draw a map showing the location of various areas. Include a map key explaining any symbols or colors you use. Also include a scale bar explaining the size of your map compared to the real area. Finally, add a compass rose and title to your map.

Glencoe's **Skillbuilder Interactive Workbook CD-ROM, Level 1,** provides instruction and practice in key social studies skills.

SECTION 3 North American Peoples

Guide to Reading

Main Idea
Many different cultures lived in North America before the arrival of the Europeans.

Key Terms
pueblo, drought, adobe, federation

Reading Strategy
Taking Notes As you read Section 3, re-create the diagram below and identify locations and ways of living for each culture.

Culture	Where they lived	How they lived
Anasazi		
Mound Builders		
Inuit		

Read to Learn
• what early people lived in North America.
• how different Native American groups adapted to their environments.

Section Theme
Culture and Traditions Early North Americans developed new societies.

Preview of Events

| ♦ 1000 B.C. | ♦ B.C./A.D. | ♦ A.D. 1000 | ♦ A.D. 1300 |

C. 1000 B.C.
First ceremonial mounds built

C. A.D. 1000
Anasazi build pueblos in North America

C. A.D. 1100
Cahokia is built

C. A.D. 1300
Hohokam civilization begins to decline

✦✦✦✦✦✦✦✦✦
AN
American Story
✦✦✦

Ancient jar, American Southwest

In the summer of 1991, a helicopter passenger made an amazing discovery in Arizona's Coconino National Forest. As the helicopter hovered among the sandstone cliffs, the sun shone into a cave 200 feet (61 m) below the rim of one cliff. Standing in the opening of the cave were three large pottery jars. The three jars had been sitting, untouched and unseen, for more than 700 years. The jars and other objects found in the cave were left there by the Sinagua. These people lived hundreds of years ago in what we now call Arizona. The Sinagua are just one of many Native American peoples who are now being studied by archaeologists and historians.

Early Native Americans

Many Native American cultures rose, flourished, and disappeared in North America long before Europeans arrived in the 1500s. Among the most advanced of these early cultures were the Hohokam and Anasazi of the Southwest and the Mound Builders of the Ohio River valley.

The Hohokam

The dry, hot desert of present-day Arizona was home to the **Hohokam** people. They may have come from Mexico about 300 B.C. The Hohokam culture flourished from about A.D. 300 to A.D. 1300 in an area bordered by the Gila and Salt River valleys.

The Hohokam were experts at squeezing every drop of available water from the sun-baked soil. Their way of life depended on the irrigation channels they dug to carry river water into their fields. In addition to hundreds of miles of irrigation channels, the Hohokam left behind pottery, carved stone, and shells etched with acid. The shells came from trade with coastal peoples.

The Anasazi

The **Anasazi** lived around the same time as the Hohokam, roughly A.D. 1 to A.D. 1300, in the area known as the Four Corners (the meeting place of the present-day states of Utah, Colorado, Arizona, and New Mexico). There they built great stone dwellings that the Spanish explorers later called pueblos (PWEH•blohs), or villages. **Pueblo Bonito,** one of the most spectacular of the Anasazi pueblos, can still be seen in New Mexico. The huge semicircular structure of stone and sun-dried earth resembles an apartment building. It is four stories high and has hundreds of rooms. Archaeologists have found traces of a complex road system linking Pueblo Bonito with other villages. This suggests that Pueblo Bonito was an important trade or religious center for the Anasazi.

The Anasazi also built dwellings in the walls of steep cliffs. Cliff dwellings were easy to defend and offered protection from winter weather. **Mesa Verde** in Colorado, one of the largest and most elaborate cliff dwellings, held several thousand inhabitants.

In about 1300 the Anasazi began leaving the pueblos and cliff dwellings to settle in smaller communities. Their large villages may have been abandoned because of droughts, long periods of little rainfall, during which their crops dried up.

Kivas at Pueblo Bonito

Picturing **History**

Pueblo Bonito had more than 800 rooms and 32 kivas, or underground ceremonial chambers. Today, the ruins of Pueblo Bonito are part of Chaco Culture National Historical Park in northwestern New Mexico. **What other kind of dwellings were built by the Anasazi?**

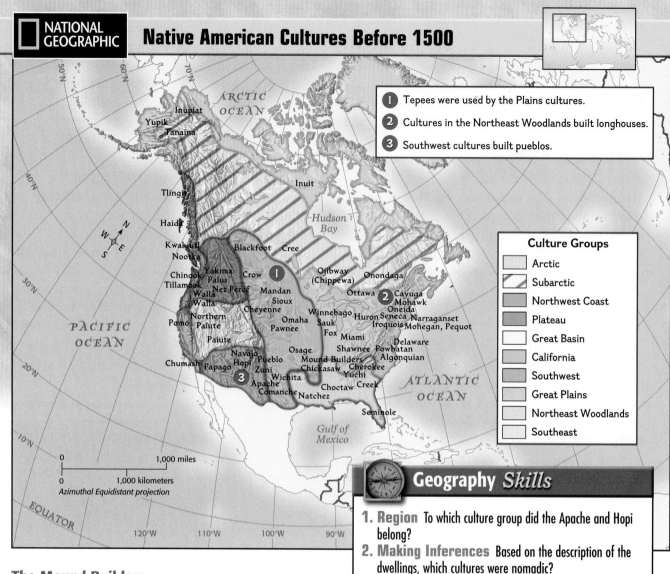

1 Tepees were used by the Plains cultures.

2 Cultures in the Northeast Woodlands built longhouses.

3 Southwest cultures built pueblos.

Culture Groups

- Arctic
- Subarctic
- Northwest Coast
- Plateau
- Great Basin
- California
- Southwest
- Great Plains
- Northeast Woodlands
- Southeast

0   1,000 miles

0   1,000 kilometers
Azimuthal Equidistant projection

Geography *Skills*

1. Region To which culture group did the Apache and Hopi belong?

2. Making Inferences Based on the description of the dwellings, which cultures were nomadic?

The Mound Builders

The early cultures of Mexico and Central America appear to have influenced people living in lands to the north. In central North America, prehistoric Native Americans built thousands of mounds of earth that look very much like the stone pyramids of the Maya and the Aztec. Some of the mounds contained burial chambers. Some were topped with temples, as in the Mayan and Aztec cultures.

The mounds are dotted across the landscape from present-day Pennsylvania to the Mississippi River valley. They have been found as far north as the Great Lakes and as far south as Florida. Archaeologists think that the first mounds were built about 1000 B.C. They were not the work of a single group but of many different peoples, who are referred to as the **Mound Builders.**

Among the earliest Mound Builders were the **Adena,** hunters and gatherers who flourished in the Ohio Valley by 800 B.C. They were followed by the **Hopewell** people, who lived between 200 B.C. and A.D. 500. Farmers and traders, the Hopewell built huge burial mounds in the shape of birds, bears, and snakes. One of them, the **Great Serpent Mound,** looks like a giant snake winding across the ground. Archaeologists have found freshwater pearls, shells, cloth, and copper in the mounds. The objects indicate a widespread pattern of trade.

Cahokia

The largest settlement of the Mound Builders was **Cahokia** (kuh•HOH•kee•uh) in present-day Illinois. This city, built after A.D. 900 by a

Native American Population

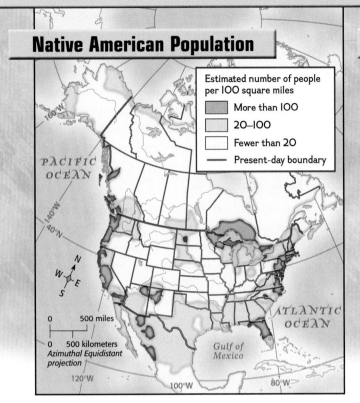

Estimated number of people per 100 square miles
- More than 100
- 20–100
- Fewer than 20
- Present-day boundary

PACIFIC OCEAN

0   500 miles
0   500 kilometers
Azimuthal Equidistant projection

ATLANTIC OCEAN

Gulf of Mexico

Hunters, Gatherers, and Fishers

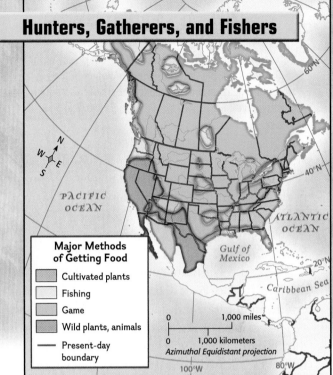

Major Methods of Getting Food
- Cultivated plants
- Fishing
- Game
- Wild plants, animals
- Present-day boundary

PACIFIC OCEAN

ATLANTIC OCEAN

Gulf of Mexico

Caribbean Sea

0   1,000 miles
0   1,000 kilometers
Azimuthal Equidistant projection

people called the Mississippians, may have had 16,000 or more residents. The largest mound in Cahokia, the Monks Mound, rises nearly 100 feet (30 m). When it was built, it was probably the highest structure north of Mexico.

Cahokia resembled the great cities of Mexico, even though it was nearly 2,000 miles away. The city was dominated by the great pyramid-shaped mound. A temple crowned the summit—perhaps a place where priests studied the movements of the sun and stars or where the priest-ruler of Cahokia lived. A legend of the Natchez people, descendants of the Mississippians, hints of a direct link to Mexico:

❝Before we came into this land we lived yonder under the sun [the speaker pointed southwest toward Mexico]. . . . Our nation extended itself along the great water [the Gulf of Mexico] where this large river [the Mississippi] loses itself.❞

✔Reading Check **Identifying** In what area did the Anasazi live?

Other Native North Americans

Although the civilizations of the Hohokam, the Anasazi, and the Mound Builders eventually faded away, other Native American cultures arose to take their place. Around the time that Europeans began arriving, North America was home to many different societies.

Peoples of the North

The people who settled in the northernmost part of North America, in the lands around the Arctic Ocean, are called the **Inuit.** Some scientists think the Inuit were the last migrants to cross the land bridge into North America.

The Inuit had many skills that helped them survive in the cold Arctic climate. They may have brought some of these skills from northern Siberia, probably their original home. In the winter the Inuit built igloos, low-lying structures of snow blocks, which protected them from severe weather. Their clothing of furs and sealskins was both warm and waterproof. The Inuit were hunters and fishers. In the coastal waters, they pursued whales, seals, and walruses in small,

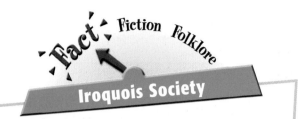

Fact Fiction Folklore

Iroquois Society

Powerful Iroquois Women did hold great power among the Iroquois people. Iroquois women owned houses, crops, and fields and chose the members of the Iroquois governing council.

skin-covered boats. On land they hunted caribou, large deerlike animals that lived in the far north. The Inuit made clothing from caribou skins and burned seal oil in lamps.

Peoples of the West

The mild climate and dependable food sources of the West Coast created a favorable environment for many different groups.

The peoples of the northwestern coast, such as the **Tlingit** (TLIHNG•kuht), **Haida,** and **Chinook,** developed a way of life that used the resources of the forest and the sea. They built wooden houses and made canoes, cloth, and baskets from tree bark. Using spears and traps, they fished for salmon along the coast and in rivers such as the Columbia. This large fish was the main food of the northwestern people. They preserved the salmon by smoking it over fires.

Salmon was also important for the people of the plateau region, the area between the Cascade Mountains and the Rocky Mountains. The **Nez Perce** (NEHZ PUHRS) and **Yakima** peoples fished the rivers, hunted deer in forests, and gathered roots and berries. The root of the camas plant, a relative of the lily, was an important part of their diet. The plateau peoples lived in earthen houses.

Present-day California was home to a great variety of cultures. Along the northern coast, Native Americans fished for their food. In the more barren environment of the southern deserts, nomadic groups wandered from place to place collecting roots and seeds. In the central valley, the **Pomo** gathered acorns and pounded them into flour. As in many Native American cultures, the women of the Pomo did most of the gathering and flour making.

In the Great Basin between the Sierra Nevada and the Rocky Mountains, Native Americans found ways to live in the dry climate. The soil was too hard and rocky for farming, so peoples such as the **Ute** (YOOT) and **Shoshone** (shuh•SHOHN) traveled in search of food. They ate small game, pine nuts, juniper berries, roots, and some insects. Instead of making permanent settlements, the Great Basin people created temporary shelters of branches and reeds.

Peoples of the Southwest

Descendants of the Anasazi formed the **Hopi,** the **Acoma,** and the **Zuni** peoples of the Southwest. They built their homes from a type of sun-dried mud brick called adobe. They raised corn or maize as their basic food. They also grew beans, squash, melons, pumpkins, and fruit. The people of the Southwest also took part in a sophisticated trade network that extended throughout the Southwest and into Mexico.

In the 1500s two new groups settled in the region—the **Apache** and the **Navajo.** Unlike the other peoples of the Southwest, the Apache and Navajo were hunters and gatherers. They hunted deer and other game. Eventually the Navajo settled into stationary communities and built square houses called hogans. In addition to hunting and gathering, they began to grow maize and beans. They also began raising sheep in the 1600s.

Peoples of the Plains

The peoples of the Great Plains were nomadic; villages were temporary, lasting only for a growing season or two. When the people moved from place to place, they dragged their homes—cone-shaped skin tents called tepees—behind them. The men hunted antelope, deer, and buffalo. The women tended plots of maize, squash, and beans.

When the Spanish brought horses to Mexico in the 1500s, some got loose. In time horses made their way north. Native Americans captured and tamed the wild horses, and the Comanche, the **Dakota,** and other Plains peoples became skilled riders. They learned to hunt on horseback and to use the horses in warfare, attacking their enemies with long spears, bows and arrows, clubs, and knives.

Citizenship

Peoples of the East and Southeast

The people who lived in the woodlands of eastern North America formed complex political systems to govern their nations. The **Iroquois** (IHR•uh•KWAWIH) and **Cherokee** had formal law codes and formed federations, governments that linked different groups.

The Iroquois lived near Canada in what is now northern New York State. There were five Iroquois groups or nations: the **Onondaga,** the **Seneca,** the **Mohawk,** the **Oneida,** and the **Cayuga.** These groups warred with each other until the late 1500s, when they joined to form the Iroquois League, also called the Iroquois Confederacy.

Iroquois women occupied positions of power in their communities. According to the constitution of the Iroquois League, women chose the 50 men who served on the league council.

The Iroquois constitution was written down after the Europeans came to North America. It describes the Iroquois peoples' desire for peace:

❝I am Dekanawidah and with the Five Nations' Confederate Lords I plant the Tree of Great Peace. . . . Roots have spread out from the Tree of the Great Peace, one to the north, one to the east, one to the south and one to the west. ❞

The Southeast was also a woodlands area, but with a warmer climate than the eastern woodlands. The Creek, Chickasaw, and Cherokee were among the region's Native American peoples. Many Creek lived in loosely knit farming communities in present-day Georgia and Alabama. There they grew corn, tobacco, squash, and other crops. The Chickasaw, most of whom lived farther west in what is now Mississippi, farmed the river bottomlands. The Cherokee farmed in the mountains of Georgia and the Carolinas.

Wherever they lived in North America, the first Americans developed ways of life that were well suited to their environments. In the 1500s, however, the Native Americans met people whose cultures, beliefs, and ways of life were different from anything they had known or ever seen. These newcomers were the Europeans, and their arrival would change the Native Americans' world forever.

HISTORY Online

Student Web Activity
Visit tarvol1.glencoe.com and click on **Chapter 1— Student Web Activities** for an activity on Native American cultures.

✓ **Reading Check** **Describing** How did the use of the horse change the lifestyle of Native Americans on the Great Plains?

SECTION 3 ASSESSMENT

Checking for Understanding

1. **Key Terms** Use each of these terms in a complete sentence that will help explain its meaning: pueblo, drought, adobe, federation.

2. **Reviewing Facts** Identify clues that led archaeologists to believe that the Mound Builders were influenced by other cultures.

Reviewing Themes

3. **Culture and Traditions** What organization did the Iroquois form to promote peace among their people?

Critical Thinking

4. **Making Generalizations** Why was the environment of the West Coast favorable for settlement by so many groups of Native Americans?

5. **Comparing** Re-create the diagram below and explain how Native American cultures differed from one another by describing their locations and ways of living.

Culture	Region	Shelter
Tlingit		
Zuni		
Dakota		

Analyzing Visuals

6. **Geography Skills** Study the map on page 30. What groups lived in California? What groups lived in the Southeast?

Interdisciplinary Activity

Geography Create or sketch a model of a home that a Native American might have built. Use natural materials that exist in the area where you live and label the materials on your diagram. Consider the climate of your area in your design.

Chapter Summary

The First Americans

The first Americans begin to adapt to their surroundings.

Societies in South and Central America and in Mexico create powerful empires.

The Inca, Maya, and Aztec

- The **Inca** develop a complex political system. They also build a large network of paved roads.

- The **Maya** create a written language and develop new ways of farming.

- The **Aztec** build a large empire, stretching from north-central Mexico to the border of Guatemala, and from the Atlantic Ocean to the Pacific Ocean.

People of North America

- The people of North America do not develop empires as large as those of the Inca, Maya, and Aztec.

- Among the most advanced of the early cultures are the Hohokam and Anasazi of the Southwest and the Mound Builders of the Ohio River valley.

- People who settle in a particular region develop a common culture.

- In the **Southwest,** Native American peoples adapt to their harsh environment by improving techniques of irrigation to farm the land.

- Most of the people of the **Great Plains** were nomadic. They lived in tepees, and used horses, spears, and bows and arrows to hunt deer, antelope, and buffalo.

- Native Americans of the Northeast form the **Iroquois League** to solve disputes.

Reviewing Key Terms

On a sheet of paper, define the following terms.

1. archaeology
2. artifact
3. Ice Age
4. nomad
5. carbon dating
6. culture
7. civilization
8. hieroglyphics
9. pueblo
10. federation

Reviewing Key Facts

11. For what reasons did Asians cross the land bridge to the Americas?
12. What regions did the land bridge connect?
13. What was the first crop raised by Native Americans in Mexico?
14. What does carbon dating measure?
15. What are hieroglyphics?
16. What regions were under Inca control?
17. What were two advantages of living in dwellings built into the side of cliffs?
18. What type of dwelling was common among the people of the Southwest?
19. In what region did the Tlingit, Haida, and the Chinook peoples live?
20. What groups formed the Iroquois League?

Critical Thinking

21. **Comparing** Re-create the diagram below and explain how the environment of Native Americans who lived in the Northwest differed from the environment of those who lived in the Southwest.

Location	Environment
Northwest	
Southwest	

22. **Analyzing Themes: Culture and Traditions** Religion was an important part of life in many Native American civilizations. What role did priests play in Mayan society?

23. **Analyzing Information** In what ways did the Inca and Aztec use war to increase their power?

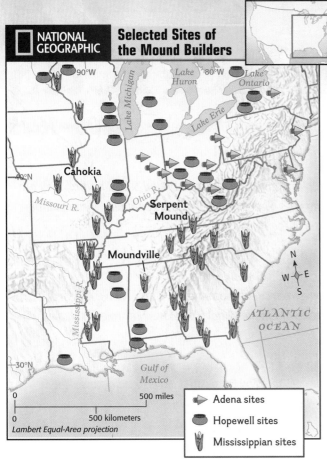

NATIONAL GEOGRAPHIC **Selected Sites of the Mound Builders**

Cahokia

Serpent Mound

Moundville

Missouri R.

Ohio R.

Mississippi R.

Lake Michigan

Lake Huron

Lake Erie

Lake Ontario

ATLANTIC OCEAN

Gulf of Mexico

90°W 80°W

40°N

30°N

N W E S

0   500 miles
0   500 kilometers
Lambert Equal-Area projection

 Adena sites
Hopewell sites
Mississippian sites

 Geography and History Activity

Study the map above and answer the questions that follow.

24. Location Along what two major rivers did many of the Mound Builders settle?

25. Place Near which river did the Adena build most of their settlements?

26. Movement Of the Adena, Hopewell, and Mississippian cultures, which settled the farthest east?

Practicing Skills

Understanding the Parts of a Map *Use the key, compass rose, and scale bar on the map of Native American cultures on page 30 to answer these questions.*

27. What does the map key highlight?

28. About how far from the Gulf of Mexico did the Omaha people live?

29. Which Native American peoples settled in the Southwest region?

30. Which people lived farthest west—the Pawnee or the Miami?

Self-Check Quiz
Visit tarvol1.glencoe.com and click on **Chapter 1—Self-Check Quizzes** to prepare for the chapter test.

Technology Activity

31. Using the Internet Search the Internet for a Web site created by a modern Native American group. Based on information you find at the site, explain the group's goals.

Citizenship Cooperative Activity

32. Research Work with a partner to investigate the early history of your community using primary and secondary sources. Find out when and why it was founded. Who were the first settlers and early leaders? How did the government change over the years? Prepare a report for your class about what you have discovered.

Economics Activity

33. Create a cause-and-effect chart. Write on your chart: *Cause: The development of farming changed the way early nomads lived.* Then, describe at least two effects.

Alternative Assessment

34. Portfolio Writing Activity Research information about one aspect of Aztec or Iroquois life. Present your information in a report to the other students.

Standardized Test Practice

Directions: Choose the *best* answer to the following question.

Because the Mayan civilization was a theocracy, the most powerful Maya were

A warriors.   **C** priests.

B craftsmen.   **D** enslaved people.

Test-Taking Tip:
This question asks you to draw an inference. What is the meaning of the word *theocracy*? Understanding the definition will help to answer the question.

Exploring the Americas

1400–1625

Why It Matters

Although the English have been the major influence on United States history, they are only part of the story. Beginning with Native Americans and continuing through time, people from many cultures came to the Americas.

The Impact Today

The Americas today consist of people from cultures around the globe. Native Americans, Spanish, Africans, and others discussed in Chapter 2 have all played key roles in shaping the culture we now call American.

The American Republic to 1877 *Video The chapter 2 video, "Exploring the Americas," presents the challenges faced by European explorers, and discusses the reasons they came to the Americas.*

1492
• Christopher Columbus reaches America

1497
• John Cabot sails to Newfoundland

1513
• Balboa crosses the Isthmus of Panama

The Americas

1400   1450   1500

World

1429
• Joan of Arc defeats the English at French town of Orléans

c. 1456
• Johannes Gutenberg uses movable metal type in printing

c. 1500
• Songhai Empire rises in Africa
• Rome becomes a major center of Renaissance culture

Founding of Maryland by Emanuel Leutze Native Americans lived in North America long before the Europeans arrived.

1534
- Cartier claims Canada for France

c. 1570
- Iroquois form League of Five Nations

1607
- Jamestown settled

1620
- Pilgrims found Plymouth

1550   1600

1517
- Martin Luther promotes Church reform

1522
- Magellan's crew completes first world voyage

1588
- England defeats Spanish Armada

HISTORY Online

Chapter Overview
Visit tarvol1.glencoe.com and click on **Chapter 2— Chapter Overviews** to preview chapter information.

SECTION 1 A Changing World

Guide to Reading

Main Idea
New knowledge and ideas led Europeans to explore overseas.

Key Terms
classical, Renaissance, technology, astrolabe, caravel, pilgrimage, mosque

Reading Strategy
Determining Cause and Effect As you read the section, re-create the diagram below and identify three reasons Europeans increased overseas exploration.

Causes of European exploration

Read to Learn
• how technology made long sea voyages possible.
• how great civilizations flourished in Africa.

Section Theme
Culture and Traditions The spirit of the Renaissance changed the way Europeans thought about the world.

Preview of Events

♦1200	♦1300	♦1400
1271 Marco Polo travels to China from Italy	**1324** Mansa Musa makes a pilgrimage to Makkah	**c. 1400** Renaissance spreads throughout Europe

Marco Polo

A European Story

In 1271 Marco Polo set off from the city of Venice on a great trek across Asia to China. Only 17 years old at the time, Polo journeyed with his father and uncle, both Venetian merchants. Traveling on camels for more than three years, the merchants crossed almost 7,000 miles (11,265 km) of mountains and deserts. Finally they reached the palace of Kublai Khan (KOO•bluh KAHN), the Mongol emperor of China. There Marco Polo spent 17 years working for the Khan and learning much about China's advanced culture.

Expanding Horizons

For centuries after the fall of the Roman Empire, the people of western Europe were isolated from the rest of the world. Their world, dominated by the Catholic Church, was divided into many small kingdoms and city-states.

Meanwhile, the religion known as Islam swept across the Middle East and Africa. The followers of Islam are known as Muslims. As Muslim power grew,

European Christians became fearful of losing access to the Holy Land, the birthplace of Christianity, in what is now Israel.

Beginning in 1095, the Europeans launched the first of nine expeditions, known as the Crusades, to regain control of their holy sites. The Crusades brought west Europeans into contact with the Middle East. Arab merchants sold spices, sugar, silk and other goods from China and India to the Europeans. As European interest in Asia grew, Marco Polo returned from China. In 1296, he began writing an account of his trip describing the marvels of Asia. Polo's *Travels* was widely read in Europe. Little did he realize that 200 years later his book about the East would inspire Christopher Columbus and others to sail in the opposite direction to reach the same destination.

$ Economics

The Growth of Trade

Merchants could make a fortune selling goods from the Orient. Wealthy Europeans clamored for cinnamon, pepper, cloves, and other spices. They also wanted perfumes, silks, and precious stones. Buying the goods from Arab traders in the Middle East, the merchants sent them overland by caravan to the **Mediterranean Sea** and then by ship to Italian ports. The cities of Venice, Genoa, and Pisa prospered and became centers of the growing East-West trade. The Arab merchants, however, charged very high prices. As demand for Asian goods increased, Europeans began looking for a route to the East that bypassed the Arab merchants.

The Growth of Ideas

In the 1300s a powerful new spirit emerged in the Italian city-states and spread throughout Europe. The development of banking and the expansion of trade with Asia made Italian merchants wealthy. These citizens were able to pursue an interest in the region's past and learn more about the glorious civilizations of ancient Rome and Greece.

Because they wanted to improve their knowledge of people and of the world, Italians studied the classical—ancient Greek and Roman—works with new interest. Scholars translated Greek manuscripts on philosophy, poetry, and science. Many thinkers of this period began to take a more experimental approach to science; they tested new and old theories and evaluated the results.

Influenced by the classical texts, a great many authors began to write about the individual and the universe. Artists studied the sculpture and architecture of the classical world. They particularly admired the harmony and balance in Greek art, with its realistic way of portraying people.

The Renaissance

This period of intellectual and artistic creativity became known as the Renaissance (REH•nuh•SAHNTS). A French word meaning "rebirth," it refers to the renewed interest in classical Greek and Roman learning. Over the next two centuries, the Renaissance spread north, south, and west, reaching Spain and northern Europe in the 1400s.

The spirit of the Renaissance dramatically changed the way Europeans thought about themselves and the world. It encouraged them to pursue new ideas and set new goals; it paved the way for an age of exploration and discovery.

✓ **Reading Check** **Describing** What cultures influenced the Renaissance?

Powerful Nations Emerge

During the 1400s the population of western Europe began to increase. Merchants and bankers in the growing cities wanted to expand their businesses through foreign trade. If they could buy spices and silks from the East directly, without going through the Arab and Italian cities, they could earn huge profits. They looked for alternatives to the overland route through the Middle East.

The development of large nation-states in western Europe helped expand trade and interest in overseas exploration. For many years Europe had been a patchwork of small states. Political power was divided among local lords, and few people traveled outside their region.

By the 1400s, however, a new type of centralized state was emerging in western Europe. Strong monarchs came to power in Spain, Portugal, England, and France. They began to establish national laws, courts, taxes, and armies to replace those of local lords. These ambitious kings and queens sought ways to increase trade and make their countries stronger and wealthier.

Reading Check **Explaining** What resulted from the emergence of large nation-states?

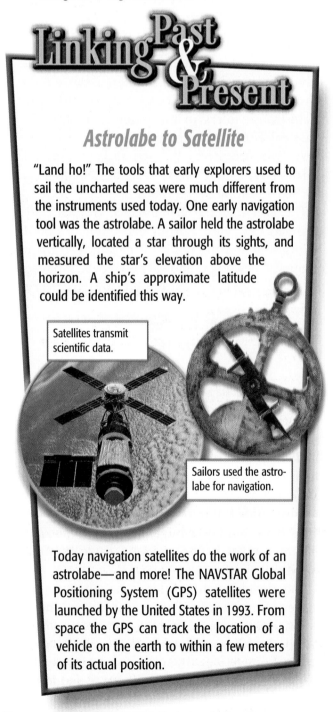

Linking Past & Present

Astrolabe to Satellite

"Land ho!" The tools that early explorers used to sail the uncharted seas were much different from the instruments used today. One early navigation tool was the astrolabe. A sailor held the astrolabe vertically, located a star through its sights, and measured the star's elevation above the horizon. A ship's approximate latitude could be identified this way.

Satellites transmit scientific data.

Sailors used the astrolabe for navigation.

Today navigation satellites do the work of an astrolabe—and more! The NAVSTAR Global Positioning System (GPS) satellites were launched by the United States in 1993. From space the GPS can track the location of a vehicle on the earth to within a few meters of its actual position.

Technology's Impact

Advances in technology—the use of scientific knowledge for practical purposes—paved the way for European voyages of exploration. In the 1450s the introduction of movable type and the printing press made it much easier to print books. Now more people could have access to books and to new information. After its publication in print form in 1477, many Europeans read Marco Polo's *Travels*.

Geography

Better Maps

Maps were a problem for early navigators. Most maps were inaccurate because they were drawn from the often-mistaken impressions of traders and travelers. Little by little, cartographers, or mapmakers, gradually improved their skills.

Using the reports of explorers and information from Arab geographers, mapmakers made more accurate land and sea maps. These maps showed the direction of ocean currents. They also showed lines of latitude, which measured the distance north and south of the Equator.

Better instruments were developed for navigating the seas. Sailors could determine their latitude while at sea with an astrolabe, an instrument that measured the position of stars. Europeans also acquired the magnetic compass, a Chinese invention that began to be widely used in Europe and the Middle East in the 1200s. The compass allowed sailors to determine their direction when they were far from land.

Better Ships

Advances in ship design allowed shipbuilders to build sailing vessels capable of long ocean voyages. The stern rudder and the triangular sail made it possible for ships to sail into the wind. Both of these new features came from the Arabs. In the late 1400s, the Portuguese developed the three-masted caravel. The caravel sailed faster than earlier ships and carried more cargo and food supplies. It also could float in shallow water, which allowed sailors to explore inlets and to sail their ships up to the beach to make repairs. A Venetian sailor called the caravels "the best ships that sailed the seas."

By the mid-1400s the Italian ports faced increased competition for foreign trade. Powerful countries like Portugal and Spain began searching for sea routes to Asia, launching a new era of exploration. Portugal began its exploration by sending ships down the west coast of Africa, which Europeans had never visited before.

✔ **Reading Check** **Explaining** How did the caravel affect overseas exploration in the fifteenth and sixteenth centuries?

African Kingdoms

Powerful kingdoms flourished in Africa south of the Sahara between 400 and 1600. The region was rich with natural resources. Africans mined gold, copper, and iron ore. Trade with Islamic societies in North Africa brought both wealth and Islamic ideas and customs to the West African kingdoms.

City-states on the east coast of Africa also benefited from trade. There Arab traders from the Middle East brought cotton, silk, and porcelain from India and China to exchange for ivory and metals from the African interior.

As the Portuguese sailed south along the African coastline in the mid-1400s, they set up trading posts. From these, they traded for gold and for slaves.

Ghana—A Trading Empire

Between 400 and 1100, a vast trading empire called **Ghana** emerged in West Africa. Well located between the salt mines of the Sahara and the gold mines to the south, Ghana prospered from the taxes the leaders of the empire imposed on trade.

Caravans with gold, ivory, and slaves from Ghana crossed the Sahara to North Africa. Muslim traders from North Africa loaded caravans

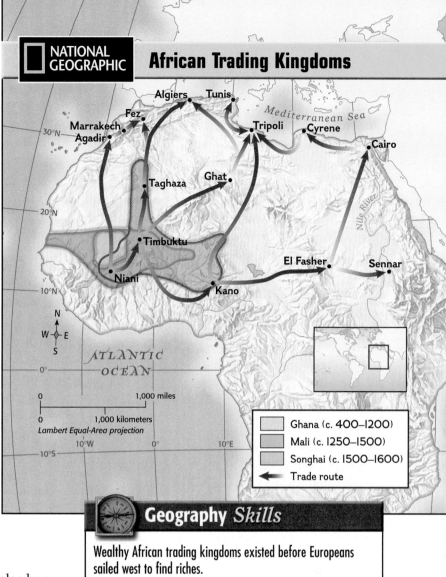

National Geographic — African Trading Kingdoms

Ghana (c. 400–1200)
Mali (c. 1250–1500)
Songhai (c. 1500–1600)
← Trade route

Geography Skills

Wealthy African trading kingdoms existed before Europeans sailed west to find riches.
1. Location What direction is Ghat from Timbuktu?
2. Comparing What African kingdom covered the smallest area?

with salt, cloth, and brass and headed back to Ghana. As a result of their trading contacts, many West Africans became Muslims.

In 1076 people from North Africa called Almoravids attacked Ghana and disrupted its trade routes. While Ghana fought the Almoravids, new trade routes and gold mines opened up to the east, bypassing Ghana. Ghana then began to decline, and new states emerged in the region.

Mali—A Powerful Kingdom

Mali, one of the new states, grew into a powerful kingdom. The people of Mali developed their own trade routes across the desert to North Africa. By the late 1200s, Mali's expanded territory included the former kingdom of Ghana. The country was mainly agricultural, but gold mines enriched the kingdom.

Mali's greatest king, **Mansa Musa,** ruled from 1312 to 1337. He was described at the time as "the most powerful, the richest, the most fortunate, the most feared by his enemies, and the most able to do good to those around him."

In 1324 Musa, a Muslim, made a grand pilgrimage to the Muslim holy city of **Makkah** (also spelled Mecca) in western Saudi Arabia. A pilgrimage is a journey to a holy place. Arab writers reported that Musa traveled with a huge military escort. Ahead of him marched 500 royal servants who carried gold to distribute along the way. Musa returned to Mali with an Arab architect who built great mosques, Muslim houses of worship, in the capital of **Timbuktu.** Under Mansa Musa, Timbuktu became an important center of Islamic art and learning.

The Songhai Empire

Some years later the Songhai (SAWNG•hy) people, who lived along the **Niger River,** rose up against Mali rule. They built a navy to control the Niger and in 1468 captured Timbuktu. In the late 1400s, **Askìya Muhammad** brought the Songhai empire to the height of its power. Askìya strengthened his country and made it the largest in the history of West Africa. He built many schools and encouraged trade with Europe and Asia.

HISTORY Online

Student Web Activity
Visit tarvol1.glencoe.com and click on **Chapter 2— Student Web Activities** for an activity on African kingdoms.

Plan of Government

Devoted to Islam, Askìya introduced laws based on the teachings of the holy book of Islam, the Quran. He appointed Muslim judges to uphold Islamic laws. Askìya also developed a sophisticated plan for his country's government. He divided Songhai into five provinces. For each province he appointed a governor, a tax collector, a court of judges, and a trade inspector. Everyone in Songhai used the same weights and measures and followed the same legal system.

In the late 1500s, the North African kingdom of Morocco sent an army across the Sahara to attack Songhai gold-trading centers. Armed with guns and cannons, the Moroccans easily defeated the Songhai.

Reading Check **Identifying** Which African kingdom thrived between A.D. 400 and A.D. 1100?

SECTION 1 ASSESSMENT

Checking for Understanding

1. **Key Terms** Write sentences in which you use the following groups of terms: classical and Renaissance; technology, astrolabe, and caravel; pilgrimage and mosque.

2. **Reviewing Facts** Name three technological advances that furthered European exploration. Describe how these advances helped explorers.

Reviewing Themes

3. **Culture and Traditions** How did the Islamic religion spread to the early kingdoms of Africa? What is the name of the holy book of Islam?

Critical Thinking

4. **Drawing Conclusions** Why do you think the Renaissance began in Italy and not in another part of Europe?

5. **Comparing** Re-create the diagram below and compare three African kingdoms. In the outer spaces, describe each kingdom. In the shared space, identify similarities between them.

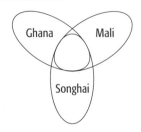

Analyzing Visuals

6. **Geography Skills** Review the map of the African trading kingdoms on page 41. Which of the trading kingdoms was established earliest? In which region of Africa did the three trading kingdoms develop?

Interdisciplinary Activity

Science Select a technological advance that has occurred during your lifetime. Compare its effects to the effects of one of the technological advances described in Section 1. Which has had the greater impact on society? Explain.

SECTION 2 · Early Exploration

Main Idea
In search of trade routes, Portuguese explorers ushered in an era of overseas exploration.

Key Terms
line of demarcation, strait, circumnavigate

Reading Strategy
Organizing Information As you read the section, re-create the diagram below and identify explorers, when they traveled, and where they went.

Explorer	Date(s)	Region

Read to Learn
- how Portugal led the way in overseas exploration.
- about Columbus's plan for sailing to Asia.

Section Theme
Geography and History In 1400 Europeans had a limited knowledge of the geography of the world.

Preview of Events

1000	1200	1400	1600

c. 1000
Leif Eriksson lands in present-day Newfoundland

1488
Bartholomeu Dias reaches the Indian Ocean

1492
Columbus lands in the Americas

1498
Vasco da Gama reaches India

1519
Magellan begins circumnavigation of the world

A European Story

Compass

More than 150 years after the death of Marco Polo, a young Italian sea captain—Christopher Columbus—sat down to read Polo's *Travels* with interest. Columbus read what Polo had to say about the islands of Cipangu, or present-day Japan. According to Polo, Cipangu lay some 1,500 miles (2,414 km) off the eastern shore of Asia. Because the earth is round, Columbus reasoned, a person sailing west from Europe should quickly reach Cipangu. It could be much closer than anyone thought.

Unfortunately, Marco Polo—and therefore Columbus—was wrong.

Seeking New Trade Routes

The maps that Columbus and the first European explorers used did not include America. They showed three continents—Europe, Asia, and Africa—merged together in a gigantic landmass, or large area of land. This landmass was bordered by oceans. Some explorers thought that the Western (Atlantic) and Eastern (Pacific) Oceans ran together to form what they called the **Ocean Sea.** At the time, no one realized that another huge landmass was missing from the maps. They also did not realize that the oceans were as large as they are.

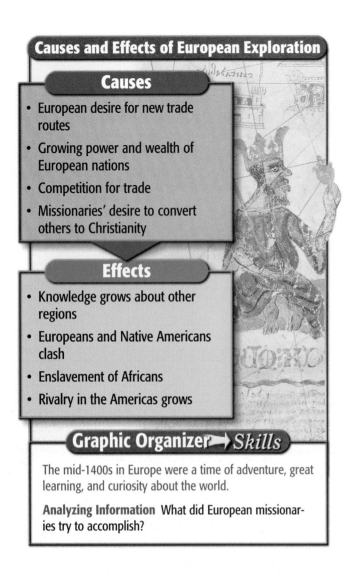

Causes and Effects of European Exploration

Causes

- European desire for new trade routes
- Growing power and wealth of European nations
- Competition for trade
- Missionaries' desire to convert others to Christianity

Effects

- Knowledge grows about other regions
- Europeans and Native Americans clash
- Enslavement of Africans
- Rivalry in the Americas grows

Graphic Organizer ➔ Skills

The mid-1400s in Europe were a time of adventure, great learning, and curiosity about the world.

Analyzing Information What did European missionaries try to accomplish?

Portugal took the lead in exploring the boundaries of the known world. Because Portugal lacked a Mediterranean port, it could not be part of the profitable trade between Asia and Europe. The country's ambitious rulers wanted to find a new route to China and India.

The Portuguese also hoped to find a more direct way to get West African gold. The gold traveled by caravan across the desert to North Africa, then by ship across the Mediterranean. Portuguese traders needed a better route.

Early Portuguese Voyages

Prince Henry of Portugal laid the groundwork for a new era of exploration. He was fascinated by what lay beyond the known boundaries of the world. In about 1420 he set up a center for exploration on the southwestern tip of Portugal, "where endeth land and where beginneth sea." Known as **Henry the Navigator,** the prince brought astronomers, geographers, and mathematicians to share their knowledge with Portuguese sailors and shipbuilders.

As Portuguese ships moved south along the coast of West Africa, they traded for gold and ivory and established trading posts. Because of its abundance of gold, the area came to be known as the **Gold Coast.** In the mid-1400s the Portuguese began buying slaves there as well.

King John II of Portugal launched new efforts to realize the Portuguese dream of a trading empire in Asia. If the Portuguese could find a sea route around Africa, they could trade directly with India and China. In the 1480s the king urged Portuguese sea captains to explore farther south along the African coast.

Bartholomeu Dias

In 1487 the king sent **Bartholomeu Dias** to explore the southernmost part of Africa. As Dias approached the area, he ran into a terrible storm that carried him off course and around the southern tip of Africa. Dias wrote that he had been around the "Cape of Storms." On learning of Dias's discovery, King John II renamed this southern tip of land the Cape of Good Hope—he hoped that the passage around Africa might lead to a new route to India.

Vasco da Gama

The first Portuguese voyages to India were made years later. In July 1497, after much preparation, **Vasco da Gama** set out from Portugal with four ships. Da Gama sailed down the coast of West Africa, rounded the Cape of Good Hope, and visited cities along the coast of East Africa. He engaged an Arab pilot who knew the Indian Ocean well. With the pilot's help, Da Gama sailed on to India. He reached the port of Calicut in 1498, completing the long-awaited eastern sea route to Asia.

The Portuguese Empire

Events moved quickly after that. Pedro Alvares Cabral, following Da Gama's route, swung so wide around Africa that he touched Brazil. By claiming the land for his king, he gave

Portugal a stake in the Americas. Meanwhile, Portuguese fleets began to make annual voyages to India returning with cargoes that made Lisbon the marketplace of Europe.

✓ **Reading Check** **Analyzing** Why was Portugal interested in exploration?

Columbus Crosses the Atlantic

Christopher Columbus had a different plan for reaching Asia. He thought he could get there by sailing west. Born in Genoa, Italy, in 1451, Columbus became a sailor for Portugal. He had traveled as far north as the Arctic Circle and as far south as the Gold Coast.

In the 1400s most educated people believed the world was round. A more difficult matter was determining its size. Columbus was among those who based their estimates of the earth's size on the work of Ptolemy, an ancient Greek astronomer. Columbus believed Asia was about 2,760 miles (4,441 km) from Europe—a voyage of about two months by ship. Ptolemy, however, had underestimated the size of the world.

The Viking Voyages

Several centuries before Columbus, northern Europeans called **Vikings** had sailed west and reached North America. In the 800s and 900s, Viking ships visited Iceland and Greenland and established settlements. According to Norse

TECHNOLOGY & History

Spanish Galleon

In the late 1500s and early 1600s, Spanish galleons carried gold and silver from the West Indies to Spain. That's not all these ships carried, however. The threat of pirates prompted the Spanish galleons to carry weapons as part of their cargo. *What powered the Spanish galleons?*

The crow's nest served as a lookout.

1 Two or three sails on the **foremast** and **mainmast** allowed the ship to "catch the wind."

2 Elaborate living quarters for the captain were placed within the high **sterncastle**. The rest of the crew slept on deck.

3 Strong hands were needed to climb the rigging into the **crow's nest**, or lookout platform.

4 Stones and bricks provided **ballast** to keep the ship from tipping over. These stones would be replaced with cargo in the Americas. Many colonial streets and sidewalks were paved with ballast stones.

Spanish galleons were about 140 feet (43 meters) long.

5 Food and water were stored in the **hold**.

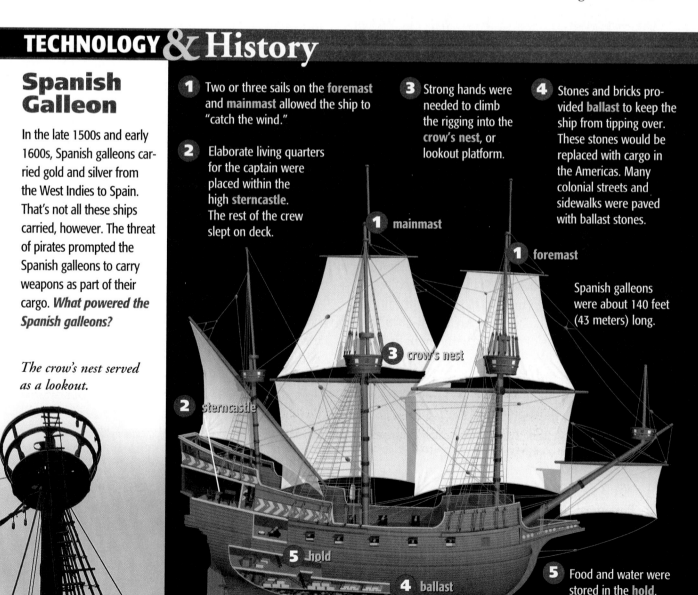

1 mainmast
1 foremast
3 crow's nest
2 sterncastle
5 hold
4 ballast

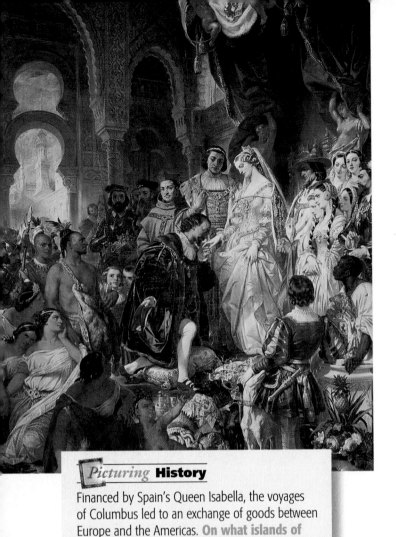

the seafaring and trading successes of neighboring Portugal with envy. They, too, wanted to share in the riches of Asian trade. Columbus needed a sponsor to finance his ambitious project of a westward voyage to Asia. He visited many European courts looking for support. After years of frustration, he finally found a sponsor in Spain.

Queen Isabella, a devout Christian, was finally persuaded by her husband's minister of finance to support the expedition for two reasons. First, Columbus had promised to bring Christianity to any lands he found. Second, if he found a way to Asia, Spain would become very wealthy. She promised Columbus a share of any riches gained from lands he discovered on his way to Asia.

Columbus's First Voyage

On August 3, 1492, Columbus set out from Palos, Spain. He had two small ships, the *Niña* and the *Pinta,* and a larger one, the *Santa María,* carrying a total of about 90 sailors. The small fleet stopped at the Canary Islands for repairs and to stock up on supplies, then sailed westward into the unknown.

The ships had good winds, but after a month at sea the sailors began to worry. Columbus wrote that he was

> ❝having trouble with the crew . . . . I am told that if I persist in going onward, the best course of action will be to throw me into the sea.❞

Columbus, however, was determined. He told the men, "I made this voyage to go to the Indies, and [I] shall continue until I find them, with God's help." To convince the crew that they had not traveled too far from home, Columbus altered the distances in his ship's log. 📖 *(See page 593 of the Primary Sources Library for another log entry by Columbus.)*

"Tierra! Tierra!"

On October 12, 1492, at 2:00 in the morning, a lookout shouted, *"Tierra! Tierra!"*—"Land! Land!" He had spotted a small island, part of the group now called the Bahamas. Columbus went ashore, claimed the island for Spain, and named it San Salvador. Although he did not know it, Columbus had reached the Americas.

sagas, or traditional stories, a Viking sailor named Leif Eriksson explored a land west of Greenland—known as Vinland—about the year 1000. Other Norse sagas describe failed attempts by the Vikings to settle in Vinland. Historians think that Vinland was North America. Archaeologists have found the remains of a Viking settlement in Newfoundland. No one is sure what other parts of North America the Vikings explored.

The Viking voyages to other lands were not well known in the rest of Europe. Europeans did not "discover" the Americas until Columbus made his great voyage.

Spain Backs Columbus

For most of the 1400s, Spanish monarchs devoted their energy to driving the Muslims out of their country. With the fall of the last Muslim kingdom in southern Spain in 1492, **King Ferdinand** and **Queen Isabella** of Spain could focus on other goals. The Spanish had been watching

Columbus explored the area for several months, convinced he had reached the East Indies, the islands off the coast of Asia. Today the **Caribbean Islands** are often referred to as the **West Indies.** Columbus called the local people Indians. He noted that they regarded the Europeans with wonder and often touched them to find out "if they were flesh and bones like themselves."

When Columbus returned to Spain in triumph, Queen Isabella and King Ferdinand received him with great honor and agreed to finance his future voyages. Columbus had earned the title of Admiral of the Ocean Sea.

Columbus's Later Voyages

Columbus made three more voyages from Spain in 1493, 1498, and 1502. He explored the Caribbean islands of Hispaniola (present-day Haiti and the Dominican Republic), Cuba, and Jamaica, and he sailed along the coasts of Central America and northern South America. He claimed the new lands for Spain and established settlements.

Columbus originally thought the lands he had found were in Asia. Later explorations made it clear that Columbus had not reached Asia at all. He had found a part of the globe unknown to Europeans, Asians, and Africans. In the following years, the Spanish explored most of the Caribbean region. In time their voyages led to the establishment of the Spanish Empire in the Americas.

Dividing the World

Both Spain and Portugal wanted to protect their claims, and they turned to Pope Alexander VI for help. In 1493 the pope drew a line of demarcation, an imaginary line running down the

TWO VIEWPOINTS

Who Had the Right to Claim the Americas?

Who owned the land of the Americas before the Europeans arrived? Did it belong to the people who already lived there, or was it there to be taken by the Europeans? While reading the excerpts below, notice the difference in opinions about who owned the rights to the land of the Americas.

Christopher Columbus

Letter from Christopher Columbus to the King and Queen of Spain, March 4, 1493

. . . I come from the Indies with the armada Your Highnesses gave me . . . . I found innumerable [many] people and very many islands, of which I took possession in Your Highnesses' name, by royal crier and with Your Highnesses' royal banner unfurled, and it was not contradicted . . . .

And I continued to enter very many harbors, in each of which I placed a very large cross in the most appropriate spot, as I had done in all the other [harbors] of the other islands. . . .

Speech by Chief Red Jacket, leader of the Seneca Nation, to a white missionary, 1805

There was a time when our forefathers owned this great island. Their seats extended from the rising to the setting of the sun. The Great Spirit had made it for the use of Indians. He had created buffalo, the deer, and other animals for food. He had made the bear and beaver, and their skins served us for clothing . . . .

The white people, brother, had now found our country. Tidings were carried back and more came amongst us. Yet we did not fear them. We took them to be friends. . . .

Brother, our seats were once large, and yours were very small. You have now become a great people, and we have scarcely a place left to spread our blankets. You have got our country, but you are not satisfied. You want to force your religion upon us . . . .

Learning From History

1. According to Christopher Columbus, who owned the land that he explored in the Americas?
2. How did the relationship between Europeans and Native Americans seem to change as more and more Europeans came to America?

middle of the Atlantic from the North Pole to the South Pole. Spain was to control all the lands to the west of the line. Portugal was to have control of all lands to the east of the line. Portugal, however, protested that the division favored Spain. As a result, in 1494 the two countries signed the Treaty of Tordesillas (TOHR•day•SEE•yuhs), an agreement to move the line farther west. The treaty divided the entire unexplored world between Spain and Portugal.

✦Geography

Exploring America

In 1499 explorer Amerigo Vespucci began mapping South America's coastline. Vespucci concluded that South America was a continent, not part of Asia. By the early 1500s, European geographers had begun to call the continent America, in honor of Amerigo Vespucci. While European geographers discussed Vespucci's findings, others continued to explore America.

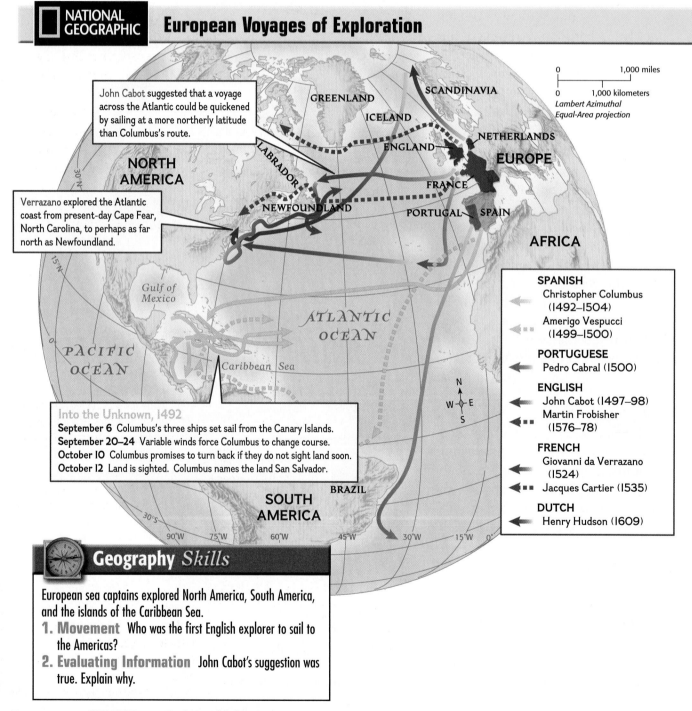

NATIONAL GEOGRAPHIC

European Voyages of Exploration

John Cabot suggested that a voyage across the Atlantic could be quickened by sailing at a more northerly latitude than Columbus's route.

Verrazano explored the Atlantic coast from present-day Cape Fear, North Carolina, to perhaps as far north as Newfoundland.

Into the Unknown, 1492
September 6 Columbus's three ships set sail from the Canary Islands.
September 20–24 Variable winds force Columbus to change course.
October 10 Columbus promises to turn back if they do not sight land soon.
October 12 Land is sighted. Columbus names the land San Salvador.

0   1,000 miles
0   1,000 kilometers
Lambert Azimuthal Equal-Area projection

SPANISH
Christopher Columbus (1492–1504)
Amerigo Vespucci (1499–1500)

PORTUGUESE
Pedro Cabral (1500)

ENGLISH
John Cabot (1497–98)
Martin Frobisher (1576–78)

FRENCH
Giovanni da Verrazano (1524)
Jacques Cartier (1535)

DUTCH
Henry Hudson (1609)

Geography *Skills*

European sea captains explored North America, South America, and the islands of the Caribbean Sea.
1. **Movement** Who was the first English explorer to sail to the Americas?
2. **Evaluating Information** John Cabot's suggestion was true. Explain why.

Vasco Núñez de Balboa (bal•BOH•uh), governor of a Spanish town in present-day Panama, had heard stories of the "great waters" beyond the mountains. In 1513 he formed an exploring party and hiked through the steaming jungles. After many days of difficult travel, the Spaniard climbed a hill and saw a vast body of water. When he reached the water's edge, Balboa waded in and claimed it and the adjoining lands for Spain. Balboa was the first European to see the Pacific Ocean from the Americas.

Sailing Around the World

The Spanish wanted to find a sea route through or around South America to Asia. In 1519 they hired **Ferdinand Magellan,** a Portuguese mariner, to lead an expedition of five ships. Sailing from Spain, Magellan headed west across the Atlantic Ocean and then south along the eastern coast of South America.

By late November 1520, Magellan had found and sailed through the narrow, twisting sea passage to the Pacific. This strait still bears his name. At the end of the strait, Magellan exclaimed: "We are about to stand [go] into an ocean where no ship has ever sailed before." He named the ocean the Pacific, which means "peaceful."

Fact Fiction Folklore

America's Flags

Spanish banner, 1492 Christopher Columbus proudly carried the Spanish banner of Castile and León to the shores of the Bahamas. The flag's castle represented Queen Isabella. The lion symbolized her husband, King Ferdinand.

Magellan expected to reach Asia in just a few weeks after rounding South America, but the voyage across the Pacific lasted four months. The crew ran out of food and ate sawdust, rats, and leather to stay alive. Magellan was killed in a skirmish in the Philippines, but some of his crew continued. Their trip had taken almost three years. Only one of the five original ships and 18 of the more than 200 crew members completed the difficult journey. These men were the first to circumnavigate, or sail around, the world.

✓ **Reading Check** **Describing** Why did Spain finance Columbus's voyage?

SECTION 2 ASSESSMENT

Checking for Understanding

1. **Key Terms** Write a short paragraph in which you use the following terms: line of demarcation, strait, circumnavigate.
2. **Reviewing Facts** Who were the first Europeans to reach the Americas and when did they arrive?

Reviewing Themes

3. **Geography and History** What nations signed the Treaty of Tordesillas? What was the purpose of the line of demarcation? How did the treaty affect European exploration of the Americas?

Critical Thinking

4. **Making Inferences** For years, many history books have claimed that "Columbus discovered America." Why do you think Native Americans might disagree with the choice of the word "discovered" in this statement? What might be a better word?
5. **Organizing Information** Re-create the diagram below and identify the regions Columbus explored.

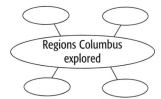

Regions Columbus explored

Analyzing Visuals

6. **Geography Skills** Review the map of European voyages of exploration on page 48; then answer the questions that follow. When did Verrazano make his voyage? For what country did he sail? How did Cabot's route to the Americas differ from that of Columbus?

Interdisciplinary Activity

Geography Draw a map of the world as you think Columbus might have seen it in 1492. Remember his error in calculating distance.

America's LITERATURE

Michael Dorris (1945–1997)

A Modoc Native American, Michael Dorris was an educator, a social activist, and an award-winning author. *Morning Girl,* his first book for young adults, portrays the lives of the Taino people of the Bahamas.

READ TO DISCOVER

Morning Girl is the fictional story of a young Native American woman who meets Columbus and his crew as they arrive in the Bahamas in 1492. While reading this passage, think about the ways that Morning Girl's life might change as a result of Columbus's visit.

READER'S DICTIONARY

backward: undeveloped
Morning Girl: a young Taino woman

Chief's chair, Taino people

Morning Girl

I swam closer to get a better look and had to stop myself from laughing. The strangers had wrapped every part of their bodies with colorful leaves and cotton. Some had decorated their faces with fur and wore shiny rocks on their heads. Compared to us, they were very round. Their canoe was short and square, and, in spite of all their dipping and pulling, it moved so slowly. What a **backward,** distant island they must have come from. But really, to laugh at guests, no matter how odd, would be impolite, especially since I was the first to meet them. If I was foolish, they would think they had arrived at a foolish place. . . .

I kicked toward the canoe and called out the simplest thing.

"Hello!". . .

The man stared at me as though he'd never seen a girl before, then shouted something to his relatives. They all stopped paddling and looked in my direction.

"Hello," I tried again. "Welcome to home. My name is **Morning Girl. . . .**"

All the fat people in the canoe began pointing at me and talking at once. In their excitement they almost turned themselves over, and I allowed my body to sink beneath the waves for a moment in order to hide my smile. . . .

When I came up they were still watching, the way babies do: wide eyed and with their mouths uncovered. They had much to learn about how to behave. . . . It was clear that they hadn't traveled much before.

From *Morning Girl* by Michael Dorris. Text © 1992 by Michael Dorris. Reprinted with permission from Hyperion Books for Children.

ANALYZING LITERATURE

1. **Recall and Interpret** How does Morning Girl describe the strangers' appearance?
2. **Evaluate and Connect** Are Morning Girl's impressions of the visitors positive or negative? Explain your reasoning.

Interdisciplinary Activity

Descriptive Writing Imagine that you are an explorer who arrived in America with Columbus. Describe the people and climate you encounter in America. Compare the way people live in America to your way of life in Europe.

Spain in America

Guide to Reading

Main Idea
In the sixteenth century, Spain established and governed a vast empire in the Americas.

Key Terms
conquistador, tribute, pueblo, mission, presidio, *encomienda*, plantation

Reading Strategy
Organizing Information As you read the section, re-create the diagram below and identify Spanish conquistadors, along with the regions they explored.

Conquistador	Region Explored

Read to Learn
- how the great Aztec and Inca Empires came to an end.
- how Spain governed its empire in the Americas.

Section Theme
Culture and Traditions The conquistadors conquered mighty empires in the Americas.

Preview of Events

♦1500	♦1530	♦1560

1519
Hernán Cortés lands in Mexico

1532
Francisco Pizarro captures Atahualpa

1541
De Soto crosses the Mississippi River

1565
Spain establishes fort at St. Augustine, Florida

Conquistador's armor

✦ AN American Story

Would you like to visit a place described in the following way? "A river . . . [stretched] two leagues wide, in which there were fishes as big as horses. . . . The lord of the country took his afternoon nap under a great tree on which were hung a great number of little gold bells. . . . The jugs and bowls were [made] of gold."

"[It was] a land rich in gold, silver, and other wealth . . . great cities . . . and civilized people wearing woolen clothes."

Spanish Conquistadors

Stories of gold, silver, and kingdoms wealthy beyond belief greeted the early Spanish explorers in the Americas. The reports led them far and wide in search of fabulous riches.

Known as **conquistadors** (kahn•KEES•tuh•dawrs), these explorers received grants from the Spanish rulers. They had the right to explore and establish settlements in the Americas. In exchange they agreed to give the Spanish crown one-fifth of any gold or treasure discovered. This arrangement allowed Spanish rulers to launch expeditions with little risk. If a conquistador failed, he lost his own fortune. If he succeeded, both he and Spain gained wealth and glory.

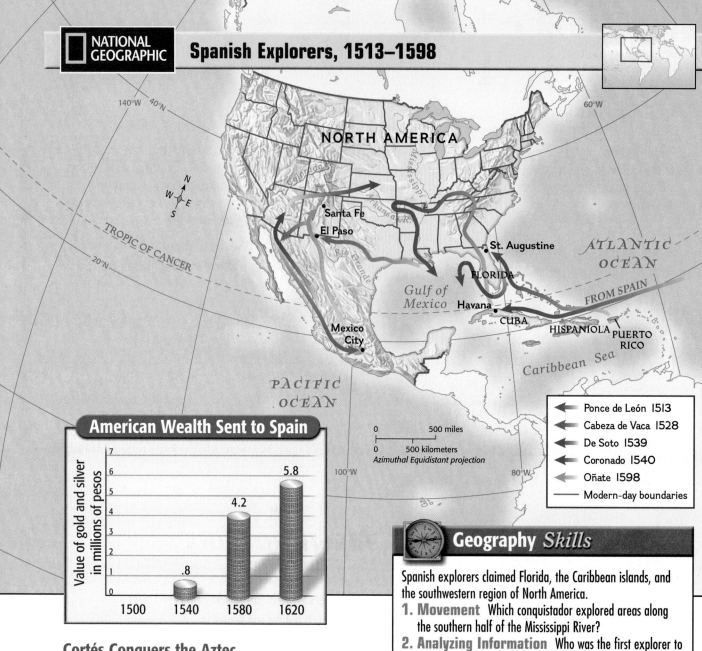

NORTH AMERICA

ATLANTIC OCEAN

FROM SPAIN

Santa Fe

El Paso

St. Augustine

FLORIDA

Gulf of Mexico

Havana

CUBA

HISPANIOLA PUERTO RICO

Mexico City

Caribbean Sea

PACIFIC OCEAN

TROPIC OF CANCER

Rio Grande

Arkansas R.

Mississippi R.

140°W 40°N

20°N

60°W

100°W

80°W

N W E S

0   500 miles
0   500 kilometers
Azimuthal Equidistant projection

←	Ponce de León 1513
←	Cabeza de Vaca 1528
←	De Soto 1539
←	Coronado 1540
←	Oñate 1598
—	Modern-day boundaries

American Wealth Sent to Spain

Value of gold and silver in millions of pesos

7
6
5.8
5
4.2
4
3
2
1
.8
0

1500   1540   1580   1620

Geography *Skills*

Spanish explorers claimed Florida, the Caribbean islands, and the southwestern region of North America.
1. **Movement** Which conquistador explored areas along the southern half of the Mississippi River?
2. **Analyzing Information** Who was the first explorer to cross the Rio Grande?

Cortés Conquers the Aztec

When **Hernán Cortés** landed on the east coast of what we now know as Mexico in 1519, he was looking for gold and glory. He came with about 500 soldiers, some horses, and a few cannons. Cortés soon learned about the great Aztec Empire and its capital of Tenochtitlán.

In building their empire, the Aztec had conquered many cities in Mexico. These cities were forced to give crops, clothing, gold, and precious stones to the Aztec as tribute. Cortés formed alliances with nearby cities against the Aztec.

Cortés marched into Tenochtitlán in November with his small army and his Native American allies. The Aztec emperor **Montezuma** (MAHN •tuh•ZOO•muh)—also spelled Moctezuma—

welcomed Cortés and his soldiers and provided them with food and a fine palace. However, Cortés took advantage of the Aztec's hospitality and made Montezuma his prisoner.

In the spring of 1520, the Aztec rebelled against the Spanish. During the fighting Montezuma was hit by stones and later died. The battle lasted for days. Eventually, the Spanish were forced to leave Tenochtitlán. Cortés, however, was determined to retake the city. He waited until more Spanish troops arrived, then attacked and destroyed the Aztec capital in 1521. An Aztec poem describes the awful scene:

> **“**Without roofs are the houses,
> And red are their walls with blood. . . .
> Weep, my friends,
> Know that with these disasters
> We have lost our Mexican nation.**”**

The Aztec Empire disintegrated, and Spain seized control of the region.

Pizarro Conquers Peru

The conquistador **Francisco Pizarro** sailed down the Pacific coast of South America with about 180 Spanish soldiers. Pizarro had heard tales of the incredibly wealthy Inca Empire in what is now Peru. In 1532 Pizarro captured the Inca ruler, **Atahualpa** (ah•tah•WAHL•pah), and destroyed much of the Incan army.

The following year, the Spanish falsely accused Atahualpa of crimes and executed him. The Inca were used to obeying commands from their rulers. Without leadership they were not able to fight effectively. Within a few years, Pizarro had gained control of most of the vast Inca Empire.

Why Spain Succeeded

The conquistadors' victories in Mexico and Peru were quick and lasting. How could Cortés and Pizarro, with only a few hundred Spanish soldiers, conquer such mighty empires?

First, the Spanish arrived with strange weapons—guns and cannons—and fearsome animals. They rode horses and had huge, ferocious dogs. To the Native Americans, the Spanish seemed almost like gods. Second, many Native Americans hated their Aztec overlords and assisted the conquistadors in overthrowing them.

Finally, disease played an extremely large role in the Spanish conquest. Native Americans had no immunity to the diseases the Europeans had, unknowingly, brought with them. Epidemics of smallpox and other diseases wiped out entire communities in the Americas and did much to weaken the resistance of the Aztec and Inca.

Reading Check **Analyzing** How were the Spanish able to defeat mighty Native American empires?

Spain in North America

Mexico and Peru were rich in silver and gold. Hoping to find similar wealth to the north, conquistadors explored the southeastern and southwestern parts of North America.

Juan Ponce de León made the first Spanish landing on the mainland of North America, arriving on the east coast of present-day Florida in 1513. According to legend, Ponce de León hoped to find not only gold, but the legendary fountain of youth, "a spring of running water of such marvelous virtue" that drinking it "makes old men young again." Ponce de León's exploration led to the first Spanish settlement in what is now the United States. In 1565 the Spanish established a fort at **St. Augustine,** Florida.

The Seven Cities of Cibola

Many other conquistadors searched for quick riches. None ever achieved this goal, and several lost their lives trying. **Álvar Núñez Cabeza de Vaca** (cah•BAY•sah day VAH•cah) was part of a Spanish expedition to Florida in 1528.

After encountering troubles in Florida, the expedition, led by **Pánfilo de Narváez,** sailed along the coast toward Mexico. However, in November 1528, three of the five boats were lost in a storm. The two boats that survived went aground on an island near present-day Texas. Within a few months, only a handful of the shipwrecked explorers were still alive.

The First Thanksgiving

Who celebrated the first Thanksgiving? We all know that the Pilgrims celebrated the first Thanksgiving. Or did they? On April 30, 1598, long before the Pilgrims came to North America, Spanish colonists held a thanksgiving feast near present-day El Paso, Texas. Juan de Oñate had led 400 men and their families across the desert from Mexico. After they reached the Rio Grande, Oñate told them to feast and give thanks for the abundance of the new land.

Juana Inés de la Cruz 1651–1695

A Mexican nun, Juana Inés de la Cruz, may have been the first woman in the Americas to write about women's rights. What is remarkable about Sor Juana ("Sister" Juana) is that she was a famous writer at a time when most women were not taught to read. Her poems and stories were well known in Mexico; her plays were performed in the royal palace of Mexico, and her books were popular in Spain.

An archbishop of the Church, however, did not approve of women freely expressing their opinions. He threatened to put her on trial for violating Church rules unless she followed a strict vow of poverty and sold her books and belongings.

Although she gave the appearance of obedience, an unfinished poem found in her belongings after her death showed that she continued to exercise her talent.

To survive, Cabeza de Vaca and an enslaved African named **Estevanico** became medicine men. Cabeza de Vaca later wrote that their method of healing was "to bless the sick, breathing on them" and to recite Latin prayers.

In 1533 the Spaniards set off on foot on a great 1,000-mile journey across the Southwest. Arriving in Mexico in 1536, Cabeza de Vaca related tales he had heard of seven cities with walls of emerald and streets of gold.

The stories inspired **Hernando de Soto,** who led an expedition to explore Florida and lands to the west. For three years De Soto and his troops wandered around the southeastern area of the present-day United States, following stories of gold. As the Spaniards traveled, they took advantage of the native peoples. Their usual method was to enter a village, take the chief hostage, and demand food and supplies.

De Soto crossed the **Mississippi River** in 1541, describing it as "swift, and very deep." After traveling as far west as present-day Oklahoma, De Soto died of fever. His men buried him in the waters of the Mississippi.

Francisco Vásquez de Coronado also wanted to find the legendary "Seven Cities of Cibola." After traveling through areas of northern Mexico and present-day Arizona and New Mexico, the expedition reached a town belonging to the Zuni people in early summer 1540. They realized at once that there was no gold. Members of the expedition traveled west to the Colorado River and east into what is now Kansas. They found nothing but "windswept plains" and strange "shaggy cows" (buffalo). Disappointed, Coronado returned to Mexico.

Reading Check **Explaining** How did stories of the "Seven Cities of Cibola" affect Spanish exploration?

Spanish Rule

Spanish law called for three kinds of settlements in the Americas—pueblos, missions, and presidios. Pueblos, or towns, were established as centers of trade. Missions were religious communities that usually included a small town, surrounding farmland, and a church. A presidio, or fort, was usually built near a mission.

Juan de Oñate (day ohn • YAH • tay) was sent from Mexico to gain control over lands to the north and to convert the inhabitants. In 1598 Oñate founded the province of New Mexico and introduced cattle and horses to the Pueblo people.

Social Classes

A class system developed in Spain's empire. The upper class consisted of people who had been born in Spain, called *peninsulares.* The *peninsulares* owned the land, served in the Catholic Church, and ran the local government. Below them were the creoles, people born in the Americas to Spanish parents. Lower in the class structure were the mestizos (meh•STEE•zohs), people with Spanish and Native American parents. Still lower were the Native Americans, most of whom lived in great poverty. At the very bottom were enslaved Africans.

In the 1500s the Spanish government granted each conquistador who settled in the Americas an *encomienda,* the right to demand taxes or labor from Native Americans living on the land. This system turned the Native Americans into slaves. Grueling labor in the fields and in the gold and silver mines took its toll. Many Native Americans died from malnutrition and disease.

A Spanish priest, **Bartolomé de Las Casas,** condemned the cruel treatment of the Native Americans. He pleaded for laws to protect them. Las Casas claimed that millions had died because the Spanish "made gold their ultimate aim, seeking to load themselves with riches in the shortest possible time."

Because of Las Casas's reports, in 1542 the Spanish government passed the New Laws, which forbade making slaves of Native Americans. Although not always enforced, the laws did correct the worst abuses.

The Plantation System

Some Spanish settlers made large profits by exporting crops and raw materials back to Spain. In the West Indies, the main exports were tobacco and sugarcane. To raise these crops, the Spanish developed the plantation system. A plantation was a large estate. The Spanish used Native Americans to work their plantations.

Las Casas suggested replacing them with enslaved Africans—a suggestion he bitterly regretted later. He thought the Africans could endure the labor better than the Native Americans.

By the mid-1500s the Spanish were bringing thousands from West Africa to the Americas. The Portuguese did the same in Brazil. The Africans who survived the brutal ocean voyage were sold to plantation owners. By the late 1500s, plantation slave labor was an essential part of the economy of the colonies.

Reading Check **Describing** Whom did Las Casas try to protect?

SECTION 3 ASSESSMENT

Checking for Understanding

1. **Key Terms** Write three true and three false statements using each of the following terms once: conquistador, tribute, pueblo, mission, presidio, plantation. Indicate which statements are false.
2. **Reviewing Facts** What three kinds of settlements did Spain establish in the Americas? How did they differ?

Reviewing Themes

3. **Culture and Traditions** What groups made up the class system in Spanish America?

Critical Thinking

4. **Analyzing Primary Sources** One conquistador explained, "We came to serve God and the king, and also to get rich." In what way do you think conquistadors planned to serve "God and the king"?
5. **Determining Cause and Effect** Re-create the diagram below and list causes of Spain's success in conquering Native American empires.

```
┌──────────┐
│          │──┐
└──────────┘  │
┌──────────┐  │   ┌─────────┐
│          │──┼──▶│ Spain's │
└──────────┘  │   │ success │
┌──────────┐  │   └─────────┘
│          │──┘
└──────────┘
```

Analyzing Visuals

6. **Geography Skills** Review the map of Spanish exploration on page 52. What expedition traveled from Florida to the Mississippi River? Through what regions did the Coronado expedition travel?

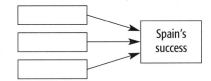

Interdisciplinary Activity

Geography Using cookbooks as references, create an all-American dinner menu that features only foods introduced to Europeans by Native Americans.

GEOGRAPHY&HISTORY

Using an astrolabe like this one to establish latitude, Father Kino carefully mapped the region.

PASSAGE PAR TERRE A LA CALIFORNIE

United States
Mexico

Gila River

Santa Cruz River

San Pedro River

Gulf of California

Baja California

Magdalena River

Altar River

Nuestra Señora de los Dolores

San Miguel River

Sonora River

A typical Spanish mission surrounded a large open courtyard.

Crops

Living quarters

Workshop

Church

Granary

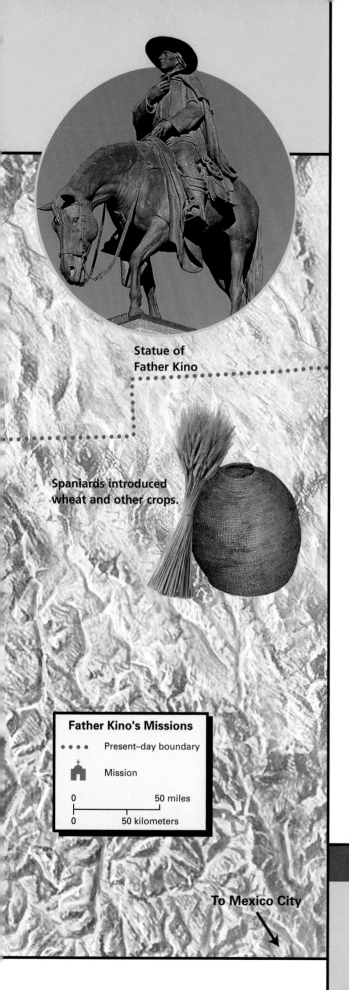

Statue of
Father Kino

Spaniards introduced
wheat and other crops.

Father Kino's Missions

• • • • Present–day boundary

⛪ Mission

0   50 miles

0   50 kilometers

To Mexico City

PADRE ON HORSEBACK

MISSIONARY AND EXPLORER Eusebio Kino
(yoo•SAY•be•oh KEE•no) was an Italian who studied
astronomy, mapmaking, and mathematics before
becoming a Jesuit priest. In 1681 he went to Mexico
with the Spaniards to map the area and convert
Native Americans to Catholicism.

MISSIONARY IN THE PIMERÍA ALTA

After several years in Mexico City and Baja
California, Father Kino was sent to establish missions
in the "Pimería Alta"—the Upper Pima Country—part
of present-day Sonora, Mexico, and southern Arizona.

In March 1687 Father Kino established his first
mission, Nuestra Señora de los Dolores at Cosari. He
helped start more than 20 missions along the San
Miguel, Magdalena, and Altar rivers.

Father Kino and other missionaries changed the face
of Pimería Alta forever. The priests converted thousands
of Native Americans to Christianity. By introducing livestock, wheat, European fruit, and other new crops, the
missionaries altered the economy of the region.

EXPLORER AND MAPMAKER

Kino traveled so much he was
known as the "padre on horseback." He covered thousands of
miles tending to the needs of his
converts and exploring and
mapping the Sonoran Desert
and California.

San Xavier del Bac, a mission started by Father
Kino in 1700, still stands
today outside of Tucson.

LEARNING from GEOGRAPHY

1. **Where did Father Kino establish his missions? Why?**

2. **How did the introduction of food crops and domestic
animals affect the development of the Southwest?**

57

Exploring North America

Guide to Reading

Main Idea

Rivalries between countries, the search for a Northwest Passage to Asia, and early trading activities led to increased exploration of North America.

Key Terms

mercantilism, Columbian Exchange, Northwest Passage, coureur de bois

Reading Strategy

Determining Cause and Effect As you read the section, re-create the diagram below and provide an effect for each cause.

Exploration of North America	
Causes	Effects
Protestant Reformation	
Search for NW passage	
Early trading activities	

Read to Learn

• how the Protestant Reformation affected North America.
• why the activities of early traders encouraged exploration.

Section Theme

Global Connections European nations competed for overseas land and resources.

Preview of Events

♦1450	♦1500	♦1550	♦1600

1497
John Cabot lands in Newfoundland

1517
Martin Luther starts the Protestant Reformation

1535
Jacques Cartier sails up the St. Lawrence River to Montreal

1609
Henry Hudson sails the Hudson River

Martin Luther

A European Story

In 1517 Martin Luther, a German priest, nailed a list of complaints about the Catholic Church on the door of a local church. Luther declared that the Bible was the only true guide for Christians. He rejected many Church practices—even the authority of the pope—because they were not mentioned in the Bible. Luther also believed that faith rather than good deeds was the way to salvation.

Church officials tried to get Luther to take back his statements. "I cannot go against my conscience," he replied. "Here I stand. I cannot do otherwise. God help me."

A Divided Church

Martin Luther's actions led to incredible changes in Europe. Before he voiced his beliefs, the countries of Europe had their differences, but they were bound together by a common church. For centuries, Catholicism had been the main religion of western Europe. In the 1500s, however, Luther's opposition to the policies of the Roman Catholic Church emerged.

Within a few years, Luther had many followers. They broke away from Catholicism to begin their own Christian churches. Martin Luther's protests were the start of a great religious and historical movement known as the **Protestant Reformation.**

Protestantism Spreads in Europe

From Germany Luther's ideas spread rapidly. **John Calvin,** a French religious thinker, also broke away from the Catholic Church. Like Luther, Calvin rejected the idea that good works would ensure a person's salvation. He believed that God had already chosen those who would be saved.

In England, King Henry VIII also left the Catholic Church, but not for religious reasons. Pope Clement VII had refused Henry's request to declare his first marriage invalid. In 1534 the English Parliament, working with the king,

Picturing **History**

In 1676 Kateri Tekakwitha, a 20-year-old Mohawk woman, accepted Christianity from French Catholic missionaries. **What region of North America was settled by the French?**

denied the authority of the pope and recognized the king as the head of the Church of England. During the rule of Henry's daughter, Queen Elizabeth I, further reforms firmly established England as a Protestant nation.

Religious Rivalries in the Americas

Throughout western Europe, people and nations divided into Catholics and Protestants. When these Europeans crossed the Atlantic, they took along their religious differences.

Spanish and French Catholics worked to spread their faith to the Native Americans. The Spanish settled in the southwestern and southeastern regions of North America, and the French settled in the northeast. Dutch and English Protestants established colonies in lands along the Atlantic coast between the French and the Spanish settlements. Some of the English settlements were founded by Protestants who wanted to practice their beliefs in peace.

✓ **Reading Check** **Explaining** What role did religion play in the exploration of North America?

$ **Economics**

Economic Rivalry

Religion was only one of the factors that pushed European nations across the Atlantic Ocean. The promise of great wealth was equally strong, especially as other Europeans watched Spain gain riches from its colonies.

According to the economic theory of mercantilism, a nation's power was based on its wealth. Rulers tried to increase their nation's total wealth by acquiring gold and silver and by developing trade. Mercantilism provided great opportunities for individual merchants to make money. It also increased rivalry between nations.

Several countries in Europe competed for overseas territory that could produce wealth. They wanted to acquire colonies in the Americas that could provide valuable resources, such as gold and silver, or raw materials. The colonies would also serve as a place to sell European products.

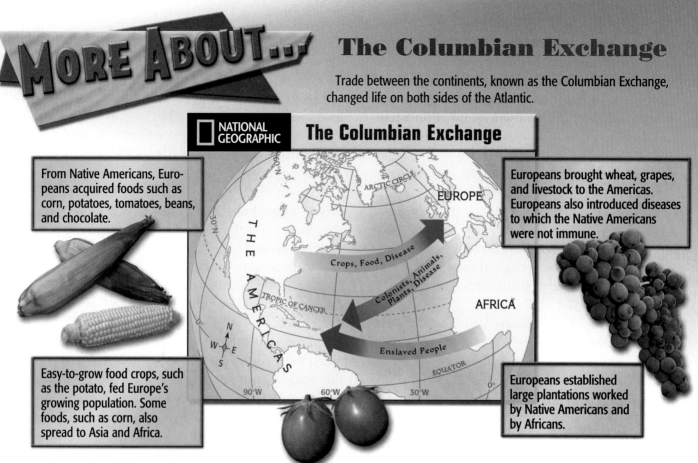

MORE ABOUT... The Columbian Exchange

Trade between the continents, known as the Columbian Exchange, changed life on both sides of the Atlantic.

NATIONAL GEOGRAPHIC — The Columbian Exchange

From Native Americans, Europeans acquired foods such as corn, potatoes, tomatoes, beans, and chocolate.

Europeans brought wheat, grapes, and livestock to the Americas. Europeans also introduced diseases to which the Native Americans were not immune.

Easy-to-grow food crops, such as the potato, fed Europe's growing population. Some foods, such as corn, also spread to Asia and Africa.

Europeans established large plantations worked by Native Americans and by Africans.

Crops, Food, Disease — Colonists, Animals, Plants, Disease — Enslaved People

The Columbian Exchange

The voyages of Columbus and other explorers brought together two parts of the globe that previously had had no contact: the continents of Europe, Asia, and Africa in one hemisphere and the Americas in the other. The contact led to an exchange of plants, animals, and diseases that altered life on both sides of the Atlantic. Scholars refer to this as the Columbian Exchange.

A Northwest Passage

The Treaty of Tordesillas had divided the Americas between Spain and Portugal. It did not allow for claims by other nations—so England, France, and the Netherlands ignored the treaty. During the 1500s and early 1600s, these countries sent explorers to chart the coast of North America. They wanted to profit from trade and colonization as well. The voyage to Asia—either around the southern tip of Africa or around South America—was long and difficult. For this reason, the three countries hoped to discover a Northwest Passage to Asia—a more direct water route through the Americas.

In 1497 England sent **John Cabot,** an Italian, to look for a northern route to Asia. Cabot prob-ably landed on the coast of present-day New-foundland. England used Cabot's voyage as the basis for its claims to North America.

In 1524 France hired an Italian, **Giovanni da Verrazano,** to look for the northern sea route. Ver-razano explored the coast of North America from present-day Nova Scotia down to the Carolinas.

In 1535 French explorer **Jacques Cartier** (KAR•tyay) sailed up the St. Lawrence River hoping it would lead to the Pacific. He got as far as the Huron village of Hochelaga. Cartier wrote that from the mountain next to the village, "one sees a very great distance." He named the peak Mont-Royal, which means "royal mountain." This is the site of the city now called **Montreal.** Cartier had heard stories about gold, but he found neither gold nor a sea route to Asia.

Hudson's Discoveries

The Netherlands, too, wanted to find a passage through the Americas. They hired **Henry Hudson,** an English sailor, to explore. In 1609 he discovered the river that now bears his name. In his ship, the *Half Moon,* Hudson sailed north on the Hudson River as far as the site of present-day Albany. Deciding that he had not found a passage to India, he turned back. The following year Hudson tried again, this time sent by England.

Sailing almost due west from northern England, Henry Hudson and his crew discovered a huge bay, now called **Hudson Bay.** Hudson thought he had reached the Pacific Ocean. After months of searching for an outlet from the bay, however, the crew rebelled. Hudson, his son John, and a few sailors were set adrift in a small boat—and never seen again.

French Open Trading Posts

France had shown little interest in building an empire in the Americas. Its rulers were preoccupied by political and religious conflicts at home. The French viewed North America as an opportunity for profits from fishing and fur trading rather than as a place to settle.

Furs were popular in Europe, and traders could make large profits from beaver pelts acquired in North America. A group of French

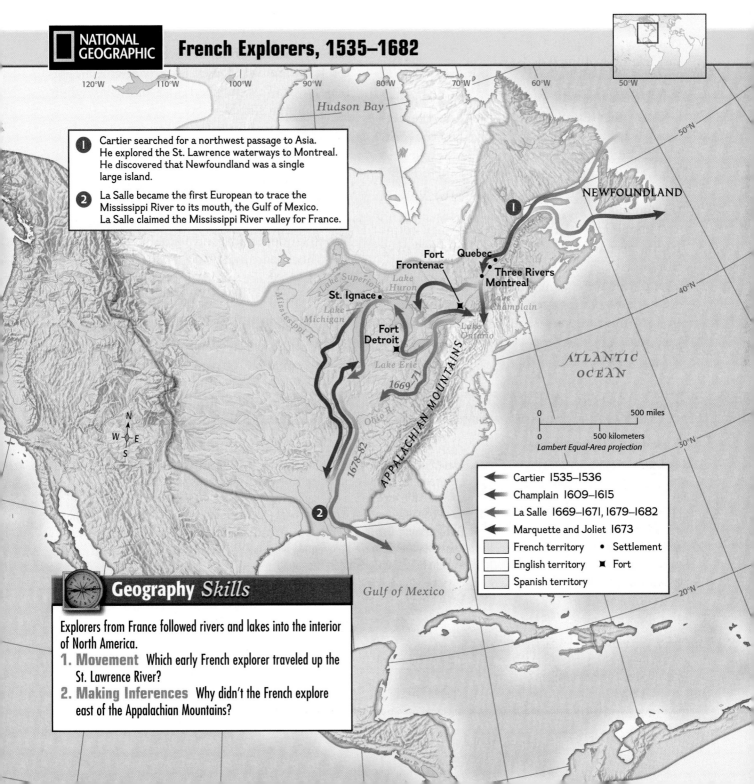

NATIONAL GEOGRAPHIC

French Explorers, 1535–1682

1. Cartier searched for a northwest passage to Asia. He explored the St. Lawrence waterways to Montreal. He discovered that Newfoundland was a single large island.

2. La Salle became the first European to trace the Mississippi River to its mouth, the Gulf of Mexico. La Salle claimed the Mississippi River valley for France.

Cartier 1535–1536
Champlain 1609–1615
La Salle 1669–1671, 1679–1682
Marquette and Joliet 1673
French territory • Settlement
English territory ✖ Fort
Spanish territory

Geography *Skills*

Explorers from France followed rivers and lakes into the interior of North America.
1. **Movement** Which early French explorer traveled up the St. Lawrence River?
2. **Making Inferences** Why didn't the French explore east of the Appalachian Mountains?

traders made an agreement with the Native Americans to trade fur. In 1608 the group sent **Samuel de Champlain** to establish a settlement in **Quebec** in what is now Canada. Champlain made several trips to the region and discovered Lake Champlain. He described the beautiful scenery and abundant wildlife and the Native Americans he met there.

From Quebec the French moved into other parts of Canada, where they built trading posts to collect furs gathered by Native Americans and French trappers. The trappers were called coureurs de bois (ku•RUHR duh BWAH), meaning "runners of the woods."

Dutch Settlements

Like other European countries, the Netherlands was also eager to claim its share of world trade. Until Hudson's voyage, there had been no Dutch exploration in North America. Hudson's voyage became the start for Dutch claims on the continent.

Although the Netherlands was a small country, its large fleet of trading ships sailed all over the world. In 1621 the Dutch West India Company set up a trading colony—New Netherland—in the area Hudson had explored. In 1624 the company sent 30 families to settle the area. They settled at Fort Orange (later

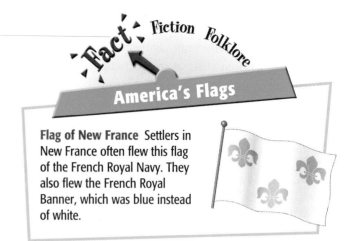

America's Flags

Flag of New France Settlers in New France often flew this flag of the French Royal Navy. They also flew the French Royal Banner, which was blue instead of white.

Albany) on the Hudson River and on Burlington Island in New Jersey. Shortly after that, Fort Nassau was established just opposite where Philadelphia stands today.

The center of the new colony was New Amsterdam, located on the tip of Manhattan Island where the Hudson River enters New York Harbor. In 1626 Peter Minuit, the governor of the colony, paid the Manhates people 60 Dutch guilders in goods for the island. The goods probably included cloth, and valuable tools such as axes, hoes, and awls. Like Portugal, Spain, and France, the Netherlands started colonies in the Americas.

✓ **Reading Check** **Analyzing** Why was the idea of a Northwest Passage important?

SECTION 4 ASSESSMENT

Checking for Understanding

1. **Key Terms** Write a sentence in which you correctly use each of the following terms: mercantilism, Columbian Exchange, Northwest Passage, coureur de bois
2. **Reviewing Facts** What were English, French, and Dutch explorers searching for while charting the coast of North America?

Reviewing Themes

3. **Global Connections** How did French goals in the Americas differ from the goals of other European nations?

Critical Thinking

4. **Identifying Central Issues** How did the economic theory of mercantilism influence the exploration and settlement of North America by Europeans?
5. **Determining Cause and Effect** Re-create the diagram below and explain how the Columbian Exchange affected both sides of the Atlantic Ocean.

Columbian Exchange	
Effects on the Americas	Effects on Europe

Analyzing Visuals

6. **Geography Skills** Review the map, *French Explorers, 1535–1682,* on page 61. Which of the French explorers traveled farthest south? Along what river did Marquette and Joliet travel?

Interdisciplinary Activity

Persuasive Writing Write a letter to one of the explorers who searched for a Northwest Passage. In the letter, explain why it is important for your nation to find a Northwest Passage.

Social Studies SKILLBUILDER

Reading a Time Line

Why Learn this Skill?

Knowing the relationship of time to events is important in studying history. A time line is a visual way to show chronological order within a time period. Most time lines are divided into sections representing equal time intervals. For example, a time line showing 1,000 years might be divided into ten 100-year sections. Each event on a time line appears beside the date when the event took place.

Learning the Skill

To read a time line, follow these steps:
- Find the dates on the opposite ends of the time line to know the time span. Also note the intervals between dates on the time line.
- Study the order of events.
- Analyze relationships among events or look for trends.

Magellan

Practicing the Skill

Analyze the time line of Magellan's voyage below. Use it to answer the questions that follow.

1. What time span is represented?

2. How many years do each of the sections represent?

3. Did Magellan's voyage to the Spice Islands occur before or after his voyage to the Philippines?

4. How long did Magellan's voyage around the world take?

Applying the Skill

Making a Time Line List 10 key events that have occurred in your life and the dates on which these events occurred. Write the events in chronological order on a time line.

GO TO
Glencoe's **Skillbuilder Interactive Workbook CD-ROM, Level 1,** provides instruction and practice in key social studies skills.

1510
Promoted to captain

1517
Offers services to king of Spain

c. 1506
Travels to Spice Islands on exploratory expeditions

◆1480   ◆1490   ◆1500   ◆1510   ◆1520

c. 1480
Magellan is born in Sabrosa, Portugal

Sept. 20, 1519
Sails from Spain with five ships

April 7, 1521
Lands in the Philippines

c. 1490
Spends early years as a page at Portuguese court

April 27, 1521
Magellan is killed during an inter-island dispute

Sept. 6, 1522
One ship reaches Spain with valuable cargo

Chapter Summary
Exploring the Americas

c. 1000
- Leif Eriksson lands in present-day Newfoundland

1488
- Bartholomeu Dias reaches Indian Ocean

1492
- Columbus lands in the Americas

1498
- Vasco da Gama reaches India

1519
- Magellan begins circumnavigation of the world
- Hernán Cortés lands in Mexico

1532
- Francisco Pizarro captures Atahualpa

1535
- Jacques Cartier sails up the St. Lawrence River to Montreal

1541
- De Soto crosses the Mississippi River

1565
- Spain establishes fort at St. Augustine, Florida

1609
- Henry Hudson sails the Hudson River

Reviewing Key Terms

Examine the groups of words below. Then write sentences explaining what each group has in common.

1. Renaissance, astrolabe, caravel
2. conquistador, mission, presidio
3. mercantilism, Northwest Passage

Reviewing Key Facts

4. Why were Europeans interested in Asia?
5. What three large African kingdoms south of the Sahara flourished between 300 and 1600?
6. What European leader set up a center for exploration in Portugal?
7. Where did the earliest Portuguese explorers sail?
8. Which country supported Columbus on his quest to find a water route to Asia?
9. List the major accomplishments of Vasco da Gama, Juan Ponce de León, and John Cabot.
10. What was the main reason the Spanish wanted to conquer the Aztec and the Inca?
11. How did the Spanish colonial system of *encomiendas* affect Native Americans?
12. What movement created religious rivalries in Europe that carried over into exploration of the Americas?
13. What were explorers searching for during their explorations of the North American coast?

Critical Thinking

14. **Analyzing Primary Sources** Read the Two Viewpoints on page 47. What does Red Jacket mean by "this great island"?
15. **Drawing Conclusions** Why do you think the Caribbean Islands are often referred to as the West Indies?
16. **Analyzing Information** Study the feature on the Columbian Exchange on page 60. What foods were shipped to Europe?
17. **Determining Cause and Effect** Re-create the diagram below and identify three reasons for voyages of exploration and three effects that resulted from the exploration.

Voyages of exploration

NATIONAL GEOGRAPHIC
Missions in New Spain by the 1800s

0 300 miles
0 300 kilometers
Lambert Equal-Area projection

- City
- Mission
- Present-day boundary

 Geography and History Activity

Study the map above and answer the questions that follow.

18. **Place** In what present-day states were the Spanish missions located?

19. **Location** Near what city was the northernmost Spanish mission located?

20. **Location** In which direction would a traveler leaving Mexico City journey to reach San Diego?

Practicing Skills

Reading a Time Line *Study the time line on pages 36–37, then answer the following questions.*

21. What is the time span covered on this time line?

22. In which century does the greatest number of events take place on this time line?

23. What event occurred in 1522?

 Technology Activity

24. **Using Word Processing Software** Search the library for information on boats and sailing. Using word processing software, prepare a report about a navigational instrument that is in use today. Describe how it would have been helpful to an explorer such as Magellan.

Citizenship Cooperative Activity

25. **Interviewing** In a group of three, find out if any people in your community have come from Great Britain, Spain, France, or other countries. Try to interview these people and ask them about the political system of the country they came from. Prepare an oral report for the class.

Economics Activity

26. Ask family members and other adults about prices paid for common products in years past. Ask about grocery items, haircuts, cars, and so on. Compare these prices with current prices. Share your findings with the class.

 Alternative Assessment

27. **Portfolio Writing Activity** Choose an explorer discussed in this chapter. Use library resources to research the explorer's life and achievements. Prepare an interview with that explorer. Plan the questions to ask and the answers you would expect the explorer to give. Write the interview as a magazine article.

Standardized Test Practice

Directions: Choose the *best* answer to the following question.

Juana Inés de la Cruz was an unusual woman because she was famous as a

A writer.
B prince.
C farmer.
D warrior.

Test-Taking Tip:
Eliminate answers that don't make sense. For instance, a woman could not be a prince, so **B** could not be the correct answer.

UNIT

2 Colonial Settlement

1587–1770

Why It Matters

As you study Unit 2, you will learn that in the 1600s and 1700s the English established colonies in the Americas—some for profit and others by religious groups seeking freedom. In time, a distinctly new American society emerged.

Pewter pitcher,
Plymouth plantation

Primary Sources Library

See pages 594–595 for primary source readings to accompany Unit 2.

 *Use the **American History Primary Source Document Library CD-ROM** to find additional primary sources about the European colonies.*

*Signing the
Mayflower Compact by
Edward Percy Moran*

"*The Indians brought us great store both of Corne and bread ready made. . . .*"

— John Smith, 1608

CHAPTER 3

Colonial America

1587–1770

Why It Matters

The early North American colonies were a meeting place of cultures. The Europeans who settled these colonies included Protestants, Catholics, and Jews.

The Impact Today

The colonies influenced values and beliefs many Americans cherish today. For example:
- *Many people still come to the Americas in search of economic opportunity and religious freedom.*
- *Representative government remains an important part of the American political system.*

 The American Republic to 1877 Video *The chapter 3 video, "The Lost Colony," examines the colony of Roanoke and how conditions were much harsher than settlers were led to believe.*

The Americas

1607
- English establish first permanent settlement at Jamestown

1620
- Pilgrims land at Plymouth Rock

1630
- Puritans begin settling Massachusetts Bay

1550　　　*1600*　　　*1650*

World

1588
- England defeats Spanish Armada

c. 1605
- Shakespeare writes *King Lear*

1660
- King Charles II is restored to the English throne

Pilgrims Going to Church by George Boughton George Boughton painted many scenes about American colonial life.

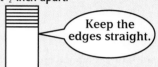

Comparison Study Foldable When you group facts into categories, it is easier to make comparisons. Make this foldable to compare and contrast the 13 colonies and their regions.

Step 1 Collect 7 sheets of paper and place them about $\frac{1}{2}$ inch apart.

> Keep the edges straight.

Step 2 Fold up the bottom edges of the paper to form 14 tabs.

> This makes all tabs the same size.

Step 3 When all the tabs are the same size, crease the paper to hold the tabs in place and staple the sheets together. Label each tab with the name of a colony and color-code each region.

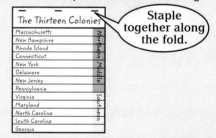

> Staple together along the fold.

The Thirteen Colonies

Massachusetts	Northern
New Hampshire	
Rhode Island	
Connecticut	
New York	Middle
Delaware	
New Jersey	
Pennsylvania	
Virginia	Southern
Maryland	
North Carolina	
South Carolina	
Georgia	

Reading and Writing As you read, write what you learn about each of the 13 colonies under each tab and compare the colonies.

1675
- King Philip's War begins

1718
- French establish port of New Orleans

1763
- British tighten enforcement of Navigation Acts

1769
- Mission of San Diego founded

1700

1750

1670
- Alafin Ajagbo founds Oyo Empire in Nigeria

1702
- England and France go to war

HISTORY Online

Chapter Overview
Visit tarvol1.glencoe.com and click on **Chapter 3— Chapter Overviews** to preview chapter information.

Early English Settlements

Guide to Reading

Main Idea
Jamestown became the first successfully established English colony in North America.

Key Terms
charter, joint-stock company, burgesses

Reading Strategy
Organizing Information As you read Section 1, re-create the diagram below and describe the economy and government of Jamestown.

Jamestown	Description
Economy	
Government	

Read to Learn
- what crop saved the people of Jamestown.
- how the colonists received political rights.

Section Theme
Economic Factors Many settlers journeyed to America with the hope of making a fortune.

Preview of Events

♦1580	♦1590	♦1600	♦1610	♦1620

1583
Sir Humphrey Gilbert claims Newfoundland for Queen Elizabeth

c. 1590
Settlers of Roanoke Island vanish

1607
Colonists settle at Jamestown

1619
House of Burgesses meets in Jamestown

English soldier's helmet, Jamestown

A European Story

In the summer of 1588, Spanish warships sailed toward the coast of England. King Philip II of Spain had sent the armada, or war fleet, of 132 ships to invade England. With 30,000 troops and 2,400 guns, the Spanish Armada was the mightiest naval force the world had ever seen. Yet the smaller, swifter English ships won the battle. The Spanish Armada fled north to Scotland, where violent storms destroyed and scattered the fleet. Only about one-half of the Spanish ships straggled home.

England in America

England and Spain had been heading toward war for years. Trading rivalry and religious differences divided the two countries. King Philip II, who ruled Spain from 1556 to 1598, was a powerful monarch and a strong defender of the Catholic faith. He wanted to put a Catholic ruler on the throne of England and bring the country back to the Catholic Church. King Philip did not consider Queen Elizabeth, a Protestant, the rightful ruler of England.

Attacks on Spanish ships and ports by such English adventurers as **Sir Francis Drake** angered Philip. He thought that Queen Elizabeth should punish Drake for his raids. Instead, she honored Drake with a knighthood. Philip sent the Spanish Armada to conquer England—but it failed completely.

Although war between England and Spain continued until 1604, the defeat of the armada marked the end of Spanish control of the seas. Now the way was clear for England and other nations to start colonies in North America.

The Lost Colony of Roanoke

The English had made several attempts to establish a base on the other side of the Atlantic before their victory over Spain. In 1583 **Sir Humphrey Gilbert** claimed Newfoundland for Queen Elizabeth. Then he sailed south along the coast looking for a place to establish a colony. Before finding a site, he died at sea.

The following year, Queen Elizabeth gave **Sir Walter Raleigh** the right to claim land in North America. Raleigh sent an expedition to look for a good place to settle. His scouts returned with an enthusiastic report of **Roanoke Island,** off the coast of present-day North Carolina.

In 1585 Raleigh sent about 100 men to settle on Roanoke Island. After a difficult winter on the island, the unhappy colonists decided to return to England. In 1587 Raleigh tried again, sending 91 men, 17 women, and 9 children to Roanoke. **John White,** a mapmaker and artist, led the group. Shortly after arriving on the island, White's daughter gave birth. This baby, named Virginia Dare, was the first English child born in North America. White explored the area and drew pictures of what he saw. He and other explorers described the towns of the Native Americans who lived in the area:

> ❝Their towns are small and few . . . a village may contain but ten or twelve houses—some perhaps as many as twenty. . . . ❞

The new settlers began building a colony. They needed many supplies, however, and White sailed to England for the supplies and to recruit more settlers. Although he had hoped to be back within a few months, the war with Spain delayed his return for nearly three years.

When White finally returned to Roanoke, he found it deserted. The only clue to the fate of the settlers was the word *Croatoan* carved on a gatepost. White thought the colonists must have gone to Croatoan Island, about 50 miles to the south. Bad weather kept White from investigating. The Roanoke colonists were never seen again.

✔**Reading Check** **Describing** Why did Raleigh choose Roanoke as the site for the colony?

Jamestown Settlement

Roanoke was Sir Walter Raleigh's last attempt to establish a colony. For a time his failure discouraged others from planning English colonies in North America. However, the idea emerged again in 1606. Several groups of merchants sought charters, the right to organize settlements in an area, from King James I.

The Virginia Company

One group of merchants, the Virginia Company of London, received a charter to "make habitation . . . into that part of America, commonly called Virginia." The Virginia Company was a joint-stock company. Investors bought stock, or part ownership, in the company in return for a share of its future profits.

The company acted quickly. In December 1606, it sent 144 settlers in 3 ships to build a new colony in North America. The settlers were supposed to look for gold and attempt to establish trade in fish and furs. Forty of them died during the voyage.

In April 1607, the ships entered **Chesapeake Bay** and then sailed up a river flowing into the bay. The colonists named the river the James and their new settlement **Jamestown** to honor their king. The settlers built Jamestown on a peninsula so they could defend it from attack. The site had major drawbacks, however. The swampy land swarmed with mosquitoes that carried disease. Jamestown also lacked good farmland.

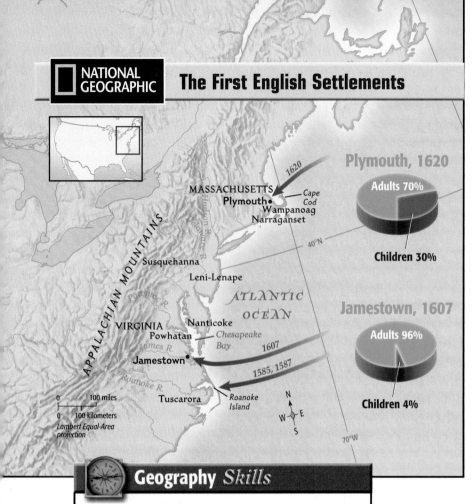

NATIONAL GEOGRAPHIC

The First English Settlements

Plymouth, 1620

Adults 70%

Children 30%

Jamestown, 1607

Adults 96%

Children 4%

MASSACHUSETTS
Plymouth
Cape Cod
Wampanoag
Narraganset

APPALACHIAN MOUNTAINS

Susquehanna

Leni-Lenape

ATLANTIC OCEAN

Nanticoke

VIRGINIA
Powhatan
Chesapeake Bay

Jamestown

1607

1585, 1587

Tuscarora
Roanoke Island

40°N

70°W

0   100 miles
0   100 kilometers
Lambert Equal-Area projection

Geography *Skills*

Many Native American groups lived near the first English settlements in the late 1500s and early 1600s.
1. Location Which colony was located farthest north?
2. Location Which Native American groups lived nearest to the Jamestown colonists?

The colonists faced more hardships over the next several months. Many of them were not accustomed to hard labor. Because the London investors expected a quick profit from their colony, the settlers searched for gold and silver when they should have been growing food. In addition, disease and hunger took a huge toll on the colonists. By spring 1608, when ships arrived with supplies and more settlers, only 38 of the Jamestown colonists remained alive.

Captain John Smith

Governing Jamestown was perhaps the biggest obstacle the colonists faced. The colony survived its first two years because of 27-year-old **Captain John Smith,** an experienced soldier and explorer. Smith forced the settlers to work,

explored the area, and managed to get corn from the local Native Americans led by Chief Powhatan. In August 1609, 400 new settlers arrived. Two months later, John Smith returned to England. Without strong leadership, the colony could not feed so many people. The winter of 1609–1610 became known as "the starving time." Fighting broke out with the Native Americans. When more settlers arrived in the spring they found only 60 survivors.

Economics

Farming the Land

Although the Virginia colonists did not find any gold or silver, they did discover another way to make money for the investors. One colonist, **John Rolfe,** learned to grow a type of tobacco using seeds from the West Indies. The first crop was sold in England in 1614. Soon planters all along the James River were raising tobacco, and the colony of Virginia began to prosper and grow. Relations with the Native Americans also improved after Rolfe married **Pocahontas,** the daughter of Chief Powhatan.

In 1614 some of the colonists were allowed to rent plots of land. Most of what they grew on their plots was their own. This move toward private ownership encouraged the colonists to grow food crops to sell—and work harder. One of the colonists explained that the colonists often avoided work when

❝our people were fed out of the common store, and labored jointly together.❞

Now that the colonists could farm their own land and operate for profit in a competitive system, they made greater efforts to succeed.

Pocahontas

Private land ownership was expanded in 1618. All the colonists who had paid their own way to America were granted 100 acres of land. In order to attract more colonists, the company gave a land grant called a **headright** of 50 acres to those who paid their own way. A settler also received 50 acres for each family member over 15 years of age and for each servant brought to Virginia. This system convinced thousands of people to move to Virginia.

Citizenship
Representative Government
At first nearly all of Jamestown's settlers were men. They worked for the Virginia Company and lived under strict rules. As the colony grew, the settlers complained about taking orders from the Virginia Company in London. In 1619 the company agreed to let the colonists have some say in their government. Ten towns in the colony each sent two representatives called burgesses to an assembly. The assembly had the right to make local laws for the colony. On July 30, 1619, the **House of Burgesses** met for the first time in a church in Jamestown.

New Arrivals in Jamestown
In 1619 the Virginia Company sent 90 women to Jamestown. As a company report noted: "The plantation can never flourish till families be planted, and the respect of wives and children fix the people on the soil." Colonists who wanted to marry one of the women had to pay a fee of 120 pounds of tobacco. Men still outnumbered women in the colony, but marriage and children became a part of life in Virginia.

A Dutch ship brought another group of newcomers to Jamestown in 1619—twenty Africans who were sold to Virginia planters to labor in the tobacco fields. These first Africans may have come as servants—engaged to work for a set period of time—rather than as slaves.

Until about 1640 some African laborers in Jamestown were free and even owned property. William Tucker, the first African American born in the American colonies, was a free man. In the years to follow, however, many more shiploads of Africans would arrive in North America, and those unwilling passengers would be sold as slaves. Slavery was first recognized in Virginia law in the 1660s.

In the early 1620s, the Virginia Company faced financial troubles. The company had poured all its money into Jamestown, but little profit was returned. The colony also suffered an attack by the Native Americans. In 1624 King James canceled the company's charter and made Jamestown the first royal colony for England in America.

Reading Check **Analyzing** Why was the House of Burgesses important?

SECTION 1 ASSESSMENT

Checking for Understanding
1. **Key Terms** Write a short paragraph in which you use the following key terms: charter, burgesses, joint-stock company.
2. **Reviewing Facts** Why did the Virginia Company establish settlements in North America?

Reviewing Themes
3. **Economic Factors** What economic activity helped save the Jamestown settlement?

Critical Thinking
4. **Making Inferences** Why do you think the king of England was willing to let a group of merchants try to establish a colony in North America?
5. **Determining Cause and Effect** Re-create the diagram below and list two effects of Jamestown's growth.

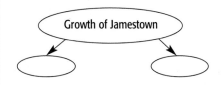

Growth of Jamestown

Analyzing Visuals
6. **Geography Skills** Study the map and graphs on page 72. What percentage of settlers in Plymouth were children?

Interdisciplinary Activity
Geography Create a poster that might have attracted early colonists to the area where you live. Focus on the location as well as natural features in your area such as good farmland, forests, waterways, and mineral resources.

FOOTHOLD IN THE NEW WORLD

JAMESTOWN: THE FIRST PERMANENT ENGLISH COLONY In the spring of 1607, three ships carrying more than a hundred English settlers sailed into the Chesapeake Bay to establish a colony and find gold. The settlers built a fort on a marshy island in the James River and named it in honor of King James I.

THE EXPEDITIONS

Captain John Smith emerged as a leader of the group. An avid explorer, he led four expeditions in the area:

- Shortly after arriving, he and Captain Christopher Newport sailed up the James River to search for gold. Powhatan's followers made them turn back at the falls.

- In December 1607 Smith and a small band of settlers set out looking for gold and food along the Chickahominy River. According to Smith, he was captured and about to be clubbed to death by Powhatan's followers when Pocahontas (the chief's daughter) saved him.

- In 1608 Smith headed up two voyages to explore the northern reaches of Chesapeake Bay. He searched futilely for gold and an outlet to the Pacific Ocean.

THE SETTLEMENT

The colonists endured many terrible hardships. Bad water, disease, starvation, and conflict with the Native Americans took a heavy toll. By early 1608 only 38 hardy souls remained alive.

Settlers learned to grow crops in the new land. When tobacco from the West Indies was introduced, it became a commercial success and guaranteed Jamestown's future.

Jamestown

■ Native American settlement

▨ Powhatan's territory

Expeditions

— May 1607

— December 1607 – January 1608

— January – July 1608

— July – September 1608

0 _____ 25 miles

0 _____ 25 kilometers

Appalachian

The Native Americans taught the settlers to cultivate native crops such as corn, beans, and squash. Corn quickly became the staple food.

LEARNING *from* GEOGRAPHY

1. **Compare the dwellings of the colonists and the Native Americans.**

2. **How did the introduction of tobacco affect the development of the colony?**

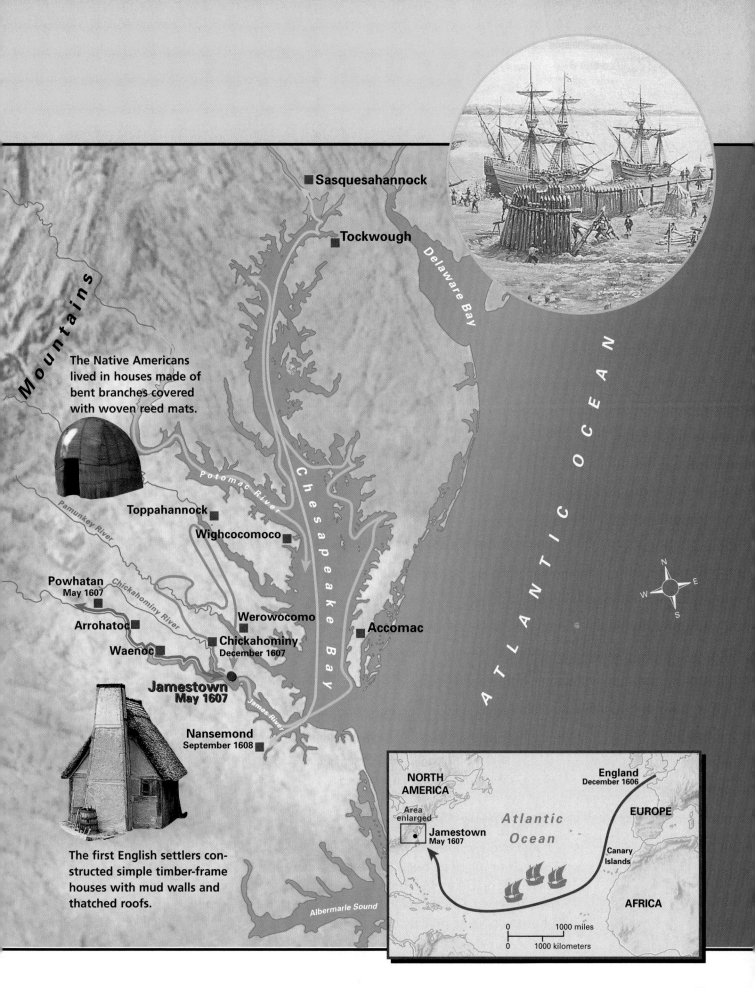

Sasquesahannock

Tockwough

Delaware Bay

Mountains

The Native Americans lived in houses made of bent branches covered with woven reed mats.

Pamunkey River

Potomac River

Chesapeake Bay

Toppahannock

Wighcocomoco

Chickahominy River

Powhatan
May 1607

Arrohatoc

Waenoc

Werowocomo

Chickahominy
December 1607

Accomac

Jamestown
May 1607

James River

Nansemond
September 1608

ATLANTIC OCEAN

N
W   E
S

The first English settlers constructed simple timber-frame houses with mud walls and thatched roofs.

Albermarle Sound

NORTH
AMERICA

Area
enlarged

Jamestown
May 1607

England
December 1606

Atlantic
Ocean

EUROPE

Canary
Islands

AFRICA

0   1000 miles

0   1000 kilometers

New England Colonies

Guide to Reading

Main Idea
Settlers begin to form the New England Colonies.

Key Terms
dissent, persecute, Puritan, Separatist, Pilgrim, Mayflower Compact, toleration

Reading Strategy
Classifying Information As you read Section 2, re-create the diagram below and explain why different colonies in New England were settled.

Colony	Reasons the colony was settled
Massachusetts	
Connecticut	
Rhode Island	

Read to Learn
- why the Pilgrims and the Puritans came to America.
- how the Connecticut, Rhode Island, and New Hampshire colonies began.

Section Theme
Civic Rights and Responsibilities
Puritan and Pilgrim colonists settled in America in search of religious freedom.

Preview of Events

◆1620 ———————————— ◆1630 ———————————— ◆1640

1620
Pilgrims land at Plymouth

1630
Puritans settle the Massachusetts Bay Colony

1636
Thomas Hooker founds Hartford

1638
Anne Hutchinson founds Portsmouth

AN American Story

Shoes, Plymouth Colony

The young man looked around at the other passengers aboard the *Mayflower.* He and the other passengers sailed to the new world not knowing what they would find. They had muskets but knew little about shooting. They planned to fish but knew nothing about fishing. They had hoped to settle in Virginia but instead landed in New England without enough supplies to last the winter. The only thing these people had plenty of was courage. They would need it.

Religious Freedom

Unlike the Jamestown settlers, the next wave of colonists would arrive in search of religious freedom. England had been a Protestant country since 1534, when King Henry VIII broke away from the Roman Catholic Church and formed the Anglican Church. Not everyone in England was happy with the new church, however. Many people dissented—they disagreed with the beliefs or practices of the Anglicans. English Catholics, for example, still considered the pope the head of the church, and they were often persecuted, or treated harshly, for that reason.

At the same time, some Protestants wanted to change—or reform—the Anglican Church, while others wanted to break away from it altogether. The Protestants who wanted to reform the Anglican Church were called Puritans. Those who wanted to leave and set up their own churches were known as Separatists.

The Separatists were persecuted in England, and some fled to the Netherlands. Though they found religious freedom there, the Separatists had difficulty finding work. They also worried that their children were losing their religious values and their English way of life.

The Pilgrims' Journey

Some Separatists in the Netherlands made an arrangement with the Virginia Company. The Separatists could settle in Virginia and practice their religion freely. In return they would give the company a share of any profits they made.

The Separatists considered themselves Pilgrims because their journey had a religious purpose. Only 35 of the 102 passengers who boarded the *Mayflower* in September 1620 were Pilgrims. The others were called "strangers." They were common people—servants, craftspeople, and poor farmers—who hoped to find a better life in America. Because Pilgrim beliefs shaped life in the Plymouth colony, however, all the early settlers are usually called Pilgrims.

The Mayflower Compact

The *Mayflower*'s passengers planned to settle in the Virginia colony. The first land they sighted was **Cape Cod,** well north of their target. Because it was November and winter was fast approaching, the colonists decided to drop anchor in Cape Cod Bay. They went ashore on a cold, bleak day in December at a place called Plymouth. **William Bradford,** their leader and historian, reported that "all things stared upon them with a weather-beaten face."

Plymouth was outside the territory of the Virginia Company and its laws. Before going ashore, the Pilgrims drew up a formal document called the Mayflower Compact. The compact pledged their loyalty to England and declared their intention of forming "a civil body politic, for our better

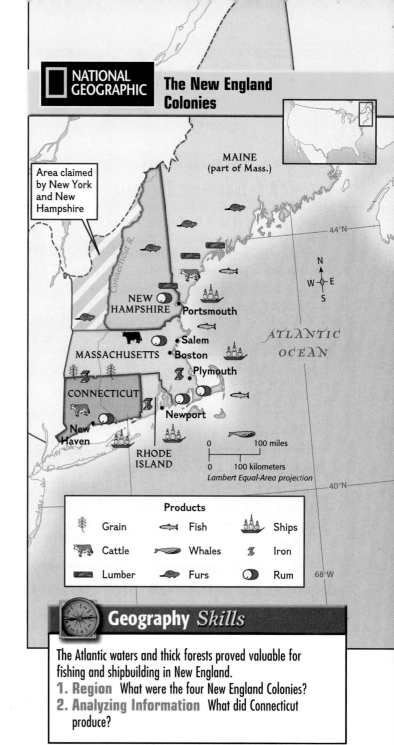

The New England Colonies

NATIONAL GEOGRAPHIC

Products

- Grain
- Cattle
- Lumber
- Fish
- Whales
- Furs
- Ships
- Iron
- Rum

Geography *Skills*

The Atlantic waters and thick forests proved valuable for fishing and shipbuilding in New England.
1. **Region** What were the four New England Colonies?
2. **Analyzing Information** What did Connecticut produce?

ordering and preservation." The signers also promised to obey the laws passed "for the general good of the colony." The Mayflower Compact was a necessary step in the development of representative government in America.

📖 *(See page 612 of the Appendix for the entire text of the Mayflower Compact.)*

Help From the Native Americans

Their first winter in America, almost half the Pilgrims died of malnutrition, disease, and

MORE ABOUT...

The First Thanksgiving

In the autumn of 1621 the Pilgrims invited the Native Americans to celebrate the peace between them. After the struggle through the first winter, the Pilgrims also felt relieved to be raising food. During the feast the Pilgrims thanked God for the harvest and for their survival.

First Thanksgiving by Jennie A. Brownscombe

Who took part? About 50 men, women, and children colonists and 90 Wampanoag Native Americans took part in the three-day feast.

What did they do? Dancing, singing, and playing games were part of the celebration. The Wampanoag demonstrated their skills with the bow and arrow.

When was it held? Exactly when the festival took place is uncertain, but it is believed the celebration occurred sometime between September 21 and November 9.

What did they eat? They most likely ate wild fowl, duck, and turkey shot by the colonists and deer provided by the Wampanoag.

---

cold. In the spring a few Native Americans approached the settlement. Two of them, **Squanto** and **Samoset,** befriended the colonists. Squanto was a Pawtuxet who had been kidnapped to Europe and had learned English.

Squanto and Samoset showed the Pilgrims how to grow corn, beans, and pumpkins and where to hunt and fish. Without their help the Pilgrims might not have survived. Squanto and Samoset also helped the Pilgrims make a treaty with the Wampanoag people who lived in the area. **Massasoit,** a Wampanoag leader, signed a treaty with the Pilgrims in March 1621, and the two groups lived in harmony.

✓ Reading Check **Summarizing** Why was the Mayflower Compact an important step toward representative government?

New Settlements

In 1625 the English throne passed to Charles I. Charles objected to the Puritans' calls for reform in the Anglican Church, and persecution of Puritans increased again. Some Puritans looked for a way to leave England.

In 1629 a group of Puritans formed the Massachusetts Bay Company and received a royal charter to establish a colony north of Plymouth. This was the Puritans' chance to create a new society in America—a society based on the Bible.

The company chose a well-educated Puritan named **John Winthrop** to be the colony's governor. In 1630 Winthrop led about 900 men, women, and children to **Massachusetts Bay.** Most of them settled in a place they called Boston.

Citizenship

Growth and Government

During the 1630s, more than 15,000 Puritans journeyed to Massachusetts to escape religious persecution and economic hard times in England. This movement of people became known as the **Great Migration.**

At first, John Winthrop and his assistants made the colony's laws. They were chosen by the General Court, which was made up of the colony's stockholders. In 1634, settlers demanded a larger role in the government. The General Court became an elected assembly. Adult male church members were allowed to vote for the governor and for their town's representatives to the General Court. In later years, they also had to own property to vote.

The Puritans came to America to put their religious beliefs into practice. The Puritans had little toleration—they criticized or persecuted people who held other religious views. This lack of toleration led to the creation of new colonies.

Connecticut and Rhode Island

The fertile Connecticut River valley, south of Massachusetts, was much better for farming than was the stony soil around Boston. In the 1630s colonists began to settle in this area.

A minister named Thomas Hooker became dissatisfied with Massachusetts. He did not like the way that Winthrop and the other Puritan leaders ran the colony. In 1636 Hooker led his congregation through the wilderness to Connecticut, where he founded the town of **Hartford.** Three years later Hartford and two other towns, Windsor and Wethersfield, agreed to form a colony. They adopted a plan of government called the **Fundamental Orders of Connecticut.** This was the first written constitution in America, and it described the organization of representative government in detail.

Good land drew colonists to Connecticut, but Rhode Island was settled by colonists who were forced out of Massachusetts. The first of these was **Roger Williams,** a minister. Williams felt that people should not be persecuted for their religious practices. In his view the government should not force people to worship in a certain way. Williams also believed it was wrong for settlers to take land away from the Native Americans.

The ideas of Roger Williams caused Massachusetts leaders to banish him in 1635. He took refuge with the Narraganset people, who later

People In History

Anne Hutchinson 1591–1643

Anne Hutchinson came to Massachusetts with her husband in 1634. She began questioning the religious authority of the colony's ministers.

As Hutchinson gained followers, she was seen as a danger to the colony's stability. In 1637 the Massachusetts leaders put her on trial for speaking false ideas.

Hutchinson defended herself well, but she claimed God spoke to her directly. This disagreed with Puritan beliefs that God spoke only through the Bible. Her accusers found her guilty and ordered her to leave the colony. With her family and some followers, Hutchinson moved to Rhode Island.

sold Williams land where he founded the town of Providence. Williams received a charter in 1644 for a colony east of Connecticut called **Rhode Island and Providence Plantations.** With its policy of religious toleration, Rhode Island became a safe place for dissenters. It was the first place in America where people of all faiths—including Jews—could worship freely.

Others followed Williams's example, forming colonies where they could worship as they pleased. In 1638 **John Wheelwright** led a group of dissidents from Massachusetts to the north. They founded the town of Exeter in **New Hampshire.** The same year, a group of Puritans settled Hampton. The colony of New Hampshire became fully independent of Massachusetts in 1679.

Conflict With Native Americans

Native Americans traded with the settlers, exchanging furs for goods such as iron pots, blankets, and guns. In Virginia the colonists had frequent encounters with the many tribes of the Powhatan confederacy. In New England the settlers met the Wampanoags, Narragansets, and other groups.

Conflicts arose, however. Usually settlers moved onto Native American lands without permission or payment. Throughout the colonial period, English settlers and Native Americans competed fiercely for control of the land.

HISTORY Online

Student Web Activity
Visit tarvol1.glencoe.com and click on **Chapter 3— Student Web Activities** for an activity on King Philip's War.

In 1636 war broke out between the settlers and the Pequot people. After two traders were killed in Pequot territory, Massachusetts sent troops to punish the Pequot. The Pequot then attacked a town in Connecticut killing nine people. In May 1637, troops from Connecticut attacked the main Pequot fort with the help of the Narraganset people. They burned the fort, killing hundreds.

In 1675 New England went to war against the Wampanoag people and their allies. Metacomet, the Wampanoag chief, was known to settlers as King Philip. He wanted to stop the settlers from moving onto Native American lands. The war began after settlers executed three Wampanoags for murder. Metacomet's forces attacked towns across the region, killing hundreds of people.

The settlers and their Native American allies fought back. King Philip's War, as the conflict was called, ended in defeat for the Wampanoag and their allies. The war destroyed the power of the Native Americans in New England, leaving the colonists free to expand their settlements.

✔ **Reading Check** **Evaluating** Describe the significance of the Fundamental Orders of Connecticut.

SECTION 2 ASSESSMENT

Checking for Understanding

1. **Key Terms** Write a short paragraph in which you use the following terms: dissent, persecute, Puritan, Separatist, Pilgrim, Mayflower Compact, toleration.

2. **Reviewing Facts** Identify the reasons why the Separatists left Europe for the Americas.

Reviewing Themes

3. **Civic Rights and Responsibilities** What freedom did Rhode Island offer that other colonies did not?

Critical Thinking

4. **Comparing** What did the Mayflower Compact and the Fundamental Orders of Connecticut have in common?

5. **Determining Cause and Effect** Re-create the diagram below and describe the effects as colonists interacted with Native Americans.

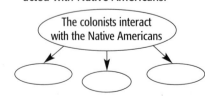

The colonists interact with the Native Americans

Analyzing Maps

6. **Geography Skills** Study the map on page 77. What products came from New Hampshire?

Interdisciplinary Activity

Government Research and write a one-page paper about the life of Roger Williams. Explain why he left Massachusetts to found a new colony. Describe how his religious ideals contributed to the growth of the representative government in Rhode Island.

Social Studies
SKILLBUILDER

Reading a Bar Graph

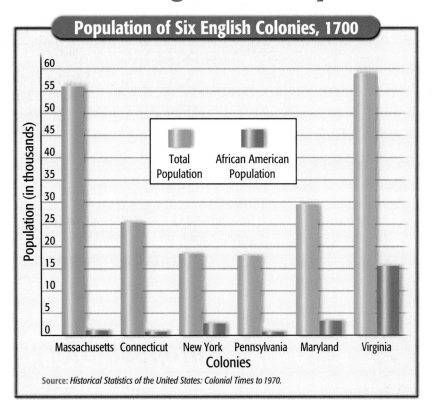

Population of Six English Colonies, 1700

Source: *Historical Statistics of the United States: Colonial Times to 1970.*

Why Learn This Skill?

A bar graph presents numerical information in a visual way. Bars of various lengths stand for different quantities. A bar graph lets you see a lot of information in an organized way. Bars may be drawn vertically—up and down—or horizontally—left to right. Labels along the left axis and the bottom axis explain what the bars represent.

Learning the Skill

To read a bar graph:
- Read the title to learn the subject of the graph.
- Look at the horizontal and vertical axes to find out what information the graph presents.
- Compare the lengths of the bars on the graph.

Practicing the Skill

Study the bar graph on this page and answer the following questions.

1. Which colony had the largest total population in 1700? The smallest?

2. Did Virginia or Maryland have a larger African American population?

Applying the Skill

Reading a Bar Graph Create a bar graph to represent the number of students in each American history class in your school.

 Glencoe's **Skillbuilder Interactive Workbook CD-ROM, Level 1,** provides instruction and practice in key social studies skills.

Middle Colonies

Main Idea
People from many different countries settled in the Middle Colonies for a variety of reasons, including religious freedom.

Key Terms
patroon, proprietary colony, pacifist

Reading Strategy
Classifying Information As you read the section, re-create the diagram below and describe how the Middle Colonies were founded.

Colony	Founder	Why settlers came
New York		
New Jersey		
Pennsylvania		

Read to Learn
- why the Middle Colonies had the most diverse populations in colonial America.
- who was America's first town planner.

Section Theme
Individual Action Leaders such as Peter Stuyvesant and William Penn helped the Middle Colonies grow.

Preview of Events

♦1600 — ♦1650 — ♦1700

1626
Manhattan Island purchased from the Manhates people

1664
New Amsterdam becomes New York

1681
William Penn founds Pennsylvania

1702
New Jersey becomes a royal colony

A
European Story

English royal plate

In 1649, 17-year-old Philip Henry stood near the back of the crowd gathered around a public platform near Whitehall Palace in London. There he watched Charles I, the king of England, prepare to die. The king made a short speech, prayed silently, and then knelt with his head on the block.

With just one blow, the executioner severed the king's head from his body. At that moment, the crowd uttered "such a groan as I never heard before, and desire I may never hear again," Henry wrote in his diary.

England and the Colonies

In England the Puritans who controlled Parliament were engaged in a struggle for power against King Charles I. In 1642 a civil war began. Led by Oliver Cromwell, a Puritan, the Parliamentary forces defeated the king. Charles I was beheaded in 1649 after a parliamentary court declared him guilty of treason.

A new government was established with Cromwell as Protector. During these years of unrest, many Puritans left New England and returned to England to fight with Parliament's forces. After the war ended, English men and women loyal to the king went to royal colonies like Virginia.

After Cromwell died in 1658, Parliament brought back the monarchy, but placed new limits on the ruler's powers. Charles II, son of Charles I, became king in 1660. His reign is called the *Restoration* because the monarchy had been restored.

In 1660 England had two clusters of colonies in what is now the United States—Massachusetts, New Hampshire, Connecticut, and Rhode Island in the north and Maryland and Virginia in the south. Between the two groups of English colonies were lands that the Dutch controlled.

In 1621 a group of Dutch merchants had formed the Dutch West India Company to trade in the Americas. Their posts along the Hudson River grew into the colony of New Netherland. The main settlement of the colony was **New Amsterdam,** located on **Manhattan Island.** In 1626 the company bought Manhattan from the Manhates people for small quantities of beads and other goods. Blessed with a good seaport, the city of New Amsterdam soon became a center of shipping to and from the Americas.

To increase the number of permanent settlers in its colony, the Dutch West India Company sent over families from the Netherlands, Germany, Sweden, and Finland. The company gave a large estate to anyone who brought at least 50 settlers to work the land. The wealthy landowners who acquired these riverfront estates were called patroons. The patroons ruled like kings. They had their own courts and laws. Settlers owed the patroon labor and a share of their crops.

England Takes Over

New Netherland boasted an excellent harbor and thriving river trade. The English wanted to acquire the valuable Dutch colony that lay between England's New England and Southern Colonies. In 1664 the English sent a fleet to attack New Amsterdam.

At the time **Peter Stuyvesant** was governor of the colony. His strict rule and heavy taxes turned many of the people in New Netherland against him. When the English ships sailed into New Amsterdam's harbor, the governor was unprepared for a battle and surrendered the colony to the English forces.

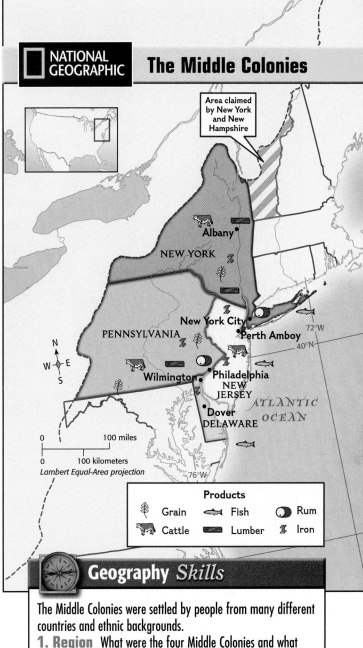

NATIONAL GEOGRAPHIC | **The Middle Colonies**

Area claimed by New York and New Hampshire

NEW YORK
Albany

PENNSYLVANIA
New York City
Perth Amboy
Wilmington
Philadelphia
NEW JERSEY
Dover
DELAWARE

ATLANTIC OCEAN

72°W
40°N
76°W

0   100 miles
0   100 kilometers
Lambert Equal-Area projection

Products
🌾 Grain   🐟 Fish   ⬤ Rum
🐄 Cattle   ▭ Lumber   Iron

Geography *Skills*

The Middle Colonies were settled by people from many different countries and ethnic backgrounds.

1. **Region** What were the four Middle Colonies and what were their main products?
2. **Drawing Conclusions** What geographic features made Philadelphia and New York City centers for trade?

King Charles II gave the colony to his brother, the **Duke of York,** who renamed it **New York.** New York was a proprietary colony, a colony in which the owner, or proprietor, owned all the land and controlled the government. It differed from the New England Colonies, where voters elected the governor and an assembly.

Most of New York's settlers lived in the Hudson River valley. The Duke of York promised the diverse colonists freedom of religion. In 1654, 23 Brazilian Jews had settled in New Amsterdam.

Penn's Treaty with the Indians In 1682 William Penn made his first treaty with the Delaware people. **Why did Penn see Pennsylvania as a "holy experiment"?**

They were the first Jews to settle in North America. In 1664 New York had about 8,000 inhabitants. Most were Dutch, but Germans, Swedes, Native Americans, and Puritans from New England lived there as well. The population also included at least 300 enslaved Africans. New Amsterdam, which was later called New York City, was one of the fastest-growing locations in the colony.

By 1683 the colony's population had swelled to about 12,000 people. A governor and council appointed by the Duke of York directed the colony's affairs. The colonists demanded a representative government like the governments of the other English colonies. The duke resisted the idea, but the people of New York would not give up. Finally, in 1691, the English government allowed New York to elect a legislature.

New Jersey

The Duke of York gave the southern part of his colony, between the Hudson and Delaware Rivers, to **Lord John Berkeley** and **Sir George Carteret.** The proprietors named their colony New Jersey after the island of Jersey in the English Channel, where Carteret was born.

To attract settlers, the proprietors offered large tracts of land and generous terms. They also promised freedom of religion, trial by jury, and a representative assembly. The assembly would make local laws and set tax rates.

Like New York, New Jersey was a place of ethnic and religious diversity. Because New Jersey had no natural harbors, however, it did not develop a major port or city like New York.

The proprietors of New Jersey did not make the profits they had expected. Berkeley sold his share, West Jersey, in 1674. Carteret's share, East Jersey, was sold in 1682.

By 1702 New Jersey had passed back into the hands of the king, becoming a royal colony. The colonists still continued to make local laws.

Reading Check **Explaining** Why did no major port develop in New Jersey?

Pennsylvania

In 1680 **William Penn,** a wealthy English gentleman, presented a plan to King Charles. Penn's father had once lent the king a great deal of money. Penn had inherited the king's promise to repay the loan. Instead of money, however, Penn asked for land in America. Pleased to get rid of his debt so easily, the king gave Penn a tract of land stretching inland from the Delaware River. The new colony, named Pennsylvania, was nearly as large as England.

William Penn belonged to a Protestant group of dissenters called the Society of Friends, or **Quakers.** The Quakers believed that every individual had an "inner light" that could guide him or her to salvation. Each person could experience religious truth directly, which meant that church services and officials were unnecessary. Everyone was equal in God's sight. Though firm in their beliefs, the Quakers were tolerant of the views of others.

Many people in England found the Quakers' ideas a threat to established traditions. Quakers would not bow or take off their hats to lords and ladies because of their belief that everyone was equal. In addition they were pacifists, people who refuse to use force or to fight in wars. Quakers were fined, jailed, and even executed for their beliefs.

William Penn saw Pennsylvania as a "holy experiment," a chance to put the Quaker ideals of toleration and equality into practice. In 1682 he sailed to America to supervise the building of **Philadelphia,** the "city of brotherly love." Penn believed that

❝any government is free to the people under it . . . where the laws rule, and the people are a party to those laws.❞

Penn had designed the city himself, making him America's first town planner. Penn also wrote Pennsylvania's first constitution.

Penn believed that the land belonged to the Native Americans and that settlers should pay for it. In 1682 he negotiated the first of several treaties with local Native Americans.

To encourage European settlers to come to Pennsylvania, Penn advertised the colony throughout Europe with pamphlets in several languages. By 1683 more than 3,000 English, Welsh, Irish, Dutch, and German settlers had arrived. In 1701, in the Charter of Liberties, Penn granted the colonists the right to elect representatives to the legislative assembly.

The southernmost part of Pennsylvania was called the Three Lower Counties. Settled by Swedes in 1638, the area had been taken over by the Dutch and the English before becoming part of Pennsylvania. The Charter of Privileges allowed the lower counties to form their own legislature, which they did in 1704. Thereafter the counties functioned as a separate colony known as Delaware, supervised by Pennsylvania's governor.

✓**Reading Check** **Summarizing** How did William Penn encourage self-government?

SECTION 3 ASSESSMENT

Checking for Understanding

1. **Key Terms** Write a short paragraph in which you use the following key terms: patroon, proprietary colony, pacifist

2. **Reviewing Facts** What did the Charter of Liberties grant to Pennsylvania colonists?

Reviewing Themes

3. **Individual Action** How did William Penn earn the respect of Native Americans?

Critical Thinking

4. **Compare and Contrast** How was the Quaker religion different from that of the Puritans?

5. **Organizing Information** Re-create the diagram below and describe how each of the Middle Colonies was governed.

Colony	Type of government
New York	
New Jersey	
Pennsylvania	

Analyzing Visuals

6. **Geography Skills** Review the map on page 83. What is the title of the map? What items are shown in the key? What products were important to Pennsylvania?

Interdisciplinary Activity

Art Design a flag for one of the Middle Colonies. Decide what symbols and colors would be appropriate to represent that colony. Display your flags in class.

Guide to Reading

Main Idea
The Southern Colonies relied on cash crops to survive, while the French and Spanish tried to establish their own settlements.

Key Terms
indentured servant, constitution, debtor, tenant farmer, mission

Reading Strategy
Classifying Information As you read the section, re-create the diagram below and identify the main crops of three of the Southern Colonies.

Colony	Main crop
Maryland	
North Carolina	
South Carolina	

Read to Learn
• how the Southern Colonies were established.
• how French and Spanish colonies differed from the English colonies.

Section Theme
Groups and Institutions Spanish and French settlements developed in different ways from English settlements.

Preview of Events

♦1600   ♦1650   ♦1700   ♦1750

c. 1610
Spanish establish Santa Fe

1676
Bacon's Rebellion occurs

1718
French establish city of New Orleans

1733
First settlers arrive in Georgia

Slave drum, Virginia

AN American Story

How did it feel to be enslaved on the plantations of the South? In the 1930s, interviewers put this question to African Americans once under slavery. Many of them were approaching 100 years old, and some still carried deep scars on their backs from whippings. To be a slave meant to have no human rights. Elderly Roberta Mason remembered, "Once they whipped my father 'cause he looked at a slave they killed, and cried."

Coming to America

By 1660, while tobacco prices fell, large plantations continued to prosper because they were better able to maintain high profits than were small farms. Along with the growth of plantations, there was an increasing need for workers in the newly settled Southern Colonies.

Establishing colonies in North America involved a great deal of work. The settlers had to clear the land, construct homes and churches, plant crops, and tend the fields. As the colonies expanded, the demand for capable workers grew.

Not all people came to work in the colonies of their own free will. English criminals and Scottish and Irish prisoners of war were also shipped to the colonies. They could earn their release by working for a period of time—often seven years. Some colonists complained that their settlements were dumping grounds for "His Majesty's seven-year passengers." African rulers took prisoners during wars and raids. They enslaved the captives and sold them to European slave traders who took them to the colonies. Many people came to the colonies as indentured servants. To pay for their passage to America, they agreed to work without pay for a certain period of time.

Establishing Maryland

Maryland arose from the dream of **Sir George Calvert, Lord Baltimore,** a Catholic. Calvert wanted to establish a safe place for his fellow Catholics, who were being persecuted in England. He also hoped that a colony would bring him a fortune.

Calvert's dream came true in 1632 when King Charles I gave him a proprietary colony north of Virginia. Calvert died before receiving the grant. His son Cecilius Calvert inherited the colony. It was named Maryland either after the English queen, Henrietta Maria, or after the Virgin Mary.

The younger Calvert—the new Lord Baltimore—never lived in Maryland. Instead, he sent two of his brothers to run the colony. They reached America in 1634 with two ships and more than 200 settlers. Entering the Chesapeake Bay, they sailed up the **Potomac River** through fertile countryside. A priest in the party described the Potomac as "the sweetest and greatest river I have ever seen." The colonists chose a site for their settlement, which they called St. Marys.

Knowing that tobacco had saved the Virginia colony, the Maryland colonists turned first to tobacco farming. To keep the colony from becoming too dependent on one crop, however, a Maryland law declared that "every person planting tobacco shall plant and tend two acres of corn." In addition to corn, most Maryland tobacco farmers produced wheat, fruit, vegetables, and livestock to feed their families and

their workers. **Baltimore,** founded in 1729, was Maryland's port. Before long Baltimore became the colony's largest settlement.

Aristocrats and Farmers

Lord Baltimore gave large estates to his relatives and other English aristocrats. By doing so he created a wealthy and powerful class of landowners in Maryland.

The colony needed people to work in the plantation fields. To bring settlers to the colony, Lord Baltimore promised land—100 acres to each

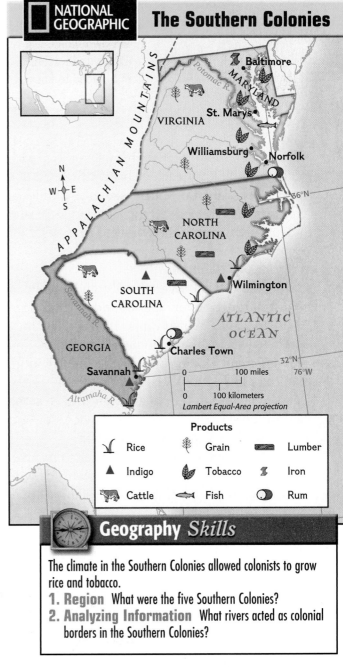

NATIONAL GEOGRAPHIC The Southern Colonies

Products

Rice		Grain		Lumber	
Indigo		Tobacco		Iron	
Cattle		Fish		Rum	

Geography *Skills*

The climate in the Southern Colonies allowed colonists to grow rice and tobacco.
1. **Region** What were the five Southern Colonies?
2. **Analyzing Information** What rivers acted as colonial borders in the Southern Colonies?

People In History

Margaret Brent c.1601–1671

Born in England, Margaret Brent moved to Maryland in 1638. She quickly accumulated several thousand acres of land and became one of the largest landowners. According to colonial records, she was also the first woman to own land in her own name.

Brave and forceful, Brent helped to put down a rebellion from neighboring Virginia, and she took charge of paying Maryland's troops. Refusing to follow the restricted life of most colonial women, she later served as attorney for Lord Baltimore, Maryland's proprietor.

In January 1648 Brent came into conflict with the colonial government when she appeared before the assembly. She demanded two votes, one for herself as a landowner and one as Lord Baltimore's legal representative. After the government denied her claim, she moved to a large plantation in Virginia. There, America's first woman lawyer lived the rest of her life.

---

male settler, another 100 for his wife, 100 for each servant, and 50 for each of his children. As the number of plantations increased and additional workers were needed, the colony imported indentured servants and enslaved Africans.

The Mason-Dixon Line

For years the Calvert family and the Penn family argued over the boundary between Maryland and Pennsylvania. In the 1760s they hired two British astronomers, Charles Mason and Jeremiah Dixon, to map the line dividing the colonies. It took the two scientists many years to lay out the boundary stones. Each stone had the crest of the Penn family on one side and the crest of the Calverts on the other.

Another conflict was even harder to resolve. The Calverts had welcomed Protestants as well as Catholics in Maryland. Protestant settlers outnumbered Catholics from the start.

Act of Toleration

To protect the Catholics from any attempt to make Maryland a Protestant colony, Baltimore passed a law called the **Act of Toleration** in 1649. The act granted Protestants and Catholics the right to worship freely but tensions continued between Protestants and Catholics. In 1692, with the support of the English government, the Protestant-controlled assembly made the Anglican Church the official church in Maryland, and imposed the same restrictions on Catholics that existed in England.

Reading Check **Explaining** Why did George Calvert establish the colony of Maryland?

Virginia Expands

While other colonies were being founded, Virginia continued to grow. Wealthy tobacco planters held the best land near the coast, so new settlers pushed inland. As the settlers moved west, they found the lands inhabited by Native Americans. In the 1640s, to avoid conflicts, Virginia's governor William Berkeley worked out an arrangement with the Native Americans. In exchange for a large piece of land, he agreed to keep settlers from pushing farther into their lands.

Bacon's Rebellion

Nathaniel Bacon, a wealthy young planter, was a leader in the western part of Virginia. He and other westerners opposed the colonial government because it was dominated by easterners. Many of the westerners resented Governor Berkeley's pledge to stay out of Native American territory. Some of them settled in the forbidden lands and then blamed the government in Jamestown for not protecting them from Native American raids.

In 1676 Bacon led the angry westerners in attacks on Native American villages. Governor Berkeley declared Bacon "the greatest rebel that ever was in Virginia." Bacon's army marched to Jamestown, set fire to the capital, and drove Berkeley into exile. Only Bacon's sudden illness and death kept him from taking charge of Virginia. England then recalled Berkeley and sent troops to restore order.

Bacon's Rebellion had shown that the settlers were not willing to be restricted to the coast. The colonial government created a militia force to control the Native Americans and opened up more land to settlement.

Nathaniel Bacon

Reading Check **Analyzing** Why did Bacon oppose the colonial government?

Settling the Carolinas

In 1663 King Charles II created a large proprietary colony south of Virginia. The colony was called Carolina, which means "Charles's land" in Latin. The king gave the colony to a group of eight prominent members of his court who had helped him regain his throne.

The Carolina proprietors carved out large estates for themselves and hoped to make money by selling and renting land. The proprietors provided money to bring colonists over from England. Settlers began arriving in Carolina in 1670. By 1680 they had founded a city, which they called Charles Town after the

king. The name later became **Charleston.**

John Locke, an English political philosopher, wrote a constitution for the Carolina colony. This constitution, or plan of government, covered such subjects as land distribution and social ranking. Locke was concerned with principles and rights. He argued that

❝every man has a property in his own person. This nobody has any right to but himself. The labour of his body, and the work of his hands, we may say, are properly his. . . .❞

Carolina, however, did not develop according to plan. The people of northern and southern Carolina soon went their separate ways, creating two colonies.

$ Economics
Northern and Southern Carolina

The northern part of Carolina was settled mostly by farmers from Virginia's backcountry. They grew tobacco and sold forest products such as timber and tar. Because the northern Carolina coast did not have a good harbor, the farmers relied on Virginia's ports and merchants to conduct their trade.

The southern part of the Carolinas was more prosperous, thanks to fertile farmland and a good harbor at Charles Town. Settlements spread, and the trade in deerskin, lumber, and beef flourished. In the 1680s planters discovered that rice grew well in the wet coastal lowlands. Rice soon became the colony's leading crop.

In the 1740s a young Englishwoman named **Eliza Lucas** developed another important Carolina crop—indigo. Indigo, a blue flowering plant, was used to dye textiles. After experimenting with seeds from the West Indies, Lucas succeeded in growing and processing indigo, the "blue gold" of Carolina.

Slave Labor in the Carolinas

Most of the settlers in southern Carolina came from another English colony—the island of Barbados in the West Indies. In Barbados the colonists used enslaved Africans to produce sugar. The colonists brought these workers with them.

Many enslaved Africans who arrived in the Carolinas worked in the rice fields. Some of them knew a great deal about rice cultivation because they had come from the rice-growing areas of West Africa. Growing rice required much labor, so the demand for slaves increased. By 1708 more than half the people living in southern Carolina were enslaved Africans.

By the early 1700s, Carolina's settlers were angry at the proprietors. They wanted a greater role in the colony's government. In 1719 the settlers in southern Carolina seized control from its proprietors. In 1729 Carolina became two royal colonies—North and South Carolina.

Reading Check **Explaining** Who was John Locke? What did he do for Carolina?

Picturing **History**

A rice plantation included the owner's large house surrounded by the small dwellings of enslaved Africans. **Why did rice cultivation increase the demand for enslaved labor?**

Georgia

Georgia, the last of the British colonies in America to be established, was founded in 1733. A group led by General **James Oglethorpe** received a charter to create a colony where English debtors and poor people could make a fresh start. In Great Britain, debtors—those who are unable to repay their debts—were generally thrown into prison.

The British government had another reason for creating Georgia. This colony could protect the other British colonies from Spanish attack. Great Britain and Spain had been at war in the early 1700s, and new conflicts over territory in North America were always breaking out. Located between Spanish Florida and South Carolina, Georgia could serve as a military barrier.

Oglethorpe's Town

Oglethorpe led the first group of "sober, industrial, and moral persons" to Georgia in 1733. They built a town called **Savannah,** as well as forts to defend themselves from the Spanish.

Oglethorpe wanted the people of Georgia to be hardworking, independent, and Protestant. He kept the size of farms small and banned slavery, Catholics, and rum.

Founding the Thirteen Colonies

Colony	1st Permanent Settlement	Reasons Founded	Founders or Leaders
New England Colonies			
Massachusetts Plymouth Mass. Bay Colony	1620 1630	Religious freedom Religious freedom	John Carver, William Bradford, John Winthrop
New Hampshire	c. 1620	Profit from trade and fishing	Ferdinando Gorges, John Mason
Rhode Island	1636	Religious freedom	Roger Williams
Connecticut	1635	Profit from fur trade, farming; religious and political freedom	Thomas Hooker
Middle Colonies			
New York	1624	Expand trade	Dutch settlers
Delaware	1638	Expand trade	Swedish settlers
New Jersey	1638	Profit from selling land	John Berkeley, George Carteret
Pennsylvania	1682	Profit from selling land; religious freedom	William Penn
Southern Colonies			
Virginia	1607	Expand trade	John Smith
Maryland	1634	To sell land; religious freedom	Cecil Calvert
North Carolina	c. 1660s	Profit from trade and selling land	Group of eight aristocrats
South Carolina	1670	Profit from trade and selling land	Group of eight aristocrats
Georgia	1733	Religious freedom; protection against Spanish Florida; safe home for debtors	James Oglethorpe

Chart Skills

The thirteen colonies were founded over a span of 125 years.

Sequencing What colony was the first to be settled? Which was the last?

Although Georgia had been planned as a debtors' colony, it actually received few debtors. Hundreds of poor people came from Great Britain. Religious refugees from Germany and Switzerland and a small group of Jews also settled there. Georgia soon had a higher percentage of non-British settlers than any other British colony in the Americas.

The Colony Changes

Many settlers complained about the limits on the size of landholdings and the law banning slave labor. They also objected to the many rules Oglethorpe made regulating their lives. The colonists referred to Oglethorpe as "our perpetual dictator."

Oglethorpe grew frustrated by the colonists' demands and the colony's slow growth. He agreed to let people have larger landholdings and lifted the bans against slavery and rum. In 1751 he gave up altogether and turned the colony back over to the king.

By that time British settlers had been in what is now the eastern United States for almost a century and a half. They had lined the Atlantic coast with colonies.

Reading Check **Explaining** How did Georgia serve as protection for the English colonies?

New France

The British were not the only Europeans who were colonizing North America, however. Elsewhere on the continent, the Spanish and the French had built settlements of their own.

The French had founded **Quebec** in 1608. At first they had little interest in large-scale settlement in North America. They were mainly concerned with fishing and trapping animals for their fur. French trappers and missionaries went far into the interior of North America. French fur companies built forts and trading posts to protect their profitable trade.

In 1663 **New France** became a royal colony. King Louis XIV limited the privileges of the fur companies. He appointed a royal governor who strongly supported new explorations.

Down the Mississippi River

In the 1670s two Frenchmen—a fur trader, **Louis Joliet,** and a priest, **Jacques Marquette**—explored the Mississippi River by canoe. Joliet and Marquette hoped to find gold, silver, or other precious metals. They were also looking for a water passage to the Pacific Ocean. The two explorers reached as far south as the junction of the Arkansas and Mississippi Rivers. When they realized that the Mississippi flowed south into the Gulf of Mexico rather than west into the Pacific, they turned around and headed back upriver.

A few years later, **René-Robert Cavelier, Sieur de La Salle,** followed the Mississippi River all the way to the Gulf of Mexico. La Salle claimed the region around the river for France. He called this territory Louisiana in honor of King Louis XIV. In 1718 the French governor founded the port of **New Orleans** near the mouth of the Mississippi River. Later French explorers, traders, and missionaries traveled west to the Rocky Mountains and southwest to the Rio Grande.

Growth of New France

French settlement in North America advanced very slowly. Settlement in New France consisted of a system of estates along the St. Lawrence River. The estate holders received land in exchange for bringing settlers to the colony. Known as tenant farmers, the settlers paid their lord an annual rent and worked for him for a fixed number of days each year.

The French had better relations with the Native Americans than did other Europeans. French trappers and missionaries traveled deep into Indian lands. They lived among the Native American peoples, learned their languages, and respected their ways.

Although the missionaries had come to convert Native Americans to Catholicism, they did not try to change the Indians' customs. Most important, the French colony grew so slowly that Native Americans were not pushed off their lands.

Reading Check **Describing** What region did La Salle explore?

New Spain

In the early 1600s, England, France, and the Netherlands began their colonization of North America. The Spanish, however, still controlled most of Mexico, the Caribbean, and Central and South America. They also expanded into the western and southern parts of what would one day be the United States.

Spain was determined to keep the other European powers from threatening its empire in America. To protect their claims, the Spanish sent soldiers, missionaries, and settlers north into present-day New Mexico.

In late 1609 or early 1610, Spanish missionaries, soldiers, and settlers founded **Santa Fe.** Another group of missionaries and settlers went to what is now Arizona in the late 1600s. When France began exploring and laying claim to lands around the Mississippi River, the Spanish moved into what is now Texas. Spain wanted to control the area between the French territory and their own colony in Mexico. In the early 1700s, Spain established San Antonio and seven other military posts in Texas.

Missions in California

Spanish priests built a string of missions along the Pacific coast. Missions are religious settlements established to convert people to a particular faith. The missions enabled the Spanish to lay claim to California.

The Spanish did more than convert Native Americans to Christianity. Spanish missionaries and soldiers also brought them to the missions—often by force—to serve as laborers in fields and workshops.

In 1769 **Junípero Serra,** a Franciscan monk, founded a mission at **San Diego.** Over the next 15 years, Father Serra set up eight more missions in California along a route called *El Camino Real* (The Royal Highway)—missions that would grow into such cities as Los Angeles and Monterey.

The distance from one mission to the next was usually a day's walk, and Serra traveled on foot to visit each one and advise the missionaries. Serra also championed the rights of the Native Americans. He worked to prevent Spanish army commanders in the region from mistreating them.

European Conflicts in North America

The rivalries between European nations carried over into the Americas. Britain and France fought several wars in the 1700s. When the two countries were at war in Europe, fighting often broke out between British colonists in America and French colonists in New France.

"[The natives] treated us with much confidence and good-will."

—*Junípero Serra, 1769*

France and Great Britain were the principal rivals of the colonial period. Both nations were expanding their settlements in North America. In the late 1700s and early 1800s, wars in Europe between the British and the French would shape events across the Atlantic even more decisively.

✓ **Reading Check** **Explaining** Why did Spain establish missions in California?

SECTION 4 ASSESSMENT

Checking for Understanding

1. **Key Terms** Write a short paragraph in which you use all of the following terms: indentured servant, constitution, debtor, tenant farmer, mission.

2. **Reviewing Facts** Explain why French settlement in North America was slower than in the English colonies.

Reviewing Themes

3. **Groups and Institutions** What role did Margaret Brent play in the government and economy of Maryland?

Critical Thinking

4. **Analyzing Information** Do you think uprisings such as Bacon's Rebellion were a sign of more unrest to come? Explain your answer.

5. **Organizing Information** Re-create the diagram below and describe the regions that these countries controlled in North America.

Country	Region
Spain	
France	

Analyzing Visuals

6. **Geography Skills** Review the map on page 87. Which of the Southern Colonies included the city of Norfolk? What were the main products in Georgia? What was the major city in South Carolina?

Interdisciplinary Activity

Art Work with a group to create a bulletin board display titled "The Southern Colonies." Include slogans and pictures to show the colonies' origins, climate, natural resources, and products.

Chapter Summary
Colonial America

1587–1650

- English settle Roanoke Island, 1587
- First permanent English colony at Jamestown, 1607
- Champlain founds Quebec, 1608
- Spanish settlers found Santa Fe, c. 1610
- House of Burgesses meets, 1619
- First Africans arrive at Jamestown, 1619
- Mayflower Compact signed, 1620
- Puritans settle Massachusetts Bay Colony, 1630
- Thomas Hooker founds Hartford, 1636
- Anne Hutchinson founds Portsmouth, 1638
- Maryland passes religious Toleration Act, 1649

1650–1700

- Marquette and Joliet explore Mississippi River, 1673
- King Philip's War, 1675
- Bacon's Rebellion, 1676
- William Penn receives charter for Pennsylvania, 1681

1700–1769

- French found city of New Orleans, 1718
- Carolina is divided into separate colonies, 1729
- Georgia settled, last of 13 English colonies, 1733
- Father Serra establishes mission at San Diego, 1769

Reviewing Key Terms

Examine the pairs of words below. Then write a sentence explaining what each of the pairs have in common.

1. charter, joint-stock company
2. dissent, persecute
3. patroon, proprietary colony
4. indentured servant, debtor
5. Pilgrim, Mayflower Compact

Reviewing Key Facts

6. Why did settlers choose a peninsula on which to build Jamestown?
7. Why did the Virginia Company create the House of Burgesses?
8. How did the Puritans' and the Pilgrims' view of the Anglican Church differ?
9. How did the Native Americans help the Pilgrims?
10. What is important about the year 1607?
11. Name two things that colonial leaders offered to attract settlers.
12. What were Sir George Calvert's two main reasons for establishing Maryland?
13. Why was there a high demand for slave labor in the Carolinas?
14. Describe the relationship between the French and the Native Americans.
15. Why did Spain send missionaries to the Pacific coast and the Southwest?

Critical Thinking

16. **Comparing** How did the economic activities of the French differ from those of the English in North America?
17. **Analyzing Themes: Civic Rights and Responsibilities** What role did religious freedom play in the founding of Rhode Island and Pennsylvania?
18. **Synthesizing Information** Re-create the diagram below. List three religious groups that left England and describe their beliefs.

Geography and History Activity

Study the map below and answer the questions that follow.

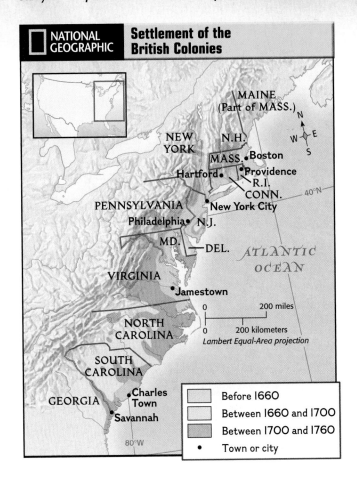

NATIONAL GEOGRAPHIC
Settlement of the British Colonies

MAINE (Part of MASS.)
NEW YORK
N.H.
MASS. • Boston
Hartford • • Providence
R.I.
CONN.
40°N
PENNSYLVANIA
• New York City
Philadelphia • N.J.
MD.
DEL.
ATLANTIC OCEAN
VIRGINIA
• Jamestown
0   200 miles
0   200 kilometers
Lambert Equal-Area projection
NORTH CAROLINA
SOUTH CAROLINA
GEORGIA • Charles Town
• Savannah
80°W

	Before 1660
	Between 1660 and 1700
	Between 1700 and 1760
•	Town or city

19. Location Which colonies had the largest areas of settlement before 1660?

20. Place During what time period was Boston settled?

Practicing Skills

Reading a Bar Graph *Study the bar graph on page 81; then answer these questions:*

21. Which colonies had passed 35,000 in population by 1700?

22. Which colony had the largest African American population?

 ## Technology Activity

23. Using the Internet Search the Internet for information about the Canadian cities of Quebec and Montreal. Find historical sites that show the French presence in these cities. Then, create a travel brochure.

Self-Check Quiz
Visit tarvol1.glencoe.com and click on **Chapter 3— Self-Check Quizzes** to prepare for the chapter test.

Citizenship Cooperative Activity

24. When you become 18 years old, you can begin to exercise one of your most important rights—the right to vote. First, however, you must register. Work with a partner to find out where you can obtain a voter registration card. Make a list of the information you will need for the card. Share your information with the class.

Economics Activity

25. Most societies use a medium of exchange—something accepted in return for goods and services. Money is one medium of exchange. In the colonies, however, the people never had a form of money that had the same value everywhere and was accepted by everyone. Since using money presented problems, colonists often traded goods without the use of money. This is called barter. Research to find out more about barter. Then answer: What are the advantages of barter?

 ## Alternative Assessment

26. Portfolio Writing Activity Examine the painting on page 84. What ideas is the artist presenting? Write a paragraph that answers the question.

Standardized Test Practice

Directions: Choose the *best* answer to the following question.

Which colony was founded to put Quaker ideas into practice?

A Plymouth   **C** Georgia
B Virginia   **D** Pennsylvania

Test-Taking Tip:

As you read the stem of each multiple-choice question, try to anticipate the answer before you look at the choices. If your answer is one of the choices, it is probably correct.

Navigate or Get Lost!

Sailing techniques were mastered long before sailors knew the earth was round. Chinese sailors probably first developed and used the compass—an instrument that shows north, south, east, and west—in the early 1000s or 1100s to guide their ships. The Arabs then used this technology and passed it on to the Europeans. The Europeans improved the magnetic compass, and during the Age of Exploration, European sailors used it to navigate their way across the unknown seas.

Analyzing the Issue

Imagine standing on board your ship. You are the captain and are in charge of the lives of about 150 crewmembers. Now your ship is in the middle of the ocean, and you have to navigate. All you can see is water—water everywhere. How in the world will you know where to find land? You are facing the same navigation problem that Christopher Columbus, Vasco da Gama, and other explorers faced. What is the solution? One way to navigate would be to use a compass to find direction. Are there other ways?

Believe It or Not!

In the late 1800s, some shipbuilders built ships with iron and steel. However, these metals interfered with the magnetic compasses sailors used. Eventually navigators learned to make the necessary adjustments to the compass so it would work properly.

Compasses

Landing of Columbus

What To Do

After you have organized into groups of six, follow the directions to explore different methods of navigation. You will need one compass per group. Each team will write three methods of getting across the classroom and then challenge classmates to follow and evaluate those methods.

1 Each group of students should pick 3 destinations across the classroom.

2 Within the group, one pair of students will write directions to one of the destinations using *compass* directions. These directions must include direction and distance, such as "go north four steps, then west three steps," and so on until the destination is reached.

3 Another pair of students will write directions to a second destination using *landmarks* for direction. Use large objects in your classroom as landmarks, such as "go to the brown bookshelf and turn left," and so on.

4 Another pair of students will write directions using *direction words* such as "left," "right," and "straight" *and number of steps.* An example might be "go straight for 3 steps and turn left," and so on.

5 Next, exchange directions with another group and navigate the room using them.

Presentation

6 Once all of the teams have finished, each group should discuss the advantages and disadvantages of each navigation method. Then have one person per group give a report to the class of what they decided was the best method and why. Keep track on the board which of the three methods got the best results.

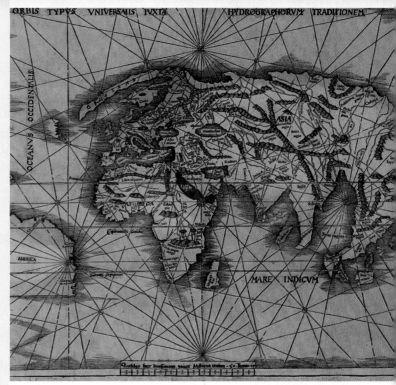

World map, 1507

Go a Step Further

Navigational tools as they developed made sailing a ship easier, but they were not foolproof. Even the explorer Christopher Columbus made some questionable navigational conclusions. His flawed measurements put China roughly where the city of San Diego, California, is now. Research information about different navigational tools that have been used. Create a chart describing the various tools, including the astrolabe, sextant, and gyrocompass. Add illustrations and present your chart to the class.

CHAPTER 4

The Colonies Grow

1607–1770

Why It Matters

Independence was a spirit that became evident early in the history of the American people. The spirit of independence contributed to the birth of a new nation, one with a new government and a culture that was distinct from those of other countries.

The Impact Today

Americans continue to value independence. For example:
- *The right to practice one's own religion freely is safeguarded.*
- *Americans value the right to express themselves freely and to make their own laws.*

The American Republic to 1877 Video *The chapter 4 video, "Middle Passage: Voyages of the Slave Trade," examines the beginnings of the slave trade, focusing on the Middle Passage.*

c. 1570
- Iroquois Confederacy formed

1651
- First Navigation Act regulates colonial trade

1676
- Bacon's Rebellion

The Americas

1550　　　　　　　　　1600　　　　　　　　　1650

World

1603
- Tokugawa Shogunate emerges in Japan

1610
- Galileo observes planets and stars with telescope

1644
- Qing Dynasty established in China

The South Side of St. John's Street by **Joseph B. Smith** This painting shows a quiet neighborhood in New York City during the late 1760s.

FOLDABLES™
Study Organizer

Compare-Contrast Study Foldable Make the following (Venn diagram) foldable to compare and contrast the peoples involved in the French and Indian War.

Step 1 Fold a sheet of paper from side to side, leaving a 2-inch tab uncovered along the side.

> Fold it so the left edge lies 2 inches from the right edge.

Step 2 Turn the paper and fold into thirds.

Step 3 Unfold and cut along the two inside fold lines.

> Cut along the two folds on the front flap to make 3 tabs.

Step 4 Label the foldable as shown.

The French and Indian War

French and Native Americans | Both | British and Colonists

Reading and Writing As you read about the participants of the war, write facts about them under the appropriate tabs of your foldable.

- **1700s**
  - Enslaved Africans brought to America

- **c. 1740**
  - Great Awakening peaks

- **1754**
  - French and Indian War begins

- **1763**
  - Proclamation of 1763

1700   **1750**

- **1689**
  - English Bill of Rights signed

- **1690**
  - Locke's *Two Treatises of Government*

- **1702**
  - England and France at war

- **1748**
  - Montesquieu's *The Spirit of Laws*

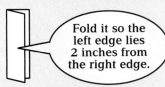

HISTORY Online

Chapter Overview
Visit tarvol1.glencoe.com and click on **Chapter 4— Chapter Overviews** to preview chapter information.

Life in the Colonies

SECTION

Guide to Reading

Main Idea
Each region developed a unique way of life.

Key Terms
subsistence farming, triangular trade, cash crop, diversity, Tidewater, backcountry, overseer

Reading Strategy
Classifying Information As you read Section 1, re-create the diagram below and describe the differences in the economies of the New England, Middle, and Southern Colonies.

Economic Development		
New England	Middle Colonies	Southern Colonies

Read to Learn
- what the triangular trade was and how it affected American society.
- how the regions in the colonies differed from one another.
- why the use of enslaved workers increased in the colonies.

Section Theme
Economic Factors Ways of earning a living varied among the colonies.

Preview of Events

| ♦1700 | | ♦1750 | | ♦1800 |

1700s
Thousands of enslaved Africans are brought to America

1750
South Carolina and Georgia have the fastest-growing colonial economies

c. 1760
New York City's population reaches 18,000

Colonial spinning wheel

AN
American Story

In 1760 Englishman Andrew Burnaby traveled throughout the North American colonies, observing American life. He could not imagine that these colonies would ever join in union for they were as different from one another as "fire and water," and each colony was jealous of the other. "In short, such is the difference of character, of manners, of religion, of interest, of the different colonies, that I think . . . were they left to themselves, there would soon be a civil war, from one end of the continent to the other."

New England Colonies

Although Burnaby believed that the colonies would never unite, the colonies continued to grow. The number of people living in the colonies rose from about 250,000 in 1700 to approximately 2.5 million by the mid-1770s. The population of African Americans increased at an even faster rate—from about 28,000 to more than 500,000.

Immigration was important to this growth. Between 1607 and 1775, almost a million people—an estimated 690,000 Europeans and 278,000 Africans—came to live in the colonies. By 1775 about 2,500 Jews lived in the colonies. Most lived in the cities of New York, Philadelphia, Charles Town, Savannah, and Newport, where they were allowed to worship as they pleased.

Another reason for the growing population was that colonial women tended to marry early and have large families. In addition, America, especially New England, turned out to be an unusually healthy place to live.

Most people in New England lived in well-organized towns. In the center of the town stood the meetinghouse, a building used for both church services and town meetings. The meetinghouse faced a piece of land called the green, or common, where cows grazed and the citizen army trained. Farmers lived in the town and worked in fields on its outskirts.

Farming was the main economic activity in all the colonies, but New England farms were smaller than those farther south. Long winters and thin, rocky soil made large-scale farming difficult. Farmers in New England practiced subsistence farming, which means that they generally produced just enough to meet the needs of their families, with little left over to sell or exchange. Most Northern farmers relied on their children for labor. Everyone in the family worked—spinning yarn, preserving fruit, milking cows, fencing in fields, and sowing and harvesting grain.

Economics
Commerce in New England

New England also had many small businesses. Some people used the waterpower from the streams on their land to run mills for grinding grain or sawing lumber. Women who made cloth, garments, candles, or soap for their families sometimes made enough of these products to sell or trade. Large towns attracted skilled craftspeople who set themselves up as blacksmiths, shoemakers, furniture makers, gunsmiths, metalsmiths, and printers.

Shipbuilding was an important industry. The lumber for building ships came from the forests of New England and was transported down rivers to the shipyards in coastal towns.

America's *Architecture*

A house design called a "salt box" became popular in many areas. The design featured a square or rectangular house, often with an addition in the back that provided more living space. These houses were called salt boxes because they were similar in shape to the wooden box in which salt was kept in colonial kitchens. **Where was the meetinghouse located in many towns?**

Pineapples symbolized hospitality in colonial America.

The region also relied on fishing. New Englanders fished for cod, halibut, crabs, oysters, and lobsters. Some ventured far out to sea to hunt whales for oil and whalebone.

Colonial Trade

As the center of the shipping trade in America, northern coastal cities linked the northern colonies with the Southern Colonies, and linked America to other parts of the world. New England ships sailed south along the Atlantic coast, trading with the colonies and with islands in the **West Indies.** They crossed the Atlantic carrying fish, furs, and fruit to trade for manufactured goods in England and Europe.

These colonial merchant ships followed many different trading routes. Some went directly to England and back. Others followed routes that came to be called the triangular trade because the routes formed a triangle. On one leg of such a route, ships brought sugar and molasses from the West Indies to the New England colonies. In New England, the molasses would be made into rum. Next, the rum and other goods were shipped to West Africa and traded for enslaved Africans. Slavery was widely practiced in West Africa.

Many West African kingdoms enslaved those they defeated in war. Some of the enslaved were sold to Arab slave traders. Others were forced to mine gold or work in farm fields. With the arrival of the Europeans, enslaved Africans also began to be shipped to America in exchange for trade goods. On the final leg of the route, the enslaved Africans were taken to the West Indies where they were sold to planters. The profit was used to buy more molasses—and the process started over.

The Middle Passage

The inhumane part of the triangular trade, shipping enslaved Africans to the West Indies, was known as the **Middle Passage.** Olaudah Equiano, a young African forced onto a ship to America, later described the voyage:

> 66 I was soon put down under the decks, . . . The closeness of the place, and the heat of the climate, added to the number in the ship, which was so crowded that each had scarcely room to turn himself, almost suffocated us. . . . The shrieks of the women, and the groans of the dying, rendered [made] the whole a scene of horror. 99

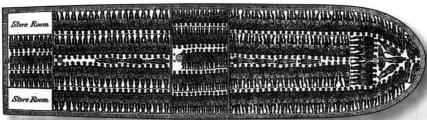

Slaves packed in a ship

 **History**

A deck plan (above) reveals tightly packed ranks of slaves on a ship bound from Africa to the Americas. Once docked, the ship's human cargo was replaced with rum or molasses. **What does the term "Middle Passage" refer to?**

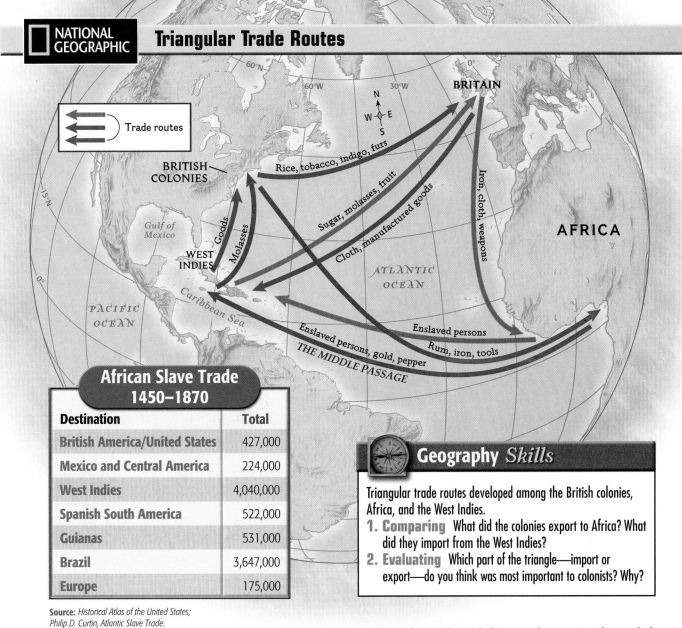

Triangular Trade Routes

Trade routes

BRITISH COLONIES

Rice, tobacco, indigo, furs

Sugar, molasses, fruit

Cloth, manufactured goods

Iron, cloth, weapons

BRITAIN

AFRICA

Goods

Molasses

WEST INDIES

Gulf of Mexico

ATLANTIC OCEAN

PACIFIC OCEAN

Caribbean Sea

Enslaved persons, gold, pepper

THE MIDDLE PASSAGE

Enslaved persons

Rum, iron, tools

African Slave Trade 1450–1870

Destination	Total
British America/United States	427,000
Mexico and Central America	224,000
West Indies	4,040,000
Spanish South America	522,000
Guianas	531,000
Brazil	3,647,000
Europe	175,000

Source: *Historical Atlas of the United States; Philip D. Curtin, Atlantic Slave Trade.*

Geography *Skills*

Triangular trade routes developed among the British colonies, Africa, and the West Indies.

1. **Comparing** What did the colonies export to Africa? What did they import from the West Indies?
2. **Evaluating** Which part of the triangle—import or export—do you think was most important to colonists? Why?

With its trade, shipbuilding, and fishing, New England's economy flourished. Although good farmland was lacking in much of the region, New England's population grew and towns and cities developed.

Reading Check **Explaining** Where was the shipping hub in America?

The Middle Colonies

The Middle Colonies enjoyed fertile soil and a slightly milder climate than New England's. Farmers in this region cultivated larger areas of land and produced bigger harvests than did New Englanders. In New York and Pennsylvania, farmers grew large quantities of wheat and other cash crops, crops that could be sold easily in markets in the colonies and overseas.

Farmers sent cargoes of wheat and livestock to New York City and Philadelphia for shipment, and these cities became busy ports. By the 1760s New York, with 18,000 people, and Philadelphia, with 24,000 people, were the largest cities in the American colonies.

Industries of the Middle Colonies

Like the New England Colonies, the Middle Colonies also had industries. Some were home-based crafts such as carpentry and flour

making. Others included larger businesses such as lumbering, mining, and small-scale manufacturing.

One iron mill in northern New Jersey employed several hundred workers, many of them from Germany. Other smaller ironworks operated in New Jersey and Pennsylvania.

German Immigrants

Most of the nearly 100,000 German immigrants who came to America in the colonial era settled in Pennsylvania. Using agricultural methods developed in Europe, these immigrants became successful farmers.

The Germans belonged to a number of Protestant groups. Together with the Dutch, Swedish, and other non-English immigrants, they gave the Middle Colonies a cultural diversity, or variety, that was not found in New England. With the diversity came tolerance for religious and cultural differences.

✓ **Reading Check** **Explaining** What are cash crops?

The Southern Colonies

With their rich soil and warm climate, the Southern Colonies were well suited to certain kinds of farming. Southern farmers could cultivate large areas of land and produce harvests of cash crops. Because most settlers in the Southern Colonies made their living from farming the land, they did not have the need to develop commerce or industry. For the most part, London merchants rather than local merchants managed Southern trade.

⑤ Economics
Tobacco and Rice

Tobacco was the principal cash crop of Maryland and Virginia. Most tobacco was sold in Europe, where the demand for it was strong. Growing tobacco and preparing it for sale required a good deal of labor. At first planters used indentured servants to work in the fields. When indentured servants became scarce and expensive, Southern planters used enslaved Africans instead.

Slaveholders with large properties became rich on tobacco. Sometimes, however, a surplus, or extra amounts, of tobacco on the market caused prices to fall and then the growers' profits also fell. In time, some tobacco planters switched to growing other crops such as corn and wheat.

The main cash crop in South Carolina and Georgia was rice. In low-lying areas along the coast, planters built dams to create rice fields, called paddies. These fields were flooded when the rice was young and drained when the rice was ready to harvest. Work in the rice paddies involved standing knee-deep in the mud all day with no protection from the blazing sun or the biting insects.

Because rice harvesting required so much strenuous work, rice growers relied on slave labor. Rice proved to be even more profitable than tobacco. As it became popular in southern Europe, the price of rice rose steadily. By the 1750s South Carolina and Georgia had the fastest-growing economies in the colonies.

Tidewater and Backcountry

Most of the large Southern plantations were located in the Tidewater, a region of flat, low-lying plains along the seacoast. Plantations, or large farms, were often located on rivers so crops could be shipped to market by boat.

Each plantation was a self-contained community with fields stretching out around a cluster of buildings. The planter's wife supervised the main house and the household servants. A plantation also included slave cabins, barns and stables, and outbuildings such as carpenter and blacksmith shops and storerooms. Even kitchens were in separate buildings. A large plantation might also have its own chapel and school.

West of the Tidewater lay a region of hills and forests climbing up toward the **Appalachian Mountains.** This region was known as the backcountry and was settled in part by hardy newcomers to the colonies. The backcountry settlers grew corn and tobacco on small farms. They usually worked alone or with their families, although some had one or two enslaved Africans to help.

In the Southern Colonies, the independent small farmers of the backcountry outnumbered the large plantation owners. The plantation owners, however, had greater wealth and more influence. They controlled the economic and political life of the region.

Reading Check **Comparing** How were the settlers of the Tidewater different from those of the backcountry?

History *Through Art*

The Old Plantation by an unknown artist
This watercolor from the 1700s shows a traditional African celebration on a Southern plantation. **Where would you be more likely to find enslaved African laborers—in the Tidewater or backcountry? Why?**

Slavery

Most enslaved Africans lived on plantations. Some did housework, but most worked in the fields and often suffered great cruelty. The large plantation owners hired overseers, or bosses, to keep the slaves working hard.

By the early 1700s, many of the colonies had issued **slave codes,** strict rules governing the behavior and punishment of enslaved Africans. Some codes did not allow slaves to leave the plantation without written permission from the master. Some made it illegal to teach enslaved people to read or write. They usually allowed slaves to be whipped for minor offenses and hanged or burned to death for serious crimes. Those who ran away were often caught and punished severely.

African Traditions

Although the enslaved Africans had strong family ties, their families were often torn apart. Slaveholders could sell a family member to another slaveholder. Slaves found a source of strength in their African roots. They developed a culture that drew on the languages and customs of their West African homelands.

Some enslaved Africans learned trades such as carpentry, blacksmithing, or weaving. Skilled workers could sometimes set up shops, sharing

Banning Slavery

Slavery was first outlawed in the northern colonies. This is not true. Slavery was first outlawed in the colony of Georgia in 1735. Georgia eventually made slavery legal again.

their profits with the slaveholders. Those lucky enough to be able to buy their freedom joined the small population of free African Americans.

Criticism of Slavery

Although the majority of white Southerners were not slaveholders, slavery played an important role in the economic success of the Southern Colonies. That success, however, was built on the idea that one human being could own another. Some colonists did not believe in slavery. Many Puritans refused to hold enslaved people. In Pennsylvania, Quakers and Mennonites condemned slavery. Eventually the debate over slavery would erupt in a bloody war, pitting North against South.

✓ **Reading Check** **Describing** What did slave codes do?

SECTION 1 ASSESSMENT

Checking for Understanding

1. **Key Terms** Use each of these terms in a sentence that will help explain its meaning: subsistence farming, triangular trade, cash crop.
2. **Reviewing Facts** Identify the various economic activities carried on in the Middle Colonies.

Reviewing Themes

3. **Economic Factors** How did New England's natural resources help its commerce?

Critical Thinking

4. **Comparing** How did farming in New England compare with farming in the Southern Colonies? Use a chart like the one below to answer the question.

	Similarities	Differences
New England		
Southern Colonies		

5. **Making Inferences** How do you think plantation owners in the Southern Colonies justified their use of enslaved Africans?

Analyzing Visuals

6. **Geography Skills** Study the map on page 103. What goods were traded from the British Colonies to Great Britain? From the West Indies to the British Colonies?

Interdisciplinary Activity

Informative Writing Imagine you live in New England in the 1750s and are visiting cousins on a farm in the Carolinas. Write a letter to a friend at home describing your visit to the farm.

America's LITERATURE

Olaudah Equiano
(c. 1750–1797)

Olaudah Equiano was 11 years old when he and his sister were kidnapped by slave traders. Olaudah was taken to the West Indies and sold into slavery. His life story includes memories of his childhood in Africa. He wrote his story after receiving the name Gustavus Vassa from one of his masters and buying his freedom. Published during the time of the movement to end slavery, Equiano's work became a best-seller.

READ TO DISCOVER

This selection begins after Olaudah has been kidnapped and forced to endure the terrifying trip across the Atlantic Ocean aboard a slave ship. As you read, think about what life must have been like for Africans who were sold into slavery.

READER'S DICTIONARY

parcel: group
lots: groups
toil: work

The Kidnapped Prince

Right away we were taken to a merchant's yard, where we were all penned up together like so many sheep. When I looked out at the town, everything was new to me. The houses were built with bricks, in stories, and were completely different from any I had seen in Africa. I was still more astonished at seeing people on horseback. . . .

We were not many days in the merchant's custody before we were sold—like this:

Someone beat a drum. Then all the buyers rushed at once into the yard where we were penned to choose the **parcel** of us that they liked best. They rushed from one group of us to another, with tremendous noise and eager faces, terrifying us all.

Three men who were sold were brothers. They were sold in different **lots.** I still remember how they cried when they were parted. Probably they never saw each other again.

I didn't know it, but this happened all the time in slave sales. Parents lost their children; brothers lost their sisters. Husbands lost their wives.

We had already lost our homes, our countries, and almost everyone we loved. The people who did the selling and buying could have done it without separating us from our very last relatives and friends. They already could live in riches from our misery and **toil.** What possible advantage did they gain from this refinement of cruelty?

From *The Kidnapped Prince* by Olaudah Equiano. Adapted by Ann Cameron. Copyright © 1995 by Ann Cameron. Reprinted by permission of Alfred A. Knopf, Inc.

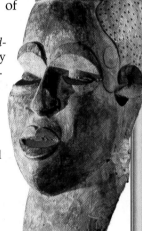

ANALYZING LITERATURE

1. **Recall and Interpret** How did the Africans feel as they were being sold?
2. **Evaluate and Connect** Do you think Olaudah Equiano supports slavery? Explain.

Interdisciplinary Activity

Descriptive Writing Re-read the excerpt and think about what it must have been like to be separated from family members. Write a dialogue you think might occur between two family members as they are about to be separated from each other.

Government, Religion, and Culture

Guide to Reading

Main Idea
The ideals of American democracy and freedom of religion took root during the colonial period.

Key Terms
mercantilism, export, import, smuggling, charter colony, proprietary colony, royal colony, apprentice, literacy

Reading Strategy
Organizing Information As you read the section, re-create the diagram below and identify the three types of English colonies.

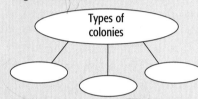

Types of colonies

Read to Learn
- why the Navigation Acts angered the colonists.
- who had the right to vote in colonial legislatures.

Section Theme
Continuity and Change The roots of American democracy, freedom of religion, and public education are found in the American colonial experience.

Preview of Events

♦1630	♦1670	♦1710	♦1750

1636
Harvard College is established

1693
College of William and Mary is founded

1732
Benjamin Franklin publishes *Poor Richard's Almanack*

c. 1740
Great Awakening sweeps through the colonies

From Poor Richard's Almanack

AN American Story

"Fish and Visitors stink after three days."

"Beware of little Expenses: a small Leak will sink a great Ship."

"No gains without pains."

Benjamin Franklin wrote these and other witty sayings for his annual book, *Poor Richard's Almanack*. The last saying—"No gains without pains"—was particularly true in the American colonies in the late 1600s.

English Colonial Rule

In his writings, Benjamin Franklin celebrated a new American spirit. This spirit signaled that Americans were beginning to view themselves differently from the way Great Britain viewed them.

Trouble was brewing in England—and in the colonies—during the mid-1600s. England's monarchy had been restored with Charles II on the throne, but many people were not satisfied with his rule. James II, Charles's successor, attempted to take back the powers Parliament had won during the English Civil War. He also tried to tighten royal control over the colonies.

In 1688 Parliament took action. It forced out James and placed his daughter Mary and her Dutch husband, William of Orange, on the throne. This change, which showed the power of the elected representatives over the monarch, came to be known as the **Glorious Revolution.**

William and Mary signed an **English Bill of Rights** in 1689 guaranteeing certain basic rights to all citizens. This document became part of the heritage of English law that the American colonists shared. It later inspired the people who created the American Bill of Rights.

England viewed its North American colonies as an economic resource. The colonies provided England with raw materials. English manufacturers used these materials to produce finished goods, which they sold to the colonists. This process followed an economic theory called mercantilism. This theory states that as a nation's trade grows, its gold reserves increase,

and the nation becomes more powerful. To make money from its trade, England had to export, or sell abroad, more goods than it imported, or bought from foreign markets.

To make certain that only England benefited from trade with the colonies, Parliament passed a series of laws between 1651 and 1673. These laws, called the **Navigation Acts,** directed the flow of goods between England and the colonies. Colonial merchants who had goods to send to England could not use foreign ships—even if those ships offered cheaper rates. The Navigation Acts also prevented the colonists from sending certain products, such as sugar or tobacco, outside England's empire.

Some colonists ignored these laws and began smuggling, or trading illegally with other nations. Controls on trade would later cause even more conflict between the American colonies and England.

✓ **Reading Check** **Examining** Under mercantilism, who controlled trade and who supplied raw materials?

People In History

Benjamin Franklin 1706–1790

Ben Franklin learned the printer's trade as a young man. By the time he was 23, he owned his own newspaper in Philadelphia. Soon afterward he began publishing *Poor Richard's Almanack*, a calendar filled with advice, philosophy, and wise sayings, such as "Early to bed, early to rise, makes

a man healthy, wealthy, and wise."

Franklin was deeply interested in science. He invented the lightning rod, bifocal eyeglasses, and the Franklin stove for heating. Energetic and open-minded, Franklin served in the Pennsylvania Assembly for many years. He founded a hospital, a fire department,

America's first lending library, and an academy of higher learning that later became the University of Pennsylvania.

Franklin's greatest services to his fellow Americans would come during the 1770s. As a statesman and patriot, Franklin would help guide the colonies toward independence.

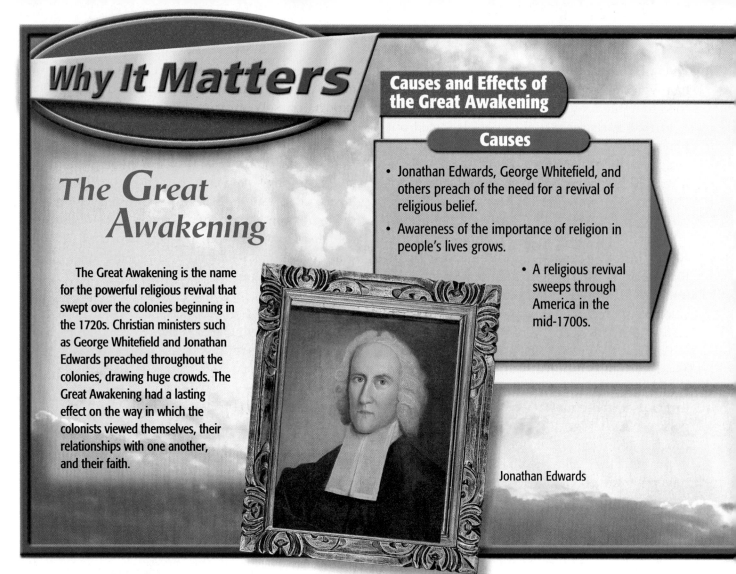

Why It Matters

Causes and Effects of the Great Awakening

Causes

- Jonathan Edwards, George Whitefield, and others preach of the need for a revival of religious belief.
- Awareness of the importance of religion in people's lives grows.
  - A religious revival sweeps through America in the mid-1700s.

The Great Awakening

The Great Awakening is the name for the powerful religious revival that swept over the colonies beginning in the 1720s. Christian ministers such as George Whitefield and Jonathan Edwards preached throughout the colonies, drawing huge crowds. The Great Awakening had a lasting effect on the way in which the colonists viewed themselves, their relationships with one another, and their faith.

Jonathan Edwards

🔲Citizenship

Colonial Government

The English colonists brought with them ideas about government that had been developing in England for centuries. By the 1600s the English people had won political liberties, such as trial by jury, that were largely unknown elsewhere. At the heart of the English system were two principles of government. These principles—limited government and representative government—greatly influenced the development of the United States.

By the time the first colonists reached North America, the idea that government was not all-powerful had become an accepted part of the English system of government. The idea first appeared in the Magna Carta that King John was forced to sign in 1215. The Magna Carta established the principle of limited government, in which the power of the king, or government, was limited. This document provided for protection against unjust punishment and against the loss of life, liberty, and property, except according to law. 📖 *(See page 611 of the Appendix for excerpts from the Magna Carta.)*

As the colonies grew, they relied more and more on their own governments to make local laws. By the 1760s there were three types of colonies in America—charter colonies, proprietary colonies, and royal colonies.

Charter Colonies

Connecticut and Rhode Island, the charter colonies, were established by settlers who had been given a charter, or a grant of rights and privileges. These colonists elected their own governors and the members of the legislature. Great Britain had the right to approve the governor, but the governor could not veto the acts of the legislature.

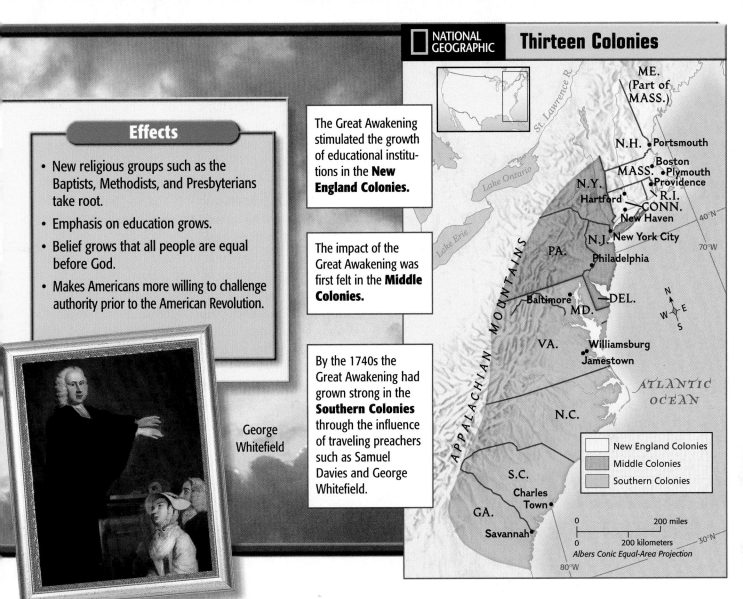

Effects

- New religious groups such as the Baptists, Methodists, and Presbyterians take root.
- Emphasis on education grows.
- Belief grows that all people are equal before God.
- Makes Americans more willing to challenge authority prior to the American Revolution.

George Whitefield

The Great Awakening stimulated the growth of educational institutions in the **New England Colonies.**

The impact of the Great Awakening was first felt in the **Middle Colonies.**

By the 1740s the Great Awakening had grown strong in the **Southern Colonies** through the influence of traveling preachers such as Samuel Davies and George Whitefield.

Thirteen Colonies

New England Colonies
Middle Colonies
Southern Colonies

ATLANTIC OCEAN

Albers Conic Equal-Area Projection

Proprietary Colonies

The proprietary colonies—Delaware, Maryland, and Pennsylvania—were ruled by proprietors. These were individuals or groups to whom Britain had granted land. Proprietors were generally free to rule as they wished. They appointed the governor and members of the upper house of the legislature, while the colonists elected the lower house.

Royal Colonies

By the 1760s Georgia, Massachusetts, New Hampshire, New Jersey, New York, North Carolina, South Carolina, and Virginia were royal colonies. Britain directly ruled all royal colonies. In each, the king appointed a governor and council, known as the upper house. The colonists elected an assembly, called the lower house. The governor and members of the council usually did what the British leaders told them to do. However, this often led to conflict with the colonists in the assembly, especially when officials tried to enforce tax laws and trade restrictions.

Voting Rights

Colonial legislatures gave only some people a voice in government. Generally, white men who owned property had the right to vote; however, most women, indentured servants, landless poor, and African Americans could not vote. In spite of these limits, a higher proportion of people was involved in government in the colonies than anywhere in the European world. This strong participation gave Americans training that was valuable when the colonies became independent.

Reading Check **Drawing Inferences** How did the Magna Carta affect government in the colonies?

An Emerging Culture

From the 1720s through the 1740s, a religious revival called the **Great Awakening** swept through the colonies. In New England and the Middle Colonies, ministers called for "a new birth," a return to the strong faith of earlier days. One of the outstanding preachers was **Jonathan Edwards** of Massachusetts. People thought that his sermons were powerful and convincing.

The English preacher **George Whitefield,** who arrived in the colonies in 1739, helped spread the religious revival. Whitefield inspired worshipers in churches and open fields from New England to Georgia. The Great Awakening led to the formation of many new churches.

Family Roles

Throughout the colonies, people adapted their traditions to the new conditions of life in America. Religion, education, and the arts contributed to a new American culture. The family formed the foundation of colonial society.

A colonial farm was both home and workplace. Mothers and fathers cared for their children. Women cooked, made butter and cheese, and preserved food. They spun yarn, made clothes, and tended chickens and cows. Men worked in the fields and built barns, houses, and fences. In many areas, women worked in the fields next to their husbands.

Men were the formal heads of the households. They managed the farms and represented the family in community affairs. In most churches, women could attend church meetings, but could not speak, vote, or serve as clergy. Families often arranged for their sons to work as indentured servants for farmers or to serve as apprentices, or learning assistants, to craft workers who taught them a trade. Married women were considered under their husbands' authority and had few rights.

TECHNOLOGY & History

Colonial Printing Press

Life in the colonies often revolved around local printers who produced pamphlets, small flyers, books, and newspapers. The first printing press in the American colonies was established by Stephen Daye in 1639.

Type is made up of large numbers of single letters that can be moved and reused.

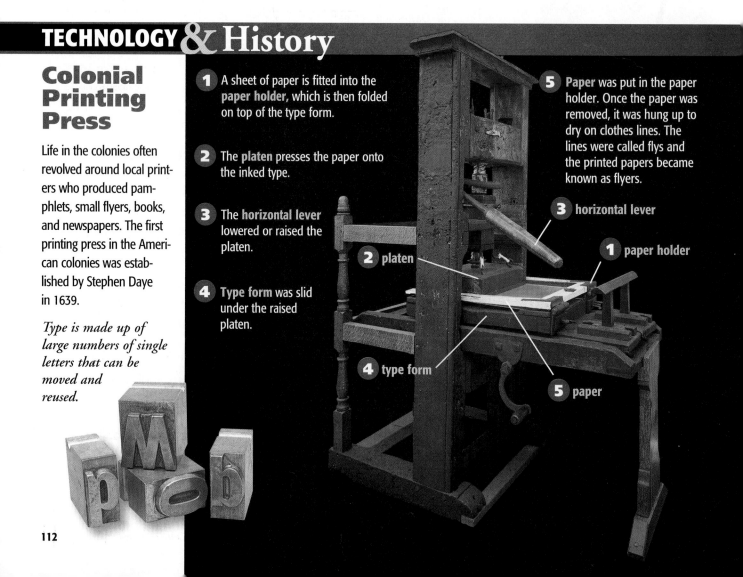

1. A sheet of paper is fitted into the **paper holder**, which is then folded on top of the type form.

2. The **platen** presses the paper onto the inked type.

3. The **horizontal lever** lowered or raised the platen.

4. **Type form** was slid under the raised platen.

5. **Paper** was put in the paper holder. Once the paper was removed, it was hung up to dry on clothes lines. The lines were called flys and the printed papers became known as flyers.

3 horizontal lever

1 paper holder

2 platen

4 type form

5 paper

Women in cities and towns sometimes held jobs outside the home. Young unmarried women might work for wealthy families as maids, cooks, and nurses. Widows might work as teachers, nurses, and seamstresses. They also opened shops and inns. Widows and women who had never married could run businesses and own property, even though they could not vote. 📖 *(See page 594 of the Primary Sources Library for the selection, "What is an American?")*

Education

Most colonists valued education. Children were often taught to read and write at home by their parents. In New England and Pennsylvania, in particular, school systems were set up to make sure that everyone could read and study the Bible. In 1647 the Massachusetts Puritans passed a public education law. Each community with 50 or more households had to have a school supported by taxes.

By 1750, New England had a very high level of literacy, the ability to read and write. Approximately 85 percent of the men and about half of the women could read. Many learned to read from *The New England Primer,* which combined lessons in good conduct with reading and writing.

Many colonial schools were run by widows or unmarried women. In the Middle Colonies, some schools were run by Quakers and other religious groups. In the towns and cities, craftspeople set up night schools for their apprentices.

The colonies' early colleges were founded to train ministers. The first was Harvard College, established in 1636 by the Puritans in Cambridge, Massachusetts. Anglicans founded William and Mary College in Virginia in 1693.

The Enlightenment

By the middle of the 1700s, many educated colonists were influenced by the **Enlightenment.** This movement, which began in Europe, spread the idea that knowledge, reason, and science could improve society. In the colonies, the Enlightenment increased interest in science. People observed nature, staged experiments, and published their findings. The best known American scientist was Benjamin Franklin.

Freedom of the Press

In 1735 John Peter Zenger of the *New York Weekly Journal* faced charges of libel for printing a critical report about the royal governor of New York. Andrew Hamilton argued that free speech was a basic right of English people. He defended Zenger by asking the jury to base its decision on whether Zenger's article was true, not whether it was offensive. The jury found Zenger not guilty. At the time the case attracted little attention, but today it is regarded as an important step in the development of a free press in America.

Reading Check **Analyzing** What was the impact of the Great Awakening?

SECTION 2 ASSESSMENT

Checking for Understanding

1. **Key Terms** Use each of these terms in a complete sentence that will help explain its meaning: export, charter colony, proprietary colony, apprentice, literacy.

2. **Reviewing the Facts** Identify some contributions of women inside and outside the home.

Reviewing Themes

3. **Continuity and Change** Why did the Navigation Acts anger the colonists?

Critical Thinking

4. **Drawing Conclusions** Why did Andrew Hamilton defend John Peter Zenger and free speech?

5. **Determining Cause and Effect** Re-create the diagram below and describe the effects of the Great Awakening.

Great Awakening

Analyzing Visuals

6. **Picturing History** Examine the printing press on page 112. Who established the first printing press in the colonies? How do you think the colonists communicated their ideas before printed material was widely used?

Interdisciplinary Activity

Government Draw a chart that shows the structure of a royal colony, a proprietary colony, and a charter colony.

What were people's lives like in the past?

What—and who—were people talking about? What did they eat? What did they do for fun? These two pages will give you some clues to everyday life in the U.S. as you step back in time with TIME Notebook.

Profile

EDWARD WINSLOW *was 25 when he sailed on the* Mayflower *to Massachusetts. Winslow helped found Plymouth Colony, served as the colony's governor three times—and still found time to sit down to the very first Thanksgiving celebrated in the British colonies in the fall of 1621. Here's part of what he wrote about the first big feast:*

"OUR HARVEST BEING GOTTEN IN, OUR GOVERNOR sent four men on the fowling (*hunt for fowl*), that we might … rejoice together after we had gathered the fruits of our labors. In one day, they killed as much fowl as … served the company almost a week. At which time, … many of the Indians came amongst us … with some ninety men whom for three days we entertained and feasted…."

Edward Winslow

BETTMANN/CORBIS

INSECTS ARRIVE

New Pests on the Dock

The Pilgrims had company on the *Mayflower*. At least three pests made their first visit to the New World on the famous ship—and decided to stay. We hope they won't be around too long.

- **cockroaches**
- **flies**
- **gray rats**

BETTMANN/CORBIS

COLONIAL EVENTS
Virginia Is Number 1

Here's a list of events that happened first in 1619 in Virginia. One of the facts is wrong. Can you figure out the one that doesn't belong?

1. First boatload of African slaves
2. First labor strike
3. First elected lawmakers
4. First time English settlers can own land
5. First daily newspaper
6. First boatload of women who agreed to marry colonists in exchange for a ticket across the Atlantic

answer: 5

POPULAR FOOD
Have Your Corn Cake – and Eat It Too!

This New World meal is all the rage in the colonies.

Stir one cup of coarse cornmeal grits into three cups of water.

Place on stove. Simmer.

Remove from heat when all the water is absorbed. Let it cool.

Shape the mixture into two round, flat cakes on a floured work surface.

Bake it in a hot oven for 45 minutes.

Serve warm or cold with freshly churned butter.

VERBATIM
WHAT PEOPLE ARE SAYING

❝...I found some black people about me, and I believe some were those who had brought me on board and had been receiving their pay....I asked them if we were not to be eaten by those white men with horrible looks, red faces, and long hair.❞

OLAUDAH EQUIANO,
11-year-old kidnapped from his home in what is now Nigeria and brought to America as an enslaved person, on his first day on the slave ship

❝For pottage and puddings and custards and pies / Our pumpkins and parsnips are common supplies. We have pumpkins at morning and pumpkins at noon, / If it were not for pumpkin, / We should be undone.❞

AMERICAN FOLK SONG,
a tribute to the pumpkin

NUMBERS
THE COLONIES AT THE TIME

1,500 Number of English children in 1627 who were kidnapped and sent to work as servants in Virginia

80% Percentage of colonists who died in Jamestown, Virginia, during the winter of 1609–10 after getting so hungry they ate rats, snakes, and horsehide

65% Percentage of colonists who could read in 1620

2,500 Number of trees needed to build a ship the size of the *Mayflower*

NORTH WIND PICTURES

0 Number of chairs set at the dinner table for children— only adults sat while eating

50 Number of pounds of tobacco colonists in Virginia were fined if they did not go to church in the early 1600s

France and Britain Clash

Guide to Reading

Main Idea
Rivalry between Great Britain and France led to a long-lasting conflict.

Key Terms
Iroquois Confederacy, militia

Reading Strategy
Organizing Information As you read the section, re-create the diagram below and describe the events that led to conflict in North America.

☐ → ☐ → ☐ → Conflict in North America

Read to Learn
• how wars in Europe spread to the American colonies.
• about the purpose of the Albany Plan of Union.

Section Theme
Continuity and Change American colonists and Native American groups were drawn into the clash between France and Britain.

Preview of Events

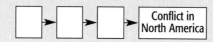

♦1740　　　　　　　♦1750　　　　　　　♦1760

1745
New England troops seize Fort Louisbourg from France

1753
George Washington sent to Ohio country to protest French actions

1754
Benjamin Franklin proposes Albany Plan of Union

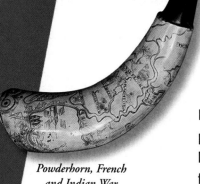

Powderhorn, French and Indian War

AN American Story

In 1689 England and France began competing to be the most powerful nation in Europe. This contest for power went on for generations, with only short intervals of peace. In 1758 writer Nathaniel Ames noted, "The parts of North America which may be claimed by Great Britain or France are of as much worth as either kingdom. That fertile country to the west of the Appalachian Mountains [is the] 'Garden of the World'!"

British-French Rivalry

Britain and France had been competing for wealth for centuries. By 1700 they were two of the strongest powers in Europe. Their long rivalry aroused bitter feelings between British and French colonists in North America.

As the growing population of the American colonies pushed up against French-held territory, hostility between England and France increased. At the same time, some land companies wanted to explore opportunities in the **Ohio River valley.** However, the French, who traded throughout the Ohio country, regarded this territory as their own. They had no intention of letting British colonists share in their profitable fur trade.

In the 1740s British fur traders went into the Ohio country. They built a fort deep in the territory of the Miami people at a place called Pickawillany. Acting quickly, the French attacked Pickawillany and drove the British traders out of Ohio. The French then built a string of forts along the rivers of the upper Ohio Valley, closer to the British colonies than ever before. Two mighty powers—Great Britain and France—were headed for a showdown in North America.

In the early 1700s, Britain had gained control of Nova Scotia, Newfoundland, and the Hudson Bay region. In the 1740s French troops raided towns in Maine and New York. In response a force of New Englanders went north and captured the important French fortress at **Louisbourg** on Cape Breton Island, north of Nova Scotia. Later Britain returned Louisbourg to France, much to the disgust of the New England colonists.

Native Americans Take Sides

The French traders and the British colonists knew that Native American help would make a difference in their struggle for North America. The side that received the best trade terms from Native Americans and the most help in the war would probably win the contest for control of North America.

The French had many Native American allies. Unlike the British, the French were interested mainly in trading for furs—not in taking over Native American land. The French also had generally better relations with Native Americans. French trappers and fur traders often married Native American women and followed their customs. French missionaries traveled through the area, converting many Native Americans to Catholicism.

During the wars between Great Britain and France, Native Americans often helped the French by raiding British settlements. In 1704, for example, the Abenaki people joined the French in an attack on the British frontier outpost at Deerfield, Massachusetts, in which almost 50 settlers were killed.

NATIONAL GEOGRAPHIC

North America in 1754

Claimed by Britain
Claimed by Spain
Claimed by France

0   500 miles
0   500 kilometers
Azimuthal Equidistant projection

Geography Skills

1. **Analyzing Information** What power claimed the territory of Florida?
2. **Region** What three rivers were located within French territory?

The Iroquois Confederacy

The most powerful group of Native Americans in the East was the Iroquois Confederacy, based in New York. When the confederacy was first formed in about 1570, it included five nations—the Mohawk, Seneca, Cayuga, Onondaga, and Oneida. Other groups later joined or were conquered by the Iroquois.

The Iroquois managed to remain independent by trading with both the British and the French. By skillfully playing the British and French against each other, the Iroquois dominated the area around the Great Lakes.

By the mid-1700s, however, the Iroquois came under greater pressure as the British moved into the Ohio Valley. Eventually the leaders of the confederacy gave certain trading rights to the

TWO VIEWPOINTS

I Claim This Land!

In the sixteenth century, Europeans became aware of a larger world around them—a world where they could claim new lands and profits. Soon a desire arose in England and France to conquer these lands and the people in them, and a race began to be the first to make those claims.

Drake Claims South and North America for England, June 1579

This country our general named Albion, and that for two causes; the one in respect of the white banks and cliffs, . . . that it might have some affinity [similarity], even in name also, with our own country, which was sometime so called.

Before we went from there, our general caused to be set up, a monument of our being there; as also of her majesties, and successors right and title to that kingdom, namely, a plate of brass, fast nailed to a great and firm post; whereon is [carved] her graces name, and the day and year of our arrival there, and of the free giving up, of the province and kingdom, both by the king and people, into her majesties hands. . . .

Sieur de St. Lusson Claims West and Northwest America for France, 1671

In the name of the Most High, Mighty, and Redoubted Monarch, Louis the Fourteenth of that name, Most Christian King of France and Navarre, I take possession of this place, Ste. Marie of the Sault, as also of Lakes Huron and Superior, the Island of Manitoulin, and all countries, rivers, lakes, and streams . . . both those which have been discovered and those which may be discovered hereafter, in all their length and breadth, bounded on the one side by the seas of the North and of the West, and on the other by the South Sea: Declaring to the nations thereof that from this time forth they are vassals [servants] of his Majesty, bound to obey his laws and follow his customs. . . .

Francis Drake

Learning From History

1. How are the two accounts similar?
2. Why do you think these men held such formal ceremonies when claiming a piece of land?

British and reluctantly became their allies. By taking this step, the Iroquois upset the balance of power between the French and British that had been so difficult to establish.

Reading Check Explaining Why were Native Americans more likely to help the French than help the British?

American Colonists Take Action

A group of Virginians had plans for settling the Ohio Valley. In the fall of 1753 Governor Robert Dinwiddie of Virginia sent a 21-year-old planter and surveyor named **George Washington** into the Ohio country. Washington's mission was to tell the French that they were trespassing on territory claimed by Great Britain and demand that they leave.

Washington delivered the message, but it did no good. "The French told me," Washington said later, "that it was their absolute design to take possession of the Ohio, and by God they would do it."

Washington's First Command

In the spring of 1754, Dinwiddie made Washington a lieutenant colonel and sent him back to the Ohio country with a militia—a group of civilians trained to fight in emergencies—of 150 men. The militia had instructions to build a fort where the Allegheny and Monongahela Rivers meet to form the Ohio River—the site of present-day Pittsburgh. When Washington and his troops arrived, they found the French were already building Fort Duquesne (doo•KAYN) on that spot.

Washington established a small post nearby called **Fort Necessity.** Although greatly outnumbered, the forces of the inexperienced Washington attacked a French scouting party. The French surrounded Washington's soldiers and forced them to surrender, but the soldiers were later released and they returned to Virginia. Washington's account of his experience in the Ohio country was published, and his fame spread throughout the colonies and Europe. In spite of his defeat, the colonists regarded Washington as a hero who struck the first blow against the French.

The Albany Plan of Union

While Washington struggled with the French, representatives from New England, New York, Pennsylvania, and Maryland met to discuss the threat of war. In June 1754, the representatives gathered in Albany, New York. They wanted to find a way for the colonies to defend themselves against the French. They also hoped to persuade the Iroquois to take their side against the French.

The representatives adopted a plan suggested by Benjamin Franklin. Known as the **Albany Plan of Union,** Franklin's plan called for "one general government" for 11 of the American colonies. An elected legislature would govern these colonies and would have the power to collect taxes, raise troops, and regulate trade. Not a single colonial assembly approved the plan. None of the colonies were willing to give up any

The Albany Plan

The Albany Plan was the first colonial constitution. Actually it was not the first. In 1639, settlers in Connecticut drew up America's first formal constitution, or charter, called the Fundamental Orders of Connecticut. This document laid out a plan for government that gave the people the right to elect the governor, judges, and representatives to make laws.

of their power. The Albany meeting failed to unite the colonists to fight the French. Disappointed, Franklin wrote,

> 66Everyone cries, a union is necessary, but when they come to the manner and form of the union, their weak noodles [brains] are perfectly distracted.99

Washington's defeat at Fort Necessity marked the start of a series of clashes and full-scale war. The colonists called it the French and Indian War because they fought two enemies—the French and their Native American allies.

Reading Check **Analyzing** What was the purpose of the Albany Plan of Union?

SECTION 3 ASSESSMENT

Checking for Understanding

1. **Key Terms** Write a short paragraph that uses the terms Iroquois Confederacy and militia.
2. **Reviewing Facts** List two reasons the French felt threatened by British interest in the Ohio River valley.

Reviewing Themes

3. **Continuity and Change** Why did colonists consider George Washington a hero, even after he was defeated by the French?

Critical Thinking

4. **Analyzing Primary Sources** Re-read Benjamin Franklin's quote on this page. What was his reaction to the colonies' refusal to accept the Albany Plan of Union?
5. **Evaluating Information** Re-create the diagram below and explain the powers the legislature would have under the Albany Plan.

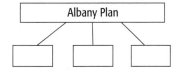

Analyzing Visuals

6. **Geography Skills** Study the map on page 117. What countries claimed land in North America? What power controlled most of what is present-day Canada? If you live in North America, what country controlled the region in which you live?

Interdisciplinary Activity

Expository Writing Make a list of five questions that a reporter might have asked Iroquois leaders after they reluctantly sided with the British.

Critical Thinking
SKILLBUILDER

Understanding Cause and Effect

Why Learn This Skill?

You know that if you watch television instead of completing your homework you will receive poor grades. This is an example of a cause-and-effect relationship. The cause—watching television instead of doing homework—leads to an effect—poor grades.

Learning the Skill

A *cause* is any person, event, or condition that makes something happen. What happens as a result is known as an *effect*. These guidelines will help you identify cause and effect.

- Identify two or more events.
- Ask questions about why events occur.
- Look for "clue words" that alert you to cause and effect, such as *because, led to, brought about, produced,* and *therefore.*
- Identify the outcome of events.

Practicing the Skill

Study the cause-and-effect chart about the slave trade on this page. Think about the guidelines listed above. Then answer the questions below.

1 What were some causes of the development of slavery in the colonies?

2 What were some of the short-term effects of enslaving Africans?

3 What was the long-term effect of the development of slavery?

Causes and Effects of the Slave Trade

Causes

- Colonists need to grow cash crops, such as tobacco and rice.
- European demand for tobacco and rice increases.
- Growing tobacco and rice requires large labor force.

Effects

- Africans are robbed of basic human rights.
- Population of enslaved Africans grows.
- Slavery creates feelings of injustice and plants seeds of regional conflict.

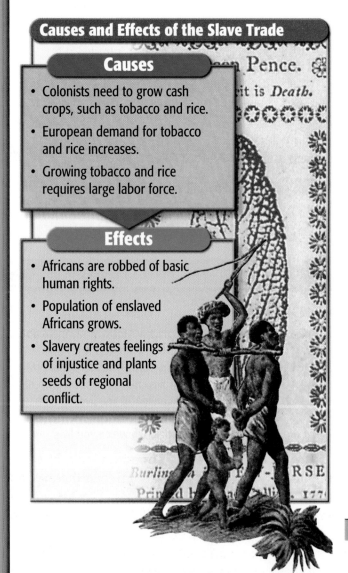

Applying the Skill

Understanding Cause and Effect Read an account of a recent event or chain of events in your community newspaper. Determine at least one cause and one effect of that event. Show the cause-and-effect relationship in a chart.

GO TO Glencoe's **Skillbuilder Interactive Workbook CD-ROM, Level 1,** provides instruction and practice in key social studies skills.

The French and Indian War

Native American maize mask

AN American Story

"These lakes, these woods, and mountains were left [to] us by our ancestors. They are our inheritances, and we will part with them to no one. . . . [Y]ou ought to know that He, the Great Spirit and Master of Life, has provided food for us in these spacious lakes and on the woody mountains. . . ."

These words, spoken by Chief Pontiac, served as a warning to the British colonists who wanted to take Native American lands.

The British Take Action

During the French and Indian War, some Native Americans fought on the side of the British. Many others fought against the British. The war that raged in North America through the late 1750s and early 1760s was one part of a larger struggle between England and France for control of world trade and power on the seas.

In 1754 the governor of Massachusetts announced to the colonial assembly that the French were on the way to "making themselves masters of this Continent."

The British colonists knew that the French were building well-armed forts throughout the Great Lakes region and the Ohio River valley. Their network of alliances, or unions, with Native Americans allowed the French to control large areas of land, stretching from the St. Lawrence River in Canada all the way south to New Orleans. The French and their Native American allies seemed to be winning control of the American frontier. The final showdown was about to begin.

During the early stages of the French and Indian War, the British colonists fought the French and the Native Americans with little help from Britain. In 1754, however, the government in London decided to intervene in the conflict. It was alarmed by the new forts the French were building and by George Washington's defeat at Fort Necessity. In the fall of 1754, Great Britain appointed **General Edward Braddock** commander in chief of the British forces in America and sent him to drive the French out of the Ohio Valley.

Braddock Marches to Duquesne

In June 1755, Braddock set out from Virginia with about 1,400 red-coated British soldiers and a smaller number of blue-coated colonial militia. George Washington served as one of his aides. It took Braddock's army several weeks to trek through the dense forest to **Fort Duquesne.** Washington reported that Braddock

❝halted to level every mole-hill and to erect bridges over every brook, by which means we were four days in getting twelve miles.❞

Washington tried to tell Braddock that his army's style of marching was not well suited to fighting in frontier country. Lined up in columns and rows, the troops made easy targets. Braddock ignored the advice.

On July 9 a combined force of Native American warriors and French troops ambushed the British. The French and Native Americans were hidden, firing from behind trees and aiming at the bright uniforms. The British, confused and frightened, could not even see their attackers. One of the survivors of Braddock's army, Captain Orne, later described the "great confusion"

Picturing **History**

Native American warriors and French troops, protected by rocks and trees, fire into General Braddock's army, who were crammed together on a forest trail. **What weakness of the British army contributed to Braddock's defeat?**

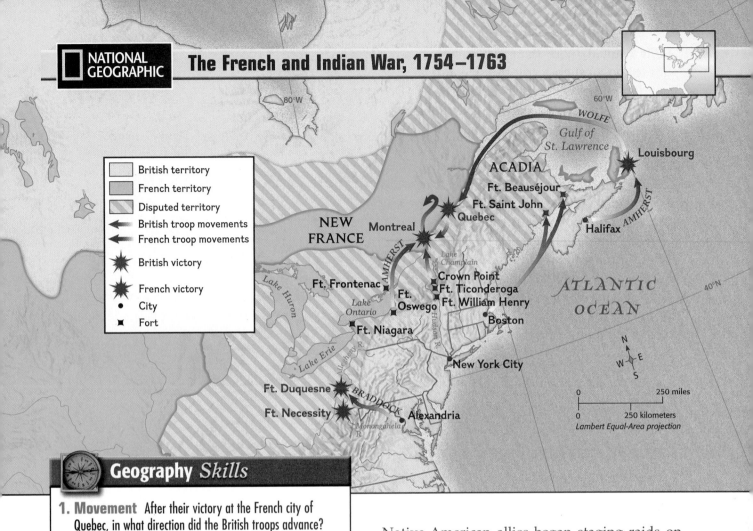

The French and Indian War, 1754–1763

British territory
French territory
Disputed territory
British troop movements
French troop movements
British victory
French victory
City
Fort

NEW FRANCE

WOLFE

Gulf of St. Lawrence

ACADIA

Louisbourg

Ft. Beauséjour

Ft. Saint John

Quebec

Montreal

AMHERST

Halifax

AMHERST

Lake Champlain

Crown Point

Ft. Ticonderoga

Ft. William Henry

Boston

ATLANTIC OCEAN

Lake Huron

Lake Ontario

Ft. Frontenac

Ft. Oswego

Ft. Niagara

Hudson R.

Lake Erie

Allegheny R.

New York City

Ft. Duquesne

BRADDOCK

Ft. Necessity

Monongahela R.

Alexandria

N
W E
S

0   250 miles

0   250 kilometers

Lambert Equal-Area projection

Geography Skills

1. Movement After their victory at the French city of Quebec, in what direction did the British troops advance?

2. Drawing Conclusions Why would Ft. Duquesne be a valuable fort to control?

---

that overcame Braddock's troops when they were attacked. Braddock called for an orderly retreat, "but the panic was so great he could not succeed." Braddock was killed, and the battle ended in a bitter defeat for the British, who suffered nearly 1,000 casualties. Washington led the survivors back to Virginia.

Britain Declares War on France

The fighting in America helped start a new war in Europe, known as the **Seven Years' War.** After arranging an alliance with Prussia, Britain declared war on France in 1756. Prussia fought France and its allies in Europe while Britain fought France in the Caribbean, India, and North America.

The first years of the war were disastrous for the British and their American colonies. French troops captured several British forts, and their Native American allies began staging raids on frontier farms from New York to Pennsylvania. They killed settlers, burned farmhouses and crops, and drove many families back toward the coast. French forces from Canada captured British forts at Lake Ontario and at Lake George.

Pitt Takes Charge

Great Britain's prospects in America improved after **William Pitt** came to power as secretary of state and then as prime minister. An outstanding military planner, Pitt knew how to pick skilled commanders. He oversaw the war effort from London.

To avoid having to deal with constant arguments from the colonies about the cost of the war, Pitt decided that Great Britain would pay for supplies needed in the war—no matter the cost. In doing so Pitt ran up an enormous debt. After the French and Indian War, the British raised the colonists' taxes to help pay this debt. Pitt had only delayed the moment when the colonists had to pay their share of the bill.

Pitt wanted more than just a clear path to the Western territories. He also intended to conquer French Canada. He sent British troops to North America under the command of such energetic officers as **Jeffrey Amherst** and **James Wolfe.**

In 1758 Amherst and Wolfe led a British assault that recaptured the fortress at Louisbourg. That same year a group of New Englanders, led by British officers, captured Fort Frontenac at Lake Ontario. Still another British force marched across Pennsylvania and forced the French to abandon Fort Duquesne, which was renamed Fort Pitt.

✓**Reading Check** **Describing** What abilities did William Pitt bring to the post of prime minister?

The Fall of New France

The year 1759 brought so many British victories that people said the church bells of London wore thin with joyous ringing. The British captured several French islands in the West Indies and the city of Havana in Cuba. They defeated the French in India, and destroyed a French fleet that had been sent to reinforce Canada. The greatest victory of the year, though, took place in the heart of New France.

The Battle of Quebec

Perched high on a cliff overlooking the St. Lawrence River, **Quebec,** the capital of New France, was thought to be impossible to attack. In September 1759, British general James Wolfe found a way.

One of Wolfe's scouts spotted a poorly guarded path up the back of the cliff. Wolfe's soldiers overwhelmed the guards posted on the path and then scrambled up the path during the night. The British troops assembled outside the fortress of Quebec on a field called the **Plains of Abraham.** There they surprised and defeated the French army. James Wolfe died in the battle. The French commander, the Marquis de Montcalm, was wounded and died the next day.

"If you are French . . . join us. If you are English, we declare war against you. Let us have your answer."

—Pontiac, 1763

The Treaty of Paris

The fall of Quebec and General Amherst's capture of Montreal the following year brought the fighting in North America to an end. In the **Treaty of Paris** of 1763, France was permitted to keep some of its sugar-producing islands in the West Indies, but it was forced to give Canada and most of its lands east of the Mississippi River to Great Britain. From Spain, France's ally, Great Britain gained Florida. In return, Spain received French lands west of the Mississippi River—the Louisiana Territory—as well as the port of New Orleans.

The Treaty of Paris marked the end of France as a power in North America. The continent was now divided between Great Britain and Spain, with the Mississippi River marking the boundary. While the Spanish and British were working out a plan for the future of North America, many Native Americans still lived on the lands covered by the European agreement.

✓**Reading Check** **Summarizing** What lands did Spain receive under the Treaty of Paris?

Trouble on the Frontier

The British victory over the French dealt a blow to the Native Americans of the Ohio River valley. They had lost their French allies and trading partners. Although they continued to trade with the British, the Native Americans regarded them as enemies. The British raised the prices of their goods and, unlike the French, refused to pay the Native Americans for the use of their land. Worst of all, British settlers began moving into the valleys of western Pennsylvania.

Pontiac's War

Pontiac, chief of an Ottawa village near Detroit, recognized that the British settlers threatened the Native American way of life. Just as Benjamin Franklin had tried to bring the colonies together with the Albany Plan, Pontiac wanted to join Native American groups to fight the British.

In the spring of 1763, Pontiac put together an alliance. He attacked the British fort at Detroit while other war parties captured most of the other British outposts in the Great Lakes region. That summer Native Americans killed settlers along the Pennsylvania and Virginia frontiers in a series of raids called **Pontiac's War.**

The Native Americans, however, failed to capture the important strongholds of Niagara, Fort Pitt, and Detroit. The war ended in August 1765 after British troops defeated Pontiac's allies, the Shawnee and Delaware people. In July 1766, Pontiac signed a peace treaty and was pardoned by the British.

HISTORY Online

Student Web Activity
Visit tarvol1.glencoe.com and click on **Chapter 4— Student Web Activities** for an activity on the French and Indian War.

★ Geography
The Proclamation of 1763

To prevent more fighting, Britain called a halt to the settlers' westward expansion. In the **Proclamation of 1763,** King George III declared that the Appalachian Mountains were the temporary western boundary for the colonies. The proclamation angered many people, especially those who owned shares in land companies. These speculators, or investors, had already bought land west of the mountains. They were furious that Britain ignored their land claims.

Although the end of the French and Indian War brought peace for the first time in many years, the Proclamation of 1763 created friction. More conflicts would soon arise between Britain and the colonists in North America.

Reading Check **Examining** Why were many colonists angered by the Proclamation of 1763?

SECTION 4 ASSESSMENT

Checking for Understanding

1. **Key Terms** Use the terms alliance and speculator in a short paragraph to explain their meaning.
2. **Reviewing the Facts** Name the three nations that were involved in the Seven Years' War.

Reviewing Themes

3. **Individual Action** How did Pontiac plan to defend Native Americans from British settlers? Was his plan successful?

Critical Thinking

4. **Analyzing Information** What did the British hope to gain by issuing the Proclamation of 1763?
5. **Analyzing Information** What actions do you think General Braddock could have taken to increase his army's chances of defeating the French? Re-create the diagram below to organize your answer.

Other strategies and tactics

Analyzing Visuals

6. **Geography Skills** Study the map of the French and Indian War on page 123. What was the result of the battle at Fort Duquesne? What route did British General Wolfe take to reach Quebec?

Interdisciplinary Activity

Geography Sketch a map showing the land claims of Great Britain, France, and Spain in North America after the Treaty of Paris.

Chapter Summary

The Colonies Grow

- Between the 1600s and early 1700s, thirteen American colonies are established—some for profit and others by religious groups seeking freedom.

- New England, the Middle Colonies, and the Southern Colonies develop diverse economies.

- Although many different people live in the colonies, their values and beliefs, government, and educational institutions grow out of English traditions.

- Between 1650 and 1750, Parliament passes laws regulating colonial trade.

- In 1754 the French and Indian War begins.

- From 1689 to 1763, France and Britain fight a series of wars.

- Under the terms of the Treaty of Paris, Britain obtains control of much of the continent.

- North America is divided between Great Britain and Spain.

JOIN, or DIE.

Reviewing Key Terms

Use all the terms below in one of three paragraphs, each about one of the following: trade, farming, organization of the colonies.

1. subsistence farming
2. cash crop
3. export
4. mercantilism
5. charter colony
6. proprietary colony
7. import

Reviewing Key Facts

8. Why did the colonial population grow rapidly?
9. What differences existed between the Tidewater planters and the backcountry farmers of the South?
10. What was the Great Awakening?
11. What immigrant groups settled in Pennsylvania?
12. How did the soil in the Middle Colonies differ from that in New England? What did that mean for the two regions?
13. What was the Iroquois Confederacy?
14. What was England's reason for the Navigation Acts?
15. What was the Enlightenment?
16. What North American land claims were the French forced to give up in the Treaty of Paris?
17. Why did the Proclamation of 1763 cause friction?

Critical Thinking

18. **Comparing** How did the economies of the New England and Southern Colonies differ? Re-create the chart below to answer the question.

Northern economy	Southern economy

19. **Drawing Conclusions** Re-read the People in History feature on page 109. In what ways did Benjamin Franklin represent the Enlightenment way of thinking?

20. **Determining Cause and Effect** How did the French relationship with Native Americans help them in their conflicts with the British?

21. **Analyzing Information** Re-read the Two Viewpoints feature on page 118. Why did Drake give the name 'Albion' to the land?

Geography and History Activity

Study the map of North America in 1754 on page 117; then answer these questions.

22. What countries controlled land on the continent?

23. What regions were under Spain's control?

24. Who controlled the land that is now Mexico?

25. What nation controlled the Mississippi River?

Practicing Skills

Determining Cause and Effect *Each of the following three sentences illustrates a cause-and-effect relationship. On a separate sheet of paper, identify the cause(s) and effect(s) in each sentence.*

26. During the 1700s the population of the English colonies grew dramatically as a result of high immigration.

27. To make certain that only England benefited from trade with the colonies, Parliament passed the Navigation Acts.

28. Because worship was so central to the Puritans, they built their towns around the church.

Citizenship Cooperative Activity

29. **Community Volunteers** Work with a partner to make a list of places in your community that need the services of volunteers. These can include libraries, nursing homes, and day care centers. Call each place and ask what the volunteers do, what times of the day and week they are needed, and how a volunteer can get started. Share your findings with the class. Then volunteer some of your time at one of the places you contacted.

Economics Activity

30. Working with a partner, create a map showing a trade route that colonial merchants might use. To get started, examine maps and information from your text and from encyclopedias and historical atlases. Include the physical features that the colonial merchants had to face, including rivers, mountains, lakes, and so on.

Alternative Assessment

31. **Portfolio Writing Activity** Research and write a report in which you identify racial, ethnic, and religious groups that immigrated to the United States. Choose one group from the 17th century, one group from the 18th century, and one from the 19th century. Identify their reasons for immigrating.

Self-Check Quiz
Visit **tarvol1.glencoe.com** and click on **Chapter 4— Self-Check Quizzes** to prepare for the chapter test.

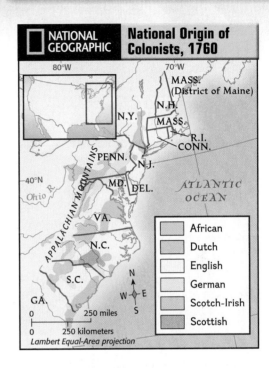

NATIONAL GEOGRAPHIC **National Origin of Colonists, 1760**

Standardized Test Practice

Directions: Use the map above to answer the following question.

According to the map, which of the following statements is true?

F The Appalachian Mountains divided North Carolina and South Carolina.

G Virginia had the largest population.

H Most of Delaware's people were English.

J Dutch communities were widespread throughout South Carolina.

Test-Taking Tip:

Make sure that you look at the map's *title* and *key* so that you understand what it represents. Since the map does not show *total population* of the colonies, you can eliminate answer **G**.

UNIT
3

Creating a Nation

1763–1791

Why It Matters

As you study Unit 3, *you will learn that the purpose of the Declaration of Independence was to justify the American Revolution and to explain the founding principles of the new nation. You will also learn that the Constitution established a republic, in which power is held by voting citizens through their representatives.*

Primary Sources Library

See pages 596–597 for primary source readings to accompany Unit 3.

◉ *Use the **American History Primary Source Document Library CD-ROM** to find additional primary sources about the American move toward independence.*

American flag, Revolutionary War

Washington Crossing the Delaware by Emanuel Gottlieb Leutze

"Give me liberty, or give me death!"

—Patrick Henry, 1775

CHAPTER 5

Road to Independence

1763–1776

Why It Matters

A spirit of independence became evident early in the history of the American people. Far from the established rules and restrictions they had faced in their home countries, the new settlers began to make their own laws and develop their own ways of doing things.

The Impact Today

The ideals of revolutionary America still play a major role in shaping the society we live in. For example:
- *Americans still exercise their right to protest laws they view as unfair.*
- *Citizens have the right to present their views freely.*

The American Republic to 1877 *Video* *The chapter 5 video, "Loyalists and Tories," portrays events leading up to the Revolutionary War from a Loyalist's point of view, as well as a Patriot's.*

The Americas

1763
- Treaty of Paris

1765
- Stamp Act protests

1770
- Boston Massacre

1763　　　　　　　　　*1766*　　　　　　　　　*1769*

World

1764
- Mozart (aged eight) writes first symphony

1762
- Rousseau publishes *The Social Contract*

1769
- Watt patents steam engine

1770
- Russians destroy Ottoman fleet

Bunker Hill by Don Troiani Low on ammunition, Colonel William Prescott gives the order, "Don't fire until you see the whites of their eyes."

1773
• Boston Tea Party

1774
• First Continental Congress meets

1776
• Declaration of Independence signed

1775
• Battles fought at Lexington and Concord

1772

1775

1772
• Poland partitioned among Russia, Prussia, and Austria

1774
• Louis XVI becomes king of France

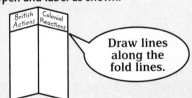

Taxation Without Representation

St. Edward's crown, worn by George III

AN
American Story

Huron and Ottawa warriors silently peered from the woods. They watched about 100 British soldiers camped on Lake Erie's shore. The soldiers—sent by the British Crown—had just stopped to rest on their way to Fort Detroit. They were worried about rumors of Native Americans planning war.

Suddenly the warriors rushed from the forest. The British managed to escape in two boats. War raged on the frontier—and the British were in the thick of it!

Relations with Britain

After winning the French and Indian War, Great Britain controlled a vast territory in North America. To limit settlement of this territory, Britain issued the Proclamation of 1763. Parts of the land acquired through the Treaty of Paris became the provinces of Quebec, East Florida, West Florida, and Grenada (a combination of several Caribbean islands). Most importantly, the Proclamation prohibited colonists from moving west of the Appalachian Mountains.

Stopping western settlement provided several advantages for Britain. It allowed the British government, not the colonists, to control westward movement. In this way, westward expansion would go on in an orderly way, and conflict with Native Americans might be avoided. Slower western settlement would also slow colonists moving away from the colonies on the coast—where Britain's important markets and investments were. Finally, closing western settlement protected the interests of British officials who wanted to control the lucrative fur trade. The British planned to keep 10,000 troops in America to protect their interests.

These plans alarmed the colonists. Many feared that the large number of British troops in North America might be used to interfere with their liberties. They saw the Proclamation of 1763 as a limit on their freedom. These two measures contributed to the feeling of distrust that was growing between Great Britain and its colonies.

The financial problems of Great Britain complicated the situation. The French and Indian War left Britain with a huge public debt. Desperate for new revenue, or incoming money, the king and Parliament felt it was only fair that the colonists pay part of the cost. They began plans to tax them. This decision set off a chain of events that enraged the American colonists and surprised British authorities.

Britain's Trade Laws

In 1763 **George Grenville** became prime minister of Britain. He was determined to reduce Britain's debt. He decided to take action against smuggling in the colonies. When the colonists smuggled goods to avoid taxes, Britain lost revenue that could be used to pay debts.

Grenville knew that American juries often found smugglers innocent. In 1763 he convinced Parliament to pass a law allowing smugglers to be sent to vice-admiralty courts. Vice-admiralty courts were run by officers and did not have juries. In 1767 Parliament decided to authorize writs of assistance. These legal documents allowed customs officers to enter any location to search for smuggled goods.

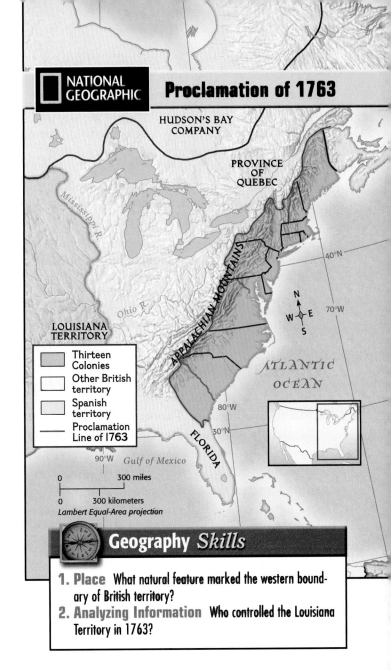

NATIONAL GEOGRAPHIC **Proclamation of 1763**

HUDSON'S BAY COMPANY

PROVINCE OF QUEBEC

Mississippi R.

APPALACHIAN MOUNTAINS

Ohio R.

LOUISIANA TERRITORY

ATLANTIC OCEAN

FLORIDA

Gulf of Mexico

- Thirteen Colonies
- Other British territory
- Spanish territory
- — Proclamation Line of 1763

0 — 300 miles
0 — 300 kilometers
Lambert Equal-Area projection

Geography Skills

1. **Place** What natural feature marked the western boundary of British territory?
2. **Analyzing Information** Who controlled the Louisiana Territory in 1763?

The Sugar Act

With a new law in place to stop smuggling, Grenville tried to increase tax revenue. In 1764 Parliament passed the **Sugar Act**. The act lowered the tax on molasses imported by the colonists. Grenville hoped the lower tax would convince the colonists to pay the tax instead of smuggling. The act also let officers seize goods from smugglers without going to court.

The Sugar Act and the new laws to control smuggling angered the colonists. They believed their rights as Englishmen were being violated. Writs of assistance violated their right to be secure in their home. Vice-admiralty courts violated their right to a jury trial. Furthermore, in trials at vice-admiralty courts, the burden of proof was on defendants to prove their innocence. This contradicted British law, which states that the accused is "innocent until proved guilty."

These measures alarmed the colonists. **James Otis,** a young lawyer in Boston, argued that

> ❝no parts of [England's colonies] can be taxed without their consent . . . every part has a right to be represented.❞

In his speeches and pamphlets, Otis defined and defended colonial rights.

✓ **Reading Check** **Analyzing** Why did Parliament pass the Sugar Act?

The Stamp Act

In 1765 Parliament passed another law in an effort to raise money. This law, the **Stamp Act,** placed a tax on almost all printed material in the colonies—everything from newspapers and pamphlets to wills and playing cards. All printed material had to have a stamp, which was applied by British officials. Because so many items were taxed, it affected almost everyone in the colonial cities. The Stamp Act convinced many colonists of the need for action.

Opposition to the Stamp Act centered on two points. Parliament had interfered in colonial affairs by taxing the colonies directly. In addition, it taxed the colonists without their consent. In passing the Stamp Act without consulting the colonial legislatures, Parliament ignored the colonial tradition of self-government.

Protesting the Stamp Act

A young member of the Virginia House of Burgesses, **Patrick Henry,** persuaded the burgesses to take action against the Stamp Act. According to tradition, when he was accused of treason, Henry replied,

> ❝If this be treason, make the most of it!❞

The Virginia assembly passed a resolution—a formal expression of opinion—declaring it had "the only and sole exclusive right and power to lay taxes" on its citizens.

In Boston **Samuel Adams** helped start an organization called the **Sons of Liberty.** Members took to the streets to protest the Stamp Act. People in other cities also organized Sons of Liberty groups.

Throughout the summer of 1765, protesters burned effigies—rag figures—representing unpopular tax collectors. They also raided and destroyed houses belonging to royal officials and marched through the streets shouting that only Americans had the right to tax Americans.

The Stamp Act Congress

In October delegates from nine colonies met in New York at the **Stamp Act Congress.** They drafted a petition to the king and Parliament declaring that the colonies could not be taxed except by their own assemblies.

In the colonial cities, people refused to use the stamps. They urged merchants to boycott—refuse to buy—British and European goods in protest. Thousands of merchants, artisans, and farmers signed nonimportation agreements. In these agreements they pledged not to buy or use goods imported from Great Britain. As the boycott spread, British merchants lost so much business that they begged Parliament to repeal, or cancel, the Stamp Act.

Revenue stamp

The Act Is Repealed

In March 1766, Parliament gave in to the colonists' demands and repealed the Stamp Act. Yet the colonists' trust in the king and Parliament was never fully restored.

While the colonists celebrated their victory over the Stamp Act, Parliament passed another act on the same day it repealed the Stamp Act. The **Declaratory Act** of 1766 stated that Parliament had the right to tax and make decisions for the British colonies "in all cases." The colonists might have won one battle, but the war over making decisions for the colonies had just begun.

✓ **Reading Check** **Evaluating** What role did Samuel Adams play in colonial protests?

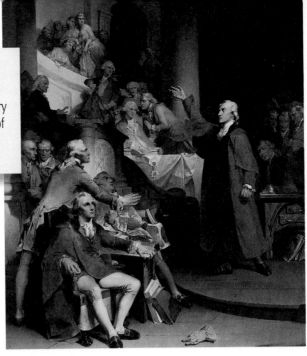

History *Through Art*

Patrick Henry Before the Virginia House of Burgesses by Peter F. Rothermel Patrick Henry gave a fiery speech before the Virginia House of Burgesses in 1765. **Why did Henry deliver the speech?**

New Taxes

Soon after the Stamp Act crisis, Parliament passed a set of laws in 1767 that came to be known as the **Townshend Acts.** In these acts the British leaders tried to avoid some of the problems the Stamp Act caused. They understood that the colonists would not tolerate internal taxes—those levied or paid inside the colonies. As a result the new taxes applied only to imported goods, with the tax being paid at the port of entry. The goods taxed, however, included basic items—such as glass, tea, paper, and lead—that the colonists had to import because they did not produce them.

By this time the colonists were outraged by *any* taxes Parliament passed. They believed that only their own representatives had the right to levy taxes on them. The colonists responded by bringing back the boycott that had worked so well against the Stamp Act. The boycott proved to be even more widespread this time.

Women took an active role in the protest against the Townshend Acts. In towns throughout the colonies, women organized groups to support the boycott of British goods, sometimes calling themselves the **Daughters of Liberty.** They urged Americans to wear homemade fabrics and produce other goods that were available only from Britain before. They believed this would help the American colonies become economically independent.

Reading Check **Comparing** How did the Townshend Acts differ from the Stamp Act?

SECTION 1 ASSESSMENT

Checking for Understanding

1. **Key Terms** Write sentences or short paragraphs in which you use the following groups of terms correctly: (1) revenue and writs of assistance; (2) resolution, effigy, boycott, nonimportation, and repeal.

2. **Reviewing Facts** State two reasons for the deterioration of relations between the British and the colonists.

Reviewing Themes

3. **Civic Rights and Responsibilities** Why did the colonists think the writs of assistance violated their rights?

Critical Thinking

4. **Identifying Central Issues** Why did British policies following the French and Indian War lead to increased tensions with American colonists?

5. **Determining Cause and Effect** Re-create the diagram below and describe the effects of these British actions.

British Actions	Effects
Sugar Act ⇨	
Stamp Act ⇨	
Townshend Acts ⇨	

Analyzing Visuals

6. **Geography Skills** Review the map on page 133. The Proclamation of 1763 banned colonists from settling west of the Appalachian Mountains. Why did the British government want to halt western movement?

Interdisciplinary Activity

Persuasive Writing Write a letter to the editor of a colonial newspaper in which you attempt to persuade fellow colonists to boycott British goods. Use standard grammar, spelling, sentence structure and punctuation.

Building Colonial Unity

Guide to Reading

Main Idea
As tensions between colonists and the British government increased, protests grew stronger.

Key Terms
propaganda, committee of correspondence

Reading Strategy
Organizing Information As you read the section, re-create the diagram below and describe how the Intolerable Acts changed life for colonists.

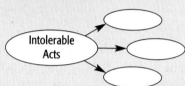

Read to Learn
- why Boston colonists and British soldiers clashed, resulting in the Boston Massacre.
- how the British government tried to maintain its control over the colonies.

Section Theme
Groups and Institutions Colonists banded together to protest British laws.

Preview of Events

♦1770 — ♦1773 — ♦1776

1770
Boston Massacre takes place

1772
Samuel Adams sets up a committee of correspondence

1773
Boston Tea Party occurs

1774
Parliament passes the Intolerable Acts

American protest banner

★★★★★★
AN
American Story

In the spring of 1768, British customs officials in Boston seized the *Liberty,* a ship belonging to John Hancock, a merchant and protest leader. The ship had docked in Boston Harbor to unload a shipment of wine and take on new supplies. The customs officials, however, charged that Hancock was using the ship for smuggling. As news of the ship's seizure spread through Boston, angry townspeople filled the streets. They shouted against Parliament and the taxes it had imposed on them. The *Liberty* affair became one of the events that united the colonists against British policies.

Trouble in Boston

Protests like the *Liberty* affair made British colonial officials nervous. In the summer of 1768, worried customs officers sent word back to Britain that the colonies were on the brink of rebellion. Parliament responded by sending two regiments of troops to Boston. As angry Bostonians jeered, the newly arrived "redcoats" set up camp right in the center of the city.

Many colonists, especially those living in Boston, felt that the British had pushed them too far. First the British had passed a series of laws that violated colonial rights. Now they had sent an army to occupy colonial cities.

To make matters worse, the soldiers stationed in Boston acted rudely and sometimes even violently toward the colonists. Mostly poor men, the redcoats earned little pay. Some of them stole goods from local shops or scuffled with boys who taunted them in the streets. The soldiers competed off-hours for jobs that Bostonians wanted. The townspeople's hatred for the soldiers grew stronger every day.

The Boston Massacre

Relations between the redcoats and the Boston colonists grew more tense. Then on March 5, 1770, the tension finally reached a peak. That day a fight broke out between townspeople and soldiers. While some British officers tried to calm the crowd, one man shouted,

> ❝We did not send for you. We will not have you here. We'll get rid of you, we'll drive you away!❞

The angry townspeople moved through the streets, picking up any weapon they could find—sticks, stones, shovels, and clubs. They pushed forward toward the customshouse on King Street.

As the crowd approached, the sentry on duty panicked and called for help. The crowd responded by throwing stones, snowballs, oyster shells, and pieces of wood at the soldiers. "Fire, you bloodybacks, you lobsters," the crowd screamed. "You dare not fire."

After one of the soldiers was knocked down, the nervous and confused redcoats did fire. Several shots rang out, killing five colonists. One Bostonian cried out:

> ❝Are the inhabitants to be knocked down in the streets? Are they to be murdered in this manner?❞

Among the dead was **Crispus Attucks,** a dockworker who was part African, part Native American. The colonists called the tragic encounter the **Boston Massacre.**

The Word Spreads

Colonial leaders used news of the killings as propaganda—information designed to influence opinion—against the British. Samuel Adams put up posters describing the "Boston Massacre" as a slaughter of innocent Americans by bloodthirsty redcoats. An engraving by Paul Revere showed a British officer giving the order to open fire on an orderly crowd. Revere's powerful image strengthened anti-British feeling.

The Boston Massacre led many colonists to call for stronger boycotts on British goods. Aware of the growing opposition to its policies, Parliament repealed all the Townshend Acts taxes except the one on tea. Many colonists believed they had won another victory. They ended their boycotts, except on the taxed tea, and started to trade with British merchants again.

Some colonial leaders, however, continued to call for resistance to British rule. In 1772 Samuel Adams revived the Boston committee of correspondence, an organization used in earlier protests. The committee circulated writings about colonists' grievances against Britain. Soon other committees of correspondence sprang up throughout the colonies, bringing together protesters opposed to British measures. 📖 *(See page 596 of the Primary Sources Library for readings about colonial resistance.)*

✓ **Reading Check** **Explaining** How did the Boston Massacre contribute to the repeal of the Townshend Acts?

Fact • Fiction • Folklore

The Boston Massacre

The British soldiers never stood trial for the massacre. Eight soldiers and the commanding officer at the Boston Massacre *were* jailed and tried for murder. Many Patriots thought it was an act of disloyalty to defend the soldiers. The soldiers' hopes for justice rested in the hands of John Adams, who believed that even the enemy should be given a fair trial. Two of the soldiers were found guilty of manslaughter. The others were found not guilty on grounds of self-defense. Some Patriots questioned Adams's loyalty; others argued that the trial showed even the hated redcoats could receive a fair trial.

MORE ABOUT... The Boston Tea Party

The Boston Tea Party is one of the significant events leading ultimately to American independence.

Most of the Townshend Acts are repealed. The tax on tea remains.

In November 1773, the citizens of Boston refuse to allow three British ships to unload 342 chests of tea.

On the evening of December 16, Boston citizens disguised as Native Americans board the ships and empty the tea into Boston Harbor.

King George III and Parliament respond by closing the city port.

TEA THROWN INTO BOSTON HARBOR DEC 16 1773.

"Fellow countrymen, we cannot afford to give a single inch! If we retreat now, everything we have done becomes useless!"

— Samuel Adams,
December 1773

A Crisis Over Tea

In the early 1770s, some Americans considered British colonial policy a "conspiracy against liberty." The British government's actions in 1773 seemed to confirm that view.

The British East India Company faced ruin. To save the East India Company, Parliament passed the **Tea Act** of 1773. This measure gave the company the right to ship tea to the colonies without paying most of the taxes usually placed on tea. It also allowed the company to bypass colonial merchants and sell its tea directly to shopkeepers at a low price. This meant that East India Company tea was cheaper than any other tea in the colonies. The Tea Act gave the company a very favorable advantage over colonial merchants.

Colonial Demands

Colonial merchants immediately called for a new boycott of British goods. Samuel Adams and others denounced the British monopoly. The Tea Act, they argued, was just another attempt to crush the colonists' liberty.

At large public meetings in Boston and Philadelphia, colonists vowed to stop the East India Company's ships from unloading. The Daughters of Liberty issued a pamphlet declaring that rather than part with freedom, "we'll part with our tea."

Parliament ignored warnings that another crisis was brewing. The East India Company shipped tea to Philadelphia, New York, Boston, and Charles Town. The colonists forced the ships sent to New York and Philadelphia to turn back. The tea sent to Charles Town was seized and stored in a warehouse. In Boston, a showdown began.

The Boston Tea Party

Three tea ships arrived in Boston Harbor in late 1773. The royal governor, whose house had been destroyed by Stamp Act protesters, refused to let the ships turn back. When he ordered the tea unloaded, Adams and the Boston Sons of Liberty acted swiftly. On December 16, a group of men disguised as Mohawks and armed with hatchets marched to the wharves. At midnight they boarded the ships and threw 342 chests of tea overboard, an event that became known as the **Boston Tea Party.**

Word of this act of defiance spread throughout the colonies. Men and women gathered in the streets to celebrate the bravery of the Boston Sons of Liberty. Yet no one spoke of challenging British rule, and colonial leaders continued to think of themselves as members of the British empire.

The Intolerable Acts

When news of the Boston Tea Party reached London, the reaction was quite different. King **George III** realized that Britain was losing control of the colonies. "We must master them or totally leave them alone." Not prepared to give up, the king and Parliament vowed to punish Boston. In the spring of 1774, Parliament passed the **Coercive Acts,** very harsh laws intended to punish the people of Massachusetts for their resistance.

The Coercive Acts closed Boston Harbor until the Massachusetts colonists paid for the ruined tea. This action prevented the arrival of food and other supplies that normally came by ship. Worse,

the laws took away certain rights of the Massachusetts colonists. For example, the laws banned most town meetings, an important form of self-government in New England. Another provision permitted royal officers to be tried in other colonies or in Britain when accused of crimes.

The Coercive Acts also forced Bostonians to shelter soldiers in their own homes. Parliament planned to isolate Boston with these acts. Instead the other colonies sent food and clothing to demonstrate their support for Boston. The colonists maintained that the Coercive Acts violated their rights as English citizens. These included the rights to no quartering of troops in private homes and no standing army in peacetime without their consent.

The Quebec Act, passed shortly after the Coercive Acts, further angered the colonists. This act set up a permanent government for Quebec and granted religious freedom to French Catholics. Colonists strongly objected to the provision that gave Quebec the area west of the Appalachians and north of the Ohio River. This provision ignored colonial claims to the area. The feelings of the colonists were made clear by *their* name for the new laws—the Intolerable Acts.

✓ Reading Check **Summarizing** List the effects of the Coercive Acts on the citizens of Boston.

SECTION 2 ASSESSMENT

Checking for Understanding

1. **Key Terms** Use these terms in sentences that relate to the Boston Massacre: propaganda, committee of correspondence.
2. **Reviewing Facts** How did colonial leaders use the Boston Massacre to their advantage?

Reviewing Themes

3. **Groups and Institutions** Why were the committees of correspondence powerful organizations?

Critical Thinking

4. **Drawing Conclusions** Do you think the Boston Tea Party was a turning point in the relationship between the British and the colonists? Explain.
5. **Organizing Information** Re-create the diagram below and describe how colonists showed their opposition to British policies.

Increased colonial opposition			

Analyzing Visuals

6. **Picturing History** Examine the material about the Boston Tea Party on page 138. What artifacts are shown? When did the "tea party" take place?

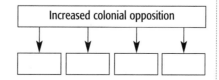
Interdisciplinary Activity

Art Draw a cartoon strip showing the story of the Boston Tea Party. Use at least four cartoon frames to present the sequence of events from your point of view. Compare your cartoon to a classmate's and describe his or her point of view.

America's LITERATURE

Esther Forbes (1891–1967)

Esther Forbes wrote a number of books; among them is the prize-winning biography *Paul Revere and the World He Lived In*. As she researched Paul Revere's life, Forbes learned that many young apprentices played a role in the American Revolution. *Johnny Tremain*, a fictional work, tells the story of such an apprentice.

READ TO DISCOVER

In this passage from *Johnny Tremain*, 14-year-old Johnny and his friend Rab have disguised themselves as Mohawks. They join the crowd at Griffin's Wharf in Boston Harbor, where three English ships carrying tea are docked and are unable to leave or unload their cargo.

READER'S DICTIONARY

boatswain: officer on a ship
warped: roped
jargon: strange language
hold: place where cargo is stored on a ship
winch: machine for hauling

Johnny Tremain

There was a **boatswain's** whistle, and in silence one group boarded the *Dartmouth*. The *Eleanor* and the *Beaver* had to be **warped** in to the wharf. Johnny was close to Mr. Revere's heels. He heard him calling for the captain, promising him, in the **jargon** everyone talked that night, that not one thing should be damaged on the ship except only the tea, but the captain and all his crew had best stay in the cabin until the work was over.

Captain Hall shrugged and did as he was told, leaving his cabin boy to hand over the keys to the **hold.** The boy was grinning with pleasure. The "tea party" was not unexpected. . . .

The **winches** rattled and the heavy chests began to appear—one hundred and fifty of them. As some men worked in the hold, others broke open the chests and flung the tea into the harbor. But one thing made them unexpected difficulty. The tea inside the chests was wrapped in heavy canvas. The axes went through the wood easily enough—the canvas made endless trouble. Johnny had never worked so hard in his life.

Then Mr. Revere called the captain to come up and inspect. The tea was utterly gone, but Captain Hall agreed that beyond that there had not been the slightest damage.

It was close upon dawn when the work on all three ships was done. And yet the great, silent audience on the wharf, men, women, and children, had not gone home. As the three groups came off the

Paul Revere

ships, they formed in fours along the wharf, their axes on their shoulders. Then a hurrah went up and a fife began to play.

ANALYZING LITERATURE

1. **Recall and Interpret** Why was the "tea party" expected?
2. **Evaluate and Connect** What does the conduct of the "tea party" participants suggest about the protest? Explain your answer.

Interdisciplinary Activity

Expository Writing Write a one-page paper about how you think you would react in Johnny's situation.

A Call to Arms

Guide to Reading

Main Idea
Colonial leaders met at Philadelphia in 1774 to discuss a united response to British policies. Seven months later American and British troops met in battle for the first time.

Key Terms
militia, minutemen, Loyalist, Patriot

Reading Strategy
Sequencing Information As you read the section, re-create the diagram below and list six events leading to the Battle of Bunker Hill.

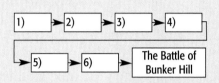

1) → 2) → 3) → 4)
5) → 6) → The Battle of Bunker Hill

Read to Learn
• what happened at the Continental Congress in Philadelphia.
• how the colonists met British soldiers in the first battle.

Section Theme
Groups and Institutions With the establishment of the Continental Congress, the colonies continued to protest.

Preview of Events

♦1774   ♦1775   ♦1776

September 1774
First Continental Congress meets

April 19, 1775
Battles of Lexington and Concord are fought

May 10, 1775
Ethan Allen captures Fort Ticonderoga

June 17, 1775
Battle of Bunker Hill is fought

Revolutionary War drum and fife

AN American Story

At first few colonists wanted a complete break with Britain. One of the most popular songs of the time, "The Bold Americans," called for *both* liberty and continued loyalty to the British king:

> We'll honor George, our sovereign, while he sits on the throne.
> If he grants us liberty, no other king we'll own.
> If he will grant us liberty, so plainly shall you see,
> We are the boys that fear no noise! Success to liberty.

As tensions mounted, however, a peaceful compromise was no longer possible.

The Continental Congress

Colonial leaders realized they needed more than boycotts to gain the liberty they sang about in "The Bold Americans." They needed the colonies to act together in their opposition to British policies.

In September 1774, 55 men arrived in the city of Philadelphia. Sent as delegates from all the colonies except Georgia, these men had come to establish a political body to represent American interests and challenge British control. They called the new organization the **Continental Congress.**

Causes and Effects of the Revolutionary War

Causes

- Colonists' tradition of self-government
- Americans' desire for a separate identity from Britain
- Proclamation of 1763
- Harsh British policies toward North America after 1763

Effects

- A long war with Great Britain
- Self-government for the United States
- World recognition of United States independence

Graphic Organizer → Skills

Relations between Britain and America worsened during the 1760s and the 1770s.

Analyzing Information Why did the colonists fight for self-government?

Delegates to the Congress

Major political leaders from all the colonies attended the Congress. Massachusetts sent fiery Samuel Adams and his younger cousin **John Adams,** a successful lawyer. New York sent **John Jay,** another lawyer. From Virginia came **Richard Henry Lee** and **Patrick Henry,** two of the most outspoken defenders of colonial rights, as well as **George Washington.**

Patrick Henry summed up the meaning of the gathering:

> ❝The distinctions between Virginians, Pennsylvanians, New Yorkers, and New Englanders are no more. . . . I am not a Virginian, but an American.❞

Decisions of the Congress

Although the delegates were hardly united in their views, they realized they needed to work together. First they drafted a statement of grievances calling for the repeal of 13 acts of Parliament passed since 1763. They declared that these laws violated the colonists' rights. Their rights were based on the "laws of nature, the principles of the English constitution, and the several charters" of the colonies. The delegates also voted to boycott all British goods and trade. No British products could be brought into or consumed in the colonies, and no colonial goods could be shipped to Britain.

One of Congress's major decisions was to endorse the Suffolk Resolves. These resolutions had been prepared by Bostonians and others who lived in Suffolk County, Massachusetts. They called on the people of Suffolk County to arm themselves against the British. The people responded by forming militias—groups of citizen soldiers. Many wondered if war was coming. The answer came the following spring.

Reading Check **Explaining** What was the purpose of the Continental Congress?

The First Battles

Colonists expected that if fighting against the British broke out, it would begin in New England. Militia companies in Massachusetts held frequent training sessions, made bullets, and stockpiled rifles and muskets. Some companies, known as minutemen, boasted they would be ready to fight on a minute's notice. In the winter of 1774–1775, a British officer stationed in Boston noted in his diary:

> ❝The people are evidently making every preparation for resistance. They are taking every means to provide themselves with arms.❞

Britain Sends Troops

The British also prepared for conflict. King George announced to Parliament that the New England colonies were "in a state of rebellion" and said that "blows must decide" who would control America. By April 1775, British general Sir Thomas Gage had several thousand soldiers under his command in and around Boston, with many more on the way. Gage had instructions to take away the weapons of the Massachusetts militia and arrest the leaders.

Gage learned that the militia was storing arms and ammunition at **Concord,** a town about 20 miles northwest of Boston. He ordered 700 troops under Lieutenant-Colonel Francis Smith to march

66to Concord, where you will seize and destroy all the artillery and ammunition you can find.99

Alerting the Colonists

On the night of April 18, 1775, Dr. Joseph Warren walked the streets of Boston, looking for any unusual activity by the British army. He saw a regiment form ranks in Boston Common and then begin to march out of the city.

Warren rushed to alert **Paul Revere** and **William Dawes,** leading members of the Sons of Liberty. Revere and Dawes rode to Lexington, a town east of Concord, to warn Samuel Adams and John Hancock that the British were coming.

Revere galloped off across the moonlit countryside, shouting, "The regulars are out!" to the people and houses he passed along the way. When he reached Lexington, he raced to tell Adams and Hancock his news. Adams could barely control his excitement. "What a glorious morning this is!" Adams was ready to fight for American independence.

Fighting at Lexington and Concord

At dawn the redcoats approached Lexington. When they reached the center of the town they discovered a group of about 70 minutemen who had been alerted by Revere and Dawes. Led by Captain John Parker, the minutemen had positioned themselves on the town common with muskets in hand. A minuteman reported,

66There suddenly appeared a number of the King's troops, about a thousand . . . the foremost of which cried, 'Throw down your arms, ye villains, ye rebels.'99

A shot was fired, and then both sides let loose with an exchange of bullets. When the fighting was over, eight minutemen lay dead.

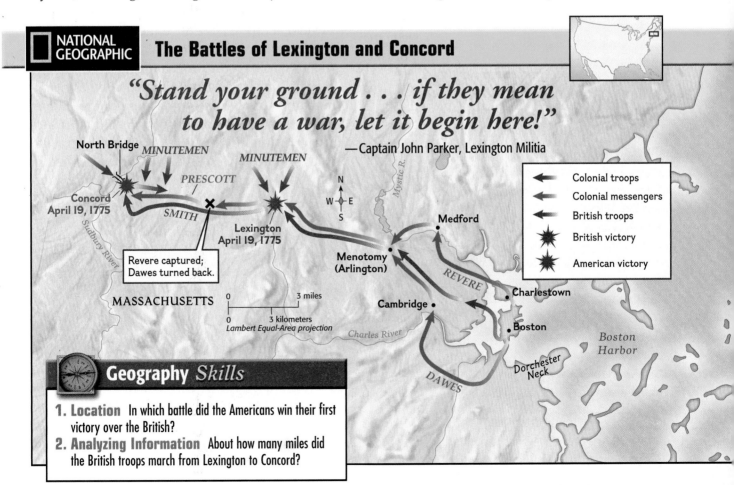

NATIONAL GEOGRAPHIC

The Battles of Lexington and Concord

"Stand your ground . . . if they mean to have a war, let it begin here!"
—Captain John Parker, Lexington Militia

North Bridge MINUTEMEN
MINUTEMEN
PRESCOTT
Concord April 19, 1775
SMITH
Lexington April 19, 1775

Revere captured; Dawes turned back.

MASSACHUSETTS

0   3 miles
0   3 kilometers
Lambert Equal-Area projection

Mystic R.
Medford
Menotomy (Arlington)
REVERE
Charlestown
Cambridge
Boston
DAWES
Dorchester Neck
Charles River
Boston Harbor

N
W - E
S

← Colonial troops
← Colonial messengers
← British troops
✹ British victory
✹ American victory

Geography *Skills*

1. **Location** In which battle did the Americans win their first victory over the British?
2. **Analyzing Information** About how many miles did the British troops march from Lexington to Concord?

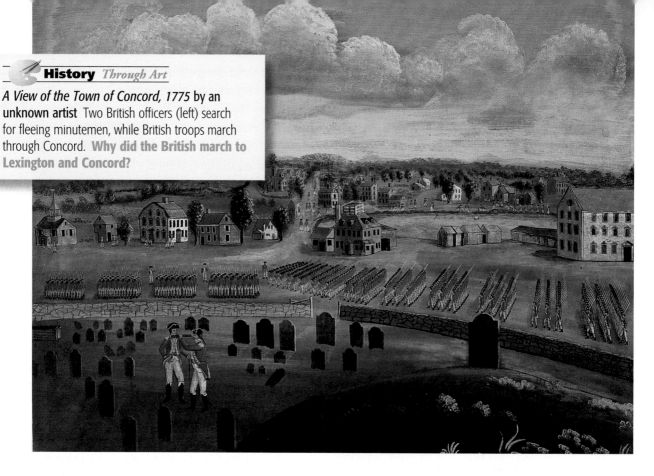

History *Through Art*

A View of the Town of Concord, 1775 by an **unknown artist** Two British officers (left) search for fleeing minutemen, while British troops march through Concord. **Why did the British march to Lexington and Concord?**

The British troops continued their march to Concord. When they arrived there, they discovered that most of the militia's gunpowder had already been removed. They destroyed the remaining supplies. At Concord's North Bridge, the minutemen were waiting for them.

Messengers on horseback had spread word of the British movements. All along the road from Concord to Boston, farmers, blacksmiths, saddle makers, and clerks hid behind trees, rocks, and stone fences. As the British marched down the road, the militia fired. A British officer wrote, "These fellows were generally good marksmen, and many of them used long guns made for duck shooting." By the time the redcoats reached Boston, at least 174 were wounded and 73 were dead.

Looking back, the poet Ralph Waldo Emerson wrote in "The Concord Hymn" that the Americans at Lexington and Concord had fired the "shot heard 'round the world." The battle for America's independence from Great Britain had begun.

Reading Check **Describing** What tactics did the colonists use against the British troops on their march back from Concord to Boston?

More Military Action

Shortly after Lexington and Concord, Benedict Arnold, a captain in the Connecticut militia, was authorized to raise a force of 400 to seize Fort Ticonderoga on Lake Champlain. Ticonderoga was not only strategically located but was rich in military supplies. Arnold learned that Ethan Allen was also mounting an expedition in Vermont to attack the fort. Arnold joined with Allen's force, known as the Green Mountain Boys, and together they caught the British by surprise. The garrison surrendered on May 10, 1775.

Later during the war, Arnold conspired to surrender the key fort of West Point to the British and led British raids against the Americans in Virginia and Connecticut. Arnold became a general in the British army.

Building Forces

After the battles of Lexington and Concord, the committees of correspondence sent out calls for volunteers to join the militias. Soon the colonial militia assembled around Boston was about 20,000 strong. For several weeks, the American and British armies waited nervously to see who would make the next move.

The Battle of Bunker Hill

On June 16, 1775, about 1,200 militiamen under the command of Colonel William Prescott set up fortifications at Bunker Hill and nearby Breed's Hill, across the harbor from Boston.

The British decided to drive the Americans from their strategic locations overlooking the city. The next day the redcoats crossed the harbor and assembled at the bottom of Breed's Hill. Bayonets drawn, they charged up the hill. With his forces low on ammunition, Colonel Prescott reportedly shouted the order, "Don't fire until you see the whites of their eyes." The Americans opened fire, forcing the British to retreat. The redcoats charged two more times, receiving furious fire. In the end the Americans ran out of gunpowder and had to withdraw.

The British won the **Battle of Bunker Hill** but suffered heavy losses—more than 1,000 dead and wounded. As one British officer wrote in his diary, "A dear bought victory, another such would have ruined us." The British had learned that defeating the Americans on the battlefield would not be quick or easy.

Choosing Sides

As American colonists heard about these battles, they faced a major decision. Should they join the rebels or remain loyal to Britain? Those who

Fact Fiction Folklore

The Battle of Bunker Hill

The Battle of Bunker Hill was fought on Breed's Hill. Most of the fighting did actually take place on Breed's Hill. The Patriot soldiers received instructions to set up defensive positions on Bunker Hill. For reasons that are unclear, they set up the positions on nearby Breed's Hill.

chose to stay with Britain, the Loyalists, did not consider unfair taxes and regulations good reasons for rebellion. Some remained loyal to the king because they were officeholders who would lose their positions as a result of the Revolution. Others were people who lived in relative isolation and who had not been part of the wave of discontent that turned so many Americans against Britain. Still others expected Britain to win the war and wanted to gain favor with the British. The Patriots, on the other hand, were determined to fight the British to the end—until American independence was won.

✓ **Reading Check** **Describing** What did the British learn from the Battle of Bunker Hill?

SECTION 3 ASSESSMENT

Checking for Understanding

1. **Key Terms** One of the following terms does not belong with the other three. Identify the term that does not belong and explain why. Terms: militia, minutemen, Loyalist, Patriots.
2. **Reviewing Facts** What decisions were made by the First Continental Congress?

Reviewing Themes

3. **Groups and Institutions** Why did the Continental Congress pass a resolution to form militias?

Critical Thinking

4. **Making Inferences** What reasons might Loyalists have had to support Great Britain?
5. **Comparing** Re-create the diagram below and list the differing beliefs of Patriots and Loyalists and those shared by both.

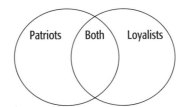

Patriots Both Loyalists

Analyzing Visuals

6. **Chart Skills** Review the cause-and-effect chart on page 142. What event in 1763 was significant to the independence movement?

Interdisciplinary Activity

Expressive Writing Write a one-act play in which a small group of ordinary men, women, and children in a small town react to news of the Battle of Lexington. Remember that reactions varied from colony to colony and that not all colonists wanted independence from Great Britain.

Critical Thinking SKILLBUILDER

Distinguishing Fact From Opinion

Why Learn This Skill?

Suppose a friend says, "Our school's basketball team is awesome. That's a fact." Actually, it is not a fact; it is an opinion. Knowing how to tell the difference between a fact and an opinion can help you analyze the accuracy of political claims, advertisements, and many other kinds of statements.

Paul Revere's ride

Learning the Skill

A **fact** answers a specific question such as: What happened? Who did it? When and where did it happen? Why did it happen? Statements of fact can be checked for accuracy and proven.

An **opinion,** on the other hand, expresses beliefs, feelings, and judgments. Although it may reflect someone's thoughts, we cannot prove or disprove it.

An opinion often begins with phrases such as *I believe, I think, probably, it seems to me,* or *in my opinion.* It often contains words such as *might, could, should,* and *ought* and superlatives such as *best, worst,* and *greatest.* Judgment words that express approval or disapproval—such as *good, bad, poor,* and *satisfactory*—also usually indicate an opinion.

To distinguish between facts and opinions, ask yourself these questions:
- Does this statement give specific information about an event?
- Can I check the accuracy of this statement?
- Does this statement express someone's feelings, beliefs, or judgment?
- Does it include phrases such as *I believe,* superlatives, or judgment words?

Practicing the Skill

Read each numbered statement below. Tell whether each is a fact or an opinion, and explain how you arrived at your answer.

1 Paul Revere rode to Lexington with the news that the British redcoats were coming.

2 The redcoats were the most feared soldiers in the world at that time.

3 The Daughters of Liberty opposed the Tea Act of 1773.

4 The Boston Tea Party raiders should have sunk the tea ships.

5 George III was a foolish king.

Applying the Skill

Distinguishing Fact from Opinion Analyze 10 advertisements. List at least three facts and three opinions presented in the ads.

 Glencoe's **Skillbuilder Interactive Workbook CD-ROM, Level 1,** provides instruction and practice in key social studies skills.

Moving Toward Independence

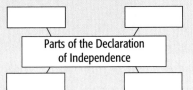

Guide to Reading

Main Idea
The Second Continental Congress voted to approve the Declaration of Independence.

Key Terms
petition, preamble

Reading Strategy
Organizing Information As you read the section, re-create the diagram below and describe the parts of the Declaration of Independence.

```
┌──────┐        ┌──────┐
└──────┘        └──────┘
    ┌─────────────────────┐
    │ Parts of the Declaration │
    │   of Independence    │
    └─────────────────────┘
        ┌──────┐
        └──────┘
```

Read to Learn
• what happened at the Second Continental Congress.
• why the colonists drafted the Declaration of Independence.

Section Theme
Government and Democracy The Declaration of Independence declared the colonies free and independent.

Preview of Events

♦1775	♦1776	♦1777

May 10, 1775
Second Continental Congress meets

July 1775
The Congress sends Olive Branch Petition to George III

March 1776
George Washington takes Boston from the British

July 4, 1776
Declaration of Independence is approved

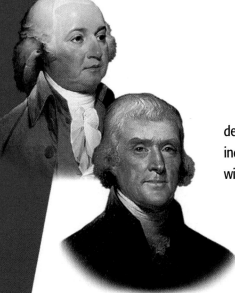

Adams and Jefferson

AN American Story

In June 1776, delegates to the Second Continental Congress came to a momentous decision. They agreed to have a committee draw up a document declaring America's independence from Great Britain. Many years later John Adams recalled a conversation with Thomas Jefferson about the writing of the document.

Jefferson: You should do it.

Adams: Oh! no.

Jefferson: Why will you not? You ought to do it. . . .

Adams: You can write ten times better than I can.

Jefferson: Well, if you are decided, I will do as well as I can.

Colonial Leaders Emerge

On May 10, 1775, the **Second Continental Congress** assembled for the first time, declaring independence was a long way off. The conversation between Jefferson and Adams did not occur until more than a year after that first meeting.

The Second Continental Congress acted as a central government for the colonies.

The delegates to the Second Continental Congress included some of the greatest political leaders in America. Among those attending were John and Samuel Adams, Patrick Henry, Richard Henry Lee, and George Washington—all delegates to the First Continental Congress held in 1774. Several distinguished new delegates came as well.

Benjamin Franklin, one of the most accomplished and respected men in the colonies, had been an influential member of the Pennsylvania legislature. In 1765, during the Stamp Act Crisis, he represented the colonies in London and helped secure the repeal of the act.

America's Flags

Continental Colors, 1775–1777 The Continental Colors, or Grand Union flag, was the first to represent all the colonies. Its 13 stripes stood for the thirteen colonies. The crosses represented the British flag and symbolized the colonists' loyalty to Great Britain at that time.

John Hancock of Massachusetts, 38 years old, was a wealthy merchant. He funded many Patriot groups, including the Sons of Liberty. The delegates chose Hancock as president of the Second Continental Congress.

Thomas Jefferson, only 32 when the Congress began, had already acquired a reputation as a brilliant thinker and writer. As a member of the Virginia House of Burgesses, Jefferson had become associated with the movement toward independence.

The Second Continental Congress began to govern the colonies. It authorized the printing of money and set up a post office with Franklin in charge. It established committees to communicate with Native Americans and with other countries. Most important, the Congress created the **Continental Army** to fight against Britain in a more organized way than the colonial militias could. On John Adams's recommendation, the Congress unanimously chose George Washington to be the army's commander.

After Washington left to take charge of the colonial forces in Boston, the delegates offered Britain one last chance to avoid all-out war. In July the Congress sent a petition, or formal request, to George III. Called the **Olive Branch Petition,** it assured the king of the colonists' desire for peace. It asked the king to protect the colonists' rights, which Parliament seemed determined to destroy. George III refused to receive the Olive Branch Petition. Instead he prepared for war, hiring more than 30,000 German troops to send to America and fight beside British troops.

The Colonies Take the Offensive

Meanwhile the Congress learned that British troops stationed in what is now Canada were planning to invade New York. The Americans decided to strike first. Marching north from Fort Ticonderoga, a Patriot force captured Montreal in November. An American attack on Quebec led by Benedict Arnold failed, however. The American forces stayed outside the city of Quebec through the long winter and returned to Fort Ticonderoga in 1776.

Washington reached Boston in July 1775, a few weeks after the Battle of Bunker Hill. He found the members of the militia growing in number every day, but he realized they lacked discipline, organization, and leadership. He began the hard work of shaping these armed civilians into an army.

By March 1776, Washington judged the Continental Army ready to fight. He positioned the army in a semicircle around Boston and gave the order for its cannons to bombard the British forces. The redcoats, under Sir William Howe, hurriedly withdrew from the city and boarded their ships. On March 17 Washington led his jubilant troops into Boston. The British troops sailed to Halifax, Nova Scotia.

Moving Toward Independence

Throughout the colonies in late 1775 and early 1776, some Americans still hoped to avoid a complete break with Britain. Support for the position of absolute independence was growing, however.

In January 1776, **Thomas Paine** published a pamphlet called *Common Sense* that captured the attention of the American colonists. In bold language, Paine called for complete independence from Britain. He argued that it was simply

HISTORY Online

Student Web Activity
Visit tarvol1.glencoe.com and click on **Chapter 5— Student Web Activities** for an activity on the Declaration of Independence.

People In History

Abigail Adams 1744–1818

Born into a comfortable Massachusetts household, Abigail Smith spent her youth reading and studying. At age 19 she married 28-year-old lawyer John Adams, who became a leader in the independence movement. Through her letters to family and friends, Abigail left us a record of her thoughts about the revolution as it developed. She also shared her hopes for the new nation.

As Congress considered a declaration of independence, she teasingly —but seriously—wrote to her husband:

"I long to hear that you have declared an independency . . . I desire you would Remember the Ladies, and be more generous and favorable to them than your ancestors."

Their correspondence during the times they spent apart showed a thoughtful exchange of ideas and a strong respect for one another. Abigail Adams would later become the second of the new nation's first ladies.

Picturing **History**

Thomas Jefferson prepared the draft of the Declaration, while Benjamin Franklin and John Adams made suggestions. **Why is July 2, 1776, a historic day?**

"common sense" to stop following the "royal brute," King George III. Paine told the colonists their cause was not just a squabble over taxes but a struggle for freedom—"in a great measure the cause of all mankind." *Common Sense* inspired thousands of Americans. 📖 *(See page 596 of the Primary Sources Library for another excerpt from* Common Sense.*)*

Reading Check **Explaining** Why was Thomas Paine important to the independence movement?

The Colonies Declare Independence

At the Second Continental Congress in Philadelphia, the meeting hall was filled with spirited debate. One central issue occupied the delegates: Should the colonies declare themselves an independent nation, or should they stay under British rule?

In April 1776, North Carolina instructed its delegates to support independence. On June 7 Virginia's Richard Henry Lee proposed a bold resolution:

❝That these United Colonies are, and of right ought to be, free and independent States . . . and that all political connection between them and the State of Great Britain is, and ought to be, totally dissolved.❞

The Congress debated the resolution. Some delegates still thought the colonies were not ready to form a separate nation. Others argued that war already had begun and a large portion of the American population wanted to separate from Great Britain. Still others feared Great Britain's power to hold down the rebellion.

While the delegates debated the issue, the Congress chose a committee to draft a **Declaration of Independence.** Jefferson was selected to write the document. Jefferson drew on the ideas of thinkers such as English philosopher John Locke to set out the colonies' reasons for proclaiming their freedom. Locke wrote that people were born with certain natural rights to life, liberty, and property; that people formed governments to protect these rights; and that a government interfering with these rights might rightfully be overthrown.

On July 2, 1776, the Congress finally voted on Lee's resolution for independence. Twelve colonies voted for it. New York did not vote but later announced its support. Next the delegates took up Jefferson's draft of the Declaration of Independence. After making some changes, they approved the document on July 4, 1776.

John Hancock, the president of the Congress, was the first to sign the Declaration of Independence. Hancock remarked that he wrote his name large enough for King George to read it without his glasses. Hancock's bold signature stands out on the original document. Eventually 56 delegates signed the paper announcing the birth of the United States.

Copies of the Declaration went out to the newly declared states. Washington had it read to his troops on July 9. In New York American soldiers tore down a statue of George III in celebration. In Worcester, Massachusetts, the reading of the Declaration of Independence was followed by "repeated huzzas [cheers], firing of musketry and cannon, bonfires, and other demonstrations of joy."

The Declaration of Independence

The Declaration has four major sections. The preamble, or introduction, states that people who wish to form a new country should explain their reasons for doing so. The next two sections list the rights the colonists believed they should have and their complaints against Britain. The final section proclaims the existence of the new nation.

The Declaration of Independence states what Jefferson and many Americans thought were universal principles. It begins with a description of traditional English political rights.

> 66 We hold these truths to be self-evident, that all men are created equal, that they are endowed by their Creator with certain unalienable Rights, that among these are Life, Liberty, and the pursuit of Happiness. 99

The Declaration states that government exists to protect these rights. If it does not, it goes on to state that "it is the Right of the People to alter or to abolish it and to institute new Government."

The Declaration goes on to list the many grievances Americans held against the king and Parliament. The crimes of George III included "cutting off our trade with all parts of the world" and "imposing taxes on us without our

Independence Day

Congress voted for independence on July 4, 1776. Actually, Congress voted for independence on July 2, 1776. Why, then, is Independence Day celebrated on the fourth? On that day the delegates voted to accept Jefferson's statement, the Declaration of Independence, as the reason why they had voted for independence two days earlier.

consent." Americans, the Declaration says, had "Petitioned for Redress" of these grievances. These petitions, however, were ignored or rejected by Britain.

The Declaration ends by announcing America's new status. Now pledging "to each other our Lives, our Fortunes, and our sacred Honor," the Americans declared themselves a new nation. The struggle for American independence—the American Revolution—had begun. 📖 *(See pages 154–157 for the entire text of the Declaration of Independence.)*

✓ **Reading Check** **Summarizing** What grievances against King George III were included in the Declaration of Independence?

SECTION 4 ASSESSMENT

Checking for Understanding

1. **Key Terms** Connect the terms below with the proper document. Then write a sentence in which you use each term. Terms: petition, preamble. Documents: Declaration of Independence, Olive Branch Petition
2. **Reviewing Facts** What was King George III's response to the Olive Branch Petition?

Reviewing Themes

3. **Government and Democracy** Why was the Second Continental Congress more like a government than the First Continental Congress?

Critical Thinking

4. **Analyzing Primary Sources** Based on the quote from the Declaration of Independence on this page, what are the "unalienable Rights" to which Jefferson referred? Give examples.
5. **Organizing Information** Re-create the diagram below and describe each individual's role in the movement toward independence.

	Role
Thomas Jefferson	
Thomas Paine	
Samuel Adams	
Benjamin Franklin	

Analyzing Visuals

6. **Picturing History** Compare the flag on page 148 with the flag on page 128. How are the two flags similar? How are they different? Which of the flags more closely resembles the American flag of today?

Interdisciplinary Activity

Expository Writing Prepare a help-wanted ad to locate a person qualified to write the Declaration of Independence. Describe the responsibilities of the job as well as the experience and character traits that are needed.

EVE OF REVOLUTION

IN THE EARLY 1770s most colonists thought of themselves as British subjects. However, they also thought of themselves as Virginians or Georgians or New Yorkers. It wasn't until colonists began to unite in opposition to harsh British policies that they began to consider themselves Americans.

STIRRINGS OF REVOLT

In 1772 Samuel Adams convinced a group of Bostonians to join a Committee of Correspondence to communicate with other towns in Massachusetts. Soon, the idea spread. In colony after colony, Americans joined Committees of Correspondence. In this era before radios or telephones, the committees spread opposition to British policies into nearly every county, town, and city.

In 1774 delegates gathered at the Continental Congress in Philadelphia to form an organization to represent their interests as Americans. In addition to stating their grievances and voting to boycott British products, the Patriots decided to organize their own militias.

THE SHOT HEARD 'ROUND THE WORLD

The Revolution's first blow fell early on the morning of April 19, 1775. British redcoats clashed with colonial minutemen at Lexington and Concord. This clash, later called the "shot heard 'round the world," was the first battle of the Revolutionary War. The Battle of Bunker Hill in June showed that the war would be hard, long, and expensive on both sides.

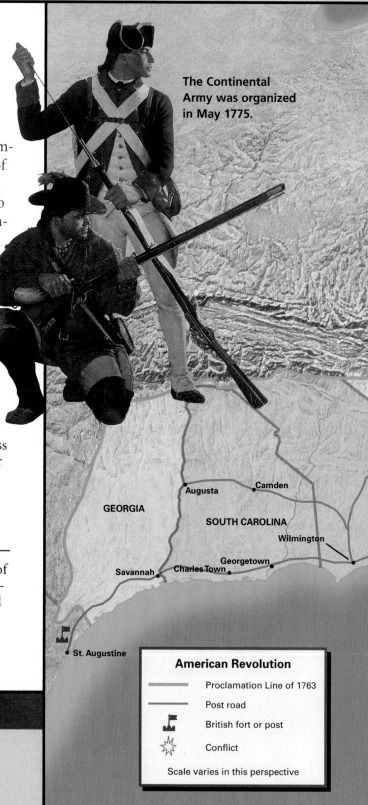

The Continental Army was organized in May 1775.

GEORGIA

Augusta

Camden

SOUTH CAROLINA

Wilmington

Savannah

Charles Town

Georgetown

St. Augustine

American Revolution

— Proclamation Line of 1763

— Post road

⚑ British fort or post

✳ Conflict

Scale varies in this perspective

LEARNING from GEOGRAPHY

1. **How do you think the geography of the colonies made communication difficult?**

2. **Near what cities did the early battles take place?**

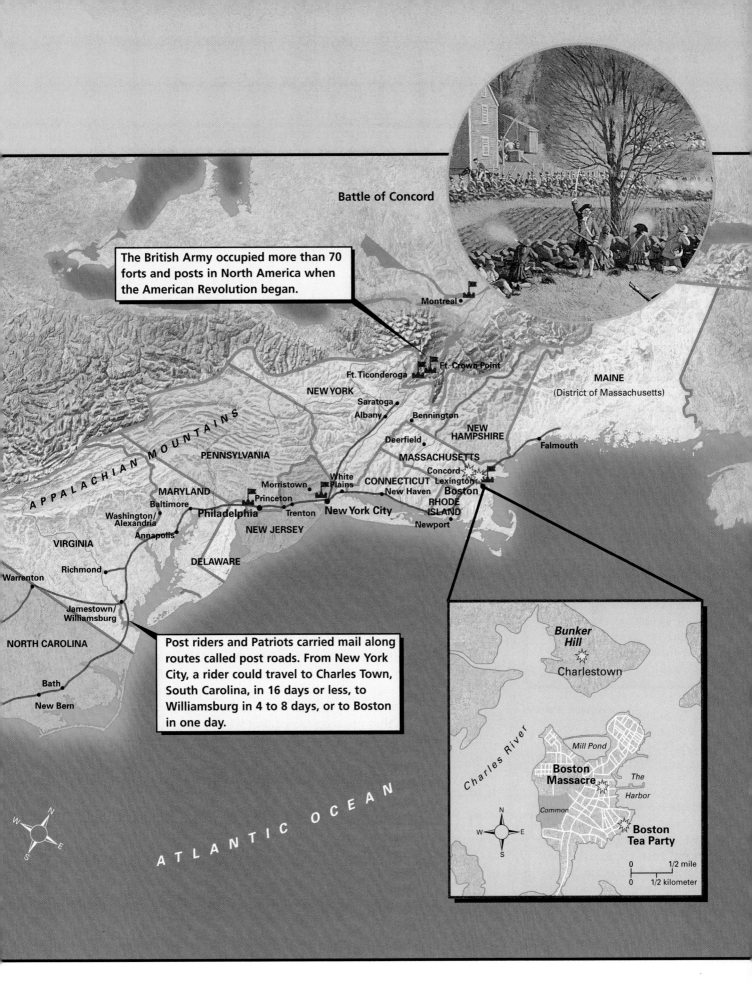

Battle of Concord

The British Army occupied more than 70 forts and posts in North America when the American Revolution began.

Montreal

Ft. Crown Point

Ft. Ticonderoga

NEW YORK

Saratoga

Albany

Bennington

Deerfield

NEW HAMPSHIRE

MAINE
(District of Massachusetts)

Falmouth

PENNSYLVANIA

APPALACHIAN MOUNTAINS

MARYLAND

Morristown

White Plains

Princeton

MASSACHUSETTS

Concord

Lexington

New Haven

CONNECTICUT

Boston

RHODE ISLAND

Baltimore

Washington/ Alexandria

Philadelphia

Trenton

New York City

Annapolis

NEW JERSEY

Newport

VIRGINIA

DELAWARE

Richmond

Warrenton

Jamestown/ Williamsburg

NORTH CAROLINA

Post riders and Patriots carried mail along routes called post roads. From New York City, a rider could travel to Charles Town, South Carolina, in 16 days or less, to Williamsburg in 4 to 8 days, or to Boston in one day.

Bath

New Bern

ATLANTIC OCEAN

W N E S

Bunker Hill

Charlestown

Charles River

Mill Pond

Boston Massacre

The Harbor

Common

Boston Tea Party

N W E S

0   1/2 mile
0   1/2 kilometer

The Declaration of Independence

In Congress, July 4, 1776. The unanimous Declaration of the thirteen united States of America,

[Preamble]

When in the Course of human events, it becomes necessary for one people to dissolve the political bands which have connected them with another, and to assume among the Powers of the earth, the separate and equal station to which the Laws of Nature and of Nature's God entitle them, a decent respect to the opinions of mankind requires that they should declare the causes which **impel** them to the separation.

[Declaration of Natural Rights]

We hold these truths to be self-evident, that all men are created equal, that they are **endowed** by their Creator with certain unalienable Rights, that among these are Life, Liberty, and the pursuit of Happiness.

That to secure these rights, Governments are instituted among Men, deriving their just powers from the consent of the governed,

That whenever any Form of Government becomes destructive of these ends, it is the Right of the People to alter or to abolish it, and to institute new Government, laying its foundation on such principles and organizing its powers in such form, as to them shall seem most likely to effect their Safety and Happiness. Prudence, indeed, will dictate that Governments long established should not be changed for light and transient causes; and accordingly all experience hath shown, that mankind are more disposed to suffer, while evils are sufferable, than to right themselves by abolishing the forms to which they are accustomed. But when a long train of abuses and usurpations, pursuing invariably the same Object evinces a design to reduce them under absolute **Despotism,** it is their right, it is their duty, to throw off such Government, and to provide new Guards for their future security.

[List of Grievances]

Such has been the patient sufferance of these Colonies; and such is now the necessity which constrains them to alter their former Systems of Government. The history of the present King of Great Britain is a history of repeated injuries and **usurpations,** all having in direct object the establishment of an absolute Tyranny over these States. To prove this, let Facts be submitted to a candid world.

He has refused his Assent to Laws, the most wholesome and necessary for the public good.

What It Means

The Preamble The Declaration of Independence has four parts. The Preamble explains why the Continental Congress drew up the Declaration.

impel *force*

What It Means

Natural Rights The second part, the Declaration of Natural Rights, lists the rights of the citizens. It goes on to explain that, in a republic, people form a government to protect their rights. The Declaration refers to these rights as *unalienable rights.* The word unalienable means nontransferable. An unalienable right is a right that cannot be surrendered.

endowed *provided*

despotism *unlimited power*

What It Means

List of Grievances The third part of the Declaration lists the colonists' complaints against the British government. Notice that King George III is singled out for blame.

usurpations *unjust uses of power*

He has forbidden his Governors to pass Laws of immediate and pressing importance, unless suspended in their operation till his Assent should be obtained; and when so suspended, he has utterly neglected to attend to them.

He has refused to pass other Laws for the accommodation of large districts of people, unless those people would **relinquish** the right of Representation in the Legislature, a right **inestimable** to them and formidable to tyrants only.

He has called together legislative bodies at places unusual, uncomfortable, and distant from the depository of their Public Records, for the sole purpose of fatiguing them into compliance with his measures.

He has dissolved Representative Houses repeatedly, for opposing with manly firmness his invasions on the rights of the people.

He has refused for a long time, after such dissolutions, to cause others to be elected; whereby the Legislative Powers, incapable of **Annihilation,** have returned to the People at large for their exercise; the State remaining in the mean time exposed to all the dangers of invasion from without, and **convulsions** within.

He has endeavoured to prevent the population of these States; for that purpose obstructing the Laws for **Naturalization of Foreigners;** refusing to pass others to encourage their migrations hither, and raising the conditions of new Appropriations of Lands.

He has obstructed the Administration of Justice, by refusing his Assent to Laws for establishing Judiciary Powers.

He has made Judges dependent on his Will alone, for the **tenure** of their offices, and the amount and payment of their salaries.

He has erected a multitude of New Offices, and sent hither swarms of Officers to harass our people, and eat out their substance.

relinquish *give up*
inestimable *priceless*

annihilation *destruction*

convulsions *violent disturbances*

Naturalization of Foreigners *process by which foreign-born persons become citizens*

tenure *term*

He has kept among us, in times of peace, Standing Armies without the Consent of our legislature.

He has affected to render the Military independent of and superior to the Civil Power.

He has combined with others to subject us to a jurisdiction foreign to our constitution, and unacknowledged by our laws; giving his Assent to their acts of pretended legislation:

quartering *lodging*

For **quartering** large bodies of troops among us:

For protecting them, by a mock Trial, from Punishment for any Murders which they should commit on the Inhabitants of these States:

For cutting off our Trade with all parts of the world:

For imposing taxes on us without our Consent:

For depriving us in many cases, of the benefits of Trial by Jury:

For transporting us beyond Seas to be tried for pretended offences:

For abolishing the free System of English Laws in a neighbouring Province, establishing therein an Arbitrary government, and enlarging its

render *make*

Boundaries so as to **render** it at once an example and fit instrument for introducing the same absolute rule into these Colonies:

For taking away our Charters, abolishing our most valuable Laws, and altering fundamentally the Forms of our Governments:

For suspending our own Legislature, and declaring themselves invested with Power to legislate for us in all cases whatsoever.

abdicated *given up*

He has **abdicated** Government here, by declaring us out of his Protection and waging War against us.

He has plundered our seas, ravaged our Coasts, burnt our towns, and destroyed the lives of our people.

He is at this time transporting large armies of foreign mercenaries to compleat the works of death, desolation and tyranny, already begun with

perfidy *violation of trust*

circumstances of Cruelty & **perfidy** scarcely paralleled in the most barbarous ages, and totally unworthy the Head of a civilized nation.

He has constrained our fellow Citizens taken Captive on the high Seas to bear Arms against their Country, to become the executioners of their friends and Brethren, or to fall themselves by their Hands.

insurrections *rebellions*

He has excited domestic **insurrections** amongst us, and has endeavoured to bring on the inhabitants of our frontiers, the merciless Indian Savages, whose known rule of warfare, is an undistinguished destruction of all ages, sexes and conditions.

petitioned for redress *asked formally for a correction of wrongs*

In every stage of these Oppressions We have **Petitioned for Redress** in the most humble terms: Our repeated Petitions have been answered only by repeated injury. A Prince, whose character is thus marked by every act which may define a Tyrant, is unfit to be the ruler of a free People.

Nor have We been wanting in attention to our British brethren. We have warned them from time to time of attempts by their legislature to extend an

unwarrantable jurisdiction *unjustified authority*

unwarrantable jurisdiction over us. We have reminded them of the circumstances of our emigration and settlement here. We have appealed to their native justice and magnanimity, and we have conjured them by the ties of our common kindred to disavow these usurpations, which, would inevitably interrupt our connections and correspondence. They too have been deaf to the voice of justice and of **consanguinity**. We must, therefore,

consanguinity *originating from the same ancestor*

acquiesce in the necessity, which denounces our Separation, and hold them, as we hold the rest of mankind, Enemies in War, in Peace Friends.

[Resolution of Independence by the United States]

We, therefore, the Representatives of the united States of America, in General Congress, Assembled, appealing to the Supreme Judge of the world for the **rectitude** of our intentions, do, in the Name, and by Authority of the good People of these Colonies, solemnly publish and declare, That these United Colonies are, and of Right ought to be Free and Independent States; that they are Absolved from all Allegiance to the British Crown, and that all political connection between them and the State of Great Britain, is and ought to be totally dissolved; and that as Free and Independent States, they have full Power to levy War, conclude Peace, contract Alliances, establish Commerce, and to do all other Acts and Things which Independent States may of right do.

And for the support of this Declaration, with a firm reliance on the Protection of Divine Providence, we mutually pledge to each other our Lives, our Fortunes and our sacred Honor.

John Hancock
    President from
    Massachusetts

Georgia
Button Gwinnett
Lyman Hall
George Walton

North Carolina
William Hooper
Joseph Hewes
John Penn

South Carolina
Edward Rutledge
Thomas Heyward, Jr.
Thomas Lynch, Jr.
Arthur Middleton

Maryland
Samuel Chase
William Paca
Thomas Stone
Charles Carroll
    of Carrollton

Virginia
George Wythe
Richard Henry Lee
Thomas Jefferson
Benjamin Harrison
Thomas Nelson, Jr.
Francis Lightfoot Lee
Carter Braxton

Pennsylvania
Robert Morris
Benjamin Rush
Benjamin Franklin
John Morton
George Clymer
James Smith
George Taylor
James Wilson
George Ross

Delaware
Caesar Rodney
George Read
Thomas McKean

New York
William Floyd
Philip Livingston
Francis Lewis
Lewis Morris

New Jersey
Richard Stockton
John Witherspoon
Francis Hopkinson
John Hart
Abraham Clark

New Hampshire
Josiah Bartlett
William Whipple
Matthew Thornton

Massachusetts
Samuel Adams
John Adams
Robert Treat Paine
Elbridge Gerry

Rhode Island
Stephen Hopkins
William Ellery

Connecticut
Samuel Huntington
William Williams
Oliver Wolcott
Roger Sherman

Chapter Summary
Road to Independence

Follow the arrows to review the causes and the effects that led to the colonies declaring independence.

Cause: French and Indian War leaves Great Britain in debt

Effect: Britain taxes colonies; Parliament passes Sugar Act and Stamp Act ➝ **Becomes Cause**

Effect: Colonists boycott British goods ➝ **Becomes Cause**

Effect: British send troops to Boston, resulting in the Boston Massacre ➝ **Becomes Cause**

Effect: British repeal import taxes ➝ **Becomes Cause**

Effect: Colonists respond with Boston Tea Party ➝ **Becomes Cause**

Effect: Parliament passes the Coercive Acts ➝ **Becomes Cause**

Effect: First Continental Congress drafts a statement of grievances ➝ **Becomes Cause**

Effect: British troops fight colonists at battles of Lexington and Concord; British defeat colonial forces at Bunker Hill

Congress signs Declaration of Independence

Reviewing Key Terms

Write five true and four false statements using the terms below. Use only one term in each statement. Indicate which statements are true and which are false. Below each false statement explain why it is false.

1. revenue
2. boycott
3. repeal
4. propaganda
5. militia
6. minutemen
7. Patriot
8. preamble
9. unalienable rights

Reviewing Key Facts

10. What did the British do to keep colonists from moving westward?
11. How did the British government use the colonies to raise revenue? Why did this anger the colonists?
12. What incident caused the British Parliament to pass the Coercive Acts?
13. What was the purpose of the First Continental Congress?
14. How did the events of 1776 move the colonists closer to self-government?
15. According to the Declaration of Independence, if a government does not protect the basic rights of the people it governs, what do people have the right to do?
16. Identify the four sections of the Declaration of Independence.

Critical Thinking

17. **Drawing Conclusions** Why did the colonists think that the Stamp Act ignored the colonial tradition of self-government?
18. **Organizing Information** Re-create the diagram below and show ways the colonists, by working in groups, resisted the British during the revolutionary period.

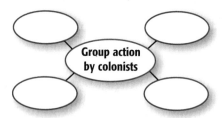

Group action by colonists

19. **Analyzing Primary Sources** What did Patrick Henry mean when he said, "I am not a Virginian, but an American"?
20. **Analyzing Information** According to the Declaration of Independence, what are the three basic freedoms to which every person is entitled?

Practicing Skills

Distinguishing Fact From Opinion *Read the following statements. Tell whether each is a fact or an opinion.*

21. Great Britain should not have tried to stop the colonists from settling west of the Appalachians.

22. The Stamp Act placed a tax on almost all printed material in the colonies.

23. The Daughters of Liberty urged Americans to wear home-made fabrics.

24. Thomas Jefferson was a better writer than John Adams.

 ## Geography and History Activity

Study the map on page 133; then answer the following questions.

25. What bodies of water did the Proclamation of 1763 prevent colonists from reaching?

26. What nation claimed the land west of the Mississippi River?

27. The land west of the Appalachian Mountains became part of what province?

28. What natural feature was cited in the Proclamation of 1763 as an approximate boundary?

Citizenship Cooperative Activity

29. Work with a group of classmates to create your own "Declaration of Independence." Use the original Declaration of Independence on pages 154–157 as a guide to create your document. Outline the basic freedoms that you expect to have as a citizen and describe why these freedoms are important to you. Then write at least three responsibilities and/or sacrifices that citizens should be willing to make to enjoy the freedoms you listed. After your group has completed its Declaration of Independence, have the groups come together as a class. Share all the groups' documents and compare the ideas expressed in each.

 ## Technology Activity

30. **Using the Internet** On the Internet, locate the computer address for the National Archives or the Library of Congress in Washington, D.C. Search each site for documents concerning the drafting of the Declaration of Independence and/or photos of pamphlets produced by the colonies in the 1700s. Print a copy of what you find or sketch a likeness to share with the class.

Self-Check Quiz
Visit **tarvol1.glencoe.com** and click on **Chapter 5— Self-Check Quizzes** to prepare for the chapter test.

Economics Activity

31. How did laws passed by the British after 1763 affect American trade and industry? Write your answer in a one-page paper.

 ## Alternative Assessment

32. **Persuasive Writing** What do you think a good citizen is? Is it someone who follows the law? Or might it be someone who breaks the law in order to stand up for an ideal? Do you think that people like the Sons of Liberty acted as good citizens? Write a persuasive paper explaining your views.

Standardized Test Practice

Read the following passage and choose the *best* answer to the question that follows.

An English philosopher named John Locke wrote about his belief that people had natural rights. These included the right to life, liberty, and property. In *Two Treatises of Government,* Locke wrote that people created government to protect natural rights. If a government failed in its basic duty of protecting natural rights, people had the right to overthrow the government.

Locke's ideas contributed to the

A Proclamation of 1763.

B Intolerable Acts.

C Declaration of Independence.

D Articles of Confederation.

Test-Taking Tip:

Look for clues in the passage to support your answer. For example, the passage refers to *life, liberty and property.* It also states that *people had the right to overthrow the government.* Which answer does this information best support?

The American Revolution

1776–1783

Why It Matters

Although the United States declared its independence in 1776, no country recognized it as an independent nation at that time. It took a war and the efforts of American diplomats to win this recognition.

The Impact Today

In fighting for the principles set forth in the Declaration of Independence, the American Patriots laid the foundation for the United States of America we know today.

 The American Republic to 1877 *Video* *The chapter 6 video, "The American Revolution," details how the American Patriots were able to defeat a powerful British military.*

1778
• France and U.S. form an alliance

1777
• Battle of Saratoga

1777–1778
• Patriot troops winter at Valley Forge

1776
• U.S. Declaration of Independence written

 The Americas

1774   *1776*   *1778*

World

1774
• Joseph Priestley discovers oxygen

1776
• Adam Smith's *Wealth of Nations* published

Study Organizer

Organizing Information Study Foldable
When you group information into categories on a table, it is easier to compare characteristics of items. Make this foldable to help you compare the attitudes and actions of the Patriots and Loyalists.

Step 1 Fold a sheet of paper into thirds from top to bottom.

This forms three rows.

Step 2 Open the paper and refold it into fourths from side to side.

Fold it in half, then in half again.

This forms four columns.

Step 3 Unfold, turn the paper, and draw lines along the folds.

Step 4 Label your table as shown.

The American Revolution	Patriots	Loyalists
Beginning		
Middle		
End		

Reading and Writing As you read about the American Revolution, write down facts about the attitudes and actions of the Patriots and Loyalists at different times during the war.

Molly Pitcher at the Battle of Monmouth by Dennis Malone Carter
According to legend, when her husband collapsed, Molly Pitcher immediately took his place in the gun crew and continued firing his cannon.

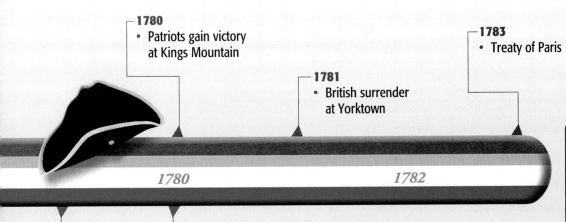

1780
• Patriots gain victory at Kings Mountain

1781
• British surrender at Yorktown

1783
• Treaty of Paris

1780   *1782*

1779
• Spain declares war on Britain

1780
• Britain declares war on Holland

HISTORY Online

Chapter Overview
Visit tarvol1.glencoe.com and click on Chapter 6—Chapter Overviews to preview chapter information.

SECTION 1 The Early Years

Guide to Reading

Main Idea
The British and the Americans each had advantages and disadvantages as they faced one another in war.

Key Terms
neutral, mercenary, recruit

Reading Strategy
Classifying Information As you read the section, re-create the chart below and describe British and American advantages and disadvantages in the spaces provided.

	Advantages	Disadvantages
British		
American		

Read to Learn
- why some Americans supported the British.
- how the Battle of Saratoga marked a turning point of the war.

Section Theme
Groups and Institutions Although British forces won several battles early in the war, Patriot victories slowed their progress.

Preview of Events

◆1776　　　　　　　　　　◆1777　　　　　　　　◆1778

July 1776
American colonies declare independence

December 1776
Patriots capture Hessians at Trenton

October 1777
Burgoyne surrenders at Saratoga

1778
African American regiment forms in Rhode Island

AN American Story

The mighty British troops sailed to America, confident that they would quickly and easily crush the rebellious colonists. A British officer wrote to his friend, describing a military skirmish:

September 3, 1776

We landed on Long-Island. . . . [I]t was a fine sight to see with what [eagerness] they dispatched the Rebels with their bayonets after we had surrounded them so that they could not resist. . . . The island is all ours, and we shall soon take New-York, for the Rebels dare not look us in the face. I expect the affair will be over [after] this campaign. . . .

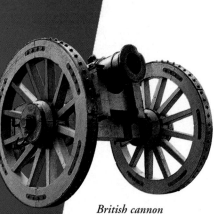

British cannon

The Opposing Sides

Following years of disagreement and negotiation, the tensions between the colonies and England had reached a critical point. After the colonies declared independence from England in July 1776, the war for freedom was unavoidable.

Both the British and the Americans expected the war for independence to be short. The British planned to crush the rebellion by force. Most of the Patriots—Americans who supported independence—believed the British would give up after losing one or two major battles. Few Patriots believed John Adams when he predicted in April 1776:

> 66We shall have a long . . .
> and bloody war to go through.99

At first glance the British had an overwhelming advantage in the war. They had the strongest navy in the world; an experienced, well-trained army; and the wealth of a worldwide empire. Britain also had a much larger population than the United States—over 8 million people in Britain compared to only 2.5 million in the United States.

The colonists suffered serious disadvantages. They lacked a regular army and a strong navy. American soldiers also lacked military experience, and weapons and ammunition were in short supply. Many Patriots belonged to militia groups—local forces—but they were volunteer soldiers who fought for short periods of time before returning home.

The Patriots faced another obstacle. Not all Americans supported the struggle for independence. Some people were neutral, taking neither side in the conflict. The Quakers, for example, would not participate in the war because they opposed all armed conflict. Still other Americans remained loyal to Britain.

The Loyalists

Those who remained loyal to Britain and opposed the war for independence were called Loyalists or Tories. At least one American in five was a Loyalist—perhaps as many as one in three. Some people changed sides during the war, depending on which army was closer. Loyalist strength varied

Two ViewPoints

The War Between Americans

The American Revolution was not only a war between the British and the Americans. It also divided Americans themselves. While American Patriots fought passionately for independence, Loyalists fought just as fiercely for their British king.

Loyalist Views
The Congress—1776 song

Ye Tories all rejoice and sing
Success to George our gracious King,
The faithful subjects tribute bring
And [denounce] the Congress.

Prepare, prepare, my friends prepare
For scenes of blood, the field of war;
To royal standard we'll repair,
And curse the haughty Congress.

Huzza! Huzza! and thrice Huzza!
Return peace, harmony and law!
Restore such times as once we saw
And bid adieu to Congress.

Patriot Views
Patrick Henry of Virginia, 1775 —
"Has Great Britain any enemy in this quarter of the world, to call for all this accumulation of navies and armies? No, sir, she has none. They are meant for us; they can be meant for no other. They are sent over to bind and rivet upon us those chains which the British ministry have been so long forging. And what have we to oppose to them? Shall we try argument? Sir, we have been trying that for the last ten years . . . but it has been all in vain."

Learning From History

1. Why did Patrick Henry believe that war was necessary?
2. Which argument—Loyalist or Patriot—would convince you if you had been an American at this time? Explain your answer.

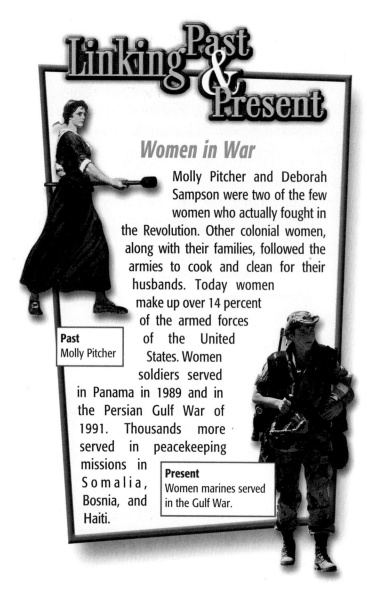

Linking Past & Present

Women in War

Molly Pitcher and Deborah Sampson were two of the few women who actually fought in the Revolution. Other colonial women, along with their families, followed the armies to cook and clean for their husbands. Today women make up over 14 percent of the armed forces of the United States. Women soldiers served in Panama in 1989 and in the Persian Gulf War of 1991. Thousands more served in peacekeeping missions in Somalia, Bosnia, and Haiti.

Past
Molly Pitcher

Present
Women marines served in the Gulf War.

66Neighbor was against neighbor, father against son and son against father. He that would not thrust his own blade through his brother's heart was called an infamous villain.99

African Americans in the War

Some African Americans also sided with the Loyalists. At the start of the war, the British appealed to enslaved Africans to join them. Lord Dunmore, the royal governor of Virginia, announced that enslaved people who fought on the British side would be freed, and many men answered his call. Eventually some of them ended up free in Canada, and others settled the British colony of Sierra Leone in Africa.

Patriot Advantages

The Americans possessed some advantages. They were fighting on their own ground and fought with great determination to protect it. The British, on the other hand, had to wage war in a faraway land and were forced to ship soldiers and supplies thousands of miles across the Atlantic Ocean.

The makeup of the British army in America also helped the Patriots. The British relied on mercenaries—hired soldiers—to fight. The Americans called the mercenaries **Hessians,** after the region in Germany where most of them lived. To gain support for the war effort, Patriots compared their own troops, who were fighting for the freedom of their own land, to the Hessians, who fought for money. The Patriots had a much greater stake in winning the war than the hired soldiers did. This personal stake gave the Americans an edge over the Hessians in battle.

The Americans' greatest advantage was probably their leader, George Washington. Few could match him for courage, honesty, and determination. The war might have taken a different turn without Washington steering its course.

Raising an Army

The Americans placed great value on liberty and personal freedom for citizens. After throwing off the rule of the British Parliament, they

from region to region. In general it was strongest in the Carolinas and Georgia and weakest in New England.

Loyalists supported Britain for different reasons. Some remained loyal because they were members of the Anglican Church, headed by the British king. Some depended on the British for their jobs. Many feared the disorder that would come from challenging the established government. Others simply could not understand what all the commotion was about. No other country, one Loyalist complained, "faced a rebellion arising from such trivial causes."

The issue of independence disrupted normal relations. Friends and families were divided over their loyalty to Britain. For example, William Franklin, son of Patriot Benjamin Franklin, was a Loyalist who had served as a royal governor. As one Connecticut Loyalist observed:

were unwilling to transfer power to their own Continental Congress. In some ways the American Revolution was really 13 separate wars, with each state pursuing its own interests. As a result Congress experienced difficulty enlisting soldiers and raising money to fight the war.

Although the militia played an essential role in the Patriots' forces, the Americans also needed a regular army—well-trained soldiers who could fight anywhere in the colonies. The Congress established the Continental Army but depended on the states to recruit, or enlist, soldiers.

At first soldiers signed up for one year of army service. General Washington appealed for longer terms. "If we ever hope for success," he said, "we must have men enlisted for the whole term of the war." Eventually the Continental Congress offered enlistments for three years or for the length of the war. Most soldiers, however, still signed up for only a year.

Women also fought with the Patriot forces. **Margaret Corbin** of Pennsylvania accompanied her husband when he joined the Continental Army. After he died in battle, she took his place. Mary Ludwig Hays McCauley also accompanied her husband in battle. The soldiers called her "Moll of the Pitcher," or **Molly Pitcher,** because she carried water pitchers to the soldiers. As a teenager, **Deborah Sampson** of Massachusetts watched her brothers and their friends go off to war. Moved by a sense of adventure, she disguised herself as a boy and enlisted.

✓ **Reading Check** **Summarizing** What disadvantages did the Patriots face?

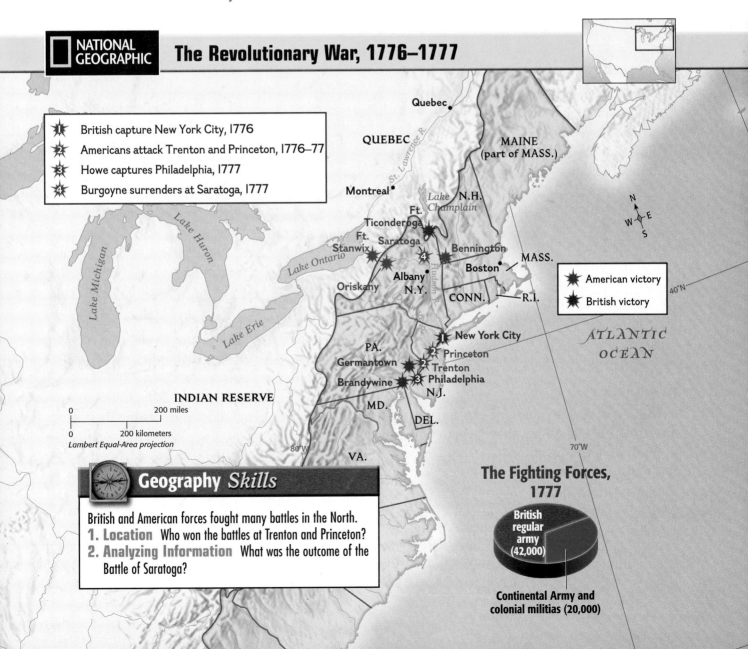

NATIONAL GEOGRAPHIC
The Revolutionary War, 1776–1777

- 1. British capture New York City, 1776
- 2. Americans attack Trenton and Princeton, 1776–77
- 3. Howe captures Philadelphia, 1777
- 4. Burgoyne surrenders at Saratoga, 1777

✦ American victory
✦ British victory

Quebec
QUEBEC
MAINE (part of MASS.)
St. Lawrence R.
Montreal
Lake Champlain
N.H.
Ft. Ticonderoga
Ft. Stanwix
Saratoga
Bennington
MASS.
Boston
Oriskany
Albany
N.Y.
CONN.
R.I.
Hudson R.
New York City
PA.
Princeton
Germantown
Trenton
Brandywine
Philadelphia
N.J.
INDIAN RESERVE
MD.
DEL.
VA.
ATLANTIC OCEAN
40°N
70°W
80°W

Lake Michigan
Lake Huron
Lake Ontario
Lake Erie

0   200 miles
0   200 kilometers
Lambert Equal-Area projection

Geography Skills

British and American forces fought many battles in the North.
1. **Location** Who won the battles at Trenton and Princeton?
2. **Analyzing Information** What was the outcome of the Battle of Saratoga?

The Fighting Forces, 1777

British regular army (42,000)

Continental Army and colonial militias (20,000)

People In History

Thomas Paine 1737–1809

In early 1776 Thomas Paine published a pamphlet titled *Common Sense.* The pamphlet moved many American colonists toward independence. After taking part in the retreat across New York and New Jersey, Paine published another pamphlet to help boost Americans' lagging spirits. In *The American Crisis,* written in December 1776, he warned: "These are the times that try men's souls. The summer soldier and the sunshine patriot will in this crisis shrink from the service of their country; but he that stands it now deserves the love and thanks of man and woman."

He reminded Americans that "the harder the conflict, the more glorious the triumph."

Washington had Paine's stirring words read to his troops to inspire them to continue the fight for independence. Throughout the colonies people passed copies of *The American Crisis* from hand to hand and discussed Paine's patriotic ideas.

Fighting in New York

Most of the early battles involved few troops. At Bunker Hill, for example, about 2,200 British soldiers fought 1,200 Americans. The British had not yet won a decisive victory over the Patriots, however, and they realized they would need more troops to end the war quickly.

During the summer of 1776, Britain sent 32,000 troops across the Atlantic to New York. The British commander, **General William Howe,** hoped the sheer size of his army would convince the Patriots to give up. He was soon disappointed.

Defeat on Long Island

Although Washington and the Patriots had fewer than 20,000 troops, they were determined to fight. In late August the two sides clashed in the **Battle of Long Island.** Outnumbered and outmaneuvered, the Continental Army suffered a serious defeat at the hands of the British forces.

One Patriot, **Nathan Hale,** proved himself a hero at Long Island. A teacher from Connecticut, Hale volunteered to spy on British troops and disguised himself as a Dutch schoolteacher. The British discovered his true identity, however, and hanged him. According to tradition, just before his hanging, Hale's last words were,

> **❝**I only regret that I have but one life to lose for my country.**❞**

Although the Americans showed bravery, they ran short of supplies for the army. In the autumn of 1776, a British officer wrote that many of the Patriot soldiers killed on Long Island had not been wearing shoes, socks, or jackets. "They are also in great want of blankets," he said, predicting that the rebels would suffer greatly when "the severe weather sets in."

After the defeat on Long Island, Washington retreated to Manhattan, pursued by the British. By late November, the Continental Army had retreated across New Jersey into Pennsylvania.

A Low Point

In the winter of 1776–1777, the Patriots' cause was near collapse. The size of the Continental Army had dwindled. Some soldiers completed their terms of service and went home. Other soldiers ran away.

Washington wrote his brother that, if new soldiers were not recruited soon, "I think the game is pretty near up." Still, Washington could not believe that the fight for liberty would truly fail.

✓ Reading Check **Describing** Why was the total number of soldiers in the Continental Army decreasing?

Patriot Gains

Washington pleaded with the Continental Congress for more troops. He asked the Congress to enlist free African Americans. Early in the war, the Southern states had persuaded the Congress to not allow African Americans in the Continental Army. Many white people in the South felt uncomfortable about giving guns to African Americans and allowing them to serve as soldiers. In Southern states with large enslaved populations, whites feared revolts.

African Americans Join the Fight

As the need for soldiers grew, some states ignored the ban and enlisted African Americans. Rhode Island raised an all-African American regiment in 1778. By the war's end, every state except South Carolina enlisted African Americans to fight.

Historians estimate that as many as 5,000 African Americans joined the Patriots. Among them were **Lemuel Hayes** and **Peter Salem,** who fought at Concord. African Americans fought for the same reasons as other Americans. They believed in the Patriot cause or they needed the money. Some soldiers were enslaved Africans who had run away from slaveholders. Others fought to earn their freedom.

American Victories in New Jersey

The British army settled in New York for the winter of 1776, leaving some troops in New Jersey at **Trenton** and **Princeton.** Armies usually called a halt to their wars during the winter, and the British did not expect to fight.

Stationed across the Delaware River from the British camp in New Jersey, Washington saw a chance to catch the British off guard. On Christmas night 1776, Washington took 2,400 troops

Fact · Fiction · Folklore

America's Flags

First Stars and Stripes, 1777–1795 On June 14, 1777, the Continental Congress designed the first Stars and Stripes. The Congress determined that "the Flag of the United States be 13 stripes, alternate red and white; that the Union be 13 stars, white in a blue field representing a new constellation." For Americans past and present, the color red symbolizes courage; white, purity of ideals; and blue, strength and unity of the states.

across the icy river and surprised the enemy at Trenton the next day. The Americans captured more than 900 Hessians. The British sent reinforcements under Lord Charles Cornwallis, but Washington led his troops away from Cornwallis's men. Washington then marched the army to Princeton, where they drove away the British. One discouraged British soldier wrote in his diary,

❝A few days ago [the Americans] had given up the cause for lost. Their late successes have turned the scale and now they are all liberty mad again.❞

✓ Reading Check **Explaining** What was the outcome of the battle at Trenton?

A British Plan for Victory

The British worked out a battle plan for 1777. They would take Albany, New York, and gain control of the Hudson River. This would separate New England from the Middle Colonies.

The plan involved a three-pronged attack. General John Burgoyne would lead nearly 8,000 troops south from Canada. A second force, under Lieutenant Colonel Barry St. Leger, would move east from Lake Ontario. A third group, under General Howe, would move north from New York City. The three British forces would meet at Albany and destroy the Patriot troops.

The British Capture Philadelphia

Howe planned to take Philadelphia, the American capital, before marching to Albany. After winning battles in September 1777 at Brandywine and Paoli near Philadelphia, Howe's troops captured the city itself, forcing the Continental Congress to flee. In early October Washington attacked the main British camp at nearby Germantown, but he was forced to withdraw. Howe postponed the move north to Albany and decided to spend the winter in Philadelphia.

Patriots Slow the British

Meanwhile problems delayed the British plans to take Albany. In August American soldiers halted St. Leger's advance at Fort Stanwix, New York. Led by **Benedict Arnold,** the Americans forced the British to retreat.

General Burgoyne's army was not making much progress toward Albany either. In July Burgoyne captured Fort Ticonderoga, but trouble followed. Burgoyne, a dashing general who enjoyed good food and fine clothes, traveled with 30 wagons of luxury goods. Loaded down with this heavy baggage, Burgoyne's army moved slowly through the dense forests. To make matters worse, the Americans blocked the British by chopping down trees across their path.

In need of food and supplies, Burgoyne sent 800 troops and Native Americans to capture the American supply base at Bennington, Vermont.

The British troops' brightly colored uniforms made the soldiers easy targets in the woods. A local militia group, the **Green Mountain Boys,** attacked and defeated them. Having lost part of his army and desperately short of supplies, Burgoyne retreated in October to the town of **Saratoga** in New York.

The Battle of Saratoga

At Saratoga Burgoyne faced serious trouble. He expected British forces from the west and south to join him, but they had not arrived. The Americans had stopped St. Leger's army at Fort Stanwix, and Howe's forces were still in Philadelphia. In addition, American troops under the command of **General Horatio Gates** blocked his path to the south. Burgoyne found himself surrounded by an army about three times as large as his own. Burgoyne made a last desperate attack on October 7, but the Americans held firm.

On October 17, 1777, General Burgoyne surrendered. As a Patriot band played "Yankee Doodle," over 5,700 British soldiers handed their weapons to the Americans. The British plan to separate New England from the Middle Colonies had failed. Soon afterward, General Howe resigned as commander of the British troops in America. He was replaced by General Henry Clinton.

✔ **Reading Check** **Analyzing** Why was the Battle of Saratoga an important victory for the Americans?

SECTION 1 ASSESSMENT

Checking for Understanding

1. **Key Terms** Write a short paragraph in which you define the following terms: neutral, mercenary, recruit.
2. **Reviewing Facts** Compare the strengths of the British and American military forces.

Reviewing Themes

3. **Groups and Institutions** What problems did the Continental Congress face in raising an army to fight during the American Revolution?

Critical Thinking

4. **Analyzing Information** Explain why African Americans were willing to enlist in the Continental Army.
5. **Organizing Information** Re-create the chart below and describe each battle, including its outcome, in the space provided.

Battle	Description
Long Island	
Trenton/Princeton	

Analyzing Visuals

6. **Geography Skills** Examine the map on page 165. Which event came first—the British capture of New York or the British capture of Philadelphia?

Interdisciplinary Activity

Descriptive Writing Write a newspaper article that describes the Battle of Saratoga. Include details about British and American strategies and troop movements.

Reading a Military Map

Why Learn This Skill?

In your study of American history, you often have to read maps. A military map shows the areas where battles occurred, routes soldiers took, who won the battles, and who controlled various sites.

Learning the Skill

Military maps use colors, symbols, and arrows to show major battles, troop movements, and defensive positions during a particular battle or over a period of time.

When reading a military map, follow these steps:

• Read the map title. This will indicate the location and time period covered on the map.

• Read the map key. This tells what the symbols on the map represent. For example, battle sites may be symbolized by crossed swords, a burst shell, or a star.

• Study the map itself. This will reveal the actual events or sequence of events that took place. Notice the geography of the area and try to determine how it could affect military strategy.

Practicing the Skill

Analyze the information on the map on this page; then answer the following questions.

❶ What troops surrounded Boston Harbor? How do you know this?

❷ What action did the American forces take after fighting the Battle of Bunker Hill?

❸ Which commander led the British troops to Breed's Hill?

❹ In which direction did the British forces move when they left Boston? What parts of the map help you find this information?

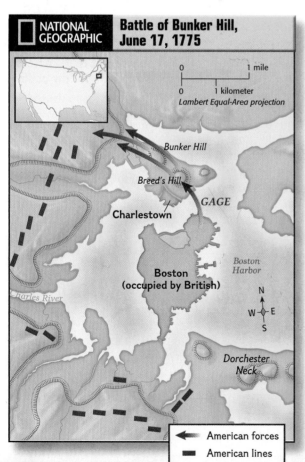

NATIONAL GEOGRAPHIC

Battle of Bunker Hill, June 17, 1775

0 ——— 1 mile
0 ——— 1 kilometer
Lambert Equal-Area projection

Bunker Hill
Breed's Hill
GAGE
Charlestown
Boston (occupied by British)
Boston Harbor
Charles River
Dorchester Neck

N
W ◆ E
S

◀— American forces
▬▬ American lines
◀— British forces

Applying the Skill

Reading a Military Map Find a map of a specific battle of the American Revolution in an encyclopedia or other reference book. Create a three-dimensional model of the battle and use moveable pieces to represent troops. Then demonstrate troop movements over the course of the battle.

 Glencoe's **Skillbuilder Interactive Workbook CD-ROM, Level 1,** provides instruction and practice in key social studies skills.

What were people's lives like in the past?

What—and who—were people talking about? What did they eat? What did they do for fun? These two pages will give you some clues to everyday life in the U.S. as you step back in time with TIME Notebook.

Eyewitness
The Boston Tea Party

BETTMANN/CORBIS

GEORGE HEWES *is one of hundreds of people roused by Sam Adams on December 16, 1773. Adams whipped the crowd into a rage, resulting in the dumping of 342 cases of untaxed British tea into Boston Harbor. Hewes boarded one of the ships that night and here is what he remembers:*

"IT WAS NOW EVENING, AND I IMMEDIATELY DRESSED MYSELF IN THE costume of an Indian, equipped with a small hatchet . . . and a club, with which, after having painted my face and hands with coal dust in the shop of a blacksmith, I [went] to Griffin's Wharf, where the ships lay that contained the tea. . . .I fell in with many who were dressed, equipped and painted as I was, and who fell in with me and marched in order to the place of our destination. . . .We then were ordered by our commander to open the hatches and take out all the chests of tea and throw them overboard, and we immediately proceeded to execute his orders, first cutting and splitting the chests with our tomahawks, so as to thoroughly expose them to the effects of the water."

Benjamin Banneker

NORTH WIND PICTURES

How to Load and Shoot a Cannon

Here are the steps that soldiers follow before firing their cannons at the British:

1 As the officer in charge, you must be loud enough to be heard above the noise of cannon shot.

2 Have six or seven strong people help you as the cannon is difficult to load and shoot. Then you must call out the following commands:

"WORM!" The **wormer**, a soldier with a long piece of iron, must step forward to clean out the barrel of the cannon.

"SPONGE!" The **sponger** must stick a wet sheepskin into the cannon barrel to cool it off and put out any sparks from the last use.

"LOAD!" The **loader** then stuffs a bag of powder into the barrel and adds ammunition—a big iron ball or smaller grapeshot.

"RAM!" The **rammer** will push and pack the ammunition down the barrel with a pole.

"PICK AND PRIME!" The **gunner** must now open a bag of gun powder. He puts a little powder in a vent hole.

"GIVE!" The **gunner** must light a fuse.

"FIRE!" The **gunner** lights the powder on top of the barrel with the fuse. The flame jumps through the air vent and ignites the powder inside the cannon.

"STAND BACK!" The **cannon ball** will explode out of the barrel at about 1,000 feet per second.

BROWN BROTHERS

NUMBERS

THE COLONIES AT THE TIME

60 Seconds it takes a Minuteman soldier to get ready to fight

16 Age of Sibyl Ludington, who in 1777 made a 40-mile midnight ride like Paul Revere's, shouting "The British are coming!"

10,000 The approximate number of enslaved persons who earned their freedom by fighting against the British

200 Number of American doctors with actual medical degrees in 1776

BROWN BROTHERS

COLONIAL GAMES

Nine Man Morris Scores a Ten!

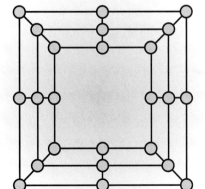

What are all the colonial kids playing?
It's that entertaining game **Nine Man Morris**.

1. Get nine copper coins, nine silver coins, and a friend to play with you.

2. Make a drawing like the one shown on a piece of paper.

3. Give yourself the copper coins and your friend the silver ones.

4. Take turns placing your coins on the dots in the drawing.

5. Be the first to line up three of your coins in a row.

6. Capture one of the other player's coins when you get three in a row.

7. Keep playing until one player is down to two coins. The other player wins!

The War Continues

Main Idea
As the Revolutionary War continued, the Americans received support from European countries.

Key Terms
desert, inflation

Reading Strategy
Classifying Information As you read the section, re-create the chart below and describe how each person helped the Americans fight for independence.

Person	Contribution
Lafayette	
Pulaski	
Von Steuben	
De Miralles	

Read to Learn
• why other nations helped the Patriots.
• how Washington's troops survived the winter at Valley Forge.
• what challenges Americans faced at home as a result of the war.

Section Theme
Groups and Institutions Patriots faced hardships but were encouraged by help from Europeans.

Preview of Events

♦1777   ♦1778   ♦1779

October 1777
Americans win
Battle of Saratoga

Winter 1777–1778
Patriot troops suffer
at Valley Forge

February 1778
France and U.S.
form an alliance

1779
Spain declares
war on Britain

*French medal showing
Benjamin Franklin*

★ ★ ★ ★ ★ ★ ★ ★
AN
American Story

The Continental Congress sent Jonathan Austin of Boston to France to deliver the news of the American victory at Saratoga. Benjamin Franklin was already in France trying to get that country to help the Americans against the British. As soon as Austin arrived, Franklin nervously inquired, "Is Philadelphia taken?" Austin answered, "It is, sir. But, sir, I have greater news than that. General Burgoyne and his whole army are prisoners of war."

Gaining Allies

The victory at Saratoga in October 1777 boosted American spirits. Even more, Saratoga marked a turning point in the war. The European nations, especially France, realized that the United States might actually win its war against Great Britain.

Now was the time for the Americans to seek support from Great Britain's rivals. By late 1777 Benjamin Franklin had been in Paris for a year, trying to get the French to support the Americans' fight for independence. With his skill and charm, Franklin gained many friends for the United States. The French gave the Americans money secretly, but they had not committed to an alliance.

France

News of the American victory at Saratoga caused a shift in France's policy. Realizing that the Americans had a chance of defeating Britain, the French announced support for the United States openly. In February 1778, the French and the Americans worked out a trade agreement and an alliance. France declared war on Britain and sent money, equipment, and troops to aid the American Patriots.

Spain

Other European nations also helped the American cause, mostly because they hated the British. Although Spain did not recognize American independence until after the Revolution, Spain declared war on Britain in 1779. The Spanish governor of Louisiana, **Bernardo de Gálvez** (GAHL•vez), raised an army. Gálvez's soldiers forced British troops from Baton Rouge and Natchez. Then the army captured British forts at Mobile in 1780 and Pensacola in 1781. Gálvez's campaign through hundreds of miles of wilderness diverted British troops from other fronts.

Winter at Valley Forge

Word of the French-American alliance did not reach the United States until the spring of 1778. Meanwhile British general Howe and his forces spent the winter in comfort in Philadelphia. Washington set up camp at **Valley Forge,** about 20 miles to the west of the British. Washington and his troops endured a winter of terrible suffering, lacking decent food, clothing, and shelter. Washington's greatest challenge at Valley Forge was keeping the Continental Army together.

Joseph Martin, a young private from Connecticut, spent the winter at Valley Forge. "We had a hard duty to perform," he wrote years later, "and little or no strength to perform it with." Most of the men lacked blankets, shoes, and shirts. Martin made a rough pair of moccasins for himself out of a scrap of cowhide. Although the moccasins hurt his feet, they were better than going barefoot, "as hundreds of my companions had to do, till they might be tracked by their bloods upon the rough, frozen ground."

📖 *(See page 597 for more accounts of the winter at Valley Forge.)*

Not surprisingly, many men deserted, or left without permission, while the Continental Army was camped at Valley Forge. Some officers resigned. The army seemed to be falling apart.

History *Through Art*

The March to Valley Forge by William B.T. Trego
While waiting for French aid, American soldiers spent a brutal winter at Valley Forge, Pennsylvania.
What were the soldiers' living conditions at Valley Forge?

Yet somehow, with strong determination, the Continental Army survived the winter, and conditions gradually improved. The troops built huts and gathered supplies from the countryside. Volunteers—including Washington's wife, Martha—made clothes for the troops and cared for the sick. Washington declared that no army had ever suffered "such uncommon hardships" with such "patience and fortitude." New soldiers joined the ranks in the spring.

66The army grows stronger every day," one officer wrote. "There is a spirit of discipline among the troops that is better than numbers.99

In April 1778 Washington told his troops of the Patriots' alliance with France. Everyone's spirits rose at the thought of help from overseas. The Continental Army celebrated with a religious service and a parade.

Help From Overseas

Among the hardy soldiers who spent the winter at Valley Forge was a French nobleman, the **Marquis de Lafayette** (lah•fay•EHT). Filled with enthusiasm for the ideas expressed in the Declaration of Independence, Lafayette had bought a ship and set sail for America. He rushed to join the battle for freedom. Lafayette wrote to his wife and children in France,

66The future of America is closely bound up with the future of all mankind.99

Upon his arrival in Philadelphia, Lafayette offered his services and those of his followers to General Washington. Lafayette became a trusted aide to Washington.

Other Europeans also volunteered to work for the Patriot cause. Two Poles—Thaddeus Kosciusko (kawsh•CHUSH•koh), an engineer, and Casimir Pulaski, a cavalry officer—contributed to the American efforts. Pulaski died in 1779, fighting for the Continental Army.

Friedrich von Steuben (STOO•buhn), a former army officer from Germany, also came to help Washington. Von Steuben drilled the Patriot troops at Valley Forge, teaching them military discipline. He turned the ragged Continental Army into a more effective fighting force.

Juan de Miralles (mee•RAH•yays) arrived in Philadelphia in 1778 as a representative of Spain. At his urging, Spain, Cuba, and Mexico sent financial aid to the colonies. Miralles befriended many Patriot leaders and lent money to the cause.

$ Economics
Money Problems

Getting money to finance the war was a major problem. The Continental Congress had no power to raise money through taxes. Although

---

Causes and Effects of French-American Alliance in 1778

Causes

- Longstanding hostility between Britain and France
- Conflict between Britain and France during French and Indian War
- Victory at Saratoga boosts French confidence in Patriots

Effects

- France lends money to the Continental Congress
- France sends soldiers and ships to help American forces
- Americans win independence

Graphic Organizer → Skills

In 1777 Benjamin Franklin negotiated with French leaders for money and support for the American cause.

Drawing Conclusions Why was it important for France to recognize the independence of the American colonies?

the Congress received some money from the states and from foreign countries, much more money was needed.

To pay for the war, the Congress and the states printed hundreds of millions of dollars worth of paper money. These bills quickly lost their value, however, because the amount of bills in circulation grew faster than the supply of gold and silver backing them. This led to inflation, which means that it took more and more money to buy the same amount of goods. The Congress stopped issuing the paper money because no one would use it. However, the Americans had no other way to finance the fighting of their war for independence.

✓ **Reading Check** **Describing** How did Lafayette help the Patriot cause?

Life on the Home Front

The war changed the lives of all Americans, even those who stayed at home. With thousands of men away in military service, women took over the duties that had once been the responsibility of their husbands or fathers. Other women ran their husbands' or their own businesses.

Changing Attitudes

The ideals of liberty and freedom that inspired the American Revolution caused some women to question their place in society. In an essay on education, **Judith Sargeant Murray** of Massachusetts argued that women's minds are as good as men's. Girls, therefore, should get as good an education as boys. At a time when most girls received little schooling, this was a radical idea.

Abigail Adams also championed women's interests. She wrote to her husband, John Adams, who was a member of the Second Continental Congress:

❝I cannot say that I think you are very generous to the ladies, for, whilst you are proclaiming peace and good will to men, emancipating all nations, you insist upon retaining an absolute power over wives.❞

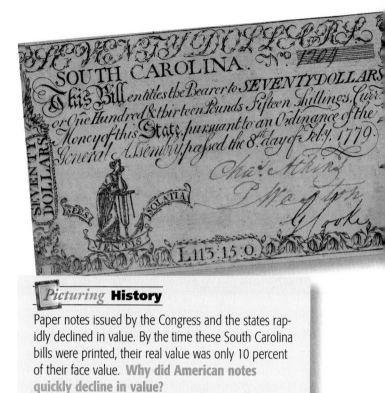

Picturing **History**

Paper notes issued by the Congress and the states rapidly declined in value. By the time these South Carolina bills were printed, their real value was only 10 percent of their face value. **Why did American notes quickly decline in value?**

Treatment of Loyalists

Every state had some Loyalists. Thousands of them fought with the British against the Patriots. To prove their loyalty to Britain, some Loyalists spied and informed on the Patriots.

Many Loyalists, however, fled the American colonies during the Revolutionary War. They packed their belongings and sold whatever they could. Some left hurriedly for England. Others took off for Florida. Still others journeyed to the frontier beyond the Appalachian Mountains and to Canada.

Loyalists who remained in the United States faced difficult times. Their neighbors often shunned them. Some became victims of mob violence. Loyalists who actively helped the British could be arrested and tried as traitors. Patriots executed a few Loyalists, but such extreme measures were unusual.

🖳Citizenship
Hopes for Equality

The Revolutionary War ideals of freedom and liberty inspired some white Americans to question slavery. As early as the Stamp Act crisis,

Analyzing *Political Cartoons*

This cartoon, drawn in 1779, shows a rider being thrown by a horse. Cartoonists often use animals as symbols. For example, an eagle is often used to symbolize the United States. The Republican Party is often represented by an elephant, while the Democratic Party symbol is the donkey. **Who do the horse and rider represent? What idea is the cartoon presenting?**

religious groups and other groups had voted to condemn slavery. In 1778 Governor William Livingston of New Jersey asked the legislature to free all enslaved people in the state. Slavery, Livingston said, was "utterly inconsistent with the principles of Christianity and humanity."

African Americans made similar arguments. In New Hampshire enslaved Africans asked the legislature for their freedom

❝so that the name of *slave* may not be heard in a land gloriously contending for the sweets of freedom.❞

From the beginning of the war—at Lexington, Concord, and Bunker Hill—African American soldiers fought for the American cause. To some fighting for freedom, both African American and white, the Revolution seemed to bring nearer the day when slavery would be abolished. Vermont, New Hampshire, Massachusetts, and Pennsylvania attempted to end slavery in their states. The issue of slavery would remain unsettled for many years, however.

Reading Check **Explaining** What contributions did women make during the war?

SECTION 2 ASSESSMENT

Checking for Understanding

1. **Key Terms** Write a short paragraph in which you define the terms desert and inflation correctly. Use standard sentence structure and spelling in your paragraph.
2. **Reviewing Facts** Explain why the French did not publicly support the Americans until after the Battle of Saratoga.

Reviewing Themes

3. **Groups and Institutions** How were the Loyalists treated by the Patriots during the war?

Critical Thinking

4. **Making Inferences** The Americans claimed to fight for liberty and freedom. How did these ideals make women and enslaved Africans question their positions in society?
5. **Determining Cause and Effect** Re-create the diagram below and describe what happened when the Continental Congress tried to finance the war by printing money.

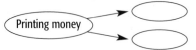

Printing money

Analyzing Visuals

6. **Graphic Organizer Skills** Study the cause-and-effect chart on page 174. In what ways did France help the Americans in their fight for independence? What event led France to aid the Americans in the first place?

Interdisciplinary Activity

Expository Writing Why was Washington such an effective leader? Write a one-page paper describing both his personal and professional characteristics.

The War Moves West and South

Guide to Reading

Main Idea
Revolutionary War fighting spreads to the West and South.

Key Terms
blockade, privateer, guerrilla warfare

Reading Strategy
Organizing Information As you read the section, re-create the chart below and describe the significance of key battles in the West and South.

Battle	Significance
Vincennes	
Camden	
Kings Mountain	
Guilford Courthouse	

Read to Learn
• how the war involved Native Americans.
• how a new kind of fighting developed in the South.

Section Theme
Geography and History As the war continued, Patriot victories were won in the West, in the South, and at sea.

Preview of Events

◆1778   ◆1779   ◆1780   ◆1781

July 1778
George Rogers Clark captures Vincennes

September 1779
The *Serapis* surrenders to John Paul Jones

May 1780
British troops take Charles Town

January 1781
Patriots defeat British at Cowpens

AN American Story

The Swamp Fox and his troops

Francis Marion organized a small but expert fighting force in South Carolina. Living off the land, Marion's soldiers harassed British troops by staging daring surprise attacks, sabotaging communication and supply lines, and rescuing American prisoners. After these attacks, Marion withdrew his men to swamps and forests. His habit of disappearing into the swamps to get away from the British earned him his nickname, the Swamp Fox.

War in the West

At the same time Francis Marion was staging his daring raids in the South, important battles of the Revolutionary War were taking place along the western frontier. Much of this fighting involved Native Americans. Although some helped the Patriots, more sided with the British. For many Native Americans, the British seemed to present less of a threat than the Americans did.

West of the Appalachian Mountains, the British and their Native American allies were raiding American settlements. Mohawk chief **Joseph Brant** led a number of brutal attacks in southwestern New York and northern Pennsylvania. After the war, Brant served as a representative of the Mohawk people to the Continental Congress and tried to get a fair land settlement for his people. Unable to reach an agreement, Brant and his people moved to Canada.

Henry Hamilton commanded Detroit, the main British base in the West. Some called Hamilton the "hair buyer" because of rumors that he paid Native Americans for the scalps of settlers.

★ Geography

Victory at Vincennes

George Rogers Clark, a lieutenant colonel in the Virginia militia, set out to end the British attacks on western settlers. In June 1778, Clark and 175 soldiers sailed down the Ohio River to the mouth of the Tennessee River. After march-ing 120 miles, the Patriots seized the British post at Kaskaskia (ka•SKAS•kee•uh) in present-day Illinois. Then, in February 1779, they captured the British town of **Vincennes** (vihn•SEHNZ) in present-day Indiana.

During Clark's absence in December, British troops under Henry Hamilton's command recaptured Vincennes. Clark vowed to get it back. In February, after marching for days through countrysides flooded with icy waters, Clark and his troops surprised the British, forcing Hamilton to surrender. George Rogers Clark's victory at Vincennes strengthened the American position in the West.

✓ **Reading Check** **Explaining** What British outposts did George Rogers Clark's troops capture?

Glory at Sea

As fighting continued on the western frontier, other battles raged at sea. Great Britain used its powerful navy to patrol American waterways,

What If...

Washington Had Stepped Down?

Throughout the Revolutionary War, Washington succeeded in holding his army together, despite many difficulties. He had to deal with low morale among soldiers who lived on poor rations and received low pay. The Continental Congress often interfered with his conduct of military operations. During the gloomy winter at Valley Forge, some congressmen and army officers plotted to replace Washington as commander in chief.

One of his critics was Dr. Benjamin Rush, who served for a time as surgeon general of the Continental Army. In a letter to John Adams, Rush compared Washington unfavorably to the hero of Saratoga, Horatio Gates.

❝I am more convinced than ever of the necessity of discipline and system in the management of our affairs. I have heard several officers who have served under General Gates compare his army to a well-regulated family. The same gentlemen have compared Gen'l Washington's imitation of an army to an unformed mob. Look at the characters of both! The one [Gates] on the pinnacle of military glory—exulting in the success of schemes planned with wisdom, and executed with vigor and bravery. . . . See the other [Washington] outgeneraled and twice beaten. . . .❞

—Dr. Benjamin Rush, October 21, 1777

keeping the ships of the Patriots and the ships of their allies from entering or leaving American harbors. This British blockade prevented supplies and reinforcements from reaching the Continental Army.

Privateers

To break the British naval blockade, the Second Continental Congress ordered the construction of 13 American warships. Only two of these, however, sailed to sea. The Americans destroyed four of their own ships to keep them out of British hands. Others were quickly captured by the British. Several states maintained their own small fleets, but the American navy was too weak to operate effectively.

American privateers captured more British vessels at sea than did the American navy. The privateers were privately owned merchant ships equipped with weapons. The Congress authorized approximately 2,000 ships to sail as privateers and attack enemy shipping. Finding crews for these ships was not difficult. Sailors

from the whaling and fishing ports of New England signed on eagerly for the profitable privateering trade.

John Paul Jones

A daring American naval officer, **John Paul Jones,** began raiding British ports in 1777. He sailed in an old French ship that Benjamin Franklin had obtained for him. Jones gave the ship a French name, *Bonhomme Richard,* in honor of Franklin's *Poor Richard's Almanack.*

Sailing near the coast of Great Britain in September 1779, the *Bonhomme Richard* met a large fleet of British merchant ships escorted by the warship *Serapis.* The *Bonhomme Richard* moved close to the *Serapis* before attacking. The two ships fought for more than three hours. At one point Jones's ship was so badly damaged that the British captain asked whether Jones wished to surrender. Jones is said to have answered, "I have not yet begun to fight."

In the end the *Serapis* surrendered, but the *Bonhomme Richard* sank not long after the battle. Still, his victory made John Paul Jones a naval hero to the American Patriots.

Reading Check **Describing** How did John Paul Jones contribute to the war effort?

Struggles in the South

In the early years of the war, the Americans had won some battles in the South. In 1776 they had crushed Loyalists at the Battle of Moore's Creek, near Wilmington, North Carolina, and had saved **Charles Town,** South Carolina, from the British. Although a small battle, its impact was great.

By 1778 the British realized that bringing the American colonies back into the empire would not be easy. As a result they changed their strategy and planned a hard-hitting offensive to finish the war.

The British concentrated their efforts in the South, where there were many Loyalists. They hoped to use British sea power and the support of the Loyalists to win decisive victories in the Southern states. Initially the strategy worked.

What might have happened?

1. How do you think the soldiers might have reacted to Washington stepping down?

2. Washington wrote that he would resign his post if he could not count on support. Would the American Revolution have taken a different course with another commander? Explain your answer.

The Revolutionary War in the West, 1778–1779

American victory

British troops

American troops

Fort

Present-day boundaries

Fort Detroit

Fort Miami

Fort Pitt

Lake Erie

Wabash R.

HAMILTON

CLARK

Cahokia (1778)

Vincennes (Feb. 1779)

Ohio R.

APPALACHIAN MOUNTAINS

N W E S

Kaskaskia (July 1778)

0   200 miles

0   200 kilometers

Lambert Equal-Area projection

Geography *Skills*

The Revolutionary War spread west of the Appalachian Mountains where American troops won key victories.

1. **Region** What victories did the American forces win in the West?
2. **Analyzing Information** From what fort did Clark's troops set out?

> "*I know the case is desperate, sir . . . no time is to be lost.*"
>
> —letter to Patrick Henry, February 1779

George Rogers Clark captured the key points of Kaskaskia, Cahokia, and Vincennes, saving the west region for the United States.

British Victories

In late 1778 General Henry Clinton sent 3,500 British troops from New York to take Savannah, on the coast of Georgia. The British occupied the city and overran most of the state.

Clinton himself headed south with a large army in early 1780 to attack the port of Charles Town, South Carolina. Charles Town surrendered in May, and the British took thousands of prisoners. It marked the worst American defeat of the war. A member of Britain's Parliament gloated, "We look on America as at our feet."

Clinton returned to New York, leaving **General Charles Cornwallis** in command of British forces in the South. The Continental Congress sent forces under General Horatio Gates to face Cornwallis. The two armies met at **Camden,** South Carolina, in August 1780. Although the British won, Cornwallis soon found that he could not control the area he had conquered. He and his troops faced a new kind of warfare.

Guerrilla Warfare

The British received less help than they had expected from Loyalists in Southern states. Instead, as British troops moved through the countryside, small forces of Patriots attacked them. These bands of soldiers appeared suddenly, struck their blows, and then disappeared. This hit-and-run technique of guerrilla warfare caught the British off guard.

One successful guerrilla leader, **Francis Marion,** operated out of the swamps of eastern South Carolina. Known as the Swamp Fox, Marion was quick and smart. One British colonel grumbled that "the devil himself" could not catch Marion.

Help From Spain

When 30-year-old Bernardo de Gálvez became governor of the Spanish territory of Louisiana in January 1777, Spain was neutral. That did not stop Gálvez from helping the colonists. He loaned thousands of dollars to the Americans and opened the port of New Orleans to free trade on the part of the colonists. Gálvez also organized the shipment of tons of supplies and ammunition up the Mississippi River to the army of George Rogers Clark in the Northwest Territory. With this help from Gálvez, Clark was able to capture the key points of Kaskaskia, Cahokia, and Vincennes.

In the summer of 1779, Spain declared war on Britain. Gálvez raised an army of Spanish soldiers along with Creoles, Native Americans, and African Americans and marched on British posts along the lower Mississippi. Striking quickly, he captured British forts at Baton Rouge and Natchez. Then, in March 1780, Gálvez forced British Mobile to surrender. In May 1781 he took Pensacola, the British capital of West Florida.

These victories opened supply lines for military goods from Spain, France, Cuba, and Mexico. According to historian Buchanan Parker Thomson, Gálvez had given

❝the most vital aid contributed by any one man to the struggling American colonies. In winning this triumphant victory over the last great British outpost, he had not only served his King to the limit of his strength but had made to the United States the most important gift an ally could offer: the security of their southeastern and western frontiers.❞

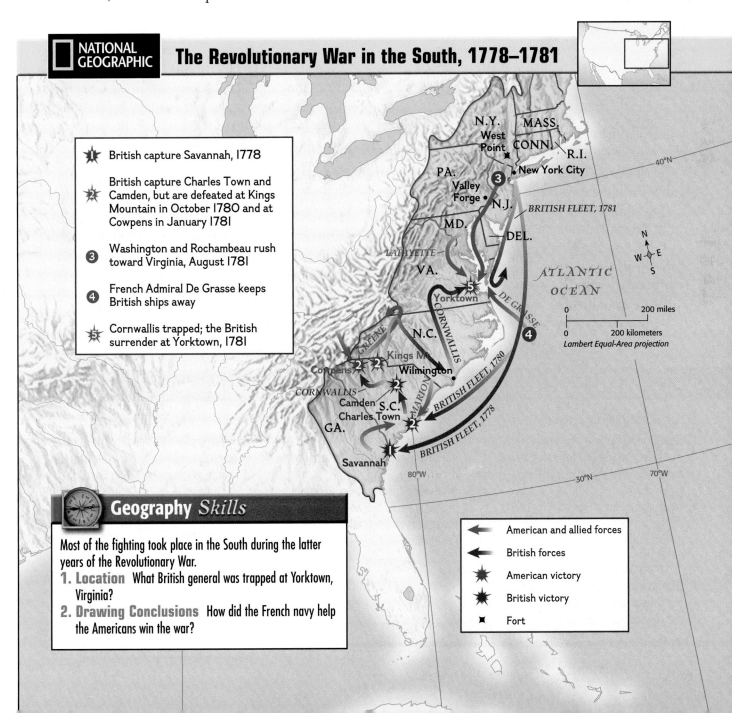

NATIONAL GEOGRAPHIC

The Revolutionary War in the South, 1778–1781

1. British capture Savannah, 1778

2. British capture Charles Town and Camden, but are defeated at Kings Mountain in October 1780 and at Cowpens in January 1781

3. Washington and Rochambeau rush toward Virginia, August 1781

4. French Admiral De Grasse keeps British ships away

5. Cornwallis trapped; the British surrender at Yorktown, 1781

American and allied forces
British forces
American victory
British victory
Fort

Geography Skills

Most of the fighting took place in the South during the latter years of the Revolutionary War.

1. Location What British general was trapped at Yorktown, Virginia?

2. Drawing Conclusions How did the French navy help the Americans win the war?

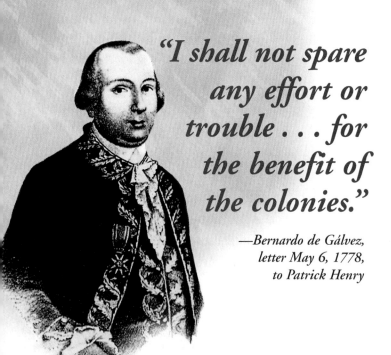

"I shall not spare any effort or trouble . . . for the benefit of the colonies."

—*Bernardo de Gálvez,*
letter May 6, 1778,
to Patrick Henry

Patriot Victories

After the British victory at Camden, South Carolina, the British moved northward through the Carolinas in September 1780. At **Kings Mountain,** a British officer and more than 1,000 Loyalists defended an outpost against the attack of Patriot sharpshooters. The Patriots forced the British to retreat. The victory brought new support for independence from Southerners. They wanted to see an end to the war that was destroying their homes and farms.

In October 1780, **Nathanael Greene** replaced Gates as commander of the Continental forces in the South. Rather than lead an all-out attack on Cornwallis's forces, Greene split his army in two. In January 1781, one section of the army, led by General Daniel Morgan, defeated the British at **Cowpens,** South Carolina. Another section joined Marion's guerrilla raids. In March Greene reunited his forces to meet Cornwallis's army at **Guilford Courthouse,** in present-day Greensboro, North Carolina. Greene's army was forced to retreat, but the British sustained great losses in the process. General Cornwallis abandoned the Carolina campaign.

British Retreat

Cornwallis decided to march north to Virginia in April 1781. His troops carried out raids throughout the state, nearly capturing Governor Thomas Jefferson and the Virginia legislature in June. Jefferson fled on horseback, just ahead of the advancing British troops.

General Washington sent Lafayette and General Anthony Wayne south to fight Cornwallis. Meanwhile Cornwallis set up camp at Yorktown, which was located on the Virginia coast, and awaited further orders from Clinton in New York. The battle for control of the South was entering its final phase.

✓ **Reading Check** **Evaluating** What effect did the Patriot victory at Kings Mountain produce?

SECTION 3 ASSESSMENT

Checking for Understanding

1. **Key Terms** Write a short paragraph in which you use the following terms: blockade, privateer, guerrilla warfare.
2. **Reviewing Facts** Explain why most Native Americans sided with the British in the conflict.

Reviewing Themes

3. **Geography and History** How did the British navy use the location of the colonies to their advantage?

Critical Thinking

4. **Drawing Conclusions** Why was guerrilla warfare effective against the British?
5. **Analyzing Information** Re-create the diagram below and describe the results of the battle at Guilford Courthouse.

Analyzing Visuals

6. **Geography Skills** Study the maps on pages 180 and 181. Who won the battle at Cowpens, South Carolina? At Kings Mountain, South Carolina? Whose forces did George Rogers Clark face at Vincennes?

Interdisciplinary Activity

Art Create a symbol or emblem that captures the spirit of the Patriot soldiers.

Guide to Reading

Main Idea
The American colonies overcame many disadvantages to win independence.

Key Terms
ratify, ambush

Reading Strategy
Organizing Information As you read the section, re-create the diagram below and list the reasons why the Americans were able to defeat the British in the Revolutionary War.

Reasons for the British defeat

Read to Learn
- how George Washington changed his military strategy.
- why the Americans won the Revolutionary War despite many disadvantages.

Section Theme
Groups and Institutions A combined Patriot force secured final victory, ensuring an independent United States.

Preview of Events

♦1780   ♦1781   ♦1782   ♦1783

July 1780
French troops arrive in colonies

August 1781
Washington advances toward British at Yorktown

October 1781
Cornwallis surrenders at Yorktown

September 1783
Treaty of Paris is signed

General Rochambeau, French commander

AN American Story

A popular children's tune in eighteenth-century Britain went like this:

"If ponies rode men and if grass ate the cows,
And cats should be chased into holes by the mouse . . .
If summer were spring and the other way 'round,
Then all the world would be upside down."

This song would hold special meaning for the British troops in America as the Revolution reached its peak.

Victory at Yorktown

The Revolutionary War was at a critical point. Both armies needed a victory to win the war. While General Washington made plans to attack the British at Yorktown, Virginia, rather than New York City, the Patriots hoped for help from the French.

In July 1780, French warships appeared in the waters off **Newport,** Rhode Island. The ships carried more than 5,000 soldiers under the command of the French general, the **Comte de Rochambeau** (ROH•SHAM•BOH). Cheering crowds greeted the French soldiers, who were well armed and clad in colorful uniforms and plumed caps. The promised French aid had arrived at last. Unfortunately the British fleet arrived soon afterward and trapped the French ships in Newport.

In the autumn of 1780, Washington camped north of New York City waiting for a second fleet of French ships. From this position he could keep a close eye on the British army based in New York that General Clinton commanded. Washington planned to attack Clinton's army as soon as this second French fleet arrived from the West Indies. He had to wait a year to put his plan into action, however, because the fleet did not set sail for America until the summer of 1781.

Change in Plans

Washington had followed reports of the fighting in the South during 1780 and 1781. He knew that the British army commanded by Cornwallis was camped in **Yorktown,** Virginia. Washington also knew that Patriot forces under the Marquis de Lafayette were keeping Cornwallis and his troops bottled up on the Yorktown peninsula.

In August 1781, Washington learned that **Admiral François de Grasse,** the French naval

commander, was heading toward Chesapeake Bay instead of New York. Washington quickly changed his plans. He would advance on the British at Yorktown rather than at New York City.

Washington took steps to keep the new American strategy secret. He wanted Clinton to think the Patriots still planned to attack New York. This, he hoped, would keep Clinton from sending aid to Cornwallis.

General Rochambeau had marched his troops from Newport to join General Washington in July. Washington and Rochambeau then rushed south with their armies. The secrecy was so strict that most of the soldiers did not know where they were going. One soldier wrote,

> ❝We do not know the object of our march, and are in perfect ignorance whether we are going against New York, or . . . Virginia.❞

Washington's troops marched 200 miles in 15 days. General Clinton in New York did not detect the forces heading south toward Virginia. Three groups—Lafayette's troops, Washington's and Rochambeau's main American-French army, and the French fleet under Admiral De Grasse—would meet at Yorktown.

The Siege of Yorktown

Washington wondered whether his complicated plan had fooled Clinton, and whether the French fleet would reach Yorktown in time. On September 5, to his great relief, Washington received news that Admiral De Grasse's ships were nearing Yorktown.

The plan worked perfectly, and the British were thoroughly confused. By the end of September, 14,000 American and French troops had trapped Cornwallis's 7,500 British and Hessian troops at Yorktown. Meanwhile, De Grasse's

Picturing **History**

The Marquis de Lafayette (left) relied on James Armistead (right), an enslaved African American, to gather military information about the British. Armistead was later freed and took the name James Armistead Lafayette.
How did the French help the Patriots win the war?

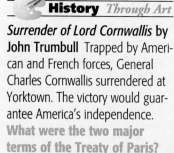

History *Through Art*

Surrender of Lord Cornwallis by **John Trumbull** Trapped by American and French forces, General Charles Cornwallis surrendered at Yorktown. The victory would guarantee America's independence. **What were the two major terms of the Treaty of Paris?**

fleet kept Cornwallis from escaping by sea. General Clinton and the rest of the British army waited in New York, unable to help Cornwallis.

Cornwallis's Defeat

On October 9 the Americans and French began a tremendous bombardment. A Hessian soldier described the dreadful scene in his diary:

> ❝One saw men lying nearly everywhere who were mortally wounded and whose heads, arms, and legs had been shot off. . . . Likewise on watch and on post in the lines, on trench and work details, they were wounded by the fearfully heavy fire.❞

British supplies began running low, and many soldiers were wounded or sick. Cornwallis realized the hopelessness of his situation. On October 19 he surrendered. The Patriots had won the **Battle of Yorktown.**

Handing over their weapons, the British marched between rows of French and American troops—the French in fancy white uniforms on one side and the raggedly clothed Continental Army on the other. A French band played "Yankee Doodle," and a British band responded with a children's tune called "The World Turned Upside Down." Indeed it had.

✔ Reading Check **Explaining** Why did Washington decide to advance on the British camp at Yorktown?

Independence

The fighting did not really end with Yorktown. The British still held Savannah, Charles Town, and New York, and a few more clashes took place on land and sea. The Patriot victory at Yorktown, however, convinced the British that the war was too costly to pursue.

The two sides sent delegates to Paris to work out a treaty. **Benjamin Franklin, John Adams,** and **John Jay** represented the United States. The American Congress ratified, or approved, the preliminary treaty in April 1783. The final **Treaty of Paris** was signed on September 3, 1783. By that time Britain had also made peace with France and Spain.

The Treaty of Paris was a triumph for the Americans. Great Britain recognized the United States as an independent nation. The territory that the new nation claimed extended from the Atlantic Ocean west to the Mississippi River and from Canada in the north to Spanish Florida in the south. The British promised to withdraw all their troops from American territory. They also agreed to give Americans the right to fish in the waters off the coast of Canada.

The United States, in turn, agreed that British merchants could collect

HISTORY Online

Student Web Activity
Visit tarvol1.glencoe.com and click on **Chapter 6— Student Web Activities** for an activity on the Battle of Yorktown.

People In History

Peter Francisco 1760–1831

Peter Francisco was found abandoned in Colonial America in 1765 when he was about five years old. It was later learned that he was from an island in the Portuguese Azores. The abandoned boy was adopted by an uncle of Patrick Henry.

When the Revolution began, 16-year-old Francisco joined the Tenth Virginia Regiment and earned a reputation for bravery and dedication to the revolutionary cause. George Washington was reported to have said about Francisco, "Without him we would have lost two crucial battles, perhaps the war, and with it our freedom. He was truly a one-man army."

After the war, Francisco served as sergeant at arms in the Virginia House of Delegates. In 1974 the Portuguese Continental Union of the United States of America began bestowing a "Peter Francisco Award" upon distinguished Americans who have contributed to the Portuguese cause.

---

debts owed by Americans. The treaty also stated that the Congress would advise the states that property taken from Loyalists was to be returned to them.

The Newburgh Conspiracy

After the British surrender, Washington maintained a strong army with headquarters at Newburgh, New York, planning to disband it when the peace treaty was signed. The period following the British surrender at Yorktown was not easy for American soldiers. Anger mounted when Congress refused to fund their pensions and failed to provide other pay. In disgust some officers circulated a letter in March 1783. If their demands were not met, the letter said, the army should refuse to disband.

Shocked and worried, General Washington realized that such an action could lead to a revolt that would threaten to destroy the new nation. He persuaded the angry officers to be patient with Congress. Then he urged Congress to meet the soldiers' just demands: "If, retiring from the field, they [the officers] are to grow old in poverty...then shall I have learned what ingratitude is."

Washington's leadership ended the threat to the new nation, and Congress soon acted on the demands.

Washington's Farewell

British troops left New York City in late November 1783. The war had truly ended, and George Washington could at last give up his command. On December 4 Washington said farewell to his officers at Fraunces' Tavern in Manhattan. "With a heart full of love and gratitude, I now take my leave of you."

Nearly three weeks later Washington formally resigned from the army at a meeting of the Second Continental Congress in Annapolis, Maryland. A witness described the scene: "The spectators all wept, and there was hardly a member of Congress who did not drop tears." Washington said,

> 66Having now finished the work assigned me I retire . . . and take my leave of all the employments of public life.99

He returned to his home, Mount Vernon, in time for Christmas. There he planned to live quietly with his family.

Why the Americans Won

How had the Americans managed to win the Revolutionary War? How had they defeated Britain, the world's strongest power?

The Americans had several advantages in the war. They fought on their own land, while the British had to bring troops and supplies from thousands of miles away. The siege of Yorktown showed how the British depended on support from the sea. When their ships were blocked, the British troops were without support.

The British succeeded in occupying cities but had difficulty controlling the countryside. They had not been successful at Saratoga or in the Carolinas. The Patriots, however, knew the local terrain and where to lay an ambush— a surprise attack.

Help from other nations contributed to the American victory. The success at Yorktown would not have been possible without French soldiers and ships. Loans from France helped the Americans win the war. The Spanish also aided the Patriots by attacking the British in the Mississippi Valley and along the Gulf of Mexico.

Perhaps most important, the American Revolution was a people's movement. Its outcome depended not on any one battle or event but on the determination and spirit of all the Patriots. As the Continental Army marched from New York to Yorktown, crowds came out to watch and wish the troops well. Washington pointed to the crowd and said,

> ❝We may be beaten by the English . . . but here is an army they will never conquer.❞

The Influence of the American Revolution

In 1776 the American colonists began a revolution, making clear the principles of freedom and rights outlined in the Declaration of Independence. These ideas bounded back across the Atlantic to influence the French Revolution. French rebels in 1789 fought in defense of "Liberty, Equality, and Fraternity." French revolutionaries repeated the principles of the American Declaration of Independence: "Men are born and remain free and equal in rights."

In 1791 the ideals of the American and French Revolutions traveled across the Caribbean and the Atlantic to the French-held island colony of Saint Domingue. Inspired by talk of freedom, enslaved Africans took up arms. Led by Toussaint-Louverture, they shook off French rule. In 1804, Saint Domingue—present-day Haiti—became the second nation in the Americas to achieve independence from colonial rule. "We have asserted our rights," declared the revolutionaries. "We swear never to yield them to any power on earth."

✓ **Reading Check** **Summarizing** What were three reasons the Americans were successful in their fight?

SECTION 4 ASSESSMENT

Checking for Understanding

1. **Key Terms** Use each of these terms in a sentence that will help explain its meaning: ratify, ambush.
2. **Reviewing Facts** Describe how the French navy helped George Washington at Yorktown.

Reviewing Themes

3. **Groups and Institutions** What influence did the American Revolution have around the world?

Critical Thinking

4. **Predicting Consequences** What might have happened if the French fleet had not arrived at Yorktown?
5. **Organizing Information** Re-create the diagram below and describe the terms that the Americans agreed to in the Treaty of Paris.

Analyzing Visuals

6. **Picturing History** Look at the painting on page 185. How does the artist focus attention on the figures in the center of the painting?

> **Interdisciplinary Activity**
>
> **Geography** Create a map of the United States that shows the boundaries of the country at the time of the Treaty of Paris. Use colored pencils to show the lands that the British gave to the Americans.

Chapter Summary
The American Revolution

1776
- Thomas Paine writes the inspiring *Common Sense*.
- The Continental Army is defeated at the Battle of Long Island.
- George Washington leads troops across the Delaware River to surprise the British at Trenton.

1777
- The Patriots defeat the British at Saratoga, New York.
- The British capture Philadelphia.

1778
- France provides money, troops, and equipment to the Patriots.
- The Continental Army suffers from the lack of supplies at Valley Forge.

1779
- John Paul Jones forces the surrender of the British warship *Serapis*.

1780
- The British capture Charles Town and take thousands of prisoners.

1781
- The Americans win the Battle of Yorktown.

1783
- The Treaty of Paris is signed, marking the end of the Revolution.

Reviewing Key Terms
Examine the pairs of words below. Then write a sentence explaining what each of the pairs has in common.
1. mercenary, recruit
2. blockade, privateer
3. guerrilla warfare, ambush

Reviewing Key Facts
4. Why did the British think their military forces were superior to those of the Americans?
5. Why did Loyalists support Britain?
6. How did Thomas Paine help the Patriots during the Revolutionary War?
7. What European nations fought with the Americans against the British?
8. What were some of the problems that troops faced during the winter at Valley Forge?
9. What ideas did Judith Sargeant Murray promote about education?
10. Why did many Native Americans give their support to the British?
11. What fighting method did the Americans use to keep the British from taking the Southern Colonies?
12. Which battle convinced the British that fighting the Americans was too costly?
13. Why was fighting on their own land an advantage for the Patriots?

Critical Thinking
14. **Compare and Contrast** What advantage did the Patriots have over the British mercenaries?
15. **Analyzing Information** How did women help in the war effort?
16. **Drawing Conclusions** Why do you think the British found it easier to capture American cities than to take over the American countryside?
17. **Determining Cause and Effect** Re-create the diagram below and describe two ways America's fight for independence influenced other countries.

Geography and History Activity

The Treaty of Paris in 1783 established the boundaries of the new United States. The newly independent nation shared land claims on the North American continent with several nations. Study the map below and answer the questions that follow.

18. **Location** What natural landmark formed the new western boundary of the United States?

19. **Region** Which country claimed the most land in North America in 1783? The least land?

Land Claims in North America, 1783

NATIONAL GEOGRAPHIC

Hudson Bay

50°N

CANADA

SPANISH LOUISIANA

Mississippi R.

UNITED STATES

40°N

N
W E
S

30°N

0   500 miles

0   500 kilometers
Azimuthal Equidistant projection

NEW SPAIN

Gulf of Mexico

20°N

10°N

80°W

100°W   90°W

United States	Disputed
British	Spanish
French	Russian

Practicing Skills

Reading a Military Map *Study the military map on page 181. Then answer the questions that follow.*

20. What color symbolizes British troop movement?

21. What symbol represents battles?

22. When did the British capture the city of Savannah?

23. Who was victorious at the Battle of Cowpens?

Self-Check Quiz
Visit **tarvol1.glencoe.com** and click on **Chapter 6—Self-Check Quizzes** to prepare for the chapter test.

Citizenship Cooperative Activity

24. **Expository Writing** As citizens, we have responsibilities to our communities. For a community to be successful, its citizens must take an active role in it. Write a one-page paper in which you discuss the topic, "My responsibilities to my community."

Economics Activity

25. Look up the word *inflation* in a dictionary or another reference book. Write a definition of the term in your own words. Then write answers to these questions:
   • What happens to the price of goods during periods of inflation?
   • How would inflation affect your standard of living?

Alternative Assessment

26. **Portfolio Writing Activity** Scan the chapter for details about people who came to the United States from other countries to help in the war effort. Record the names in your journal. Then create a chart that shows the people's names, their home countries, and what they did to aid the Americans.

Standardized Test Practice

Directions: Choose the *best* answer to the following question.

What American victory convinced the French to form an alliance with the United States?
A Saratoga   C Bunker Hill
B Ticonderoga   D Trenton

Test-Taking Tip

Remember to eliminate answers that you know are wrong. For example, the Patriots did not win the battle of Bunker Hill; therefore, choice **C** is not correct.

A More Perfect Union

1777–1790

Why It Matters

When the American colonies broke their political ties with Great Britain, they faced the task of forming independent governments at both the state and national levels. In 1788 the Constitution became the official plan of American government.

The Impact Today

Created to meet the needs of a changing nation, the Constitution has been the fundamental law of the United States for more than 200 years. It has served as a model for many constitutions all over the world.

 The American Republic to 1877 *Video* *The chapter 7 video, "Discovering Our Constitution," examines how the Constitution has preserved our government and the rights of citizens for over two hundred years.*

1777
• Articles of Confederation written

1783
• Treaty of Paris

United States
PRESIDENTS

1776

1779

1782

World

1778
• France goes to war against Britain

1780
• League of Armed Neutrality formed

1784
• Russians found colony on Kodiak Island, Alaska

FOLDABLES™
Study Organizer

Comparison Study Foldable Make this foldable to help you compare the Articles of Confederation to the U.S. Constitution.

Step 1 Fold a sheet of paper from side to side, leaving a 2-inch tab uncovered along the side.

Fold it so the left edge lies 2 inches from the right edge.

Step 2 Turn the paper and fold it into thirds.

Step 3 Unfold and cut along the two inside fold lines.

Cut along the two folds on the front flap to make 3 tabs.

Step 4 Label the foldable as shown.

A More Perfect Union
Articles of Confederation | Both | U.S. Constitution

Reading and Writing As you read the chapter, write what you learn about these documents under the appropriate tabs.

George Washington Addressing the Constitutional Convention by J.B. Stearns The Constitution created the basic form of American government.

1787
- Shays's Rebellion
- U.S. Constitution signed
- Northwest Ordinance passed

1788
- U.S. Constitution ratified

Washington 1789–1797

1785

1788

1791

1785
- First hot air balloon crosses English Channel

1788
- British establish penal colony in Australia

1789
- French Revolution begins

HISTORY Online

Chapter Overview
Visit tarvol1.glencoe.com and click on **Chapter 7— Chapter Overviews** to preview chapter information.

The Articles of Confederation

Guide to Reading

Main Idea
The leaders of the new United States worked to define the powers of government.

Key Terms
constitution, bicameral, republic, petition, ordinance, depreciate

Reading Strategy
Organizing Information As you read the section, re-create the diagram below and in the ovals list the powers you think a national government should have.

Powers of government

Read to Learn
- how the weaknesses of the Articles of Confederation led to instability.
- how Congress dealt with the western lands.

Section Theme
Government and Democracy At both state and national levels, the government of the United States tried to define its powers.

Preview of Events

◆1775	◆1780	◆1785	◆1790

1777
Articles of Confederation are written

1781
All states approve Confederation government

1783
Treaty of Paris officially ends American Revolution

1787
Northwest Ordinance is passed

Phillis Wheatley

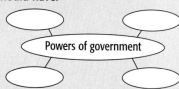

AN American Story

Many Americans, from colonial times on, spoke out for liberty. One who lent her voice to the pursuit of freedom was poet Phillis Wheatley. Celebrated as the founder of the African American literary tradition, Wheatley wrote many poems supporting the colonists in the Revolutionary War. For many Americans, like Wheatley, the end of the Revolution was a reason for joy. American liberty had survived the challenge of war. But could it meet the demands of peace?

Thirteen Independent States

Although the Americans won their independence, they had trouble winning Britain's respect. Ignoring the terms of the Treaty of Paris, the British kept troops at frontier posts in American territory. The British believed the new American government was weak and ineffective. While Americans were fighting for their independence on the battlefield, they were also creating new governments. After rejecting British rule, they needed to establish their own political institutions.

State Constitutions

In May 1776 the Continental Congress asked the states to organize their governments, and each moved quickly to adopt a state constitution, or plan of government. By the end of 1776, eight states had drafted constitutions. New York and Georgia followed suit in 1777, and Massachusetts in 1780. Connecticut and Rhode Island retained their colonial charters as state constitutions.

Their experience with British rule made Americans cautious about placing too much power in the hands of a single ruler. For that reason the states adopted constitutions that limited the power of the governor. Pennsylvania even replaced the office of governor with an elected council of 12 members.

Limiting Power

The states took other measures against concentration of power. They divided government functions between the governor (or Pennsylvania's council) and the legislature. Most states established two-house, or bicameral, legislatures to divide the power even further.

The writers of the constitutions not only wanted to prevent abuses of power in the states, but they also wanted to keep power in the hands of the people. State legislators were popularly elected, and elections were frequent. In most states, only white males who were at least 21 years old could vote. These citizens also had to own a certain amount of property or pay a certain amount of taxes. Some states allowed free African American males to vote.

The state constitutions restricted the powers of the governors, which made the legislatures the most powerful branch of government. The state legislatures struggled to make taxes more fair, but there were many disagreements. Going from dependent colonies to self-governing states brought new challenges.

✔ **Reading Check** **Explaining** Why did some states choose a bicameral legislature?

The Articles of Confederation

Forming a Republic

For Americans, establishing separate state governments was a much easier task than creating a central government. They agreed that their country should be a republic, a government in which citizens rule through elected representatives. They could not agree, however, on the organization and powers of their new republic.

At first most Americans favored a weak central government. They assumed the states would be very much like small, independent countries—similar to the way that the colonies had been set up. The states would act independently on most issues, working together through a central government only to wage war and handle relations with other nations.

Planning a New Government

In 1776 the Second Continental Congress appointed a committee to draw up a plan for a new government. The delegates in the Congress realized they needed a central government to coordinate the war effort against Britain. After much debate the Congress adopted the committee's plan, the **Articles of Confederation**, in November 1777.

The Articles, America's first constitution, provided for a new central government under which the states gave up little of their power. For the states, the Articles of Confederation were "a firm league of friendship" in which each state retained "its sovereignty, freedom and independence."

Under the Articles of Confederation, the government—consisting of the Congress—had the authority to conduct foreign affairs, maintain armed forces, borrow money, and issue currency. Yet it could not regulate trade, force citizens to join the army, or impose taxes. If Congress needed to raise money or troops, it had to ask the state legislatures—but the states were not required to contribute. In addition the govern-

ment lacked a chief executive. The Confederation government carried on much of its business, such as selling western lands, through congressional committees.

Under the new plan, each state had one vote in Congress, regardless of its population, and all states had to approve the Articles as well as any amendments. Despite this arrangement, the larger states believed that their population warranted having more votes. The states were also divided by whether or not they claimed land in the West. Maryland refused to approve the Articles until New York, Virginia, and other states abandoned claims to lands west of the Appalachian Mountains. Finally the states settled their differences. With Maryland's ratification, all 13 states had approved the Articles. On March 1, 1781, the Confederation formally became the government of the United States.

Why It Matters

Surveying the Land

When the Revolution began, only a few thousand white settlers lived west of the Appalachian Mountains. By the 1790s their numbers had increased to about 120,000. Through the Ordinance of 1785, Congress created a system for surveying—taking a detailed measurement of an area of land—and selling the western lands.

The Ordinance at first applied only to what was then called the Northwest Territory—present-day Ohio, Indiana, Michigan, Illinois, and Wisconsin. It established a system of land survey and settlement that we still use today.

The Land Ordinance led to the sale of large amounts of land and speeded settlement of the Northwest Territory.

The Confederation Government

The years between 1781 and 1789 were a critical period for the young American republic. The Articles of Confederation did not provide a government strong enough to handle the problems facing the United States. The Congress had limited authority. It could not pass a law unless nine states voted in favor of it. Any attempt to change the Articles required the consent of all 13 states, making it difficult for the Congress to pass laws when there was any opposition. Despite its weaknesses, the Confederation did accomplish some important things. Under the Confederation government, Americans won their independence and expanded foreign trade. The Confederation also provided for settling and governing the nation's western territories.

✓**Reading Check** **Explaining** What powers did the Confederation government have?

New Land Policies

At the beginning of the Revolutionary War, only a few thousand settlers lived west of the Appalachian Mountains. By the 1790s the number was approaching 120,000. These western settlers hoped to organize their lands as states and join the union, but the Articles of Confederation contained no provision for adding new states. Congress realized that it had to extend its national authority over the frontier and bring order to this territory.

During the 1780s all of the states except Georgia gave up their claims to lands west of the Appalachians, and the central government took control of these lands. In 1784 Congress, under

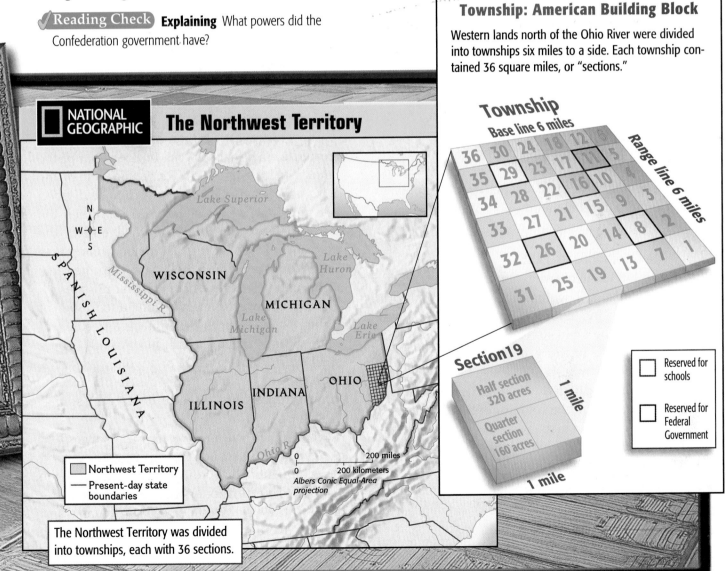

NATIONAL GEOGRAPHIC

The Northwest Territory

Lake Superior

WISCONSIN

MICHIGAN

Lake Huron

Lake Michigan

Lake Erie

SPANISH LOUISIANA

Mississippi R.

ILLINOIS

INDIANA

OHIO

Ohio R.

0   200 miles
0   200 kilometers
Albers Conic Equal-Area projection

☐ Northwest Territory
— Present-day state boundaries

The Northwest Territory was divided into townships, each with 36 sections.

Township: American Building Block

Western lands north of the Ohio River were divided into townships six miles to a side. Each township contained 36 square miles, or "sections."

Township
Base line 6 miles

Range line 6 miles

36	30	24	18	12	6
35	29	23	17	11	5
34	28	22	16	10	4
33	27	21	15	9	3
32	26	20	14	8	2
31	25	19	13	7	1

Section 19

Half section 320 acres

Quarter section 160 acres

1 mile

1 mile

☐ Reserved for schools

☐ Reserved for Federal Government

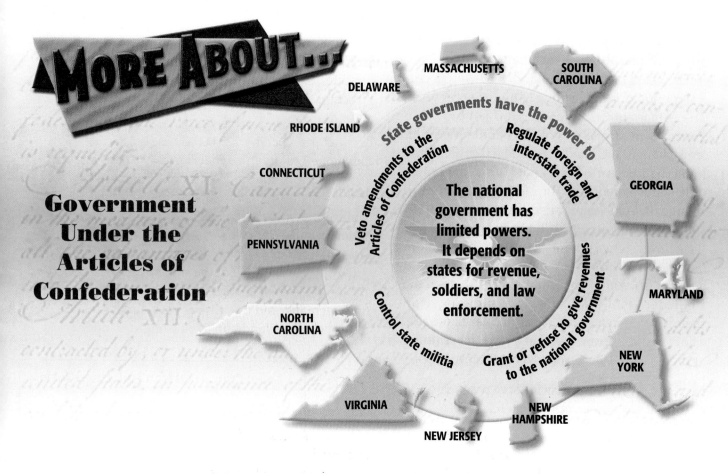

MORE ABOUT...

Government Under the Articles of Confederation

MASSACHUSETTS · **SOUTH CAROLINA** · **DELAWARE** · **RHODE ISLAND** · **CONNECTICUT** · **GEORGIA** · **PENNSYLVANIA** · **MARYLAND** · **NORTH CAROLINA** · **NEW YORK** · **VIRGINIA** · **NEW HAMPSHIRE** · **NEW JERSEY**

State governments have the power to:
- Veto amendments to the Articles of Confederation
- Regulate foreign and interstate trade
- Control state militia
- Grant or refuse to give revenues to the national government

The national government has limited powers. It depends on states for revenue, soldiers, and law enforcement.

a plan proposed by Thomas Jefferson, divided the western territory into self-governing districts. When the number of people in a district reached the population of the smallest existing state, that district could petition, or apply to, Congress for statehood.

The Ordinance of 1785

In 1785 the Confederation Congress passed an ordinance, or law, that established a procedure for surveying and selling the western lands north of the Ohio River. The new law divided this massive territory into townships six miles long and six miles wide. These townships were to be further divided into 36 sections of 640 acres each that would be sold at public auction for at least a dollar an acre.

Land speculators viewed the law as an opportunity to cheaply accumulate large tracts of land. Concerned about lawless people moving into western lands, Richard Henry Lee, the president of Congress, urged that "the rights of property be clearly defined" by the government. Congress drafted another ordinance to protect the interests of hard-working settlers.

The Northwest Ordinance

The Northwest Ordinance, passed in 1787, created a single **Northwest Territory** out of the lands north of the Ohio River and east of the Mississippi River. The lands were to be divided into three to five smaller territories. When the population of a territory reached 60,000, the people could petition for statehood. Each new state would come into the Union with the same rights and privileges as the original 13 states.

The Northwest Ordinance included a bill of rights for the settlers, guaranteeing freedom of religion and trial by jury. It also stated, "There shall be neither slavery nor involuntary servitude in said territory." This clause marked the United States's first attempt to stop the spread of slavery.

The Confederation's western ordinances had an enormous effect on American expansion and development. The Ordinance of 1785 and the Northwest Ordinance opened the way for settlement of the Northwest Territory in a stable and orderly manner.

Reading Check **Explaining** What was the purpose of the Northwest Ordinance?

Trouble on Two Fronts

Despite its accomplishments, the Confederation government had so little power that it could not deal with the country's financial problems. It also failed to resolve problems with Britain and Spain.

$ Economics

Financial Problems

By 1781 the money printed during the Revolutionary War had depreciated, or fallen in value, so far that it was almost worthless. Unable to collect taxes, both the Continental Congress and the states had printed their own paper money. No gold or silver backed up these bills. The value of the bills plummeted, while the price of food and other goods soared. Between 1779 and 1781, the number of Continental dollars required to buy one Spanish silver dollar rose from 40 to 146. In Boston and some other areas, high prices led to food riots.

Fighting the war left the Continental Congress with a large debt. Congress had borrowed money from American citizens and foreign governments during the war. It still owed the Revolutionary soldiers their pay for military service. Lacking the power to tax, the Confederation could not pay its debts. It requested funds from the states, but the states contributed only a small portion of the money needed.

Robert Morris's Import Tax

In 1781, faced with a total collapse of the country's finances, Congress created a department of finance under Philadelphia merchant **Robert Morris.** While serving in Congress, Morris had proposed a 5 percent tax on imported goods to help pay the national debt.

The plan required that the Articles of Confederation be changed to give Congress the power to levy the tax. Although 12 states approved the plan, Rhode Island's opposition killed the measure. A second effort in 1783 also failed to win unanimous approval. The financial crisis only worsened.

Problems with Britain

The weaknesses of the new American government became more evident as the United States encountered problems with other countries. In the Treaty of Paris of 1783, Britain had promised to withdraw from the lands east of the Mississippi River. Yet British troops continued to occupy several strategic forts in the Great Lakes region.

Picturing History

Pennsylvania merchant and banker Robert Morris became Superintendent of Finance in May 1781. **What reform did Morris propose to help the nation's finances?**

Continental currency

Robert Morris

Fact · Fiction · Folklore

John Hanson

The Forgotten President? Who was the first president of the United States? Was it George Washington—or John Hanson? Some historians consider Hanson the first United States president because he was the first to serve in the office in 1781 under the Articles of Confederation. Other historians argue that Hanson was the head of Congress, but not until George Washington began his term in 1789 did the nation have a "true" president.

British trade policy caused other problems. American merchants complained that the British were keeping Americans out of the West Indies and other profitable British markets.

In 1785 Congress sent **John Adams** to London to discuss these difficulties. The British, however, were not willing to talk. They pointed to the failure of the United States to honor *its* promises made in the Treaty of Paris. The British claimed that Americans had agreed to pay Loyalists for the property taken from them during the Revolutionary War. The Congress had, in fact, recommended that the states pay the Loyalists, but the states had refused.

Problems With Spain

If American relations with Great Britain were poor, affairs with Spain were worse. Spain, which held Florida as well as lands west of the Mississippi River, was anxious to halt American expansion into the territory it claimed. As a result, Spain closed the lower Mississippi River to American shipping in 1784. Western settlers depended on the Mississippi River for commerce. As **John Jay,** the American secretary of foreign affairs, had noted a few years earlier:

66 The Americans, almost to a man, believed that God Almighty had made that river a highway for the people of the upper country to go to sea by. 99

In 1786 American diplomats reached an agreement with Spain. Representatives from the Southern states, however, blocked the agreement because it did not include the right to use the Mississippi River.

The weakness of the Confederation and its inability to deal with problems worried many leaders. George Washington described the government as "little more than the shadow without the substance." Many Americans began to agree that the country needed a stronger government.

✓ **Reading Check** **Analyzing** Why did Spain close the lower Mississippi River to American trade?

SECTION 1 ASSESSMENT

Checking for Understanding

1. **Key Terms** Use each of these terms in a complete sentence that will help explain its meaning: constitution, bicameral, republic, petition, ordinance, depreciate.

2. **Reviewing Facts** Describe the country's financial problems after the Revolutionary War.

Reviewing Themes

3. **Government and Democracy** Why did most states limit the power of their governors and divide the legislature into two bodies?

Critical Thinking

4. **Predicting Consequences** What effect do you think the Northwest Ordinance had on Native Americans?

5. **Organizing Information** Re-create the diagram below and summarize the strengths and weaknesses of the Confederation government.

The Articles of Confederation	
Strengths	Weaknesses

Analyzing Visuals

6. **Geography Skills** Study the material on pages 194 and 195 about the Ordinance of 1785. Then answer these questions. What present-day states were created from the Northwest Territory? How many sections are in a township?

Interdisciplinary Activity

Citizenship Imagine you are an American citizen in the 1780s. Create a poster that defends the Articles of Confederation. Be sure to include reasons the Confederation Congress is needed.

Convention and Compromise

Guide to Reading

Main Idea
The new Constitution corrected the weaknesses of government under the Articles of Confederation.

Key Terms
depression, manumission, proportional, compromise

Reading Strategy
Organizing Information As you read the section, re-create the diagram below. In the boxes, describe the role each individual played in creating the new plan of government.

	Role
Edmund Randolph	
James Madison	
Roger Sherman	

Read to Learn
• how the Constitutional Convention broke the deadlock over the form the new government would take.
• how the delegates answered the question of representation.

Section Theme
Groups and Institutions National leaders worked to produce a new constitution for the United States.

Preview of Events

♦1783	♦1785	♦1787	♦1789

1784
Rhode Island passes plan to end slavery

September 1786
Daniel Shays leads rebellion

May 1787
Delegates meet to revise Articles of Confederation

September 1787
Delegates sign draft of Constitution

AN American Story

George Washington

By 1786 many Americans observed that the Confederation was not working. George Washington himself agreed that the United States was really "thirteen Sovereignties pulling against each other."

In the spring of 1787, Washington joined delegates from Virginia and 11 other states who gathered in Philadelphia to address this problem. Rhode Island decided not to participate. The delegates came "for the sole and express purpose of revising the Articles of Confederation."

Economic Depression

The call to revise the Articles of Confederation came while the young nation faced difficult problems. Many Americans believed that the Confederation government was too weak to deal with these challenges.

After the Revolutionary War ended, the United States went through a depression, a period when economic activity slowed and unemployment

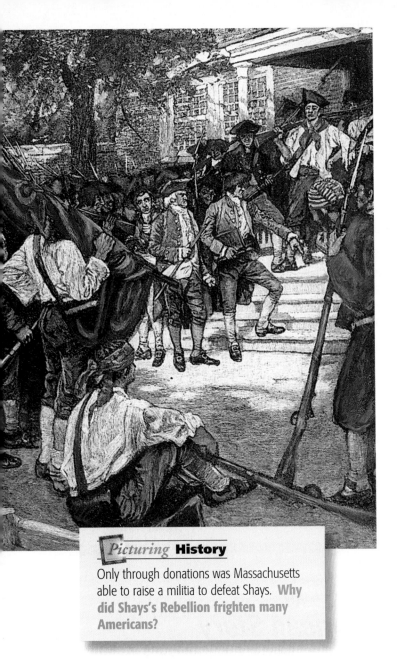

Picturing History

Only through donations was Massachusetts able to raise a militia to defeat Shays. **Why did Shays's Rebellion frighten many Americans?**

Shays's Rebellion

Resentment grew especially strong in Massachusetts. Farmers viewed the new government as just another form of tyranny. They wanted the government to issue paper money and make new policies to relieve debtors. In a letter to state officials, some farmers proclaimed:

    ❝Surely your honours are not strangers to the distresses [problems] of the people but . . . know that many of our good inhabitants are now confined in [jail] for debt and taxes.❞

In 1786 angry farmers lashed out. Led by **Daniel Shays,** a former Continental Army captain, they forced courts in western Massachusetts to close so judges could not confiscate farmers' lands.

In January 1787 Shays led more than 1,000 farmers toward the federal arsenal in **Springfield,** Massachusetts, for arms and ammunition. The state militia ordered the advancing farmers to halt, then fired over their heads. The farmers did not stop, and the militia fired again, killing four rebels. Shays and his followers scattered, and the uprising was over.

Shays's Rebellion frightened many Americans. They worried that the government could not control unrest and prevent violence. On hearing of the rebellion, George Washington wondered whether "mankind, when left to themselves, are unfit for their own government." Thomas Jefferson, minister to France at the time, had a different view. "A little rebellion, now and then," he wrote, "is a good thing."

The Issue of Slavery

The Revolutionary War brought attention to the contradiction between the American battle for liberty and the practice of slavery. Between 1776 and 1786, 11 states—all except South Carolina and Georgia—outlawed or heavily taxed the importation of enslaved people.

Although slavery was not a major source of labor in the North, it existed and was legal in all the Northern states. Many individuals and groups began to work to end the institution of slavery. In 1774 Quakers in Pennsylvania organized the first American antislavery society. Six

increased. Southern plantations had been damaged during the war, and rice exports dropped sharply. Trade also fell off when the British closed the profitable West Indies (Caribbean) market to American merchants. What little money there was went to pay foreign debts, and a serious currency shortage resulted.

Difficult Times for Farmers

American farmers suffered because they could not sell their goods. They had problems paying the requests for money that the states levied to meet Revolutionary War debts. As a result state officials seized farmers' lands to pay their debts and threw many farmers into jail. Grumblings of protest soon grew into revolt.

years later Pennsylvania passed a law that provided for the gradual freeing of enslaved people.

Between 1783 and 1804, Connecticut, Rhode Island, New York, and New Jersey passed laws that gradually ended slavery. Still, free African Americans faced discrimination. They were barred from many public places. Few states gave free African Americans the right to vote. The children of most free blacks had to attend separate schools. Free African Americans established their own institutions—churches, schools, and mutual-aid societies—to seek opportunity.

The states south of Pennsylvania clung to the institution of slavery. The plantation system of the South had been built on slavery, and many Southerners feared that their economy could not survive without it. Nonetheless, an increasing number of slaveholders began freeing the enslaved people that they held after the war. Virginia passed a law that encouraged manumission, the freeing of individual enslaved persons, and the state's population of free African Americans grew.

The abolition of slavery in the North divided the new country on the critical issue of whether people should be allowed to hold other human beings in bondage. This division came at the time when many American leaders had decided that the Articles of Confederation needed strengthening. In the summer of 1787, when state representatives assembled to plan a new government, they compromised on this issue. It would take years of debate, bloodshed, and ultimately a war to settle the slavery question.

Reading Check **Explaining** Why did Southern states support slavery?

A Call for Change

The American Revolution had led to a union of 13 states, but it had not yet created a nation. Some leaders were satisfied with a system of independent state governments that resembled the old colonial governments. Others saw a strong national government as the solution to America's problems. They demanded a reform of the Articles of Confederation.

Two Americans active in the movement for change were **James Madison,** a Virginia planter, and **Alexander Hamilton,** a New York lawyer. In September 1786, Hamilton proposed calling a convention in Philadelphia to discuss trade issues. He also suggested that this convention consider what possible changes were needed to make

❝the Constitution of the Federal Government adequate to the exigencies [needs] of the Union.❞

At first George Washington was not enthusiastic about the movement to revise the Articles of Confederation. When he heard the news of Shays's Rebellion, Washington changed his mind. After Washington agreed to attend the Philadelphia convention, the meeting took on greater significance.

Reading Check **Evaluating** Why did Madison and Hamilton call for a convention in 1787?

Picturing **History**

Philadelphia preachers Richard Allen (left) and Absalom Jones (right) founded the Free African Society and later set up the first African American churches. **What challenges did free African Americans face?**

The Constitutional Convention

The Philadelphia meeting began in May 1787 and continued through one of the hottest summers on record. The 55 delegates included planters, merchants, lawyers, physicians, generals, governors, and a college president. Three of the delegates were under 30 years of age, and one, Benjamin Franklin, was over 80. Many were well educated. At a time when only one white man in 1,000 went to college, 26 of the delegates had college degrees. Native Americans, African Americans, and women were not considered part of the political process, so none attended.

Several men stood out as leaders. The presence of George Washington and Benjamin Franklin ensured that many people would trust the Convention's work. Two Philadelphians also played key roles. James Wilson often read Franklin's speeches and did important work on the details of the Constitution. Gouverneur Morris, a powerful speaker and writer, wrote the final draft of the Constitution.

From Virginia came Edmund Randolph and James Madison. Both were keen supporters of a strong national government. Madison's careful notes are the major source of information about the Convention's work. Madison is often called the **Father of the Constitution** because he was the author of the basic plan of government that the Convention adopted.

Organization

The Convention began by unanimously choosing George Washington to preside over the meetings. It also decided that each state would have one vote on all questions. A simple majority vote of those states present would make decisions. No meetings could be held unless delegates from at least seven of the 13 states were present. The delegates decided to close their doors to the public and keep the sessions secret. This was a key decision because it made it possible for the delegates to talk freely.

The Virginia Plan

After the rules were adopted, the Convention opened with a surprise. It came from the Virginia delegation. Edmund Randolph proposed

America's *Architecture*

Independence Hall The Pennsylvania State House, later known as Independence Hall, was the site of the signing of the Declaration of Independence and of the Constitutional Convention. Independence Hall was restored in 1950 and is now maintained as a museum. **Why do you think this site was used for many important events?**

People In History

James Madison 1751–1836

James Madison, only 36 at the time of the Constitutional Convention, was the best prepared of the delegates. In the months before the convention, he had made a detailed study of government. He read hundreds of books on history, politics, and economics. He also corresponded with Thomas Jefferson.

Madison looked for ways to build a strong but fair system of government. He knew that republics were considered weaker than monarchies because kings or queens could use their authority to act quickly and decisively. Who would provide the same leadership in a republic? At the same time, Madison was concerned about protecting the people from misuse of power. As he searched for solutions, Madison worked out a new plan that included a system of balances among different functions of government. The delegates adopted many of Madison's ideas in what would become the United States Constitution.

that the delegates create a strong national government instead of revising the Articles of Confederation. He introduced the **Virginia Plan,** which was largely the work of James Madison. The plan called for a two-house legislature, a chief executive chosen by the legislature, and a court system. The members of the lower house of the legislature would be elected by the people. The members of the upper house would be chosen by the lower house. In both houses the number of representatives would be proportional, or corresponding in size, to the population of each state. This would give Virginia many more delegates than Delaware, the state with the smallest population.

Delegates from Delaware, New Jersey, and other small states immediately objected to the plan. They preferred the Confederation system in which all states were represented equally.

Delegates unhappy with the Virginia Plan rallied around **William Paterson** of New Jersey. On June 15 he presented an alternative plan that revised the Articles of Confederation, which was all the convention was empowered to do.

The New Jersey Plan

The **New Jersey Plan** kept the Confederation's one-house legislature, with one vote for each state. Congress, however, could set taxes and regulate trade—powers it did not have under the Articles. Congress would elect a weak executive branch consisting of more than one person.

Paterson argued that the Convention should not deprive the smaller states of the equality they had under the Articles. Thus, his plan was designed simply to amend the Articles.

✓ **Reading Check** **Explaining** Why did some delegates criticize the Virginia Plan?

Compromise Wins Out

The convention delegates had to decide whether they were simply revising the Articles of Confederation or writing a constitution for a new national government. On June 19 the states voted to work toward a national government based on the Virginia Plan, but they still had to resolve the thorny issue of representation that divided the large and small states.

Picturing **History**
Delegates to the Constitutional Convention met in this room at Independence Hall. **How many states had to ratify the Constitution before it went into effect?**

Discussion and Disagreement

As the convention delegates struggled to deal with difficult questions, tempers and temperatures grew hotter. How were the members of Congress to be elected? How would state representation be determined in the upper and lower houses? Were enslaved people to be counted as part of the population on which representation was based?

⬛Citizenship
The Great Compromise

Under Franklin's leadership, the convention appointed a "grand committee" to try to resolve their disagreements. **Roger Sherman** of Connecticut suggested what came to be known as the **Great Compromise.** A compromise is an agreement between two or more sides in which each side gives up some of what it wants.

Sherman proposed a two-house legislature. In the lower house—the House of Representatives—the number of seats for each state would vary according to the state's population. In the upper house—the Senate—each state would have two members.

The Three-Fifths Compromise

Another major compromise by the delegates dealt with counting enslaved people. Southern states wanted to include the enslaved in their population counts to gain delegates in the House of Representatives. Northern states objected to this idea because enslaved people were legally considered property. Some delegates from Northern states argued that the enslaved, as property, should be counted for the purpose of taxation but not representation. However, neither side considered giving enslaved people the right to vote.

The committee's solution, known as the **Three-Fifths Compromise,** was to count each enslaved person as three-fifths of a free person for both taxation and representation. In other words, every five enslaved persons would equal three free persons. On July 12 the convention delegates voted to approve the Three-Fifths Compromise. Four days later, they agreed that each state should elect two senators.

Slave Trade

The convention needed to resolve another difficult issue that divided the Northern and Southern states. Having banned the slave trade within their borders, Northern states wanted to prohibit it throughout the nation. Southern states considered slavery and the slave trade essential to their economies. To keep the Southern states in the nation, Northerners agreed that the Congress could not interfere with the slave trade until 1808. Beginning that year Congress could limit the slave trade if it chose to.

Bill of Rights

George Mason of Virginia proposed a bill of rights to be included in the Constitution. Some delegates worried that without the protection of a bill of rights the new national government might abuse its power. However, most of the delegates believed that the Constitution, with its carefully defined listing of government powers, provided adequate protection of individual rights. Mason's proposal was defeated.

Approving the Constitution

The committees finished their work on the Constitution in late summer. On September 17, 1787, the delegates assembled in the Philadelphia State House to sign the document. Franklin made a final plea for approval:

❝ I consent to this Constitution because I expect no better, and because I am not sure, that it is not the best. ❞

Three delegates refused to sign—Elbridge Gerry of Massachusetts, and Edmund Randolph and George Mason of Virginia. Gerry and Mason would not sign without a bill of rights.

The Confederation Congress then sent the approved draft of the Constitution to the states for consideration. To amend the Articles of Confederation had required unanimous approval of the states. Getting a unanimous vote had proved slow and frustrating. Therefore, the delegates agreed to change the approval process for the Constitution. When 9 of the 13 states had approved, the new government of the United States would come into existence. 📖 *(See pages 232–253 for the entire text of the Constitution.)*

✓ **Reading Check** **Analyzing** Who refused to sign the Constitution? Explain why.

HISTORY Online

Student Web Activity
Visit tarvol1.glencoe.com and click on **Chapter 7— Student Web Activities** for an activity on the Constitutional Convention.

SECTION 2 ASSESSMENT

Checking for Understanding

1. **Key Terms** Use the terms that follow to write a newspaper article about the main events of the Constitutional Convention: depression, manumission, proportional, compromise.

2. **Reviewing Facts** Explain what caused Shays's Rebellion. What was one effect?

Reviewing Themes

3. **Groups and Institutions** How did the Great Compromise satisfy both the small and the large states on the question of representation?

Critical Thinking

4. **Summarizing Information** You are asked to write a 30-second news broadcast to announce the agreement made in the Great Compromise. What would you include in the broadcast?

5. **Analyzing Information** Re-create the diagram below and identify arguments for and against ratifying the Constitution.

Ratification	
Arguments for	Arguments against

Analyzing Visuals

6. **Picturing History** Examine the images that appear on pages 202 and 204. What do they show? Where are they located? Why are these places important in the nation's history?

Interdisciplinary Activity

Government Create a political cartoon that illustrates the view of either the Northern states or the Southern states on how enslaved people should be counted for representation.

Critical Thinking SKILLBUILDER

Making Comparisons

Why Learn This Skill?

Suppose you want to buy a portable compact disc (CD) player, and you must choose among three models. You would probably compare characteristics of the three models, such as price, sound quality, and size, to figure out which model is best for you. When you study American history, you often compare people or events from one time period with those from a different time period.

Learning the Skill

When making comparisons, you examine two or more groups, situations, events, or documents. Then you identify similarities and differences. For example, the chart on this page compares two documents, specifically the powers each gave the federal government. The Articles of Confederation were implemented before the United States Constitution, which replaced the Articles.

When making comparisons, you first decide what items will be compared and determine which characteristics you will use to compare them. Then you identify similarities and differences in these characteristics.

Powers of the Federal Government	Articles of Confederation	United States Constitution
Declare war; make peace	✔	✔
Coin money	✔	✔
Manage foreign affairs	✔	✔
Establish a postal system	✔	✔
Impose taxes		✔
Regulate trade		✔
Organize a court system		✔
Call state militias for service		✔
Protect copyrights		✔
Take other necessary actions to run the federal government		✔

Practicing the Skill

Analyze the information on the chart on this page. Then answer the following questions.

1 What items are being compared?

2 Which document allowed the government to organize state militias?

3 Which document allowed the government to coin money? Regulate trade?

4 In what ways are the two documents different?

5 In what ways are the two documents similar?

Applying the Skill

Making Comparisons On the editorial page of your local newspaper, find two letters to the editor that express different viewpoints on the same issue. Read the letters and identify the similarities and differences between the two points of view.

 Glencoe's **Skillbuilder Interactive Workbook CD-ROM, Level 1,** provides instruction and practice in key social studies skills.

A New Plan of Government

Guide to Reading

Main Idea
The United States system of government rests on the Constitution.

Key Terms
Enlightenment, federalism, article, legislative branch, executive branch, Electoral College, judicial branch, checks and balances, ratify, Federalist, Antifederalist, amendment

Reading Strategy
Organizing Information Re-create the diagram below. In the boxes explain how the system of checks and balances works.

	Has check or balance over:	Example
President		
Congress		
Supreme Court		

Read to Learn
- about the roots of the Constitution.
- how the Constitution limits the power of government.

Section Theme
Civic Rights and Responsibilities
The Constitution outlines the responsibilities and the limits of the three branches of the national government.

Preview of Events

♦1680   ♦1720   ♦1760   ♦1800

1689
English Bill of Rights established

1690
Locke publishes *Two Treatises of Civil Government*

1748
Montesquieu writes *The Spirit of Laws*

1787
Constitutional Convention meets in Philadelphia

AN American Story

As Benjamin Franklin was leaving the last session of the Constitutional Convention, a woman asked, "What kind of government have you given us, Dr. Franklin? A republic or a monarchy?" Franklin answered, "A republic, Madam, if you can keep it." Franklin's response indicated that a republic—a system of government in which the people elect representatives to exercise power for them—requires citizens to take an active role.

Washington's chair, Constitutional Convention

Roots of the Constitution

After four long and difficult months, Franklin and the other delegates had produced a new constitution. The document provided the framework for a strong central government for the United States.

Although a uniquely American document, the Constitution has roots in many other civilizations. The delegates had studied and discussed the history of political development at length—starting with ancient Greece—so that their new government could avoid the mistakes of the past.

Many ideas embedded in the Constitution came from the study of European political institutions and political writers. British ideas and institutions particularly influenced the delegates.

The Framers who shaped the document were familiar with the parliamentary system of Britain, and many had participated in the colonial assemblies or their state assemblies. They valued the individual rights guaranteed by the British judicial system. Although the Americans had broken away from Britain, they respected many British traditions.

British System of Government

The **Magna Carta** (1215) had placed limits on the power of the monarch. England's lawmaking body, Parliament, emerged as a force that the king had to depend on to pay for wars and to finance the royal government. Like Parliament, the colonial assemblies controlled their colony's funds. For that reason the assemblies had some control over colonial governors.

The English Bill of Rights of 1689 provided another important model for Americans. Many Americans felt that the Constitution also needed a bill of rights.

Framers of the Constitution got many ideas on the nature of people and government from European writers of the Enlightenment. The Enlightenment was a movement of the 1700s that promoted knowledge, reason, and science as the means to improve society. James Madison and other architects of the Constitution were familiar with the work of **John Locke** and **Baron de Montesquieu** (MAHN•tuhs•KYOO), two important philosophers.

Locke, an English philosopher, believed that all people have **natural rights.** These natural rights include the rights to life, liberty, and property. In his *Two Treatises of Civil Government* (1690), he wrote that government is based on an agreement, or contract, between the people and the ruler. Many Americans interpreted natural rights to mean the rights of Englishmen defined in the Magna Carta and the English Bill of Rights. The Framers viewed the Constitution as a contract between the American people and their government. The contract protected the people's natural rights by limiting the government's power.

"[E]very man has a property in his own person. This nobody has any right to but himself."

—*John Locke*, **The Second Treatise of Government** *(1690)*

In *The Spirit of Laws* (1748), the French writer Montesquieu declared that the powers of government should be separated and balanced against each other. This separation would keep any one person or group from gaining too much power. The powers of government should also be clearly defined and limited to prevent abuse. Following the ideas of Montesquieu, the Framers of the Constitution carefully specified and divided the powers of government.

Reading Check **Describing** How did the English Bill of Rights influence Americans?

The Federal System

The Constitution created a federal system of government that divided powers between the national, or federal, government and the states. Under the Articles of Confederation the states retained their sovereignty. Under the Constitution the states gave up some of their powers to the federal government while keeping others.

Shared Powers

Federalism, or sharing power between the federal and state governments, is one of the distinctive features of the United States government.

Under the Constitution, the federal government gained broad powers to tax, regulate trade, control the currency, raise an army, and declare war. It could also pass laws that were "necessary and proper" for carrying out its responsibilities.

However, the Constitution left important powers in the hands of the states. The states had the power to pass and enforce laws and regulate trade within their borders. They could also establish local governments, schools, and other institutions affecting the welfare of their citizens. Both federal and state governments also had the power to tax and to build roads.

The Constitution Becomes Supreme Law of the Land

The Constitution and the laws that Congress passed were to be "the supreme law of the land." No state could make laws or take actions that went against the Constitution. Any dispute between the federal government and the states was to be settled by the federal courts on the basis of the Constitution. Under the new federal system, the Constitution became the final and supreme authority.

✓ **Reading Check** **Describing** What is the principle of federalism?

The Organization of Government

Influenced by Montesquieu's idea of a division of powers, the Framers divided the federal government into three branches—legislative, executive, and judicial. The first three articles, or parts, of the Constitution describe the powers and responsibilities of each branch.

America's *Architecture*

The Old Senate Chamber The U.S. Senate met in the Old Senate Chamber from 1810 until 1859. The two-story chamber is semicircular in shape and measures 75 feet long and 50 feet wide. Two visitors galleries overlook the chamber. After the Senate moved to its present location, the room was occupied by the Supreme Court, from 1860 to 1935. **What branches of government conducted business in the chamber?**

The Legislative Branch

Article I of the Constitution establishes Congress, the legislative branch, or lawmaking branch, of the government. Congress is composed of the House of Representatives and the Senate. As a result of the Great Compromise between large and small states, each state's representation in the House is proportional to its population. Representation in the Senate is equal—two senators for each state.

The powers of Congress include collecting taxes, coining money, and regulating trade. Congress can also declare war and "raise and support armies." Finally it makes all laws needed to fulfill the functions given to it as stated in the Constitution.

The Executive Branch

Memories of King George III's rule made some delegates reluctant to establish a powerful executive, or ruler. Others believed that the

Picturing History
The Supreme Court has the final say in deciding what the Constitution means. **What types of cases does the Supreme Court hear?**

Confederation had failed, in part, because it lacked an executive branch or president. They argued that a strong executive would serve as a check, or limit, on Congress.

Article II of the Constitution established the executive branch, headed by the president, to carry out the nation's laws and policies. The president serves as commander in chief of the armed forces and conducts relations with foreign countries.

The president and a vice president are elected by a special group called the Electoral College, made up of presidential electors. Each state's voters select electors to cast their votes for the president and vice president. Each state has as many electors as it has senators and representatives in Congress. The president and vice president chosen by the electors serve a four-year term.

The Judicial Branch

Article III of the Constitution deals with the judicial branch, or court system, of the United States. The nation's judicial power resides in "one supreme Court" and any other lower federal courts that Congress might establish. The

Supreme Court and the federal courts hear cases involving the Constitution, laws passed by Congress, and disputes between states.

System of Checks and Balances

The most distinctive feature of the United States government is the separation of powers. The Constitution divides government power among the legislative, executive, and judicial branches. To keep any one branch from gaining too much power, the Framers built in a system of checks and balances. The three branches of government have roles that check, or limit, the others so that no single branch can dominate the government.

Both the House and the Senate must pass a bill for it to become law. The president can check Congress by vetoing, or rejecting, the bill. However, Congress can then check the president by overriding, or voting down, the veto. To override a veto, two-thirds of the members of both houses of Congress must vote for the bill.

The system of checks and balances also applies to the Supreme Court. The president appoints Supreme Court justices, and the Senate must approve the appointments.

Over time, the Court became a check on Congress and the president by ruling on the constitutionality of laws and presidential acts. The system has been successful in maintaining a balance of power among the branches of the federal government and limiting abuses of power.

National Citizens

The Constitution created citizens of the United States. It set up a government in which the people choose their officials—directly or indirectly. Officials answer to the people rather than to the states. The new government pledged to protect the personal freedoms of its citizens.

With these revolutionary changes, Americans showed the world that it was possible for a people to change its form of government through discussion and choice—rather than through chaos, force, or war. The rest of the world watched the new nation with interest to see whether its experiment in self-government would really work.

Reading Check **Explaining** Why does the Constitution divide government power among the legislative, executive, and judicial branches?

🗣 Citizenship

The Constitutional Debate

The delegates at Philadelphia had produced the Constitution, but its acceptance depended upon the will of the people. Gaining approval of the Constitution, with its radical new plan of government, was not going to be easy. Supporters and opponents prepared to defend their positions.

Before the Constitution could go into effect, nine states needed to ratify, or approve, it. State legislatures set up special ratifying conventions to consider the document. By late 1787 these conventions started to meet. Rhode Island stood apart. Its leaders opposed the Constitution from the beginning and therefore did not call a convention to approve it.

A great debate now took place throughout the country. In newspapers, at public meetings, and in ordinary conversations, Americans discussed the arguments for and against the new Constitution.

Linking Past & Present

Great Seal of the United States

The Great Seal of the United States is the official seal of the United States government. The seal appears on important government documents. First adopted in 1782, it remains in use today. The face of the seal shows an American eagle with its wings spread. The seal also includes the motto *E pluribus unum* ("From many, one"). Most Americans don't know it, but they often carry around the seal. The one-dollar bill has both sides of the Great Seal on its back.

The United States has had several versions of the Great Seal.

The Great Seal and the number thirteen

On the Great Seal are
13 stars in the crest above the eagle
13 stripes on the eagle's shield
13 arrows in the eagle's left claw
13 olives and leaves in the eagle's right claw
13 letters in *E Pluribus Unum*
13 letters in the motto above the eye, *Annuit Coeptis*

Federalists

Supporters of the new Constitution were called Federalists. Better organized than their opponents, Federalists enjoyed the support of two of the most respected men in America—George Washington and Benjamin Franklin.

Three of the nation's most gifted political thinkers—James Madison, Alexander Hamilton, and **John Jay**—also backed the Constitution.

Madison, Hamilton, and Jay teamed up to write a series of essays explaining and defending the Constitution. These essays appeared in newspapers around the country and were widely read by Americans of every persuasion. Called *The Federalist Papers*, they were later published as a book and sent to delegates at the remaining ratifying conventions. (See pages 614–615 of the Appendix for excerpts from The Federalist Papers.) Jefferson described the series of essays as

66the best commentary on the principles of government which was ever written.99

Antifederalists

The Federalists called those who opposed ratification **Antifederalists**. Although not as well organized as the Federalists, the Antifederalists

Picturing **History**

Antifederalist Mercy Otis Warren feared that the Constitution would make the central government too powerful. **What was the biggest criticism of the Constitution by Antifederalists?**

had some dedicated supporters. They responded to the Federalists with a series of their own essays, now known as the *Antifederalist Papers*. Their main argument was that the new Constitution would take away the liberties Americans had fought to win from Great Britain. The Constitution would create a strong central government, ignore the will of the states and the people, and favor the wealthy few over the common people. Antifederalists preferred local government close to the people. An energetic central government, they feared, would be government by a small, educated group of individuals. They agreed with Patrick Henry, who warned that the Constitution was "incompatible with the genius of republicanism."

Protecting Rights

Perhaps the strongest criticism of the Constitution was that it lacked a bill of rights to protect individual freedoms. Antifederalists believed that no government could be trusted to protect the freedom of its citizens. Several state conventions took a stand and announced that they would not ratify the Constitution without the addition of a bill of rights.

Mercy Otis Warren, a Massachusetts opponent of the Constitution, expressed the problem faced by many Antifederalists. She admitted the need for a strong government but feared it.

66We have struggled for liberty and made costly sacrifices . . . and there are still many among us who [value liberty] too much to relinquish . . . the rights of man for the dignity of government.99

In many ways the debate between Federalists and Antifederalists came down to their different fears. Federalists feared disorder without a strong central government. They believed that more uprisings like Shays's Rebellion would occur. They looked to the Constitution to create a national government capable of maintaining order. The Antifederalists feared oppression more than disorder. They worried about the concentration of power that would result from a strong national government.

Reading Check **Explaining** According to the Antifederalists, why was a bill of rights important?

Analyzing *Political Cartoons*

A cartoon published in 1788 celebrates New Hampshire becoming the ninth state to ratify the Constitution. **From the cartoon, which was the first state to ratify?**

Adopting the Constitution

On December 7, 1787, Delaware became the first state to approve the Constitution. On June 21, 1788, the ninth state—New Hampshire—ratified it. In theory that meant that the new government could go into effect. However, without the support of the two largest states—New York and Virginia—the future of the new government was not promising. Neither state had ratified yet, and both had strong Antifederalist groups.

In Virginia, **Patrick Henry** gave fiery speeches against the proposed Constitution. It did not, he charged, sufficiently limit the power of the federal government. Still, Virginia ratified the Constitution at the end of June 1788, after being assured that the Constitution would include a bill of rights amendment. An amendment is something added to a document.

That left three states—New York, North Carolina, and Rhode Island—to ratify. In July 1788, New York finally ratified it by a narrow margin. North Carolina ratified in November 1789, and Rhode Island ratified in May 1790.

After ratification came the celebrations. Boston, New York, and Philadelphia held big parades accompanied by cannon salutes and ringing church bells. Smaller celebrations took place in hundreds of American towns.

The task of creating the Constitution had ended. The Bill of Rights would be added in 1791, after the new government took office. Now it was time for the nation to elect leaders and begin the work of government.

✓ **Reading Check** **Explaining** Why was the support of New York and Virginia vital to ratifying the Constitution?

big states w/ strong antifederalist groups

SECTION 3 ASSESSMENT

Checking for Understanding

1. **Key Terms** Define the following terms: Enlightenment, federalism, article, Electoral College, checks and balances, ratify, Federalist, Antifederalist, amendment.

2. **Reviewing Facts** What influence did John Locke have on American government?

Reviewing Themes

3. **Civic Rights and Responsibilities** Why did the Framers of the Constitution believe that a division of powers and a system of checks and balances were necessary in a government?

Critical Thinking

4. **Finding the Main Idea** What do you think was the most important reason for establishing a strong central government under the Constitution?

5. **Comparing** Re-create the diagram below. Describe the differences between Hamilton's and Henry's views on the Constitution.

Views on the Constitution	
Hamilton	Henry

Analyzing Visuals

6. **Political Cartoons** Study the political cartoon on this page. Then answer the questions that follow. What do the pillars represent? How do the last two pillars appear?

Interdisciplinary Activity

Citizenship Refer to the Bill of Rights on pages 244–245. Collect photographs from newspapers or magazines that illustrate the freedoms guaranteed in the Bill of Rights. Put your photos on a poster entitled "Pictures of Liberty."

Chapter Summary

A More Perfect Union

1777
- Congress adopts the Articles of Confederation to coordinate the war effort against Britain.

1781
- The Articles of Confederation formally become the government of the United States.

1784
- Spain closes the lower Mississippi River to American shipping.

1785
- The Land Ordinance provides a method for settlement of public lands north of the Ohio River.

1787
- Congress provides for the organization of the Northwest Territory and outlines the steps that a territory must take in order to become a state.
- Delegates meet in Philadelphia and draft the Constitution.
- Delaware becomes the first state to ratify the Constitution.

1788
- New Hampshire becomes the ninth state to vote for ratification.

1790
- The last of the 13 states—Rhode Island—votes for ratification.

1791
- Bill of Rights is added to the Constitution.

Reviewing Key Terms

For each of the pairs of terms below, write a sentence or short paragraph showing how the two are related.

1. constitution, ratify
2. bicameral, legislative branch
3. executive branch, Electoral College

Reviewing Key Facts

4. Summarize the strengths and weaknesses of the Articles of Confederation.
5. What caused the depression after the Revolution?
6. How did the Northwest Ordinance provide for the country's expansion?
7. According to the Virginia Plan, how was the legislature to be set up?
8. Who supported the New Jersey Plan?
9. What was the Three-Fifths Compromise?
10. What powers did the Constitution leave in the hands of the state governments? *p209*
11. Why did some states want a bill of rights added to the Constitution?
12. How did the *Federalist Papers* and the *Antifederalist Papers* influence ideas on systems of U.S. government?
13. How does the system of checks and balances work?

Critical Thinking

14. **Comparing** Who had the most power under the Articles of Confederation? Re-create the diagram below. In the boxes, describe the powers given to the state and national governments.

State Governments	National Government

15. **Analyzing Themes: Groups and Institutions** Were the people who attended the Constitutional Convention representative of the American public? Explain.
16. **Drawing Conclusions** Why did Madison want checks and balances built into the Constitution?
17. **Analyzing Information** Refer to the grievances listed in the Declaration of Independence on pages 154–157. How were these grievances addressed in the Constitution?

Geography and History Activity

Examine the map of the Northwest Territory on page 195. Then answer the questions that follow.

18. How many miles long and wide was a township?
19. How many miles long and wide was a section?
20. How many acres were in a section?

Practicing Skills

Making Comparisons *The two statements that follow reflect the opinions of an Antifederalist and a Federalist toward the ratification of the Constitution. Read the opinions; then answer the questions.*

"These lawyers and men of learning, and moneyed men . . . make us poor illiterate people swallow down the pill, expect to get into Congress themselves; they expect to be the managers of this Constitution, and get all the power and all the money into their own hands, and then they will swallow up all of us little folks. . . . This is what I am afraid of."

— Amos Singletary, farmer

"I am a plain man, and get my living by the plough. . . . I did not go to any lawyer, to ask his opinion; I formed my own opinion, and was pleased with this Constitution. . . . I don't think the worse of the Constitution because lawyers, and men of learning, and moneyed men, are fond of it."

— Jonathan Smith, farmer

21. Who is the Antifederalist? How do you know?
22. How are the two opinions similar? How are they different?
23. In your opinion, does the Antifederalist or the Federalist make the stronger argument? Explain.

Citizenship Cooperative Activity

24. **Interviewing** In groups of three, interview students from your school and adults from your community to find out what they know about the powers of government specified in the Constitution. Prepare a list of questions to use in your interviews. To keep the interviews brief, you might use yes/no questions, such as "Does the Constitution give the government the power to regulate highways?" Compile the answers and present a report to your class.

Self-Check Quiz

Visit tarvol1.glencoe.com and click on **Chapter 7—Self-Check Quizzes** to prepare for the chapter test.

Economics Activity

25. For a week, keep track of the number of times that you read about or hear about the topics of unemployment and inflation. Write down the source from which you heard or read this information. After each entry, indicate whether the economic news was good.

Alternative Assessment

26. **Portfolio Writing Activity** Review the Bill of Rights to the Constitution (first 10 amendments) on pages 244–245. Summarize each in your journal. Next, choose the amendment from the Bill of Rights that you think is the most important. Write a paragraph in which you explain your choice. Finally, knowing what you know about today's society, write a short description of a right you think the Framers of the Constitution should have included.

Standardized Test Practice

Directions: Choose the *best* answer to the following multiple choice question.

Each of the states enacted state constitutions in the late 1700s. All state constitutions

A established equal rights for all persons living in the state.

B set up legislative and executive branches of state government.

C granted women the right to vote.

D agreed that states would be supervised by the federal government.

Test-Taking Tip:

Eliminate answers that do not make sense. For example, *equal rights for all* (choice A) is a fairly new concept. During the 1700s, women and enslaved people had few rights.

Civics in Action
A Citizenship Handbook

The Constitution

Guide to Reading

Main Idea

For more than 200 years, the Constitution has provided the framework for the United States government and has helped preserve the basic rights of American citizens.

Key Terms

preamble, domestic tranquility, popular sovereignty, republicanism, federalism, enumerated powers, reserved powers, concurrent powers, amendment, implied powers, judicial review

Read to Learn

- why the Constitution is the nation's most important document.
- the goals of the Constitution.
- the principles that form the basis of the Constitution.

Goals of the Constitution

The Preamble, or introduction, to the Constitution reflects the basic principle of American government—the right of the people to govern themselves. It also lists six goals for the United States government:

> 66...to form a more perfect Union, establish Justice, insure domestic Tranquility, provide for the common defence [defense], promote the general Welfare, and secure the Blessings of Liberty to ourselves and our Posterity. 99

These goals guided the Constitution's Framers as they created the new government. They remain as important today as they were when the Constitution was written.

To Form a More Perfect Union Under the Articles of Confederation, the states functioned almost like independent nations. For the most part, they did not work together on important matters such as defense and finances. This lack of unity could have been dangerous for the nation during times of crisis. To form "a more perfect Union" the Framers believed the states needed to agree to operate as a single country and cooperate on major issues.

To Establish Justice For the Framers, treating each citizen equally was one of the fundamental principles on which to build the new nation.

The Constitution provides a national system of courts to protect the people's rights, and to hear cases involving violations of federal law and disputes between the states.

To Insure Domestic Tranquility Shays's Rebellion began in 1786 and shocked Americans. The United States had become a self-governing nation, yet a group of people had resorted to violence to express their anger over government policies. The Constitution provides a strong central government to "insure domestic Tranquility"—that is, to keep peace among the people.

To Provide for the Common Defense The Articles of Confederation required nine states to approve any decision by the Confederation Congress to build an army or navy. The Constitution gives the federal government the power to maintain armed forces to protect the country and its citizens from attack.

To Promote the General Welfare The Declaration of Independence states that the purpose of government is to promote "Life, Liberty, and the pursuit of Happiness" for the people of the nation. The Constitution includes ways to "promote the general Welfare"—or well-being—of the people by maintaining order, protecting individual liberties, regulating commerce and bankruptcies, and promoting science and technology by granting patents.

To Secure the Blessings of Liberty The American colonists fought the Revolutionary War to gain their liberty. The Framers believed that preserving liberty should also be a major goal of the Constitution. The Constitution guarantees that no American's basic rights will be taken away now or for posterity (generations not yet born).

✓**Reading Check** **Analyzing** What is the purpose of the Preamble?

Major Principles

The principles outlined in the Constitution were the Framers' solution to the problems of a representative government. The Constitution rests on seven major principles: (1) popular sovereignty, (2) republicanism, (3) limited government, (4) federalism, (5) separation of powers, (6) checks and balances, and (7) individual rights.

Popular Sovereignty The Declaration of Independence states that governments derive their powers from "the consent of the governed." The opening words of the Constitution, "We the people," reinforce this idea of popular sovereignty—or "authority of the people."

Republicanism Under republicanism, voters hold sovereign power. The people elect representatives and give them the responsibility to make laws and conduct government. For most Americans today, the terms *republic* and *representative democracy* mean the same thing: a system of limited government where the people are the ultimate source of governmental power.

Limited Government The Framers saw both benefits and risks in creating a powerful national government. They agreed that the nation needed strong central authority but feared misuse of power. They wanted to prevent the government from using its power to give one

Voting is a basic political right of all citizens.

Major Principles of the Constitution

Popular Sovereignty	People are the source of the government's power.
Republicanism	People elect their political representatives.
Limited Government	The Constitution limits the actions of government by specifically listing powers it does and does not have.
Federalism	In this government system, power is divided between national and state governments.
Separation of Powers	Each of the three branches of government has its own responsibilities.
Checks and Balances	Each branch of government holds some control over the other two branches.
Individual Rights	Basic liberties and rights of all citizens are guaranteed in the Bill of Rights.

Chart *Skills*

The Principles outlined in the Constitution were the Framers' solution to the complex problems presented by a representative government.

Analyzing Information What is the relationship between checks and balances and separation of powers?

REGISTER TO VOTE HERE

The Federal System

National Government

Enumerated Powers
- Regulate trade
- Coin Money
- Provide an army and navy
- Conduct Foreign affairs
- Set up federal courts

National & State Governments

Concurrent Powers
- Enforce the laws
- Establish courts
- Collect taxes
- Borrow money
- Provide for the general welfare

State Governments

Reserved Powers
- Regulate trade within the state
- Establish local government systems
- Conduct elections
- Establish public school systems

group special advantages or to deprive another group of its rights. By creating a limited government, they made certain the government would have only those powers granted by the people.

Article I of the Constitution states the powers that the government has and the powers that it does not have. Other limits on government appear in the Bill of Rights, which guarantees certain rights and liberties to the people.

Limited government can be described as the "rule of law." No people or groups are above the law. Government officials must obey the law.

Federalism When the states banded together under the Constitution, they gave up some independence. States could no longer print their own money or tax items imported from other states. Nevertheless, each state governed itself much as it had in the past.

This system, in which the power to govern is shared between the national government and the states, is called the federal system, or federalism. Our federal system allows the people of each state to deal with their needs in their own way. At the same time, it lets the states act together to deal with matters that affect all Americans.

The Constitution defines three types of government powers. Enumerated powers belong only to the federal government. These include the power to coin money, regulate interstate and foreign trade, maintain the armed forces, and create federal courts (Article I, Section 8).

The second kind of powers are those retained by the states, known as reserved powers. They include such rights as the power to establish

schools, pass marriage and divorce laws, and regulate trade within a state. Although reserved powers are not listed specifically in the Constitution, the Tenth Amendment says that all powers not specifically granted to the federal government "are reserved to the States."

The third set of powers defined by the Constitution are concurrent powers—powers shared by the state and federal governments. Among these powers are the right to raise taxes, borrow money, provide for public welfare, and administer criminal justice.

When conflicts arise between state law and federal law, the Constitution declares that the Constitution is "the supreme Law of the Land." Conflicts between state law and federal law must be settled in a federal court.

Separation of Powers To prevent any single group or institution in government from gaining too much authority, the Framers divided the federal government into three branches: **legislative, executive,** and **judicial.** Each branch has its own functions and powers. The legislative branch, Congress, makes the laws. The executive branch, headed by the president, carries out the laws. The judicial branch, consisting of the Supreme Court and other federal courts, interprets and applies the laws.

Checks and Balances As an additional safeguard, the Framers established a system of **checks and balances** in which each branch of government can check, or limit, the power of the other branches. This system helps maintain a

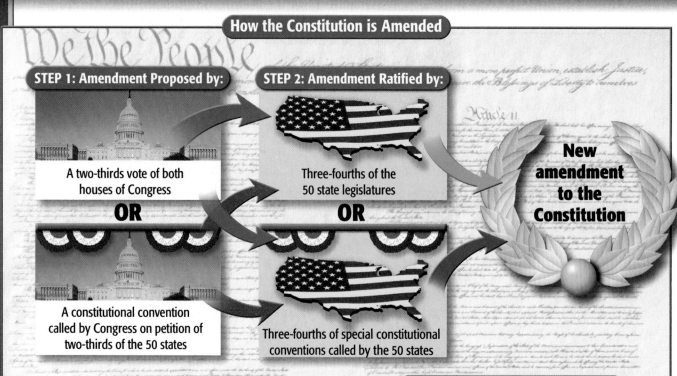

How the Constitution is Amended

STEP 1: Amendment Proposed by:

A two-thirds vote of both houses of Congress

OR

A constitutional convention called by Congress on petition of two-thirds of the 50 states

STEP 2: Amendment Ratified by:

Three-fourths of the 50 state legislatures

OR

Three-fourths of special constitutional conventions called by the 50 states

New amendment to the Constitution

Graphic Organizer → Skills

Amending the Constitution allows it to be able to adapt to changing times.

Analyzing Information What role do the states play in the amendment process?

balance in the power of the three branches. For example, Congress can pass a law. Then the president can reject the law by vetoing it. However, Congress can override, or reverse, the president's veto if two-thirds of the members of both houses vote again to approve the law.

Over the years, the Supreme Court has acquired the power to determine the meaning of the Constitution and to declare that a law or a government policy goes against the Constitution. In doing so, the Court provides a check on the powers of Congress and the president. Judicial decisions—those made by the courts—can be overruled by amending the Constitution. The president and the Senate provide a check on the judicial branch through their power to appoint and approve federal judges. Congress can also change a law so that it no longer conflicts with the Constitution, or it can amend the Constitution. The Fourteenth Amendment, passed by Congress in 1866, overturned the Supreme Court's ruling in the *Dred Scott* decision, which had ruled that enslaved African Americans were not citizens.

Individual Rights The Bill of Rights became part of the Constitution in 1791. These first 10 amendments protect basic liberties and rights

that you may take for granted—including freedom of speech, freedom of the press, freedom of assembly, freedom of religion, and the right to a trial by jury.

The 17 amendments that follow the Bill of Rights expand the rights of Americans and adjust certain provisions of the Constitution. Included among them are amendments that abolish slavery, define citizenship, guarantee the right to vote to all citizens, authorize an income tax, and set a two-term limit on the presidency.

✓**Reading Check** **Explaining** What is popular sovereignty?

A Living Constitution

Two years after the Constitutional Convention, Benjamin Franklin wrote, "Our Constitution is in actual operation; everything appears to promise that it will last; but in this world nothing is certain but death and taxes."

Despite Franklin's uncertainty about the Constitution's future, it is still very much alive today. The Constitution has survived because the Framers wrote a document that the nation could alter and adapt to meet changing needs. The result is a flexible document that can be interpreted in different ways in keeping with the conditions of a particular time. The Constitution's flexibility allows the government to deal with matters the Framers never anticipated—such as regulating nuclear power plants or developing a space program. In addition the Constitution contains a provision for amending—changing or adding to—the document.

Amending the Constitution The Framers intentionally made the amendment process difficult to discourage minor or frequent changes being made. Although thousands of amendments—changes to the Constitution—have been proposed since 1788, only 27 of them have actually become part of the Constitution.

An amendment may be proposed in two ways: by the vote of two-thirds of both houses of Congress or by two-thirds of the state legislatures asking for a special convention on the amendment. The second method has never been used. Ratification of an amendment requires approval by three-fourths of the states. The Constitution can be ratified by the approval of state legislatures or by special state conventions.

Only the Twenty-first Amendment—which repealed the Eighteenth Amendment, banning the sale of alcoholic beverages—was ratified by state conventions. Voters in each state chose the delegates to the special conventions.

Interpreting the Constitution The Constitution includes two provisions that give Congress the power to act as needed to meet changing conditions. The first of these provisions is what is known as the "elastic clause" (Article I, Section 8). It directs Congress to "make all Laws which shall be necessary and proper" for executing all the powers of government. Congress has interpreted this clause to mean that it has certain implied powers, powers not specifically defined in the Constitution. Over the years,

Congress has drawn on its implied powers to pass laws to deal with the needs of society.

The second provision used to expand congressional authority, the "commerce clause" (Article I, Section 8), gives Congress the power to "regulate Commerce with foreign Nations, and among the several States." Congress has used this clause to expand its powers into a number of areas, such as regulation of the airline industry, radio and television, and nuclear energy.

Powers of the Presidency The Constitution describes the role and the powers of the president in general terms. This has allowed the executive branch to extend its powers. In 1803, for example, President Thomas Jefferson approved a treaty with France that enabled the United States to buy an enormous tract of land.

The Bill of Rights

1	Guarantees freedom of religion, speech, assembly, and press, and the right of people to petition the government
2	Protects the rights of states to maintain a militia and of citizens to bear arms
3	Restricts quartering of troops in private homes
4	Protects against "unreasonable searches and seizures"
5	Assures the right not to be deprived of "life, liberty, or property, without due process of law"
6	Guarantees the right to a speedy and public trial by an impartial jury
7	Assures the right to a jury trial in cases involving the common law (the law established by previous court decisions)
8	Protects against excessive bail, or cruel and unusual punishment
9	Provides that people's rights are not restricted to those specified in the first eight Amendments
10	Restates the Constitution's principle of federalism by providing that powers not granted to the national government nor prohibited to the states are reserved to the states and to the people

"I have finally been included in 'We the people.'"

—*Barbara Jordan, U.S. representative from Texas, 1972–1978*

The Courts The role of the judicial branch has also grown as powers implied in the Constitution have been put into practice. In 1803 Chief Justice John Marshall expanded the powers of the Supreme Court by striking down an act of Congress in the case of *Marbury* v. *Madison*. In that decision the Court defined its right to determine whether a law violates the Constitution. Although not mentioned in the Constitution, judicial review has become a major power of the judicial branch.

The process of amending the Constitution and applying its principles in new areas helps keep our government functioning well. In 1974 Barbara Jordan, an African American member of Congress and a constitutional scholar, spoke in ringing tones of her faith in the Constitution:

❝I felt somehow for many years that George Washington and Alexander Hamilton just left me out by mistake. But through the process of amendment, interpretation, and court decision I have finally been included in 'We the people.'❞

✓ **Reading Check** **Explaining** What are implied powers?

SECTION 1 ASSESSMENT

Checking for Understanding

1. **Key Terms** Write complete sentences using each group of terms below. Group 1: republicanism, federalism. Group 2: enumerated powers, concurrent powers. Group 3: preamble, amendment.
2. **Reviewing Facts** Explain the origin of judicial review.

Reviewing Themes

3. **Government and Democracy** What is the importance of federalism in the Constitution?

Critical Thinking

4. **Analyzing Information** Why was it so important for basic freedoms to be guaranteed in the Constitution?
5. **Comparing** Re-create the diagram below and describe how each branch of government has power over another branch.

Branch	Power
Legislative	
Executive	
Judicial	

Analyzing Visuals

6. **Reading a Table** Refer to the table on page 218. How are popular sovereignty and republicanism related?

Interdisciplinary Activity

Civics The Bill of Rights guarantees certain basic rights to all Americans. Select one of the 10 amendments that make up the Bill of Rights (see page 221) and research its history. Present your findings in a one-page essay.

SECTION 2 The Federal Government

Guide to Reading

Main Idea
The government of the United States has three branches: the legislative branch, the executive branch, and the judicial branch.

Key Terms
appropriate, impeach, constituents

Read to Learn
- the goals of the three branches of the government.
- the powers of the three branches of the government.

The Legislative Branch

Congress, the legislative branch of the government, makes the nation's laws. It also has the power to "lay and collect taxes" and to declare war. Congress has two houses, the House of Representatives and the Senate.

The House and Senate Today the House of Representatives has 435 voting members and five nonvoting delegates from the District of Columbia, Puerto Rico, Guam, American Samoa, and the Virgin Islands. The number of representatives from each state is determined by the state's population. Representatives, who must be at least 25 years old, serve two-year terms.

The Senate consists of 100 senators, two from each state. Senators, who must be at least 30 years old, serve six-year terms. The senators' terms are staggered, which means that one-third of the Senate seats come up for election every two years.

Seal of the U.S. Congress

The Role of Congress Congress has two primary functions: to make the nation's laws and to control government spending. The government cannot spend any money unless Congress appropriates, or sets aside, funds. All tax and spending bills must originate in the House of Representatives and gain approval in both the House and the Senate before moving on to the president for signature.

Congress also serves as a watchdog over the executive branch, monitoring its actions and investigating possible abuses of power. The House of Representatives can impeach, or bring formal charges against, any federal official it suspects of wrongdoing or misconduct. If an official is impeached, the Senate acts as a court and tries the accused official. Officials who are found guilty may be removed from office.

The Senate also holds certain special powers. Only the Senate can ratify treaties made by the president and confirm presidential appointments of federal officials, such as department heads, ambassadors, and federal judges.

All members of Congress have the responsibility of representing their constituents, the people of their home states and districts. As a constituent you can expect your senators and representatives to promote and protect your state's interests as well as those of the nation.

Congress at Work Thousands of **bills**, or proposed laws, are introduced in Congress every year. Because individual members of Congress

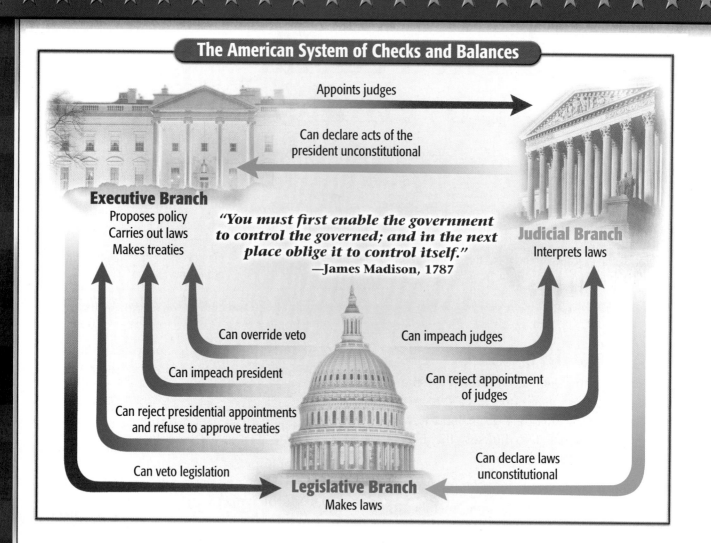

The American System of Checks and Balances

Appoints judges

Can declare acts of the president unconstitutional

Executive Branch
Proposes policy
Carries out laws
Makes treaties

"You must first enable the government to control the governed; and in the next place oblige it to control itself."
—James Madison, 1787

Judicial Branch
Interprets laws

Can override veto

Can impeach judges

Can impeach president

Can reject appointment of judges

Can reject presidential appointments and refuse to approve treaties

Can veto legislation

Can declare laws unconstitutional

Legislative Branch
Makes laws

---

cannot possibly study all these bills carefully, both houses use committees of selected members to evaluate proposed legislation.

Standing committees are permanent committees in both the House and the Senate that specialize in a particular topic, such as agriculture, commerce, or veterans' affairs. These committees usually are broken down into **subcommittees** that focus on a particular aspect of a problem or issue.

The House and the Senate sometimes form temporary **select committees** to deal with issues requiring special attention. These committees meet only until they complete their task.

Occasionally the House and the Senate form **joint committees** with members from both houses. These committees meet to consider specific issues, such as the system of federal taxation. One type of joint committee, a **conference committee,** has a special function. If the House

and the Senate pass different versions of the same bill, a conference committee tries to work out a compromise bill acceptable to both houses.

When it receives a bill, a committee can kill it by rejecting it outright, "pigeonhole" it by setting it aside without reviewing it, or prepare it for consideration by the full House or Senate. While preparing bills, committees hold public hearings at which citizens can present arguments and documents supporting or opposing the bills.

Once a bill is approved by a committee in either house of Congress, it is sent to the full Senate or House for debate. After debate the bill may be passed, rejected, or returned to committee for further changes.

When both houses pass a bill, the bill goes to the president. If the president approves the bill and signs it, it becomes law. If the president vetoes the bill, it does not become law, unless Congress **overrides** (cancels) the presidential veto by a vote of two-thirds of the members in each house.

✓ Reading Check **Sequencing** List the basic steps of how a bill becomes a law.

The Executive Branch

The executive branch of government includes the president, the vice president, and various executive offices, departments, and agencies. The executive branch carries out the laws that Congress passes.

Chief Executive The president plays a number of different roles in government, each of which has specific powers and responsibilities. These roles include the nation's chief executive, chief diplomat, commander in chief, chief of state, and legislative leader.

As chief executive, the president is responsible for carrying out the nation's laws. Many executive departments and agencies assist the president in this job.

Chief Diplomat As chief diplomat, the president directs foreign policy, appoints ambassadors, and negotiates treaties with other nations. Treaties must be approved by a two-thirds vote of the Senate before they go into effect.

Commander in Chief As commander in chief of the armed forces, the president can use the military to intervene or offer assistance in crises at home and around the world. The president cannot declare war; only Congress holds this power. The president can send troops to other parts of the world for up to 60 days but must notify Congress when doing so. The troops may remain longer only if Congress gives approval or declares war.

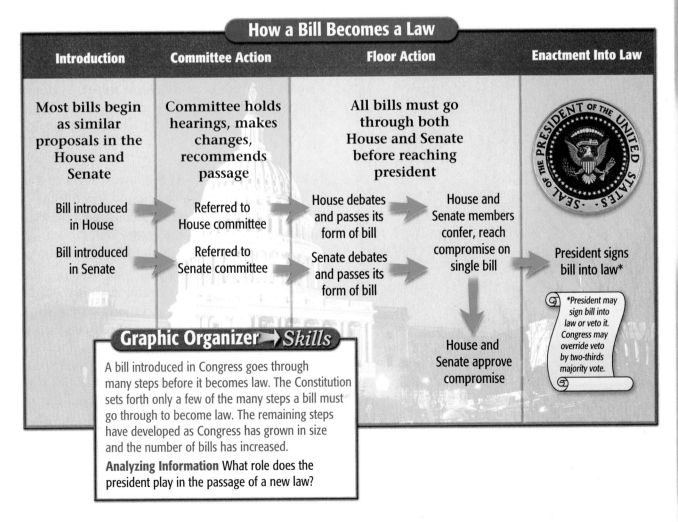

How a Bill Becomes a Law

Introduction	Committee Action	Floor Action	Enactment Into Law
Most bills begin as similar proposals in the House and Senate	Committee holds hearings, makes changes, recommends passage	All bills must go through both House and Senate before reaching president	
Bill introduced in House	Referred to House committee	House debates and passes its form of bill	House and Senate members confer, reach compromise on single bill
Bill introduced in Senate	Referred to Senate committee	Senate debates and passes its form of bill	President signs bill into law*
		House and Senate approve compromise	

*President may sign bill into law or veto it. Congress may override veto by two-thirds majority vote.

Graphic Organizer → Skills

A bill introduced in Congress goes through many steps before it becomes law. The Constitution sets forth only a few of the many steps a bill must go through to become law. The remaining steps have developed as Congress has grown in size and the number of bills has increased.

Analyzing Information What role does the president play in the passage of a new law?

Chief of State As chief of state, the president serves a symbolic role as the representative of all Americans. The president fulfills this role when receiving foreign ambassadors or heads of state, visiting foreign nations, or bestowing honors on Americans.

Legislative Leader The president serves as a legislative leader by proposing laws to Congress and working to see that they are passed. In the annual State of the Union address, the president presents goals for legislation.

The Executive Branch at Work Many executive offices, departments, and independent agencies help the president carry out and enforce the nation's laws. The Executive Office of the President (EOP) is made up of individuals and agencies that directly assist the president. Presidents rely heavily on the EOP for advice and for gathering information.

The executive branch also includes 14 executive departments, each responsible for a different area of government. For example, the

Department of State plans and carries out foreign policy, and the Department of the Interior manages and protects the nation's public lands and natural resources. The heads, or secretaries, of these departments are members of the president's **cabinet,** a group that helps the president make decisions and set government policy.

The independent agencies manage federal programs in many fields. These include aeronautics and space, banking, communications, farm credit, and trade. Government corporations are government agencies that are run like privately owned businesses. One government corporation whose services you may often use is the United States Postal Service.

✓**Reading Check** **Describing** What is the president's cabinet?

The Judicial Branch

Article III of the Constitution called for the creation of a Supreme Court and "such inferior [lower] courts as Congress may from time to time ordain and establish." In 1789 Congress passed a **Judiciary Act,** which added a series of district courts to the federal court system. Congress added appeals courts, sometimes called circuit courts, in 1891 to ease the workload of the Supreme Court.

Lower Federal Courts At the lowest level of the federal court system are the United States **district courts.** These courts consider criminal and civil cases that come under federal, rather than state, authority. The criminal cases include such offenses as kidnapping and federal tax evasion. Civil cases cover claims against the federal government and cases involving constitutional rights, such as free speech. There are 91 district courts in the nation, with at least one in every state.

The next level of federal courts, the **appeals courts,** reviews district court decisions in which the losing side has asked for a review of the verdict. If an appeals court disagrees with the lower court's decision, it can either overturn the verdict or order a retrial. There are 14 appeals courts in the United States.

Picturing **History**

President George W. Bush describes a legislative program in the annual State of the Union message to Congress. **What powers does the president hold in his role as commander in chief?**

The Supreme Court The **Supreme Court** stands at the top of the American legal system. Article III of the Constitution created the Supreme Court as one of three coequal branches of the national government, along with Congress and the president.

The Supreme Court is composed of nine justices: the chief justice of the United States and eight associate justices. Congress sets this number and has the power to change it. Over the years it has varied from 5 to 10, but it has been 9 since 1869.

The Constitution does not describe the duties of the justices. Instead, the duties have developed from laws, through tradition, and as the needs and circumstances of the nation have developed. The main duty of the justices is to hear and rule on cases. This duty involves them in three decision-making tasks: deciding which cases to hear from among the thousands appealed to the Court each year; deciding the case itself; and determining an explanation for the decision, called the Court's **opinion.**

Shaping Public Policy The Supreme Court is both a political and a legal institution. It is a legal institution because it is responsible for settling disputes and interpreting the meaning of laws. The Court is a political institution because when it applies the law to specific disputes, it often determines what national policy will be. For example, when the Court rules that certain parts of the Social Security Act must apply to men and women equally, it is determining government policy.

Judicial Review As you have read, the Supreme Court's power to examine the laws and actions of local, state, and national governments and to cancel them if they violate the Constitution is called judicial review. The Supreme Court first assumed the power of judicial review in the case of *Marbury* v. *Madison* (1803). Since then, the Court has invalidated, or canceled, nearly 200 provisions of federal law.

The Supreme Court may also review presidential policies. In the case of *Ex parte Milligan* (1866), the Court ruled President Lincoln's suspension of certain civil rights during the Civil War was unconstitutional.

Judicial review of state laws and actions may have as much significance as the Court's activities at the federal level. In *Brown* v. *Board of Education of Topeka* (1954), the Court held that laws requiring or permitting racially segregated schools in four states were unconstitutional. The *Brown* decision cleared the way for the end of segregated schools throughout the nation.

✓ Reading Check **Describing** How was the court system set up?

SECTION 2 ASSESSMENT

Checking for Understanding

1. **Key Terms** Use each of these terms in a complete sentence that helps explain its meaning: appropriate, impeach, constituents.

2. **Reviewing Facts** List three responsibilities of the president.

Reviewing Themes

3. **Government and Democracy** Why is Congress's power to appropriate money important?

Critical Thinking

4. **Analyzing Information** Which branch of government do you think is most powerful? Explain why you think so.

5. **Analyzing Information** Re-create the diagram below and provide five different kinds of Congressional committees.

Analyzing Visuals

6. **Reading a Flowchart** Refer to the flowchart on page 225. What do committees do to a bill?

Interdisciplinary Activity

Current Events Research in newspapers and news magazines about bills that are being debated in Congress. Find out what the bill will do if it is passed. Write a one-page paper about the bill and what has happened to it as it has gone through Congress.

SECTION 3 Citizens' Rights and Responsibilities

Guide to Reading

Main Idea
Citizens of the United States have both rights and responsibilities.

Key Terms
due process of law, citizen, naturalization

Read to Learn
- where the rights of citizens come from.
- the rights and responsibilities of United States citizens.

The Rights of American Citizens

❝We hold these truths to be self-evident, that all men are created equal, that they are endowed by their Creator with certain unalienable Rights, that among these are Life, Liberty, and the pursuit of Happiness.❞

These words from the Declaration of Independence continue to inspire Americans. They have encouraged Americans to pursue the ideals expressed in the Declaration and to create a Constitution and a Bill of Rights that protect these rights. The rights of Americans fall into three broad categories: the right to be protected from unfair actions of the government, to have equal treatment under the law, and to have basic freedoms.

Due Process The Fifth Amendment states that no person shall "be deprived of life, liberty, or property, without due process of law." Due process of law means that the government must follow procedures established by law and guaranteed by the Constitution, treating all people according to these principles.

Equal Protection All Americans, regardless of race, religion, or political beliefs, have the right to be treated the same under the law. The Fourteenth Amendment requires every state to grant its citizens "equal protection of the laws."

Basic Freedoms The basic freedoms involve the liberties outlined in the First Amendment—freedom of speech, freedom of religion, freedom of the press, freedom of assembly, and the right to petition. In a democratic society, power exists in the hands of the people. Therefore, its citizens must be free to exchange ideas freely.

The First Amendment allows citizens to criticize the government, in speech or in the press, without fear of punishment. It also states that the government cannot endorse a religion, nor can it prohibit citizens from practicing a religion if they choose to do so. In addition, the Ninth Amendment states that the rights of Americans are not limited to those mentioned in the Constitution. This has allowed basic freedoms to expand over the years through the passage of other amendments and laws. The Twenty-sixth Amendment, for example, extends the right to vote to American citizens 18 years of age.

Limits on Rights Our rights are not unlimited. The government can establish laws or rules to restrict certain standards to protect the health, safety, security, and moral standards of a community. Moreover, rights may be limited to prevent one person's rights from interfering with the rights of others. The restrictions of rights, however, must be reasonable and must apply to everyone equally.

✓ **Reading Check** Summarizing What is due process of law?

Citizen Participation

A citizen is a person who owes loyalty to and is entitled to the protection of a state or nation. How do you become an American citizen? Generally, citizenship is granted to anyone born within the borders of the United States. Citizenship is also granted to anyone born outside the United States if one parent is a United States citizen. A person of foreign birth can also become a citizen through the process of naturalization.

To qualify, applicants must be at least 18 years old. They must have been lawfully admitted for permanent residence and have lived in the United States for at least five years. They must possess good moral character and accept the principles of the Constitution. Applicants must also understand English and demonstrate an understanding of the history and principles of the government of the United States. Before being admitted to citizenship, applicants must be willing to give up any foreign allegiance and must promise to obey the Constitution and the laws of the United States.

As citizens of the United States, we are expected to carry out certain duties and responsibilities. **Duties** are things we are required to do by law. **Responsibilities** are things we should do. Fulfilling both our duties and our responsibilities helps ensure that we have a good government and that we continue to enjoy our rights.

Duties One of the duties of all Americans is to obey the law. Laws serve three important functions. They help maintain order; they protect the health, safety, and property of all citizens; and they make it possible for people to live together peacefully. If you disobey laws, for example, you endanger others and interfere with the smooth functioning of society. If you believe a law needs to be changed, you can work through your elected representatives to improve it.

Americans also have a duty to pay taxes. The government uses tax money to defend the nation, provide health insurance for people over 65, and build roads and bridges. Americans benefit from services provided by the government.

Flag Etiquette

★ The flag should be raised and lowered by hand and displayed only from sunrise to sunset. On special occasions, it may be displayed at night.

★ The flag may be displayed on all days, weather permitting, particularly on national and state holidays and on historic and special occasions.

★ No flag should be flown above the American flag or to the right of it at the same height.

★ The flag may be flown at half-mast to mourn the death of public officials.

★ The flag should never touch the ground or floor beneath it.

★ The flag may be flown upside down only to signal distress.

★ When the flag becomes old and tattered, it should be destroyed by burning. According to an approved custom, the Union (the white stars on the blue field) is first cut from the flag; then the two pieces, which no longer form a flag, are burned.

Another duty of citizens is to defend the nation. All males aged 18 and older must register with the government in case they are needed for military service. The nation no longer has a **draft,** or required military service, but a war could make the draft necessary again.

The Constitution guarantees all Americans the right to a trial by a jury of their peers (equals). For this reason you should be prepared to serve on a jury when you become eligible at the age of 18. Having a large group of jurors on hand is necessary to guarantee the right to a fair and speedy trial. You also have a duty to serve as a witness at a trial if called to do so.

Responsibilities The responsibilities of citizens are not as clear-cut as their duties. Because responsibilities are voluntary, people are not arrested or punished if they do not fulfill these obligations. The quality of our government and of our lives will diminish, however, if our responsibilities are not carried out.

Keep in mind that government exists to serve you. Therefore, one of your responsibilities as a citizen is to know what the government is doing and to voice your opinion when you feel strongly about something the government has done or has failed to do. When the government learns that most people favor or oppose an action, it usually follows their wishes.

You also need to be informed about your rights and to exercise them when necessary. Knowing your rights helps preserve them. Other responsibilities include respecting diversity, accepting responsibility for your actions, and supporting your family.

Citizens taking part in a town meeting

Vote, Vote, Vote! Perhaps your most important responsibility as an American citizen will be to vote when you reach the age of 18. Voting allows you to participate in government and guide its direction. When you vote for people to represent you in government, you will be exercising your right of self-government. If you disapprove of the job your representatives are doing, it will be your responsibility to help elect other people in the next election. You can also let your representatives know how you feel about issues through letters, telephone calls, and petitions.

While not everyone holds public office, everyone can participate in government in other ways. Working on a political campaign, volunteering

to help in a hospital or a library, and participating in a local park cleanup are all ways to take responsibility and to make a contribution to good government and a well-run community.

Respecting Others' Rights To enjoy your rights to the fullest, you must be prepared to respect the rights of others. Respecting the rights of others also means respecting the rights of people with whom you disagree. Respecting and accepting others regardless of race, religion, beliefs, or other differences is essential in a democracy. All Americans are entitled to the same respect and good treatment.

✓ **Reading Check** **Identifying** What is naturalization?

SECTION 3 ASSESSMENT

Checking for Understanding

1. **Key Terms** Use each of these terms in a complete sentence that helps explain its meaning: due process of law, citizen, naturalization.

2. **Reviewing Facts** Why are personal responsibilities important?

Reviewing Themes

3. **Government and Democracy** Summarize three of the freedoms granted in the First Amendment.

Critical Thinking

4. **Analyzing Information** The Fifth Amendment states that people have the right of "due process of law." Why is this phrase important?

5. **Analyzing Information** Re-create the diagram below and provide the three categories of American rights.

```
        Rights
       /   |   \
      O    O    O
```

Analyzing Visuals

6. **Analyzing a Chart** Refer to the chart on page 229. For what reason may the flag be flown at half-mast?

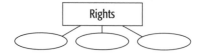

Civics One responsibility of being an American citizen is to become involved in the democratic system. Make a poster showing how students can get involved in their community's democracy. Display your poster in a prominent place in school.

Handbook Assessment

✓ Reviewing Key Terms

Write the key term that completes each sentence. Then write a sentence for each term not chosen.

a. popular sovereignty

b. enumerated powers

c. reserved powers

d. amendment

e. implied powers

f. judicial review

1. A(n)_____ is a change to the Constitution.

2. Those powers that are suggested but not directly stated in the Constitution are called _____.

3. _____ is the Supreme Court's power to review all congressional acts and executive actions.

4. Those powers mentioned specifically in the Constitution are called _____.

✓ Reviewing Key Facts

5. List the six goals of government stated in the Preamble.

6. How does one become a naturalized citizen?

7. Explain why the amendment process is so difficult.

8. Explain why responsible citizenship is important. Provide examples of responsible citizenship.

9. How does the Constitution protect individual rights?

10. Summarize the basic freedoms outlined in the First Amendment.

✓ Critical Thinking

11. **Analyzing Information** Analyze how limited government, republicanism, and popular sovereignty are important parts of the Constitution.

12. **Identifying Options** Describe five possible ways a person can fulfill his or her responsibilities in society and at home.

13. **Comparing** Some people argue that there should be a limit on the number of terms a senator or representative can serve. What are some of the advantages of the present system, which does not limit these terms? What are some of the disadvantages?

14. **Predicting Consequences** Re-create the diagram below and predict what might have happened to the U.S. if the Framers had not provided for a system of checks and balances.

✓ Citizenship Cooperative Activity

15. **Examining Citizens' Rights** Working with a partner, choose one of the following rights and trace its historical development in the United States from the time the Constitution was ratified to the present:

   suffrage

   freedom of religion

   freedom of speech

   equal protection of law

16. **Civic Planning** Constitutions provide a plan for organizing and operating governments. What plan provides the rules for your local government? Contact a local government official to find out about the basic plan of your city or town. Share your findings with the class.

✓ Alternative Assessment

17. **Portfolio Writing Activity** Part of your responsibility as an American citizen is to be informed about what the government is doing and to voice your opinion about its actions. Compose a letter to the editor of your local newspaper. In your letter, express your opinion about an issue in your community.

Standardized Test Practice

Directions: Choose the *best* answer to the following question.

Under the Constitution, the president chooses judges to serve on the Supreme Court, but each choice must be approved by the Senate. This is an example of what principle of government?

A Checks and balances

B Federalism

C Separation of powers

D Judicial Review

Test-Taking Tip:

What do you think would happen if the president could choose all judges without anyone else's approval? The writers of the Constitution wanted to make sure that none of the three branches of government became too powerful. Which answer shows this idea?

The Constitution of the United States

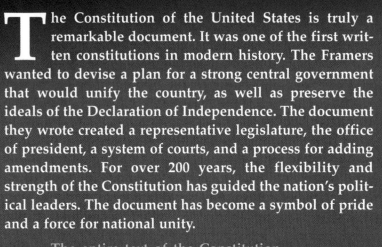

The Constitution of the United States is truly a remarkable document. It was one of the first written constitutions in modern history. The Framers wanted to devise a plan for a strong central government that would unify the country, as well as preserve the ideals of the Declaration of Independence. The document they wrote created a representative legislature, the office of president, a system of courts, and a process for adding amendments. For over 200 years, the flexibility and strength of the Constitution has guided the nation's political leaders. The document has become a symbol of pride and a force for national unity.

The entire text of the Constitution and its amendments follows. Those passages that have been set aside, outdated by the passage of time, or changed by the adoption of amendments are printed in blue. Also included are explanatory notes that will help clarify the meaning of each article and section.

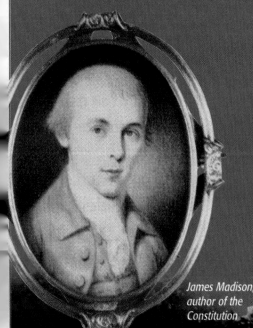

James Madison, author of the Constitution

Preamble

We the People of the United States, in Order to form a more perfect Union, establish Justice, insure domestic Tranquility, provide for the common defence, promote the general Welfare, and secure the Blessings of Liberty to ourselves and our Posterity, do ordain and establish this Constitution for the United States of America.

The Preamble introduces the Constitution and sets forth the general purposes for which the government was established. The Preamble also declares that the power of the government comes from the people.

The printed text of the document shows the spelling and punctuation of the parchment original.

Article I

Section 1

All legislative Powers herein granted shall be vested in a Congress of the United States, which shall consist of a Senate and House of Representatives.

Section 2

[1.] The House of Representatives shall be composed of Members chosen every second Year by the People of the several States, and the Electors in each State shall have the Qualifications requisite for Electors of the most numerous Branch of the State Legislature.

[2.] No person shall be a Representative who shall not have attained to the Age of twenty five Years, and been seven Years a Citizen of the United States, and who shall not, when elected, be an Inhabitant of that State in which he shall be chosen.

[3.] Representatives and direct Taxes shall be apportioned among the several States which may be included within this Union, according to their respective Numbers, which shall be determined by adding to the whole Number of free Persons, including those bound to Service for a Term of Years, and excluding Indians not taxed, three fifths of all other Persons. The actual Enumeration shall be made within three Years after the first Meeting of the Congress of the United States, and within every subsequent Term of ten Years, in such Manner as they shall by Law direct. The Number of Representatives shall not exceed one for every thirty Thousand, but each State shall have at Least one Representative; and until such enumeration shall be made, the State of New Hampshire shall be entitled to chuse three; Massachusetts eight, Rhode-Island and Providence Plantations one, Connecticut five, New-York six, New Jersey four, Pennsylvania eight, Delaware one, Maryland six, Virginia ten, North Carolina five, South Carolina five, and Georgia three.

[4.] When vacancies happen in the Representation from any State, the Executive Authority thereof shall issue Writs of Election to fill such Vacancies.

[5.] The House of Representatives shall chuse their Speaker and other Officers; and shall have the sole Power of Impeachment.

Article I. The Legislative Branch

The Constitution contains seven divisions called articles. Each article covers a general topic. For example, Articles I, II, and III create the three branches of the national government—the legislative, executive, and judicial branches. Most of the articles are divided into sections.

Section 2. House of Representatives

Division of Representatives Among the States The number of representatives from each state is based on the size of the state's population. Each state is entitled to at least one representative. *What are the qualifications for members of the House of Representatives?*

Vocabulary

preamble: *introduction*
constitution: *principles and laws of a nation*
enumeration: *census or population count*
impeachment: *bringing charges against an official*

Section 3. The Senate

Number of Members, Terms of Office, and Voting Procedure Originally, senators were chosen by the state legislators of their own states. The Seventeenth Amendment changed this, so that senators are now elected by the people. There are 100 senators, 2 from each state. The vice president serves as president of the Senate.

John Adams, the first vice president

Section 3. The Senate

Trial of Impeachment One of Congress's powers is the power to impeach—to accuse government officials of wrongdoing, put them on trial, and if necessary remove them from office. *Which body has the power to decide the official's guilt or innocence?*

Vocabulary

president pro tempore: *presiding officer of Senate who serves when the vice president is absent*
indictment: *charging a person with an offense*
quorum: *minimum number of members that must be present to conduct sessions*
adjourn: *to suspend a session*
immunity privilege: *members cannot be sued or prosecuted for anything they say in Congress*
emoluments: *salaries*
bill: *draft of a proposed law*
revenue: *income raised by government*

Section 3

[1.] The Senate of the United States shall be composed of two Senators from each State, chosen by the Legislature thereof, for six Years; and each Senator shall have one Vote.

[2.] Immediately after they shall be assembled in Consequence of the first Election, they shall be divided as equally as may be into three Classes. The Seats of the Senators of the first Class shall be vacated at the Expiration of the second Year, of the second Class at the Expiration of the fourth Year, and of the third Class at the Expiration of the sixth Year, so that one third may be chosen every second Year; and if Vacancies happen by Resignation, or otherwise, during the Recess of the Legislature of any State, the Executive thereof may make temporary Appointments until the next Meeting of the Legislature, which shall then fill such Vacancies.

[3.] No Person shall be a Senator who shall not have attained to the Age of thirty Years, and been nine Years a Citizen of the United States, and who shall not, when elected, be an Inhabitant of that State for which he shall be chosen.

[4.] The Vice President of the United States shall be President of the Senate, but shall have no Vote, unless they be equally divided.

[5.] The Senate shall chuse their other Officers, and also a President pro tempore, in the Absence of the Vice President, or when he shall exercise the Office of the President of the United States.

[6.] The Senate shall have the sole Power to try all Impeachments. When sitting for that Purpose, they shall be on Oath or Affirmation. When the President of the United States is tried, the Chief Justice shall preside: And no Person shall be convicted without the Concurrence of two thirds of the Members present.

[7.] Judgment in Cases of Impeachment shall not extend further than to removal from Office, and disqualification to hold and enjoy any Office of honor, Trust or Profit under the United States: but the Party convicted shall nevertheless be liable and subject to Indictment, Trial, Judgment and Punishment, according to Law.

Section 4

[1.] The Times, Places and Manner of holding Elections for Senators and Representatives, shall be prescribed in each State by the Legislature thereof; but the Congress may at any time by Law make or alter such Regulations, except as to the Places of chusing Senators.

[2.] The Congress shall assemble at least once in every Year, and such Meeting shall be on the first Monday in December, unless they shall by Law appoint a different Day.

Section 5

[1.] Each House shall be the Judge of the Elections, Returns and Qualifications of its own Members, and a Majority of each shall constitute a Quorum to do Business; but a smaller Number may adjourn from day to day, and may be authorized to compel the Attendance of absent Members, in such Manner, and under such Penalties as each House may provide.

[2.] Each House may determine the Rules of its Proceedings, punish its Members for disorderly Behaviour, and, with the Concurrence of two thirds, expel a Member.

[3.] Each House shall keep a Journal of its Proceedings, and from time to time publish the same, excepting such Parts as may in their Judgment require Secrecy; and the Yeas and Nays of the Members of either House on any question shall, at the Desire of one fifth of those Present, be entered on the Journal.

[4.] Neither House, during the Session of Congress, shall, without the Consent of the other, adjourn for more than three days, nor to any other Place than that in which the two Houses shall be sitting.

Senate gavel

Section 6

[1.] The Senators and Representatives shall receive a Compensation for their Services, to be ascertained by Law, and paid out of the Treasury of the United States. They shall in all Cases, except Treason, Felony and Breach of the Peace, be privileged from Arrest during their Attendance at the Session of their respective Houses, and in going to and returning from the same; and for any Speech or Debate in either House, they shall not be questioned in any other Place.

[2.] No Senator or Representative shall, during the Time for which he was elected, be appointed to any civil Office under the Authority of the United States, which shall have been created, or the Emoluments whereof shall have been encreased during such time; and no Person holding any Office under the United States, shall be a Member of either House during his Continuance in Office.

Section 6. Privileges and Restrictions

Pay and Privileges To strengthen the federal government, the Founders set congressional salaries to be paid by the United States Treasury rather than by members' respective states. Originally, members were paid $6 per day. In 2002, all members of Congress received a base salary of $150,000.

Section 7

[1.] All Bills for raising Revenue shall originate in the House of Representatives; but the Senate may propose or concur with Amendments as on other Bills.

[2.] Every Bill which shall have passed the House of Representatives and the Senate, shall, before it become a Law, be presented to the President of the United States; If he approve he shall sign it, but if not he shall return it, with his Objections to that House in which it shall have originated, who shall enter the Objections at large on their Journal, and proceed to reconsider it. If after such Reconsideration two thirds of that House shall agree to pass the Bill, it shall be sent, together with the Objections, to the other House, by which it shall likewise be reconsidered, and if approved by two thirds

Section 7. Passing Laws

Revenue Bills All tax laws must originate in the House of Representatives. This ensures that the branch of Congress that is elected by the people every two years has the major role in determining taxes.

Section 7. Passing Laws

How Bills Become Laws A bill may become a law only by passing both houses of Congress and by being signed by the president. The president can check Congress by rejecting—vetoing—its legislation. *How can Congress override the president's veto?*

of that House, it shall become a Law. But in all such Cases the Votes of both Houses shall be determined by yeas and Nays, and the Names of the Persons voting for and against the Bill shall be entered on the Journal of each House respectively. If any Bill shall not be returned by the President within ten Days (Sundays excepted) after it shall have been presented to him, the Same shall be a Law, in like Manner as if he had signed it, unless the Congress by their Adjournment prevent its Return, in which Case it shall not be a Law.

[3.] Every Order, Resolution, or Vote to which the Concurrence of the Senate and House of Representatives may be necessary (except on a question of Adjournment) shall be presented to the President of the United States; and before the Same shall take Effect, shall be approved by him, or being disapproved by him, shall be repassed by two thirds of the Senate and House of Representatives, according to the Rules and Limitations prescribed in the Case of a Bill.

Section 8

[1.] The Congress shall have the Power To lay and collect Taxes, Duties, Imposts and Excises, to pay the Debts and provide for the common Defence and general Welfare of the United States; but all Duties, Imposts and Excises shall be uniform throughout the United States;

[2.] To borrow Money on the credit of the United States;

[3.] To regulate Commerce with foreign Nations, and among the several States, and with the Indian Tribes;

[4.] To establish an uniform Rule of Naturalization, and uniform Laws on the subject of Bankruptcies throughout the United States;

[5.] To coin Money, regulate the Value thereof, and of foreign Coin, and fix the Standard of Weights and Measures;

[6.] To provide for the Punishment of counterfeiting the Securities and current Coin of the United States;

[7.] To establish Post Offices and post Roads;

[8.] To promote the Progress of Science and useful Arts, by securing for limited Times to Authors and Inventors the exclusive Right to their respective Writings and Discoveries;

[9.] To constitute Tribunals inferior to the supreme Court;

[10.] To define and punish Piracies and Felonies committed on the high Seas, and Offences against the Law of Nations;

[11.] To declare War, grant Letters of Marque and Reprisal, and make Rules concerning Captures on Land and Water;

Section 8. Powers Granted to Congress

Expressed Powers Expressed powers are those powers directly stated in the Constitution. Most of the expressed powers of Congress are listed in Article I, Section 8. These powers are also called enumerated powers because they are numbered 1–18. *Which clause gives Congress the power to declare war?*

Civil War money

Vocabulary

resolution: *legislature's formal expression of opinion*

naturalization: *procedure by which a citizen of a foreign nation becomes a citizen of the United States*

tribunal: *a court*

letter of marque: *authority given to a citizen to outfit an armed ship and use it to attack enemy ships in time of war*

reprisal: *taking by force property or territory belonging to another country or to its citizens*

insurrection: *rebellion*

[12.] To raise and support Armies, but no Appropriation of Money to that Use shall be for a longer Term than two Years;

[13.] To provide and maintain a Navy;

[14.] To make Rules for the Government and Regulation of the land and naval Forces;

[15.] To provide for calling forth the Militia to execute the Laws of the Union, suppress Insurrections and repel Invasions;

[16.] To provide for organizing, arming, and disciplining, the Militia, and for governing such Part of them as may be employed in the Service of the United States, reserving to the States respectively, the Appointment of the Officers, and the Authority of training the Militia according to the discipline prescribed by Congress;

[17.] To exercise exclusive Legislation in all Cases whatsoever, over such District (not exceeding ten Miles square) as may, by Cession of particular States, and the Acceptance of Congress, become the Seat of Government of the United States, and to exercise like Authority over all Places purchased by the Consent of the Legislature of the State in which the Same shall be, for the Erection of Forts, Magazines, Arsenals, dock-Yards, and other needful Buildings;—And

[18.] To make all Laws which shall be necessary and proper for carrying into Execution the foregoing Powers, and all other Powers vested by this Constitution in the Government of the United States, or in any Department or Officer thereof.

Section 9

[1]. The Migration or Importation of such Persons as any of the States now existing shall think proper to admit, shall not be prohibited by the Congress prior to the Year one thousand eight hundred and eight, but a Tax or duty may be imposed on such Importation, not exceeding ten dollars for each Person.

[2.] The Privilege of the Writ of Habeas Corpus shall not be suspended, unless when in Cases of Rebellion or Invasion the public Safety may require it.

[3.] No Bill of Attainder or ex post facto Law shall be passed.

[4.] No Capitation, or other direct, Tax shall be laid, unless in Proportion to the Census or Enumeration herein before directed to be taken.

[5.] No Tax or Duty shall be laid on Articles exported from any State.

[6.] No Preference shall be given by any Regulation of Commerce or Revenue to the Ports of one State over those of another: nor shall Vessels bound to, or from, one State, be obliged to enter, clear, or pay Duties in another.

Seal of the U.S. Navy

Section 8. Powers Granted to Congress

Elastic Clause The final enumerated power is often called the "elastic clause." This clause gives Congress the right to make all laws "necessary and proper" to carry out the powers expressed in the other clauses of Article I. It is called the elastic clause because it lets Congress "stretch" its powers to meet situations the Founders could never have anticipated.

What does the phrase "necessary and proper" in the elastic clause mean? Almost from the beginning, this phrase was a subject of dispute. The issue was whether a strict or a broad interpretation of the Constitution should be applied. The dispute was first addressed in 1819, in the case of *McCulloch* v. *Maryland*, when the Supreme Court ruled in favor of a broad interpretation.

Section 9. Powers Denied to the Federal Government

Habeas Corpus A writ of habeas corpus issued by a judge requires a law official to bring a prisoner to court and show cause for holding the prisoner. A bill of attainder is a bill that punished a person without a jury trial. An "ex post facto" law is one that makes an act a crime after the act has been committed. *What does the Constitution say about bills of attainder?*

[7.] No Money shall be drawn from the Treasury, but in Consequence of Appropriations made by Law; and a regular Statement and Account of the Receipts and Expenditures of all public Money shall be published from time to time.

[8.] No Title of Nobility shall be granted by the United States: And no Person holding any Office of Profit or Trust under them, shall, without the Consent of the Congress, accept of any present, Emolument, Office, or Title, of any kind whatever, from any King, Prince, or foreign State.

Section 10. Powers Denied to the States

Limitations on Power Section 10 lists limits on the states. These restrictions were designed, in part, to prevent an overlapping in functions and authority with the federal government.

Section 10

[1.] No State shall enter into any Treaty, Alliance, or Confederation; grant Letters of Marque and Reprisal; coin Money; emit Bills of Credit; make any Thing but gold and silver Coin a Tender in Payment of Debts; pass any Bill of Attainder, ex post facto Law, or Law impairing the Obligation of Contracts, or grant any Title of Nobility.

[2.] No State shall, without the Consent of the Congress, lay any Imposts or Duties on Imports or Exports, except what may be absolutely necessary for executing it's inspection Laws: and the net Produce of all Duties and Imposts, laid by any State on Imports and Exports, shall be for the Use of the Treasury of the United States; and all such Laws shall be subject to the Revision and Controul of the Congress.

[3.] No State shall, without the Consent of Congress, lay any Duty of Tonnage, keep Troops, or Ships of War in time of Peace, enter into any Agreement or Compact with another State, or with a foreign Power, or engage in War, unless actually invaded, or in such imminent Danger as will not admit of delay.

United States coins

Article II. The Executive Branch

Article II creates an executive branch to carry out laws passed by Congress. Article II lists the powers and duties of the presidency, describes qualifications for office and procedures for electing the president, and provides for a vice president.

Article II

Section 1

[1.] The executive Power shall be vested in a President of the United States of America. He shall hold his Office during the Term of four Years, and, together with the Vice President, chosen for the same Term, be elected, as follows

[2.] Each State shall appoint, in such Manner as the Legislature thereof may direct, a Number of Electors, equal to the whole Number of Senators and Representatives to which the State may be entitled in the Congress: but no Senator or Representative, or Person holding an Office of Trust or Profit under the United States, shall be appointed an Elector.

[3.] The Electors shall meet in their respective States, and vote by Ballot for two Persons, of whom one at least shall not be an Inhabitant of the same State with

Vocabulary

appropriations: *funds set aside for a specific use*
emolument: *payment*
impost: *tax*
duty: *tax*

themselves. And they shall make a List of all the Persons voted for, and of the Number of Votes for each; which List they shall sign and certify, and transmit sealed to the Seat of the Government of the United States, directed to the President of the Senate. The President of the Senate shall, in the Presence of the Senate and House of Representatives, open all the Certificates, and the Votes shall then be counted. The Person having the greatest Number of Votes shall be the President, if such Number be a Majority of the whole Number of Electors appointed; and if there be more than one who have such Majority, and have an equal Number of Votes, then the House of Representatives shall immediately chuse by Ballot one of them for President; and if no person have a Majority, then from the five highest on the List the said House shall in like Manner chuse the President. But in chusing the President, the Votes shall be taken by States, the Representation from each State having one Vote; A quorum for this Purpose shall consist of a Member or Members from two thirds of the States, and a Majority of all the States shall be necessary to a Choice. In every Case, after the Choice of the President, the Person having the greatest Number of Votes of the Electors shall be the Vice President. But if there should remain two or more who have equal Votes, the Senate shall chuse from them by Ballot the Vice President.

[4.] The Congress may determine the Time of chusing the Electors, and the Day on which they shall give their Votes; which Day shall be the same throughout the United States.

[5.] No Person except a natural born Citizen, or a Citizen of the United States, at the time of the Adoption of this Constitution, shall be eligible to the Office of President; neither shall any Person be eligible to that Office who shall not have attained to the Age of thirty five Years, and been fourteen Years a Resident within the United States.

[6.] In Case of the Removal of the President from Office, or of his Death, Resignation, or Inability to discharge the Powers and Duties of the said Office, the Same shall devolve on the Vice President, and the Congress may by Law provide for the Case of Removal, Death, Resignation or Inability, both of the President and Vice President, declaring what Officer shall then act as President, and such Officer shall act accordingly, until the Disability be removed, or a President shall be elected.

[7.] The President shall, at stated Times, receive for his Services, a Compensation, which shall neither be increased nor diminished during the Period for which he shall have been elected, and he shall not receive within that Period any other Emolument from the United States, or any of them.

[8.] Before he enter on the Execution of his Office, he shall take the following Oath or Affirmation:—"I do solemnly swear (or affirm) that I will faithfully execute the Office of President of the United States, and will to the best of my Ability, preserve, protect and defend the Constitution of the United States."

Section 1. President and Vice President

Former Method of Election The Twelfth Amendment, added in 1804, changed the method of electing the president stated in Article II, Section 1, paragraph 3. The Twelfth Amendment requires that the electors cast separate ballots for president and vice president.

George Washington, the first president

Section 1. President and Vice President

Qualifications The president must be a citizen of the United States by birth, at least 35 years of age, and a resident of the United States for 14 years.

Section 1. President and Vice President

Vacancies If the president dies, resigns, is removed from office by impeachment, or is unable to carry out the duties of the office, the vice president assumes the duties of the president. The Twenty-Fifth Amendment sets procedures for presidential succession.

Section 1. President and Vice President

Salary Originally, the president's salary was $25,000 per year. The president's current salary is $400,000 plus a $50,000 nontaxable expense account per year. The president also receives living accommodations in two residences—the White House and Camp David.

Section 2. Powers of the President

Military, Cabinet, Pardons Mention of "the principal officer in each of the executive departments" is the only suggestion of the president's cabinet to be found in the Constitution. The cabinet is an advisory body, and its power depends on the president. Section 2, Clause 1 also makes the president—a civilian—the head of the armed services. This established the principle of civilian control of the military.

Section 2. Powers of the President

Treaties and Appointments An executive order is a command issued by a president to exercise a power which he has been given by the U.S. Constitution or by a federal statute. In times of emergency, presidents sometimes have used the executive order to override the Constitution of the United States and the Congress. During the Civil War, President Lincoln suspended many fundamental rights guaranteed in the Constitution and the Bill of Rights. He closed down newspapers that opposed his policies and imprisoned some who disagreed with him. Lincoln said that these actions were justified to preserve the Union.

Impeachment ticket

Article III. The Judicial Branch

The term *judicial* refers to courts. The Constitution set up only the Supreme Court but provided for the establishment of other federal courts. The judiciary of the United States has two different systems of courts. One system consists of the federal courts, whose powers derive from the Constitution and federal laws. The other includes the courts of each of the 50 states, whose powers derive from state constitutions and laws.

Section 2

[1.] The President shall be Commander in Chief of the Army and Navy of the United States, and of the Militia of the several States, when called into the actual Service of the United States; he may require the Opinion, in writing, of the principal Officer in each of the executive Departments, upon any Subject relating to the Duties of their respective Offices, and he shall have Power to grant Reprieves and Pardons for Offences against the United States, except in Cases of Impeachment.

[2.] He shall have Power, by and with the Advice and Consent of the Senate, to make Treaties, provided two thirds of the Senators present concur; and he shall nominate, and by and with the Advice and Consent of the Senate, shall appoint Ambassadors, other public Ministers and Consuls, Judges of the supreme Court, and all other Officers of the United States, whose Appointments are not herein otherwise provided for, and which shall be established by Law: but the Congress may by Law vest the Appointment of such inferior Officers, as they think proper, in the President alone, in the Courts of Law, or in the Heads of Departments.

[3.] The President shall have Power to fill up all Vacancies that may happen during the Recess of the Senate, by granting Commissions which shall expire at the End of their next Session.

Section 3

He shall from time to time give to the Congress Information of the State of the Union, and recommend to their Consideration such Measures as he shall judge necessary and expedient; he may, on extraordinary Occasions, convene both Houses, or either of them, and in Case of Disagreement between them, with Respect to the Time of Adjournment, he may adjourn them to such Time as he shall think proper; he shall receive Ambassadors and other public Ministers; he shall take Care that the Laws be faithfully executed, and shall Commission all the Officers of the United States.

Section 4

The President, Vice President and all civil Officers of the United States, shall be removed from Office on Impeachment for, and Conviction of, Treason, Bribery, or other high Crimes and Misdemeanors.

Article III

Section 1

The judicial Power of the United States, shall be vested in one supreme Court, and in such inferior Courts as the Congress may from time to time ordain and establish. The Judges, both of the supreme and inferior Courts, shall hold their Offices during good Behaviour, and shall, at stated Times, receive for their Services, a Compensation, which shall not be diminished during their Continuance in Office.

Section 2

[1.] The judicial Power shall extend to all Cases, in Law and Equity, arising under this Constitution, the Laws of the United States, and Treaties made, or which shall be made, under their Authority;—to all Cases affecting Ambassadors, other public Ministers and Consuls;—to all Cases of admiralty and maritime Jurisdiction;—to Controversies to which the United States shall be a Party;—to Controversies between two or more States;—between a State and Citizens of another State;—between Citizens of different States,—between Citizens of the same State claiming Lands under Grants of different States, and between a State, or the Citizens thereof, and foreign States, Citizens or Subjects.

[2.] In all Cases affecting Ambassadors, other public Ministers and Consuls, and those in which a State shall be Party, the supreme Court shall have original Jurisdiction. In all the other Cases before mentioned, the supreme Court shall have appellate Jurisdiction, both as to Law and Fact, with such Exceptions, and under such Regulations as the Congress shall make.

[3.] The Trial of all Crimes, except in Cases of Impeachment, shall be by Jury; and such Trial shall be held in the State where the said Crimes shall have been committed; but when not committed within any State, the Trial shall be at such Place or Places as the Congress may by Law have directed.

Section 3

[1.] Treason against the United States, shall consist only in levying War against them, or in adhering to their Enemies, giving them Aid and Comfort. No Person shall be convicted of Treason unless on the Testimony of two Witnesses to the same overt Act, or on Confession in open Court.

[2.] The Congress shall have Power to declare the Punishment of Treason, but no Attainder of Treason shall work Corruption of Blood, or Forfeiture except during the Life of the Person attainted.

Article IV

Section 1

Full Faith and Credit shall be given in each State to the public Acts, Records, and judicial Proceedings of every other State. And the Congress may by general Laws prescribe the Manner in which such Acts, Records and Proceedings shall be proved, and the Effect thereof.

Section 2. Jurisdiction
Statute Law Federal courts deal mostly with "statute law," or laws passed by Congress, treaties, and cases involving the Constitution itself.

Section 2. Jurisdiction
The Supreme Court A Court with "original jurisdiction" has the authority to be the first court to hear a case. The Supreme Court primarily has "appellate jurisdiction" and mostly hears cases appealed from lower courts.

Article IV. Relations Among the States

Article IV explains the relationship of the states to one another and to the national government. This article requires each state to give citizens of other states the same rights as its own citizens, addresses admitting new states, and guarantees that the national government will protect the states.

Vocabulary

original jurisdiction: *authority to be the first court to hear a case*

appellate jurisdiction: *authority to hear cases that have been appealed from lower courts*

treason: *violation of the allegiance owed by a person to his or her own country, for example, by aiding an enemy*

Section 3. New States and Territories

New States Congress has the power to admit new states. It also determines the basic guidelines for applying for statehood. Two states, Maine and West Virginia, were created within the boundaries of another state. In the case of West Virginia, President Lincoln recognized the West Virginia government as the legal government of Virginia during the Civil War. This allowed West Virginia to secede from Virginia without obtaining approval from the Virginia legislature.

Section 4. Federal Protection for States

Republic Government can be classified in many different ways. The ancient Greek philosopher Aristotle classified government based on the question: Who governs? According to Aristotle, all governments belong to one of three major groups: (1) autocracy—rule by one person; (2) oligarchy—rule by a few persons; or (3) democracy—rule by many persons. A republic is a form of democracy in which the people elect representatives to make laws and conduct government.

Article V. The Amendment Process

Article V spells out the ways that the Constitution can be amended, or changed. All of the 27 amendments were proposed by a two-thirds vote of both houses of Congress. Only the Twenty-first Amendment was ratified by constitutional conventions of the states. All other amendments have been ratified by state legislatures. *What is an amendment?*

Vocabulary

extradition: *surrender of a criminal to another authority*
amendment: *a change to the Constitution*
ratification: *process by which an amendment is approved*

Section 2

[1.] The Citizens of each State shall be entitled to all Privileges and Immunities of Citizens in the several States.

[2.] A Person charged in any State with Treason, Felony, or other Crime, who shall flee from Justice, and be found in another State, shall on Demand of the executive Authority of the State from which he fled, be delivered up, to be removed to the State having Jurisdiction of the Crime.

[3.] No Person held to Service of Labour in one State, under the Laws thereof, escaping into another, shall, in Consequence of any Law or Regulation therein, be discharged from such Service or Labour, but shall be delivered up on Claim of the Party to whom such Service or Labour may be due.

Section 3

[1.] New States may be admitted by the Congress into this Union; but no new State shall be formed or erected within the Jurisdiction of any other State; nor any State be formed by the Junction of two or more States, or Parts of States, without the Consent of the Legislatures of the States concerned as well as of the Congress.

[2.] The Congress shall have Power to dispose of and make all needful Rules and Regulations respecting the Territory or other Property belonging to the United States; and nothing in this Constitution shall be so construed as to Prejudice any Claims of the United States, or of any particular State.

Section 4

The United States shall guarantee to every State in this Union a Republican Form of Government, and shall protect each of them against Invasion; and on Application of the Legislature, or of the Executive (when the Legislature cannot be convened) against domestic Violence.

Article V

The Congress, whenever two thirds of both Houses shall deem it necessary, shall propose Amendments to this Constitution, or, on the Application of the Legislatures of two thirds of the several States, shall call a Convention for proposing Amendments, which, in either Case, shall be valid to all Intents and Purposes, as Part of this Constitution, when ratified by the Legislatures of three fourths of the several States, or by Conventions in three fourths thereof, as the one or the other Mode of Ratification may be proposed by the Congress; Provided that no Amendment which may be made prior to the Year One thousand eight hundred and eight shall in any Manner affect the first and fourth Clauses in the Ninth Section of the first Article; and that no State, without its Consent, shall be deprived of its equal Suffrage in the Senate.

Article VI

[1.] All Debts contracted and Engagements entered into, before the Adoption of this Constitution, shall be as valid against the United States under this Constitution, as under the Confederation.

[2.] This Constitution, and the Laws of the United States which shall be made in Pursuance thereof; and all Treaties made, or which shall be made, under the Authority of the United States, shall be the supreme Law of the Land; and the Judges in every State shall be bound thereby, any Thing in the Constitution or Laws of any State to the Contrary notwithstanding.

[3.] The Senators and Representatives before mentioned, and the Members of the several State Legislatures, and all executive and judicial Officers, both of the United States and of the several States, shall be bound by Oath or Affirmation, to support this Constitution; but no religious Test shall ever be required as a Qualification to any Office or public Trust under the United States.

Article VII

The Ratification of the Conventions of nine States, shall be sufficient for the Establishment of this Constitution between the States so ratifying the Same.

Done in Convention by the Unanimous Consent of the States present the Seventeenth Day of September in the Year of our Lord one thousand seven hundred and Eighty seven and of the Independence of the United States of America the Twelfth. In witness whereof We have hereunto subscribed our Names,

Article VI. National Supremacy

Article VI contains the "supremacy clause." This clause establishes that the Constitution, laws passed by Congress, and treaties of the United States "shall be the supreme Law of the Land." The "supremacy clause" recognized the Constitution and federal laws as supreme when in conflict with those of the states.

Article VII. Ratification

Article VII addresses ratification and declares that the Constitution would take effect after it was ratified by nine states.

Signers

*George Washington, **President and Deputy from Virginia***

New Hampshire
John Langdon
Nicholas Gilman

Massachusetts
Nathaniel Gorham
Rufus King

Connecticut
William Samuel Johnson
Roger Sherman

New York
Alexander Hamilton

New Jersey
William Livingston
David Brearley
William Paterson
Jonathan Dayton

Pennsylvania
Benjamin Franklin
Thomas Mifflin
Robert Morris
George Clymer
Thomas FitzSimons
Jared Ingersoll
James Wilson
Gouverneur Morris

Delaware
George Read
Gunning Bedford, Jr.
John Dickinson
Richard Bassett
Jacob Broom

Maryland
James McHenry
Daniel of St. Thomas Jenifer
Daniel Carroll

Virginia
John Blair
James Madison, Jr.

North Carolina
William Blount
Richard Dobbs Spaight
Hugh Williamson

South Carolina
John Rutledge
Charles Cotesworth Pinckney
Charles Pinckney
Pierce Butler

Georgia
William Few
Abraham Baldwin

Attest: *William Jackson,*
Secretary

Bill of Rights

The first 10 amendments are known as the Bill of Rights (1791). These amendments limit the powers of government. The First Amendment protects the civil liberties of individuals in the United States. The amendment freedoms are not absolute, however. They are limited by the rights of other individuals. *What freedoms does the First Amendment protect?*

Amendment 2

Right to Bear Arms This amendment is often debated. Originally, it was intended to prevent the national government from repeating the actions of the British, who tried to take weapons away from the colonial militia, or armed forces of citizens. This amendment seems to support the right of citizens to own firearms, but the Supreme Court has ruled that it does not prevent Congress from regulating the interstate sale of weapons. *Why is the Second Amendment's meaning debated?*

Amendment 5

Rights of Accused Persons This amendment contains important protections for people accused of crimes. One of the protections is that government may not deprive any person of life, liberty, or property without due process of law. This means that the government must follow proper constitutional procedures in trials and in other actions it takes against individuals. *According to Amendment V, what is the function of a grand jury?*

Vocabulary

quarter: *to provide living accommodations*
probable cause: *police must have a reasonable basis to believe a person is linked to a crime*
warrant: *document that gives police particular rights or powers*
common law: *law established by previous court decisions*
bail: *money that an accused person provides to the court as a guarantee that he or she will be present for a trial*

Amendment I

Congress shall make no law respecting an establishment of religion, or prohibiting the free exercise thereof; or abridging the freedom of speech, or of the press; or the right of the people peaceably to assemble, and to petition the Government for a redress of grievances.

Amendment II

A well regulated Militia, being necessary to the security of a free State, the right of the people to keep and bear Arms, shall not be infringed.

Amendment III

No Soldier shall, in time of peace be quartered in any house, without the consent of the Owner, nor in time of war, but in a manner to be prescribed by law.

Amendment IV

The right of the people to be secure in their persons, houses, papers, and effects, against unreasonable searches and seizures, shall not be violated, and no Warrants shall issue, but upon probable cause, supported by Oath or affirmation, and particularly describing the place to be searched, and the persons or things to be seized.

Amendment V

No person shall be held to answer for a capital, or otherwise infamous crime, unless on a presentment or indictment of a Grand Jury, except in cases arising in the land or naval forces, or in the Militia, when in actual service in time of War or public danger; nor shall any person be subject for the same offence to be twice put in jeopardy of life or limb; nor shall be compelled in any criminal case to be a witness against himself, nor be deprived of life, liberty, or property, without due process of law; nor shall private property be taken for public use without just compensation.

Amendment VI

In all criminal prosecutions, the accused shall enjoy the right to a speedy and public trial, by an impartial jury of the State and district wherein the crime shall have been committed, which district shall have been previously ascertained by law, and to be informed of the nature and cause of the accusation; to be confronted with the witnesses against him; to have compulsory process for obtaining Witnesses in his favor, and to have the assistance of counsel for his defence.

Amendment VII

In Suits at common law, where the value in controversy shall exceed twenty dollars, the right of trial by jury shall be preserved, and no fact tried by a jury, shall be otherwise reexamined in any Court of the United States, than according to the rules of common law.

Amendment VIII

Excessive bail shall not be required, nor excessive fines imposed, nor cruel and unusual punishments inflicted.

Amendment IX

The enumeration in the Constitution, of certain rights, shall not be construed to deny or disparage others retained by the people.

Amendment X

The powers not delegated to the United States by the Constitution, nor prohibited by it to the States, are reserved to the States respectively, or to the people.

Amendment XI

The Judicial power of the United States shall not be construed to extend to any suit in law or equity, commenced or prosecuted against one of the United States by Citizens of another State, or by Citizens or Subjects of any Foreign State.

Amendment 6

Right to a Speedy, Fair Trial A basic protection is the right to a speedy, public trial. The jury must hear witnesses and evidence on both sides before deciding the guilt or innocence of a person charged with a crime. This amendment also provides that legal counsel must be provided to a defendant. In 1963, the Supreme Court ruled, in *Gideon* v. *Wainwright*, that if a defendant cannot afford a lawyer, the government must provide one to defend him or her. *Why is the right to a "speedy" trial important?*

Amendment 9

Powers Reserved to the People This amendment prevents government from claiming that the only rights people have are those listed in the Bill of Rights.

Amendment 10

Powers Reserved to the States The final amendment of the Bill of Rights protects the states and the people from an all-powerful federal government. It establishes that powers not given to the national government—or denied to the states—by the Constitution belong to the states or to the people.

Amendment 11

Suits Against States The Eleventh Amendment (1795) limits the jurisdiction of the federal courts. The Supreme Court had ruled that a federal court could try a lawsuit brought by citizens of South Carolina against the state of Georgia. This case, *Chisholm* v. *Georgia*, decided in 1793, raised a storm of protest, leading to passage of the Eleventh Amendment.

Amendment 12

Election of President and Vice President The Twelfth Amendment (1804) corrects a problem that had arisen in the method of electing the president and vice president. This amendment provides for the Electoral College to use separate ballots in voting for president and vice president. *If no candidate receives a majority of the electoral votes, who elects the president?*

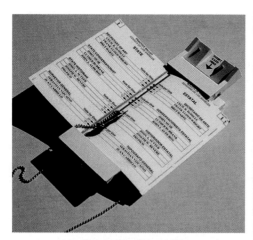

Ballot and ballot marker

Amendment 13

Abolition of Slavery Amendments Thirteen (1865), Fourteen (1868), and Fifteen (1870) often are called the Civil War amendments because they grew out of that great conflict. The Thirteenth Amendment outlaws slavery.

Vocabulary

majority: *more than half*
devolve: *to pass on*
abridge: *to reduce*
insurrection: *rebellion against the government*
emancipation: *freedom from slavery*

Amendment XII

The electors shall meet in their respective states and vote by ballot for President and Vice-President, one of whom, at least, shall not be an inhabitant of the same state with themselves; they shall name in their ballots the person voted for as President, and in distinct ballots the person voted for as Vice-President, and they shall make distinct lists of all persons voted for as President, and of all persons voted for as Vice-President, and of the number of votes for each, which lists they shall sign and certify, and transmit sealed to the seat of the government of the United States, directed to the President of the Senate;—The President of the Senate shall, in the presence of the Senate and House of Representatives, open all the certificates and the votes shall then be counted;—The person having the greatest number of votes for President, shall be the President, if such number be a majority of the whole number of Electors appointed; and if no person have such majority, then from the persons having the highest numbers not exceeding three on the list of those voted for as President, the House of Representatives shall choose immediately, by ballot, the President. But in choosing the President, the votes shall be taken by states, the representation from each state having one vote; a quorum for this purpose shall consist of a member or members from two-thirds of the states, and a majority of all the states shall be necessary to a choice. And if the House of Representatives shall not choose a President whenever the right of choice shall devolve upon them, before the fourth day of March next following, then the Vice-President shall act as President, as in the case of the death or other constitutional disability of the President. The person having the greatest number of votes as Vice-President, shall be the Vice-President, if such number be a majority of the whole number of Electors appointed, and if no person have a majority, then from the two highest numbers on the list, the Senate shall choose the Vice-President; a quorum for the purpose shall consist of two-thirds of the whole number of Senators, and a majority of the whole number shall be necessary to a choice. But no person constitutionally ineligible to the office of President shall be eligible to that of Vice-President of the United States.

Amendment XIII

Section 1

Neither slavery nor involuntary servitude, except as a punishment for crime whereof the party shall have been duly convicted, shall exist within the United States, or any place subject to their jurisdiction.

Section 2

Congress shall have power to enforce this article by appropriate legislation.

Amendment XIV

Section 1

All persons born or naturalized in the United States, and subject to the jurisdiction thereof, are citizens of the United States and of the State wherein they reside. No State shall make or enforce any law which shall abridge the privileges or immunities of citizens of the United States; nor shall any State deprive any person of life, liberty, or property, without due process of law; nor deny to any person within its jurisdiction the equal protection of the laws.

Section 2

Representatives shall be apportioned among the several States according to their respective numbers, counting the whole number of persons in each State, excluding Indians not taxed. But when the right to vote at any election for the choice of electors for President and Vice President of the United States, Representatives in Congress, the Executive and Judicial officers of a State, or the members of the Legislature thereof, is denied to any of the male inhabitants of such State, being twenty-one years of age, and citizens of the United States, or in any way abridged, except for participation in rebellion, or other crime, the basis of representation therein shall be reduced in the proportion which the number of such male citizens shall bear to the whole number of male citizens twenty-one years of age in such State.

Section 3

No person shall be a Senator or Representative in Congress, or elector of President and Vice President, or hold any office, civil or military, under the United States, or under any State, who, having previously taken an oath, as a member of Congress, or as an officer of the United States, or as a member of any State legislature, or as an executive or judicial officer of any State, to support the Constitution of the United States, shall have engaged in insurrection or rebellion against the same, or given aid or comfort to the enemies thereof. But Congress may by a vote of two-thirds of each House, remove such disability.

Section 4

The validity of the public debt of the United States, authorized by law, including debts incurred for payment of pensions and bounties for service in suppressing insurrection or rebellion, shall not be questioned. But neither the United States nor any State shall assume or pay any debt or obligation incurred in aid of insurrection or rebellion against the United States, or any claim for the loss or emancipation of any slave; but all such debts, obligations and claims shall be held illegal and void.

Amendment 14
Rights of Citizens The Fourteenth Amendment (1868) originally was intended to protect the legal rights of the freed slaves. Today it protects the rights of citizenship in general by prohibiting a state from depriving any person of life, liberty, or property without "due process of law." In addition, it states that all citizens have the right to equal protection of the law in all states.

Amendment 14. Section 2
Representation in Congress This section reduced the number of members a state had in the House of Representatives if it denied its citizens the right to vote. Later civil rights laws and the Twenty-Fourth Amendment guaranteed the vote to African Americans.

Amendment 14. Section 3
Penalty for Engaging in Insurrection The leaders of the Confederacy were barred from state or federal offices unless Congress agreed to remove this ban. By the end of Reconstruction all but a few Confederate leaders were allowed to return to public life.

Amendment 14. Section 4
Public Debt The public debt acquired by the federal government during the Civil War was valid and could not be questioned by the South. However, the debts of the Confederacy were declared to be illegal. *Could former slaveholders collect payment for the loss of their slaves?*

Amendment 15
Right to Vote The Fifteenth Amendment (1870) prohibits the government from denying a person's right to vote on the basis of race. Despite the law, many states denied African Americans the right to vote by such means as poll taxes, literacy tests, and white primaries. During the 1950s and 1960s, Congress passed successively stronger laws to end racial discrimination in voting rights.

Internal Revenue Service

Amendment 17
Direct Election of Senators The Seventeenth Amendment (1913) states that the people, instead of state legislatures, elect United States senators. *How many years are in a Senate term?*

Vocabulary

apportionment: *distribution of seats in House based on population*
vacancy: *an office or position that is unfilled or unoccupied*

Section 5
The Congress shall have power to enforce, by appropriate legislation, the provisions of this article.

Amendment XV

Section 1
The right of citizens of the United States to vote shall not be denied or abridged by the United States or by any State on account of race, color, or previous condition of servitude.

Section 2
The Congress shall have power to enforce this article by appropriate legislation.

Amendment XVI
The Congress shall have power to lay and collect taxes on incomes, from whatever source derived, without apportionment among the several States and without regard to any census or enumeration.

Amendment XVII

Section 1
The Senate of the United States shall be composed of two Senators from each State, elected by the people thereof, for six years; and each Senator shall have one vote. The electors in each State shall have the qualifications requisite for electors of the most numerous branch of the State legislatures.

Section 2
When vacancies happen in the representation of any State in the Senate, the executive authority of such State shall issue writs of election to fill such vacancies: *Provided,* That the legislature of any State may empower the executive thereof to make temporary appointments until the people fill the vacancies by election as the legislature may direct.

Section 3
This amendment shall not be so construed as to affect the election or term of any Senator chosen before it becomes valid as part of the Constitution.

Amendment XVIII

Section 1
After one year from ratification of this article, the manufacture, sale, or transportation of intoxicating liquors within, the importation thereof into, or the exportation thereof from the United States and all territory subject to the jurisdiction thereof for beverage purposes is hereby prohibited.

Section 2
The Congress and the several States shall have concurrent power to enforce this article by appropriate legislation.

Section 3
This article shall be inoperative unless it shall have been ratified as an amendment to the Constitution by the legislatures of the several States, as provided in the Constitution, within seven years from the date of the submission hereof to the States by the Congress.

Amendment XIX

Section 1
The right of citizens of the United States to vote shall not be denied or abridged by the United States or by any State on account of sex.

Section 2
Congress shall have power by appropriate legislation to enforce the provisions of this article.

Amendment XX

Section 1
The terms of the President and Vice President shall end at noon on the 20th day of January, and the terms of the Senators and Representatives at noon on the 3d day of January, of the years in which such terms would have ended if this article had not been ratified; and the terms of their successors shall then begin.

Section 2
The Congress shall assemble at least once in every year, and such meeting shall begin at noon on the 3d day of January, unless they shall by law appoint a different day.

Amendment 18
Prohibition of Alcoholic Beverages The Eighteenth Amendment (1919) prohibited the production, sale, or transportation of alcoholic beverages in the United States. Prohibition proved to be difficult to enforce. This amendment was later repealed by the Twenty-first Amendment.

Amendment 19
Woman Suffrage The Nineteenth Amendment (1920) guaranteed women the right to vote. By then women had already won the right to vote in many state elections, but the amendment put their right to vote in all state and national elections on a constitutional basis.

Amendment 20
"Lame-Duck" Amendment The Twentieth Amendment (1933) sets new dates for Congress to begin its term and for the inauguration of the president and vice president. Under the original Constitution, elected officials who retired or who had been defeated remained in office for several months. For the outgoing president, this period ran from November until March. Such outgoing officials had little influence and accomplished little, and they were called lame ducks because they were so inactive. *What date was fixed as Inauguration Day?*

Section 3

If, at the time fixed for the beginning of the term of the President, the President elect shall have died, the Vice President elect shall become President. If a President shall not have been chosen before the time fixed for the beginning of his term, or if the President elect shall have failed to qualify, then the Vice President elect shall act as President until a President shall have qualified; and the Congress may by law provide for the case wherein neither a President elect nor a Vice President elect shall have qualified, declaring who shall then act as President, or the manner in which one who is to act shall be selected, and such person shall act accordingly until a President or Vice President shall have qualified.

Section 4

The Congress may by law provide for the case of the death of any of the persons from whom the House of Representatives may choose a President whenever the right of choice shall have devolved upon them, and for the case of the death of any of the persons from whom the Senate may choose a Vice President whenever the right of choice shall have devolved upon them.

Section 5

Sections 1 and 2 shall take effect on the 15th day of October following the ratification of this article.

Section 6

This article shall be inoperative unless it shall have been ratified as an amendment to the Constitution by the legislatures of three-fourths of the several States within seven years from the date of its submission.

> **Amendment 20. Section 3**
> **Succession of President and Vice President** This section provides that if the president-elect dies before taking office, the vice president-elect becomes president.

John Tyler was the first vice president to become president when a chief executive died.

> **Amendment 21**
> **Repeal of Prohibition Amendment** The Twenty-first Amendment (1933) repeals the Eighteenth Amendment. It is the only amendment ever passed to overturn an earlier amendment. It is also the only amendment ratified by special state conventions instead of state legislatures.

Amendment XXI

Section 1

The eighteenth article of amendment to the Constitution of the United States is hereby repealed.

Section 2

The transportation or importation into any State, Territory, or possession of the United States for delivery or use therein of intoxicating liquors, in violation of the laws thereof, is hereby prohibited.

Section 3

This article shall be inoperative unless it shall have been ratified as an amendment to the Constitution by conventions in the several States, as provided in the Constitution, within seven years from the date of the submission hereof to the States by the Congress.

Vocabulary

president-elect: *individual who is elected president but has not yet begun serving his or her term*
District of Columbia: *site of nation's capital, occupying an area between Maryland and Virginia*

Amendment XXII

Section 1

No person shall be elected to the office of the President more than twice, and no person who had held the office of President, or acted as President, for more than two years of a term to which some other person was elected President shall be elected to the office of the President more than once. But this Article shall not apply to any person holding the office of President when this Article was proposed by the Congress, and shall not prevent any person who may be holding the office of President, or acting as President, during the term within which this Article becomes operative from holding the office of President or acting as President during the remainder of such term.

Section 2

This article shall be inoperative unless it shall have been ratified as an amendment to the Constitution by the legislatures of three-fourths of the several States within seven years from the date of its submission to the States by the Congress.

Amendment XXIII

Section 1

The District constituting the seat of Government of the United States shall appoint in such manner as the Congress may direct:

A number of electors of President and Vice President equal to the whole number of Senators and Representatives in Congress to which the District would be entitled if it were a State, but in no event more than the least populous State; they shall be in addition to those appointed by the States, but they shall be considered, for the purposes of the election of President and Vice President, to be electors appointed by a State; and they shall meet in the District and perform such duties as provided by the twelfth article of amendment.

Section 2

The Congress shall have power to enforce this article by appropriate legislation.

Presidential campaign buttons

President Gerald Ford

Amendment XXIV

Section 1

The right of citizens of the United States to vote in any primary or other election for President or Vice President, for electors for President or Vice President, or for Senator or Representative in Congress, shall not be denied or abridged by the United States or any State by reason of failure to pay any poll tax or other tax.

Section 2

The Congress shall have power to enforce this article by appropriate legislation.

Amendment XXV

Section 1

In case of the removal of the President from office or his death or resignation, the Vice President shall become President.

Section 2

Whenever there is a vacancy in the office of the Vice President, the President shall nominate a Vice President who shall take the office upon confirmation by a majority vote of both Houses of Congress.

Section 3

Whenever the President transmits to the President pro tempore of the Senate and the Speaker of the House of Representatives his written declaration that he is unable to discharge the powers and duties of his office, and until he transmits to them a written declaration to the contrary, such powers and duties shall be discharged by the Vice President as Acting President.

Section 4

Whenever the Vice President and a majority of either the principal officers of the executive departments or of such other body as Congress may by law provide, transmit to the President pro tempore of the Senate and the Speaker of the House of Representatives their written declaration that the President is unable to discharge the powers and duties of his office, the Vice President shall immediately assume the power and duties of the office of Acting President.

Thereafter, when the President transmits to the President pro tempore of the Senate and the Speaker of the House of Representatives his written declaration that no inability exists, he shall resume the powers and duties of his office unless the Vice President and a majority of either the principal officers of the executive department or of such other body as Congress may by law provide, transmit within four days to the President pro tempore of the Senate and the Speaker of the House of Representatives their written declaration that the President is unable to discharge the powers and duties of his office. Thereupon Congress shall decide the issue, assembling within forty-eight hours for that purpose if not in session. If the Congress, within twenty-one days after receipt of the latter written declaration, or, if Congress is not in session, within twenty-one days after Congress is required to assemble, determines by two-thirds vote of both Houses that the President is unable to discharge the powers and duties of his office, the Vice President shall continue to discharge the same as Acting President; otherwise, the President shall resume the power and duties of his office.

Amendment XXVI

Section 1
The right of citizens of the United States, who are eighteen years of age or older, to vote shall not be denied or abridged by the United States or by any State on account of age.

Section 2
The Congress shall have power to enforce this article by appropriate legislation.

Amendment XXVII
No law, varying the compensation for the services of Senators and Representatives, shall take effect, until an election of representatives shall have intervened.

Amendment 26
Eighteen-Year-Old Vote The Twenty-sixth Amendment (1971) guarantees the right to vote to all citizens 18 years of age and older.

Amendment 27
Restraint on Congressional Salaries The Twenty-seventh Amendment (1992) makes congressional pay raises effective during the term following their passage. James Madison offered the amendment in 1789, but it was never adopted. In 1982 Gregory Watson, then a student at the University of Texas, discovered the forgotten amendment while doing research for a school paper. Watson made the amendment's passage his crusade.

Joint meeting of Congress

The New Republic

1789–1825

Why It Matters

As you study Unit 4, you will learn how the young United States chose its leaders and established its policies. The following resources offer more information about this period in American history.

Primary Sources Library

See pages 598–599 for primary source readings to accompany Unit 4.

*Use the **American History Primary Source Document Library CD-ROM** to find additional primary sources about the new republic.*

Pitcher honoring Washington's inauguration, 1789

Daniel Boone Escorting Settlers Through the Cumberland Gap by George Caleb Bingham

"Observe good faith and justice toward all nations."

—George Washington, 1796

CHAPTER 8

A New Nation

1789–1800

Why It Matters

George Washington's administration faced the huge task of making the new government work. The Constitution had created the office of the presidency, but Washington established many procedures and customs.

The Impact Today

President Washington set many examples that presidents still follow. These include creating a cabinet, directing foreign affairs, and serving as chief legislator.

 The American Republic to 1877 Video The chapter 8 video, "George Washington," examines the issues that arose upon the establishment of the office of president.

1789
- Washington becomes first president
- Judiciary Act passed

1791
- Bill of Rights added to Constitution

1794
- Whiskey Rebellion

United States
PRESIDENTS

Washington
1789–1797

1790   *1792*   *1794*

World

1792
- France declares war on Austria

1793
- Louvre opens as public museum in Paris

1794
- Slavery abolished in all French colonies

Boston Harbor as Seen From Constitution Wharf by Robert Salmon
Salmon recorded the emerging cities and scenic harbors of the young nation.

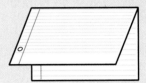
1795
• Nation's first chief justice, John Jay, retires from court

1798
• Alien and Sedition Acts passed
• XYZ affair

1800
• Convention of 1800 resolves U.S./French conflicts

Adams 1797–1801

1796   *1798*

1796
• Jenner develops smallpox vaccine

1799
• Rosetta stone discovered

Guide to Reading

Guide to Reading

Main Idea
President Washington and the first Congress tackled the work of establishing a new government.

Key Terms
precedent, cabinet, national debt, bond, speculator, unconstitutional, tariff

Reading Strategy
Classifying Information As you read the section, re-create the diagram below and list the actions taken by Congress and Washington's first administration.

Actions	
Washington	Congress

Read to Learn
• what actions were taken to launch the new government.
• how Hamilton proposed to strengthen the economy.

Section Theme
Government and Democracy President Washington and Congress took actions that shaped the future of government in our nation.

Preview of Events

♦1789   ♦1790   ♦1791   ♦1792

April 6, 1789
George Washington is elected president

April 30, 1789
Washington takes the oath of office

September 1789
Judiciary Act sets up federal court system

December 1791
Bill of Rights added to the Constitution

AN American Story

Celebrations erupted in the streets of Philadelphia, New York, Boston, and Charleston in 1789. News of the Constitution's ratification was greeted with relief and enthusiasm. All that was needed now was a leader to guide the new nation.

On April 6 the new Senate counted the presidential ballots. To no one's surprise, the votes were unanimous. Senator John Langdon wrote to General George Washington: "Sir, I have the honor to transmit to Your Excellency the information of your unanimous election to the office of President of the United States of America." Washington was ready to begin the difficult task of leading the country.

February 22nd, 1732
December 14th, 1799

Washington banner

President Washington

The 57-year-old president-elect made his way slowly toward New York City, then the nation's capital. After the Constitutional Convention, George Washington had looked forward to a quiet retirement. Instead his fellow citizens elected him to the highest office in the land. On April 30, 1789, Washington took the oath of office as the first president of the United States under the federal Constitution (there had been several presidents under the Articles of Confederation). John Adams became vice president. 📖 *(See page 598 of the Primary Sources Library for an excerpt of an account of Washington's First Inaugural.)*

Perhaps no office in the new government created more suspicion among the people than the office of president. Many Americans feared that a president would try to become king, but they trusted Washington. They believed that his leadership had brought them victory in the Revolutionary War.

Washington was aware of the difficulties he faced. He knew that the precedents, or traditions, he established as the nation's first president would shape the future of the United States. "No slip will pass unnoticed," he remarked. One precedent he established concerned the way people should address him. Vice President Adams supported "His Highness the President of the United States," but ultimately it was decided that "Mr. President" would be more appropriate.

Washington and the new Congress also had many decisions to make about the structure of government. For example, the Constitution gave Congress the power to establish executive departments, but it did not state whether the department heads would report to the president or to Congress.

The First Congress

During the summer of 1789, Congress set up three departments in the executive branch of government. The State Department would handle relations with other nations, the Treasury Department would deal with financial matters, and the War Department would provide for the nation's defense. Congress also created the office of attorney general to handle the government's legal affairs and the office of postmaster general to direct the postal service.

To head the departments, Washington chose prominent political figures of the day—**Thomas Jefferson** as secretary of state, **Alexander Hamilton** as secretary of the treasury, and **Henry Knox** as secretary of war. He appointed **Edmund Randolph** as attorney general. Washington met regularly with the three department heads and the attorney general, who together became known as the cabinet.

Congress created the executive departments; opinion was divided, however, on how much power the president should have over them. For example, should the president be able to replace an official that he had appointed and the Senate had confirmed? Senators were evenly divided in voting on the issue.

Vice President Adams broke the tie by voting to allow the president the authority to dismiss cabinet officers without the Senate's approval. This decision strengthened the president's position. It also helped create a greater separation between the legislative and executive branches of government by establishing the president's authority over the executive branch.

Judiciary Act

The first Congress also had to decide how to set up the nation's court system. The Constitution briefly mentioned a supreme court but had left further details about the courts to Congress.

Disagreements arose between those favoring a uniform, national legal system and those favoring state courts. The two groups reached a compromise in the **Judiciary Act of 1789.** With this act, Congress established a federal court system with 13 district courts and three circuit courts to serve the nation. State laws would remain, but the federal courts would have the power to reverse state decisions.

The Supreme Court would be the final authority on many issues. Washington nominated **John Jay** to lead the Supreme Court as chief justice, and the Senate approved Jay's nomination. With the Judiciary Act, Congress had taken the first steps toward creating a strong and independent national judiciary.

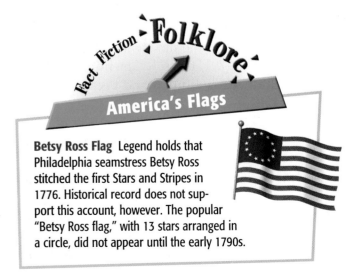

America's Flags

Betsy Ross Flag Legend holds that Philadelphia seamstress Betsy Ross stitched the first Stars and Stripes in 1776. Historical record does not support this account, however. The popular "Betsy Ross flag," with 13 stars arranged in a circle, did not appear until the early 1790s.

People In History

Benjamin Banneker 1731–1806

Benjamin Banneker

Black Heritage USA 15¢

Benjamin Banneker was born into a free African American family in Maryland. He attended a private Quaker school, but was largely self-educated. When his father died, Banneker sold the family farm and devoted the rest of his life to mathematics and natural sciences.

Banneker's skill in mathematics prompted Thomas Jefferson to give him a job surveying the land for the new national capital at Washington, D.C. When French architect Pierre L'Enfant was removed from the project, he took his detailed maps with him. Banneker amazed everyone

by redrawing the missing maps from memory! From 1792 to 1802 he made astronomical and tide calculations for a yearly almanac. Banneker became a symbol for racial justice in a land not yet ready to grant him the rights of citizenship, granted to others in the Bill of Rights.

The Bill of Rights

Americans had long feared strong central governments. They had fought a revolution to throw off one and did not want to replace it with another. Many people insisted the Constitution needed to include guarantees of personal liberties. Some states had supported the Constitution on the condition that a bill of rights be added.

To fulfill the promises made during the fight for ratification of the Constitution, James Madison introduced a set of amendments during the first session of Congress. Congress passed 12 amendments, and the states ratified 10 of them. In December 1791, these 10 amendments were added to the Constitution and became known as the **Bill of Rights.**

The Bill of Rights limits the powers of government. Its purpose is to protect the rights of individual liberty, such as freedom of speech, and rights of persons accused of crimes, including trial by jury. The Tenth Amendment protects the rights of states and individuals by saying that powers not specifically given to the federal government "are reserved to the States

respectively, or to the people." With the Tenth Amendment, Madison hoped to use the states as an important line of defense against a too-powerful national government. 📖 *(See pages 244–245 for the entire text of the Bill of Rights.)*

✓**Reading Check** **Describing** Why was the Bill of Rights created? *To guarantee personal liberties To fulfill promise made before ratification*

💲**Economics**

Financial Problems

Washington himself rarely proposed laws, and he almost always approved the bills that were passed by Congress. The first president concentrated on foreign affairs and military matters and left the government's economic policies to his dynamic secretary of the treasury, Alexander Hamilton.

The new nation faced serious financial problems. The national debt—the amount the nation's government owed—was growing. Hamilton tried to find a way to improve the government's financial reputation and to strengthen the nation at the same time.

Hamilton's Plan

In 1790 Hamilton proposed that the new government pay off the millions of dollars in debts owed by the Confederation government to other countries and to individual American citizens. The states had fought for the nation's independence, Hamilton argued, so the national government should pay for the cost of their help. Hamilton also believed that federal payment of state debts would give the states a strong interest in the success of the national government.

Opposition to the Plan

Congress agreed to pay money owed to other nations, but Hamilton's plan to pay off the debt to American citizens unleashed a storm of protest. When the government had borrowed money during the American Revolution, it had issued bonds—paper notes promising to repay the money in a certain length of time. While waiting for the payment, many of the original bond owners—shopkeepers, farmers, and soldiers—had sold the bonds for less than their value. They were purchased by speculators, people who risk money in order to make a larger profit. Hamilton proposed that these bonds be paid off at their original value. Opponents believed that Hamilton's plan would make speculators rich, and

> 66established at the expense of national justice, gratitude, and humanity.99

The original bond owners felt betrayed by the government because they had lost money on their bonds while new bond owners profited.

Even stronger opposition came from the Southern states, which had accumulated much less debt than the Northern states. Southern states complained that they would have to pay more than their share under Hamilton's plan.

Compromise Results in a Capital

To win support for his plan, Hamilton compromised. He agreed to a proposal from Southern leaders to locate the new nation's capital in the South after moving to Philadelphia while workmen prepared the new city for the federal government. A special district would be laid out between Virginia and Maryland along the banks of the Potomac River. This district became **Washington, D.C.** In return, Southerners supported his plan to pay off the state debts.

Reading Check **Explaining** Why did Hamilton's plan to pay off the debt to American citizens cause such a storm of protest? *The original bond owners felt that speculators would benefit.*

America's *Architecture*

The Capitol is the seat of the United States Congress in Washington, D.C. Built on a hill popularly called Capitol Hill, the Capitol contains floor space equivalent to over 16 acres. The dome of the United States Capitol, finished in 1863, is one of the most famous landmarks in the United States. Other important parts of the Capitol include the Rotunda directly under the dome, the Senate Chamber in the north wing, the House Chamber in the south wing, and the National Statuary Hall.

Building the Economy

Hamilton made other proposals for building a strong national economy. He asked Congress to create a national bank, the Bank of the United States. Both private investors and the national government would own the Bank's stock.

The Fight Over the Bank

In 1792 there were only eight other banks in the nation. All eight had been established by state governments. Madison and Jefferson opposed the idea of a national bank. They believed it would benefit the wealthy. They also charged that the Bank was unconstitutional—that it was inconsistent with the Constitution. Hamilton argued that although the Constitution did not specifically say that Congress could create a bank, Congress still had the power to do so. In the end the president agreed with Hamilton and signed the bill creating the national bank.

Tariffs and Taxes

At the time, most Americans earned their living by farming. Hamilton thought the development of manufacturing would make America's economy stronger. He proposed a tariff—a tax on imports—to encourage people to buy American products. This protective tariff would protect American industry from foreign competition.

The South, having little industry to protect, opposed protective tariffs. Hamilton did win support in Congress for some low tariffs to raise money rather than to protect industries. By the 1790s the revenue from tariffs provided 90 percent of the national government's income.

The final portion of Hamilton's economic program concerned the creation of national taxes. The government needed additional funds to operate and to make interest payments on the national debt. At Hamilton's request Congress approved a variety of taxes, including one on whiskey distilled in the United States.

Hamilton's economic program gave the national government new financial powers. However, his proposals split Congress and the nation. The opponents—including Jefferson and Madison—feared a national government with strong economic powers dominated by the wealthy class. They had a very different vision of what America should become.

✔ **Reading Check** **Comparing** Summarize the arguments for and against protective tariffs.

Hamilton wanted to encourage the development of domestic manufacturing by imposing a tariff on imported items. The South had little industry to protect

SECTION 1 ASSESSMENT

Checking for Understanding

1. **Key Terms** Write a paragraph for each group of terms below. Group 1: precedent, cabinet. Group 2: national debt, bond, speculator. Group 3: unconstitutional, tariff.

2. **Reviewing Facts** Name three things that Hamilton wanted to do to create a stable economic system and strengthen the economy.

Reviewing Themes

3. **Government and Democracy** What compromise did Congress reach in establishing a court system?

Critical Thinking

4. **Analyzing Primary Sources** Hamilton said about Washington, "He consulted much, pondered much, resolved slowly, resolved surely." Did this make Washington a good first president? Explain.

5. **Comparing** Re-create the diagram below. Compare the views of Hamilton and Jefferson. In the boxes, write "for" or "against" for each issue.

Issue	Hamilton	Jefferson
National bank		
Protective tariff		
National taxes		

Analyzing Visuals

6. **Picturing History** Examine the picture of the U.S. Capitol on page 261. The Capitol is one of the most widely recognized buildings in the world. What members of the government serve in the Capitol? What does the U.S. Capitol symbolize to you?

Interdisciplinary Activity

Expository Writing You have been given the task of choosing the first cabinet members. Write a job description for the secretaries of state, treasury, and war. Then interview classmates to see who would be best suited for each position.

Main Idea

In the 1790s, the new government struggled to keep peace at home and avoid war abroad.

Key Terms

neutrality, impressment

Reading Strategy

Classifying Information As you read the section, re-create the diagram below and list results of government actions during the early Republic.

Government action	Results
Treaty of Greenville	
Proclamation of Neutrality	
Jay's Treaty	
Pinckney's Treaty	

Read to Learn

• how the federal government asserted its power in the West.
• how the United States tried to stay out of European conflicts.

Section Theme

Geography and History The new government clashed over control of the Northwest Territory.

Preview of Events

♦1790   ♦1792   ♦1794   ♦1796

November 1791
Little Turtle defeats St. Clair's forces

March 1793
Washington begins second term

July 1794
Western farmers revolt in Whiskey Rebellion

August 1794
Battle of Fallen Timbers occurs

October 1795
Spain opens Mississippi River to American shipping

Drawing of tax collector

AN
American Story

Far removed from the bustle of trade and shipping along the Atlantic coast, farmers on the western frontier lived quite differently. In fact, western ways seemed almost primitive to travelers from the East. They seemed to notice only the poor roads and the boring diet of corn and salted pork. Living in scattered, isolated homesteads, frontier farmers were proud of their self-reliance. They wanted no "eastern" tax collectors heading their way.

The Whiskey Rebellion

Hamilton's taxes led to rebellion in western Pennsylvania. The farmers were in an uproar over having to pay a special tax on the whiskey they made from surplus corn. In the backcountry most farmers lived by bartering—exchanging whiskey and other items they produced for goods they needed. They rarely had cash. How could they pay a tax on whiskey?

The farmers' resistance was mostly peaceful—until July 1794, when federal officers stepped up efforts to collect the tax. Then a large mob of people armed with swords, guns, and pitchforks attacked tax collectors and burned down buildings.

The armed protest, called the **Whiskey Rebellion,** alarmed government leaders. President Washington and his advisers decided to crush the challenge. The rebellion collapsed as soon as the army crossed the Appalachian Mountains.

By his action, Washington served notice to those who opposed government actions. If citizens wished to change the law, they had to do so peacefully, through constitutional means. Government would use force when necessary to maintain the social order.

✓ Reading Check **Explaining** How did the Whiskey Rebellion affect the way government handled protesters?

Government used necessary force to maintain social order.

★ Geography

Struggle Over the West

The new government faced difficult problems in the West. The Native Americans who lived between the Appalachian Mountains and the Mississippi River denied that the United States had any authority over them. On many occasions Native Americans turned to Britain and Spain to help them in their cause. Both countries welcomed the opportunity to prevent American settlement of the region.

Washington worried about European ambitions in the Northwest Territory. He hoped that signing treaties with the Native American tribes in the area would lessen the influence of the British and Spanish. American settlers ignored the treaties and continued to move onto lands promised to the Native Americans. Fighting broke out between the two groups.

Washington sent an army under General Arthur St. Clair to restore order in the Northwest Territory. In November 1791, St. Clair's forces were badly beaten by Little Turtle, chief of the Miami people. More than 600 American soldiers died in a battle by the Wabash River.

Many Americans believed that an alliance with France would enable them to defeat the combined forces of the British, Spanish, and Native Americans in the West. The British, who still had forts in the region, wanted to hold on to the profitable fur trade. The possibility of French involvement in the region pushed the British to make a bold bid for control of the West. In 1794 the British government urged Native Americans to destroy American settlements west of the Appalachians. The British also began building a new fort in Ohio.

Battle of Fallen Timbers

The Native Americans demanded that all settlers north of the Ohio River leave the territory. Washington sent another army headed by Anthony Wayne, a former Revolutionary War general, to challenge their demands. In August 1794 his army defeated over 1,000 Native Americans under Shawnee chief Blue Jacket at the **Battle of Fallen Timbers** (near present-day Toledo, Ohio). The Battle of Fallen Timbers crushed the Native Americans' hopes of keeping their land. In the **Treaty of Greenville** (1795), the Native Americans agreed to surrender most of the land in present-day Ohio.

✓ Reading Check **Describing** What did Native American groups do to fight more effectively in the Northwest?

They turned to Britain & Spain for help.

Problems With Europe

Shortly after Washington was inaugurated in 1789, the French Revolution began. At first most Americans cheered upon hearing the news. The French had helped the Americans in their struggle for independence, and their revolution seemed to embody many of the ideals of the American Revolution.

By 1793 the French Revolution had turned bloody. The leaders had executed the king and queen of France and thousands of French citizens. Public opinion in the United States started to divide. The violence of the French Revolution, as well as its attack on religion and disregard of individual liberties, offended many Americans. Others hailed the new republic as a copy of the United States.

When Britain and France went to war in 1793, some Americans, particularly in the South, sympathized with France. Others, especially manufacturers and merchants who traded with the British, favored Britain. Hamilton, Adams, and their supporters generally sided with the

British. Jefferson was pro-French. A French victory, Jefferson reasoned, would help drive the British out of North America.

Washington hoped that the nation could maintain its neutrality—that is, that it would not take sides in the conflict between France and Britain. As time went on, however, neutrality became increasingly difficult.

Washington Proclaims Neutrality

The French tried to involve the United States in their conflict with Britain. In April 1793, they sent diplomat **Edmond Genêt** (zhuh•NAY) to the United States. His mission was to recruit American volunteers to attack British ships.

President Washington took action to discourage American involvement. On April 22 he issued a **Proclamation of Neutrality.** It prohibited American citizens from fighting in the war and barred French and British warships from American ports. Genêt's plans eventually failed, but he did manage to sign up a few hundred Americans to serve on French ships. These ships seized British vessels and stole their cargoes before Washington ended their adventures by closing American ports.

Outraged by the French attacks at sea, the British began capturing American ships that traded with the French. The British also stopped American merchant ships and forced their crews into the British navy. This practice, known as impressment, infuriated the Americans. British attacks on American ships and sailors, along with the challenge in the West, pushed the nation closer to war with Great Britain.

A Controversial Treaty

President Washington decided to make one last effort to come to a peaceful solution with Britain. He sent John Jay, chief justice of the Supreme Court, to negotiate.

The British were willing to listen to Jay's proposals. War with the United States would only make it harder to carry on the war with France, and the United States was Britain's best market.

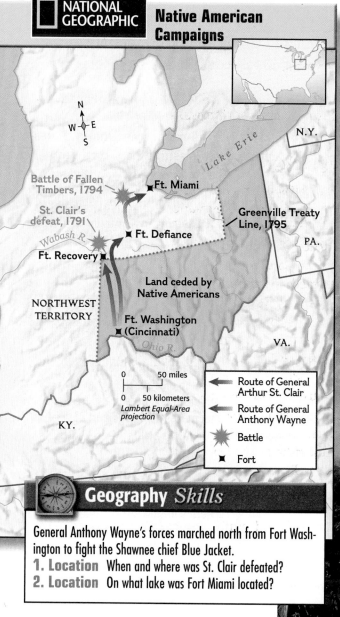

NATIONAL GEOGRAPHIC

Native American Campaigns

N.Y.

Lake Erie

Battle of Fallen Timbers, 1794

Ft. Miami

St. Clair's defeat, 1791

Wabash R.

Ft. Defiance

Greenville Treaty Line, 1795

Ft. Recovery

PA.

Land ceded by Native Americans

NORTHWEST TERRITORY

Ft. Washington (Cincinnati)

Ohio R.

VA.

KY.

0   50 miles
0   50 kilometers
Lambert Equal-Area projection

← Route of General Arthur St. Clair
← Route of General Anthony Wayne
✸ Battle
▪ Fort

Geography *Skills*

General Anthony Wayne's forces marched north from Fort Washington to fight the Shawnee chief Blue Jacket.

1. Location When and where was St. Clair defeated?
2. Location On what lake was Fort Miami located?

Picturing **History**

Upon signing the Treaty of Greenville, 12 Native American nations received $20,000 worth of goods to share. **How did the treaty affect white settlement?**

Chief Justice John Jay

In **Jay's Treaty** the British agreed to withdraw from American soil, to pay damages for ships they had seized, and to allow some American ships to trade with British colonies in the Caribbean. The treaty also provided for settlement of debts from before 1776.

Despite these gains few Americans approved of Jay's Treaty. They protested that the treaty did not deal with the issue of impressment and did not mention British interference with American trade. Although Washington found fault with the treaty, he realized it would end an explosive crisis with Great Britain. He sent the treaty to the Senate, which narrowly approved it after a fierce debate.

Treaty With Spain

When Jay's Treaty was made, Spanish leaders realized that the United States and Great Britain could work together against the Spanish Empire in North America. Thomas Pinckney was sent to Spain to try to settle the differences between the two nations. In 1795 **Pinckney's Treaty** gave the Americans free navigation of the Mississippi River and the right to trade at New Orleans.

✓ **Reading Check** **Describing** Why did many Americans protest Jay's Treaty? *It did not deal with impressment or British interference in American trade.*

Washington's Farewell

In September 1796, Washington announced he would not seek a third term. By choosing to serve only two terms, Washington set a precedent that later presidents would follow.

Plagued with a variety of ailments, the 64-year-old president looked forward to retirement at Mount Vernon. He also felt troubled over the divisions that had developed in American politics and with what he considered a grave danger to the new nation—the growth of political parties.

Washington's "Farewell Address" was published in a Philadelphia newspaper. In it he attacked the evils of political parties and entanglement in foreign affairs. He also urged his fellow citizens to

❝observe good faith and justice toward all nations . . . Tis our policy to steer clear of permanent alliances.❞

Washington's parting words influenced the nation's foreign policy for more than 100 years. The text is still read aloud in the United States Senate each year on Washington's birthday. 📖
(See page 615 of the Appendix for an excerpt from Washington's Farewell Address.)

✓ **Reading Check** **Explaining** What was the impact of Washington's Farewell Address?

SECTION 2 ASSESSMENT

Checking for Understanding

1. **Key Terms** Use the terms neutrality and impressment in a sentence about Washington's administration.
2. **Reviewing Facts** What message was Washington sending to the American people when he used force to stop the Whiskey Rebellion?

Reviewing Themes

3. **Geography and History** How did the Treaty of Greenville affect the land claims of Native Americans in the Northwest Territory?

Critical Thinking

4. **Predicting Consequences** What did the United States have to gain by remaining neutral in foreign affairs?
5. **Determining Cause and Effect** Re-create the diagram below. In the boxes, list the cause and effects of the Whiskey Rebellion.

Cause	Cause/Effect	Effects
	Whiskey Rebellion	

Analyzing Visuals

6. **Geography and History** Review the map on page 265. The Native American nations surrendered land that makes up a large part of what present-day state?

Interdisciplinary Activity

Descriptive Writing A tribute is a speech showing respect and gratitude. Write a one-paragraph tribute that you might have delivered if you had been asked to speak at George Washington's funeral.

SECTION 3 The First Political Parties

Guide to Reading

Main Idea
By the election of 1796, two distinct political parties with different views about the role of the national government had formed.

Key Terms
partisan, implied powers, caucus, alien, sedition, nullify, states' rights

Reading Strategy
Classifying Information As you read Section 3, create a diagram like the one below and list the differences between the Federalists and the Democratic-Republicans.

Issue	Federalists	Democratic-Republicans
Role of federal government		

Read to Learn
- how political parties got started and what positions they supported.
- how John Adams and Thomas Jefferson became candidates of opposing parties in the election of 1796.

Section Theme
Government and Democracy Different values fueled the rise of the nation's first political parties.

Preview of Events

♦1796	♦1798	♦1800

1796 Federalists nominate Adams for president; Democratic-Republicans nominate Jefferson

1797 John Adams becomes president

1798 Congress passes Alien and Sedition Acts

1800 Convention of 1800

George Washington

AN American Story

The Washington presidency was known for its dignity and elegance. The president rode in a coach drawn by horses and accompanied by mounted attendants. He and his wife, Martha, lived in the finest house in Philadelphia, the new nation's capital. They entertained a great deal, holding weekly receptions. Each year a ball was held on Washington's birthday. The president wore a black velvet suit with gold buckles, yellow gloves, powdered hair, an ostrich plume in his hat, and a sword in a white leather sheath. Despite these extravagances, Washington's character and military record were admired by most Americans.

Opposing Views

Although hailed by Americans as the nation's greatest leader, George Washington did not escape criticism during his two terms as president. From time to time, harsh attacks on his policies and on his personality appeared in newspapers. One paper even called Washington "the scourge and the misfortune of his country."

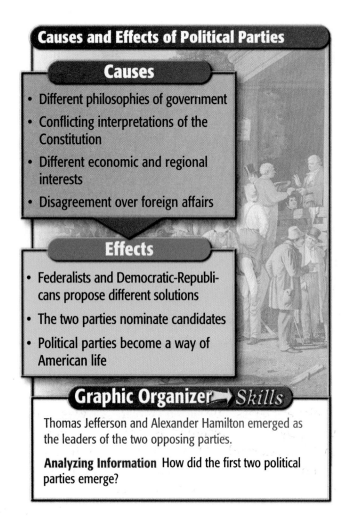

Causes and Effects of Political Parties

Causes

- Different philosophies of government
- Conflicting interpretations of the Constitution
- Different economic and regional interests
- Disagreement over foreign affairs

Effects

- Federalists and Democratic-Republicans propose different solutions
- The two parties nominate candidates
- Political parties become a way of American life

Graphic Organizer ➔ Skills

Thomas Jefferson and Alexander Hamilton emerged as the leaders of the two opposing parties.

Analyzing Information How did the first two political parties emerge?

Most attacks on Washington had come from supporters of Thomas Jefferson. They were trying to discredit the policies of Washington and Hamilton by attacking the president. By 1796 Americans were beginning to divide into opposing groups and to form political parties.

At that time, many Americans considered political parties harmful. Parties—or "factions" as they were called—were to be avoided as much as strong central government. The nation's founders did not even mention political parties in the Constitution.

Washington had denounced political parties and warned that they would divide the nation. To others it seemed natural that people would disagree about issues and that those who held similar views would band together.

In Washington's cabinet Hamilton and Jefferson often took opposing sides on issues. They disagreed on economic policy and foreign relations, on the power of the federal government, and on interpretations of the Constitution. Even

Washington had been partisan—favoring one side of an issue. Although he believed he stood above politics, Washington usually supported Hamilton's positions.

Political Parties Emerge

In Congress and the nation at large, similar differences existed. By the mid-1790s, two distinct political parties had taken shape.

The name **Federalist** had first described someone who supported ratification of the Constitution. By the 1790s the word was applied to the group of people who supported the policies of the Washington administration.

Generally Federalists stood for a strong federal government. They admired Britain because of its stability and distrusted France because of the violent changes following the French Revolution. Federalist policies tended to favor banking and shipping interests. Federalists received the strongest support in the Northeast, especially in New England, and from wealthy plantation owners in the South.

Efforts to turn public opinion against Federalist policies began seriously in late 1791 when Philip Freneau (Freh•NOH) began publishing the *National Gazette.* Jefferson, then secretary of state, helped the newspaper get started. Later he and Madison organized people who disagreed with Hamilton. They called their party the **Republicans,** or the **Democratic-Republicans.**

The Republicans wanted to limit government's power. They feared that a strong federal government would endanger people's liberties. They supported the French and condemned what they regarded as the Washington administration's pro-British policies. Republican policies appealed to small farmers and urban workers, especially in the Middle Atlantic states and the South.

🞂Citizenship

Views of the Constitution

One difference between Federalists and Republicans concerned the basis of government power. In Hamilton's view the federal government had implied powers, powers that were not expressly forbidden in the Constitution.

Hamilton used the idea of implied powers to justify a national bank. He argued that the Constitution gave Congress the power to issue money and regulate trade, and a national bank would clearly help the government carry out these responsibilities. Therefore, creating a bank was within the constitutional power of Congress.

Jefferson and Madison disagreed with Hamilton. They believed in a strict interpretation of the Constitution. They accepted the idea of implied powers, but in a much more limited sense than Hamilton did: Implied powers are those powers that are "absolutely necessary" to carry out the expressed powers.

The People's Role

The differences between the parties, however, went even deeper. Federalists and Republicans had sharply opposing views on the role ordinary people should play in government.

Federalists supported representative government, in which elected officials ruled in the people's name. They did not believe that it was wise to let the public become too involved in politics. Hamilton said:

> 66The people are turbulent and changing. . . . They seldom judge or determine right.99

Public office, Federalists thought, should be held by honest and educated men of property who would protect everyone's rights. Ordinary people were too likely to be swayed by agitators.

In contrast, the Republicans feared a strong central government controlled by a few people. They believed that liberty would be safe only if ordinary people participated in government. As Jefferson explained:

> 66I am not among those who fear the people; they, and not the rich, are our dependence [what we depend on] for continued freedom.99

Washington's Dilemma

Washington tried to get his two advisers to work out their differences. Knowing Jefferson was discontented, Washington wrote:

> 66I have a great sincere esteem and regard for you both, and ardently wish that some line could be marked out by which both [of] you could walk.99

Nevertheless, by 1793 Jefferson was so unhappy that he resigned as secretary of state. In 1795, Alexander Hamilton resigned, too, as secretary of the treasury. The rival groups and their points of view moved further apart.

The Election of 1796

In the presidential election of 1796, candidates sought office for the first time as members of a party. To prepare for the election, the Federalists and the Republicans held meetings called caucuses. At the caucuses members of

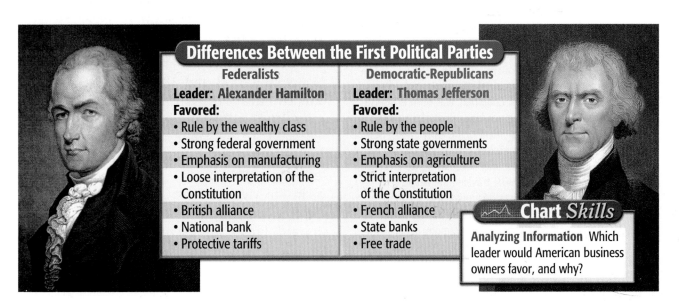

Differences Between the First Political Parties	
Federalists	**Democratic-Republicans**
Leader: Alexander Hamilton	**Leader: Thomas Jefferson**
Favored:	**Favored:**
• Rule by the wealthy class	• Rule by the people
• Strong federal government	• Strong state governments
• Emphasis on manufacturing	• Emphasis on agriculture
• Loose interpretation of the Constitution	• Strict interpretation of the Constitution
• British alliance	• French alliance
• National bank	• State banks
• Protective tariffs	• Free trade

Chart Skills

Analyzing Information Which leader would American business owners favor, and why?

Congress and other leaders chose their party's candidates for office.

The Federalists nominated Vice President John Adams as their candidate for president and Charles Pinckney for vice president. The Republicans put forth former secretary of state Jefferson for president and Aaron Burr for vice president. Adams and Jefferson, who had been good friends, became rivals. The Federalists expected to carry New England. The Republicans' strength lay in the South, which would give most of its votes to Jefferson.

In the end Adams received 71 electoral votes, winning the election. Jefferson finished second with 68 votes. Under the provisions of the Constitution at that time, the person with the second-highest number of electoral votes became vice president. Jefferson therefore became the new vice president. The administration that took office on March 4, 1797, had a Federalist president and a Republican vice president.

Reading Check **Explaining** Which political party would a Boston factory owner most likely support?

American Heroes

Did Johnny Appleseed scatter apple seeds in the wilderness? There was a real Johnny Appleseed. Johnny, whose real name was John Chapman, was born in Massachusetts in 1774. When the rich lands west of the Ohio River were opened for settlement in the early 1800s, he was the among the first to explore the new territory. Johnny Appleseed did not scatter seeds as he wandered, as many people believe. As he traveled, he would spot good sites for planting. There he would clear the land and plant the seeds. His orchards varied in size. Some covered about an acre. Others covered many acres. When settlers arrived, they found Johnny Appleseed's young apple trees ready for sale.

President John Adams

John Adams had spent most of his life in public service. One of Massachusetts's most active patriots, he later became ambassador to France and to Great Britain. He helped to negotiate the Treaty of Paris that ended the Revolution. Under Washington, he served two terms as vice president.

The XYZ Affair

When Adams took office, he inherited the dispute with France. The French regarded Jay's Treaty, signed in 1794, as an American attempt to help the British in their war with France. To punish the United States, the French seized American ships that carried cargo to Britain.

Adams wanted to avoid war with France. In the fall of 1797, he sent a delegation to Paris to try to resolve the dispute. French foreign minister **Charles de Talleyrand,** however, refused to meet with the Americans. Instead, Talleyrand sent three agents who demanded a bribe and a loan for France from the Americans. "Not a sixpence," the Americans replied and sent a report of the incident to the United States. Adams was furious. Referring to the three French agents as X, Y, and Z, the president urged Congress to prepare for war. The incident became known as the **XYZ affair.**

Undeclared War With France

Congress responded with a program to strengthen the armed forces. It established the Navy Department in April 1798 and set aside money for building warships. Congress also increased the size of the army. George Washington was appointed commanding general.

Between 1798 and 1800, United States and French naval vessels clashed on a number of occasions, although war was not formally declared. Adams's representatives negotiated an agreement with France in September 1800 that ensured peace.

In the view of most Americans, France had become an enemy. The Republican Party, friendly toward France in the past, hesitated to turn around and condemn France. As a result, in the 1798 elections, Americans voted some Republicans out of office.

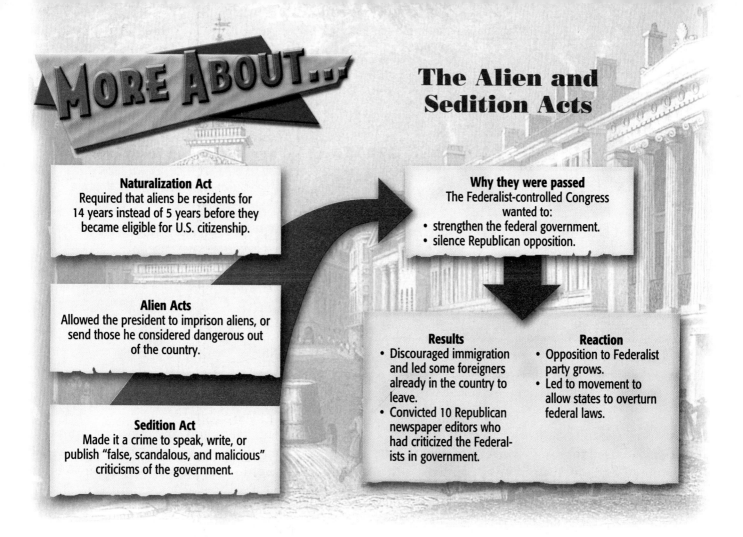

MORE ABOUT...

The Alien and Sedition Acts

Naturalization Act
Required that aliens be residents for 14 years instead of 5 years before they became eligible for U.S. citizenship.

Alien Acts
Allowed the president to imprison aliens, or send those he considered dangerous out of the country.

Sedition Act
Made it a crime to speak, write, or publish "false, scandalous, and malicious" criticisms of the government.

Why they were passed
The Federalist-controlled Congress wanted to:
• strengthen the federal government.
• silence Republican opposition.

Results
• Discouraged immigration and led some foreigners already in the country to leave.
• Convicted 10 Republican newspaper editors who had criticized the Federalists in government.

Reaction
• Opposition to Federalist party grows.
• Led to movement to allow states to overturn federal laws.

Alien and Sedition Acts

The threat of war with France made Americans more suspicious of aliens, immigrants living in the country who were not citizens. Many Europeans who came to the United States in the 1790s supported the ideals of the French Revolution. Some Americans questioned whether these aliens would remain loyal if the United States went to war with France.

Federalists in Congress responded with strict laws to protect the nation's security. In 1798 they passed a group of measures known as the **Alien and Sedition Acts.** Sedition refers to activities aimed at weakening established government.

🔲Citizenship

Domestic and Foreign Affairs

For some Americans, fears of a strong central government abusing its power seemed to be coming true. The Republicans looked to the states to preserve the people's liberties and stand

up to what they regarded as Federalist tyranny. Madison and Jefferson drafted documents of protest that were passed by the Virginia and Kentucky legislatures.

The Virginia and Kentucky Resolutions of 1798 and 1799 claimed that the Alien and Sedition Acts could not be put into action because they violated the Constitution. The Kentucky Resolutions further suggested that states might nullify—legally overturn—federal laws considered unconstitutional.

The resolutions affirmed the principle of states' rights—limiting the federal government to those powers clearly assigned to it by the Constitution and reserving to the states all other powers not expressly forbidden to them. The issue of states' rights would arise again and again in the nation's early history.

As the election of 1800 approached, the Federalists found themselves under attack. They urged Adams to step up the war with France. They hoped to benefit politically from the

Analyzing *Political Cartoons*

Fighting in Congress *The Sedition Act led to hard feelings, even violence. This cartoon provides a humorous look at a fight in Congress. Federalist Roger Griswold attacks Republican Matthew Lyon with a cane. Lyon seizes a pair of fire tongs and fights back. On the wall is a painting named "Royal Sport" showing animals fighting.* **How are the other members of Congress reacting to the fight?**

1 Matthew Lyon **2** Roger Griswold **3** painting

patriotic feelings that war would unleash. Adams refused to rush to war, especially for his own political gain. Instead he appointed a new commission to seek peace with France.

In 1800 the French agreed to a treaty and stopped attacks on American ships. Although the agreement with France was in the best interest of the United States, it hurt Adams's chance for re-election. Rather than applauding the agreement, Hamilton and his supporters now opposed their own president. With the Federalists split, the Republican prospects for capturing the presidency improved. The way was prepared for Thomas Jefferson in the election of 1800.

✓ **Reading Check** **Summarizing** *How did the peace agreement with France affect the Federalists?*

SECTION 3 ASSESSMENT

Checking for Understanding

1. **Key Terms** Write a short newspaper article about the election of 1796 in which you use the following terms: *partisan, implied powers, caucus.*
2. **Reviewing Facts** Who was elected president in 1796, and who became vice president?

Reviewing Themes

3. **Government and Democracy** How were the Federalists different from the Republicans in how they felt about a powerful central government?

Critical Thinking

4. **Drawing Conclusions** Do you think the development of political parties was necessary? Why or why not?
5. **Classifying Information** Re-create the diagram below. Provide information about the election of 1796 in the spaces provided.

Presidential Election of 1796		
Candidate		
Party		
Electoral votes		
Winner (check column)		
Vice President (check column)		

Analyzing Visuals

6. **Graphic Organizer Skills** Study the diagram on page 271. Who are aliens? Why were the Alien and Sedition Acts passed? How did their passage affect the Federalist Party?

Interdisciplinary Activity

Art Choose the presidential candidate for whom you would have voted in 1796. Design a campaign poster or button using words and illustrations to help promote your candidate.

Social Studies
SKILLBUILDER

Reading a Flowchart

Why Learn This Skill?

Sometimes determining a sequence of events can be confusing, particularly when many events occur at the same time. A flowchart can help you understand what is going on in a series of events.

Learning the Skill

Flowcharts show the steps in a process or a sequence of events. For example, a flowchart could be used to show the movement of goods through a factory, of people through a training program, or of a bill through Congress. The following steps explain how to read a flowchart:

- Read the title or caption of the flowchart to find out what you are studying.
- Read all of the labels or sentences on the flowchart.
- Look for numbers indicating a sequence, or arrows showing the direction of movement.

Practicing the Skill

Read the flowchart on this page. It shows a sequence of events that took place in the Northwest Territory. Analyze the information in the flowchart; then answer the following questions.

1 What symbol is used to show the sequence of the events?

2 What actions taken by the British set off the sequence of events that are reflected in the title of the chart?

3 What action did Washington take in response to trouble in the Ohio Valley?

4 What information from the chapter could you add to the flowchart to continue the sequence of events?

Conflicts in the Northwest Territory

1790s
Great Britain holds forts in the Ohio Valley.

British stir up trouble between Native Americans and American settlers in the Ohio Valley.

President Washington sends troops into the Northwest Territory.

Federal troops are defeated by Miami chief Little Turtle.

Applying the Skill

Making a Flowchart Imagine that a student who is new to your school asks you how to sign up for a sport or social club. Draw a flowchart outlining the steps the student should follow.

 Glencoe's **Skillbuilder Interactive Workbook CD-ROM, Level 1,** provides instruction and practice in key social studies skills.

Chapter Summary

A New Nation

Federal Government

- First Congress establishes three executive departments
- Judiciary Act of 1789 passes
- Bill of Rights added to the Constitution
- Nation's capital moves to Washington, D.C.
- National bank created
- Congress approves tariffs

Early Challenges

- Whiskey Rebellion put down
- Force and treaties slow Native American resistance to settlement
- Washington maintains American neutrality
- Treaty with Spain allows access to the Mississippi River

The New Nation

First Political Parties

- Federalists emerge, promoting a strong central government
- Republicans want to leave more power in the hands of the states.

President John Adams

- Federalist John Adams becomes second president
- American and French naval forces fight an undeclared war
- Federalists in Congress pass the Alien and Sedition Acts
- Virginia and Kentucky Resolutions advocate states' rights

Reviewing Key Terms

On graph paper, create a word search puzzle using the following terms. Crisscross the terms vertically and horizontally, then fill in the remaining squares with extra letters. List the definition of each term below the puzzle as clues. Share your puzzle with a classmate.

1. precedent
2. cabinet
3. tariff
4. neutrality
5. impressment
6. caucus
7. sedition
8. states' rights

Reviewing Key Facts

9. Why did Hamilton want national taxes? Why did some oppose the taxes?
10. What was the importance of the Judiciary Act of 1789?
11. What caused farmers in western Pennsylvania to revolt during the Whiskey Rebellion?
12. According to Hamilton, what are implied powers?
13. What actions by France led to an undeclared war with the United States?
14. Who was elected president in 1796? Who was elected vice president?

Critical Thinking

15. **Analyzing Themes: Government and Democracy** Refer to the grievances listed in the Declaration of Independence. How were these grievances addressed in the Bill of Rights?
16. **Analyzing Information** What did President Washington say in his Farewell Address about political parties and foreign policy?
17. **Comparing** Re-create the diagram below. Compare the positions of the Federalists and Democratic-Republicans on the national bank. In the boxes list the leaders and their positions.

National Bank	
Federalists	**Democratic-Republicans**
Leader:	Leader:
Position:	Position:

Practicing Skills

Reading a Flowchart *Alexander Hamilton promoted the creation of a national bank. Study the flowchart below. Then answer the questions that follow.*

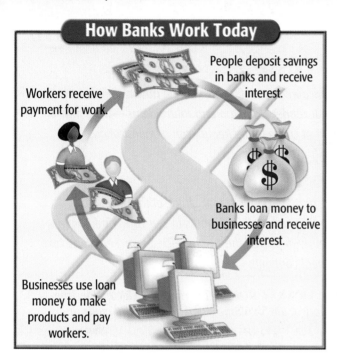

How Banks Work Today

Workers receive payment for work.

People deposit savings in banks and receive interest.

Banks loan money to businesses and receive interest.

Businesses use loan money to make products and pay workers.

18. What is used to show the sequence of events?
19. What happens after workers receive payment for work?
20. What two parts on this flowchart show who receives interest on their money?

Geography and History Activity

Study the map on page 265. Then answer the questions that follow.

21. **Movement** In which direction did St. Clair's troops move?
22. **Location** Along what river was Ft. Washington located?

Citizenship Cooperative Activity

23. **Researching** Work in groups of four to discuss and develop answers to these questions:
   • How does the Bill of Rights reflect the principle of limited government?
   • What are two individual rights protected in the Bill of Rights?
   • Why would it be necessary to change the Constitution?

HISTORY Online

Self-Check Quiz
Visit **tarvol1.glencoe.com** and click on **Chapter 8— Self-Check Quizzes** to prepare for the chapter test.

Economics Activity

24. **Math Practice** When you deposit money in a bank, you receive interest—a payment for lending money to the bank. To figure simple interest, you need to know what the interest rate is. Say, for example, a local bank is offering simple interest on savings accounts at 6 percent per year. If you deposit $100, how much will you have in the account at the end of one year? At the end of four years?

Technology Activity

25. **Using a Computerized Card Catalog** Search your local library's computerized card catalog for sources on Mount Vernon, George Washington's home. Find the sources on the library shelves, then use the information you found to write a two-paragraph description that Washington might have written if he had ever wanted to sell his home.

Alternative Assessment

26. Review the chapter and make a list of the differences between the Federalist and Republican parties. Based on your list, create a symbol to represent each of the parties.

Standardized Test Practice

Directions: Choose the *best* answer to the following question.

Certain grievances listed in the Declaration of Independence were addressed in the Bill of Rights. Which amendment addressed the quartering of troops?

A 1st Amendment   C 8th Amendment

B 3rd Amendment   D 12th Amendment

Test-Taking Tip
Read the question carefully. The 12th Amendment was not part of the Bill of Rights, so it can be eliminated as a possibility.

CHAPTER 9

The Jefferson Era

1800–1816

Why It Matters

In 1801 the Democratic-Republican Party took control of the nation's government. The Federalists—the party of Alexander Hamilton and John Adams—were now on the sidelines and played the role of critics to the Republican administration.

The Impact Today

Politicians today operate within the party system that took shape at that time.
- *While the two main parties have changed, each still works to win votes and gain power.*
- *If the people vote to change the party in power, the newly elected representatives take office peacefully and the government continues.*

The American Republic to 1877 Video *The chapter 9 video, "The True Story of Sacagawea," tells the story of the Shoshone woman who helped guide the Lewis and Clark expedition.*

1803
- Supreme Court establishes judicial review

1804
- Lewis and Clark begin expedition

1807
- Congress passes Embargo Act

United States PRESIDENTS

Jefferson 1801–1809

1800

1804

1808

World

1804
- Napoleon names himself emperor of France

1808
- Beethoven's *Fifth Symphony* performed

Battle of North Point by Don Troiani American soldiers battled British forces advancing on Baltimore.

FOLDABLES™
Study Organizer

Organizing Information Study Foldable
Make this foldable to organize information and sequence events about the Jefferson era into a flowchart.

Step 1 Fold a sheet of paper in half from side to side.

Fold it so the left edge lies about $\frac{1}{2}$ inch from the right edge.

Step 2 Turn the paper and fold it into thirds.

Step 3 Unfold and cut the top layer only along both folds. Then cut each of the three tabs in half.

This will make six tabs.

Step 4 Label your foldable as shown.

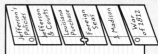

Reading and Writing As you read, select key facts about the events of the Jefferson era and write them under the tabs of your foldable.

1811
• Battle of Tippecanoe

1812
• U.S. declares war on Britain

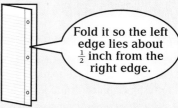

1815
• Battle of New Orleans

Madison 1809–1817

1812   *1816*

1812
• Napoleon invades Russia

1814
• Congress of Vienna meets

1815
• Napoleon defeated at Waterloo

HISTORY
Online

Chapter Overview
Visit tarvol1.glencoe.com and click on **Chapter 9—Chapter Overviews** to preview chapter information.

The Republicans Take Power

Main Idea
The election of 1800 marked the transfer of power from one political party to another through a democratic election.

Key Terms
laissez-faire, customs duties, judicial review

Reading Strategy
Organizing Information As you read the section, use a diagram like the one shown here to identify ways Republicans tried to reduce the role of government.

Ways the Republicans reduced government

Read to Learn
• how the election deadlock of 1800 was resolved.
• how John Marshall strengthened the Supreme Court.

Section Theme
Government and Democracy Jefferson believed that a large federal government threatened liberty.

Preview of Events

| ♦1800 | ♦1801 | ♦1802 | ♦1803 |

1800
Thomas Jefferson and John Adams contend for presidency

1801
Judiciary Act expands court system

March 1801
Jefferson is inaugurated

1803
Marbury v. *Madison* sets precedent for judicial review

AN American Story

Abigail Adams in the unfinished White House

In 1801 Washington, D.C., was slowly rising from a swampy site on the Potomac River. The nation's new capital had only two noteworthy buildings—the president's mansion (later called the White House) and the still-unfinished Capitol. Between them stretched about two miles of muddy streets on which pigs and chickens roamed freely.

Very few people liked being in Washington. It was hot and steamy in the summer, and the river and swamps were a breeding ground for mosquitoes. Abigail Adams called the new capital "the very dirtiest Hole."

The Election of 1800

The Federalist and Republican parties fought a bitter election campaign in 1800. Federalists supported President Adams for a second term and Charles Pinckney of South Carolina for vice president. Republicans nominated **Thomas Jefferson** for president and **Aaron Burr** of New York as his running mate.

The election campaign of 1800 differed greatly from campaigns of today. Neither Adams nor Jefferson traveled around the country making speeches about why he should be elected. That would have been considered in bad taste. Instead the candidates and their allies wrote hundreds of letters to leading citizens and friendly newspapers to publicize their views. The letter-writing campaign, however, was not polite.

Federalists charged the Republican Jefferson, who believed in freedom of religion, as being "godless." Republicans warned that the Federalists would bring back monarchy. Federalists, they claimed, represented the interests of wealthy people with property.

Election Deadlock

When members of the Electoral College voted, Jefferson and Burr each received 73 votes. Because of this tie, the House of Representatives had to decide the election. At the time the electors voted for each presidential and vice-presidential candidate individually rather than voting for a party's candidates as a team.

In the House, Federalists saw a chance to prevent the election of Jefferson by supporting Burr. For 35 ballots, the election remained tied. Finally, at Alexander Hamilton's urging, one Federalist decided not to vote for Burr. Jefferson became president, and Burr became vice president.

To prevent another showdown between a presidential and a vice-presidential candidate, Congress passed the Twelfth Amendment to the Constitution in 1803. This amendment, ratified in 1804, requires electors to vote for the president and vice president on separate ballots. 📖
(See page 246 for the entire text of the Twelfth Amendment.)

Jefferson's Inauguration

On March 4, 1801, the day of the inauguration, Jefferson dressed in everyday clothes. He left his boardinghouse and walked to the Senate to be sworn in as president. President Adams did not attend the ceremony. He had slipped out of the presidential mansion and left the city so he would not have to watch Thomas Jefferson become president.

In his Inaugural Address, Jefferson tried to bridge the gap between the developing political parties and reach out to Federalists with healing words. "We are all Republicans, we are all Federalists," he said. Then he outlined some of his goals, which included "a wise and frugal government" and "the support of state governments in all their rights." Jefferson had long been a supporter of states' rights. He believed that a large federal government threatened liberty and that vigilant states could best protect freedom.

Jefferson believed in reducing the power and size of the federal government. These ideas were similar to the French philosophy of laissez-faire (leh•say FEHR), which means "let (people) do (as they choose)."

✓ **Reading Check** **Describing** What does the Twelfth Amendment to the Constitution require?

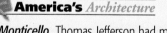

America's *Architecture*

Monticello Thomas Jefferson had many talents, including being a skilled architect. He designed buildings at the University of Virginia and his home at Monticello. Construction on Monticello began in 1769, following Jefferson's first design. Remodeling and enlarging the house began in 1796 and was completed by 1809.

"All my wishes end, where I hope my days will end, at Monticello."

—*Thomas Jefferson*

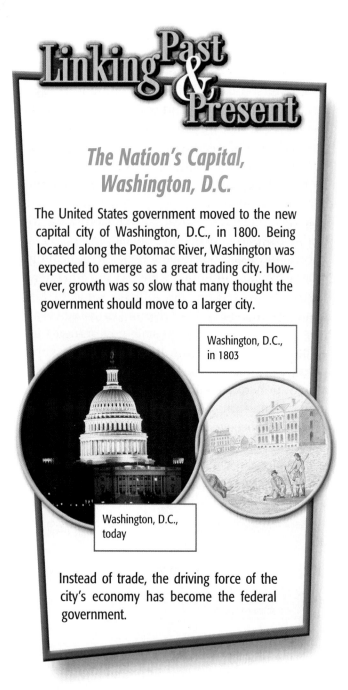
Jefferson's Policies

Thomas Jefferson had strong ideas about how to make the United States a success. He believed that the strength of the United States was its independent farmers. As long as most people owned their own property, they would fight to protect their rights and to preserve the republic. For this reason, Jefferson favored expanding the nation westward to acquire more land. He also believed the federal government should be kept small. He distrusted standing armies and wanted to reduce the size of the military.

Jefferson's Cabinet

When Jefferson entered office, he surrounded himself with men who shared his Republican principles. His secretary of state was his friend and fellow Virginian, James Madison. For secretary of the treasury, he chose **Albert Gallatin.** This Pennsylvanian had a grasp of financial matters that equaled Alexander Hamilton's.

The new government soon ended two unpopular Federalist measures. It allowed the Alien and Sedition acts to expire and repealed the Naturalization Act. For Republicans both acts were symbols of a federal government that threatened individual liberties.

Cutting Costs

Jefferson and Gallatin aimed to reduce the national debt that the Federalists had left. They scaled down military expenses. They cut the army by one-third and reduced the navy from 25 to 7 ships. By slashing spending Jefferson and Gallatin significantly lowered the national debt within a few years.

Jefferson and Gallatin also persuaded Congress to repeal all federal internal taxes, including the hated whiskey tax. At that point government funds would come only from customs duties—taxes on foreign imported goods—and from the sale of western lands.

The entire federal government in 1801 consisted of only a few hundred people. This was exactly how Jefferson thought it should be. In his view the responsibilities of the national government should be limited to delivering the mail, collecting customs duties, and conducting a census every 10 years.

Reading Check **Explaining** How did the changes that Jefferson made when he became president reflect his views about government?

Jefferson and the Courts

Jefferson hoped that some Federalists would support his policies. However, bitter feelings between the parties continued during his administration. Much of the ill will resulted from a fight over control of the federal courts.

Judiciary Act of 1801

Before Jefferson took office, the Federalists passed the Judiciary Act of 1801. The act set up regional courts for the United States with 16 judges and many other judicial officials. In his last days as president, John Adams made hundreds of appointments to these positions, and the Federalist-controlled Congress approved them. Adams also asked **John Marshall,** his secretary of state, to serve as chief justice of the United States. By these actions Adams shut President-elect Jefferson out of the appointment process and ensured that Federalists would control the courts.

Adams and Marshall worked around the clock in the final hours of the Federalist government, processing the papers for these judicial appointments. The appointments could not take effect, however, until the papers (commissions) for these last-minute "midnight judges" were delivered. When Jefferson became president on March 4, a few of the commissions had not yet been delivered. He told Secretary of State Madison not to deliver them. One commission was addressed to William Marbury.

Marbury v. *Madison*

To force the delivery of his commission, Marbury took his case directly to the Supreme Court, which he claimed had jurisdiction as a result of the Judiciary Act of 1789. John Marshall wrote an opinion turning down Marbury's claim. He noted that the Constitution did not give the Court jurisdiction to decide Marbury's case.

In his opinion, Marshall set out three principles of judicial review: (a) The Constitution is the supreme law of the land. (b) When there is a conflict between the Constitution and any other law, the Constitution must be followed. (c) The judicial branch has a duty to uphold the Constitution. It must be able to determine when a federal law conflicts with the Constitution and to nullify, or cancel, unconstitutional laws.

Marshall not only extended the power of the Court, he also broadened federal power at the expense of the states. In *McCulloch* v. *Maryland* (1819), the Court held that the elastic clause allows Congress to do more than the Constitution expressly authorizes it to do. In *Gibbons* v. *Ogden* (1824) the Court held that federal law takes precedence over state law in interstate transportation. 📖 *(See the Supreme Court Case Summaries beginning on page 624 for more on these cases.)*

Reading Check **Summarizing** Summarize the court case that established judicial review.

SECTION 1 ASSESSMENT

Checking for Understanding

1. **Key Terms** Write a short paragraph in which you explain the terms laissez-faire, customs duties, and judicial review.
2. **Reviewing Facts** Explain how Jefferson cut government spending.

Reviewing Themes

3. **Government and Democracy** How did the judicial branch under Jefferson serve as a check on the executive and legislative branches?

Critical Thinking

4. **Identifying Central Issues** How was the deadlock in the presidential election of 1800 finally resolved?
5. **Determining Cause and Effect** Re-create the diagram below. In the boxes list the effects that came from the appointment of the "midnight judges."

Adams appoints judges → □ → □ → □

Analyzing Visuals

6. **Analyzing Architecture** Examine the photograph of Monticello on page 279. Who lived there? What do you think gives Monticello its unique look? Explain.

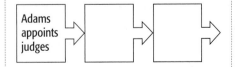

Expository Writing A letter of recommendation is written to discuss the positive qualities of a person. Write a letter from John Adams to Thomas Jefferson about John Marshall. Address Marshall's skills and leadership qualities.

The Louisiana Purchase

Guide to Reading

Main Idea

The Louisiana Purchase opened a vast area to exploration and settlement.

Key Terms

Conestoga wagon, secede

Reading Strategy

Classifying Information As you read, re-create the diagram below and describe the areas that Lewis and Clark, and Zebulon Pike explored.

Explorer	Region explored
Meriwether Lewis and William Clark	
Zebulon Pike	

Read to Learn

- how the United States expanded in the early 1800s.
- how Lewis and Clark led an expedition to explore the Louisiana Territory.

Section Theme

Geography and History The purchase of the Louisiana Territory doubled the nation's size.

Preview of Events

♦1804	♦1805	♦1806	♦1807
October 1803 Senate ratifies Louisiana Purchase treaty	**May 1804** Lewis and Clark begin expedition	**September 1806** Lewis and Clark return to St. Louis	**November 1806** Zebulon Pike sights Pikes Peak

AN
American Story

Why did Americans risk everything they had to travel west? An English visitor, Harriet Martineau, observed: "The pride and delight of Americans is in their quantity of land. . . . The possession of land is the aim of all action . . . and the cure for all social evils. . . . If a man is disappointed in politics or love, he goes and buys land. If he disgraces himself, he betakes himself to a lot in the West. . . ."

Conestoga wagon

Western Territory

During the early 1800s, more and more Americans moved west in search of land and adventure. These pioneers headed over the mountains into Kentucky and Tennessee and the less settled areas of the Northwest Territory. Most of these pioneers were farmers. They made a long and exhausting journey over the Appalachian Mountains. Pioneers had to trudge along crude, muddy roads or cut their way through dense forests.

Settlers loaded their household goods into Conestoga wagons, sturdy vehicles topped with white canvas. For these westward-bound pioneers, their two most valued possessions were a rifle for protection and hunting and an ax to hack their way through the dense forests.

In 1800 the territory of the United States extended only as far west as the Mississippi River. The area to the west of the river—known as the **Louisiana Territory**—belonged to Spain. It was an enormous area of land, anchored to the south by the city of New Orleans and extending west to the Rocky Mountains. Its northern boundaries remained undefined.

Many of the pioneers settled down and established farms along rivers that fed into the upper Mississippi River. They needed the river to ship their crops to markets. The Spanish allowed the Americans to sail on the lower Mississippi and trade in **New Orleans.** For the western farmers, this right was vital. The goods they sent downriver were unloaded in New Orleans and sent by ship to markets on the East Coast.

The French Threat

In 1802 the Spanish suddenly changed their policy. They refused to allow American goods to move into or past New Orleans. That same year, President Jefferson confirmed that Spain and France had made a secret agreement that transferred the Louisiana Territory to France.

This agreement posed a serious threat for the United States. France's leader, **Napoleon Bonaparte,** had plans for empires in Europe and the Americas. Jefferson was alarmed. He believed French control would jeopardize American trade on the Mississippi River. Jefferson authorized Robert Livingston, the new minister to France, to offer as much as $10 million for New Orleans and West Florida in order to gain control of the territory. Jefferson believed that France had gained Florida as well as Louisiana in its secret agreement with Spain.

Revolt in Santo Domingo

Napoleon had recognized the importance of Santo Domingo as a Caribbean naval base from which he could control an American empire. Events in Santo Domingo ended Napoleon's dream of a Western empire. Inspired by the ideas of the French Revolution, enslaved Africans and other laborers in Santo Domingo had revolted against the island's plantation owners. After fierce and bitter fighting, the rebels, led by **Toussaint-Louverture** (TOO•SA LOO•vuhr•TYUR), declared the colony an independent republic. Toussaint set up a new government.

In 1802 Napoleon sent troops to regain control. The French captured Toussaint but could not regain control of the island. By 1804, the French were driven out of Santo Domingo and the country regained its original name of Haiti.

✓**Reading Check** **Explaining** Why was the Mississippi River important to western farmers?

The Nation Expands

Without Santo Domingo, Napoleon had little use for Louisiana. The French also needed money to finance Napoleon's plans for war against Britain. The French believed they had something to sell that the United States might want to buy.

French foreign minister Charles de Talleyrand informed the American diplomats that the entire Louisiana Territory was for sale. Livingston and James Monroe, Jefferson's new special representative, were taken completely by surprise. Accepting the offer went far beyond what they were authorized to do, but the deal was too good to pass up. After a few days of negotiation, the parties agreed on a price of $15 million.

The Louisiana Purchase pleased Jefferson. The new territory would provide cheap and abundant land for farmers for generations to come. He worried, however, whether the purchase was legal. The Constitution said nothing about acquiring new territory. By what authority could he justify the purchase? Livingston wrote from Paris, urging Jefferson to accept the deal before Napoleon changed his mind. Jefferson decided the government's treaty-making powers allowed the purchase of the new territory. The Senate gave its approval in October 1803. With the ratification of the treaty, the size of the United States doubled.

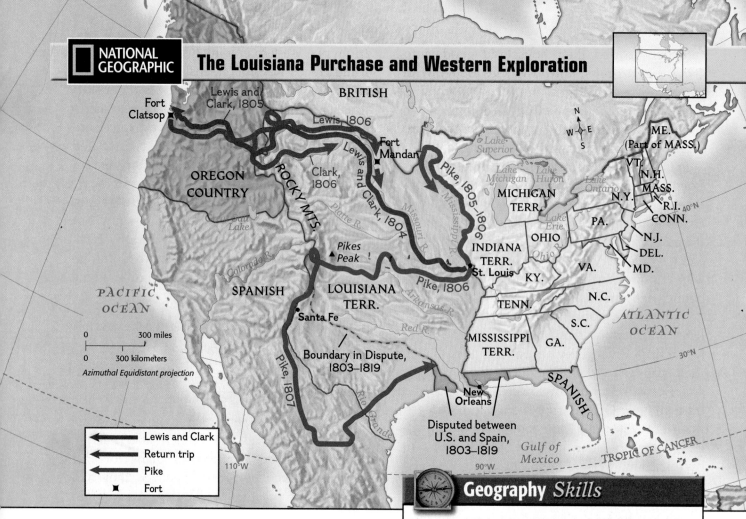

The Louisiana Purchase and Western Exploration

Fort Clatsop

Lewis and Clark, 1805

BRITISH

Lewis, 1806

Fort Mandan

Pike, 1805–1806

OREGON COUNTRY

ROCKY MTS.

Clark, 1806

Lewis and Clark, 1804

Platte R.

Missouri R.

Mississippi R.

Lake Superior

Lake Michigan

Lake Huron

Lake Ontario

Lake Erie

MICHIGAN TERR.

N
W E
S

ME. (Part of MASS.)

VT.
N.H.
MASS.
N.Y.
R.I. 40°N
CONN.
N.J.
DEL.
MD.

PA.

OHIO

INDIANA TERR.

St. Louis

Ohio R.

Pike, 1806

KY.

VA.

N.C.

PACIFIC OCEAN

Salt Lake

Colorado R.

Pikes Peak

SPANISH

LOUISIANA TERR.

Santa Fe

Arkansas R.

Red R.

Pike, 1807

Boundary in Dispute, 1803–1819

Rio Grande

TENN.

MISSISSIPPI TERR.

GA.

S.C.

ATLANTIC OCEAN

30°N

SPANISH

New Orleans

Disputed between U.S. and Spain, 1803–1819

Gulf of Mexico

TROPIC OF CANCER

110°W

90°W

0   300 miles

0   300 kilometers

Azimuthal Equidistant projection

Lewis and Clark
Return trip
Pike
Fort

Geography Skills

The purchase of the Louisiana Territory doubled the size of the United States. Americans quickly set out to explore the region and lands farther west.

1. Place What geographical barrier did Lewis and Clark have to cross in order to reach the Pacific Ocean?

2. Region What rivers flowed through the Louisiana Territory?

Geography

Lewis and Clark

Jefferson wanted to know more about the mysterious lands west of the Mississippi. Even before the Louisiana Purchase was complete, he persuaded Congress to sponsor an expedition to explore the new territory. Jefferson was particularly interested in the expedition as a scientific venture. Congress was interested in commercial possibilities and in sites for future forts.

To head the expedition, Jefferson chose his private secretary, 28-year-old **Meriwether Lewis.** Lewis was well qualified to lead this journey of exploration. He had joined the militia during the Whiskey Rebellion and had been in the army since that time. The expedition's co-leader was **William Clark,** 32, a friend of Lewis's from military service. Both Lewis and Clark were knowledgeable amateur scientists and had conducted business with Native Americans. Together they assembled a crew that included expert river men, gunsmiths, carpenters, scouts, and a cook. Two

men of mixed Native American and French heritage served as interpreters. An African American named York rounded out the group.

The expedition left **St. Louis** in the spring of 1804 and slowly worked its way up the **Missouri River.** Lewis and Clark kept a journal of their voyage and made notes on what they saw and did.

Along their journey they encountered Native American groups. One young Shoshone woman named **Sacagawea** (SA•kuh•juh•WEE•uh) joined their group as a guide. After 18 months and nearly 4,000 miles, Lewis and Clark reached the Pacific Ocean. After spending the winter there, both explorers headed back east along separate routes.

INTO THE UNKNOWN

LEWIS AND CLARK In 1803 President Jefferson set up the Corps of Discovery to find a water route to the Pacific and explore the recently acquired Louisiana Purchase. In the spring of 1804, William Clark and Meriwether Lewis, with a company of recruits, set off from St. Louis.

1804 THE JOURNEY WEST

1 MAY 14 The members of the Corps of Discovery, which number over 45, embark on the expedition, which would eventually cover nearly 7,700 miles.

2 NOVEMBER The explorers set up a winter camp near the villages of the Mandans and Hidatsas. Sacagawea, a Shoshone woman who had been kidnapped by the Hidatsa, joins the expedition.

1805

3 APRIL 7 Lewis and Clark send a group back on the keelboat with reports and specimens of some of the plants and animals that were unknown in the East. The expedition continues in smaller boats.

4 AUGUST 12 Lewis realizes that there is no Northwest Passage—or river route—to the Pacific. The Corps continues on horseback.

5 DECEMBER 25 The expedition celebrates Christmas in its new winter quarters, Fort Clatsop.

1806 THE RETURN TRIP

6 JULY 3 The expedition splits into smaller units to explore more of the Louisiana Territory. They reunite on August 12.

7 SEPTEMBER 23 The Corps of Discovery finally arrives back in St. Louis. The explorers had established peaceful contact with many Native Americans and accumulated a wealth of geographic information. Fur traders and others, armed with the new knowledge, soon start heading west.

Map legend
- Route west (1804-1805)
- Return route east (1806)
- Continental divide
- Fort
- Travel by keel boat
- Travel by horseback
- Travel by dugout canoe

0   100 miles
0   100 kilometers

ST. LOUIS

The explorers travel up the Missouri River in a large keelboat and smaller boats called pirogues.

LEARNING from GEOGRAPHY

1. What obstacles do you think would have been the most difficult for the expedition?

2. Write a paragraph that describes the importance of teamwork in helping the Corps of Discovery reach its goals.

A Time of Conflict

Guide to Reading

Main Idea
Between 1800 and 1815 the United States experienced rapid expansion as well as the challenge of war.

Key Terms
tribute, neutral rights, impressment, embargo, War Hawks, nationalism

Reading Strategy
Organizing Information As you read the section, re-create the diagram below and describe in the box the actions the United States took in each of these situations.

```
                    Demand for tribute
U.S. actions  <---- Attack on Chesapeake
                    Tecumseh's confederation
```

Read to Learn
• why Tecumseh built a confederacy among Native American nations.
• why the War Hawks wanted to go to war.

Section Theme
Global Connections The nation's neutrality was challenged.

Preview of Events

♦1804	♦1808	♦1812

1804
Barbary pirates seize the U.S. warship *Philadelphia*

1807
The British navy attacks the American vessel *Chesapeake;* Congress passes the Embargo Act

1811
Harrison defeats the Prophet at Tippecanoe

1812
Madison asks Congress to declare war on Britain

★★★★★★★ AN
American Story

American sailors

The floors of the oceans are littered with the remains of once-mighty ships and the unmarked graves of unlucky sailors who sank with them in the 1700s. Seafarer Francis Rogers described the terror of a storm in this journal entry: "The sky seemed all on fire and [all around] were such swift darting rays of lightning, flying in long bright veins, with inexpressible fury as was very frightful."

Americans in Foreign Seas

Despite the dangers of sea travel in the early 1800s, the livelihoods of many Americans depended on trade with foreign nations. In 1785 the American ship *Empress of China* returned to New York from China with a highly prized cargo of tea and silk. The goods sold for a fabulous profit. Soon ships from New York, Philadelphia, and especially New England were sailing regularly to China and India carrying furs and other goods. In the following years, American merchant ships sailed far and wide, making calls in South America, Africa, and lands along the Mediterranean Sea.

War between the French and British in the mid-1790s gave an additional boost to American shipping. Rather than risk capture or destruction by the enemy, many French and British merchant ships remained at home. American shippers profited from the situation and increased their trade. By 1800 the United States had almost 1,000 merchant ships trading around the world.

Barbary Pirates

Sailing in foreign seas was not without danger. In the Mediterranean, for example, ships had to be on guard for pirates from Tripoli and the other **Barbary Coast states** of North Africa. For years these Barbary pirates had been terrorizing the Mediterranean. They demanded tribute, or protection money, from European governments to let their ships pass safely.

War With Tripoli

The United States, too, had paid tribute for safe passage—but not enough. In 1801 the ruler of Tripoli asked for more money from the United States. When President Jefferson refused, the ruler chopped down the flagpole of the American consulate—a declaration of war. Jefferson sent ships to the Mediterranean and blockaded, or closed off, Tripoli. The American fleet, however, was not powerful enough to defeat the Barbary pirates, and the conflict continued.

In 1804 the pirates seized the U.S. warship *Philadelphia* and towed it into Tripoli Harbor. They threw the captain and crew into jail. **Stephen Decatur,** a 25-year-old United States Navy captain, took action. Slipping into the heavily guarded harbor with a small raiding party, Decatur burned the captured ship to prevent the pirates from using it. A British admiral praised the deed as the "most bold and daring act of the age."

Negotiations finally ended the conflict with Tripoli in June 1805. Tripoli agreed to stop demanding tribute, but the United States had to pay a ransom of $60,000 for the release of the American prisoners.

Reading Check **Explaining** Why did Tripoli declare war on the United States?

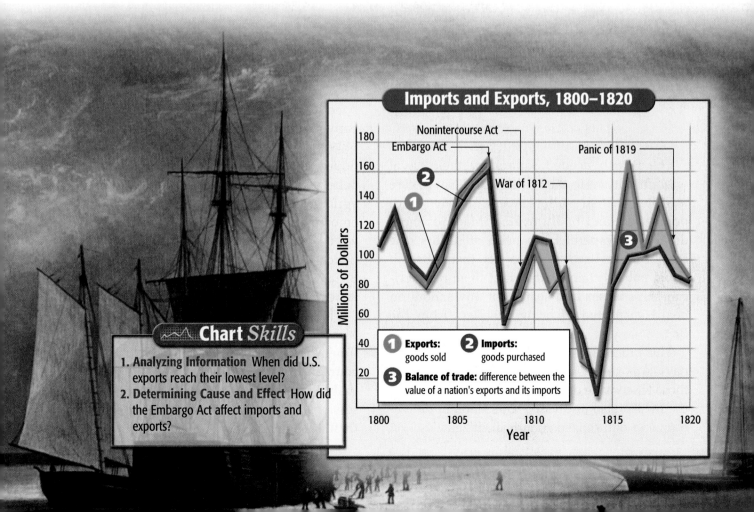

Imports and Exports, 1800–1820

Nonintercourse Act
Embargo Act
War of 1812
Panic of 1819

1 Exports: goods sold
2 Imports: goods purchased
3 Balance of trade: difference between the value of a nation's exports and its imports

Millions of Dollars

Chart *Skills*

1. **Analyzing Information** When did U.S. exports reach their lowest level?
2. **Determining Cause and Effect** How did the Embargo Act affect imports and exports?

Freedom of the Seas

Riding the wave of four successful years as president, Jefferson won reelection easily in 1804. Jefferson received 162 electoral votes to only 14 for his Federalist opponent, Charles Pinckney. His second term began with the nation at peace. Across the sea, however, Great Britain and France were already involved in a war that threatened to interfere with American trade.

The thriving foreign trade of the United States depended on being able to sail the seas freely. The nation had resolved the threat from the Barbary pirates. Now it was challenged at sea by the two most powerful nations in Europe.

Neutral Rights Violated

When Britain and France went to war in 1803, America enjoyed a prosperous commerce with both countries. As long as the United States remained neutral, shippers could continue doing business. A nation not involved in a conflict had neutral rights—the right to sail the seas and not take sides.

For two years American shipping continued to prosper. By 1805, however, the warring nations had lost patience with American "neutrality." Britain blockaded the French coast and threatened to search all ships trading with France. France later announced that it would search and seize ships caught trading with Britain.

American Sailors Kidnapped

The British needed sailors for their naval war. Conditions in the British Royal Navy were terrible. British sailors were poorly paid, poorly fed, and badly treated. Many of them deserted. Desperately in need of sailors, the British often used force to get them. British naval patrols claimed the right to stop American ships at sea and search for any sailors on board suspected of being deserters from the British navy.

This practice of forcing people to serve in the navy was called impressment. While some of those taken were deserters from the British navy, the British also impressed thousands of native-born and naturalized American citizens.

Attack on the *Chesapeake*

Quite often the British would lie in wait for American ships outside an American harbor. This happened in June 1807 off the coast of **Virginia.** A British warship, the *Leopard,* intercepted the American vessel *Chesapeake* and demanded to search the ship for British deserters. When the *Chesapeake*'s captain refused, the British opened fire, killing 3, wounding 18, and crippling the American ship.

As news of the attack spread, Americans reacted with an anti-British fury not seen since the Revolutionary War. Secretary of State **James Madison** called the attack an outrage. Many demanded war against Britain. Although President Jefferson did not intend to let Great Britain's actions go unanswered, he sought a course of action other than war.

A Disastrous Trade Ban

Britain's practice of impressment and its violation of America's neutral rights had led Jefferson to ban some trade with Britain. The attack on the *Chesapeake* triggered even stronger measures. In December 1807, the Republican Congress passed the **Embargo Act.** An embargo prohibits trade with another country. Although Great Britain was the target of this act, the embargo banned imports from and exports to *all* foreign countries. Jefferson wanted to prevent Americans from using other countries as go-betweens in the forbidden trade.

With the embargo, Jefferson and Madison hoped to hurt Britain but avoid war. They believed the British depended on American agricultural products. As it turned out, the embargo of 1807 was a disaster. The measure wiped out all American commerce with other nations. Worse, it proved ineffective against Britain. The British simply traded with Latin America for its agricultural goods.

The embargo clearly had not worked. On March 1, 1809, Congress repealed it. In its place Congress enacted the much weaker **Nonintercourse Act.** The new act prohibited trade only with Britain and France and their colonial possessions. It was no more popular or successful than the Embargo Act.

Jefferson Leaves Office

Following Washington's precedent, Jefferson made it clear in mid-1808 that he would not be a candidate for a third term. With Jefferson's approval the Republicans chose James Madison as their candidate for president. The Federalists nominated Charles Pinckney and hoped that anger over the embargo would help their party. Pinckney carried most of New England, but the Federalist ticket collected little support from the other regions. Madison won with 122 electoral votes to Pinckney's 47 votes.

Reading Check **Evaluating** How effective was the Embargo Act?

War Fever

James Madison did not take office as president under the most favorable conditions. At home and abroad, the nation was mired in the embargo crisis. Meanwhile Britain continued to claim the right to halt American ships, and cries for war with Britain grew louder.

Closer to War

In 1810 Congress passed a law permitting direct trade with either France or Britain, depending on which country first lifted its trade restrictions against America. Napoleon seized the opportunity and promised to end France's trade restrictions.

Unfortunately for Madison, Napoleon had tricked the American administration. The French continued to seize American ships, selling them and pocketing the proceeds. Americans were deeply divided. To some it seemed as if the nation was on the verge of war—but it was hard to decide if the enemy should be Britain or France. Madison knew that France had tricked him, but he continued to see Britain as the bigger threat to the United States.

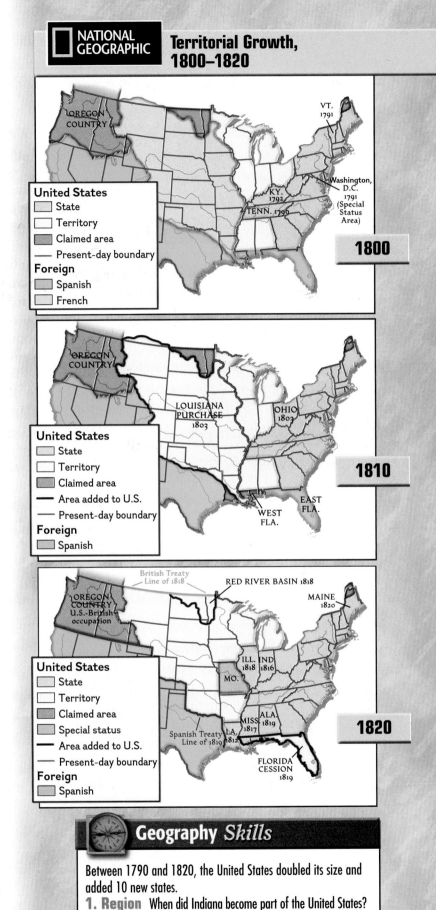

NATIONAL GEOGRAPHIC

Territorial Growth, 1800–1820

1800

United States
- State
- Territory
- Claimed area
- Present-day boundary

Foreign
- Spanish
- French

1810

United States
- State
- Territory
- Claimed area
- Area added to U.S.
- Present-day boundary

Foreign
- Spanish

1820

United States
- State
- Territory
- Claimed area
- Special status
- Area added to U.S.
- Present-day boundary

Foreign
- Spanish

Geography *Skills*

Between 1790 and 1820, the United States doubled its size and added 10 new states.

1. **Region** When did Indiana become part of the United States?
2. **Human-Environment Interaction** Describe the changes in French territory between 1800 and 1820.

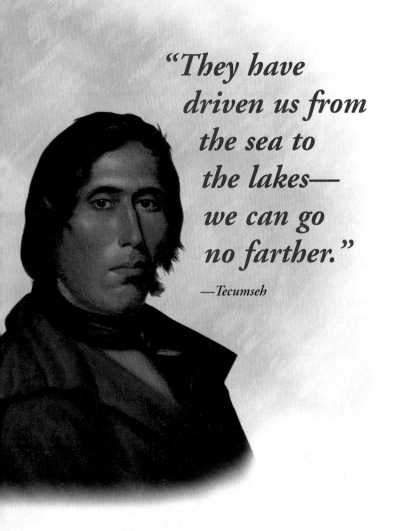

"They have driven us from the sea to the lakes— we can go no farther."

—Tecumseh

Frontier Conflicts

While Madison was trying to decide how to resolve the difficulties with European powers, news arrived about problems in the West. **Ohio** had become a state in 1803. Between 1801 and 1810, white settlers continued to press for more land in the Ohio Valley. Native Americans had given up many millions of acres. Now the settlers were moving onto lands that had been guaranteed to Native Americans by treaty.

As tensions increased, some Native Americans began renewing their contacts with British agents and fur traders in Canada. Others pursued a new strategy. A powerful Shawnee chief named **Tecumseh** (tuh•KUHM•suh) built a confederacy among Native American nations in the Northwest. Tecumseh believed that a strong alliance—with the backing of the British in Canada—could put a halt to white movement onto Native American lands.

A commanding speaker, Tecumseh possessed great political skills. In his view, the United States

government's treaties with separate Native American nations were worthless. "The Great Spirit gave this great island to his red children," he said. No one nation had the right to give it away.

Tecumseh had a powerful ally—his brother, known as **the Prophet.** The Prophet urged Native Americans everywhere to return to the customs of their ancestors. They should, he said, give up practices learned from the white invaders—wearing western dress, using plows and firearms, and especially drinking alcohol. The Prophet attracted a huge following among Native Americans. He founded a village at a site in northern Indiana, near present-day Lafayette, where the Tippecanoe and Wabash Rivers meet. It was called Prophetstown.

A Meeting With Harrison

The American governor of the Indiana Territory, **General William Henry Harrison,** became alarmed by the growing power of the two Shawnee brothers. He feared they would form an alliance with the British.

In a letter to Tecumseh, Harrison warned that the United States had many more warriors than all the Indian nations could put together. "Do not think that the redcoats can protect you; they are not able to protect themselves." Tecumseh sent word that he would reply in person.

A few weeks later, Tecumseh came to Harrison and spoke to the white people assembled there:

❝Brothers: Since the peace was made, you have killed some of the Shawnees, Winnebagoes, Delawares, and Miamis, and you have taken our land from us; and I do not see how we can remain at peace if you continue to do so. You try to force the red people to do some injury; it is you who are pushing them on to do mischief. You try to keep the tribes apart, and make distinctions among them. You wish to prevent the Indians from uniting.❞

The Battle of Tippecanoe

In 1811 while Tecumseh was in the South trying to expand his confederacy, Harrison decided to attack Prophetstown on the

Tippecanoe River. After more than two hours of battle, the Prophet's forces fled the area in defeat. The **Battle of Tippecanoe** was proclaimed a glorious victory for the Americans. Harrison acquired the nickname "Tippecanoe" and used it as a patriotic rallying cry when he ran for president in 1840.

Harrison's victory at the Battle of Tippecanoe, however, resulted in something the American people had hoped to prevent. Tecumseh now joined forces with the British troops. White settlers in the region claimed that the British had supplied Tecumseh's confederacy with guns. As a result, the rallying cry of the settlers became "On to Canada!"

War Hawks

Back in the nation's capital, President Madison faced demands for a more aggressive policy toward the British. The most insistent voices came from a group of young Republicans elected to Congress in 1810. Known as the War Hawks, they came from the South and the West. The War Hawks pressured the president to declare war against Britain.

While the War Hawks wanted to avenge British actions against Americans, they were also eager to expand the nation's power. Their nationalism—or loyalty to their country—appealed to a renewed sense of American patriotism. The leading War Hawks were **Henry**

TECHNOLOGY & History

The Conestoga Wagon

By the mid-1700s, sturdy Conestoga wagons transported settlers and their freight over the Appalachian Mountains. These wagons were first built in the Conestoga Creek region of Lancaster, Pennsylvania. As people pushed even farther westward, the Conestoga was seen rolling across the plains toward Oregon and California. *Why did Conestoga wagons have a high front and back?*

1 Six to eight draft horses or a dozen oxen pull the wagon. The driver rides or walks beside the animals.

2 The boat-shaped wagon's high front and back keep goods from falling out on steep mountain trails.

3 A **toolbox** attached to the side of the wagon holds spare parts for needed repairs.

4 A white canvas cloth stretches over the hoops, or **wagon bows**. This cover protects passengers and cargo from heat, rain, and snow.

5 Broad **wheels** help keep the heavy wagon from being mired in the mud.

The average Conestoga wagon was 21 feet long, 11 feet high, and 4 feet in width and depth. It could carry up to 12,000 pounds of cargo.

3 toolbox **4** wagon bows

2

1

5 wheels

Clay from Kentucky and **John Calhoun** from South Carolina, both in their 30s. Hunger for land heightened war fever. Westerners wanted to move north into the fertile forests of southern Canada. A war with Britain might make Canadian land available. Southerners wanted Spanish Florida.

The War Hawks urged major military spending. Through their efforts Congress quadrupled the army's size. The Federalists in the Northeast, however, remained strongly opposed to the war.

Declaring War

By the spring of 1812, Madison concluded that war with Britain was inevitable. In a message to Congress on June 1, he cited "the spectacle of injuries and indignities which have been heaped on our country" and asked for a declaration of war.

In the meantime the British had decided to end their policy of search and seizure of American ships. Unfortunately, because of the amount of time it took for news to travel across the Atlantic, this change in policy was not known in Washington. Word of the breakthrough arrived too late. Once set in motion, the war machine could not be stopped.

✓ **Reading Check** **Explaining** Why did the War Hawks call for war with Britain?

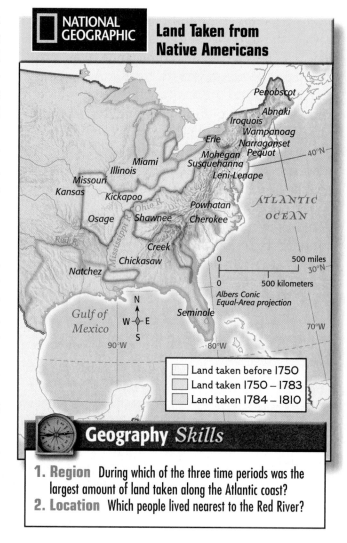

NATIONAL GEOGRAPHIC **Land Taken from Native Americans**

Geography *Skills*

1. **Region** During which of the three time periods was the largest amount of land taken along the Atlantic coast?
2. **Location** Which people lived nearest to the Red River?

Land taken before 1750
Land taken 1750 – 1783
Land taken 1784 – 1810

SECTION 3 ASSESSMENT

Checking for Understanding

1. **Key Terms** Write two paragraphs in which you use all of the following terms: tribute, neutral rights, impressment, embargo, War Hawks, nationalism.
2. **Reviewing Facts** Describe the negotiations that ended the war between the United States and Tripoli.

Reviewing Themes

3. **Global Connections** How did the conflict in Europe help the American shipping industry prosper?

Critical Thinking

4. **Determining Cause and Effect** How did frontier battles with Native Americans intensify Americans' anti-British feelings?
5. **Sequencing Information** Re-create the diagram below and list key events in the nation's effort to remain neutral in the war between France and Britain.

```
              June        Dec.
1805         1807        1807        1809
 |------------|------------|------------|
```

Analyzing Visuals

6. **Geography Skills** Examine the maps that appear on page 291. When did Tennessee gain statehood? Which of the maps shows the territory gained from the Louisiana Purchase? In what year was Florida ceded to the United States?

Interdisciplinary Activity

Art Choose a side in the argument about war with Great Britain. Draw a political cartoon supporting your point of view.

America's LITERATURE

Ignatia Broker (1919–1987)

Ignatia Broker was born on the White Earth Ojibway Reservation in Minnesota. She grew up hearing the stories of her people. She decided that one day she would tell others about Ojibway traditions. Through her writing, Broker passed on many Ojibway tales about "the purity of man and nature and keeping them in balance."

READ TO DISCOVER

Night Flying Woman tells the story of Oona, Ignatia Broker's great-great-grandmother. Oona was still a child when the Ojibway were forced to leave their land and find a new home. As you read, look for the ways in which Oona overcomes her fear of her latest home. What gives the Ojibway people faith that they will continue as a people?

READER'S DICTIONARY

fretful: worrisome, anxious, uneasy

A-wa-sa-si: a storyteller traveling with Oona's people

Ojibway: a Native American nation

Night Flying Woman

The next morning, very early, Grandfather, Oldest Uncle, and Father walked into the thick forest. Oona did not see them leave, for she was sleeping soundly. When Mother told her that they were gone, Oona looked at the forest fearfully. It seemed very unfriendly. She thought, "It has swallowed up my grandfather and father." She became **fretful.**

Mother said, "Daughter, look at the forest again but do not look and see only the dark and shadows. Instead, look at the trees, each one, as many as you can. Then tell me what you think.". . .

As Oona looked at the trees, she heard the si-si-gwa-d—the murmuring that the trees do when they brush their branches together. It was a friendly sound, and the sun sent sparkles through the si-si-gwa-d that chased the shadows. Suddenly the forest seemed different to Oona, and she knew that Grandfather, Oldest Uncle, and Father had gone into a friendly place. . . .

A-wa-sa-si said, "The forests have never failed the **Ojibway.** . . . As long as the Ojibway are beneath, the trees will murmur with contentment. When the Ojibway and the Animal Brothers are gone, the forest will weep and this will be reflected in the sound of the si-si-gwa-d. . . . In each generation of

Ojibway there will be a person who will hear the si-si-gwa-d, who will listen and remember and pass it on to the children. Remembering our past and acting accordingly will ensure that we, the Ojibway, will always people

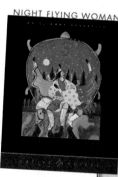

the earth. The trees have patience and so they have stood and have seen many generations of Ojibway. Yet will there be more, and yet will they see more."

From *Night Flying Woman: An Ojibway Narrative* by Ignatia Broker. Copyright © 1983 by the Minnesota Historical Society. Reprinted by permission.

ANALYZING LITERATURE

1. **Recall and Interpret** What sound did Oona hear in the forest? How did the sound affect Oona's feelings about the forest?

2. **Evaluate and Connect** What does Ignatia Broker in *Night Flying Woman* say about the importance of the past? Explain your answer.

Interdisciplinary Activity

Art Create a painting or drawing that shows the forest as Oona saw it. Use symbols to hint at the coming of the Europeans.

The War of 1812

Guide to Reading

Main Idea
Beginning in 1812 the United States was at war with Britain. Fighting took place in the United States, in Canada, and at sea.

Key Terms
frigate, privateer

Reading Strategy
Taking Notes As you read the section, re-create the diagram below and in the boxes describe each battle's outcome.

Battle	Outcome
Lake Erie	
Washington, D.C.	
New Orleans	

Read to Learn
- how the British seized and set fire to Washington, D.C.
- why Andrew Jackson fought a battle after the war was over.

Section Theme
Government and Democracy The end of the War of 1812 produced a new spirit of nationalism.

Preview of Events

♦1812   ♦1813   ♦1814   ♦1815

June 1812
United States declares war on Britain

September 1813
Perry defeats the British navy on Lake Erie

August 1814
The British burn Washington, D.C.

January 1815
American forces win the Battle of New Orleans

Madison peace medal

AN American Story

While President Madison awarded peace medals to Native Americans who supported the United States against the British, Congressional War Hawks could be heard singing:

Ye Parliaments of England,
Ye lords and commons, too,
Consider well what you're about,
And what you're goin' to do;

You're now at war with Yankees,
And I'm sure you'll rue the day
Ye roused the sons of liberty,
In North Americay.

War Begins

Despite their swaggering songs, the War Hawks did not achieve the quick victory they boldly predicted. The Americans committed a series of blunders that showed how unprepared they were for war. The regular army now consisted of fewer than 7,000 troops. The states had between 50,000 and 100,000 militia, but the units were poorly trained, and many states opposed "Mr. Madison's war." The military commanders, veterans of the American Revolution, were too old for warfare, and the government in Washington provided no leadership. The Americans also underestimated the strength of the British and their Native American allies.

The war started in July 1812, when **General William Hull** led the American army from **Detroit** into Canada. Hull was met by Tecumseh and his warriors. Fearing a massacre by the Native Americans, Hull surrendered Detroit to a small British force in August. Another attempt by General William Henry Harrison was unsuccessful as well. Harrison decided that the Americans could make no headway in Canada as long as the British controlled Lake Erie.

Naval Battles

Oliver Hazard Perry, commander of the **Lake Erie** naval forces, had his orders. He was to assemble a fleet and seize the lake from the British. From his headquarters in Put-in-Bay, Ohio, Perry could watch the movements of the enemy ships. The showdown came on September 10, 1813, when the British ships sailed out to face the Americans. In the bloody battle that followed, Perry and his ships defeated the British naval force. After the battle, Perry sent General William Henry Harrison the message, "We have met the enemy and they are ours."

With Lake Erie in American hands, the British and their Native American allies tried to pull back from the Detroit area. Harrison and his troops cut them off. In the fierce **Battle of the Thames** on October 5, the great leader Tecumseh was killed.

The Americans also attacked the town of York (present-day Toronto, Canada), burning the parliament buildings. Canada remained unconquered, but by the end of 1813 the Americans had won some victories on land and at sea.

To lower the national debt, the Republicans had reduced the size of the navy. However, the navy still boasted three of the fastest frigates, or warships, afloat. Americans exulted when the *Constitution*, one of these frigates, destroyed two British vessels—the *Guerrière* in August 1812 and the *Java* four months later. After seeing a shot bounce off the *Constitution*'s hull during battle, a sailor nicknamed the ship "Old Ironsides."

American privateers, armed private ships, also staged spectacular attacks on British ships and captured numerous vessels. These victories were more important for morale than for their strategic value.

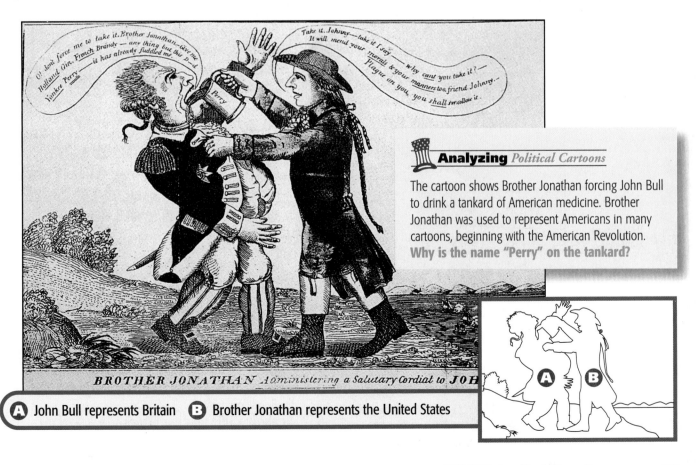

BROTHER JONATHAN *Administering a Salutary Cordial to JOH*

Ⓐ John Bull represents Britain　**Ⓑ Brother Jonathan represents the United States**

Analyzing *Political Cartoons*

The cartoon shows Brother Jonathan forcing John Bull to drink a tankard of American medicine. Brother Jonathan was used to represent Americans in many cartoons, beginning with the American Revolution. **Why is the name "Perry" on the tankard?**

Setbacks for Native Americans

With the death of Tecumseh in 1813, hopes for a Native American confederation died. In his travels two years before his death, Tecumseh had discussed plans for a confederation with the Creeks in the Mississippi Territory.

In March 1814, a lanky Tennessee planter named **Andrew Jackson** attacked the Creeks. Jackson's forces slaughtered more than 550 of the Creek people. Known as the **Battle of Horseshoe Bend,** the defeat broke the Creeks' resistance and forced them to give up most of their lands to the United States.

✓ **Reading Check** **Evaluating** Do you think the United States was prepared to wage war? Explain.

The British Offensive

British fortunes improved in the spring of 1814. They had been fighting a war with Napoleon and had won. Now they could send more forces to America.

Attack on Washington, D.C.

In August 1814, the British sailed into Chesapeake Bay. Their destination was Washington, D.C. On the outskirts of Washington, D.C., the British troops quickly overpowered the American militia and then marched into the city. "They proceeded, without a moment's delay, to burn and destroy everything in the most distant degree connected with government," reported a British officer.

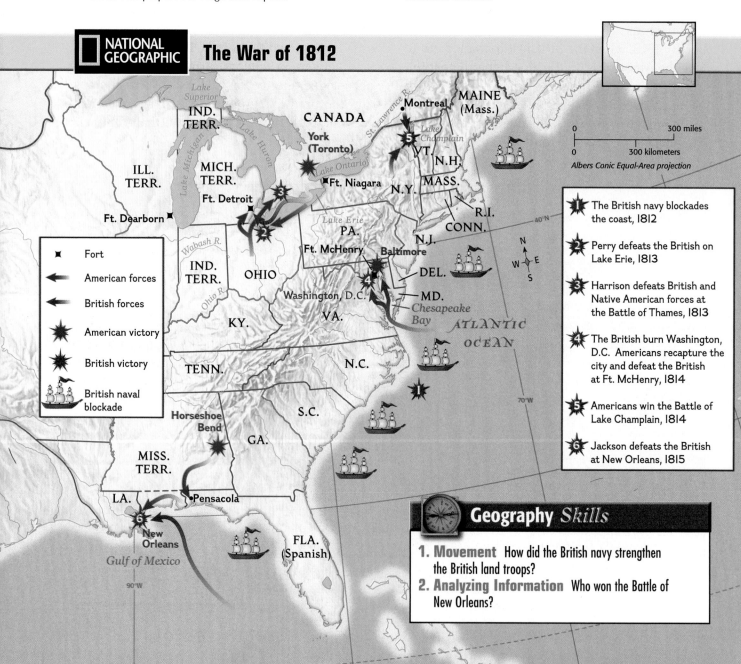

NATIONAL GEOGRAPHIC

The War of 1812

Legend:
- ✶ Fort
- ← American forces
- ← British forces
- ✷ American victory
- ✷ British victory
- British naval blockade

1. The British navy blockades the coast, 1812
2. Perry defeats the British on Lake Erie, 1813
3. Harrison defeats British and Native American forces at the Battle of Thames, 1813
4. The British burn Washington, D.C. Americans recapture the city and defeat the British at Ft. McHenry, 1814
5. Americans win the Battle of Lake Champlain, 1814
6. Jackson defeats the British at New Orleans, 1815

Geography *Skills*

1. **Movement** How did the British navy strengthen the British land troops?
2. **Analyzing Information** Who won the Battle of New Orleans?

People In History

Dolley Madison 1768–1849

Born in North Carolina, Dolley Payne grew up in Virginia until, at age 15, her family moved to Philadelphia. There she married John Todd, Jr. As Dolley Todd, she gave birth to two children, but lost her husband and one child in 1793 during a yellow fever epidemic.

The following year she married James Madison. While her husband was secretary of state, Dolley Madison served as unofficial first lady for the widower president, Thomas Jefferson. She became the nation's official first lady when James Madison was elected president in 1808. During the War of 1812

she showed remarkable bravery. In 1814, as the British approached the capital, she refused to leave the executive mansion until she had packed up many valuable government documents, a painting of George Washington, and other priceless valuables.

The Capitol and the president's mansion were among the buildings burned. Watching from outside the city, President Madison and his cabinet saw the night sky turn orange. Fortunately a violent thunderstorm put out the fires before they could do more damage. August 24, 1814, was a low point for the Americans.

Baltimore Holds Firm

Much to everyone's surprise, the British did not try to hold Washington. They left the city and sailed north to Baltimore. Baltimore, however, was ready and waiting—with barricaded roads, a blocked harbor, and some 13,000 militiamen. The British attacked in mid-September. They were kept from entering the town by a determined defense and ferocious bombardment from Fort McHenry in the harbor.

During the night of September 13–14, a young attorney named **Francis Scott Key** watched as the bombs burst over Fort McHenry. Finally "by the dawn's early light," Key was able to see that the American flag still flew over the fort. Deeply moved by patriotic feeling, Key wrote a poem called "The Star-Spangled Banner." In 1931, Congress designated "The Star-Spangled Banner" as the National Anthem. 📖 *(See page 616 of the Appendix for an excerpt from "The Star-Spangled Banner.")*

Defeat at Plattsburgh

Meanwhile, in the north, General Sir George Prevost led more than 10,000 British troops into New York State from Canada. The first British goal was to capture Plattsburgh, a key city on the shore of Lake Champlain. The invasion was stopped when an American naval force on Lake Champlain defeated the British fleet on the lake in September 1814. Knowing the American ships could use their control of the lake to bombard them and land troops behind them, the British retreated to Canada.

After the Battle of Lake Champlain, the British decided the war in North America was too costly and unnecessary. Napoleon had been defeated in Europe. To keep fighting the United States would gain little and was not worth the effort.

The War Ends

American and British representatives signed a peace agreement in December 1814 in Ghent, Belgium. The **Treaty of Ghent** did not change any existing borders. Nothing was mentioned about the impressment of sailors, but, with Napoleon's defeat, neutral rights had become a dead issue.

Before word of the treaty had reached the United States, one final—and ferocious—battle occurred at New Orleans. In December 1814, British army troops moved toward New Orleans. Awaiting them behind earthen fortifications was an American army led by Andrew Jackson.

On January 8, 1815, the British troops advanced. The redcoats were no match for Jackson's soldiers, who shot from behind bales of cotton. In a short but gruesome battle, hundreds of British soldiers were killed. At the **Battle of New Orleans,** Americans achieved a decisive victory. Andrew Jackson became a hero, and his fame helped him win the presidency in 1828.

American Nationalism

New England Federalists had opposed "Mr. Madison's war" from the start. In December 1814, unhappy New England Federalists gathered in Connecticut at the **Hartford Convention.** A few favored secession. Most wanted to remain within the Union, however. To protect their interests, they drew up a list of proposed amendments to the Constitution.

After the convention broke up, word came of Jackson's spectacular victory at New Orleans, followed by news of the peace treaty. In this moment of triumph, the Federalist grievances seemed unpatriotic. The party lost respect in the eyes of the public. Most Americans felt proud and self-confident at the end of the War of 1812.

America's Flags

The First Star-Spangled Banner, 1779–1818 The Stars and Stripes flag gained two more stars and two more stripes in 1795, after Kentucky and Vermont joined the Union.

Congress realized that the flag would become too large if a stripe were added for every new state. It decided in 1818 to keep the stripes at 13—for the thirteen original colonies—and to add a star for each new state.

The young nation had gained new respect from other nations in the world. Americans felt a new sense of patriotism and a strong national identity.

Although the Federalist Party weakened, its philosophy of strong national government was carried on by the War Hawks who were part of the Republican Party. They favored trade, western expansion, the energetic development of the economy, and a strong army and navy.

Reading Check **Analyzing** Did the Treaty of Ghent resolve any major issues? Explain.

SECTION 4 ASSESSMENT

Checking for Understanding

1. **Key Terms** Write a short paragraph in which you use the terms frigate and privateer.

2. **Reviewing Facts** Who won the Battle of Lake Champlain? Why was it an important victory?

Reviewing Themes

3. **Government and Democracy** Why did the Federalist Party lose support after the War of 1812?

Critical Thinking

4. **Drawing Conclusions** Why did people from the North, South, and the West feel differently about going to war with Britain?

5. **Determining Cause and Effect** Recreate the diagram below. In the ovals, list four effects that the War of 1812 had on the United States.

Effects of the War of 1812

Analyzing Visuals

6. **Geography Skills** Study the map on page 298. On what lake did Perry defeat the British? Which battle—Lake Champlain or Thames—took place later in time?

Interdisciplinary Activity

Music Imagine if Francis Scott Key had been at the Battle of New Orleans instead of in Baltimore. Rewrite the first verse of "The Star-Spangled Banner" based on what occurred in that battle.

Writing a Journal

Why Learn This Skill?

Journal writing is personal writing with a casual style. What you write *on* is not as important as what you write *about*—your experiences, interests, and even your feelings.

Learning the Skill

A journal is a written account that records what you have learned or experienced. In the journal you can express your feelings about a subject, summarize key topics, describe difficulties or successes in solving particular problems, and draw maps or other visuals. To help you get started writing in your journal, follow these steps:

- As you read your textbook, jot down notes or questions about a specific topic or event. Then look for details and answers about it as you continue reading.
- Describe your feelings as you read a selection or look at a photograph. Are you angry, happy, frustrated, sad? Explain why.
- Ask yourself if drawing a map or flowchart would help you understand an event better. If so, draw in your journal.

Practicing the Skill

The following excerpt describes the burning of Washington, D.C., during the War of 1812. Read the excerpt, then use the following questions to help you write entries in your own journal.

66 [T]his was a night of dismay to the inhabitants of Washington. They were taken completely by surprise. . . . The first impulse of course tempted them to fly. . . . [T]he streets were . . . crowded with soldiers and senators, men, women, and children, horses, carriages, and carts loaded with household furniture, all hastening towards a wooden bridge which crosses the Potomac. The confusion . . . was terrible, and the crowd upon the bridge was such to endanger its giving way. 99

1 What is particularly interesting about this description?

2 What are your feelings as you read the excerpt?

3 Draw a map or other visual to help you understand the situation described here.

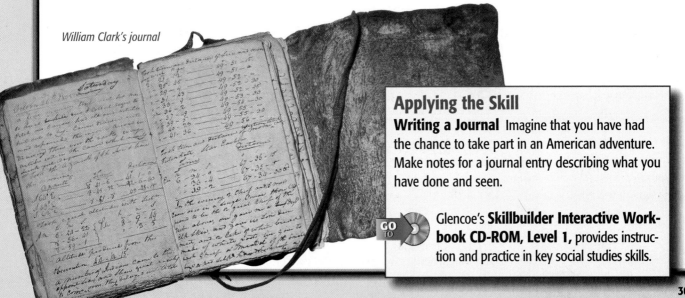

William Clark's journal

Applying the Skill

Writing a Journal Imagine that you have had the chance to take part in an American adventure. Make notes for a journal entry describing what you have done and seen.

GO TO

Glencoe's **Skillbuilder Interactive Workbook CD-ROM, Level 1,** provides instruction and practice in key social studies skills.

Chapter Summary

The Jefferson Era

1801
- Thomas Jefferson inaugurated as third president

1803
- *Marbury* v. *Madison* sets precedent for judicial review
- Louisiana Territory purchased from France
- Ohio becomes a state

1804
- Twelfth Amendment ratified
- Lewis and Clark expedition sets off from St. Louis
- Thomas Jefferson wins reelection

1807
- American ship *Chesapeake* attacked by British navy
- Congress passes the Embargo Act

1809
- James Madison becomes president

1811
- Harrison defeats the Prophet at Tippecanoe

1812
- U.S. declares war on Britain
- British navy blockades coast

1813
- Perry defeats British navy on Lake Erie
- Tecumseh killed at the Battle of the Thames

1814
- British burn Washington, D.C.
- Treaty of Ghent ends war with Britain

Reviewing Key Terms

On a sheet of paper, use all of the following terms to write several short, historically accurate paragraphs related to the information in the chapter. Use standard grammar and punctuation.

1. laissez-faire
2. impressment
3. embargo
4. nationalism
5. judicial review
6. secede

Reviewing Key Facts

7. What did Congress do to prevent a deadlock in presidential elections?
8. How did events in Santo Domingo (Haiti) influence American expansion?
9. How did the Embargo Act of 1807 hurt the United States?
10. Who were the War Hawks?
11. What effect did Tecumseh's death have on Native Americans?

Critical Thinking

12. **Analyzing Themes: Government and Democracy** Summarize the importance of the *Marbury* v. *Madison* decision.
13. **Analyzing Information** What were the boundaries of the Louisiana Territory?
14. **Comparing** Re-create the diagram below. In the boxes, describe the differences between the War Hawks and Federalists in their views of the War of 1812.

War of 1812	
View of War Hawks	View of Federalists

 Geography and History Activity

Study the maps of territorial growth on page 291 and answer the following questions.

15. **Location** In what year did Mississippi become a state?
16. **Region** What three Southern states were admitted to the nation between 1810 and 1820?

Practicing Skills

17. Writing a Journal By the late 1700s, more than 55,000 Americans had crossed the mountains into Kentucky and Tennessee. Write entries for a journal for such a trip. Explain why you are enduring such hardships to move to new land.

Citizenship Cooperative Activity

18. Analyzing Current Events With a partner, choose a recent event for which you will be able to locate primary and secondary sources of information. Compare the primary source with one secondary source. Prepare a report for the class in which you describe the event and compare the information in the primary and secondary sources.

Economics Activity

19. Work in small groups to prepare an international trade map. Your map should show United States imports during the early 1800s from each of the major continents. What major ports were merchants sailing to during this time? What products were they bringing back to the United States? Your map should include the names of important ports, the countries where they were located, symbols to represent the different products, a map key to explain the symbols, and other information such as distances or major shipping routes.

 Technology Activity

20. Using a Spreadsheet Search the library for information about the modern city of New Orleans. Make a database using the spreadsheet. Beginning in column B, label four columns as follows: 1) Street names; 2) Buildings; 3) Foods; 4) Sites. Beginning in row two, label rows as follows: 1) Spanish; 2) French. Fill in the spreadsheet with the information you find.

 Alternative Assessment

21. Portfolio Writing Activity Review the chapter for information about the expedition of Lewis and Clark. Imagine that you had the chance to accompany them on their adventure. Write a letter home describing what you have done and seen. Be sure to include how you were affected by the land and the people you encountered.

Self-Check Quiz
Visit tarvol1.glencoe.com and click on **Chapter 9—Self-Check Quizzes** to prepare for the chapter test.

Standardized Test Practice

Use the map below to choose the *best* answer to the question.

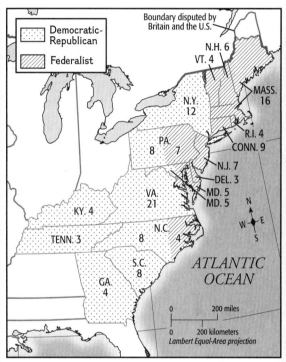

Which of the following statements about the election of 1800 is true?

F Federalists won Georgia's electoral votes.

G New Hampshire supported the Democratic-Republican ticket.

H Connecticut had seven electoral votes.

J Pennsylvania was one of the states that split its votes.

Test-Taking Tip:

Double-check all answer choices to make sure that you have chosen the best answer. Make sure that your answer choice is supported by information on the map. Check each choice against the map. Only one is correct.

CHAPTER 10

Growth and Expansion

1790–1825

Why It Matters

During the early 1800s, manufacturing took on a stronger role in the American economy. During the same period, people moved westward across the continent in larger and larger numbers. In 1823 the United States proclaimed its dominant role in the Americas with the Monroe Doctrine.

The Impact Today

These developments were important factors in shaping the nation. Today the United States is one of the leading economic and military powers in the world.

The American Republic to 1877 *Video* *The chapter 10 video, "The One-Room Schoolhouse," depicts a typical school day in the nineteenth century.*

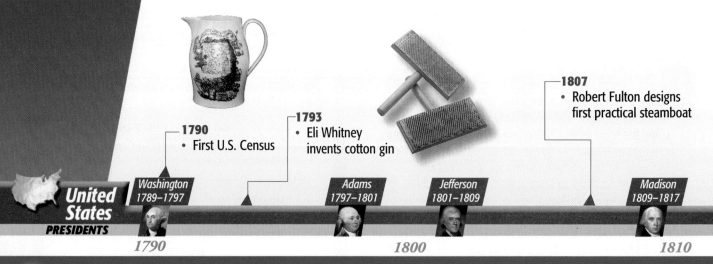

1790
• First U.S. Census

1793
• Eli Whitney invents cotton gin

1807
• Robert Fulton designs first practical steamboat

United States PRESIDENTS

Washington 1789–1797

Adams 1797–1801

Jefferson 1801–1809

Madison 1809–1817

1790   *1800*   *1810*

World

1792
• Russia invades Poland

1804
• Haiti claims independence from France

Valley of the Yosemite by Albert Bierstadt Bierstadt's panoramic scenes of the American West capture the vastness of the landscape.

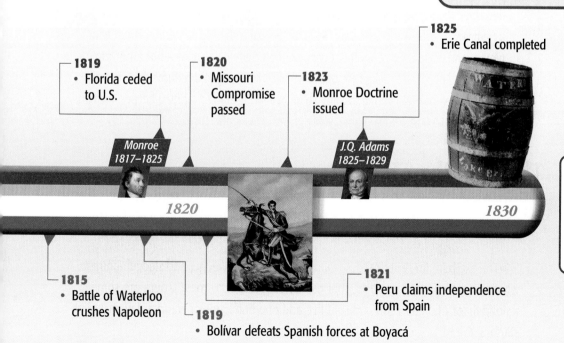

1825
• Erie Canal completed

1819
• Florida ceded to U.S.

1820
• Missouri Compromise passed

1823
• Monroe Doctrine issued

Monroe 1817–1825

J.Q. Adams 1825–1829

1820

1830

1815
• Battle of Waterloo crushes Napoleon

1821
• Peru claims independence from Spain

1819
• Bolívar defeats Spanish forces at Boyacá

Economic Growth

Guide to Reading

Main Idea
The rise of industry and trade led to the growth of cities.

Key Terms
Industrial Revolution, capitalism, capital, free enterprise, technology, cotton gin, patent, factory system, interchangeable parts

Reading Strategy
Organizing Information As you read the section, re-create the diagram below and describe in the ovals changes brought about by the Industrial Revolution.

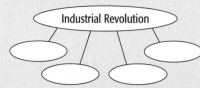

Industrial Revolution

Read to Learn
• how the Industrial Revolution began in the United States.
• how the United States changed as it became more economically independent.

Section Theme
Economic Factors The Industrial Revolution changed the way goods were made.

Preview of Events

♦1790   ♦1800   ♦1810   ♦1820

1793
Eli Whitney invents the cotton gin

1807
Congress passes Embargo Act

1814
Francis Lowell opens textile plant in Massachusetts

1816
Second National Bank is chartered

AN American Story

American blacksmith, early 1800s woodcut

Both men and women in the early 1800s valued hard work. An English journalist described the farmers of Long Island in 1818: "Every man can use an axe, a saw, and a hammer. Scarcely one who cannot do any job at rough carpentering, and mend a plough and wagon. . . ." Another European noted the daily activities of American women in 1823: "They take care of everything pertaining to the domestic economy, for example, making candles, boiling soap, preparing starch, canning berries, fruit and cucumbers, baking, and spinning, sewing, and milking the cows."

The Growth of Industry

During the colonial era, workers were in short supply. Americans learned to develop tools that made work easier and more efficient. American methods and inventions won the admiration of Europeans. One observer exclaimed:

❝The axe here [in America] . . . is a combination axe, wedge, and sledgehammer; what an accomplished woodchopper can do with this instrument! There are some among them who can chop and split five and one-half loads of wood a day, including stacking them.❞

People working in their homes or in work-shops made cloth and most other goods. Using hand tools, they produced furniture, farm equipment, household items, and clothing.

In the mid-1700s, however, the way goods were made began to change. These changes appeared first in Great Britain. British inventors created machinery to perform some of the work involved in cloth making, such as spinning. The machines ran on waterpower, so British cloth makers built mills along rivers and installed the machines in these mills. People left their homes and farms to work in the mills and earn wages. The changes this system brought about were so great that this historic development is known as the Industrial Revolution.

The Industrial Revolution in New England

The Industrial Revolution began to take root in the United States around 1800, appearing first in New England—Massachusetts, Rhode Island, Connecticut, Vermont, and New Hampshire. New England's soil was poor, and farming was difficult. As a result, people were willing to leave their farms to find work elsewhere. Also, New England had many rushing rivers and streams. These provided the waterpower necessary to run the machinery in the new factories.

New England's geographic location also proved to be an advantage. It was close to other resources, including coal and iron from nearby Pennsylvania. New England also had many ports. Through these ports passed the cotton

TECHNOLOGY & History

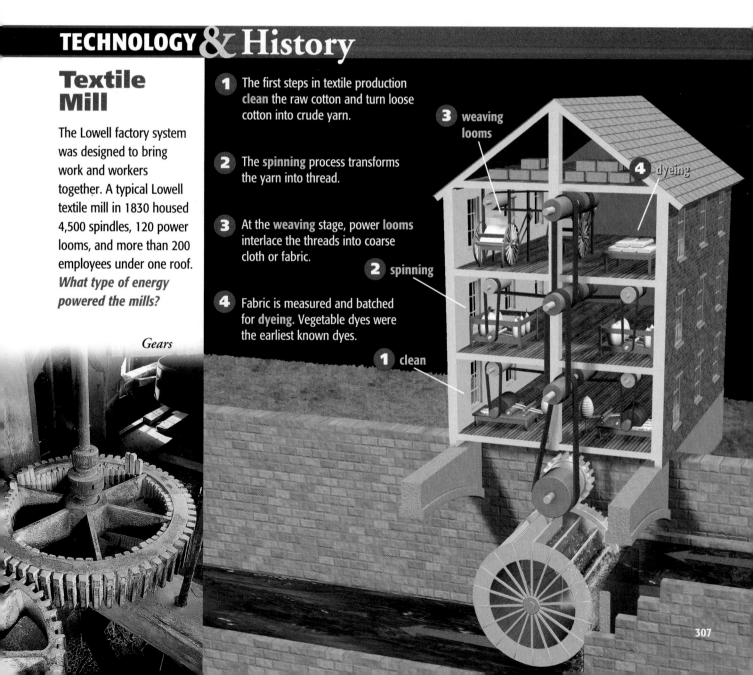

Textile Mill

The Lowell factory system was designed to bring work and workers together. A typical Lowell textile mill in 1830 housed 4,500 spindles, 120 power looms, and more than 200 employees under one roof. *What type of energy powered the mills?*

Gears

1 The first steps in textile production **clean** the raw cotton and turn loose cotton into crude yarn.

2 The **spinning** process transforms the yarn into thread.

3 At the **weaving** stage, power **looms** interlace the threads into coarse cloth or fabric.

4 Fabric is measured and batched for **dyeing**. Vegetable dyes were the earliest known dyes.

3 weaving looms

4 dyeing

2 spinning

1 clean

307

shipped from Southern states to New England factories, as well as the finished cloth bound for markets throughout the nation.

Also necessary to strong industrial growth is an economic system that allows competition to flourish with a minimum of government interference. The economic system of the United States is called capitalism. Under capitalism, individuals put their capital, or money, into a business in hopes of making a profit.

Free enterprise is another term used to describe the American economy. In a system of free enterprise, people are free to buy, sell, and produce whatever they want. They can also work wherever they wish. The major elements of free enterprise are competition, profit, private property and economic freedom. Business owners have the freedom to produce the products that they think will be the most profitable. Buyers also compete to find the best products at the lowest prices.

New Technology

Workers, waterpower, location, and capital all played roles in New England's Industrial Revolution. Yet without the invention of new machines and technology—scientific discoveries that simplify work—the Industrial Revolution could not have taken place.

Inventions such as the spinning jenny and the water frame, which spun thread, and the power loom, which wove the thread into cloth, made it possible to perform many steps in making cloth by machine, saving time and money. Because these new machines ran on waterpower, most mills were built near rivers. In 1785, for the first time, a steam engine provided power for a cotton mill.

In 1793 **Eli Whitney** of Massachusetts invented the cotton gin, a simple machine that quickly and efficiently removed the seeds from the cotton fiber. The cotton gin enabled one worker to clean cotton as fast as 50 people working by hand.

In 1790 Congress passed a patent law to protect the rights of those who developed "useful and important inventions." A patent gives an inventor the sole legal right to the invention and

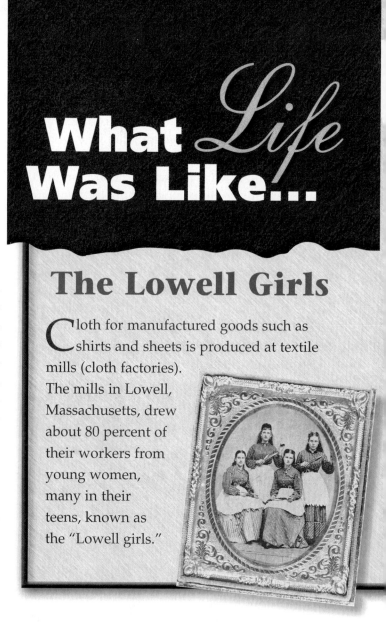

What Life Was Like...

The Lowell Girls

Cloth for manufactured goods such as shirts and sheets is produced at textile mills (cloth factories). The mills in Lowell, Massachusetts, drew about 80 percent of their workers from young women, many in their teens, known as the "Lowell girls."

its profits for a certain period of time. One of the first patents went to Jacob Perkins for a machine to make nails.

✓ **Reading Check** Analyzing Why were the first mills in Great Britain built near rivers?

New England Factories

The British tried to keep their new industrial technology a secret. They even passed laws prohibiting their machinery as well as their skilled mechanics from leaving the country. However, a few enterprising workers managed to slip away to the United States.

In Britain **Samuel Slater** had worked in a factory that used machines invented by Richard Arkwright for spinning cotton threads. Slater

Working Conditions

The young women who worked in Lowell's mills endured difficult working conditions. They put in long hours—from sunrise to sunset—for low wages. The volume of the factory machinery was earsplitting and the work was monotonous. The women usually performed one task over and over again.

Magazine

The Lowell Offering was a magazine written for and about the mill girls.

On the Job

Lucy Larcom started working in the mills when she was 11 years old. She later recalled her life at Waltham:

❝We did not call ourselves ladies. We did not forget that we were working girls, wearing aprons suitable to our work, and that there was some danger of our becoming drudges.❞

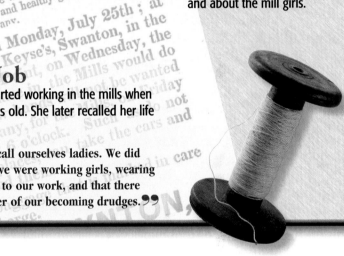

---

memorized the design of Arkwright's machines and slipped out of Britain in 1789. Once in the United States, Slater took over the management of a cotton mill in Pawtucket, Rhode Island. There he duplicated Arkwright's machines. Using these machines the mill made cotton thread. Women working in their homes wove the thread into cloth. Slater's mill marked an important step in the Industrial Revolution in America.

In 1814 **Francis Cabot Lowell** opened a textile plant in Waltham, Massachusetts. The plan he implemented went several steps beyond Slater's mill. For the first time, all the stages of cloth making were performed under one roof. Lowell's mill launched the factory system, a system bringing manufacturing steps together in one place to increase efficiency. The factory system

was a significant development in the way goods were made—and another important part of the Industrial Revolution.

Interchangeable Parts

The inventor Eli Whitney started the use of interchangeable parts. These were identical machine parts that could be quickly put together to make a complete product. Because all the parts were alike, they could be manufactured with less-skilled labor, and they made machine repair easier. Interchangeable parts opened the way for producing many different kinds of goods on a mass scale and for reducing the price of the goods.

✔**Reading Check** **Describing** How did the factory system work?

Population of the United States, 1820

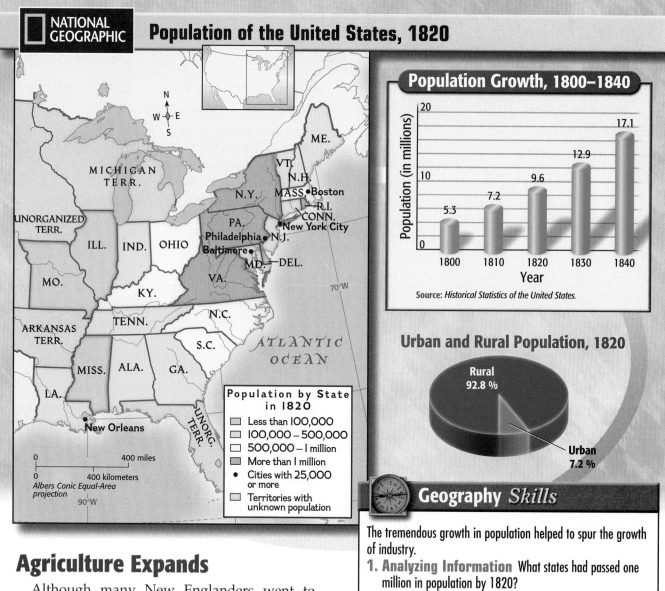

Population by State in 1820
- ☐ Less than 100,000
- ☐ 100,000 – 500,000
- ☐ 500,000 – 1 million
- ☐ More than 1 million
- ● Cities with 25,000 or more
- ☐ Territories with unknown population

0 — 400 miles
0 — 400 kilometers
Albers Conic Equal-Area projection

Population Growth, 1800–1840

Year	Population (in millions)
1800	5.3
1810	7.2
1820	9.6
1830	12.9
1840	17.1

Source: *Historical Statistics of the United States.*

Urban and Rural Population, 1820

Rural 92.8 %

Urban 7.2 %

Geography *Skills*

The tremendous growth in population helped to spur the growth of industry.

1. **Analyzing Information** What states had passed one million in population by 1820?
2. **Comparing** Which state had the larger population—Missouri or Alabama?

Agriculture Expands

Although many New Englanders went to work in factories, most Americans still lived and worked on farms. In the 1820s more than 65 percent of Americans were farmers.

In the Northeast, farms tended to be small, and the produce was usually marketed locally. In the South, cotton production increased dramatically. The demand for cotton had grown steadily with the development of the textile industries of New England and Europe. Southern plantation owners used enslaved workers to plant, tend, and pick the cotton. The cotton gin—which made it possible to clean the cotton faster and less expensively than by hand—encouraged the planters to raise larger crops. Between 1790 and 1820, cotton production soared from 3,000 to more than 300,000 bales a year.

In the West, agriculture also expanded. Southern farmers seeking new land moved west to plant cotton. Western farmers north of the Ohio River concentrated on raising pork and cash crops such as corn and wheat.

Reading Check **Describing** How was the Northeast different from the South in what it produced?

Economic Independence

Most new industries were financed by small investors—merchants, shopkeepers, and farmers. These people invested some of their money in the hope of earning profits if the new businesses succeeded. Low taxes, few government regulations, and competition encouraged people to invest in new industries.

Large businesses called **corporations** began to develop rapidly in the 1830s, when some legal obstacles to their formation were removed. The rise of these new corporations made it easier to sell **stock**—shares of ownership in a company—to finance improvement and development.

The charter of the First Bank of the United States had expired in 1811. In 1816 Congress chartered the **Second Bank of the United States,** also chartered for 20 years. The Bank had the power to make large loans to businesses. State banks and frontier people criticized the Bank on the grounds that it was a monopoly used by the rich and powerful for their own gain. Those who believed in strict interpretation of the Constitution also criticized it because they believed Congress did not have the power to charter such a bank.

Cities Come of Age

The growth of factories and trade spurred the growth of towns and cities. The new industrial towns grew quickest. Many developed along rivers and streams to take advantage of the waterpower. Older cities like New York, Boston, and Baltimore also grew as centers of commerce and trade. In the West, towns like Pittsburgh, Cincinnati, and Louisville profited from their locations on major rivers. As farmers in the West shipped more and more of their products by water, these towns grew rapidly.

Cities and towns looked quite different from modern urban areas. Buildings were made of wood or brick. Streets and sidewalks were unpaved, and barnyard animals often roamed freely. There were no sewers to carry waste and dirty water away, so the danger of diseases such as cholera and yellow fever was very real. In 1793, for example, a yellow fever epidemic in Philadelphia killed thousands of people.

Fire posed another threat to cities. Sparks from a fireplace or chimney could easily ignite a wooden building and spread to others. Few towns or cities had organized fire companies, and fires could be disastrous.

Cities and towns of the period also had advantages, however. Some people left farming because cities and towns offered a variety of jobs and steady wages. As cities grew they added libraries, museums, and shops that were unavailable in the countryside. For many, the jobs and attractions of city life outweighed any of the dangers.

Reading Check **Analyzing** Why did cities such as Pittsburgh and Louisville grow?

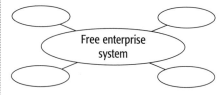

SECTION 1 ASSESSMENT

Checking for Understanding

1. **Key Terms** Use each of these terms in a sentence that will help explain its meaning: Industrial Revolution, capital, technology, cotton gin, patent, factory system, interchangeable parts.

2. **Reviewing Facts** Describe the reasons New England was ideal for the development of factories.

Reviewing Themes

3. **Economic Factors** How did the cotton gin affect cotton production?

Critical Thinking

4. **Categorizing Information** Re-create the diagram below and describe the characteristics and benefits of the free enterprise system.

Free enterprise system

5. **Determining Cause and Effect** Was new technology necessary for the Industrial Revolution? Explain.

Analyzing Visuals

6. **Geography Skills** Study the map and the graphs on page 310. What do the cities shown on the map have in common? Which state had the larger population in 1820—Georgia or Ohio?

Interdisciplinary Activity

Expository Writing Study the map and graphs on page 310. Create a quiz for your classmates based on the information presented. Trade quizzes with a classmate and answer those questions.

What were people's lives like in the past?

What—and who—were people talking about? What did they eat? What did they do for fun? These two pages will give you some clues to everyday life in the U.S. as you step back in time with **TIME Notebook**.

Profile

SAGOYEWATHA *is the great Iroquois leader some call Red Jacket. Why? Because he fought with the British in the Revolutionary War. Sagoyewatha means "He Causes Them to Be Awake." Below is part of a speech Sagoyewatha delivered in 1805 to a group of religious leaders from Boston:*

"BROTHERS, OUR (*NATIVE AMERICAN*) SEATS were once large and yours (colonists) were small. You have now become a great people, and we have scarcely a place left to spread our blankets. You have got our country but are not satisfied; you want to force your religion upon us....

Brothers, continue to listen. You say there is but one way to worship and serve the Great Spirit. If there is but one religion, why do you white people differ so much about it?...

Brothers, we...also have a religion which was given to our forefathers and has been handed down to us, their children...."

Sagoyewatha

1790s WORD PLAY

Ahoy There!

U.S. FRIGATE CONSTITUTION

The U.S.S. Constitution, the world's largest frigate, or warship, was launched in 1797 with a crew of 450 and 54 cannons. Want to join the crew? First, you must prove you can understand a sailor's vocabulary. Match each word or phrase in the first column with its original meaning.

1. Keel over
2. Try a new tack
3. Let the cat out of the bag
4. Mind your p's and q's
5. Shipshape

a. Sailors who do wrong are disciplined with a cat-o'-nine-tails whip that's kept in a red sack

b. Putting a ship in for repair

c. Bartenders keep track of what sailors drink and owe by marking numbers under "pints" and "quarts"

d. The course or direction boats take into the wind

e. Good condition

answers: 1. b; 2. d; 3. a; 4. c; 5. e

NATIVE AMERICAN LIFE

Sports Story

GEORGE CATLIN *is a white man with a strong interest in Native American life. This lawyer has made a name for himself as an artist, painting portraits of Native American leaders, families, and everyday Western life. Here he paints with words, telling us about a game (one the French call lacrosse) played by Choctaw men:*

"EACH PARTY (TEAM) HAD THEIR GOAL MADE WITH TWO UPRIGHT POSTS, about 25 feet high and six feet apart, set firm in the ground, with a pole across at the top. These goals were about 40 to 50 rods (660–825 feet) apart. At a point just halfway between was another small stake, driven down, where the ball was to be thrown up at the firing of a gun, to be struggled for by the players ... who were some 600 or 700 in numbers, and were (trying) to catch the ball in their sticks, and throw it home and between their respective stakes....For each time that the ball was passed between the stakes of either party, one was counted for their game...until the successful party arrived to 100, which was the limit of the game, and accomplished at an hour's sun."

RIGHT: George Catlin *painted this picture of a 15-year-old Native American girl. Her name, Ka-te-qua, means "female eagle."*

BELOW: *Painting by* **George Catlin** *of* **Choctaw athletes** *playing their version of lacrosse.*

NATIONAL GALLERY OF ART

NUMBERS

U.S. AT THE TIME

30 Number of treaties that took away Native American land or moved their borders. The treaties were between the U.S. and the Creeks, Choctaws, and Chickasaws between 1789 and 1825

$158 million The price the U.S. spent to fight the War of 1812

First Elizabeth Seton founds the Sisters of Charity, a Roman Catholic order, in 1809

First Mary Kies becomes the first woman to receive a U.S. patent in 1809 for a method of weaving straw with silk

$3,820.33 Amount paid to Paul Revere for providing the U.S.S. *Constitution* with copper parts and a ship's bell in 1797

45 feet Length of the dinosaur dug up by Lewis and Clark on their 1804 expedition

Westward Bound

Pioneer homestead, Smoky Mountains

AN American Story

During the 1800s, settlers poured into the frontier west of the Appalachians. The typical frontier family moved from place to place as the line of settlement pushed ever westward. Their home often consisted of a three-sided shack or a log cabin with a dirt floor and no windows or door. A pile of leaves in the loft of the cabin often served as a bed. Loneliness, poverty, and an almost primitive lifestyle were daily companions to many frontier people.

Moving West

The first census—the official count of a population—of the United States in 1790 revealed a population of nearly four million. Most of the Americans counted lived east of the Appalachian Mountains and within a few hundred miles of the Atlantic coast.

Within a few decades this changed. The number of settlers heading west increased by leaps and bounds. In 1811 a Pennsylvania resident reported seeing 236 wagons filled with people and their possessions on the road to Pittsburgh. A man in Newburgh, New York, counted 60 wagons rolling by in a single day. In 1820, just 30 years after the first census, the population of the

United States had more than doubled, to about 10 million people, with nearly 2 million living west of the Appalachians.

Traveling west was not easy in the late 1790s and early 1800s. The 363-mile trip from **New York City** to **Buffalo** could take as long as three weeks. A pioneer family heading west with a wagonload of household goods faced hardship and danger along the way.

Roads and Turnpikes

The nation needed good inland roads for travel and for the shipment of goods. Private companies built many turnpikes, or toll roads. The fees travelers paid to use those roads helped to pay for construction. Many of the roads had a base of crushed stone. In areas where the land was often muddy, companies built "corduroy roads," consisting of logs laid side by side, like the ridges of corduroy cloth. 📖 *(See page 599 of the Primary Sources Library for an account of a typical stagecoach journey.)*

When Ohio joined the Union in 1803, the new state asked the federal government to build a road to connect it with the East. In 1806 Congress approved funds for a **National Road** to the West and five years later agreed on the route. Because work on the road stopped during the War of 1812, the first section, from Maryland to western Virginia, did not open until 1818. In later years the National Road reached Ohio and continued on to Vandalia, Illinois. Congress viewed the National Road as a military necessity, but it did not undertake other road-building projects.

✦Geography
River Travel

River travel had definite advantages over wagon and horse travel. It was far more comfortable than travel over the bumpy roads, and pioneers could load all their goods on river barges—if they were heading downstream in the direction of the current.

River travel had two problems, however. The first related to the geography of the eastern United States. Most major rivers in the region flowed in a north-south direction, not east to west, where most people and goods were headed. Second, traveling upstream by barge against the current was extremely difficult and slow.

People In History

Robert Fulton 1765–1815

Robert Fulton grew up in Lancaster, Pennsylvania. At an early age he created his own lead pencils and rockets. While living in Europe in the late 1790s, Fulton designed and built a submarine called the *Nautilus* to be used in France's war against Britain. Submarine warfare became common later.

Fulton returned to the United States and developed a steamboat engine that was more powerful and provided a smoother ride than previous engines. On August 17, 1807, Fulton's *Clermont* made its first successful run. By demonstrating the usefulness of two-way river travel, Fulton launched the steamboat era. Although his engine was considered a great success, trouble followed after Fulton received a monopoly and government money. Eventually, the collapse of the monopoly led to lower prices, growth of competition, and introduction of new technology to improve the steamboat.

Steam engines were already being used in the 1780s and 1790s to power boats in quiet waters. Inventor James Rumsey equipped a small boat on the Potomac River with a steam engine. John Fitch, another inventor, built a steamboat that navigated the Delaware River. Neither boat, however, had enough power to withstand the strong currents and winds found in large rivers or open bodies of water.

In 1802 Robert Livingston, a political and business leader, hired **Robert Fulton** to develop a steamboat with a powerful engine. Livingston wanted the steamboat to carry cargo and passengers up the **Hudson River** from New York City to **Albany.**

In 1807 Fulton had his steamboat, the **Clermont,** ready for a trial. Powered by a newly designed engine, the *Clermont* made the 150-mile trip from New York to Albany in the unheard-of time of 32 hours. Using only sails, the trip would have taken four days.

About 140-feet long and 14-feet wide, the *Clermont* offered great comforts to its passengers. They could sit or stroll about on deck, and at

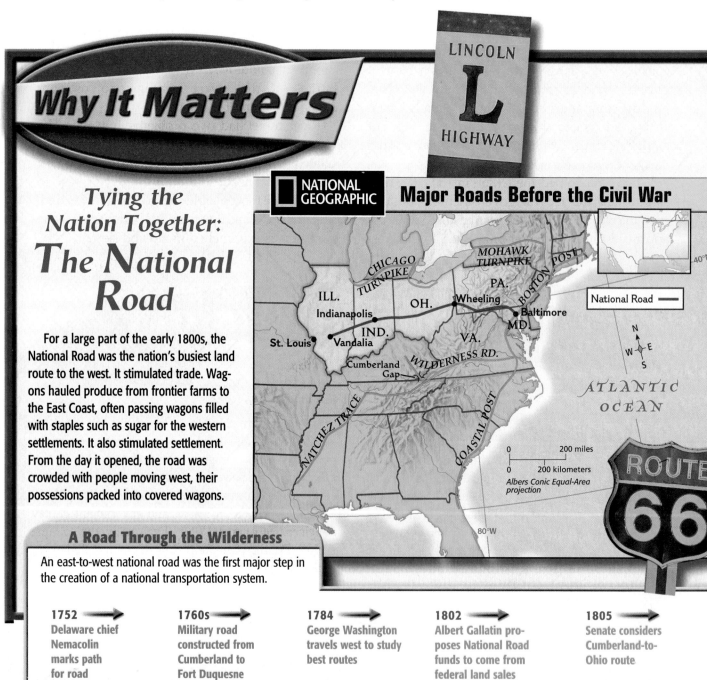

Why It Matters

Tying the Nation Together:
The National Road

For a large part of the early 1800s, the National Road was the nation's busiest land route to the west. It stimulated trade. Wagons hauled produce from frontier farms to the East Coast, often passing wagons filled with staples such as sugar for the western settlements. It also stimulated settlement. From the day it opened, the road was crowded with people moving west, their possessions packed into covered wagons.

NATIONAL GEOGRAPHIC   **Major Roads Before the Civil War**

National Road ———

A Road Through the Wilderness

An east-to-west national road was the first major step in the creation of a national transportation system.

1752 ➡
Delaware chief Nemacolin marks path for road

1760s ➡
Military road constructed from Cumberland to Fort Duquesne

1784 ➡
George Washington travels west to study best routes

1802 ➡
Albert Gallatin proposes National Road funds to come from federal land sales

1805 ➡
Senate considers Cumberland-to-Ohio route

night they could relax in the sleeping compartments below deck. The engine was noisy, but its power provided a fairly smooth ride.

Steamboats ushered in a new age in river travel. They greatly improved the transport of goods and passengers along major inland rivers. Shipping goods became cheaper and faster. Steamboats also contributed to the growth of river cities like Cincinnati and St. Louis.

✓ **Reading Check** **Comparing** What advantages did steamboat travel have over wagon and horse travel?

Canals

Although steamboats represented a great improvement in transportation, their routes depended on the existing river system. Steamboats could not effectively tie the eastern and western parts of the country together.

In New York, business and government officials led by De Witt Clinton came up with a plan to link New York City with the Great Lakes

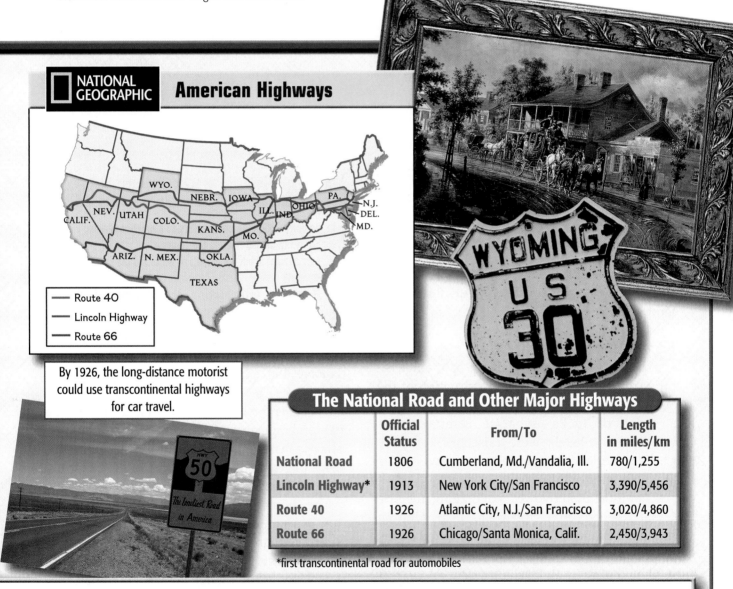

NATIONAL GEOGRAPHIC American Highways

Route 40
Lincoln Highway
Route 66

By 1926, the long-distance motorist could use transcontinental highways for car travel.

The National Road and Other Major Highways

	Official Status	From/To	Length in miles/km
National Road	1806	Cumberland, Md./Vandalia, Ill.	780/1,255
Lincoln Highway*	1913	New York City/San Francisco	3,390/5,456
Route 40	1926	Atlantic City, N.J./San Francisco	3,020/4,860
Route 66	1926	Chicago/Santa Monica, Calif.	2,450/3,943

*first transcontinental road for automobiles

1811 Construction begins at Cumberland

1818 Cumberland-to-Wheeling section completed

1825 Construction in Ohio begins

1833 Route to Columbus, Ohio, completed

1850 National Road stops at Vandalia

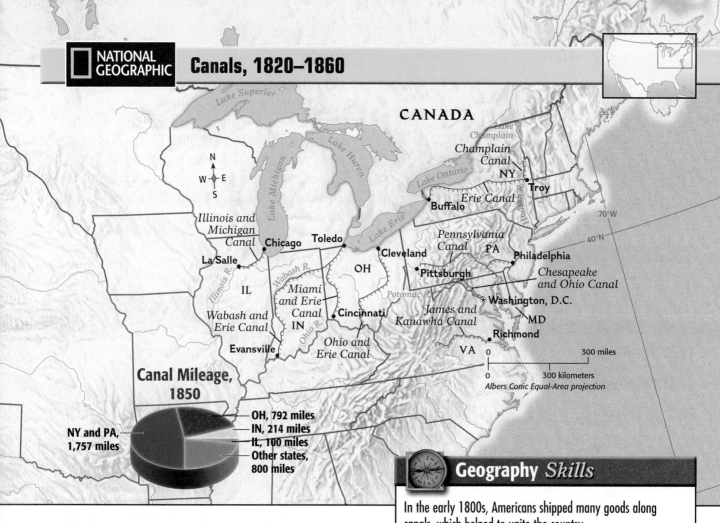

NATIONAL GEOGRAPHIC Canals, 1820–1860

CANADA

Lake Superior

Lake Michigan

Lake Huron

Lake Ontario

Lake Erie

Lake Champlain

Champlain Canal

NY

Troy

Erie Canal

Buffalo

Illinois and Michigan Canal

Chicago

Toledo

Cleveland

La Salle

Illinois R.

Wabash R.

Pennsylvania Canal

PA

Philadelphia

Pittsburgh

Chesapeake and Ohio Canal

IL

OH

Miami and Erie Canal

Cincinnati

Potomac R.

Washington, D.C.

Wabash and Erie Canal

IN

Ohio R.

James and Kanawha Canal

MD

Evansville

Ohio and Erie Canal

Richmond

VA

70°W

40°N

0   300 miles

0   300 kilometers

Albers Conic Equal-Area projection

Canal Mileage, 1850

NY and PA, 1,757 miles

OH, 792 miles
IN, 214 miles
IL, 100 miles
Other states, 800 miles

Geography Skills

In the early 1800s, Americans shipped many goods along canals, which helped to unite the country.
1. **Location** What two bodies of water did the Erie Canal connect?
2. **Analyzing Information** About how many miles long was the Erie Canal?

region. They would build a canal—an artificial waterway—across New York State, connecting Albany on the Hudson River with Buffalo on **Lake Erie.**

Building the Erie Canal

Thousands of laborers, many of them Irish immigrants, worked on the construction of the 363-mile **Erie Canal.** Along the canal they built a series of locks—separate compartments where water levels were raised or lowered. Locks provided a way to raise and lower boats at places where canal levels changed.

After more than two years of digging, the Erie Canal opened on October 26, 1825. Clinton boarded a barge in Buffalo and journeyed on the canal to Albany. From there, he headed down the Hudson River to New York City. As crowds cheered, the officials poured water from Lake Erie into the Atlantic. The East and Midwest were joined.

In its early years, the canal did not allow steamboats because their powerful engines could

damage the earthen embankments along the canal. Instead, teams of mules or horses hauled the boats and barges. A two-horse team pulled a 100-ton barge about 24 miles in one day—astonishingly fast compared to travel by wagon. In the 1840s the canal banks were reinforced to accommodate steam tugboats pulling barges.

The success of the Erie Canal led to an explosion in canal building. By 1850 the United States had more than 3,600 miles of canals. Canals lowered the cost of shipping goods. They brought prosperity to the towns along their routes. Perhaps most important, they helped unite the growing country.

Reading Check **Identifying** What two cities did the Erie Canal connect?

Western Settlement

Americans moved westward in waves. The first wave began before the 1790s and led to the admission of four new states between 1791 and 1803—Vermont, Kentucky, Tennessee, and Ohio. A second wave of westward growth began between 1816 and 1821. Five new western states were created—Indiana, Illinois, Mississippi, Alabama, and Missouri.

The new states reflected the dramatic growth of the region west of the Appalachians. Ohio, for example, had only 45,000 settlers in 1800. By 1820 it had 581,000.

Pioneer families tended to settle in communities along the great rivers, such as the Ohio and the Mississippi, so that they could ship their crops to market. The expansion of canals, which criss-crossed the land in the 1820s and 1830s, allowed people to live farther away from the rivers.

People also tended to settle with others from their home communities. Indiana, for example, was settled mainly by people from Kentucky and Tennessee, while Michigan's pioneers came mostly from New England.

Western families often gathered together for social events. Men took part in sports such as wrestling. Women met for quilting and sewing parties. Both men and women participated in cornhuskings—gatherings where farm families

Legendary Heroes

Paul Bunyan and John Henry Legends have grown around mythical figures like Paul Bunyan. Imaginary stories were passed along about how this giant lumberjack dug the Mississippi River and performed other incredible feats. Yet some of the famous characters in American folklore were real people. There was a John Henry who worked on the railroads. He was an African American renowned for his strength and skill in driving the steel drills into solid rock. He is best remembered for something that probably never happened. According to legend, John Henry defeated a steel-driving machine, but the effort killed him.

shared the work of stripping the husks from ears of corn.

Life in the West did not include the conveniences of Eastern town life, but the pioneers had not come west to be pampered. They wanted to make a new life for themselves and their families. America's population continued to spread westward in the years ahead.

✓ **Reading Check** **Identifying** What states were formed between 1791 and 1803?

SECTION 2 ASSESSMENT

Checking for Understanding

1. **Key Terms** Use the following terms to write a short newspaper article about the opening of the Erie Canal: turnpike, canal, lock.
2. **Reviewing Facts** Describe the improvements for transportation in the westward expansion during the early 1800s.

Reviewing Themes

3. **Science and Technology** How did steam-powered boats improve river travel?

Critical Thinking

4. **Drawing Conclusions** How did better transportation affect westward expansion?
5. **Comparing** What forms of communication and transportation linked East to West in the early 1800s? What links exist today? Re-create the diagram below and compare the links.

Links	
Early 1800s	Today

Analyzing Visuals

6. **Geography Skills** Study the information on the National Road on pages 316 and 317. When did construction of the National Road begin? To what city did it extend? How long was the National Road?

Interdisciplinary Activity

Geography Create a chart that lists the major means of transportation that helped the United States grow. Include the advantages and disadvantages of each type of transportation.

Social Studies SKILLBUILDER

Reading a Diagram

Why Learn This Skill?

Suppose you buy a new bicycle and discover that you must assemble the parts before you can ride it. A *diagram,* or a drawing that shows how the parts fit together, would make this job much easier.

Learning the Skill

To read a diagram, follow these steps:
- Read the title to find out what the diagram shows.
- Read all labels carefully to clearly determine their meanings.
- Read the legend and identify symbols and colors used in the diagram.
- Look for numbers indicating a sequence of steps, or arrows showing movement.

Practicing the Skill

Analyze the diagram of the Clermont, *then answer the following questions.*

1. What type of energy was used to power this ship?

2. What was the purpose of the paddle wheels?

Applying the Skill
Making a Diagram Draw a diagram showing either how to make macaroni and cheese or how to tie a pair of shoes. Label your diagram.

 Glencoe's **Skillbuilder Interactive Workbook CD-ROM, Level 1,** provides instruction and practice in key social studies skills.

The *Clermont* Steamboat

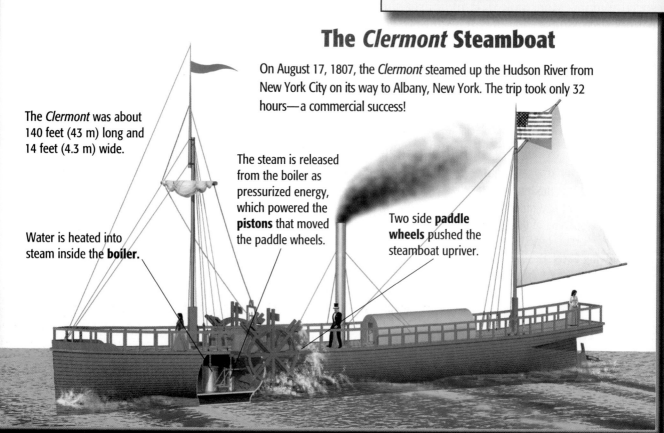

On August 17, 1807, the *Clermont* steamed up the Hudson River from New York City on its way to Albany, New York. The trip took only 32 hours—a commercial success!

The *Clermont* was about 140 feet (43 m) long and 14 feet (4.3 m) wide.

The steam is released from the boiler as pressurized energy, which powered the **pistons** that moved the paddle wheels.

Water is heated into steam inside the **boiler.**

Two side **paddle wheels** pushed the steamboat upriver.

Unity and Sectionalism

Guide to Reading

Main Idea
As the nation grew, differences in economic activities and needs increased sectionalism.

Key Terms
sectionalism, internal improvements, American System, disarmament, demilitarize, court-martial

Reading Strategy
Organizing Information As you read the section, re-create the diagram below and list four issues that created sectional conflict.

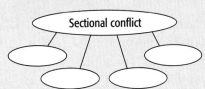

Sectional conflict

Read To Learn
- why sectional differences grew in the 1820s.
- what effect the Monroe Doctrine had on foreign policy.

Section Theme
Individual Action Senators Calhoun, Webster, and Clay represented different regions and different interests.

Preview of Events

♦1815   ♦1820   ♦1825

1816
James Monroe elected president

1820
Missouri Compromise passed

1823
Monroe Doctrine issued

AN American Story

Following the War of 1812, Americans felt buoyed by a new sense of pride and faith in the United States. In his Inaugural Address on March 4, 1817, President James Monroe expressed this feeling of proud nationalism: "If we look to the history of other nations, ancient or modern, we find no example of a growth so rapid, so gigantic, of a people so prosperous and happy."

James Monroe pocket watch

The Era of Good Feelings

The absence of major political divisions after the War of 1812 helped forge a sense of national unity. In the 1816 presidential election, James Monroe, the Republican candidate, faced almost no opposition. The Federalists, weakened by doubts of their loyalty during the War of 1812, barely existed as a national party. Monroe won the election by an overwhelming margin.

Although the Federalist Party had almost disappeared, many of its programs gained support. Republican president James Madison, Monroe's predecessor, had called for tariffs to protect industries, for a national bank, and for other programs.

Political differences seemed to fade away, causing a Boston newspaper to call these years the **Era of Good Feelings.** The president himself symbolized these good feelings.

Monroe had been involved in national politics since the American Revolution. He wore breeches and powdered wigs—a style no longer in fashion. With his sense of dignity, Monroe represented a united America, free of political strife.

Early in his presidency, Monroe toured the nation. No president since George Washington had done this. He paid his own expenses and tried to travel without an official escort. Everywhere Monroe went, local officials greeted him and celebrated his visit.

Monroe arrived in Boston, the former Federalist stronghold, in the summer of 1817. About 40,000 well-wishers cheered him, and John Adams, the second president, invited Monroe to his home. Abigail Adams commended the new president's "unassuming manner."

Monroe did not think the demonstrations were meant for him personally. He wrote Madison that they revealed a "desire in the body of the people to show their attachment to the union."

Two years later Monroe continued his tour, traveling as far south as Savannah and as far west as Detroit. In 1820 President Monroe won reelection, winning all but one electoral vote.

Reading Check **Describing** Why was this period called the Era of Good Feelings?

Sectionalism Grows

The Era of Good Feelings did not last long. Regional differences soon came to the surface, ending the period of national harmony.

Most Americans felt a strong allegiance to the region where they lived. They thought of themselves as Westerners or Southerners or Northerners. This sectionalism, or loyalty to their region, became more intense as differences arose over national policies.

The conflict over slavery, for example, had always simmered beneath the surface. Most white Southerners believed in the necessity and value of slavery. Northerners increasingly opposed it. To

protect slavery, Southerners stressed the importance of states' rights. States' rights are provided in the Constitution. Southerners believed they had to defend these rights against the federal government infringing on them.

The different regions also disagreed on the need for tariffs, a national bank, and internal improvements. Internal improvements were federal, state, and privately funded projects, such as canals and roads, to develop the nation's transportation system. Three powerful voices emerged in Congress in the early 1800s as spokespersons for their regions: John C. Calhoun, Daniel Webster, and Henry Clay.

John C. Calhoun

John C. Calhoun, a planter from South Carolina, was one of the War Hawks who had called for war with Great Britain in 1812. Calhoun remained a nationalist for some time after the war. He favored support for internal improvements and developing industries, and he backed a national bank. At the time, he believed these programs would benefit the South.

In the 1820s, however, Calhoun's views started to change, and he emerged as one of the chief supporters of **state sovereignty,** the idea that states have autonomous power. Calhoun

Fact • Fiction • Folklore

America's Flags

Flag of 1818 By 1818 the number of states had reached 20. In April President Monroe signed a bill that set the basic design of the flag. Each newly admitted state added a star to the field of blue. The addition of a new star took place on the Fourth of July following the state's year of entry.

The Great Star Flag Congress did not state how the stars should be arranged, so flagmakers used various designs. The Great Star Flag placed the stars in the form of a five-pointed star.

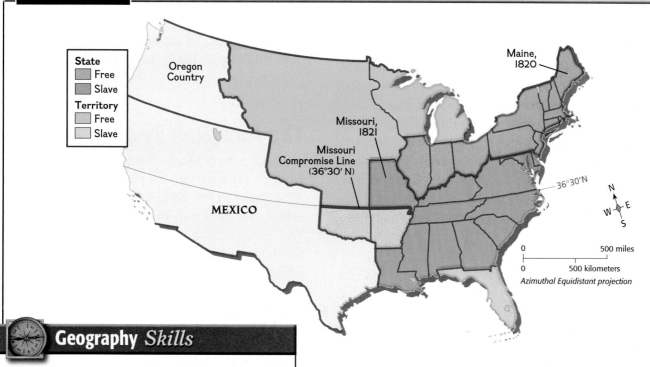

Geography *Skills*

After 1820 all new states north of 36°30'N were to be admitted as free states.

1. **Region** Did Missouri enter the Union as a free state or a slave state?
2. **Analyzing Information** Was Maine a slave state or a free state in 1820?

became a strong opponent of nationalist programs such as high tariffs. Calhoun and other Southerners argued that tariffs raised the prices that they had to pay for the manufactured goods they could not produce for themselves. They also argued that high tariffs protected inefficient manufacturers.

Daniel Webster

First elected to Congress in 1812 to represent his native New Hampshire, **Daniel Webster** later represented Massachusetts in both the House and the Senate. Webster began his political career as a supporter of free trade and the shipping interests of New England. In time, Webster came to favor the Tariff of 1816—which protected American industries from foreign competition—and other policies that he thought would strengthen the nation and help the North.

Webster gained fame as one of the greatest orators of his day. As a United States senator, he spoke eloquently in defense of the nation as a whole against sectional interests. In one memorable speech Webster declared, "Liberty and Union, now and forever, one and inseparable!"

Henry Clay

Another leading War Hawk, **Henry Clay** of Kentucky, became Speaker of the House of Representatives in 1811 and a leader who represented the interests of the Western states. He also served as a member of the delegation that negotiated the Treaty of Ghent, ending the War of 1812. Above all, Henry Clay became known as the national leader who tried to resolve sectional disputes through compromise.

The Missouri Compromise

Sectional tension reached new heights in 1820 over the issue of admitting new states to the Union. The problem revolved around slavery. The South wanted Missouri, part of the Louisiana Purchase, admitted as a slave state. Northerners wanted Missouri to be free of slavery. The issue became the subject of debate throughout the country, exposing bitter regional divisions that would plague national politics for decades.

While Congress considered the Missouri question, Maine—still part of Massachusetts—also applied for statehood. The discussions about Missouri now broadened to include Maine.

Some observers feared for the future of the Union. Eventually Henry Clay helped work out a compromise that preserved the balance between North and South. The **Missouri Compromise,** reached in March 1820, provided for the admission of Missouri as a slave state and Maine as a free state. The agreement banned slavery in the remainder of the Louisiana Territory north of the 36°30'N parallel.

✔ Reading Check **Identifying** What issue did the Missouri Compromise address? How did the Northern and Southern attitudes towards slavery differ?

The American System

Though he was a spokesperson for the West, Henry Clay believed his policies would benefit *all* sections of the nation. In an 1824 speech, he called his program the "American System." The American System included a protective tariff; a program of internal improvements, especially the building of roads and canals, to stimulate trade; and a national bank to control inflation and to lend money to build developing industries.

Clay believed that the three parts of his plan would work together. The tariff would provide the government with money to build roads and canals. Healthy businesses could use their profits to buy more agricultural goods from the South, then ship these goods northward along the nation's efficient new transportation system.

Not everyone saw Clay's program in such positive terms. Former president Jefferson believed the American System favored the wealthy manufacturing classes in New England. Many people in the South agreed with Jefferson. They saw no benefits to the South from the tariff or internal improvements.

In the end, little of Clay's American System went into effect. Congress eventually adopted some internal improvements, though not on the scale Clay had hoped for. Congress had created the Second National Bank in 1816, but it remained an object of controversy.

McCulloch v. Maryland

The Supreme Court also became involved in sectional and states' rights issues at this time. The state of Maryland imposed a tax on the Baltimore branch of the Second Bank of the United States—a federal institution. The Bank refused to pay the state tax, and the case, *McCulloch v. Maryland,* reached the Court in 1819.

Linking Past & Present

Past

"Modern" Medicine

In the mid-1800s, a visit to the doctor's office was viewed with suspicion. Faced with "cures" that were often fatal, people started using patent medicines—those they could buy in stores. One popular remedy, Snake Oil, was a mixture of wintergreen and white gasoline.

Today artificial hearts, cameras that move through veins, and other products have greatly improved Americans' health.

Present
Genetic engineer

Speaking for the Court, Chief Justice **John Marshall** ruled that Maryland had no right to tax the Bank because it was a federal institution. He argued that the Constitution and the federal government received their authority directly from the people, not by way of the state governments. Those who opposed the *McCulloch* decision argued that it was a "loose construction" of the Constitution, which says that the federal government can "coin" money—gold, silver, and other coins—but the Constitution does not mention paper money. In addition, the Constitutional Convention had voted *not* to give the federal government the authority to charter corporations, including banks. 📖 *(See page 625 of the Appendix for a summary of McCulloch v. Maryland.)*

Gibbons v. *Ogden*

Another Supreme Court case, *Gibbons* v. *Ogden,* established that states could not enact legislation that would interfere with Congressional power over interstate commerce. The Supreme Court's rulings strengthened the national government. They also contributed to the debate over sectional issues. People who supported states' rights believed that the decisions increased federal power at the expense of state power. Strong nationalists welcomed the rulings' support for national power. 📖 *(See page 624 of the Appendix for a summary of Gibbons v. Ogden.)*

✓ **Reading Check** **Examining** Why was the Court's decision in *Gibbons* v. *Ogden* significant?

Foreign Affairs

The War of 1812 heightened Americans' pride in their country. Abigail Adams, wife of John Adams, wrote from England to her sister back in Massachusetts:

❝Do you know that European birds have not half the melody of ours? Nor is their fruit half so sweet, nor their flowers half so fragrant, nor their manners half so pure, nor their people half so virtuous.❞

At the same time, many Americans realized that the United States needed peace with Britain to grow and develop. It had to put differences aside and establish a new relationship with the "Old World."

Relations With Britain

In the years following the War of 1812, President Monroe and his secretary of state, John Quincy Adams, moved to resolve long-standing disputes with Great Britain and Spain.

In 1817, in the **Rush-Bagot Treaty,** the United States and Britain agreed to set limits on the number of naval vessels each could have on the Great Lakes. The treaty provided for the disarmament—the removal of weapons—along an important part of the border between the United States and British **Canada.**

The second agreement with Britain, the **Convention of 1818,** set the boundary of the Louisiana Territory between the United States and Canada at the 49th parallel. The convention created a secure and demilitarized border—a border without armed forces. Through Adams's efforts, Americans also gained the right to settle in the **Oregon Country.**

Relations With Spain

Spain owned East Florida and also claimed West Florida. The United States contended that West Florida was part of the Louisiana Purchase. In 1810 and 1812, Americans simply added parts of West Florida to Louisiana and Mississippi. Spain objected but took no action.

In April 1818, General **Andrew Jackson** invaded Spanish East Florida, seizing control of two Spanish forts. Jackson had been ordered to stop Seminole raids on American territory from Florida. In capturing the Spanish forts, however, Jackson went beyond his instructions.

Luis de Onís, the Spanish minister to the United States, protested forcefully and demanded the punishment of Jackson and his officers. Secretary of War Calhoun said that Jackson should be court-martialed—tried by a military court—for overstepping instructions. Secretary of State John Quincy Adams disagreed.

★ Geography
Adams-Onís Treaty

Although Secretary of State Adams had not authorized Jackson's raid, he did nothing to stop it. Adams guessed that the Spanish did not want war and that they might be ready to settle the Florida dispute. He was right. For the Spanish the raid had demonstrated the military strength of the United States.

Already troubled by rebellions in **Mexico** and South America, Spain signed the **Adams-Onís Treaty** in 1819. Spain gave East Florida to the United States and abandoned all claims to West Florida. In return the United States gave up its claims to Spanish Texas and took over responsibility for paying the $5 million that American citizens claimed Spain owed them for damages.

The two countries also agreed on a border between the United States and Spanish possessions in the West. The border extended northwest from the Gulf of Mexico to the 42nd parallel and then west to the Pacific, giving the United States a large piece of territory in the Pacific Northwest. America had become a transcontinental power.

✔ **Reading Check** **Identifying** What areas did the United States obtain from Spain?

Latin American Republics

While the Spanish were settling territorial disputes with the United States, they faced a series of challenges within their empire. In the early

Miguel Hidalgo

1800s, Spain controlled a vast colonial empire that included what is now the southwestern United States, Mexico and Central America, and all of South America except Brazil.

In the fall of 1810 a priest, **Miguel Hidalgo** (ee• DAHL• goh), led a rebellion against the Spanish government of Mexico. Hidalgo called for racial equality and the redistribution of land. The Spanish defeated the revolutionary forces and executed Hidalgo. In 1821 Mexico gained its independence, but independence did not bring social and economic change.

Bolívar and San Martín

Independence in South America came largely as a result of the efforts of two men. **Simón Bolívar,** also known as "the Liberator," led the movement that won freedom for the present-day countries of Venezuela, Colombia, Panama, Bolivia, and Ecuador. **José de San Martín** successfully achieved independence for Chile and Peru. By 1824 the revolutionaries' military victory was complete, and most of South America had liberated itself from Spain. Portugal's large colony of Brazil gained its independence peacefully in 1822. Spain's empire in the Americas had shrunk to Cuba, Puerto Rico, and a few other islands in the Caribbean.

The Monroe Doctrine

In 1822 Spain had asked France, Austria, Russia, and Prussia—the Quadruple Alliance—for help in its fight against revolutionary forces in South America. The possibility of increased European involvement in North America led President Monroe to take action.

The president issued a statement, later known as the **Monroe Doctrine,** on December 2, 1823. While the United States would not interfere with any existing European colonies in the Americas, Monroe declared, it would oppose any new ones. North and South America "are henceforth not to be considered as subjects for future colonization by any European powers."

In 1823 the United States did not have the military power to enforce the Monroe Doctrine. The Monroe Doctrine nevertheless became an important element in American foreign policy and has remained so for more than 170 years. 📖 *(See page 616 of the Appendix for an excerpt from the Monroe Doctrine.)*

✓ **Reading Check** **Evaluating** How did the Monroe Doctrine affect foreign policy?

HISTORY Online
Student Web Activity
Visit tarvol1.glencoe.com and click on **Chapter 10—Student Web Activities** for an activity on the democratic movements in the Americas.

SECTION 3 ASSESSMENT

Checking for Understanding

1. **Key Terms** Write a short paragraph in which you use the following key terms: sectionalism, internal improvements, American System, disarmament, demilitarize.
2. **Reviewing Facts** Describe the disagreement between the North and South that resulted in the Missouri Compromise.

Reviewing Themes

3. **Individual Action** What action did Daniel Webster take that shows he placed his concerns for the nation above his sectional interests?

Critical Thinking

4. **Identifying Central Issues** Explain the debate involved in *Gibbons* v. *Ogden* and the final decision.
5. **Determining Cause and Effect** Describe the chain of events in Latin America and Europe that led to the adoption of the Monroe Doctrine. Show your answers in a diagram like the one below.

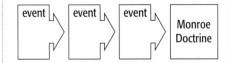

event → event → event → Monroe Doctrine

Analyzing Visuals

6. **Geography Skills** Use the map on page 323 to answer these questions. Which parallel did the Missouri Compromise line follow? How many slave states were there in 1820? How many free states?

Interdisciplinary Activity

Art Design a flag to represent either the North, South, or West during the early 1800s. Use photos, symbols, or mottoes that might have been popular with the people who lived in these regions.

Chapter Summary

Growth and Expansion

1790
- Samuel Slater builds first cotton mill in America

1793
- Eli Whitney invents the cotton gin

1801
- John Marshall is appointed chief justice of the Supreme Court

1807
- Robert Fulton builds the *Clermont*

1811
- National Road is begun

1816
- James Monroe elected president
- Second National Bank is chartered

1817
- Rush-Bagot Treaty is signed

1818
- Convention of 1818 agreement is signed

1819
- Adams-Onís Treaty is signed
- Supreme Court rules on *McCulloch* v. *Maryland*

1820
- Missouri Compromise is adopted

1823
- Monroe Doctrine is announced

1825
- Erie Canal is opened

Reviewing Key Terms

On a sheet of paper, create a crossword puzzle using the following terms. Use the terms' definitions as your crossword clues.

1. Industrial Revolution
2. factory system
3. sectionalism
4. disarmament
5. demilitarize
6. court-martial

Reviewing Key Facts

7. What problems did cities face as a result of rapid growth during the Industrial Revolution?

8. How did the landscape of New England affect how and where people lived in the late 1700s and early 1800s?

9. How did canals boost the economy of the Great Lakes region?

10. How did North and South differ on the issue of tariffs?

11. Identify factors in the United States that made it ideal for the free enterprise system.

12. What was the American System?

13. Explain the debate involved in *McCulloch* v. *Maryland* and the final decision in the case. Why was the decision significant?

14. How did James Monroe change the nation's foreign policy?

Critical Thinking

15. **Analyzing Themes: Economic Factors** How did the Industrial Revolution help to make the United States more economically independent in the early 1800s?

16. **Analyzing Themes: Global Connections** Why did Secretary of State John Quincy Adams allow General Jackson's invasion into Spanish East Florida in 1818?

17. **Determining Cause and Effect** How did the development of roads boost the growth of the United States? Use a diagram like the one shown to organize your answer.

Roads

Geography and History Activity

In 1819 Spain ceded Florida to the United States in the Adams-Onís Treaty. The Spanish had established colonies in Florida beginning in the 1500s. Study the map and answer the questions that follow.

NATIONAL GEOGRAPHIC
Acquisition of Florida, 1819

MISSISSIPPI
ALABAMA
Natchez
GEORGIA
80°W
Baton Rouge
Pensacola
New Orleans
St. Augustine
30°N
Annexed by U.S., 1812
Annexed by U.S., 1810
Gulf of Mexico
Ceded by Spain, 1819
N W E S
0   200 miles
0   200 kilometers
Albers Conic Equal-Area projection
90°W

18. **Region** When was the largest portion of Florida acquired from Spain?

19. **Location** What body of water blocked further expansion of Florida to the west?

20. **Movement** In what direction did the United States acquire the various parts of Florida?

Practicing Skills

Reading a Diagram *Study the diagram of the textile mill on page 307. Use the diagram to answer these questions.*

21. What is the first step in the production of textiles?

22. At what stage does the thread become cloth?

23. What process turns the yarn into thread?

24. When would a cotton gin be necessary in this process?

25. Now choose one of the inventions mentioned in the chapter. Prepare a diagram that traces the development of that invention to a similar device in use today. For example, you might diagram the development of a modern cruise ship, showing all the improvements made from start to finish.

HISTORY Online

Self-Check Quiz
Visit tarvol1.glencoe.com and click on **Chapter 10—Self-Check Quizzes** to prepare for the chapter test.

Citizenship Cooperative Activity

26. **Exploring Your Community's Past** Working with two other students, contact a local historical society to learn about your community's history. Then interview people in your neighborhood to learn about their roots in the community. Find out when their families first settled there. Write a history of the community and give a copy of it to the historical society.

Economics Activity

27. **Using the Internet** Search the Internet for information about how to apply for a patent for an invention. Create a step-by-step list of directions describing the process.

Alternative Assessment

28. **Portfolio Writing Activity** Review Section 2 of the chapter for information about what it was like to live in the West in the early 1800s. Record your notes in your journal. Use your notes to write a postcard to a friend describing your social life.

Standardized Test Practice

Directions: Choose the *best* answer to the following question.

The South opposed protective tariffs for which reason?

A They thought tariffs would not work.

B They had very little industry to protect.

C They thought foreign goods were better.

D Their main business was smuggling.

Test-Taking Tip:
Eliminate answers that do not make sense. For example, it is not realistic that the main business for the entire South was smuggling. Therefore, answer **D** cannot be correct.

Why It Matters

As you study Unit 5, you will learn how growth, migration, and conflict increased following the Industrial Revolution. The following resources offer more information about this period in American history.

Primary Sources Library

See pages 600–601 for primary source readings to accompany Unit 5.

 Use the **American History Primary Source Document Library CD-ROM** to find additional primary sources about the developing nation.

Goblet showing Jackson's log cabin

Advice on the Prairie
by William T. Ranney

"Liberty and Union, now and forever. . . ."

—Daniel Webster, 1830

CHAPTER 11

The Jackson Era

1824–1845

Why It Matters

The struggle for political rights took shape in the 1820s and 1830s, when many people questioned the limits of American democracy.

The Impact Today

In the years since the Jackson era:
- *Women, African Americans, and other minorities have won the right to vote and to participate in the political process.*
- *Today every United States citizen aged 18 or older, regardless of gender, race, or wealth, has the right to vote.*

The American Republic to 1877 *Video* *The chapter 11 video, "Old Hickory," chronicles events in Andrew Jackson's military and political careers.*

1833
- Force Bill passed

1823
- President Monroe outlines Monroe Doctrine

1830
- Indian Removal Act passed
- Webster-Hayne debate

United States PRESIDENTS

Monroe 1817–1825

J. Q. Adams 1825–1829

Jackson 1829–1837

1820   *1825*   *1830*

World

1822
- Brazil gains independence from Portugal

1826
- French scientist Niépce produces first photograph

1829
- Louis Braille publishes reading system for the blind

1833
- Slavery abolished in British colonies

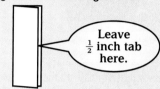

Stump Speaking by George Caleb Bingham Bingham's series of election paintings expressed faith in the growth of democracy.

FOLDABLES™
Study Organizer

Evaluating Information Study Foldable
Make this foldable to help you ask and answer questions about the Jackson era.

Step 1 Fold a sheet of paper in half from side to side, leaving a $\frac{1}{2}$ inch tab along the side.

> Leave $\frac{1}{2}$ inch tab here.

Step 2 Turn the paper and fold it into fourths.

> Fold in half, then fold in half again.

Step 3 Unfold and cut up along the three fold lines.

> Make four tabs.

Step 4 Label your foldable as shown.

> Who? What? When? Why?

Reading and Writing As you read, ask yourself "who" Andrew Jackson was, "what" he did, "when" he did it, and "why" it happened. Write your thoughts and facts under each appropriate tab.

1834
- Indian Territory created by Congress

1837
- Panic of 1837

1838
- Cherokee forced to move west

1840
- Harrison elected president

Van Buren 1837–1841

W. H. Harrison 1841

Tyler 1841–1845

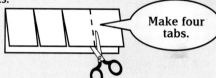

1835   1840   1845

1839
- Scottish blacksmith, Kirkpatrick Macmillian, produces first bicycle

1843
- Charles Dickens writes "A Christmas Carol"

1845
- Deadly fungus destroys much of Ireland's potato crop

HISTORY Online

Chapter Overview
Visit tarvol1.glencoe.com and click on **Chapter 11—Chapter Overviews** to preview chapter information.

Jacksonian Democracy

Guide to Reading

Main Idea
The United States's political system changed under Andrew Jackson.

Key Terms
favorite son, majority, plurality, mudslinging, landslide, suffrage, bureaucracy, spoils system, caucus, nominating convention, tariff, nullify, secede

Reading Strategy
As you read Section 1, create a chart like the one below and in the boxes describe the political parties in 1828.

	Candidate	Views
Democratic Republicans		
National Republicans		

Read to Learn
- why the nation's sixth president was chosen by the House.
- what political changes came under President Jackson.

Section Theme
Continuity and Change James Monroe's decision not to seek a third term was followed by two hotly contested presidential elections.

Preview of Events

♦1825   ♦1830   ♦1835

1825
John Quincy Adams wins presidency in House election

1828
Andrew Jackson elected president

1830
Webster and Hayne debate

1832
South Carolina threatens to secede

Jackson sewing box

AN American Story

The presidential campaign of 1828 was one of the most vicious in American history. Supporters of John Quincy Adams in Philadelphia distributed a pamphlet titled "Some Account of Some of the Bloody Deeds of General Jackson." One illustration in the pamphlet showed a ferocious-looking Andrew Jackson plunging his sword through the body of a helpless civilian. Meanwhile Jackson's supporters falsely accused John Quincy Adams of kidnapping a young American girl and selling her to the ruler of Russia.

The Election of 1824

From 1816 to 1824, the United States had only one political party, the Jeffersonian Republicans. Within the party, however, differences arose among various groups that had their own views and interests. In 1824 James Monroe was finishing his second term as president but declined to run for a third term. Four candidates from the Republican Party competed for the presidency.

The four candidates' opinions differed on the role of the federal government. They also spoke for different parts of the country. The Republican Party nominated **William H. Crawford,** a former congressman from Georgia. However, Crawford's poor health weakened him as a candidate.

The other three Republicans in the presidential race were favorite son candidates, meaning they received the backing of their home states rather than that of the national party. Two of these candidates—**Andrew Jackson** and **Henry Clay**—came from the West. Clay, of Kentucky, was Speaker of the House of Representatives. He fought for his program of internal improvements, high tariffs, and a stronger national bank.

General Andrew Jackson of Tennessee was not a Washington politician, but he was a hero of the War of 1812. Raised in poverty, he claimed to speak for the Americans who had been left out of politics.

John Quincy Adams of Massachusetts, son of former president John Adams, received support from merchants of the Northeast.

Striking a Bargain

In the election Jackson received the largest number of popular votes. However, no candidate received a majority, or more than half, of the electoral votes. Jackson won 99 electoral votes, which gave him a plurality, or largest single share. Under the terms of the Twelfth Amendment to the Constitution, when no candidate receives a majority of electoral votes, the House of Representatives selects the president.

While the House was preparing to vote on the next president, Henry Clay met with Adams. Clay agreed to use his influence as Speaker of the House to defeat Jackson. In return Clay may have hoped to gain the position of secretary of state.

With Clay's help Adams was elected president in the House. Adams quickly named Clay as secretary of state, traditionally the stepping-stone to the presidency. Jackson's followers accused the two men of making a **"corrupt bargain"** and stealing the election.

The Adams Presidency

In **Washington, D.C.,** the "corrupt bargain" had cast a shadow over Adams's presidency. Outside the capital Adams's policies ran against popular opinion. Adams wanted a stronger navy and government funds for scientific expeditions. Adams also wanted the federal government to direct economic growth.

Such ideas horrified those who desired a more limited role for the federal government, and Congress turned down many of Adams's proposals. This was especially true after the congressional elections of 1826, when enemies of Adams controlled both the House and Senate.

Reading Check **Describing** Why were Adams and Clay accused of making a "corrupt bargain"?

The Election of 1828

By the election of 1828, the party had divided into two separate parties: the **Democratic-Republicans,** who supported Jackson, and the **National Republicans,** who supported Adams. Jackson's Democratic-Republicans, or Democrats, favored states' rights and mistrusted

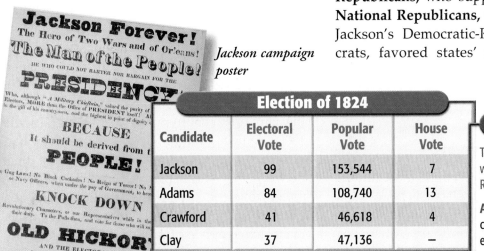

Jackson campaign poster

Election of 1824

Candidate	Electoral Vote	Popular Vote	House Vote
Jackson	99	153,544	7
Adams	84	108,740	13
Crawford	41	46,618	4
Clay	37	47,136	–

Chart Skills

The presidential election of 1824 was decided in the House of Representatives.

Analyzing Information Which candidate received the most electoral votes?

strong central government. Many Democrats were individualists from the frontier, immigrants, or laborers in the big cities.

The National Republicans wanted a strong central government. They supported federal measures, such as road building and the Bank of the United States, that would shape the nation's economy. Many were merchants or farmers.

During the campaign both parties resorted to mudslinging, attempts to ruin their opponent's reputation with insults. The Democratic-Republicans accused Adams of betraying the people. They put out a handbill calling the election a contest "between an honest patriotism, on the one side, and an unholy, selfish ambition, on the other."

The National Republicans fought back. They created a vicious campaign song to play up embarrassing incidents in Jackson's life. One involved Jackson's order in the War of 1812 to execute several soldiers who had deserted.

Mudslinging was not the only new element introduced in the 1828 campaign. Election slogans, rallies, buttons, and events such as barbecues were also used to arouse enthusiasm. All of these new features became a permanent part of American political life.

Jackson Triumphs

In the election of 1828, Jackson received most of the votes cast by voters of the new frontier states. He also received many votes in the South, where his support for states' rights was popular. John C. Calhoun of South Carolina, who had served as Adams's vice president, switched parties to run with Jackson. Calhoun also championed states' rights. Jackson won the election in a landslide, an overwhelming victory, with 56 percent of the popular vote and 178 electoral votes.

Reading Check **Summarizing** How did Jackson try to get the support of people in the election of 1828?

Jackson as President

Andrew Jackson was everything most Americans admired—a patriot, a self-made man, and a war hero. On March 4, 1829, thousands of farmers, laborers, and other ordinary Americans crowded into the nation's capital to hear Jackson's Inaugural Address. After Jackson's speech a crowd joined him at a White House reception. They filled the elegant rooms of the mansion, trampling on the carpets with muddy shoes, spilling food on sofas and chairs. They were there to shake the hand of the general who seemed just like them.

"Old Hickory"

Like many of his supporters, Andrew Jackson had been born in a log cabin. His parents, poor farmers, died before he was 15. As a teenager Jackson fought with the Patriots in the American Revolution. Before he was 30, he was elected to Congress from Tennessee.

Jackson gained fame during the War of 1812. He defeated the Creek Nation in the Battle of Horseshoe Bend and defeated the British at the Battle of New Orleans. His troops called him "Old Hickory" because he was as tough as a hickory stick.

Small farmers, craft workers, and others who felt left out of the expanding American economy loved Jackson. They felt that his rise from a log cabin to the White House demonstrated the American success story. His popularity with the common man changed politics in Washington, D.C.

☐ Citizenship
New Voters

President Andrew Jackson promised "equal protection and equal benefits" for all Americans—at least for all white American men. During his first term, a spirit of equality spread through American politics.

In the nation's early years, most states had limited suffrage, or the right to vote, for men who owned property or paid taxes. By 1815 many states had loosened or soon would loosen the property requirements for voting. In the 1820s democracy expanded as people who had not been allowed to vote voted for the first time. Between 1824 and 1828, the percentage of white males voting in presidential elections increased from 26.9 to 57.6 percent. For the first time, white male sharecroppers, factory workers, and many others were brought into the political process.

Analyzing *Political Cartoons*

A Political Card Game Andrew Jackson plays a card game with his political enemies. **Why did Jackson's opponents criticize the spoils system?**

Ⓐ Andrew Jackson **Ⓑ** Nicholas Biddle **Ⓒ** Henry Clay **Ⓓ** John C. Calhoun

The expansion of suffrage continued, and in 1840 more than 80 percent of white males voted in the presidential election. However, women still could not vote, and African Americans and Native Americans had few rights of any kind.

Another development in the broadening of democracy involved presidential electors. By 1828, 22 of the 24 states changed their constitutions to allow the people, rather than the state legislatures, to choose presidential electors.

The Spoils System

Democrats carried the spirit of democracy into government. They wanted to open up government jobs to people from all walks of life. They were disturbed that the federal government had become a bureaucracy, a system in which nonelected officials carry out laws. Democrats argued that ordinary citizens could handle any government job.

President Jackson fired many federal workers and replaced them with his supporters. The discharged employees protested vehemently. They charged that Jackson was acting like a tyrant, hiring and firing people at will. Jackson responded that a new set of federal employees would be good for democracy.

One Jackson supporter explained it another way: "To the victors belong the spoils." In other words, because the Jacksonians had won the election, they had the right to the spoils—benefits of victory—such as handing out government jobs to supporters. The practice of replacing government employees with the winning candidate's supporters became known as the spoils system.

Electoral Changes

Jackson's supporters worked to make the political system more democratic as well. They abandoned the unpopular caucus system. In this system major political candidates were chosen by committees made up of members of Congress. The caucuses were replaced by nominating conventions in which delegates from the states selected the party's presidential candidate.

The Democrats held their first national party convention in 1832 in **Baltimore, Maryland.** The convention drew delegates from each state in the Union. The delegates decided to nominate the candidate who could gather two-thirds of the vote, and Jackson won the nomination. This system allowed many people to participate in the selection of political candidates.

✓ **Reading Check** **Describing** What is a caucus system?

$ Economics

The Tariff Debate

Americans from different parts of the country disagreed strongly on some issues. One such issue was the tariff, a fee paid by merchants who imported goods. While president, Jackson faced a tariff crisis that tested the national government's powers.

In 1828 Congress passed a very high tariff on manufactured goods from Europe. Manufacturers in the United States—mostly in the Northeast—welcomed the tariff. Because tariffs made European goods more expensive, American consumers were more likely to buy American-made goods.

Southerners, however, hated the new tariff. They called it the Tariff of Abominations— something hateful. These critics argued that, while tariffs forced consumers to buy American goods, tariffs also meant higher prices.

The South Protests

Southern politicians and plantation owners were ready to act. Vice President John C. Calhoun argued that a state or group of states had the right to nullify, or cancel, a federal law it considered against state interests. Some Southerners called for the Southern states to secede, or break away, from the United States and form their own government. When Calhoun explored this idea, troubling questions arose. The United States had been a nation for nearly 50 years. What if a state disagreed with the federal government? Did a state have the right to go its own way?

Calhoun drew from the ideas that Madison and Jefferson wrote in the Virginia and Kentucky Resolutions of 1798–1799. Calhoun argued that since the federal government was a creation of the states, the states themselves are the final authority of the constitutionality of federal laws. The alternative to state sovereignty, Calhoun pointed out, is to allow the Supreme Court or Congress to tell the people what our Constitution means and what orders we must obey.

The Webster–Hayne Debate

In January 1830, Senator Daniel Webster delivered a stinging attack on nullification. Webster stood on the floor of the Senate to challenge a speech given by Robert Hayne, a young senator from South Carolina. Hayne had defended the idea that the states had a right to nullify acts of the federal government, and even to secede.

In his response, Webster defended the Constitution and the Union. He argued that nullification could only mean the end of the Union. Webster closed with the ringing statement, "Liberty and Union, now and forever, one and inseparable!"

Jackson Takes a Stand

Nobody knew exactly where President Jackson stood on the issue of nullification. Many Southerners hoped that Jackson might side with them. In April 1830 supporters of states' rights invited the president to speak at a dinner. The guests, including Calhoun, waited anxiously for Jackson to speak. Finally, the president rose to his feet and spoke directly to Calhoun.

66Our federal union . . . must be preserved!99

The states' rights supporters were shocked and disappointed, but Calhoun answered the president's challenge. He raised his glass and said,

66The Union—next to our liberty, most dear.99

He meant that the fate of the Union must take second place to a state's liberty to overrule the Constitution if its interests were threatened.

Calhoun realized that Jackson would not change his views. Wishing to return to Congress to speak for Southern interests, Calhoun won election to the Senate in December 1832. Not long after, he resigned the vice presidency.

The Nullification Crisis

Southern anger over the tariff continued to build. The Union seemed on the verge of splitting apart. In 1832 Congress passed a new, lower tariff, hoping that the protest in the South would die down. It did not.

South Carolina, Calhoun's home state, had led the fight against the so-called Tariff of Abominations. Now South Carolina took the

battle one step further. The state legislature passed the **Nullification Act,** declaring that it would not pay the "illegal" tariffs of 1828 and 1832. The South Carolina legislators threatened to secede from the Union if the federal government tried to interfere with their actions.

To ease the crisis, Jackson supported a compromise bill proposed by Henry Clay that would gradually lower the tariff over several years. At the same time, Jackson made sure that the South would accept Clay's compromise. Early in 1833 he persuaded Congress to pass the **Force Bill,** which allowed the president to use the United States military to enforce acts of Congress.

In response, South Carolina accepted the new tariff. However, to show that they had not been defeated, state leaders voted to nullify the Force Act. Calhoun and his followers claimed a victory for nullification, which had, they insisted, forced the revision of the tariff. For the time being, the crisis between a state and the federal government was over. Yet South Carolina and the rest of the South would remember the lesson of the nullification crisis—that the federal government would not allow a state to go its own way without a fight.

Reading Check **Summarizing** Why did South Carolina pass the Nullification Act?

SECTION 1 ASSESSMENT

Check for Understanding

1. **Key Terms** Use each of these terms in a complete sentence that will help explain its meaning: favorite son, majority, plurality, mudslinging, landslide, suffrage, spoils system, secede.
2. **Reviewing Facts** Why did the House of Representatives select the president in the 1824 presidential election?

Reviewing Themes

3. **Continuity and Change** What election practices used in the 1828 presidential campaign are still used today?

Critical Thinking

4. **Drawing Conclusions** What was the main reason President Adams was not popular with the Democratic-Republicans?
5. **Organizing Information** Re-create the diagram below and describe the changes that took place in the political system under Andrew Jackson.

Changes

Analyzing Visuals

6. **Analyzing Political Cartoons** Look at the cartoon on page 338. What symbols are used to represent the United States? How does the cartoonist use labels? What does the cartoonist want readers to think of President Jackson?

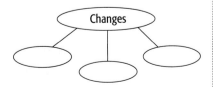

Interdisciplinary Activity

Interviewing Prepare a list of five questions that you might have asked President Jackson if you had interviewed him.

Analyzing Primary Sources

Why Learn This Skill?

Historians determine what happened in the past by combing through bits of evidence to reconstruct events. This evidence—both written and illustrated—is called *primary sources.* Examining primary sources can help you understand history.

Choctaw forced from their land

Learning the Skill

Primary sources are records of events made by the people who witnessed them. They include letters, diaries, photographs and pictures, news articles, and legal documents. To analyze primary sources, follow these steps:

- Identify when and where the document was written.
- Read the document for its content and try to answer the five "W" questions: <u>W</u>ho is it about? <u>W</u>hat is it about? <u>W</u>hen did it happen? <u>W</u>here did it happen? <u>W</u>hy did it happen?
- Identify the author's opinions.

Practicing the Skill

The primary source that follows comes from Speckled Snake, an elder of the Creek Nation, in 1829. He was more than 100 years old at the time

he said these words. Read the quote, then answer the questions that follow.

  ❝Brothers! I have listened to many talks from our Great Father. When he first came over the wide waters, he was but a little man. . . . But when the white man had warmed himself before the Indians' fire and filled himself with their hominy, he became very large. With a step he bestrode the mountains and his feet covered the plains and the valleys. His hand grasped the eastern and the western sea, and his head rested on the moon. Then he became our Great Father. Brothers, I have listened to a great many talks from our Great Father. But they always began and ended in this—'Get a little further; you are too near me.'❞

1 What events are described?

2 Who was affected by these events?

3 What is the general feeling of the person who stated this opinion?

Applying the Skill

Analyzing Primary Sources Find a primary source from your past—a photograph, a report card, an old newspaper clipping, or your first baseball card. Bring this source to class and explain what it shows about that time in your life.

Glencoe's **Skillbuilder Interactive Workbook CD-ROM, Level 1,** provides instruction and practice in key social studies skills.

SECTION 2 Conflicts Over Land

Guide to Reading

Main Idea

As more white settlers moved into the Southeast, conflict arose between the Native Americans who lived there and the United States government.

Key Terms

relocate, guerrilla tactics

Reading Strategy

As you read Section 2, create a chart like the one below that describes what happened to each group of Native Americans as the United States expanded.

	Description
Cherokee	
Sauk/Fox	
Seminole	

Read to Learn

• how Native American peoples were forced off their lands in the Southeast.
• how President Jackson defied the Supreme Court.

Section Theme

Groups and Institutions In the 1830s many Native American peoples were forced to relocate.

Preview of Events

```
     ◆1830              ◆1833              ◆1836              ◆1839
```

1830
Congress passes the Indian Removal Act

1832
Black Hawk leads Sauk and Fox people to Illinois

1835
Seminole refuse to leave Florida

1838
Cherokee driven from their homelands on the Trail of Tears

Sequoya

AN American Story

The Cherokee held their land long before European settlers arrived. Through treaties with the United States government, the Cherokee became a sovereign nation within Georgia. By the early 1800s the Cherokee had their own schools, their own newspaper, and their own written constitution. Sequoya's invention of a Cherokee alphabet enabled many of the Cherokee to read and write in their own language. The Cherokee farmed some of Georgia's richest land, and in 1829 gold was discovered there. Settlers, miners, and land speculators began trespassing on Cherokee territory in pursuit of riches.

Moving Native Americans

While the United States had expanded westward by the 1830s, large numbers of Native Americans still lived in the eastern part of the country. In Georgia, Alabama, Mississippi, and Florida lived the "Five Civilized Tribes"—the Cherokee, Creek, Seminole, Chickasaw, and Choctaw. The tribes had established farming societies with successful economies.

Because the area west of the Mississippi was dry and seemed unsuitable for farming, few white Americans lived there. Many settlers wanted the federal government to relocate Native Americans living in the Southeast. They proposed to force the Native Americans to leave their land and move west of the Mississippi River. President Andrew Jackson, a man of the frontier himself, supported the settlers' demand for Native American land.

Indian Removal Act

Congress responded by passing the **Indian Removal Act** in 1830. The act allowed the federal government to pay Native Americans to move west. Jackson then sent officials to negotiate treaties with Native Americans of the Southeast. Most felt compelled to accept payment for their lands. In 1834 Congress created the **Indian Territory,** an area in present-day Oklahoma, for Native Americans from the Southeast.

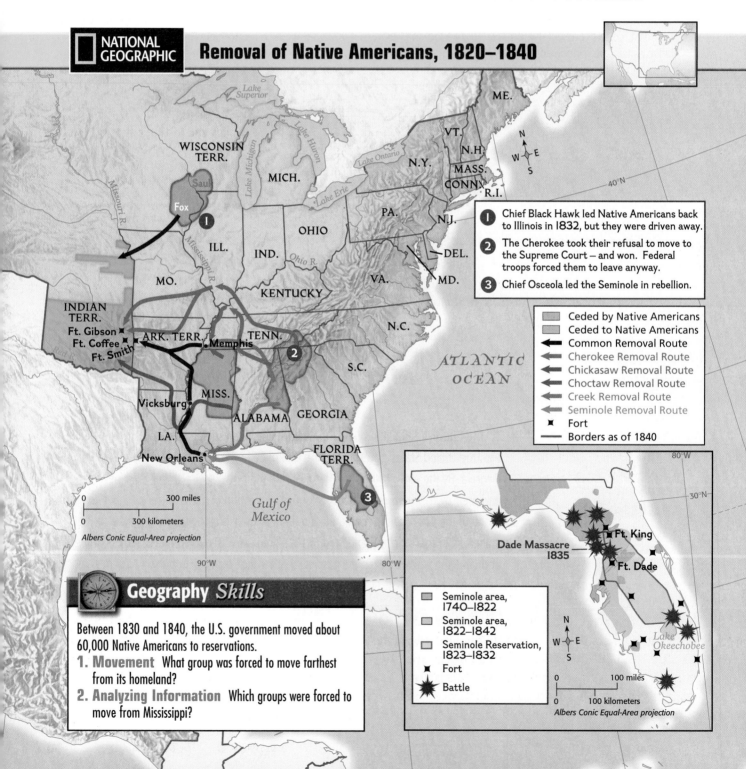

NATIONAL GEOGRAPHIC

Removal of Native Americans, 1820–1840

1. Chief Black Hawk led Native Americans back to Illinois in 1832, but they were driven away.
2. The Cherokee took their refusal to move to the Supreme Court — and won. Federal troops forced them to leave anyway.
3. Chief Osceola led the Seminole in rebellion.

- Ceded by Native Americans
- Ceded to Native Americans
- Common Removal Route
- Cherokee Removal Route
- Chickasaw Removal Route
- Choctaw Removal Route
- Creek Removal Route
- Seminole Removal Route
- ✶ Fort
- Borders as of 1840

Dade Massacre 1835 · Ft. King · Ft. Dade · Lake Okeechobee

- Seminole area, 1740–1822
- Seminole area, 1822–1842
- Seminole Reservation, 1823–1832
- ✶ Fort
- ✹ Battle

Albers Conic Equal-Area projection

Geography *Skills*

Between 1830 and 1840, the U.S. government moved about 60,000 Native Americans to reservations.

1. **Movement** What group was forced to move farthest from its homeland?
2. **Analyzing Information** Which groups were forced to move from Mississippi?

The Cherokee Nation

The Cherokee Nation, however, refused to give up its land. In treaties of the 1790s, the federal government had recognized the Cherokee people in the state of Georgia as a separate nation with their own laws. Georgia, however, refused to recognize Cherokee laws.

The Cherokee sued the state government and eventually took their case to the Supreme Court. In *Worcester* v. *Georgia* (1832), Chief Justice John Marshall ruled that Georgia had no right to interfere with the Cherokee. Only the federal government had authority over matters involving the Cherokee. *(See page 627 of the Appendix for a summary of* Worcester v. Georgia.)

President Jackson had supported Georgia's efforts to remove the Cherokee. He vowed to ignore the Supreme Court's ruling. "John Marshall has made his decision," Jackson reportedly said. "Now let him enforce it."

The Trail of Tears

In 1835 the federal government persuaded a few Cherokee to sign a treaty giving up their people's land. Yet most of the 17,000 Cherokee refused to honor the treaty. They wrote a protest letter to the government and people of the United States.

"We are aware that some persons suppose it will be for our advantage to [re]move beyond the Mississippi. . . . Our people universally think otherwise. . . . We wish to remain on the land of our fathers."

The Cherokee plea for understanding did not soften the resolve of President Jackson or the white settlers of the area. In 1838 **General Winfield Scott** and an army of 7,000 federal troops came to remove the Cherokee from their homes and lead them west.

Scott threatened to use force if the Cherokee did not leave. He told them he had positioned troops all around the country so that resistance and escape were both hopeless. "Chiefs, head men, and warriors—Will you then, by resistance, compel us to resort to arms?" The Cherokee knew that fighting would only lead to their destruction. Filled with sadness and anger, their leaders gave in, and the long march to the West began. One man in Kentucky wrote of seeing hundreds of Cherokee marching by:

People In History

Osceola 1804–1838

Osceola was born in 1804. His ancestors were Creek, African American, British, Irish, and Scottish. After President Jackson signed the Indian Removal Act in 1830, Osceola became the leader of the Seminoles and led successful attacks on United States forts. Hiding in the swampy lands of the Everglades, the Seminoles grew tired, sick, and hungry. Osceola attempted to surrender but was captured. He and his family were imprisoned at Fort Moultrie, South Carolina, where he died of a throat infection in 1838. Although he had waged a war against the United States, the public considered Osceola an honorable hero and a victim of trickery, and he was given a funeral with full military honors.

66Even [the] aged . . . nearly ready to drop in the grave, were traveling with heavy burdens attached to their backs, sometimes on frozen ground and sometimes on muddy streets, with no covering for their feet.99

Brutal weather along the way claimed thousands of Cherokee lives. Their forced journey west became known to the Cherokee people as the Trail Where They Cried. Historians call it the **Trail of Tears.**

Reading Check **Explaining** What was the purpose of the Indian Removal Act?

Native American Resistance

In 1832 the Sauk chieftain, **Black Hawk,** led a force of Sauk and Fox people back to Illinois, their homeland. They wanted to recapture this area, which had been given up in a treaty. The Illinois state militia and federal troops responded with force, gathering nearly 4,500 soldiers. They chased the Fox and Sauk to the Mississippi River and slaughtered most of the Native Americans as they tried to flee westward into present-day Iowa.

The Seminole people of Florida were the only Native Americans who successfully resisted their removal. Although they were pressured in the early 1830s to sign treaties giving up their land, the Seminole chief, **Osceola,** and some of his people refused to leave Florida. The Seminole decided to go to war against the United States instead.

In 1835 the Seminole joined forces with a group of African Americans who had run away to escape slavery. Together they attacked white settlements along the Florida coast. They used guerrilla tactics, making surprise attacks and then retreating back into the forests and swamps. In December 1835, Seminole ambushed soldiers under the command of Major Francis Dade. Only a few of the 110 soldiers survived the attack. The Dade Massacre pressured the call for more troops and equipment to fight the Seminole.

By 1842 more than 1,500 American soldiers had died in the Seminole wars. The government gave up and allowed some of the Seminole to remain in Florida. Many Seminole, however,

HISTORY Online

Student Web Activity
Visit tarvol1.glencoe.com and click on **Chapter 11—Student Web Activities** for an activity on the Trail of Tears.

"We told them to let us alone and keep away from us; but they followed on."

—*Black Hawk, Sauk leader* (far right), *pictured here with his son, Whirling Thunder*

had died in the long war, and many more were captured and forced to move westward. After 1842 only a few scattered groups of Native Americans lived east of the Mississippi. Most had been removed to the West. Native Americans had given up more than 100 million acres of eastern land to the federal government. They had received in return about $68 million and 32 million acres in lands west of the Mississippi River. There they lived, divided by tribes, in reservations. Eventually, these reservations, too, would face intrusion from white civilization.

The area of present-day Oklahoma became part of the United States in 1803 with the Louisiana Purchase. The United States set aside this area as the home for various Native American groups.

The Five Civilized Tribes were relocated in the eastern half of present-day Oklahoma on lands claimed by several Plains groups, including the Osage, Comanche, and Kiowa. United States Army leaders got agreements from the Plains groups to let the Five Civilized Tribes live in peace. Settled in their new homes, the Five Tribes developed their governments, improved their farms, and built schools. The Five Tribes also developed a police force called the Lighthorsemen. This law enforcement unit maintained safety for the region.

Reading Check **Comparing** How was the response of the Seminoles different from that of the Cherokee when they were removed from their lands?

SECTION 2 ASSESSMENT

Checking for Understanding

1. **Key Terms** Use the terms relocate and guerrilla tactics in complete sentences that will explain their meanings.
2. **Analyzing** Analyze how President Jackson reacted to the Supreme Court decision supporting the Cherokees' rights.

Reviewing Themes

3. **Groups and Institutions** How were the Seminole able to resist relocation?

Critical Thinking

4. **Drawing Conclusions** How was Georgia's policy toward the Cherokee different from the previous federal policy?
5. **Organizing Information** Re-create the diagram below to show how the Cherokee were eventually removed from their land.

```
1835           →  [   ]  →  [   ]  →  [   ]
treaty
with
Cherokee
```

Analyzing Visuals

6. **Geography Skills** Study the maps on page 342. Which groups of Native Americans were located in Alabama? What does the inset map show? In what area of Florida was the Seminole reservation?

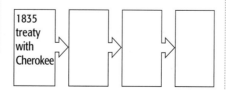

Interdisciplinary Activity

Persuasive Writing Write a letter to Andrew Jackson telling him why the Native Americans should or should not be allowed to stay in their homelands.

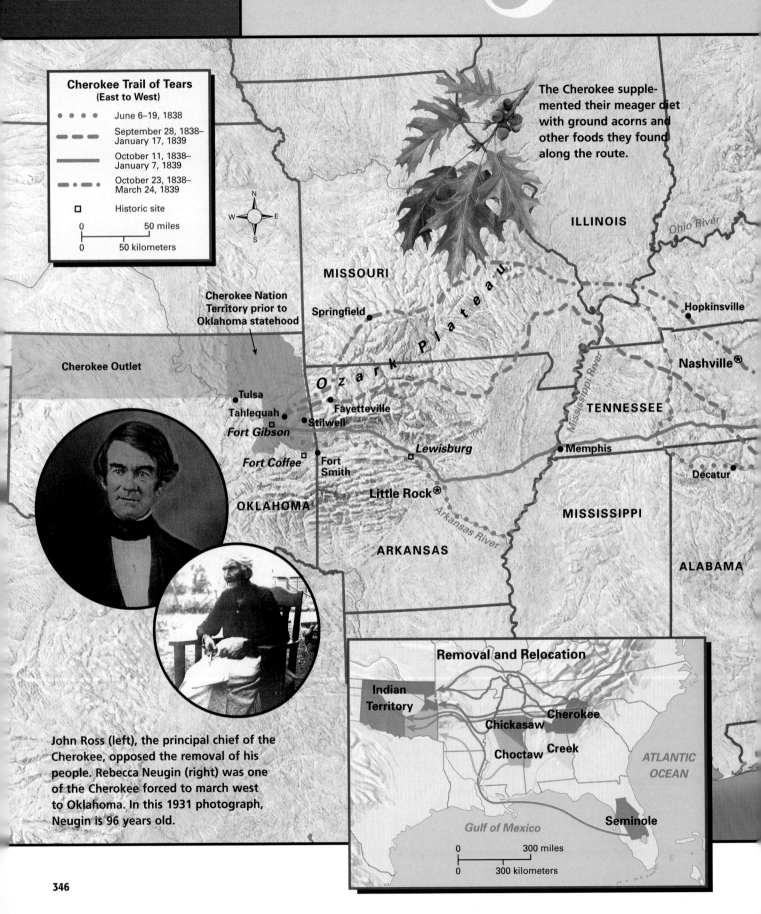

Cherokee Trail of Tears
(East to West)

• • • • June 6–19, 1838

– – – September 28, 1838–
January 17, 1839

——— October 11, 1838–
January 7, 1839

–•–•– October 23, 1838–
March 24, 1839

▢ Historic site

0   50 miles
0   50 kilometers

The Cherokee supplemented their meager diet with ground acorns and other foods they found along the route.

ILLINOIS

Ohio River

MISSOURI

Hopkinsville

Cherokee Nation Territory prior to Oklahoma statehood

Springfield

Ozark Plateau

Nashville ⊗

Cherokee Outlet

Tulsa

Mississippi River

TENNESSEE

Tahlequah
Fort Gibson

Fayetteville
Stilwell

Memphis

Lewisburg

Fort Coffee

Fort Smith

Decatur

Little Rock ⊗

OKLAHOMA

Arkansas River

MISSISSIPPI

ARKANSAS

ALABAMA

John Ross (left), the principal chief of the Cherokee, opposed the removal of his people. Rebecca Neugin (right) was one of the Cherokee forced to march west to Oklahoma. In this 1931 photograph, Neugin is 96 years old.

Removal and Relocation

Indian Territory

Cherokee

Chickasaw

Choctaw   Creek

ATLANTIC OCEAN

Seminole

Gulf of Mexico

0   300 miles
0   300 kilometers

TRAIL OF TEARS

LONG BEFORE EUROPEAN EXPLORERS ARRIVED, the Cherokee, Chickasaw, Choctaw, Creek, and Seminole were living in eastern North America. The Native Americans built permanent communities, practiced agriculture, and developed complex tribal governments—thereby earning the name of Five Civilized Tribes.

REMOVAL

As white settlers moved into the southeastern states, they began demanding the land held by Native Americans. In 1830, Congress passed the Indian Removal Act to move the Five Civilized Tribes west of the Mississippi. Under pressure, the Choctaw, Chickasaw, and Creek moved west while the Cherokee and the Seminole resisted.

RESISTANCE

Despite protests from the Cherokee people, they were forced to march west. In 1838, 13 ragged groups trekked to Fort Gibson in the newly created Indian Territory (see maps). Along the journey, which became known as the "Trail of Tears," 4,000 Cherokee died of cold, hunger, or disease.

Some of the Seminole refused to abandon their homeland and waged a guerrilla war in the Florida Everglades until the government gave up its efforts to resettle them in 1842.

KENTUCKY

APPALACHIAN MOUNTAINS

NORTH CAROLINA

Cherokee

Fort Cass

Chattanooga

SOUTH CAROLINA

New Echota

Fort Payne

Atlanta

GEORGIA

Most Cherokee farmers lived in log cabins.

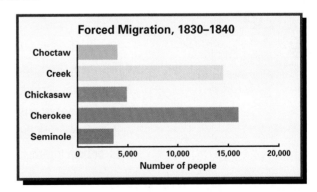

Forced Migration, 1830–1840

	Number of people
Choctaw	
Creek	
Chickasaw	
Cherokee	
Seminole	

0   5,000   10,000   15,000   20,000
Number of people

LEARNING *from* GEOGRAPHY

1. To what present-day state were the Five Civilized Tribes forced to move?

2. Through what cities did the Cherokee travel during the removal that began on June 6, 1838?

Jackson and the Bank

Guide to Reading

Main Idea

Economic issues affected the presidencies of Andrew Jackson and Martin Van Buren.

Key Terms

veto, depression, laissez-faire, log cabin campaign

Reading Strategy

Sequencing Information As you read the section, re-create the diagram below. In the spaces provided, describe the steps Andrew Jackson took that put the Bank of the United States out of business.

```
[   ] → [   ] → [ Jackson stops Bank ]
```

Read to Learn

• why Jackson wanted to destroy the Bank of the United States.
• how the Whigs came to power in 1840.

Section Theme

Economic Factors Economic issues influenced politics in the mid-1800s.

Preview of Events

♦1830   ♦1835   ♦1840   ♦1845

1832
Andrew Jackson challenges the Bank of the United States

1836
Martin Van Buren is elected president

1837
Panic of 1837 strikes the nation

1841
Vice President John Tyler becomes president

Bank note issued in the mid-1800s

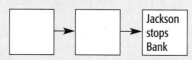

AN American Story

President Andrew Jackson made many enemies. His most outspoken rivals, the Whigs, were strong in Congress. They accused "King Andrew" of increasing his power and spreading corruption with the spoils system. In response, Jackson declared that the president was responsible for the protection of "the liberties and rights of the people and the integrity of the Constitution against the Senate, or the House of Representatives, or both together."

War Against the Bank

Jackson had another great battle during his presidency. For years, he had attacked the Bank of the United States as being an organization of wealthy Easterners over which ordinary citizens had no control. The Bank of the United States was a powerful institution. It held the federal government's money and controlled much of the country's money supply. Although the Bank had been chartered by Congress, it was run by private bankers rather than elected officials.

The Bank's president, **Nicholas Biddle,** represented everything Jackson disliked. Jackson prided himself on being a self-made man who started with nothing. Biddle, on the other hand, came from a wealthy family and had a good education and social standing.

In 1832 Jackson's opponents gave him the chance to take action against the Bank. Senators **Henry Clay** and **Daniel Webster,** friends of Biddle, planned to use the Bank to defeat Jackson in the 1832 presidential election. They persuaded Biddle to apply early for a new charter—a government permit to operate the Bank—even though the Bank's current charter did not expire until 1836.

Clay and Webster believed the Bank had popular support. They thought that an attempt by Jackson to veto its charter would lead to his defeat and allow Henry Clay to be elected president.

When the bill to renew the Bank's charter came to Jackson for signature, he was sick in bed. Jackson told his friend **Martin Van Buren,** "The bank, Mr. Van Buren, is trying to kill me. But I will kill it!" Jackson vetoed, or rejected, the bill.

Jackson, like many others, still felt the Bank was unconstitutional despite the Supreme Court's decision to the contrary in *McCulloch* v. *Maryland* (1819). In a message to Congress, Jackson angrily denounced the Bank, arguing that

   ❝. . . when laws . . . make the rich richer and the potent more powerful, the humble members of society—the farmers, mechanics, and laborers—who have neither the time nor the means of securing like favors to themselves, have a right to complain of the injustice of their Government.❞

The Election of 1832

Webster and Clay were right about one thing. The Bank of the United States did play a large part in the campaign of 1832. Their strategy for

Analyzing *Political Cartoons*

Many cartoons from the period depicted Jackson's battle against the Second Bank of the United States. **Does this cartoon support the president or the Bank? Explain.**

Ⓐ The Bank   Ⓑ President Jackson   Ⓒ American people

Picturing **History**

In the 1840 election campaign, the Whigs marched in street parades, often carrying miniature log cabins on poles. **Why did Harrison's supporters make the log cabin their symbol?**

William Henry Harrison

Miniature log cabin

gaining support for Clay as president, however, backfired. Most people supported Jackson's veto of the bank charter bill. Jackson was re-elected, receiving 55 percent of the popular vote and collecting 219 electoral votes to Clay's 49. Martin Van Buren was elected vice president.

Once re-elected, Jackson decided on a plan to "kill" the Bank ahead of the 1836 schedule. He ordered the withdrawal of all government deposits from the Bank and placed the funds in smaller state banks. In 1836 he refused to sign a new charter for the Bank, and it closed.

Economics

The Panic of 1837

When Jackson decided not to run for a third term in 1836, the Democrats selected Martin Van Buren of New York, Jackson's friend and vice president, as their candidate. Van Buren faced bitter opposition from the Whigs, a new political party that included former National Republicans and other anti-Jackson forces. Jackson's great popularity and his personal support helped Van Buren easily defeat several Whig opponents. Van Buren was inaugurated in 1837.

Shortly after Van Buren's election, the country entered a severe economic depression, a period in which business and employment fall to a very low level. The depression began with the **Panic of 1837,** a time when land values dropped sharply, investments declined suddenly, and banks failed. Thousands of businesses closed and hundreds of thousands of people lost their jobs. In the South, cotton prices fell to record lows. Farmers plunged into debt and lost their land. In the cities, many people could not afford food or rent. In February 1837, people in New York put up signs voicing their anger:

> 66Bread, Meat, Rent, and Fuel!
> Their prices must come down!
> The Voice of the People shall be heard
> and will prevail!99

President Van Buren believed in the principle of laissez-faire—that government should interfere as little as possible in the nation's economy. Van Buren did persuade Congress to establish an independent federal treasury in 1840. The government would no longer deposit its money with private individual banks as it had started to do during President Jackson's war with the Bank of the United States. Instead the government would store its money in the federal treasury. The private banks had used government funds to back their banknotes. The new treasury system would prevent banks from using government funds in this way and so help guard against further bank crises.

Van Buren and his supporters hailed the new law as a "second declaration of independence." However, criticism of the act came from members of Van Buren's own Democratic Party as well as from Whigs. The split in the Democratic Party meant the Whigs had a chance to win the presidency in 1840.

✓ **Reading Check** **Explaining** What was the new treasury system supposed to prevent?

The Whigs Come to Power

The Democrats had controlled the presidency for 12 years. However, with the country still in the depths of depression, the Whigs thought they had a chance to win the election in 1840. They nominated **William Henry Harrison,** a hero of the War of 1812, to run against President Van Buren. **John Tyler**, a planter from Virginia, was Harrison's running mate. Because Harrison had gained national fame defeating Tecumseh's followers in the Battle of Tippecanoe, the Whigs' campaign slogan was "Tippecanoe and Tyler Too."

To win the election, Harrison had to gain the support of the laborers and farmers who had voted for Jackson. The Whigs adopted a log cabin as their symbol. Political cartoons in newspapers showed Harrison, a wealthy man from Virginia, in front of a log cabin. The Whigs wanted to show that their candidate was a "man of the people."

The Whigs also ridiculed Van Buren as "King Martin," a wealthy snob who had spent the people's money on fancy furniture for the White House. The log cabin campaign seemed to work, and Harrison went on to defeat Van Buren by a wide margin.

William Henry Harrison was inaugurated in 1841 as the first Whig president. The Whigs were still celebrating their victory when Harrison died of pneumonia on April 4, 1841. John Tyler of Virginia became the first vice president to gain the presidency because the elected president died in office.

Although Tyler had been elected vice president as a Whig, he had once been a Democrat. As president, Tyler, a strong supporter of states' rights, vetoed several bills sponsored by Whigs in Congress, including a bill to recharter the Bank of the United States. His lack of party loyalty outraged Whigs. Most of Tyler's cabinet resigned, and Whig leaders in Congress expelled Tyler from the party.

It seemed that the Whigs could not agree on their party's goals. Increasingly, Whigs voted according to sectional ties—North, South, and West—not party ties. This division may explain why the Whig candidate, Henry Clay, lost the election of 1844 to Democratic candidate **James Polk.** After only four years, the Whigs were out of power again.

✓ **Reading Check** **Describing** How did John Tyler become president?

SECTION 3 ASSESSMENT

Checking for Understanding

1. **Key Terms** Use each of these terms in a complete sentence that will help explain its meaning: veto, depression, laissez-faire, log cabin campaign.
2. **Reviewing Facts** List Jackson's reasons for wanting to "kill" the Bank of the United States.

Reviewing Themes

3. **Economic Factors** Why did President Van Buren do little to solve the nation's economic problems during the depression?

Critical Thinking

4. **Analyzing Information** What tactics did the Whigs borrow from Jackson's campaign to win the election of 1840?
5. **Organizing Information** Re-create the diagram below to show how the Panic of 1837 affected the presidency of Martin Van Buren.

Panic of 1837 → ☐ → ☐

Analyzing Visuals

6. **Analyzing Political Cartoons** Study the cartoon on page 349. Do you think the Bank of the United States is portrayed positively or negatively? Explain your answer.

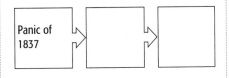

Interdisciplinary Activity

Art Write a campaign slogan for Van Buren or Harrison in the election of 1840. Then design a campaign button that incorporates your slogan.

Chapter Summary

The Jackson Era

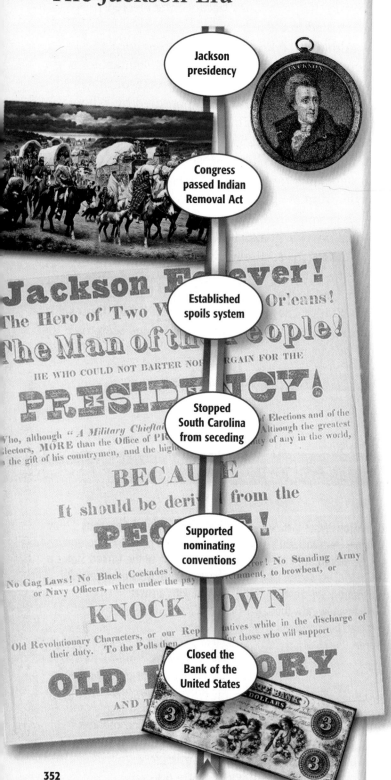

- Jackson presidency
- Congress passed Indian Removal Act
- Established spoils system
- Stopped South Carolina from seceding
- Supported nominating conventions
- Closed the Bank of the United States

Reviewing Key Terms

On graph paper, create a word search puzzle using the following terms. Crisscross the terms vertically and horizontally. Then fill in the remaining squares with extra letters. List the definitions below the puzzle as clues. Share your puzzle with a classmate.

1. plurality
2. landslide
3. suffrage
4. majority
5. nullify
6. secede
7. depression

Reviewing Key Facts

8. How did the supporters of Jackson and Adams differ in their beliefs?
9. What were some of the political tactics used by Democratic-Republicans and the National Republicans in the election of 1828?
10. Which Americans were prohibited from voting in most states before the 1800s?
11. How did nominating conventions make the selection of political candidates more democratic?
12. Why was the South against high tariffs?
13. Who did the Seminoles join forces with as they fought against forced removal from their land?
14. How did the Panic of 1837 affect the nation's economy?
15. Why was Harrison's log cabin campaign successful?

Critical Thinking

16. **Drawing Conclusions** President Andrew Jackson promised "equal protection and equal benefits" for all Americans. Do you think he included Native Americans in his promise? Why or why not?
17. **Analyzing Themes: Groups and Institutions** What agreement did the Cherokee Nation make with the federal government that Georgia refused to recognize?
18. **Organizing Information** Re-create the chart below. List the issues that Jackson dealt with during his presidency. Then describe how he responded to each issue.

Issues	Jackson's response

Self-Check Quiz
Visit tarvol1.glencoe.com and click on **Chapter 11—Self-Check Quizzes** to prepare for the chapter test.

Geography and History Activity

The issue of states' rights was debated in the election of 1828. Study the map below and answer the questions that follow.

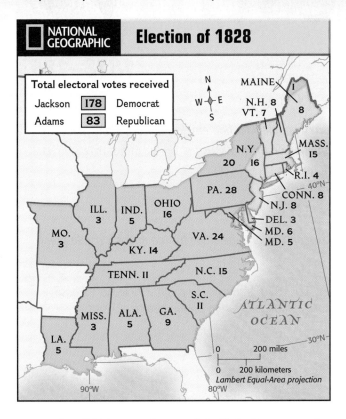

NATIONAL GEOGRAPHIC **Election of 1828**

Total electoral votes received

Jackson **178** Democrat
Adams **83** Republican

19. **Region** Which general areas of the United States voted for Andrew Jackson in the election of 1828?

20. **Location** Which candidate won more votes in Adams's home state of Massachusetts?

21. **Place** Which three states divided their total electoral count between the two candidates?

Practicing Skills

Analyzing Primary Sources *In an annual message to Congress in 1835, President Andrew Jackson spoke the words below. Read the excerpt and answer the questions that follow.*

66All preceding experiments for the improvement of the Indians have failed. It seems now to be an established fact that they cannot live in contact with a civilized community and prosper. . . . A country west of Missouri and Arkansas has been assigned to them, into which the white settlements are not to be pushed.99

22. Whose opinion is stated in the excerpt?

23. What is the speaker's attitude toward Native Americans?

24. According to the speaker, why should Native Americans be assigned to a country west of Missouri and Arkansas?

Citizenship Cooperative Activity

25. **Becoming an Informed Voter** With a partner, choose an election in your community. Outline how you would become informed on the candidates and/or the issues. Then follow your outline and become an informed voter. Share your outline and your findings with the class.

Economics Activity

26. Look in a dictionary to find definitions of "recession" and "depression." Write a paragraph to explain the difference between the two.

Standardized Test Practice

Directions: Choose the *best* answer to the following question.

Which of the following statements expresses an opinion about Andrew Jackson?

A Jackson served two terms as president.

B He spoke out against South Carolina's Nullification Act.

C Because of Jackson, the United States has the best system of filling government positions.

D Jackson supported the Indian Removal Act.

Test-Taking Tip

An opinion is a person's belief. It is not a proven fact (such as answer A). Opinions often contain subjective words, like *easier* or *best.*

CHAPTER 12

Manifest Destiny

1818–1853

Why It Matters

The United States was made up of people who had emigrated from many places in the world. Many Americans remained on the move as the United States extended its political borders and grew economically.

The Impact Today

The United States grew in size and wealth, setting the stage for the nation's rise to great economic and political power.

 The American Republic to 1877 *Video* *The chapter 12 video, "Whose Destiny?," chronicles the influence of Manifest Destiny on the history of Texas.*

1820
• Missouri Compromise

1809
• Elizabeth Ann Seton founds Sisters of Charity

1824
• Russia surrenders land south of Alaska

United States PRESIDENTS

| Madison 1809–1817 | Monroe 1817–1825 | | J.Q. Adams 1825–1829 | Jackson 1829–1837 |

1810   *1820*   *1830*

World

1821
• Mexico declares independence from Spain

1828
• Russia declares war on Ottoman Empire

1830
• France occupies Algeria

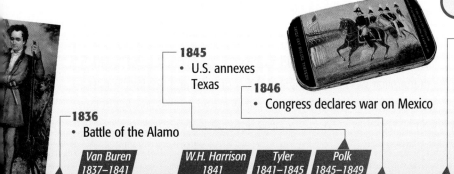

War News from Mexico by Richard Caton Woodville Many of Woodville's paintings show scenes of everyday life.

FOLDABLES™
Study Organizer

Organizing Information Study Foldable
Make this foldable to organize information from the chapter to help you learn more about how Manifest Destiny led to western expansion.

Step 1 Collect three sheets of paper and place them on top of one another about 1 inch apart.

Keep the edges straight.

Step 2 Fold up the bottom edges of the paper to form 6 tabs.

This makes all tabs the same size.

Step 3 When all the tabs are the same size, fold the paper to hold the tabs in place and staple the sheets together. Turn the paper and label each tab as shown.

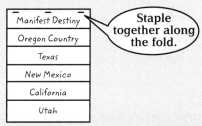

| Manifest Destiny |
| Oregon Country |
| Texas |
| New Mexico |
| California |
| Utah |

Staple together along the fold.

Reading and Writing As you read, use your foldable to write under each appropriate tab what you learn about Manifest Destiny and how it affected the borders of the United States.

1836
• Battle of the Alamo

1845
• U.S. annexes Texas

1846
• Congress declares war on Mexico

1848
• Treaty of Guadalupe Hidalgo signed

1850
• California becomes a state

| Van Buren 1837–1841 | W.H. Harrison 1841 | Tyler 1841–1845 | Polk 1845–1849 | Taylor 1849–1850 |

1840   *1850*

1839
• Opium War between Britain and China

1844
• The Dominican Republic secedes from Haiti

1846
• The planet Neptune is discovered

HISTORY Online

Chapter Overview
Visit tarvol1.glencoe.com and click on **Chapter 12— Chapter Overviews** to preview chapter information.

The Oregon Country

Main Idea
Manifest Destiny is the idea that the United States was meant to extend its borders from the Atlantic Ocean to the Pacific Ocean.

Key Terms
joint occupation, mountain man, rendezvous, emigrant, Manifest Destiny

Reading Strategy
Sequencing Information As you read Section 1, re-create the diagram below and in the boxes list key events that occurred.

1819	1825	1836	1846

Read to Learn
- why large numbers of settlers headed for the Oregon Country.
- how the idea of Manifest Destiny contributed to the nation's growth.

Section Theme
Economic Factors Many fur traders and pioneers moved to Oregon for economic opportunities.

Preview of Events

♦1820	♦1830	♦1840	♦1850
1819 Adams-Onís Treaty is signed	**1836** Marcus Whitman builds mission in Oregon	**1840s** "Oregon fever" sweeps through Mississippi Valley	**1846** U.S. and Britain set the Oregon Boundary at 49°N

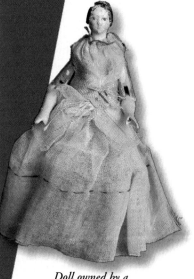

Doll owned by a young pioneer

★★★★★★★★
AN
American Story

On an April morning in 1851, 13-year-old Martha Gay said good-bye to her friends, her home, and the familiar world of Springfield, Missouri. She and her family were beginning a long, hazardous journey. The townsfolk watched as the Gays left in four big wagons pulled by teams of oxen. "Farewell sermons were preached and prayers offered for our safety," Martha wrote years later. "All places of business and the school were closed . . . and everybody came to say good-bye to us." This same scene occurred many times in the 1840s and 1850s as thousands of families set out for the Oregon Country.

Rivalry in the Northwest

The **Oregon Country** was the huge area that lay between the Pacific Ocean and the Rocky Mountains north of **California.** It included all of what is now Oregon, Washington, and Idaho plus parts of Montana and Wyoming. The region also contained about half of what is now the Canadian province of British Columbia.

In the early 1800s, four nations laid claim to the vast, rugged land known as the Oregon Country. The United States based its claim on Robert Gray's discovery of the **Columbia River** in 1792 and on the Lewis and Clark expedition. Great Britain based its claim on British explorations of the Columbia River. Spain, which had also explored the Pacific coast in the late 1700s, controlled California to the south. Russia had settlements that stretched south from **Alaska** into Oregon.

Adams-Onís Treaty

Many Americans wanted control of the Oregon Country to gain access to the Pacific Ocean. Secretary of State **John Quincy Adams** played a key role in promoting this goal. In 1819 he negotiated the **Adams-Onís Treaty** with Spain. In the treaty the Spanish agreed to set the limits of their territory at what is now California's northern border and gave up any claim to Oregon. In 1824 Russia also surrendered its claim to the land south of Alaska. Only Britain remained to challenge American control of Oregon.

In 1818 Adams had worked out an agreement with Britain for joint occupation of the area. This meant that people from both the United States and Great Britain could settle there. When Adams became president in 1825, he proposed that the two nations divide Oregon along the 49°N line of latitude. Britain refused, insisting on a larger share of the territory. Unable to resolve their dispute, the two countries agreed to extend the joint occupation. In the following years, thousands of Americans streamed into Oregon, and they pushed the issue toward resolution.

Mountain Men

The first Americans to reach the Oregon Country were not farmers but fur traders. They had come to trap beaver, whose skins were in great demand in the eastern United States and in Europe. The British established several trading posts in the region, as did merchant **John Jacob Astor** of New York. In 1808 Astor organized the American Fur Company. The American Fur Company soon became the most powerful of the fur companies in America. It allowed him to build up trade with the East Coast, the Pacific Northwest, and China.

At first the merchants traded for furs that the Native Americans supplied. Gradually American adventurers joined the trade. These people, who spent most of their time in the Rocky Mountains, came to be known as mountain men.

The tough, independent mountain men made their living by trapping beaver. Many had Native American wives and adopted Native American ways. They lived in buffalo-skin lodges and dressed in fringed buckskin pants, moccasins, and beads.

Some mountain men worked for fur-trading companies; others sold their furs to the highest bidder. Throughout the spring and early summer they ranged across the mountains, setting traps and then collecting the beaver pelts. In late summer they gathered for a rendezvous (RAHN•dih•voo), or meeting.

For the mountain men, the annual rendezvous was the high point of the year. They met with the trading companies to exchange their "hairy

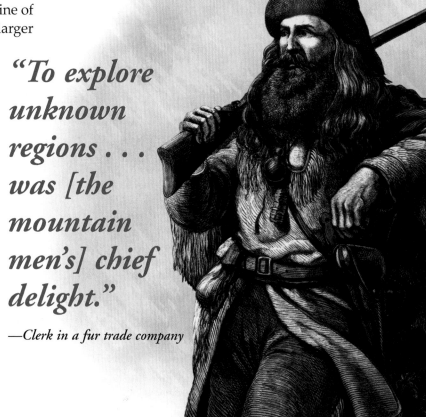

"To explore unknown regions . . . was [the mountain men's] chief delight."

—*Clerk in a fur trade company*

banknotes"—beaver skins—for traps, guns, coffee, and other goods. They met old friends and exchanged news. They relaxed by competing in races and various other contests—including swapping stories about who had been on the most exciting adventures.

As they roamed searching for beaver, the mountain men explored the mountains, valleys, and trails of the West. Jim Beckwourth, an African American from Virginia, explored Wyoming's Green River. Robert Stuart and Jedediah Smith both found the **South Pass,** a broad break through the Rockies. South Pass later became the main route that settlers took to Oregon.

To survive in the wilderness, a mountain man had to be skillful and resourceful. Trapper Joe Meek told how, when faced with starvation, he once held his hands "in an anthill until they were covered with ants, then greedily licked them off." The mountain men took pride in joking about the dangers they faced.

In time the mountain men killed off most of the beaver and could no longer trap. Some went to settle on farms in Oregon. With their knowledge of the western lands, though, some mountain men found new work. Jim Bridger, Kit Carson, and others acted as guides to lead the parties of settlers now streaming west.

☑ **Reading Check** **Identifying** What North American territories did Russia control in the early 1800s?

Alaska

Is Alaska the largest state? If you calculate by area, Alaska is far and away the largest state, with more than 570,000 square miles. It is approximately 2,000 miles from east to west. If placed on top of the mainland area of the United States, it would stretch from Atlanta to Los Angeles. Population is another matter. Alaska's population of 626,932 makes it the third least populous state. There is about 1.0 person per square mile in Alaska, compared to more than 79 people per square mile for the rest of the United States.

Settling Oregon

Americans began traveling to the Oregon Country to settle in the 1830s. Reports of the fertile land persuaded many to make the journey. Economic troubles at home made new opportunities in the West look attractive.

The Whitman Mission

Among the first settlers of the Oregon Country were missionaries who wanted to bring Christianity to the Native Americans. Dr. Marcus Whitman and his wife, Narcissa, went to Oregon in 1836 and built a mission among the Cayuse people near the present site of Walla Walla, Washington.

New settlers unknowingly brought measles to the mission. An epidemic killed many of the Native American children. Blaming the Whitmans for the sickness, the Cayuse attacked the mission in November 1847 and killed them and 11 others. Despite this, the flood of settlers continued into Oregon.

The Oregon Trail

In the early 1840s, "Oregon fever" swept through the Mississippi Valley. The depression caused by the Panic of 1837 had hit the region hard. People formed societies to gather information about Oregon and to plan to make the long trip. The "great migration" had begun. Tens of thousands of people made the trip. These pioneers were called emigrants because they left the United States to go to Oregon.

Before the difficult 2,000-mile journey, these pioneers stuffed their canvas-covered wagons, called **prairie schooners,** with supplies. From a distance these wagons looked like schooners (ships) at sea. Gathering in Independence or other towns in Missouri, they followed the **Oregon Trail** across the Great Plains, along the Platte River, and through the South Pass of the Rocky Mountains. On the other side, they took the trail north and west along the Snake and Columbia Rivers into the Oregon Country.

☑ **Reading Check** **Explaining** How did most pioneers get to Oregon?

The Oregon Trail

The Importance of the Trail The Oregon Trail was much more than just a trail to Oregon. It served as the most practical route to the western United States. The pioneers traveled in large groups, often of related families. Some went all the way to Oregon in search of farmland. Many others split off for California in search of gold.

The Journey The trip west lasted five or six months. The pioneers had to start in the spring and complete the trip before winter snows blocked the mountain passes. The trail crossed difficult terrain. The pioneers walked across seemingly endless plains, forded swift rivers, and labored up high mountains.

"We are creeping along slowly, one wagon after another, the same old gait, the same thing over, out of one mud hole into another all day."

—*Amelia Stewart Knight, 1853*

Problems Along the Way Although the pioneers feared attacks by Native Americans, such attacks did not often occur. More often Native Americans assisted the pioneers, serving as guides and trading necessary food and supplies. About 1 in 10 of the pioneers died on the trail, perishing from disease, overwork, hunger, or accidents.

When did use of the trail stop? With the building of a transcontinental railroad in 1869, the days of using the Oregon Trail as a corridor to the West were over.

"After Laramie we entered the great American desert, which was hard on the teams. Sickness became common. . . ."

—*Catherine Sager Pringle, 1844*

The Division of Oregon

Most American pioneers headed for the fertile **Willamette Valley** south of the Columbia River. Between 1840 and 1845, the number of American settlers in the area increased from 500 to 5,000, while the British population remained at about 700. The question of ownership of Oregon arose again.

Expansion of Freedom

Since colonial times many Americans had believed their nation had a special role to fulfill. For years people thought the nation's mission should be to serve as a model of freedom and democracy. In the 1800s that vision changed. Many believed that the United States's mission was to spread freedom by occupying the entire continent. In 1819 John Quincy Adams expressed what many Americans were thinking when he said expansion to the Pacific was as inevitable "as that the Mississippi should flow to the sea."

Manifest Destiny

In the 1840s New York newspaper editor John O'Sullivan put the idea of a national mission in more specific words. O'Sullivan declared it was

Who was the first "dark horse" president? A dark horse is a little-known contender who unexpectedly wins. In 1844 the Democrats passed over Martin Van Buren, John C. Calhoun, and other party leaders. Instead, they nominated James K. Polk, the governor of Tennessee. The Whigs were confident that their candidate, the celebrated Henry Clay, would win the election easily. Contrary to all expectations, Polk won the election, becoming at age 49 the youngest president in American history up to that time.

James K. Polk received the Democratic Party's nomination for president, partly because he supported American claims for sole ownership of Oregon. Democrats campaigned using the slogan "Fifty-four Forty or Fight." The slogan referred to the line of latitude that Democrats believed should be the nation's northern border in Oregon.

Henry Clay of the Whig Party, Polk's principal opponent, did not take a strong position on the Oregon issue. Polk won the election because the antislavery Liberty Party took so many votes from Clay in New York that Polk won the state. Polk won 170 electoral votes to 105 for Clay.

Reaching a Settlement

Filled with the spirit of Manifest Destiny, President Polk was determined to make Oregon part of the United States. Britain would not accept a border at "Fifty-four Forty," however. To do so would have meant giving up its claim entirely. Instead, in June 1846, the two countries compromised, setting the boundary between the American and British portions of Oregon at latitude 49°N.

During the 1830s Americans sought to fulfill their Manifest Destiny by looking much closer to home than Oregon. At that time much attention was also focused on Texas.

America's "Manifest Destiny to overspread and to possess the whole of the continent which Providence has given us." O'Sullivan meant that the United States was clearly destined—set apart for a special purpose—to extend its boundaries all the way to the Pacific.

"Fifty-four Forty or Fight"

The settlers in Oregon insisted that the United States should have sole ownership of the area. More and more Americans agreed. As a result Oregon became a significant issue in the 1844 presidential election.

☑ **Reading Check** **Explaining** In what way did some people think of Manifest Destiny as a purpose?

SECTION 1 ASSESSMENT

Checking for Understanding

1. **Key Terms** Use each of these terms in a complete sentence that will help explain its meaning: joint occupation, mountain man, rendezvous, emigrant, Manifest Destiny.
2. **Reviewing Facts** Name the four countries that claimed parts of the Oregon Country.

Reviewing Themes

3. **Economic Factors** How did the fur trade in Oregon aid Americans who began settling there?

Critical Thinking

4. **Making Generalizations** How did the idea of Manifest Destiny help Americans justify their desire to extend the United States to the Pacific Ocean?
5. **Determining Cause and Effect** Re-create the diagram below. In the box, describe how the fur trade led to interest in Oregon.

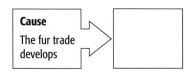

Cause
The fur trade develops

Analyzing Visuals

6. **Picturing History** Study the painting on page 359. Do you think it provides a realistic portrayal of the journey west?

Interdisciplinary Activity

Informative Writing Imagine you and your family are traveling to the Oregon Country in the 1840s. A friend will be making the same trip soon. Write a letter telling your friend what to expect on the journey.

Understanding Latitude and Longitude

Why Learn This Skill?

Your new friend invites you to her house. In giving directions, she says, "I live on Summit Street at the southwest corner of Indiana Avenue." She has pinpointed her exact location. We use a similar system of lines of latitude and longitude to pinpoint locations on maps and globes.

Learning the Skill

The imaginary horizontal lines that circle the globe from east to west are called lines of **latitude.** Because the distance between the lines of latitude is always the same, they are also called *parallels.* The imaginary vertical lines that intersect the parallels are lines of **longitude,** also called *meridians.*

Lines of longitude run from the North Pole to the South Pole. They are numbered in degrees east or west of a starting line called the Prime Meridian, which is at 0° longitude. On the opposite side of the earth from the Prime Meridian is the International Date Line, or 180° longitude.

The point at which parallels and meridians intersect is the grid address, or coordinates, of an exact location. The coordinates for Salt Lake City, for example, are 41°N and 112°W.

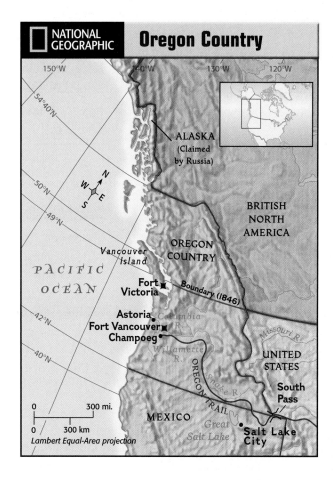

NATIONAL GEOGRAPHIC **Oregon Country**

Practicing the Skill

Analyze the information on the map on this page, then answer the following questions.

1 What are the approximate coordinates of Fort Victoria?

2 At what line of latitude was the Oregon Country divided between the United States and Britain?

3 What geographic feature lies at about 42°N and 115°W?

Applying the Skill

Understanding Latitude and Longitude Turn to the atlas map of the United States on pages RA2 and RA3. Find your city or the city closest to it. Identify the coordinates as closely as possible. Now list the coordinates of five other cities and ask a classmate to find the cities based on your coordinates.

Glencoe's **Skillbuilder Interactive Workbook CD-ROM, Level 1,** provides instruction and practice in key social studies skills.

SECTION 2 Independence for Texas

Guide to Reading

Main Idea
Texans won their independence from Mexico and asked to be admitted to the United States.

Key Terms
Tejano, empresario, decree, annex

Reading Strategy
Sequencing Information As you read Section 2, re-create the diagram below and, in the boxes, list key events that occurred in Texas.

1835		1836		
Oct.	Dec.	Mar.	May	
	Feb.	Apr.	Sept.	

Read to Learn
- why problems arose between the Mexican government and the American settlers in Texas.
- how Texas achieved independence and later became a state.

Section Theme
Geography and History Mexico's offers of huge tracts of fertile land brought American settlers to Texas.

Preview of Events

♦1820	♦1830		♦1840

1821
Moses Austin receives land grant in Texas

1833
Santa Anna becomes president of Mexico

March 1836
The Alamo falls to Mexican troops

September 1836
Sam Houston is elected president of Texas

Davy Crockett

AN American Story

Davy Crockett was a backwoodsman from Tennessee. His skill as a hunter and story-teller helped get him elected to three terms in Congress. But when he started his first political campaign, Crockett was doubtful about his chances of winning. "The thought of having to make a speech made my knees feel mighty weak and set my heart to fluttering." Fortunately for Crockett, the other candidates spoke all day and tired out the audience. "When they were all done," Crockett boasted, "I got up and told some laughable story, and quit. . . . I went home, and didn't go back again till after the election was over." In the end, Crockett won the election by a wide margin.

A Clash of Cultures

Davy Crockett of Tennessee won notice for his frontier skills, his sense of humor, and the shrewd common sense he often displayed in politics. When he lost his seat in Congress in 1835, he did not return to Tennessee. Instead he went southwest to Texas.

Crockett thought he could make a new start there. He also wanted to help the Texans win their independence from Mexico. Little did he know his deeds in Texas would bring him greater fame than his adventures on the frontier or his years in Congress.

Conflict over Texas began in 1803, when the United States bought the Louisiana Territory from France. Americans claimed that the land in present-day Texas was part of the purchase. Spain protested. In 1819, in the **Adams-Onís Treaty,** the United States agreed to drop any further claim to the region.

Land Grants

At the time, few people lived in Texas. Most residents—about 3,000—were Tejanos (teh•HAH•nohs), or Mexicans who claimed Texas as their home. Native Americans, including Comanches, Apaches, and Kiowas, also lived in the area.

Because the Spanish wanted to promote the growth of Texas, they offered vast tracts of land to people who agreed to bring families to settle on the land. The people who obtained these grants from the government and recruited the settlers were called empresarios.

Moses Austin, a businessman who had developed a mining operation in Missouri, applied for and received the first land grant in 1821. Before he could establish his colony, however, Moses contracted pneumonia and died. After Mexico declared independence from Spain, Austin's son, **Stephen F. Austin,** asked the Mexican government to confirm his father's land grant. Once he received confirmation, he began to organize the colony.

Stephen F. Austin recruited 300 American families to settle the fertile land along the Brazos River and the Colorado River of Texas. The first settlers came to be called the **Old Three Hundred.** Many received 960 acres, with additional acres for each child. Others received larger ranches. Austin's success made him a leader among the American settlers in Texas.

From 1823 to 1825, Mexico passed three colonization laws. All these laws offered new settlers large tracts of land at extremely low prices and

People In History

Stephen F. Austin 1793–1836

Stephen F. Austin earned the name "Father of Texas" because of his leadership in populating the Mexican territory of Texas. After attending college he worked as a businessperson. Austin organized the first land grant colony in Texas in 1821. Austin offered large tracts of land to settlers, and his colony grew quickly.

Austin often played the role of spokesperson with the Mexican government, sometimes on behalf of colonists who were not part of his settlement. He served as their advocate, even when he disagreed with their opinions. For example, he negotiated for permission to continue slavery in the province of Texas after it was banned by Mexican law. He also served

nearly a year in prison for promoting independence for the Texans.

After Texas won its war for independence, Austin ran for the office of president. He was defeated but was appointed secretary of state. He died just a few months later. The state of Texas honored Stephen F. Austin by naming its capital city—Austin—after its founding father.

What If...

The Defenders Had Not Stayed at the Alamo?

William Travis and almost 200 other defenders were determined to hold the Alamo. Travis wrote several messages to the people of Texas and the United States asking them for assistance. Travis's appeal was unsuccessful. Texas military forces were not yet well organized and were badly scattered. Travis's letter of February 24, 1836, is one of the finest statements of courage in American history.

The defenders—mostly volunteers—were free to leave whenever they chose. But they decided to defend the Alamo for a cause in which they believed.

Santa Anna hoped the fall of the Alamo would convince other Texans that it was useless to resist his armies. Instead, the heroism of those in the Alamo inspired other Texans to carry on the struggle. "Remember the Alamo!" became the battle cry of Houston's army.

Travis's Appeal for Aid at the Alamo, February 24, 1836

To the People of Texas and All Americans in the World—

Fellow Citizens and Compatriots:

I am besieged by a thousand or more of the Mexicans under Santa Anna. I have sustained a continual Bombardment & cannonade for 24 hours & have not lost a man. The enemy has demanded a surrender at discretion, otherwise the garrison are to be put to the sword if the fort is taken. I have answered the demand with a cannon shot, and our flag still waves proudly from the walls. I shall never surrender or retreat.

Then, I call on you in the name of Liberty, of patriotism, & of everything dear to the American character, to come to our aid with all dispatch. The enemy is receiving reinforcements daily & will no doubt increase to three or four thousand in four or five days. If this call is neglected I am determined to sustain myself as long as possible & die like a soldier who never forgets what is due to his honor & that of his country.

Victory or Death
William Barret Travis
Lt. Col. Comdt.

---

reduced or no taxes for several years. In return the colonists agreed to learn Spanish, become Mexican citizens, convert to Catholicism—the religion of Mexico—and obey Mexican law.

Mexican leaders hoped to attract settlers from all over, including other parts of Mexico. Most Texas settlers, however, came from the United States.

Growing Tension

By 1830 Americans in Texas far outnumbered Mexicans. Further, these American colonists had not adopted Mexican ways. In the meantime the United States had twice offered to buy Texas from Mexico.

The Mexican government viewed the growing American influence in Texas with alarm. In 1830 the Mexican government issued a decree, or official order, that stopped all immigration

from the United States. At the same time, the decree encouraged the immigration of Mexican and European families with generous land grants. Trade between Texas and the United States was discouraged by placing a tax on goods imported from the United States.

These new policies angered the Texans. The prosperity of many citizens depended on trade with the United States. Many had friends and relatives who wanted to come to Texas. In addition, those colonists who held slaves were uneasy about the Mexican government's plans to end slavery.

Attempt at Reconciliation

Some of the American settlers called for independence. Others hoped to stay within Mexico but on better terms. In 1833 **General Antonio López de Santa Anna** became president of

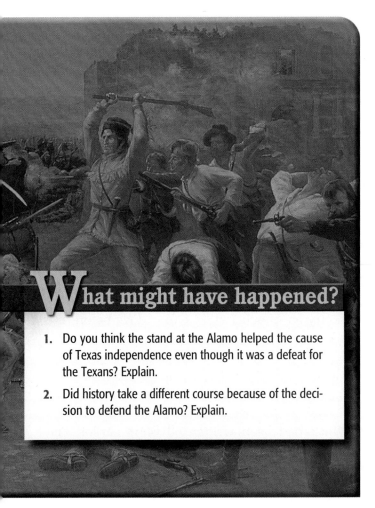

What might have happened?

1. Do you think the stand at the Alamo helped the cause of Texas independence even though it was a defeat for the Texans? Explain.

2. Did history take a different course because of the decision to defend the Alamo? Explain.

Mexico. Stephen F. Austin traveled to Mexico City with the Texans' demands, which were to remove the ban on American settlers and to make Texas a separate state.

Santa Anna agreed to the first request but refused the second. Austin sent a letter back to Texas, suggesting that plans for independence get underway. The Mexican government intercepted the letter and arrested Austin. While Austin was in jail, Santa Anna named himself dictator and overthrew Mexico's constitution of 1824. Without a constitution to protect their rights, Texans felt betrayed. Santa Anna reorganized the government, placing greater central control over Texas. This loss of local power dismayed many people.

Reading Check **Explaining** What role did empresarios play in colonization?

The Struggle for Independence

During 1835 unrest grew among Texans and occasionally resulted in open conflict. Santa Anna sent an army into Texas to punish the Texans for criticizing him. In October some Mexican troops tried to seize a cannon held by Texans at the town of **Gonzales.** During the battle the Texans decorated the front of the cannon with a white flag that bore the words "Come and Take It." After a brief struggle, Texans drove back the Mexican troops. Texans consider this to be the first fight of the Texan Revolution.

The Texans called on volunteers to join their fight. They offered free land to anyone who would help. Davy Crockett and many others—including a number of African Americans and Tejanos—answered that call.

In December 1835, the Texans scored an important victory. They liberated **San Antonio** from the control of a larger Mexican force. The Texas army at San Antonio included more than 100 Tejanos. Many of them served in a scouting company commanded by Captain Juan Seguín. Born in San Antonio, Seguín was an outspoken champion of the Texans' demand for independence.

Despite these victories, the Texans encountered problems. With the Mexican withdrawal, some Texans left San Antonio, thinking the war was won. Various groups argued over who was in charge and what course of action to follow. In early 1836, when Texas should have been making preparations to face Santa Anna, nothing was being done.

The Battle of the Alamo

Santa Anna marched north, furious at the loss of San Antonio. When his army reached San Antonio in late February 1836, it found a small Texan force barricaded inside a nearby mission called the **Alamo.**

Although the Texans had cannons, they lacked gunpowder. Worse, they had only about 180 soldiers to face Santa Anna's army of several thousand. The Texans did have brave leaders, though, including Davy Crockett, who had arrived with a band of sharpshooters from Tennessee, and a tough Texan named Jim Bowie. The commander, William B. Travis, was only 26

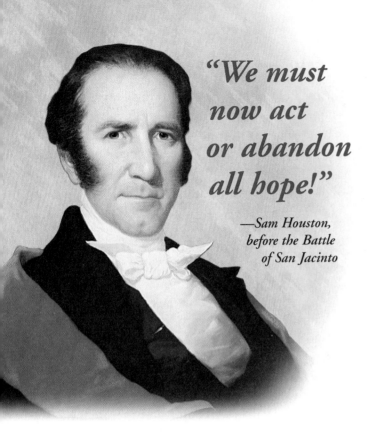

"We must now act or abandon all hope!"

—Sam Houston,
before the Battle
of San Jacinto

years old, but he was determined to hold his position. Travis managed to send messages out through Mexican lines. He wrote several messages to the people of Texas and the United States, asking them for assistance. In his last message, Travis described the fighting that had already taken place and repeated his request for assistance. He warned that

66the power of Santa Anna is to be met here, or in the colonies; we had better meet them here than to suffer a war of devastation to rage in our settlements.99

Travis concluded with the statement that he and his troops were determined to hold the Alamo.

For 12 long days, the defenders of the Alamo kept Santa Anna's army at bay with rifle fire. The Mexicans launched two assaults but had to break them off. During the siege, 32 volunteers from Gonzales slipped through the Mexican lines to join the Alamo's defenders.

On March 6, 1836, Mexican cannon fire smashed the Alamo's walls, and the Mexicans launched an all-out attack. The Alamo defenders killed many Mexican soldiers as they crossed open land and tried to mount the Alamo's walls. The Mexicans were too numerous to hold back, however, and they finally entered the fortress, killing William Travis, Davy Crockett, Jim Bowie, and all the other defenders. Only a few women and children and some servants survived to tell of the battle.

In the words of Santa Anna's aide, "The Texans fought more like devils than like men." The defenders of the Alamo had killed hundreds of Mexican soldiers. But more important, they had bought Texans some much needed time.

Texas Declares Its Independence

During the siege of the Alamo, Texan leaders were meeting at Washington-on-the-Brazos, where they were drawing up a new constitution. There, on March 2, 1836—four days before the fall of the Alamo—American settlers and Tejanos firmly declared independence from Mexico and established the Republic of Texas.

The Texas Declaration of Independence was similar to the Declaration of the United States, which had been written 60 years earlier. The Texas Declaration stated that the government of Santa Anna had violated the liberties guaranteed under the Mexican Constitution. The declaration charged that Texans had been deprived of freedom of religion, the right to trial by jury, the right to bear arms, and the right to petition. It noted that the Texans' protests against these policies were met with force. The Mexican government had sent a large army to drive Texans from their homes. Because of these grievances, the declaration proclaimed the following:

66The people of Texas, in solemn convention assembled, appealing to a candid world for the necessities of our condition, do hereby resolve and declare that our political connection with the Mexican nation has forever ended; and that the people of Texas do now constitute a free, sovereign, and independent republic....99

HISTORY Online

Student Web Activity
Visit tarvol1.glencoe.com
and click on **Chapter 12—Student Web Activities** for an activity on the fight for Texas independence.

With Mexican troops in Texas, it was not possible to hold a general election to ratify the constitution and vote for leaders of the new republic. Texas leaders set up a temporary government. They selected officers to serve until regular elections could be held.

David G. Burnet, an early pioneer in Texas, was chosen president and Lorenzo de Zavala, vice president. De Zavala had worked to establish a democratic government in Mexico. He moved to Texas when it became clear that Santa Anna would not make reforms.

The government of the new republic named **Sam Houston** as commander in chief of the Texas forces. Houston had come to Texas in 1832. Raised among the Cherokee people, he became a soldier, fighting with Andrew Jackson against the Creek people. A politician as well, Houston had served in Congress and as governor of Tennessee.

Houston wanted to prevent other forts from being overrun by the Mexicans. He ordered the troops at **Goliad** to abandon their position. As they retreated, however, they came face to face with Mexican troops led by General Urrea. After a fierce fight, several hundred Texans surrendered. On Santa Anna's orders, the Texans were executed a few days later. This action outraged Texans, who called it the "Goliad Massacre."

The Battle of San Jacinto

Houston moved his small army eastward about 100 miles, watching the movements of Santa Anna and waiting for a chance to strike. Six weeks after the Alamo, he found the opportunity.

After adding some new troops, Houston gathered an army of about 900 at **San Jacinto** (SAN juh•SIHN•toh), near the site of present-day Houston. Santa Anna was camped nearby with an army of more than 1,300. On April 21 the Texans launched a surprise attack on the Mexican camp, shouting, "Remember the Alamo! Remember Goliad!" They killed more than 600 soldiers and captured about 700 more—including Santa Anna. On May 14, 1836, Santa Anna signed a treaty that recognized the independence of Texas.

Reading Check **Identifying** Who was commander in chief of the Texas forces?

The Lone Star Republic

Texans elected Sam Houston as their president in September 1836. Mirabeau Lamar, who had built a fort at Velasco and had fought bravely at the Battle of San Jacinto, served as vice president. Houston sent a delegation to Washington, D.C., asking the United States to annex—take control of—Texas. The nation's president Andrew Jackson refused, however, because the addition of another slave state would upset the balance of slave and free states in Congress. For the moment Texas would remain an independent country.

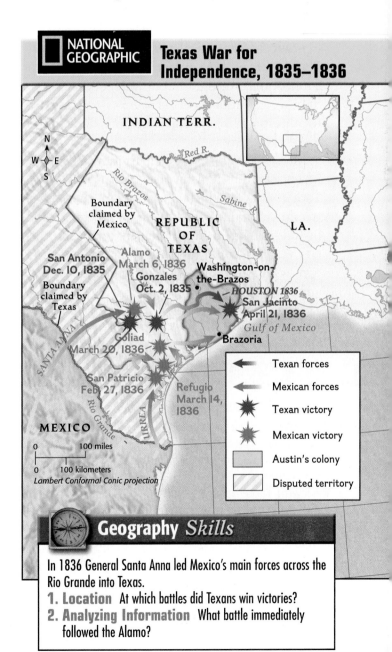

NATIONAL GEOGRAPHIC

Texas War for Independence, 1835–1836

INDIAN TERR.

Red R.

Rio Brazos

Sabine R.

Boundary claimed by Mexico

REPUBLIC OF TEXAS

LA.

San Antonio Dec. 10, 1835

Alamo March 6, 1836

Gonzales Oct. 2, 1835

Washington-on-the-Brazos

Boundary claimed by Texas

HOUSTON 1836

San Jacinto April 21, 1836

SANTA ANNA

Goliad March 20, 1836

Gulf of Mexico

Brazoria

San Patricio Feb. 27, 1836

Rio Grande

URREA

Refugio March 14, 1836

MEXICO

0   100 miles

0   100 kilometers

Lambert Conformal Conic projection

Texan forces

Mexican forces

Texan victory

Mexican victory

Austin's colony

Disputed territory

Geography *Skills*

In 1836 General Santa Anna led Mexico's main forces across the Rio Grande into Texas.
1. **Location** At which battles did Texans win victories?
2. **Analyzing Information** What battle immediately followed the Alamo?

America's Flags

Texas Republic, 1839 For its first six years, this Lone Star flag symbolized the independent nation of the Republic of Texas. Texans kept the Lone Star banner as their official state flag after joining the Union in 1845.

The Question of Annexation

Despite rapid population growth, the new republic faced political and financial difficulties. The Mexican government refused to honor Santa Anna's recognition of independence, and fighting continued between Texas and Mexico. In addition Texas had an enormous debt and no money to repay it.

Many Texans still hoped to join the United States. Southerners favored the annexation of Texas, but Northerners objected that Texas would add another slave state to the Union. President Martin Van Buren, like Jackson, did not want to inflame the slavery issue or risk war with Mexico. He put off the question of annexing Texas.

John Tyler, who became the nation's president in 1841, was the first vice president to become president upon the death of a chief executive. He succeeded William Henry Harrison, who died in April, just one month after taking office. Tyler supported adding Texas to the Union and persuaded Texas to reapply for annexation. However, the Senate was divided over slavery and failed to ratify the annexation treaty.

Texas Becomes a State

The situation changed with the 1844 presidential campaign. The feeling of Manifest Destiny was growing throughout the country. The South favored annexation of Texas. The North demanded that the United States gain control of the Oregon country from Britain. The Democratic candidate, James K. Polk, supported both actions. The Whig candidate, Henry Clay, initially opposed adding Texas to the Union. When he finally came out for annexation, it lost him votes in the North—and the election.

After Polk's victory, supporters of annexation pressed the issue in Congress. They proposed and passed a resolution to annex Texas. On December 29, 1845, Texas officially became a state of the United States.

✓ **Reading Check** **Identifying** Who was president of the Texas Republic?

SECTION 2 ASSESSMENT

Checking for Understanding

1. **Key Terms** Write a short history about events in Texas using the following terms: Tejano, empresario, decree, annex.
2. **Reviewing Facts** Name the four things that American settlers agreed to do in exchange for receiving land in Texas.

Reviewing Themes

3. **Geography and History** Why did Northerners and Southerners disagree on the annexation of Texas?

Critical Thinking

4. **Analyzing Information** How did the fall of the Alamo help the cause of Texas independence, even though it was a defeat for the Texans?
5. **Categorizing Information** Re-create the diagram below. In the boxes, describe two causes of the war between Mexico and Americans in Texas.

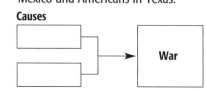

Causes → War

Analyzing Visuals

6. **Sequencing** Study the map on page 367. Place these battles in order, starting with the earliest: Gonzales, San Jacinto, the Alamo, Goliad.

Interdisciplinary Activity

Descriptive Writing Look at the painting of the Battle of the Alamo on page 365. Write one paragraph that describes what is happening in the picture.

War with Mexico

AN American Story

Long lines of covered wagons stretched as far as the eye could see. "All's set!" a driver called out. "All's set!" everyone shouted in reply.

"Then the 'Heps!' of drivers—the cracking of whips—the trampling of feet—the occasional creak of wheels—the rumbling of wagons—form a new scene of [intense] confusion," reported Josiah Gregg. Gregg was one of the traders who traveled west on the Santa Fe Trail in the 1830s to sell cloth, knives, and other goods in New Mexico.

Wagon wheel

The New Mexico Territory

In the early 1800s, **New Mexico** was the name of a vast region sandwiched between the Texas and California territories. It included all of present-day New Mexico, Arizona, Nevada, and Utah and parts of Colorado and Wyoming.

Native American peoples had lived in the area for thousands of years. Spanish conquistadors began exploring there in the late 1500s and made it part of Spain's colony of Mexico. In 1610 the Spanish founded the settlement of **Santa Fe.** Missionaries followed soon after.

When Mexico won its independence in 1821, it inherited the New Mexico province from Spain. The Mexicans, however, had little control over the distant province. The inhabitants of New Mexico mostly governed themselves.

The Spanish had tried to keep Americans away from Santa Fe, fearing that Americans would want to take over the area. The Mexican government changed this policy, welcoming American traders into New Mexico. It hoped that the trade would boost the economy of the province.

The Santa Fe Trail

William Becknell, the first American trader to reach Santa Fe, arrived in 1821 with a pack of mules loaded with goods. Becknell sold the merchandise he brought for many times what he would have received for it in St. Louis.

Becknell's route came to be known as the **Santa Fe Trail.** The trail left the Missouri River near Independence, Missouri, and crossed the prairies to the Arkansas River. It followed the river west toward the Rocky Mountains before turning south into New Mexico Territory. Because the trail was mostly flat, on later trips Becknell used wagons to carry his merchandise.

Other traders followed Becknell, and the Santa Fe Trail became a busy trade route for hundreds of wagons. Americans brought cloth and firearms, which they exchanged in Santa Fe for silver, furs, and mules. The trail remained in use until the arrival of the railroad in 1880.

As trade with New Mexico increased, Americans began settling in the region. In the United States, the idea of Manifest Destiny captured the popular imagination, and many people saw New Mexico as territory worth acquiring. At the same time, they eyed another prize—the Mexican territory of California, which would provide access to the Pacific.

Reading Check **Describing** Where did the Santa Fe Trail end?

California's Spanish Culture

Spanish explorers and missionaries from Mexico had been the first Europeans to settle in California. In the 1760s Captain Gaspar de Portolá and Father Junípero Serra began building a string of missions that eventually extended from San Diego to Sonoma.

The mission system was a key part of Spain's plan to colonize California. The Spanish used the missions to convert Native Americans to Christianity. By 1820, California had 21 missions, with about 20,000 Native Americans living in them.

In 1820 American mountain man Jedediah Smith visited the San Gabriel Mission east of present-day Los Angeles. Smith reported that the Native Americans farmed thousands of acres and worked at weaving and other crafts. He described the missions as "large farming and grazing establishments." Another American in Smith's party called the Native Americans "slaves in every sense of the word."

History *Through Art*

Vaqueros in a Horse Corral by James Walker
Mexican American cowhands, or vaqueros, work on a ranch in the Southwest. **Why did the number of ranchos grow in the 1820s and 1830s?**

California After 1821

After Mexico gained its independence from Spain in 1821, **California** became a state in the new Mexican nation. At the time only a few hundred Spanish settlers lived in California, but emigrants began arriving from Mexico. The wealthier settlers lived on ranches devoted to raising cattle and horses.

In 1833 the Mexican government passed a law abolishing the missions. The government gave some of the lands to Native Americans and sold the remainder. Mexican settlers bought these lands and built huge properties called ranchos.

The Mexican settlers persuaded Native Americans to work their lands and tend their cattle in return for food and shelter. The California ranchos were similar to the plantations of the South, and the rancheros—ranch owners—treated Native American workers almost like slaves.

Manifest Destiny and California

Americans had been visiting California for years. Most arrived on trading or whaling ships, although a few hardy travelers like Jedediah Smith came overland from the East. Soon more began to arrive.

At first the Mexican authorities welcomed Americans in California. The newcomers included agents for American shipping companies, fur traders from Oregon, and merchants from New Mexico. In the 1840s families began to arrive in California to settle. They made the long journey from Missouri on the Oregon Trail and then turned south after crossing the Rocky Mountains. Still, by 1845 the American population of California numbered only about 700. Most Americans lived in the Sacramento River valley.

Some American travelers wrote glowing reports of California. **John C. Frémont,** an army officer who made several trips through California in the 1840s, wrote of the region's mild climate, scenic beauty, and abundance of natural resources.

Americans began to talk about adding California to the nation. Shippers and manufacturers hoped to build ports on the Pacific coast for trade with China and Japan. Many Americans

John C. Frémont's strong belief in westward expansion advanced the cause of Manifest Destiny.

saw the advantage of extending United States territory to the Pacific. That way the nation would be safely bordered by the sea instead of by a foreign power. In 1845 Secretary of War William Marcy wrote that

❝if the people [of California] should desire to unite their destiny with ours, they would be received as brethren [brothers].❞

President James Polk twice offered to buy California and New Mexico from Mexico, but Mexico refused. Soon, the United States would take over both regions by force.

☑ **Reading Check** **Examining** What was the purpose of the California missions?

War With Mexico

President James K. Polk was determined to get the California and New Mexico territories from Mexico. Their possession would guarantee that the United States had clear passage to the Pacific Ocean—an important consideration because the British still occupied part of Oregon. Polk's main reason, though, involved fulfilling the nation's Manifest Destiny. Like many Americans, Polk saw California and New Mexico as rightfully belonging to the United States.

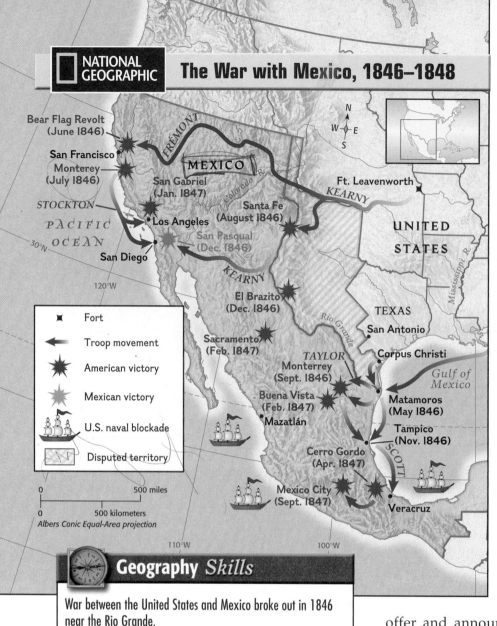

Bear Flag Revolt
(June 1846)

San Francisco
Monterey
(July 1846)

STOCKTON

PACIFIC

OCEAN

30°N

San Diego

120°W

FREMONT

MEXICO

San Gabriel
(Jan. 1847)

Los Angeles

Colorado

San Pasqual
(Dec. 1846)

KEARNY

Santa Fe
(August 1846)

Ft. Leavenworth

KEARNY

UNITED

STATES

Mississippi R.

N
W E
S

El Brazito
(Dec. 1846)

Rio Grande

TEXAS

San Antonio

Corpus Christi

Fort

Troop movement

American victory

Mexican victory

U.S. naval blockade

Disputed territory

Sacramento
(Feb. 1847)

TAYLOR
Monterrey
(Sept. 1846)

Buena Vista
(Feb. 1847)

Mazatlán

Cerro Gordo
(Apr. 1847)

Gulf of
Mexico

Matamoros
(May 1846)

Tampico
(Nov. 1846)

SCOTT

0   500 miles

0   500 kilometers
Albers Conic Equal-Area projection

Mexico City
(Sept. 1847)

Veracruz

110°W   100°W

Geography Skills

War between the United States and Mexico broke out in 1846
near the Rio Grande.
1. **Location** Which battle occurred farthest north?
2. **Making Inferences** What information on the map
can you use to infer which side won the war?

After Mexico refused to sell California and
New Mexico, President Polk plotted to pull the
Mexican provinces into the Union through war.
He wanted, however, to provoke Mexico into tak-
ing military action first. This way Polk could jus-
tify the war to Congress and the American people.

Relations between Mexico and the United
States had been strained for some years. When
the United States annexed Texas in 1845, the situation worsened. Mexico, which had never recognized the independence of Texas, charged
that the annexation was illegal.

Another dispute con-
cerned the Texas-Mexico
border. The United States
insisted that the **Rio
Grande** formed the border.
Mexico claimed that the
border lay along the **Nueces**
(nu•AY•suhs) **River,** 150
miles farther north. Because
of this dispute, Mexico had
stopped payments to Amer-
ican citizens for losses suffered during Mexico's war
for independence.

Polk sent an agent, John
Slidell, to Mexico to propose a deal. Slidell was
authorized to offer $30 mil-
lion for California and New
Mexico in return for Mex-
ico's acceptance of the Rio
Grande as the Texas boundary. In addition, the United
States would take over payment of Mexico's debts to
American citizens.

Conflict Begins

The Mexican govern-
ment refused to discuss the
offer and announced its intention to reclaim
Texas for Mexico. In response Polk ordered
General Zachary Taylor to march his soldiers
across the disputed borderland between the
Nueces River and the Rio Grande. Taylor followed the order and built a fort there on his
arrival. On April 24, Mexican soldiers
attacked a small force of Taylor's soldiers.
Taylor sent the report the president wanted to
hear: "Hostilities may now be considered as
commenced."

Polk called an emergency meeting of his cabinet, and the cabinet agreed that the attack was
grounds for war with Mexico. On May 11, 1846,
the president told Congress that Mexico had
"invaded our territory and shed American
blood upon the American soil." Congress
passed a declaration of war against Mexico.

American Attitudes Toward the War

The American people were divided over the war with Mexico. Polk's party, the Democrats, generally supported the war. Many Whigs opposed it, calling Polk's actions aggressive and unjust. Northerners accused Democrats of waging the war to spread slavery.

Illinois congressman Abraham Lincoln demanded to know the exact spot where the first attack against American troops had occurred. Lincoln, like many who opposed the war, claimed that the spot was clearly in Mexico and that Polk therefore had no grounds for blaming the war on Mexico.

Frederick Douglass, an African American leader in the antislavery movement, called the war "disgraceful" and "cruel." Douglass shared the belief that if the United States expanded into the West, the Southern states would carry slavery into the new territories.

Newspapers generally supported the war, and volunteers quickly signed up for military service. As time went on, however, antiwar feeling grew, particularly in the North.

Polk's War Plan

President Polk had a three-part plan for the war with Mexico. First, American troops would drive Mexican forces out of the disputed border region in Texas and make the border secure. Second, the United States would seize New Mexico and California. Finally, American forces would take **Mexico City,** the capital of Mexico.

Zachary Taylor accomplished the first goal. His army captured the town of Matamoros in May 1846 and **Monterrey** in September 1846. The Americans pushed forward and entered the bishop's palace. The Mexican flag was lowered, and a mighty cheer erupted from American forces remaining on the plain below. In February 1847, Taylor defeated the Mexicans again at Buena Vista. The Texas border was secure.

While Taylor made progress in northern Mexico, American forces also advanced farther west. General **Stephen Watts Kearny** led his troops to New Mexico and California. In the summer of 1846, Kearny led about 1,500 cavalry soldiers along the Santa Fe Trail from Fort Leavenworth to New Mexico. The Mexican governor fled, allowing the Americans to capture New Mexico's capital, Santa Fe, on August 18, 1846, without firing a shot. Kearny and his army then headed across the deserts of New Mexico and Arizona to California.

California and the Bear Flag Republic

In June 1846, a small group of Americans had seized the town of Sonoma north of San Francisco and proclaimed the independent Republic of California. They called the new country the **Bear Flag Republic** because their flag showed a bear and a star on a white background. John C. Frémont and mountain man **Kit Carson,** who were already out West on a military expedition in California, joined the Americans in Sonoma.

Though unaware of the outbreak of war with Mexico, Frémont declared that he would conquer California. Frémont's actions outraged many Californios, the Mexicans who lived in California. They might have supported a revolt for local control of government, but they opposed what looked like an attempt by a band of Americans to seize land.

Naval Intervention

In July 1846, a United States Navy squadron under Commodore John Sloat captured the ports of Monterey and San Francisco. Sloat declared California annexed to the United States, and the American flag replaced the Bear Flag in California.

Sloat's fleet sailed for San Diego, carrying Frémont and Carson. The Americans captured San Diego and moved north to Los Angeles. Carson

California Bear Flag

headed east with the news of California's annexation. On his way he met and joined Kearny's force, marching west from Santa Fe.

After Sloat's ships left, many Californios in San Diego rose up in arms against the Americans who had taken over the city. General Kearny and his troops arrived in the midst of the rebellion. They faced a stiff fight but eventually won. By January 1847, California was fully controlled by the United States.

The Capture of Mexico City

With their victories in New Mexico and California, the Americans met their first two goals in the war. President Polk then launched the third part of his war plan—an attack on Mexico City.

Polk gave the task of capturing Mexico City to General **Winfield Scott.** In March 1847, Scott's army landed on the coast of the Gulf of Mexico, near the Mexican port of **Veracruz.** Scott captured Veracruz after a three-week siege and then set out to march the 300 miles to Mexico City.

The Americans had to fight their way toward Mexico City, battling not only the Mexican army but also bands of armed citizens. Scott reached the outskirts of Mexico City with his troops towards the end of August 1847. By mid-September the Americans had taken Mexico City. The Mexican government surrendered.

The United States lost 1,721 men to battle and more than 11,000 to disease in the war with Mexico. Mexico's losses were far greater. The war cost the United States nearly $100 million, but here, too, Mexico paid a higher price. The war would cost Mexico half its territory.

The Peace Treaty

Peace talks between the United States and Mexico began in January 1848. The **Treaty of Guadalupe Hidalgo** (GWAH•duhl•OOP hih•DAL•goh) was signed in February 1848.

In the treaty Mexico gave up all claims to Texas and agreed to the Rio Grande as the border between Texas and Mexico. Furthermore, in what was called the **Mexican Cession,** Mexico ceded—gave—its provinces of California and New Mexico to the United States. In return the United States gave Mexico $15 million.

In 1853 the United States paid Mexico an additional $10 million for the **Gadsden Purchase,** a strip of land along the southern edge of the present-day states of Arizona and New Mexico. With the Gadsden Purchase, the United States mainland reached its present size. All that remained was to settle the newly acquired territories.

✓ **Reading Check** **Describing** What lands did Mexico cede to the United States?

SECTION 3 ASSESSMENT

Checking for Understanding

1. **Key Terms** Write a short paragraph in which you use the following terms: rancho, ranchero, Californios, cede.

2. **Reviewing Facts** According to the Mexican government, where did the border between Texas and Mexico lie?

Reviewing Themes

3. **Culture and Traditions** Why did the Spanish establish missions in the Southwest? What happened to the mission land after Mexico gained its independence?

Critical Thinking

4. **Analyzing Primary Sources** Explain the meaning of this sentence in your own words: "If the people [of California] should desire to unite their destiny with ours, they would be received as brethren [brothers]."

5. **Categorizing Information** Re-create the diagram below and describe the three parts of Polk's strategy and how they were accomplished.

Analyzing Visuals

6. **Geography Skills** List the battles that appear on the map on page 372 in order from first to last. Identify whether each was a Mexican victory or a U.S. victory.

Interdisciplinary Activity

Science Settlers traveling west encountered new wildlife, vegetation, and landforms. Choose one region of the west and investigate as a traveling scientist would. List plants and animals you would see there. Write a report summarizing what you have observed.

New Settlers in California and Utah

Guide to Reading

Main Idea
The lure of gold and the promise of religious freedom drew many settlers westward.

Key Terms
forty-niners, boomtown, vigilante

Reading Strategy
Organizing Information As you read Section 4, re-create the diagram below. In the boxes, describe who these groups and individuals were and what their role was in the settlement of California and Utah.

	What was their role?
Forty-niners	
Mormons	
Brigham Young	

Read to Learn
- how the hopes of getting rich drew thousands of people to California.
- how the search for religious freedom led to the settlement of Utah.

Section Theme
Groups and Institutions In the mid-1800s, people went to California in search of gold, and Mormons settled in Utah in search of religious freedom.

Preview of Events

♦1846   ♦1848   ♦1850

1846
Mormons migrate to the Great Salt Lake area

1848
Gold is discovered at Sutter's Mill

1850
California applies for statehood

Gold miner's cradle

AN American Story

James Marshall was building a sawmill on the South Fork of the American River in California. He worked for John Sutter, who owned a vast tract of land about 35 miles from present-day Sacramento. On January 24, 1848, Marshall saw something shining in a ditch. "I reached my hand down and picked it up," he wrote later. "It made my heart thump, for I was certain it was gold." Looking around, he found other shiny pieces. Marshall rushed to show the glittering pieces to Sutter, who determined that they were gold. Sutter tried to keep the discovery a secret, but word soon leaked out. The great California Gold Rush was underway!

California Gold Rush

People from all over the world flocked to California in search of quick riches. More than 80,000 people came to California looking for gold in 1849 alone. Those who arrived in 1849 were called forty-niners. An official in Monterey reported that "the farmers have thrown aside their plows, the lawyers their

Linking Past & Present

Jeans

In 1873 Levi Strauss, a dry goods merchant living in San Francisco, and Jacob Davis, a Nevada tailor, developed and began to market denim pants reinforced with small copper tacks called rivets. Levi's popular denims—called blue jeans today—are known for their durability and quality.

Early Levi ads were aimed at miners and farmers.

LEVI STRAUSS & Co's
COPPER RIVETED
OVERALLS: SPRING BOTTOM PANTS
AND
BLANKET LINED
CLOTHING

At one time, jeans were associated exclusively with hard work. Now they're worn everywhere.

briefs, the doctors their pills, the priests their prayer books, and all are now digging gold." By the end of 1848, they had taken $6 million in gold from the American River.

Many of the gold seekers came to California by sea. Others came overland, traveling on the Oregon Trail or the Santa Fe Trail and then pushing westward through California's **Sierra Nevada** mountain range.

Americans made up about 80 percent of the forty-niners. Others came from Mexico, South America, Europe, and Australia. About 300 men arrived from China, the first large group of Asian immigrants to come to America. Although some eventually returned to China, others remained, establishing California's Chinese American community.

The Californios

The Treaty of Guadalupe Hidalgo ending the war with Mexico made **Californios** (Mexican Californians) citizens of the United States. The treaty also guaranteed them the rights to their lands. But these rights would soon be weakened.

The Land Law of 1851 set up a group of people to review the Californios' land rights. The Californios had to prove what land they owned. When a new settler claimed the rights to a Californio's land, the two parties would go to court. Some Californios were able to prove their claims. Many, however, lost their land.

Life in California

As people rushed to a new area to look for gold, they built new communities, called boomtowns, almost overnight. At one site on the Yuba River where only two houses stood in September 1849, a miner arrived the next year to find a town of 1,000 people "with a large number of hotels, stores, groceries, bakeries, and . . . gambling houses." The miners gave some of the boomtowns colorful names such as Shinbone Peak and You Bet.

Cities also flourished during the Gold Rush. As ships arrived daily with gold seekers and adventurers, San Francisco grew from a tiny village to a city of about 20,000 people.

Most of the hopeful forty-niners had no experience in mining. Rushing furiously from place to place, they attacked hillsides with pickaxes and shovels and spent hours bent over streambeds, "washing" or "panning" the water to seek gold dust and nuggets.

The California Gold Rush more than doubled the world's supply of gold. For all their effort, however, very few of the forty-niners achieved lasting wealth. Most of the miners found little or no gold. Many of those who did lost their riches through gambling or wild spending.

Merchants, however, made huge profits. They could charge whatever they liked because the miners had no place else to go to buy food and other essential items. Eggs sold for $10 a dozen. A Jewish immigrant named **Levi Strauss** sold the miners sturdy pants made of denim. His "Levi's" made him rich.

Gold Rush Society

Very few women lived in the mining camps, which were populated by men of all races and walks of life. Lonely and suffering from the hardships of mining, many men spent their free hours drinking, gambling, and fighting.

Mining towns had no police or prisons, so lawbreakers posed a real threat to business owners and miners. One miner wrote,

> 66 Robberies and murders were of daily occurrence. Organized bands of thieves existed in the towns and in the mountains. 99

Concerned citizens formed vigilance committees to protect themselves. The vigilantes (VIH•juh•LAN•tees) took the law into their own hands, acting as police, judge, jury, and sometimes executioner.

Economic and Political Progress

The Gold Rush ended within a few years but had lasting effects on California's economy. Agriculture, shipping, and trade expanded to meet the miners' needs for food and other goods. Many people who had come looking for gold stayed to farm or run a business. California's population soared, increasing from about 20,000 in 1848 to more than 220,000 only four years later.

Such rapid growth brought the need for more effective government. Zachary Taylor, the Mexican War hero and now president, urged the people of California to apply for statehood. They did so, choosing representatives in September 1849 to write a constitution. Once their constitution was approved, Californians elected a governor and state legislators.

California applied to Congress for statehood in March 1850. Because California's constitution banned slavery, however, the request caused a crisis in Congress. The Southern states objected to making California a state because it would upset the balance of free and slave states. California did not become a state until Congress worked out a compromise six months later.

✓ Reading Check **Explaining** Why did the forty-niners come to California?

A Religious Refuge in Utah

A visitor to the Utah Territory in the 1850s wrote admiringly: "The whole of this small nation occupy themselves as usefully as the working bees of a hive." This account described the **Mormons,** or members of the Church of Jesus Christ of Latter-day Saints. Mormons had come to Utah to fulfill their vision of the godly life.

The First Mormons

Joseph Smith founded the church in 1830 in New York State. He had visions that led him to launch a new Christian church. He hoped to use these visions to build an ideal society.

Smith believed that property should be held in common. He also supported polygamy, the idea that a man could have more than one wife. This angered a large number of people. Mormons eventually gave up this practice.

Smith formed a community in New York, but unsympathetic neighbors disapproved of the

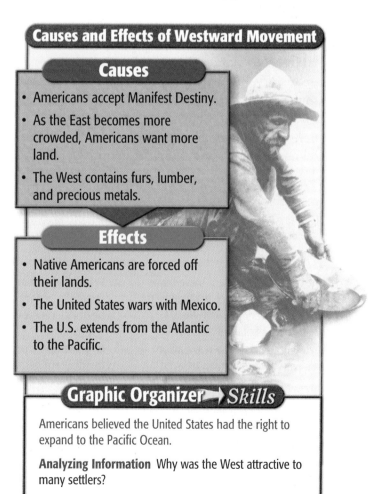

Causes and Effects of Westward Movement

Causes

- Americans accept Manifest Destiny.
- As the East becomes more crowded, Americans want more land.
- The West contains furs, lumber, and precious metals.

Effects

- Native Americans are forced off their lands.
- The United States wars with Mexico.
- The U.S. extends from the Atlantic to the Pacific.

Graphic Organizer → Skills

Americans believed the United States had the right to expand to the Pacific Ocean.

Analyzing Information Why was the West attractive to many settlers?

Cartoons of the period often showed Americans rushing to California in hopes of striking it rich. **What idea do you think the cartoonist is presenting?**

Mormons' religion. They forced the Mormons to move on. From New York the Mormons went to Ohio, then to Missouri, and then Illinois.

In 1844 a mob in Illinois killed Smith, and **Brigham Young** took over as head of the Mormons. Young decided the Mormons should move again, this time near the **Great Salt Lake** in present-day Utah. Although part of Mexico at that time, no Mexicans had settled in the region because of its harsh terrain.

A Haven in the Desert

The Mormon migration to the Great Salt Lake area began in 1846. About 12,000 Mormons made the trek—the largest single migration in American history. In the midst of the desert they set up communities in an area they called **Deseret.**

With hard work and determination, the Mormons made Deseret flourish. They planned their towns carefully and built irrigation canals to water their farms. They also founded industries so they could be self-sufficient. Mormon merchants sold supplies to the forty-niners who passed through Utah on their way to California.

In 1848 the United States acquired the Salt Lake area as part of the settlement of the war with Mexico. In 1850 Congress established the Utah Territory, and President Millard Fillmore made Brigham Young its governor.

Utah was not easily incorporated into the United States. The Mormons often had conflicts with federal officials. In 1857 and 1858, war almost broke out between the Mormons and the United States Army. Utah did not become a state until 1896.

Reading Check **Explaining** Why was Deseret able to grow economically?

SECTION 4 ASSESSMENT

Checking for Understanding

1. **Key Terms** Use each of these terms in a complete sentence that will help explain its meaning: forty-niners, boomtown, vigilante.

2. **Reviewing Facts** Why was California's entry into the Union delayed?

Reviewing Themes

3. **Groups and Institutions** What steps did Californians take to apply for statehood? When was California admitted?

Critical Thinking

4. **Predicting Consequences** How might the history of California have been different if the Gold Rush had not happened?

5. **Organizing Information** Re-create the diagram below. In the boxes, describe how the Gold Rush helped California's economy grow.

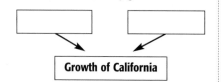

Growth of California

Analyzing Visuals

6. **Graphic Organizer Skills** Study the cause-and-effect chart on page 377. Are each of the effects of the westward movement positive? Explain.

Interdisciplinary Activity

Art Boomtowns sprang up almost overnight as gold seekers flocked to the West. Draw a scene of a boomtown. Include a written description of the activities that took place in the town.

America's LITERATURE

Hamlin Garland (1860–1940)

Hamlin Garland was born in rural Wisconsin and grew up on farms in Iowa and South Dakota. At the age of 24, he moved to Boston to begin his writing career. Although he gave up the life of a prairie farmer, Garland's work—fiction and nonfiction—reflects his background and his concern for the hard, lonely lives of pioneer men and women.

READ TO DISCOVER

A Son of the Middle Border is Garland's autobiography. The following excerpt describes one of the many westward moves that the Garland family made. As you read, pay attention to the emotions that the author expresses when he sees the plains for the first time.

READER'S DICTIONARY

middle border: the advancing frontier across the Mississippi River
habitation: residence
blue-joint: type of prairie grass

A Son of the Middle Border

Late in August my father again loaded our household goods into wagons, and with our small herd of cattle following, set out toward the west, bound once again to overtake the actual line of the **middle border.**

This journey has an unforgettable epic charm as I look back upon it. Each mile took us farther and farther into the unsettled prairie, until in the afternoon of the second day, we came to a meadow so wide that its western rim touched the sky without revealing a sign of man's **habitation** other than the road in which we travelled.

The plain was covered with grass tall as ripe wheat and when my father stopped his team and came back to us and said, "Well, children, here we are on The Big Prairie," we looked about us with awe, so endless seemed this spread of wild oats and waving **blue-joint.**

Far away dim clumps of trees showed, but no chimney was in sight, and no living thing moved save our own cattle and the hawks lazily wheeling in the air. My heart filled with awe as well as wonder. . . .

Sunset came at last, but still he drove steadily on through the sparse settlements. Just at nightfall we came to a beautiful little stream and stopped to let the horses drink.

I heard its rippling, reassuring song on the pebbles. Thereafter all is dim and vague to me until my mother called out sharply, "Wake up, children! Here we are!"

Struggling to my feet I looked about me. Nothing could be seen but the dim form of a small house. On every side the land melted into blackness, silent and without boundary.

Child's doll made of cornhusks

ANALYZING LITERATURE

1. **Recall and Interpret** Give two details that Garland uses to describe "The Big Prairie."
2. **Evaluate and Connect** How does Garland feel about the prairie and the move west? Explain.

Interdisciplinary Activity

Descriptive Writing Write a poem about a vast empty place that you know, or base your poem on a place you have read about.

Chapter Summary
Manifest Destiny

Through war and negotiations, the United States acquires Texas, Oregon, California, Utah, and the remainder of the Southwest. By 1850 thousands and thousands of settlers cross the Great Plains for new homes.

CALIFORNIA

OREGON TERR.

UTAH TERR.

NEW MEXICO TERR.

GADSDEN PURCHASE

TEXAS

Reviewing Key Terms

Use the vocabulary terms to create a newspaper article in which you describe events in the Southwest during this era.

1. emigrant
2. Tejano
3. empresario
4. ranchero
5. forty-niner

Reviewing Key Facts

6. What agreement did the United States and Great Britain reach about the Oregon Territory?
7. Why did President Jackson refuse to annex Texas?
8. Why did some Americans think that making California part of the United States would strengthen the security of the nation?
9. Explain the two main causes of the United States's war with Mexico.
10. Why did merchants earn such large profits during the Gold Rush?
11. **Analyzing Information** Reread the feature on page 363 about Stephen F. Austin. Why was Austin a good spokesperson for American settlers in Texas?

Critical Thinking

12. **Determining Cause and Effect** How did economic troubles in the East affect settlement in the Oregon area?
13. **Analyzing Themes: Geography and History** How did the war with Mexico change the U.S. border and its land holdings?
14. **Drawing Conclusions** What reactions do you think the governments of Great Britain and Mexico had to the American idea of Manifest Destiny?
15. **Comparing** How did the negotiations between the United States and Britain over the Oregon Territory differ from those between the United States and Mexico over the Southwest?
16. **Determining Cause and Effect** Re-create the diagram below. In the box, explain what led to the need for a more effective government in California.

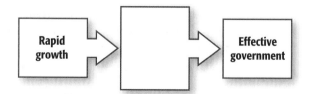

Rapid growth → → Effective government

Self-Check Quiz
Visit tarvol1.glencoe.com and click on **Chapter 12—Self-Check Quizzes** to prepare for the chapter test.

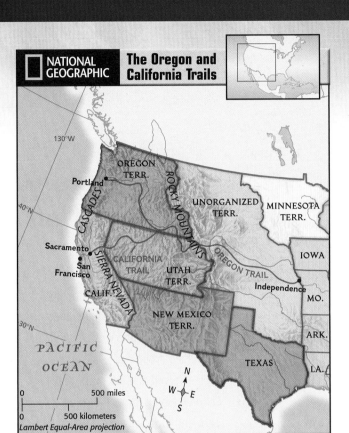

NATIONAL GEOGRAPHIC **The Oregon and California Trails**

130°W

OREGON TERR.

Portland

40°N

ROCKY MOUNTAINS

UNORGANIZED TERR.

MINNESOTA TERR.

CASCADES

Sacramento

CALIFORNIA TRAIL

SIERRA NEVADA

San Francisco

OREGON TRAIL

IOWA

UTAH TERR.

CALIF.

Independence

MO.

30°N

NEW MEXICO TERR.

ARK.

PACIFIC OCEAN

N
W E
S

TEXAS

LA.

0   500 miles
0   500 kilometers
Lambert Equal-Area projection

Technology Activity

21. Using a Database Search your library's card catalog for books and reports containing information about Salt Lake City and the state of Utah. Use this information to make an alphabetical directory of historic sites to visit. Your list might include museums, sites of businesses, or other places of interest.

Alternative Assessment

22. Portfolio Writing Activity If you were asked to make a film about one event described in this chapter, what would it be? In your journal describe the event and make a list of at least three people from history who would be in your movie. Then suggest the names of modern movie or TV stars you think would be suitable for these roles.

Geography and History Activity

Study the routes of the western trails shown on the map above. Then answer the questions that follow.

17. Region Which mountains did settlers have to cross to reach Oregon's Pacific coast? California's Pacific coast?

18. Location In what city did the Oregon Trail begin? In what city did it end?

Citizenship Cooperative Activity

19. Analyzing Issues With a partner, read the newspaper to find out what problems your state faces. Perhaps your state has a large budget deficit, or the crime rate has increased sharply. List the problems and describe what you would do if you were governor. List your options and the advantages and disadvantages of each one. Choose a solution and explain why it is the best option.

Practicing Skills

20. Understanding Latitude and Longitude Turn to the map of the world on pages RA14–RA15 of the Reference Atlas. What is the largest land area both west of the Prime Meridian and entirely north of the Equator?

Standardized Test Practice

Directions: Choose the *best* answer to the following question.

The discovery of gold in California led to which of the following?

A Discovery of gold in the Black Hills of the Dakotas

B Increased western expansion and foreign immigration

C Annexation of California as a slave state

D War with Mexico over the independence of California

Test-Taking Tip:

This question is a good example of *cause and effect*. Think about other times in history when people have discovered something of value in an area. What effect did this discovery have on people's behavior?

Let's Go West

Put yourself on a farm in Missouri in the 1840s. You work hard, but this year has been the most difficult. The crops have failed, and surviving winter will be a challenge. You meet other farmers traveling past your home on their way to the Oregon country or California. They speak of free, fertile land and new opportunities. Married settlers can claim a square mile, 640 acres, of the Oregon country at no cost. After much thought, you too decide to move your family west.

Analyzing the Issue

You, together with your spouse and two children, have decided to join a wagon train—a group of other families moving west. You will be traveling about 2,000 miles over rough country, finding your way with only the aid of natural landmarks. You will travel to either the Oregon country or to California. The trip will take about five months and must be completed before winter. Your goal is to survive and to make sure your family survives. Not knowing exactly what to expect, you have some research to do and decisions to make.

Believe It or Not!

Along the Oregon Trail, travelers lacked firewood for fuel over long parts of the trail. Looking for an alternative, they discovered dried buffalo dung burned well and was plentiful. The buffalo droppings—called chips—served another purpose too. Children would throw the chips back and forth for fun—the first, pioneer-type Frisbees?

Advice on the Prairie by William T. Ranney, 1853

Inside of Conestoga Wagon

What To Do

After you have organized into groups of four to six, follow the directions to make decisions about your trip. Decide upon specific tasks for each member of your group and who will research the following items.

Research the following:

1 Your destination and departure date

2 What route you should follow (A map will need to be drawn.)

3 A set of "rules for the road" (For example, up at dawn, on the road by seven, careful use of water, drive at least 15 miles per day, walk nearly all the way, etc.)

4 What supplies you will carry with you (You will need to research and estimate the weights of supplies because you may only take with you what you can carry in your wagon. The wagon dimensions are 4 feet by 10 feet, and at least 1,000 pounds of food is needed for a four-person family. Be careful not to overload your wagon—you do not want the wagon to break down or your animals to become exhausted.)

5 What mode of power will your wagon use?
- mules (most sure-footed, but expensive and hard to control)
- horses (can pull wagons faster, but can easily become ill)
- oxen (slowest, strongest, and have most endurance)

Presentation

6 Once you have collected your data, make your decisions and prepare your presentation. The format of the presentation is up to the group.

Go a Step Further

The Oregon Trail is the nation's longest graveyard. In 25 years, thousands died from illness, accidents, and drownings. Using your experience with this activity, answer this question: What do you think was the major cause for failure for wagon trains traveling west? Answer the question by writing the story of one such possible failure.

Why It Matters

At the same time that national spirit and pride were growing throughout the country, a strong sectional rivalry was also developing. Both North and South wanted to further their own economic and political interests.

The Impact Today

Differences still exist between the regions of the nation but are no longer as sharp. Mass communication and the migration of people from one region to another have lessened the differences.

 The American Republic to 1877 *Video The chapter 13 video, "Young People of the South," describes what life was like for children in the South.*

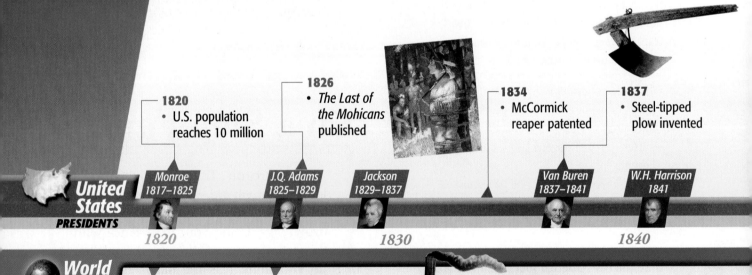

1820
• U.S. population reaches 10 million

1826
• *The Last of the Mohicans* published

1834
• McCormick reaper patented

1837
• Steel-tipped plow invented

United States PRESIDENTS

Monroe
1817–1825

J.Q. Adams
1825–1829

Jackson
1829–1837

Van Buren
1837–1841

W.H. Harrison
1841

1820

1830

1840

World

1820
• Antarctica discovered

1825
• World's first public railroad opens in England

Compare-and-Contrast Study Foldable
Make this foldable to help you analyze the similarities and differences between the development of the North and the South.

Step 1 Mark the midpoint of the side edge of a sheet of paper.

Draw a mark at the midpoint.

Step 2 Turn the paper and fold the outside edges in to touch at the midpoint.

Step 3 Turn and label your foldable as shown.

Northern
Economy & People
Economy & People
Southern

Reading and Writing As you read the chapter, collect and write information under the appropriate tab that will help you compare and contrast the people and economics of the Northern and Southern states.

The Oliver Plantation by unknown artist During the mid-1800s, plantations in southern Louisiana were entire communities in themselves.

1845
• Alexander Cartwright sets rules for baseball

1849
• Thoreau writes "Civil Disobedience"

1860
• U.S. population climbs to over 30 million

| Tyler 1841–1845 | Polk 1845–1849 | Taylor 1849–1850 | Fillmore 1850–1853 | Pierce 1853–1857 | Buchanan 1857–1861 |

1850 *1860*

1845
• Beginning of Irish potato famine

1848
• Revolution in Austrian Empire

1857
• Sepoy Rebellion begins in India

1859
• Darwin's *On the Origin of Species* published

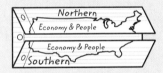

HISTORY Online

Chapter Overview
Visit tarvol1.glencoe.com and click on **Chapter 13— Chapter Overviews** to preview chapter information.

The North's Economy

Main Idea
During the 1800s, advances in technology and transportation shaped the North's economy.

Key Terms
clipper ship, telegraph, Morse code

Reading Strategy
Organizing Information As you read the section, re-create the diagram below and list examples of advances in transportation and technology.

Advances

Read to Learn
• how advances in technology shaped the economy of the North.
• how new kinds of transportation and communication spurred economic growth.

Section Theme
Economic Factors Advances in technology and transportation shaped the North's economy.

Preview of Events

♦1830   ♦1840   ♦1850   ♦1860

1834
Cyrus McCormick patents reaper

1844
Samuel Morse sends first telegraph message

1846
Elias Howe patents a sewing machine

1860
About 3,000 steamboats are operating

Samuel Morse's telegraph key

AN American Story

In the 1840s, telegraph wires and railroads began to cross the nation. But traveling by rail had its discomforts, as writer Charles Dickens describes: "[T]here is a great deal of jolting, a great deal of noise, a great deal of wall, not much window, a locomotive engine, a shriek, and a bell. . . . In the center of the carriage there is usually a stove . . . which is for the most part red-hot. It is insufferably close; and you see the hot air fluttering between yourself and any other object you may happen to look at, like the ghost of smoke. . . ."

Technology and Industry

In 1800 most Americans worked on farms. Items that could not be made at home were manufactured—by hand, one at a time—by local blacksmiths, shoemakers, and tailors. By the early 1800s, changes took place in the Northern states. Power-driven machinery performed many tasks that were once done by hand. Industrialization and technology were changing the way Americans worked, traveled, and communicated.

Industrialization

The industrialization of the North developed in three phases. In the first, manufacturers made products by dividing the tasks involved among the workers. One worker would spin thread all day and another would weave cloth—instead of having one person spin and then weave. During the second phase, manufacturers built factories to bring specialized workers together. This allowed products to be made more quickly than before.

In the third phase, factory workers used machinery to perform some of their work. Many of the new machines ran on waterpower or steam power. For example, power-driven looms took over the task of weaving. The worker's job changed from weaving to tending the machine, which produced more fabric in less time.

Mass production of cotton textiles began in New England in the early 1800s. After **Elias Howe** invented the sewing machine in 1846, machine operators could produce clothing on a large scale from fabrics made by machine. Other types of industries developed during the same period. By 1860 the Northeast's factories produced at least two-thirds of the country's manufactured goods.

Improved Transportation

Improvements in transportation contributed to the success of many of America's new industries. Between 1800 and 1850, construction crews built thousands of miles of roads and canals. The canals opened new shipping routes by connecting many lakes and rivers. The growth of the railroads in the 1840s and 1850s also helped to speed the flow of goods. Inventor **Robert Fulton** demonstrated a reliable steamboat in 1807. Steamboats carried goods and passengers more cheaply and quickly along inland waterways than could flatboats or sail-powered vessels.

In the 1840s canal builders began to widen and deepen canals to accommodate steamboats. By 1860 about 3,000 steamboats traveled the major rivers and canals of the country as well as the Great Lakes. Steamboats spurred the growth of cities such as Cincinnati, Buffalo, and Chicago.

In the 1840s sailing ships were improved. The clipper ships—with sleek hulls and tall sails—were the pride of the open seas. They could sail 300 miles per day, as fast as most steamships of the day. The ships got their name because they "clipped" time from long journeys. Before the clippers, the voyage from New York to Great Britain took about 21 to 28 days. A clipper ship could usually make that trip in half the time.

Picturing **History**

A clipper ship, the *Flying Cloud,* set a new record by sailing from New York to California in less than 90 days. **How did clipper ships get their name?**

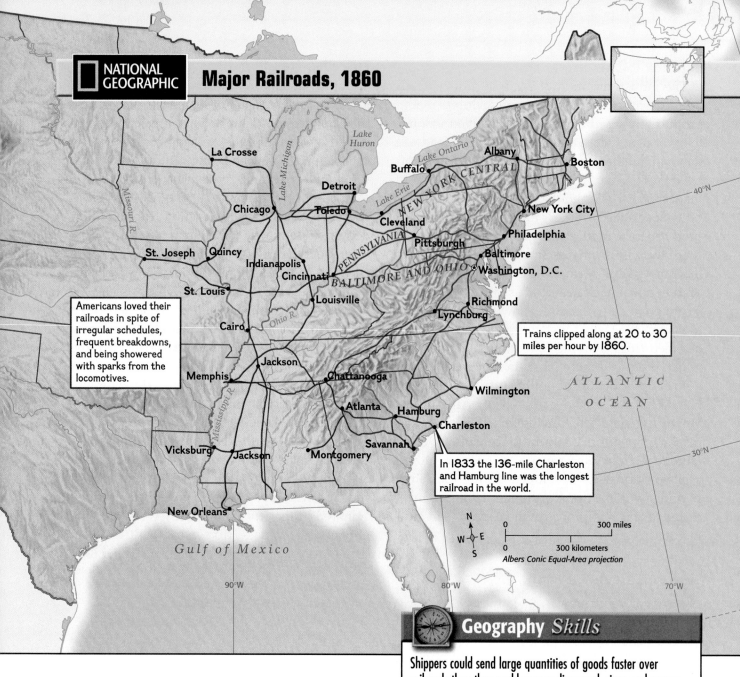

Major Railroads, 1860

NATIONAL GEOGRAPHIC

Americans loved their railroads in spite of irregular schedules, frequent breakdowns, and being showered with sparks from the locomotives.

Trains clipped along at 20 to 30 miles per hour by 1860.

In 1833 the 136-mile Charleston and Hamburg line was the longest railroad in the world.

300 miles

300 kilometers
Albers Conic Equal-Area projection

Geography *Skills*

Shippers could send large quantities of goods faster over railroads than they could over earlier canal, river, and wagon routes.
1. **Location** To what westernmost city did the railroads extend by 1860?
2. **Location** What cities might a train traveler pass through on a trip from Chicago to New Orleans?

Locomotives

The development of railroads in the United States began with short stretches of tracks that connected mines with nearby rivers. Early trains were pulled by horses rather than by locomotives. The first steam-powered passenger locomotive, the *Rocket*, began operating in Britain in 1829.

Peter Cooper designed and built the first American steam locomotive in 1830. Called the *Tom Thumb*, it got off to a bad start. In a race against a horse-drawn train in **Baltimore**, the *Tom Thumb*'s engine failed. Engineers soon improved the engine, and within 10 years steam locomotives were pulling trains in the United States.

A Railway Network

In 1840 the United States had almost 3,000 miles of railroad track. By 1860 it had almost 31,000 miles, mostly in the North and the **Midwest.** One railway linked New York City and Buffalo. Another connected Philadelphia and Pittsburgh. Yet another linked Baltimore with Wheeling, Virginia (now West Virginia).

Railway builders connected these eastern lines to lines being built farther west in Ohio, Indiana, and Illinois. By 1860 a network of railroad track united the Midwest and the East.

Moving Goods and People

Along with canals, the railways transformed trade in the nation's interior. The changes began with the opening of the Erie Canal in 1825 and the first railroads of the 1830s. Before this time agricultural goods were carried down the Mississippi River to New Orleans and then shipped to other countries or to the East Coast of the United States.

The development of the east-west canal and the rail network allowed grain, livestock, and dairy products to move directly from the Midwest to the East. Because goods now traveled faster and more cheaply, manufacturers in the East could offer them at lower prices.

The railroads also played an important role in the settlement and industrialization of the Midwest. Fast, affordable train travel brought people into Ohio, Indiana, and Illinois. As the populations of these states grew, new towns and industries developed.

Picturing **History**

The defeat of the train *Tom Thumb* in 1830 did not mean the end of the steam engine. The first successful use of a steam locomotive in the United States took place in South Carolina in 1831. **In 1860 which regions of the United States had the most miles of railroad track?**

Faster Communication

The growth of industry and the new pace of travel created a need for faster methods of communication. The telegraph—an apparatus that used electric signals to transmit messages— filled that need.

Samuel Morse, an American inventor, had been seeking support for a system of telegraph lines. On May 24, 1844, Morse got the chance to demonstrate that he could send messages instantly along wires. As a crowd in the U.S. capital watched, Morse tapped in the words, "What hath God wrought!" A few moments later, the telegraph operator in Baltimore sent the same message back in reply. The telegraph worked! Soon telegraph messages were flashing back and forth between Washington and Baltimore.

Morse transmitted his message in Morse code, a series of dots and dashes representing the letters of the alphabet. A skilled Morse code operator could rapidly tap out words in the dot-and-dash alphabet. Americans adopted the telegraph eagerly. A British visitor marveled at the speed with which Americans formed telegraph companies and erected telegraph lines. Americans, he wrote, were driven to "annihilate [wipe out] distance" in their vast country. By 1852 the United States was operating about 23,000 miles of telegraph lines.

Reading Check **Explaining** How did canals and railways change transportation?

Samuel Morse

Agriculture

The railroads gave farmers access to new markets to sell their products. Advances in technology allowed farmers to greatly increase the size of the harvest they produced.

In the early 1800s, few farmers had ventured into the treeless **Great Plains** west of Missouri, Iowa, and Minnesota. Even areas of mixed forest and prairie west of Ohio and Kentucky seemed too difficult for farming. Settlers worried that their wooden plows could not break the prairie's matted sod and that the soil was not fertile.

Revolution in Agriculture

Three revolutionary inventions of the 1830s changed farming methods and encouraged settlers to cultivate larger areas of the West. One was the steel-tipped plow that **John Deere** invented in 1837. Far sturdier than the wooden plow, Deere's plow easily cut through the hard-packed sod of the prairies. Equally important was the mechanical reaper, which sped up the harvesting of wheat, and the thresher, which quickly separated the grain from the stalk.

McCormick's Reaper

Born on a Virginia farm, **Cyrus McCormick** became interested in machines that would ease the burden of farmwork. After years of tinkering, McCormick designed and constructed the mechanical reaper and made a fortune manufacturing and selling it.

For hundreds of years, farmers had harvested grain with handheld sickles. McCormick's reaper could harvest grain much faster than a hand-operated sickle. Because farmers could harvest wheat so quickly, they began planting more of it. Growing wheat became profitable.

McCormick's reaper ensured that raising wheat would remain the main economic activity in the Midwestern prairies. New machines and railroads helped farmers plant more acres in "cash" crops—crops planted strictly for sale. Midwestern farmers began growing more wheat and shipping it east by train and canal barge. Farmers in the Northeast and Middle Atlantic states increased their production of fruits and vegetables that grew well in Eastern soils.

Despite improvements in agriculture, however, the North turned away from farming and increasingly toward industry. It was difficult making a living farming the rocky soil of New England, but industry flourished in the area. The number of people who worked in factories continued to rise—and so did problems connected with factory labor.

Reading Check **Identifying** What innovation sped the harvesting of wheat?

SECTION 1 ASSESSMENT

Checking for Understanding

1. **Key Terms** Use each of these terms in a sentence that will help explain its meaning: clipper ship, telegraph, Morse code.
2. **Reviewing Facts** Identify and describe the three phases of industrialization in the North.

Reviewing Themes

3. **Economic Factors** How did improvements in transportation affect the price of goods?

Critical Thinking

4. **Determining Cause and Effect** How did the steel-tipped plow aid settlers on the Great Plains?
5. **Analyzing Consequences** How might failure to improve transportation have affected the economic and social development of the nation? Re-create the diagram below and list the possible effects.

Effects	
Social	Economic

Analyzing Visuals

6. **Geography Skills** Study the map on page 388, then answer this question: Through what two cities in Mississippi did major rail lines pass?

Interdisciplinary Activity

Math Research the number of acres of wheat harvested in the United States before and after McCormick introduced his reaper. Then create a chart or graph to illustrate your findings.

SECTION 2 The North's People

Main Idea
Many cities grew tremendously during this period.

Key Terms
trade union, strike, prejudice, discrimination, famine, nativist

Reading Strategy
Determining Cause and Effect As you read the section, re-create the diagram below and list two reasons for the growth of cities.

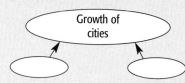

Growth of cities

Read to Learn
• how working conditions in industries changed.
• how immigration affected American economic, political, and cultural life.

Section Theme
Geography and History Growth of industry and an increase in immigration changed the North.

Preview of Events

♦1820	♦1830	♦1840	♦1850	♦1860
1827 *Freedom's Journal,* first African American newspaper, is published	**1833** The General Trades Union of New York is formed		**1854** American Party (Know-Nothings) forms	**1860** Population of New York City passes 800,000

AN American Story

"At first the hours seemed very long, but I was so interested in learning that I endured it very well; when I went out at night the sound of the mill was in my ears," a Northern mill worker wrote in 1844. The worker compared the noise of the cotton mill to the ceaseless, deafening roar of Niagara Falls. The roar of machinery was only one feature of factory life workers had to adjust to. Industrialization created new challenges for the men, women, and children who worked in the nation's factories.

12-year-old factory worker

Northern Factories

Between 1820 and 1860, more and more of America's manufacturing shifted to mills and factories. Machines took over many of the production tasks.

In the early 1800s, in the mills established in **Lowell, Massachusetts,** the entire production process was brought together under one roof—setting up the factory system. In addition to textiles and clothing, factories now produced such items as shoes, watches, guns, sewing machines, and agricultural machinery.

Working Conditions

As the factory system developed, working conditions worsened. Factory owners wanted their employees to work longer hours in order to produce more goods. By 1840 factory workers averaged 11.4 hours a day. As the workday grew longer, on-the-job accidents became more and more common.

Factory work involved many dangerous conditions. For example, the long leather belts that connected the machines to the factory's water-powered driveshaft had no protective shields. Workers often suffered injuries such as lost fingers and broken bones from the rapidly spinning belts. Young children working on machines with powerful moving parts were especially at risk.

Workers often labored under unpleasant conditions. In the summer, factories were miserably hot and stifling. The machines gave off heat, and air-conditioning had not yet been invented. In the winter, workers suffered because most factories had no heating.

Factory owners often showed more concern for profits than for the comfort and safety of their employees. Employers knew they could easily replace an unhappy worker with someone else eager for a job. No laws existed to regulate working conditions or to protect workers.

Attempts to Organize

By the 1830s workers began organizing to improve working conditions. Fearing the growth of the factory system, skilled workers had formed trade unions—organizations of workers with the same trade, or skill. Steadily deteriorating working conditions led unskilled workers to organize as well.

In the mid-1830s skilled workers in New York City staged a series of strikes, refusing to work in order to put pressure on employers. Workers wanted higher wages and to limit their workday to 10 hours. Groups of skilled workers formed the General Trades Union of New York.

In the early 1800s going on strike was illegal. Striking workers could be punished by the law, or they could be fired from their jobs. In 1842 a Massachusetts court ruled that workers did have the right to strike. It would be many years, however, before workers received other legal rights.

African American Workers

Slavery had largely disappeared from the North by the 1830s. However, racial prejudice—an unfair opinion not based on facts—and discrimination—unfair treatment of a group—remained in Northern states. For example, in 1821 New York eliminated the requirement that white men had to own property in order to vote—yet few African Americans were allowed to vote. Both Rhode Island and Pennsylvania passed laws prohibiting free African Americans from voting.

Most communities would not allow free African Americans to attend public schools and barred them from public facilities as well. Often African Americans were forced into segregated, or separate, schools and hospitals.

History *Through Art*

Young Man in White Apron by John Mackie Falconer The artist of this painting was known for his watercolors depicting New York City workers such as this African American clerk. **How did prejudice affect the lives of African Americans in the North?**

A few African Americans rose in the business world. Henry Boyd owned a furniture manufacturing company in Cincinnati, Ohio. In 1827 Samuel Cornish and John B. Russwurm founded *Freedom's Journal*, the first African American newspaper, in New York City. In 1845 Macon B. Allen became the first African American licensed to practice law in the United States. The overwhelming majority of African Americans, however, were extremely poor.

Women Workers

Women had played a major role in the developing mill and factory systems. However, employers discriminated against women, paying them less than male workers. When men began to form unions, they excluded women. Male workers wanted women kept out of the workplace so that more jobs would be available for men.

Some female workers attempted to organize in the 1830s and 1840s. In Massachusetts the Lowell Female Labor Reform Organization, founded by a weaver named **Sarah G. Bagley**, petitioned the state legislature for a 10-hour workday in 1845. Because most of the petition's signers were women, the legislature did not consider the petition.

Most of the early efforts by women to achieve equality and justice in the workplace failed. They paved the way, however, for later movements to correct the injustices against female workers.

✓**Reading Check** **Describing** How did conditions for workers change as the factory system developed?

The Rise of Cities

The growth of factories went hand in hand with the growth of Northern cities. People looking for work flocked to the cities, where most of the factories were located. The population of New York City, the nation's largest city, passed 800,000, and Philadelphia, more than 500,000 in 1860.

Between 1820 and 1840, communities that had been small villages became major cities, including St. Louis, Pittsburgh, Cincinnati, and Louisville. All of them profited from their location on the

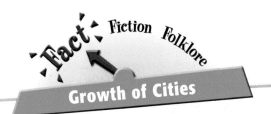

Growth of Cities

Cities grow along fall lines A "fall line" is the boundary between an upland region and a lower region where rivers and streams move down over rapids or waterfalls to the lower region. Cities sprang up along fall lines for a number of reasons. Boats could not travel beyond the fall line, so travelers and merchants had to transfer their goods to other forms of transportation there. Early manufacturers also took advantage of the falls to power their mills. Fall-line cities include Richmond, Virginia; Trenton, New Jersey; and Augusta, Georgia.

Mississippi River or one of the river's branches. These cities became centers of the growing trade that connected the farmers of the Midwest with the cities of the Northeast. After 1830 the Great Lakes became a center for shipping, creating major new urban centers. These centers included Buffalo, Detroit, Milwaukee, and Chicago.

Immigration

Immigration—the movement of people into a country—to the United States increased dramatically between 1840 and 1860. American manufacturers welcomed the tide of immigrants, many of whom were willing to work for long hours and for low pay.

The largest group of immigrants to the United States at this time traveled across the Atlantic from Ireland. Between 1846 and 1860 more than 1.5 million Irish immigrants arrived in the country, settling mostly in the Northeast.

The Irish migration to the United States was brought on by a terrible potato famine. A famine is an extreme shortage of food. Potatoes were the main part of the Irish diet. When a devastating blight, or disease, destroyed Irish potato crops in the 1840s, starvation struck the country. More than one million people died.

Although most of the immigrants had been farmers in Ireland, they were too poor to buy land in the United States. For this reason many Irish immigrants took low-paying factory jobs in

MORE ABOUT...

Immigration

Newcomers came to America from many different countries in the mid-1800s, but the overwhelming majority came from Ireland and Germany.

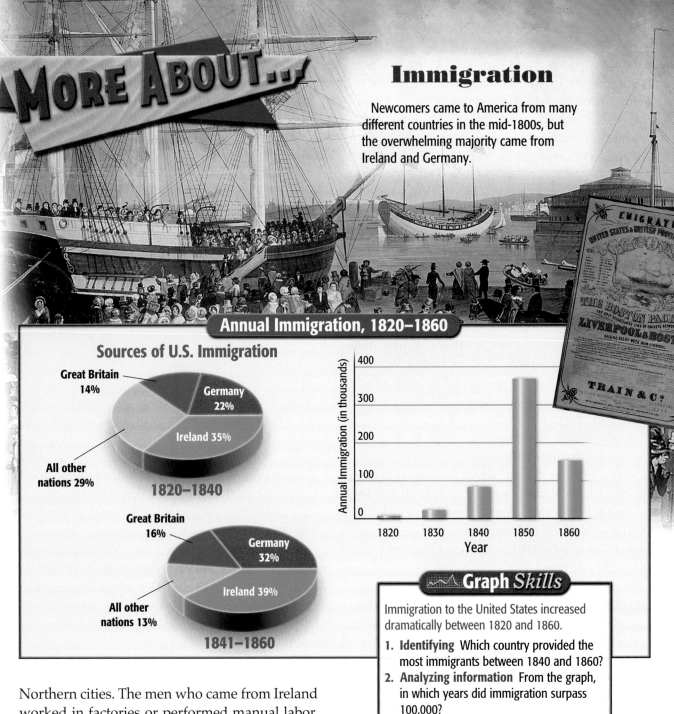

Annual Immigration, 1820–1860

Sources of U.S. Immigration

1820–1840
- Great Britain 14%
- Germany 22%
- Ireland 35%
- All other nations 29%

1841–1860
- Great Britain 16%
- Germany 32%
- Ireland 39%
- All other nations 13%

Annual Immigration (in thousands): 400, 300, 200, 100, 0 — Year: 1820, 1830, 1840, 1850, 1860

Graph Skills

Immigration to the United States increased dramatically between 1820 and 1860.

1. **Identifying** Which country provided the most immigrants between 1840 and 1860?
2. **Analyzing information** From the graph, in which years did immigration surpass 100,000?

Northern cities. The men who came from Ireland worked in factories or performed manual labor, such as working on the railroads. The women, who accounted for almost half of the immigrants, became servants and factory workers.

The second-largest group of immigrants in the United States between 1820 and 1860 came from Germany. Some sought work and opportunity. Others had left their homes because of the failure of a democratic revolution in Germany in 1848.

Between 1848 and 1860 more than one million German immigrants—many in family groups—settled in the United States. Many arrived with enough money to buy farms or open their own businesses. They prospered in many parts of the country, founding their own communities and self-help organizations. Some German immigrants settled in New York and Pennsylvania, but many moved to the Midwest and the western territories.

The Impact of Immigration

The immigrants who came to the United States between 1820 and 1860 changed the character of the country. These people brought their languages, customs, religions, and ways of life with them, some of which filtered into American culture.

Before the early 1800s, the majority of immigrants to America had been either Protestants from Great Britain or Africans brought forcibly to America as slaves. At the time, the country had relatively few Catholics, and most of these lived around Baltimore, New Orleans, and St. Augustine. Most of the Irish immigrants and about one-half of the German immigrants were Roman Catholics.

Many Catholic immigrants settled in cities of the Northeast. The Church gave the newcomers more than a source of spiritual guidance. It also provided a center for the community life of the immigrants.

The German immigrants brought their language as well as their religion. When they settled, they lived in their own communities, founded German-language publications, and established musical societies.

Immigrants Face Prejudice

In the 1830s and 1840s, anti-immigrant feelings rose. Some Americans feared that immigrants were changing the character of the United States too much.

People opposed to immigration were known as **nativists** because they felt that immigration threatened the future of "native"—American-born—citizens. Some nativists accused immigrants of taking jobs from "real" Americans and were angry that immigrants would work for lower wages. Others accused the newcomers of bringing crime and disease to American cities. Immigrants who lived in crowded slums served as likely targets of this kind of prejudice.

The Know-Nothing Party

The nativists formed secret anti-Catholic societies, and in the 1850s they joined to form a new political party: the American Party. Because members of nativist groups often answered questions about their organization with the statement "I know nothing," their party came to be known as the **Know-Nothing Party.**

The Know-Nothings called for stricter citizenship laws—extending the immigrants' waiting period for citizenship from 5 to 21 years—and wanted to ban foreign-born citizens from holding office.

In the mid-1850s the Know-Nothing movement split into a Northern branch and a Southern branch over the question of slavery. At this time the slavery issue was also dividing the Northern and Southern states of the nation.

Reading Check **Identifying** What two nations provided the largest number of immigrants to the United States during this era?

SECTION 2 ASSESSMENT

Checking for Understanding

1. **Key Terms** Use each of these terms in a complete sentence that will help explain its meaning: trade union, strike, prejudice, discrimination, famine, nativist.

2. **Reviewing Facts** What was the nation's largest city in 1860?

Reviewing Themes

3. **Geography and History** How did German and Irish immigrants differ in where they settled?

Critical Thinking

4. **Making Inferences** How do you think nativists would have defined a "real" American?

5. **Determining Cause and Effect** Re-create the diagram below and list reasons workers formed labor unions.

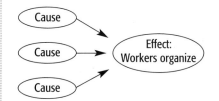

Analyzing Visuals

6. **Graph Skills** Study the graphs on page 394. What country provided about 1 of 4 immigrants to the U.S. between 1820 and 1840?

Social Studies SKILLBUILDER

Reading a Circle Graph

Why Learn This Skill?

Have you ever watched someone dish out pieces of pie? When the pie is cut evenly, everybody gets the same size slice. If one slice is cut a little larger, however, someone else gets a smaller piece. A **circle graph** is like a pie cut in slices. Often, a circle graph is called a *pie chart*.

Learning the Skill

In a circle graph, the complete circle represents a whole group—or 100 percent. The circle is divided into "slices," or wedge-shaped sections representing parts of the whole.

The size of each slice is determined by the percentage it represents.

To read a circle graph, follow these steps:
- Study the labels or key to determine what the parts or "slices" represent.
- Compare the parts of the graph to draw conclusions about the subject.
- When two or more circle graphs appear together, read their titles and labels. Then compare the graphs for similarities and differences.

Practicing the Skill

Read the graphs on this page. Then answer the following questions.

❶ What do the four graphs represent?

❷ What percentage of workers were in agriculture in 1840? In 1870?

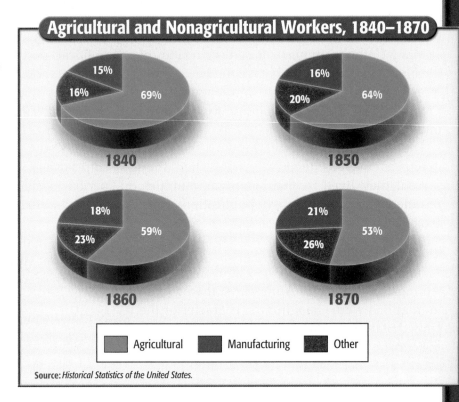

Agricultural and Nonagricultural Workers, 1840–1870

1840 — 69%, 16%, 15%
1850 — 64%, 20%, 16%
1860 — 59%, 23%, 18%
1870 — 53%, 26%, 21%

Agricultural   Manufacturing   Other

Source: *Historical Statistics of the United States.*

❸ During what decade did the percentage of workers in manufacturing increase the most?

❹ What can you conclude from the graphs about the relationship between manufacturing and agricultural workers from 1840 to 1870?

Applying the Skill

Reading a Circle Graph Find a circle graph related to the economy in a newspaper or magazine. Compare its sections. Then draw a conclusion about the economy.

 Glencoe's **Skillbuilder Interactive Workbook CD-ROM, Level 1,** provides instruction and practice in key social studies skills.

SECTION 3 Southern Cotton Kingdom

Guide to Reading

Main Idea

Cotton was vital to the economy of the South.

Key Terms

cotton gin, capital

Reading Strategy

Comparing As you read the section, re-create the diagram. In the ovals, give reasons why cotton production grew while industrial growth was slower.

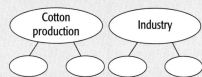

Cotton production   Industry

Read to Learn

• how settlement expanded in the South.
• why the economy of the South relied on agriculture.

Section Theme

Science and Technology Technology, a favorable climate, and rising demand led to the cotton boom in the Deep South.

Preview of Events

| 1780 | 1800 | 1820 | 1840 | 1860 |

1793
Eli Whitney invents cotton gin

1800s
Removal of Native Americans spurs expansion of cotton production

1860
The South remains largely rural and dependent on cotton

AN American Story

Cotton was "king" in the South before 1860. "Look which way you will, you see it; and see it moving," wrote a visitor to Mobile, Alabama. "Keel boats, ships, brigs, schooners, wharves, stores, and press-houses, all appeared to be full." Cotton was also the main topic of conversation: "I believe that in the three days that I was there . . . I must have heard the word *cotton* pronounced more than 3,000 times."

Stem of cotton

Rise of the Cotton Kingdom

In 1790 the South seemed to be an underdeveloped agricultural region with little prospect for future growth. Most Southerners lived along the Atlantic coast in Maryland, Virginia, and North Carolina in what came to be known as the **Upper South.**

By 1850 the South had changed. Its population had spread inland to the states of the **Deep South**—Georgia, South Carolina, Alabama, Mississippi, Louisiana, and Texas. The economy of the South was thriving. Slavery, which had disappeared from the North, grew stronger than ever in the South.

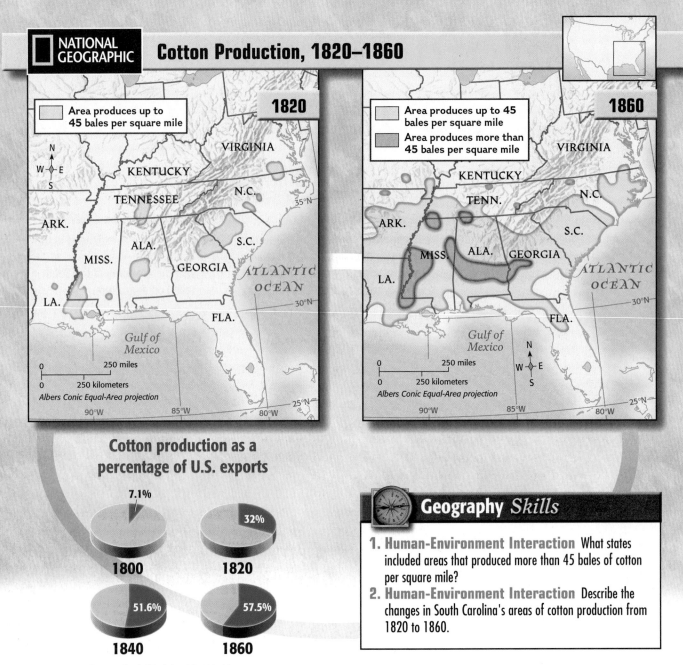

Cotton Production, 1820–1860

1820

Area produces up to 45 bales per square mile

1860

Area produces up to 45 bales per square mile

Area produces more than 45 bales per square mile

Cotton production as a percentage of U.S. exports

7.1% — 1800
32% — 1820
51.6% — 1840
57.5% — 1860

Source: *Historical Statistics of the United States.*

Geography *Skills*

1. **Human-Environment Interaction** What states included areas that produced more than 45 bales of cotton per square mile?
2. **Human-Environment Interaction** Describe the changes in South Carolina's areas of cotton production from 1820 to 1860.

Cotton Rules the Deep South

In colonial times, rice, indigo, and tobacco made up the South's main crops. After the American Revolution, demand for these crops decreased. European mills, however, wanted Southern cotton. But cotton took time and labor to produce. After harvest, workers had to painstakingly separate the plant's sticky seeds from the cotton fibers.

Cotton production was revolutionized when **Eli Whitney** invented the cotton gin in 1793. The cotton gin was a machine that removed seeds from cotton fibers, dramatically increasing the amount of cotton that could be processed. A worker could clean 50 pounds of cotton a day with the machine—instead of 1 pound by hand. Furthermore the gin was small enough for one person to carry from place to place.

Whitney's invention had important consequences. The cotton gin led to the demand for more workers. Because the cotton gin processed cotton fibers so quickly, farmers wanted to grow more cotton. Many Southern planters relied on slave labor to plant and pick the cotton.

By 1860 the economies of the Deep South and the Upper South had developed in different ways. Both parts of the South were agricultural, but the Upper South still produced tobacco, hemp, wheat, and vegetables. The Deep South was committed to cotton and, in some areas, to rice and sugarcane.

The value of enslaved people increased because of their key role in producing cotton and sugar. The Upper South became a center for the sale and transport of enslaved people throughout the region.

✓ **Reading Check** **Describing** What effect did the cotton gin have on the South's economy?

Industry in the South

The economy of the South prospered between 1820 and 1860. Unlike the industrial North, however, the South remained overwhelmingly rural, and its economy became increasingly different from the Northern economy. The South accounted for a small percentage of the nation's manufacturing value by 1860. In fact, the entire South had a lower value of manufactured goods than the state of Pennsylvania.

Barriers to Industry

Why was there little industry in the South? One reason was the boom in cotton sales. Because agriculture was so profitable, Southerners remained committed to farming rather than starting new businesses.

Another stumbling block was the lack of capital—money to invest in businesses—in the South. To develop industries required money, but many Southerners had their wealth invested in land and slaves. Planters would have had to sell slaves to raise the money to build factories. Most wealthy Southerners were unwilling to do this. They believed that an economy based on cotton and slavery would continue to prosper.

In addition the market for manufactured goods in the South was smaller than it was in the North. A large portion of the Southern

TECHNOLOGY & History

The Cotton Gin

In 1793 Eli Whitney visited Catherine Greene, a Georgia plantation owner. She asked him to build a device that removed the seeds from cotton pods. Whitney called the machine the cotton gin—"gin" being short for engine. *How did the invention of the cotton gin affect slavery?*

Eli Whitney

1 Cotton bolls are dumped into the **hopper.**

2 A hand **crank** turns a **cylinder** with wire teeth. The teeth pull the cotton past a grate.

1 hopper

3 grate

2 cylinder

2 crank

4 brushes

3 Slots in the **grate** allow the cotton but not its seeds to pass through.

4 A second cylinder with **brushes** pulls the cotton off the toothed cylinder and sends it out of the gin

population consisted of enslaved people with no money to buy merchandise. So the limited local market discouraged industries from developing.

Yet another reason for the lack of industry is that some Southerners did not want industry to flourish there. One Texas politician summed up the Southerners' point of view this way:

66We want no manufactures; we desire no trading, no mechanical or manufacturing classes. As long as we have our rice, our sugar, our tobacco and our cotton, we can command wealth to purchase all we want.99

Southern Factories

While most Southerners felt confident about the future of the cotton economy, some leaders wanted to develop industry in the region. They argued that, by remaining committed to cotton production, the South was becoming dependent on the North for manufactured goods. These Southerners also argued that factories would revive the economy of the Upper South, which was less prosperous than the cotton states.

One Southerner who shared this view was **William Gregg,** a merchant from Charleston, South Carolina. After touring New England's textile mills in 1844, Gregg opened his own textile factory in South Carolina.

In Richmond, Virginia, **Joseph Reid Anderson** took over the Tredegar Iron Works in the 1840s and made it one of the nation's leading producers of iron. Years later during the Civil War, Tredegar provided artillery and other iron products for the Southern forces.

The industries that Gregg and Anderson built stood as the exception rather than the rule in the South. In 1860 the region remained largely rural and dependent on cotton.

Southern Transportation

Natural waterways provided the chief means for transporting goods in the South. Most towns were located on the seacoast or along rivers. There were few canals, and roads were poor.

Like the North, the South also built railroads, but to a lesser extent. Southern rail lines were short, local, and did not connect all parts of the region in a network. As a result Southern cities grew more slowly than cities in the North and Midwest, where railways provided the major routes of commerce and settlement. By 1860 only about one-third of the nation's rail lines lay within the South. The railway shortage would have devastating consequences for the South during the Civil War.

☑ **Reading Check** **Explaining** What is capital? Why is it important for economic growth?

SECTION 3 ASSESSMENT

Checking for Understanding

1. **Key Terms** Use each of these terms in a sentence that will help explain its meaning: cotton gin, capital.
2. **Reviewing Facts** How did the lack of capital affect industrial growth?

Reviewing Themes

3. **Science and Technology** Why did the invention of the cotton gin increase the demand for enslaved Africans?

Critical Thinking

4. **Predicting Consequences** If slavery had been outlawed, how do you think it would have affected the South's economy?
5. **Comparing** How did agriculture in the Upper South differ from agriculture in the Deep South? Re-create the diagram below and describe the differences.

Agriculture	
Upper South	Deep South

Analyzing Visuals

6. **Geography Skills** Look at the maps and the graphs on page 398. What area of Florida specialized in cotton? Did cotton make up more than 50 percent of U.S. exports in 1820?

Interdisciplinary Activity

Informative Writing Research and write a report on a machine mentioned in the chapter—perhaps the steam locomotive, steamboat, or another steam-driven machine. Illustrate your report if you wish. Keep the report in your portfolio.

SECTION 4 The South's People

Guide to Reading

Main Idea
The South's population consisted of wealthy slaveholding planters, small farmers, poor whites, and enslaved African Americans.

Key Terms
yeoman, tenant farmer, fixed cost, credit, overseer, spiritual, slave code

Reading Strategy
Organizing Information As you read the section, re-create the diagram below and describe the work that was done on Southern plantations.

Working on a plantation

Read to Learn
- about the way of life on Southern plantations.
- how enslaved workers maintained strong family and cultural ties.

Section Theme
Culture and Traditions Most of the people in the South worked in agriculture in the first half of the 1800s.

Preview of Events

♦1800	♦1820	♦1840	♦1860
1808 Congress outlaws the slave trade	**1831** Nat Turner leads rebellion in Virginia	**1859** Arkansas orders free blacks to leave	**1860** Population of Baltimore reaches 212,000

AN American Story

Planters gathered in the bright Savannah sunshine. They were asked to bid on a strong slave who could plow their fields. Fear and grief clouded the enslaved man's face because he had been forced to leave his wife and children. Later, he wrote this letter: "My Dear wife I [write] . . . with much regret to inform you that I am Sold to a man by the name of Peterson. . . . Give my love to my father and mother and tell them good Bye for me. And if we Shall not meet in this world, I hope to meet in heaven. My Dear wife for you and my Children my pen cannot express the [grief] I feel to be parted from you all."

Plow

Small Farms

Popular novels and films often portray the South before 1860 as a land of stately plantations owned by rich white slaveholders. In reality most white Southerners were either small farmers without slaves or planters with a handful of slaves. Only a few planters could afford the many enslaved Africans and the lavish mansions shown in fictional accounts of the Old South. Most white Southerners fit into one of four categories: yeomen, tenant farmers, the rural poor, or plantation owners.

Small Farmers and the Rural Poor

The farmers who did not have slaves—yeomen—made up the largest group of whites in the South. Most yeomen owned land. Although they lived throughout the region, they were most numerous in the Upper South and in the hilly rural areas of the Deep South, where the land was unsuited to large plantations.

A yeoman's farm usually ranged from 50 to 200 acres. Yeomen grew crops both for their own use and to sell, and they often traded their produce to local merchants and workers for goods and services.

Most Southern whites did not live in elegant mansions or on large plantations. They lived in far simpler homes, though the structure of their homes changed over time. In the early 1800s many lived in cottages built of wood and plaster with thatched roofs. Later many lived in one-story frame houses or log cabins.

Not all Southern whites owned land. Some rented land, or worked as tenant farmers, on landlords' estates. Others—the rural poor—lived in crude cabins in wooded areas where they could clear a few trees, plant some corn, and keep a hog or a cow. They also fished and hunted for food.

The poor people of the rural South were stubbornly independent. They refused to take any job that resembled the work of enslaved people. Although looked down on by other whites, the rural poor were proud of being self-sufficient.

Reading Check **Identifying** What group made up the largest number of whites in the South?

Plantations

A large plantation might cover several thousand acres. Well-to-do plantation owners usually lived in comfortable but not luxurious farmhouses. They measured their wealth partly by the number of enslaved people they controlled and partly by such possessions as homes, furnishings, and clothing. A small group of plantation owners—about 4 percent—held 20 or more slaves in 1860. The large majority of slaveholders held fewer than 10 enslaved workers.

A few free African Americans possessed slaves. The Metoyer family of Louisiana owned thousands of acres of land and more than 400 slaves. Most often, these slaveholders were free African Americans who purchased their own family members in order to free them.

Picturing **History**
Wealthy Southerners pose for the camera in front of an elegant plantation home. **What were the duties of the wife of a plantation owner?**

Atlanta, Georgia, business street, c. 1860

$ Economics

Plantation Owners

The main economic goal for large plantation owners was to earn profits. Such plantations had fixed costs—regular expenses such as housing and feeding workers and maintaining cotton gins and other equipment. Fixed costs remained about the same year after year.

Cotton prices, however, varied from season to season, depending on the market. To receive the best prices, planters sold their cotton to agents in cities such as **New Orleans, Charleston,** Mobile, and Savannah. The cotton exchanges, or trade centers, in Southern cities were of vital importance to those involved in the cotton economy. The agents of the exchanges extended credit—a form of loan—to the planters and held the cotton for several months until the price rose. Then the agents sold the cotton. This system kept the planters always in debt because they did not receive payment for their cotton until the agents sold it.

Plantation Wives

The wife of a plantation owner generally was in charge of watching over the enslaved workers who toiled in her home and tending to them when they became ill. Her responsibilities also included supervising the plantation's buildings and the fruit and vegetable gardens. Some wives served as accountants, keeping the plantation's financial records.

Women often led a difficult and lonely life on the plantation. When plantation agriculture spread westward into Alabama and Mississippi, many planters' wives felt they were moving into a hostile, uncivilized region. Planters traveled frequently to look at new land or to deal with agents in New Orleans or **Memphis.** Their wives spent long periods alone at the plantation.

Work on the Plantation

Large plantations needed many different kinds of workers. Some enslaved people worked in the house, cleaning, cooking, doing laundry, sewing, and serving meals. They were called domestic slaves. Other African Americans were trained as blacksmiths, carpenters, shoemakers,

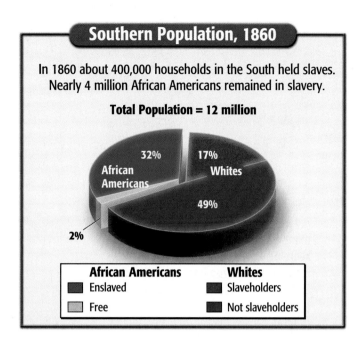

Southern Population, 1860

In 1860 about 400,000 households in the South held slaves. Nearly 4 million African Americans remained in slavery.

Total Population = 12 million

32% African Americans

17% Whites

49%

2%

African Americans	Whites
■ Enslaved	■ Slaveholders
▢ Free	■ Not slaveholders

or weavers. Still others worked in the pastures, tending the horses, cows, sheep, and pigs. Most of the enslaved African Americans, however, were field hands. They worked from sunrise to sunset planting, cultivating, and picking cotton and other crops. They were supervised by an overseer—a plantation manager.

✓ **Reading Check** **Explaining** Why were many slaves needed on a plantation?

Life Under Slavery

Enslaved African Americans endured hardship and misery. They worked hard, earned no money, and had little hope of freedom. One of their worst fears was being sold to another planter and separated from their loved ones. In the face of these brutal conditions, enslaved African Americans maintained their family life as best they could and developed a culture all their own. They resisted slavery through a variety of ingenious methods, and they looked to the day when they would be liberated.

Life in the Slave Cabins

Enslaved people had few comforts beyond the bare necessities. Josiah Henson, an African American who escaped from slavery, described the quarters where he had lived.

MORE ABOUT...

Living Under Slavery

Enslaved workers reached the fields before the sun came up, and they stayed there until sundown. Planters wanted to keep the slaves busy all the time, which meant long and grueling days in the fields. Enslaved women as well as men were required to do heavy fieldwork. Young children carried buckets of water. By the age of 10, they were considered ready for fieldwork.

Cabins were usually made of small logs, about 10 to 20 feet square. Often, two or three families shared a cabin.

Heavy iron leg shackles were used to punish workers, especially those who tried to run away.

Enslaved people had few personal possessions.

When rented to other masters, enslaved people wore identification tags.

66We lodged in log huts and on the bare ground. Wooden floors were an unknown luxury. In a single room were huddled, like cattle, ten or a dozen persons, men, women and children. . . .

Our beds were collections of straw and old rags, thrown down in the corners and boxed in with boards, a single blanket the only covering. . . . The wind whistled and the rain and snow blew in through the cracks, and the damp earth soaked in the moisture till the floor was miry [muddy] as a pigsty.99

Family Life

Enslaved people faced constant uncertainty and danger. American law in the early 1800s did not protect enslaved families. At any given time a husband or wife could be sold away, or a slaveholder's death could lead to the breakup of an enslaved family. Although marriage between enslaved people was not recognized by law, many couples did marry. Their marriage ceremonies included the phrase "until death or separation do us part"—recognizing the possibility that a marriage might end with the sale of one spouse.

To provide some measure of stability in their lives, enslaved African Americans established a network of relatives and friends, who made up their extended family. If a father or mother were sold away, an aunt, uncle, or close friend could raise the children left behind. Large, close-knit extended families became a vital feature of African American culture.

African American Culture

Enslaved African Americans endured their hardships by extending their own culture, fellowship, and community. They fused African and American elements into a new culture.

The growth of the African American population came mainly from children born in the United States. In 1808 Congress had outlawed the slave trade. Although slavery remained legal in the South, no new slaves could enter the United States. By 1860 almost all the enslaved people in the South had been born there.

These native-born African Americans held on to their African customs. They continued to practice African music and dance. They passed traditional African folk stories to their children. Some wrapped colored cloths around their heads in the African style. Although a large number of enslaved African Americans accepted Christianity, they often followed the religious beliefs and practices of their African ancestors as well.

African American Christianity

For many enslaved African Americans, Christianity became a religion of hope and resistance. They prayed fervently for the day when they would be free from bondage.

The passionate beliefs of the Southern slaves found expression in the spiritual, an African American religious folk song. The song "Didn't My Lord Deliver Daniel," for example, refers to the biblical story of Daniel who was saved from the lions' den.

> ❝Didn't my Lord deliver Daniel,
> deliver Daniel, deliver Daniel,
> Didn't my Lord deliver Daniel,
> An' why not every man?❞

Spirituals provided a way for the enslaved African Americans to communicate secretly among themselves. Many spirituals combined Christian faith with laments about earthly suffering.

Slave Codes

Between 1830 and 1860 life under slavery became even more difficult because the slave codes—the laws in the Southern states that controlled enslaved people—became more severe. In existence since the 1700s, slave codes aimed to prevent the event white Southerners dreaded most—the slave rebellion. For this reason slave codes prohibited slaves from assembling in large groups and from leaving their master's property without a written pass.

Slave codes also made it a crime to teach enslaved people to read or write. White Southerners feared that a literate slave might lead other African Americans in rebellion. A slave who did not know how to read and write, whites believed, was less likely to rebel.

Resistance to Slavery

Some enslaved African Americans did rebel openly against their masters. One was **Nat Turner,** a popular religious leader among his fellow slaves. Turner had taught himself to read and write. In 1831 Turner led a group of followers on a brief, violent rampage in Southhampton County, Virginia. Before being captured Turner and his followers killed at least 55 whites. Nat Turner was hanged, but his rebellion frightened white Southerners and led them to pass more severe slave codes.

Armed rebellions were rare, however. African Americans in the South knew that they would only lose in an armed uprising. For the most part enslaved people resisted slavery by working slowly or by pretending to be ill. Occasionally resistance took more active forms, such as setting fire to a plantation building or breaking tools. Resistance helped enslaved African Americans endure their lives by striking back at white masters—and perhaps establishing boundaries that white people would respect.

People In History

Harriet Tubman 1820–1913

Born as a slave in Maryland, Harriet Tubman worked in plantation fields until she was nearly 30 years old. Then she made her break for freedom, escaping to the North with the help of the Underground Railroad.

Realizing the risks of being captured, Tubman courageously made 19 trips back into the South during the 1850s to help other enslaved people escape. Altogether she assisted more than 300 individuals—including her parents—to escape from slavery.

While she did not establish the Underground Railroad, she certainly became its most famous and successful conductor. Tubman was known as the "Moses of her people." Despite huge rewards offered in the South for her capture and arrest, Tubman always managed to elude her enemies.

Escaping Slavery

Some enslaved African Americans tried to run away to the North. A few succeeded. **Harriet Tubman** and **Frederick Douglass,** two African American leaders who were born into slavery, gained their freedom when they fled to the North.

Yet for most enslaved people, getting to the North was almost impossible, especially from the Deep South. Most slaves who succeeded in running away escaped from the Upper South. **The Underground Railroad**—a network of "safe houses" owned by free blacks and whites who opposed slavery—offered assistance to runaway slaves.

Some slaves ran away to find relatives on nearby plantations or to escape punishment. Rarely did they plan to make a run for the North. Moses Grandy, who did escape, spoke about the problems runaways faced:

> ❝They hide themselves during the day in the woods and swamps; at night they travel. . . . [I]n these dangerous journeys they are guided by the north-star, for they only know that the land of freedom is in the north.❞

Most runaways were captured and returned to their owners. Discipline was severe; the most common punishment was whipping.

✓ **Reading Check** Explaining How did the African American spiritual develop?

City Life and Education

Although the South was primarily agricultural, it was the site of several large cities by the mid-1800s. By 1860 the population of **Baltimore** had reached 212,000 and the population of New Orleans had reached 168,000. The ten largest cities in the South were either seaports or river ports.

With the coming of the railroad, many other cities began to grow as centers of trade. Among the cities located at the crossroads of the railways were Columbia, South Carolina; Chattanooga, Tennessee; Montgomery, Alabama; Jackson, Mississippi; and Atlanta, Georgia. The population of Southern cities included white city dwellers, some enslaved workers, and many of the South's free African Americans.

The cities provided free African Americans with opportunities to form their own communities. African American barbers, carpenters, and small traders offered their services throughout their communities. Free African Americans founded their own churches and institutions. In New Orleans they formed an opera company.

Although some free African Americans prospered in the cities, their lives were far from secure. Between 1830 and 1860 Southern states passed laws that limited the rights of free African Americans. Most states would not allow them to migrate from other states. Although spared the horrors of slavery, free African Americans were denied an equal share in economic and political life.

Education

Plantation owners and those who could afford to do so often sent their children to private schools. One of the best known was the academy operated by Moses Waddel in Willington, South Carolina. Students attended six days a week. The Bible and classical literature were stressed, but the courses also included mathematics, religion, Greek, Latin, and public speaking.

During this era, no statewide public school systems existed. However, cities such as Charleston, Louisville, and Mobile did establish excellent public schools.

By the mid-1800s, education was growing. Hundreds of public schools were operating in North Carolina by 1860. Even before that, the Kentucky legislature set up a funding system for public schools. Many states also had charity schools for students whose parents could not afford to pay.

Although the number of schools and teachers in the South grew, the South lagged behind other sections of the country in **literacy,** the number of people who can read and write. One reason for this was the geography of the South. Even in the more heavily populated Southern states there were few people per square mile. Virginia and North Carolina had fewer than 15 white inhabitants per square mile. In contrast, Massachusetts had 124 inhabitants per square mile.

It was too great a hardship for many Southern families to send their children great distances to attend school. In addition, many Southerners believed education was a private matter, not a state function; therefore, the state should not spend money on education.

Reading Check **Describing** What Southern city had surpassed 200,000 in population by the year 1860?

HISTORY Online

Student Web Activity
Visit tarvol1.glencoe.co and click on **Chapter 13— Student Web Activities** for an activity on family life in the South.

SECTION 4 ASSESSMENT

Checking for Understanding

1. **Key Terms** Use the following terms to create a newspaper article about life in the South during this period of time: yeoman, tenant farmer, overseer, spiritual, slave code.

2. **Reviewing Facts** List two differences between yeomen and plantation owners.

Reviewing Themes

3. **Culture and Traditions** Why were extended families vital to African American culture?

Critical Thinking

4. **Making Generalizations** If you were a plantation owner, what would you tell your son or daughter if he or she asked why you held slaves?

5. **Classifying Information** Re-create the diagram below and in the boxes briefly explain how the slave codes operated.

Slave codes	
Control education	Control assembly

Analyzing Visuals

6. Look at the pictures on pages 402 and 404. Write a paragraph explaining what you think the pictures portray about life in the South.

Interdisciplinary Activity

Geography Research the economic activity of one of the Southern states. Draw a map of the state, and use symbols to represent each resource and show its location in the state.

Chapter Summary
North and South

North	South

Economy

- Growth of industrialization.
- Specialization and machinery allow for mass production.

- Cotton is leading cash crop.
- Industry limited due to lack of capital and market demand.

Transportation

- Roads, canals, and railroads being built.
- Locomotives improve during this era.

- Natural waterways chief means of transportation.
- Canals and roads are poor.
- Railroads are limited.

Way of Life

- Many people move to cities to find work.
- Cities grow crowded and many live in unhealthy and unsafe conditions.
- African Americans suffer discrimination and have few rights.

- Plantation owners farm large tracts of land; plantations are generally self-sufficient.
- Yeomen make up the largest group of whites.
- Tenant farmers farm small tracts of land.
- Enslaved African Americans do most of the work on plantations.

Reviewing Key Terms

On graph paper, create a word search puzzle using the following terms. Crisscross the terms vertically and horizontally, then fill in the remaining squares with extra letters. Use the terms' definitions as clues to find the words in the puzzle.

1. telegraph
2. nativist
3. overseer
4. yeoman
5. credit

Reviewing Key Facts

6. How did the development of the canal and rail network alter the trade route between the Midwest and the East Coast?
7. How did the the telegraph influence long-distance communication?
8. Provide three reasons why cities grew in the early 1800s.
9. What was the goal of workers going on strike?
10. In what ways were women in the workforce discriminated against?
11. Why did immigration from Germany increase after 1848?
12. How did the cotton gin affect cotton production?
13. Why was there little industry in the South?
14. What was the Underground Railroad?
15. What was the purpose of the slave codes?

Critical Thinking

16. **Analyzing Themes: Economic Factors** How did improvements in transportation affect the economy of the North?
17. **Comparing** Discuss one advantage and one disadvantage of city life in the North.
18. **Comparing** Re-create the diagram below and compare the use of railroads in the North and South before 1860.

	North	South
Use of railroads		

19. **Analyzing Information** Describe ways in which enslaved African Americans held on to their African customs.

HISTORY Online

Self-Check Quiz
Visit tarvol1.glencoe.com and click on **Chapter 13—Self-Check Quizzes** to prepare for the chapter test.

Practicing Skills

Reading a Circle Graph *Study the circle graphs below; then answer these questions.*

Populations of the North and South in 1860

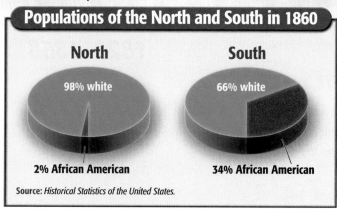

North
98% white
2% African American

South
66% white
34% African American

Source: *Historical Statistics of the United States.*

20. What does the information in the two graphs represent?

21. In what part of the country did African Americans make up more than one-third of the population?

22. Can you use the graphs to draw a conclusion about the total population of each region? Why or why not?

 Geography and History Activity

Study the map on page 388 and answer the questions that follow.

23. **Movement** In which direction would a train travel from Chattanooga, Tennessee, to Lynchburg, Virginia?

24. **Location** What was the easternmost city on the New York Central line?

25. **Movement** What cities would a train passenger pass through taking the most direct Memphis-to-Baltimore route?

Citizenship Cooperative Activity

26. **Community Issues** Working with two other students, contact the office of your local government to find out what is being done to solve local problems and how volunteers can help. Find out when the town board or city council meets. After you obtain the information, interview people in the neighborhood to find out what they think about various problems the community faces. Tell them about the town board or city council meetings, and encourage them to attend or to become involved in community activities. Compare your findings about community issues with the other groups.

Economics Activity

27. Although railroads helped the economy, why might investors in turnpikes and canals view them as a threat?

 Technology Activity

28. **Research and Writing** Use your text, encyclopedias, and other library resources for information about the lives of enslaved and free African Americans during this era. Write a report at least two pages in length in which you identify various political, economic, and social factors that affected their lives. Compare the effects these factors had on their lives.

 Alternative Assessment

29. **Portfolio Writing Activity** Write a conversation between a Southerner and Northerner who meet on a train in the mid-1800s. Have them talk about the differences between their lives. Use the notes from your journal in the script.

Standardized Test Practice

Directions: Choose the *best* answer to the following question.

Organizations of workers having the same skills or working within the same trade are called

A nativists.

B trade unions.

C yeomen.

D congressional committees.

Test-Taking Tip

Use the process of elimination to answer this question: Which answers can you rule out as definitely wrong?

CHAPTER 14

The Age of Reform

1820–1860

Why It Matters

The idea of reform—the drive to improve society and the lives of Americans—grew during the mid-1800s. Reformers set out to improve the lives of the disadvantaged, especially enslaved people and the urban poor.

The Impact Today

The spirit of reform is alive and well in the modern world. Individual freedom became a key goal during the last half of the twentieth century. Civil rights movements have advanced racial equality. In many countries the women's movement has altered traditional female roles and opportunities.

The American Republic to 1877 *Video* *The chapter 14 video, "Women and Reform," chronicles the role of women in the reform movements of the 1800s.*

1827
- New York bans slavery

1825
- New Harmony, Indiana, established

1836
- Texas gains independence

1830
- *Book of Mormon* published

United States PRESIDENTS	Monroe 1817–1825	J.Q. Adams 1825–1829	Jackson 1829–1837	Van Buren 1837–1841	W.H. Harrison 1841

1820   1830   1840

World

1821
- Mexico becomes independent nation

1837
- Victoria becomes queen of England

The Country School by Winslow Homer By the mid-1800s, the number of public elementary schools was growing.

1848
- Seneca Falls Convention

1851
- Maine bans sale of alcohol

1862
- Mary Jane Patterson is first African American woman to earn a college degree

| *Tyler* 1841–1845 | *Polk* 1845–1849 | *Taylor* 1849–1850 | *Fillmore* 1850–1853 | *Pierce* 1853–1857 | | *Buchanan* 1857–1861 |

1850   *1860*

1847
- Liberia claims independence

1850
- Taiping Rebellion begins in China

1853
- Crimean War begins

1859
- Lenoir builds first practical internal-combustion engine

HISTORY Online

Chapter Overview
Visit tarvol1.glencoe.com and click on **Chapter 14— Chapter Overviews** to preview chapter information.

Social Reform

Guide to Reading

Main Idea

During the early 1800s, many religious and social reformers attempted to improve American life and education and help people with disabilities.

Key Terms

utopia, revival, temperance, normal school, transcendentalist

Reading Strategy

Taking Notes As you read section 1, re-create the diagram below and identify these reformers' contributions.

	Contributions
Lyman Beecher	
Horace Mann	
Thomas Gallaudet	
Dorothea Dix	

Read to Learn

- how religious and philosophical ideas inspired various reform movements.
- why educational reformers thought all citizens should go to school.

Section Theme

Civic Rights and Responsibilities Many reformers worked for change during this era.

Preview of Events

◆1820	◆1830	◆1840	◆1850
1825 Robert Owen establishes New Harmony, Indiana	**1835** Oberlin College admits African Americans	**1837** Horace Mann initiates education reform	**1843** Dorothea Dix reveals abuses of mentally ill

Henry David Thoreau

AN American Story

According to folklore, Henry David Thoreau sat on the hard, wooden bench in the jail cell, but he did not complain about its stiffness. He felt proud that he had stood up for his beliefs. Thoreau had refused to pay a one-dollar tax to vote, not wanting his money to support the Mexican War. As he looked through the cell bars, he heard a voice. "Why are you here?" asked his friend Ralph Waldo Emerson. Thoreau replied, "Why are you *not* here?" He would later write, "Under a government which imprisons any unjustly, the true place for a just man is also a prison."

The Reforming Spirit

Thoreau represented a new spirit of reform in America. The men and women who led the reform movement wanted to extend the nation's ideals of liberty and equality to all Americans. They believed the nation should live up to the noble goals stated in the Declaration of Independence and the Constitution.

The spirit of reform brought changes to American religion, politics, education, art, and literature. Some reformers sought to improve society by forming utopias, communities based on a vision of a perfect society. In 1825 Robert Owen established New Harmony, Indiana, a village dedicated to cooperation rather than competition among its members.

chained to the walls with little or no clothing, often in unheated cells. To her further horror, she learned that some of the inmates were guilty of no crime—they were mentally ill persons. Dix made it her life's work to educate the public as to the poor conditions for both the mentally ill and for prisoners.

Reading Check **Identifying** How did Dr. Samuel Howe help the visually impaired?

Cultural Trends

The changes in American society influenced art and literature. Earlier generations of American painters and writers looked to Europe for their inspiration and models. Beginning in the 1820s American artists developed their own style and explored American themes.

The American spirit of reform influenced transcendentalists. Transcendentalists stressed the relationship between humans and nature as well as the importance of the individual conscience. Writers such as Margaret Fuller, Ralph Waldo Emerson, and Henry David Thoreau were leading transcendentalists. Through her writings, Fuller supported rights for women. In his poems and essays, Emerson urged people to listen to the inner voice of conscience and to break the bonds of prejudice. Thoreau put his beliefs into practice through **civil disobedience** —refusing to obey laws he thought were unjust. In 1846 Thoreau went to jail rather than pay a tax to support the Mexican War.

The transcendentalists were not the only important writers of the period. Many poets created impresive works during this period. Henry Wadsworth Longfellow wrote narrative, or story, poems, such as the *Song of Hiawatha*. Poet Walt Whitman captured the new American spirit and confidence in his *Leaves of Grass*. Emily Dickinson wrote simple, deeply personal poems. In a poem called "Hope," written in 1861, she compares hope with a bird:

> 66 'Hope' is the thing with feathers—
> That perches in the soul—
> And sings the tune without the words—
> And never stops—at all— 99

Women writers of the period were generally not taken seriously, yet they were the authors of the most popular fiction. Harriet Beecher Stowe wrote the most successful best-seller of the mid-1800s, *Uncle Tom's Cabin*. Stowe's novel explores the injustice of slavery—an issue that took on new urgency during the age of reform.

Reading Check **Describing** What was one of the subjects that Margaret Fuller wrote about?

SECTION 1 ASSESSMENT

Checking for Understanding

1. **Key Terms** Use each of these terms in a sentence that helps explain its meaning: utopia, revival, temperance, normal school, transcendentalist.
2. **Reviewing Facts** What were the three accepted principles of public education in the 1850s?

Reviewing Themes

3. **Civic Rights and Responsibilities** How did Thoreau act on his beliefs? What impact might such acts have had on the government?

Critical Thinking

4. **Drawing Conclusions** What did Thomas Jefferson mean when he said that the United States could not survive as a democracy without educated and well-informed citizens?
5. **Determining Cause and Effect** Re-create the diagram below and describe two ways the religious movement influenced reform.

```
Religious        ┌──────────┐
movement ────────┤          │
                 └──────────┘
                 ┌──────────┐
           ──────┤          │
                 └──────────┘
```

Analyzing Visuals

6. **Picturing History** Study the painting of the school room on page 414. What is pictured that you still use in school today?

Interdisciplinary Activity

Research Interview your grandparents or other adults who are over 50 years old to find out what they remember about their public school days. Before you do the interview, write six questions about the information that interests you.

What were people's lives like in the past?

What—and who—were people talking about? What did they eat? What did they do for fun? These two pages will give you some clues to everyday life in the U.S. as you step back in time with TIME Notebook.

Profile

"My best friends solemnly regard me as a madman." That's what the artist **JOHN JAMES AUDUBON** (left) writes about himself in his journal. And he does seem to be a bit peculiar. After all, he put a band around a bird's foot so he could tell if it returned from the South in the spring. No one's ever done that before. Audubon is growing more famous thanks to his drawings. His love of the wild and his skill as an artist have awakened a new sense of appreciation for American animal life both here and in Europe. Here is what he wrote recently while on a trip to New Orleans:

"I TOOK A WALK WITH MY GUN THIS afternoon to see… millions of Golden Plovers [medium-sized shorebirds] coming from the northeast and going nearly south— the destruction… was really astonishing—the Sportsmen here are more numerous and at the same time more expert at shooting on the wing than anywhere in the United States."

Baseball for Beginners

Want to take up the new game of baseball? Keep your eye on the ball—because the rules keep changing!

1845
- canvas bases are set 90 feet apart in a diamond shape
- only nine men play on each side
- pitches are thrown underhanded
- a ball caught on the first bounce is an "out"

1846
- at first base, a fielder can tag the bag before the runner reaches it and so make an out

1847
- players may no longer throw the ball at a runner to put him out

Americans Living on Farms

1790: 95% of Americans live on farms

1820: 93% live on farms

1850: 85% live on farms

Personalities Meet Some Concord Residents

YEARS AGO, ONE OF THE FIRST BATTLES OF THE REVOLUTIONARY WAR was fought at Concord, Massachusetts. But now the sparks that fly are of a more intellectual variety. If you want to visit Concord, you should read some of the works of its residents.

Nathaniel Hawthorne
This writer's novel *The Scarlet Letter* moved some readers, and outraged others.

Henry Wadsworth Longfellow
Writes poems about Paul Revere, Hiawatha, and a village blacksmith.

Louisa May Alcott
Author of *Little Women* who published her first book at age 16.

Louisa May Alcott

MILESTONES

PEOPLE AND EVENTS OF THE TIME

Frederick Douglass

EMIGRATED. In 1845, to England, **FREDERICK DOUGLASS**, former slave, author, and abolitionist leader, to escape danger in reaction to his autobiography, *Narrative of the Life of Frederick Douglass.*

MOVED. HENRY DAVID THOREAU, writer, to Walden Pond, Concord, Massachusetts, in 1845. Thoreau intends to build his own house on the shore of the pond and earn his living by the labor of his hands only. "Many of the so-called comforts of life," writes Thoreau, "are not only not indispensable, but positive hindrances to the elevation of mankind."

AILING. EDGAR ALLAN POE, in Baltimore, 1847, following the death of his wife, Virginia. Other than a poem on death, Poe has written little this year, devoting his dwindling energies to lawsuits against other authors he claims copied his work.

INVENTED. Samuel F.B. Morse has revolutionized communications with a series of dots and dashes in 1844.

Edgar Allan Poe

NUMBERS

U.S. AT THE TIME

9,022 Miles of railways operating in 1850

- - - - - - - - - - - - - - -

3 Number of U.S. Presidents in 1841—Van Buren's term ended, Harrison died, and Tyler took his place

- - - - - - - - - - - - - - -

29 Number of medical schools Elizabeth Blackwell, a woman, applied to before being accepted at one in 1847

- - - - - - - - - - - - - - -

700 Number of New England whaling ships at sea in 1846

- - - - - - - - - - - - - - -

$8 Approximate yearly cost for a newspaper subscription in 1830

- - - - - - - - - - - - - - -

50% Approximate percentage of the American workforce in 1820 under the age of 10

CHILD LABOR

Letter From a Mill Worker

Mary Paul is a worker in her teens at a textile mill in Lowell, Massachusetts. Mary works 12 hours a day, 6 days a week. She sent this letter to her father:

Dear Father,

I am well which is one comfort. My life and health are spared while others are cut off. Last Thursday one girl fell down and broke her neck which caused instant death. Last Tuesday we were paid. In all I had six dollars and sixty cents, paid $4.68 for board [rent and food]....At 5 o'clock in the morning the bell rings for the folks to get up and get breakfast. At half past six it rings for the girls to get up and at seven they are called into the mill. At half past 12 we have dinner, are called back again at one and stay till half past seven. . . . If any girl wants employment, I advise them to come to Lowell.

Guide to Reading

Main Idea
Many reformers turned their attention to eliminating slavery.

Key Terms
abolitionist, Underground Railroad

Reading Strategy
Organizing Information As you read Section 2, identify five abolitionists. Below each name, write a sentence describing his or her role in the movement.

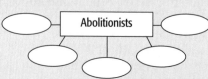

Abolitionists

Read to Learn
• how some Americans worked to eliminate slavery.
• why many Americans feared the end of slavery.

Section Theme
Individual Action Leaders such as Harriet Tubman and William Lloyd Garrison strengthened the abolitionist movement.

Preview of Events

◆1815   ◆1830   ◆1845   ◆1860

1816
American Colonization Society is formed

1822
First African Americans settle in Liberia

1831
William Lloyd Garrison founds *The Liberator*

1847
Liberia becomes an independent country

William Lloyd Garrison

AN American Story

William Lloyd Garrison, a dramatic and spirited man, fought strongly for the right of African Americans to be free. On one occasion Garrison was present when Frederick Douglass, an African American who had escaped from slavery, spoke to a white audience about life as a slave. Douglass electrified his listeners with a powerful speech. Suddenly Garrison leaped to his feet. "Is this a man," he demanded of the audience, "or a thing?" Garrison shared Douglass's outrage at the notion that people could be bought and sold like objects.

Early Efforts to End Slavery

The spirit of reform that swept the United States in the early 1800s was not limited to improving education and expanding the arts. It also included the efforts of abolitionists like Garrison and Douglass—members of the growing band of reformers who worked to abolish, or end, slavery.

Even before the American Revolution, some Americans had tried to limit or end slavery. At the Constitutional Convention in 1787, the delegates had reached a compromise on the difficult issue, agreeing to let each state decide whether to allow slavery. By the early 1800s, Northern states had ended slavery, but it continued in the South.

The religious revival and the reform movement of the early and mid-1800s gave new life to the antislavery movement. Many Americans came to believe that slavery was wrong. Yet not all Northerners shared this view. The conflict over slavery continued to build.

Many of the men and women who led the antislavery movement came from the Quaker faith. One Quaker, Benjamin Lundy, wrote:

❝I heard the wail of the captive. I felt his pang of distress, and the iron entered my soul.❞

Lundy founded a newspaper in 1821 to spread the abolitionist message.

American Colonization Society

The first large-scale antislavery effort was not aimed at abolishing slavery but at resettling African Americans in Africa or the Caribbean. The **American Colonization Society,** formed in 1816 by a group of white Virginians, worked to free enslaved workers gradually by buying them from slaveholders and sending them abroad to start new lives.

The society raised enough money from private donors, Congress, and a few state legislatures to send several groups of African Americans out of the country. Some went to the west coast of Africa, where the society had acquired land for a colony. In 1822 the first African American settlers arrived in this colony, called **Liberia,** Latin for "place of freedom."

In 1847 Liberia became an independent country. American emigration to Liberia continued until the Civil War. Some 12,000 to 20,000 African Americans settled in the new country between 1822 and 1865.

The American Colonization Society did not halt the growth of slavery. The number of enslaved people continued to increase at a steady pace, and the society could only resettle a small number of African Americans. Furthermore, most African Americans did not want to go to Africa. Many were from families that had lived in America for several generations. They simply wanted to be free in American society. African Americans feared that the society aimed to strengthen slavery.

✓ **Reading Check** **Explaining** How did the American Colonization Society fight slavery?

The Movement Changes

Reformers realized that the gradual approach to ending slavery had failed. Moreover, the numbers of enslaved persons had sharply increased because the cotton boom in the Deep South made planters increasingly dependent on slave labor. Beginning in about 1830, the American antislavery movement took on new life. Soon it became the most pressing social issue for reformers.

William Lloyd Garrison

Abolitionist **William Lloyd Garrison** stimulated the growth of the antislavery movement. In 1829 Garrison left Massachusetts to work for the country's leading antislavery newspaper in Baltimore. Impatient with the paper's moderate position, Garrison returned to Boston in 1831 to found his own newspaper, *The Liberator.*

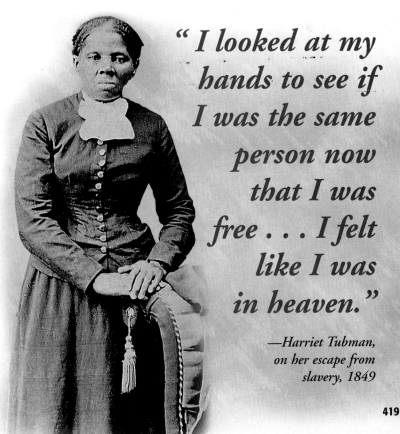

" *I looked at my hands to see if I was the same person now that I was free . . . I felt like I was in heaven.*"

—*Harriet Tubman, on her escape from slavery, 1849*

TWO VIEWPOINTS

Is American Slavery Compassionate or Cruel?

More than any other factor, slavery isolated the South from the rest of the United States. While abolitionists cried out to bring the cruel practice to an end, Southern slaveholders defended the only way of life they knew.

Sojourner Truth, former slave, 1851

Look at me! Look at my arm! I have ploughed, and planted, and gathered into barns, and no man could head me! . . . I could work as much and eat as much as a man—when I could get it—and bear the lash as well! And ain't I a woman?

I have borne thirteen children, and seen them most all sold off to slavery, and when I cried out with my mother's grief, none but Jesus heard me! And ain't I a woman?

Sojourner Truth

Jeremiah Jeter, Southern slaveholder, c. 1820

I could not free them, for the laws of the State forbade it. Yet even if they had not forbidden it, the slaves in my possession were in no condition to support themselves. It was simple cruelty to free a mother with dependent children. Observation, too, had satisfied me that the free negroes were, in general, in a worse condition than the slaves. The manumission [setting free] of my slaves to remain in the State was not to be thought of. Should I send them to Liberia? Some of them were in a condition to go, but none of them desired to. If sent, they [would] be forced to leave wives and children belonging to other masters [on nearby plantations], to dwell in a strange land.

Learning From History

1. Why do you think Sojourner Truth was an effective speaker?
2. Why didn't Jeremiah Jeter just free his slaves?
3. Do the two excerpts contradict each other? In what way?

Garrison was one of the first white abolitionists to call for the "immediate and complete emancipation [freeing]" of enslaved people. Promising to be "as harsh as truth, and as uncompromising as justice," he denounced the slow, gradual approach of other reformers. In the first issue of his paper he wrote: "I will not retreat a single inch—AND I WILL BE HEARD."

Garrison *was* heard. He attracted enough followers to start the New England Antislavery Society in 1832 and the American Antislavery Society the next year. The **abolitionist movement** grew rapidly. By 1838 the antislavery societies Garrison started had more than 1,000 chapters, or local branches.

The Grimké Sisters

Among the first women who spoke out publicly against slavery were **Sarah** and **Angelina Grimké.** Born in South Carolina to a wealthy slaveholding family, the sisters moved to Philadelphia in 1832.

In the North the Grimké sisters lectured and wrote against slavery. At one antislavery meeting, Angelina Grimké exclaimed,

> 66As a Southerner, I feel that it is my duty to stand up . . . against slavery. I have seen it! I have seen it!99

The Grimkés persuaded their mother to give them their share of the family inheritance. Instead of money or land, the sisters asked for several of the enslaved workers, whom they immediately freed.

Angelina Grimké and her husband, abolitionist Theodore Weld, wrote *American Slavery As It Is* in 1839. This collection of firsthand accounts of life under slavery was one of the most influential abolitionist publications of its time.

African American Abolitionists

Although white abolitionists drew public attention to the cause, African Americans themselves played a major role in the abolitionist movement from the start. The abolition of slavery was an especially important goal to the free African Americans of the North.

Most African Americans in the North lived in poverty in cities. Although they were excluded from most jobs and were often attacked by white mobs, a great many of these African Americans were intensely proud of their freedom and wanted to help those who were still enslaved.

African Americans took an active part in organizing and directing the American Antislavery Society, and they subscribed in large numbers to William Lloyd Garrison's *The Liberator.* In 1827 Samuel Cornish and John Russwurm started the country's first African American newspaper, *Freedom's Journal.* Most of the other newspapers that African Americans founded before the Civil War also promoted abolition.

Born a free man in North Carolina, writer **David Walker** of Boston published an impassioned argument against slavery, challenging African Americans to rebel and overthrow slavery by force. "America is more our country than it is the whites'—we have enriched it with our blood and tears," he wrote.

In 1830 free African American leaders held their first convention in Philadelphia. Delegates met "to devise ways and means for the bettering of our condition." They discussed starting an African American college and encouraging free African Americans to emigrate to Canada.

Frederick Douglass

Frederick Douglass, the most widely known African American abolitionist, was born enslaved in Maryland. After teaching himself to read and write, he escaped from slavery in Maryland in 1838 and settled first in Massachusetts and then in New York.

As a runaway, Douglass could have been captured and returned to slavery. Still, he joined the Massachusetts Antislavery Society and traveled widely to address abolitionist meetings. A powerful speaker, Douglass often moved listeners to tears with his message. At an Independence Day gathering he told the audience:

HISTORY Online

Student Web Activity
Visit tarvol1.glencoe.com and click on **Chapter 14— Student Web Activities** for an activity on the abolitionist movement.

66What, to the American slave, is your Fourth of July? I answer: a day that reveals to him, more than all other days in the year, the gross injustice and cruelty to which he is the constant victim. To him, your celebration is a sham . . . your national greatness, swelling vanity; your sounds of rejoicing are empty and heartless . . . your shouts of liberty and equality, hollow mockery.99

For 16 years, Douglass edited an antislavery newspaper called the *North Star.* Douglass won admiration as a powerful and influential speaker and writer. He traveled abroad, speaking to huge antislavery audiences in London and the West Indies.

Douglass returned to the United States because he believed abolitionists must fight slavery at its source. He insisted that African Americans receive not just their freedom but full equality with whites as well. In 1847 friends helped Douglass purchase his freedom from the slaveholder from whom he had fled in Maryland.

Sojourner Truth

"I was born a slave in Ulster County, New York," Isabella Baumfree began when she told her story to audiences. Called "Belle," she lived in the cellar of a slaveholder's house. She escaped in 1826 and gained official freedom in 1827 when New York banned slavery. She eventually settled in New York City.

In 1843 Belle chose a new name. "**Sojourner Truth** is my name," she said, "because from this day I will walk in the light of [God's] truth." She began to work in the movements for abolitionism and for women's rights.

✓ **Reading Check** **Explaining** Why did Frederick Douglass return to the United States?

MORE ABOUT...

The Underground Railroad

The Underground Railroad was neither "underground" nor a "railroad." It was a secret organization to help African Americans escape from slavery. The escape of Henry Brown is one of the most remarkable stories in the history of the Underground Railroad.

Henry Brown Henry "Box" Brown escaped slavery by having himself sealed into a small box and shipped from Richmond to Philadelphia. Although "this side up" was marked on the crate, he spent a good part of the trip upside down. When news of his escape spread, he wrote an autobiography and spoke to many anti-slavery groups.

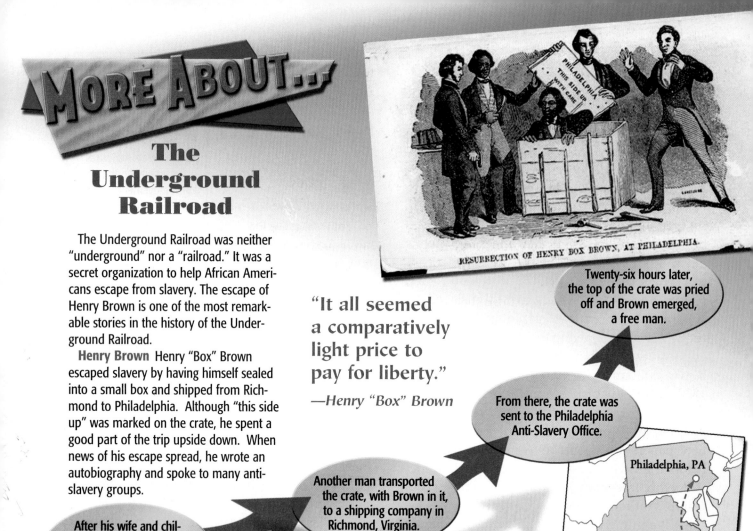

RESURRECTION OF HENRY BOX BROWN, AT PHILADELPHIA.

"It all seemed a comparatively light price to pay for liberty."
—Henry "Box" Brown

After his wife and children were sold to a slaveholder in another state, Brown was determined to escape.

Another man transported the crate, with Brown in it, to a shipping company in Richmond, Virginia.

From there, the crate was sent to the Philadelphia Anti-Slavery Office.

Twenty-six hours later, the top of the crate was pried off and Brown emerged, a free man.

Philadelphia, PA

Richmond, VA

The Underground Railroad

Some abolitionists risked prison—even death—by secretly helping African Americans escape from slavery. The network of escape routes from the South to the North came to be called the Underground Railroad.

The Underground Railroad had no trains or tracks. Instead, passengers on this "railroad" traveled through the night, often on foot, and went north—guided by the North Star. The runaway slaves followed rivers and mountain chains, or felt for moss growing on the north side of trees.

Songs such as "Follow the Drinkin' Gourd" encouraged runaways on their way to freedom. A hollowed-out gourd was used to dip water for drinking. Its shape resembled the Big Dipper, which pointed to the North Star.

66When the river ends in between two hills,
Follow the drinkin' gourd,
For the Ole Man's waitin' for to carry you
to freedom.
Follow the drinkin' gourd.99

During the day passengers rested at "stations"—barns, attics, church basements, or other places where fugitives could rest, eat, and hide until the next night's journey. The railroad's "conductors" were whites and African Americans who helped guide the escaping slaves to freedom in the North.

In the early days, many people made the journey north on foot. Later they traveled in wagons, sometimes equipped with secret compartments. African Americans on the Underground Railroad hoped to settle in a free state in the North or to move on to Canada. Once in the North, however, fugitives still feared capture. Henry Bibb, a runaway who reached Ohio, arrived at "the place where I was directed to call on an Abolitionist, but I made no stop: so great were my fears of being pursued."

After her escape from slavery, Harriet Tubman became the most famous conductor on the Underground Railroad. Slaveholders offered a large reward for Tubman's capture or death.

The Underground Railroad helped only a tiny fraction of the enslaved population. Most who used it as a route to freedom came from the states located between the northern states and the Deep South. Still, the Underground Railroad gave hope to those who suffered in slavery. It also provided abolitionists with a way to help some enslaved people to freedom.

Clashes Over Abolitionism

The antislavery movement led to an intense reaction against abolitionism. Southern slaveholders—and many Southerners who did not have slaves—opposed abolitionism because they believed it threatened the South's way of life, which depended on enslaved labor. Many people in the North also opposed the abolitionist movement.

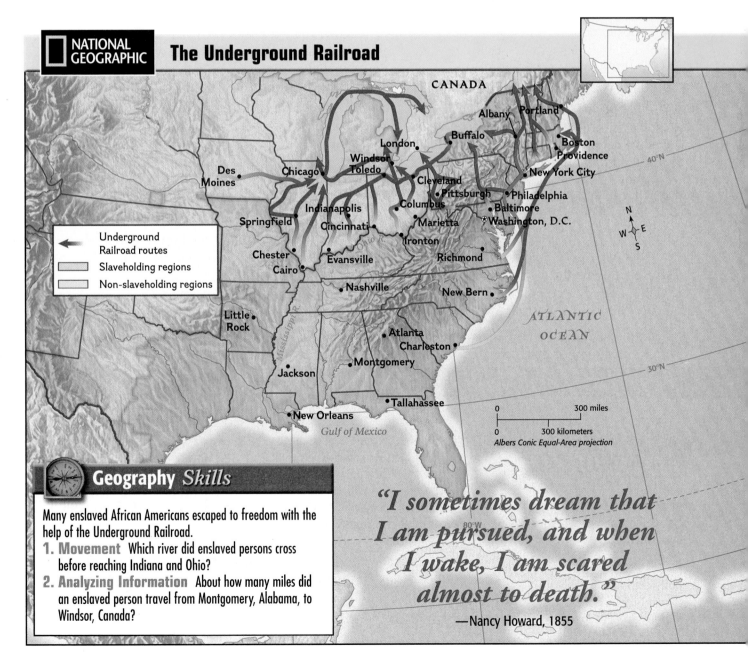

NATIONAL GEOGRAPHIC

The Underground Railroad

Underground Railroad routes

Slaveholding regions

Non-slaveholding regions

CANADA

Albany · Portland · Buffalo · London · Windsor · Toledo · Cleveland · Pittsburgh · Philadelphia · Columbus · Baltimore · Marietta · Washington, D.C. · Boston · Providence · New York City · Chicago · Des Moines · Indianapolis · Springfield · Cincinnati · Ironton · Chester · Evansville · Richmond · Cairo · Nashville · New Bern · Little Rock · Atlanta · Charleston · Montgomery · Jackson · Tallahassee · New Orleans

ATLANTIC OCEAN

Gulf of Mexico

40°N
30°N
80°W

0   300 miles
0   300 kilometers
Albers Conic Equal-Area projection

Geography *Skills*

Many enslaved African Americans escaped to freedom with the help of the Underground Railroad.

1. **Movement** Which river did enslaved persons cross before reaching Indiana and Ohio?

2. **Analyzing Information** About how many miles did an enslaved person travel from Montgomery, Alabama, to Windsor, Canada?

"I sometimes dream that I am pursued, and when I wake, I am scared almost to death."

—Nancy Howard, 1855

Opposition in the North

Even in the North, abolitionists never numbered more than a small fraction of the population. Many Northerners saw the antislavery movement as a threat to the nation's social order. They feared the abolitionists could bring on a destructive war between the North and the South. They also claimed that, if the enslaved African Americans were freed, they could never blend into American society.

Economic fears further fed the backlash against abolitionism. Northern workers worried that freed slaves would flood the North and take jobs away from whites by agreeing to work for lower pay.

Opposition to abolitionism sometimes erupted into violence against the abolitionists themselves. In the 1830s a Philadelphia mob burned the city's antislavery headquarters to the ground and set off a bloody race riot. In Boston a mob attacked abolitionist William Lloyd Garrison and threatened to hang him. Authorities saved his life by locking him in jail.

Elijah Lovejoy was not so lucky. Lovejoy edited an abolitionist newspaper in Illinois. Three times angry whites invaded his offices and wrecked his presses. Each time Lovejoy installed new presses and resumed publication. The fourth time the mob set fire to the building. When Lovejoy came out of the blazing building, he was shot and killed.

The South Reacts

Southerners fought abolitionism by mounting arguments in defense of slavery. They claimed that slavery was essential to the South. Slave labor, they said, had allowed Southern whites to reach a high level of culture.

Southerners also argued that they treated enslaved people well. Some Southerners argued that Northern workers were worse off than slaves. The industrial economy of the North employed factory workers for long hours at low wages. These jobs were repetitive and often dangerous, and Northern workers had to pay for their goods from their small earnings. Unlike the "wage slavery" of the North, Southerners said that the system of slavery provided food, clothing, and medical care to the workers.

Other defenses of slavery were based on racism. Many whites believed that African Americans were better off under white care than on their own. "Providence has placed [the slave] in our hands for his own good," declared one Southern governor.

The conflict between proslavery and antislavery groups continued to mount. At the same time, a new women's rights movement was growing, and many leading abolitionists were involved in that movement as well.

Reading Check **Explaining** Why did many Northerners oppose the abolition of slavery?

SECTION 2 ASSESSMENT

Checking for Understanding

1. **Key Terms** Write a short paragraph in which you use these key terms: abolitionist, Underground Railroad.

2. **Reviewing Facts** Describe the American Colonization Society's solution to slavery.

Reviewing Themes

3. **Individual Action** What role did Harriet Tubman play in the antislavery movement?

Critical Thinking

4. **Comparing** Compare the arguments of Northerners with Southerners who opposed abolitionism.

5. **Organizing Information** Use a diagram like the one below to identify actions that abolitionists took to free enslaved people.

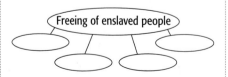
Freeing of enslaved people

Analyzing Visuals

6. **Geography Skills** Study the map of the Underground Railroad on page 423. Why do you think more enslaved people escaped from the border states than from the Deep South?

The Women's Movement

Guide to Reading

Main Idea
Women reformers campaigned for their own rights.

Key Terms
suffrage, coeducation

Reading Strategy
Taking Notes As you read the section, use a chart like the one below to identify the contributions these individuals made to women's rights.

	Contributions
Lucretia Mott	
Elizabeth Cady Stanton	
Susan B. Anthony	
Elizabeth Blackwell	

Read to Learn
• how the antislavery and the women's rights movements were related.
• what progress women made toward equality during the 1800s.

Section Theme
Groups and Institutions Women in the 1800s made some progress toward equality.

Preview of Events

♦1830　　　　　　　　　　　♦1860　　　　　　　　　　　♦1890

1837
Mary Lyon establishes Mount Holyoke Female Seminary

1848
First women's rights convention held in Seneca Falls, New York

1857
Elizabeth Blackwell founds the New York Infirmary for Women and Children

1869
Wyoming Territory grants women the right to vote

Mary Lyon, pioneer in higher education for women

AN American Story

Women who fought to end slavery began to recognize their own bondage. On April 19, 1850, about 400 women met at a Quaker meetinghouse in the small town of Salem, Ohio. They came together "to assert their rights as independent human beings." One speaker stated: "I use the term *Woman's Rights,* because it is a technical phrase. I like not the expression. It is not Woman's *Rights* of which I design to speak, but of Woman's *Wrongs.* I shall claim nothing for ourselves because of our sex. . . . [W]e should demand *our* recognition as equal members of the human family. . . ."

Women and Reform

Many women abolitionists also worked for women's rights. They launched a struggle to improve women's lives and win equal rights. Like many of the women reformers, **Lucretia Mott** was a Quaker. Quaker women enjoyed a certain amount of equality in their own communities. Mott gave lectures in Philadelphia calling for temperance, peace, workers' rights, and abolition. Mott

Raising the Status of Women

The Seneca Falls Convention

Throughout the nation's history, women had fought side by side with the men to build a new nation and to ensure freedom. Even though the Declaration of Independence promised equality for all, the promise rang hollow for women.

Female reformers began a campaign for their own rights. In 1848 Lucretia Mott and Elizabeth Cady Stanton organized the Seneca Falls Convention. One of the resolutions demanded suffrage, or the right to vote, for women. This marked the beginning of a long, hard road to gain equal rights.

Lucretia Mott (below) and Susan B. Anthony were leaders in the effort to allow women a greater role in American society.

"We hold these truths to be self-evident: that all men and women are created equal."
— *Declaration of the Seneca Falls Convention, 1848*

Gaining the Right to Vote, 1848–1920

The Seneca Falls Convention led to the growth of the woman suffrage movement.

1848	1850	1866	1869	1878	1884
Seneca Falls Convention	First national women's rights convention held in Worcester, Massachusetts	Susan B. Anthony forms Equal Rights Association	Women granted voting rights in Wyoming Territory	Woman suffrage amendment first introduced in U.S. Congress	Belva Lockwood runs for president

also helped fugitive slaves and organized the Philadelphia Female Anti-Slavery Society. At the world antislavery convention in London, Mott met **Elizabeth Cady Stanton.** There the two female abolitionists joined forces to work for women's rights.

The Seneca Falls Convention

In July 1848, Elizabeth Cady Stanton, Lucretia Mott, and a few other women organized the first women's rights convention in **Seneca Falls, New York.** About 200 women and 40 men attended.

The convention issued a Declaration of Sentiments and Resolutions modeled on the Declaration of Independence. The women's document declared: "We hold these truths to be self-evident: that all men and women are created equal."

The women's declaration called for an end to all laws that discriminated against women. It demanded that women be allowed to enter the all-male world of trades, professions, and businesses. The most controversial issue at the Seneca Falls Convention concerned suffrage, or the right to vote.

Elizabeth Stanton insisted that the declaration include a demand for woman suffrage, but delegates thought the idea of women voting was too radical. Lucretia Mott told her friend, "Lizzie, thee will make us ridiculous." Frederick Douglass stood with Stanton and argued powerfully for women's right to vote. After a heated debate the convention voted to include the demand for woman suffrage in the United States. (See page 617 of the Appendix for excerpts of the Seneca Falls Declaration.)

Maria Mitchell gained world renown when she discovered a comet in 1847. She became a professor of astronomy and the first woman elected to the American Academy of Arts and Sciences.

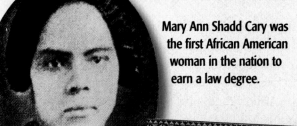

Mary Ann Shadd Cary was the first African American woman in the nation to earn a law degree.

Elizabeth Blackwell was the first woman to receive a medical degree in the United States.

Helen Keller overcame the challenges of an illness that left her deaf, blind, and mute to help others with similar disabilities.

Susette La Flesche was a member of the Omaha tribe and campaigned for Native American rights.

1893 ➔ Colorado adopts woman suffrage

1896 ➔ Utah joins the Union, granting women full suffrage

1910–1918 ➔ States including Washington, Kansas, and Michigan adopt woman suffrage

1919 ➔ House and Senate pass the federal woman suffrage amendment

1920 ➔ Tennessee ratifies the Nineteenth Amendment, called the Susan B. Anthony Amendment. It becomes law on August 26, 1920.

The Movement Grows

The Seneca Falls Convention paved the way for the growth of the **women's rights movement.** During the 1800s women held several national conventions. Many reformers—male and female—joined the movement.

Susan B. Anthony, the daughter of a Quaker abolitionist in rural New York, worked for women's rights and temperance. She called for equal pay for women, college training for girls, and coeducation—the teaching of boys and girls together. Anthony organized the country's first women's temperance association, the Daughters of Temperance.

Susan B. Anthony met Elizabeth Cady Stanton at a temperance meeting in 1851. They became lifelong friends and partners in the struggle for women's rights. For the rest of the century, Anthony and Stanton led the women's movement. They worked with other women to win the right to vote. Beginning with Wyoming in 1890, several states granted women the right to vote. It was not until 1920, however, that woman suffrage became a reality everywhere in the United States.

✓ Reading Check **Explaining** What is suffrage?

Progress by American Women

Pioneers in women's education began to call for more opportunity. Early pioneers such as Catherine Beecher and Emma Hart Willard believed that women should be educated for their traditional roles in life. They also thought that women could be capable teachers. The Milwaukee College for Women set up courses based on Beecher's ideas "to train women to be healthful, intelligent, and successful wives, mothers, and housekeepers."

Education

After her marriage Emma Willard educated herself in subjects considered suitable only for boys, such as science and mathematics. In 1821 Willard established the Troy Female Seminary in upstate New York. Willard's Troy Female Seminary taught mathematics, history, geography, and physics, as well as the usual homemaking subjects.

Mary Lyon established Mount Holyoke Female Seminary in Massachusetts in 1837. She modeled its curriculum on that of nearby Amherst College. Some young women began to make their own opportunities. They broke the barriers to female education and helped other women do the same.

Marriage and Family Laws

During the 1800s women made some gains in the area of marriage and property laws. New York, Pennsylvania, Indiana, Wisconsin, Mississippi, and the new state of California recognized the right of women to own property after their marriage.

Some states passed laws permitting women to share the guardianship of their children jointly with their husbands. Indiana was the first of several states that allowed women to seek divorce if their husbands were chronic abusers of alcohol.

Breaking Barriers

In the 1800s women had few career choices. They could become elementary teachers—although school boards often paid lower salaries to women than to men. Breaking into fields such as medicine and the ministry was more difficult. Some strong-minded women, however, succeeded in entering these all-male professions.

Hoping to study medicine, **Elizabeth Blackwell** was turned down by more than 20 schools. Finally accepted by Geneva College in New York, Blackwell graduated at the head of her class. She went on to win acceptance and fame as a doctor.

Despite the accomplishments of notable women, gains in education, and changes in state laws, women in the 1800s remained limited by social customs and expectations. The early feminists—like the abolitionists, temperance workers, and other activists of the age of reform—had just begun the long struggle to achieve their goals.

Reading Check **Identifying** Who established the Troy Female Seminary?

SECTION 3 ASSESSMENT

Checking for Understanding

1. **Key Terms** Define the following terms: suffrage, coeducation.
2. **Reviewing Facts** How did the fight to end slavery help spark the women's movement?

Reviewing Themes

3. **Groups and Institutions** Discuss three specific goals of the women's rights movement.

Critical Thinking

4. **Making Generalizations** What qualities do you think women such as Sojourner Truth, Susan B. Anthony, Elizabeth Cady Stanton, and Elizabeth Blackwell shared?
5. **Organizing Information** Re-create the diagram below and list the areas where women gained rights.

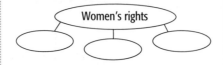

Women's rights

Analyzing Visuals

6. **Sequencing Information** Study the information on the feature on the Seneca Falls Convention on pages 426–427. When did Wyoming women gain the right to vote? What "first" did Elizabeth Blackwell accomplish?

Interdisciplinary Activity

Music Write and record a song designed to win supporters for the women's rights movement. Include lyrics that will draw both men and women supporters.

SKILLBUILDER

Evaluating a Web Site

Why Learn This Skill?

The Internet has become a valuable research tool. It is convenient to use, and the information contained on the Internet is plentiful. However, some Web site information is not necessarily accurate or reliable. When using the Internet as a research tool, the user must distinguish between quality information and inaccurate or incomplete information.

Learning the Skill

There are a number of things to consider when evaluating a Web site. Most important is to check the accuracy of the source and content. The author and publisher or sponsor of the site should be clearly indicated. The user must also determine the usefulness of the site. The information on the site should be current, and the design and organization of the site should be appealing and easy to navigate.

To evaluate a Web site, ask yourself the following questions:
- Are the facts on the site documented?
- Is more than one source used for background information within the site?
- Does the site contain a bibliography?
- Are the links within the site appropriate and up-to-date?
- Is the author clearly identified?
- Does the site explore the topic in-depth?
- Does the site contain links to other useful resources?
- Is the information easy to access? Is it properly labeled?
- Is the design appealing?

Practicing the Skill

Visit the Web site featured on this page at www. nationalgeographic.com/features/99/railroad/ and answer the following questions.

1. Who is the author or sponsor of the Web site?

2. What links does the site contain? Are they appropriate to the topic?

3. Does the site explore the topic in-depth? Why or why not?

4. Is the design of the site appealing? Why or why not?

5. What role did William Still play on the Underground Railroad? How easy or difficult was it to locate this information?

Applying the Skill

Comparing Web Sites Locate two other Web sites about the Underground Railroad. Evaluate them for accuracy and usefulness. Then compare them to the site featured above.

Chapter Summary
The Age of Reform

Utopian communities
- Groups start small voluntary communities to put their idealistic ideas into practice.

Religion
- Great revival meetings, the building of new churches, and the founding of scores of colleges and universities mark the Second Great Awakening.

Temperance
- Reformers work to control consumption of alcohol.

Education
- A movement grows to improve education, make school attendance compulsory, and help students with special needs.

Abolition
- Reformers work to help enslaved people escape to freedom and to ban slavery.

Women's rights
- Reformers call for equal rights, including the right to vote.

The Arts
- Writers and painters turn their attention to the American scene.

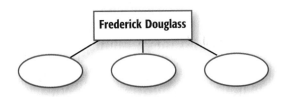

Reviewing Key Terms

On graph paper, create a word search puzzle using the following terms. Crisscross the terms vertically and horizontally, then fill in the remaining squares with extra letters. Use the terms' definitions as clues to find the words in the puzzle. Share your puzzle with a classmate.

1. utopia
2. revival
3. temperance
4. normal school
5. transcendentalist
6. civil disobedience
7. abolitionist
8. Underground Railroad
9. suffrage
10. women's rights movement
11. coeducation

Reviewing Key Facts

12. What were the founders of utopias hoping to achieve?
13. What problems in society did reformers in the temperance movement blame on the manufacture and sale of alcoholic beverages?
14. What were the basic principles of public education?
15. What was unique about the subject matter that American artists and writers of the mid-1800s used?
16. How did William Lloyd Garrison's demands make him effective in the anti-slavery movement?
17. What was the purpose of the Underground Railroad?
18. What role did Catherine Beecher play in education for women?

Critical Thinking

19. **Analyzing Information** What role did Dorothea Dix play regarding prison inmates and people with mental illness?
20. **Making Generalizations** What was the significance of the Seneca Falls Convention?
21. **Organizing Information** Re-create the diagram below and describe the contributions Frederick Douglass made to the abolitionist movement.

```
        Frederick Douglass
        |       |       |
      (   )   (   )   (   )
```

Practicing Skills

Evaluating a Web Site *Review the information about evaluating a Web site on page 429. Visit the Web site* www.greatwomen.org/index.php *and answer the following questions.*

22. What information is presented on this Web site?

23. What categories are used to organize the information?

24. What links does the site contain? Are they appropriate to the topic?

25. Do you think the site explores the topic in depth? Explain.

Geography and History Activity

Use the map on page 423 to answer the following questions.

26. **Region** What other country did passengers on the Underground Railroad travel to?

27. **Location** From what Southern ports did African Americans flee by ship?

28. **Location** What kinds of places were used as "stations" of the Underground Railroad?

29. **Human-Environment Interaction** Why do you think the routes of the Underground Railroad included many coastal cities?

Technology Activity

30. **Using the Internet** Search the Internet for a modern organization founded to support women's rights. Write a brief description of the organization, including its name, location, and a description of its purpose or activities.

Citizenship Cooperative Activity

31. **The Importance of Voting** Work with a partner to complete this activity. You know that the right to vote belongs to every United States citizen. In your opinion, what do citizens forfeit if they do not exercise their right to vote? Write a one-page paper that answers this question and share your paper with the other students.

Economics Activity

32. Goods are the items people buy. Services are activities done for others for a fee. List five goods you have purchased in the past month. List five services you purchased.

Self-Check Quiz
Visit tarvol1.glencoe.com and click on **Chapter 14— Self-Check Quizzes** to prepare for the chapter test.

Alternative Assessment

33. **Portfolio Writing Activity** Write a poem designed to win supporters for one of the reform movements discussed in Chapter 14.

Standardized Test Practice

Directions: Choose the *best* answer to the following question.

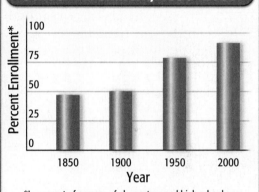

School Enrollment, 1850–2000

In percent of persons of elementary and high school age
Source: *Historical Statistics of the United States; Statistical Abstract.*

According to the graph above, the greatest increase in the percentage of school enrollment occurred between

F 1850 and 1880.   **H** 1900 and 1950.

G 1850 and 1900.   **J** 1950 and 2000.

Test-Taking Tip

Use the information on the *graph* to help you answer this question. Look carefully at the information on the bottom and the side of a bar graph to understand what the bars represent. Process of elimination is helpful here. For example, answer F cannot be correct because this time period is not shown on the graph.

6 Civil War and Reconstruction

1846–1896

Why It Matters

As you study Unit 6, you will learn how social, economic, and political differences between the North and South grew. As compromises failed, the country plunged into civil war. The following resources offer more information about this period in American history.

Confederate soldier's cap (upper left) and Union soldier's cap (lower right)

Primary Sources Library

See pages 602–603 for primary source readings to accompany Unit 6.

Use the *American History Primary Source Document Library* **CD-ROM** to find additional primary sources about the Civil War and Reconstruction.

General Patrick R. Cleburne
by Don Troiani

"A house divided
against itself
cannot stand."

—Abraham Lincoln, 1858

CHAPTER 15

Road to Civil War

1820–1861

Why It Matters

Slavery was a major cause of the worsening division between the North and South in the period before the Civil War. The struggle between the North and South turned more hostile, and talk grew of separation and civil war.

The Impact Today

"If slavery is not wrong, nothing is wrong," Abraham Lincoln wrote in a letter to A.G. Hodges in 1864. By studying this era of our history, we can better understand the state of racial relations today and develop ways for improving them.

The American Republic to 1877 *Video* *The chapter 15 video, "Secrets of the Underground Railroad," tells how enslaved African Americans escaped to freedom.*

1850
- Compromise of 1850 passed

1852
- *Uncle Tom's Cabin* published

1845
- Texas becomes a state

United States PRESIDENTS

W.H. Harrison 1841	Tyler 1841–1845	Polk 1845–1849	Taylor 1849–1850	Fillmore 1850–1853

1840　　　　*1845*　　　　*1850*

World

1845
- Many people begin emigrating to escape potato famine in Ireland

1848
- Marx publishes *The Communist Manifesto*

African Americans in 1850 About 425,000 African Americans in the United States were free while 3.2 million lived in slavery.

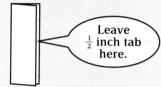

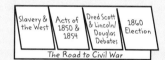
1854
• Kansas-Nebraska Act passed

1857
• *Dred Scott* decision

1859
• Raid on Harpers Ferry

1860
• Lincoln elected president

1861
• Civil War begins

Pierce
1853–1857

Buchanan
1857–1861

1855

1860

1856
• Bessemer patents steel process

1861
• Alexander II frees serfs in Russia

1863
• French troops occupy Mexico City

HISTORY Online

Chapter Overview
Visit tarvol1.glencoe.com and click on **Chapter 15—Chapter Overviews** to preview chapter information.

Slavery and the West

Guide to Reading

Main Idea

As new states entered the Union, the question of whether to admit them as free states or slave states arose.

Key Terms

sectionalism, fugitive, secede, abstain

Reading Strategy

Organizing Information As you read the section, re-create the table below and describe how these compromises answered the question of admitting new states.

Admission of new states	
The Missouri Compromise	The Compromise of 1850

Read to Learn

- how the debate over slavery was related to the admission of new states.
- what the Compromise of 1850 accomplished.

Section Theme

Government and Democracy Controversy over slavery grew during the early and mid-1800s.

Preview of Events

◆1820 ◆1830 ◆1840 ◆1850

1820 Missouri Compromise is passed

1845 Texas becomes a state

1848 Free-Soil Party nominates Martin Van Buren

1850 Compromise of 1850 diverts war

CAUTION!!

COLORED PEOPLE
OF BOSTON, ONE & ALL,

You are hereby respectfully CAUTIONED and advised, to avoid conversing with the

Watchmen and Police Officers
of Boston,

For since the recent ORDER OF THE MAYOR & ALDERMEN, they are empowered to act as

KIDNAPPERS
AND

Slave Catchers,

And they have already been actually employed in KIDNAPPING, CATCHING, AND KEEPING SLAVES. Therefore, if you value your LIBERTY, and the Welfare of the Fugitives among you, Shun them in every possible manner, as so many HOUNDS on the track of the most unfortunate of your race.

Keep a Sharp Look Out for KIDNAPPERS, and have TOP EYE open.

APRIL 24, 1851.

Poster warning African Americans

AN American Story

"The deed is done. The . . . chains of slavery are forged for [many] yet unborn. Humble yourselves in the dust, ye high-minded citizens of Connecticut. Let your cheeks be red as crimson. On *your* representatives rests the stigma of this foul disgrace." These biting, fiery words were published in a Connecticut newspaper in 1820. They were in response to members of Congress who had helped pave the way for the admission of Missouri as a slaveholding state.

The Missouri Compromise

The request by slaveholding **Missouri** to join the Union in 1819 caused an angry debate that worried former president Thomas Jefferson and Secretary of State John Quincy Adams. Jefferson called the dispute "a fire-bell in the night" that "awakened and filled me with terror." Adams accurately predicted that the bitter debate was "a mere preamble—a title-page to a great tragic volume."

Many Missouri settlers had brought enslaved African Americans into the territory with them. By 1819 the Missouri Territory included about 50,000 whites and 10,000 slaves. When Missouri applied to Congress for admission as a state, its constitution allowed slavery.

In 1819, 11 states permitted slavery and 11 did not. The Senate—with two members from each state—was therefore evenly balanced between slave and free states. The admission of a new state would upset that balance.

In addition, the North and the South, with their different economic systems, were competing for new lands in the western territories. At the same time, a growing number of Northerners wanted to restrict or ban slavery. Southerners, even those who disliked slavery, opposed these antislavery efforts. They resented the interference by outsiders in Southerners' affairs. These differences between the North and the South grew into sectionalism—an exaggerated loyalty to a particular region of the country.

Clay's Proposal

The Senate suggested a way to resolve the crisis by allowing Missouri's admittance as a slave state while simultaneously admitting Maine as a free state. Maine, formerly part of Massachusetts, had also applied for admission to the Union. The Senate also sought to settle the issue of slavery in the territories for good. It proposed prohibiting slavery in the remainder of the Louisiana Purchase north of 36°30'N latitude.

Speaker of the House **Henry Clay** of Kentucky skillfully maneuvered the Senate bill to passage in 1820 by dividing it into three proposals. The **Missouri Compromise** preserved the balance between slave and free states in the Senate and brought about a lull in the bitter debate in Congress over slavery.

Reading Check **Explaining** What is sectionalism?

New Western Lands

For the next 25 years, Congress managed to keep the slavery issue in the background. In the 1840s, however, this heated debate moved back into Congress. Once again the cause of the dispute was the issue of slavery in new territories. The territories involved were **Texas,** which had won its independence from Mexico in 1836, and **New Mexico** and **California,** which were still part of Mexico.

Many Southerners hoped to see Texas, where slavery already existed, join the Union. As a result, the annexation of Texas became the main issue in the presidential election of 1844. Democrat **James Polk** of Tennessee won the election and pressed forward on acquiring Texas, and Texas became a state in 1845. At the same time, support for taking over New Mexico and California also grew in the South. The federal government's actions on these lands led to war with Mexico.

Conflicting Views

Just months after the Mexican War began, Representative David Wilmot of Pennsylvania introduced a proposal in Congress. Called the **Wilmot Proviso,** it specified that slavery should be prohibited in any lands that might be acquired from Mexico. Southerners protested furiously. They wanted to keep open the possibility of introducing slavery to California and New Mexico.

Senator **John C. Calhoun** of South Carolina countered with another proposal. It stated that neither Congress nor any territorial government had the authority to ban slavery from a territory or regulate it in any way.

Polk campaign banner

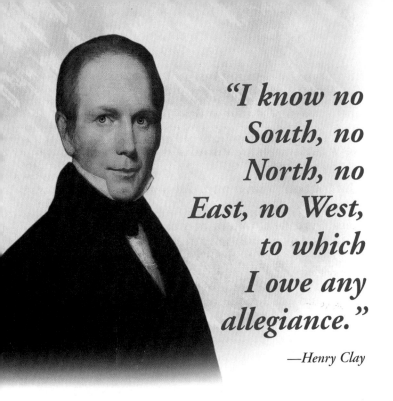

"I know no South, no North, no East, no West, to which I owe any allegiance."

—Henry Clay

Neither Wilmot's nor Calhoun's proposal passed, but both caused bitter debate. By the time of the 1848 presidential election, the United States had gained the territories of California and New Mexico from Mexico but had taken no action on the issue of slavery in those areas.

The Free-Soil Party

The debate over slavery led to the formation of a new political party. In 1848 the Whigs chose **Zachary Taylor,** a Southerner and a hero of the Mexican War, as their presidential candidate. The Democrats selected Senator Lewis Cass of Michigan. Neither candidate took a stand on slavery in the territories.

This failure to take a position angered voters. Many antislavery Democrats and Whigs left their parties and joined with members of the old Liberty Party to form the **Free-Soil Party.** The new party proclaimed "Free Soil, Free Speech, Free Labor, and Free Men," and endorsed the Wilmot Proviso. The party nominated former president **Martin Van Buren** as its presidential candidate.

Whig candidate Zachary Taylor won the election by successfully appealing to both slave and free states. Taylor defeated Cass 163 to 127 in electoral votes. Van Buren captured only 14 percent of the popular vote in the North, but several candidates of the Free-Soil Party won seats in Congress.

California

Once in office President Taylor urged leaders in the two territories of California and New Mexico to apply for statehood immediately. Once these lands had become states, he reasoned, their citizens could decide whether to allow slavery. New Mexico did not apply for statehood, but California did in 1850.

Taylor's plan ran into trouble when California's statehood became tangled up with other issues before Congress. Antislavery forces wanted to abolish slavery in the District of Columbia, the nation's capital. Southerners wanted a strong national law requiring states to return fugitive, or runaway, slaves to their masters. Another dispute involved the New Mexico–Texas border.

The greatest obstacle to Taylor's plan was concern over the balance of power in the Senate. In 1849 the nation included 15 slave states and 15 free states. If California entered as a free state—and New Mexico, Oregon, and Utah followed as free states, which seemed likely—the South would be hopelessly outvoted in the Senate. As tension grew, some Southerners began talking about having their states secede from, or leave, the United States.

Reading Check **Explaining** How was John C. Calhoun's proposal different from the Wilmot Proviso?

A New Compromise

In January 1850, Henry Clay, now a senator, presented a multi-part plan to settle all the issues dividing Congress. First, California would be admitted as a free state. Second, the New Mexico Territory would have no restrictions on slavery. Third, the New Mexico–Texas border dispute would be settled in favor of New Mexico. Fourth, the slave trade, but not slavery itself, would be abolished in the District of Columbia. Finally, Clay pushed for a stronger fugitive slave law.

Clay's proposal launched an emotional debate in Congress that raged for seven months. Opening that debate were Clay and two other distinguished senators—John C. Calhoun of South Carolina and **Daniel Webster** of Massachusetts.

Calhoun opposed Clay's plan. He believed that the only way to save the Union was to protect slavery. If Congress admitted California as a free state, Calhoun warned, the Southern states had to leave the Union.

Three days later Webster gave an eloquent speech in support of Clay's plan. He argued that antislavery forces lost little in agreeing to the compromise:

> ❝I would rather hear of natural blasts and mildews, war, pestilence, and famine, than to hear gentlemen talk of secession.❞

Webster reasoned that geography would prevent slavery from taking root in the new territories, since most of the land was not suited for plantations. What was most important was to preserve the Union.

The Compromise of 1850

Clay's plan could not pass as a complete package. Too many members of Congress objected to one part of it or another. President Taylor also opposed the plan and threatened to use force against the South if states tried to secede.

Then in July President Taylor suddenly died. The new president, **Millard Fillmore,** supported some form of compromise. At the same time, **Stephen A. Douglas,** a young senator from Illinois, took charge of efforts to resolve the crisis. Douglas divided Clay's plan into a series of

Before They Were Presidents

Like Zachary Taylor, did most presidents make the military their profession? Some presidents *did* make the military their principal profession. Washington, William Henry Harrison, Grant, and Eisenhower, as well as Taylor, all made a career in the military. However, more presidents came from the ranks of attorneys than from any other profession. More than half of all presidents, including Jefferson and Lincoln, made their living in the practice of law.

measures that Congress could vote on separately. In this way members of Congress would not have to support proposals they opposed.

President Fillmore persuaded several Whig representatives to abstain—not to cast votes—on measures they opposed. Congress finally passed a series of five separate bills in August and September of 1850. Taken together these laws, known as the **Compromise of 1850,** contained the five main points of Clay's original plan. Fillmore called the compromise a "final settlement" of the conflict between North and South. The president would soon be proved wrong.

✓ **Reading Check** **Explaining** How did the Compromise of 1850 affect the New Mexico Territory?

SECTION 1 ASSESSMENT

Checking for Understanding

1. **Key Terms** Use each of these social studies terms in a sentence that will help explain its meaning: sectionalism, fugitive, secede, abstain.
2. **Reviewing Facts** List the provisions of the Missouri Compromise.

Reviewing Themes

3. **Government and Democracy** Why was the Free-Soil Party created?

Critical Thinking

4. **Analyzing Information** What was the Wilmot Proviso? Why was it controversial?
5. **Comparing** Re-create the table below and describe what the North and South each gained from the Compromise of 1850.

Compromise of 1850	
Northern gains	Southern gains

Analyzing Visuals

6. **Examining Artifacts** Look at the campaign banner on page 437. Compare it to a modern political button or advertisement you have seen. In what ways are they similar? In what ways are they different?

Interdisciplinary Activity

Government Create a poster for the Free-Soil Party presidential candidate. Include slogans or symbols to gain popular support.

Critical Thinking
SKILLBUILDER

Recognizing Bias

Why Learn This Skill?

Cats make better pets than dogs. If you say this, then you are stating a bias. A bias is a prejudice. It can prevent you from looking at a situation in a reasonable or truthful way.

Learning the Skill

Most people have feelings and ideas that affect their point of view. This viewpoint, or *bias,* influences the way they interpret events. For this reason, an idea that is stated as a fact may really be only an opinion. Recognizing bias will help you judge the accuracy of what you read. There are several things you should look for that will help you recognize bias. Identify the author of the statement and examine his or her views and possible reasons for writing the material. Look for language that reflects an emotion or opinion—words such as *all, never, best, worst, might,* or *should.* Examine the writing for imbalances— leaning only to one viewpoint and failing to provide equal coverage of other possible viewpoints.

Practicing the Skill

Read the excerpts on this page. The first excerpt is from an 1858 newspaper editorial. The second is from a speech by Senator John C. Calhoun of South Carolina. Then answer the four questions that follow.

❝Popular sovereignty for the territories will never work. Under this system, each territory would decide whether or not to legalize slavery. This method was tried in the territory of Kansas and all it produced was bloodshed and violence.❞

—*The Republican Leader,* 1858

❝. . . [T]he two great divisions of society are not rich and poor, but white and black; and all the former, the poor as well as the rich, belong to the upper classes, and are respected and treated as such.❞

—Senator Calhoun

❶ Is Senator Calhoun expressing a proslavery or antislavery bias?

❷ What statements indicate the racism in Calhoun's bias?

❸ What political party's view does the editorial represent?

❹ What biases or beliefs are expressed in the editorial?

Applying the Skill

Recognizing Bias Look through the letters to the editor in your local newspaper. Write a short report analyzing one of the letters for evidence of bias.

 Glencoe's **Skillbuilder Interactive Workbook CD-ROM, Level 1,** provides instruction and practice in key social studies skills.

A Nation Dividing

Guide to Reading

Main Idea
Growing tensions led to differences that could not be solved by compromise.

Key Terms
popular sovereignty, border ruffians, civil war

Reading Strategy
As you read the section, re-create the table below and describe how Southerners and Northerners reacted to the Kansas-Nebraska Act.

Kansas-Nebraska Act	
Southern reaction	Northern reaction

Read to Learn
- how the Fugitive Slave Act and the Kansas-Nebraska Act further divided the North and South.
- how popular sovereignty led to violence.

Section Theme
Continuity and Change As they grew farther apart, Northerners and Southerners sought compromise.

Preview of Events

1850	1853	1856
1850 Fugitive Slave Act is passed	**1852** *Uncle Tom's Cabin* is published	**1854** Kansas-Nebraska Act is passed	**1856** Charles Sumner attacked in Senate

AN American Story

On May 24, 1854, the people of Boston erupted in outrage. Federal officers had seized Anthony Burns, a runaway slave who lived in Boston, to send him back to slavery. Abolitionists tried to rescue Burns from the federal courthouse, and city leaders attempted to buy his freedom. All efforts failed. Local militia units joined the marines and cavalry in Boston to keep order. Federal troops escorted Burns to a ship that would carry him back to Virginia and slavery. In a gesture of bitter protest, Bostonians draped buildings in black and hung the American flag upside down.

Anthony Burns

The Fugitive Slave Act

The **Fugitive Slave Act** of 1850 required all citizens to help catch runaways. Anyone who aided a fugitive could be fined or imprisoned. People in the South believed the law would force Northerners to recognize the rights of Southerners. Instead, enforcement of the law led to mounting anger in the North, convincing more people of the evils of slavery.

After passage of the Fugitive Slave Act, slaveholders stepped up their efforts to catch runaway slaves. They even tried to capture runaways who had lived in freedom in the North for years. Sometimes they seized African Americans who were not escaped slaves and forced them into slavery.

People In History

Harriet Beecher Stowe 1811–1896

Writer Harriet Beecher Stowe called the Fugitive Slave Act a "nightmare abomination." Stowe, the daughter of a New England minister, spent part of her childhood in Cincinnati. There, on the banks of the Ohio River, she saw enslaved people being loaded onto ships to be taken to slave markets. As an adult and the wife of a religion professor, she wrote many books and stories about social reform. Her most famous work was a novel about the evils of slavery. *Uncle Tom's Cabin* was published in 1852. Packed with dramatic incidents and vivid characters, the novel shows slavery as a cruel and brutal system.

Uncle Tom's Cabin quickly became a sensation, selling over 300,000 copies in the first year of publication. The book had such an impact on public feelings about slavery that when Abraham Lincoln was introduced to Stowe during the Civil War, he said, so, you "wrote the book that started this great war."

Resistance to the Law

In spite of the penalties, many Northerners refused to cooperate with the law's enforcement. The Underground Railroad, a network of free African Americans and whites, helped runaways make their way to freedom. Antislavery groups tried to rescue African Americans who were being pursued or to free those who were captured. In Boston, members of one such group followed federal agents shouting, "Slave hunters—there go the slave hunters." People contributed funds to buy the freedom of African Americans. Northern juries refused to convict those accused of breaking the Fugitive Slave Law.

Reading Check **Explaining** What was the purpose of the Underground Railroad?

The Kansas–Nebraska Act

Franklin Pierce, a New Hampshire Democrat who supported the Fugitive Slave Act, became president in 1853. Pierce intended to enforce the Fugitive Slave Act, and his actions hardened the opposition.

In 1854 the dispute over slavery erupted in Congress again. The cause was a bill introduced by Stephen A. Douglas, the Illinois senator who had forged the Compromise of 1850.

Hoping to encourage settlement of the West and open the way for a transcontinental railroad, Douglas proposed organizing the region west of Missouri and Iowa as the territories of **Kansas** and **Nebraska.** Douglas was trying to work out a plan for the nation to expand that both the North and the South would accept. Instead his bill reopened the conflict about slavery in the territories.

Because of their location, Kansas and Nebraska seemed likely to become free states. Both lay north of 36°30'N latitude, the line established in the Missouri Compromise as the boundary of slavery. Douglas knew that Southerners would object to having Kansas and Nebraska become free states because it would give the North an advantage in the Senate. As a result Douglas proposed abandoning the Missouri Compromise and letting the settlers in each territory vote on whether to allow slavery. He called this popular sovereignty—allowing the people to decide.

Passage of the Act

Many Northerners protested strongly. Douglas's plan to repeal the Missouri Compromise would allow slavery into areas that had been free for more than 30 years. Opponents of the bill demanded that Congress vote down the bill.

Southerners in Congress, however, provided solid support for the bill. They expected that Kansas would be settled in large part by slaveholders from Missouri who would vote to keep slavery legal. With some support from Northern Democrats and the backing of President Pierce, Congress passed the **Kansas–Nebraska Act** in May 1854.

Division Grows

Northern Democrats in the House split almost evenly on the vote, revealing deep divisions in the party. Many Northerners became convinced that compromise with the South was no longer possible. Sam Houston, senator from Texas, predicted that the bill "will convulse [upset] the country from Maine to the Rio Grande."

 **Reading Check** **Describing** Write a definition of "popular sovereignty" in your own words.

Conflict in Kansas

Right after passage of the Kansas–Nebraska Act, proslavery and antislavery groups rushed supporters into Kansas. In the spring of 1855, when elections took place in Kansas, a proslavery legislature was elected.

Although only about 1,500 voters lived in Kansas at the time, more than 6,000 people cast ballots in the elections. Thousands of proslavery supporters from Missouri had crossed the border just to vote in the election. These Missourians traveled in armed groups and became known as border ruffians. Soon after the election, the new Kansas legislature passed laws supporting slavery. One law even restricted political office to proslavery candidates.

The antislavery people refused to accept these laws. Instead they armed themselves, held their own elections, and adopted a constitution that banned slavery. By January 1856, rival governments existed in Kansas, one for and one against slavery. Each asked Congress for recognition. To confuse matters further, President Pierce and the Senate favored the proslavery government, while the House backed the forces opposed to slavery.

NATIONAL GEOGRAPHIC **Slavery and Sectionalism**

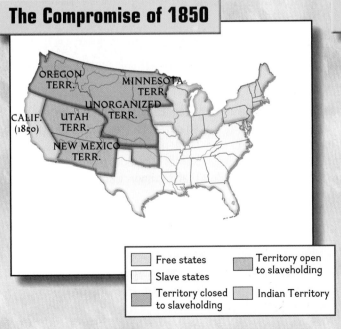

The Compromise of 1850

Free states
Slave states
Territory closed to slaveholding
Territory open to slaveholding
Indian Territory

Kansas–Nebraska Act, 1854

Geography Skills

1. **Region** How did the Kansas–Nebraska Act change the amount of territory open to slaveholding?
2. **Analyzing Information** What territories were non-slaveholding in 1854?

John Brown

"Bleeding Kansas"

With proslavery and antislavery forces in Kansas arming themselves, the outbreak of violence became inevitable. In May 1856, 800 slavery supporters attacked the town of Lawrence, the antislavery capital. They sacked the town, burned the hotel and the home of the governor, and destroyed two newspaper offices. Soon after, forces opposed to slavery retaliated.

John Brown, a fervent abolitionist, believed God had chosen him to end slavery. When he heard of the attack on Lawrence, Brown went into a rage. He vowed to "strike terror in the hearts of the proslavery people." One night Brown led four of his sons and two other men along Pottawatomie Creek, where they seized and killed five supporters of slavery.

More violence followed as armed bands roamed the territory. Newspapers began referring to "Bleeding Kansas" and "the Civil War in Kansas." A **civil war** is a conflict between citizens of the same country. Not until October of 1856 did John Geary, the newly appointed territorial governor, stop the bloodshed in Kansas. He suppressed guerrilla forces and used 1,300 federal troops.

Violence in Congress

The violence that erupted in Kansas spilled over to the halls of Congress as well. Abolitionist senator **Charles Sumner** of Massachusetts delivered a speech entitled "The Crime Against Kansas." Sumner lashed out against proslavery forces in Kansas. He also criticized proslavery senators, repeatedly attacking Andrew P. Butler of South Carolina.

Two days after the speech, Butler's distant cousin, Representative **Preston Brooks,** walked into the Senate chamber. He hit Sumner again and again over the head and shoulders with a cane. Sumner fell to the floor, unconscious and bleeding. He suffered injuries so severe that he did not return to the Senate for several years. The Brooks-Sumner incident and the fighting in "Bleeding Kansas" revealed the rising level of hostility between North and South.

✓ **Reading Check** **Explaining** What is a civil war?

SECTION 2 ASSESSMENT

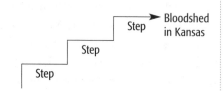

Checking for Understanding

1. Key Terms Use each of these terms in a sentence that will help explain its meaning: popular sovereignty, border ruffians, civil war.

2. Reviewing Facts Describe how Northern abolitionists reacted to the Fugitive Slave Act.

Reviewing Themes

3. Continuity and Change How did popular sovereignty lead to violence in Kansas?

Critical Thinking

4. Predicting Consequences Could the violence in Kansas have been prevented if Congress had not abandoned the Missouri Compromise? Explain.

5. Organizing Information Re-create the diagram below and list the steps that led to bloodshed in Kansas.

```
                          ┌─→ Bloodshed
                   Step ──┘    in Kansas
            Step ──┘
      Step ──┘
```

Analyzing Visuals

6. Geography Skills Study the maps on page 443. From which territory or territories were the Nebraska and Kansas Territories formed? Was the Utah territory closed to slaveholding?

Interdisciplinary Activity

Descriptive Writing With members of your class, choose a scene from *Uncle Tom's Cabin* to portray in a one-act play. Write a short script, assign roles, and present it to the class.

SECTION 3 Challenges to Slavery

Guide to Reading

Main Idea
Social, economic, and political differences divided the North and South.

Key Terms
arsenal, martyr

Reading Strategy
Sequencing Information As you read the section, re-create the diagram below and list major events for each year.

1846	1854	1856	1858

Read to Learn
- why the Republican Party was formed.
- how the *Dred Scott* decision, the Lincoln-Douglas debates, and John Brown's raid affected Americans.

Section Theme
Continuity and Change The slavery issues continued to drive the North and South further apart.

Preview of Events

♦1854   ♦1856   ♦1858   ♦1860

1854
Republican Party is formed

1856
James Buchanan is elected president

1857
Dred Scott decision states that all slaves are property

1859
John Brown raids Harpers Ferry, Virginia

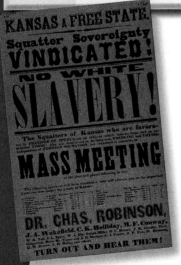

Kansas Free-Soil poster

AN American Story

Many people considered John Brown to be a radical murderer, while others viewed him as a fighter for the cause of freedom. When he was executed in 1859, the *Anglo-African Magazine* wrote that, as John Brown left the jail, "a black woman, with a little child in her arms, stood near his way. . . . He stopped for a moment in his course, stooped over, and with the tenderness of one whose love is as broad as the brotherhood of man, kissed the child affectionately."

A New Political Party

Even before Brown's raid, other events had driven the North and South further apart. After the Kansas–Nebraska Act, the Democratic Party began to divide along sectional lines, with Northern Democrats leaving the party. Differing views over the slavery issue destroyed the Whig Party.

In 1854 antislavery Whigs and Democrats joined forces with Free-Soilers to form the **Republican Party.** The new party was determined to rally "for the establishment of liberty and the overthrow of the Slave Power."

CHAPTER 15   Road to Civil War   **445**

The Republicans challenged the proslavery Whigs and Democrats, choosing candidates to run in the state and congressional elections of 1854. Their main message was that the government should ban slavery from new territories.

The Republican Party quickly showed its strength in the North. In the election, the Republicans won control of the House of Representatives and of several state governments. In the South the Republicans had almost no support.

Northern Democrats suffered a beating. Almost three-fourths of the Democratic candidates from free states lost in 1854. The party was increasingly becoming a Southern party.

The Election of 1856

Democrats and Republicans met again in the presidential election of 1856. The Whig Party, disintegrating over the slavery issue, did not offer a candidate of its own.

The Republicans chose **John C. Frémont** of California as their candidate for president. Frémont had gained fame as an explorer in the West. The party platform called for free territories and its campaign slogan became "Free soil, free speech, and Frémont."

The Democratic Party nominated **James Buchanan** of Pennsylvania, an experienced diplomat and former member of Congress. The party endorsed the idea of popular sovereignty.

The American Party, or Know Nothings, had grown quickly between 1853 and 1856 by attacking immigrants. The Know Nothings nominated former president Millard Fillmore.

The presidential vote divided along rigid sectional lines. Buchanan won the election, winning all of the Southern states except Maryland and received 174 electoral votes compared to 114 for Frémont and 8 for Fillmore. Frémont did not receive a single electoral vote south of the Mason-Dixon line, but he carried 11 of the 16 free states.

Reading Check **Explaining** What stand did the new Republican party take on the issue of slavery?

The *Dred Scott* Decision

President Buchanan took office on March 4, 1857. Two days later the Supreme Court announced a decision about slavery and the territories that shook the nation.

Dred Scott was an enslaved African American bought by an army doctor in Missouri, a slave state. In the 1830s the doctor moved his household to Illinois, a free state, and then to the Wisconsin Territory, where slavery was banned by the Northwest Ordinance of 1787. Later the family returned to Missouri, where the doctor died. In 1846, with the help of antislavery lawyers, Scott sued for his freedom. He claimed he should be free because he had once lived on free soil. Eleven years later, in the midst of growing anger over the slavery issue, the case reached the Supreme Court.

The case attracted enormous attention. While the immediate issue was Dred Scott's status, the

Picturing **History**

Family members (left) honor the memory of Dred Scott. Scott (above), who lived in slavery, had appealed to the Supreme Court in hopes of being granted his freedom. **How did the Court rule?**

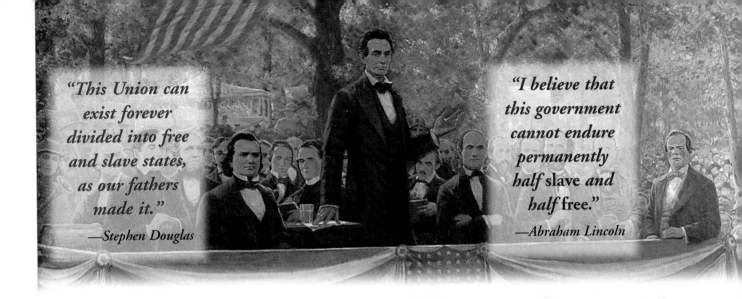

"This Union can exist forever divided into free and slave states, as our fathers made it."
—Stephen Douglas

"I believe that this government cannot endure permanently half slave and half free."
—Abraham Lincoln

Court also had the opportunity to rule on the question of slavery in territories. Many Americans hoped that the Court would resolve the issue for good.

The Court's Decision

The Court's decision electrified the nation. Chief Justice **Roger B. Taney** (TAW•nee) said that Dred Scott was still a slave. As a slave, Scott was not a citizen and had no right to bring a lawsuit. Taney could have stopped there, but he decided to address the broader issues.

Taney wrote that Scott's residence on free soil did not make him free. An enslaved person was property, and the Fifth Amendment prohibits Congress from taking away property without "due process of law."

Finally, Taney wrote that Congress had no power to prohibit slavery in any territory. The Missouri Compromise—which had banned slavery north of 36°30'N latitude—was unconstitutional. For that matter, so was popular sovereignty. Not even the voters in a territory could prohibit slavery because that would amount to taking away a person's property. In effect, the decision meant that the Constitution protected slavery. 📖 *(See page 624 of the Appendix for a summary of the Dred Scott decision.)*

Reaction to the Decision

Rather than settling the issue, the Supreme Court's decision divided the country even more. Many Southerners were elated. The Court had reaffirmed what many in the South had always maintained: Nothing could legally prevent the spread of slavery. Northern Democrats were pleased that the Republicans' main issue—restricting the spread of slavery—had been ruled unconstitutional.

Republicans and other antislavery groups were outraged, calling the *Dred Scott* decision "a wicked and false judgment" and "the greatest crime" ever committed in the nation's courts.

Lincoln and Douglas

In the congressional election of 1858, the Senate race in Illinois was the center of national attention. The contest pitted the current senator, Democrat Stephen A. Douglas, against Republican challenger **Abraham Lincoln.** People considered Douglas a likely candidate for president in 1860. Lincoln was nearly an unknown.

Douglas, a successful lawyer, had joined the Democratic Party and won election to the House in 1842 and to the Senate in 1846. Short, stocky, and powerful, Douglas was called "the Little Giant." He disliked slavery but thought that the controversy over it would interfere with the nation's growth. He believed the issue could be resolved through popular sovereignty.

Born in the poor backcountry of Kentucky, Abraham Lincoln moved to Indiana as a child, and later to Illinois. Like Douglas, Lincoln was intelligent, ambitious, and a successful lawyer. He had little formal education—but excellent political instincts. Although Lincoln saw slavery as morally wrong, he admitted there was no easy way to eliminate slavery where it already existed. He was certain, though, that slavery should not be allowed to spread.

The Lincoln–Douglas Debates

Not as well known as Douglas, Lincoln challenged the senator to a series of debates. Douglas reluctantly agreed. The two met seven times in August, September, and October of 1858 in cities and villages throughout Illinois. Thousands came to these debates. The main topic, of course, was slavery.

During the debate at Freeport, Lincoln pressed Douglas about his views on popular sovereignty. Could the people of a territory legally exclude slavery before achieving statehood? Douglas replied that the people could exclude slavery by refusing to pass laws protecting slaveholders' rights. Douglas's response, which satisfied antislavery followers but lost him support in the South, became known as the **Freeport Doctrine.**

Douglas claimed that Lincoln wanted African Americans to be fully equal to whites. Lincoln denied this. Still, Lincoln said, "in the right to eat the bread . . . which his own hand earns, [an African American] is my equal and the equal of [Senator] Douglas, and the equal of every living man." The real issue, Lincoln said, is "between the men who think slavery a wrong and those who do not think it wrong. The Republican Party thinks it wrong."

Following the debates, Douglas won a narrow victory in the election. Lincoln lost the election but gained a national reputation.

The Raid on Harpers Ferry

After the 1858 elections, Southerners began to feel threatened by growing Republican power. In late 1859, an act of violence greatly increased their fears. On October 16 the abolitionist John Brown led 18 men, both whites and African Americans, on a raid on Harpers Ferry, Virginia. His target was an arsenal, a storage place for weapons and ammunition. Brown—who had killed five proslavery Kansans in 1856—hoped to start a rebellion against slaveholders by arming enslaved African Americans. His raid had been financed by a group of abolitionists.

Brown and his men were quickly defeated by local citizens and federal troops. Brown was convicted of treason and murder and was sentenced to hang. His execution caused an uproar in the North. Some antislavery Northerners, including Republican leaders, denounced Brown's use of violence. Others viewed Brown as a hero. Writer Ralph Waldo Emerson called Brown a martyr—a person who dies for a great cause.

John Brown's death became a rallying point for abolitionists. When Southerners learned of Brown's connection to abolitionists, their fears of a great Northern conspiracy against them seemed to be confirmed. The nation was on the brink of disaster.

Reading Check **Explaining** How did the *Dred Scott* decision regulate the spread of slavery?

SECTION 3 ASSESSMENT

Checking for Understanding

1. **Key Terms** Use the terms arsenal and martyr in a paragraph about John Brown's raid on Harpers Ferry.
2. **Reviewing Facts** Discuss stages in the development of the Republican Party.

Reviewing Themes

3. **Continuity and Change** How did the *Dred Scott* decision reverse a previous decision made by Congress? What was the reaction of Republicans?

Critical Thinking

4. **Making Inferences** Why did Lincoln emerge as a leader after the Lincoln-Douglas debates?
5. **Organizing Information** Re-create the table shown here, and describe the positions taken by Lincoln and Douglas in their debates.

Lincoln–Douglas Debates	
Lincoln's position	Douglas's position

Analyzing Visuals

6. **Examining Artifacts** Examine the poster on page 445. What is the poster advertising? Explain why some of the phrases are in larger type.

Interdisciplinary Activity

Government Draw a political cartoon that illustrates Lincoln's statement "A house divided against itself cannot stand."

Secession and War

Guide to Reading

Main Idea
In 1860 Abraham Lincoln's election as president of the United States was followed by Southern states leaving the Union.

Key Terms
secession, states' rights

Reading Strategy
Sequencing Information As you read the section, re-create the time line below and list the major events at each time.

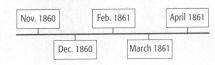

| Nov. 1860 | Feb. 1861 | April 1861 |

| Dec. 1860 | March 1861 |

Read to Learn
• how the 1860 election led to the breakup of the Union.
• why secession led to the Civil War.

Section Theme
Geography and History The election of 1860 clearly divided the nation along sectional lines.

Preview of Events

♦1860   ♦1861   ♦1862

Nov. 1860
Abraham Lincoln is elected president

Dec. 1860
South Carolina secedes

February 1861
Southern states form the Confederate States of America

April 1861
Confederate forces attack Fort Sumter; the Civil War begins

Secessionist ribbon

★ AN ★ American Story

After John Brown's raid on Harpers Ferry, calls for secession grew. South Carolina's *Charleston Mercury* declared "The day of compromise is passed . . . [T]here is no peace for the South in the Union." The *Nashville Union and American* said, "The South will hold the whole party of Republicans responsible for the bloodshed at Harpers Ferry." Republicans refused to take the threat of secession seriously. Secession is only a scare tactic, they argued, aimed at frightening voters from casting their ballot for Abraham Lincoln. To many Southerners, however, the election of Lincoln would be a final signal that their position in the Union was hopeless.

The Election of 1860

Would the Union break up? That was the burning question in the months before the presidential election of 1860. The issue of slavery was seriously discussed and eventually caused a break in the Democratic Party. As the election approached, a northern wing of the Democratic Party nominated Stephen

TWO VIEWPOINTS

Union or Secession?

President Abraham Lincoln and Jefferson Davis, president of the Confederacy, were inaugurated just several weeks apart. These excerpts from their Inaugural Addresses will help you understand differing points of view about secession from the United States in 1861.

Abraham Lincoln's Inaugural Address, March 4, 1861

One section of our country believes slavery is *right* and ought to be extended, while the other believes it is *wrong* and ought not to be extended. This is the only substantial dispute . . . .

Physically speaking, we can not separate. We can not remove our respective sections from each other nor build an impassable wall between them. A husband and wife may be divorced and go out of the presence and beyond the reach of each other; but the different parts of our country can not do this. . . .

In *your* hands, my dissatisfied fellow countrymen, and not in *mine*, is the momentous issue of civil war.

Abraham Lincoln

Jefferson Davis's Inaugural Address, February 18, 1861

As a necessity, not a choice, we have resorted to the remedy of separation, and henceforth our energies must be directed to the conduct of our own affairs, and the [continuation] of the Confederacy which we have formed. If a just perception of mutual interest shall permit us peaceably to pursue our separate political career, my most earnest desire will have been fulfilled. But if this be denied to us . . . [we will be forced] to appeal to arms. . . .

Jefferson Davis

Learning From History

1. According to Lincoln, what was the only substantial disagreement between the North and the South?
2. What did Lincoln compare the United States to?
3. Did Lincoln and Davis say anything in their inaugural addresses that was similar?

Douglas for the presidency and supported popular sovereignty. Southern Democrats—vowing to uphold slavery—nominated John C. Breckinridge of Kentucky and supported the *Dred Scott* decision. Moderates from both the North and South who had formed the Constitutional Union Party nominated John Bell of Tennessee. This party took no position on slavery.

Lincoln Nominated

The Republicans nominated Abraham Lincoln. Their platform, designed to attract voters from many quarters, was that slavery should be left undisturbed where it existed, but that it should be excluded from the territories. Many Southerners feared, however, that a Republican victory would encourage slave revolts.

Lincoln Elected

With the Democrats divided, Lincoln won a clear majority of the electoral votes—180 out of 303. He received only 40 percent of the popular vote, but this was more than any other candidate. Douglas was second with 30 percent of the vote.

The vote was along purely sectional lines. Lincoln's name did not even appear on the ballot in most Southern states, but he won every Northern state. Breckinridge swept the South, and Bell took most border states. Douglas won only the state of Missouri and three of New Jersey's seven electoral votes.

In effect, the more populous North had outvoted the South. The victory for Lincoln was a short-lived one, however, for the nation Lincoln was to lead would soon disintegrate.

✓ **Reading Check** **Examining** What caused the split in the Democratic Party in 1860?

The South Secedes

Lincoln and the Republicans had promised not to disturb slavery where it already existed. Many people in the South, however, did not trust the party, fearing that the Republican administration would not protect Southern rights. On December 20, 1860, the South's long-standing threat to leave the Union became a reality when South Carolina held a special convention and voted to secede.

Attempt at Compromise

Even after South Carolina's action, many people still wished to preserve the Union. The question was *how*. As other Southern states debated secession—withdrawal from the Union—leaders in Washington, D.C., worked frantically to fashion a last-minute compromise. On December 18, 1860, Senator **John Crittenden** of Kentucky proposed a series of amendments to the Constitution. Central to Crittenden's plan was a provision to protect slavery south of 36°30'N latitude—the line set by the Missouri Compromise—in all territories "now held or hereafter acquired."

Republicans considered this unacceptable. They had just won an election on the principle that slavery would not be extended in any territories. "Now we are told," Lincoln said,

66the government shall be broken up, unless we surrender to those we have beaten.99

Leaders in the South also rejected the plan. "We spit upon every plan to compromise," exclaimed one Southern leader. "No human power can save the Union," wrote another.

The Confederacy

By February 1861, Texas, Louisiana, Mississippi, Alabama, Florida, and Georgia had joined South Carolina and also seceded. Delegates from these states and South Carolina met in Montgomery, Alabama, on February 4 to form a new nation and government. Calling themselves the **Confederate States of America,** they chose **Jefferson Davis,** a senator from Mississippi, as their president.

Southerners justified secession with the theory of states' rights. The states, they argued, had voluntarily chosen to enter the Union. They defined the Constitution as a contract among the independent states. Now because the national government had violated that contract—by refusing to enforce the Fugitive Slave Act and by denying the Southern states equal rights in the territories—the states were justified in leaving the Union.

Reactions to Secession

Many Southerners welcomed secession. In Charleston, South Carolina, people rang church bells, fired cannons, and celebrated in the streets. A newspaper in Atlanta, Georgia, said the South "will never submit" and would defend its liberties no matter what the cost.

Other Southerners, however, were alarmed. A South Carolinian wrote,

66My heart has been rent [torn] by . . . the destruction of my country—the dismemberment of that great and glorious Union.99

Virginian Robert E. Lee expressed concern about the future. "I see only that a fearful calamity is upon us," he wrote.

In the North some abolitionists preferred to allow the Southern states to leave. If the Union could be kept together only by compromising on slavery, they declared, then let the Union be destroyed. Most Northerners, however, believed that the Union must be preserved. For Lincoln the issue was "whether in a free government the minority have the right to break up the government whenever they choose."

Presidential Responses

Lincoln had won the election, but he was not yet president. James Buchanan's term ran until March 4, 1861. In December 1860, Buchanan sent a message to Congress saying that the Southern states had no right to secede. Then he added that he had no power to stop them from doing so.

As Lincoln prepared for his inauguration on March 4, 1861, people in both the North and the South wondered what he would say and do. They wondered, too, what would happen in Vir-

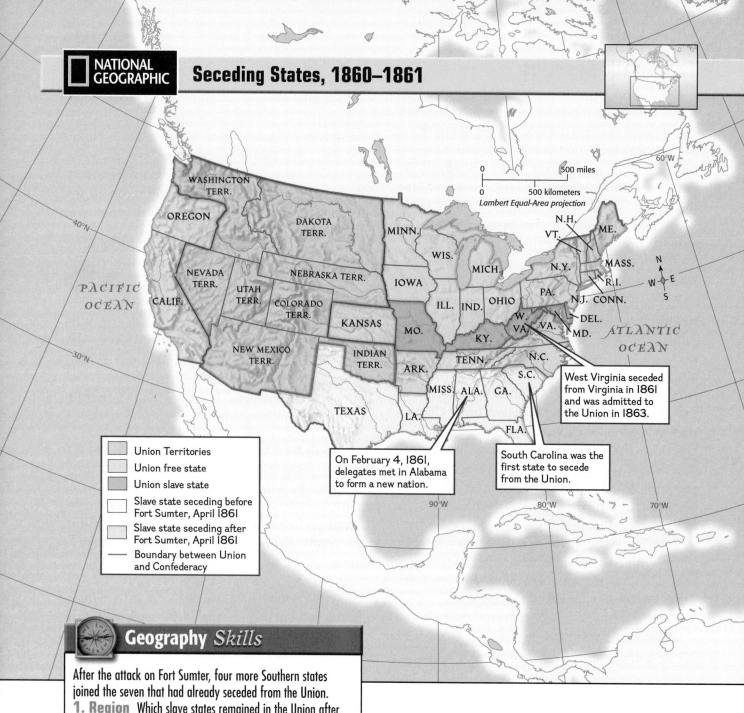

0 ___ 500 miles
0 ___ 500 kilometers
Lambert Equal-Area projection

WASHINGTON TERR.

OREGON

DAKOTA TERR.

MINN.

N.H.

VT.

ME.

WIS.

MICH.

N.Y.

MASS.

R.I.

NEVADA TERR.

NEBRASKA TERR.

IOWA

PA.

N.J. CONN.

PACIFIC OCEAN

CALIF.

UTAH TERR.

COLORADO TERR.

ILL. IND.

OHIO

W. VA.

VA.

DEL.

MD.

KANSAS

MO.

KY.

ATLANTIC OCEAN

NEW MEXICO TERR.

INDIAN TERR.

ARK.

TENN.

N.C.

S.C.

MISS. ALA. GA.

West Virginia seceded from Virginia in 1861 and was admitted to the Union in 1863.

TEXAS

LA.

FLA.

On February 4, 1861, delegates met in Alabama to form a new nation.

South Carolina was the first state to secede from the Union.

Union Territories
Union free state
Union slave state
Slave state seceding before Fort Sumter, April 1861
Slave state seceding after Fort Sumter, April 1861
Boundary between Union and Confederacy

Geography *Skills*

After the attack on Fort Sumter, four more Southern states joined the seven that had already seceded from the Union.

1. Region Which slave states remained in the Union after the Fort Sumter attack?

2. Analyzing Information Which states did not secede until after the Fort Sumter attack?

ginia, North Carolina, Kentucky, Tennessee, Missouri, and Arkansas. These slave states had chosen to remain in the Union, but the decision was not final. If the United States used force against the Confederate States of America, the remaining slave states also might secede. In his Inaugural Address, the new president mixed toughness and words of peace. He said that

secession would not be permitted, vowing to hold federal property in the South and to enforce the laws of the United States. At the same time, Lincoln pleaded with the people of the South for reconciliation:

❝We are not enemies, but friends. We must not be enemies. Though passion may have strained, it must not break our bonds of affection.❞

Reading Check **Explaining** How did the seceding states justify their right to leave the Union?

Fort Sumter

The South soon tested President Lincoln's vow to hold federal property. Confederate forces had already seized some United States forts within their states. Although Lincoln did not want to start a war by trying to take the forts back, allowing the Confederates to keep them would amount to admitting their right to secede.

On the day after his inauguration, Lincoln received a dispatch from the commander of **Fort Sumter,** a United States fort on an island guarding Charleston Harbor. The message warned that the fort was low on supplies and that the Confederates demanded its surrender.

The War Begins

Lincoln responded by sending a message to Governor Francis Pickens of South Carolina. He informed Pickens that he was sending an unarmed expedition with supplies to Fort Sumter. Lincoln promised that Union forces would not "throw in men, arms, or ammunition" unless they were fired upon. The president thus left the decision to start shooting up to the Confederates.

Confederate president Jefferson Davis and his advisers made a fateful choice. They ordered their forces to attack Fort Sumter before the Union supplies could arrive. Confederate guns opened fire on the fort early on April 12, 1861. Union captain Abner Doubleday witnessed the attack from inside the fort:

> 66Showers of balls . . . and shells . . . poured into the fort in one incessant stream, causing great flakes of masonry to fall in all directions.99

High seas had prevented Union relief ships from reaching the besieged fort. The Union garrison held out for 33 hours before surrendering on April 14. Thousands of shots were exchanged during the siege, but there was no loss of life on either side. The Confederates hoisted their flag over the fort, and all the guns in the harbor sounded a triumphant salute.

News of the attack galvanized the North. President Lincoln issued a call for 75,000 troops to fight to save the Union, and volunteers quickly signed up. Meanwhile, Virginia, North Carolina, Tennessee, and Arkansas voted to join the Confederacy. The Civil War had begun.

✓ **Reading Check** **Explaining** What action did Lincoln take after the attack on Fort Sumter?

HISTORY Online

Student Web Activity
Visit tarvol1.glencoe.com and click on **Chapter 15— Student Web Activities** for an activity on the period leading up to the Civil War.

SECTION 4 ASSESSMENT

Checking for Understanding

1. **Key Terms** Write a newspaper article about the election of 1860, using the terms states' rights and secession.
2. **Reviewing Facts** Who served as the president of the Confederate States of America?

Reviewing Themes

3. **Geography and History** What role did sectionalism play in Lincoln's winning the 1860 election?

Critical Thinking

4. **Drawing Conclusions** Do you think either Northerners or Southerners believed that secession would *not* lead to war? Explain.
5. **Organizing Information** Re-create the diagram below. In the ovals, describe the events leading to the firing on Fort Sumter.

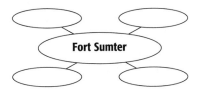

Fort Sumter

Analyzing Visuals

6. **Geography Skills** Examine the map on page 452. How many states made up the Confederacy? Which state seceded earlier—Mississippi or Arkansas?

Interdisciplinary Activity

Expository Writing Reread the excerpts on pages 450 and 452 from Lincoln's first inaugural address. Write a paragraph expressing in your own words what Lincoln said about government, union, liberty, and equality.

What were people's lives like in the past?

What—and who—were people talking about? What did they eat? What did they do for fun? These two pages will give you some clues to everyday life in the U.S. as you step back in time with TIME Notebook.

Profile

It's 1853, and **AMELIA STEWART** *is heading west to Oregon with her husband and seven children in a covered wagon. How hard can the five-month trip be? Here are two entries from her diary:*

MONDAY, AUGUST 8 We have to make a drive of 22 miles without water today. Have our cans filled to drink. Here we left, unknowingly, our [daughter] Lucy behind, not a soul had missed her until we had gone some miles, when we stopped a while to rest the cattle; just then another train drove up behind us, with Lucy. She was terribly frightened and said she was sitting under the bank of the river when we started, busy watching some wagons cross, and did not know that we were ready....It was a lesson for all of us.

FRIDAY, AUGUST 12 Lost one of our oxen. We were traveling slowly along, when he dropped dead in the yoke....I could hardly help shedding tears, when we drove round this poor ox who had helped us along thus far, and had given us his very last step.

MILESTONES
EVENTS OF THE TIME

CLOTHED. Hundreds of miners in 1850 by **LEVI STRAUSS**. Using canvas he originally intended to make into tents, Levi made sturdy, tough pants with lots of pockets—perfect clothing for the rough work of mining. Can you imagine anyone in the city ever wearing them?

BETTMANN/CORBIS

MARCHED. Just under 100 camels in 1857, from San Antonio to Los Angeles, led by hired Turkish, Greek, and Armenian camel drivers. It is hoped the desert beasts will help the U.S. Army open the West.

MAILED. Thousands of letters carried by **PONY EXPRESS** in 1860 from Missouri to California in an extremely short time—only 10 days! Riders switch to fresh horses every 10 or 15 miles and continue through the night, blizzards, and attacks by outlaws.

FRONTIER FOOD

Trail Mix

Hard Tack for a Hard Trip

INGREDIENTS: • **3 cups flour** • **3 tsp. salt** • **1 cup water**

Mix all ingredients and stir until it becomes too difficult. Knead the dough; add more flour until mixture is very dry. Roll to 1/2-inch thickness and cut into 3" squares, poke with a skewer [pin] to make several holes in each piece (for easy breaking). Bake 30 minutes in a hot oven until hard. Store for up to 10 years.

WESTERN WORD PLAY
Word Watch

Can you talk "Western"? Match the words below to their meaning.

1. maverick
2. Hangtown fry
3. grubstake
4. bonanza
5. palo alto
6. pard or rawwheel

a. gold rush favorite, made of eggs, bacon, and oysters

b. inexperienced '49er; eastern type not used to wearing boots

c. a lucky discovery of gold; a source of sudden wealth

d. a style of hat worn by gold rush miners

e. an individual who takes an independent stand, from the name of a Texas cattleman who left his herd unbranded

f. food provided by an investor to a gold prospector in exchange for a share of whatever gold the prospector finds

answers: 1. e; 2. a; 3. f, 4. c; 5. d, 6. b

The Price of a Life

This notice appeared in 1852.

CREDIT SALE OF A CHOICE GANG OF 41
SLAVES!
COMPRISING MECHANICS, LABORERS, ETC,
FOR THE SETTLEMENT OF A CO-PARTNERSHIP OF RAILROAD CONTRACTORS.
BY J. A. BEARD & MAY, J. A. BEARD, AUCT'R.
WILL BE SOLD AT AUCTION, AT BANKS' ARCADE, MAGAZINE STREET.

SALE OF SLAVES AND STOCK

The Negroes and Stock listed below are a Prime Lot, and belong to the ESTATE OF THE LATE LUTHER McGOWAN, and will be sold on Monday, Sept. 22nd, 1852, at the Fair Grounds, in Savannah, Georgia, at 1:00 P.M. The Negroes will be taken to the grounds two days previous to the Sale, so that they may be inspected by prospective buyers.

On account of the low prices listed below, they will be sold for cash only, and must be taken into custody within two hours after sale.

No.	Name	Age	Remarks	Price
1	Lunesta	27	Prime Rice Planter	
2	Violet	16	Housework and Nursemaid	$1,275.00
3	Lizzie	30	Rice, Unsound	900.00
4	Minda	27	Cotton, Prime Woman	300.00
5	Adam	28	Cotton, Prime Young Man	1,200.00
6	Abel	41	Rice Hand, Eyesight Poor	1,100.00
7	Tanney	22	Prime Cotton Hand	675.00
8	Flementina	39	Good Cook	950.00

CHICAGO HISTORICAL SOCIETY/PHOTO RESEARCHERS INC.

NUMBERS
U.S. AT THE TIME

$81,249,700
Estimated value of gold mined in 1852

89 Days it takes the American clipper ship, the *Flying Cloud*, to go from Boston around Cape Horn to San Francisco in 1851—a trip that normally takes eight or nine months

12 Poems included in Walt Whitman's new collection, called *Leaves of Grass* (1855)

33 Number of states in 1859 after Oregon enters the union

100 Seats in Congress won by the Republicans in 1854, the year the party was created

300,000 Copies of Harriet Beecher Stowe's novel, *Uncle Tom's Cabin*, sold in 1852

UNCLE TOM'S CABIN;
OR,
LIFE AMONG THE LOWLY.
BY
HARRIET BEECHER STOWE.

VOL. I.
SIXTEENTH THOUSAND.
BOSTON:
JOHN P. JEWETT & COMPANY.
CLEVELAND, OHIO:
JEWETT, PROCTOR & WORTHINGTON.
1852.

Chapter Summary

Road to Civil War

1820
- Missouri Compromise passed

1844
- Polk elected president

1845
- Texas becomes a state

1848
- Free-Soil Party nominates Van Buren

1850
- Compromise of 1850 passed

1852
- *Uncle Tom's Cabin* published

1854
- Kansas-Nebraska Act passed
- Republican Party formed

1856
- Violence erupts in Kansas
- Buchanan elected president

1857
- *Dred Scott* decision handed down

1858
- Lincoln-Douglas debates held

1859
- John Brown attacks Harpers Ferry

1860
- Lincoln is elected president
- South Carolina becomes first state to secede

1861
- Confederate States of America formed
- Fort Sumter attacked

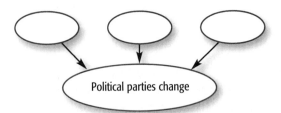

Reviewing Key Terms

Write five true *and five* false *statements using the terms below. Use only one term in each statement. Indicate which statements are true and which are false. Below each false statement explain why it is false.*

1. sectionalism
2. secede
3. border ruffians
4. arsenal
5. secession
6. fugitive
7. popular sovereignty
8. civil war
9. martyr
10. states' rights

Reviewing Key Facts

11. What was the purpose of the Missouri Compromise?
12. List the five parts of the Compromise of 1850.
13. What was Stephen Douglas's solution to the slavery issue in the Kansas and Nebraska territories?
14. How did Abraham Lincoln become a national figure in politics?
15. What was the *Dred Scott* decision? What did it mean for those opposed to slavery?
16. Why were there four parties and candidates in the presidential election of 1860?
17. How did Lincoln plan to prevent secession?

Critical Thinking

18. **Finding the Main Idea** Why was the balance of free and slave states in the Senate such an important issue?
19. **Drawing Conclusions** Why did Northerners protest Douglas's plan to repeal the Missouri Compromise?
20. **Determining Cause and Effect** Re-create the diagram below. List three ways pro- or antislavery groups changed the structure of political parties in the 1850s.

```
 ◯        ◯        ◯
    ↘      ↓      ↙
    ◯ Political parties change ◯
```

21. **Analyzing Themes: Geography and History** How did the North's larger population give it an edge over the South in the 1860 election?

Geography and History Activity

The election of 1860 divided the nation along sectional lines. Study the map below; then answer the questions that follow.

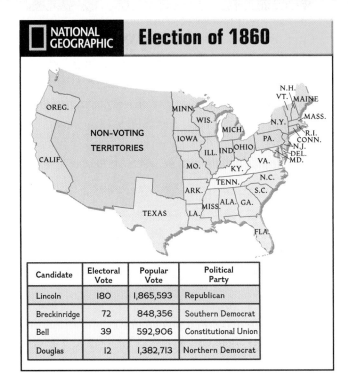

NATIONAL GEOGRAPHIC **Election of 1860**

Candidate	Electoral Vote	Popular Vote	Political Party
Lincoln	180	1,865,593	Republican
Breckinridge	72	848,356	Southern Democrat
Bell	39	592,906	Constitutional Union
Douglas	12	1,382,713	Northern Democrat

22. **Location** Which states supported Douglas?

23. **Region** In what region(s) was the Republican Party strongest?

24. **Region** In what region did Breckinridge find support?

Practicing Skills

25. **Recognizing Bias** Find written material about a topic of interest in your community. Possible sources include editorials, letters to the editor, and pamphlets from political candidates and interest groups. Write a short report analyzing the material for evidence of bias.

Technology Activity

26. **Using the Internet** Search the Internet for a list of political parties in existence today. Make a table that briefly summarizes each party's current goals. Then research to find the date that the party was founded. Include this information on your table, too. Then compare your table to the political parties discussed in Chapter 15.

HISTORY Online

Self-Check Quiz
Visit tarvol1.glencoe.com and click on **Chapter 15—Self-Check Quizzes** to prepare for the chapter test.

Citizenship Cooperative Activity

27. **Making Compromises** With a partner, think of a controversial issue that is a source of disagreement today. Take opposite sides on the issue; then work together to come up with a list of three compromises that would make the solution to this problem acceptable to both sides. Share the issue and your compromises with the class.

Alternative Assessment

28. **Portfolio Writing Activity** Write a report that answers these questions: Why was Congress in conflict over the question of statehood for California? How did the Compromise of 1850 address this question? What role did Clay, Calhoun, and Webster play in the Compromise?

Standardized Test Practice

Directions: Use the map of the Compromise of 1850 on page 443 to choose the *best* answer to the following question.

Which of the following statements is true?

A The Compromise of 1850 allowed the Oregon Territory to be open to slaveholding.

B The Compromise of 1850 did not make any land on the Pacific Ocean open to slaveholding.

C The Compromise of 1850 made every state touching the southern border of the United States open to slaveholding.

D The Compromise of 1850 gave the Minnesota Territory the authority to choose whether it would allow slaveholding.

Test-Taking Tip

Remember to use the information on the map to support your answer. Don't rely only on your memory. Check each answer choice against the map. Only one choice is correct.

CHAPTER 16 The Civil War
1861–1865

Why It Matters

The Civil War—a war in which Americans fought other Americans—transformed the United States. It shattered the economy of the South while contributing to the rapid economic growth of the North and the West. African Americans gained freedom when slavery was abolished, but the war left a legacy of bitterness between North and South that lasted for generations.

The Impact Today

Key events during this era still shape our lives today. For example:
* *The institution of slavery was abolished.*
* *The war established the power of the federal government over the states.*

The American Republic to 1877 *Video* *The chapter 16 video, "The Face of War," gives insight into the realities of the Civil War.*

1861
* Confederate States of America formed
* Conflict at Fort Sumter, South Carolina, begins Civil War

1863
* Emancipation Proclamation issued
* Battle of Gettysburg

1862
* Robert E. Lee named commander of Confederate armies

United States PRESIDENTS

Lincoln 1861–1865

1861   1862   1863

World

1861
* Charles Dickens's *Great Expectations* published
* Victor Emmanuel II recognized as king of unified Italy

1862
* Otto von Bismarck named premier of Prussia

1863
* Discovery of Lake Victoria as source of Nile River
* International Red Cross established

Fight for the Colors by **Don Troiani** Troiani has painted many dramatic war scenes, such as this one of the Battle of Gettysburg.

FOLDABLES™
Study Organizer

Organizing Information Study Foldable
Make this foldable to help you organize what you learn about the Civil War.

Step 1 Fold a sheet of paper in half from side to side.

Fold it so the left edge lies about ½ inch from the right edge.

Step 2 Turn the paper and fold it into thirds.

Step 3 Unfold and cut the top layer only along both folds.

This will make three tabs.

Step 4 Label your foldable as shown.

Before the War | During the War | After the War

The Civil War

Reading and Writing As you read the chapter, list events that occurred before, during, and after the Civil War under the appropriate tabs of your foldable.

1864
• Sherman's "march to the sea" begins
• Lincoln reelected president

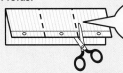

1865
• Civil War ends
• Lincoln assassinated

1864

1865

1864
• Maximilian installed as emperor of Mexico

1865
• Lewis Carroll publishes *Alice's Adventures in Wonderland*

HISTORY
Online

Chapter Overview
Visit tarvol1.glencoe.com and click on **Chapter 16—Chapter Overviews** to preview chapter information.

SECTION 1 The Two Sides

Guide to Reading

Main Idea
Both the North and the South had strengths and weaknesses that helped determine their military strategies.

Key Terms
border state, blockade, offensive, Rebel, Yankee

Reading Strategy
Classifying Information As you read the section, complete a chart like the one shown here by listing the strengths and weaknesses of the Union and the Confederacy.

	Union	Confederacy
Strengths		
Weaknesses		

Read to Learn
- why the border states played an important part in the war.
- how the North and South compared in terms of population, industry, resources, and war aims.

Section Theme
Government and Democracy The Southern states seceded from the Union to protect states' rights.

Preview of Events

♦1861   ♦1862   ♦1863

February 1861
The Confederacy forms

April 1861
Four more states join the Confederacy

Summer 1861
Confederate forces total 112,000; Union 187,000

June 1863
West Virginia joins Union

AN American Story

Confederate soldier, 1861

Union sergeant Driscoll directed his troops at Malvern Hill on July 1, 1862. The enemy fought fiercely, especially one young Confederate soldier. Driscoll raised his rifle, took aim, and shot the boy. As he passed the spot where the boy had fallen, Driscoll turned the daring soldier over to see what he looked like. The boy opened his eyes and faintly murmured, "Father," then his eyes fluttered shut, never to open again. A Union captain later wrote, "I will forever recollect the frantic grief of Driscoll; it was harrowing to witness. He [had killed] his son, who had gone South before the war."

Like the Driscolls, many families were divided by the war. Neither side imagined, however, that the war would cost such a terrible price in human life. During the four years of fighting, hundreds of thousands of Americans were killed in battle.

Choosing Sides

By February 1861, seven states had left the Union and formed the Confederacy. After the Confederate bombardment of Fort Sumter, President Abraham Lincoln issued a call for troops to save the Union. His action caused Virginia, North Carolina, Tennessee, and Arkansas to join the Confederacy. These four states brought needed soldiers and supplies to the Confederacy. For its capital, the Confederacy chose **Richmond,** Virginia, a city only about 100 miles from the Union capital of Washington, D.C.

Four states that allowed slavery—Missouri, Kentucky, Maryland, and Delaware—remained in the Union. The people of these border states were divided over which side to support. Missouri, Kentucky, and Maryland had such strong support for the South that the three states teetered on the brink of secession.

Losing the border states would seriously damage the North. All had strategic locations. Missouri could control parts of the Mississippi River and major routes to the West. Kentucky controlled the Ohio River. Delaware was close to the important Northern city of Philadelphia.

Maryland, perhaps the most important of the border states, was close to Richmond. Vital railroad lines passed through Maryland. Most significantly, Washington, D.C., lay within the state. If Maryland seceded, the North's government would be surrounded.

Maryland's key role became clear in April 1861. A mob in Baltimore attacked Northern troops; Confederate sympathizers burned railroad bridges and cut the telegraph line to Washington, isolating the capital from the rest of the North. Northern troops soon arrived, but the nation's capital had suffered some anxious days.

Remaining With the Union

Lincoln had to move cautiously to avoid upsetting people in the border states. If he announced that he aimed to end slavery, for instance, groups supporting the Confederacy might take their states out of the Union. If he ordered Northern troops into Kentucky, Confederate sympathizers there would claim the state had been invaded and swing it to the South.

In some ways Lincoln acted boldly. He suspended some constitutional rights and used his power to arrest people who supported secession. In the end Lincoln's approach worked. The border states stayed in the Union, but many of their citizens joined armies of the South.

A Secession From the South

Most white Southerners favored secession. Still, pockets of Union support existed in parts of Tennessee and Virginia. People in the

History *Through Art*

7th New York Militia at Jersey City on April 19, 1861 by E.L. Henry The 7th New York Militia was one of the first fully equipped and trained units at the outbreak of the war. **Why were troops ordered to the nation's capital in early 1861?**

Appalachian region generally opposed secession. In western Virginia a movement to secede from the state and rejoin the Union grew. In 1861, 48 Virginia counties organized themselves as a separate state called **West Virginia.** Congress admitted this state to the Union in 1863.

✓ **Reading Check** **Explaining** Why was Maryland strategically important?

Comparing North and South

When the war began, both sides had advantages and disadvantages. How they would use those strengths and weaknesses would determine the war's outcome.

The North enjoyed the advantages of a larger population, more industry, and more abundant resources than the South. It had a better banking system, which helped to raise money for the war. The North also possessed more ships, and almost all the members of the regular navy remained loyal to the Union. Finally, the North had a larger and more efficient railway network.

The North also faced disadvantages. Bringing the Southern states back into the Union would be difficult. The North would have to invade and hold the South—a large area filled with a hostile population. Furthermore, the Southern people's support for the war remained strong. Recalling the example of the American Revolution, when the smaller, weaker colonies had won independence from wealthy Great Britain, many believed the South had a good chance of winning.

One Northern advantage was not obvious until later. Both sides greatly underestimated Abraham Lincoln. His dedication, intelligence, and humanity would lead the North to victory.

One of the main advantages of the South was the strong support its white population gave the war. Southerners also had the advantage of fighting in familiar territory—defending their land, their homes, and their way of life.

The military leadership of the South, at least at first, was superior to the North's. Southern families had a strong tradition of military training and service, and military college graduates provided the South with a large pool of officers. Overseeing the Southern effort was Confederate president **Jefferson Davis,** a West Point graduate and an experienced soldier.

The South faced material disadvantages. It had a smaller population of free men to draw upon in building an army. It also possessed very few factories to manufacture weapons and other supplies, and it produced less than half as much food as the North. With less than half the miles of railroad tracks and vastly fewer trains than the North, the Confederate government had difficulty delivering food, weapons, and other supplies to its troops.

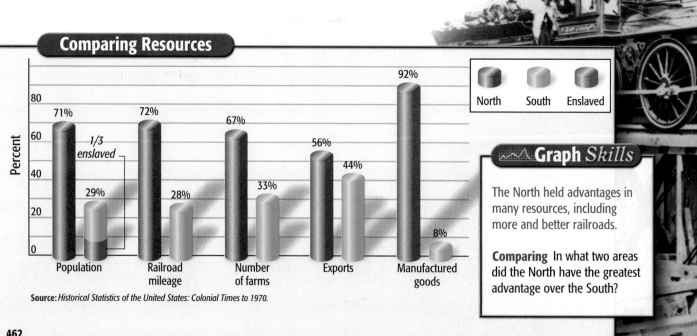

Comparing Resources

Percent

| Population | Railroad mileage | Number of farms | Exports | Manufactured goods |

71% — 1/3 enslaved — 29%
72% — 28%
67% — 33%
56% — 44%
92% — 8%

North South Enslaved

Source: *Historical Statistics of the United States: Colonial Times to 1970.*

📈 **Graph** *Skills*

The North held advantages in many resources, including more and better railroads.

Comparing In what two areas did the North have the greatest advantage over the South?

The belief in **states' rights**—a founding principle of the Confederacy—also hampered the South's efforts. The individual states refused to give the Confederate government sufficient power. As a result, the government found it difficult to fight the war effectively.

War Aims and Strategy

The North and the South entered the Civil War with different aims. The main goal of the North at the outset was to bring the Southern states back into the Union. Ending slavery was not a major Northern goal at first, but this changed as the war continued.

The Union's plan for winning the war included three main strategies. First the North would blockade, or close, Southern ports to prevent supplies from reaching the South—and to prevent the South from earning money by exporting cotton. Second, the Union intended to gain control of the Mississippi River to cut Southern supply lines and to split the Confederacy. Third, the North planned to capture Richmond, Virginia, the Confederate capital.

For the South, the primary aim of the war was to win recognition as an independent nation. Independence would allow Southerners to preserve their traditional way of life—a way of life that included slavery.

To achieve this goal, the South worked out a defensive strategy. It planned to defend its homeland, holding on to as much territory as possible until the North tired of fighting. The South expected that Britain and France, which imported large quantities of Southern cotton, would pressure the North to end the war to restore their cotton supply.

During the war Southern leaders sometimes changed strategy and took the offensive—went on the attack. They moved their armies northward to threaten Washington, D.C., and other Northern cities, hoping to persuade the North it could not win the war.

Reading Check **Explaining** What role did Jefferson Davis play in the war?

American People at War

The Civil War was more than a war between the states. It often pitted brother against brother, parents against their children, and neighbor against neighbor.

American Against American

The leaders from both North and South—and their families—felt these divisions. President Lincoln's wife, Mary Todd Lincoln, had several relatives who fought in the Confederate army. John Crittenden, a senator from Kentucky, had two sons who became generals in the war—one for the Confederacy and one for the Union. Officers on both sides—including Confederate general Robert E. Lee, and Union generals George McClellan and William Tecumseh Sherman—had attended the United States Military Academy at West Point, never dreaming that they would one day command forces against each other.

Who Were the Soldiers?

Most of the soldiers were young. The average age of a recruit was 25 years old, but about 40 percent were 21 or younger. Ted Upson of Indiana was only 16 when he begged his father to let him join the Union army. His father replied, "This Union your ancestors and mine helped to make must be saved from destruction." *(See page 603 for an additional primary source reading about Civil War soldiers.)*

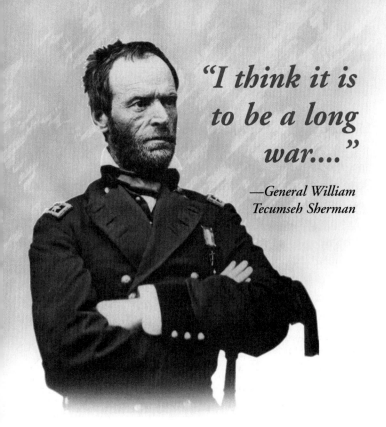

"I think it is to be a long war...."

—*General William Tecumseh Sherman*

William Stone from Louisiana rushed to join the Confederate army after the attack on Fort Sumter. His sister Kate wrote that he was

66 . . . wild to be off to Virginia. He so fears that the fighting will be over before he can get there. 99

Soldiers came from every region and all walks of life. Most, though, came from farms. Almost half of the North's troops and more than 60 percent of the South's had owned or worked on farms. The Union army did not permit African Americans to join at first, but they did serve later. Lincoln's early terms of enlistment asked governors to supply soldiers for 90 days. When the conflict did not end quickly, soldiers' terms became longer.

By the summer of 1861 the Confederate army had about 112,000 soldiers, who were sometimes called **Rebels.** The Union had about 187,000 soldiers, or **Yankees,** as they were also known. By the end of the war, about 850,000 men fought for the Confederacy and about 2.1 million men fought for the Union. The Union number included just under 200,000 African Americans. About 10,000 Hispanic soldiers fought in the conflict.

False Hopes

When the war began, each side expected an early victory. A Confederate soldier from a town in Alabama expected the war to be over well within a year because "we are going to kill the last Yankee before that time if there is any fight in them still." Northerners were just as confident that they would beat the South quickly.

Some leaders saw the situation more clearly. Northern general William Tecumseh Sherman wrote, "I think it is to be a long war—very long—much longer than any politician thinks." The first spring of the war proved that Sherman's prediction was accurate.

✓ **Reading Check** **Comparing** Which side had the larger fighting force?

SECTION 1 ASSESSMENT

Checking for Understanding

1. **Key Terms** Write a short paragraph in which you use all of the following key terms: border state, blockade, offensive, Rebel, Yankee.

2. **Reviewing Facts** Why were the border states important to the North?

Reviewing Themes

3. **Government and Democracy** How did a strong belief in states' rights affect the South during the war?

Critical Thinking

4. **Predict** What do you think would be the South's greatest advantage in the war?

5. **Comparing** Create a diagram like the one shown here. Then compare Northern and Southern aims and strategies.

	North	South
Aims		
Strategies		

Analyzing Visuals

6. **Making Generalizations** Review the graph on page 462 and write a general conclusion based on the data presented in the graph.

Interdisciplinary Activity

Expository Writing You are a Southerner (or a Northerner) in 1861. Write a journal entry that explains your reasons for joining the Confederate (or Union) army.

America's LITERATURE

Stephen Crane (1871–1900)

Stephen Crane began his career in journalism while still in his teens. Later, as a reporter, Crane covered several wars in the late 1890s. He had not yet seen a battlefield, however, when he wrote *The Red Badge of Courage.* Even so, he described the experience of war so realistically that even combat veterans admired his work.

READ TO DISCOVER

What is it like to be a soldier facing battle for the first time? Henry Fleming, the young recruit in *The Red Badge of Courage,* offers some answers as he thinks about his role in the war. What battle does Henry fight with himself before he fights in an actual Civil War battle?

READER'S DICTIONARY

Huns: soldiers known for their fierce fighting
haversack: bag soldiers used to carry personal items
obliged: felt it necessary to do something
confronted: faced
lurking: lying in wait
tumult: uproar

The Red Badge of Courage

Various veterans had told him tales. Some talked of . . . tremendous bodies of fierce soldiery who were sweeping along like the **Huns.** Others spoke of tattered and eternally hungry men. . . . "They'll charge through hell's fire an' brimstone t' git a holt on a **haversack . . .**" he was told. From the stories, the youth imagined the red, live bones sticking out through slits in the faded uniforms.

Still, he could not put a whole faith in veterans' tales, for recruits were their prey. They talked much of smoke, fire, and blood, but he could not tell how much might be lies. They persistently yelled "Fresh fish!" at him, and were in no wise to be trusted.

However, he perceived now that it did not greatly matter what kind of soldiers he was going to fight. . . . There was a more serious problem. He lay in his bunk pondering upon it. He tried to mathematically prove to himself that he would not run from a battle.

Previously he had never felt **obliged** to wrestle too seriously with this question. In his life he had taken certain things for granted, never challenging his belief in ultimate success. . . . But here he was **confronted** with a thing of moment. It had suddenly appeared to him that perhaps in a battle he might run.

He was forced to admit that as far as war was concerned he knew nothing of himself. . . .

A little panic-fear grew in his mind. As his imagination went forward to a fight, he saw hideous possibilities. He contemplated the **lurking** menaces of the future, and failed in an effort to see himself standing stoutly in the midst of them. He recalled his visions of broken-bladed glory, but in the shadow of the impending **tumult** he suspected them to be impossible pictures.

Medal of Honor

ANALYZING LITERATURE

1. **Recall and Interpret** How did Henry view the veterans and their war tales?
2. **Evaluate and Connect** What feelings do you think you might have just before going into battle?

Interdisciplinary Activity

Descriptive Writing Write a conversation between two young soldiers before their first battle. Save your work for your portfolio.

Guide to Reading

Main Idea

Neither the Union nor the Confederate forces gained a strong advantage during the early years of the war.

Key Terms

blockade runner, ironclad, casualty

Reading Strategy

Classifying Information As you read, describe the outcome of each of these battles on a chart like the one shown.

Battle	Outcome
First Battle of Bull Run (Manassas)	
Monitor v. *Merrimack*	
Antietam	

Read to Learn

- what successes and failures the North and the South had in the early years of the war.
- how the North's naval blockade hurt the South.

Section Theme

Geography and History The North and the South fought the war differently in different geographic regions.

Preview of Events

♦1861	♦1862	♦1863

July 1861
First Battle of Bull Run (Manassas)

February 1862
Grant captures Fort Henry and Fort Donelson

April 1862
Battle of Shiloh

September 1862
Battle of Antietam

AN American Story

Sunday, July 21, 1861, was a pleasant, sunny day in Washington, D.C. Hundreds of cheerful residents, food baskets in hand, left the city and crossed the Potomac River to spend the day in Virginia. They planned to picnic while watching the first battle between the Union and the Confederate armies. Expecting to see Union troops crush the Rebels, they looked forward to a quick victory. The Confederate soldiers also expected a quick victory. They "carried dress suits with them, and any quantity of fine linen. Every soldier, nearly, had a servant with him, and a whole lot of spoons and forks, so as to live comfortably and elegantly in camp...."

Civil War cannon

First Battle of Bull Run

This first major battle of the Civil War was fought in northern Virginia, about five miles from a town called Manassas Junction near Bull Run—a small river in the area. Usually called the **First Battle of Bull Run,** it began when about 30,000 inexperienced Union troops commanded by General Irvin McDowell attacked a smaller, equally inexperienced Confederate force led by General P.G.T. Beauregard.

President Lincoln meets General McClellan and other Union officers.

The Yankees drove the Confederates back at first. Then the Rebels rallied, inspired by reinforcements under General Thomas Jackson. Jackson, who was seen holding out heroically "like a stone wall," became known thereafter as **"Stonewall" Jackson.** The Confederates unleashed a savage counterattack that forced the Union lines to break.

The Confederates surged forward with a strange, unearthly scream that came to be known as the Rebel yell. Terrified, the Northern soldiers began to drop their guns and packs and run. One observer, Representative Albert Riddle, reported:

   ❝ A cruel, crazy, mad, hopeless panic possessed them. . . . The heat was awful . . . the men were exhausted—their mouths gaped, their lips cracked and blackened with the powder of the cartridges they had bitten off in the battle, their eyes staring in frenzy. **❞**

The Union army began an orderly retreat that quickly became a mad stampede when the retreating Union troops collided with the civilians, fleeing in panic back to Washington, D.C. The Confederates, though victorious, were too disorganized and weakened to pursue the retreating Yankees. Regardless, the South rejoiced. Edmund Ruffin of Virginia thought it meant "the close of the war."

A Shock for the North

The outcome of the battle shocked the North. Northerners began to understand that the war could be a long, difficult, and costly struggle. Although discouraged by the results, President Abraham Lincoln was also determined. Within days he issued a call for more volunteers for the army. He signed two bills requesting a total of one million soldiers, who would serve for three years. Volunteers soon crowded into recruiting offices. Lincoln also appointed a new general, **George B. McClellan,** to head the Union army of the East—called the **Army of the Potomac—** and to organize the troops.

✓ Reading Check **Explaining** How did the First Battle of Bull Run change people's views about the war?

War at Sea

Even before Bull Run, Lincoln had ordered a naval blockade of Southern ports. An effective blockade would prevent the South from exporting its cotton and from importing the supplies necessary to continue the war.

Enforcing the Blockade

When the war began, the North did not have enough ships to blockade the South's entire 3,500-mile coastline. Many Confederate ships, called blockade runners, could sail in and out of Southern ports. In time, the North built more ships and became better able to enforce the blockade.

The blockade caused serious problems for the South. Although the blockade could never close off all Southern trade, it did reduce the trade by more than two-thirds. Goods such as coffee, shoes, nails, and salt—as well as guns and ammunition—were in short supply throughout the war.

The *Monitor* Versus the *Merrimack*

The South did not intend to let the blockade go unchallenged. Southerners salvaged the *Merrimack,* a Union warship that Northern forces had abandoned when Confederate forces seized the naval shipyard in **Norfolk, Virginia.** The Confederates rebuilt the wooden ship, covered it with thick iron plates, and renamed it the *Virginia.*

On March 8, 1862, this ironclad warship attacked a group of Union ships off the coast of Virginia. The North's wooden warships could not damage the Confederate ship—shells simply bounced off its sides.

Some Northern leaders feared the South would use the ironclad warship to destroy much of the Union navy, steam up the Potomac River, and bombard Washington, D.C. However, the North had already built an ironclad ship of its own, the *Monitor.* Described as looking like a "tin can on a shingle," the *Monitor* rushed south to engage the Confederate ship in battle.

On March 9, the two ironclads exchanged fire, but neither ship could sink the other. The Union succeeded in keeping the *Merrimack* in the harbor, so it never again threatened Northern ships. The battle marked a new age in naval warfare—the first battle between two metal-covered ships.

Reading Check **Explaining** What was significant about the battle between the *Merrimack* and the *Monitor?*

War in the West

After the First Battle of Bull Run in July 1861, the war in the East settled into a stalemate as each side built its strength. Generals focused on training raw recruits, turning civilians into soldiers. For a while the action shifted to the West.

Early Victories for the North

One of the North's primary goals in the West was to gain control of the Mississippi and Tennessee Rivers. This would split the Confederacy and hinder Southern efforts to transport goods.

The Union launched its operations in the West from Cairo, Illinois. The city was strategically located where the Ohio and Mississippi Rivers meet. In addition, Cairo was only a short distance from the Cumberland and Tennessee Rivers. The Union commander at Cairo was **Ulysses S. Grant.**

Ironclads marked the beginning of the modern, armored, self-propelled warship.

Early in 1862, Grant was ordered to move against Confederate forces under General Albert Sidney Johnson in Kentucky and Tennessee. On February 6, with the aid of a fleet of newly made ironclads under Andrew Foote, Grant captured Fort Henry on the Tennessee River. Ten days later Grant captured Fort Donelson on the Cumberland. When the Confederate commander at Fort Donelson realized he was trapped, he asked Grant for his terms. Grant's reply was,

❝No terms except unconditional and immediate surrender can be accepted.❞

"Unconditional Surrender" Grant became the North's new hero.

Grant's victories helped secure the lower Tennessee River. They also opened a path for Union troops to march into Tennessee, Mississippi, and Alabama. The victories drove the Confederates out of Kentucky, where the South had been attempting to persuade Kentuckians to secede from the Union.

⭐ Geography
The Battle of Shiloh

General Grant and about 40,000 troops then headed south along the Tennessee River toward Corinth, Mississippi, an important railroad junction. In early April 1862, the Union army camped at Pittsburg Landing, 20 miles from Corinth. Nearby was a church named Shiloh. Additional Union forces came from Nashville to join Grant.

Confederate leaders decided to strike first, before the reinforcements arrived. Early in the morning of April 6, Confederate forces led by Albert Sidney Johnston and P.G.T. Beauregard launched a surprise attack on the Union troops. The **Battle of Shiloh** lasted two days, with some of the most bitter, bloody fighting of the war. The first day, the Confederates drove Grant and his troops back to the Tennessee River. The second day, the Union forces recovered. Aided by the 25,000 troops from Nashville and shelling by gunboats on the river, they defeated the Confederates, who withdrew to Corinth.

Names of Battles

Many Civil War battles have two names. The Union named battles after the nearest body of water. The Confederacy named them after the nearest settlement. Therefore, the battle called the Battle of Bull Run (a river) in the North was known as the Battle of Manassas (a settlement) in the South.

The losses in the Battle of Shiloh were enormous. Together the two armies suffered more than 20,000 casualties—people killed or wounded. Confederate general Johnston also died in the bloodbath. One Confederate soldier lamented that the battle "was too shocking [and] too horrible."

After their narrow victory at Shiloh, Union forces gained control of Corinth on May 30. Memphis, Tennessee, fell to Union armies on June 6. The North seemed well on its way to controlling the Mississippi River.

New Orleans Falls

A few weeks after Shiloh, the North won another important victory. On April 25, 1862, Union naval forces under **David Farragut** captured New Orleans, Louisiana, the largest city in the South. Farragut, who was of Spanish descent, had grown up in the South but remained loyal to the Union. His capture of New Orleans, near the mouth of the Mississippi River, meant that the Confederacy could no longer use the river to carry its goods to sea. Together with Grant's victories to the north, Farragut's capture of New Orleans gave Union forces control of almost all the Mississippi River.

Reading Check **Analyzing** Why was control of the Mississippi River important to the Union?

War in the East

In the East, General McClellan was training the Army of the Potomac to be an effective fighting force. An expert at training soldiers,

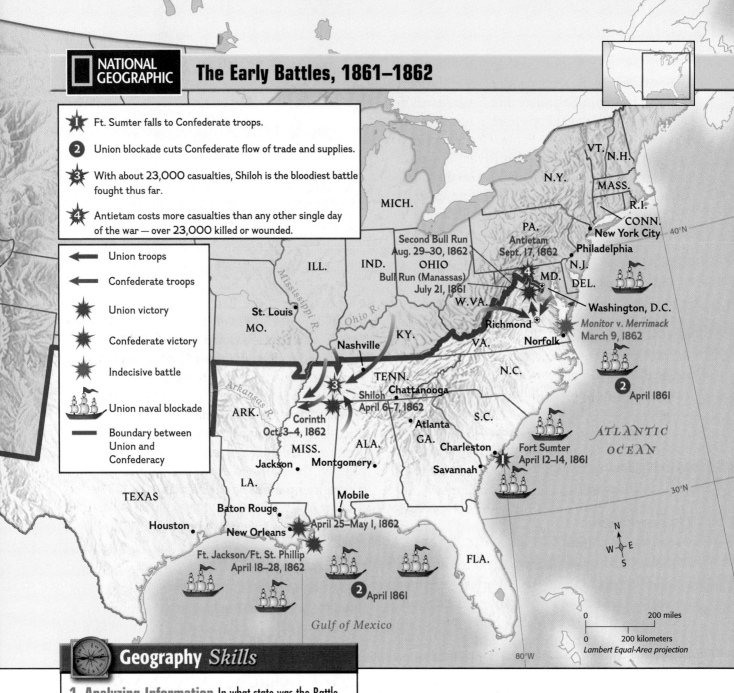

The Early Battles, 1861–1862

NATIONAL GEOGRAPHIC

1. Ft. Sumter falls to Confederate troops.

2. Union blockade cuts Confederate flow of trade and supplies.

3. With about 23,000 casualties, Shiloh is the bloodiest battle fought thus far.

4. Antietam costs more casualties than any other single day of the war — over 23,000 killed or wounded.

Union troops
Confederate troops
Union victory
Confederate victory
Indecisive battle
Union naval blockade
Boundary between Union and Confederacy

Second Bull Run Aug. 29–30, 1862
Antietam Sept. 17, 1862
Bull Run (Manassas) July 21, 1861
Monitor v. Merrimack March 9, 1862
Shiloh April 6–7, 1862
Corinth Oct. 3–4, 1862
Fort Sumter April 12–14, 1861
Ft. Jackson/Ft. St. Phillip April 18–28, 1862
April 25–May 1, 1862

ATLANTIC OCEAN

Gulf of Mexico

0   200 miles
0   200 kilometers
Lambert Equal-Area projection

Geography Skills

1. **Analyzing Information** In what state was the Battle of Shiloh fought?
2. **Summarizing** In what battles were Confederate forces victorious?

McClellan thoroughly reorganized and drilled the Army of the Potomac. However, when faced with the prospect of battle, McClellan was cautious and worried that his troops were not ready. He hesitated to fight because of reports that overestimated the size of the Rebel forces. Finally, in March 1862, the Army of the Potomac was ready for action. Its goal was to capture Richmond, the Confederate capital.

Union Defeat at Richmond

Instead of advancing directly overland to Richmond as Lincoln wished, McClellan moved his huge army by ship to a peninsula between the York and the James Rivers southeast of the city. From there he began a major offensive known as the **Peninsular Campaign.** The operation took many weeks. Time passed and opportunities to attack slipped away as General McClellan readied his troops and tried to evaluate the enemy's strength. Lincoln, constantly prodding McClellan to fight, ended one message with an urgent plea: "You must act." Complaining of his difficult situation, McClellan did not act. His delays allowed the Confederates to prepare their defense of Richmond.

McClellan and his army inched slowly toward Richmond, getting so close that the troops could hear the city's church bells. At the end of June, the Union forces finally met the Confederates in a series of encounters known as the Seven Days' Battles. In these battles Confederate general **Robert E. Lee** took command of the army opposing McClellan. Before the battles began, Lee's cavalry leader, **James E.B. (J.E.B.) Stuart,** performed a daring tactic. He led his 1,200 troops in a circle around the Union army, gathering vital information about Union positions and boosting Southern morale. Stuart lost only one man in the action. General Lee then boldly countered Union advances and eventually drove the Yankees back to the James River. The Union troops had failed to capture Richmond.

Gloom in the North

Reports from Richmond disheartened the North. Despite the good news of Union victories in the West, failure to take the Confederate capital left Northerners with little hope. There was another call for volunteers—300,000 this time—

but the response was slow. The Southern strategy of making the North weary of war seemed to be working.

The defeat had not been complete, however. McClellan's army had been pushed back, but it was larger than Lee's and still only 25 miles from Richmond. When McClellan failed to renew the attack, President Lincoln ordered him to move his army back to northern Virginia and join the troops led by Major General John Pope.

Stonewall Jackson's forces moved north to attack Pope's supply base at Manassas. Jackson's troops marched 50 miles in two days and were then joined by the rest of Lee's army. On August 29, 1862, Pope attacked the approaching Confederates and started the Second Battle of Bull Run. The battle ended in a Confederate victory. Richmond was no longer threatened. Indeed, the situation of the two sides was completely reversed. Lee and the Confederates now stood only 20 miles from Washington, D.C.

The Battle of Antietam

Following these Southern victories, Confederate president **Jefferson Davis** ordered Lee to launch an offensive into Maryland, northwest of

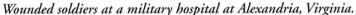

Wounded soldiers at a military hospital at Alexandria, Virginia.

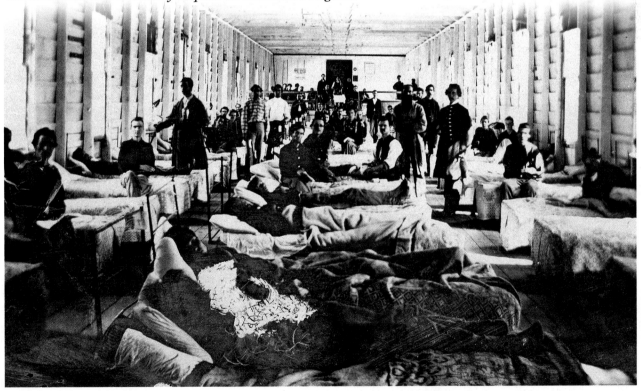

HISTORY
Online

Student Web Activity
Visit tarvol1.glencoe.com
and click on **Chapter 16—
Student Web Activities**
for an activity on the
Second Battle of Bull Run.

Washington. He hoped another victory would win aid from Great Britain and France. Lee also issued a proclamation urging the people of Maryland to join the Confederacy, but he received no response.

As Lee's army marched into Maryland in September 1862, McClellan and 80,000 Union troops moved slowly after them. On September 13 the North had an extraordinary piece of good luck. In a field near Frederick, Maryland, two Union soldiers found a copy of Lee's orders for his army wrapped around three cigars. The bundle had probably been dropped by a Southern officer.

Now McClellan knew exactly what Lee planned to do. He also learned that Lee's army was divided into four parts. This provided McClellan with an opportunity to overwhelm Lee's army one piece at a time.

Once again, McClellan was overly cautious. He waited four days before he decided to attack the Confederates. This enabled Lee to gather most of his forces together near Sharpsburg, Maryland, along the Antietam Creek.

The Union and the Confederate armies clashed on September 17 in the **Battle of Antietam.** It was the single bloodiest day of the entire war. A Union officer wrote that

66In the time that I am writing, every stalk of corn in [cornfields to the north] was cut as closely as could have been with a knife, and the slain lay in rows precisely as they had stood in their ranks a few minutes before.99

By the time the fighting ended, close to 6,000 Union and Confederate soldiers lay dead or dying, and another 17,000 were seriously wounded. Although both armies suffered heavy losses, neither was destroyed.

The day after the battle, Lee withdrew to Virginia. The Confederate retreat allowed the Union troops to claim victory. However, McClellan, who had been ordered by President Lincoln to "destroy the rebel army," did not pursue the Confederate troops. The president, disgusted with McClellan's failure to follow up his victory, removed McClellan from his command in November. Lincoln placed General **Ambrose Burnside** in command.

Antietam had a profound impact on the war. The Army of the Potomac finally gained some confidence, having forced Lee and his soldiers back south. More important, the battle marked a major change in Northern war aims. President Lincoln used the battle to take action against slavery.

Reading Check **Summarizing** What was the outcome of the Seven Days' Battles?

SECTION 2 ASSESSMENT

Checking for Understanding

1. **Key Terms** Use each of these terms in a sentence that will help explain its meaning: blockade runner, ironclad, casualty.

2. **Reviewing Facts** Explain why the North wanted to blockade the South.

Reviewing Themes

3. **Geography and History** What was the North's main goal in the western campaign?

Critical Thinking

4. **Analyzing Information** Why was Union general McClellan not effective as a military commander?

5. **Drawing Conclusions** Why was control of the Mississippi River important? Use a web like the one shown here.

Control of the Mississippi River

Analyzing Visuals

6. **Geography Skills** Study the map on page 470. Who claimed victory at the First Battle of Bull Run? When was the Battle of Shiloh fought?

Interdisciplinary Activity

Art Draw a cartoon that would accompany a front-page newspaper story describing the battle between the *Merrimack* and the *Monitor.*

A Call for Freedom

Guide to Reading

Main Idea
The Civil War provided opportunities for African Americans to contribute to the war effort.

Key Terms
emancipate, ratify

Reading Strategy
Classifying Information As you read the section, complete a table like the one shown describing what the Emancipation Proclamation and the Thirteenth Amendment to the Constitution were meant to accomplish.

	Goal
Emancipation Proclamation	
Thirteenth Amendment	

Read to Learn
- why Lincoln issued the Emancipation Proclamation.
- what role African Americans played in the Civil War.

Section Theme
Groups and Institutions The North's main goal from the start of the war was to preserve the Union, not to abolish slavery.

Preview of Events

1862	1863	1864	1865

1862
African Americans allowed to serve in the Union army

January 1863
Lincoln signs the Emancipation Proclamation

July 1863
Nearly half of the 54th Massachusetts Regiment is wiped out

1865
Thirteenth Amendment is ratified

Lincoln portrait, by artist Peter Baumgras

AN American Story

President Lincoln shook many hands on New Year's Day of 1863, as a reception was held to commemorate the official signing of the Emancipation Proclamation. Diplomats, cabinet members, and army officers filed past the president, and when he finally left the reception he noted that his arm was very stiff. As the document was presented, Lincoln remarked, "Now, this signature is one that will be closely examined and if they find my hand trembled, they will say 'he had some compunctions [second thoughts].' But, any way, it is going to be done!"

Emancipation

From the start of the war through the brutal Battle of Antietam, the Northerners' main goal was to preserve the Union rather than to destroy slavery. Abolitionists did not control the North, or even the Republican Party. Abraham Lincoln and other Republican leaders insisted on many occasions that they would act only to prevent the expansion of slavery.

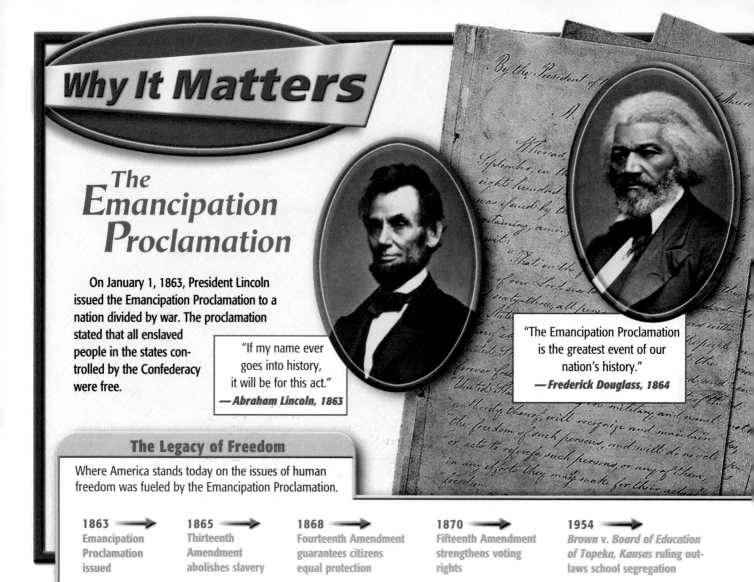

Why It Matters

The Emancipation Proclamation

On January 1, 1863, President Lincoln issued the Emancipation Proclamation to a nation divided by war. The proclamation stated that all enslaved people in the states controlled by the Confederacy were free.

"If my name ever goes into history, it will be for this act."
— *Abraham Lincoln, 1863*

"The Emancipation Proclamation is the greatest event of our nation's history."
— *Frederick Douglass, 1864*

The Legacy of Freedom

Where America stands today on the issues of human freedom was fueled by the Emancipation Proclamation.

1863 → Emancipation Proclamation issued

1865 → Thirteenth Amendment abolishes slavery

1868 → Fourteenth Amendment guarantees citizens equal protection

1870 → Fifteenth Amendment strengthens voting rights

1954 → *Brown* v. *Board of Education of Topeka, Kansas* ruling outlaws school segregation

---

Although Lincoln considered slavery immoral, he hesitated to move against slavery because of the border states. Lincoln knew that making an issue of slavery would divide the people and make the war less popular. In August 1862, Abraham Lincoln responded to pressure to declare an end to slavery.

❝ If I could save the Union without freeing *any* slave, I would do it; and if I could save it by freeing *all* the slaves, I would do it; and if I could save it by freeing some and leaving others alone, I would also do that. ❞

That was his official position. His personal wish was "that all men everywhere could be free."

As the war went on, attitudes toward slavery began to change. More Northerners believed that slavery was helping the war effort in the South. Enslaved people in the Confederacy raised crops used to feed the armies and did the heavy work in the trenches at the army camps. In the North's view, anything that weakened slavery struck a blow against the Confederacy.

As early as May 1861, some African Americans in the South escaped slavery by going into territory held by the Union army. In 1861 and 1862, Congress passed laws that freed enslaved people who were held by those active in the rebellion against the Union.

🏛 Citizenship
The Emancipation Proclamation

Lincoln was keenly aware of the shift in public opinion. He also knew that striking a blow against slavery would make Britain and France

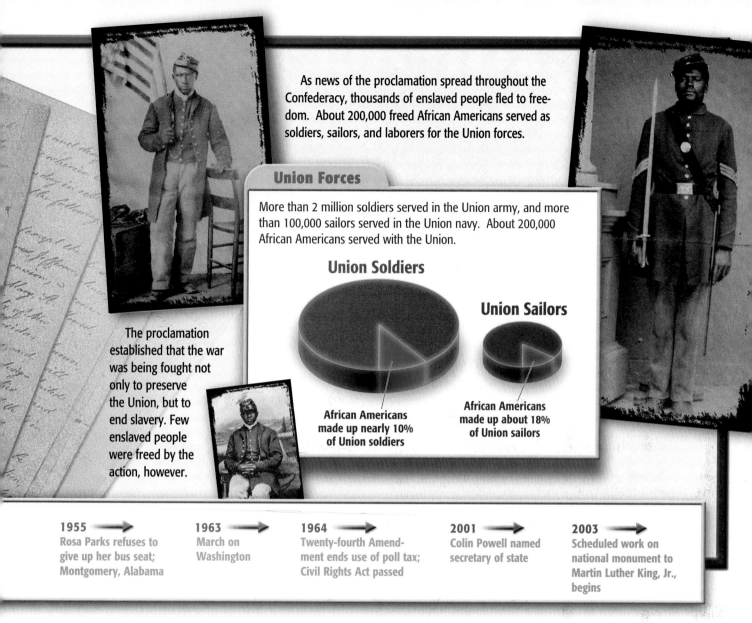

As news of the proclamation spread throughout the Confederacy, thousands of enslaved people fled to freedom. About 200,000 freed African Americans served as soldiers, sailors, and laborers for the Union forces.

Union Forces

More than 2 million soldiers served in the Union army, and more than 100,000 sailors served in the Union navy. About 200,000 African Americans served with the Union.

Union Soldiers

Union Sailors

African Americans made up nearly 10% of Union soldiers

African Americans made up about 18% of Union sailors

The proclamation established that the war was being fought not only to preserve the Union, but to end slavery. Few enslaved people were freed by the action, however.

1955 → Rosa Parks refuses to give up her bus seat; Montgomery, Alabama

1963 → March on Washington

1964 → Twenty-fourth Amendment ends use of poll tax; Civil Rights Act passed

2001 → Colin Powell named secretary of state

2003 → Scheduled work on national monument to Martin Luther King, Jr., begins

less likely to aid the South. Moreover, Lincoln became convinced that slavery helped the South continue fighting. Every enslaved person who worked enabled a white Southerner to fight in the Confederate army.

Lincoln also had political reasons for taking action on slavery. He believed it was important that the president rather than the antislavery Republicans in Congress make the decision on ending slavery. Lincoln told the members of his cabinet, "I must do the best I can, and bear the responsibility."

By the summer of 1862, Lincoln had decided to emancipate—or free—all enslaved African Americans in the South. He waited for the right moment so that he would not appear to be acting in desperation when the North seemed to be losing the war. On September 22, 1862, five days

after the Union forces turned back the Confederate troops at the Battle of Antietam, Lincoln announced his plan to issue an order freeing all enslaved people in the Confederacy. On January 1, 1863, Lincoln signed the **Emancipation Proclamation,** which said that

66 …all persons held as slaves within any state…in rebellion against the United States, shall be then, thenceforward, and forever free. 99

Effects of the Proclamation

Because the Emancipation Proclamation applied only to areas that the Confederacy controlled, it did not actually free anyone. Lincoln knew, however, that many enslaved people would hear about the proclamation. He hoped

Nearly 200,000 African Americans joined Union forces.

that knowledge of it would encourage them to run away from their slaveholders. Even before the Emancipation Proclamation, some 100,000 African Americans had left slavery for the safety of Union lines. 📖 *(See page 617 of the Appendix for the text of the Emancipation Proclamation.)*

Despite the limitations of the Emancipation Proclamation, African Americans in the North greeted it joyfully. On the day it was signed, a crowd of African Americans gathered at the White House to cheer the president. Frederick Douglass wrote, "We shout for joy that we live to record this righteous decree."

The proclamation had the desired effect in Europe as well. The Confederacy had been seeking support from its trading partners, Britain and France. However, the British took a strong position against slavery. Once Lincoln proclaimed emancipation, Britain and France decided to withhold recognition of the Confederacy.

In 1864 Republican leaders in Congress prepared a constitutional amendment to abolish slavery in the United States. In 1865 Congress passed the **Thirteenth Amendment,** which was ratified, or approved, the same year by states loyal to the Union. It was this amendment that truly freed enslaved Americans. 📖 *(See page 246 for the complete text of the Thirteenth Amendment.)*

✓ **Reading Check** **Explaining** What did the Thirteenth Amendment do?

African Americans in the War

Early in the war, Lincoln opposed enlisting African Americans as soldiers. The Emancipation Proclamation announced Lincoln's decision to permit African Americans to join the Union army. In the South, as well as in the North, the Civil War was changing the lives of all African Americans.

In the South

When the war began, over 3.5 million enslaved people lived in the Confederacy. Making up more than 30 percent of the region's population and the bulk of its workforce, enslaved workers labored on plantations and in vital iron, salt, and lead mines. Some worked as nurses in military hospitals and cooks in the army. By the end of the war, about one-sixth of the enslaved population had fled to areas controlled by Union armies.

The possibility of a slave rebellion terrified white Southerners. For this reason most Southerners refused to use African Americans as soldiers—for then they would be given weapons.

Near the end of the war, however, the Confederate military became desperate. Robert E. Lee and some others supported using African Americans as soldiers and believed that those who fought should be freed. The Confederate Congress passed a law in 1865 to enlist enslaved people, although the law did not include automatic freedom. The war ended before any regiments could be organized.

Helping the North

The story was different in the North. At the start of the war, African Americans were not permitted to serve as soldiers in the Union army. This disappointed many free African Americans who had volunteered to fight for the Union.

Yet African Americans who wished to help the war effort found ways to do so. Although the army would not accept them, the Union navy did. African Americans who had escaped slavery often proved to be especially useful as guides and spies because of their knowledge of the South. Some women, such as **Harriet Tubman,** who had helped hundreds escape slavery by way of the Underground Railroad, repeatedly spied behind Confederate lines.

In 1862 Congress passed a law allowing African Americans to serve in the Union army. As a result both free African Americans and those who had escaped slavery began enlisting. In the Emancipation Proclamation, Lincoln supported the use of African American soldiers, and more African Americans began enlisting.

By the end of the war, African American volunteers made up nearly 10 percent of the Union army and about 18 percent of the navy. In all, nearly 200,000 African Americans served. About 37,000 lost their lives defending the Union. By becoming soldiers, African Americans were taking an important step toward securing civil rights.

African American Soldiers

African American soldiers were organized into regiments separate from the rest of the Union army. Most commanding officers of these regiments were white. African Americans received lower pay than white soldiers at first, but protests led to equal pay in 1864.

One of the most famous African American regiments was the **54th Massachusetts,** led by white abolitionists. On July 18, 1863, the 54th spearheaded an attack on a Confederate fortification near Charleston, South Carolina. Under heavy fire, the troops battled their way to the top of the fort. The Confederates drove them back with heavy fire. Nearly half of the 54th were wounded, captured, or killed. Their bravery won respect for African American troops.

Lincoln's political opponents criticized the use of African American soldiers. Lincoln replied by quoting General Grant, who had written to Lincoln that "[they] will make good soldiers and taking them from the enemy weakens him in the same proportion they strengthen us."

Many white Southerners, outraged by African American soldiers, threatened to execute any they captured. In a few instances, this threat was carried out. However, enslaved workers were overjoyed when they saw that the Union army included African American soldiers. As one African American regiment entered Wilmington, North Carolina, a soldier wrote, "Men and women, old and young, were running throughout the streets, shouting and praising God. We could then truly see what we have been fighting for."

✔ **Reading Check** **Comparing** How were African American soldiers treated differently than white soldiers?

SECTION 3 ASSESSMENT

Checking for Understanding

1. **Key Terms** Use the vocabulary terms that follow to write a paragraph about the Thirteenth Amendment: emancipate, ratify.
2. **Reviewing Facts** Summarize President Lincoln's reasons for issuing the Emancipation Proclamation.

Reviewing Themes

3. **Groups and Institutions** How did African Americans help the war effort in the North? What roles did they play in the South?

Critical Thinking

4. **Comparing** How did President Lincoln's political stand on slavery differ from his personal stand during the war?
5. **Determining Cause and Effect** Re-create the diagram below and list the factors that caused Lincoln to change his war goals to include freeing enslaved persons.

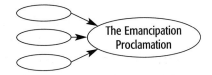

The Emancipation Proclamation

Analyzing Visuals

6. **Picturing History** Study the pictures of the African American soldiers on pages 475 and 476. Do you think that these soldiers have fought in battle? Explain your reasoning.

Interdisciplinary Activity

Citizenship It is 1865 and you have heard about the passage of the Thirteenth Amendment. Using material, thread, beads, and/or felt letters, create a banner that you anticipate carrying in a parade after the Civil War is over.

Life During the Civil War

Guide to Reading

Main Idea

Civilians as well as soldiers had an impact on the war effort.

Key Terms

habeas corpus, draft, bounty, greenback, inflation

Reading Strategy

Classifying Information As you read the section, complete a table like the one shown by describing the roles of these individuals during the war.

	Role
Loretta Janeta Velázquez	
Dorothea Dix	
Clara Barton	

Read to Learn

- what life was like for the soldiers.
- what role women played in the war.
- how the war affected the economies of the North and the South.

Section Themes

Economic Factors The Civil War strained the Northern and Southern economies.

Preview of Events

♦1861	♦1862	♦1863	♦1864
1861 Union Congress passes income tax	**April 1862** Confederate Congress passes draft law	**March 1863** The Union passes draft law	**July 1863** Angry mobs oppose the draft in New York City

AN American Story

A soldier's life was not easy—whether in battle or in the mess tent! A Louisiana soldier wrote, "No soldier will forget his first horse-meat breakfast. It was comical to see the facial expression as they viewed the platters of hot steak fried in its own grease or the "chunk" of boiled mule as it floated in a bucket of "stew." However, there seemed to be perfect good humor as they one after the other 'tackled the job.'. . .Occasionally would some stalwart fellow throw back his head and utter a long and loud 'Ye-ha, ye-ha, yehaw!' in imitation of a . . . mule."

Union soldier and family, 1861

The Lives of Soldiers

In both the North and the South, civilians and soldiers suffered terrible hardships and faced new challenges. In touching letters to their families and friends at home, soldiers described what they saw and how they felt—their boredom, discomfort, sickness, fear, and horror.

At the start of the war, men in both the North and the South rushed to volunteer for the armies. Their enthusiasm did not last.

Most of the time the soldiers lived in camps. Camp life had its pleasant moments of songs, stories, letters from home, and baseball games. Often, however, a soldier's life was dull, a routine of drills, bad food, marches, and rain.

During lulls between battles, Confederate and Union soldiers sometimes forgot that they were enemies. A Southern private described a Fourth of July on the front lines in 1862:

66 Our boys and Yanks made a bargain not to fire at each other . . . and talked over the fight, and traded tobacco and coffee and newspaper as peacefully and kindly as if they had not been engaged . . . in butchering one another. 99

The Reality of War

In spite of fleeting moments of calm, the reality of war was never far away. Both sides suffered terrible losses. The new rifles used during the Civil War fired with greater accuracy than the muskets of earlier wars.

Medical facilities were overwhelmed by the thousands of casualties in each battle. After the Battle of Shiloh, many wounded soldiers lay in the rain for more than 24 hours waiting for medical treatment. A Union soldier recalled, "Many had died there, and others were in the last agonies as we passed. Their groans and cries were heart-rending."

Faced with such horrors, many men deserted. About one of every 11 Union soldiers and one of every 8 Confederates ran away because of fear, hunger, or sickness.

Rebel soldiers suffered from a lack of food and supplies. One reason for Lee's invasion of Maryland in 1862 was to allow his army to feed off Maryland crops. A woman who saw the Confederates march to Antietam recalled the "gaunt starvation that looked from their cavernous eyes."

Reading Check **Explaining** Why did many soldiers desert from the armies?

Women and the War

Many Northern and Southern women took on new responsibilities during the war. They became teachers, office workers, salesclerks, and government workers. They worked in factories

Picturing **History**

Some paintings offered an idealized picture of the Civil War. Photographs provided a chilling account of life—and death—at the front lines. **In what ways might photographs have affected Americans' view of the war in a way that paintings did not?**

People In History

Clara Barton 1821–1921

When the Civil War began, Clara Barton, a U.S. Patent Office clerk, began collecting provisions for the Union army. In 1862 she began to deliver supplies directly to the front and to tend to the wounded and dying during battle.

Arriving at Antietam, Barton watched as surgeons dressed the soldiers' wounds with cornhusks because they did not have bandages. Barton was able to give the doctors a wagonload of bandages and other medical supplies. As the battle raged around her, Barton comforted the wounded and helped the doctors with their work.

As night neared, the medical staff had trouble working. From her supply wagon, Barton fetched lanterns and the doctors went back to work.

At Antietam and many other battles, Barton showed courage on the battlefield and gave aid to many. In 1881 Barton organized the American Red Cross and served as its first president for more than 20 years.

---

and managed farms. They also suffered the loss of husbands, fathers, sons, and brothers. As **Mary Chesnut** of South Carolina wrote:

> 66 Does anyone wonder [why] so many women die? Grief and constant anxiety kill nearly as many women at home as men are killed on the battle-field. 99

Women performed many jobs that helped the soldiers and the armies. They rolled bandages, wove blankets, and made ammunition. Many women collected food, clothing, and medicine to distribute to the troops. They also raised money for supplies.

Life at Home

For the most part, Northerners saw the war from a distance, since most of the battles took place in the South. News from the battlefront and letters home from the soldiers kept the war in people's minds.

Almost every woman who stayed at home was touched in some way by the war. But while everyday life in the North suffered little disruption, life in the South was dramatically changed. The fighting and the ever-tightening blockade disrupted everyday life. Those who lived in the paths of marching armies lost crops and homes. As one Southerner noted: the South had depended upon the outside world "for everything from a hairpin to a toothpick, and from a cradle to a coffin." As the war dragged on, shortages became more commonplace.

The South ran out of almost everything. Shortages in feed for animals and salt for curing meant that little meat was available. Shortages in meat were matched by shortages in clothing, medicine, and even shelter.

Spies

Some women were spies. While Harriet Tubman spied for the North, **Rose O'Neal Greenhow** entertained Union leaders in Washington, D.C., picking up information about Union plans that she passed to the South. Greenhow was caught, convicted of treason, and exiled.

Belle Boyd, of Front Royal, Virginia, informed Confederate generals of Union army movements in the Shenandoah Valley. Some women disguised themselves as men and became soldiers. **Loretta Janeta Velázquez** fought for the South at the First Battle of Bull Run and at Shiloh. Later she became a Confederate spy.

Treating the Sick and Wounded

In the Civil War, for the first time, thousands of women served as nurses. At first many doctors did not want women nurses on the grounds that women were too delicate for such work. Men also disapproved of women doing what was considered male work, and felt it was improper for women to tend the bodies of unknown men.

Strong-minded women disregarded these objections. In the North **Dorothea Dix** organized large numbers of women to serve as military nurses. Another Northerner, **Clara Barton**, became famous for her work with wounded soldiers. In the South **Sally Tompkins** established a hospital for soldiers in Richmond, Virginia.

Nursing was hard work. Kate Cummings of Alabama, who nursed the wounded in Corinth after the Battle of Shiloh, wrote, "Nothing that I had ever heard or read had given me the faintest idea of the horrors witnessed here." Yet women did a remarkable job in the war.

✓ **Reading Check** **Describing** What role did Sally Tompkins play in the war effort?

Opposition to the War

The war efforts of the Union and the Confederate governments faced opposition. Politicians objected to wartime policies, and ordinary citizens protested the way the war affected their lives.

When the war began, Northern Democrats split into two groups. One group supported most of Lincoln's wartime policies. The other, the "Peace Democrats," favored negotiating with the Confederacy. The Peace Democrats warned that continuing the war would lead to "terrible social change and revolution." They also appealed to racist feelings among Northern whites. Republican newspapers called the Peace Democrats "Copperheads." When Union armies fared poorly, support for the Copperheads rose.

Some Republicans suspected Copperheads of aiding the Confederates. The president ordered the arrest of anyone interfering with the war effort, such as discouraging men from enlisting in the army. Several times Lincoln suspended the right of habeas corpus, which guarantees accused individuals the right to a hearing before being jailed. Lincoln defended his actions, asking "Must I shoot a simple-minded soldier boy who deserts while I must not touch a hair of a wily agitator who induces him to desert?"

Enlistments Decline

As the war dragged on, the number of volunteers declined. Enlisting enough soldiers became a problem, and both the Confederacy and the Union tried new measures.

In April 1862, the Confederate Congress passed a draft law that required men between ages 18 and 35 to serve in the army for three years. A person could avoid the draft by hiring a

Picturing **History**

This 1862 photo shows a Union soldier with his family at the front near Washington, D.C. Most soldiers on both sides, however, faced long separations from their families. **What other hardships did Civil War soldiers face?**

substitute. Later, Congress exempted one white man on every plantation with 20 or more enslaved people. This led ordinary people to complain of "a rich man's war but a poor man's fight." In reality people from all levels of society served in both armies.

Union states encouraged enlistment by offering bounties—payments to encourage volunteers. In March 1863, when this system failed, the North turned to a draft. All men from age 20 to 45 had to register, and the army drew the soldiers it needed from this pool of names. A person could avoid the draft by hiring a substitute or by paying the government $300.

Draft laws aroused opposition, with protests erupting into riots in several Northern cities. The worst disturbance took place in New York City in July 1863. Angry mobs, opposed to the draft and to fighting to free African Americans, went on a rampage of burning, looting, and killing. After four days of terror, more than 100 people were dead. Troops from the Army of the Potomac had to be rushed in to end the rioting.

No disturbance as severe took place in the South, but many opposed the draft. The strong opposition led Jefferson Davis, the president of the Confederacy, to proclaim military law and suspend habeas corpus as Lincoln had done early in the war. Davis's action outraged Southerners who feared that they would lose the liberties for which they had gone to war.

Reading Check **Examining** Why did the governments institute a draft?

S Economics

War and the Economy

The Civil War strained the Northern and the Southern economies. The North, with its greater resources, was better able to cope with wartime demands than the South was.

TECHNOLOGY & History

Civil War Camera

Photographer Mathew Brady and his many assistants recorded the camps, lives, and deaths of soldiers in more than 10,000 photos. *What is the biggest difference between this camera and a more modern one?*

Photographer Mathew Brady

1 The photographer looks at the subject through a glass plate.

2 A plate holder is inserted into the back panel.

3 The photographer opens the lens. The lens creates a reversed, upside-down image on the "wet" plate.

4 The body of the camera protects the wet plate.

The plate holder and the exposed wet plate are removed from the back panel, then developed into a negative in the photographer's "traveling" darkroom.

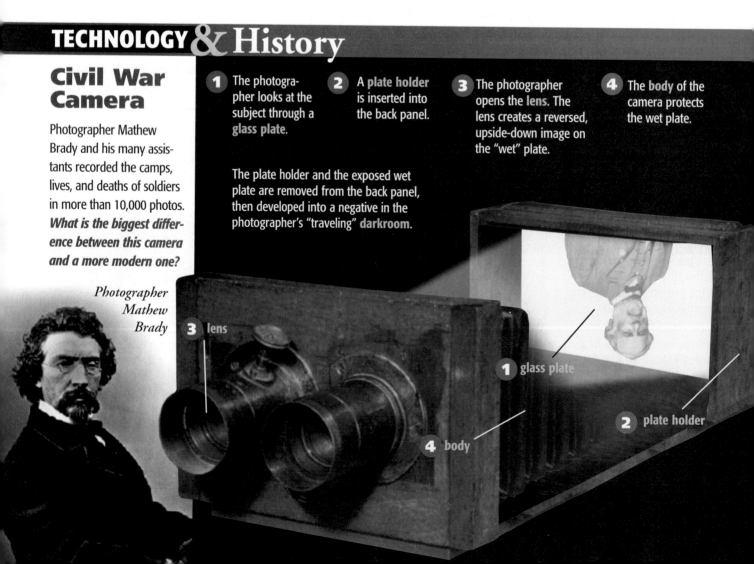

3 lens

1 glass plate

2 plate holder

4 body

Both the Union and the Confederacy financed the war by borrowing money, increasing taxes, and printing paper money. The North borrowed more than $2 billion, mainly by selling war bonds that promised high interest. The South borrowed more than $700 million. It issued so many bonds that people stopped buying them.

Both sides imposed new taxes as well. The Union passed an income tax in 1861. When Southern states did not provide sufficient funds, the Confederacy also imposed an income tax.

Because neither borrowing nor taxes raised enough money, both sides began printing paper money. Northern money was called greenbacks because of its color. The Confederacy also issued paper money—several times the amount printed in the North.

The North Prospers

During the war prices rose faster than wages in the North. This inflation—a general increase in prices—caused great hardship for working people. Overall, however, the Northern economy boomed. The need for a steady supply of food for Union troops helped farmers prosper.

Factory production grew as manufacturers responded to the demands of war. The army needed many items, from guns and ammunition to shoes and uniforms. Greater use of machinery and the standardization of parts made it possible for the North to produce what it needed.

Economic Troubles in the South

The Civil War is often called the first "modern" war because it required the total commitment of resources. Such a war has an impact on every part of life. However, the impact was more devastating on the South than on the North.

The South struggled to carry out its war effort. Its government encouraged factories to supply arms and ammunition, but the South lacked the industry to provide other necessities.

The economy of the South suffered far more than that of the North. Because most fighting occurred in the South, Southern farmland was overrun and rail lines were torn up. By the end of the war, large portions of the South lay in ruins and thousands of people were homeless.

The North's blockade of Southern ports caused severe shortages of essential goods. A scarcity of food led to riots in Atlanta, Richmond, and other cities. Inflation, too, was much worse in the South. During the course of the war, prices rose 9,000 percent—compared to a rise of 80 percent in the North.

These conditions affected soldiers. Worries about their families caused many men to desert. A Mississippi soldier who overstayed his leave to help his family wrote the governor: "We are poor men and are willing to defend our country but our families [come] first."

✓ Reading Check **Explaining** What is inflation?

SECTION 4 ASSESSMENT

Checking for Understanding

1. **Key Terms** Use each of these terms in a complete sentence that will help explain its meaning: habeas corpus, draft, bounty, greenback, inflation.

2. **Reviewing Facts** Why was life on the home front more difficult for Southerners?

Reviewing Themes

3. **Economic Factors** How did the war affect the economy of the South?

Critical Thinking

4. **Making Inferences** Why do you think President Lincoln believed the Copperheads were a threat to the Union war effort?

5. **Analyzing Information** Describe three ways that both the North and South raised money for the war. Use a chart like the one shown below.

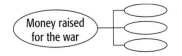

Money raised for the war

Analyzing Visuals

6. **Picturing History** Study the photograph of the family on page 481. Why do you think some families accompanied the armies in the field?

Interdisciplinary Activity

Economics List three sectors of the economy that welcomed women during the Civil War. Describe the jobs women held and the contributions they made.

Taking Notes

Why Learn This Skill?

One of the best ways to remember something is to write it down. Taking notes—writing down information in a brief and orderly form—not only helps you remember, but it also makes your studying easier.

Learning the Skill

There are several styles of note taking, but all explain and put information in a logical order. When you are taking notes, it will help to keep in mind these guidelines:

Identify the subject and write it at the top of the page. In your text, for example, look at the chapter title, section title, and other headings.

Select specific information for your notes. For example, anything your teacher writes on the chalkboard or shows you from a transparency should be included. If your teacher emphasizes a point or spends a large amount of time on a topic, this is also a clue to its importance.

Paraphrase the information. That means putting the information in your own words rather than trying to take it down word for word. Doing so helps you think about what the speaker or writer means.

To save time, you might want to develop different strategies. One way is to create a personal "shorthand." For example, use symbols, arrows, or rough drawings: "+" for "and." Practice your shorthand in all of your classes.

Write legible and neat notes so that you will be able to understand them when you read them again.

Practicing the Skill

Review the guidelines for taking notes. Then read Section 5, entitled "The Way to Victory." After you have carefully read the section, follow the guidelines and create shorthand notes for the subsection entitled "The Tide of War Turns," which begins on page 486.

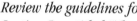

Applying the Skill

Taking Notes Scan a local newspaper for a short editorial or article about your local government. Take notes by using shorthand or by creating an outline. Summarize the article, using only your notes.

Glencoe's **Skillbuilder Interactive Workbook CD-ROM, Level 1,** provides instruction and practice in key social studies skills.

The Way to Victory

AN American Story

"My shoes are gone; my clothes are almost gone. I'm weary, I'm sick, I'm hungry. My family have been killed or scattered, and may be now wandering helpless and unprotected in a strange country. And I have suffered all this for my country. I love my country. I would die—yes, I would die willingly because I love my country. But if this war is ever over, I'll…[n]ever love another country!" A Confederate soldier expressed these thoughts during difficult times in 1863.

Confederate soldier

Southern Victories

Gone were the parades and masses of volunteers, the fancy uniforms and optimism of the first years of the war. From 1862 until 1865, the soldiers and civilians faced a grim conflict marked by death, destruction, and wrenching change. What endured on each side was a fierce dedication to its own cause.

The winter of 1862–1863 saw gloom in the North and hope in the South. Robert E. Lee's **Army of Northern Virginia** seemed unbeatable. Lee's grasp of strategy made him more than a match for weak Union generals.

Fredericksburg and Chancellorsville

Lee needed little skill to win the **Battle of Fredericksburg.** On December 13, 1862, Union general **Ambrose Burnside** clashed with Lee near the Virginia town. Burnside had the larger army, but the Confederates were entrenched, or set up in a strong position, on a number of hills south of the town. Repeated attacks failed to overcome Lee's troops as thousands of Union soldiers fell on the hillside. Devastated by his failure, Burnside resigned his command and was replaced by General **Joseph Hooker.**

Hooker rebuilt the army and in early May 1863, launched a campaign against Lee. Before Hooker could mount a major attack, Lee struck at **Chancellorsville,** Virginia, a few miles west of Fredericksburg. Boldly dividing his troops for an assault on the Union forces, Lee won another victory—but it proved costly. The battle's heavy casualties included General Stonewall Jackson.

On May 2, Jackson and his troops attacked Union troops at dusk. One of the Confederate companies fired on Jackson's party by mistake, wounding the general in the left arm. Jackson's arm had to be amputated and he died a week later.

✓ **Reading Check** **Describing** At what Virginia town did Lee defeat Burnside's forces?

America's Flags

Confederate Battle Flag, 1861 During the early Civil War battles, soldiers had difficulty distinguishing between the Confederate and Union flags. As a result, Southern soldiers began to carry this battle flag. It had 13 stars, although there were only 11 states in the Confederacy. The other two stars represented the border states of Kentucky and Missouri.

Seventeenth Flag of the Union, 1863 The Union flag of 1863 held 35 stars. Like all the Union flags of the Civil War, it retained stars for the seceded Southern states.

The Tide of War Turns

Despite his own heavy losses, Lee decided to invade the North. Another victory—one on Northern soil—might persuade Britain and France to aid the Confederacy.

The Battle of Gettysburg

In June, Lee began moving north with an army of 75,000. Union general Hooker wanted to advance against Richmond, but Lincoln told him to attack Lee's army. When Hooker failed to do this, Lincoln replaced him with General **George Meade.** Meade's mission was to find and fight Lee's forces and to protect Washington and Baltimore from Confederate attack.

The two armies met by accident on July 1, 1863, near the small town of Gettysburg, Pennsylvania. The three-day **Battle of Gettysburg** began when Union cavalry surprised Rebel infantry raiding the town for shoes. Outnumbered, the Northerners fought desperately to hold the town before retreating to Cemetery Ridge, a line of hills south of Gettysburg. The next day the Rebels launched another assault, but a counterattack saved the Union position.

On the third and final day of battle, Lee decided to launch an attack, determined to "create a panic and virtually destroy the [Union] army."

This last attack, led by General George Pickett, is remembered as **Pickett's Charge.** About 14,000 Confederate soldiers advanced across about one-half mile of open ground toward the Union lines. They made easy targets for Union fire as they marched. Barely half of the Rebels returned from the charge. Lee knew the battle was lost. "It's all my fault," he told his troops as they retreated to Virginia.

Victory at Vicksburg

Meanwhile, a great battle was taking place at **Vicksburg, Mississippi.** Vicksburg stood on a high bluff above the Mississippi River. To gain control of the river, one of the North's major war goals, the Union needed to seize Vicksburg. For several months, Union forces under **Ulysses S. Grant** had laid siege to the town. Finally, on July 4, 1863, Vicksburg surrendered.

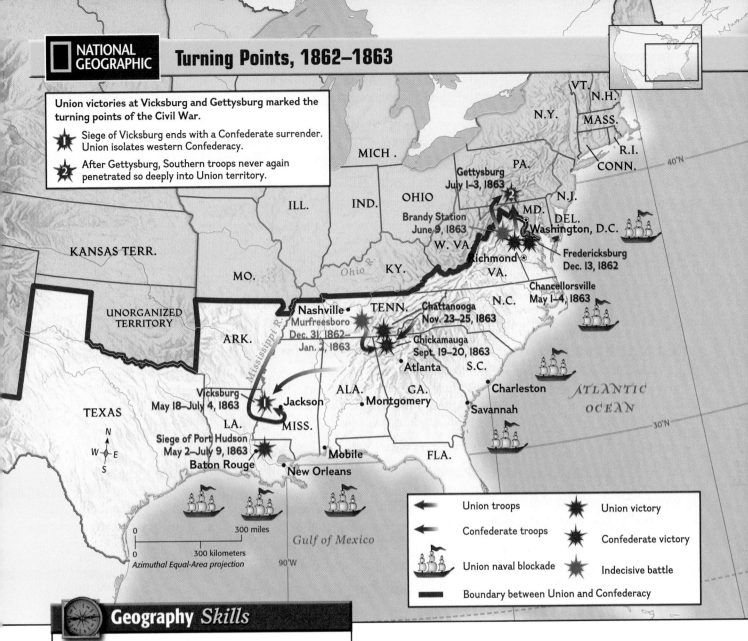

NATIONAL GEOGRAPHIC

Turning Points, 1862–1863

Union victories at Vicksburg and Gettysburg marked the turning points of the Civil War.

1 Siege of Vicksburg ends with a Confederate surrender. Union isolates western Confederacy.

2 After Gettysburg, Southern troops never again penetrated so deeply into Union territory.

Gettysburg
July 1–3, 1863

Brandy Station
June 9, 1863

Washington, D.C.

Fredericksburg
Dec. 13, 1862

Richmond

Chancellorsville
May 1–4, 1863

Nashville
Murfreesboro
Dec. 31, 1862–
Jan. 2, 1863

Chattanooga
Nov. 23–25, 1863

Chickamauga
Sept. 19–20, 1863

Atlanta

Vicksburg
May 18–July 4, 1863

Jackson

Montgomery

Charleston

Savannah

ATLANTIC OCEAN

Siege of Port Hudson
May 2–July 9, 1863

Baton Rouge

Mobile

New Orleans

Gulf of Mexico

KANSAS TERR.

UNORGANIZED TERRITORY

TEXAS

ARK.

LA.

MISS.

ALA.

GA.

FLA.

TENN.

MO.

ILL.

IND.

OHIO

KY.

W. VA.

VA.

N.C.

S.C.

MICH.

PA.

N.Y.

VT.

N.H.

MASS.

R.I.

CONN.

N.J.

MD.

DEL.

40°N

30°N

90°W

0 — 300 miles
0 — 300 kilometers
Azimuthal Equal-Area projection

← Union troops	✸ Union victory
← Confederate troops	✸ Confederate victory
⛵ Union naval blockade	✸ Indecisive battle
▬ Boundary between Union and Confederacy	

Geography Skills

1. Location What was the only major battle fought on Union soil?

2. Analyzing Information Why was success at Vicksburg so important to the Union?

With the surrender of Vicksburg and then Port Hudson—a Confederate fort in Louisiana—the Union now held the entire Mississippi River. Texas, Louisiana, and Arkansas were sealed off from the Confederacy.

The Union victories at Gettysburg and Vicksburg marked a turning point in the war. They drove Lee's army out of Pennsylvania, secured the Mississippi as a Union highway, and cut the South in two. Nevertheless, the South still had troops and a will to fight. The war would continue for two more terrible years.

Lincoln at Gettysburg

On November 19, 1863, at a ceremony dedicating a cemetery at Gettysburg, scholar Edward Everett spoke for two hours. Then in a two-minute speech, called the **Gettysburg Address,** President Lincoln beautifully expressed what the war had come to mean:

66 It is for us the living . . . to be here dedicated to the great task remaining before us . . . that these dead shall not have died in vain— that this nation, under God, shall have a new birth of freedom—and that government of the people, by the people, for the people shall not perish from the earth. 99

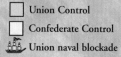

☐ Union Control
☐ Confederate Control
🚢 Union naval blockade

The Anaconda Plan From the beginning the Northern war strategy was to invade the South and divide it. As the plan—called the Anaconda Plan—progressed, the North blocked Southern supply lines and isolated Confederate troops.

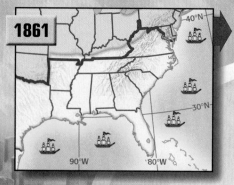

1861

Early Stages Confederate troops won most of the battles in the first year of the Civil War.

1863

Union Gains Union control of the Mississippi River cut off Texas and Arkansas, the South's leading food producers, from the Confederacy.

1865

Final Stages By 1865 the Union controlled large parts of the Confederacy.

Lives Lost
More lives were lost in the Civil War than in any other major American conflict. Deadly weapons, poor medical practices, infection and disease all contributed to this.

Civil War 620,000
World War II 407,000
World War I 107,000
Vietnam War 58,000
Korean War 54,000
Revolutionary War 25,000
Mexican War 13,000
Other major wars 5,000

The speech helped war-weary Americans look beyond the images of the battlefield and focus on their shared ideals. 📖 *(See page 618 of the Appendix for the entire text of the Gettysburg Address.)*

✓ **Reading Check** **Identifying** What battle victories gave the Union control of the Mississippi River?

Final Phases of the War

In November 1863, Grant and General **William Tecumseh Sherman** won an important victory at Chattanooga, Tennessee. Following the Northern triumphs at Vicksburg and Gettysburg, Chattanooga further weakened the Confederates. The following March, President Lincoln turned to Grant for help.

Ulysses S. Grant was small and unimpressive in appearance. His early army career was not impressive either, and in 1854 he had been forced to resign because of a drinking problem. When the war began, he rejoined the army. His victories in the West and his willingness to attack hard impressed President Lincoln. "I can't spare this man," the president said. "He fights." After the victory at Chattanooga, Lincoln named Grant commander of all the Union armies.

Grant devised a plan to attack the Confederacy on all fronts. The Army of the Potomac would try to crush Lee's army in Virginia. The western army, under Sherman, would advance to Atlanta, Georgia, and crush the Confederate forces in the Deep South. If the plan succeeded, they would destroy the Confederacy.

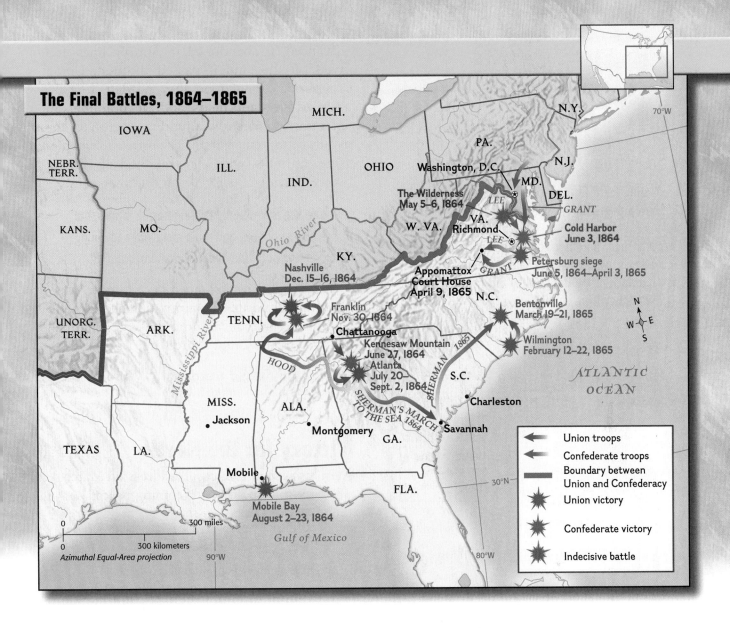

The Final Battles, 1864–1865

Union troops
Confederate troops
Boundary between Union and Confederacy
Union victory
Confederate victory
Indecisive battle

Grant soon put his strategy into effect. In May and June of 1864, Grant's army of 115,000 men smashed into Lee's 64,000 troops in a series of three battles near Richmond, Virginia—the Battles of the Wilderness, Spotsylvania Courthouse, and Cold Harbor. Each time, Confederate lines held, but each time Grant quickly resumed the attack.

The battles cost the North thousands of men. Critics called Grant a butcher, but he said, "I propose to fight it out on this line if it takes all summer." Lincoln supported Grant.

After Cold Harbor, Grant swung south of Richmond to attack **Petersburg,** an important railroad center. If it fell, Richmond would be cut off from the rest of the Confederacy. Grant's assault turned into a nine-month siege.

The Election of 1864

To the war-weary North, the events of the first half of 1864 were discouraging. Grant was stuck outside Richmond and Petersburg, and Sherman was stuck outside Atlanta. Sentiment for a negotiated peace grew. The Democrats wanted to make peace with the South, even though that might result in Confederate independence. Lincoln was determined to push for restoring the Union.

In the summer of 1864, Lincoln's chances for reelection did not look good. "I am going to be beaten and unless some great change takes place, badly beaten," he said.

Great changes did take place. In August, David Farragut led a Union fleet into **Mobile Bay**. The Union now controlled the Gulf of Mexico. In September, news arrived that Sherman

Linking Past & Present

From Hardtack to MREs

During the Civil War, food rations usually included hardtack—a hard, saltless, flour biscuit.

With age, hardtack could become infested with weevils. Some soldiers said it was better to eat hardtack in the dark—they did not want to see what they were eating!

POTATOES AU GRATIN

OMELET WITH HAM

Hardtack was fried in pork fat and dipped in coffee.

MREs can last five years or longer if stored in a cool environment.

Rations for today's soldiers are far different. They are called Meals Ready to Eat (MREs). MREs are dehydrated foods in airtight containers.

had captured Atlanta. Then in October, General Sheridan's Union forces completed a campaign that drove the Rebels out of the Shenandoah Valley in Virginia. With these victories the end of the war was in sight. Lincoln easily won reelection, taking 55 percent of the popular vote.

Total War

Leaving Atlanta in ruins, Sherman convinced Grant to let him try a bold plan. Sherman's army began the historic "march to the sea" to **Savannah, Georgia.** As the army advanced, it abandoned its supply lines and lived off the land it passed through. Union troops took what food they needed, tore up railroad lines and fields, and killed animals in an effort to destroy anything useful to the South. They cut a path of destruction sometimes 50 miles wide. This method of waging war was known as total war. Sherman said:

66 We are not only fighting hostile armies, but a hostile people, and must make old and young, rich and poor, feel the hard hand of war. 99

After capturing Savannah in December, Sherman turned north. The army marched through South Carolina, devastating the state. Sherman planned to join Grant's forces in Virginia.

☑ **Reading Check** **Describing** What was the "march to the sea"?

Victory for the North

In his second Inaugural Address on March 4, 1865, Lincoln spoke of the coming peace:

66 With malice toward none, with charity for all . . . let us strive on to finish the work we are in, to bind up the nation's wounds . . . to do all which may achieve and cherish a just and lasting peace among ourselves and with all nations. 99

Throughout the fall and winter of 1864, Grant continued the siege of Petersburg. Lee and his troops defended the town, but sickness, hunger, casualties, and desertion weakened them. Finally, on April 2, 1865, the Confederate lines broke and Lee withdrew his troops.

Richmond fell the same day. Rebel troops, government officials, and many residents fled the Confederate capital. As they left, they set fire to much of the city to keep it from falling into Union hands.

On April 4 Lincoln visited Richmond and walked its streets. One elderly African American man approached the president, took off his hat, and bowed. Tearfully, he said, "May God bless you." Lincoln removed his own hat and bowed in return.

Surrender at Appomattox

Lee moved his army west of Richmond, hoping to link up with the small Confederate force that was trying to stop Sherman's advance. But the Union army blocked his escape route. Realizing the situation was hopeless, Lee said:

> ❝ There is nothing left for me to do but go and see General Grant, and I would rather die a thousand deaths. ❞

On April 9, 1865, Lee and his troops surrendered to Grant in a small Virginia village called **Appomattox Court House.** Grant's terms were generous. The Confederate soldiers had to lay down their arms, but then were free to go home. Grant allowed them to keep their horses so that they could, as he said, "put in a crop to carry themselves and their families through the next winter." Grant also ordered three days' worth of food sent to Lee's hungry troops.

Several days after Lee's surrender, the Confederate forces in North Carolina surrendered to General Sherman. Jefferson Davis, the president of the Confederacy, was captured in Georgia on May 10. The Civil War was over at last.

Results of the War

The Civil War was the most devastating conflict in American history. More than 600,000 soldiers died, and the war caused billions of dollars of damage, most of it in the South. The war also created bitter feelings among defeated Southerners that lasted for generations.

The war had other consequences as well. The North's victory saved the Union. The federal government was strengthened and was now clearly more powerful than the states. Finally, the war freed millions of African Americans. How the nation would treat these new citizens remained to be seen.

✓ Reading Check **Identifying** Where did General Lee surrender?

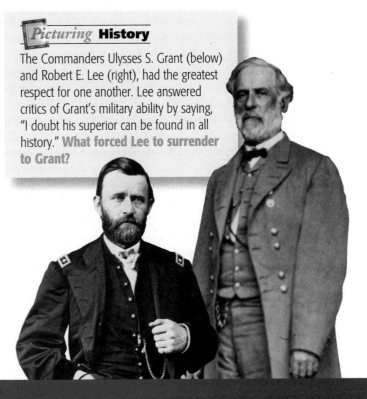

Picturing History

The Commanders Ulysses S. Grant (below) and Robert E. Lee (right), had the greatest respect for one another. Lee answered critics of Grant's military ability by saying, "I doubt his superior can be found in all history." **What forced Lee to surrender to Grant?**

SECTION 5 ASSESSMENT

Checking for Understanding

1. **Key Terms** Use the following terms in complete sentences that will help explain their meaning: entrenched, total war.
2. **Reviewing Facts** Identify the reasons that Gettysburg and Vicksburg were important battles.

Reviewing Themes

3. **Individual Action** What thoughts about peace did Lincoln express in his second Inaugural Address?

Critical Thinking

4. **Drawing Conclusions** How did the Union's victory strengthen the federal government?
5. **Analyzing Information** Use a chart like the one shown to explain the significance of each battle listed.

Battle	Importance
Gettysburg	
Vicksburg	
Mobile Bay	
Richmond	

Analyzing Visuals

6. **Geography Skills** Study the map of the final battles on page 489. In which directions did Sherman's army travel from Atlanta to Savannah and then to Bentonville?

Interdisciplinary Activity

Expository Writing Refer to Lincoln's Gettysburg Address on page 618. Write three paragraphs discussing Lincoln's ideas on liberty, equality, union, and government.

NATIONAL GEOGRAPHIC

GEOGRAPHY & HISTORY

West Woods

Hagerstown Pike

Dunker Church

This is the area that is shown above.

Potomac River

Hagerstown Pike

Dunker Church

Bloody Lane

Union Headquarters

SHARPSBURG

Antietam Creek

Confederate Headquarters

0   1/2 mile
0   1/2 kilometer

ANTIETAM: THE BLOODIEST DAY

FOUGHT ON SEPTEMBER 17, 1862, the Battle of Antietam, or Sharpsburg, was the bloodiest day in American history, with over 23,000 soldiers killed or wounded. Antietam changed the course of the Civil War. McClellan's Union forces stopped Lee's invasion of the North and forced him on the defensive. This strategic victory encouraged Lincoln to issue the Emancipation Proclamation.

MORNING

The battle began at dawn when Union artillery fired on Stonewall Jackson's forces in Miller Cornfield north of town. Union troops attacked the Confederates north of Dunker Church. For three hours, the battle lines swept back and forth along the West and East Woods, the Cornfield, and along Hagerstown Pike.

MIDDAY

Union soldiers emerged from the East Woods and were turned back by the Confederates in the West Woods. Later, the Yankees advanced toward "Bloody Lane," a sunken farm road held by the Confederates just south of Dunker Church. The Confederates held their line until midday, when the fighting stopped briefly.

AFTERNOON

After much fighting, the Union troops crossed Antietam Creek and slowly drove the Confederate forces back toward Sharpsburg. Just when all hope seemed lost, Confederate forces arrived from Harpers Ferry and stopped the Union advance. The day ended in a standoff that halted Lee's march northward. The next day, Lee began his retreat along the Potomac River.

LEARNING from GEOGRAPHY

1. How do you think Bloody Lane got its name?
2. Why do you think Lee retreated after the Battle of Antietam?

Chapter Summary

The Civil War

Secession

1860
- South Carolina secedes from Union

1861
- Lincoln inaugurated
- Confederate States of America formed
- Fort Sumter falls—Civil War begins
- Confederate forces win at Bull Run

1862
- Union victorious at Shiloh
- Union captures New Orleans
- Union wins at Antietam
- Lee named commander of Confederate armies

1863
- Lincoln issues Emancipation Proclamation
- Lee's forces turn back at Gettysburg
- Vicksburg surrenders

1864
- Petersburg, Virginia, under siege
- Sherman captures Atlanta
- March to the sea begins
- Lincoln reelected president

1865
- Lee surrenders to Grant at Appomattox
- Lincoln assassinated
- Thirteenth Amendment abolishing slavery is ratified

Reconstruction

Reviewing Key Terms

Examine the pairs of words below. Then write a sentence explaining what each of the pairs has in common.

1. blockade, offensive
2. ironclad, blockade runner
3. border state, Union
4. draft, habeas corpus

Reviewing Key Facts

5. During what years was the Civil War fought?
6. What three advantages did the Confederate states have in the war?
7. Who were the presidents of the United States and of the Confederate States of America?
8. What role did Clara Barton play in the Civil War?
9. Why did the Union blockade Southern ports?
10. What was the outcome of the Battle of Gettysburg?
11. What did the Emancipation Proclamation state?
12. In what ways did African Americans contribute to the war efforts?
13. How did the Civil War hurt the South's economy?
14. What terms of surrender did Grant offer to Lee?

Critical Thinking

15. **Analyzing Themes: Government and Democracy** How did the people of western Virginia respond to Virginia's secession from the Union?
16. **Determining Cause and Effect** Why was controlling the Mississippi River vital to the North and the South?
17. **Analyzing Themes: Groups and Institutions** Why do you think many leaders called for African Americans to be allowed to fight in the Civil War?
18. **Making Inferences** Why do you think General Lee was such an effective military leader?
19. **Analyzing Information** Re-create the diagram below. Fill in the year for each event. Then explain the significance of each event.

Event	Year	Significance
Attack on Fort Sumter		
Monitor v. *Merrimack*		
Emancipation Proclamation issued		
Lincoln is reelected		
Appomattox Court House		

Self-Check Quiz
Visit tarvol1.glencoe.com and click on **Chapter 16—Self-Check Quizzes** to prepare for the chapter test.

Geography and History Activity

Study the map below and answer the questions.

20. Along what ridge were the Union troops positioned?
21. Who led forces across Rock Creek?
22. What five Confederate commanders are shown?

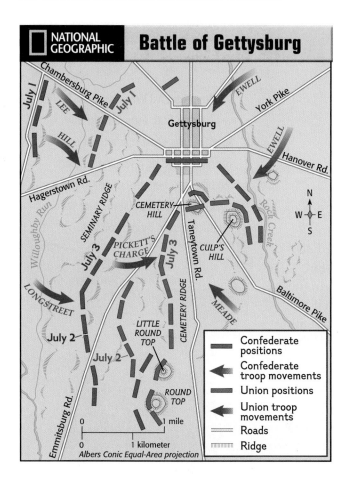

NATIONAL GEOGRAPHIC **Battle of Gettysburg**

Chambersburg Pike · July 1 · July 1 · LEE · HILL · EWELL · York Pike · Gettysburg · EWELL · Hanover Rd. · Hagerstown Rd. · SEMINARY RIDGE · Willoughby Run · CEMETERY HILL · Taneytown Rd. · Rock Creek · N W E S · PICKETT'S CHARGE · July 3 · July 3 · CULP'S HILL · LONGSTREET · CEMETERY RIDGE · MEADE · Baltimore Pike · LITTLE ROUND TOP · July 2 · July 2 · ROUND TOP · Emmitsburg Rd.

Confederate positions
Confederate troop movements
Union positions
Union troop movements
Roads
Ridge

0 ─── 1 mile
0 ─── 1 kilometer
Albers Conic Equal-Area projection

Practicing Skills

23. **Taking Notes** Review the guidelines for taking notes on page 484. Then reread Section 5 about the last years of the Civil War. Create a time line showing the dates of battles and other important events discussed in the section.

 ## Technology Activity

24. **Using the Internet** Search the Internet for museums that specialize in Civil War artifacts and photo collections. Make a map showing the names and locations of these museums.

Citizenship Cooperative Activity

25. **Debating Issues** A writ of habeas corpus is a court order that guarantees a person who is arrested the right to appear before a judge in a court of law. During the Civil War, President Lincoln suspended habeas corpus. Do you think that action was justified? Debate the issue as a group, with one side supporting and one side criticizing Lincoln's actions.

Economics Activity

26. Economic differences had always existed between the North and the South. From your reading of Chapter 16, would you say that the North or the South was better equipped economically for war? Explain your reasoning.

 ## Alternative Assessment

27. **Portfolio Writing Activity** To explain his reelection, Lincoln stated, "it is not best to swap horses while crossing the river." Write a paragraph that explains Lincoln's quotation and how it applied to him. Save your work for your portfolio.

Standardized Test Practice

Directions: Choose the *best* answer to the following question.

By gaining control of the Mississippi and Tennessee rivers, the Union was able to

A   capture Fort Sumter.
B   force the Confederacy to surrender.
C   split the Confederacy.
D   defeat the Confederate forces at Gettysburg.

Test-Taking Tip:

Eliminate answers that don't make sense. For example, Confederate forces, not Union forces, captured Fort Sumter. Therefore, choice **A** is incorrect.

Quilting History

Quilts were not just used for comfort and protection during the Civil War. They also served as patriotic symbols, and they helped raise money for war materials. Northern quilts often reflected abolition themes. Patterns were created that were named "North Star" and "Underground Railroad." In the South, enslaved people made most of the quilts and designed them using colors and patterns inspired by African traditions.

Analyzing the Issue

In this activity, your group will be making a memorial quilt about the Civil War.

The group must decide how large of a quilt to make. Each panel—or square—in the quilt will have a different design, so the group must decide what they want to represent on the quilt. The panels should reflect your interests in the Civil War or how you feel about it. Keep in mind the experiences of all Americans during the war, such as soldiers, women, enslaved persons, and politicians.

Believe It or Not!

When the Civil War was over, fabric was hard to find, especially in the South. Quilts were made from uniforms of dead or returning soldiers. Family members inscribed on the quilts the dates and names of the battles fought by the soldiers.

Civil War quilt

What To Do

After you have organized into groups, decide what role each member will play and what materials to use. Suggested materials are sheets of paper, drawing tools, and yarn.

1. As a group, select topics to be depicted on your Civil War memorial quilt panels. You can re-create whatever setting you choose—a battle scene, a scene at home, or any event that took place during the war.

2. Use colored pencils or markers to draw the scenes on pieces of construction paper. If possible, and with teacher supervision, laminate your drawing using a laminating machine.

3. When the panels are finished, make a quilt. Take a paper puncher and place holes at the four corners of each piece of paper.

4. String the yarn loosely through the holes so that each drawing is connected to the ones around it. Pull out the slack and tie the loose ends.

5. Hang your completed Civil War memorial quilt in your classroom.

Presentation

6. Once all of the quilts are finished, have one person per quilt group give a report of what their quilt represents. The group can also discuss how certain panels contribute to the overall meaning.

Go a Step Further

During the Civil War, Americans had to be very careful with any money that they did have. That is why they recycled old clothing to make quilts and made their food supplies last as long as possible. The cost of food rose dramatically in 1864. For example, the following costs were common: a dozen eggs, $6.00; a pound of butter, $6.25; a quart of milk, $10.00; and a pound of coffee, $12.00. Prepare a bar graph that compares those prices with prices today. Summarize what conclusions you can draw from your graph.

CHAPTER 17

Reconstruction and Its Aftermath

1865–1896

Why It Matters

We had survived our worst war, but the end of the Civil War left Americans to deal with a set of pressing issues. The status of some 3.5 million former enslaved people had yet to be decided. Nor had the terms by which the former Confederate states would rejoin the union been decided. How Americans would handle these issues would shape the future of our country.

The Impact Today

Debate over the rightful power of the federal government and the states continues to this day. Americans continue to wrestle with the problem of providing civil rights and equal opportunity to all citizens.

 The American Republic to 1877 Video *The chapter 17 video, "Life After the War," tells the story of Reconstruction through the eyes of writers and artists of the period.*

1870
- Fifteenth Amendment ratified

1867
- First Reconstruction Act passed

1877
- Reconstruction ends

United States
PRESIDENTS

| Lincoln 1861–1865 | A. Johnson 1865–1869 | Grant 1869–1877 | Hayes 1877–1881 | Garfield 1881 |

1860   1870   1880

World

1868
- Meiji era begins in Japan

1871
- Bismarck unifies Germany

1874
- First major exhibit of impressionist art in Paris

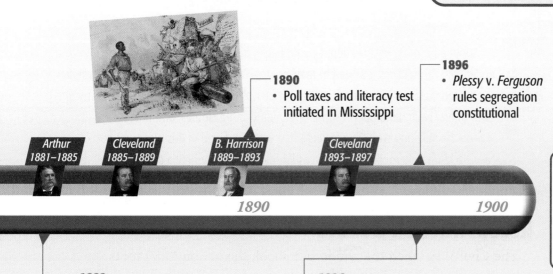

Ruins of the North Eastern Depot, Charleston, South Carolina Southerners faced the task of rebuilding cities, industries, and farms devastated by war.

Comparison Study Foldable Make this foldable to help you compare and contrast Reconstruction in the Northern and Southern states.

Step 1 Mark the midpoint of the side edge of a sheet of paper.

Draw a mark at the midpoint.

Step 2 Turn the paper and fold the edges in to touch at the midpoint.

Step 3 Turn and label your foldable as shown.

North Reconstruction
South

Reading and Writing As you read the chapter, write facts that show how Reconstruction differed and was the same in the Northern states and Southern states. Write the facts in the appropriate places inside your foldable.

1890
• Poll taxes and literacy test initiated in Mississippi

1896
• *Plessy* v. *Ferguson* rules segregation constitutional

| Arthur 1881–1885 | Cleveland 1885–1889 | B. Harrison 1889–1893 | Cleveland 1893–1897 |

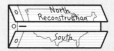

1890   1900

1882
• Beginning of British occupation of Egypt

1896
• Ethiopia defeats invading Italians

HISTORY Online

Chapter Overview
Visit tarvol1.glencoe.com and click on **Chapter 17— Chapter Overviews** to preview chapter information.

SECTION 1 Reconstruction Plans

Guide to Reading

Main Idea
Differences over how Reconstruction should be carried out divided the government.

Key Terms
Reconstruction, amnesty, radical, freedmen

Reading Strategy
Taking Notes As you read the section, re-create the diagram below and describe each of the Reconstruction plans.

Plan	Description
Ten Percent Plan	
Wade-Davis Plan	
Restoration	

Read to Learn
• how the Reconstruction plans of Lincoln and the Radical Republicans differed.
• what President Johnson's Reconstruction plans were.

Section Theme
Groups and Institutions The South worked to rebuild its economy and its institutions.

Preview of Events

♦1864   ♦1865   ♦1866

July 1864
Congress passes
Wade-Davis Bill

March 1865
Freedmen's Bureau
is established

April 9, 1865
Lee surrenders

April 14, 1865
President Lincoln
is assassinated

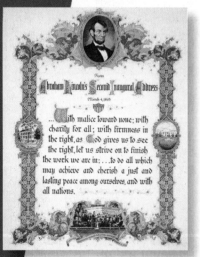

*Lincoln's second
Inaugural Address*

AN American Story

About a month after President Lincoln began his second term of office, the Civil War ended and the soldiers returned to their homes. One Illinois veteran wrote upon reaching the family farm, "The morning after my arrival, September 29th, I [took off] my uniform of first lieutenant, put on some of my father's old clothes, and proceeded to wage war on the standing corn. The feeling I had while engaged in this work was sort of [odd]. It almost seemed, sometimes, as if I had been away only a day or two, and had just taken up the farm work where I had left off."

Reconstruction Debate

The Civil War saved the Union but shook the nation to its roots. As Americans attempted to reunite their shattered nation, they faced many difficult questions. For example, should the slaveholding Southerners be punished or forgiven? What rights should be granted to the freed African Americans? How could the war-torn nation be brought back together?

The war had left the South with enormous problems. Most of the major fighting had taken place in the South. Towns and cities were in ruin, plantations had been burned, and roads, bridges, and railroads destroyed.

More than 258,000 Confederate soldiers had died in the war, and illness and wounds weakened thousands more. Many Southern families faced the task of rebuilding their lives with few resources and without the help of adult males.

People in all parts of the nation agreed that the devastated Southern economy and society needed rebuilding. They disagreed bitterly, however, over how to accomplish this. This period of rebuilding is called Reconstruction. This term also refers to the various plans for accomplishing the rebuilding.

Lincoln's Plan

President Lincoln offered the first plan for accepting the Southern states back into the Union. In December 1863, during the Civil War, the president announced what came to be known as the Ten Percent Plan. When 10 percent of the voters of a state took an oath of loyalty to the Union, the state could form a new government and adopt a new constitution—a constitution banning slavery.

Lincoln wanted to encourage Southerners who supported the Union to take charge of the state governments. He believed that punishing the South would serve no useful purpose and would only delay healing the torn nation.

The president offered amnesty—a pardon—to all white Southerners, except Confederate leaders, who were willing to swear loyalty to the Union. Lincoln also supported granting the right to vote to African Americans who were educated or had served in the Union army. However, he would not force the Southern states to give rights held by white Americans to African Americans.

In 1864 three states that the Union army occupied—Louisiana, Arkansas, and Tennessee—established governments under Lincoln's plan. These states then became caught in a struggle between the president and Congress when Congress refused to seat the states' representatives.

A Rival Plan

A group of Republicans in Congress considered Lincoln's plan too mild. They argued that Congress, not the president, should control Reconstruction policy. Because these Republicans favored a tougher and more radical, or extreme, approach to Reconstruction, they were called **Radical Republicans.** A leading Radical Republican, **Thaddeus Stevens,** declared that Southern institutions "must be broken up and relaid, or all our blood and treasure have been spent in vain."

Controlled by the Radical Republicans, Congress voted to deny seats to representatives from any state reconstructed under Lincoln's plan. Then Congress began to create its own plan.

The Wade-Davis Bill

In July 1864, Congress passed the **Wade-Davis Bill.** The bill offered a plan much harsher than Lincoln's. First, a majority of white males in a state had to swear loyalty to the Union. Second, a state constitutional convention could be held,

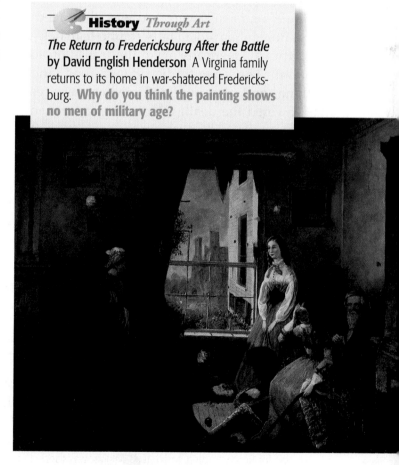

History *Through Art*

The Return to Fredericksburg After the Battle **by David English Henderson** A Virginia family returns to its home in war-shattered Fredericksburg. **Why do you think the painting shows no men of military age?**

but only white males who swore they had never taken up arms against the Union could vote for delegates to this convention. Former Confederates were also denied the right to hold public office. Finally, the convention had to adopt a new state constitution that abolished slavery. Only then could a state be readmitted to the Union.

Lincoln refused to sign the bill into law. He wanted to encourage the formation of new state governments so that order could be restored quickly. Lincoln realized that he would have to compromise with the Radical Republicans.

The Freedmen's Bureau

More progress was made on the other great issue of Reconstruction—helping African Americans freed from slavery. In March 1865, during the final weeks of the war, Congress and the president established a new government agency to help former enslaved persons, or freedmen. Called the **Freedmen's Bureau,** this agency was actually part of the war department.

In the years following the war, the Freedmen's Bureau played an important role in helping African Americans make the transition to freedom. The agency distributed food and clothing, and also provided medical services that lowered the death rate among freed men and women.

The Freedmen's Bureau achieved one of its greatest successes in the area of education. The bureau established schools, staffed mostly by teachers from the North. It also gave aid to new African American institutions of higher learning, such as Atlanta University, Howard University, and Fisk University.

The bureau helped freed people acquire land that had been abandoned by owners or seized by Union armies. It offered African Americans free transportation to the countryside where laborers were needed, and it helped them obtain fair wages. Although its main goal was to aid African Americans, the bureau also helped Southerners who had supported the Union.

✓ **Reading Check** **Examining** Why did Lincoln offer his plan for Reconstruction before the Civil War was over?

Picturing **History**

Actor John Wilkes Booth used this pistol to shoot Lincoln at Ford's Theater. The "wanted" poster promises a large reward for help in capturing Booth. **How was Booth finally captured?**

Lincoln Assassinated!

A terrible event soon threw the debates over Reconstruction into confusion. On the evening of April 14, 1865, President and Mrs. Lincoln attended the play *Our American Cousin* at Ford's Theater in **Washington, D.C.** It was just five days after the surrender of Lee's army and four years to the day after the fall of Fort Sumter.

As the Lincolns watched the play from a private box in the balcony, **John Wilkes Booth,** an actor and Confederate sympathizer, entered the box without anyone seeing him. Booth shot the president in the back of the head, then leaped to the stage and escaped during the chaos that followed the shooting. Aides carried the wounded president to the nearby house of William Petersen, a tailor. Lincoln died there a few hours later, without ever regaining consciousness.

After escaping from Ford's Theater, Booth fled on horseback to Virginia. Union troops tracked him down and on April 26 cornered him in a barn near Port Royal, Virginia. When Booth refused to surrender, he was shot to death.

Booth was part of a small group that plotted to kill high officials of the United States government. A military court convicted eight people of taking part in the plot. Four were hanged and the others imprisoned for life.

News of Lincoln's assassination shocked the nation. African Americans mourned the death of the man who had helped them win their freedom. Northern whites grieved for the leader who had saved the Union.

A New President

When Lincoln died, Vice President **Andrew Johnson** became president. Formerly a Democratic senator from Tennessee, Johnson had been the only Southern senator to support the Union during the Civil War.

Soon after taking office, President Johnson revealed his plan for Reconstruction. He resented the slaveholders who had dominated the South and wished to punish them. As a result Radicals thought Johnson would create a harsh plan they could accept. Johnson, however, believed in giving the states control over many decisions, and he had no desire to help African Americans.

"Restoration"

Johnson announced his plan, which he preferred to call "Restoration," in May of 1865. Under his plan, most Southerners would be granted amnesty once they swore an oath of loyalty to the Union. High-ranking Confederate officials and wealthy landowners, however, could be pardoned only by applying personally to the president. This provision was Johnson's attack on the wealthy leaders who he believed had tricked the people of the South into seceding.

Johnson also appointed governors to Southern states and required them to hold elections for state constitutional conventions. Only whites who had sworn their loyalty and been pardoned would be allowed to vote. Johnson opposed granting all freed African Americans equal rights or letting them vote. He believed that each Southern state should decide what to do about freed people, saying, "White men alone must manage the South."

Before a state could reenter the Union, its constitutional convention had to denounce secession and abolish slavery. States also had to ratify the **Thirteenth Amendment** to the Constitution, which Congress had passed in January 1865. This amendment abolished slavery in all parts of the United States. By the end of 1865, all the former Confederate states except Texas had formed new governments and were ready to rejoin the Union. President Johnson declared that "Restoration" was almost complete.

Reading Check **Comparing** How did President Johnson's plan for Reconstruction differ from that of the Radical Republicans?

SECTION 1 ASSESSMENT

Check for Understanding

1. **Key Terms** Use each of these terms in a sentence that will help explain its meaning: Reconstruction, amnesty, radical, freedmen.
2. **Reviewing Facts** What did the Thirteenth Amendment provide?

Reviewing Themes

3. **Groups and Institutions** Why do you think both Lincoln and the Radical Republicans excluded former Confederate officers from their Reconstruction plans?

Critical Thinking

4. **Drawing Conclusions** Do you think President Johnson's early ties to the South influenced his treatment of African Americans in his Reconstruction plans? Explain your answer.
5. **Comparing** Re-create the diagram below and compare Lincoln's Ten Percent Plan to the Radical Republicans' Wade-Davis Bill.

Reconstruction Plans	
Ten Percent Plan	Wade-Davis Bill

Analyzing Visuals

6. **Picturing History** Study the painting on page 501. What words would you use to describe the mood of the people?

Interdisciplinary Activity

Math Use the *Statistical Abstract of the United States* or another reference book to find information on the percentages of African American students enrolled in schools in 1860, 1870, and 1880. Use this information to create a bar graph.

SECTION 2 Radicals in Control

Guide to Reading

Main Idea
Radical Republicans were able to put their version of Reconstruction into action.

Key Terms
black codes, override, impeach

Reading Strategy
Organizing Information As you read the section, re-create the diagram below and provide information about impeachment.

Impeachment	
What is it?	
Who was impeached?	
Outcome of the trial?	

Read to Learn
• what some Southerners did to deprive freed people of their rights, and how Congress responded.
• what the main features of Radical Reconstruction were.

Section Theme
Civic Rights and Responsibilities Southern states created new governments and elected new representatives.

Preview of Events

♦1865	♦1867	♦1869	♦1871

1865
First black codes passed

March 1867
Radical Reconstruction begins

November 1868
Ulysses S. Grant elected president

February 1870
Fifteenth Amendment extends voting rights

Ku Klux Klan flag

AN American Story

For three days in May 1866, white mobs in Memphis, Tennessee, burned African American churches, schools, and homes. Close to fifty people, nearly all of them African American, were killed in the rioting. Many Northerners saw the rampage as an attempt by whites to terrorize African Americans and keep them from exercising their new freedoms. This incident and similar riots in other Southern cities helped convince Radical Republicans that President Johnson's Reconstruction plans were not strong enough.

African Americans' Rights

During the fall of 1865, the Southern states created new governments that met the rules President Johnson laid down, and Southern voters elected new representatives to Congress. More than one dozen of these representatives had been high-ranking officials in the Confederacy—including the Confederacy's vice president, Alexander H. Stephens. When the newly elected Southern representatives arrived in Washington, D.C., Congress refused to seat them. Many Republicans refused to readmit the Southern states on such easy terms and rejected Johnson's claim that Reconstruction was complete.

To many in the North, it seemed that Johnson's plan for Reconstruction was robbing the Union of its hard-won victory. In addition Northerners realized that the treatment of African Americans in Southern states was not improving.

Black Codes

In 1865 and early 1866, the new Southern state legislatures passed a series of laws called black codes. Key parts of these laws aimed to control freed men and women and to enable plantation owners to exploit African American workers.

Modeled on laws that had regulated free African Americans before the Civil War, the black codes of each Southern state trampled the rights of African Americans. Some laws allowed local officials to arrest and fine unemployed African Americans and make them work for white employers to pay off their fines. Other laws banned African Americans from owning or renting farms. One law allowed whites to take orphaned African American children as unpaid apprentices. To freed men and women and many Northerners, the black codes reestablished slavery in disguise.

Challenging the Black Codes

In early 1866 Congress extended the life of the Freedmen's Bureau and granted it new powers. The Freedmen's Bureau now had authority to set up special courts to prosecute individuals charged with violating the rights of African Americans. These courts provided African Americans with a form of justice where they could serve on juries.

Congress also passed the **Civil Rights Act of 1866.** This act granted full citizenship to African Americans and gave the federal government the power to intervene in state affairs to protect their rights. The law overturned the black codes. It also contradicted the 1857 *Dred Scott* decision of the Supreme Court, which had ruled that African Americans were not citizens.

President Johnson vetoed both the Freedmen's Bureau bill and the Civil Rights Act, arguing that the federal government was overstepping its proper authority. He also said that the laws were unconstitutional because they were passed by a Congress that did not include representatives from all the states. By raising the issue of representation, Johnson indirectly threatened to veto any law passed by this Congress.

Republicans in Congress had enough votes to override, or defeat, both vetoes, and the bills became law. As the split between Congress and the president grew, the possibility of their working together faded. The Radical Republicans abandoned the idea of compromise and drafted a new Reconstruction plan—one led by Congress.

Citizenship
The Fourteenth Amendment

Congress wanted to ensure that African Americans would not lose the rights that the Civil Rights Act granted. Fearing it might be

History *Through Art*

His First Vote by Thomas Waterman Wood
Wood's oil painting emphasized the importance of the ballot to African American voters. **How did African American males gain the right to vote?**

challenged and overturned in court, Congress in June 1866 passed a new amendment to the Constitution.

The **Fourteenth Amendment** granted full citizenship to all individuals born in the United States. Because most African Americans in the United States had been born there, they became full citizens. The amendment also stated that no state could take away a citizen's life, liberty, and property "without due process of law," and that every citizen was entitled to "equal protection of the laws." States that prevented any adult male citizen from voting could lose part of their representation in Congress. 📖 *(See pages 247–248 for the entire text of the Fourteenth Amendment.)*

The amendment barred prominent former Confederates from holding national or state office unless pardoned by a vote of two-thirds of Congress. The Fourteenth Amendment was interpreted as not including members of the Native American tribes. Not until 1924 did Congress make all Native Americans citizens of the United States.

Congress declared that Southern states had to ratify the amendment to be readmitted to the Union. Of the 11 Southern states, only Tennessee ratified the Fourteenth Amendment. The refusal of the other states to ratify the amendment delayed its adoption until 1868.

Republican Victory

The Fourteenth Amendment became a major issue in the congressional elections of 1866. Johnson urged Northern and Southern state legislatures to reject it. He also campaigned vigorously against Republican candidates. Many Northerners were disturbed by the nastiness of Johnson's campaign. They also worried about violent clashes between whites and African Americans, such as the riots that erupted in Memphis, Tennessee, and New Orleans, Louisiana.

The Republicans won a decisive victory, increasing their majorities in both houses of Congress. The Republicans also gained control of the governments in every Northern state. The election gave Congress the signal to take Reconstruction into its own hands.

✓ **Reading Check** **Describing** What does the Fourteenth Amendment provide?

Radical Reconstruction

The Republicans in Congress quickly took charge of Reconstruction. Most Radicals agreed with Congressman James Garfield of Ohio that

❝we must compel obedience to the Union, and demand protection for its humblest citizen.❞

President Johnson could do little to stop them because Congress could easily override his vetoes. Thus began a period known as Radical Reconstruction.

Reconstruction Act of 1867

On March 2, 1867, Congress passed the **First Reconstruction Act.** The act called for the creation of new governments in the 10 Southern states that had not ratified the Fourteenth Amendment. Tennessee, which had ratified the amendment, kept its government, and the state was quickly readmitted to the Union.

The act divided the 10 Southern states into five military districts and placed each under the authority of a military commander until new governments were formed. The act also guaranteed African American males the right to vote in state elections, and it prevented former Confederate leaders from holding political office.

To gain readmission to the Union, the states had to ratify the Fourteenth Amendment and submit their new state constitutions to Congress for approval. A **Second Reconstruction Act,** passed a few weeks later, required the military commanders to begin registering voters and to prepare for new state constitutional conventions.

Readmission of States

Many white Southerners refused to take part in the elections for constitutional conventions and state governments. Thousands of newly registered African American voters did use their right to vote. In the elections, Republicans gained control of Southern state governments. By 1868, seven Southern states—Alabama, Arkansas, Florida, Georgia, Louisiana, North Carolina, and South Carolina—had established new governments and met the conditions for readmission to the Union. By 1870, Mississippi, Virginia, and Texas were restored to the Union.

Military Reconstruction Districts, 1867

NATIONAL GEOGRAPHIC

Military district boundary
Union general in command

1st District
★ John Schofield

VA.

Tennessee rejoined the Union in 1866.

TENN.

N.C.

4th District
★ Edward Ord

S.C.

2nd District
★ Daniel Sickles

ARK.

MISS. ALA. GA.

TEXAS

LA.

3rd District
★ John Pope

FLA.

ATLANTIC OCEAN

30°N

MEXICO

0   250 miles

0   250 kilometers
Lambert Equal-Area projection

5th District
★ Philip Sheridan

Gulf of Mexico

Geography Skills

After taking control of Reconstruction, Congress divided the South into five districts under the command of military officers.
1. **Region** Which two states made up the largest district?
2. **Analyzing Information** Why did no Union troops occupy Tennessee?

Challenge to Johnson

Strongly opposed to Radical Reconstruction, President Johnson had the power as commander in chief of the army to direct the actions of the military governors. For this reason Congress passed several laws to limit the president's power.

One of these laws, the **Tenure of Office Act** of March 1867, was a deliberate challenge. It prohibited the president from removing government officials, including members of his own cabinet, without the Senate's approval. The act violated the tradition that presidents controlled their cabinets, and it threatened presidential power.

Impeaching the President

The conflict between Johnson and the Radicals grew more intense. In August 1867—when Congress was not in session—Johnson suspended Secretary of War **Edwin Stanton** without the Senate's approval. When the Senate met

again and refused to approve the suspension, Johnson removed Stanton from office—a deliberate violation of the Tenure of Office Act. Johnson angered the Republicans further by appointing some generals the Radicals opposed as commanders of Southern military districts.

Outraged by Johnson's actions, the House of Representatives voted to impeach—formally charge with wrongdoing—the president. The House accused Johnson of misconduct and sent the case to the Senate for trial.

The trial began in March 1868 and lasted almost three months. Johnson's defenders claimed that the president was exercising his right to challenge laws he considered unconstitutional. The impeachment, they argued, was politically motivated and thus contrary to the spirit of the Constitution. Samuel J. Tilden, a Democrat from New York, claimed that Congress was trying to remove the president from office without accusing him of a crime "or anything more than a mere difference of opinion."

Johnson's accusers argued that Congress should retain the supreme power to make the laws. Senator Charles Sumner of Massachusetts declared that Johnson had turned

> ❝the veto power conferred by the Constitution as a remedy for ill-considered legislation . . . into a weapon of offense against Congress.❞

In May the senators cast two votes. In both instances the result was 35 to 19 votes to convict the president—one vote short of the two-thirds majority required by the Constitution for conviction. Several moderate Republicans voted for a verdict of not guilty because they did not believe a president should be removed from office for political differences. As a result, Johnson stayed in office until the end of his term in March 1869.

Election of 1868

By the presidential election of 1868, most Southern states had rejoined the Union. Many Americans hoped that conflicts over Reconstruction and sectional divisions were behind them.

Abandoning Johnson, the Republicans chose General **Ulysses S. Grant,** the Civil War hero, as their presidential candidate. The Democrats nominated Horatio Seymour, a former governor of New York.

Grant won the election, gaining 214 of 294 electoral votes. He also received most of the votes of African Americans in the South. The 1868 election was a vote on Reconstruction, and the voters supported the Republican approach to the issue.

The Fifteenth Amendment

After the election Republicans developed their last major piece of Reconstruction legislation. In February 1869, Congress passed the **Fifteenth Amendment.** It prohibited the state and federal governments from denying the right to vote to any male citizen because of "race, color, or previous condition of servitude."

African American men won the right to vote when the Fifteenth Amendment was ratified and became law in February 1870. Republicans thought that the power of the ballot would enable African Americans to protect themselves. That belief, it turned out, was too optimistic.

📖 *(See page 248 for the entire text of the Fifteenth Amendment.)*

✓ **Reading Check** **Explaining** What was the outcome of the impeachment trial of President Johnson?

SECTION 2 ASSESSMENT

Checking for Understanding

1. **Key Terms** Write a short paragraph in which you use these key terms: black codes, override, impeach.
2. **Reviewing Facts** Discuss two ways Southerners violated Lincoln's plan for Reconstruction.

Reviewing Themes

3. **Civic Rights and Responsibilities** How did Congress challenge the black codes set up by Southern states?

Critical Thinking

4. **Drawing Conclusions** If you had been a member of the Senate, would you have voted for or against convicting President Johnson? Why?
5. **Summarizing Information** Re-create the diagram below and answer the questions about these amendments.

	Date ratified	Impact on life
Fourteenth Amendment		
Fifteenth Amendment		

Analyzing Visuals

6. **Geography Skills** Examine the map that appears on page 507; then answer these questions. What are the geographic divisions of the South shown on the map? Which military district was composed of only one state? Which states made up the Third District?

Interdisciplinary Activity

Expository Writing Write a one-page essay in which you argue for or argue against the Radical Republicans' plan for Reconstruction.

SECTION 3 The South During Reconstruction

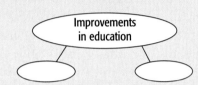

Guide to Reading

Main Idea
After the Civil War the South had to rebuild not only its farms and roads, but its social and political structures as well.

Key Terms
scalawag, carpetbagger, corruption, integrate, sharecropping

Reading Strategy
Organizing Information As you read the section, re-create the diagram below and describe improvements in the South in the field of education.

Improvements in education

Read to Learn
• what groups participated in Reconstruction in the South.
• how Southern life changed during Reconstruction.

Section Theme
Continuity and Change The Republican Party dominated Southern politics during Reconstruction.

Preview of Events

♦1865	♦1867	♦1869	♦1871

1865
Freedmen's Bank is established

1866
Ku Klux Klan is formed

1869
African Americans serve in House of Representatives

1870
First African American is elected to the Senate

AN American Story

"The dust of our fathers mingles with yours in the same graveyards. . . . This is your country, but it is ours too." So spoke an emancipated African American after the Civil War. Most formerly enslaved people did not seek revenge or power over whites, only respect and equality. The petition of an African American convention in 1865 stated: "We simply ask that we shall be recognized as *men;* . . . that the same laws which govern *white men* shall govern *black men;* . . . that, in short, we be dealt with as others are—in equity and justice."

Mississippi Senator Hiram Revels

New Groups Take Charge

During Reconstruction the Republican Party came to dominate Southern politics. Support for the Republican Party came mainly from three groups. One group was African Americans who were overwhelmingly Republican. Support also came from white Southerners who supported Republican policies, and white settlers from the North. These groups dominated the state constitutional conventions and state governments.

CHAPTER 17 Reconstruction and Its Aftermath **509**

African Americans in Government

African Americans played an important role in Reconstruction politics both as voters and as elected officials. In states where African American voters were the majority, they contributed heavily to Republican victories.

African Americans did not control the government of any state, although they briefly held a majority in the lower house of the South Carolina legislature. In other Southern states they held important positions, but never in proportion to their numbers.

At the national level, 16 African Americans served in the House of Representatives and 2 in the Senate between 1869 and 1880. **Hiram Revels,** one of the African American senators, was an ordained minister. During the Civil War he had recruited African Americans for the Union army, started a school for freed African Americans in St. Louis, Missouri, and served as chaplain of an African American regiment in Mississippi. Revels remained in Mississippi after the war and was elected to the Senate in 1870. He served a year in the Senate, where he declared he received "fair treatment."

Blanche K. Bruce, the other African American senator, also came from Mississippi. A former runaway slave, Bruce had taught in a school for African Americans in Missouri when the war began. In 1869 he went to Mississippi, entered politics, and became a superintendent of schools. He was elected to the Senate in 1874, serving there for six years.

Scalawags and Carpetbaggers

Some Southern whites supported Republican policy throughout Reconstruction. Many were nonslaveholding farmers or business leaders who had opposed secession in the first place. Former Confederates despised them for siding with the Republicans and called them scalawags, a term meaning "scoundrel" or "worthless rascal."

Many Northern whites who moved to the South after the war also supported the Republicans and served as Republican leaders during Reconstruction. Critics called these Northerners carpetbaggers because they arrived with all their belongings in cheap suitcases made of carpet fabric. Although some of the carpetbaggers were greedy and took advantage of the situation in the South, most did not. Many carpetbaggers were former Union army soldiers or members of the Freedmen's Bureau who liked the South and wanted to settle there. Others were reformers from the North—including lawyers, doctors, and teachers—who wanted to help reshape Southern society.

Many Southerners ridiculed the Reconstruction governments and accused them of corruption—dishonest or illegal actions—and financial mismanagement. While some officials made money illegally, the practice was hardly widespread. Indeed, there was probably less corruption in the South than in the North.

Resistance to Reconstruction

Most white Southerners opposed efforts to expand African Americans' rights. Carl Schurz, a Republican from Missouri who toured the South right after the war, reported:

> 66Wherever I go—the street, the shop, the house, the hotel, or the steamboat—I hear the people talk in such a way as to indicate that they are yet unable to conceive of the Negro as possessing any rights at all.99

Plantation owners tried to maintain control over freed people in any way they could. Many told African Americans they could not leave the plantations. Most white land owners refused to rent land to freedmen.

Other white Southerners also made life difficult for African Americans. Store owners refused them credit, and employers refused to give them work. Some whites also used fear and force to keep freedmen in line.

The Ku Klux Klan

Violence against African Americans and their white supporters became commonplace during Reconstruction. Much of this violence

HISTORY *Online*

Student Web Activity
Visit tarvol1.glencoe.com and click on **Chapter 17— Student Web Activities** for an activity on the first African American members of Congress.

People In History

Frederick Douglass 1817–1895

Frederick Douglass escaped slavery in 1838 and quickly emerged as a leader of the movement for liberty for African Americans. During the Civil War, he urged President Lincoln to free the enslaved people, and he helped organize African American troops to fight for freedom.

After Lincoln was assassinated, Douglass opposed President Johnson's Reconstruction program. Instead he supported the Radical Republican plan. A skilled and powerful speaker, Douglass traveled throughout the nation insisting on full equality for African Americans. He was particularly outspoken in support of the Fifteenth Amendment, guaranteeing African American men the right to vote. To Douglass, the vote meant that African Americans would not only be full citizens but would also have a weapon to protect their rights.

was committed by secret societies organized to prevent freed men and women from exercising their rights and to help whites regain power.

The most terrifying of these societies, the **Ku Klux Klan,** was formed in 1866. Wearing white sheets and hoods, members of the Klan launched "midnight rides" against African Americans, burning their homes, churches, and schools. The Klan killed as well. In Jackson County, Florida, the Klan murdered more than 150 people over a three-year period. Klan violence often increased before elections, as the group tried to scare African Americans to keep them from voting. The Klan also attacked white supporters of Reconstruction.

The tactics of the Klan and other violent groups had the support of many Southerners, especially planters and Democrats. These Southerners, who had the most to gain from the reestablishment of white supremacy, saw violence as a defense against Republican rule.

Taking Action Against Violence

Southerners opposed to terrorism appealed to the federal government to do something. In 1870 and 1871, Congress passed several laws to try to stop the growing violence of the Klan. These laws had limited success. Most white Southerners refused to testify against those who attacked African Americans and their white supporters. Still, enough arrests were made to restore order for the 1872 presidential election.

✓ **Reading Check** **Explaining** Why did laws to control the Ku Klux Klan have little effect?

Some Improvements

Despite the violence, Reconstruction brought important changes throughout the South. This was especially true in education.

Education improved for both African Americans and whites. African Americans saw education as an important step to a better life. In many regions they created their own schools, contributing both labor and money to build the schools.

The Freedmen's Bureau and private charities played a major role in spreading education. Northern women and free African Americans came South to teach in these schools. By 1870 about 4,000 schools had been established, with 200,000 students. More than half the teachers in these schools were African American.

Mother and daughter reading

advanced education for African Americans. Some academies developed into colleges and universities, such as Morehouse College and Atlanta University.

Generally, African American and white students attended different schools. Only Louisiana, South Carolina, and Florida required that schools be integrated—include both whites and African Americans—but the laws were not enforced.

Public Schools

In the 1870s Reconstruction governments began creating public school systems for both races, which had not existed in the South before the war. Within a few years, more than 50 percent of the white children and about 40 percent of African American children in the South were enrolled in public schools. Northern missionary societies also established academies offering

Farming the Land

Along with education, most freed people wanted land. Some African Americans were able to buy land with the assistance of the Freedmen's Bank, established in 1865. Most, however, failed to get their own land.

The most common form of farmwork for freed individuals was sharecropping. In this system a landowner rented a plot of land to a sharecropper, or farmer, along with a crude shack, some seeds and tools, and perhaps a mule. In return sharecroppers shared a percentage of their crop with the landowner.

After paying the landowners, sharecroppers often had little left to sell. Sometimes there was barely enough to feed their families. For many, sharecropping was little better than slavery.

✓ Reading Check **Explaining** How did sharecroppers get land to farm?

SECTION 3 ASSESSMENT

Checking for Understanding

1. **Key Terms** Define each term using a complete sentence: scalawag, carpetbagger, corruption, integrate, sharecropping.
2. **Reviewing Facts** How did some Southerners try to maintain control over freed people?

Reviewing Themes

3. **Continuity and Change** How did the state governments under Reconstruction reform education?

Critical Thinking

4. **Drawing Conclusions** Why was voting and owning land so important to newly freed African Americans?
5. **Organizing Information** Re-create the diagram below and identify the three groups that made up the Southern Republican Party.

Southern Republican Party

Analyzing Visuals

6. **Picturing History** Study the picture above. Write a paragraph that explains who the people are and why reading is important to them.

Interdisciplinary Activity

Reading Bring newspapers to class and search for stories that show groups of people struggling for their rights throughout the world. After reading the articles aloud in class, post the items on the bulletin board with the heading "Let Freedom Ring."

and withdraw all remaining troops from Southern states. The Democrats, in turn, promised to maintain African Americans' rights.

In his Inaugural Address, Hayes declared that what the South needed most was the restoration of "wise, honest, and peaceful local self-government." During a goodwill trip to the South, Hayes announced his intention of letting Southerners handle racial issues. In Atlanta he told an African American audience:

> 66. . . your rights and interests would be safer if this great mass of intelligent white men were left alone by the general government. 99

Hayes's message was clear. The federal government would no longer attempt to reshape Southern society or help Southern African Americans. Reconstruction was over.

✔ Reading Check **Summarizing** What effect did the Compromise of 1877 have on Reconstruction?

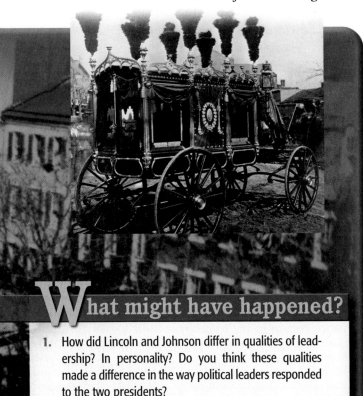

Lincoln's funeral carriage

What might have happened?

1. How did Lincoln and Johnson differ in qualities of leadership? In personality? Do you think these qualities made a difference in the way political leaders responded to the two presidents?

2. Would Reconstruction have taken a different course if Lincoln had not been assassinated? Explain.

Change in the South

> 66I am treated not as an American citizen, but as a brute. . . . [A]nd for what? Not that I am unable to or unwilling to pay my way; not that I am obnoxious in my personal appearance or disrespectful in my conduct; but simply because I happen to be of a darker complexion. 99

John Lynch, a member of Congress who had once been enslaved, spoke these words. At the end of Reconstruction, many African Americans faced lives of poverty, indignity, and despair.

A New Ruling Party

Many Southern whites hated Republicans because of their role in the Civil War and in Reconstruction. When Reconstruction ended, political power in the South shifted from the Republicans to the Democrats.

In some regions, the ruling Democrats were the large landowners and other groups that had held power before the Civil War. In most areas, however, a new ruling class took charge. Among their ranks were merchants, bankers, industrialists, and other business leaders who supported economic development and opposed Northern interference. These Democrats called themselves **"Redeemers"** because they had "redeemed," or saved, the South from Republican rule.

The Redeemers adopted conservative policies such as lower taxes, less public spending, and reduced government services. They drastically cut, or even eliminated, many social services started during Reconstruction, including public education. Their one-party rule and conservative policies dominated Southern politics well into the 1900s.

Rise of the "New South"

By the 1880s forward-looking Southerners were convinced that their region must develop a strong industrial economy. They argued that the South had lost the Civil War because its industry and manufacturing did not match the North's. **Henry Grady,** editor of the *Atlanta Constitution,* headed a group that urged Southerners to "out-

Yankee the Yankees" and build a "New South." This New South would have industries based on coal, iron, tobacco, cotton, lumber, and the region's other abundant resources. Southerners would create this new economy by embracing a spirit of hard work and regional pride. In 1886 Grady told a Boston audience that industrial development would allow the New South to match the North in a peaceful competition.

Southern Industries

Industry in the South made dramatic gains after Reconstruction. Some of the strongest advances were in the textile industry. Before the Civil War, Southern planters had shipped cotton to textile mills in the North or in Europe. In the 1880s textile mills sprang up throughout the South. Many Northern mills would later close as companies built new plants in the South.

Other important industries were lumbering and tobacco processing. The tobacco industry was developed largely through the efforts of **James Duke** of North Carolina. Duke's American Tobacco Company eventually controlled almost all tobacco manufacturing in the nation.

The iron and steel industry also grew rapidly. In the mid-1800s William Kelly, an American ironworker, and Henry Bessemer, a British engineer, had developed methods—called the **Bessemer process**—to inexpensively produce steel from iron. Steel answered industry's need for a sturdy, workable metal. By 1890 Southern mills produced nearly 20 percent of the nation's iron and steel. Much of the industry was in Alabama near deposits of iron ore.

Presidential Elections

Hayes was the only president to win the electoral vote, but lose the popular vote. Actually, three other times in American history—in the elections of John Quincy Adams in 1824, Benjamin Harrison in 1888, and George W. Bush in 2000—the candidate who lost the popular vote won the election.

Factors in Growth

A cheap and reliable workforce helped Southern industry grow. Most factory workers put in long hours for low wages. Sometimes whole families, including children, worked in factories. African Americans got few opportunities in industry except in the lowest-paying jobs.

A railroad-building boom also aided industrial development. By 1870 the Southern railroad system, which had been destroyed during the war, was largely rebuilt. The miles of track more than doubled between 1880 and 1890.

Still, the South did not develop an industrial economy as strong as the North's. The North was still industrializing more rapidly. The South remained primarily agricultural.

Economics
Rural Economy

Supporters of the New South hoped to change Southern agriculture as well as industry. They pictured small, profitable farms raising a variety of crops rather than large plantations devoted to growing cotton.

A different economy emerged, however. Some plantations were broken up, but many large landowners kept control of their property. When estates were divided, much of the land went to sharecropping and tenant farming, neither of which was profitable.

Debt caused problems as well. Poor farmers had to buy on credit to get the food and supplies they needed. The merchants who sold on credit charged high prices for their goods, increasing the farmers' debt. The quickest way for farmers to repay that debt, they thought, was to grow cash crops—crops that could be sold for money. As in the past, the biggest cash crop was cotton. An oversupply of cotton forced prices down, however. The farmers then had to grow even more cotton to try to recover their losses.

Sharecropping and reliance on a single cash crop hampered the development of a more modern agricultural economy. Instead, the rural South sank deeper into poverty and debt.

Reading Check Describing What happened to prices when more cotton was produced than could be sold?

A Divided Society

As Reconstruction ended, African Americans' dreams for justice faded. In the last 20 years of the 1800s, racism became firmly entrenched, and individuals took steps to keep African Americans separated from whites and to deny them basic rights.

Voting Restrictions

The Fifteenth Amendment prohibited any state from denying an individual the right to vote because of race. Southern leaders, however, found ways to get around the amendment and prevent African Americans from voting.

Many Southern states required a poll tax, a fee that people had to pay before voting. Because many African Americans could not afford the tax, they could not vote. The tax also prevented many poor whites from voting. Another approach was to make prospective voters take a literacy test in which they had to read and explain difficult parts of state constitutions or the federal Constitution. Because most African Americans had little education, literacy tests prevented many from voting.

Literacy tests could also keep some whites from voting. For this reason some states passed grandfather clauses. These laws allowed individuals who did not pass the literacy test to vote if their fathers or grandfathers had voted before Reconstruction. Because African Americans could not vote until 1867, they were excluded. Georgia enacted a poll tax and other limits as early as 1870. Such laws, however, did not become widespread until after 1889. African Americans continued to vote in some states until the end of the 1800s. Then, voting laws and the constant threat of violence caused African American voting to drastically decline.

Jim Crow Laws

Another set of laws hurt African Americans. By the 1890s segregation, or the separation of the races, was a prominent feature of life in the South.

The Southern states formed a segregated society by passing so-called **Jim Crow laws.** Taking their name from a character in a song, Jim Crow

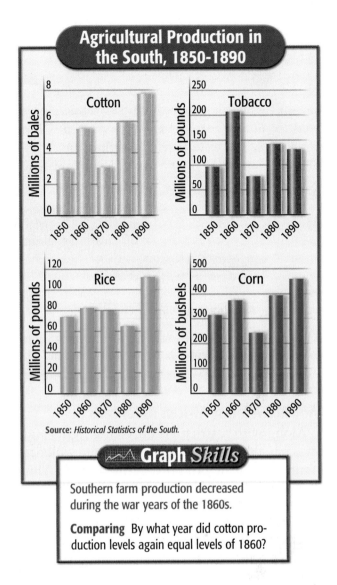

Agricultural Production in the South, 1850-1890

Cotton — Millions of bales

Tobacco — Millions of pounds

Rice — Millions of pounds

Corn — Millions of bushels

Source: *Historical Statistics of the South.*

Graph *Skills*

Southern farm production decreased during the war years of the 1860s.

Comparing By what year did cotton production levels again equal levels of 1860?

laws required African Americans and whites to be separated in almost every public place where they might come in contact with each other.

In 1896 the Supreme Court upheld Jim Crow laws and segregation in *Plessy v. Ferguson.* The case involved a Louisiana law requiring separate sections on trains for African Americans. The Court ruled that segregation was legal as long as African Americans had access to public facilities or accommodations equal to those of whites. ⌑
(See page 626 of the Appendix for a summary of Plessy v. Ferguson.*)*

The problem, however, was that the facilities were separate but in no way equal. Southern states spent much more money on schools and other facilities for whites than on those for African Americans. This "separate but equal" doctrine provided a legal foundation for segregation in the South that lasted for more than 50 years.

Violence Against African Americans

Along with restrictions on voting rights and laws passed to segregate society, white violence against African Americans increased. This violence took many terrible forms, including lynching, in which an angry mob killed a person by hanging. African Americans were lynched because they were suspected of committing crimes—or because they did not behave as whites thought they should.

Reconstruction's Impact

Reconstruction was both a success and a failure. It helped the South recover from the war and begin rebuilding its economy. Yet economic recovery was far from complete. Although Southern agriculture took a new form, the South was still a rural economy, and that economy was still very poor.

Under Reconstruction African Americans gained greater equality and began creating their own institutions. They joined with whites in new governments, fairer and more democratic than the South had ever seen. This improvement for African Americans did not last long, however. In the words of African American writer and civil rights leader **W.E.B. Du Bois,**

❝The slave went free; stood a brief moment in the sun; then moved back again toward slavery.❞

The biggest disappointment of Reconstruction was that it did not make good on the promise of true freedom for freed African Americans. The South soon created a segregated society.

✓ **Reading Check** **Describing** What is segregation?

SECTION 4 ASSESSMENT

Checking for Understanding

1. **Key Terms** Define the following terms: reconciliation, commission, cash crop, poll tax, literacy test, grandfather clause, segregation, lynching.
2. **Reviewing Facts** How did the Bessemer process affect Southern industry?

Reviewing Themes

3. **Continuity and Change** In what industries did the South make great gains after Reconstruction?

Critical Thinking

4. **Determining Cause and Effect** Explain how the Amnesty Act helped the Democratic Party regain its strength.
5. **Organizing Information** Re-create the diagram below and describe how the poll tax and literacy tests restricted voting rights.

Poll tax ⟶ ◯

Literacy tests ⟶ ◯

Analyzing Visuals

6. Study the election map on page 515. Which candidate received the greater number of popular votes? Who won the election?

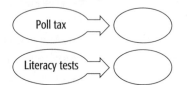

Interdisciplinary Activity

Government Research to find out how many African Americans hold seats in Congress today. Make a list of their names and states of residence. Be sure to include members of both the House of Representatives and the Senate.

Critical Thinking SKILLBUILDER

Identifying the Main Idea

Why Learn This Skill?

Historical details, such as names, dates, and events, are easier to remember when they are connected to a main idea. Understanding the main idea allows you to grasp the whole picture or story.

Learning the Skill

Follow these steps to identify a main idea:

- Before you read the material, find out the setting of the article or document: the time, the place, and who the writer is.
- Read the material and ask, "What is the purpose of this information?"
- Identify supporting details.
- Identify the main idea or central issue.

Practicing the Skill

In the passage below, W.E.B. Du Bois, an African American scholar, describes the attitudes of people in Charleston, South Carolina, just after the Civil War. Read the passage and answer the questions that follow.

66 The economic loss which came through war was great, but not nearly as influential as the psychological change, the change in habit and thought….

The hatred of the Yankees was increased. The defeated Southern leaders were popular heroes. Numbers of Southerners planned to leave the country and go to South America or Mexico….

The labor situation, the prospect of free Negroes, caused great apprehension. It was accepted as absolutely true by most planters that the Negro could not work without a white master. 99

A plantation owner meets her former slaves following emancipation.

1 Du Bois begins by naming two kinds of losses from the war. What are they? Which does he say was greater?

2 What is the main idea of the passage?

3 What details support the main idea?

4 Does the painting support or negate Du Bois's main idea?

Applying the Skill

Identifying the Main Idea Bring a news article about a current event to class. Identify the main idea and supporting details in the article.

 GO TO

Glencoe's **Skillbuilder Interactive Workbook CD-ROM, Level 1,** provides instruction and practice in key social studies skills.

Chapter Summary

Reconstruction and Its Aftermath

Reconstruction Plans

- Ten Percent Plan
- Wade-Davis Bill
- "Restoration"

Radicals in Control

- Civil Rights Act of 1866
- The Fourteenth Amendment
- President Johnson is impeached
- The Fifteenth Amendment

End of Reconstruction

- Interest in Reconstruction declines
- Amnesty Act
- Election of 1876
- Compromise of 1877

Change in the South

- Southern industry grows
- Economy remains agricultural
- Many white and African American farmers turn to sharecropping
- Jim Crow laws promote segregation

Reviewing Key Terms

Explain why each of these terms is used in a chapter about Reconstruction.

1. amnesty
2. black codes
3. poll tax
4. freedmen
5. impeach
6. segregation

Reviewing Key Facts

7. What services did the Freedmen's Bureau provide?
8. Who succeeded Lincoln as president?
9. How was the Fourteenth Amendment supposed to help African Americans?
10. What verdict did the Senate reach in the trial of President Johnson?
11. What right does the Fifteenth Amendment protect?
12. What role did African Americans play in early Reconstruction politics in the South?
13. What tactic did the Ku Klux Klan use to influence elections in the South?
14. Why was a special commission needed to decide the presidential election of 1876?
15. What Supreme Court decision upheld the legality of segregation so long as "separate but equal" facilities were provided?

Critical Thinking

16. **Analyzing Themes: Civic Rights and Responsibilities** How did the black codes deny rights?
17. **Analyzing Primary Sources** Explain the following quote as it applies to Reconstruction: "The slave went free; stood a brief moment in the sun; then moved back again toward slavery."
18. **Analyzing Themes: Economic Factors** Why did growing cotton after the Civil War send many Southern farmers into debt?
19. **Organizing Information** Re-create the diagram below and explain two important concessions that were made in the Compromise of 1877.

```
         Compromise of 1877
         /              \
   [          ]      [          ]
```

Practicing Skills

The excerpt below was written by Charlotte Forten, one of many African American teachers who went South to teach freed individuals during the period of Reconstruction. Read the excerpt, which describes her first days of teaching school. Then answer the questions that follow.

> . . . I never before saw children so eager to learn, although I had had several years' experience in New England schools. Coming to school is a constant delight and recreation to them. They come here as other children go to play. The older ones, during the summer, work in the fields from early morning until eleven or twelve o'clock, and then come to school, after their hard toil in the hot sun, as bright and as anxious to learn as ever. **99**

20. What is the main idea of this passage?
21. What details support the main idea of this passage?

Citizenship Cooperative Activity

22. **Registering to Vote** Laws about voter registration vary from place to place. Working with a partner, contact your local election board to find out what the requirements for voter registration are in your community. Then design a brochure that encourages citizens to register to vote.

Economics Activity

23. What happened to the price of cotton when an oversupply of cotton was on the market? How do you think prices would change if the demand for cotton were greater than the supply? Explain.

Geography and History Activity

Turn to the map on page 515 to answer the following questions.

24. **Location** Electoral votes are based on population. What were the six most populous states in 1876?
25. **Region** Which political party gained the most votes in the western states?
26. **Place** How many electoral votes were in dispute?

Self-Check Quiz

Visit tarvol1.glencoe.com and click on **Chapter 17— Self-Check Quizzes** to prepare for the chapter test.

Alternative Assessment

27. **Portfolio Writing Activity** Review the chapter to make a list of specific ways that Southern states tried to deny equal rights to African Americans after the war. Then decide which amendment(s)—Thirteenth, Fourteenth, or Fifteenth—should have prevented each action. Put this information in an essay using standard grammar and spelling.

Standardized Test Practice

Directions: Read the passage below. It is an excerpt from the Fifteenth Amendment to the Constitution. Then answer the question that follows.

> The right of citizens of the United States to vote shall not be denied or abridged by the United States or any State on account of race, color, or previous condition of servitude.
>
> The Congress shall have power to enforce this article by appropriate legislation.

The main idea of the Fifteenth Amendment is that

A enslaved people convicted of crimes had the right to a fair trial.

B slavery was made illegal in every state of the Union.

C the government was not allowed to deny a person's right to vote on the basis of race.

D Congress had the right to set voting restrictions in whatever state it chose.

Test-Taking Tip

This question asks for the *main idea* of the passage—in this case, of the Fifteenth Amendment. Read through all the answer choices before choosing the best one. Make sure you look for information in the passage to support your answer.

UNIT 7

Modern America Emerges

1877–Present

Why It Matters

As you study Unit 7, you will learn how new technology and industries thrust the United States into the modern era. America's role in two world wars during the twentieth century made the nation a superpower. Today, the United States continues as a leading nation that strives to meet challenges at home and abroad.

Primary Sources Library

See pages 604–605 for primary source readings to accompany Unit 7.

Use the American history **Primary Source Document Library CD-ROM** for primary sources about Modern America.

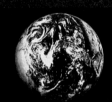

Decorative flag, computer art

The International
Space Station

524

"America, at its best, is compassionate."

—President George W. Bush,
2001 Inaugural Address

CHAPTER 18 Reshaping the Nation

1877–1929

Why It Matters

Growth has been a constant part of the American experience. Beginning as a small cluster of colonies on the Atlantic coast, the nation expanded beyond the Mississippi River to the Pacific Ocean. As it became powerful, the United States moved beyond its territorial limits in search of new markets and colonies. The United States also began to take a major role in shaping world affairs.

The Impact Today

The nation's responsibilities as an international power demand open attitudes to new ideas. Americans adjust to these ideas in ways that assure the future of a free and democratic society.

The American Republic to 1877 *Video* *The chapter 18 video, "The Builders of Our Railroads," examines the life and hardships that immigrants faced as workers on the railroads.*

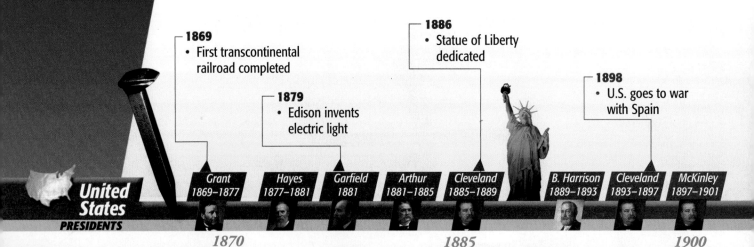

1869
• First transcontinental railroad completed

1879
• Edison invents electric light

1886
• Statue of Liberty dedicated

1898
• U.S. goes to war with Spain

United States PRESIDENTS

| Grant 1869–1877 | Hayes 1877–1881 | Garfield 1881 | Arthur 1881–1885 | Cleveland 1885–1889 | B. Harrison 1889–1893 | Cleveland 1893–1897 | McKinley 1897–1901 |

1870   1885   1900

World

1866
• Transatlantic telegraph line successfully completed

1869
• Suez Canal opens

1895
• José Martí leads revolt in Cuba

New York City, East Side 1900 New arrivals crowded into America's cities and brought with them the cultural heritage of their homelands.

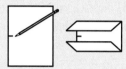
1901
• President McKinley assassinated

1917
• U.S. enters World War I

1920
• Nineteenth Amendment grants woman suffrage

1927
• Charles Lindbergh flies across Atlantic

| T. Roosevelt 1901–1909 | Taft 1909–1913 | Wilson 1913–1921 | Harding 1921–1923 | Coolidge 1923–1929 |

1915   *1930*

1905
• Albert Einstein announces theory of relativity

1914
• World War I begins

1919
• Treaty of Versailles signed

1928
• Alexander Fleming discovers penicillin

HISTORY
Online

Chapter Overview
Visit tarvol1.glencoe.com and click on **Chapter 18— Chapter Overviews** to preview chapter information.

The Western Frontier

Guide to Reading

Main Idea
Following the Civil War, settlers began to move west, which led to conflict with Native Americans.

Key Terms
boomtown, transcontinental, vaqueros, reservation

Reading Strategy
Organizing Information As you read the section, re-create the diagram below and describe the significance of each of the following.

	Significance
Promontory Point	
Homestead Act	
Farmers' Alliance	

Read to Learn
• why settlers moved west.
• why settlers came into conflict with Native Americans.

Section Theme
Geography and History Railroads led the way west and opened the Great Plains to settlement.

Preview of Events

♦1870	♦1880	♦1890	♦1900

1869
First transcontinental railroad completed

1876
Battle of Little Bighorn

1890
Populist Party organized

1896
McKinley elected president

Gold nuggets

AN American Story

"We'll cross the bold Missouri, and we'll steer for the West,
And we'll take the road we think is the shortest and the best,
We'll travel over plains where the wind is blowing bleak,
And the sandy wastes shall echo with—Hurrah for Pikes Peak."
                                    —"The Gold Seekers' Song"
Miners sang this hopeful song in 1859 as they headed for Pikes Peak, Colorado, where gold had been discovered.

There remained one last frontier for Americans to settle—the Trans-Mississippi West. This area lay between the Mississippi River and the Sierra Nevada Mountains and included the Great Plains, the Rocky Mountains, and the Great Basin. The first white settlers were fur traders who had started moving into the West in the early 1800s. By the time of the Civil War, however, mineral discoveries had drawn another type of pioneer to the West—the miner. Soon, the whole region was a mining frontier.

Settling the West

Miners, ranchers, and farmers settled on the Great Plains, despite resistance from Native Americans. With the closing of this last frontier, the United States fulfilled the dream of Manifest Destiny.

The Mining Boom

In 1858, prospectors found gold in Colorado and Nevada. The gold strikes created boomtowns—towns that grew up almost overnight near mining sites—as thousands of prospectors headed to the region. The miners soon found other metals as well, including copper, lead, and zinc.

The discovery of valuable minerals helped bring the railroads west. Gold, silver, and other ore had little value unless it could be shipped east to factories. Miners also needed food and supplies. Wagons and stagecoaches could not move goods fast enough, but railroads could.

Railroad construction was often supported by large government subsidies—loans and land grants from the government. The first task facing the railroads was to build a transcontinental rail line—one that would span the continent and connect the Atlantic and Pacific coasts. The Union Pacific Company began laying track westward from Nebraska, while the Central Pacific worked eastward from California. On May 10, 1869, the two sets of tracks met at **Promontory Point,** Utah. The railroads brought a wave of new settlers to the West—ranchers and farmers.

The Cattle Kingdom

When the Spanish settled the Southwest, they brought with them a breed of cattle called **longhorns** that gradually spread across Texas. At the same time, the Civil War had caused a shortage of beef in the east, driving prices up. To get the cattle to market, the Texas ranchers organized cattle drives—herding hundreds of thousands of cattle north to the railroad.

The sudden increase in the longhorns' value set off what became known as the **Long Drive**—the herding of cattle 1,000 miles or more to meet the railroads. In the late 1860s, the **Chisholm Trail** extended from San Antonio, Texas, to Abilene, Kansas. The **Goodnight-Loving Trail,** named for ranchers Charlie Goodnight and Oliver Loving, swung west through New Mexico Territory and then turned north. During the peak years of the "Cattle Kingdom," from the late 1860s to the mid-1880s, the trails carried millions of cattle north:

> 66At the end of the trail, cattle crowded the stockyards. Railroad cities—Omaha, Abilene, Kansas City, Chicago—flourished during the 20-year heyday of cattle driving.99

Life on the Trail

Cattle driving was hard work. Cowhands rode in the saddle up to 15 hours every day, in driving rain, dust storms, and blazing sun. The life was lonely, too. Cowhands saw few outsiders.

Many cowhands were veterans of the Confederate army. Some, like **Nat Love,** were African Americans who moved west in search of a better life after the Civil War. Others were Hispanics. In fact, the tradition of cattle herding began with Hispanic ranch hands in the Spanish Southwest. These vaqueros developed many of the skills—riding, roping, and branding—that cowhands used on the drives.

Nat Love was one of many African Americans who rode the cattle trails.

✦ Geography
The Cattle Kingdom Ends

The open-range cattle industry collapsed even more quickly than it had risen. Too many animals on open ranges resulted in overgrazing, depriving both livestock and wild animals of food. Overproduction drove prices down, and sheepherders and farmers competed with ranchers for land. Finally, two severe winters in the mid- and late-1880s killed thousands of animals. The cattle industry survived, but the day of large herds on the open range ended. From then on, ranchers raised herds on fenced-in ranches. With the end of the Cattle Kingdom, another group of settlers arrived on the Plains—the farmers.

Farmers Settle the Plains

The early pioneers who reached the Great Plains did not believe they could farm the dry, treeless area. In the late 1860s, however, farmers began settling there and planting crops. In a short time, the Plains changed from "wilderness" to farmland. In 1872 a Nebraska settler wrote,

❝One year ago this was a vast houseless, uninhabitable prairie. . . . Today I can see more than thirty dwellings from my door.❞

Several factors brought settlers to the Plains. The railroads made the journey west easier and cheaper. Above-average rainfall made the Plains better suited to farming. New laws offered free land.

In 1862 Congress passed the **Homestead Act,** which gave 160 free acres of land to any settler who paid a filing fee and lived on the land for 5 years.

Homesteading lured thousands of new settlers to the Great Plains. Some were immigrants who had begun the process of becoming American citizens and were eligible to file for land. Others were women. Although married women could not claim land, single women and widows had the same rights as men—and they took advantage of the Homestead Act to acquire property.

To survive on the Plains, the farmers—known as **sodbusters**—had to find new ways of doing things. Lacking wood, they cut sod into bricks to build houses. They used windmills to pump water and barbed wire to fence in their property.

The Oklahoma Land Rush

The last part of the Plains to be settled was the Oklahoma Territory, which Congress had designated as "Indian Territory" in the 1830s. After years of pressure from land dealers and white settlers, the federal government opened Oklahoma to homesteaders in 1889. Settlement had changed the Plains dramatically. No one felt these changes more keenly than the Native Americans who had lived on the Plains for centuries.

✔️ Reading Check **Explaining** What was the purpose of the Long Drive?

On the Great Plains *Living on the Plains meant settlers had to build houses that did not require lumber on this treeless land. A Plains family's first home was usually made of sod.*

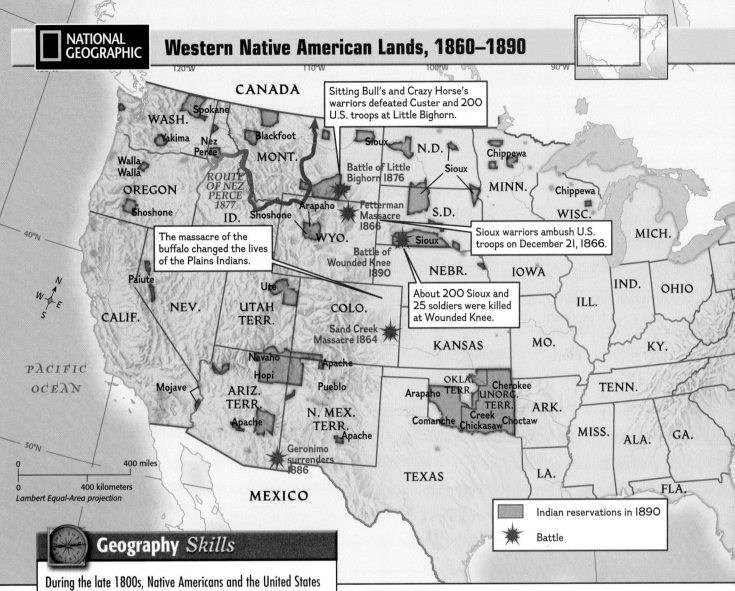

Western Native American Lands, 1860–1890

Sitting Bull's and Crazy Horse's warriors defeated Custer and 200 U.S. troops at Little Bighorn.

CANADA

WASH.
Spokane
Yakima
Nez Perce
Blackfoot
MONT.
Walla Walla
OREGON
ROUTE OF NEZ PERCE 1877
Shoshone
ID.
Shoshone
Arapaho
Battle of Little Bighorn 1876
Fetterman Massacre 1866
WYO.
Battle of Wounded Knee 1890
NEBR.

Sioux
N.D.
Sioux
S.D.

Chippewa
MINN.
Chippewa
WISC.
MICH.

Sioux warriors ambush U.S. troops on December 21, 1866.

The massacre of the buffalo changed the lives of the Plains Indians.

Paiute
Ute
NEV.
UTAH TERR.
COLO.
Sand Creek Massacre 1864
KANSAS
MO.
IOWA
ILL.
IND.
OHIO
KY.

About 200 Sioux and 25 soldiers were killed at Wounded Knee.

CALIF.
Mojave
Navaho
Hopi
ARIZ. TERR.
Apache
Pueblo
Apache
N. MEX. TERR.
Apache
Geronimo surrenders 1886

OKLA. TERR.
Arapaho
Comanche
Chickasaw
Creek
Cherokee
UNORG. TERR.
Choctaw
ARK.
TENN.
MISS.
ALA.
GA.

PACIFIC OCEAN

TEXAS
LA.
FLA.

MEXICO

0 — 400 miles
0 — 400 kilometers
Lambert Equal-Area projection

N W E S

120°W   110°W   100°W   90°W   40°N   30°N

Indian reservations in 1890
✴ Battle

Geography Skills

During the late 1800s, Native Americans and the United States Army fought many battles over land.
1. **Location** In what present-day state was the Battle of Little Bighorn fought?
2. **Analyzing Information** Which Native American nations resettled in or near the Oklahoma Territory?

Native American Struggles

Many Native American groups lived on the Plains. The buffalo that roamed there provided most of the essentials the Plains peoples needed for daily living. As railroads, miners, ranchers, and farmers spread west, however, vast numbers of buffalo were slaughtered.

The federal government recommended moving the Native Americans to reservations. Reservations were tracts of land set aside for Native Americans. Many refused to accept the reserva-

tion policy. Some clashed with settlers. Soon, fighting began between the United States Army and various Native American groups.

Little Bighorn

The Sioux received lands in the Black Hills of South Dakota. Yet soon crews and settlers discovered gold in the Black Hills, and miners swarmed onto the reservation.

The government reduced the size of most reservations or moved the Native Americans to lands less desirable. The Sioux decided they should not have to honor government policy when whites did not. **Sitting Bull** and **Crazy Horse** led their people off the reservation. Near the Little Bighorn River in southern Montana Territory, they joined forces with several thousand other Sioux and Cheyenne.

In June 1876 Lieutenant Colonel **George Custer** and more than 200 troops sent to round up the Sioux faced an unexpected group of several thousand. In the battle, the Native Americans killed Custer and all of his troops. The Sioux and Cheyenne won the battle, but within months government soldiers had forced them to surrender.

The Nez Perce and the Apache

In the 1870s other Native American people beside the Sioux and Cheyenne resisted the move to reservations. One of these was the Nez Perce of eastern Oregon. In 1877 the government ordered the Nez Perce to move to a smaller reservation in Idaho. The Nez Perce attempted to flee, led by **Chief Joseph.** They evaded capture for nearly two months before surrendering to United States troops just 40 miles from the Canadian border. In advising his people to give up, Chief Joseph said:

> 66 ….I am tired. My heart is sick and sad. From where the sun now stands, I will fight no more forever. 99

The government forced the Nez Perce onto an Oklahoma reservation instead of resettling them in their native Northwest. Unused to the climate and terrain, many of them died.

A group of Apache, led by **Geronimo,** became the last Native American nation to resist. By the time the Americans captured Geronimo in 1886, American troops had confined every Native American nation to reservations.

Wounded Knee

One final episode of Native American resistance took place in the Dakota Territory. In December 1890 United States soldiers tried to disarm a large band of Plains Native Americans gathered at **Wounded Knee** on the Pine Ridge Reservation in South Dakota. The result was a massacre in which more than 200 Native Americans and 25 soldiers lost their lives. Wounded Knee marked the end of armed conflict between the United States government and Native Americans.

New Policies

During the 1880s the plight of Native Americans led to calls for more humane policies. Sentiment for reform grew with the publication of Helen Hunt Jackson's book, *A Century of Dishonor.* Jackson wrote about the broken treaties and mistreatment Native Americans endured at the hands of the government and settlers.

Congress changed government policy in the Dawes Act in 1887. The act proposed to break up the reservations and to end individual identification with a tribal group. Each Native American would receive a plot of reservation land. The goal was to encourage the Native American people to become farmers. Eventually, they would become American citizens. Native American children would be sent to white-run boarding schools. Some of the reservation lands would be sold to support this schooling.

Over the next 50 years, the government divided up the reservations. Speculators acquired most of the valuable land. With Native American resistance at an end, nothing remained to stop white settlers. In 1890 the census report stated that the Trans-Mississippi West was so broken up by acres of settlement that a frontier line could no longer be identified. The last frontier, and with it the Old West, had disappeared.

"If we must die, we die defending our rights."

—*Sitting Bull*

Reading Check **Identifying** Who led the Nez Perce on their journey of escape?

Farmers in Protest

After the Civil War, farming expanded in the West and South. The supply of crops grew faster than the demand for them, however, and prices fell steadily. At the same time, farmers' expenses—for transporting their goods, for seed, and for equipment—remained high.

Organizing

Farmers blamed their troubles on the high shipping rates of the railroads. To solve their problems, farmers formed self-help groups, such as the **Farmers' Alliance.** In 1890, members of the Alliance established the **Populist Party.**

The Party urged the federal government to help keep prices for farmers' crops high. It also called on government to nationalize, or take over, public transportation and communication. Populists hoped that nationalization would finally end the railroads' high rates.

Most important, the Populists demanded that the government expand the money supply by permitting silver to become, along with gold, the basis for money. America maintained the gold standard in which each paper dollar was redeemable in gold. To make sure it had enough gold, the government limited the amount of paper money. This limited the amount of money available. Meanwhile, the population increased. As each dollar gained in value, farmers earned less as prices dropped and the value of their debts increased.

Poster celebrating the farmer, 1876

Election of 1896

In the presidential election of 1896, the major issue was whether the government should accept silver for making coins. The Democrats nominated **William Jennings Bryan,** a strong supporter of silver. The Republicans nominated **William McKinley,** a strong supporter of gold. The Populists also endorsed Bryan, but the Democrat lost. Big business backed the Republican McKinley, as did factory workers. Urban America now had more political strength than rural America. America was changing from a farming nation to an industrial nation.

Reading Check **Describing** What actions did the Populist Party want government to take regarding the railroad industry?

SECTION 1 ASSESSMENT

Checking for Understanding

1. **Key Terms** Use each of these terms in a sentence that will help explain its meaning: boomtown, transcontinental, vaquero, reservation.

2. **Reviewing Facts** Who was Chief Joseph?

Reviewing Themes

3. **Geography and History** What was the transcontinental railroad? How did it influence settlement?

Critical Thinking

4. **Drawing Conclusions** In what ways did the government reservation policy ignore the needs of Native Americans?

5. **Organizing Information** Re-create the diagram below and list new ways farmers adapted to life on the Plains.

Analyzing Visuals

6. **Geography Skills** Study the map of Western Native American Lands on page 531. When did the Battle of Wounded Knee occur? Where were the Shoshone reservations located?

Interdisciplinary Activity

Art Create a poster that the United States government might have used to encourage farmers to move west. Display your posters in class.

Invention and Industry

Guide to Reading

Main Idea
During the late 1800s, the United States experienced tremendous industrial growth.

Key Terms
horizontal integration, trust, monopoly, vertical integration, collective bargaining, settlement house

Reading Strategy
Organizing Information As you read the section, re-create the diagram below and explain the importance of these individuals.

	Importance
Thomas Edison	
Samuel Gompers	
Jane Addams	

Read to Learn
• how American cities and industries had changed at the turn of the century.
• what challenges immigrants to the United States faced.

Section Theme
Science and Technology New inventions promoted economic growth.

Preview of Events

♦1880   ♦1890   ♦1900   ♦1910

1879
Thomas Edison develops first practical lightbulb

1886
American Federation of Labor forms

1889
Jane Addams founds Hull House

1903
Wright brothers fly at Kitty Hawk

Train song sheet

AN American Story

Rugged construction gangs labored on the Union Pacific and other railways during the transportation boom of the late 1800s. A favorite song was:

*Well, every morning at seven
    o'clock
There were 20 tarriers [drillers]
    a-workin' at the rock,
And the boss comes round and he
    says "Kape still!"
And come down heavy on the cast
    iron drill,*

*And drill, ye tarriers, drill!"
Drill, ye tarriers, drill!
For it's work all day for sugar in
    your tay,
Down behind of the railway and,
Drill, ye tarriers, drill!
And blast!
And fire!*

Even as settlers moved west to farm the last American frontier, farmers in other parts of the country moved to the cities. They took jobs in the new urban industries that recent inventions made possible. The United States was changing from a rural nation into a modern, industrial nation.

The Growth of Industry

The nation's rich farmlands, great forests, and mighty rivers helped the early colonists develop a strong agricultural economy. As the nation grew, Americans developed resources of a different kind. In addition to talented inventors, they had eager investors, willing workers, and a pro-business government. These new resources made the expansion of American industry possible.

⭐ Geography

Rich Natural Resources

The United States also possessed other necessary ingredients for industry—plenty of natural resources. Large deposits of coal lay in western Pennsylvania, the Mississippi Valley, and Appalachia. The shores of Lake Superior held major supplies of iron ore. Mines in western states contained gold, silver, lead, zinc, and copper.

These minerals formed the base of heavy industry in the United States. A heavy industry produces materials such as iron or steel. Out of these materials, Americans built railroads, bridges, skyscrapers, and machinery for the factories that transformed the nation. By the late 1800s, the United States had become the world's number one manufacturing nation.

Railroads Lead the Way

During the Civil War, trains carried troops, weapons, and supplies to the front. After the war, railroads became a driving force behind America's economic growth. Railroad construction increased the demand for iron, steel, coal, timber, and other goods, which created thousands of new jobs for Americans.

The railroads allowed American industry to expand into the West. They moved rural people to the cities and brought homesteaders to the Plains. They united the nation's regions and helped bring American society together.

American Inventions

During the late 1800s, an invention boom spurred the growth of industry. The government granted many **patents**—licenses protecting people's rights to make, sell, or use their inventions.

Two discoveries revolutionized the iron and steel industries. The first was the use of coke (soft coal with the impurities removed). Coke was an excellent fuel for iron-smelting blast furnaces. The second was the Bessemer Process, discovered independently by William Kelly and Henry Bessemer. The process used blasts of cold air to burn off impurities from heated iron. Because steel could now be made cheaply, steel production soared.

Cheap, durable steel then became the basis for other industrial advances. Train rails made of steel lasted much longer than iron rails. Steel beams supported bigger, heavier bridges and buildings. Steel was used for making new machinery and many other products.

Americans also developed new sources of power. Thomas Alva Edison led others in building the first large power plant to furnish elec-

Their first flight at Kitty Hawk, North Carolina, encouraged the Wright brothers to continue their experiments. Soon, they would have a practical aircraft and the world would have a new form of transportation.

1912 Model T Ford

tricity to entire cities. By the turn of the century, electric power lit homes and offices and ran streetcars, elevators, and factories.

Communications

Important inventions appeared in communications. The telegraph had already brought rapid changes before the Civil War. Then in 1866, **Cyrus Field** laid a transatlantic telegraph cable. Now a message sent to someone in Europe arrived in minutes instead of weeks. The telephone was developed by **Alexander Graham Bell,** a young teacher of the deaf, who filed for a patent in 1876. A few years later, the American Bell Telephone Company was established.

Experiments were beginning in radio communication as well. In 1895 Italian inventor **Guglielmo Marconi** transmitted the first messages, and, by 1902, radio messages were being sent for thousands of miles.

Transportation

Two other inventions began a transportation revolution in the United States—the automobile and the airplane. In the early 1900s, **Henry Ford** developed a gasoline-powered automobile that could be built cheaply using an assembly line. In 1903, **Orville** and **Wilbur Wright** built and tested the first successful engine-powered aircraft at **Kitty Hawk, North Carolina.** Their success marked the beginning of the modern aircraft industry.

Economics

An Age of Big Business

With the economy growing, many railroads and other businesses looked for ways to expand. To do so, they needed to raise **capital,** or money, to buy equipment and hire workers. One way a company could raise capital was by becoming a **corporation**—a company that sold shares, or stock, of its business.

One major industry that grew rapidly during this era was the oil industry. In 1870, **John D. Rockefeller** organized the Standard Oil Company. To build Standard Oil, Rockefeller used horizontal integration—the combining of competing companies into one corporation. Rockefeller also increased his control of the oil industry by forming a trust—a group of companies managed by the same board of directors. Using a trust enabled Rockefeller to create a monopoly—almost total control of an industry by one company.

The steel industry also became a huge business in the late 1800s. The leading figure in the early steel industry was **Andrew Carnegie.** His company became powerful through vertical integration—acquiring companies that provided the materials he needed. Carnegie bought coal and iron mines, warehouses, ships, and railroads to gain control of all parts of the steel-making process.

Industrial Workers

Industrial growth in the late 1800s created new jobs and raised the standard of living for many workers. Laborers, however, worked 10 to 12 hours a day, six days a week. Factories and mines were often noisy, polluted, and unsafe.

Dissatisfied workers organized into groups, called labor unions, to demand better pay and working conditions. In 1869, America's first large industrial union, called the **Knights of Labor,** was organized and grew to more than 700,000 members. After some of its members were accused of using violence, the Knights lost members and influence in the 1890s.

In 1886, a group of unions joined together to form the **American Federation of Labor** (AFL). The AFL represented skilled workers. Its first leader was **Samuel Gompers.** The AFL pushed for higher wages, better working conditions, and the right to bargain collectively. In collective bargaining, unions represent workers in bargaining with management.

Many workers used strikes to achieve their goals. They refused to do their jobs until their employers agreed to certain demands. In 1877 a national railroad strike became the first of many violent confrontations between workers and employers. Few strikes succeed between 1865 and 1900, however. Employers usually hired other workers or waited until the strikers ran out of money and returned to work. Most Americans viewed labor unions in a negative manner and government authorities usually sided with employers against strikers.

By the end of the 1800s most workers found themselves with less political power and control of the workplace. Meanwhile, the big businesses managed to protect their interests and wealth.

Reading Check **Identifying** Who developed the telephone?

The Growing Cities

As people moved to the cities to take factory jobs, they transformed America from a rural country into an urban nation. The cities also grew because of the arrival of new immigrants.

The New Immigrants

After the Civil War, many immigrants arrived from southern and eastern Europe. Others came from China, Japan, and Mexico. When they arrived they were processed at government reception centers. The two most famous were **Ellis Island** in New York Harbor, and **Angel Island** in San Francisco Bay.

Most immigrants settled in cities and looked for factory work. People of the same **ethnic group**—with the same language and customs—tended to form communities. Neighborhoods of Jewish, Italian, Polish, Chinese, and other groups developed in large cities.

HISTORY Online
Student Web Activity
Visit tarvol1.glencoe.com and click on **Chapter 18—Student Web Activities** for an activity on immigrant life.

Immigrant children learned American ways in the classroom.

Immigrants Face Discrimination

Not all Americans welcomed newcomers to their country. The immigrants' languages and customs seemed strange to some Americans and aroused distrust and discrimination.

Many Americans wondered if immigrants could ever be assimilated into American life. Some people, especially workers, blamed immigrants for low wages. Employers found that immigrants would accept lower wages than native Americans. Others resented the different cultures and religions of the many immigrants.

In the late 1800s hostility grew toward many of the new racial and ethnic groups coming into the country. Immigrants became easy targets of hostility for Americans disturbed by the rapid social changes.

Life in the Cities

Cities were exciting places that offered jobs, stores, and entertainment. However, there was also substandard housing and desperate poverty. The gap between the rich and the poor was staggering.

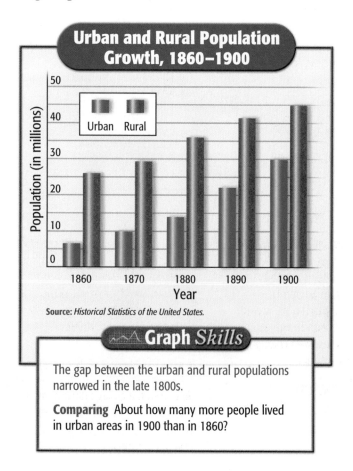

Urban and Rural Population Growth, 1860–1900

Source: *Historical Statistics of the United States.*

Graph *Skills*

The gap between the urban and rural populations narrowed in the late 1800s.

Comparing About how many more people lived in urban areas in 1900 than in 1860?

Tenement Life

People poured into the cities faster than housing could be built. The poor often lived in **tenements**—huge apartment buildings—with as many as four people living in each of the small, dark rooms. The rapid growth of cities produced other serious problems as well, including disease, crime, and poor sanitation.

The Middle Class and the Upper Class

The cities also had a growing middle class. The middle class included the families of professional people such as doctors, lawyers, and ministers. An increasing number of managers and salaried office clerks also became part of the middle class.

The middle class enjoyed a comfortable life. Many families began moving from cities to the suburbs, residential areas that sprang up outside of city centers.

At the top of the economic and social ladder stood the very rich. Wealthy people lived very differently than did most Americans. They built enormous mansions in the cities and huge estates in the country. The term **"Gilded Age"**—'gilded' refers to something covered with a thin layer of gold—became associated with America of the late 1800s. The Gilded Age suggested both the extravagant wealth of the time and the terrible poverty that lay underneath.

Cities in Crisis

The rapid growth of the cities produced serious problems. Terrible overcrowding in tenement districts created sanitation and health problems. Garbage accumulated in city streets. Filth created a breeding ground for disease.

The poverty in the cities also led to crime. Orphans and homeless children sometimes resorted to picking pockets and other crimes. Gangs roaming the poor neighborhoods committed more serious crimes.

Seeking Solutions

Religious groups, such as the Salvation Army, set up soup kitchens to feed the hungry and opened shelters for the homeless. The poor also received help from settlement houses.

These houses provided education, medical care, playgrounds, nurseries, and libraries to the poor. One famous settlement house was **Hull House** in Chicago, founded by **Jane Addams** in 1889. Addams explained:

Jane Addams

❝We were ready to perform the humblest neighborhood serv-ices. We were asked to wash the new-born babies, and to prepare the dead for burial, to nurse the sick, and to 'mind the children.'❞

A Danish immigrant named Jacob Riis shocked many Americans with his photographs of the horrible living conditions in New York. He chal-lenged his readers to renew the face of the cities.

During the 1880s and 1890s, many reformers accepted Riis's challenge. They campaigned for clean water and better sewage systems. They demanded better ventilation, plumbing in all new buildings, and mandatory vaccinations. These improvements meant that fewer people died of diseases like typhoid and smallpox.

Education

Most Americans in 1865 had attended school for an average of only four years. Government and business leaders and reformers believed that for the nation to progress, the people needed more schooling. Toward the end of the 1800s, education became more widely available to Americans.

By 1914 nearly every state required children to have at least some schooling. More than 80 percent of all children between the ages of 5 and 17 were enrolled in elementary and secondary schools.

A Changing American Culture

Many Americans began to enjoy increasing amounts of leisure time. The large crowds in the cities increased the popularity of spectator sports—including baseball, football, basketball, and boxing. People also flocked to nickelodeon theaters, which charged 5 cents to see a movie.

New types of music and literature developed at the turn of the century. Band music, jazz, and ragtime became popular. Writers such as Mark Twain, Stephen Crane, and Jack London pro-duced stories that described the real lives of peo-ple at the time. More and more people began to read newspapers and magazines.

✔**Reading Check** **Describing** What did settlement houses provide?

SECTION 2 ASSESSMENT

Checking for Understanding

1. **Key Terms** Write a paragraph about American corporations. Use the fol-lowing terms: horizontal integra-tion, vertical integration, trust.
2. **Reviewing Facts** Where is Ellis Island? What purpose did it serve?

Reviewing Themes

3. **Science and Technology** Which of the inventions in Section 2 do you think is the most valuable to today's world? Explain.

Critical Thinking

4. **Making Comparisons** Explain how the Knights of Labor and the Ameri-can Federation of Labor were alike and how they were different.
5. **Organizing Information** Re-create the diagram below and write three ways in which cities were changing at the turn of the century.

Analyzing Visuals

6. **Graph Skills** According to the graph on page 538, about how many more people lived in rural than in urban areas in 1860? What conclusion can you draw about total population between 1860 and 1900?

Interdisciplinary Activity

Art Create a collage illustrating the origins of immigrants who came to the United States in the late 1800s and early 1900s.

Reform at Home, Expansion Abroad

Guide to Reading

Main Idea
Progressive reform affected many areas of life and the United States took a more active role in international affairs.

Key Terms
muckraker, suffragist, imperialism, yellow journalism

Reading Strategy
Organizing Information As you read the section, re-create the diagram below and describe these amendments and laws.

	Contributions
Seventeenth Amendment	
Nineteenth Amendment	
Sherman Antitrust Act	

Read to Learn
- how the Progressive movement changed America.
- why the United States sought to expand overseas.

Section Theme
Groups and Institutions Progressive reformers worked to extend voting rights, improve working conditions, and promote temperance.

Preview of Events

♦1890   ♦1900   ♦1910   ♦1920

1890
Sherman Antitrust
Act passed

1909
W.E.B. Du Bois helps
found the NAACP

1920
Nineteenth Amendment gives
women the right to vote

✯✯✯✯✯✯✯ AN
American Story

Jacob Riis

Newspaper reporter Jacob Riis shocked Americans in 1890 with his book *How the Other Half Lives.* With words and powerful photographs, Riis vividly portrayed immigrant life in New York City's crowded tenements. Said Riis: "We used to go in the small hours of the morning into the worst tenements to count noses and see if the law against overcrowding was violated and the sights I saw gripped my heart until I felt that I must tell of them, or burst."

The reform spirit gained strength during the late 1800s and flourished during the early 1900s. Some reformers believed that rapid social and economic change had resulted in a disordered and corrupt society. These reformers, called **progressives,** believed that the efforts of individuals and government could make society better and more fair. As progressive leaders reached positions of power in government, they passed laws affecting government employees, business practices and public health. These progressive laws form the basis for modern ideas of the role of government.

The Progressive Movement

Progressives believed that urban problems were caused by corruption. **Political machines**—powerful organizations linked to political parties—controlled many cities. Political bosses gained votes for their parties by doing favors for people. Although some did help people, many bosses were dishonest. To break the power of political bosses, reformers founded groups that worked to make city governments more honest and efficient.

Cities troubled by poor management or corruption tried new forms of government. After the tidal wave of a hurricane devastated Galveston, Texas, in 1900, the task of rebuilding the city overwhelmed the mayor and city council. Galveston's citizens persuaded the state legislature to approve a new charter that placed the city government in the hands of five commissioners. The new commission efficiently rebuilt the city. By 1917 commissions governed nearly 400 cities.

Controlling Business

Progressives also believed that government had to keep large combinations of companies from becoming too powerful. In 1890, Congress passed the **Sherman Antitrust Act,** making it illegal for companies to limit competition. During the 1890s, the government rarely used the Sherman Act to curb business. Instead, it applied the act against labor unions, claiming that union strikes interfered with trade. Not until the early 1900s did the government win cases against trusts with the Sherman Act.

Reformers also called for regulations on railroad rates. In 1887 Congress passed the Interstate Commerce Act, which required railroads to charge "reasonable and just" rates. The act also created the **Interstate Commerce Commission** (ICC) to supervise the railroad industry and, later, the trucking industry.

The New Reformers

Some journalists, nicknamed muckrakers, helped progressives by exposing injustices. Magazine writer **Lincoln Steffens** was one of the most effective muckrakers. Steffens exposed corrupt political machines in New York, Chicago, and other cities. His articles strengthened the demand for urban reform.

Another writer, **Ida Tarbell,** described the unfair practices of the oil trust. Her articles led to public pressure for more government control over big business.

In his novel *The Jungle* (1906), **Upton Sinclair** described the horrors of the meatpacking industry. His shocking descriptions of unhealthful practices in meatpacking spurred Congress to pass the Meat Inspection Act and the Pure Food and Drug Act.

Reading Check **Identifying** What are trusts?

Expanding Democracy

In the early 1900s, progressives backed a number of reforms to expand the people's direct control of the government. Oregon took the lead in giving voters more power. The reforms included a direct primary election, and the initiative, the referendum, and the recall.

The **initiative** allowed citizens to place a measure or issue on the ballot in a state election. The **referendum** gave voters the opportunity to accept or reject measures that the state legislature enacted. The **recall** enabled voters to remove

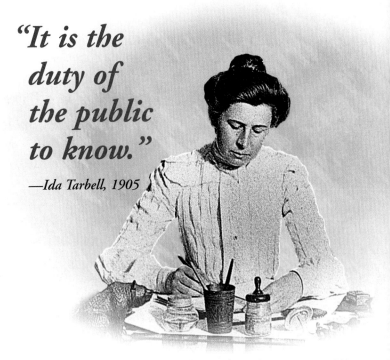

"It is the duty of the public to know."

—*Ida Tarbell, 1905*

unsatisfactory elected officials from their jobs. These reforms were called the Oregon system. Other western states soon adopted the reforms.

Progressives also changed the way United States senators are elected. The Constitution had given state legislatures the responsibility, but party bosses and business interests often controlled the process. The **Seventeenth Amendment** provided for the direct election of senators. Ratified in 1913, the amendment gave the people a voice in selecting their representatives.

🗣 Citizenship

The Fight for Suffrage

Women at the Seneca Falls Convention in 1848 had called for the right to vote. After the Civil War, Congress passed the Fifteenth Amendment, giving voting rights to freed men—but not to women. Some leading abolitionists became suffragists—men and women who fought for woman suffrage, or women's right to vote.

Suffragists won their first victories in the West. Wyoming led the nation in giving women the vote. Between 1910 and 1913, five other states adopted woman suffrage. In the meantime suffragists continued their struggle to win the vote everywhere.

In 1919 the Senate voted in favor of the **Nineteenth Amendment,** which allowed woman suffrage. The amendment was ratified in 1920, in time for women to vote in that year's presidential election. For the first time, American women were able to participate in the election of their national leaders.

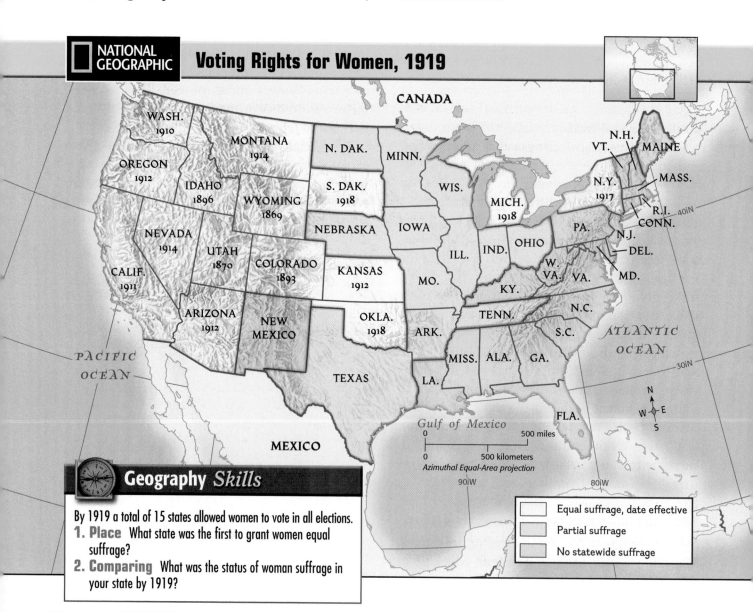

NATIONAL GEOGRAPHIC

Voting Rights for Women, 1919

WASH. 1910
MONTANA 1914
N. DAK.
MINN.
CANADA
N.H.
VT.
MAINE
OREGON 1912
IDAHO 1896
WYOMING 1869
S. DAK. 1918
WIS.
N.Y. 1917
MASS.
R.I.
40ÎN
CONN.
NEVADA 1914
UTAH 1870
NEBRASKA
IOWA
MICH. 1918
PA.
N.J.
DEL.
CALIF. 1911
COLORADO 1893
KANSAS 1912
ILL.
IND.
OHIO
W. VA.
VA.
MD.
MO.
KY.
ARIZONA 1912
NEW MEXICO
OKLA. 1918
TENN.
N.C.
ARK.
S.C.
ATLANTIC OCEAN
PACIFIC OCEAN
MISS.
ALA.
GA.
30ÎN
TEXAS
LA.
N
W E
S
FLA.
Gulf of Mexico
0   500 miles
0   500 kilometers
Azimuthal Equal-Area projection
MEXICO
90ÎW
80ÎW

Geography *Skills*

By 1919 a total of 15 states allowed women to vote in all elections.

1. Place What state was the first to grant women equal suffrage?

2. Comparing What was the status of woman suffrage in your state by 1919?

Legend:
☐ Equal suffrage, date effective
☐ Partial suffrage
☐ No statewide suffrage

A Progressive in the White House

The wave of progressive reform that began to sweep across the United States eventually reached the level of presidential politics. The first progressive president was Republican **Theodore Roosevelt**, who took office after President McKinley was assassinated. Beginning in 1902, Roosevelt began to take action against companies that had violated the Sherman Antitrust Act. His administration sued trusts in the railroad, beef, tobacco, and oil industries. Roosevelt also believed strongly in the need for **conservation**—the protection and preservation of natural resources.

Reform Continues

Roosevelt's successor, **William Howard Taft,** continued many of Roosevelt's policies. **Woodrow Wilson,** who became president after Taft, introduced his own progressive reforms. He convinced Congress to create the **Federal Reserve**—a system of 12 regional banks supported by a central board based in Washington. Wilson also established the **Federal Trade Commission** to investigate corporations for unfair trade practices.

Prejudice and Discrimination

Despite progressive reforms, many Americans still faced **discrimination**—unequal treatment because of their race, religion, ethnic background, or place of birth.

Some Americans faced discrimination because of their religion. Many Americans feared that Catholic immigrants threatened the American way of life.

Many Jewish immigrants came to America to escape prejudice in their homelands. Some found the same anti-Semitic attitudes in the United States. Landlords, employers, and schools discriminated against Jews.

Discrimination was also based on race. In California and other western states, Asians struggled against prejudice and resentment. White Americans claimed that Chinese immigrants, who worked for lower wages, were taking away jobs. Legislation limited the rights of immigrants from Japan as well as China.

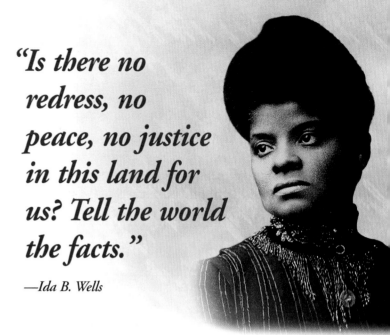

"Is there no redress, no peace, no justice in this land for us? Tell the world the facts."

—*Ida B. Wells*

African Americans Seek Justice

African Americans faced discrimination in both the North and the South. Although officially free, African Americans were denied basic rights and restricted to second-class citizenship. In 1896, the Supreme Court, in *Plessy* v. *Ferguson,* legalized segregation, which recognized the legality of "separate but equal" facilities.

African Americans rose to the challenge of achieving equality. **Booker T. Washington** founded the Tuskegee Institute to teach African Americans technical skills to help them escape poverty. **Ida B. Wells,** editor of an African American newspaper, began a crusade to end lynching.

W.E.B. Du Bois was one of the most important African American leaders of the time. Du Bois urged African Americans to fight for civil rights. Under no circumstances, he said, should they accept segregation. Du Bois helped found the **National Association for the Advancement of Colored People** (NAACP) in 1909. This interracial group has remained at the forefront of efforts to gain legal and economic equality for African Americans.

Mexican Americans Work Together

Immigrants from Mexico had long come to the United States as laborers, especially in the West and Southwest. Between 1900 and 1914,

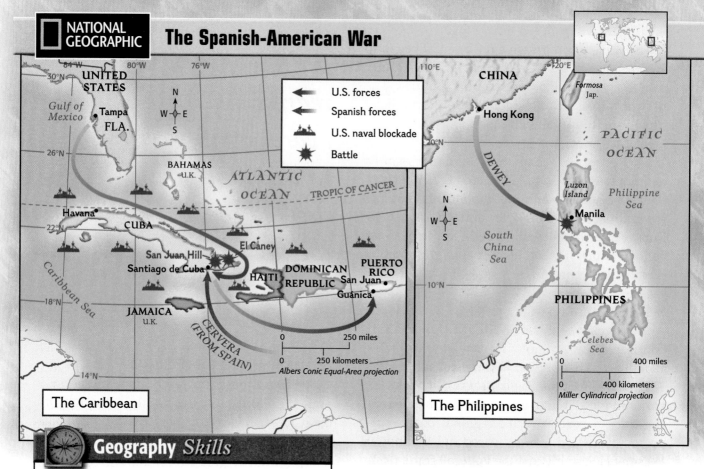

U.S. forces

Spanish forces

U.S. naval blockade

Battle

The Caribbean

The Philippines

Geography Skills

American troops sailed from Tampa, Florida, to the south coast of Cuba in June 1898. Admiral Dewey had already sailed from Hong Kong to Manila.

1. Movement According to the two maps, in which area did more of the fighting take place?

2. Analyzing Information On what two Caribbean islands did United States forces land?

the Mexican American population grew dramatically as people crossed the border to escape revolution and economic troubles in Mexico.

Like other immigrant groups, Mexican Americans encountered discrimination and violence. Relying on themselves to solve their problems, they formed self-defense associations to raise money for insurance and legal help. In labor camps and Mexican neighborhoods, they organized self-help groups to deal with overcrowding, poor sanitation, and inadequate public services.

✓ Reading Check **Describing** How did the Seventeenth Amendment extend the people's role in the democratic process?

Overseas Expansion

By 1890, the United States spanned the continent from the Atlantic to the Pacific. Americans now began to look west across the Pacific for new frontiers. They wanted to expand America's trade and power.

Expanding Horizons

Americans knew that they faced competition from other nations overseas. The late 1800s and early 1900s were an age of imperialism—a time when powerful European nations, as well as Japan, created large empires. The search for markets and raw materials in Asia and Africa drove imperialism.

Imperialism convinced many Americans that if the United States wanted to keep its economy growing, it too had to expand its power overseas. Some Americans also had a sense of mission. They wanted to share Christianity and Western civilization with the people of Asia.

Many American settlers in Hawaii set up sugarcane plantations and began selling sugar to the United States. In the early 1890s, they decided that Hawaii should join the United States so that they would not have to pay tariffs on their exports. In 1893, the sugar planters overthrew the Hawaiian queen, and five years later the United States annexed Hawaii.

The Spanish-American War

The people of Cuba had lived under Spanish rule for centuries. In 1895, Cubans, led by **José Martí,** began a war of independence against Spain. Many Americans sympathized with the Cubans. American support was intensified by yellow journalism—sensational, biased, and often false reporting by many of the nation's leading newspapers.

In early 1898, President McKinley sent the battleship *Maine* to protect Americans living in Cuba. On February 15, 1898, the *Maine* exploded, killing 266 people. American papers blamed the Spanish. On April 25, 1898, Congress declared war on Spain.

The opening of the Spanish-American War found the United States unprepared to fight. In 1898 the U.S. Army had only 28,000 soldiers. To correct the situation, Congress approved the addition of over 30,000 soldiers to the regular, or permanent, army and authorized a large volunteer force. Among the volunteers was a cavalry unit called the "Rough Riders," led by Colonel Leonard Wood and his second in command, Lieutenant Theodore Roosevelt.

The first battle of the Spanish-American War happened thousands of miles away in the Spanish colony of the **Philippines.** In May 1898 shortly after war was declared, Commodore George Dewey sailed his fleet into Manila. With his command, "You may fire when ready, Mr. Gridley," the onslaught began. When the firing was over, the Spanish fleet was destroyed. Not a single American vessel was lost.

At the time Dewey did not have the support needed for a land attack. He decided to block Manila until help arrived. In July support troops arrived in the Philippines. American forces, backed by Filipino rebels under General Emilio Aguinaldo, captured Manila in August.

Meanwhile, the rest of the Spanish fleet was blockaded in Santiago Harbor in the Caribbean. By the end of June, Americans forces, including the Rough Riders, had landed in Cuba and were pushing toward the city of Santiago. After fierce fighting, American troops won at El Caney and San Juan Hill. The Spanish surrendered.

✓**Reading Check** **Describing** What happened to the *Maine?*

SECTION 3 ASSESSMENT

Checking for Understanding

1. **Key Terms** Define: muckraker, suffragist, imperialism, yellow journalism.
2. **Reviewing Facts** Name five groups who were the targets of discrimination in the late 1800s and early 1900s.

Reviewing Themes

3. **Groups and Institutions** Who were suffragists? What right does the Nineteenth Amendment provide?

Critical Thinking

4. **Identifying Assumptions** Some who favored American expansion believed it was the nation's mission to "civilize" the "uncivilized" people of the world. What do you think they meant by *uncivilized* ?
5. **Organizing Information** Re-create the diagram below and list two reasons for American expansion overseas.

Reasons for expansion

Analyzing Visuals

6. **Geography Skills** Examine the map on page 542. Why do you think the percentage of states allowing woman suffrage was so much higher in the West than in the East?

Interdisciplinary Activity

Expository Writing Find a newspaper article that deals with the role of women today. Rewrite the article to reflect how this information might have been presented in the late 1800s and early 1900s.

World War I and Its Aftermath

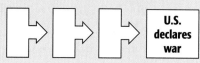

Guide to Reading

Main Idea
The United States entered World War I and helped the Allies win.

Key Terms
nationalism, propaganda, reparations, Prohibition

Reading Strategy
Organizing Information As you read the section, re-create the diagram below and list events that prompted the United States to enter the war.

U.S. declares war

Read to Learn
• what role the United States played in World War I.
• how the nation changed during the 1920s.

Section Theme
Global Connections The entry of the United States into the war eventually led to Germany's surrender.

Preview of Events

♦1910   ♦1915   ♦1920

1914
World War I begins

1917
United States enters war

1920
Prohibition begins

Jeannette Rankin

AN American Story

The swift chain of events that led to war in Europe in 1914 stunned Americans. Most agreed with Jeannette Rankin—the first woman to serve in the U.S. Congress, at a time when women could not even vote in most states—that "You can no more win a war than you can win an earthquake." Most Americans wanted the country to stay out of other countries' affairs. They saw no good reason to get involved in a conflict that they believed grew out of national pride and greed. As time went on, however, the United States found it more and more difficult to remain neutral.

The people of the time called the conflict the World War, or the Great War, because they believed that never again would there be another like it. The conflict, which began in Europe, soon spread. Although the United States tried to remain neutral, it was drawn into the conflict. Over the next few years, nearly 30 nations were at war. The main campaigns were fought in Europe, but armies also fought in the Middle East, Africa, and China, and navies clashed worldwide.

World War

The tensions that led to World War I went back many years. The conflicts grew as European nations pursued dreams of empire, built up their armies, and formed alliances.

War Erupts in Europe

Nationalism—a feeling of intense loyalty to one's country or group—caused much of the tension in Europe. Because of nationalism, Britain and Germany raced to build the largest navy. To protect themselves, European nations began to form **alliances**—defense agreements among nations.

In June 1914, a Serbian terrorist named Gavrilo Princip assassinated Archduke Franz Ferdinand, heir to the throne of the Austro-Hungarian Empire. Austria-Hungary blamed Serbia's government for the attack, and declared war on Serbia.

At this point, the alliance system brought about a world war. Russia decided to help Serbia, which caused Austria-Hungary's ally Germany to declare war on Russia as well as on Russia's ally France. Germany then invaded Belgium, so Britain, which had promised to protect Belgium, declared war on Germany.

The "Great War" had begun. On the one side were the **Allied Powers**—Great Britain, France, and Russia. On the other side were the **Central Powers**—Germany, Austria-Hungary, and the Ottoman (Turkish) Empire. Japan and Italy joined the Allies as well.

The British and French stopped the German attack on France at the **Battle of the Marne.** For the next three years, the two sides faced each other across an elaborate network of trenches. The war had reached a stalemate.

America Enters the War

When World War I began, President Wilson declared the United States to be neutral. To gain the support of Americans, both the Allies and the Central Powers used propaganda—information designed to influence opinion. As the war went on, Americans began to side with the Allies. At the same time, American trade with the Allies soared.

To stop the American assistance to the Allies, Germany began using submarines, known as U-boats, to sink cargo ships headed to Britain. In May 1915, a U-boat sank the passenger ship *Lusitania,* killing more than 1,000 people, including 128 Americans. After Wilson denounced the attack, Germany promised to warn neutral ships before attacking.

Picturing **History**

The *Lusitania* left New York for England on May 1, 1915. Germany had placed a warning notice in American newspapers, but few people took it seriously. **How did the United States respond to German U-boat attacks?**

In 1917, Germany broke its promise and ordered its U-boats to attack without warning. In mid-March, U-boats sank three American ships. President Wilson asked Congress to declare war on Germany on April 2, 1917.

Americans Join the Allies

Shortly after declaring war, Congress passed the **Selective Service Act,** establishing a military draft. By the end of the war, about 3 million American men had been drafted, and another 2 million had volunteered. More than 300,000 African Americans joined the military.

As America prepared to enter the war, Russia withdrew. In November 1917, the **Bolsheviks**— a group of Communists led by Vladimir Lenin— overthrew Russia's government. In March 1918, they signed a treaty ending the war with Germany. Shortly afterward, the Germans launched a massive offensive in France. Their goal was to smash the British and the French armies before the Americans could fully mass their strength. As a result, shortly after the Americans were assigned their first divisional area north of Paris at Cantigny, the German army was about 40 miles from Paris.

American Troops in Battle

At Cantigny about 4,000 soldiers of the First Division made the first American offensive action of the war. After a bitter battle, these troops won the first victory ever by Americans fighting in Europe.

In June 1918, American divisions were ordered to the Marne River. The objective was to recapture **Belleau Wood.** For 24 hours a day for the next two weeks, U.S. marines fought their way through the forest. The Americans finally took the forest—but at a cost of thousands of casualties.

The Germans launched a massive offensive at **Château-Thierry** along the Marne in July. Together the Americans and the French fought back the Germans, breaking their offensive strength, and for the first time, the Allies held the upper hand.

In late September, the United States First Army under the command of General **John J. Pershing,** attacked German military forces along the Meuse River and Argonne Forest in northeastern France. Victory at the battle of **Meuse-Argonne,** after 47 days of heavy fighting, caused the German lines to crumble.

Much of World War I was fought from trenches where soldiers spent weeks at a time.

With their troops in retreat, German military leaders realized they had little chance of winning the war. On October 4, 1918, the German government appealed for an **armistice.** An armistice is an agreement to end the fighting. On November 11, 1918, an armistice based on Allied demands was signed by both sides. The fighting was over, and plans began to build a lasting peace.

Searching for Peace

In January 1919, President Wilson and other world leaders met in Paris to negotiate a treaty ending the war. The **Treaty of Versailles,** as it was known, set up the **League of Nations**—an international organization to preserve the peace. It required Germany to make reparations—or payments—for the damage it had caused. The treaty also created new nations including Czechoslovakia, Yugoslavia, and Poland.

When Wilson presented the Treaty of Versailles to the Senate for ratification, Republicans argued that the League of Nations would limit America's independence. The Senate rejected the treaty. The United States never did join the League of Nations.

✓ Reading Check **Describing** What happened in April 1917?

The 1920s

Tired of war and world responsibilities, Americans were ready to seek enjoyment. It was a time of new pastimes and new heroes. Crossword puzzles and the Chinese game of Mah Jongg became national obsessions. Athletes like base-

NATIONAL GEOGRAPHIC **Europe After World War I**

New Nations

0   300 miles
0   300 kilometers
Azimuthal Equidistant projection

Geography *Skills*

1. **Region** What new nations bordered Germany?
2. **Analyzing Information** Which new nations did not have any coastline along a sea or an ocean?

ball's **Babe Ruth** and golf's **Bobby Jones** became larger-than-life heroes. Americans gloried in the feat of **Charles Lindbergh,** who completed the first nonstop solo flight across the Atlantic.

A Time of Turmoil

Labor and management had put aside their differences during the war years. A sense of patriotism, high wages, and wartime laws helped keep conflict to a minimum. Once the war was over, conflict flared anew. The war-stimulated economy cooled down, and veterans found they had to compete for a declining number of jobs. Workers in general wanted to preserve and, if possible, hike the wages paid during the war. When management refused to cooperate many workers resorted to their chief bargaining tool—the strike. Although strikes had been in use in America since the 1870s, those which took place after World War I were numerous and violent. In 1919 alone there were more than 3,600 strikes involving millions of workers.

The Red Scare

Many Americans believed there was a strong tie between union activism and radicalism. The belief helped fuel a movement to fight radicalism in the United States. Known as the **Red Scare,** the movement began with a general concern with communism. **Communism** is a theory that advocates the elimination of private property. It is also a totalitarian system of government in which a single party controls the citizens.

The fears many Americans felt also led to an increase in **nativism**—or anti-immigrant feelings. World War I had dramatically slowed the huge flow of immigration that had begun in the 1880s. After the war ended, heavy immigration resumed. Many Americans saw the newcomers as a threat to their jobs and their security.

Prohibition

In 1920, Prohibition began. This was a total ban on the manufacture, sale, and transportation of alcohol. People began making and selling alcohol illegally, however. Prohibition also contributed to the rise of organized crime. Prohibition was finally repealed in 1933 with the passage of the **Twenty-first Amendment.**

A Booming Economy

With the end of World War I and the start of the 1920s came another industrial revolution. As energy poured into industry, goods poured out. Among the products that gained popularity in the 1920s were telephones, vacuum cleaners, refrigerators, and canned goods. While these items and others like them made it possible for Americans to spend less time on household chores and more time on recreation another product had an even greater impact. The product was the automobile.

The automobile industry revolutionized American society. The industry used so much steel, glass, wood, gas, and rubber that it provided jobs for millions of workers. It transformed American buying habits, making installment buying a way of life. It promoted highway construction and travel.

Reading Check **Identifying** What is Prohibition? When did it go into effect?

SECTION 4 ASSESSMENT

Checking for Understanding

1. **Key Terms** Write headlines for events during World War I using each of the following terms: nationalism, propaganda, reparations.
2. **Reviewing Facts** What did the Selective Service Act do?

Reviewing Themes

3. **Global Connections** What was the Treaty of Versailles? Why did the U.S. Senate reject it?

Critical Thinking

4. **Analyzing Information** Why did the United States experience an economic boom in the early 1920s?
5. **Organizing Information** Re-create the diagram below and describe how nationalism led to war.

Nationalism

Analyzing Visuals

6. **Geography Skills** Examine the map showing European borders following World War I on page 549. Which of the following was not a new nation—Poland, Latvia, or Bulgaria?

Interdisciplinary Activity

Descriptive Writing Make a list of three to five adjectives that you think describe the mood of the nation during World War I. Draw or paint these adjectives on poster board in a way that expresses the words' meanings.

Technology SKILLBUILDER

Building a Database

Why Learn This Skill?

Have you ever collected baseball cards or catalogued the CDs in your collection? Have you ever kept a list of the names and addresses of your friends and relatives? If you have collected information and kept some sort of list or file, then you have created a database.

Learning the Skill

An electronic database is a collection of facts that are stored in files on the computer. The information is organized in fields.

A database can be organized and reorganized in any way that is useful to you. By using a database management system (DBMS)—special software developed for record keeping—you can easily add, delete, change, or update information. You give commands to the computer telling it what to do with the information and it follows your commands. When you want to retrieve information, the computer searches through the files, finds the information, and displays it on the screen.

Practicing the Skill

Theodore Roosevelt is one of the presidents discussed in this chapter. Follow these steps to build a database of the political and cultural events that took place during his presidency.

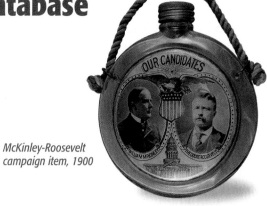

McKinley-Roosevelt campaign item, 1900

① Find information about the events during this period from encyclopedias, histories, and the Internet. Determine what facts you want to include in your database.

② Follow instructions in the DBMS you are using to set up fields. Then enter each item of data into its assigned field.

③ Determine how you want to organize the facts in the database—chronologically by the date of the event, or alphabetically by the name of the event.

④ Follow the instructions in your computer program to place the information in order of importance.

⑤ Check that the information in your database is all correct. If necessary, add, delete, or change information or fields.

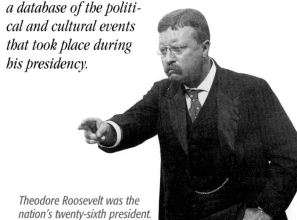

Theodore Roosevelt was the nation's twenty-sixth president.

Applying the Skill

Building a Database Bring current newspapers to class. Using the steps just described, build a database of political figures mentioned in the newspapers. For example, you may wish to build a database of national leaders or government officials in your community. Explain to a partner why the database is organized the way it is and how it might be used in this class.

Chapter Summary

Reshaping the Nation

1869
- First transcontinental railroad completed

1870
- Rockefeller organizes Standard Oil Company

1876
- Sioux defeat Custer's forces at Little Bighorn

1886
- Trade unions form AFL

1886
- Statue of Liberty is dedicated

1890
- Massacre at Wounded Knee

1892
- Populist Party formed

1901
- Theodore Roosevelt becomes president after assassination of McKinley

1903
- Wright Brothers fly motorized airplane

1908
- Ford introduces the Model T

1909
- NAACP is formed

1914
- World War I begins

1917
- U.S. enters World War I

1919
- Eighteenth Amendment prohibits alcohol

1920
- Nineteenth Amendment grants woman suffrage

1927
- Lindbergh flies across the Atlantic

Reviewing Key Terms

On a sheet of paper, define the following terms.

1. transcontinental
2. reservation
3. collective bargaining
4. suffragist
5. imperialism
6. nationalism
7. propaganda
8. Prohibition

Reviewing Key Facts

9. What are boomtowns?
10. When was the transcontinental rail line completed?
11. What did the Populist Party call for government to do?
12. Why does a corporation sell shares of its business?
13. What industry did Andrew Carnegie lead? How did his company become so powerful?
14. What are political machines?
15. Why did Booker T. Washington start the Tuskegee Institute?
16. Where was the Spanish-American War fought?
17. When did the United States enter World War I?
18. What amendment to the Constitution granted women the right to vote?

Critical Thinking

19. **Making Inferences** Another name for the Populist Party was the People's Party. Why do you think the Populists considered themselves to be a party of the people?

20. **Evaluating** Which of the inventions described in the chapter do you think brought about the most dramatic change in people's lives? Explain.

21. **Drawing Conclusions** Why do you think the right to vote was important to women?

22. **Analyzing Themes: Culture and Traditions** Re-create the diagram below and describe two ways you think immigrants try to preserve their cultural heritage.

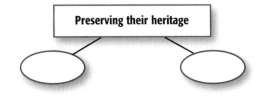

Preserving their heritage

 Geography and History Activity

Reading a Thematic Map *Study the thematic map below; then answer the questions that follow.*

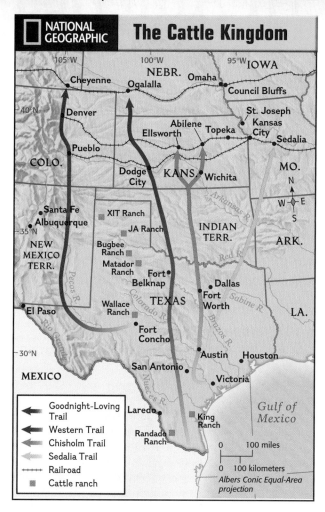

The Cattle Kingdom

23. What geographic region is shown?

24. In what part of Texas were most of the large cattle ranches located?

25. What did the towns where the trails ended have in common? Why was this important?

Practicing Skills

Making Inferences

26. Many Americans wanted the United States to remain neutral during World War I. Why do you think many Americans feared war?

27. How might economic interests get in the way of the nation remaining neutral?

Citizenship Cooperative Activity

28. **Community Service** Working in groups of three, interview one of your community's officials to learn how you can begin taking an active role in the community. Members of your group may wish to volunteer for some sort of community service, then perform the service and report your experiences to your classmates.

Economics Activity

29. **History and Economics** Today many Native Americans still live on reservations. Some reservations have developed their own businesses and industries to help make them more self-sufficient. With a partner, research to find information about a reservation in the United States today. Write a report describing one of the major businesses on that reservation.

 Alternative Assessment Activity

30. **Portfolio Writing Activity** Research the life of one of the men or women from the chapter. Prepare a one-page biography of that person and share it with the class.

Standardized Test Practice

Directions: Choose the *best* answer to the following question.

People in the late 1800s took advantage of the open grasslands of the West to develop which of these industries?

A Banking

B Manufacturing

C Ranching

D Mining

Test-Taking Tip

The important words in this question are *open grasslands.* Banking and manufacturing do not need open grasslands, so you can easily eliminate answers **A** and **B**.

CHAPTER 19

The Making of Modern America

1929–Present

Why It Matters

During the twentieth century, Americans suffered through wars and economic and political unrest. The end of the Cold War brought about communism's fall in many parts of the world and the triumph of democracy. A new world was at hand—or so it seemed. Long-hidden national and ethnic rivalries flared into violence in various parts of the world. The threats to peace included acts of terrorism.

Its Impact Today

In the twenty-first century, the world faces great challenges. Acts of terrorism present a threat to freedom and security. Although most nations condemn such acts, terrorism is likely to remain a global concern.

The American Republic to 1877 Video *The chapter 19 video, "America Responds to Terrorism," focuses on how Americans united after the events of September 11, 2001.*

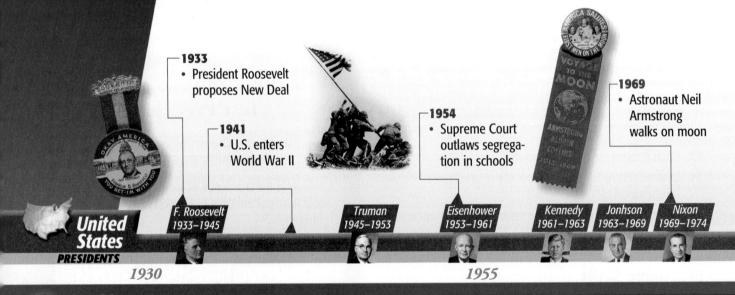

1933
• President Roosevelt proposes New Deal

1941
• U.S. enters World War II

1954
• Supreme Court outlaws segregation in schools

1969
• Astronaut Neil Armstrong walks on moon

United States PRESIDENTS

F. Roosevelt 1933–1945 | Truman 1945–1953 | Eisenhower 1953–1961 | Kennedy 1961–1963 | Jonhson 1963–1969 | Nixon 1969–1974

1930   *1955*

World

1933
• Hitler comes to power in Germany

1939
• World War II begins

1945
• World War II ends

1953
• Korean War ends

1961
• Berlin Wall erected

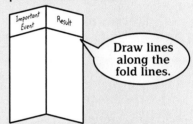

Inauguration 2001 George W. Bush takes the oath of office as the nation's forty-third president.

FOLDABLES™
Study Organizer

Cause-Effect Information Study Foldable
Make this foldable to help you organize events and facts about the history of modern America from 1929 to the present.

Step 1 Fold one sheet of paper in half from side to side.

> Fold the sheet vertically.

Step 2 Fold it again, 1 inch from the top. (**Tip:** The middle knuckle of your index finger is about 1 inch long.)

Step 3 Open and label as shown.

> Important Event   Result

> Draw lines along the fold lines.

Reading and Writing As you read this chapter, write down important events in the first column of your foldable. Then, in the second column, list some major results of each event listed in the first column.

1974
• President Nixon resigns

1991
• Persian Gulf War begins

1998
• President Clinton impeached

2000
• George W. Bush elected president

2001
• Terrorists kill thousands in attack on America

2003
• Space shuttle *Columbia* is lost

Ford 1974–1977	Carter 1977–1981	Reagan 1981–1989	G. Bush 1989–1993	Clinton 1993–2001	G. W. Bush 2001–

1980   *2005*

1981
• Scientists identify AIDS

1989
• Communism begins to fall in Eastern Europe

1991
• Breakup of Soviet Union

2000
• Millions celebrate new millenium

HISTORY Online

Chapter Overview
Visit tarvol1.glencoe.com and click on **Chapter 19— Chapter Overviews** to preview chapter information.

CHAPTER 19   The Making of Modern America   **555**

Depression and a Second World War

Guide to Reading

Main Idea
The United States maintained its free enterprise system during the Great Depression and won victory in a global conflict at great cost.

Key Terms
dictator, genocide, Holocaust, island hopping

Reading Strategy
Organizing Information Re-create the diagram below to identify three causes of World War II.

Causes

World War II

Read to Learn
- how President Roosevelt responded to the Great Depression.
- what actions led to the outbreak of World War II.

Section Theme
Global Connections The United States joined with allied nations to fight a world war to protect rights and freedoms.

Preview of Events

1925	1935	1945

1929
Stock market crashes, triggering Great Depression

1939
World War II begins in Europe

1941
Japanese attack Pearl Harbor; U.S. enters the war

1945
World War II ends

Unemployed man seeking work

AN American Story

During the early years of the Great Depression, the number of homeless people in the United States skyrocketed. One woman described her amazement when she first saw how people had to live outside one Midwestern city: "Here were all these people living in old, rusted-out car bodies. There were people living in shacks made of orange crates. . . . This wasn't just a little section, this was maybe ten miles wide and ten miles long. People living in what ever they could junk together."

The Great Depression

The severe economic crisis of the 1930s was called the **Great Depression.** It marked the longest, deepest, and most devastating economic depression ever experienced by the United States.

The bubble of American prosperity burst when the New York stock market collapsed in October 1929. Thousands of investors lost all their savings. Wall Street—the nation's financial center—was in a state of shock. In the booming economy of the 1920s, many people invested money in the stock market. As the value of stocks rose, people began borrowing to buy stocks.

In October 1929, stock prices fell dramatically. Investors panicked and began selling their stocks. Many could not pay back their loans, which weakened the banks. Millions of people lost their savings and their jobs.

The Economy Crumbles

The stock market crash shook people's confidence in the economy. Other factors, working together, sent the economy into a long tailspin.

Farm income shrank. For many farmers, years of dry weather made the situation even worse. In parts of the Great Plains a long drought turned fertile land into a **Dust Bowl.** Many farmers had to give up their land. Many industries declined. In the months before the stock market crash, the automobile and construction industries suffered from lagging orders. As a result, employers cut wages and laid off workers. With their incomes slashed, many Americans could no longer afford the consumer goods that the nation's industries had been churning out.

Borrowed money had fueled much of the economy in the 1920s. Farmers, plagued by low prices since the end of World War I, bought land, equipment, and supplies on credit. Consumers used credit to buy cars. Investors borrowed to buy stocks. Many small banks suffered when consumers defaulted, or failed to meet loan payments. Large banks, which had bought stocks as an investment, suffered huge losses in the stock market crash. These losses forced thousands of banks across the nation to close between 1930 and 1933, and many depositors lost their money.

Weaknesses also sapped the strengths of foreign economies. During the late 1920s, bank funds for loans dried up. International trade slowed down because, without American loans, other nations had less money to spend.

Joblessness and Poverty

As the Depression tightened its grip on the United States, millions lost their jobs. In 1932, about one out of every four workers were out of work. The unemployed felt devastated. One out-of-work man wrote about developing:

> ❝a feeling of worthlessness—and loneliness; I began to think of myself as a freak and misfit.❞

Long lines of hungry people snaked through the streets of cities, waiting for hours to receive a slice of bread or a bowl of soup donated by local government or charities.

Those who had lost their homes built shelters out of old boxes and other debris. Some referred to these shantytowns as **Hoovervilles** after President Hoover. As the Depression dragged on, many Americans lost faith in their government. They blamed President Hoover for their hard times because none of his policies eased the suffering of massive unemployment.

Roosevelt's New Deal

During the 1932 presidential election, Franklin Delano Roosevelt promised a "new deal for the American people." With the nation's economy crumbling, the American people elected Democrat **Franklin Delano Roosevelt** as president. Roosevelt sent Congress proposals to fight the Depression that collectively became known as the **New Deal**.

Dorothea Lange photographed a homeless Oklahoma family during Dust Bowl days.

The New Deal created the **Civilian Conservation Corps** (CCC). The CCC put about 3 million young men to work on projects such as planting trees and building levees to prevent floods. It also established the **Public Works Administration** (PWA). The PWA provided jobs by building huge public works, such as roads, hospitals, and schools. The New Deal's **Agricultural Adjustment Administration** (AAA) raised farm prices and controlled farm production.

Roosevelt then asked Congress to pass the **Social Security Act.** This created a tax paid by all employers and workers that was used to pay pensions to retired people. Another tax funded **unemployment insurance**—payments to people who lost their jobs.

Americans seemed better off in 1936 than they had been when Roosevelt took office in 1933. Even so, when FDR began his second term, the Great Depression had not ended. He continued to push for more reform. In 1937 business slowed and another recession hit the nation. This time Americans blamed Roosevelt and the New Deal. When FDR proposed numerous programs after this, Congress would not cooperate with the President.

Although reform under Roosevelt ended, the New Deal produced lasting effects. It greatly increased the power of the presidency and the size of the federal government. It also established the idea that the federal government is responsible for the welfare of needy Americans. By the late 1930s, the economy had almost recovered. Just as the domestic problems seemed to be ending, however, World War II began.

☑ **Reading Check** **Explaining** What was the New Deal?

World War II

Less than 25 years after World War I, the United States found itself at war again. This war, though, was different from World War I. It was a

The plight of flood victims standing in a relief line contrasts sharply with the family shown on the billboard.

fight for survival, and, before it was over, it involved almost every country in the world. By the end of 1941, 22 countries had already declared their support for the **Allies**—the United States, Great Britain, France, China, and the Soviet Union. The **Axis** Powers—Germany, Italy, and Japan—were also supported by Romania, Bulgaria, and Hungary.

The Road to War

The events leading to World War II began in the 1920s. Several dictators—leaders who control their nations by force—seized power by playing on the fear and anger people felt after World War I and during the Great Depression.

The first dictator to take power was **Benito Mussolini** in Italy. In Germany, many people rallied around **Adolf Hitler**—leader of the National Socialist Worker's Party, or Nazi Party. The Depression also brought military leaders to power in Japan. In 1940, Germany, Italy, and Japan signed a pact and became allies.

In September 1939, Hitler sent his armies into Poland. Two days later, Britain and France declared war on Germany. World War II had begun. Germany's armed forces quickly overran Poland. The following spring, Hitler's troops invaded France, which surrendered a few weeks later. Then, in June 1941, Hitler ordered a massive attack on the Soviet Union.

Japan Attacks Pearl Harbor

Americans watched the war in Europe with concern, but did not want to become involved. Roosevelt promised to stay neutral. He asked Congress to pass the **Lend-Lease Act,** allowing America to sell, lease, or lend weapons to nations whose security was vital to America's defense. Britain and the Soviet Union began receiving lend-lease aid.

While Roosevelt tried to help Britain, Japanese troops seized France's colony of Indochina and threatened nearby British colonies. The United States tried to stop Japan by applying economic pressure. Desperate for resources and confident of Japan's military might, the Japanese government began planning an attack on the United States.

Picturing **History**

Franklin D. Roosevelt, who was paralyzed by polio as a young man, is shown with Ruth Bie, the daughter of the caretaker at FDR's estate. **Through what two of the nation's great crises did Roosevelt serve as president?**

On December 7, 1941, Japanese warplanes attacked the American naval base at **Pearl Harbor,** Hawaii. The attack enraged Americans. The next day, Roosevelt went before Congress. Calling December 7 "a day which will live in infamy," he asked for a declaration of war on Japan. On December 11, Germany and Italy declared war on the United States. The United States then joined the Allies—Great Britain, France, and the Soviet Union—against the Axis powers.

On the Home Front

By the time the United States entered the war, the fighting had already been going on for more than two years, and it was to continue for almost four more. The war years had a deep effect on Americans and on the nation as a whole. Out of the war came new technology, a new prosperity, and a new sense of power and strength.

500 miles
500 kilometers
Lambert Azimuthal
Equal-Area projection

← Allied Forces
Major Axis powers
Greatest extent of Axis control
Allied or Ally-controlled
Neutral nations

GREENLAND
Den.

ICELAND

ARCTIC CIRCLE

ATLANTIC
OCEAN

SWEDEN
FINLAND
NORWAY
ESTONIA
Moscow

North
Sea
DENMARK
LATVIA
IRELAND UNITED
KINGDOM
LITHUANIA

London NETH. GERMANY
Dunkirk BELG. Berlin
Paris Warsaw
POLAND

SOVIET UNION

Aral
Sea

D-Day
June 6, 1944

Vienna CZECH.
SWITZ. AUSTRIA
FRANCE HUNGARY
ITALY

FINAL SOVIET DRIVE
July-Aug., 1944

Stalingrad

Caspian Sea

PORTUGAL
Aug. 15, 1944
Rome
Naples ALBANIA

ROMANIA
Black Sea
YUGOSLAVIA
BULGARIA

Nov. 8, 1942 SPAIN
GREECE

TURKEY

IRAN

Sicily
TUNISIA July 10, 1943
Mediterranean Sea

SYRIA
Fr.
LEBANON
PALESTINE
U.K.
TRANS-
JORDAN
U.K.

IRAQ
KUWAIT

THE
TRUCIAL
STATES

MOROCCO

El Alamein Cairo

RIO DE ORO
Sp.

ALGERIA

LIBYA

EGYPT

1942 - The British
defeat the German
tank division at
El Alamein.

SAUDI
ARABIA

MUS
AND
OMA

FRENCH WEST
AFRICA
Fr.

Red Sea

ADEN
PROTECTORA
U.K.

FRENCH
EQUATORIAL
AFRICA
Fr.

ANGLO-EGYPTIAN
SUDAN
U.K. and Egypt

YEMEN

Geography *Skills*

1. **Place** Where did the Allied forces land on D-Day?
2. **Analyzing Information** When did Allied forces invade Sicily?

After Pearl Harbor, millions of Americans rushed to enlist in the armed forces. Those who remained at home had to provide food, shelter, training, and medical care for all those in uniform.

During the war, industry expanded rapidly. Incomes rose and unemployment fell. For the first time, a large number of women—about 350,000—served in the military. At the same time, far more women than ever before entered the work force.

The war also created new opportunities for African Americans—in the armed forces and in the nation's war factories. Although many minority groups made gains during the war, Japanese Americans experienced discrimination after the attack on Pearl Harbor. Worried about their loyalty, the government forced Japanese Americans on the West Coast to relocate to **internment camps.**

The War in Europe and the Mediterranean

Until late in 1942, the Axis held the upper hand in Eastern and Western Europe and in North Africa. In November, British and American

American forces now closed in on Japan itself. In March 1945 they seized the island of **Iwo Jima** and in June the island of **Okinawa,** the last stop before invading Japan itself. Before the invasion took place, however, the United States decided to use a new weapon—the atomic bomb.

At the urging of Albert Einstein, President Roosevelt had begun the **Manhattan Project,** a top-secret attempt to build an atomic bomb. After the bomb was ready, President Truman demanded that Japan surrender. When Japan refused, Truman ordered the use of the bomb.

The United States dropped two atomic bombs in August 1945. The first destroyed the city of Hiroshima. The second destroyed the city of Nagasaki. After the bombings, Japan agreed to surrender. August 15—**V-J Day,** for "Victory over Japan"—marked the end of World War II.

After the War

World War II was the costliest and most destructive war ever. At least 50 million soldiers and civilians died—more than during any other war. The war devastated billions of dollars worth of property. Life in some countries would not return to normal for many years.

Hitler had appealed to national pride and racial hatred in Germany, using force to silence all opposition. Hitler's Nazi party blamed Ger-

Raising the flag at Iwo Jima

many's economic problems on its Jewish population and killed nearly 6 million Jews and millions of other people in concentration camps.

People from all over the world looked for ways to prevent such a terrible conflict from happening again. Many believed that an international organization dedicated to freedom and cooperation could ensure peace. The American people looked forward to a future in which peace would be preserved. However, they would soon be disappointed.

✓ **Reading Check** **Identifying** What event occurred on December 7, 1941? What did this event lead to?

SECTION 1 ASSESSMENT

Checking for Understanding

1. **Key Terms** Write a short paragraph in which you use all of the following key terms: dictator, genocide, Holocaust.

2. **Reviewing Facts** Who was president of the United States when World War II began? Who was president when it ended?

Reviewing Themes

3. **Global Connections** What did the Lend-Lease Act, supported by Roosevelt, provide?

Critical Thinking

4. **Determining Cause and Effect** How did the role of government in American democracy change as a result of the Depression and the New Deal?

5. **Organizing Information** Create a diagram like the one shown here and identify three causes of the Great Depression.

Analyzing Visuals

6. **Geography Skills** Examine the maps on page 560 and page 562. What are the topics of the maps? Did Japanese control in 1942 include the Philippine Islands? The Hawaiian Islands? Was Finland under Axis control at one time or another? Was France? How can you tell?

Interdisciplinary Activity

Language Arts Write newspaper headlines about three important events covered in Section 1.

Turning Points

Guide to Reading

Main Idea

During the second half of the twentieth century, Americans struggled with communism abroad and civil rights at home.

Key Terms

stalemate, affluence, segregation, civil disobedience, feminist

Reading Strategy

Sequencing Information Create a time line like the one below and identify key events in the postwar world.

1948   1953   1954   1964   1973

Read to Learn

- how the United States attempted to stop the spread of communism.
- what actions African Americans took to secure their rights.

Section Theme

Civic Rights and Responsibilities American minorities and women intensified their efforts to secure their full rights as citizens.

Preview of Events

♦1945   ♦1955   ♦1965   ♦1975

1950
Korean War begins

1959
Fidel Castro takes over Cuba

1963
President Kennedy is assassinated

1973
U.S. ends role in Vietnam

Big Three at Yalta

AN American Story

The three most powerful men in the world met around a conference table in Yalta to discuss the fate of the postwar world. President Roosevelt hoped to promote his vision of postwar cooperation. Prime Minister Churchill spoke elegantly and forcefully. Soviet leader Stalin remained stubbornly opposed to much of what was proposed. Stalin said to his aides: "They want to force us to accept their plans on Europe and the world. Well, that's not going to happen." As the Allies discovered, Stalin had his own plans.

The Cold War Era

As World War II ended, a bitter rivalry developed between the United States and the Soviet Union. It was known as the **Cold War.** The problems leading to the Cold War began when Stalin refused to allow promised free elections in Eastern Europe. Instead, the Soviets set up communist governments. In response, the new American president, Harry S Truman, announced a new policy in 1947. The **Truman Doctrine** was a commitment to help nations resist communism.

In June 1948, the United States, Great Britain, and France united the zones of Germany they controlled to form a new nation, which became West Germany. To protest this decision, the Soviet Union sealed off Berlin, which was in the East

German sector. President Truman responded with an airlift to bring food, fuel, and other supplies to Berlin. In April 1949, the United States, Canada, and the countries of Western Europe created the **North Atlantic Treaty Organization** (NATO)—a mutual defense pact.

The Korean War

The Cold War was not limited to Europe. In 1949, **Mao Zedong** formed a new communist government in China. Shortly afterward, American troops found themselves fighting Mao's forces in Korea.

In June 1950, the communist nation of North Korea invaded South Korea. American and United Nations (UN) forces came to South Korea's

Korean Service Medal

defense. As they pushed the North Koreans back, China intervened. Huge numbers of Chinese troops drove the UN troops back into South Korea.

The UN forces eventually stopped the Chinese, then pushed them back to the border between North and South Korea. The war then became a stalemate—a situation in which neither side could win. A cease-fire agreement was finally reached in July 1953. After years of fighting, Korea remained divided. By fighting in Korea, the United States showed that it would willingly fight to halt communist expansion.

Eisenhower's Administration

Although international relations between the United States and the Soviet Union remained tense in the 1950s, the American economy generated a new level of prosperity.

In 1952, Republican Dwight D. Eisenhower won the presidential election. Eisenhower wanted to make the federal government smaller, but he believed that the government should protect the basic welfare of all Americans. He expanded Social Security and approved greater funding for public housing for poor people.

The Nation Expands

The greatest domestic program of the Eisenhower presidency involved building a network of interstate highways. In June 1956 Congress passed the Federal Highway Act to provide easy transportation for military forces in case of an attack. The law funded the construction of more than 40,000 miles of highways that tied the nation together.

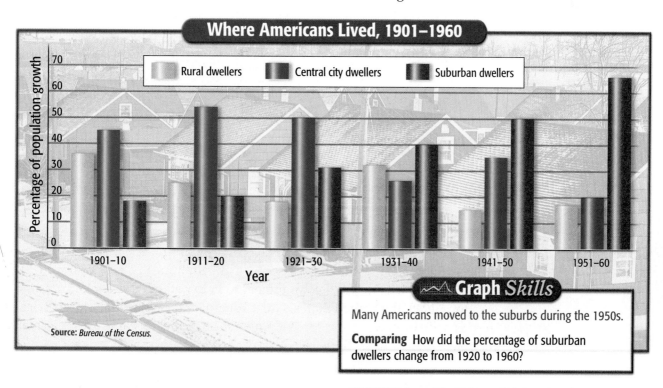

Where Americans Lived, 1901–1960

Percentage of population growth

Legend: Rural dwellers — Central city dwellers — Suburban dwellers

Year: 1901–10, 1911–20, 1921–30, 1931–40, 1941–50, 1951–60

Source: *Bureau of the Census.*

Graph Skills

Many Americans moved to the suburbs during the 1950s.

Comparing How did the percentage of suburban dwellers change from 1920 to 1960?

The nation itself also grew during Eisenhower's presidency. In 1959 Alaska and Hawaii entered the Union, bringing the number of states to 50.

1950s Prosperity

After World War II, the American economy began to grow very rapidly. This rapid growth increased Americans' affluence, or wealth, and also led to the baby boom—a dramatic increase in the nation's birthrate.

During the 1950s, many new homes were built in the suburbs. Usually located on the fringes of major cities, suburban housing developments appealed to many Americans. In addition to affordable homes, they offered privacy, space, and a sense of belonging to a community.

✔ **Reading Check** **Identifying** What does NATO stand for? What is its purpose?

The Civil Rights Era

After World War II, many African Americans began to fight for equal opportunity in jobs, housing, and education, and for an end to segregation—the separation of people of different races.

The Civil Rights Movement

The modern civil rights movement began in the early 1950s. **Thurgood Marshall,** an African American lawyer, brought a case to the Supreme Court challenging segregation in schools. In 1954, in the case of *Brown* v. *Board of Education,* the Supreme Court ruled that segregation in schools was unconstitutional.

In December 1955, a woman named **Rosa Parks** was arrested in Montgomery, Alabama, for refusing to leave a section of a bus reserved for white people. Shortly afterward, African Americans in Montgomery began to **boycott**— to refuse to use—the city's buses. Finally, in 1956, the Supreme Court ruled that all segregated buses were unconstitutional.

At the meeting to organize the boycott, a young minister named **Dr. Martin Luther King, Jr.,** emerged as one of the leaders of the civil rights movement. King believed that African Americans should use nonviolent protests and civil disobedience, or the refusal to obey laws that are considered unjust.

Kennedy and Johnson

As the civil rights movement grew, Americans prepared for the 1960 presidential election. The Republicans nominated Vice President **Richard Nixon,** the Democrats Senator **John F. Kennedy.** The election was close, but Kennedy won.

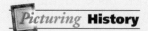
Picturing **History**

The Supreme Court ruled that it was unconstitutional to separate schoolchildren by race, but African American students faced difficulties trying to attend previously all-white schools. **What Court ruling said that segregated schools were against the law?**

Dr. Martin Luther King, Jr.

Kennedy proposed more government spending on education and a program to help poor people get jobs. Congress refused to pass most of Kennedy's proposals, believing they cost too much money. On November 22, 1963, during a visit to Dallas, Texas, President Kennedy was shot and killed. Vice President **Lyndon Johnson** became president.

Lyndon Johnson outlined a set of programs called the **"Great Society."** Perhaps the most important laws passed as part of the Great Society were those establishing **Medicare** and **Medicaid.** Medicare helped pay for medical care for senior citizens. Medicaid helped poor people pay their hospital bills.

The Struggle Continues

During Kennedy's and Johnson's administrations, the civil rights movement continued to grow. In February 1960, four African American students refused to leave a lunch counter in Greensboro, North Carolina, that was reserved for white people. This was the beginning of the **sit-in** movement. Protestors would show up where they were excluded and refuse to leave.

In 1963, Dr. Martin Luther King, Jr., led a march in Birmingham, Alabama. After police attacked the marchers, President Kennedy sent a civil rights bill to Congress to outlaw segregation. To rally support for the bill, many civil rights organizations organized a march on Washington, D.C., in August 1963. Late in the afternoon, King spoke to the crowd in ringing words of his desire to see America transformed:

> **❝**I have a dream that one day this nation will rise up and live out the true meaning of its creed: 'We hold these truths to be self-evident; that all men are created equal.'…**❞**

Southern Democrats blocked Kennedy's civil rights bill. Johnson eventually persuaded Congress to pass the **Civil Rights Act of 1964,** which outlawed discrimination in hiring and banned segregation. The next year, African Americans organized a march in Selma, Alabama, to demand the right to vote. Police again attacked the marchers, and President Johnson asked Congress to pass the **Voting Rights Act of 1965.**

Other Voices

By the mid-1960s the civil rights movement had won many victories. Yet a growing number of African Americans grew tired of the slow pace of change.

Malcolm X, a leader in the Nation of Islam (or Black Muslims), emerged as an important new voice. He criticized integration, declaring that the best way to achieve justice was for African Americans to separate themselves from whites. Later, instead of racial separation, Malcolm X called for "a society in which there could exist honest white-black brotherhood." He was shot and killed in February 1965.

Riots broke out in many major cities during the mid-1960s. In the summer of 1965 violent conflict broke out in the Watts section of Los Angeles. In a week of rioting 34 people died and much of Watts burned to the ground. Between 1965 and 1967 riots broke out in many American cities, including San Francisco and Chicago. In July 1967 urban riots devastated neighborhoods and buildings in Newark, New Jersey, and Detroit, Michigan.

On April 4, 1968, racial tension took another tragic turn. An assassin shot and killed Dr. Martin Luther King, Jr. King's assassination set off angry rioting in more than 100 cities.

Other Groups Seek Rights

Women, Hispanics, and Native Americans found inspiration in the struggle of African Americans for equal rights. In 1966, feminists—activists for women's rights—formed the National Organization for Women. NOW fought for equal rights for women in all aspects of life. They campaigned for an **Equal Rights Amendment** (ERA) to the Constitution, but were unable to get the states to ratify it.

Despite the defeat of the ERA, women did make progress. In 1972 the federal government outlawed discrimination against women in educational programs receiving federal funds.

In the 1960s the rapidly growing Hispanic population sought equal rights. The term Hispanic American refers to those Americans who have come, or are descended from others who have come, to the United States from the nations of Latin America and Spain. In the early 1960s, migrant workers formed unions to fight for better wages and working conditions. Their leader, **César Chávez,** organized thousands of farmworkers into the United Farm Workers (UFW). The efforts of Chávez called attention to the migrant workers' cause. Others besides Chávez worked to secure equal rights for Hispanic Americans. Hispanic men and women organized to fight discrimination and to elect Hispanics to government posts. The League of United Latin American Citizens won suits in federal court to guarantee Hispanic Americans the right to serve on juries and to send their children to unsegregated schools.

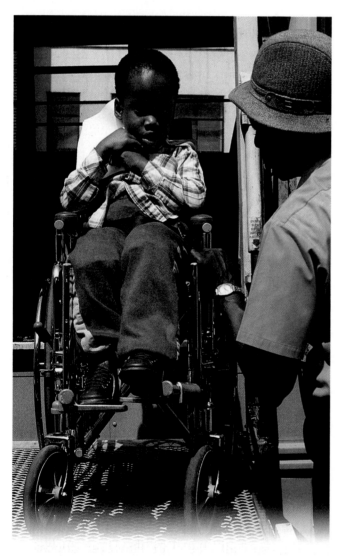

The Americans with Disabilities Act of 1990 requires institutions to provide disabled people with easier access to public transportation.

Native Americans

In the 1960s Native Americans demanded political power. In 1968 Congress passed the Indian Civil Rights Act, which formally protected the constitutional rights of all Native Americans. At the same time, the new law recognized the right of Native American nations to make laws on their own reservations.

Believing the process of change too slow, some Native Americans began taking stronger action. In February 1973 members of the **American Indian Movement** (AIM) seized Wounded Knee, South Dakota, the site of the 1890 massacre of the Sioux by federal troops. Wounded Knee was part of a large Sioux reservation. The people there suffered from terrible poverty and ill health. After several months, the siege ended, but it focused national attention on the terrible living conditions of many Native Americans.

Americans With Disabilities

People with disabilities also sought equal treatment in the 1960s and 1970s. Congress responded by passing a number of laws. One law concerned the removal of barriers that prevented some people from gaining access to public facilities. Another law required employers to offer more opportunities for disabled people in the workplace. Yet another asserted the right of children with disabilities to equal educational opportunities.

Reading Check **Analyzing** What did the Supreme Court rule in *Brown* v. *Board of Education*?

The Vietnam Era

Even as the civil rights movement tried to remake American society at home, the United States continued to struggle against communism abroad, particularly in Vietnam.

Kennedy's Foreign Policy

In 1959, **Fidel Castro** seized power in Cuba. The following year, Castro allied with the Soviet Union. In April 1961, President Kennedy allowed approximately 1,500 Cubans, trained by the Central Intelligence Agency, to land in Cuba at the **Bay of Pigs.** Their mission to overthrow Castro's government failed.

Two months later, Soviet leader **Nikita Khrushchev** told Kennedy that the West must get out of Berlin. Kennedy refused. Shortly afterward, the East German government, with Soviet support, built a wall dividing East Berlin from West Berlin. The **Berlin Wall** became a symbol of communist repression.

In October 1962, Kennedy decided to **blockade**—or close off—Cuba, until the Soviets removed the nuclear missiles they were installing there. As Soviet ships headed toward the blockade, the world waited to see if nuclear war would break out. Abruptly, the Soviet ships turned back. After days of negotiations, the Soviets agreed to pull their missiles out of Cuba.

War in Vietnam

In the late 1950s, President Eisenhower had sent military supplies and advisers to South Vietnam. President Kennedy continued this policy. Despite American aid, the **Vietcong**—the communist forces in South Vietnam—grew stronger. The Vietcong received weapons and supplies from North Vietnam.

The War Escalates

In August 1964, North Vietnam allegedly attacked American ships in the Gulf of Tonkin. In response, Congress authorized the president to use force to defend Americans against attack. Gradually, the American troops shifted from defending their bases to trying to find and destroy the Vietcong. In mid-February 1965, Johnson ordered sustained bombing of North Vietnam. Then, on March 8, the first United States combat troops landed in Vietnam. Next, in April Johnson decided to increase American forces in South Vietnam and to use combat troops for offensive actions.

As the war escalated, North Vietnam increased its support of the Vietcong. To meet the situation, American commander General William Westmoreland asked for additional troops and a commitment to a land war. By the end of 1965, there were more than 180,000 American troops in Vietnam. By the end of 1968, the total had increased to more than 500,000.

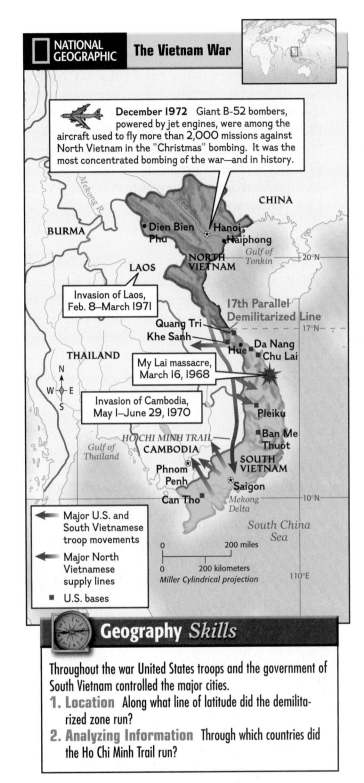

NATIONAL GEOGRAPHIC The Vietnam War

December 1972 Giant B-52 bombers, powered by jet engines, were among the aircraft used to fly more than 2,000 missions against North Vietnam in the "Christmas" bombing. It was the most concentrated bombing of the war—and in history.

CHINA

BURMA

Dien Bien Phu

Hanoi

Haiphong

Gulf of Tonkin

20°N

NORTH VIETNAM

LAOS

Invasion of Laos, Feb. 8–March 1971

17th Parallel Demilitarized Line

17°N

Quang Tri

Khe Sanh

Hue

Da Nang

Chu Lai

THAILAND

My Lai massacre, March 16, 1968

Invasion of Cambodia, May 1–June 29, 1970

Pleiku

Ban Me Thuot

HO CHI MINH TRAIL

Gulf of Thailand

CAMBODIA

SOUTH VIETNAM

Phnom Penh

Saigon

Can Tho

Mekong Delta

10°N

South China Sea

⬅ Major U.S. and South Vietnamese troop movements

⬅ Major North Vietnamese supply lines

■ U.S. bases

0 200 miles

0 200 kilometers

Miller Cylindrical projection

110°E

Geography *Skills*

Throughout the war United States troops and the government of South Vietnam controlled the major cities.

1. **Location** Along what line of latitude did the demilitarized zone run?
2. **Analyzing Information** Through which countries did the Ho Chi Minh Trail run?

Opposition to the War

The American people disagreed sharply over the Vietnam War. Many young people opposed the war, especially the draft. However, opposition to the war was not limited to the young. Members of Congress and the news media became critical of Johnson's policies, too.

As the 1968 election approached, President Johnson announced he would not run for reelection. The violence of the 1960s led many Americans to support candidates who promised to restore order. The Republican Party nominated Richard Nixon, Eisenhower's vice president. Nixon narrowly defeated Democrat Hubert Humphrey. Nixon promised to find a way to end the Vietnam War, pledging America would have "peace with honor."

Nixon and Vietnam

President Nixon's plan to achieve "peace with honor" was called Vietnamization. As American troops were withdrawn, the United States would step up efforts to train and equip South Vietnamese forces. In time these forces would take over total responsibility for the war.

Nixon's hope was that ultimately the North Vietnamese would grow tired of the war and negotiate peace. To hasten that end, Nixon secretly ordered the bombing of Cambodia because the Vietcong and North Vietnamese were using sanctuaries—safe places—there as springboards for offensives into South Vietnam. Then in the spring of 1970 Nixon announced the invasion of Cambodia.

The Cambodian invasion sparked demonstrations on college campuses throughout the nation. Many demonstrations were accompanied by violence. Four students were killed at Kent State University in Ohio and two were killed at Jackson State College in Mississippi. Antiwar protests increased.

The End of American Involvement

Previous attempts at negotiations had stalled. Then in late 1972 a breakthrough came. The final agreement was reached in January 1973. The last American troops pulled out of South Vietnam. Despite the peace agreement, North Vietnam's army launched a full-scale invasion of South Vietnam in early 1975. By May 1975, South Vietnam had fallen. Vietnam was united into one country, under the control of a communist government. America's longest war was over.

The Vietnam War took a staggering toll of lives and caused great suffering. More than 58,000 Americans were dead. Over 1 million Vietnamese—civilians as well as soldiers on one side or the other—died between 1965 and 1975. The relatives of the American soldiers who had been classified as missing in action, or as **MIAs,** continued to demand that the government press the Vietnamese for information. As the years passed, however, the likelihood of finding anyone alive faded.

Reading Check **Identifying** Who succeeded Lyndon Johnson to the presidency?

SECTION 2 ASSESSMENT

Checking for Understanding

1. **Key Terms** Define: stalemate, affluence, segregation, civil disobedience, feminist
2. **Reviewing Facts** What role did Rosa Parks play in the struggle for civil rights?

Reviewing Themes

3. **Civic Rights and Responsibilities** Describe the various actions taken by African Americans to secure civil rights at this time.

Critical Thinking

4. **Drawing Inferences** Do you think President Nixon succeeded in attaining "peace with honor?" Explain.
5. **Organizing Information** Re-create the chart shown here, and describe each.

	Description
Truman Doctrine	
NATO	
Brown v. Board of Education	
Great Society	

Analyzing Visuals

6. **Geography Skills** Study the map of the Vietnam War on page 569. Where did most of the United States bases lie? Why do you think those sites were chosen?

Interdisciplinary Activity

Citizenship Create a time line of the civil rights movement. Research and clip pictures from magazines and newspapers of historic and present-day civil rights events and issues. Add captions.

Critical Thinking SKILLBUILDER

Problem Solving

Why Learn This Skill?

Imagine you got a poor grade on a math test. You wonder why, since you always take notes and study for the tests. To improve your grades, you need to identify your specific problem and then take actions to solve it.

Learning the Skill

There are six key steps you should follow that will help you through the process of problem solving.

- Identify the problem. In the example in the first paragraph, you know that you are not doing well on math tests.
- Gather information. You know that you always take notes and study. You work on math problems every day for an hour. You also know that you sometimes forget details about math formulas.
- List and consider possible solutions. Instead of working on the math problems by yourself, you might try working with a friend or a group.
- Consider the advantages and disadvantages of each solution.

A wounded American soldier reaches for a fallen comrade.

- Now that you have considered the possible options, you need to choose the best solution to your problem then carry it out.
- Evaluate the effectiveness of the solution. This will help you determine if you have solved the problem. If you earn better grades on the next few math tests, you will know.

Practicing the Skill

Reread the material in Section 2 about the Vietnam War. Use that information and the steps above to answer the following questions.

1. What problems did the United States face in the Vietnam War?

2. What options were available to President Johnson? To President Nixon? What were the advantages and disadvantages?

3. Explain the solution President Nixon implemented.

4. Evaluate the effectiveness of Nixon's solution. Was it successful? How do you determine this?

Applying the Skill

Problem Solving President Roosevelt implemented a set of programs called the New Deal. Identify the problem that the New Deal was designed to deal with. List other possible solutions and their advantages and disadvantages. Then, write a short evaluation of the chosen solution.

 Glencoe's **Skillbuilder Interactive Workbook CD-ROM, Level 1,** provides instruction and practice in key social studies skills.

AN American Story

Nixon button

To improve relations with the Communist world, President Richard Nixon made a historic visit to China in February 1972. Nixon later described how he felt upon his arrival in Beijing, the Chinese capital: ". . . 'The Star Spangled Banner' had never sounded so stirring to me as on that windswept runway in the heart of Communist China. . . . As we left the airport, [Chinese leader Chou En-lai] said, 'Your handshake came over the vastest ocean in the world—twenty-five years of no communication.'"

Crisis of Confidence

Even while the Vietnam war raged on, President Nixon attempted to improve American relations with the Communist world. Nixon's efforts were one step along the way to ending the Cold War. President Nixon came to the White House with the hope of bringing America together. However, illegal activity in the administration forced him to resign. While still reeling from the scandal, Americans elected Jimmy Carter to the presidency in 1976. President Carter had some success in foreign affairs. The administration lost the American people's confidence because of its inability to pull the nation out of an economic slump and failure to secure the release of hostages in Iran.

Nixon's Administration

When President Nixon took office in 1969, he hoped to build a more stable world. The People's Republic of China played a key role in Nixon's plan. If the United States opened relations with China, it might make the Soviet Union more cooperative. The United States resumed trade with China in 1971.

America's improved relations with China convinced the Soviet Union to improve relations with the United States as well. The Soviets invited Nixon to Moscow. They agreed to sign an arms control treaty limiting the number of nuclear missiles both sides could have.

During the 1970s, the United States also became involved in the Middle East. Angry at America's support for Israel, the Arab states with oil imposed an embargo—a ban on shipments—of oil. This caused gasoline prices to skyrocket. The oil crisis ended when Secretary of State **Henry Kissinger** negotiated an agreement between Arab and Israeli leaders.

Nixon tried to reduce the federal government's role in people's lives. To give state governments more influence, he introduced revenue sharing—a plan for giving federal taxes back to the states. Although he reduced the federal government's role, Nixon did create the Environmental Protection Agency (EPA).

Nixon's policies were popular with the American people. As a result, he was reelected in a landslide in 1972. Shortly afterward, however, a scandal disrupted his presidency.

Watergate

During the election campaign, burglars were caught trying to break into the Democratic Party offices at the Watergate apartment complex. Nixon denied that his staff had ordered the break-in. After a Senate committee uncovered his staff's involvement, Nixon denied ordering a cover-up.

The House of Representatives began proceedings to **impeach,** or formally accuse, the president of abusing his power. On August 9, 1974, Richard Nixon resigned as president. His vice president, **Gerald Ford,** succeeded him.

Gerald Ford's administration faced growing economic problems, caused in part by the oil embargo. This, plus the Watergate scandal,

President Nixon leaves the White House.

turned many people against Ford. In 1976, voters elected the Democratic candidate, **Jimmy Carter,** to the presidency.

The Carter Presidency

When Jimmy Carter took office, his first priority was to fix the economy. He tried to speed economic growth by cutting taxes and increasing government spending, but his policies did little to improve the economy.

Carter spent much of his time dealing with foreign policy problems. He arranged for new negotiations between Israeli and Egyptian leaders at Camp David. These negotiations eventually led to opening Egyptian-Israeli economic and diplomatic relations. It marked the first time that an Arab nation recognized Israel's right to exist.

Carter based much of his foreign policy on human rights—a concern that governments around the world grant more freedom to their people. He withdrew economic and military aid from some of the worst offenders, including Argentina, South Africa, and Iran. In November 1979, Iranian students with the support of fundamentalists in the government seized the American embassy in Tehran. They then held 52 Americans hostage.

The hostage crisis and the nation's ongoing economic problems damaged President Carter politically. In the 1980 election, the Republican candidate, **Ronald Reagan,** easily defeated Carter. Shortly afterward, Iran released the American hostages.

Reading Check **Identifying** When did President Richard Nixon resign? Who succeeded him?

New Challenges

The 1980s and 1990s saw great changes. By the end of the 1980s, communism in Europe had collapsed. At the same time, America's economy began to rapidly expand.

(Clockwise from lower left) Leaders of Egypt, United States, and Israel celebrate 1979 peace treaty; Americans held hostage in Iran, 1979; President Reagan and Soviet leader Gorbachev meet at 1988 summit in Moscow.

The Reagan Presidency

Ronald Reagan had promised to reduce the role of the government in people's lives. He slashed taxes, eliminated many government regulations, and cut back many government programs. His policies seemed to work. After a brief recession in 1982, the economy began to grow rapidly, and the stock market boomed.

Reagan also began a rapid buildup of American military forces. By cutting taxes while increasing military spending, Reagan greatly increased the federal debt—the amount of money the government had to borrow to pay for its programs. His policies were popular with the American people. Reagan easily won reelection in 1984. Shortly after his second term began, **Mikhail Gorbachev** became the new leader of the Soviet Union.

The Soviet economy was on the edge of collapse. The American military buildup had forced the Soviet Union to respond, and it simply could not afford to keep up. Gorbachev saw that the time had come to reform the communist system.

Reagan began negotiations with Gorbachev to reduce the number of nuclear missiles under their control. Gorbachev's reforms, and Reagan's willingness to improve relations, began to change the Soviet Union.

The Bush Presidency

Ronald Reagan's popularity enabled his vice president, **George Bush,** to win the Republican nomination and defeat the Democratic nominee, Michael Dukakis, in the 1988 presidential election. Once in office, Bush continued negotiations with the Soviet Union.

(Clockwise from lower right) Celebrating the fall of the Berlin wall, 1989; Reading about the allied air strike in Iraq, 1991; President Clinton prepares to address nation after his impeachment, 1998.

In late 1989, demonstrators filled the streets of Eastern Europe demanding more democracy. Within weeks, most of the communist governments in Eastern Europe collapsed. The Berlin Wall was torn down, and the following year East Germany and West Germany reunited. By the end of 1991, the Communist Party had been outlawed in Russia, and the Soviet Union had broken up into 15 separate republics.

While communism collapsed in Europe, a serious crisis developed in the Middle East. In 1990, Iraq invaded Kuwait. President Bush persuaded European and Arab nations to join the United States in an effort to free Kuwait. Bush then launched **Operation Desert Storm**—a massive attack on Iraqi forces that freed Kuwait and destroyed much of Iraq's army.

The Clinton Presidency

George Bush's popularity soared after the war against Iraq. But the onset of an economic recession left many Americans dissatisfied. The Democrats nominated **Bill Clinton,** governor of Arkansas, to run against Bush in 1992. Many Americans decided to vote for a third party candidate—businessman Ross Perot. Perot's candidacy split the vote three ways, enabling Clinton to win the election with only 43 percent of the popular vote.

After assuming office, Clinton cut government spending to reduce the deficit. He also convinced Congress to pass the Family Medical Leave Act. In 1993, he helped reach an agreement giving Palestinians the right to their own government in Israeli territory.

Another foreign policy issue involved change in trade policy. The **North American Free Trade Agreement** (NAFTA), which took effect in 1994, called for the gradual removal of tariffs and other trade barriers on most goods produced and sold in North America.

After Clinton won reelection in 1996, the economy continued to grow rapidly. For the first time in many years, the government balanced the budget and ran a **surplus**—it took in more money than it spent. With the Cold War over, Clinton's foreign policy focused on resolving regional conflicts.

As Clinton struggled with foreign policy problems, a scandal emerged involving a personal relationship between the president and a White House intern. Some evidence suggested that the president had obstructed justice and committed perjury, or lied under oath, to conceal the relationship. The House of Representatives voted to impeach President Clinton. The Senate then held a trial and acquitted the president.

The Election of 2000

The impeachment scandal left the country divided. For the 2000 election, the Democrats nominated Vice President **Al Gore.** The Republicans nominated Governor **George W. Bush** of Texas, son of former President Bush.

The 2000 election was one of the closest in history. Gore led in the popular vote, but the results in Florida were disputed and on election night no one knew who won. Without Florida's 25 electoral votes, neither Bush nor Gore had the 270 electoral votes needed to win. As the Florida ballots were being recounted, Bush and Gore went to court to challenge the recount process. The dispute was finally resolved by the Supreme Court. On January 20, 2001, George W. Bush became the 43rd president of the United States.

A New Bush Administration

The new president quickly established his administration. One of his first responsibilities was to name cabinet members. Bush named retired General of the Army **Colin Powell** to be secretary of state. He chose **Donald Rumsfeld** to serve as secretary of defense.

Bush continued the practice of expanding the number of women in high-level positions in his administration. Included were **Gale Norton** as Secretary of Interior and **Christine Todd Whitman** as head of the Environmental Protection Agency. The new Secretary of Labor, **Elaine Chao,** was the first Asian American woman appointed to a president's cabinet. National Security Adviser, **Condoleezza Rice,** was the first African American woman to hold that post.

During the election campaign, Bush promised a tax cut and he soon presented his tax plan to Congress. The plan generated much debate.

People In History

Colin Powell 1937–

During the Persian Gulf War, the highest-ranking military officer serving was Colin Powell, the chairman of the Joint Chiefs of Staff. He was the youngest person and the first African American to hold that position. A four-star general, Powell had a very distinguished military career for thirty-five years, serving twice in Vietnam and working for four presidents.

Born to Jamaican immigrants, Powell was raised in Harlem and the South Bronx of New York City. He attended public school and the City College of New York, where he studied geology and began military training.

After the Gulf War, Powell wrote an autobiography and established a charitable organization, America's Promise—the Alliance for Youth, that helps children.

In 2001, Powell went to work for his fifth president, George W. Bush, as the first African American secretary of state.

Supporters argued that it was the people's money and that they deserved it back. They also claimed that the tax cut would help the economy. Opponents argued that the money could be used more responsibly elsewhere, such as for Social Security or for paying off the national debt. In June 2001 President Bush signed into law the largest reduction in federal taxes since 1981.

As the president's top military advisor, Colin Powell laid out a blueprint for intervention in international conflict. The Powell Doctrine called for using American troops only when a vital interest is at stake and there is a clear and realistic goal.

✓ **Reading Check** **Determining Cause and Effect**
What event sparked Operation Desert Storm?

Looking to the Future

As Americans entered a new century, they faced many uncertainties—and opportunities. New technologies and a changing society had begun to transform America in new ways.

President Bush said one of his major aims was to stimulate global economic growth:

> ❝We know that nations that open their economies to the benefits of trade are more successful in climbing out of poverty. . . . [F]ree trade encourages the habits of liberty. . . .❞

Since 1995 the World Trade Organization (WTO) has administered trade practices between many nations. The WTO has more than 146 members.

Growth of technology boosted economic growth. Personal computers were being used in homes, schools, and businesses in greater numbers than ever before. Through the Internet, a worldwide linking of computer networks, American students could communicate with students in other countries.

A Changing Society

Because Americans were living longer than in the past, elderly people formed an increasing portion of the population. The Census Bureau reported that more than 12 percent of the population was over 65 years of age in the year 2000.

An important issue facing the nation was reform of Medicare. Medicare is the federal health care program for the elderly. By the summer of 2002, both the House and the Senate had passed bills that added a benefit for prescription drugs.

Congress also reacted to an increase in corporate scandals. For example, at one large energy trading company, Enron, corporate leaders cost investors and employees billions of dollars before the company went bankrupt. The federal government tightened accounting regulations and toughened penalties for dishonest executives.

By 2002, more than 10 percent of the population was foreign-born. Asian Americans made up about 4 percent of the population; Hispanic Americans more than 12 percent. The Hispanic community is now the nation's largest minority community.

Environmental Challenges

For years, scientists noted that the earth's atmosphere was losing ozone. This layer of gas protects life on Earth from cancer-causing rays of the sun. In 1987, the United States and 24 other nations agreed to stop making chemicals that might be weakening the ozone layer.

Scientists continued to debate the effects of global warming. They warned that the steady increase in average world temperatures could bring about major changes in weather patterns, the environment, and crop production.

Threats to Peace and Security

Preserving peace remains the most pressing global issue. In the late 1900s and early 2000s, acts of terrorism multiplied.

Terrorism—the use of violence by groups against civilians to achieve a political goal—threatened the security of the nation. On April 19, 1995, a massive bomb exploded at the Murrah Federal Building in downtown Oklahoma City, leaving 168 dead. The tragedy focused national attention on the violent anti-government feelings of private American militia groups. In January 1998, Theodore Kaczynski pleaded guilty to a string of mail bombings, dating from 1978 to 1995, which killed 3 and injured 29 others. Kaczynski hoped to inspire a rebellion against modern industrial society. These are examples of **domestic terrorism.** People engage in domestic terrorism when they attack people in their own country.

In addition to concern about domestic terrorism, the United States also faced **international terrorism.** As the world's most powerful nation, the United States frequently served as a target for terrorists—either those acting independently or with the support of a hostile government. The attack on the World Trade Center and the Pentagon on September 11, 2001, was an example of international terrorism.

✓ **Reading Check** **Explaining** Describe one way in which the nation's population is changing.

SECTION 3 ASSESSMENT

Checking for Understanding

1. **Key Terms** Define: embargo, human rights, federal debt, perjury, terrorism
2. **Reviewing Facts** When did Iranian students take Americans hostage?

Section Theme

3. **Government and Democracy** What is impeachment? Was President Nixon impeached? Was President Clinton?

Critical Thinking

4. **Drawing Conclusions** Do you think President Reagan's actions proved he was committed to reducing the role of government in the lives of Americans? Explain.
5. **Sequencing** Re-create the time line below and identify important events for each of the dates.

```
1971     1979     1991     2000
  |        |        |        |
```

Analyzing Visuals

6. **Picturing History** Select one of the news photographs that appears on pages 574–575. Write one paragraph about the photo. Identify the people and describe what is happening.

Interdisciplinary Activity

Geography Illustrate a world map showing the cities and regions discussed in the section.

The War on Terrorism

Guide to Reading

Main Idea
After suffering the worst terrorist attack in its history, the United States launched an effort to fight international terrorism.

Key Terms
counter-terrorism

Reading Strategy
Organizing Information As you read about America's war on terrorism, complete a diagram like the one below to explain how Americans responded to the events of September 11, 2001.

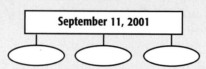

September 11, 2001

Read to Learn
• how Americans responded to terrorism.
• what actions the government took to fight terrorism.

Section Theme
Global Connections The United States called for a worldwide coalition to fight against terrorism.

Preview of Events

♦1975   ♦1985   ♦1995   ♦2005

1979
Soviet Union invades Afghanistan

1988
Al-Qaeda is organized

1998
Bombs explode at U.S. embassies in Kenya and Tanzania

2001
Attack on the Pentagon and World Trade Center

Rescue workers carry out an injured man at the World Trade Center.

AN American Story

The first airliner hit the World Trade Center's north tower in New York City at about 8:45 in the morning. Eighteen minutes later, a second plane hit the south tower. Those who died on the airplanes were the first victims. Fire and falling wreckage from the twin towers of the World Trade Center killed thousands more, and hundreds of rescuers—fire fighters, police officers, and volunteers—themselves became victims. "The smoke was so bad, I was suffocating. When the buildings toppled, it was like a volcano," one survivor noted. "We have a lot of heroes," said one firefighter, "and we lost a lot of good people."

The crash of two passenger airplanes into the World Trade Center was not an accident. Early on the morning of September 11, 2001, terrorist hijackers had seized control of the planes, then deliberately flew them into the buildings. Terrorists took control of a third plane and crashed into the Pentagon, the headquarters of the nation's Department of Defense. Hijackers also seized a fourth airplane, but passengers heroically attacked the hijackers, causing that plane to crash in Pennsylvania. In all, thousands died.

Terrorist attacks destroyed the World Trade Center (left), one of the nation's economic centers. Three New York City firefighters (right) raise the American flag amid the rubble.

Many New York City rescue workers who went to help also lost their lives when the towers collapsed. Hundreds of firefighters, police officers, and volunteers gave their lives in the line of duty trying to save others. Among those who died were Fire Department chaplain Mychal Judge and first deputy commissioner William Feehan, a 42-year veteran of the fire department. The largest number of New York City firefighters to have died in a single disaster before the terrorist attack was 12.

The Terrorist Threat

The attacks on the World Trade Center and the Pentagon were acts of terrorism. Terrorism is the use of violence by groups against civilians to achieve a political goal.

Who Was Responsible?

Intelligence sources and FBI investigators quickly identified **Osama bin Laden** as the prime suspect. Like most people in the Middle East, bin Laden is a **Muslim**—someone who believes in and practices the religion of Islam. Although the vast majority of the 1 billion Muslims worldwide believe Islam rejects terrorism, militant **fundamentalists** like bin Laden do not. They believe that any action is justified to drive American influence out of the Arab world.

Bin Laden believed that Western ideas had harmed Muslim society. His experience in Afghanistan convinced him that superpowers could be beaten.

War in Afghanistan

In 1979 the Soviet Union had invaded the nation of **Afghanistan,** in Southwest Asia, to support that nation's pro-communist government. Muslims from across the Middle East went to Afghanistan to fight against the Soviets. Among them was bin Laden, who came from one of Saudi Arabia's wealthiest families. In 1988, he founded an organization called **al-Qaeda** (al KY-duh), or "the Base." Al-Qaeda recruited Muslims to fight against the Soviets and bought arms for the Afghanistan soldiers. After Soviet forces withdrew from Afghanistan, bin Laden became a hero to many fundamentalists.

Terrorist Acts

Operating first from Sudan and then from Afghanistan—which was then under the control of Muslim fundamentalists known as the **Taliban**—bin Laden led al-Qaeda on a mission to drive Americans and other non-Muslims out of the Middle East. In 1998, terrorist truck bombs exploded at the American embassies in the African countries of **Kenya** and **Tanzania.** The bombs killed more than 200 people, including 12 Americans, and injured over 4,500. In late 1999, terrorists linked to al-Qaeda were arrested trying to smuggle explosives into the United States in an attempt to bomb targets in Seattle, Washington. In October 2000, terrorists backed by al-Qaeda crashed a boat loaded with explosives into the **USS** *Cole,* an American warship, while it was refueling in Yemen.

✔ **Reading Check** **Describing** How did Osama bin Laden become so influential in Afghanistan?

A New War Begins

Then on September 11, 2001, terrorists struck on an even greater scale. The shock was felt across the nation, and thousands of people sought a way to help.

The Spirit of America

From coast to coast, thousands attended prayer services and vigils. Across the nation, Americans lined up to donate blood. Others raised money and collected food, blankets, and other supplies for the victims and rescue workers. Firefighters and medical workers from many cities headed to New York to help.

Using a combination of imagination and hard work, young people throughout the nation volunteered to help. Students in Western Springs, a village near Chicago, Illinois, encouraged their entire community to take part in a toys, books, and games garage sale to raise money. Students at a school in Cedar Rapids, Iowa, started a project called Working for America. The students worked by doing chores for family and neighbors and donated money they earned to the Red Cross. The South Bronx Job Corps Center put

NATIONAL GEOGRAPHIC **Terrorism Against Americans, 1970–2002**

0 ——— 3,000 miles
0 ——— 3,000 kilometers
Winkel Tripel projection

1 **1970** Terrorists hijack airplanes to Jordan

2 **1979** Fifty-two Americans held hostage in Iran for more than a year

3 **1983** Bombing of U.S. Marine barracks in Beirut, Lebanon, kills 241

4 **1985** TWA flight 847 hijacked; hostages held for 17 days in Beirut, Lebanon

5 **1986** Bombing at West Berlin dance club; kills 3, injures 150

6 **1988** Bomb on Pan Am flight 103 kills 270 in Lockerbie, Scotland

7 **1993** Bomb at World Trade Center kills 6

8 **1995** Truck bomb destroys a federal building in Oklahoma City; kills 168, injures more than 500

9 **1996** Bomb at U.S. complex in Dharan, Saudi Arabia, kills 19 American soldiers

10 **1998** Bombings at U.S. embassies in Kenya and Tanzania kill more than 200

11 **2000** Bomb kills 17 American sailors and injures 39 aboard USS *Cole*

12 **2001** Hijacked airliners crash into the World Trade Center, the Pentagon, and a field in Pennsylvania, killing thousands

13 **2002** Bombs in Indonesia kill over 200

AMERICA'S HEROES

New York City Fire Department Chaplain Mychal Judge, shown here in prayer, was killed while administering last rites to a firefighter.

New York City firefighter Tony James salutes during a funeral service.

Jessica Malone, who comes from a large family of firefighters, went to New York City to help.

together canine care packages for search and rescue dogs at the World Trade Center site.

Fair Treatment

Realizing that many people might turn their anger against Muslims in the United States, President Bush visited the Islamic Center in Washington, D.C. There he issued a statement explaining that Islam is a peaceful religion. He urged all Americans to uphold the nation's values and treat Muslim Americans fairly.

President Bush created a special fund to help the children of Afghanistan. Many of the children in Afghanistan are orphans and do not have enough to eat. The president asked the children of the United States to send $1—or whatever they could—to America's Fund for Afghan Children.

New Threats

Concern over the use of biological and chemical weapons grew in the wake of the September 11 tragedy. Letters containing deadly anthrax spores were mailed to several political leaders and the news media. Anthrax is an animal disease that has existed for tens of thousands of years.

Law enforcement investigated to determine the identity and the motives of the attackers, but so far, no suspects have been identified. Officials do not think al-Qaeda sent the anthrax.

Protecting America

President Bush and his advisers began planning a response to the terrorist attacks. The president placed the armed forces on high alert. Fighter aircraft began patrolling the skies over major

In the face of all this evil, we remain strong and united, "one nation under God." —*President George W. Bush*

cities. Security at airports was increased, and the FBI began a massive investigation. The president created a new federal agency called the Office of **Homeland Security,** to coordinate counter-terrorism efforts. Counter-terrorism involves military or political activities intended to combat terrorism. He named Pennsylvania governor Tom Ridge to head the agency. 📖 *(See pages 604–605 of the Appendix for President Bush's address to Congress after the attacks.)*

The Office of Homeland Security had trouble coordinating counter-terrorism efforts. In June 2002, President Bush asked Congress to combine all of the agencies responsible for the public's safety into a new department to be called the Department of Homeland Security.

In late October 2001, Congress passed and the president signed into law new measures to combat terrorism. The **USA Patriot Act of 2001** gave federal prosecutors and FBI agents new powers to investigate those who plot or carry out acts of terrorism. The law expanded the power of federal agents to tap telephones and track Internet usage in the hunt for terrorists. It also permits agents to conduct secret searches of a suspect's home or office without giving prior notice to the owner of the property.

Attorney General **John Ashcroft** promised that government agents would waste no time putting the new tools to use in the hunt for terrorists. Although both houses of Congress passed the bill overwhelmingly, some critics expressed concern that measures could be used not only against suspected terrorists, but people and organizations engaged in lawful activity. To make sure civil liberties were not compromised by the new law, many of its powers will expire in late 2005, unless extended by Congress.

Building a Coalition

The death and devastation caused by terrorism affected not only Americans, but also people around the world. World leaders responded with statements of sympathy and outrage. NATO members promised to support the United States as did other nations including India, Pakistan, Turkey, and Israel. Some Muslim nations, including Saudi Arabia and Egypt, offered more limited support because they feared widespread protests from their people.

On the Trail of Terrorism

The war against terrorism first concentrated on Afghanistan where bin Laden was reported to be in hiding. The Taliban controlled most of Afghanistan and imposed their religious views on the Afghan people. Taliban leaders had come under criticism for discriminating against women and being intolerant of other religions. Since 1996, when the Taliban captured the Afghan capital, **Kabul,** the main opposition force, the **Northern Alliance,** had battled the Taliban but had made little headway.

President Bush demanded that the Taliban in Afghanistan turn over bin Laden and his supporters. After the Taliban refused, on October 7 the U.S. military attacked Taliban and al-Qaeda forces. Cargo jets also dropped food, medicine, and supplies to the Afghan people.

The air strikes by U.S. warplanes allowed the Northern Alliance to quickly take control of the country. After the Taliban fell from power, the United States and its allies worked with Afghan leaders to create a new government to run the country. Nations around the world pledged more than four billion dollars to help Afghanistan. Thousands of American and allied troops began arriving in Afghanistan to act as peacekeepers and to hunt for al-Qaeda terrorists. Afghan leaders selected Hamid Karzai to serve as Afghanistan's new president.

Although the war in Afghanistan was going well, terrorist attacks in South Asia and the Middle East created new problems. In December 2001, terrorists from Kashmir—a region in northern India—attacked India's parliament. India has fought many wars with Pakistan over Kashmir. India's leaders blamed Pakistan for the attack on the parliament, and began mobilizing India's army.

By June 2002, the two nations were ready to go to war. The situation was very dangerous because both sides had nuclear weapons. Although India and Pakistan eventually stepped back from the threat of nuclear war, neither side showed signs of setting aside their arms.

South Asia was not the only region where terrorism created problems. In the Middle East, Palestinian terrorists sent suicide bombers into Israel. These bombers concealed explosives under their clothing. They detonated the bombs

Americans gathered at parks, churches, and fire stations across the nation to express not only their grief but their patriotism.

in Israeli restaurants, shops, and buses, killing dozens of other people. After several suicide bombings took place in Israel, the Israeli army invaded several Palestinian cities where they believed the terrorist groups were based.

In response to the violence in the Middle East, President Bush outlined a plan for ending the Israeli-Palestinian conflict. He announced his support for the creation of a Palestinian state living in peace beside Israel. He asked Israel to stop raiding Palestinian cities. At the same time, he demanded Palestinian leaders stop terrorist attacks and reform their government to make it more democratic and less corrupt.

Continuing the War on Terrorism

President Bush made it clear that while the war on terrorism would start by targeting al-Qaeda, it would not end there. "It will not end," the president announced, "until every terrorist group of global reach has been found, stopped, and defeated." He also warned that the United States would regard "any nation that continues to harbor or support terrorism" as an enemy.

The war against terrorism, President Bush warned Americans, would not end quickly, but it was a war the people of the United States were now called to fight:

> ❝Great harm has been done to us. We have suffered great loss. And in our grief and anger we have found our mission and our moment.... We will not tire, we will not falter, and we will not fail.❞

Widening the War on Terror

The attacks of September 11, 2001, raised fears that al-Qaeda and other terrorist groups might acquire nuclear, chemical, or biological weapons. These **weapons of mass destruction** could kill tens of thousands of people all at once.

In his 2002 State of the Union address, President Bush said his goal was "to prevent regimes that sponsor terror from threatening America or our friends with weapons of mass destruction." He singled out Iraq, Iran, and North Korea, claiming these states "and their terrorist allies constitute an axis of evil arming to threaten the peace of the world."

In October 2002, North Korea announced that it had restarted its nuclear weapons program. The Bush administration used diplomatic pressure to persuade the North Koreans to stop. However, North Korea warned the U.S. that it would continue to build its nuclear power.

Confronting Iraq

Iraq's dictator Saddam Hussein had already ordered the use of chemical weapons twice, once in Iraq's war against Iran in the 1980s and again against the Kurds, an ethnic minority in northern Iraq who had rebelled against Hussein. After the Gulf War in 1991, UN inspectors found evidence that Iraq had developed biological weapons and was working on a nuclear bomb.

In the summer of 2002, President Bush increased pressure on Iraq. On September 12, he asked the UN to pass a new resolution demanding that Iraq give up its weapons of mass destruction. The president made it clear that the United States would act with or without UN support.

In mid-October, Congress voted to authorize the use of force against Iraq. Then, in early November, the United Nations set a deadline for Iraq to readmit weapons inspectors. It required Iraq to declare all of its weapons of mass destruction, to stop supporting terrorism, and to stop oppressing its people. The resolution threatened Iraq with "serious consequences" if it did not cooperate.

Iraq agreed to allow UN inspectors into the country, but questions arose over whether Iraqi officials were cooperating as they had promised. President Bush argued that the Iraqis were still hiding weapons of mass destruction. The Bush administration asked the UN Security Council to pass a resolution calling for the use of force in Iraq. When Council members France and Russia said they would veto a resolution, the United States prepared for war.

On March 20, the American military, aided by soldiers from Great Britain, attacked. Over the next six weeks, much of Iraq's army fell into disarray. American troops quickly seized control of the country. On May 1, President Bush declared the end of major combat operations. About 140 Americans, and several thousand Iraqis, had died.

The controversy over Iraq and the fighting, though, continued. While many Iraqis welcomed the fall of Saddam Hussein's regime, others did not. U.S. and British troops faced continued attacks. By the fall of 2003, more Americans had died after May 1 than had died in the six weeks of major combat. As American deaths and expenses mounted, President Bush began to seek support from the UN and other countries to rebuild Iraq. Despite the capture of Saddam Hussein in December 2003, the path toward a free and stable Iraq appeared to be long and difficult.

Reading Check **Analyzing** Why did President Bush call for military action against Saddam Hussein's regime?

SECTION 4 ASSESSMENT

Checking for Understanding

1. **Key Terms** Define: counter-terrorism.
2. **Reviewing Facts** What happened to the USS *Cole* when it was refueling in Yemen?

Reviewing Themes

3. **Global Connections** Do you think the dangers of terrorism require global cooperation? Explain and support your point of view with reasons.

Critical Thinking

4. **Drawing Conclusions** Why do you think President Bush specifically chose to visit the Islamic Center in Washington, D.C.?
5. **Organizing Information** Use a diagram like the one below to identify what you think are the three major effects of terrorism on Americans.

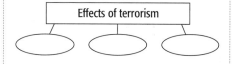

Effects of terrorism

Analyzing Visuals

6. **Geography Skills** Examine the map on terrorism on page 581. How many Americans were taken hostage in Iran? What events on the map took place in the 1990s?

Interdisciplinary Activity

Expository Writing How will world events affect your future? Write an essay entitled "The World's Future and My Own" identifying important issues and explaining how events could affect your life.

Chapter Summary

The Making of Modern America

Depression and World War

- A severe economic depression affects much of the world during the 1930s.
- Aid to the Allies and the Japanese attack on Pearl Harbor pull the United States into World War II.
- The surrender of Germany and Japan in 1945 ends the war.

The Cold War

- The desire to contain communism leads the United States to assume an active role in world affairs.
- The cold war rivalry leads to conflict in Korea and confrontation in Cuba.

The Civil Rights Era

- In the 1950s African Americans renew their struggle for full equality.
- Women and minority groups begin to work for change in their own right.

The Vietnam Era

- Unable to end the war quickly, the United States finds itself increasingly drawn into the Vietnam War.
- Illegal activities by government officials result in the Watergate scandal and the resignation of President Nixon.

Search for Solutions

- President Ronald Reagan acts quickly to limit the size of the federal government and build the nation's military.
- The United States and allies liberate Kuwait after Iraqi invasion.

New Challenges

- During the 1990s, the nation enjoys prosperous economic times, but the government is shaken by scandal and the impeachment trial of President Clinton.
- America seeks to meet the challenges of terrorism both at home and abroad.
- Saddam Hussein is deposed as Iraqi leader.

586

Reviewing Key Terms

On a sheet of paper, use all of the following terms to write several short, historically accurate paragraphs relating to the information in the chapter. Try to use more than one term in a sentence.

1. Holocaust
2. stalemate
3. segregation
4. civil disobedience
5. embargo
6. federal debt
7. terrorism
8. counter-terrorism

Reviewing Key Facts

9. What was the purpose of the Social Security Act?
10. What happened on D-Day?
11. Why was Okinawa a strategic site during World War II?
12. What states joined the nation in 1959?
13. Describe Rosa Parks's role in the struggle for civil rights.
14. Who was César Chávez?
15. Why did President Kennedy call for a blockade of Cuba in 1962?
16. Who proposed the policy of Vietnamization? What was its goal?
17. Who won the presidential election in 1976?
18. What was the purpose of Operation Desert Storm?
19. What is significant about September 11, 2001?
20. What is the Department of Homeland Security?

Critical Thinking

21. **Drawing Conclusions** Do you think the expansion of the federal government during Franklin Roosevelt's presidency was necessary? Why or why not?
22. **Explaining** What does the term "Cold War" mean and how did it apply to the post-World War II era?
23. **Organizing Information** Re-create the chart shown here and list three steps taken during Nixon's presidency to end United States involvement in Vietnam.

24. **Analyze** What are the two major challenges Americans face today? Explain why you made your choices.

Geography and History

Study the map below. Then read the statements that follow. Identify whether each statement is true or not true and explain your answer.

NATIONAL GEOGRAPHIC **Election of 2000**

Candidate	Electoral Vote	Popular Vote	Political Party
Bush	271	50,456,002	Republican
Gore	266	50,999,897	Democrat

* 1 elector from Washington, D.C., abstained.

25. A total of 438 electoral votes were cast.
26. Gore received more popular votes than Bush.
27. Gore received strong support from the southeastern states.

Practicing Skills

28. **Problem Solving** Describe a decision that you might face today or in the near future, such as the choice to go to college or to get a job after high school. List the steps of the problem-solving process. Write the questions and information you would consider at each step and what your answers might be. Evaluate what you think would be your best option.

 Technology Activity

29. **Using the Internet** Use the Internet to research the life of one of the men or women discussed in Chapter 19. Prepare a list of 10 key facts about that person. Share your list with the class.

 **HISTORY** *Online*

Self-Check Quiz
Visit tarvol1.glencoe.com and click on **Chapter 19— Self-Check Quizzes** to prepare for the chapter test.

Citizenship Cooperative Activity

30. **Serving on a Jury** With a partner, think about what happens if you receive a jury notice in the mail. Write a description of what you would do next and what you would expect to happen. Then note what you plan to tell the judge about your understanding of a juror's responsibilities. Share your writing with the class.

Economics Activity

31. Research for information, then summarize your findings in a short report that answers these questions. What field or career area interests you? What education and skills are required to enter it? What attitudes, work habits, and other qualities does it take to succeed on the job?

 Alternative Assessment

32. **Portfolio Writing Activity** Choose an event that you think has had a great impact on everyday life in the United States. Write a column for a newspaper describing how that change has affected your life.

Standardized Test Practice

The cold war between the United States and the former Soviet Union was a rivalry between what two forms of government?

F communism and socialism

G communism and dictatorships

H communism and democracy

J democracy and monarchy

Test-Taking Tip

When you are studying for an exam, use a dictionary to look up important terms. Communism, dictatorship, socialism, democracy, and monarchy are words describing different types of government. Which choices contain words that describe the U.S. government?

Appendix

Contents

What Is an Appendix and How Do I Use One?

An appendix is the additional material you often find at the end of books. The following information will help you learn how to use the appendix in **The American Republic to 1877.**

Primary Sources Library

The **Primary Sources Library** provides additional first-person accounts of historical events. Primary sources are often narratives by a person who actually experienced what is being described.

Presidents of the United States

The **presidents** have served as our nation's leaders. In this resource you will find information of interest on each of the nation's presidents, including their term in office, political affiliation, and their occupations before they became president.

Documents of American History

This is a collection of some of the most important writings in American history. Each **document** begins with an introduction describing the author and placing the selection within its historical context.

Supreme Court Case Summaries

The **Supreme Court Case Summaries** provide readable discussions of important Supreme Court cases. The summaries are listed in alphabetical order and include a summary of the facts of the case and its impact.

Gazetteer

A **gazetteer** (GA•zuh•TIHR) is a geographical dictionary. It lists some of the largest countries, cities, and several important geographic features. Each entry also includes a page number telling where this place can be found in your textbook.

Glossary

A **glossary** is a list of important or difficult terms found in a textbook. Since words sometimes have other meanings, you may wish to consult a dictionary to find other uses for the term. The glossary gives a definition of each term as it is used in the book. The glossary also includes page numbers telling you where in the textbook the term is used.

Spanish Glossary

A **Spanish glossary** contains everything that an English glossary does, but it is written in Spanish. A Spanish glossary is especially important to bilingual students, or those Spanish-speaking students who are learning the English language.

Index

An **index** is an alphabetical listing that includes the subjects of the book and the page numbers where those subjects can be found. The index in this book also lets you know that certain pages contain maps, graphs, photos, or paintings about the subject.

Acknowledgements and Photo Credits

This section lists photo credits and/or literary credits for the book. You can look at this section to find out where the publisher obtained the permission to use a photograph or to use excerpts from other books.

Test Yourself

Find the answers to these questions by using the Appendix on the following pages.

1. **What does ironclad mean?**
2. **Who was the sixth president of the United States?**
3. **On what page can I find out about Anne Hutchinson?**
4. **Where exactly is Roanoke located?**
5. **What was the Supreme Court's decision in *Marbury* v. *Madison?***

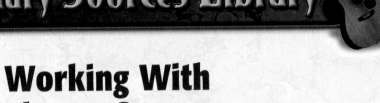
Working With Primary Sources

S uppose that you have been asked to write a report on changes in your community over the past 25 years. Where would you get the information you need to begin writing? You would draw upon two types of information—primary sources and secondary sources.

Definitions

Primary sources are often first-person accounts by someone who actually saw or lived through what is being described. In other words, if you see a fire or live through a great storm and then write about your experiences, you are creating a primary source. Diaries, journals, photographs, and eyewitness reports are examples of primary sources. **Secondary sources** are secondhand accounts. For instance, if your friend experiences the fire or storm and tells you about it, or if you read about the fire or storm in the newspaper, and then you write about it, you are creating a secondary source. Textbooks, biographies, and histories are secondary sources.

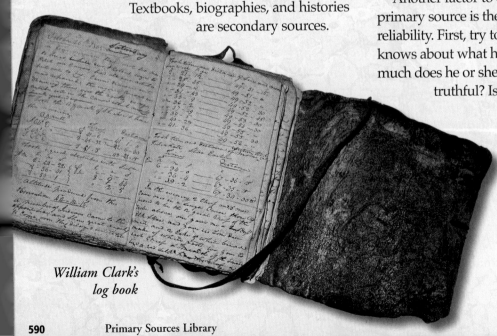

William Clark's log book

Checking Your Sources

When you read primary or secondary sources, you should analyze them to figure out if they are dependable or reliable. Historians usually prefer primary sources to secondary sources, but both can be reliable or unreliable, depending on the following factors.

Time Span

With primary sources, it is important to consider how long after the event occurred the primary source was written. Chances are the longer the time span between the event and the account, the less reliable the account is. As time passes, people often forget details and fill in gaps with events that never took place. Although we like to think we remember things exactly as they happened, the fact is we often remember them as we wanted them to occur.

Reliability

Another factor to consider when evaluating a primary source is the writer's background and reliability. First, try to determine how this person knows about what he or she is writing. How much does he or she know? Is the writer being truthful? Is the account convincing?

Opinions

When evaluating a primary source, you should also decide whether the account has been influenced by emotion, opinion, or exaggeration. Writers can have reasons to distort the truth to suit their personal purposes. Ask yourself: Why did the person write the account? Do any key words or expressions reveal the author's emotions or opinions? You may wish to compare the account with one written by another witness to the event. If the two accounts differ, ask yourself why they differ and which is more accurate.

Interpreting Primary Sources

To help you analyze a primary source, use the following steps:

- **Examine the origins of the document.**
  You need to determine if it is a primary source.

- **Find the main ideas.**
  Read the document and summarize the main ideas in your own words. These ideas may be fairly easy to identify in newspapers and journals, for example, but are much more difficult to find in poetry.

- **Reread the document.**
  Difficult ideas are not always easily understood on the first reading.

- **Use a variety of resources.**
  Form the habit of using the dictionary, the encyclopedia, and maps. These resources are tools to help you discover new ideas and knowledge and check the validity of sources.

George Washington's compass

Classifying Primary Sources

Primary sources fall into different categories:

Printed Publications

Printed publications include books such as autobiographies. Printed publications also include newspapers and magazines.

Songs & Poems

Songs and poems include works that express the personal thoughts and feelings, or political or religious beliefs, of the writer, often using rhyming and rhythmic language.

Visual Materials

Visual materials include a wide range of forms: original paintings, drawings, sculptures, photographs, film, and maps.

Oral Histories

Oral history collects spoken memories and personal observations through recorded interviews. By contrast, oral tradition involves stories that people have passed along by word of mouth from generation to generation.

Personal Records

Personal records are accounts of events kept by an individual who is a participant in, or witness to, these events. Personal records include diaries, journals, and letters.

Artifacts

Artifacts are objects such as tools or ornaments. Artifacts present information about a particular culture or a stage of technological development.

Different Worlds Meet

Until the arrival of Christopher Columbus, the lifestyle and culture of Native Americans had endured for centuries. They told stories, sang songs, and recited tales that recounted their past and their close relationship with the natural world. These stories and songs survived through oral tradition. This means that each generation passed down its stories and songs to its young people by word of mouth. As you read, think about how oral history, folklore, and tradition connect us to the past.

Reader's Dictionary

Lakota: a member of the Sioux people of central and eastern North America

prophecy: a prediction about the future

Black Hills: mountains in the western Dakotas and northeast Wyoming

elder: a person who is honored for his or her age and experience

Pinta: one of the three ships under Columbus's command during his first trip to the Americas

White Buffalo Calf Woman Brings the First Pipe

Joseph Chasing Horse of the Lakota people tells the story of the White Buffalo Calf Woman.

We **Lakota** people have a **prophecy** about the white buffalo calf. How that prophecy originated was that we have a sacred bundle, a sacred pipe, that was brought to us about 2,000 years ago by what we know as the White Buffalo Calf Woman.

The story goes that she appeared to two warriors at that time. These two warriors were out hunting buffalo . . . in the sacred **Black Hills** of South Dakota, and they saw a big body coming toward them. And they saw that it was a white buffalo calf. As it came closer to them, it turned into a beautiful young Indian girl.

[At] that time one of the warriors [had bad thoughts] and so the young girl told him to step forward. And when he did step forward, a black cloud came over his body, and when the black cloud disappeared, the warrior who had bad thoughts was left with no flesh or blood on his bones. The other warrior kneeled and began to pray.

And when he prayed, the white buffalo calf, who was now an Indian girl told him to go back to his people and warn them that in four days she was going to bring a sacred bundle.

So the warrior did as he was told. He went back to his people, and he gathered all the **elders,** and all the

Kiowa animal hide calendar

leaders, and all the people in a circle and told them what she had instructed him to do. And sure enough, just as she said she would, on the fourth day, she came.

They say a cloud came down from the sky, and off of the cloud stepped the white buffalo calf. As it rolled onto the earth, the calf stood up and became this beautiful young woman who was carrying the sacred bundle in her hand.

As she entered into the circle of the nation, she sang a sacred song and took the sacred bundle to the people who were there to take [it from] her.

. . . And she instructed our people that as long as we performed these ceremonies we would always remain caretakers and guardians of sacred land. She told us that as long as we took care of it and respected it that our people would never die and would always live.

The sacred bundle is known as the White Buffalo Calf Pipe because it was brought by the White Buffalo Calf Woman. . . .

When White Buffalo Calf Woman promised to return again, she made some prophecies at that time. One of those prophecies was that the birth of a white buffalo calf would be a sign that it would be near the time when she would return again to purify the world. What she meant by that was that she would bring back [spiritual] harmony. . . .

Astrolabe

Columbus Crosses the Atlantic

Personal Records

Christopher Columbus reached the new world on October 12, 1492. At sea for over two months, his sailors worried that they would not find land before their food and water ran out. Columbus's entries in his logs show the mood of his crew, and their impressions of the natives.

October 11:

The crew of the **Pinta** spotted some . . . reeds and some other plants; they also saw what looked like a small board or plank. A stick was recovered that looks man-made, perhaps carved with an iron tool . . . but even these few [things] made the crew breathe easier; in fact the men have even become cheerful.

October 12:

The islanders came to the ships' boats, swimming and bringing us parrots and balls of cotton thread . . . which they exchanged for . . . glass beads and hawk bells . . . they took and gave of what they had very willingly, but it seemed to me that they were poor in every way. They bore no weapons, nor were they acquainted with them, because when I showed them swords they seized them by the edge and so cut themselves from ignorance.

Analyzing Primary Sources

1. What did the Indian girl tell the Lakota warriors?
2. What prophecy did the White Buffalo Calf Woman make to the people?
3. What does the use of the animal hide tell you about the people who made the calendar?
4. Why were the members of Columbus's crew cheerful when they spied the objects at sea?

Colonial Settlement

Early America was a nation of people unafraid to experiment. Because colonists often had to learn new ways of obtaining food and shelter in a primitive country, they grew to appreciate ingenuity. Because of the need to cooperate—for companionship, and even for survival—they overlooked the differences in cultures that separated them in the old country. As you read these primary source selections, think about how the necessity to adapt affected the way the colonists approached everyday situations.

Reader's Dictionary

enlightened: informed

haughty: proud, vain

indigence: poverty

habitation: home

phial: small bottle

blunder: mistake

tolerable: satisfactory

What is an American?

 **Printed Publications**

J. Hector St. John Crevecoeur of France traveled widely in the American colonies and farmed in New York. His Letters from an American Farmer *was published in 1782.*

I wish I could be acquainted with the feelings and thoughts which must . . . present themselves to the mind of an **enlightened** Englishman, when he first lands on the continent. . . . If he travels through our rural districts he views not the hostile castle, and the **haughty** mansion, contrasted with the clay-built hut and miserable cabin, where cattle and men help to keep each other warm, and dwell in meanness, smoke, and **indigence.** A pleasing uniformity of decent competence appears throughout our **habitations.** The meanest of our log-houses is dry and comfortable. . . . What then is the American, this new man? He is either a European, or the descendant of a European, hence that strange mixture of blood, which you will find in no other country. I could point out to you a family whose grandfather was an Englishman, whose wife was Dutch, and whose son married a French woman, and whose present four sons have now four wives of different nations. . . . There is room for everybody in America; has he particular talent, or industry? He exerts it in order to produce a livelihood, and it succeeds. . . .

Butter churn

Ben Franklin

Personal Records

We often think of Benjamin Franklin as a successful diplomat and inventor. In 1750, Franklin wrote to a friend about an experiment that did not go as well as he had planned.

I have lately made an experiment in electricity, that I desire never to repeat. Two nights ago, being about to kill a turkey by the shock from two large glass jars, containing as much electrical fire as forty common **phials,** I . . . took the whole [charge] through my own arms and body, by receiving the fire from the united top wires with one hand, while the other held a chain connected with the outsides of both jars. The company present (whose talking to me, and to one another, I supposed occasioned my inattention to what I was about) say, that the flash was very great, and the crack as loud as a pistol; yet, my senses being instantly gone, I neither saw the one nor heard the other. . . . Nothing remains now of this shock, but a soreness in my breast-bone, which feels as if it had been bruised. I did not fall, but suppose I should have been knocked down, if I had received the stroke in my head. The whole was over in less than a minute.

You may communicate this to Mr. Bowdoin, as a caution to him, but do not make it more public, for I am ashamed to have been guilty of so notorious a **blunder;**. . . . I am yours . . .

    B. Franklin

P.S. The jars hold six gallons each.

Penn's Colony

Personal Records

In a letter written in 1683, William Penn describes the growth of his colony.

Our capital town is advanced to about 150 very **tolerable** houses for wooden ones; they are chiefly on both the navigable rivers that bound the ends or sides of the town. The farmers have got their winter corn in the ground. I suppose we may be 500 farmers strong. I settle them in villages, dividing 5,000 acres among ten, fifteen, or twenty families, as their ability is to plant it. . . .

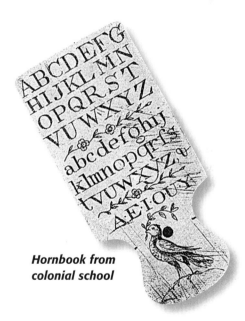

Hornbook from colonial school

Analyzing Primary Sources

1. How does de Crevecoeur describe the typical home in the colonies in the late 1700s?
2. What do you think Franklin was trying to learn with his experiment?
3. During what season of the year did Penn write this letter? How can you tell?

left

Creating a Nation

In settling North America, the colonists developed a sense that they were taking part in the birth of a new society, where people had the opportunity to better themselves. As you read these primary source selections, think about the reasons the colonists began to find fault with Great Britain. What words would you use to describe the American "spirit" that made them determined to fight for independence?

Reader's Dictionary

sovereign: king or leader

destitute: lacking

procure: gain or obtain

gall: to become sore by rubbing

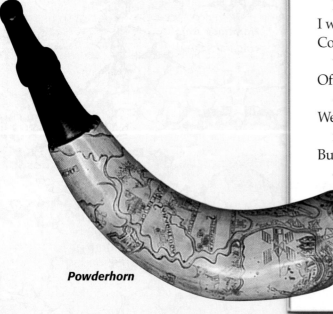

Powderhorn

Common Sense

In Common Sense, *written in January 1776, patriot Thomas Paine called upon the colonists to break away from Great Britain.*

Every thing that is right begs for separation from [Great] Britain. The Americans who have been killed seem to say, 'TIS TIME TO PART. England and America are located a great distance apart. That is itself strong and natural proof that God never expected one to rule over the other.

The Bold Americans

Broadside ballads—emotionally-charged story poems printed on a single sheet of paper—were distributed widely and helped fuel colonists' passion for freedom.

Come all you bold young Bostonians, come
    listen unto me:
I will sing you a song concerning liberty.
Concerning liberty, my boys, the truth I will
    unfold,
Of the bold Americans, who scorn to be
    controlled.
We'll honor George, our **sovereign,** on any
    reasonable terms,
But if he don't grant us liberty, we'll all lay down
    our arms.
        But if he will grant us liberty, so plainly
           shall you see,
        We are the boys that fear no noise!
           Success to liberty!

Surviving at Valley Forge

Below are excerpts from the personal records of two different people who served at Valley Forge. The first selection is by Albigence Waldo, a surgeon who tended the sick and injured.

I am sick—discontented . . . Poor food—hard lodging—cold weather—fatigue—nasty cloathes—nasty cookery. . . . I can't endure it—Why are we sent here to starve and freeze? . . .

In this selection, soldier Joseph Plumb Martin, age 16 at the time, remembers the hardships on the way to Valley Forge.

The army was not only starved but naked. The greatest part were not only shirtless and barefoot, but **destitute** of all other clothing, especially blankets. I **procured** a small piece of rawhide and made myself a pair of moccasins, which

Military drum of the American Revolution

kept my feet (while they lasted) from the frozen ground, although, as I well remember, the hard edges so **galled** my ankles, while on a march, that it was with much difficulty and pain that I could wear them afterwards; but the only alternative I had was to endure this inconvenience or to go barefoot, as hundreds of my companions had to, till they might be tracked by their bloods upon the rough frozen ground.

Immigrant Life in America

A German immigrant wrote this account of his experiences.

But during the voyage there is on board these ships terrible misery, stench, fumes, horror, vomiting, many kinds of sea-sickness, fever . . . all of which comes from old and sharply salted food and meat, also from very bad and foul water, so that many die miserably. . . .

Many parents must sell and trade away their children like so many head of cattle. . . . [I]t often happens that such parents and children, after leaving the ship, do not see each other again for many years, perhaps no more in all their lives.

Analyzing Primary Sources

1. What is the main point that Thomas Paine makes in the excerpt from *Common Sense*?
2. What do the bold Americans scorn?
3. What might have kept the soldiers from leaving Valley Forge, under such horrible conditions?

The New Republic

The Constitution established a completely new framework of government that was meant to be flexible and lasting. Along with the excitement of starting a new nation came challenges and growing pains. Many people, both American-born and foreign-born, wondered: Can this new kind of government last? As you read these primary source selections, think about how well the government served the people as the nation grew.

Reader's Dictionary

gallery: outdoor balcony

proclamation: announcement

agitated: upset and nervous

ungainly: awkward, clumsy

plainest manner: in a simple way

discord: disagreement, conflict

rapture: joy

marsh: soft, wet land

corduroy-road: a road made of logs laid side by side

Washington's First Inaugural

Personal Records

Pennsylvania Senator William Maclay was one of the many witnesses to the nation's first presidential inauguration.

The President was conducted out of the middle window into the **gallery** [overlooking Wall Street], and the oath was administered by the Chancellor [the highest judicial officer in the state of New York]. Notice that the business done was communicated to the crowd by **proclamation** . . . who gave three cheers, and repeated it on the President's bowing to them.

As the company returned into the Senate chamber, the President took the chair and the Senators and Representatives their seats. He rose, and all arose also, and [he] addressed them. This great man was **agitated** and embarrassed more than ever he was by the leveled cannon or pointed musket. He trembled, and several times could scarce make out to read, though it must be supposed he had often read it before. . . . When he came to the words *all the world*, he made a flourish with his right hand, which left rather an **ungainly** impression. I sincerely, for my part, wished all set ceremony in the hands of the dancing-masters, and that this first of men had read off his address in the **plainest manner,** without ever taking his eyes from the paper, for I felt hurt that he was not first in everything.

Copy of letter written by President Washington

Song of Liberty

Songs & Poems

The following song is one of the hundreds of anonymous patriotic songs written, printed, and distributed in little song books during the early 1800s.

The fruits of our country, our flocks and
   our fleeces,
What treasures immense, in our mountains
   that lie,
While **discord** is tearing Old Europe to
   pieces,
Shall amply the wants of the people
   supply;
New roads and canals, on their bosoms
   conveying,
Refinement and wealth through our forests
   shall roam,
And millions of freemen, with **rapture**
   surveying,
Shall shout out "O Liberty! this is thy home!"

*Flag flown at
Fort McHenry
during War of
1812*

On the Road

Printed Publications

David Stevenson described a journey by stage-coach along a typical route of the time.

Sometimes our way lay for miles through extensive **marshes,** which we crossed by **corduroy-roads.** . . . At others the coach stuck fast in mud, from which it could be [moved] only by the combined efforts of the coachman and passengers; at one place we traveled . . . through a forest flooded with water, which stood to a height of several feet. . . . The distance of the route from Pittsburgh to Erie is 128 miles, which was accomplished in forty-six hours . . . although the [stagecoach] by which I traveled carried the mail, and stopped only for breakfast, dinner and tea, but there was considerable delay by the coach being once upset and several times "mired."

A woman named Elizabeth Smith Geer wrote about winter travel in her diary:

My children gave out with cold and fatigue and could not travel, and the boys had to unhitch the oxen and bring them and carry the children on to camp. It was so cold and numb I could not tell by feeling that I had any feet at all. . . . I have not told you half we suffered.

Analyzing Primary Sources

1. What was it about Washington's public speaking manner that Maclay criticized?
2. In the song, what does the phrase "treasures immense" mean?
3. How did roads of the early 1800s differ from roads that we travel on today?

The Growing Nation

In the early 1800s, the United States had a firmly established democracy, but the freedoms it guaranteed did not extend to everyone. Native Americans were forced from their lands, while African Americans were enslaved—torn from their homelands and often separated from their families. As you read these primary source selections, think about how long these conditions existed before ideas of reform began to take hold.

Reader's Dictionary

detachment: group or body of people

inclemency: harsh conditions

auction block: site where enslaved people were bought and sold

piteous: sad, distressed

vociferously: loudly

battery: a grouping of weapons

rent: opened or parted

Trail of Tears

 **Printed Publications**

Although recognized as a separate nation by several U.S. treaties, the Cherokee people were forced to leave their lands because white people wanted it for farming. Thousands died before they reached Indian Territory, the present-day state of Oklahoma. This forced journey came to be called the Trail of Tears. A newspaper published this account.

On Tuesday evening we fell in with a **detachment** of the poor Cherokee Indians . . . about eleven hundred Indians—sixty wagons—six hundred horses, and perhaps forty pairs of oxen. We found them in the forest camped for the night by the road side . . . under a severe fall of rain accompanied by heavy wind. With their canvas for a shield from the **inclemency** of the weather, and the cold wet ground for a resting place, after the fatigue of the day, they spent the night . . . many of the aged Indians were suffering extremely from the fatigue of the journey, and the ill health consequent upon it . . . several were then quite ill, and one aged man we were informed was then in the last struggles of death.

Map of Georgia in 1826 showing Cherokee land (left) and seal of Cherokee Nation (right)

Delicia Patterson

Oral Histories

Delicia Patterson provided this look at life under slavery. She was 92 years old when she was interviewed.

I was born in Boonville, Missouri, January 2, 1845. Mother had five children but raised only two of us. I was owned by Charles Mitchell until I was fifteen years old. They were fairly nice to all of their slaves. . . .

When I was fifteen years old, I was brought to the courthouse, put up on the **auction block** to be sold. Old Judge Miller from my county was there. I knew him well because he was one of the wealthiest slave owners in the county, and the meanest one. He was so cruel all the slaves and many owners hated him because of it. He saw me on the block for sale, and he knew I was a good worker. So, when he bid for me, I spoke right out on the auction block and told him:

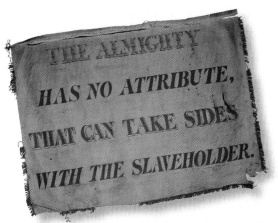

Anti-slavery banner

"Old Judge Miller, don't you bid for me, 'cause if you do, I would not live on your plantation. I will take a knife and cut my own throat from ear to ear before I would be owned by you. . . ."

So he stepped back and let someone else bid for me. . . . So I was sold to a Southern Englishman named Thomas Steele for fifteen hundred dollars. . . .

Religious Camp Meeting

Personal Records

The desire for self-improvement was closely connected to a renewed interest in religion. By the 1830s, the Second Great Awakening, the second great period of religious revival in the United States, was in full swing. The camp meeting was especially important to isolated frontier families. One preacher, James Finley, described a revival meeting:

The noise was like the roar of Niagara. . . . Some of the people were singing, others praying, some crying for mercy in the most **piteous** accents, while others were shouting most **vociferously**. . . . At one time I saw at least five hundred swept down in a moment, as if a **battery** of a thousand guns had been opened upon them, and then immediately followed shrieks and shouts that **rent** the very heavens.

Analyzing Primary Sources

1. Do you think the writer of the newspaper article feels sympathy toward the Cherokee?
2. Why did Delicia, the formerly enslaved woman, not want to serve on Judge Miller's plantation?
3. What scene is James Finley describing?

Civil War and Reconstruction

The American Civil War, or the War Between the States, was a major turning point for the American people. When the fighting ended, 600,000 Americans had lost their lives, slavery had been abolished, and most of the South lay in ruin. Leaders argued over how to reunite the shattered nation. And even though slavery had been abolished, African Americans quickly discovered that freedom did not mean equality. As you read these selections, think about the changes that took place during this era.

Reader's Dictionary

exterminating: destructive

bondage: slavery

suffrage: the right to vote

musket: soldier's rifle

Swing Low, Sweet Chariot

 Songs & Poems

Spirituals—songs of salvation—provided the enslaved African Americans who wrote and sang them with not only a measure of comfort in bleak times but with a means for communicating secretly among themselves.

Swing low, sweet chariot,
Coming for to carry me home,
Swing low, sweet chariot,
Coming for to carry me home.

I looked over Jordan and what
    did I see
Coming for to carry me home,
A band of angels coming after me.
Coming for to carry me home.

If you get there before I do,
Coming for to carry me home,
Tell all my friends I'm coming too,
Coming for to carry me home.

I'm sometimes up and sometimes down,
Coming for to carry me home,
But still my soul feels heavenly bound,
Coming for to carry me home.

The Fisk Jubilee Singers

On the Plight of African Americans

In 1867 Frederick Douglass appealed eloquently to Congress on behalf of African Americans.

. . . Yet the Negroes have marvelously survived all the **exterminating** forces of slavery, and have emerged at the end of 250 years of **bondage,** not [sad and hateful], but cheerful, hopeful, and forgiving. They now stand before Congress and the country, not complaining of the past, but simply asking for a better future.

. . . It is true that a strong plea for equal **suffrage** might be addressed to the national sense of honor. Something, too, might be said of national gratitude. A nation might well hesitate before the temptation to betray its allies. There is something . . . mean, to say nothing of the cruelty, in placing the loyal Negroes of the South under the political power of their rebel masters. . . . We asked the Negroes to [support] our cause, to be our friends, to fight for us and against their masters; and now, after they have done all that we asked them to do . . . it is proposed in some quarters to turn them over to the political control of the common enemy of the government and of the Negro. . . .

What, then, is the work before Congress? . . . In a word, it must [allow African Americans to vote], and by means of the loyal Negroes and the loyal white men of the South build up a national party there, and in time bridge the [gap] between North and South, so that our country may have a common liberty and a common civilization. . . .

The Fire of Battle

Union soldier George Sargent served in the area west of Washington, D.C., throughout the Shenandoah Valley. He wrote his impressions of how soldiers react in battle.

Can you imagine a fellow's feelings about that time, to have to face thousands of **muskets** with a prospect of having a bullet put through you? If you can, all right; I can't describe it. I've heard some say that they were not scared going into a fight, but I think it's all nonsense. I don't believe there was ever a man who went into battle but was scared, more or less. Some will turn pale as a sheet, look wild and ferocious, some will be so excited that they don't know what they are about while others will be as cool and collected as on other occasions.

Analyzing Primary Sources

1. What does "Swing Low, Sweet Chariot" show about the condition and faith of the people who sang it?
2. What did Frederick Douglass urge Congress to do?
3. What does George Sargent say happens to all soldiers in battle?

Modern America Emerges

In the years following the Civil War modern American was born. The United States became an urban industrial nation. Millions of immigrants came to the United States following the promise of freedom and economic opportunity. As its society became more diverse, Americans struggled to end discrimination at home and to preserve freedom overseas. In the twenty-first century, Americans faced the challenge of fighting terrorism to preserve freedom. As you examine these selections, think of the challenges and opportunities facing the United States today.

Reader's Dictionary

extremism: the holding of unreasonable views

humanitarian: committed to improving the lives of other people

pluralism: society with different ethnic and religious groups

tolerance: acceptance of and fairness toward people who hold different views

Proud to Be an American

"God Bless the USA," by singer Lee Greenwood, topped the country music charts in the 1980s. It was adopted as a theme song for President Reagan's 1984 reelection campaign.

I'm proud to be an American
where at least I know I'm free,
And I won't forget the men who died
who gave that right to me,
And I gladly stand up next to you
and defend her still today,
'Cause there ain't no doubt I love this land
God Bless the U.S.A.

Address to Congress

On September 20, 2001, President George W. Bush addressed Congress, nine days after New York City and Washington, D.C., were shaken by suicide aircraft attacks.

On September the eleventh, enemies of freedom committed an act of war against our country. Americans have known wars—but for the past 136 years, they have been wars on foreign soil, except for one Sunday in 1941 [the attack on Pearl Harbor]. Americans have known the casualties of war—but not at the center of a great city on a peaceful morning. Americans have known surprise attacks—but never before on thousands of civilians. All of this was brought upon us in a single day—and night fell on a different world, a world where freedom itself is under attack. . . .

The terrorists [who carried out the attack] practice a fringe form of Islamic **extremism** that has been rejected by Muslim scholars and the vast majority of Muslim clerics— a fringe movement that perverts the peaceful teachings of Islam. . . .

This group [al-Qaeda] and its leader, a person named Osama bin Laden, are linked to many other organizations in different countries. . . . The leadership of al-Qaeda has great influence in Afghanistan and supports the Taliban regime in controlling most of that country. . . .

The United States respects the people of Afghanistan—after all, we are currently its largest source of **humanitarian** aid—but we condemn the Taliban regime.

[The terrorists] hate what we see right here in this chamber—a democratically elected government. Their leaders are self-appointed. They hate our freedoms—our freedom of religion, our freedom of speech, our freedom to vote and assemble and disagree with each other. . . .

This is not, however, just America's fight. And what is at stake is not just America's freedom. This is the world's fight. This is civilization's fight. This is the fight of all who believe in progress and **pluralism, tolerance,** and freedom. . . .

The civilized world is rallying to America's side. They understand that if this terror goes unpunished, their own cities, their own citizens may be next. Terror, unanswered, can not

President Bush thanks rescue workers

only bring down buildings, it can threaten the stability of legitimate governments. And we will not allow it. . . .

I ask you to uphold the values of America, and remember why so many have come here. We are in a fight for our principles, and our first responsibility is to live by them. No one should be singled out for unfair treatment or unkind words because of their ethnic background or religious faith. . . .

Great harm has been done to us. We have suffered great loss. And in our grief and anger we have found our mission and our moment. Freedom and fear are at war. The advance of human freedom—the great achievement of our time, and the great hope of every time— now depends on us. Our Nation—this generation—will lift a dark threat of violence from our people and our future. We will rally the world to this cause, by our efforts and by our courage. We will not tire, we will not falter, and we will not fail.

Analyzing Primary Sources

1. What themes does Lee Greenwood express in his song?
2. To what other tragic event does President Bush compare the events of September 11, 2001?
3. Why does the president believe other nations should help in the fight against terrorism?

Presidents of the United States

In this resource you will find portraits of the individuals who served as presidents of the United States, along with their occupations, political party affiliations, and other interesting facts.

**The Republican Party during this period developed into today's Democratic Party. Today's Republican Party originated in 1854.

1 George Washington

Presidential term: 1789–1797
Lived: 1732–1799
Born in: Virginia
Elected from: Virginia
Occupations: Soldier, Planter
Party: None
Vice President: John Adams

2 John Adams

Presidential term: 1797–1801
Lived: 1735–1826
Born in: Massachusetts
Elected from: Massachusetts
Occupations: Teacher, Lawyer
Party: Federalist
Vice President: Thomas Jefferson

3 Thomas Jefferson

Presidential term: 1801–1809
Lived: 1743–1826
Born in: Virginia
Elected from: Virginia
Occupations: Planter, Lawyer
Party: Republican**
Vice Presidents: Aaron Burr, George Clinton

4 James Madison

Presidential term: 1809–1817
Lived: 1751–1836
Born in: Virginia
Elected from: Virginia
Occupation: Planter
Party: Republican**
Vice Presidents: George Clinton, Elbridge Gerry

5 James Monroe

Presidential term: 1817–1825
Lived: 1758–1831
Born in: Virginia
Elected from: Virginia
Occupation: Lawyer
Party: Republican**
Vice President: Daniel D. Tompkins

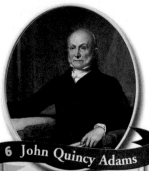

6 John Quincy Adams

Presidential term: 1825–1829
Lived: 1767–1848
Born in: Massachusetts
Elected from: Massachusetts
Occupation: Lawyer
Party: Republican**
Vice President: John C. Calhoun

7 Andrew Jackson

Presidential term: 1829–1837
Lived: 1767–1845
Born in: South Carolina
Elected from: Tennessee
Occupations: Lawyer, Soldier
Party: Democratic
Vice Presidents: John C. Calhoun, Martin Van Buren

8 Martin Van Buren

Presidential term: 1837–1841
Lived: 1782–1862
Born in: New York
Elected from: New York
Occupation: Lawyer
Party: Democratic
Vice President: Richard M.
　　Johnson

9 William H. Harrison

Presidential term: 1841
Lived: 1773–1841
Born in: Virginia
Elected from: Ohio
Occupations: Soldier, Planter
Party: Whig
Vice President: John Tyler

10 John Tyler

Presidential term: 1841–1845
Lived: 1790–1862
Born in: Virginia
Elected as V.P. from: Virginia
Succeeded Harrison
Occupation: Lawyer
Party: Whig
Vice President: None

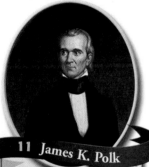

11 James K. Polk

Presidential term: 1845–1849
Lived: 1795–1849
Born in: North Carolina
Elected from: Tennessee
Occupation: Lawyer
Party: Democratic
Vice President: George M.
　　Dallas

12 Zachary Taylor

Presidential term: 1849–1850
Lived: 1784–1850
Born in: Virginia
Elected from: Louisiana
Occupation: Soldier
Party: Whig
Vice President: Millard
　　Fillmore

13 Millard Fillmore

Presidential term: 1850–1853
Lived: 1800–1874
Born in: New York
Elected as V.P. from: New York
Succeeded Taylor
Occupation: Lawyer
Party: Whig
Vice President: None

14 Franklin Pierce

Presidential term: 1853–1857
Lived: 1804–1869
Born in: New Hampshire
Elected from: New Hampshire
Occupation: Lawyer
Party: Democratic
Vice President: William R. King

15 James Buchanan

Presidential term: 1857–1861
Lived: 1791–1868
Born in: Pennsylvania
Elected from: Pennsylvania
Occupation: Lawyer
Party: Democratic
Vice President: John C.
　　Breckinridge

16 Abraham Lincoln

Presidential term: 1861–1865
Lived: 1809–1865
Born in: Kentucky
Elected from: Illinois
Occupation: Lawyer
Party: Republican
Vice Presidents: Hannibal
　　Hamlin, Andrew Johnson

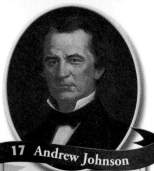

17 Andrew Johnson

Presidential term: 1865–1869
Lived: 1808–1875
Born in: North Carolina
Elected as V.P. from: Tennessee
Succeeded Lincoln
Occupation: Tailor
Party: Republican
Vice President: None

18 Ulysses S. Grant

Presidential term: 1869–1877
Lived: 1822–1885
Born in: Ohio
Elected from: Illinois
Occupations: Farmer, Soldier
Party: Republican
Vice Presidents: Schuyler Colfax,
Henry Wilson

19 Rutherford B. Hayes

Presidential term: 1877–1881
Lived: 1822–1893
Born in: Ohio
Elected from: Ohio
Occupation: Lawyer
Party: Republican
Vice President: William A.
Wheeler

20 James A. Garfield

Presidential term: 1881
Lived: 1831–1881
Born in: Ohio
Elected from: Ohio
Occupations: Laborer, Professor
Party: Republican
Vice President: Chester A.
Arthur

21 Chester A. Arthur

Presidential term: 1881–1885
Lived: 1830–1886
Born in: Vermont
Elected as V.P. from: New York
Succeeded Garfield
Occupations: Teacher, Lawyer
Party: Republican
Vice President: None

22 Grover Cleveland

Presidential term: 1885–1889
Lived: 1837–1908
Born in: New Jersey
Elected from: New York
Occupation: Lawyer
Party: Democratic
Vice President: Thomas A.
Hendricks

23 Benjamin Harrison

Presidential term: 1889–1893
Lived: 1833–1901
Born in: Ohio
Elected from: Indiana
Occupation: Lawyer
Party: Republican
Vice President: Levi P. Morton

24 Grover Cleveland

Presidential term: 1893–1897
Lived: 1837–1908
Born in: New Jersey
Elected from: New York
Occupation: Lawyer
Party: Democratic
Vice President: Adlai E.
Stevenson

25 William McKinley

Presidential term: 1897–1901
Lived: 1843–1901
Born in: Ohio
Elected from: Ohio
Occupations: Teacher, Lawyer
Party: Republican
Vice Presidents: Garret Hobart,
Theodore Roosevelt

26 Theodore Roosevelt

Presidential term: 1901–1909
Lived: 1858–1919
Born in: New York
Elected as V.P. from: New York
Succeeded McKinley
Occupations: Historian, Rancher
Party: Republican
Vice President: Charles W.
   Fairbanks

27 William H. Taft

Presidential term: 1909–1913
Lived: 1857–1930
Born in: Ohio
Elected from: Ohio
Occupation: Lawyer
Party: Republican
Vice President: James S.
   Sherman

28 Woodrow Wilson

Presidential term: 1913–1921
Lived: 1856–1924
Born in: Virginia
Elected from: New Jersey
Occupation: College Professor
Party: Democratic
Vice President: Thomas R.
   Marshall

29 Warren G. Harding

Presidential term: 1921–1923
Lived: 1865–1923
Born in: Ohio
Elected from: Ohio
Occupations: Newspaper Editor,
   Publisher
Party: Republican
Vice President: Calvin Coolidge

30 Calvin Coolidge

Presidential term: 1923–1929
Lived: 1872–1933
Born in: Vermont
Elected as V.P. from:
   Massachusetts
Succeeded Harding
Occupation: Lawyer
Party: Republican
Vice President: Charles G. Dawes

31 Herbert C. Hoover

Presidential term: 1929–1933
Lived: 1874–1964
Born in: Iowa
Elected from: California
Occupation: Engineer
Party: Republican
Vice President: Charles Curtis

32 Franklin D. Roosevelt

Presidential term: 1933–1945
Lived: 1882–1945
Born in: New York
Elected from: New York
Occupation: Lawyer
Party: Democratic
Vice Presidents: John N. Garner,
   Henry A. Wallace, Harry S
   Truman

33 Harry S Truman

Presidential term: 1945–1953
Lived: 1884–1972
Born in: Missouri
Elected as V.P. from: Missouri
Succeeded Roosevelt
Occupations: Clerk, Farmer
Party: Democratic
Vice President: Alben W.
   Barkley

34 Dwight D. Eisenhower

Presidential term: 1953–1961
Lived: 1890–1969
Born in: Texas
Elected from: New York
Occupation: Soldier
Party: Republican
Vice President: Richard M.
   Nixon

35 John F. Kennedy

Presidential term: 1961–1963
Lived: 1917–1963
Born in: Massachusetts
Elected from: Massachusetts
Occupations: Author, Reporter
Party: Democratic
Vice President: Lyndon B. Johnson

36 Lyndon B. Johnson

Presidential term: 1963–1969
Lived: 1908–1973
Born in: Texas
Elected as V.P. from: Texas
Succeeded Kennedy
Occupation: Teacher
Party: Democratic
Vice President: Hubert H. Humphrey

37 Richard M. Nixon

Presidential term: 1969–1974
Lived: 1913–1994
Born in: California
Elected from: New York
Occupation: Lawyer
Party: Republican
Vice Presidents: Spiro T. Agnew, Gerald R. Ford

38 Gerald R. Ford

Presidential term: 1974–1977
Lived: 1913–
Born in: Nebraska
Appointed as V.P. upon Agnew's resignation; succeeded Nixon
Occupation: Lawyer
Party: Republican
Vice President: Nelson A. Rockefeller

39 James E. Carter, Jr.

Presidential term: 1977–1981
Lived: 1924–
Born in: Georgia
Elected from: Georgia
Occupations: Business, Farmer
Party: Democratic
Vice President: Walter F. Mondale

40 Ronald W. Reagan

Presidential term: 1981–1989
Lived: 1911–2004
Born in: Illinois
Elected from: California
Occupations: Actor, Lecturer
Party: Republican
Vice President: George H.W. Bush

41 George H.W. Bush

Presidential term: 1989–1993
Lived: 1924–
Born in: Massachusetts
Elected from: Texas
Occupation: Business
Party: Republican
Vice President: J. Danforth Quayle

42 William J. Clinton

Presidential term: 1993–2001
Lived: 1946–
Born in: Arkansas
Elected from: Arkansas
Occupation: Lawyer
Party: Democratic
Vice President: Albert Gore, Jr.

43 George W. Bush

Presidential term: 2001–
Lived: 1946–
Born in: Connecticut
Elected from: Texas
Occupation: Business
Party: Republican
Vice President: Richard B. Cheney

The Magna Carta

The Magna Carta, signed by King John in 1215, marked a decisive step forward in the development of constitutional government in England. Later, it became a model for colonists who carried the Magna Carta's guarantees of legal and political rights to America.

1. . . . [T]hat the English Church shall be free, and shall have its rights entire, and its liberties unimpaired. . . . we have also granted for us and our heirs forever, all the liberties written out below, to have and to keep for them and their heirs, of us and our heirs:

39. No free man shall be seized or imprisoned, or stripped of his rights or possessions, or outlawed or exiled, or deprived of his standing in any other way, nor will we proceed with force against him, or send others to do so, except by the lawful judgment of his equals, or by the law of the land.

40. To no one will we sell, to no one deny or delay right or justice.

41. All merchants may enter or leave England unharmed and without fear, and may stay or travel within it, by land or water, for purposes of trade, free from all illegal exactions, in accordance with ancient and lawful customs. This, however, does not apply in time of war to merchants from a country that is at war with us. . . .

42. In future it shall be lawful for any man to leave and return to our kingdom unharmed and without fear, by land or water, preserving his allegiance to us, except in time of war, for some short period, for the common benefit of the realm. . . .

60. All these customs and liberties that we have granted shall be observed in our kingdom in so far as concerns our own relations with our subjects. Let all men of our kingdom, whether clergy or laymen, observe them similarly in their relations with their own men. . . .

63. . . . Both we and the barons have sworn that all this shall be observed in good faith and without deceit. Witness the abovementioned people and many others. Given by our hand in the meadow that is called Runnymede, between Windsor and Staines, on the fifteenth day of June in the seventeenth year of our reign.

Illuminated manuscript, Middle Ages

The Mayflower Compact

On November 21, 1620, 41 colonists aboard the Mayflower drafted this agreement. The Mayflower Compact was the first plan of self-government ever put in force in the English colonies.

In the Name of God, Amen. We, whose names are underwritten, the Loyal Subjects of our dread Sovereign Lord King James, by the Grace of God, of Great Britain, France, and Ireland, King, Defender of the Faith, etc. Having undertaken for the Glory of God, and Advancement of the Christian Faith, and the Honour of our King and Country, a Voyage to plant the first Colony in the northern Parts of Virginia; Do by these Presents, solemnly and mutually, in the Presence of God and one another, covenant and combine ourselves together into a civil Body Politick, for our better Ordering and Preservation, and Furtherance of the Ends aforesaid: And by Virtue hereof do enact, constitute, and frame, such just and equal Laws, Ordinances, Acts, Constitutions, and Officers, from time to time, as shall be thought most meet and convenient for the general Good of the Colony; unto which we promise all due Submission and Obedience. In Witness whereof we have hereunto subscribed our names at Cape-Cod the eleventh of November, in the Reign of our Sovereign Lord King James, of England, France, and Ireland, the eighteenth, and of Scotland, the fifty-fourth, Anno Domini, 1620.

The Fundamental Orders of Connecticut

In January 1639, settlers in Connecticut, led by Thomas Hooker, drew up the Fundamental Orders of Connecticut—America's first written Constitution. It is essentially a compact among the settlers and a body of laws.

Forasmuch as it has pleased the Almighty God by the wise disposition of His Divine Providence so to order and dispose of things that we, the inhabitants and residents of Windsor, Hartford, and Wethersfield are now cohabiting and dwelling in and upon the river of Conectecotte and the lands thereunto adjoining; and well knowing where a people are gathered together the Word of God requires that, to maintain the peace and union of such a people, there should be an orderly and decent government established according to God, . . . do therefore associate and conjoin ourselves to be as one public state or commonwealth. . . .

1. It is ordered . . . . that there shall be yearly two general assemblies or courts; . . . The first shall be called the Court of Election, wherein shall be yearly chosen . . . so many magistrates and other public officers as shall be found requisite. Whereof one to be chosen governor . . . and no other magistrate to be chosen for more than one year; provided always there be six chosen besides the governor . . . by all that are admitted freemen and have taken the oath of fidelity, and do cohabit within this jurisdiction. . . .

The English Bill of Rights

In 1689 William of Orange and his wife, Mary, became joint rulers of England after accepting what became known as the Bill of Rights. This document assured the people of certain basic civil rights.

. . . And thereupon the said lords spiritual and temporal and commons . . . do . . . declare That the pretended power of suspending of laws or the execution of laws by regal authority without consent of parliment is illegal. . . .

That levying money for or to the use of the crown . . . without grant of parliament for longer time or in other manner than the same is or shall be granted is illegal.

That it is the right of the subjects to petition the king and all commitments and prosecutions for such petitioning are illegal.

That the raising or keeping a standing army within the kingdom in time of peace unless it be with consent of parliament is against law. . . .

That election of members of parliament ought to be free. . . .

That excessive bail ought not to be required nor excessive fines imposed nor cruel and unusual punishments inflicted. . . .

Seal of William and Mary

The Articles of Confederation

The Continental Congress attempted to establish a federal union by drawing up the Articles of Confederation in 1777. The Articles did not go into effect until 1781, however, because some states delayed approval of the new plan of government.

Articles of Confederation and Perpetual Union Between the States of New Hampshire, Massachusetts Bay, Rhode Island and Providence Plantations, Connecticut, New York, New Jersey, Pennsylvania, Delaware, Maryland, Virginia, North Carolina, South Carolina, and Georgia.

ARTICLE I.
The style of this confederacy shall be "The United States of America."

ARTICLE II.
Each state retains its sovereignty, freedom, and independence, and every power, jurisdiction, and right which is not by this confederation expressly delegated to the United States in Congress assembled.

ARTICLE III.
The said states hereby severally enter into a firm league of friendship with each other, for their common defense, the security of their liberties, and their mutual and general welfare, binding themselves to assist each other against all force offered to, or attacks made upon them, or any of them, on account of religion, sovereignty, trade, or any other pretense whatever.

ARTICLE IV.
[T]he free inhabitants of each of these states . . . shall be entitled to all privileges and immunities of free citizens in the several states. . . .

The Federalist, No. 10

James Madison wrote several articles supporting ratification of the Constitution for a New York newspaper. In the excerpt below, Madison argues for the idea of a federal republic.

By a faction, I understand a number of citizens . . . who are united and actuated by some common impulse . . . adverse to the rights of other citizens. . . .

The inference to which we are brought is that the causes of faction cannot be removed and that relief is only to be sought in the means of controlling its *effects*. . . .

James Madison

A republic, by which I mean a government in which the scheme of representation takes place . . . promises the cure for which we are seeking. . . .

The two great points of difference between a democracy and a republic are: first, the delegation of the government, in the latter, to a small number of citizens elected by the rest; secondly, the greater number of citizens, and greater sphere of country, over which the latter may be extended.

The effect of the first difference is . . . to refine and enlarge the public views, by passing them through the medium of a chosen body of citizens, whose wisdom may best discern the true interest of their country, and whose patriotism and love of justice will be least likely to sacrifice it to temporary or partial considerations. . . .

The Federalist, No. 51

In the first of these two excerpts, the writer, either Madison or Alexander Hamilton, discusses the nature of society and government. In the second excerpt, the writer reveals his thoughts about protecting individuals and groups against the will of the majority.

If men were angels, no government would be necessary. If angels were to govern men, neither external nor internal controls on government would be necessary. In framing a government which is to be administered by men over men, the great difficulty lies in this: you must first enable the government to control the governed; and in the next place oblige it to control itself. A dependence on the people is, no doubt, the primary control on the government. . . .

It is of great importance in a republic not only to guard the society against the oppression of its rulers, but to guard one part of the society against the injustice of the other part. Different interests necessarily exist in different classes of citizens. If a majority be united by a common interest, the rights of the minority will be insecure. . . . [I]n the federal republic of the United States . . . the society itself will be broken into so many parts, interests, and classes of citizens, that the rights of individuals, or of the minority, will be in little danger from interested combinations of the majority. In a free government the security for civil rights must be the same as that for religious rights. It consists in the one case in the multiplicity of interests, and in the other in the multiplicity of sects. . . .

The Federalist, No. 59

In this federalist paper, Alexander Hamilton explains why Congress, and not the states, should have the final say in how federal elections are conducted.

The natural order of the subject leads us to consider . . . that provision of the Constitution which authorizes the national legislature to regulate, in the last resort, the election of its own members. . . . Its propriety rests upon the evidence of this plain proposition, that every government ought to contain in itself the means of its own preservation. . . . Nothing can be more evident, than that an exclusive power of regulating elections for the national government, in the hands of the state legislatures, would leave the existence of the union entirely at their mercy. They could at any moment annihilate it, by neglecting to provide for the choice of persons to administer its affairs. . . .

It is certainly true that the state legislatures, by forbearing the appointment of senators, may destroy the national government. But it will not follow that, because they have a power to do this in one instance, they ought to have it in every other. . . . it is an evil; but it is an evil which could not have been avoided without excluding the states . . . from a place in the organization of the national government. If this had been done, it would doubtless have been interpreted into an entire dereliction of the federal principle; and would certainly have deprived the state governments of that absolute safeguard which they will enjoy under this provision. . . .

Washington's Farewell Address

At the end of his second term as president, George Washington spoke of the dangers facing the young nation. He warned against the dangers of political parties and sectionalism, and he advised the nation against permanent alliances with other nations.

. . . Citizens by birth or choice of a common country, that country has a right to concentrate your affections. The name of American, which belongs to you in your national capacity, must always exalt the just pride of patriotism more than any appellation derived from local discriminations. With slight shades of difference, you have the same religion, manners, habits, and political principles. You have in a common cause fought and triumphed together. . . .

In contemplating the causes which may disturb our union it occurs as matter of serious concern that any ground should have been furnished for characterizing parties by *geographical* discriminations. . . .

No alliances, however strict, between the parts can be an adequate substitute. They must inevitably experience the infractions and interruptions which all alliances in all times have experienced. . . .

The great rule of conduct for us in regard to foreign nations is, in extending our commercial relations to have with them as little *political* connection as possible. . . .

The Star-Spangled Banner

During the British bombardment of Fort McHenry during the War of 1812, a young Baltimore lawyer named Francis Scott Key was inspired to write the words to "The Star-Spangled Banner." In 1931 Congress officially declared "The Star-Spangled Banner" as our national anthem. Below are the first and fourth verses.

O! say can you see by the dawn's
early light,
What so proudly we hailed at the twilight's
last gleaming,
Whose broad stripes and bright stars
through the perilous fight,
O'er the ramparts we watch'd, were so
gallantly streaming?
And the Rockets' red glare, the Bombs
bursting in air,
Gave proof through the night that our
Flag was still there;

O! say does that star-spangled Banner
yet wave,
O'er the Land of the free, and the home
of the brave!

O! thus be it ever when freemen shall stand,
Between their lov'd home, and the war's
desolation,
Blest with vict'ry and peace, may the
Heav'n rescued land,
Praise the Power that hath made and
preserv'd us a nation!
Then conquer we must, when our cause
it is just,
And this be our motto— "In God is our
Trust;"
And the star-spangled Banner in triumph
shall wave,
O'er the Land of the Free, and the Home of
the Brave.

The Monroe Doctrine

In 1823 President James Monroe proclaimed the Monroe Doctrine. Designed to end European influence in the Western Hemisphere, it became a cornerstone of United States foreign policy.

. . . With the existing colonies or dependencies of any European power we have not interfered and shall not interfere. But with the Governments who have declared their independence and maintained it, and whose independence we have, on great consideration and on just principles, acknowledged, we could not view any interposition for the purpose of oppressing them, or controlling in any other manner their destiny, by any European power in any other light than as the manifestation of any unfriendly disposition toward the United States. . . .

Our policy in regard to Europe, which was adopted at an early stage of the wars which have so long agitated that quarter of the globe, nevertheless remains the same, which is, not to interfere in the internal concerns of any of its powers; to consider the government *de facto* as the legitimate government for us; to cultivate friendly relations with it, and to preserve those relations by a frank, firm, and manly policy, meeting in all instances the just claims of every power, submitting to injuries from none. . . .

The Seneca Falls Declaration

One of the first documents to express the desire for equal rights for women is the Declaration of Sentiments and Resolutions, issued in 1848 at the Seneca Falls Convention in Seneca Falls, New York. Led by Elizabeth Cady Stanton, the delegates adopted a set of resolutions modeled on the Declaration of Independence.

When, in the course of human events, it becomes necessary for one portion of the family of man to assume among the people of the earth a position different from that which they have hitherto occupied, but one to which the laws of nature and of nature's God entitle them, a decent respect to the opinions of mankind requires that they should declare the causes that impel them to such a course.

We hold these truths to be self-evident: that all men and women are created equal; that they are endowed by their Creator with certain inalienable rights; that among these are life, liberty, and the pursuit of happiness; that to secure these rights governments are instituted, deriving their just powers from the consent of the governed. Whenever any form of government becomes destructive of these ends, it is the right of those who suffer from it to refuse allegiance to it, and to insist upon the institution of a new government, laying its foundation on such principles, and organizing its powers in such form as to them shall seem most likely to effect their safety and happiness.

Elizabeth Cady Stanton

Documents

The Emancipation Proclamation

On January 1, 1863, President Abraham Lincoln issued the Emancipation Proclamation, which freed all enslaved people in states under Confederate control. The Proclamation was a step toward the Thirteenth Amendment (1865), which ended slavery in all of the United States.

. . . That on the 1st day of January, in the year of our Lord 1863, all persons held as slaves within any state or designated part of a state, the people whereof shall then be in rebellion against the United States, shall be then, thenceforward, and forever free; and the Executive Government of the United States, including the military and naval authority thereof, will recognize and maintain the freedom of such persons, and will do no act or acts to repress such persons, or any of them, in any efforts they may make for their actual freedom. . . .

And I further declare and make known that such persons, of suitable condition, will be received into the armed service of the United States. . . .

And upon this act, sincerely believed to be an act of justice, warranted by the Constitution upon military necessity, I invoke the considerate judgement of man-kind and the gracious favor of Almighty God. . . .

The Gettysburg Address

On November 19, 1863, President Abraham Lincoln gave a short speech at the dedication of a national cemetery on the battlefield of Gettysburg. His simple yet eloquent words expressed his hopes for a nation divided by civil war.

Four score and seven years ago our fathers brought forth on this continent a new nation, conceived in liberty, and dedicated to the proposition that all men are created equal.

Now we are engaged in a great civil war, testing whether that nation, or any nation so conceived and so dedicated, can long endure. We are met on a great battlefield of that war. We have come to dedicate a portion of that field as a final resting place for those who here gave their lives that that nation might live. It is altogether fitting and proper that we should do this.

But, in a larger sense, we can not dedicate—we can not consecrate—we can not hallow—this ground.

The brave men, living and dead, who struggled here, have consecrated it far above our poor power to add or detract. The world will little note nor long remember what we say here, but it can never forget what they did here. It is for us, the living, rather, to be dedicated here to the unfinished work which they who fought here have thus far so nobly advanced. It is rather for us to be here dedicated to the great task remaining before us—that from these honored dead we take increased devotion to that cause for which they gave the last full measure of devotion; that we here highly resolve that these dead shall not have died in vain; that this nation, under God, shall have a new birth of freedom; and that government of the people, by the people, for the people, shall not perish from the earth.

Soldier's kit, Civil War

Gettysburg Memorial

I Will Fight No More

Shield made of buffalo hide

In 1877 the Nez Perce fought the government's attempt to move them to a smaller reservation. After a remarkable attempt to escape to Canada, Chief Joseph realized that resistance was hopeless and advised his people to surrender.

Tell General Howard I know his heart. What he told me before I have in my heart. I am tired of fighting. . . . The old men are all dead. It is the young men who say yes or no. He who led the young men is dead. It is cold and we have no blankets. The little children are freezing to death. My people, some of them have run away to the hills, and have no blankets, no food; no one knows where they are—perhaps freezing to death. I want to have time to look for my children and see how many of them I can find. Maybe I shall find them among the dead. Hear me, my chiefs. I am tired; my heart is sick and sad. From where the sun now stands I will fight no more forever.

The Pledge of Allegiance

In 1892 the nation celebrated the 400th anniversary of Columbus's landing in America. In connection with this celebration, Francis Bellamy, a magazine editor, wrote and published the Pledge of Allegiance. The words "under God" were added by Congress in 1954 at the urging of President Dwight D. Eisenhower.

I pledge allegiance to the Flag of the United States of America and to the Republic for which it stands, one Nation under God, indivisible, with liberty and justice for all.

Students in a New York City school recite the Pledge of Allegiance

The American's Creed

William Tyler Page of Friendship Heights, Maryland, wrote The American's Creed. This statement of political faith summarizes the true meaning of freedom available to all Americans. The U.S. House of Representatives adopted the creed on behalf of the American people on April 3, 1918.

I believe in the United States of America as a Government of the people, by the people, for the people; whose just powers are derived from the consent of the governed; a democracy in a republic; a sovereign Nation of many sovereign States; a perfect union, one and inseparable; established upon those principles of freedom, equality, justice, and humanity for which American patriots sacrificed their lives and fortunes.

I therefore believe it is my duty to my Country to love it; to support its Constitution; to obey its laws; to respect its flag, and to defend it against all enemies.

The Fourteen Points

On January 8, 1918, President Woodrow Wilson went before Congress to offer a statement of aims called the Fourteen Points. Wilson's plan called for freedom of the seas in peace and war, an end to secret alliances, and equal trading rights for all countries. The excerpt that follows is taken from the President's message.

. . . We entered this war because violations of right had occurred which touched us to the quick and made the life of our own people impossible unless they were corrected and the world secured once for all against their recurrence. What we demand in this war, therefore, is nothing peculiar to ourselves. It is that the world be made fit and safe to live in; and particularly that it be made safe for every peace-loving nation which, like our own, wishes to live its own life, determine its own institutions, be assured of justice and fair dealing by the other peoples of the world as against force and selfish aggression. All the peoples of the world are in effect partners in this interest, and for our own part we see very clearly that unless justice be done to others it will not be done to us. The program of the world's peace, therefore, is our program; and that program, the only possible program, as we see it, is this:

I. Open covenants of peace, openly arrived at, after which there shall be no private international understandings of any kind but diplomacy shall proceed always frankly and in the public view.

II. Absolute freedom of navigation upon the seas, outside territorial waters, alike in peace and in war, except as the seas may be closed in whole or in part by international action for the enforcement of international covenants.

XIV. A general association of nations must be formed under specific covenants for the purpose of affording mutual guarantees of political independence and territorial integrity to great and small states alike. . . .

Brown v. Board of Education

On May 17, 1954, the Supreme Court ruled in Brown v. Board of Education of Topeka, Kansas *that racial segregation in public schools was unconstitutional. This decision provided the legal basis for court challenges to segregation in every aspect of American life.*

. . . The plaintiffs contend that segregated public schools are not "equal" and cannot be made "equal" and that hence they are deprived of the equal protection of the laws. Because of the obvious importance of the question presented, the Court took jurisdiction. . . .

Our decision, therefore, cannot turn on merely a comparison of these tangible factors in the Negro and white schools involved in each of the cases. We must look instead to the effect of segregation itself on public education.

In approaching this problem, we cannot turn the clock back to 1868 when the Amendment was adopted, or even to 1896 when *Plessy* v. *Ferguson* was written. We must consider public education in the light of its full development and its present place in American life throughout the Nation. Only in this way can it be determined if segregation in public schools deprives these plaintiffs of the equal protection of the laws.

Today, education is perhaps the most important function of state and local governments. Compulsory school attendance laws and the great expenditures for education both demonstrate our recognition of the importance of education to our democratic society. . . . In these days, it is doubtful that any child may reasonably be expected to succeed in life if he is denied the opportunity of an education. Such an opportunity, where the state has undertaken to provide it, is a right which must be made available to all on equal terms.

We come then to the question presented: Does segregation of children in public schools solely on the basis of race, even though the physical facilities and other "tangible" factors may be equal, deprive the children of the minority group of equal educational opportunities? We believe that it does.

. . . We conclude that in the field of public education the doctrine of "separate but equal" has no place. Separate educational facilities are inherently unequal. Therefore, we hold that the plaintiffs and others similarly situated for whom the actions have been brought are, by reason of the segregation complained of, deprived of the equal protection of the laws guaranteed by the Fourteenth Amendment. . . .

Troops escort students to newly integrated school

John F. Kennedy's Inaugural Address

President Kennedy's Inaugural Address on January 20, 1961, set the tone for his administration. In his address Kennedy stirred the nation by calling for "a grand and global alliance" to fight tyranny, poverty, disease, and war.

We observe today not a victory of party but a celebration of freedom—symbolizing an end as well as a beginning—signifying renewal as well as change. For I have sworn before you and Almighty God the same solemn oath our forebears prescribed nearly a century and three-quarters ago.

The world is very different now. For man holds in his mortal hands the power to abolish all forms of human poverty and all forms of human life. And yet the same revolutionary beliefs for which our forebears fought are still at issue around the globe—the belief that the rights of man come not from the generosity of the state but from the hand of God.

We dare not forget today that we are the heirs of that first revolution. Let the word go forth from this time and place, to friend and foe alike, that the torch has been passed to a new generation of Americans—born in this century, tempered by war, disciplined by a hard and bitter peace, proud of our ancient heritage—and unwilling to witness or permit the slow undoing of those human rights to which this nation has always been committed, and to which we are committed today at home and around the world.

Let every nation know, whether it wishes us well or ill, that we shall pay any price, bear any burden, meet any hardship, support any friend, oppose any foe to assure the survival and the success of liberty.

This much we pledge—and more.

To those old allies whose cultural and spiritual origins we share, we pledge the loyalty of faithful friends. United, there is little we cannot do in a host of cooperative ventures. Divided, there is little we can do. . . .

Let us never negotiate out of fear. But let us never fear to negotiate.

Let both sides explore what problems unite us instead of belaboring those problems which divide us. . . .

Let both sides seek to invoke the wonders of science instead of its terrors. Together let us explore the stars, conquer the deserts, eradicate disease, tap the ocean depths, and encourage the arts and commerce. . . .

And so, my fellow Americans: ask not what your country can do for you—ask what you can do for your country.

My fellow citizens of the world: ask not what America will do for you, but what together we can do for the freedom of man. . . .

President Kennedy speaking at his inauguration

I Have a Dream

On August 28, 1963, while Congress debated wide-ranging civil rights legislation, Dr. Martin Luther King, Jr., led more than 200,000 people in a march on Washington, D.C. On the steps of the Lincoln Memorial he gave a stirring speech in which he eloquently spoke of his dreams for African Americans and for the United States. Excerpts of the speech follow.

. . . There are those who are asking the devotees of civil rights, "When will you be satisfied?"

We can never be satisfied as long as the Negro is the victim of the unspeakable horrors of police brutality. . . .

We cannot be satisfied as long as the Negro's basic mobility is from a smaller ghetto to a larger one.

We can never be satisfied as long as a Negro in Mississippi cannot vote and a Negro in New York believes he has nothing for which to vote. . . .

I say to you today, my friends, that in spite of the difficulties and frustrations of the moment I still have a dream. It is a dream deeply rooted in the American dream. I have

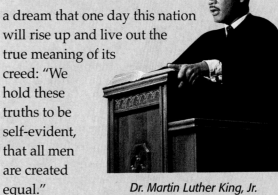

a dream that one day this nation will rise up and live out the true meaning of its creed: "We hold these truths to be self-evident, that all men are created equal."

Dr. Martin Luther King, Jr.

I have a dream that one day on the red hills of Georgia the sons of former slaves and the sons of former slaveowners will be able to sit down together at the table of brotherhood.

I have a dream that one day even the state of Mississippi, a desert state sweltering with the heat of injustice and oppression, will be transformed into an oasis of freedom and justice.

I have a dream that my four little children will one day live in a nation where they will not be judged by the color of their skin but by the content of their character. . . .

. . . When we let freedom ring, when we let it ring from every village and every hamlet, from every state and every city, we will be able to speed up that day when all of God's children, black men and white men, Jews and Gentiles, Protestants and Catholics, will be able to join hands and sing in the words of the old Negro spiritual: "Free at last! Free at last! Thank God Almighty, we are free at last!"

The March on Washington

Documents

Supreme Court Case Summaries

The following summaries give details about important Supreme Court cases.

Brown v. Board of Education (1954)

In *Brown v. Board of Education of Topeka, Kansas* the Supreme Court overruled *Plessy v. Ferguson* (1896) [see p. 626] making the separate-but-equal doctrine in public schools unconstitutional. The Supreme Court rejected the idea that truly equal but separate schools for African American and white students would be constitutional. The Court explained that the Fourteenth Amendment's requirement that all persons be guaranteed equal protection of the law is not met simply by ensuring that African American and white schools "have been equalized...with respect to buildings, curricula, qualifications and salaries, and other tangible factors."

The Court then ruled that racial segregation in public schools violates the Equal Protection Clause of the Constitution because it is inherently unequal. In other words, nothing can make racially segregated public schools equal under the Constitution because the very fact of separation marks the separated race as inferior. In practical terms, the Court's decision in this case has been extended beyond public education to virtually all public accommodations and activities.

Dred Scott v. Sandford (1857)

Dred Scott was taken by slaveholder John Sandford to the free state of Illinois and to the Wisconsin Territory, which had also banned slavery. Later they returned to Missouri, a slave state. Several years later, Scott sued for his freedom under the Missouri legal principle of "once free, always free." In other words, under Missouri law enslaved people were entitled to freedom if they had lived in a free state at any time. Missouri courts ruled against Scott, but he appealed the case all the way to the United States Supreme Court.

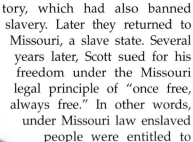

Dred Scott

The Supreme Court decided this case before the Fourteenth Amendment was added to the Constitution. (The Fourteenth Amendment provides that anyone born or naturalized in the United States is a citizen of the nation and of his or her state of residence.) The court held that enslaved African Americans were property, not citizens, and thus had no rights under the Constitution. The decision also declared that it was unconstitutional to prohibit slavery in the territories. Many people in the North were outraged by the decision, which moved the nation closer to civil war.

Furman v. Georgia (1972)

This decision put a halt to the application of the death penalty under state laws then in effect. For the first time, the Supreme Court ruled that the death penalty amounted to cruel and unusual punishment, which is outlawed in the Constitution. The Court explained that existing death penalty laws did not give juries enough guidance in deciding whether or not to impose the death penalty. As a result, the death penalty in many cases was imposed arbitrarily, that is, without a reasonable basis in the facts and circumstances of the offender or the crime.

The Furman decision halted all executions in the 39 states that had death penalty laws at that time. Since the decision, 38 states have rewritten death penalty laws to meet the requirements established in the Furman case.

Gibbons v. Ogden (1824)

Thomas Gibbons had a federal license to operate a steamboat along the coast, but he did not have a license from the state of New York to travel on New York waters. He wanted to run a steamboat line between Manhattan and New Jersey that would compete with Aaron Ogden's company. Ogden had a New York license. Gibbons sued for the freedom to use his federal license to compete against Ogden on New York waters.

Gibbons won the case. The Supreme Court made it clear that the authority of Congress to regulate interstate commerce (among states) includes the authority to regulate intrastate commerce (within a single state) that bears on, or relates to, interstate commerce.

Before this decision, it was thought that the Constitution would permit a state to close its borders to interstate commercial activity—which, in effect, would stop such activity in its tracks. This case says that a state can regulate purely internal commercial activity, but only Congress can regulate commercial activity that has both intrastate and interstate dimensions.

Gideon v. Wainwright (1963)

After being accused of robbery, Clarence Gideon defended himself in a Florida court because the judge in the case refused to appoint a free lawyer. The jury found Gideon guilty. Eventually, Gideon appealed his conviction to the United States Supreme Court, claiming that by failing to appoint a lawyer the lower court had violated his rights under the Sixth and Fourteenth Amendments.

The Supreme Court agreed with Gideon. In *Gideon v. Wainwright* the Supreme Court held for the first time that poor defendants in criminal cases have the right to a state-paid attorney under the Sixth Amendment. The rule announced in this case has been refined to apply whenever the defendant, if convicted, can be sentenced to more than six months in jail or prison.

Korematsu v. United States (1944)

After the Japanese bombing of Pearl Harbor in 1941, thousands of Japanese Americans on the West Coast were forced to abandon their homes and businesses, and they were moved to internment camps in

In 1983 Fred Korematsu (center) won a reversal of his conviction.

California, Idaho, Utah, Arizona, Wyoming, Colorado, and Arkansas. The prison-like camps offered poor food and cramped quarters.

The Supreme Court's decision in *Korematsu v. United States* upheld the authority of the federal government to move Japanese Americans, many of whom were citizens, from designated military areas that included almost the entire West Coast. The government defended the so-called exclusion orders as a necessary response to Japan's attack on Pearl Harbor. Only after his reelection in 1944 did President Franklin Roosevelt rescind the evacuation orders, and by the end of 1945 the camps were closed.

Marbury v. Madison (1803)

During his last days in office, President John Adams commissioned William Marbury and several other men as judges. This action by Federalist president Adams angered the incoming Democratic-Republican president Thomas Jefferson. Jefferson then ordered James Madison, his secretary of state, not to deliver the commissions, thus blocking the appointments. William Marbury sued, asking the Supreme Court to order Madison to deliver the commission that would make him a judge.

The Court ruled against Marbury, but more importantly, the decision in this case established one of the most significant principles of American constitutional law. The Supreme Court held that it is the Court itself that has the final say on what the Constitution means. This is known as judicial review. It is also the Supreme Court that has the final say in whether or not an act of government—legislative or executive at the federal, state, or local level—violates the Constitution.

McCulloch v. Maryland (1819)

Following the War of 1812, the United States experienced years of high inflation and general economic turmoil. In an attempt to stabilize the economy, the United States Congress chartered a Second Bank of the United States in 1816. Maryland and several other states, however, opposed the competition that the new national bank created and passed laws taxing its branches. In 1818, James McCulloch, head of the Baltimore branch of the Second Bank of the United States, refused to pay the tax to the state of Maryland. The case worked its way through the Maryland state courts all the way to the United States Supreme Court.

The Supreme Court declared the Maryland tax unconstitutional and void. More importantly, the decision established the foundation for expanded Congressional authority. The Court held that the necessary and proper clause of the Constitution allows Congress to do more than the Constitution expressly authorizes it to do. The decision allows Congress to enact nearly any law that will help it achieve any of its duties as set forth in the Constitution. For example, Congress has the express authority to regulate interstate commerce. The necessary and proper clause permits Congress to do so in ways not actually specified in the Constitution.

Miranda v. Arizona (1966)

In 1963, police in Arizona arrested Ernesto Miranda for kidnapping. The court found Miranda guilty on the basis of a signed confession. The police admitted that neither before nor during the questioning had Miranda been advised of his right to consult with an attorney before answering any questions or of his right to have an attorney present during the interrogation. Miranda appealed his conviction, claiming that police had violated his right against self-incrimination under the Fifth Amendment by not informing him of his legal rights during questioning.

Miranda won the case. The Supreme Court held that a person in police custody cannot be questioned unless told that he or she has: 1) the right to remain silent, 2) the right to an attorney (at government expense if the accused is unable to pay), and 3) that anything the person says after stating that he or she understands these rights can be used as evidence of guilt at trial. These rights have come to be called the

In 1963, the arrest of Ernesto Miranda (left) led to a landmark decision.

Miranda warning. They are intended to ensure that an accused person in custody will not unknowingly give up the Fifth Amendment's protection against self-incrimination.

New York Times Company v. United States (1971)

In June 1971, the *New York Times* published its first installment of the "Pentagon Papers," a classified document about government actions in the Vietnam War era. The secret document had been leaked to the *Times* by antiwar activist Daniel Ellsberg, who had previously worked in national security for the government. President Richard Nixon went to court to block further publication of the Pentagon Papers. The *New York Times* appealed to the Supreme Court to allow it to continue publishing without government interference.

The Supreme Court's ruling in this case upheld earlier decisions that established the doctrine of prior restraint. This doctrine protects the press (broadly defined to include newspapers, television and radio, filmmakers and distributors, etc.) from government attempts to block publication. Except in extraordinary circumstances, the press must be allowed to publish.

Plessy v. Ferguson (1896)

In the late 1800s railroad companies in Louisiana were required by state law to provide "separate-but-equal" cars for white and African American passengers. In 1890 a group of citizens in New Orleans selected Homer Plessy to challenge that law. In 1892, Plessy boarded a whites-only car and refused to move. He was arrested. Plessy appealed to the Supreme Court, arguing that the Louisiana separate-but-equal law violated his right to equal protection under the Fourteenth Amendment.

Homer Plessy lost the case. The Plessy decision upheld the separate-but-equal doctrine used by Southern states to perpetuate segregation following the Civil War. The court ruled that the Fourteenth Amendment's equal protection clause required only equal public facilities for the two races, not equal access to the same facilities. This decision was overruled in 1954 by *Brown* v. *Board of Education of Topeka, Kansas* (discussed previously).

Roe v. Wade (1973)

Roe v. *Wade* challenged restrictive abortion laws in both Texas and Georgia. The suit was brought in the name of Jane Roe, an alias used to protect the privacy of the plaintiff.

In this decision, the Supreme Court ruled that females have a constitutional right under various provisions of the Constitution—most notably, the due process clause—to decide whether or not to terminate a pregnancy. The Supreme Court's decision in this case was the most significant in a long line of decisions over a period of 50 years that recognized a constitutional right of privacy, even though the word *privacy* is not found in the Constitution.

Tinker v. Des Moines School District (1969)

During the Vietnam War, some students in Des Moines, Iowa, wore black armbands to school to protest American involvement in the conflict. Two days earlier, school officials had adopted a policy banning the wearing of armbands to school. When the students arrived at school wearing armbands, they were suspended and sent home. The students argued that school officials violated their First Amendment right to free speech.

The Supreme Court sided with the students. In a now-famous statement the court said that "it can hardly be argued that either students or teachers shed their constitutional rights of freedom of speech or expression at the schoolhouse gate." The Supreme Court went on to rule that a public school could not suspend students who wore black armbands to school to symbolize their opposition to the Vietnam War. In so holding, the Court likened the students' conduct to pure speech and decided it on that basis.

United States v. Nixon (1974)

In the early 1970s, President Nixon was named an unindicted co-conspirator in the criminal investigation that arose in the aftermath of a break-in at the offices of the Democratic Party in Washington, D.C. A federal judge had ordered President Nixon to turn over tapes of conversations he had with his advisers about the break-in. Nixon resisted the order, claiming that the conversations were entitled to absolute confidentiality by Article II of the Constitution.

The decision in this case made it clear that the president is not above the law. The Supreme Court held that only those presidential conversations and communications that relate to performing the duties of the office of president are confidential and protected from a judicial order of disclosure. The Court ordered Nixon to give up the tapes, which revealed evidence linking the president to the conspiracy to obstruct justice. He resigned from office shortly thereafter.

Worcester v. Georgia (1832)

State officials in Georgia wanted to remove the Cherokees from land that had been guaranteed to them in earlier treaties. Samuel Worcester was a Congregational missionary who worked with the Cherokee people. He was arrested for failure to have a license that the state required to live in Cherokee country and for refusing to obey an order from the Georgia militia to leave Cherokee lands. Worcester then sued the state of Georgia. He claimed that Georgia had no legal authority on Cherokee land because the United States government recognized the Cherokee in Georgia as a separate nation.

The Supreme Court agreed with Worcester by a vote of 5 to 1. Chief Justice John Marshall wrote the majority opinion which said that Native American nations were a distinct people with the right to have independent political communities and that only the federal government had authority over matters that involved the Cherokee.

President Andrew Jackson supported Georgia's efforts to remove the Cherokee to Indian Territory and refused to enforce the court's ruling. After the ruling Jackson remarked, "John Marshall has made his decision. Now let him enforce it."

Gazetteer

The gazetteer is a geographical dictionary that lists political divisions, natural features, and other places and locations. Following each entry is a description, its latitude and longitude, and a page reference that indicates where each entry may be found in this text.

A

Afghanistan country in southwestern Asia (33°N/63°E) RA13, 580

Africa continent of the Eastern Hemisphere south of the Mediterranean Sea and adjoining Asia on its northeastern border (10°N/22°E) RA15, 41

Alabama state in the southeastern United States; 22nd state to enter the Union (33°N/87°W) RA3, 319

Alamo Texas mission captured by Mexican forces in 1836 (29°N/98°W) 365

Alaska state in the United States, located in northwestern North America (64°N/150°W) RA2

Albany capital of New York State located in the Hudson Valley; site where Albany Congress proposed first formal plan to unite the 13 colonies (42°N/74°W) 119

Allegheny River river in western Pennsylvania uniting with the Monongahela River at Pittsburgh to form the Ohio River (41°N/79°W) RA5, 123

Andes mountain system extending along western coast of South America (13°S/75°W) 18

Antietam Civil War battle site in western Maryland (40°N/77°W) 472

Appalachian Mountains chief mountain system in eastern North America extending from Quebec and New Brunswick to central Alabama (37°N/82°W) RA5, 60

Appomattox Court House site in central Virginia where Confederate forces surrendered, ending the Civil War (37°N/78°W) 491

Arizona state in the southwestern United States; 48th state to enter the Union (34°N/113°W) RA2, 28

Arkansas state in the south central U.S.; acquired as part of Louisiana Purchase (35°N/94°W) RA3, 310

Asia continent of the Eastern Hemisphere forming a single landmass with Europe (50°N/100°E) RA15, 17

Atlanta capital of Georgia located in the northwest central part of the state (34°N/84°W) 423

Atlantic Ocean ocean separating North and South America from Europe and Africa (5°S/25°W) RA14, 16

Australia continent and country southeast of Asia (25°S/125°E) RA15, 42

Austria-Hungary former monarchy in central Europe (47°N/12°E) 547

B

Baltimore city on the Chesapeake Bay in central Maryland (39°N/77°W) 87

Barbary Coast north coast of Africa between Morocco and Tunisia (35°N/3°E) 289

Bay of Pigs site of 1961 invasion of Cuba by U.S.-trained Cuban exiles (22°N/79°W) 568

Beijing capital of China located in the northeastern part of the country (40°N/116°E) 572

Belgium country in northwest Europe (51°N/3°E) RA15, 668

Bering Strait waterway between North America and Asia where a land bridge once existed (65°N/170°W) 17

Beringia land bridge that linked Asia and North America during the last Ice Age (65°N/170°W) 17

Berlin city in east central Germany; former capital divided into sectors after World War II (53°N/13°E) 564

Birmingham city in north central Alabama; scene of several civil rights protests (33°N/86°W) 567

Black Hills mountains in southwestern South Dakota; site of conflict between the Sioux and white settlers during 1870s (44°N/104°W) 535

Boston capital of Massachusetts located in the eastern part of the state; founded by English Puritans in 1630 (42°N/71°W) 78

Brazil country in eastern South America (9°S/53°W) RA14, 55

Breed's Hill site near Boston where the Battle of Bunker Hill took place (42°N/71°W) 145

Buffalo industrial city and rail center in New York State (43°N/79°W) 315

Bull Run site of two Civil War battles in northern Virginia; also called Manassas (39°N/77°W) 466

C

Cahokia largest settlement of the Mound Builders, built in Illinois after A.D. 900 (39°N/90°W) 30

California state in the western United States; attracted thousands of miners during gold rush of 1849 (38°N/121°W) RA2, 371

Cambodia country in Southeastern Asia bordering Gulf of Siam; official name Democratic Kampuchea (12°N/105°E) RA15

Canada country in northern North America (50°N/100°W) RA14, 17

Cape of Good Hope southern tip of Africa (34°S/18°E) 44

Caribbean Sea tropical sea in the Western Hemisphere (15°N/75°W) RA9, 19

Central America area of North America between Mexico and South America (11°N/86°W) RA8, 17

Chancellorsville Virginia site of 1863 Confederate victory (38°N/78°W) 486

Charleston city in South Carolina on the Atlantic coast; original name Charles Town (33°N/80°W) 89

Chesapeake Bay inlet of the Atlantic Ocean in Virginia and Maryland (38°N/76°W) 72

Chicago largest city in Illinois; located in northeastern part of the state along Lake Michigan (42°N/88°W) 318

Chile South American country (35°S/72°W) RA14

China country in eastern Asia; mainland (People's Republic of China) under communist control since 1949 (37°N/93°E) RA15, 565

Chisholm Trail pioneer cattle trail from Texas to Kansas (34°N/98°W) 529

Cincinnati city in southern Ohio on the Ohio River; grew as a result of increasing steamship traffic during the mid-1800s (39°N/84°W) 265

Cleveland city in northern Ohio on Lake Erie (41°N/82°W) 423

Colombia country in South America (4°N/73°W) RA14, 26

Colorado state in the western United States (39°N/107°W) RA3, 29

Colorado River river that flows from the Colorado Rockies to the Gulf of California (36°N/113°W) RA4, 284

Columbia River river flowing through southwest Canada and northwestern United States into the Pacific Ocean (46°N/120°W) 357

Concord village northwest of Boston, Massachusetts; site of early battle of the American Revolution (42°N/ 71°W) 143

Connecticut state in the northeastern United States; one of the original 13 states (42°N/73°W) RA3, 79

Cuba country in the West Indies, North America (22°N/79°W) RA9, 52

Czechoslovakia former country in central Europe; now two countries, the Czech Republic and Slovakia (49°N/ 16°E) RA15

Dallas a leading city in Texas (33°N/ 97°W) 567

Delaware state in the northeastern United States; one of the original 13 states (39°N/75°W) RA3, 84

Detroit city in southeastern Michigan; site of significant battles during the French and Indian War and the War of 1812; center of automobile industry (42°N/83°W) 125

Dodge City Kansas cattle town during the 19th century (37°N/100°W) 535

Dominican Republic country in the West Indies on the eastern part of Hispaniola Island (19°N/71°W) RA9, 47

East Germany country in central Europe; reunified with West Germany in 1990 (52°N/12°E) 569

Egypt country in northeastern Africa (27°N/27°E) RA12, 574

England division of the United Kingdom of Great Britain and Northern Ireland (52°N/2°W) 40

Erie Canal the waterway connecting the Hudson River with Lake Erie through New York State (43°N/ 76°W) 318

Ethiopia country in eastern Africa, north of Somalia and Kenya (8°N/ 38°E) RA15

Europe continent of the northern part of the Eastern Hemisphere between Asia and the Atlantic Ocean (50°N/ 15°E) RA15, 38

Florida state in the southeastern United States (30°N/85°W) RA3, 93

Fort McHenry fort in Baltimore harbor; inspired poem that later became "The Star-Spangled Banner" (39°N/ 76°W) 299

Fort Necessity Pennsylvania fort built by George Washington's troops in 1754 (40°N/80°W) 118

Fort Sumter Union fort during the Civil War located on island near Charleston, South Carolina; site of first military engagement of Civil War (33°N/80°W) 453

Fort Ticonderoga British fort on Lake Champlain (44°N/73°W) 144

France country in western Europe (50°N/1°E) RA15, 40

Fredericksburg city and Civil War battle site in northeast Virginia (38°N/ 77°W) 486

Freeport city in northern Illinois; site of 1858 Lincoln-Douglas campaign debate (42°N/89°W) 448

Gadsden Purchase portion of present-day Arizona and New Mexico; area purchased from Mexico in 1853 (32°N/111°W) 374

Galveston city on the Gulf of Mexico coast in Texas; created nation's first commission form of city government (29°N/95°W) 541

Gaza Strip narrow coastal strip along the Mediterranean (31°N/34°E) RA12

Georgia state in the southeastern United States (33°N/84°W) RA3, 90

Germany country in central Europe; divided after World War II into East Germany and West Germany; unified in 1990 (50°N/10°E) RA15, 547

Gettysburg city and Civil War battle site in south central Pennsylvania; site where Lincoln delivered the Gettysburg Address (40°N/77°W) 486

Great Britain commonwealth comprising England, Scotland, and Wales (56°N/2°W) 559

Great Lakes chain of five lakes, Superior, Erie, Michigan, Ontario, and Huron, in central North America (45°N/87°W) RA5, 60

Great Plains flat grassland in the central United States (45°N/104°W) RA4, 390

Great Salt Lake lake in northern Utah with no outlet and strongly saline waters (41°N/113°W) RA3, 378

Greece country in southeastern Europe (39°N/21°E) RA15

Grenada country in the Caribbean (12°N/61°W) RA9

Guadalcanal island in the Solomons east of Australia (10°S/159°E) 562

Guam U.S. possession in the western Pacific Ocean (14°N/143°E) 562

Guatemala country in Central America, south of Mexico (16°N/92°W) RA8, 23

Gulf of Mexico gulf on the southeast coast of North America (25°N/94°W) RA5, 92

Gulf of Tonkin gulf in South China Sea east of northern Vietnam (20°N/ 108°E) 569

Haiti country on Hispaniola Island in the West Indies (19°N/72°W) RA9, 47

Harpers Ferry town in northern West Virginia on the Potomac River (39°N/78°W) 448

Hartford capital of Connecticut located along the Connecticut River (42°N/ 73°W) 79

Hawaii state in the United States located in the Pacific Ocean (20°N/ 157°W) RA2

Hiroshima city in southern Japan; site of first military use of atomic bomb, August 6, 1945 (34°N/132°E) 563

Hispaniola island in the West Indies in North America (17°N/73°W) RA9, 47

Horseshoe Bend Alabama site where Creek-U.S. battled in 1814 (33°N/ 86°W) 298

Hudson Bay large bay in northern Canada (60°N/86°W) RA14, 61

Hudson River river flowing through New York State (53°N/ 74°W) 316

Hungary country in central Europe (47°N/20°E) RA15

Idaho state in the northwestern U.S.; ranks among top states in silver production (44°N/115°W) RA2, 541

Illinois state in the north central United States; one of the states formed in the Northwest Territory (40°N/91°W) RA3, 195

Indian Territory land reserved by the United States government for Native Americans, now the state of Oklahoma (36°N/98°W) 342

Indiana state in the north central United States; one of the states formed in the

Northwest Territory (40°N/87°W) RA3, 195

Indochina region in Southeast Asia (17°N/105°E) 559

Iowa state in the north central U.S. acquired as part of the Louisiana Purchase (42°N/94°W) RA3, 541

Iran country in southwestern Asia (31°N/53°E) RA13, 574

Iraq country in southwestern Asia (32°N/42°E) RA13, 576

Ireland island west of England, occupied by the Republic of Ireland and by Northern Ireland (54°N/8°W) RA14

Israel country of the Middle East in southwestern Asia along the Mediterranean Sea (33°N/34°E) RA12, 574

Italy country in southern Europe along the Mediterranean (44°N/11°E) RA15, 39

Jamestown first permanent English settlement in North America; located in southeastern Virginia (37°N/77°W) 72

Japan island country in eastern Asia (36°N/133°E) RA15, 544

Kansas state in the central United States; fighting over slavery issue in 1850s gave territory the name "Bleeding Kansas" (38°N/99°W) RA3, 442

Kentucky state in the south central United States; border state that sided with the Union during the Civil War (37°N/87°W) RA3, 282

Korea peninsula in eastern Asia between China, Russia, and the Sea of Japan, on which are located the countries North Korea and South Korea (38°N/127°E) RA15, 565

Kuwait country of the Middle East in southwestern Asia between Iraq and Saudi Arabia (29°N/49°E) RA13, 576

Lake Erie one of the five Great Lakes between Canada and the U.S. (42°N/81°W) RA5, 61

Lake Huron one of the five Great Lakes between Canada and the U.S. (45°N/83°W) RA5, 61

Lake Michigan one of the five Great Lakes between Canada and the U.S. (43°N/87°W) RA5, 61

Lake Ontario the smallest of the five Great Lakes (43°N/79°W) RA5, 61

Lake Superior the largest of the five Great Lakes (48°N/89°W) RA5, 61

Laos southeast Asian country, south of China and west of Vietnam (20°N/102°E) RA15

Latin America Central and South America; settled by Spain and Portugal (14°N/90°W) RA14

Lexington Revolutionary War battle site in eastern Massachusetts; site of first clash between colonists and British, April 19, 1775 (42°N/71°W) 143

Leyte island of the east central Philippines, north of Mindanao (10°N/125°E) 562

Little Rock capital of Arkansas located in the center of the state; site of 1957 conflict over public school integration (35°N/92°W) 423

London capital of United Kingdom located in the southeastern part of England (51°N/0°) 73

Louisiana state in the south central United States (31°N/93°W) RA3, 298

Louisiana Territory region of west central United States between the Mississippi River and the Rocky Mountains purchased from France in 1803 (40°N/95°W) 124

Lowell city in Massachusetts (43°N/83°W) 391

Maine state in the northeastern United States; 23rd state to enter the Union (45°N/70°W) RA3, 324

Mali country in Western Africa (16°N/0°) RA14, 41

Manila capital and largest city of the Philippines located on southwest Luzon Island and Manila Bay (14°N/121°E) RA15, 562

Maryland state in the eastern United States; one of the original 13 states (39°N/76°W) RA3, 87

Massachusetts state in the northeastern United States; one of the original 13 states (42°N/72°W) RA3, 79

Massachusetts Bay Colony Pilgrim settlements along the Charles River (42°N/71°W) 78

Mediterranean Sea sea between Europe and Africa (36°N/13°E) RA14–15, 39

Memphis Tennessee city on the Mississippi River near the Mississippi border (35°N/90°W) 403

Mexican Cession territory gained by the United States after war with Mexico in 1848 (37°N/111°W) 374

Mexico country in North America south of the United States (24°N/104°W) RA8, 19

Mexico City capital and most populous city of Mexico (19°N/99°W) 24

Michigan state in the north central United States; one of the states formed in the Northwest Territory (45°N/85°W) RA3, 195

Midway Islands U.S. possession in the central Pacific Ocean (28°N/179°W) 562

Minnesota state in the north central United States; fur trade, good soil, and lumber attracted early settlers (46°N/96°W) RA3

Mississippi state in the southeastern United States; became English territory after French and Indian War (32°N/90°W) RA3, 319

Mississippi River river flowing through the United States from Minnesota to the Gulf of Mexico; explored by French in 1600s (29°N/89°W) RA5, 30

Missouri state in the south central U.S.; petition for statehood resulted in sectional conflict and the Missouri Compromise (41°N/93°W) RA3, 324

Missouri River river flowing through the United States from the Rocky Mountains to the Mississippi River near St. Louis (39°N/90°W) RA5

Montana state in the northwestern United States; cattle industry grew during 1850s (47°N/112°W) RA3, 503

Montgomery capital of Alabama located in the central part of the state; site of 1955 bus boycott to protest segregation (32°N/86°W) 566

Montreal city along the St. Lawrence River in southern Quebec, Canada (45°N/73°W) 60

Moscow capital of former Soviet Union and capital of Russia (56°N/37°E) 573

Nagasaki Japanese city; site of the second atom-bombing in 1945, ending World War II (32°N/130°E) 563

Nashville capital of Tennessee located in the north central part of the state (36°N/87°W) 423

Natchez city in western Mississippi along the Mississippi River (32°N/91°W) 316

National Road road from Baltimore, Maryland, to Vandalia, Illinois (40°N/81°W) 315

Gazetteer

Nebraska state in the central United States (42°N/101°W) RA3, 442

Netherlands country in northwestern Europe (53°N/4°E) RA15, 77

Nevada state in the western United States (39°N/117°W) RA2, 510

New Amsterdam town founded on Manhattan Island by Dutch settlers in 1625; renamed New York by British settlers (41°N/74°W) 83

New England region in northeastern United States (42°N/72°W) 76

New France French land claims stretching from Quebec to Louisiana (39°N/85°W) 92

New Hampshire state in the northeastern United States; one of the original 13 states (44°N/72°W) RA3, 80

New Jersey state in the northeastern United States; one of the original 13 states (40°N/75°W) RA3, 84

New Mexico state in the southwestern United States; ceded to the United States by Mexico in 1848 (34°N/107°W) RA2, 369

New Netherland Dutch Hudson River colony (42°N/72°W) 83

New Orleans city in Louisiana in the Mississippi Delta (30°N/90°W) 92

New Spain part of Spain's empire in the Western Hemisphere (35°N/110°W) 92

New York state in the northeastern United States; one of the original 13 states (43°N/78°W) RA3, 83

New York City city in southeastern New York State at the mouth of the Hudson River; first capital of nation (41°N/74°W) 84

Newfoundland province in eastern Canada (48°N/56°W) RA14, 46

Nicaragua country in Central America (13°N/86°W) RA9

Normandy region along French coast and site of D-Day invasion, June 6, 1944 (48°N/2°W) 561

North America continent in the northern part of the Western Hemisphere between the Atlantic and Pacific oceans (45°N/100°W) RA14, 16

North Carolina state in the southeastern United States; one of the original 13 states (36°N/81°W) RA3, 89

North Dakota state in the north central U.S.; Congress created Dakota Territory in 1861 (47°N/102°W) RA3, 531

North Korea Asian country on the northern Korean Peninsula (40°N/127°E) RA15, 565

North Vietnam communist nation in Southeast Asia; unified with South Vietnam in 1976 to form Vietnam (21°N/106°E) RA15, 569

Northwest Territory territory north of the Ohio River and east of the Mississippi River (47°N/87°W) 196

O

Ohio state in the north central United States; first state in the Northwest Territory (40°N/83°W) RA3, 195

Ohio River river flowing from Allegheny and Monongahela rivers in western Pennsylvania into the Mississippi River (37°N/85°W) RA5, 28

Oklahoma state in the south central United States; Five Civilized Tribes moved to territory in the period 1830–1842 (36°N/98°W) RA3, 530

Oregon state in the northwestern United States; adopted woman suffrage in 1912 (44°N/124°W) RA2, 356

Oregon Trail pioneer trail from Independence, Missouri, to the Oregon Territory (42°N/110°W) 358

P

Pacific Ocean world's largest ocean, located between Asia and the Americas (0°/175°W) RA14–15, 43

Panama country in the southern part of Central America, occupying the Isthmus of Panama (8°N/81°W) RA9

Pearl Harbor naval base at Honolulu, Hawaii; site of 1941 Japanese attack, leading to United States entry into World War II (21°N/158°W) 559

Pennsylvania state in the northeastern United States (41°N/78°W) RA3, 85

Persian Gulf gulf in southwestern Asia between Iran and the Arabian Peninsula (28°N/50°E) RA13

Peru country in South America, south of Ecuador and Colombia (10°S/75°W) RA14, 26

Philadelphia city in eastern Pennsylvania on the Delaware River; Declaration of Independence and the Constitution both adopted in city's Independence Hall (40°N/75°W) 85

Philippines island country in southeast Asia (14°N/125°E) RA15, 545

Pikes Peak mountain in Rocky Mountains in central Colorado (38°N/105°W) 285

Pittsburgh city in western Pennsylvania; one of the great steelmaking centers of the world (40°N/80°W) 423

Plymouth town in eastern Massachusetts, first successful English colony in New England (42°N/71°W) 77

Poland country on the Baltic Sea in Eastern Europe (52°N/18°E) RA15, 549

Portugal country in southwestern Europe (38°N/8°W) RA14, 44

Potomac River river flowing from West Virginia into Chesapeake Bay (38°N/77°W) RA5, 87

Providence capital of Rhode Island; site of first English settlement in Rhode Island (42°N/71°W) RA3

Puerto Rico United States commonwealth in the West Indies (18°N/67°W) RA9

Q

Quebec city in Canada, capital of Quebec Province, on the St. Lawrence River; first settlement in New France (47°N/71°W) 62

R

Rhode Island state in the northeastern United States; one of the original 13 states (41°N/72°W) RA3, 80

Richmond capital of Virginia located in the central part of the state; capital of the Confederacy during the Civil War (37°N/77°W) 388

Rio Grande river between the United States and Mexico in North America; forms the boundary between Texas and Mexico (26°N/97°W) RA4, 372

Roanoke island off the coast of present-day North Carolina that was site of early British colonizing efforts (35°N/76°W) 71

Rocky Mountains mountain range in western United States and Canada in North America (50°N/114°W) RA4, 32

Russia name of republic; former empire of eastern Europe and northern Asia-coinciding with Soviet Union (60°N/64°E) RA15, 549

S

Sacramento capital of California located in the north central part of the state (38°N/121°W) 372

Salt Lake City capital of Utah located in the northern part of the state; founded by Mormons in 1847 (41°N/112°W) 361

San Antonio city in south central Texas (29°N/98°W) 365

San Diego city in southern California (33°N/117°W) 93

San Francisco city in northern California on the Pacific coast (38°N/122°W) 372

Santa Fe capital of New Mexico located in the north central part of the state (36°N/106°W) 92

Santa Fe Trail cattle trail from Independence, Missouri, to Santa Fe, New Mexico (36°N/106°W) 370

Saratoga Revolutionary War battle site in the Hudson Valley of eastern New York State (43°N/74°W) 168

Savannah city in far eastern Georgia (32°N/81°W) 90

Seattle Washington city bordered by Puget Sound and Lake Washington (47°N/122°W) RA2

Seneca Falls town in New York State; site of women's rights convention in 1848 (43°N/77°W) 426

Shiloh site of 1862 Union victory in Tennessee (35°N/88°W) 469

Sicily Italian island in the Mediterranean (37°N/13°E) 561

Sierra Nevada mountain range in eastern California (39°N/120°W) RA4, 32

South America continent in the southern part of the Western Hemisphere lying between the Atlantic and Pacific oceans (15°S/60°W) RA14, 16

South Carolina state in the southeastern United States; one of the original 13 states (34°N/81°W) RA3, 89

South Dakota state in the north central United States; acquired through the Louisiana Purchase (44°N/102°W) RA3, 531

South Korea country in Asia on the Korean Peninsula (36°N/128°E) RA15, 565

South Vietnam country in Southeast Asia united in 1976 with North Vietnam to form Vietnam (11°N/107°E) RA15, 569

Soviet Union former country in northern Europe and Asia (60°N/64°E) 559

Spain country in southwestern Europe (40°N/4°W) RA14, 46

St. Augustine city in northeastern Florida on the Atlantic coast; oldest permanent existing European settlement in North America, founded in 1565 (30°N/81°W) 53

St. Lawrence River river flowing from Lake Ontario, between Canada and the United States, through parts of Canada to the Atlantic Ocean (48°N/69°W) 60

Stalingrad city in the former Soviet Union on the Volga River; present name Volgograd (49°N/42°E) 561

Switzerland European country in the Alps (47°N/8°E) RA15

Taiwan island country off the southeast coast of China; seat of the Chinese Nationalist government (24°N/122°E) RA15

Tehran capital of Iran (36°N/52°E) RA13, 574

Tennessee state in the south central United States; first state readmitted to the Union after the Civil War (36°N/88°W) RA3, 319

Tenochtitlán Aztec capital at the site of present-day Mexico City (19°N/99°W) 24

Texas state in the south central United States; Mexican colony that became a republic before joining the United States (31°N/101°W) RA3, 363

Tokyo capital of Japan located on the eastern coast of Honshu Island (36°N/140°E) 562

Toronto city in Canada on Lake Ontario; capital of the province of Ontario (44°N/79°W) RA14

Trenton capital of New Jersey located on the Delaware River in the central part of the state; site of Revolutionary War battle in December 1776 (40°N/75°W) 167

Union of Soviet Socialist Republics See Soviet Union.

United Kingdom country in northwestern Europe made up of England, Scotland, Wales, and Northern Ireland (56°N/2°W) RA14

United States country in central North America; fourth largest country in the world in both area and population (38°N/110°W) RA2–3, RA14

Utah state in the western United States; settled by Mormons in 1840s (39°N/113°W) RA2, 378

Valley Forge Revolutionary War winter camp northwest of Philadelphia (40°N/75°W) 173

Venezuela South American country on the Caribbean Sea (8°N/65°W) RA14

Vermont state in the northeastern United States; 14th state to enter the Union (44°N/73°W) RA3, 144

Vicksburg city and Civil War battle site in western Mississippi on the Mississippi River (42°N/85°W) 486

Vietnam country in southeastern Asia (16°N/108°E) RA15, 568

Virginia state in the eastern United States; colony of first permanent English settlement in the Americas (37°N/80°W) RA3, 72

Washington state in the northwestern United States; territory reached by Lewis and Clark in 1805 (47°N/121°W) RA2, 261

Washington, D.C. capital of the United States located on the Potomac River at its confluence with the Anacostia River, between Maryland and Virginia coinciding with the District of Columbia (39°N/77°W) RA3, 262

West Indies islands in the Caribbean Sea, between North America and South America (19°N/79°W) RA9, 47

West Virginia state in the east central United States (39°N/81°W) RA3, 462

Willamette Valley valley of the Willamette River in western Oregon (45°N/123°W) 359

Wisconsin state in the north central United States; passed first state unemployment compensation act, 1932 (44°N/91°W) RA3, 195

Wounded Knee site of massacre of Native Americans by soldiers in southern South Dakota in 1890 and of American Indian Movement protest in 1973 (43°N/102°W) 532

Wyoming state in the western United States; territory provided women the right to vote, 1869 (43°N/108°W) RA3, 531

Yorktown town in southeastern Virginia and site of final battle of Revolutionary War (37°N/76°W) 185

Yugoslavia country in southeast Europe, on the Adriatic Sea (44°N/20°E) RA15, 549

Gazetteer

Glossary

A

abolitionist a person who strongly favors doing away with slavery (p. 418)

abstain to not take part in some activity, such as voting (p. 439)

adobe a sun-dried mud brick used to build the homes of some Native Americans (p. 32)

affluence the state of having much wealth (p. 566)

alien an immigrant living in a country in which he or she is not a citizen (p. 271)

alliance a close association of nations or other groups, formed to advance common interests or causes (pp. 122, 547)

ambush a surprise attack (p. 187)

amendment an addition to a formal document such as the Constitution (pp. 213, 221)

American System policies devised by Henry Clay to stimulate the growth of industry (p. 324)

amnesty the granting of pardon to a large number of persons; protection from prosecution for an illegal act (p. 501)

annex to add a territory to one's own territory (p. 367)

Antifederalists individuals who opposed ratification of the Constitution (p. 212)

apprentice assistant who is assigned to learn the trade of a skilled craftsman (p. 112)

appropriate to set something aside for a particular purpose, especially funds (p. 223)

archaeology the study of ancient peoples (p. 17)

arsenal a storage place for weapons and ammunition (p. 448)

article a part of a document, such as the Constitution, that deals with a single subject (p. 209)

artifact an item left behind by early people that represents their culture (p. 17)

astrolabe an instrument used by sailors to observe positions of stars (p. 40)

B

backcountry a region of hills and forests west of the Tidewater (p. 105)

bicameral consisting of two houses, or chambers, especially in a legislature (p. 193)

black codes laws passed in the South just after the Civil War aimed at controlling freedmen and enabling plantation owners to exploit African American workers (p. 505)

blockade cut off an area by means of troops or warships to stop supplies or people from coming in or going out; to close off a country's ports (pp. 179, 463)

blockade runner ship that sails into and out of a blockaded area (p. 468)

bond a note issued by the government, which promises to pay off a loan with interest (p. 261)

boomtown a community experiencing a sudden growth in business or population (pp. 376, 529)

border ruffians Missourians who traveled in armed groups to vote in Kansas's election during the mid-1850s (p. 443)

border states the states between the North and the South that were divided over whether to stay in the Union or join the Confederacy (p. 461)

bounty money given as a reward, such as to encourage enlistment in the army (p. 482)

boycott to refuse to buy items from a particular country (p. 134)

bureaucracy system in which nonelected officials carry out laws and policies (p. 337)

burgesses elected representatives to an assembly (p. 73)

C

cabinet a group of advisers to the president (p. 259)

Californios Mexicans who lived in California (p. 373)

canal an artificial waterway (p. 318)

capital money for investment (pp. 308, 399, 536)

capitalism an economic system based on private property and free enterprise (p. 308)

caravel small, fast ship with a broad bow (p. 40)

carbon dating a scientific method used to determine the age of an artifact (p. 19)

carpetbaggers name given to Northern whites who moved South after the Civil War and supported the Republicans (p. 510)

cash crop farm crop raised to be sold for money (pp. 103, 518)

casualty a military person killed, wounded, or captured (p. 469)

caucus a meeting held by a political party to choose their party's candidate for president or decide policy (pp. 269, 337)

cede to give up by treaty (p. 374)

census official count of a population (p. 314)

charter a document that gives the holder the right to organize settlements in an area (p. 71)

charter colony colony established by a group of settlers who had been given a formal document allowing them to settle (p. 110)

checks and balances the system in which each branch of government has a check on the other two branches so that no one branch becomes too powerful (p. 210)

circumnavigate to sail around the world (p. 49)

citizen a person who owes loyalty to and is entitled to the protection of a state or nation (p. 229)

civil disobedience refusal to obey laws that are considered unjust as a nonviolent way to press for changes (p. 566)

civil war conflict between opposing groups of citizens of the same country (p. 444)

civilization a highly developed culture, usually with organized religions and laws (p. 22)

classical relating to ancient Greece and Rome (p. 39)

clipper ship a fast sailing ship with slender lines, tall masts, and large square sails (p. 387)

coeducation the teaching of male and female students together (p. 427)

collective bargaining discussion between an employer and union representatives of workers over wages, hours, and working conditions (p. 537)

Columbian Exchange exchange of goods, ideas, and people between Europe and the Americas (p. 60)

commission a group of persons directed to perform some duty (p. 516)

committee of correspondence an organization that used meetings, letters, and pamphlets to spread political ideas through the colonies (p. 137)

compromise agreement between two or more sides in which each side gives up some of what it wants (p. 204)

concurrent powers powers shared by the states and the federal government (p. 219)

Conestoga wagon sturdy vehicle topped with white canvas and used by pioneers to move west (p. 283)

conquistador Spanish explorer in the Americas in the 1500s (p. 51)

constituents people that members of Congress represent (p. 223)

constitution a formal plan of government (pp. 89, 193)

corruption dishonest or illegal actions (p. 510)

cotton gin a machine that removed seeds from cotton fiber (pp. 308, 398)

counter-terrorism military or political activities intended to combat terrorism (p. 583)

coureur de bois French trapper living among Native Americans (p. 62)

court-martial to try by a military court (p. 326)

credit a form of loan; ability to buy goods based on future payment (p. 403)

culture a way of life of a group of people who share similar beliefs and customs (p. 19)

customs duties taxes on foreign imported goods (p. 280)

D

debtor person or country that owes money (p. 90)

decree an order or decision given by one in authority (p. 364)

demilitarize to remove armed forces from an area (p. 326)

depreciate to fall in value (p. 197)

depression a period of low economic activity and widespread unemployment (pp. 199, 350)

desert to leave without permission (p. 173)

dictator a leader who rules with total authority, often in a cruel or brutal manner (p. 559)

disarmament removal of weapons (p. 326)

discrimination unfair treatment of a group; unequal treatment because of a person's race, religion, ethnic background, or place of birth (pp. 392, 543)

dissent disagreement with or opposition to an opinion (p. 76)

diversity variety or difference (p. 104)

domestic tranquility maintaining peace within the nation (p. 217)

draft the selection of persons for required military service (p. 481)

drought a long period of time with little rainfall (p. 29)

due process of law idea that the government must follow procedures established by law and guaranteed by the Constitution (p. 228)

E

effigy rag figure representing an unpopular individual (p. 134)

Electoral College a special group of voters selected by their state's voters to vote for the president and vice president (p. 210)

emancipate to free from slavery (p. 475)

Glossary

embargo an order prohibiting trade with another country (pp. 290, 573)

emigrant a person who leaves a country or region to live elsewhere (p. 358)

empresario a person who arranged for the settlement of land in Texas during the 1800s (p. 363)

encomienda system of rewarding conquistadors with tracts of land and the right to tax and demand labor from Native Americans who lived on the land (p. 55)

Enlightenment movement during the 1700s that spread the idea that knowledge, reason, and science could improve society (p. 208)

entrenched occupying a strong defensive position (p. 486)

enumerated powers powers belonging only to the federal government (p. 219)

executive branch the branch of government, headed by the president, that carries out the nation's laws and policies (p. 210)

export to sell goods abroad (p. 109)

factory system system bringing manufacturing steps together in one place to increase efficiency (p. 309)

famine an extreme shortage of food (p. 393)

favorite son candidate that receives the backing of his home state rather than of the national party (p. 335)

federal debt the amount of money owed by the government (p. 575)

federalism the sharing of power between federal and state governments (pp. 208, 219)

Federalists supporters of the Constitution (p. 211)

federation a type of government that links different groups together (p. 33)

feminist a person who advocates or is active in promoting women's rights (p. 567)

fixed costs regular expenses such as housing or maintaining equipment that remain about the same year after year (p. 403)

forty-niners people who went to California during the gold rush of 1849 (p. 375)

free enterprise the freedom of private businesses to operate competitively for profit with minimal government regulation (p. 308)

freedman a person freed from slavery (p. 502)

frigate warship (p. 297)

fugitive runaway or trying to run away (p. 438)

genocide the deliberate destruction of a racial, political, or cultural group (p. 561)

global warming a steady increase in average world temperatures (p. 578)

grandfather clause a clause that allowed individuals who did not pass the literacy test to vote if their fathers or grandfathers had voted before Reconstruction began; an exception to a law based on preexisting circumstances (p. 519)

greenback a piece of U.S. paper money first issued by the North during the Civil War (p. 483)

guerrilla tactics referring to surprise attacks or raids rather than organized warfare (p. 344)

guerrilla warfare a hit-and-run technique used in fighting a war; fighting by small bands of warriors using tactics such as sudden ambushes (p. 180)

habeas corpus a legal order for an inquiry to determine whether a person has been lawfully imprisoned (p. 481)

hieroglyphics an ancient form of writing using symbols and pictures to represent words, sounds, and concepts (p. 24)

Holocaust the name given to the mass slaughter of Jews and other groups by the Nazis during World War II (p. 561)

horizontal integration the combining of competing firms into one corporation (p. 536)

human rights rights regarded as belonging to all persons, such as freedom from unlawful imprisonment, torture, and execution (p. 574)

Ice Age a period of extremely cold temperatures when part of the planet's surface was covered with massive ice sheets (p. 17)

impeach to formally charge a public official with misconduct in office (pp. 223, 507, 573)

imperialism the actions used by one nation to exercise political or economic control over smaller or weaker nations (p. 544)

implied powers powers not specifically mentioned in the Constitution (pp. 221, 268)

import to buy goods from foreign markets (p. 109)

Glossary

impressment forcing people into service, as in the navy (pp. 265, 290)

indentured servant laborer who agreed to work without pay for a certain period of time in exchange for passage to America (p. 87)

Industrial Revolution the change from an agrarian society to one based on industry which began in Great Britain and spread to the United States around 1800 (p. 307)

inflation a continuous rise in the price of goods and services (pp. 175, 483)

integrate to end separation of different races and bring into equal membership in society (p. 512)

interchangeable parts uniform pieces that can be made in large quantities to replace other identical pieces (p. 309)

internal improvements federal projects, such as canals and roads, to develop the nation's transportation system (p. 322)

Internet a worldwide linking of computer networks (p. 577)

ironclad armored naval vessel (p. 468)

Iroquois Confederacy a powerful group of Native Americans in the eastern part of the United States made up of five nations: the Mohawk, Seneca, Cayuga, Onondaga, and Oneida (p. 117)

island hopping a strategy used during World War II that called for attacking and capturing certain key islands and using these islands as bases to leapfrog to others (p. 562)

joint occupation the possession and settling of an area shared by two or more countries (p. 357)

joint-stock company a company in which investors buy stock in the company in return for a share of its future profits (p. 71)

judicial branch the branch of government, including the federal court system, that interprets the nation's laws (p. 210)

judicial review the right of the Supreme Court to determine if a law violates the Constitution (pp. 222, 281)

laissez-faire policy that government should interfere as little as possible in the nation's economy (pp. 279, 350)

landslide an overwhelming victory (p. 336)

legislative branch the branch of government that makes the nation's laws (p. 209)

line of demarcation an imaginary line running down the middle of the Atlantic Ocean from the North Pole to the South Pole dividing the Americas between Spain and Portugal (p. 47)

literacy the ability to read and write (p. 113)

literacy test a method used to prevent African Americans from voting by requiring prospective voters to read and write at a specified level (p. 519)

lock in a canal, an enclosure with gates at each end used in raising or lowering boats as they pass from level to level (p. 318)

log cabin campaign name given to William Henry Harrison's campaign for the presidency in 1840, from the Whigs' use of a log cabin as their symbol (p. 351)

Loyalists American colonists who remained loyal to Britain and opposed the war for independence (p. 145)

lynching putting to death a person by the illegal action of a mob (p. 520)

maize an early form of corn grown by Native Americans (p. 19)

majority more than half (p. 335)

Manifest Destiny the idea popular in the United States during the 1800s that the country must expand its boundaries to the Pacific (p. 360)

manumission the freeing of some enslaved persons (p. 201)

martyr a person who sacrifices his or her life for a principle or cause (p. 448)

Mayflower Compact a formal document, written in 1620, that provided law and order to the Plymouth colony (p. 77)

mercantilism the theory that a state's or nation's power depended on its wealth (pp. 59, 109)

mercenary paid soldier who serves in the army of a foreign country (p. 164)

migration a movement of a large number of people into a new homeland (p. 17)

militia a group of civilians trained to fight in emergencies (pp. 118, 142)

minutemen companies of civilian soldiers who boasted that they were ready to fight on a minute's notice (p. 142)

Glossary

mission religious settlement (pp. 54, 92)

monopoly total control of an industry by one company (p. 536)

Morse code a system for transmitting messages that uses a series of dots and dashes to represent the letters of the alphabet, numbers, and punctuation (p. 389)

mosque a Muslim house of worship (p. 42)

mountain man a frontiersman living in the wilderness, as in the Rocky Mountains (p. 357)

muckraker a journalist who uncovers abuses and corruption in a society (p. 541)

mudslinging attempt to ruin an opponent's reputation with insults (p. 336)

national debt the amount of money a national government owes to other governments or its people (p. 260)

nationalism loyalty to a nation and promotion of its interests above all others (pp. 293, 547)

nativist a person who favors those born in his country and is opposed to immigrants (p. 395)

naturalization to grant full citizenship to a foreigner (p. 229)

neutral taking no side in a conflict (p. 163)

neutral rights the right to sail the seas and not take sides in a war (p. 290)

neutrality a position of not taking sides in a conflict (p. 265)

nomads people who move from place to place, usually in search of food or grazing land (p. 17)

nominating convention system in which delegates from the states selected the party's presidential candidate (p. 337)

nonimportation the act of not importing or using certain goods (p. 134)

normal school a two-year school for training high school graduates as teachers (p. 413)

Northwest Passage water route to Asia through North America sought by European explorers (p. 60)

nullify to cancel or make ineffective (pp. 271, 338)

offensive position of attacking or the attack itself (p. 463)

ordinance a law or regulation (p. 196)

override to overturn or defeat, as a bill proposed in Congress (p. 505)

overseer person who supervises a large operation or its workers (pp. 106, 403)

ozone the layer of gas composed of a form of oxygen that protects the earth and its people from cancer-causing sun rays (p. 578)

pacifist person opposed to the use of war or violence to settle disputes (p. 85)

partisan favoring one side of an issue (p. 268)

patent a document that gives an inventor the sole legal right to an invention for a period of time (pp. 308, 535)

Patriots American colonists who were determined to fight the British until American independence was won (p. 145)

patroon landowner in the Dutch colonies who ruled like a king over large areas of land (p. 83)

perjury lying when one has sworn an oath to tell the truth (p. 576)

persecute to treat someone harshly because of that person's beliefs or practices (p. 76)

petition a formal request (pp. 148, 196)

pilgrimage a journey to a holy place (p. 42)

Pilgrims Separatists who journeyed to the colonies during the 1600s for a religious purpose (p. 77)

plantation a large estate run by an owner or manager and farmed by laborers who lived there (p. 55)

plurality largest single share (p. 335)

poll tax a tax of a fixed amount per person that had to be paid before the person could vote (p. 519)

popular sovereignty political theory that government is subject to the will of the people (p. 218); before the Civil War, the idea that people living in a territory had the right to decide by voting if slavery would be allowed there (p. 442)

preamble the introduction to a formal document, especially the Constitution (pp. 151, 217)

precedent a tradition (p. 259)

prejudice an unfair opinion not based on facts (p. 392)

presidio Spanish fort in the Americas built to protect mission settlements (p. 54)

privateer armed private ship (pp. 179, 297)

Prohibition the nationwide ban on the manufacture, sale, and transportation of liquor in the United States that went into effect when the Eighteenth Amendment was ratified in 1919 (p. 550)

Glossary

propaganda ideas or information designed and spread to influence opinion (pp. 137, 547)

proportional to be the same as or corresponding to (p. 203)

proprietary colony colony run by individuals or groups to whom land was granted (pp. 83, 111)

pueblo home or community of homes built by Native Americans (pp. 29, 54)

Puritans Protestants who, during the 1600s, wanted to reform the Anglican Church (p. 77)

R

radical extreme (p. 501)

ranchero Mexican ranch owner (p. 371)

rancho huge properties for raising livestock set up by Mexican settlers in California (p. 371)

ratify to give official approval to (pp. 185, 211, 476)

Rebel Confederate soldier, so called because of opposition to the established government (p. 464)

reconciliation settling by agreement or coming together again (p. 514)

Reconstruction the reorganization and rebuilding of the former Confederate states after the Civil War (p. 501)

recruit to enlist soldiers in the army (p. 165)

relocate to force a person or group of people to move (p. 342)

Renaissance a period of intellectual and artistic creativity, c. 1300–1600 (p. 39)

rendezvous a meeting (p. 357)

reparations payment by the losing country in a war to the winner for the damages caused by the war (p. 549)

repeal to cancel an act or law (p. 134)

republic a government in which citizens rule through elected representatives (p. 193)

republicanism favoring a republic, or representative democracy, as the best form of government (p. 218)

reservation an area of public lands set aside for Native Americans (p. 531)

reserved powers powers retained by the states (p. 219)

resolution a formal expression of opinion (p. 134)

revenue incoming money (p. 133)

revival a series of meetings conducted by a preacher to arouse religious emotions (p. 413)

royal colony colony run by a governor and a council appointed by the king or queen (p. 111)

S

scalawags name given by former Confederates to Southern whites who supported Republican Reconstruction of the South (p. 510)

secede to leave or withdraw (pp. 285, 338, 438)

secession withdrawal from the Union (p. 451)

sectionalism loyalty to a region (pp. 322, 437)

sedition activities aimed at weakening established government (p. 271)

segregation the separation or isolation of a race, class, or group (p. 519, 566)

Separatists Protestants who, during the 1600s, wanted to leave the Anglican Church in order to found their own churches (p. 77)

settlement house institution located in a poor neighborhood that provided numerous community services such as medical care, child care, libraries, and classes in English (p. 538)

sharecropping system of farming in which a farmer works land for an owner who provides equipment and seeds and receives a share of the crop (p. 512)

slave code the laws passed in the Southern states that controlled and restricted enslaved people (p. 405)

smuggling trading illegally with other nations (p. 109)

speculator person who risks money in order to make a large profit (pp. 125, 261)

spiritual an African American religious folk song (p. 405)

spoils system practice of handing out government jobs to supporters; replacing government employees with the winning candidate's supporters (p. 337)

stalemate a situation during a conflict when action stops because both sides are equally powerful and neither will give in (p. 565)

states' rights rights and powers independent of the federal government that are reserved for the states by the Constitution; the belief that states' rights supersede federal rights and law (pp. 271, 451)

strait a narrow passageway connecting two larger bodies of water (p. 49)

strike a stopping of work by workers to force an employer to meet demands (p. 392)

subsistence farming farming in which only enough food to feed one's family is produced (p. 101)

suffrage the right to vote (pp. 336, 426)

suffragist a man or woman who fought for a woman's right to vote (p. 542)

tariff a tax on imports or exports (pp. 262, 338)

technology the application of scientific discoveries to practical use (pp. 40, 308)

Tejano a Mexican who claims Texas as his home (p. 363)

telegraph a device or system that uses electric signals to transmit messages by a code over wires (p. 389)

temperance the use of little or no alcoholic drink (p. 413)

tenant farmer farmer who works land owned by another and pays rent either in cash or crops (pp. 92, 402)

terrace a raised piece of land with the top leveled off to promote farming (p. 26)

terrorism the use of violence by groups against civilians to achieve a political goal (p. 578)

theocracy a form of government in which the society is ruled by religious leaders (p. 23)

Tidewater a region of flat, low-lying plains along the seacoast (p. 105)

toleration the acceptance of different beliefs (p. 79)

total war war on all aspects of the enemy's life (p. 490)

trade union organization of workers with the same trade or skill (p. 392)

Transcendentalist any of a group of New England writers who stressed the relationship between human beings and nature, spiritual things over material things, and the importance of the individual conscience (p. 415)

transcontinental extending across a continent (p. 529)

triangular trade a trade route that exchanged goods between the West Indies, the American colonies, and West Africa (p. 102)

tribute money paid for protection (pp. 52, 289)

trust a combination of firms or corporations formed by a legal agreement, especially to reduce competition (p. 536)

turnpike a road that one must pay to use; the money is used to pay for the road (p. 315)

unalienable right a right that cannot be surrendered (p. 154)

unconstitutional not agreeing or consistent with the Constitution (p. 262)

Underground Railroad a system that helped enslaved African Americans follow a network of escape routes out of the South to freedom in the North (p. 422)

utopia community based on a vision of a perfect society sought by reformers (p. 412)

vaquero Hispanic ranch hand (p. 529)

vertical integration the combining of companies that supply equipment and services needed for a particular industry (p. 536)

veto to reject a bill and prevent it from becoming a law (p. 349)

vigilantes people who take the law into their own hands (p. 377)

War Hawks Republicans during Madison's presidency who pressed for war with Britain (p. 293)

writ of assistance legal document that enabled officers to search homes and warehouses for goods that might be smuggled (p. 133)

Yankee Union soldier (p. 464)

yellow journalism a type of sensational, biased, and often false reporting (p. 545)

yeoman Southern owner of a small farm who did not have enslaved people (p. 402)

Glossary

Spanish Glossary

A

abolitionist/abolicionista una persona que favorece firmemente suprimir la esclavitud (p. 418)

abstain/abstenerse no tomar parte de una actividad, como de votar (p. 439)

adobe/adobe un ladrillo de lodo, seco al sol, usado para construir las casas de los Nativos Americanos (p. 32)

affluence/afluencia la condición de tener mucha riqueza (p. 566)

alien/extranjero una persona inmigrante que vive en un país en el cual no es ciudadano (p. 271)

alliance/alianza una asociación íntima entre naciones u otros grupos formada para avanzar intereses o causas que llevan en común (pp. 122, 547)

ambush/emboscada un ataque por sorpresa (p. 187)

amendment/enmienda una adición a un documento formal tal como la Constitución (pp. 213, 221)

American System/Sistema Americano políticas ideadas por Henry Clay para estimular el crecimiento de la industria (p. 324)

amnesty/amnistía el otorgar perdón a un número grande de personas; la protección del proceso a causa de una acción ilegal (p. 501)

annex/anexar añadir un territorio a su propio territorio (p. 367)

Antifederalists/antifederalistas personas que estaban en contra de que se ratificara la Constitución (p. 212)

apprentice/aprendiz asistente asignado para aprender el oficio de un artesano experto (p. 112)

appropriate/destinar apartar para un propósito en particular, dicho especialmente de fondos (p. 223)

archaeology/arqueología el estudio de pueblos antiguos (p. 17)

arsenal/arsenal un lugar para el almacenaje de armas y municiones (p. 448)

article/artículo una parte de un documento tal como la Constitución que trata de un solo tema (p. 209)

artifact/artefacto un artículo dejado por pueblos antiguos que representa su cultura (p. 17)

astrolabe/astrolabio un instrumento usado por los marineros para observar las posiciones de las estrellas (p. 40)

B

backcountry/monte una región de colinas y bosques al oeste de la orilla del mar (p. 105)

bicameral/bicameral que consiste de dos cámaras, especialmente dicho en una legislatura (p. 193)

black codes/códigos negros leyes establecidas en el Sur al terminar la Guerra Civil para controlar a los libertos y permitir a los dueños de plantaciones la explotación de los trabajadores afroamericanos (p. 505)

blockade/bloqueo el cerrar un área por medio de tropas o de buques de guerra para prohibir el entrar y el salir de abastos y de personas; cerrar los puertos de un país (pp. 179, 463)

blockade runner/forzador de bloqueo un buque que navega adentro y afuera de un área bloqueada (p. 468)

bond/bono una obligación hecha por el gobierno la cual promete pagar un préstamo con interés (p. 261)

boomtown/pueblo en bonanza una comunidad experimentando un auge repentino de comercio o población (p. 376, 529)

border ruffians/rufianes fronterizos hombres de Missouri que viajaban en grupos armados a votar en la elección de Kansas a mediados de los años 1850 (p. 443)

border states/estados fronterizos los estados entre el Norte y el Sur que fueron divididos sobre el problema de quedarse en la Unión o de unirse a la Confederación (p. 461)

bounty/gratificación dinero dado como recompensa, como para animar el alistamiento en el ejército (p. 482)

boycott/boicotear rehusar comprar artículos de un país en particular (p. 134)

bureaucracy/burocracia sistema en el cual oficiales no elegidos administran las leyes y políticas (p. 337)

burgesses/burgueses representantes elegidos para una asamblea (p. 73)

C

cabinet/gabinete un grupo de consejeros al presidente (p. 259)

Californios/californios mexicanos que vivían en California (p. 373)

canal/canal vía artificial de agua (p. 318)

capital/capital dinero para inversión (pp. 308, 399, 536)

capitalism/capitalismo un sistema económico basado en la propiedad particular y la empresa libre (pp. 308, 701)

caravel/carabela un buque pequeño y veloz con una proa ancha (p. 40)

carbon dating/datar con carbón un método científico usado para determinar la edad de un artefacto (p. 19)

carpetbaggers/*carpetbaggers* nombre dado a los blancos norteños que se trasladaban al Sur después de la guerra y apoyaban a los republicanos (p. 510)

cash crop/cultivo comercial cosecha cultivada para vender por dinero (pp. 103, 518)

casualty/baja un miliciano muerto, herido, o capturado (p. 469)

caucus/junta electoral una reunión llevada a cabo por un partido político para escoger el candidato a la presidencia de su partido o para decidir políticas (pp. 269, 337)

cede/ceder abandonar por tratado (p. 374)

census/censo registro oficial de una población (p. 314)

charter/carta de privilegio un documento que otorga los derechos de organizar establecimientos en una área (p. 71)

charter colony/colonia a carta colonia establecida por un grupo de colonizadores a quienes se les había dado un documento formal permitiéndoles colonizar (p. 110)

checks and balances/inspecciones y balances el sistema en el cual cada rama de gobierno refrena las otras dos ramas para que ninguna rama vuelva a ser demasiado poderosa (p. 210)

circumnavigate/circunnavegar navegar alrededor del mundo (p. 49)

citizen/ciudadano una persona que debe ser leal y tiene derecho a la protección de un estado o nación (p. 229)

civil disobedience/desobediencia civil el rehusar obedecer las leyes que uno considera injustas como una manera pacífica para inisistir en cambios (p. 566)

civil war/guerra civil conflicto entre grupos opuestos de ciudadanos del mismo país (p. 444)

civilization/civilización una cultura sumamente desarrollada, generalmente con religiones y leyes organizadas (p. 22)

classical/clásico relacionado a Grecia y Roma antigua (p. 39)

clipper ship/buque clíper un buque veloz con líneas delgadas, mástiles altos, y grandes velas cuadradas (p. 387)

coeducation/coeducación la enseñanza conjunta de estudiantes hombres y mujeres (p. 427)

collective bargaining/negociaciones colectivas discusión entre el empresario y los representantes sindicales de los trabajadores sobre salario, horas, y condiciones del taller (p. 537)

Columbian Exchange/Cambio Colombiano el cambio de productos, ideas, y personas entre Europa y las Américas (p. 60)

commission/comisión un grupo de personas dirigidas a hacer algún deber (p. 516)

committee of correspondence/comité de correspondencia una organización que usaba reuniones, cartas, y panfletos para propagar ideas políticas para las colonias (p. 137)

compromise/compromiso un acuerdo entre dos o más partidos en el cual cada partido abandona algo de lo que quiere (p. 204)

concurrent powers/poderes concurrentes poderes compartidos por los estados y el gobierno federal (p. 219)

Conestoga wagon/conestoga vehículo firme cubierto de lona blanca usado por los pioneros para moverse hacia el oeste (p. 283)

conquistador/conquistador explorador español en las Américas en los años 1500 (p. 51)

constituents/constituyentes personas representadas por miembros del Congreso (p. 223)

constitution/constitución un plan formal de gobierno (pp. 89, 193)

corruption/corrupción acciones deshonestas o ilegales (p. 510)

cotton gin/despepitadora de algodón una máquina que sacaba las semillas de las fibras de algodón (pp. 308, 398)

counter-terrorism/contraterrorismo actividades militares o políticos con el fin de combatir el terrorismo (p. 583)

coureur de bois/*coureur de bois* cazador de pieles francés viviendo entre los Nativos Americanos (p. 62)

court-martial/consejo de guerra someter a juicio por un tribunal militar (p. 326)

credit/crédito una forma de préstamo; la capacidad de comprar productos basada en pagos futuros (p. 403)

culture/cultura la manera de vivir de un grupo de personas que tienen en común sus creencias y costumbres (p. 19)

customs duties/derechos de aduana impuestos sobre productos importados del extranjero (p. 280)

debtor/deudor persona o país que debe dinero (p. 90)

decree/decreto una orden o decisión dada por alguién de autoridad (p. 364)

demilitarize/desmilitarizar quitar fuerzas armadas de un área (p. 326)

Spanish Glossary

depreciate/depreciar caer en valor (p. 197)

depression/depresión un período de poca actividad económica y de desempleo extenso (pp. 199, 350)

desert/desertar salir sin permiso (p. 173)

dictator/dictador un líder que manda con plena autoridad, a menudo de una manera cruel o brutal (p. 559)

disarmament/desarme el quitar armas (pp. 326)

discrimination/discriminación trato injusto de un grupo; trato parcial a causa de la raza, la religión, los antecedentes étnicos, o lugar de nacimiento de alguién (pp. 392, 543)

dissent/dissension desacuerdo con u oposición a una opinion (p. 76)

diversity/diversidad variedad o diferencia (p. 104)

domestic tranquility/tranquilidad doméstica mantener la paz dentro de la nación (p. 217)

draft/reclutamiento la selección de personas a servicio militar requirido (p. 481)

drought/sequía un largo período con poca lluvia (p. 29)

due process of law/proceso justo de ley idea de que el gobierno debe de seguir los procesos establecidos por ley y garantizados por la Constitución (p. 228)

effigy/efigie una figura rellenada de trapos que representa una persona impopular (p. 134)

Electoral College/Colegio Electoral un grupo especial de votantes escogidos por los votantes de sus estados para elegir al presidente y al vicepresidente (p. 210)

emancipate/emancipar liberar de la esclavitud (p. 475)

embargo/embargo una orden que prohibe el comercio con otro país (pp. 290, 573)

emigrant/emigrante una persona que sale de un país o una región para vivir en otras partes (p. 358)

empresario/empresario una persona que arregló la colonización de tierra en Texas durante los años 1800 (p. 363)

encomienda/encomienda sistema de recompensar a los conquistadores con extensiones de tierra y el derecho de recaudar impuestos y exigir mano de obra a los Nativos Americanos que vivían en la tierra (p. 55)

Enlightenment/Siglo de las Luces movimiento durante los años 1700 que propagaba la idea de que el conocimiento, la razón, y la ciencia podrían mejorar la sociedad (p. 208)

entrenched/atrincherado que ocupa una fuerte posición defensiva (p. 486)

enumerated powers/poderes enumerados poderes que pertenecen solamente al gobierno federal (p. 219)

executive branch/rama ejecutiva la rama de gobierno, dirigida por el presidente, que administra las leyes y la política de una nación (p. 210)

export/exportar vender bienes en el extranjero (p. 109)

factory system/sistema de fábrica sistema que junta en un solo lugar las categorías de fabricación para aumentar la eficiencia (p. 309)

famine/hambre una escasez extrema de comida (p. 393)

favorite son/hijo favorito candidato que recibe el apoyo de su estado natal en lugar del partido nacional (p. 335)

federal debt/deuda federal la cantidad de dinero debido por el gobierno (p. 575)

federalism/federalismo el compartir el poder entre el gobierno federal y los gobiernos estatales (pp. 208, 219)

Federalists/federalistas apoyadores de la Constitución (p. 211)

federation/federación una forma de gobierno que une grupos diferentes (p. 33)

feminist/feminista una persona que aboga por o está activa en promulgar los derechos de la mujer (p. 567)

fixed costs/costos fijos gastos regulares tal como de vivienda o mantenimiento de equipo que se quedan casi iguales año tras año (p. 403)

forty-niners/*forty-niners* personas que fueron a California durante la fiebre del oro en 1849 (p. 375)

free enterprise/libre comercio la libertad de empresas privadas para operarse competetivamente para ganancias con la mínima regulación gubernamental (p. 308)

freedman/liberto una persona liberada de la esclavitud (p. 502)

frigate/fragata buque de guerra (p. 297)

fugitive/fugitivo evadido que trata de huir (p. 438)

genocide/genocidio el eradicar un grupo racial, político, o cultural (p. 561)

global warming/calentamiento mundial un aumento contínuo del promedio de temperaturas mundiales (p. 578)

grandfather clause/cláusula de abuelo una cláusula que permitía votar a las personas que no aprobaron el examen de alfabetismo si sus padres o sus abuelos habían votado antes de que empezó la Reconstrucción; una excepción a una ley basada en circunstancias preexistentes (p. 519)

greenback/billete de dorso verde un billete de la moneda de EE.UU. expedido primeramente por el Norte durante la Guerra Civil (p. 483)

guerrilla tactics/tácticas de guerrilla referente a ataques sorpresas o incursiones en lugar de la guerra organizada (p. 344)

guerrilla warfare/contienda a guerrilleros una técnica de tirar y darse a la huída usada en combates de guerra (p. 180)

H

habeas corpus/hábeas corpus una orden legal para una encuesta para determinar si una persona ha sido encarcelada legalmente (p. 481)

hieroglyphics/jeroglíficos una forma antigua de escribir usando símbolos y dibujos para representar palabras, sonidos, y conceptos (p. 24)

Holocaust/Holocausto el nombre dado a la matanza extensa de judíos y otros grupos por los nazis durante la Segunda Guerra Mundial (p. 561)

horizontal integration/integración horizontal la asociación de firmas competitivas en una sociedad anónima (p. 536)

human rights/derechos humanos derechos, tal como la libertad de encarcelamiento ilegal, tortura, y ejecución, considerados como pertenecientes a todas las personas (p. 574)

I

Ice Age/Época Glacial un período de temperaturas extremadamente frías cuando parte de la superficie del planeta estaba cubierta de extensiones masivas de hielo (p. 17)

impeach/acusar acusación formal a un oficial público de mala conducta en la oficina (pp. 223, 507, 573)

imperialism/imperialismo las acciones usadas por una nación para ejercer control político o económico sobre naciones más pequeñas y débiles (p. 544)

implied powers/poderes implícitos poderes no mencionados específicamente en la Constitución (pp. 221, 268)

import/importar comprar bienes de mercados extranjeros (p. 109)

impressment/requisición captura de marineros para forzarlos a servir en una marina extranjera (pp. 265, 290)

indentured servant/sirviente contratado trabajador que consiente trabajar sin pago durante un cierto período de tiempo a cambio del pasaje a América (p. 87)

Industrial Revolution/Revolución Industrial el cambio de una sociedad agraria en una basada en la industria que empezó en la Gran Bretaña y se promulgó a los Estados Unidos alrededor del año 1800 (p. 307)

inflation/inflación aumento contínuo del precio de productos y servicios (pp. 175, 483)

integrate/integrar suprimir la segregación de las razas diferentes e introducir a membrecía igual y común en la sociedad (p. 512)

interchangeable parts/partes intercambiables piezas uniformes que pueden ser hechas en grandes cantidades para reemplazar otras piezas idénticas (p. 309)

internal improvements/mejoramientos internos proyectos federales, tal como canales y carreteras, para desarrollar el sistema de transportación de una nación (p. 322)

Internet/Internet enlaze a través de todo el mundo de redes de computadoras (p. 577)

ironclad/acorazado buque armado (p. 468)

Iroquois Confederacy/Confederación Iroquesa un grupo poderoso de Nativos Americanos de la región oriental de los Estados Unidos compuesto de cinco naciones: los pueblos mohawk, séneca, cayuga, onondaga y oneida (p. 117)

island hopping/saltar islas una estrategia usada durante la Segunda Guerra Mundial que demandó el atacar y capturar ciertas islas importantes para usarlas como bases para saltar por encima de otras (p. 562)

J

joint occupation/ocupación en común la posesión y colonización de un área como esfuerzo compartido por dos o más países (p. 357)

joint-stock company/compañía por acciones una compañía en la cual los inversionistas compran acciones de la compañia a cambio de una porción de las ganancias en el futuro (p. 71)

judicial branch/rama judicial la rama de gobierno, incluyendo el sistema de tribunales federales, que interpreta las leyes de una nación (p. 210)

judicial review/repaso judicial el derecho del Tribunal Supremo para determinar si una ley viola la Constitución (pp. 222, 281)

L

laissez-faire/*laissez-faire* la creencia de que el gobierno no debe de involucrarse en los asuntos comerciales y económicos del país (pp. 279, 350)

landslide/victoria arrolladora una victoria abrumadora (p. 336)

legislative branch/rama legislativa la rama de gobierno que redacta las leyes de una nación (p. 209)

Spanish Glossary

line of demarcation/línea de demarcación una línea imaginaria a lo largo del medio del Océano Atlántico desde el Polo Norte hasta el Polo Sur para dividir las Américas entre España y Portugal (p. 47)

literacy/alfabetismo la capacidad de leer y escribir (p. 113)

literacy test/examen de alfabetismo un método usado para prohibir a los afroamericanos a votar por requerir a presuntos votantes que pudieran leer y escribir a niveles especificados (p. 519)

lock/esclusa en un canal un recinto con puertas en cada extremo y usado para levantar y bajar los buques mientras pasan de un nivel al otro (p. 318)

log cabin campaign/campaña de cabaña rústica el nombre dado a la campaña para la presidencia de William Henry Harrison en 1840, debido al uso de una cabaña rústica de troncos como su símbolo por los whigs (p. 351)

Loyalists/lealistas colonizadores americanos que quedaron leales a la Bretaña y se opusieron a la guerra para la independencia (p. 145)

lynching/linchamiento matar a una persona a través de la acción ilegal de una muchedumbre airada (p. 520)

maize/maíz una forma antigua de elote cultivado por los Nativos Americanos (p. 19)

majority/mayoría más de la mitad (p. 335)

Manifest Destiny/Destino Manifiesto la idea popular en los Estados Unidos durante los años 1800 de que el país debería de extender sus fronteras hasta el Pacífico (p. 360)

manumission/manumisión el liberar a unas personas esclavizadas (p. 201)

martyr/mártir una persona que sacrifica su vida por un principio o una causa (p. 448)

Mayflower Compact/Convenio del Mayflower un documento formal escrito en 1620 que proporcionó leyes para el mantenimiento del orden público en la colonia de Plymouth (p. 77)

mercantilism/mercantilismo idea de que el poder de una nación dependía de ampliar su comercio y aumentar sus reservas de oro (pp. 59, 109)

mercenary/mercenario soldado remunerado para servir en el ejército de un país extranjero (p. 164)

migration/migración el movimiento de un gran número de personas hacia una nueva patria (p. 17)

militia/milicia un grupo de civiles entrenados para luchar durante emergencias (pp. 118, 142)

minutemen/*minutemen* compañías de soldados civiles que se jactaban de que podrían estar listos para tomar armas en sólo un minuto (p. 142)

mission/misión una comunidad religiosa (pp. 54, 92)

monopoly/monopolio control total de una industria por una persona o una compañía (p. 536)

Morse code/código Morse un sistema para transmitir mensajes que usa una serie de puntos y rayas para representar las letras del abecedario, los números, y la puntuación (p. 389)

mosque/mezquita una casa de alabanza musulmana (p. 42)

mountain man/hombre montañés colonizador que vivía en el monte, como en las Montañas Rocosas (p. 357)

muckraker/expositor de corrupción periodista que descubre abusos y corrupción en una sociedad (p. 541)

mudslinging/detractar intentar arruinar la reputación de un adversario con insultos (p. 336)

national debt/deuda nacional la cantidad de dinero que un gobierno debe a otros gobiernos o a su pueblo (p. 260)

nationalism/nacionalismo lealtad a una nación y promoción de sus intereses sobre todos los demás (pp. 293, 547)

nativist/nativista una persona que favorece a los nacidos en su patria y se opone a los inmigrantes (p. 395)

naturalization/naturalización el otorgar la plena ciudadanía a un extranjero (p. 229)

neutral/neutral que no toma partido a ninguna persona ni a ningún país en un conflicto (p. 163)

neutral rights/derechos neutrales el derecho para navegar en el mar sin tomar partido en una guerra (p. 290)

neutrality/neutralidad una posición de no tomar partido en un conflicto (p. 265)

nomads/nómadas personas que se mueven de lugar a lugar, generalmente en busca de comida o de tierras para pastar (p. 17)

nominating convention/convención nominadora sistema en el cual los diputados estatales escogieron al candidato para la presidencia de su partido (p. 337)

nonimportation/no importación la acción de evitar la importación o uso de ciertos productos (p. 134)

normal school/escuela normal una escuela con programa de dos años para entrenar a los graduados de preparatoria para ser maestros (p. 413)

Northwest Passage/Paso Noroeste ruta acuática para Asia por América del Norte buscada por exploradores europeos (p. 60)

nullify/anular cancelar o hacer sin efecto (pp. 271, 338)

O

offensive/ofensiva la posición de atacar o el mismo ataque (p. 463)

ordinance/ordenanza una ley o regulación (p. 196)

override/vencer rechazar o derrotar, como un proyecto de ley propuesto en el Congreso (p. 505)

overseer/capataz persona que supervisa una operación grande o a sus trabajadores (pp. 106, 403)

ozone/ozono el estrato de gas compuesto de una forma de oxígeno que protege la tierra y a su gente de los rayos del sol que causan el cáncer (p. 578)

P

pacifist/pacifista persona opuesta al uso de guerra o violencia para arreglar disputas (pp. 85)

partisan/partidario a favor de una parte de un asunto (p. 268)

patent/patente un documento que da al inventor el derecho exclusivo legal de una invención durante un período de tiempo (p. 308, 535)

Patriots/patriotas colonizadores americanos que estaban determinados para luchar en contra de los británicos hasta que se ganara la independencia americana (p. 145)

patroon/*patroon* terrateniente de las colonias holandesas que gobernaba áreas grandes de tierra como un rey (p. 83)

perjury/perjurio el mentir después de haber jurado decir la verdad (p. 576)

persecute/perseguir tratar cruelmente a alguién a causa de sus creencias o prácticas (p. 76)

petition/petición una solicitud formal (pp. 148, 196)

pilgrimage/peregrinación un viaje a un sitio sagrado (p. 42)

Pilgrims/peregrinos separatistas que viajaron a las colonias durante los años 1600 por un propósito religioso (p. 77)

plantation/plantación una finca grande manejada por el dueño o un gerente y cultivada por trabajadores que vivían allí (p. 55)

plurality/pluralidad el mayor número de individuos (p. 335)

poll tax/impuesto de capitación un impuesto de una cantidad fija por cada persona que tenía que ser pagada antes de que pudiera votar la persona (p. 519)

popular sovereignty/soberanía popular la teoría política de que el gobierno está sujeto a la voluntad del pueblo (p. 218); antes de la Guerra Civil, la idea de que la gente que vivía en un territorio tenía el derecho de decidir por votar si allí sería permitida la esclavitud (p. 442)

preamble/preámbulo la introducción de un documento formal, especialmente la Constitución (pp. 151, 217)

precedent/precedente una tradición (p. 259)

prejudice/prejuicio una opinión injusta no basada en los hechos (p. 392)

presidio/presidio un fuerte español en las Américas construido para proteger las colonias misioneras (p. 54)

privateer/buque corsario buque armado privado (pp. 179, 297)

Prohibition/Prohibición entredicho contra la fabricación, transportación, y venta de bebidas alcohólicas por todo los Estados Unidos (p. 550)

propaganda/propaganda ideas o información diseñadas para influenciar la opinión (pp. 137, 547)

proportional/proporcional que son iguales o que corresponden (p. 203)

proprietary colony/colonia propietaria colonia dirigida por personas o grupos a quienes se les había otorgado la tierra (pp. 83, 111)

pueblo/pueblo una casa o una comunidad de casas construidas por Nativos Americanos (pp. 29, 54)

Puritans/puritanos protestantes que, durante los años 1600, querían reformar la iglesia anglicana (p. 77)

R

radical/radical extremo (p. 501)

ranchero/ranchero dueño de rancho mexicano (p. 371)

rancho/rancho propiedades grandísimas para producir ganado establecidas por colonizadores mexicanos en California (p. 371)

ratify/ratificar dar aprobación oficial para (pp. 185, 211, 476)

Rebel/rebelde soldado confederado, así nombrado a causa de su oposición al gobierno establecido (p. 464)

reconciliation/reconciliación arreglar por acuerdo o por reunirse de nuevo (p. 514)

Reconstruction/Reconstrucción la reorganización y la reconstrucción de los anteriores estados confederados después de la Guerra Civil (p. 501)

recruit/reclutar enlistar a soldados para el ejército (p. 165)

relocate/reubicar forzar a una persona o a un grupo de personas a trasladarse (p. 342)

Renaissance/Renacimiento un período de creatividad intelectual y artística, alrededor de los años 1300–1600 (p. 39)

rendezvous/*rendezvous* una reunión (p. 357)

reparations/reparaciones pago por el país que pierde una guerra al país que gana por los daños causados por la guerra (p. 549)

Spanish Glossary

repeal/revocar cancelar un decreto o ley (p. 134)

republic/república un gobierno en el cual ciudadanos gobiernan por medio de representantes elegidos (p. 193)

republicanism/republicanismo que favorece una república, o sea una democracia representativa, como la mejor forma de gobierno (p. 218)

reservation/reservación un área de tierra pública apartada para los Nativos Americanos (p. 531)

reserved powers/poderes reservados poderes retenidos por los estados (p. 219)

resolution/resolución una expresión formal de opinión (p. 134)

revenue/ingresos entrada de dinero (p. 133)

revival/renacimiento religioso una serie de reuniones dirigidas por un predicador para animar emociones religiosas (p. 413)

royal colony/colonia real colonia administrada por un gobernador y un consejo nombrados por el rey o reina (p. 111)

scalawags/*scalawags* nombre dado por los confederados anteriores a los blancos sureños que apoyaban la Reconstrucción republicana del Sur (p. 510)

secede/separarse abandonar o retirar (pp. 285, 338, 438)

secession/secesión retiro de la Unión (p. 451)

sectionalism/regionalismo lealtad a una región (pp. 322, 437)

sedition/sedición actividades con el propósito de debilitar un gobierno establecido (p. 271)

segregation/segregación la separación o aislamiento de una raza, una clase, o un grupo (pp. 519, 566)

Separatists/separatistas protestantes que, durante los años 1600, querían dejar la iglesia anglicana para fundar sus propias iglesias (p. 77)

settlement house/casa de beneficencia institución colocada en una vecindad pobre que proveía numerosos servicios a la comunidad tal como cuidado médico, cuidado de niños, bibliotecas, y clases de inglés (p. 538)

sharecropping/aparcería sistema de agricultura en el cual un granjero labra la tierra para un dueño que provee equipo y semillas y recibe una porción de la cosecha (p. 512)

slave code/código de esclavos las leyes aprobadas en los estados sureños que controlaban y restringían a la gente esclavizada (p. 405)

smuggling/contrabandear cambiar ilegalmente con otras naciones (p. 109)

speculator/especulador persona que arriesga dinero para hacer una ganancia grande (pp. 125, 261)

spiritual/espiritual una canción popular religiosa afroamericana (p. 405)

spoils system/sistema de despojos la práctica de dar puestos gubernamentales a los partidarios; reemplazar a los empleados del gobierno con los partidarios del candidato victorioso (p. 337)

stalemate/estancamiento una situación durante un conflicto cuando la acción se para debido a que ambos partidos son igualmente poderosos y ningún de los dos lo abandonará (p. 565)

states' rights/derechos estatales derechos y poderes independientes del gobierno federal que son reservados a los estados por la Constitución (pp. 271, 451)

strait/estrecho un paso angosto que conecta dos extensiones más grandes de agua (p. 49)

strike/huelga un paro de trabajo por los trabajadores para forzar al empresario a satisfacer demandas (p. 392)

subsistence farming/agricultura para subsistencia labranza que produce solamente la comida que se necesita para dar de comer a la familia del trabajador (p. 101)

suffrage/sufragio el derecho al voto (pp. 336, 426)

suffragist/sufragista un hombre o mujer que luchaba para el derecho al voto de la mujer (p. 542)

tariff/tarifa impuesto sobre productos importados o exportados (pp. 262, 338)

technology/tecnología el uso de conocimientos científicos para propósitos prácticos (pp. 40, 308)

Tejano/tejano un mexicano que reclama Texas como su patria (p. 363)

telegraph/telégrafo un aparato o sistema que usa señales eléctricas para transmitir mensajes a códigos a través de alambres (p. 389)

temperance/templanza el uso de poca o de ninguna bebida alcohólica (p. 413)

tenant farmer/granjero arrendatario un granjero que labra la tierra de otro dueño y paga renta ya sea con la cosecha o al contado (pp. 92, 402)

terrace/terraza una parcela de tierra elevada y allanada para fomentar la agricultura (p. 26)

terrorism/terrorismo el uso de la violencia contra ciudadanos para lograr un gol político (p. 578)

theocracy/teocracia una forma de gobierno en la cual la sociedad está gobernada por líderes religiosos (p. 23)

Tidewater/Orilla del Mar una región de llanuras planas y bajas alrededor de la costa del mar (p. 105)

toleration/tolerancia el aceptar creencias diferentes (p. 79)

total war/guerra total la guerra en todo aspecto de la vida del enemigo (p. 490)

trade union/gremio una organización de artesanos con el mismo oficio o destreza (pp. 392)

Transcendentalist/transcendentalista uno de un grupo de escritores de Nueva Inglaterra que acentuaban la relación entre los seres humanos y la naturaleza, asuntos espirituales sobre asuntos materiales, y la importancia de la conciencia particular (p. 415)

transcontinental/*transcontinental* que se extiende a través del continente (p. 529)

triangular trade/trato triangular una ruta de comercio para cambiar productos entre las Antillas, las colonias americanas, y África del Oeste (p. 102)

tribute/tributo dinero pagado para protección (pp. 52, 289)

trust/cártel una combinación de firmas o sociedades anónimas formada por un acuerdo legal, especialmente para reducir la competición (pp. 536)

turnpike/autopista una carretera que uno debe de pagar para usar; el dinero se usa para pagar el costo de la carretera (p. 315)

unalienable right/derecho inalienable un derecho al que no se puede renunciar (p. 154)

unconstitutional/anticonstitucional no de acuerdo ni consistente con la Constitución (p. 262)

Underground Railroad/Ferrocarril Subterráneo un sistema que ayudó a los afroamericanos esclavizados a seguir una red de rutas de escape afuera del Sur hacia la libertad del Norte (p. 422)

utopia/utopía una comunidad basada en una visión de la sociedad perfecta buscada por los reformistas (p. 412)

vaquero/vaquero trabajador ranchero hispánico (p. 529)

vertical integration/integración vertical la asociación de compañías que abastecen con equipo y servicios necesarios para una industria particular (p. 536)

veto/vetar rechazar un proyecto de ley y prevenir que vuelva a ser una ley (p. 349)

vigilantes/vigilantes gente que toman la ley en sus propias manos (pp. 377)

War Hawks/halcones de guerra republicanos durante la presidencia de Madison que insistían en la guerra con la Bretaña (p. 293)

writ of assistance/escrito de asistencia documento legal que permitía a los oficiales que exploraran las casas y bodegas en busca de productos que tal vez pudieran ser de contrabandeado (p. 133)

Yankee/yanqui soldado de la Unión (p. 464)

yellow journalism/periodismo amarillista una clase de reportaje sensacional, prejuzgado, y a menudo falso (p. 545)

yeoman/terrateniente menor dueño sureño de una granja pequeña que no tenía esclavos (p. 402)

Spanish Glossary

Teacher, Student & Parent One-Stop Internet Resources

This textbook contains one-stop Internet resources for teachers, students and parents. Log on to tarvol1.glencoe.com for more information. Online study tools include Chapter Overviews, Self-Check Quizzes, an Interactive Tutor, and E-Flashcards. Online research tools include Student Web Activities, Beyond the Textbook Features, Current Events, Web Resources, and State Resources. The interactive online student edition includes the complete Interactive Student Edition along with textbook updates. Especially for teachers, Glencoe offers an online Teacher Forum, Web Activity Lesson Plans, and Literature Connections.

Italicized page numbers refer to illustrations. The following abbreviations are used in the index:
m = map, c = chart, p = photograph or picture, g = graph, crt = cartoon, ptg = painting, q = quote

Index

Index

Index

Index

Index

Index

Index

Index

Index

Index

Acknowledgements and Photo Credits

Acknowledgements

50 From *Morning Girl* by Michael Dorris. Text © 1992 by Michael Dorris. Reprinted with permission from Hyperion Books for Children.

107 From *The Kidnapped Prince* by Olaudah Equiano. Adapted by Ann Cameron. Copyright © 1995 by Ann Cameron. Reprinted by permission of Alfred A. Knopf, Inc.

140 Excerpt from *Johnny Tremain* by Esther Forbes. Copyright © 1943 by Esther Forbes Hoskins, © renewed 1971 by Linwood M. Erskine, Jr., Executor of the Estate of Esther Forbes Hoskins. Reprinted by permission of Houghton Mifflin Co. All rights reserved.

295 From *Night Flying Woman: An Ojibway Narrative* by Ignatia Broker. Copyright © 1983 by the Minnesota Historical Society. Reprinted by permission.

567, 623 Reprinted by arrangement with the Heirs to the Estate of Martin Luther King, Jr., c/o Writers House, Inc. as agent for the proprietor. Copyright © 1963 by Martin Luther King, Jr., copyright renewed 1991 by Coretta Scott King.

604 "God Bless the USA," words and music by Lee Greenwood. Copyright © 1984 Songs of Universal Inc. and Universal Songs of Polygram International Inc. (BMI) International Copyright Secured. All Rights Reserved.

Glencoe would like to acknowledge the artists and agencies who participated in illustrating this program: Morgan Cain & Associates; Ortelius Design, Inc.; QA Digital.

Photo Credits

COVER (tl)Corbis, (tc)PhotoDisc, (tr)Chicago Historical Society, (bl)Massachusetts Historical Society; (br)Mongerson-Wunderlich Gallery, Chicago, (flag) PhotoDisc, (background)Library of Congress; iv (t)file photo, (b)Peabody Museum of Salem; ix Stock Montage; v (t)Grant Heilman Photography, (tc)Mark Burnett, (b)PhotoDisc, (bc)Superstock; vi Michael Freeman; vii Kari Haavisto; x Field Museum of Natural History; xi Chester County Historical Society, West Chester, PA; xiv Corbis; xv (t)courtesy Ford Motor Company, (b)PhotoDisc; xvii Collection of Michael Barson; xviii Larry Kunkel/FPG RA16, RA17 PhotoDisc; 2 (t)Robert W. Madden/National Geographic Society, (b)Rich Buzzelli/Tom Stack & Associates; 4 (t)David M. Dennis, (b)Walter Meayers Edwards/National Geographic Society; 5 Private Collection; 6 (t)Museum of Ethnology, (t)Johnny Johnson (bl)Jerry Jacks/courtesy Arizona State Museum, University of Arizona, (l)Eliot Cohen; 7 Jeremy Horner/Stone; 9 Richard Alexander Cooke III, Scala/Art Resource, NY; 12 Scala/Art Resource, NY; 12-13 Brown Brothers; 14 (l)Bridgeman/Art Resource, NY; (r)Addison Doty/Morning Star Gallery, 15 (t)Ed Simpson/Stone, (bl)Michel Zabe'/Museo Templo Major; (br)Heye Foundation, National Museum of The American Indian/Smithsonian Institution; 16 file photo; 17 Heye Foundation, National Museum of The American Indian/Smithsonian Institutte; 22 Boltin Picture Library; 23 (l)Richard Alexander Cooke III, (r)David Hiser/Stone; 25 (t)DDB Stock Photo, (bl)Michel Zabe', (background)USDA, (br)N. Carter/North Wind Picture Archive, (br)Inga Spence/DDB Stock Photo; 27 Museum of Ethnology; 28 Jerry Jacka/courtesy Arizona State Museum, Arizona University; 29 David Muench; 34 (t)file photo, (b)Addison Doty/Morning Star Gallery; 36 U.S. Architect of the Capitol, (b)National Museum of African Art/Jeffrey Ploskonka, (l)Archivio Fotografico del Museo Preistorico Etnografico L. Pigorini, Roma; 37 ©Architect of the United States, (t)The Library of Congress, (b)file photo, ©National Portrait Gallery, Smithsonian Institution/Art Resource, NY; 38 Brown Brothers; 40 (l)NASA, (r)National Maritime Museum; 43 Peabody Museum of Salem; 44 Giraudon/Art Resource, NY; 45 Doug Martin; 46 Giraudon/Art Resource, NY; 47 Culver Pictures; 50 (t)Louise Erdrich, (b)Musee de L'Homme, Palais de Chateau, Paris; 51 courtesy The Oakland Museum; 52 Collection of Colonel Stuart S. Corning/Rob Huntley/Lightstream; 54 Museo de Historia, Chapultepec/Bob Schalkwijk; 56 Walter Edwards; 57 (t)Chas W. Polzer, (c)Greg Edwards, (b)Edwardo Fuss; 58 SuperStock; 59 "Kateri Tekakwitha" by Father Claude Chauchetiere, S.J., around 1690, photo by Bob Peters, St. Francis Xavier Mission, Kahnawake, Quebec; 60 Corbis; 61 courtesy The Oakland Museum; 63 Maritime Museum, Seville/Artephot/Oronoz; 64 (t)University Museum of National Antiquities, Oslo, Norway, (c)U.S. Architect of the Capitol, (b)courtresy The Oakland Museum; 66 Plimoth Plantation; 66-67 Corbis; 67 Brown Brothers; 68 (t)Hulton/Archive, (b)file photo; 69 (t)New York Historical Society, (bl)Courtesy Haffenreffer Museum of Anthropology, Brown University, (br)Courtesy The Oakland Museum; 70-71 Jamestown-Yorktown Foundation; 72 National Portrait Gallery, Smithsonian Institution/Art Resource, NY; 74 Richard T. Nowitz/National Geographic Society; 75 (t)Jamestown Foundation, (c)file photo, (b)Bob Pratt/ National Geographic Society; 76 Plimoth Plantation; 78 courtesy Pilgrim Society, Plymouth, MA; 79 Brown Brothers; 82 courtesy Winterthur Museum; 84 Glencoe file photo; 86 British Museum; 88 Corbis; 89 Courtesy of APVA Preservation Virginia; 90 Culver Pictures; 91 (t)Larry Stevens/Nawrocki Stock Photo, (b)Nawrocki Stock Photo; 92 Gibbes Museum of Art; 93 Historical Picture Collection/Stock Montage; 94 (t)National Portrait Gallery, Smithsonian Institution/Art Resource, NY, (tc)Private Collection, (bc)courtesy Haffenreffer Museum of Anthropology, Brown University, (b)Historical Picture Collection/Stock Montage; 96 (t)Smithsonian Institution, (b)Peabody Museum of Salem; 97 Timothy Fuller; 98 (l)Chicago Historical Society, (r)courtesy Historic Deerfield Inc./Amanda Merullo 99 (t)courtesy Old John Street United Methodist Church, (bl)Blue Ridge Institute & Museums/Ferrum College, (br)Yale University Art Gallery, 100 Colonial Williamsburg; 101 (l)Lee Snider/Corbis, (r)Bruce M. Wellman/Stock Boston; 102 Peabody Essex Museum/Mark Sexton, 104 courtesy American Antiquarian Society; 105 Colonial Williamsburg; 107 Royal Albert Memorial Museum, Exeter, England; 108 Yale University Art Gallery; 109-110 Yale University Art Gallery; 111 National Portrait Gallery, London/SuperStock; 111-112 PhotoDisc; 112 The Ohio Historical Village, Columbus, Ohio, Photo by Doug Martin; 116 courtesy American Antiquarian Society; 118 Culver Pictures; 120 file photo; 121 Musee de L'Homme/M. Delaplanche; 122 State Historical Society of Wisconsin Museum Collection; 124 Amanita Pictures; 126 (t)Colonial Williamsburg, (tc)courtesy American Antiquarian Society, (bc)Musee de L'Homme/M. Delaplanche (b)Library of Congress; 128 David A. Schorsch; 128-129 Corbis; 129 file photo; 130 (tl)Archive Photos, (tr)courtesy Peabody & Essex Museum, Salem, MA, (b)Stock Montage; 131 (t)Painting by Don Troianni, www.historicalartprints.com (cr)DAR Museum on loan from Boston Tea Party Chapter, (cl)courtesy American Antiquarian Society, (r)Massachusetts Historical Society; 132 Crown copyright. Historic Royal Palaces. Photograph David Chalmess; 134 Massachusetts Historical Society; 135 Patrick Henry Before the Virginia House of Burgesses (1851) by Peter F. Rothermel. Red Hill, The Patrick Henry National Memorial, Brookneal, VA; 136 file photo; 138 (tr)Corbis-Bettmann, (br)courtesy American Antiquarian Society, (c)DAR Museum on loan from Boston Tea Party Chapter, (tc)The Royal Collection, Her Majesty Queen Elizabeth II (l)Stock Montage; 140 Culver Pictures/SuperStock; 141-142 North Wind Picture Archives; 144 Concord Museum, Concord, MA; 146 Private Collection; 147 White House Historical Association; 148 Historical Society of Pennsylvania; 149 Stock Montage; 150 Virginia Historical Society, All Rights Reserved; 152 Painting by Don Troiani, www.historicalartprints.com; 155 Corbis; 157 Deposited by the City of Boston, courtesy Museum of Fine Arts, Boston; 160 (l)Virginia Historical Society, (r)Giraudon/Art Resource; 160-161 Frances Tavern Museum, New York City; 161 file; 162 West Point Museum; 163 North Wind Picture Archive; 164 (l)Corbis-Bettmann, (r)UPI/Corbis-Bettmann; 166 Brown Brothers; 172 Chicago Historical Society; 173 The Valley Forge Historical Society; 174 Corbis; 175 Eric P. Newman Numismatic Education Society; 176 file photo; 177 William T. Ranney, MARION CROSSING THE PEDEE, 1850, 1983.125; Amon Carter Museum, Fort Worth, Texas; 178-179 (background)Library of Congress; 179 (inset)Massachusettes Historical Society; 180 Stock Montage; 182 Archives Division, Texas State Library; 183 Chicago Historical Society; 184 Lafayette College Art Collection, Easton, PA. Gift of Mrs. John Hubbard; 185 Trumball Collection, Yale University Art Gallery; 186 Courtesy J. Quintus Massie on behalf of descendants; 188 Painting by Don Troiani, www.historicalartprints.com (bl)Virginia Historical Society, (tr)The Metropolitan Museum of Art, Gift of John S. Kennedy, 1897. (97.34); 190 Picture Research Consultants; 190-191 Corbis; 191(bl)Corbis Bettmann, (c) White House Historical Association, (br)New York Historical Society; 192 North Wind Picture Archive; 193 Picture Research Consultants; 194 file photo; 196 (background)PhotoDisc; 197 (r)Independence National Historic Park, (l)Chicago Historical Society; 199 Independence National Historical Park; 200 Corbis-Bettmann; 201 (r)Delaware Art Museum, Wilmington. Gift of Absalom Jones School, Wilmington, (l)Moorland Spingarn Research Center, Howard University; 202 SuperStock; 203 Library of Congress; 204 Independence National Historic Park; 207 Independence National Historical Park; 208 National Portrait Gallery; 209 Fred Maroon/Smithsonian Institution; 210 Supreme Court Historical Society; 211 file photo; 212 Bequest of Winslow Warren, courtesy Museum of Fine Arts, Boston; 213 file photo; 214 (t)Library of Congress, (c)Bettmann/Corbis, (b)Fraunces Tavern Museum; 215 Independence National Historic Park; 216 Picture Research Consultants; 220 Massachusetts Historical Society; 221 SuperStock; 224 White House/Liaison Agency; 226 Bob Daemmrich/Stone; 228 Sylvain Grandadam/Stone; 230 Mark Burnett; 244 Boltin Picture Library; 249 Cobalt Productions; 251 Paul Conklin; 252 Museum of American Textile History; 254 (inset)Smithsonian Institution; 254 Smithsonian Institution; 254-255 (t)Independence National Historic Park/Joseph Painter, 256 (t) file photo, (c) White House Historical Association, (b)Erich Lessing/Art Resource, NY; 257 (t)Boston Naval Library & Institute Collection, (bl)Yale University Art Gallery, (c)White House Historical Association, (br)Collection of David J. & Janice L. Frent; 258 Frank & Marie-Therese Wood Print Collection, Alexandria, VA; 260 Aaron Haupt; 261 David R. Frazier; 263 Atwater Kent Museum; 265 Chicago Historical Society; 268 courtesy Winterthur Museum; 269 Stock Montage; 271 Archive Photo; 272 Stock Montage; 274 Library of Congress; 276 (tl)Duke University

Archives, (tr)Royal Ontario Museum, Toronto/National Geographic Society, (c)White House Historical Association, (b)Eric Lessing/Art Resources, NY; 276-277 Don Troianni, www.historicalartprints.com; 277(t)file photo, (c)White House Historical Association, (b)North Wind Picture Archives; 278 The White House Historical Association; 279 North Wind Picture Archive; 280 (r)The Huntington - San Marino, CA/SuperStock, (l)Corbis, 282 West Virginia State Museum; 288 North Wind Picture Archives; 289 Corbis; 292 Field Museum of Natural History; 293 Brown Brothers; 295 (l)Darlene Pfister/Minneapolis Star Tribune, (r)Minnesota Historical Society; 296 Princeton University Library; 297 Library of Congress; 299 Stock Montage; 301 Missouri Historical Society; 302 (t)White House Historical Association, (background)Kendall Cross, (cl)White House Historical Association, (cr)Library of Congress, (b)New York State Historical Association, Cooperstown; 304 (l)Smithsonian Institution, Burstein Collection/Corbis, (r)Bob Mullenix; 304-305 (t)Corbis, (presidential gallery) White House Historical Association; 305 (l,r)New York Historical Society; 306 Corbis; 307 Aaron Haupt; 309 (tl)Baker Library, Harvard University, (tr)Lowell National Historical Park, (bl)file photo, (br)File photo, (background)file photo; 314 Corbis; 315 Stock Montage; 316 (tl)Michael G. Buettner, Lincoln Highway Association, (br)Douglas Kirkland/Corbis; 317 (tr)SuperStock, (l)David G. Houser/Corbis, (br)Henry Diltz/Corbis; 324 (t)Boot Hill Museum/Henry Groskinsky, (b)Peter Menzel; 325 (l)Library of Congress, (r)Collection of the Boston Public Library, Print Division, 326 file photo; 328 (t)Smithsonian Institution, (b)New York Historical Society, (r)Anthony Richardson, (bc)James Monroe Museum & Memorial Library, (l)Craig McDougal, (tc)The Metropolitan Museum of Art, Rogers Fund, 1942. (42.95.11); 328-329 St. Louis Art Museum, Eliza McMillan Fund; 329 courtesy Charleston Museum; 331 Library of Congress; 333 Boatmen's National Bank of St. Louis; 334 Collection of David J. & Janice L. Frent; 335 New York Historical Society; 337 Library Company of Philadelphia; 338 North Wind Picture Archive; 340 Archives & Manuscripts Division of the Oklahoma Historical Society; 340-341 Kevin C. Chadwick/National Geographic Society; 341 (l)White House Historical Association, (r)Archives & Manuscripts Division of the Oklahoma Historical Society; 343 SuperStock; 344 National Museum of American Art, Smithsonian Institution. Gift of Mrs. Joseph Harrison, JR/Art Resource, NY; 349 New York Historical Society; 350 (l)National Portrait Gallery, Smithsonian Institution/Art Resource, NY, (r)Smithsonian Institution; 354 (l)Stock Montage, (r)Collection of David J. & Janet L. Frent; 354-355 (t)The Manoogian Foundation, on loan to the National Gallery of Art, Washington. Photo by Lyle Peterzell, (presidential gallery) White House Historical Association; 355 (l)Collection Mrs. J. Maxwell Moran, (r)Collection of David J. & Janice L. Frent; 356 Nikki Pahl; 357 Archive Photo; 359 Henry Groskinsky; 362 Archives Division, Texas State Library; 363 Institute of Texas Culture; 364 Friends of the Governor's Mansion, Austin; 366 Archives Division, Texas State Library; 369 Panhandle Plains Historical Museum; 370 Thomas Gilcrease Institute of American Art, Tulsa, OK; 371 file photo; 373 California State Library; 375 courtesy The Oakland Museum; 376 (l)White House Historical Association, (c)Doug Martin, (l)Levi Strauss & Company; 377 Denver Public Library, Western History Collection; 378 Bettmann/Corbis; 379 (l)Corbis-Bettmann, (r)Wenham Museum; 380 courtesy Denver Public Library Western History Department; 382 American Museum, Bath,England/Bridgeman Collection/SuperStock, Inc.; 383 Timothy Fuller; 384 (t)Smithsonian Institution, (c,b)file photo; 384-385 (t)SuperStock, (presidential gallery) White House Historical Association; 385 (l)North Wind Picture Archive, (r)National Portrait Gallery, Smithsonian Institution; 386 Smithsonian Institution/Charles Phillips; 391 Jack Naylor; 392 Museum of Fine Arts, Boston, M. & M. Karolik Collection; 394 (l)Museum of the City of New York, (r)Bostonian Society/Mark Sexton; 397 Grant Heilman Photography; 399 (l)Bettmann/Corbis, (r)Smithsonian Institution; 401 John Deere Museum; 402 (l)The J. Paul Getty Museum, (r)Bettmann/Corbis; 404 (cr)Adam Woolfitt/Corbis (br)Valentine Museum, (bl)courtesy Charleston Museum, (background)New York Historical Society; 406 Stock Montage; 408 (t)John Deere Museum, (tr)Smithsonian Institution/Charles Phillips, (c)file photo (b)T.W. Wood Art Gallery, Montpelier, VT; 410 (t)The American Antiquarian Society, (br)FPG, (b)file photo, 410-411 (t)SuperStock, (presidential gallery) White House Historical Association; 411 (l)Chicago Historical Society, (r)from Fletcher's History of Oberlin College, courtesy Oberlin College; 412 National Portrait Gallery, Smithsonian Institution, Washington DC; 414 (t)City Art Museum of St. Louis/SuperStock, (bc)Brown Brothers, (bl)Museum of American Textile History; 418 Peabody Essex Museum/Mark Sexton; 419 Library of Congress; 420 Collection of William Gladstone; 422 Bettmann/Corbis; 425 Mount Holyoke College Art Museum, South Hadley, Massachusetts, 426 (l)Chicago Historical Society, (r)Meserve Collection; 427 (tr)Maria Mitchell Association, (bc)National Archives of Canada, (br)Corbis, (l)Nebraska State Historical Society, (tc)Hulton Archive; 430 (t)New York Historical Society, (c)Peabody Essex Museum/Mark Sexton, (b)Library of Congress; 432 Mark Burnett; 432-433 Painting by Don Troiani, www.historicalartprints.com; 433 PhotoDisc; 434-435 (t) Corbis, (presidential gallery) White House Historical Association; 435 (t)Medford Historical Society, courtesy Robert M. Hicklin, Jr., (bl)Missouri State Historical Society, (br)Photo Network; 436 Frank & Marie-Therese Wood Print Collection, Alexandria, VA; 437 Collection of David J. & Janice L. Frent; 438 New York Historical Society;

440 Corbis; 441 Library of Congress; 442 Schlesinger Library, Radcliffe College; 444 H. Armstrong Roberts; 445 North Wind Picture Archive; 446 (l)Corbis, (r)Missouri State Historical Society, (l)Jim Gensheimer; 446 447 Kevin C. Chadwick/National Geographic Society; 447 courtesy Illinois State Historical Library; 449 Chicago Historical Society; 450 (t)courtesy Chicago Historical Society, (b)Library of Congress; 456 (tc)Missouri State Historical Society, (bc)courtesy Chicago Historical Society, (t)NorthWind Picture Archive; 458 (l) Museum of the Confedracy, (r)Corbis; 458-459 Painting by Don Troiani, www.historicalartprints.com, (presidential gallery) White House Historical Association; 459 (l)Time-Life Books Inc. from the series "Civil War"/Edward Owen, National Archives, (r)Illinois State Historical Library; 460 PhotoDisc; 461 Seventh Regiment Fund, New York City; 463 PhotoDisc 464 National Archives; 465 (t)File photo, (l)Corbis-Bettmann; 466 Manassas National Battlefield Park/Larry Sherer; 467 National Archives; 468 PhotoDisc; 471 Medford Historical Society Collection/Corbis; 473 McLellan Lincoln Collection, The John Hay Library, Brown University/John Miller; 474-475 PhotoDisc; 476 Glencoe file photo; 478 Collection of Larry Williford; 479 (l)Museum of the Confederacy, (r)PhotoDisc 480 FPG; 481 National Archives; 482 (l)Brown Brothers, (r)Corbis; 484 MAK I; 485 Picture Research Consultants; 486 Michigan Capitol Committee, photography by Peter Glendinning; 490 (l)Matt Meadows, (r)Glencoe file photo; 491 (l)Brown Brothers, (r)Corbis; 494 (t)McLellan Lincoln Collection, The John Hay Library, Brown University/John Miller, (bc)Painting by Don Troiani, www.historicalartprints.com, (tc)Corbis, (b)National Archives; 496 ©Shelburne Museum, Shelburne, Vermont; 497 Aaron Haupt; 498 (l)North Wind Picture Archive, (r)file photo; 498-499 (t)Corbis, (presidential gallery) White House Historical Association; 499 Museum of American Political Life; 500 National Museum of American History/Smithsonian Institution; 501 Gettysburg National Military Park; 504 Chicago Historical Society; 505 Tennessee Botanical Gardens & Museum of Art, Nashville; 509 Corbis; 511 Chester County Historical Society, West Chester, PA; 512 National Museum of American History, Smithsonian Institution/Rudolf Eickmeyer; 513 North Wind Picture Archive; 514 Stock Montage; 516 file photo, Corbis; 517 Bettmann/Corbis; 520 (t)Morning Star Gallery, Addison Doty photo, Museum of American Political Life, (b)Bob Mullenix; 520-521 Collection of Mr. & Mrs. Paul Mellon, Board of Trustees, National Gallery of Art; 521 National Park Service Collection; 522 file photo, National Portrait Gallery, Smithsonian Institution/Art Resource, NY, Collection of David J. & Janice L. Frent, (b)Corcoran Gallery of Art; 523 National Museum of American Art, Washington, DC/Art Resource, NY; 524 John Sohm/Chromosohn/Stock Boston; 524-525 NASA; 525 John Sohm/Chromosohn/Corbis, 526, (l)Stanford University Museum of Art; (r)Rudi von Briel; 526-527 (t)Lisa Ades, (b)The White House Historical Association; 527 (tc)Bettmann Archive, (b)Collection of Colonel Stuart S. Corning/Rob Huntley/ Lightstream, 528 (l)courtesy The Oakland Museum; 529 Duke University; 530 (l) Nebraska State Historical Society, Lincoln, (r)Montana Historical Society, Helena, 532 Denver Public Library, Western History Collection; 533 New York Historical Society; 534 Picture Research Consultants; 535 National Air and Space Museum; 536 courtesy Ford Motor Company; 537 Jacob A. Riis Collection, Museum of the City of New York; 539 University of Illinois at Chicago, Jane Addams Memorial Collection; 540 Archive Photo; 541 Pelletier Library/Alleghany College; 543 Oscar B. Willis/The Schomburg Center for Research in Black Culture, New York Public Library; 546 Corbis; 547, (l)Corbis-Bettmann, (c)Corbis, (r)Larry O. Nighswander/National Geographic Society Image Collection; 548 Brown Brothers; 552 (b)Bettmann Archive, (t)Stanford University Museum of Art, (tc)Rudi von Briel, (bc)Collection of Colonel Stuart S. Corning/Rob Huntley/Lightstream; 554 (l, r)collection of David J. & Janice L. Frent, (c)PhotoDisc; 554-555 (t)Corbis, (b)The White House Historical Association; 555 (t)Bettmann/Corbis, (b)Peter Marlow/Magnum Photos; 556 W.H. Clark/H. Armstrong Roberts; 557 Library of Congress; 558 Margaret Bourke-White, Life Magazine, Time, Inc; 559, 561 Corbis; 562, 563 Library of Congress; 564 US Army; 565 Superstock; 566 (l)Flip Schulke/Black Star, (r)Corbis; 568 file photo; 571 Larry Burrows/Time, Inc; 572 Collection of David J. & Janice L. Frent; 573 Alex Webb/Magnum Photos; 574 (l)Liaison Agency, (r)David Burnett/Contact Press Images, (b)Dirck Halstead/Gamma Liaison; 575 (t)Greg Gibson/AP/Wide World Photos; (b)Black Star; 576, 577, 578, 579 Corbis; 580 (l) Corbis, (r)Thomas E. Franklin/Bergen Record/SABA/Corbis; 582 (l)Corbis, (c)Joe Raedle/Getty News, (r)Sygma/Corbis, (background)AFP/Corbis; 583 Library of Congress; 584 (t)Steve Liss/Time; 586 Reuters/Timepix; 588 (tr, lc)file photo, (bc)Brown Brothers, (others, background)PhotoDisc; 590 (t) PhotoDisc, (b)Missouri Historical Society; 591 Chicago Historical Society; 592 National Anthropological Archives, Smithsonian Institution; 593 National Maritime Museum; 594 W. Saunders/TimePix; 595, 596 Brown Brothers; 597 file photo; 598 Corbis; 599 Smithsonian Institution; 600 Corbis; 601 Massachusetts Historical Society, Boston; 602 courtesy Fisk University, Nashville, TN; 605 Reuters/TimePix; 606-610 The White House Historical Society; 610 (bc, br)Corbis; 611 North Wind Picture Archives; 613 courtesy Winterthur Museum; 614 Corbis; 614-615 Corbis; 617 National Portrait Gallery/ Smithsonian Institution; 618 (l)file photo, (r)Mark Burnett; 619 (t)Denver Art Museum, (b)Corbis; 621, 622 Corbis; 623 Flip Schulke/Black Star; 624 Missouri State Historical Society; 625, 626 Corbis.

Photo Credits

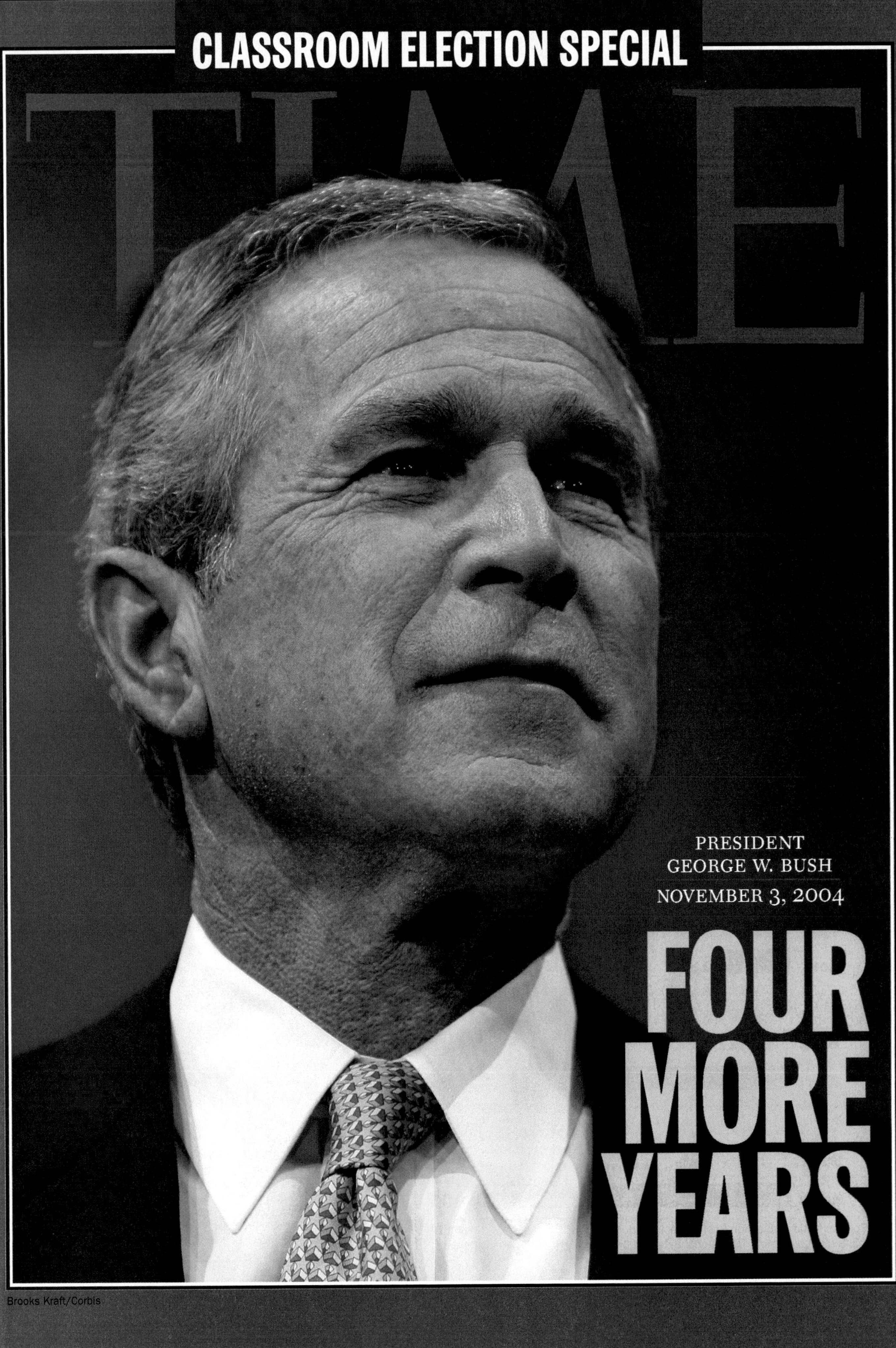
CLASSROOM ELECTION SPECIAL
TIME
PRESIDENT
GEORGE W. BUSH
NOVEMBER 3, 2004
FOUR
MORE
YEARS

Brooks Kraft/Corbis

ELECTION ★ NOTEBOOK

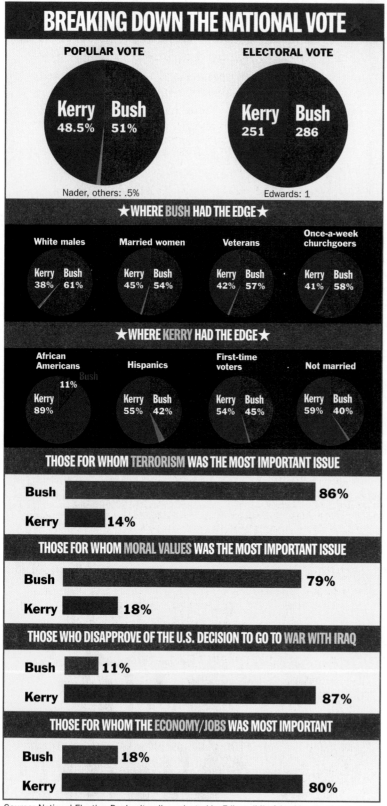

BREAKING DOWN THE NATIONAL VOTE

POPULAR VOTE

Kerry 48.5% Bush 51%

Nader, others: .5%

ELECTORAL VOTE

Kerry 251 Bush 286

Edwards: 1

★ WHERE BUSH HAD THE EDGE ★

White males
Kerry 38% Bush 61%

Married women
Kerry 45% Bush 54%

Veterans
Kerry 42% Bush 57%

Once-a-week churchgoers
Kerry 41% Bush 58%

★ WHERE KERRY HAD THE EDGE ★

African Americans
Kerry 89% Bush 11%

Hispanics
Kerry 55% Bush 42%

First-time voters
Kerry 54% Bush 45%

Not married
Kerry 59% Bush 40%

THOSE FOR WHOM TERRORISM WAS THE MOST IMPORTANT ISSUE

Bush 86%
Kerry 14%

THOSE FOR WHOM MORAL VALUES WAS THE MOST IMPORTANT ISSUE

Bush 79%
Kerry 18%

THOSE WHO DISAPPROVE OF THE U.S. DECISION TO GO TO WAR WITH IRAQ

Bush 11%
Kerry 87%

THOSE FOR WHOM THE ECONOMY/JOBS WAS MOST IMPORTANT

Bush 18%
Kerry 80%

Source: National Election Pool exit poll conducted by Edison/Mitofsky. Margin of error is ±3 percentage points for national data and ±4 percentage points for state data.

NUMBERS

34 Number of states visited by George W. Bush during the presidential campaign

41 Number of states visited by Senator John Kerry

36 Number of visits made by Kerry to Ohio, the most by any candidate to one state

630,000 Total number of TV campaign commercials aired this election season

5,480 Number of campaign ads aired in Florida's Miami-Fort Lauderdale market during October

$1.45 billion Total spent at all levels on campaign advertising this year

$140 million Amount raised during the campaign by liberal 527 groups (non-profit organizations whose goal is to influence elections)

$75 million Amount raised by conservative 527 groups

2,256 Number of lawyers the Democrats sent to Ohio to monitor voting

8 Number of U.N. electoral assistance workers in Iraq

Samantha Appleton/Aurora

VERBATIM

Gregory Heisler/Time Life Pictures/Getty Images

"My fellow Americans, this is the most important election of our lifetime."

JOHN KERRY,
Massachusetts Senator, accepting the Democratic nomination for President

"Trying to challenge the two-party dictatorship is like trying to climb a cliff with a slippery rope."

RALPH NADER,
independent candidate, who won less than 1% of national vote

"Jenna and I aren't very political, but we love our Dad too much to watch from the sidelines."

AP Photo/Susan Walsh

BARBARA BUSH,
23, on why she and her twin sister decided to campaign

"We promised ... that every vote would count and that every vote would be counted."

JOHN EDWARDS,
Democratic vice-presidential candidate, at 2:30 a.m. on Nov. 3, 2004, on why Kerry was holding back his concession

"I'll reach out to everyone who shares our goals."

GEORGE W. BUSH,
at his first post-election press conference, Nov. 5, 2004

A LOOK AT VOTER TURNOUT

More Americans voted for—and against—George W. Bush than for any other presidential candidate in U.S. history, and turnout was higher than in any election since 1968. Among 18- to 24-year-olds, turnout rose by 5.8 percentage points, with nearly 2 million more members of this age group voting than in 2000.

Turnout of Young Voters in Presidential Elections, 1972–2004

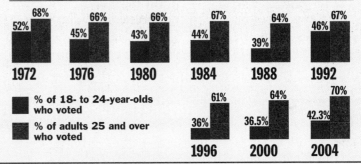

	1972	1976	1980	1984	1988	1992
% of 18- to 24-year-olds who voted	52%	45%	43%	44%	39%	46%
% of adults 25 and over who voted	68%	66%	66%	67%	64%	67%

	1996	2000	2004
% of 18- to 24-year-olds who voted	36%	36.5%	42.3%
% of adults 25 and over who voted	61%	64%	70%

Source: The Center for Information and Research on Civic Learning and Engagement; 2004 figures are preliminary estimates based on exit polls

WHAT HAPPENED IN THE SWING STATES

Three of the most intense battles between Kerry and Bush came in Pennsylvania, Ohio, and Florida, key swing states with a total of 68 electoral votes among them. While Kerry won in Pennsylvania, Bush carried Florida and Ohio. A Kerry win in either Florida or Ohio would have given him the White House.

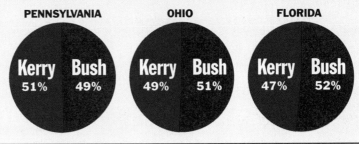

PENNSYLVANIA	OHIO	FLORIDA
Kerry 51% Bush 49%	Kerry 49% Bush 51%	Kerry 47% Bush 52%

ELECTION 2004: THE PRESIDENCY

FOUR MORE YEARS

How the Bush team orchestrated its nail-biting win

By NANCY GIBBS

IN THE END, AN ELECTION that was supposed to be about all the ways the country is divided at least brought Americans together at 193,000 polling places in democracy's messy leap of faith. Turnout was huge even in states where the result was assured. In Ohio

the polls closed at 7:30, but the lines were so long that people were still voting at midnight. Some people admitted they just did not want to face their neighbors or their children at the end of the day and say they had not bothered to show up. Others said if you don't vote, you can't complain

and did not want to be silent at a time like this.

About 120 million Americans voted, 15 million more than in 2000. When the electoral votes were tallied, Republican George W. Bush had won 286 to Democrat John Kerry's 251. Of the three most hotly contested swing states, Kerry took Pennsylvania, while

★ HOW THE ELECTORAL VOTES ADD UP ★

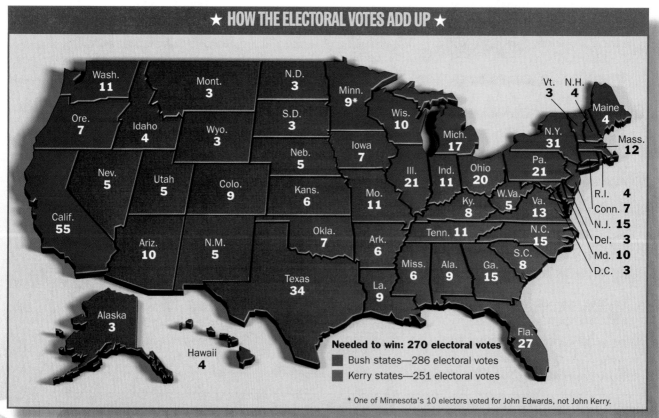

Needed to win: 270 electoral votes
Bush states—286 electoral votes
Kerry states—251 electoral votes

* One of Minnesota's 10 electors voted for John Edwards, not John Kerry.

Bush snagged Florida and Ohio. Bush also became the first president since 1988 to win a majority of the popular vote, with about 51% to 48.5% for Kerry.

So consider the obstacles Bush overcame to win the hotly contested election. Since the country previously

AP Photo/
David Anderson

SWAMPING THE POLLS: Provisional ballots gave Julie Goulis a chance to vote in Cleveland.

met at the polls, voters have encountered a record deficit, job losses, airport shoe searches, rising bankruptcies, and bruising battles over stem-cell research and the definition of marriage. On the eve of Election Day, fully 55% of voters said the country was moving in the wrong direction. Only 49% approved of the job the president was doing, and anything below 50% is supposed to be fatal to an incumbent. A war that Bush promised would cost no more than $50 billion a year

is running at nearly three times that. His character and values were attacked by well-organized detractors throughout the campaign. And he faced an opponent with a long record of public service, decorations from his service during the Vietnam War, and a Democratic base that had never been so united.

Bush says the war on terrorism is not a clash of civilizations, but this campaign was, by his careful design. He never really pretended to have much to say to Democrats beyond I will keep you safe. He relied largely instead on inspiring those who agreed with him already, who want to protect marriage as an institution, think stem-cell research has been oversold, and believe abortion is a sin. Even Republicans who disagreed with him on one or more issues—like the civil libertarians who would like the Patriot Act changed or the fiscal conservatives who worry about the massive national debt—are still willing to side with him.

His 97% approval rate within his party surpassed even Ronald Reagan's. Bush plainly understood that his best weapon against Kerry was less what Bush did than who he was. You may disagree with me, he said at every stop, but you know where I stand.

Overall, Bush succeeded in making Kerry appear an elitist defending moderation at a time when nothing less than passion would do. In Boston at their convention, the Democrats held a somber remembrance of 9/11. A month later in New York City, the Republicans unleashed a battle cry, and the contrast was plain: the party of victims vs. the party of warriors.

For Kerry supporters, there is some consolation that Bush will have to take responsibility for finishing what he started in Iraq. For Bush supporters, there is an obligation to recognize that the intense effort of the other side was as much an expression of love of country as any pledge, hymn, or flag. For people on both sides, there is relief that the day affirmed the sustaining virtue of American democracy. However fierce the battle and however high the stakes, on Election Day citizens go to the polls, close a curtain, and cast their vote—and then go home to honor the outcome because we have only one president at a time.

REPUBLICANS EXTEND CONTROL OF CONGRESS

G.O.P. Strengthens Its Decade-Long Grip on the House, Adds Senate Seats

REPUBLICANS PICKED up seats in both chambers of Congress on Election Day, leaving Speaker Dennis Hastert (R-IL) and Majority Leader Tom DeLay (R-TX) in charge of the House and toppling Tom Daschle (D-SD) from his post as Senate Minority Leader. The key to strengthening G.O.P. control of the House lay in Texas, where four incumbent Democrats lost their seats as a result of a controversial redistricting plan backed by DeLay. This is the sixth consecutive election since 1994 in which Republicans have held a majority in the House.

Democrats had hoped to regain control of the Senate this year but wound up losing ground. They were defeated in several pivotal races, including those in Georgia, South Carolina, North Carolina, Alaska, and Florida. Despite these losses, Senate Democrats will retain enough votes to make it hard for Republicans to pass legislation without opposition. That's because it takes 60 votes to end debate on a bill.

Given the makeup of the new Congress, Republicans say they'll push for approval of measures that have been stalled—including oil exploration in the Arctic National Wildlife Refuge and limits on lawsuits.

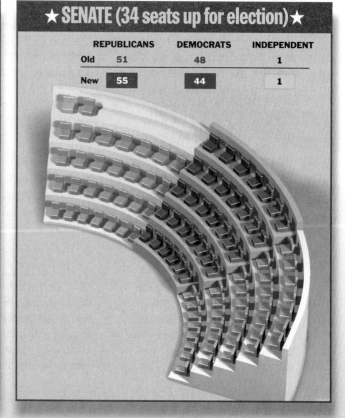

★ HOUSE (All seats up for election) ★

	REPUBLICANS	DEMOCRATS	INDEPENDENT
Old	227	205	1 (2 vacancies)
New	232	202	1

★ SENATE (34 seats up for election) ★

	REPUBLICANS	DEMOCRATS	INDEPENDENT
Old	51	48	1
New	55	44	1

Faces to watch in the 109th Congress

AP Photo/Doug Dreyer

The Giant Killer

Elections are not just about votes. They're also about symbols. And for Senate Republicans, minority leader Tom Daschle has long been Moby Dick. Here was a Democrat from a solidly Republican state, South Dakota, who not only couldn't be defeated but also seemed to emerge from each electoral and legislative battle bigger and more powerful. So when John Thune arrives in Washington, he will not be just another freshman senator. He will be a conquering hero—the man who fulfilled the G.O.P.'s 18-year quest to unseat Daschle.

Thune, a former congressman, ran a profoundly focused race, taking every opportunity to remind voters that Daschle's positions on gun control and abortion set him at odds with "South Dakota values." But he did not bag his big game alone. Majority leader Bill Frist broke with Senate etiquette by visiting South Dakota to campaign for Daschle's ouster. In fact, the last time a Senate leader visited his opposite's state to rail against him was in 1900.

"We're All Connected"

In the past year, Barack Obama, 43, has been compared, in all seriousness, to Abraham Lincoln, Martin Luther King Jr., and Bill Clinton. Democrats debate whether he should run for President in 2012 or 2016. Following a landslide victory on Election Day, Obama became the only African American in the U.S. Senate—and just the third in the past 100 years.

AP Photo/Stephan Savoia

The turning point in Obama's career came in Boston on July 27, 2004, when he delivered one of the best speeches ever heard at a political convention. Facing thousands of Democrats, he spoke of a country not pock-marked by racism or fear—a place in which an African immigrant could marry a Midwestern white woman and their middle-class son could go to Harvard Law School. And he told the cheering crowd that "we're all connected as one people. If there is a child on the South Side of Chicago who can't read, that matters to me ... If there's an Arab American family being rounded up without benefit of an attorney or due process, that threatens my civil liberties."

The Tough-Talking Cuban

When Cuban parents launched Operation Pedro Pan in 1960, they were trying to get their children safely out of Cuba and into the U.S. Nobody knew then that one of those children—Mel Martinez—would go on to become the first Cuban American elected to the U.S. Senate. Martinez, now 58, served as Secretary of Housing and Urban Development from 2001 to 2003 and received strong support from the White House and Florida Governor Jeb Bush.

AP Photo/Chris Omeara

An Advocate for Children

As a state senator, Allyson Schwartz was called the "Mother of Pennsylvania Children's Health Insurance" for devising an insurance plan that many states later copied. Now she hopes to pass similar legislation on the federal level. Schwartz is one of 65 women who will serve in the House—a gain of five from the 108th Congress. Among the new faces are Melissa Bean (D-IL), who unseated Philip Crane, the longest-serving Republican in the House; and Gwen Moore (D-WI), the first African American to represent Wisconsin.

Courtesy Allyson Schwartz

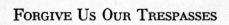

Forgive Us Our Trespasses

FORGIVE US
OUR TRESPASSES

BY

LLOYD C. DOUGLAS

Author of
'*Magnificent Obsession*'

BOSTON AND NEW YORK
HOUGHTON MIFFLIN COMPANY
The Riverside Press Cambridge
1932

The Riverside Press
CAMBRIDGE · MASSACHUSETTS
PRINTED IN THE U.S.A.

TO

BESSE IO PORCH DOUGLAS

WITH GRATITUDE FOR
VALUABLE COÖPERATION

DINNY was born to hatred: born in savage revolt against the world that had caught and crushed his too-trusting young mother.

By the time he was twenty-five he had been successively typesetter, reporter, football star, and columnist. He had rocked a small mid-Western college to its foundations by blacking the eyes of its Y.M.C.A. Secretary in defense of his college president. For this he had been expelled. But expulsion had only given him the chance to use his biting pen to better advantage.

Here in barest outline is the beginning of Lloyd C. Douglas's second book. The awakening of a human soul is a strange and rare occurrence, but it would be difficult to find a more inspiring theme or one better suited to the talents of the author of 'Magnificent Obsession.'

Forgive Us Our Trespasses

∴

CHAPTER I

THE new-laid harvest straw beneath the faded red carpet rustled crisply under Martha's shapeless felt slippers as she padded across the living-room to the cluttered mantel.

With the quizzical grimace of long-neglected astigmatism she adjusted the steel-bowed spectacles that had been her mother's, had of a notion peddler for two dozen eggs and a pound of butter.

The wooden-wheeled clock — a noisy but amazingly accurate and exquisitely ornamented product of old Ferd's, while laid up one winter with a broken leg that had kept him two months sober — clacked irascibly at Martha that another blistering August morning was nearly five hours old. High time, indeed, that the day's work began. Not much wonder the Millers were poor.

Dragging her slipper-heels to the door of the spare bedroom which, in spite of her continued protests, Susan and Greta had insisted on occupying of late, Martha vigorously rattled the latch.

Glumly appeased by assurances from within, she returned to the dingy kitchen and peered into the kettle to see if there was enough water to prime the parching pump under the pear tree.

Then, kettle in hand, she plodded to the foot of the narrow stairs, and petulantly called:

'Julia!'

* * * * * *

Outstretched on velvet moss so soft and deep it yielded to every curve of her supple young body, Julia knew that if she stirred, the least bit, she would never be able to re-capture the complete satisfaction of this luxurious languor.

Doubtless it was too much to expect that an experience so strangely sweet could be quite real. Sooner or later, something or somebody would invade her peace. A tall giraffe would saunter up and thrust his long nose into the top of the banana tree. Giraffes ate bananas, didn't they? ... Or a big man with a blue coat and shiny buttons would order her off.... Or there would be a peremptory summons from afar to come at once!

Julia's unbuckled consciousness was already troubled by the persistent echo of a distant call. It had seemed to come from the depths of this tropical forest — a faint but urgent cry for help. The voice had sounded tired, plaintive, persecuted — just like Martha's.

But what would Martha be doing away out here in... in Tasmania? Julia now readily identified her location by recalling a picture in *The Pictorial Atlas*, her omnivorous memory obliging her with phrases from the adjacent de-scriptive text: 'Mountains heavily forested... magnificent scenery... peaks of crystalline rock showing pink and blue ... frequent showers... luxuriant vegetation.' If this wasn't Tasmania, it was some-place else too far off for Martha to find. Martha never went anywhere, not even to Ligonier on Saturdays. She always saw them off, standing there under the big maple, mopping her tanned forehead with the corner of her brown apron.

'Wish you was a-goin' along, Mat,' Hiram would drawl, conscious that he only, by virtue of his clumsy champion-ship of her dour eccentricities, could nickname her without rebuke.

'No,' Martha would reply, sacrificially, 'somebody's got to stay on th' place — what with them young turkeys and all.'

Whoever was calling, Julia had an uneasy sense of guilt over her failure to respond. Whether required to go or not, she at least should have the courtesy to answer. Of course, if it did actually turn out to be Martha — a most improbable event — she would have to obey. One always came when Martha called. Sometimes one came scowling and grumbling, but one always came.

Martha had an uncanny instinct for knowing when one must on no account be disturbed. Had one reached the most exciting episode in a story, Martha needed a few dry chips immediately to revive an expiring fire. Let the sunset be at that phase where vermilion was beginning to be laced with purple, Martha's accusing voice inquired from the kitchen door whether one expected to gather the eggs, or must she go out later and do it herself in the dark and all?... But this couldn't be Martha!

In just a moment, now, Julia would reply to the entreaty. She would draw a deep breath — though deep breaths were rather disconcerting, lately, for they seemed to make her plump, round breasts so much more mature than she was, herself — and try to exhale 'Coming!' so effortlessly as not to disturb this delightful lethargy. She would wait until the cry sounded a little more distinctly, and then she would answer, 'Yes, Martha... Coming!'

Evidently someone else had gone to the rescue, for everything was blissfully quiet again. That was good. So nice not to be bothered. Julia sighed contentedly as a big drop of warm dew dripped from the tip of a sheltering fern-frond and rolled slowly down her cheek.

She opened one eye cautiously — a mere tiny slit — to make sure the tall, slim, slanting date-palm was still there. It was; plainly visible through the vertical bars of her long black lashes.

Was this the one in the *Elementary Geography* or the *Child's Natural History*? No — it couldn't be; for the date-palm in the Geography had a gray monkey in the top, and the one in the Natural History was being climbed by a brown boy with arms as long as his legs, and sharp heels, scampering up out of the tiresome paragraph that read: 'The Malay is of pigmy stature, averaging 148–149 cm., with black skin and short woolly hair.'... No — this date-palm must be the one in the magic-lantern lecture, last winter, over at Hinebaugh's Schoolhouse.

As for the dripping rubber trees, with the waxy leaves that shaded her like hands folded above her eyes, Julia could locate them certainly. They were from the little conservatory at Fort Wayne... out in Spring Fountain Park... the day she didn't go to the show. And here they were in this immense conservatory — for this really was a conservatory. Julia smiled over her silly mistake. She had fancied herself out in the open... in Tasmania, maybe; and all the time she had been lying here on the moss in this conservatory, exactly like the one in Spring Fountain Park — only twenty times bigger!

But there was no mistaking these moist rubber trees. She had sat under them for a whole hour on a sticky green iron bench, that day last summer, when their family — all but Martha, what with the plums and all — had gone to Barnum and Bailey's circus; only she hadn't seen the show. She had indignantly left them standing there giggling foolishly on the crowded courthouse steps, craning their necks to follow the last of the little elephants at the tail of the pompous parade — the little elephants whose bulbous, bobbing, nodding heads seemed to be saying, 'Yes, yes — we're coming.'... (Yes, Martha... Coming!)

Hiram and Elmer had been so noisy and silly, and had attracted so much unpleasant comment, that she had suddenly rebelled against the further humiliation of going out to the show-grounds with them.

'Aw — come on!' Elmer had shouted, against the deafening shrieks of the steam calliope. 'Don't be a sissy!'

''S'matter with yuh?' growled Hiram. ''Shamed o' yer folks?'

Greta was laughing uproariously over Susan's comment, 'Wouldn't it kill yuh, Gret?... Father a-scoldin' the boys fer drinkin' so much, and him just able to stand up.'

Julia had been very sorry for her father that day, swaying

unsteadily in the broiling sun as he morosely watched the clanking, jingling, garish, pungent parade — his tanned face screwed up into tight little wrinkles, his shaggy gray hair curled in tight little ringlets on his temples, his blue eyes, deep-set, swimming with vertigo. She couldn't bear to see him ridiculed. He belonged to her.

'Please, Greta!'

Greta had grinned, and cracked her chewing-gum.

Julia had been strongly impulsed to slip her arm through her father's, and make off with him; to offer him a hand exactly like his, only smaller and not so brown; to smile into his eyes with eyes exactly like them, only younger and not so weary; to take him along with her — anywhere to be away from these unfeeling people who were not related to either of them except by the mere unfortunate accident that they all happened to belong to the same family.

At that very moment, however, he had turned on her reproachfully, stifled a hiccough that hinted at impending nausea, and muttered, 'You'd better let yourself go and have some fun once.'

'Fun?'

'Yes: their kind o' fun. It won't do you no good to be haughty. You might as well cave in — an' like it! I done it! So kin you! I even larnt to talk like 'em. If you don't want to be lonesome all yer life, you'd better ——'

That quite settled it!... Promising to meet them at the Pennsylvania Station at seven-fifteen (they had left old Florrie and the dilapidated surrey at Larwill and had come the rest of the way by rail), Julia had slipped through the sweaty crowd, her cheeks aflame.

Three blocks away she took the street-car — No. 52, a policeman had told her — an almost empty little green street-car that banged its bell furiously at the now demobilizing throng, demanding it to drag its roly-poly, waddling wife and gawky children and their yellow balloons and pink popcorn balls off the rails; had ground dizzily around sharp corners, and lost its few passengers — all but

Julia — finally reaching almost open country, where it took the bit between its teeth, tucked its chin against its neck, and galloped over a rusty, hummocky track, the trolley-wheel singing a painfully shrill note, until it brought up with a jerk at the shabby station-shed in Spring Fountain Park.

The grass was seared and badly trampled, and the dahlias were dusty and frowsy in their prim round beds. A black-lettered board pointed an index-finger toward 'The Conservatory.'

Julia had had the steamy, sweaty, stuffy, little greenhouse all to herself, that afternoon. Everybody else had gone to the circus. She had sat there on the sticky iron bench, hoping it wouldn't come off on her new pink gingham, dreamily transporting herself to the equatorial regions where all this rank, lush, stifled vegetation belonged, finding a strange kinship with it. She sympathized with these cramped, dwarfed, imprisoned rubber trees, and the gigantic ferns with dejected, drooping arms and wings.

And now, to Julia's annoyance, the cry for help was repeated. It came from just outside the conservatory door, this time. Would she, or would she not, come immediately?

The huge dome of the conservatory lifted and disappeared. It was exactly like the glass cover that protected the plate of soggy doughnuts from the flies on the high counter in Ruggles's Restaurant and Pool Hall at Cromwell.... Martha had taken the conservatory by the handle, and lifted it off. One could hear what she was saying now, ever so distinctly. Would she come, this instant, and help get breakfast for Susan and Greta, who, as she very well knew, had promised to be ready at half-past five to go with the other huckleberry-pickers to Wadham's marsh? And wasn't it little enough for her to do, seeing she had begged off from the berryin' to study her algebry, or whatever it was, so she would be prepared for that there County Institute, week after next, which everybody knew she hadn't any right to waste their money on — even if it was her'n, a-teachin' silly paintin' lessons to women as ought to been a-keepin' their children's buttons on — what with them so hard-up and all? And didn't she have any natural feelin's of ——'

'Yes, Martha. I'm *coming!*'

Julia sat up, drenched with perspiration, stretched, inhaled an unsatisfactory draught of sultry, humid air, and gazed out through the east window at a chrome yellow sun that already threatened to break an August record. Next Thursday's *Ligonier Weekly Banner* would probably say, in big black headlines, 'HOTTEST DAY FOR TEN YEARS!... Highest Temperature Since 1885 Recorded on August the ——'

August the whath?... August the tenth! Her birthday! Would anyone else remember?

She reached out a long, slender hand for her stockings, dangling over the back of a chair, and tugged them on. After all, shouldn't she be glad she had a good excuse not to go into Wadham's snake-infested huckleberry marsh and have her arms and legs scratched with briars and nettles while she fought deer-flies with an exasperation close to tears, and shuddered with loathing at the sight of enormous caterpillars, and wiped the slimy cobwebs out of her eyes with sun-blistered, juice-smeared wrists?... Blessings on the pesky algebra!

'J-u-l-i-a!'

'Yes, Martha. I'm coming!'

* * * * * *

Her entrance into the grim little dining-room was effected with much difficulty. She could have wished that her first appearance before her household, as an adult in good and regular standing, might have been somewhat more impressive.

Circumstances had decreed that Julia must bump her way crabwise through the obstinate swinging-door from the smoky kitchen with a precariously poised platter of bacon in one hand and the big battered coffee-pot in the other, while the family, glancing up from its first round of fried mush and sorghum molasses — with which munitions Martha had preceded her — wondered, not without warrantable anxiety, whether she would make port with all her cargo.

It was not to be expected that her lazy and surly brothers, much less absent-minded old Ferd — whose fork trembled in a long, slim hand that had been obviously intended for more esteemed employment than shingling barns and blowing stumps — would spring to her rescue. That would have been 'a-puttin' on style,' an affectation held in snarling contempt by Hiram and Elmer. Indeed, their sentiment on this subject was commonly shared by the entire male species, so far as she had been able to observe.

As for Greta, who, at twenty-two, had already well developed an impish talent for the enjoyment of other people's discomfiture; and as for Susan, whose twenty-seven virginal years and one hundred and sixty-seven pounds gave such alarming promise of unarrestable progress in both dimensions that she was frankly envious of her willowy young sister, Julia's predicament was clearly no concern of theirs.

Martha, seated with her angular back to the door, which now capitulated with a savage swish and a sullen bang, cleared a place at her elbow for the brown-stained coffee-pot, and dutifully remarked that this was Julia's eighteenth birthday.

While still in her teens, Martha had accidentally lost an upper canine. Morbidly self-conscious, her misfortune had worried her grievously; but there had been no necessity for replacing the missing tooth. By skillful practice, Martha had been able to conceal this disfigurement with the corner of her lip, a technique which had produced a meticulousness of articulation oddly inconsistent with the slovenly elisions and shockingly bad syntax demanded by her righteous passion to avoid 'a-puttin' on airs.'

'Yes; your little sister,' reiterated Martha, her choice of a pronoun indicating the maternal relationship she sustained to the family, 'is came of age.'

Brief, bucolic felicitations from the boys were mumbled through the mush, to which old Ferd — so stung with remorse over having no gift for her that he did not even raise his eyes — added solemnly that Martha could always be depended on to remember the days.

Depositing her awkward burdens, Julia stiffened to a martial stance, brought her full red lips to a determined pucker, tossed her curly head airily, and swept the breakfast-table with a look of pretended challenge, as if to say that she was quite grown up now and they must all have a care how they treated her.

A moment later she was repentantly reflecting that previous experiences might have warned her against indulging in this bit of playful pantomime. Julia's sporadic efforts to dramatize some situation for the amusement of her family had been uniformly unsuccessful. It would have been very pleasant, she often thought, to belong to a household quick to interpret and enjoy a little good-natured clowning. It was not that their stodginess and lack of sparkle evoked her contempt: she was too naïve to be contemptuous. Indeed, she had never known — except in *Little Women*, long since read to rags and learned by heart — any such family as the rollicking, bantering, make-believe crew that constituted her ideal home.

On one's birthday, however, it might reasonably be hoped that the family would waive its habitual taciturnity, and humor a whim; so, quite recklessly overplaying her premeditated skit, Julia glared at her brothers and sisters with a mock severity signifying her newly acquired dignity. But they had already returned to their bacon and mush; and, noting that no one of them — not even her father — showed signs of sharing her mood, she doffed her archness, rubbed a damp wisp of blue-black hair from her low forehead with the back of a shapely wrist — astonishingly like old Ferd's, only daintier — and slipped into her accustomed place on the end of the pine bench beside Susan.

'Reckon you'll be too cocky to live with, now yer old enough t' be yer own boss,' observed Hiram, who, on second thought, had decided not to leave Julia under the impression that he, at least, was too thick-witted to have taken note of her brief charade.

Equally unwilling to be considered incapable of clever deduction, Greta remarked to her plate that Julia would probably be leaving home, one of these days, to go on the stage.

Old Ferd hitched about in his chair, and for a moment Julia thought he was going to offer a comment.

'Julia's always been a-playin' she was somethin' else besides what she is,' said Susan.

'Well — she ain't harmed no one by a-doin' that,' growled Ferd. 'She come by it honestly enough. When I was her age, er thereabouts ——'

'More coffee, paw?' inquired Martha, loudly, as if he were deaf.

'It's sure a-goin' to be a scorcher, Gret,' observed Susan, fanning her goiter with the bib of her apron, and peering through the open doorway toward the road.

'There goes old Len Bausermann with his pick 'n' shovel,' reported Elmer, following his plump sister's eyes to the highway.

'He'll be a-diggin' Granny Hartsock's grave today,' explained Hiram, without turning to look.

'A saint,' murmured Martha, unctuously, 'if they ever was one.'

'Who — Len?' chaffed Elmer. 'That consarned old chicken-thief?'

Susan and Greta laughed immoderately. Martha, easily offended when her piety was ridiculed, drew down the corners of her mouth, and pouted. Elmer explored a defective wisdom-tooth with a pointed quill, and grinned.

Old Ferd knew they didn't care to hear his story — none

of them but Julia. He could always be sure of an attentive listener in Julia, though sometimes she asked too many questions.

The family's rude indifference occasioned him no surprise. He had been on the defensive for so long in a home to which he contributed almost nothing, his small earnings claimed by Jake Heffel, that he had no right to be indignant over such discourtesies. He poured the thin coffee into his saucer with a shaky hand, crumbled bread into it, and sprinkled the dish with brown sugar, intent upon his occupation. Julia, toying absently with her food, studied his deep-lined, mobile face, confident that she was following his reminiscences as closely as if he had been given encouragement to recite them.

He was, she knew, skipping hurriedly over the Dresden part of it; the part that most interested her; the part that really mattered. She had never been able to construct a very clear picture of his boyhood home. The blurry impression she had of it was an accumulated synthesis of chance remarks accidentally dropped, and laconic answers to her importunate queries in the rare moments when he seemed willing to talk about his youth.

He would be out in his tiny shop under the big maple, standing at his home-made lathe, turning wooden pins for the mending of Squire Craig's harrow-teeth. The fine hickory shavings would come writhing and screaming from the point of his blue-hot chisel. He would pretend not to notice her, sitting on the old tool-chest, intently watching him.

'Let me treadle it, father. I like to.'

The huge oak balance-wheel overhead would lumber to a creaking stop.

'Mind you don't get yer foot caught under it, now!'

Julia would snuggle in between his arms and stand so close, her back to his breast, pumping the broad pedal that made the patched belt go snapping and crackling on the great wooden fly-wheel, threatening to bring it down on their heads; her father's warm, hairy forearm, tense on the chisel, moist with sweat and powdered with fine sawdust, brushing her cheek, almost as if he caressed her.

Panting with exertion, she would look up over her shoulder, and smile, when he signaled her to stop.

'You're more like her every day, Julia!' he would murmur, as the machinery idled to a standstill.

'Because my hair dips down to a point here in the middle?'

'That — and the deep dimple in your chin.'

'And she had the same kind of eyes that we have.'

'Exactly; that's where we got 'em.'

'The others don't have them, father.... Funny — isn't it?'

Thus drawn together in these brief intimacies, there would be some talk about her Grandmother Mueller — Ferd had changed his name to Miller, when coming to Indiana, because the people invariably mispronounced it; or was that the exact reason, Julia often wondered, when she had grown up — Grandmother Mueller who always seemed to be a mere slip of a girl, stooping over the flower-beds in the garden that was so ——

'How big was it, father — honestly: big as our potato-patch?'

He would chuckle derisively.

'Our potato-patch! Huh! Six — eight — ten times as big!'

Then there would be some vigorous prodding of memory for more information about the house. It was a great, rambling, stone house with tall, broad chimneys and many gables. Yes — his own room had a gable, and there was a window-seat with a rose-colored velvet cushion. Wrens nested in a little box under the eaves, and when it stormed, the branch of an elm swept the diamond-shaped panes of the mullioned window.

'And was there honestly a fountain in the middle of a big pool, father?'

'Yes — and lily-pads.'

'And really goldfish, like you said?'

'Yes, daughter — but don't you think you'd better go and help Martha now?'

'And you would feed them in the mornings — and they always knew when you were coming, and swam close to the edge to meet you?'

Of late Julia was becoming painfully aware of their lost heritage. Her day-dreams were bounded by the high stone wall, made warm and friendly by the tall hollyhocks his mother loved. On summer afternoons she fancied herself sitting in the rose-arbor, hard-by the large, half-timbered workshop and studio where distinguished guests were so often entertained at tea.

'Tea! — in a shop?' she had exclaimed, the first time he had told her about it.

'But it wasn't a little shop like this here, Julia. Seems to me like it had five or six big rooms. I disremember, exactly. The people came to see the carvings; almost every afternoon, somebody. And there would be exhibitions, couple o' times a year. Lots o' people came then, from long distances, Paris and London.'

'Would they talk to you, father?'

'I was just a young feller.'

'Going to school?'

'No — I had a tutor.... But I was always a-hangin' around the shop, and I can't remember when I wasn't a-playin' with chisels, and a-makin' things.... Once I heard a Count — I disremember his name — a-tellin' somebody that *Mueller* on a rood screen made it worth more 'n' its weight in gold.'

And there was a river.

Julia felt almost certain, as she sat watching her father's slow motions with his spoon, oblivious of the dull prattle of his family's table-talk, that he was dreaming of that river. You went through a thick oaken door set in the garden wall. The door had heavy wrought-iron hinges, and was always locked o' nights with a key that must have weighed all of a pound. You went through the door, and there was the river. The banks were rounded and grassy, and a long row of tall poplars grew on our side, 'their leaves always a-flutterin' whether there was any wind or not.' He disremembered the name of the river, but 'one of the swans was called "William Tell."' There were boats, too; a couple o' canoes and a dory and a punt with a red and blue canopy ——

'How much did Lafe Shock git fer his gol-danged shoats?' Elmer was inquiring of Hiram.

'Four cents, I heared,' rumbled Hiram, puffing at his sputtering pipe. ''Bout enough to pay fer th' corn he'd chucked unto 'em.'

'Corn — hell!' scoffed Elmer. 'Them shoats never seen a grain o' corn. All they ever et was swill!'

'Lot o' good the Shock swill woulda done 'em,' sneered Greta.

'They was so gol-danged poor,' expatiated Elmer, 'that I bet Lafe had to soak 'em afore they'd hold slop.'

—— and a punt with a red and blue canopy; and, sometimes, in the evening, his mother sat in the punt, with her guitar, and sang ballads to him, very sweetly. No — his father never joined them. No — he disremembered what the songs were.

Now Julia was at sea with her father, standing beside him as he stoked his way, with blistered hands, on a slow boat; she was landing with him, bewilderedly, at Castle Garden. Much had happened since the swans and the ballads in the evening; but it was quite impossible to recover intervening events. His father had whipped him savagely when he was sixteen. He wouldn't tell her why; but it had something to do with his mother. She had cried desperately, and that night he ran away. The tutor had helped him get away. The tutor had gone away, too, that same night.

Judging by the confident tightening of his lips, Julia knew he was in New York now, apprenticed to Lamb's

Studios. Four years of that passed in a few seconds. Now he was hard at work on the big walnut eagle — his first important assignment — that was to be poised on a lectern for Saint John's in Philadelphia. Lamb's had taken him in on the strength of the Mueller tradition, and had given him every possible encouragement, undisguisedly rejoicing in his budding talent. Every day he was improving his skill; every night he was poring over his new books, determined to perfect his English.

Then came the war. Julia saw the clouds gathering on the seamed old face. It was all over now. He had gone back to Lamb's in a faded uniform topped by the absurd little cap with the stiff visor that he still wore, rather rakishly, on Decoration Day — a day Julia dreaded, for he always marched unsteadily, and joked a good deal, when he should have been silent and dignified.

Now he had returned to the Lamb Studios, stubbly, fuddled, and pungent, after a fortnight's spree. All was forgiven. Soldiers would be soldiers. Lamb's were disappointed, but hopeful. Why, Mr. Joseph Lamb, himself! — (Ferd had been too proud of that recognition to keep it a secret, even if its implications were not to his own credit) — Mr. Joseph Lamb, himself, had pleaded with him to straighten up, and be a man. Surely, nobody could have asked for a better friend, Ferd often remarked, than 'Mr. Joseph,' who, it was said, had given up his plans to enter the ministry because he thought he could do more for religion by adding something to its beauty. 'Mr. Joseph Lamb was a great artist!' Ferd would say. 'Yes *sir!*'

No — it wasn't the fault of Lamb's Studios if he had drunk himself practically into the gutter at a time when a returned soldier's dissipation was easily pardoned, but not so easily capitalized in a profession demanding the utmost steadiness of eye and hand. Ferd was so proud of his erstwhile craftsmanship and its stern exactions that he was willing to admit his own inability to meet its requirements, shamelessly confessing the cause of his failure, as if his very drunkenness, at twenty-four, was to be talked about in tones of respect, seeing it had been important enough to collide successfully with an esteemed art.

So — that chapter was finished, then, and her father had ceased being an artist. Julia recognized the exact moment when he 'took to the road' en route to Pennsylvania in quest of a distant cousin who owned 'a bit of a truck-farm.' Oddly enough, no exigency of poverty had ever induced him to part with the books he had bought in the golden days when he was so brilliantly succeeding at Lamb's. He had stored them in New York; had kept himself sober long enough to save the money required for their transportation to his new home; for, now he had a home. He had married the plump, shy, awkward, yellow-haired daughter of an improvident neighbor who indifferently operated a small sawmill, 'mortgaged, by Golly, down to the last cleat in the old pulley-belt.'

Julia knew how it always amused him to repeat that phrase. He smiled, now, and glanced up furtively to make sure the family's attention was occupied. She dodged his eyes and took no further risks with them until she was sure he was in 'pardnership' with his unthrifty father-in-law, who, hearing rumors of advantages to be had by moving to Northern Indiana, 'where everybody was a-makin' big money loggin' and gettin' out railroad ties,' had suggested the immediate migration of his populous, penniless tribe.

Ferd grinned again, rather wryly. Julia was not quite sure where we were in the story, now. Perhaps he was thinking about something he had never told her — something not very pleasant, perhaps; something not much to our credit, she feared.

He had taken along to Indiana their simple, mostly home-made, household gear, the precious books — English classics — which were to become a veritable Godsend to Julia! — and his only military trophy, his little brown jug. Occasionally, of a late Saturday night in Heffel's Saloon in Cromwell, when Ferd and his cronies had passed from the bragging stage to the distinctly maudlin, nose-trumpeting phase of bland confessions and remorses over their respective might-have-beens, he would pull himself together long enough to make a pathetic joke of his own disaster.

'Yep' — Ferd would say, grinning drunkenly through his tears — 'that was my only military trophy — that there little brown jug.'

He glanced up, now, out of the tail of his eye, and found Julia regarding him with rapt interest. A bit disconcerted by this intense scrutiny (sometimes Julia's penetrating knowledge of his moods and meditations annoyed him, just a little), he pushed back his chair, and muttered, partly to himself, partly to her:

'Yep — that's the way it goes.'

He gnawed off a large bite of Horseshoe chewing-tobacco from the plug he had rummaged from the depth of his overall-pocket, and, without a backward glance, strolled out through the doorway toward his shop.

Perhaps he would continue his reminiscences while he worked on the Snell baby's pine coffin; but he had already covered everything in his story that had any interest for Julia. Except for such minor episodes as the births of his five children, and the death of Minnie, six years ago, his history was an unpunctuated monotony of trivial jobs — building corncribs, replacing timbers in the forebay at Austin's gristmill, planing and hanging Squire Craig's screendoors every April, and stowing them in the loft of the woodhouse every November — a chronicle as sterile of novelty as the legendary minstrel's redundant report that now another locust came and carried away another grain of corn.

Julia wondered, sometimes, whether her father ever missed her mother. It was obvious that he did not grieve for her. Minnie's biological contribution to Julia's character was no more in evidence than the influence of a hen on a golden pheasant's egg. Julia was all Ferd's.

Minnie had been an ignorant, whining, colorless, unimaginative creature, her quite astounding bulk disproving the adage that stout people are invariably optimistic. Save for the fact that she had been an economical housekeeper (as she had plenty of reason to be), and was thought to put up the best green-tomato pickles in the Oak Grove neighborhood, nothing important was remembered of her; not even by her own kin.

A litter of empty, overturned, glass fruit-jars on her grave in the Baptist Cemetery which, on the anniversaries of her death, the melancholy Martha stuffed with garden flowers, ironically testified to Minnie's previous relation to other natural objects in a world where she had dully foozled a chance to present society with a rehabilitated wood-carver of exceptional virtuosity, and had contented herself with the excellence of her piccalilli.

*   *   *   *   *   *

A clatter of wheels and harness drew Greta to the door.

'Fer Gosh sakes, Sue, if Bob ain't came with the hay-ladders on! Jolt the very stuffin' out of yuh!' She turned to the abstracted Julia. 'You'd better come, too, Miss Stuck-up! Here's that Schrofe boy what's so crazy about yuh.... Hoo-hoo, Bob! We'll be out in a jiffy!'

'Mebby you better go, Julia,' advised Martha, maternally.

Julia demurred. It was little enough time she had to review her algebra, even if she studied every minute.

Old Ferd, returning for a tin of water to cool his grindstone, arrived in time to take a hand in the argument.

'Give her a chance, Martha. I'd like to see one of us do somethin' to make our name a little more important than it's been.'

Martha picked up a double handful of dishes with a decisiveness of manner that promised an impressive exit, to be followed presently by a great clatter of pots and pans off stage.

'Well — all I got t' say is ——'

But the threatened tantrum was played to a thinning house. Ferd had found his tin cup, and was off with it. Susan and Greta were on the way to the wagon. The boys slouched toward the barn. Julia carried her plate to the kitchen, where Martha was sniffling ostentatiously, and vanished with a promise to make the beds, her sister's plaintive whine trailing her all the way upstairs. ''Pears like nobody in this house cares what I think about anything. Just a hired girl... without any pay.'

* * * * * *

Standing before the severely plain but expertly crafted walnut desk that her father had given her, last Christmas, Julia unlocked a drawer and re-read the precious document it contained.

The desk had become a symbol of the considerable difference between herself and her brothers and sisters. A source of anxiety and embarrassment at first, the desk had come to be a refuge and an inspiration.

On Christmas morning, having presented each member of the family with a fine, large orange, Ferd had made a mysterious trip through the snow to his shop, returning shortly with the desk. Julia's exclamations of delight had intensified the sullen silence. At supper, that evening, Greta's smouldering indignation blazed forth in an irascible comment to which Ferd quietly replied:

'She's the only one in this family that would have any use fer a desk. If any o' the rest o' yuh ever needs one, mebby I'll 'tend to it.'

This sarcastic explanation of the gift did little to conciliate them. So much constraint was traceable to the episode that Martha told Julia she had better take her new desk upstairs and keep it out of sight. Susan added that she, for one, would never darken the door of Julia's room while it was there.

But, however painful the situation, at the outset, it developed for Julia a privacy she had never enjoyed before.

By common consent, the family left her to herself, implying, a dozen times a day, that she considered the rest of them inferior, twisting her every remark into allusions to their ignorance.

'What shall I do, father?' she inquired one day, in the shop. 'They're always trying to act as if they're not as smart as I am.'

Ferd grinned, and blew the sawdust off his chisel-handle.

'They don't have t' put on, very much, t' play that.'

'But it makes me so miserable!'

'Well — don't cry.... That's what yuh get fer a-bein' smart. Smart people's always miserable. Old man Solomon said that — er somethin' about like it.'

'Was he miserable?' asked Julia, with a tearful little smile.

'Gosh, yes! He was the smartest man that ever lived!' Ferd sat down on the tool-chest, laid a dusty hand on her knee, and grinned mysteriously. 'Julia, are yuh sure you've found all the drawers in that there little desk? One of 'em ain't got no handle.'

Her eyes brightened.

'No,' she whispered, excitedly, 'I haven't found it. Will you show me?'

He had found it for her the next time the family was out of the house — a narrow drawer set in the center of a row of six open pigeon-holes and faced by a little pilaster carved to imitate a longitudinal section of a Corinthian column.

'That there's it,' pointed Ferd, hugely enjoying Julia's flutter of excitement. 'No — it don't come out that way,' he said, when she had unsuccessfully grappled with the ornament which defied the best efforts of her finger-tips. 'Nobody could ever get it out a-doin' that.'

'Do show me, father!'

He had proceeded then in leisurely fashion, immensely relishing her suspense, to demonstrate the strange magic of the secret drawer.

'Now, if you ever want to put anythin' out o' sight, Julia,' commented Ferd, with a comradely wink, 'you'll know how to do it; and it'll take a heap o' tinkerin' with this here desk fer anybody else but you to find out how that drawer opens.'

Julia was ecstatic.

Her close inspection of the desk had led to another discovery: Ferd had carved the name 'Mueller' on the beveled edge of the little receptacle for ink-bottles and pens.

'I'm so glad you did that, father. That makes the desk still more valuable, doesn't it?'

Ferd flushed with pride.

'It's the only time, Julia, since I cut the name under the wing of an eagle what holds the Bible in a big church in Philadelphia. It's the same way my father cut his name — and his father — and his father's father.... It's a good name, daughter.'

Standing now before the desk, Julia withdrew a document — much too long to fit into the secret drawer — bearing the impressive seal of the Great State of Indiana and signed with an affected flourish by the Noble County Superintendent of Public Instruction, authorizing her to teach an ungraded school for the term of One Year. Beside it, in the long envelope, was the covering letter containing a pressing suggestion that the recipient plan to attend a five-day Institute to be held in Albion, the county seat, in late August, chiefly for the benefit of inexperienced teachers.

'Please God,' whispered Julia, wistfully but shyly, for they were not very well acquainted, 'let me have a school!'

Nobody in the Miller family exhibited any piety but Martha, who was presumed to have enough for all. Martha's conversation was sprinkled with scriptural allusions, her stock of texts featuring the punitive phrases promising the ultimate rebuke of the proud, the 'froward' (whoever they were), and the stiff of neck. Julia, gifted in parody, occasionally employed these solemn exhortations herself, with *ex tempore* improvisations and amendments which amused her, and sometimes frightened her, too; for, she reflected, if there really was a hell, surely the fabricator of any such flippancies was reserving a warm berth.

When Martha, in her thin, flat voice, caroled from the kitchen, 'I'm washed in the blood of the Lamb,' Julia invariably shuddered, swallowed hard, and muttered, 'Ugh! — how nasty!'

'Please let me have the Schrofe School,' wheedled Julia, clutching her precious credentials tightly in one hand and with the other pressing her eyes hard to make sure they were closed firmly enough to satisfy the requirements of Deity, who was sure to be suspicious of her sincerity, 'so I won't have to come home except on Sundays. But — any school will do. Please, dear God, let me hear from one of them pretty soon. It would be so nice to have word on my birthday. Please!'

Somewhat startled by the inflection of this final word of entreaty, which hinted at an intimacy with the Almighty which, she was aware, impertinently presumed upon a very sketchy relationship, Julia added, humbly ' — Unless, of course, it should not be in accordance with Thy Holy Will.'

* * * * * *

What have yuh got yer Sunday hat 'n' dress on fer?' inquired Martha, when, a half-hour later, Julia passed through the kitchen, book and slate in hand, pausing to remark that she was going down by the creek where it was cooler.

'I thought I might walk over to Oak Grove, when I am tired studying, and see if there is any mail — about a school, you know.'

'Mighty sight o' studyin' you'll get done with that on yer mind. Better to a-gone berryin', like I told yuh. Anyways, all the schools are a-took by now. 'Pears to me like ——'

Without waiting for the rest of it, Julia walked out of the kitchen, quickened her steps immediately she was out of sight over the slope behind the barn, tossed her algebra and slate into the grass at the foot of the big willow that overhung the stream, climbed to the highway, and set out at a swinging stride toward the village two miles to the west — two miles by the road, but subject to considerable discount if one cut across Squire Craig's stubble-field, just beyond the Baptist Church, and took the path through the woods along the widening river, pent by the Austin milldam.

There were two high fences and a padlocked gate to climb, and occasionally the Squire's ill-tempered ram contested the audacity of trespassers, but Julia was impatient to peer into the tiny pane of dirty glass — No. 8 — in the Post Office which occupied a few square feet in the front end of Baber's General Store.

Halfway across the stubble-field, Julia's steps became shorter and less confident.

Seated, with his back to her, on the top rail of the fence that bounded the woods, was a young stranger, fashionably dressed, his shoulders slumped as if he were lost in serious thought; in trouble, perhaps.

Julia reflected that if he were to straighten himself out to full length he would be very tall.

The stranger's perch must be quite uncomfortable. Julia surmised that he would not remain there long. If she dallied, he might proceed, unconscious of her approach. She stopped, toying with the idea of retracing her steps, but the sun beat pitilessly upon the dazzling yellow field, and the cool maples promised a relief irresistible. Her heart quickened as her pace slowed. She pulled off her dowdy hat, made of cheap lace over a wire frame, and patted the damp curls at her hot temples.

Now the young stranger had turned, and, over his shoulder, was regarding her arrival with frank interest. He stepped down from the fence, on the grove side, consulted his watch, and smiled. It was almost as if he had been waiting for her, thought Julia; as if they had arranged to meet, and she was late. Had he decided to play, she wondered, that they were keeping an engagement? Could it be possible that there was anyone in the world like that? It would be such fun.

9655

Would he not think her a bit stupid if she stared stonily into his friendly eyes, pretending to be offended, pretending to be haughty? Was it not one's duty to be cordial to strangers? Even Martha, prude that she was, believed that one might be 'entertaining angels unawares.'

Julia had never seen that sort of a smile on a boy's face. It signified nothing but a proffer of friendliness from one young human being to another. It left out of consideration the negligible fact that they were not of the same sex. How different from the awkward, crooked grin of the typical gum-chewing youngster who maneuvered to one's side at a boisterous barn-dance and paid one a clumsy compliment while turning to wink at some equally boorish bystander, as if to say, 'I'm a-tryin' to see how fer I c'n git with her!' — as if their relationship implied that she was willing it should be rated an obscenity. She had often been half-ashamed she was a girl.

Julia was within a few yards of the fence, now, making no pretense of indifference to the presence of the tall, athletic chap who awaited her, watch still in hand.

His smile was so disarming that her red lips parted in an honest recognition of the first of its kind she had ever seen worn by a contemporary male. Her ingenuous response to it was quite free of self-consciousness or embarrassment. Toward this handsome, urbane, self-possessed boy — clearly not of her world at all, so far as outward appearances went — she sensed a strange kinship which, she believed, it would have been unworthy of her to deny either to herself or to him.

It was what she had been longing for, all her life, wasn't it? Hadn't she dreamed of an acquaintance with some congenial spirit in whose company she might be... herself? Why dissemble? She owed something to that dream.

'It's much cooler over here,' he said, offering her both hands, when, having lightly climbed to the top of the fence, she sat facing him, fanning her flushed cheeks with her crumpled, frumpy hat.

'I know,' said Julia.

She took his hands without hesitation or coyness, and joined him.

'But we must keep an eye out for my Uncle Jasper's pet sheep, Otto the Seventh,' he said, as they fell into step on the path. 'Otto has a vile disposition, and the run of this grove.'

'Yes,' said Julia, 'I know.'

He ventured a sidelong glance, as if to inquire whether his new friend had exhausted her conversational possibilities, and met an enigmatic smile.

'Had I kept you waiting long?' she asked, with an earnestness that puzzled him.

He turned about and faced her so soberly that Julia repented her whimsical audacity. Did nobody in the world know how to take a little joke? Was she the only one, after all, who had any instinct for impromptu drama? She took a step forward. He detained her with a light touch on her arm.

'Yes,' he said, rather huskily, 'I have been waiting a long time... for you.'

'Don't spoil it,' said Julia, entreatingly. 'We were only playing, weren't we?'

CHAPTER II

FOR the first time in the history of the Schrofe School it was being taught without benefit of whips and dunce-caps.

The innovation caused some stir. Discipline had been much less savage in recent years under a succession of female teachers, but the present policy of complete disarmament was viewed with anxiety.

'Fer the girl's own sake,' agreed the younger mothers, whose support of her had been swiftly won by the affectionate interest bestowed on their little tots, 'them bigger boys oughta be kept in hand. They'll run her out afore Thanksgivin'.'

Ham Ditzler, who had put in six exciting winters behind that desk, more than a decade earlier, and now divided his time between odd jobs of plasterin', paperin', paintin', an' butcherin', in the casual employ of his erstwhile pupils — ('danged degradin' work') — offered to bet (amount of wager unspecified) that the Miller girl would never finish out her term, a prediction which came true, though not for lack of firmness in her schoolroom.

Abner Schrofe, Chairman of the Board of Trustees, when joined in his barn by the four other members, one rainy Sunday forenoon in early October, silently shucked corn during their recital of the public's apprehension based on criticisms offered by the veteran pedagogue.

Upon the conclusion of their remarks, Chairman Schrofe listed heavily to starboard and deftly poured a considerable quantity of tobacco-juice down a convenient rat-hole, thus setting himself at liberty to express the opinion — conciliatorily phrased in terms consonant with the dignity of his office — that Ham Ditzler was nothin' but a damned old sore-head.

Encountering no opposition to this statement, not even from Zeke Trumbull, Ham's son-in-law, with whom he made his home, Abner further deposed that there was more brains in Julia Miller's little finger than Ham Ditzler had in his hull body, adding that he would respectfully entertain a motion a-sayin' it to be th' sense of this here board, duly and properly assembled, that Miss Miller's services was 'sadisfactory.'

Hez Brumbaugh said he would so move, and suggested that the Chairman inform Miss Miller of their action.

Jake Waters, who since last spring had owed Abner the final Eight Dollars on a Guernsey heifer, 'lowed that Ham Ditzler — after all's said and done, and a-takin' him by and large — was purty much of a gol-darned old blatherskike whose idears wasn't wuth hell-room.

At Zeke's suggestion, this was taken by consent. He modestly demurred, however, when delegated to convey this sentiment to his father-in-law, feeling that it would have 'more weight' coming from someone else. The decorum of the board being slightly disturbed by this remark, it grinningly adjourned to the hog-pen to inspect the new 'Poland-Chiny' sow that Abner had purchased at the recent Whitley County Fair.

'Please, Mr. Schrofe,' pleaded Julia, next morning, after Abner, delighted to have an official errand at the schoolhouse, had told her he was on his way to settle Mr. Ditzler's hash, 'leave him to me. Don't hurt him. I'll think of some way to accomplish the same thing without humiliating him.'

Ham, already silenced by a hint from Zeke to the effect that if he knowed which side his bread was buttered on he would let up on the Miller girl, bewilderedly accepted her invitation to make a little talk to the school on the afternoon of Columbus Day, on which occasion he astounded himself and the assembled mothers by confessing the difficulty that an old-timer has in a-keepin' up with th' march o' progress.

An able craftsman of home-made philosophy, Ham spent many meditative hours evolving what he thought was a brana-new theory for the achievement of this here thing they calls success, chattering so volubly about his discovery that it became a community joke.

His convictions on this subject were never better expressed than on the late afternoon of an eventful day in May when, riding home from a service at the Oak Grove Baptist Church in company with Zeke and Lola and their swollen-eyed little daughter Goldie, Ham observed:

'It all goes fer t' show that this here thing they calls success is the fruit of self-confydence.

'If yuh know yer bigger 'n' yer job, and c'n drop the dang thing whenever yuh like and do somethin' better, the people yer a-workin' fer seems t' know it without yer a-tellin' 'em. They take orders as if they was a-spoke by Jehovah, so long as they know yuh know there's sumethin' in prospec' fer yuh a dang sight more important than a-foolin' away yer time with the likes o' them!

'If a teacher, f'rinstance, thinks he's got about all that's a-comin' to him, and has to mind his p's and q's er the Board'll set on him, he just natcherly has t' whale hell outa the brats to make 'em behave.

'If he c'n get along without rules er whips er threatenin's, it's because th' scholars knows that he don't have t' care a tinker's dam whether he keeps his job er not, seein' he c'n leave 'em, if they don't like it, and do somethin' better.... And I bet that's the secret o' success in all th' walks o' life, in ev'ry day an' generation.'

Ham leaned far out of the open surrey, where he shared the back seat with Goldie, and improved his impaired articulation by relieving himself of a large quid of tobacco, wiped his stubbly lips with the back of a brown hand, and continued:

'You take this here parson, over in Wayne, what's been a-sayin' lately that th' story about Jonah ain't so, d'yuh reckon they'd let him stay there and be as honest as that if they didn't know the hull town knows as how he's had an invite to a big church in Chicago? Not by a dang sight!

They just grin when he goes after the Old Testyment fer a-sayin' that th' Lord God drownded all them heathens fer spite... 'cause they know that if they holler he'll tell 'em t' take their danged ol' church b' th' bell-clapper, 'n' go t' hell!'

'Sh! — Pap!' admonished Lola, without turning. 'What kinda talk... right afore little Goldie, too!'

'Well — I wisht I'd a-heared some talk like that when I was about her size,' muttered Ham, remorsefully. 'Mebby I'd amounted to somethin'.'

'I wonder,' inquired Zeke, 'why didn't this here smart preacher in Wayne take that there bigger job in Chi?'

Ham was fidgety with eagerness to explain.

'Now yer a-gettin' to it! That just goes fer t' show how smart this feller is! If he went to Chicago, where mebby he'd be exac'ly the size of his job, er mebby a little small-er, he wouldn't be able t' tell 'em where t' get off at. He likes a-bein' where he c'n tell 'em, if they object t' his preachin', that they c'n take their danged ol' church b' th' bell-clapper, 'n' ——'

'Pap — that'll do now!' snapped Lola, adding, growl-ingly, 'Can't we never talk about nothin' else but things as riles Pap and makes him swear, right afore little Goldie?'

'All th' same,' finished Ham, doggedly reverting to his original proposition, 'if Julia Miller hadn't 'lowed, all th' time she was a-teachin', that she was a-goin' away purty soon t' be a rich man's wife, I bet she'd a-had t' lam them sassy young rake-hells all over th' schoolhouse, five times a day!'

Little Goldie wept noisily.

'Shet up, Pap!' commanded Lola. 'Hain't yuh got no proper feelin's at all?'

* * * * * *

Sometimes, during those early autumn days, Julia's hap-piness almost suffocated her. As often, it terrified her. Was Martha's grim and hateful philosophy correct? Did people always have to pay the piper? Was this ecstasy the sort of thing you inevitably had to settle for with interest compounded?

Sudden waves of black depression briefly but increasingly inundated her dream-world. Was she living in a fool's paradise? Would the clock presently strike twelve, and send the prancing horses scampering back to rejoin their fellow-mice? Nonsense! She must pull out of this! How silly! Was ever anyone more fortunate than she?

She became very sensitive on the subject of her happiness, eager to keep her radiant spirits within bounds so that Fate would at least give her credit for all the humility and gratitude she would muster. Diligently occupied with the unaccustomed task of disciplining her emotions, sternly warning them to keep their distance from her eyes, her lips, her voice, her hands and feet, Julia was unaware of the outward effect of these suppressions.

'Julia has growed up, almost overnight,' muttered old Ferd.

'Who'd a-thought that Julia Miller would age so fast?' remarked Mrs. Abner Schrofe. 'She's a *woman!*'

The effect of Julia's self-discipline in the cause of propitiating Nemesis was an unconscious exhibition of that magnetic and covetable type of personal poise not to be had cheaper than at the price of a stoical imprisonment of kinetic energy bruising its fists against the bars and pleading for its right to shout and dance and sing.

Eager to offer any forfeit to fend off the Day of Judgment, Julia had decided to room and board at home, involving a daily tramp of nearly six miles. It was a very real sacrifice, in anticipation; for, in looking forward to her new work, its most alluring promise had been the escape it offered from an irksome home environment.

School had been in progress barely a week, however, before Julia began to doubt the efficacy of her splendid sacrifice. The atmosphere at home had improved. The boys were shaving now, every other day, in honor of the young school-mistress who appeared at their breakfast-table trimly clad for her day's work. Susan and Greta crimped their hair, starched their aprons, and conceded the boarder a right to the exclusive use of her own trinkets. Her father's gratitude for the money she had engaged to pay touched her. Martha's awkward tenderness and solicitude slightly embarrassed her. What a difference a little money made in the general line-up of human relations! Julia smiled, with new understanding, over the story that had gone the rounds about Widow Mercer, who lived near Bippus, ten miles east.

Mr. Mercer, an enthusiastic Maccabee, had left her Two Thousand Dollars in fraternal insurance. There were four sons, all concerned that this large fortune should not be dissipated. They suggested that their mother divide the money among them, and spend her time living in their homes as an honored guest.

'No,' she had replied, quietly. ''Pears to me like an elderly lady with Two Thousand Dollars would be a much more interestin' guest than an old woman with nothin'.'

It made all the difference in the world, money did!

One day you were 'Julia?... Julia!... *Julia!!* Come here, this instant, like I told yuh, and peel these potatoes!'

One short week later you were 'Julia, you just let Susan peel them potatoes, and you go set down till supper's ready.'

Nor was this refreshing change at home Julia's chief ground for satisfaction. She was grateful for the opportunity to be alone, two hours daily, with her enchanting memories and high expectations. The vigorous walk quickened her imagination. Fully a third of the trip to school was taken through tall timber on a picturesque wagon-road that negligently waived the right o' way to close-meshed clumps of flaming sumac, and an occasional obdurate oak — a narrow ribbon of a road, carpeted with freshly fallen leaves, frost-sensitized to autumnal rays filtered through the livelier half of the prism, and crisp under her nimble feet.

On the return journey, Julia was always the school-teacher, it being part of her discipline to restrict her thoughts to her professional obligations.

On the early morning trip, however, she was all Zandy's! Her capacity increased for the vivid recovery of her deliriously happy experiences with him. To the very minutia of detail, Julia reconstructed every tone, posture, and gesture associated with those dreamy, unreal afternoons under the shade of the river-willows behind the Baptist Cemetery, not more than a dozen yards from her mother's grave, and the few almost painfully rapturous hours that had transfigured dull and dusty little Albion into the City Delectable!

The first half-mile of the out-bound trip, which brought her to the Baptist Church, where she turned to the left on the busy Larwill Pike, was invariably taken, at that early hour, without encountering any traffic, either on foot or wheel.

Except for the shrill scream of some excited water-bird on the river, and the lonesome clangor of a cow-bell registering the impatience of horns entangled in a wild grapevine down in the glen, there would be no sound but the rhythmic crunch of frosty gravel under her competent heels.

Julia's precious recollections proceeded in orderly sequence. Sometimes — let her do her utmost to concentrate on the opening chapter of the almost incredible story — her memory would insist on turning whole handfuls of pages; but, tugging herself free of the culminating episodes that mattered most, she would pursue events chronologically. She always wanted to be through with the early part of the story before she reached the busier mile of pike, for the full enjoyment of their first encounter demanded a few merry roulades of bantering laughter — her own: Zandy had been so serious. And, besides, she liked to be in the thick of the dark woods when she arrived at the Albion part of it!... Dear, dear Zandy! How tender! How precious!

Julia's reminiscences always began at the fence where they had met on the morning of her birthday. Now they were ambling slowly through the grove. They had left the path, and were wandering toward the river. She was still en route to the Post Office, but they were off the path.

'You have a first name, too?' (I have told him mine.)

'Alexander.'

'Quite long and dignified.' (I think I must not do that, any more. He doesn't like teasing. He is so serious.)

'So was my grandfather. It was his name. Everyone calls me Zandy. My sister began it when she was a little tot, and I was a baby.'

'Do they call you Zandy at Dartmouth, too?'

'Mmm.' (Zandy says 'Mmm' when he means yes; not 'Umm-humm,' the way our people do. Martha thinks it queer when I say 'Mmm.') 'College students are not very formal. Even the profs have nicknames.'

'Do they know it?'

'In time. They don't seem to care. We had a big Scot in Math, last year, with an enormous mustache. He discovered that he was "The Walrus," and pared it down. When that didn't help, he shaved it off.'

'And then he wasn't a walrus, any more?'

'Oh, yes, he was still a walrus.... I say, Julia, I'm going to like you, most awfully.' (I knew, then, that it was true. Zandy was going to like me. He couldn't have said it, that way, and not mean it.)

'What is your sister's name?' (I think it better we should talk about his sister. I'm afraid my face is red, and my heart is just pounding!)

'Alison.... She's married.'

'Does she live in Cincinnati, too?'

'She lives in a Pullman car. Her husband is Roland Forsythe.'

'The famous tenor?'

'Mmm... and tanker.'

'You mean he drinks?'

'Like a fish.'

'Is that why your sister goes along?'

'Exactly — but Alison doesn't mind. She likes excitement. And she thinks Providence has appointed her to keep a great artist sober. She married him for that.'

'And she can't?'

'Not much of the time.'

'But how can he sing?'

'You don't have to be sober to sing! A good many people never do sing unless they're ——'

'It doesn't always work that way. Some people get glum and mean.'

'Roland doesn't. He's mean when he's sober. But it'll get him, some day. Leaky heart.'

'How I hate it!' (I almost tell him why, for he's sure to find out.)

Now they had reached the gate at the farther side of the woods, and Julia had climbed it, leaving Zandy to wait her return from the Post Office. She had discouraged his going along, reluctant to amuse the loafers who would be sitting in front of Eph Mumaugh's blacksmith shop.... Now she was back.

'Look, Zandy!' (How natural it seemed to call him Zandy.) 'I've got a school! — the Shrofe one! — the one I wanted!' (He takes the letter, and our hands touch.)

'Writes like a ten-year-old boy, doesn't he?'

'He probably never went to school much.'

'I'll bet he can multiply bushels by dollars.' (We are down at the river, again, sitting on the grass.)

'That's where I'm weak... figures. I think algebra's awful!' (I tell him all about having to go to Albion for the Institute.)

'I'll help you. It's easy.... Explain it to you in an hour.'

'Will you, honestly?' (Zandy gives my hand a little pat. That was the first time.)

'This afternoon!'

'But I mustn't take your time. You'll be busy!'

'What would I be busy at? It'll save my life.' (His father is sore at him because he's decided to be a writer, instead of making nails, and he's changed his course in college, and his father has sent him to the country, all summer, as a punishment, instead of taking him along to Europe, as he had promised.)

* * * * * *

Most of the early part of the story would have been covered by the time Julia reached the woods. She had walked rapidly on the pike, and could afford to take the rest of the trip more leisurely.

Now they were sitting on the river-bank behind the Baptist Cemetery. It was Thursday, late afternoon. They had known each other three days. She was reclining against the bole of a maple, using the opened algebra to protect her back from the rough bark. Zandy had just finished reading her the *Rubáiyat*. What a wonderful voice he had! So tender! Her eyes were wet.

'Let me have it a minute. I want to see that verse about ——' She reached for the book.

He took her hand.

'Anybody would know at a glance, Julia, that you were meant for some kind of creative art.'

'How would they?'

'Your thumb!'

'What's funny about my thumb?' she had asked, searching his deep-set, gray-green eyes.

'Bends back so far.... Open your hand, dear.... Wide.... See?'

'Does yours?... Let me look.... Why, the very idea!... Is that what makes you think you can write?... Our hands are very much alike, aren't they?'

A little shiver of excitement always came over Julia when she reached this part of the story.

'We're alike in more ways than that, precious!'

She had made a little effort to retrieve her hands. Zandy had taken both of them in one of his. When he kissed her, she did not resist. How everlastingly right it seemed! She had shared his kiss, a bit clumsily. They were both quite stampeded for a moment. She hoped he would kiss her again: perhaps she could do better. It was rather embarrassing to feel that one had been so awkward. She had done much better, the next time, maybe because it was not so hurried.... Zandy's kisses! They made your heart so big there wasn't room in your chest to breathe!

He had walked back with her, that day, until they could see the chimney of her house. When she stopped, meaning that he mustn't come any farther, he said, 'What are you doing, tonight?'

* * * * * *

It proved to be an eventful evening. Julia volunteered to accompany Martha to prayer-meeting. At the door of the church, however, she said, 'I think I'll run over to the Post Office, first.... I've a letter that should be mailed to Albion, about my room, you know.'

'I thought you had did that,' said Martha. 'You'll not be back afore meetin' is out!'

But Martha seemed relieved. Julia knew that her sister preferred not to have other members of the family present when she testified to the submissiveness of her burden-bearing. It reflected no credit on her home, where, it was implied, she took all the hard knocks with little to show for them but a chastened spirit.

'You'll not go through them dark woods, will yuh?' Martha cautioned. Julia promised.

Zandy was waiting for her, by the fence where she had first met him. He kissed her lips, her eyes, her hair.... They were made for each other, weren't they?... They would plan to spend their lives together.... Why not?... Didn't she love him?...

Someone was blowing out the malodorous kerosene lamps in the church when Julia returned across the stubble-field with Zandy, the shrill rendition of 'God Be With You Till

We Meet Again' warning them their tryst was over. They stopped in the darkness for a final embrace.

'It won't be long now, sweetheart.'

'Oh, Zandy; I'm so happy!'

The little group on the church porch was separating, Martha's prim voice conspicuous above the others.

They walked home almost in silence, Martha mentally putting into rehearsal the testimony she meant to give, next time; Julia wondering what Martha would be saying if she knew that Zandy Craig was going along with her to Albion where they were to be *married!*

Late in the night, Julia, wide-awake but calm, wondered if she were playing the game squarely with everybody; with her father, with Martha, with Zandy's father, who made nails and was so gruff and domineering; with Zandy's mother, who already had a girl selected for him.... But, as Zandy had said, they had their own lives to live. Her father, her sister, his father, his mother — had they not been given a chance to live their lives, as they liked?... Maybe not.... It was all very confusing. Life was complicated.

'We will do what our hearts tell us is exactly right, darling,' Zandy had said. 'Nobody in the world has a right to keep us apart. We will keep it a secret, now, but, one of these days, when they see how happy we are, and how right it all was, they will be glad.'

* * * * * *

Old Ferd remarked at supper, one Saturday evening in early November, that he had met Abner Schrofe, that afternoon.

'Ab says,' reported Ferd, proudly, 'that Julia is the best teacher they ever had. I'm a-goin' to tell her when she comes down. It's no more 'n' right she should hear it.... What's a-keepin' her?'

'She's been a-lyin' down most o' th' afternoon, paw,' said Martha. 'I'm afeard that long walk every day is a-pullin'

Julia down, now it's come rainy. She hasn't looked good fer quite a spell.'

'She was a-cryin' when I looked in to call her t' supper,' said Greta. 'Funny fer Julia to be a-cryin'.'

'I'll go up,' said Martha. 'Here, Susan, dish them turnips.'

Julia recognized her sister's step on the stairs, raised up on one elbow, dabbed at her eyes with a soggy little handkerchief, tucked a letter under her pillow.

'No — I'm quite all right, Martha. Working pretty hard, you know. Just... sort of unstrung. No — I don't believe I could eat a bite; not now. Maybe, after a while. Run along. It's nothing.'

Martha clumped down the stairs, and the letter was unfolded again.

'What a misfortune, darling, if things are as you fear. If it had happened a little later — wouldn't we have been glad? Maybe it isn't that. Try not to worry.

'All one hears about now is the big game with the Chicago Athletic Club on Thanksgiving. Father and mother are coming East for it. How I wish you could be here! Big doings!

'If it's what you think, darling, can you go on, a little while, as if nothing had happened? How long? Maybe I can have a heart-to-heart with my father. But he's pretty hard, you know. Savage old thing, when disappointed. I'm afraid he'd take me out of college. That would set us back. If I can get through this year, the rest will be easy.'

* * * * * *

Julia had fainted at the Friday afternoon program with which school closed for the Christmas holidays. The room was packed with visitors and stuffy with festal decorations. When the exercises were all but over, Julia crumpled in a pathetic heap on the floor. Young Jason Schrofe, whose attentions she had regarded so casually that he had quite lost hope, drove her home in his sleigh.

'That settles it,' said old Ferd. 'She's not a-goin' to tramp through them snowdrifts any more.... You must find a place to board, Julia, closer by th' school.'

She smiled wanly and shook her head. She would be all right. No use wasting the money.

She had hoped that the cruel exertion might... somehow ... solve the problem. In any event, the long walk daily helped to distract her mind. She might go mad, otherwise. ... How long would it be until people noticed?... What would those all-knowing young mothers think of her fainting?... How much torture could she stand in these cruel stays?

'It fairly breaks my heart, darling,' Zandy had written. 'There you are, worrying your dear little head off; and here I am, starting home for the holidays, unable to bear even a wee bit of your trouble... and discomfort, too, I suppose. I don't know much about such things.'

'The dear boy,' thought Julia. 'He doesn't know, of course. He probably thinks a woman just knows it's going to happen, on a certain day, and — when the time comes — it happens. And I don't know much more about it, except that I'm afraid I can't keep it a secret much longer... not even for Zandy's dear sake.'

* * * * * *

Zandy was in line for the Perkins Medal in oratory. On no account must that event be jeopardized.... Could Julia, he wondered, manage to carry on until the oratorical contest was over? February third, it was. How about it, Julia, darling?

Julia would certainly try. Zandy must not be disqualified for that medal. Perhaps his father would be that much more kind, if he won it. But, dear boy, let's arrange to tell them the very minute the contest is over! It's getting serious! Please!

It so happened that on the very night when Zandy was laboriously composing a letter which began, 'My dear

Father Miller (for I really want to call you Father Miller, because your Julia is my wife; though I'm afraid you will be annoyed, a little, that we haven't told you earlier about our wedding)' — Greta had whispered to Susan, and Susan, white-faced, had whispered to Martha, and Martha, trembling with fear and indignation, had entered Julia's room without knocking.

Julia was outstretched, her dark-circled eyes were closed, her hands lay supine, palms upward, on the counterpane. Martha looked at her for a long time before she spoke. She swallowed, noisily.

'You might as well make a clean breast of it,' said Martha, hoarsely.

Julia opened her eyes and smiled.

'In the drawer of my desk, Martha. Here's the key. That long paper. That's it. My marriage license.'

'So you run off and got married, did yuh?'

'Well — not exactly... run off. We were married during the County Institute.'

'And you was in Albion, a-livin' with a man, while we thought you was a-goin' to that school that cost all o' Thirty Dollars!'

'He was my husband — and it was my money.'

'Humph! He don't seem to set much store by yuh... a-leavin' yuh to face the music. What's his name?' Martha adjusted her steel-bowed spectacles, and stooped under the lamp. 'Alexander Craig... who's that? You don't mean t' say it's that rich Craig's boy what was here last summer a-visitin' at the Squire's?'

Julia nodded.

'It's a heap the Craigs would do fer a Miller! You wait til your father hears o' this. He'll make that young rascal sweat! He'll have th' law on him!'

So — at long last, Julia had no further need to punish her desperately ill-treated body. Ungirded — physically, mentally — she felt that her worst troubles were behind her. They could say what they liked, they could do what they would — she had made her last agonizing trip to the school-house. There was some comfort in that, at least.

Old Ferd was torn between grief and anger. He wanted to pour out his rage without delay. He would write to that lousy whelp and tell him, for once, what somebody should have told him long ago — that he was a low-lived coward, a dirty blackguard, and — and — if he ever darkened their door, except to bring the money to pay for Julia's sickness, he would be pitched out!... And he did write that, and more, pounded a stamp on the envelope with a fist that looked amazingly like Julia's, only not so white, and stalked, half-blind with hate, to the Post Office, where he was regarded with fresh interest, the loafers in corduroy coats and felt boots noting his state of mind and winking at one another out of the tails of their eyes. He was aware of it. Everybody knew, damn them!... There was a letter for Julia. She always got the mail, herself.... He would tear it up, and throw it in the river. The sleety gale sobered him, somewhat, on the way home. He did not destroy the letter.

* * * * * *

'A couple of years from now, darling,' wrote Zandy, a week later, 'we will have forgotten all about this. At the moment, things do look pretty dark, don't they? I was all ready to come when I had the letter from your father. He is in a great temper; hardly to be blamed, of course; talked of shooting. Anyone else but your father, I would debate that subject with him. But all I could do for you now would be to stir up a tremendous row and probably make everything more difficult for you.

'I postponed writing to my father until last Saturday; couldn't think up just the right way to approach the matter. He is always so autocratic and hair-triggery. I did the best I could to make him see things. There is a wire from him this afternoon, hundred words, saying he is done with me. That, of course, only means he is very sore. He may come around all right. But not very soon. You have no idea how stubborn he can be.

'So — meantime, I can't stay in school. My mind is too
upset, anyway. I shall be out of funds, too. In fact, I'm
out of funds now. The month's allowance is just due, and
he isn't even going to send that. I've made up my mind to
bum my way through to the Coast. This twenty is all the
money I have but five dollars. You can depend on me to
send you some more as soon as I have it. Don't be discouraged, dear. I intend to succeed. Success is more a gift
than an achievement. Some people are born to succeed. I
am one of them. You will share. Keep that in mind through
these hard days. I shall soon send for you, and we will be
happy together forever.'

*   *   *   *   *   *

With confidence unshaken, for there was a peculiar contagion associated with Zandy's optimism that gave her
courage, Julia watched the last of the snow disappear.

Everything was going to come out all right, as Zandy had
predicted. He had started West to find work and make a
little home. Then he would send for her... for *them!*

Every few days there came another postal card... from
Detroit, Chicago, Davenport, Denver, Spokane. Zandy
was on the way.

Presently the lilacs were opening, and the air was vibrant
with the hum of all sorts of awakened winged things. Julia
could hear the occasional scream of her father's chisel doing
a shrill aria to the accompanying rumble of the big wooden
fly-wheel.

'Poor old darling,' she thought, tenderly. 'He's worried
about me, and trying to keep his hands busy... dear, shaky,
old hands.'

'What's father making, Martha?'

'Will yuh let on yer surprised when he gives it t' yuh?'

'Mmm — but maybe you'd better not tell me if it's a
secret.'

'A little cradle,' whispered Martha. 'Mind yuh don't let
on.'

Julia wept a few happy tears. Her father had forgiven her, then. That was ever so much better. It would come out all right, as Zandy had said.

When Doctor Engle came, next day, he was shortly after joined by Doctor Marshall, a specialist from Fort Wayne. Jason Shrofe had driven him up from Larwill.

Doctor Marshall had quiet blue eyes and wore a brown suit that fitted him. He did not talk much, and hardly asked any questions at all. Julia had great confidence in him and felt no shyness in his strong, competent hands.

The charge was twenty-five dollars, and when Julia had counted it out — after Doctor Engle had handed her the pocket-book from her desk — she was pleased to find that there was just enough; a twenty, a two, and three ones. Doctor Marshall looked at the money and the empty pocket-book, and said not to bother about paying it until she was well. He would send her a bill, some day.

'Thank you,' said Julia, gratefully. 'I'll pay you as soon as I'm up.'

'That will be soon enough,' said Doctor Marshall.

Martha came and sat on the edge of the bed, after the doctors were gone, holding Julia's throbbing fingers. Martha had shown the doctors out, and Julia had heard them talking, downstairs, for a disturbingly long time. Martha's face, always an open book, was troubled. It twitched, as it did when she was worried.

'What is it, Martha? You talked to them. Do they think I'm very sick? They don't think I'm going to — they don't think maybe I'm not going to get well, do they?' Julia's words came slowly, and as from a considerable distance.

Martha pressed her bony knuckles hard against her cheek and swayed slowly back and forth.

'They're a-doin' everythin' they knows how, Julia. We must all put our trust in th' Lord 'n' His precious promises.... Can't yuh let yerself just rest on His Blessed Name?'

Julia turned her face away and stared hard at the white wall, her eyes wide, frightened.

'Would yuh like Brother Miner t' come over from Cromwell 'n' talk t' yuh, Julia? It might be quite comfortin'.'

Julia shook her head, and there was a little convulsive shudder of her shoulders. Sighing audibly, Martha drew up the sheet over the quivering shoulders, laid the back of her rough hand against the hot neck, and quietly left the room.

A violent storm was rising in Julia's breast — a devastating tornado of rebellion. Why had Fate played this ghastly trick on her? What had she ever done to earn this dull tragedy? What chance had she had from the beginning? Why had Destiny set her down in this stupid house — her mother a whining fool, her father a shabby old drunkard, her brothers and sisters nothing but clods and dolts?

And that wasn't the worst of it! Fate had opened the door a little way and pointed toward liberty. Love — great love — had come! Why hadn't Fate left her to the tiresome little drudgeries that were the common lot of people badly born? Why this mocking glimpse of freedom?

In her broken-dyked passion, Julia's scorn swept over everything and everybody associated with her disaster. Her father! What right had this drunken old man and his slatternly wife to bring her into the world at all? And this smug, surly, ignorant, superstititious old sister — calmly inviting her, in this hour of break-up, to like it!... to put her trust in the Lord! Mighty little He cared! Nobody cared! Least of all — the Lord! If He saw it, at all, He probably grinned! Another good joke! — saith the Lord.

Martha was back now, seated again on the edge of the bed, wetting her thumb and leafing the thin pages of a book. Julia dully turned her eyes and recognized the cheap little Bible she had earned for faithful attendance at Sunday School when she was nine or ten. Martha was doubtless hunting for some more of those precious promises. What a dull, uninteresting old thing those precious promises had made of her!

Clearing her throat and settling her spectacles more firmly on her thin nose, Martha held up the Bible at an angle that would better the light on the fine print.

'No, please, Martha,' muttered Julia. 'Not now — please!'

'I'll just leave it here, then,' said Martha, regretfully. 'Mebby it'll be a sort o' comfort just t' have it under yer pillow.'

She was gone now, leaving Julia with the precious promises within easy reach. But the storm was by no means spent. With white-knuckled little fists and tightly clenched teeth, rigid lips wide apart, Julia stared up defiantly. In a moment she gave way to the passionate indignation that was all but driving her mad. The precious promises! Bah! ... God — and the Bible — and prayer — and the angels — and miracles — and faith that would remove mountains! Bah!... She groped under the pillow, clutched the book, opened it in the middle, utterly blind with hot tears and crazed with desperate anger, and began to claw at the pages with her nails. She buried all her fingers in the book, and tore, and ripped, and crumpled, making snarling little mutterings deep in her throat.

'*That!... and that!... for You!*' she panted. (Rip!) '*And that!... and this!... for Your*... (Crunch!)... *precious ... promises!... Look!... if You can see... You cruel Thing ...what I'm doing to your Holy Word!... Now! There!... send me to hell!*'

Completely spent by her exertion, Julia lay as one dead under the litter of ragged, crumpled desecration, her shuddering sobs all but subsided; and, fatigued beyond endurance, drifted away from the shameful scene, and slept.

When she woke there was a dim light burning on the table. Her father was sitting on the low rocking-chair by the bed, elbows on knees, his fingers tangled in his shaggy gray hair. Remembering dully, she felt about on the counterpane. Nothing there. So it was only a bad dream, after all. That was good. Her fingers touched a rumpled scrap of paper. It was not a dream. She laid her hand on the torn paper and closed on it.

Roused by her stirring, Ferd glanced up, and their eyes met. Julia's were inquisitive.

Ferd shook his head, and smiled wanly.

'It's all right, Julia. I cleared it up. Nobody seen it. Guess you was a little out o' yer mind fer a spell.'

'I'm dreadfully sorry, father,' she murmured, penitently. 'It was... an awful thing to do.'

Old Ferd caressed the white hand nearest him. With the other, Julia absently rolled the fragment she had found into a tight little ball.

She fell to wondering whether there was anything still legible on the scrap; and, if so, whether it would be some frightful forecast of doom for sinners. Well — she deserved it, didn't she? She recalled her curiosity about the sentimental mottoes that came on thin, narrow, sticky strips of paper wrapped around cheap taffy at the County Fair.... Funny how people took stock in the silly fortunes told that way.... She remembered a discussion between Martha and Becky Slemmer, one day, over the 'messages' they had had by tossing the Bible open at random and reading the first verse at the top of the page.... Martha had come by many a precious promise accidentally... poor Martha.... Becky had laughed over some of hers, and Martha had hush-hushed her, warningly. Becky said you couldn't make much out of it, anyway. One time, after a big quarrel with Zelma in which they had bit, scratched, and pulled hair, she had gone to the Bible for guidance, and the magic verse at the top of the column said, 'She is loud and stubborn.' Becky was sure, at first, that the Lord referred to her sister, but she wondered afterward. Martha said: 'No — Becky. The Lord wouldn't send a message t' Zelma through you. He must 'a' meant somethin' personal.'

'Shall I get yuh a cold drink, Julia?' Ferd was inquiring.

'Please, father... and turn up the light a little, won't you, before you go down?'

* * * * * *

'You're ever so much better this morning,' said Doctor Engle, cheerily.

Julia smiled contentedly, and nodded.

'You're overcoming this toxine, Julia.'

'What's toxine, doctor?' she inquired, interestedly.

'Poison.'

'Yes,' said Julia, thoughtfully, 'I have overcome it.'

'Well — maybe not all of it yet,' he cautioned, stroking his cheek, 'but ——'

Julia's dry lips puckered determinedly, and she nodded her head with an air of deep conviction.

'All of it,' she said, firmly, 'all the poison is gone.'

That afternoon, to Martha's astonishment and disapproval, Julia demanded pen, ink, paper, and privacy. Protestingly, the weary and worried woman propped her sister up with pillows, and closed the door.

Summoning all her depleted energy, Julia wrote a long letter addressed to her unborn child. The writing was uneven and sprawling, and the lines sagged at the right end, more and more, until the last ones ran nearly off the pages in a pitiful little toboggan toward the corner.

Everything she knew about Dresden was in it; high pride for the things that were Dresden; high hopes for the heir to the Dresden tradition.

Everything she knew about Zandy was in it; poor, bewildered Zandy, so frightfully misunderstood, and showing up so badly when he really had it in his heart to do the right thing.

'I'm going to hide this letter, and hope that you find it, some day, in case anything happens to me. You'll not find it, perhaps, until you're big enough to want to take things to pieces and see how they were put together. I hope you won't find it even then. I hope you won't find it until you're old enough to have had a few harder bumps than just falling out of your cradle.

'I've discovered a secret. It's going to take me through what I have to face. If I live, it's going to make me over into something else than I've been. If I die, I'll die happy. I'm going to tell you what I've found. It's the only thing I have to leave you. If you'll take it, and make use of it, you may need no other fortune.'

It was a difficult letter to write. The uncanny experience that had been hers, during the preceding eighteen hours, was not easy to explain. But Julia did the best she could, and with the last physical resource left from the fatigue of writing, she groped her way dizzily to the little walnut desk, with a great effort opened the secret drawer, deposited her letter, and returned to her bed, exhausted.

*   *   *   *   *   *

After her grinding agony was over, Julia slept, and woke, and slept, and dreamed.

In the late afternoon, she became slightly delirious. Martha caught fragments of it, and wept quietly.... Roses overhanging a trellis at the doorway of a little bungalow... Zandy being welcomed with outstretched arms that quickly fell inert from fatigue.... Then — there was a garden... a high, gray, stone wall... and in the wall there was a door ... and beyond the door, a river.... Martha sobbed chokingly, and turned the iced towel on the hot forehead.... And on the river there was a punt... with a red and blue canopy ... and the sound of a tender voice, singing... and a guitar.

When she awoke again, it was almost dark. It was apparent to the watchers that Julia was mildly curious about the presence of the whole family.

Doctor Engle was seated at the bedside with his fingers on her wrist. Her father stood stiffly beside him, his hands clenched. Martha slowly waved a palm-leaf fan, supporting her weary weight on outspread fingers laid against the head of the bed. Susan and Greta stood at the foot, staring wide-eyed. Hiram and Elmer were in the doorway.

Julia's eyes slowly traveled over the group, finally coming to rest on old Ferd whom she inspected with gravity. She attempted a little smile for him — a solicitous little smile that seemed to say, 'What a lot of trouble I'm making you. So sorry.' Ferd couldn't face the stiff little smile any longer; closed his eyes, walked to the window; wept.

Julia had kept her secret too long. Through hot, parched lips she asked Martha if she would please take care of the baby. Greta drew a sudden racking sob, and sank to the floor. Susan raised her up and tugged her out into the hall.

'His name,' murmured Julia, valiantly battling with the oncoming fog, 'is Alexander Ferdinand.... But — Martha — if that's too long a name... for such a little boy... you may call him Zandy.'

* * * * * *

It was late afternoon. They had just returned from the service at Oak Grove Baptist Church, and its sequel in the Cemetery. The long row of hitching-racks had been quite inadequate. Barely a third of the people had been able to enter the church.

Martha had whispered to the undertaker, and he had laid one of the sprays on their mother's grave, hard-by. Jason Schrofe, observing that his flowers had been chosen for this tribute, tarried, after the others had moved away, and re-placed it.

Susan and Greta were busying themselves in the kitchen, sympathetically assisted by neighbors whose voices, re-strained but endeavoring to be cheerful, drifted up the stairs where Martha, having laid her borrowed bonnet and veil on Julia's primly made, white-counterpaned bed, was stooping over the cradle.

Old Ferd tiptoed into the room, and Martha glanced up.

'Look at them long fingers,' she said. 'Like her'n.'

Ferd handed her a yellow envelope.

'One o' the Schrofe boys fetched this over from Crom-well.'

Martha opened it, read it through, silently, her lips forming the words, and gave it back. Ferd stared hard at the message from Seattle.

COURAGE DARLING IT WILL NOT BE LONG NOW
GOOD JOB   ZANDY

He tossed the telegram on Julia's bed, and stumbled out of the room, whimpering like a punished child.

*   *   *   *   *   *

That night — as if the Millers had not already furnished enough sensation to satisfy the community — Ferd hanged himself from a rafter in the vacant stall next to Florrie.

Hiram had gone out to throw down some straw, and saw It, from the mow-ladder, slowly revolving. Martha, hearing a hoarse shout, ran from the kitchen and found her brother retching violently. It seemed a long time before they found a box high enough to stand on.

'I was a-feared o' this, all along,' groaned Martha.

Greta kept screaming, hysterically, while she tugged at the rope of the dinner-bell that clanged ominously from its perch on the roof of the milkhouse.

The barnyard filled with neighbors carrying lanterns. Milt Mumaugh volunteered to drive to Albion for the coroner, and put his three-year-old roan mare to a gallop.

It was a warm night, but they felt chilly and built a fire to sit by while they waited. About midnight, the wives of the watchers served sandwiches, cake, and coffee.

Abner Schrofe and Doc Engle sat on the doorstep of old Ferd's shop, smoking and slapping mosquitoes.

'Baby a-goin' t' live, Doc?'

'Looks like it.... Poor little devil.... Maybe better off if it died.... Not much of a future for it, I'm afraid.'

'Well — as fer that,' drawled Abner, 'yuh never c'n tell.'

CHAPTER III

'AND now, Ferdinand' — Reverend Miles Brumm pursed
a public smile — 'perhaps you had better mount your new
pony, and see how he sits.'

'Please, Uncle Miles, I don't want to.'

Ferdinand's voice was barely audible, but to the congregation assembled in the parsonage barn-lot there was no
mistaking the determined shake of his curly head.

Consternation prevailed in the audience, composed of
half the children in Zanesdale, and what Mr. Brumm would
have considered on Sunday morning as 'a goodly company'
of adults.

A medley of encouragement, ridicule, insufferable patron-
age, and downright contempt volleyed at the embarrassed
boy.

'Aw, gwan! Ride him!' ... 'Don't be scairt of him,
Ferdinand; he won't throw yuh!' ... 'He's yourn, hain't
he? Git on 'im!' ... 'Shucks! — feared of a Shetland
pony!' ... 'Yeah — tame as a kitten!'

Ferdinand hung his head, abstractedly crushed an ant
with his bare toes, and was painfully conscious of the rapid
beating of a bulging vein in his neck.

'Bet he cost a hundred dollars!' appraised Nathan Himes,
who had joined the procession when it passed his drugstore.

'Hundred dollars!' scoffed Bill Trask, the station agent;
'that there saddle 'n' bridle cost more 'n' a hundred dollars!'

'My land!' exclaimed Sophie Trask, proudly relaying her
husband's versatility to the huddle of women by the big
gate, 'Mr. Trask says the saddle and bridle alone must 'a'
cost more than a hundred dollars! What must the pony be
worth?'

Nobody paid any attention to the comment except young
Mrs. Himes (her as was one o' them Sheriff Effendorfer
girls from over beyond Maples; so stuck up — all of 'em —

their noses was out o' joint), who, behind her hand, remarked to Clara Sellars, the lately-from-Wayne peroxide-blonde milliner (less said the better), that the Trasks always knew so much, to which Miss Sellars replied, in a disgusted undertone, 'Don't they give yuh a pain?'

Mr. Brumm, aware of the unanimous curiosity about the pony, to which his young nephew had now added spice by his reluctance to exhibit a natural interest in it, felt himself in an awkward situation. He had been unprepared for the episode that had plunged his family into the public eye. No chance had been given him to collect his thoughts or confer with Ferdinand in private.

It was the lad's tenth birthday. At breakfast he had received a large, inexpensive pocket-knife from his uncle, a sticky, acrid-smelling, red-and-green *Child's Illustrated Bible* from his aunt, and three lead-pencils in a slim pasteboard box from Angela.

He had put down the apple he was munching, and had gone about, as the custom was, dutifully kissing the donors — Uncle Miles, first; for Uncle Miles was always served first with whatever happened to be in distribution; and then Aunt Martha, who moistened a finger and brushed back the unruly lock that dipped to a point in the center; and then Angela, whom he tried to kiss on the cheek, for Angela's kisses were wet, and he had a disinclination toward them which he hoped she would realize, one of these days, without too much injury to her feelings.

At that mellow moment — for, however stiffly the family ties were habitually starched, there were festal occasions when something like spontaneous affection had its innings — there was a vigorous rap at the kitchen door. Straightening his frayed cravat, Mr. Brumm had answered the summons. A stranger's business-like voice was heard.

'Mr. Brumm? ... How do you do, sir? ... Very well, sir. ... My name is Thompson. I'm from Chicago; that is, I'm from the Winnetka Stock Farm. Our people has had orders to deliver a pony here for Master Craig ——'

Through the open door came the rumble of many voices. Angela wiped her shapely lips on her sleeve and hurried to the window. Ferdinand stared hard at Aunt Martha, listening intently.

'He lives with you, don't he? ... It's a birthday gift from his father. ... It's Mr. Craig's instructions from Seattle. ... I've just got in with it, expressed from our place in Winnetka. ... The pony's out here in your lot, delivered in good shape, as you'll see, and if you, or the young gentleman, will sign these papers, I can catch the nine-seventeen back to the city. ... Right here you are, sir, on that line; and here, too, if you please. Thanks! ... Quite a crowd we gathered up, coming through the village, eh? Guess it's the first time a pony ever came to this town on a passenger train.'

Aunt Martha had taken off her brown apron and joined her husband at the back door, nervously smoothing her hair with both hands.

Ferdinand, blinking rapidly, and tapping his front teeth with a restless thumb, squeezed past his aunt, and ventured out upon the back porch, quite overawed by the gathering crowd.

Uncle Miles, with a pumped-up air of heartiness, as if he himself were being presented with a thoroughbred Shetland pony by his admiring fellow-townsmen, breezed forth to the barnyard, delightedly intoning, 'Well — well — indeed! ... A great surprise, I'm sure! ... A pony! ... Well — well!'

It was the crowd that remembered the pony was Ferdinand's.

'Heigh! Ferdinand! Come on out! Look what yuh got!'

'Must I, Aunt Martha?' asked Ferdinand, his face twitching.

'Of course, silly!' shouted Angela, clutching his hand and dragging him along.

'Fancy that great big boy having to be tugged out of the house to see a pony!' scoffed Clara Sellars.

'He's only a kid,' explained Mrs. Himes. 'Awful big for his age; tall as his half-sister, and she must be all of fourteen. I s'pose he's just shy of so many people.'

Very much embarrassed, Ferdinand allowed himself to be propelled through the crowd. He drew a stiff, reluctant smile, reached out a slim hand, stroked the pony's velvet muzzle, and was generously rewarded for the tentative caress, the pony sniffing inquisitively at his pockets and licking his hands.

'Aw — look — ain't that cute?' The women cooed appreciatively, and beamed on Aunt Martha, who had joined them, murmuring apologies for her looks and all. They told her she looked quite all right, they were sure.

Miss Sellars, pretending interest in the half-finished sweater that Mrs. Himes was carrying under her arm, whispered, 'Did yuh ever see such an old frump?'

'Awful pious, I guess.'

'Can't people be pious without ——'

'No,' said Mrs. Himes, 'Sh! — Listen!'

'Well — Ferdinand ——' said Uncle Miles.

'No, Uncle Miles.' His deep-set, gray-green eyes were perplexed, and his face was contorted as he gnawed his lips. He stepped back, and glanced about as if looking for a way of escape.

Mr. Brumm wiped his brow with a large handkerchief. It would hardly do to send these parishioners of his away with so great a mystery to discuss.

'Don't you like your pony?' he stammered, in a tone that affected to express the general surprise.

'Of course!' Ferdinand's voice was husky under the strain. 'But I mustn't have it! I can't have it! You know why!' Hot tears sprang to his eyes, and he scurried through the speechless crowd, disappearing into the house.

'Ferdinand's a little nervous and excited,' explained Mrs. Brumm, primly, but obviously shaken by the unfortunate event. 'He wasn't expecting a pony, you know, and what with so many good friends coming along, and all ——'

'That's it — that's it,' said Mr. Brumm, who, upon Ferdinand's retreat, had moved toward his wife to learn what explanation she was offering for this strange conduct. 'Ferdinand will be quite himself, presently.'

'Yeah — I bet there's a skeleton in the Brumms' closet, all right, all right!' muttered Miss Sellars. 'They're badly fussed — both of 'em!'

* * * * * *

Ferdinand, face downward on his bed, could hear the children's excited shouts as they took turns riding the pony about the barn-lot. ... It sounded now as if they had taken him out into the road. 'Please let me next, Angela!' ... 'I said first, Angela!' ... 'These stirrups is too high!'

He heard his uncle's heavy footsteps on the stairs.

'Now, my boy, what's the trouble?' Uncle Miles was serious.

Ferdinand stifled a racking sob.

'You know I can't take anything from *him!* ... Sure — I love the pony, and I want it awfully... but I wouldn't take anything from *him — not if he gave me a million trillion dollars!*'

'But you didn't have to show off like that before all our people! What do you suppose they'll think?'

'I don't care what they think,' growled Ferdinand into the damp pillow. 'It's none of their business, is it?'

'They'll make it their business to find out.'

Uncle Miles sat down on the edge of the bed, Ferdinand moving over with a great effort to make him room.

'You are a strange child, Ferdinand, to feel this way about your father.' Uncle Miles laid a hand on the twitching shoulder. 'I hardly thought it possible for a child of your years to be capable of as much hatred as you ——'

'But *you* hate him, don't you, Uncle Miles? Aunt Martha hates him!'

'Hate is an ugly word, Ferdinand. Neither your Aunt Martha nor I hate anybody in the whole wide world — not even your erring father. Whatever mistakes he may have made in letting your young mother suffer and be misunderstood and maligned...and die...it will do you no good to carry a grudge — especially now that he wants to be friendly.'

At this, Ferdinand broke down completely, and cried piteously.

'He waited for ten years!... Not one word from him! ... Even if you and Aunt Martha did hate him, I kept hoping he would write to me when I got big enough to read. ... But I swore, last Christmas morning, I would hate him... forever!'

'On Christmas morning!' Uncle Miles was horrified. 'What a day to choose for a pledge to everlasting hate!'

'Good as any,' grumbled Ferdinand.

Uncle Miles took a turn or two up and down the room, tugging at his black burnsides.

'Well — if you're sure you don't want the pony' — Uncle Miles' tone was conciliatory — 'we'll sell it. Perhaps that would be more prudent, anyway. You've shown pretty good judgment for a small boy. We can't afford a pony, and our people know it. You would only make the other children envious. It's out of keeping with everything else we have. ... Suppose we sell the pony, and put the money in bank for your college education: how's that?'

'But — Uncle Miles!' — Ferdinand's voice rose shrilly. 'That's all the same, isn't it? I don't want anything he's got! I won't have his ponies, or saddles, or colleges, or anything! He same as killed my mother! Aunt Martha said so! I'm going to write and tell him so! You see if I don't!'

'Now — now!' soothed Uncle Miles. 'You wouldn't do that.'

He patted Ferdinand on the head and walked slowly out of the room and down the hall to his study, where he slumped into the shabby morris chair by the window and meditatively twisted the burnsides into pencil-points.

Every three months since his marriage to Martha Miller

seven years ago, he had received a draft for two hundred
and fifty dollars from his prosperous brother-in-law. It
exceeded his salary.

Indeed, his decision to marry Martha Miller — which he
tried later to tell himself was based on the fact that she,
albeit unsightly and eccentric, was an excellent housekeeper, a paragon of piety, and singularly devoted to his
motherless little Angela — had been hastened upon her
confiding to him that the baby Ferdinand was something
other than a liability.

'It's very sacrificial of you, Miss Miller,' he had said,
that April afternoon on his return to the Miller home for a
brief glimpse of Angela, who, since the revival he had conducted at the Oak Grove Baptist Church in November, had
been happily in Martha's care — 'it's very fine of you to
have assumed, so cheerfully, the burden of your unfortunate sister's child: very unselfish, indeed!'

Martha had smiled, cryptically.

'I must be honest with yuh, Brother Brumm. Of course,
I would 'a' took care o' Julia's baby, like I promised, even if
young Craig had disowned it. ... But — he remembers.'

'Indeed?... Does him credit, I must say. ... Does he remember substantially, may I ask, Miss Martha?'

'Two hundred and fifty every quarter.' Martha seemed
satisfied with the effect of her announcement. 'Reg'lar as
the clock.'

'A thousand dollars a year, Martha, for the keep of a
baby?'

Martha nodded, smiled, folded her arms, rocked gently.

'I had a promise from Craig' — she leaned forward and
lowered her voice confidentially — 'shortly after our poor
Julia passed away. He had wrote a-sayin' was there anything he could do, though at the minute he hadn't much to
do with, he said, and I reckon that was true. ... Give the
devil his due, I always say ——'

'I'm sure you would, Martha!'

He recalled Martha's prompt reaction to the note of

tenderness in his voice. She had smiled appreciatively, puckered her lips self-deprecatingly, touched her hair, rather gingerly; for it was the first time she had done it up over a rat — not one of the larger rats, to be sure, such as the bulky Susan affected; a mere mouse, indeed, compared to Susan's — and was obviously not quite at ease with her graying foretop so heavily shadowing her eyes.

'But — and so — then —— Oh, yes; then I wrote him as how poor Julia had gave me th' baby t' bring up, and that I meant t' do so, well as I could. If he ever wanted t' send me anything toward its keep, all well and good, I said, but the baby was mine. I told him as how it was Julia's last words, and it was, almost. I asked him t' promise he would never try t' take little Alexander away from me, or even write to him when he grew big enough t' understand; fer it might make him discontented and all... *and he promised!*'

'Alexander? I thought the child's name was Ferdinand.'

'Well, you see Julia had wrote a letter, a couple o' days afore she died, and if the baby was a boy it was to be Alexander. So Craig always calls him Alexander. ... We just couldn't; not after what he'd done, 'n' all. ... Anyways, that's the baby's other name.'

Mr. Brumm had proposed marriage to Martha, that evening, and had been accepted with a coyness he had hardly suspected her capable of in the face of her nun-like, ascetic piety.

On the day of their wedding in December — Mr. Brumm had just returned aglow over the quite brilliant success of his three weeks' revival at Partridge Crossing, Illinois — certain small items of business were under discussion. He and Martha were out walking in the snow on the highway, safe from the hostile curiosity of the family in whose opinion that slick feller Brumm was a-tryin' t' lay his miracle-workin' hands on th' baby's money, an indictment they had hinted at, in his presence, and freely discussed within easy earshot.

Martha had beamed over the prompt victory she had

won in gaining his consent to look for a settled pastorate and discontinue his itinerant evangelistic career. Her solicitude over his endurance of cold beds, unwholesome food, and long journeys touched him, even if — as he suspected — there was another reason, quite as good, for her request. As the wife of a minister, Martha hoped to enjoy whatever refracted glory shone upon that office. There would be small comfort sitting at home, unrecognized, with the care of two small children — Angela was seven, Ferdinand three — while her crusading spouse spent blocks of weeks in distant parts.

With this triumph scored, Martha was prepared to be generous when Miles (it was becoming easier to call him Miles) suggested that he would deeply appreciate it if their future negotiations with Alexander Craig might be conducted by himself. It would be much more pleasant, all 'round, if he, as head of the household — and would not little Ferdinand be the same as his own son, now? — were entrusted with this business.

Pursuant to that agreement, Martha had promptly written to Seattle notifying her young brother-in-law of her marriage and stating that hereafter Mr. Brumm was to be considered custodian of the child's funds, adding that the arrangement would undoubtedly make Mr. Brumm even more interested in little Alexander. She hadn't said why.

Shortly before little Ferdinand was eight, Mr. Brumm had received a letter from Craig — they had always referred to him as Craig; not Mr. Craig, which would have denoted an unearned respect for him, or Alexander, which would have seemed more friendly than they felt — inquiring whether it would be considered a violation of his covenant if he wrote to his son on the occasion of his next birthday. The letter was typed on the expensively embossed stationery of *The Puget Sound —— Editorial Department.*

Mr. Brumm, who enjoyed letting himself go, a bit, with

a pen, had written a reply which, after many revisions, pleased him.

'We live very simply here, as becomes the family of a village clergyman, on small pay, ministering to a by no means well-to-do community composed of persons who for the most part make their own clothes and grow their own food. Your son's wants are few. As you are aware, we have thought it imprudent to inform him of your benefactions. Did he know that we are receiving generous amounts of money on his account, it would unquestionably alter his relation to our household, both in his mind and ours. It would make for constraint, and, perhaps, a breakdown of the discipline which every small boy, however tractable, requires.'

There was a great deal more of it, running into all of four pages, redundantly cautioning Mr. Craig that any affectionate gesture toward his son, at this time, would make the child restless in his humble home, and reminding Mr. Craig of his promise to Mrs. Brumm 'never to disturb the existing relationship while she lives.'

Mr. Brumm had had no reply to that letter which, he felt, deserved adequate recognition, considering the amount of time and labor he had spent on its composition. The quarterly remittances continued to arrive unaccompanied by any personal message. On each occasion, Mr. Brumm receipted with a brief note, reporting on the boy's health and advancement in school, always optimistically.

As for young Ferdinand's opinion of his father, they had tried to shape it properly by making the relationship seem as remote as possible. How else, indeed, were they to insure the child's contentment?

Reflecting on it now, in the light of this morning's dismaying episode, Mr. Brumm wondered if they had not slightly overdone their efforts to portray Craig as a selfish, cowardly scapegrace who had fled in terror from the gravest of obligations. He was aware that Martha had spared no ugly words in recounting for Ferdinand the pitiful details of a tragedy which had become an obsession in her cramped mind. Would this hot-headed boy actually write to his father, provoking an open breach, perhaps an investigation? It was a comfort to remember that Ferdinand did not know his father's address beyond the bare fact that he lived in Seattle. But was that a comfort? Mr. Brumm wondered if a letter addressed to Alexander Craig, Seattle, might not be delivered.

* * * * * *

Meantime, while Mr. Brumm toyed absently with his beard, there was a dull rumble of conversation drifting in from Ferdinand's room, where Aunt Martha was endeavoring to set everything right. From the boy's protests, it was to be gathered that she was not meeting with much success.

'I was just a-sayin' to Ferdinand' — Aunt Martha rose from the low rocking-chair, and leaned against the foot of the bed as Uncle Miles strolled in — 'that we mustn't have any more fuss now about this pony business. It's gone plenty far enough!'

'Well,' said Uncle Miles, casually, 'we'll think it over and decide what's the best thing to do. Ferdinand's going to be reasonable, I feel sure.'

His shoes squeaked as he went downstairs. Aunt Martha sighed audibly, and followed him. Ferdinand, fatigued by the emotional storm, yawned, stretched, slept.

After a brief conference in the kitchen, Uncle Miles harnessed the glossy bay mare to the jump-seat buggy, while Aunt Martha, in their downstairs bedroom, changed to her white lawn with the black spray.

'Angela,' she called, 'your father 'n' me are a-goin' to make a call on Sister Sprecker.'

In deference to Ferdinand's distress, Angela had cheerfully consented that the pony should be stabled, and was sitting on one foot in the porch swing deeply absorbed in *The Last Days of Pompeii*, which, after many unsuccessful attempts, she was devouring with interest. The book was lowered to her lap for a moment. Odd — making a visit on Saturday afternoon. Father always reserved Saturday for study.

Aunt Martha did not explain that she herself was to be left with Sister Sprecker, who lived on the pike halfway to Bluffton, while Uncle Miles continued to town for the purpose of sending a telegram, which he could not prudently dispatch from Zanesdale, inquiring of the Winnetka Stock Farm whether they would buy back the pony and equipment. She tiptoed upstairs, and returned to the front screen-door, bonneted and black-mitted for her journey.

'Ferdinand's asleep, Angela. He's been so stirred up 'n' all. Get him a piece when he comes down. We mayn't be back much afore sundown. You peel th' potatoes, 'n' make a good fire about five o'clock.'

Briefly disengaging herself from panic-stricken Pompeii, Angela mumbled acquiescence and hoped they would have a good time.

She was a flaxen-haired, large-eyed, precocious youngster whom her father regarded as a valuable asset in his profession. A great deal of attention had been paid to Angela when she was a mere tiny tot by the adoring widows and elderly maidens in whose indulgent care she had been lodged, in at least a score of small towns, while her father was pursuing his evangelistic ministry, previous to his second marriage.

Sometimes she sat beside him in the pulpit, an enraptured and undeniably touching picture of cherubic innocence. Not infrequently she was adverted to, with a tender gesture, when the preacher spoke feelingly of the uninquisitive faith to be found at its best in the heart of a child.

At eight, Angela had sung, 'I'll Meet Mother Over There,' in a sweet, unaffected, little voice that had utterly devastated with emotion the large crowd on the last night of Mr. Brumm's memorable revival at Unger, shortly after accepting their call.

More than a hundred souls were saved during that revival; and at least a score, already saved, experienced the second blessing. Little Angela herself had publicly professed a receipt of the second blessing, on that final night of the revival, somewhat to her parent's confusion; for this degree, while not explicitly restricted to an adult constituency, had not — at least within his own purview — been undertaken by anyone of Angela's immature years. There was nothing he could do about it, however; certainly not at the moment, seeing with what a spontaneous wave of hysterical exultation the child's bland announcement was accepted. In fact, it was Angela's second blessing that had brought the month's 'big meetin'' to an almost painfully triumphant crescendo insuring her father's standing in the community for five successful years.

As was to be expected, Angela, thereafter, was looked to, on occasions when emotion ran high, for a tender song, a fervid testimony, a sugary little prayer — demands which she met so adequately that even she herself could not have failed to realize the value of her talent, had she been infinitely more reticent than she was. Everybody predicted a bright future for Angela. It went without debate that she could expect to be mightily used by the Lord. Aunt Martha occasionally hinted to her husband that it would be a pity if Angela's head should be turned by so much praise; but, observing that his smug smile left something unsaid on the subject of envy, she did not venture to press the matter.

No endeavor had been made to capitalize Ferdinand's piety which was of a much less showy type. He had displayed no prophetic gifts. At Christmas and on Children's Day he spoke short pieces and participated in dialogues, always without enthusiasm or promise of future distinction either as an apostle or platform orator. Privately he despised these exhibitions, and consented to be a party to them only when his loyalty to his uncle was challenged. Especially did he loathe the dialogues. Overtopping by a head all the other boys of his age, he appeared the dolt in a line-up of brighter juniors, albeit some of them might be older than he. It was a sore trial, indeed, when it came his turn to hold up a little white pasteboard card bearing the letter D, and recite, shamefacedly, amid the pardonable titters of the congregation:

> ' I am the Daisy that grows in the spring,
> Sweetly adoring the love of our King. '

Presently all these letters would spell

GODS LITTLE FLOWERS

and he could stumble awkwardly to his seat beside Aunt Martha, who, smiling benignly, would wet a finger and brush back the lock that had come all the way from Dresden.

Ferdinand accepted Angela's opulent faith at face value. It never occurred to him to be jealous of the marked attentions she received, wherever they went, sometimes in quite glaring contrast to the attitude people manifested toward him. He rejoiced in her well-deserved popularity. He liked Angela. The hazard of childish quarrels between them had been reduced to a minimum by the fact that no question of property rights ever arose. Until recently, Angela had contented herself at play with her dolls and dishes. Ferdinand, when not whittling sticks, amused himself with his small set of smeary rubber-type. They kept out of each other's way.

Of late, however, Angela had been taking more interest in Ferdinand. At first he had been flattered by these friendly attentions; though, on the whole, he rather liked her better when she left him to his own devices. Sometimes she came out to the bench, behind the woodhouse, and sat by him while he whittled toy furniture out of soft pine; sat very close, often hampering him.

Angela confided in him very freely now, as if he were her own age. One of these days she was going to be an evangelist. She could do it now if they would let her. Not only would she do a great deal of good, but she could earn some money. She could have nice clothes. 'And I'll get you a really good printing-outfit, too, Ferdinand. You want one very much, don't you?'

And when he said he certainly did — very much — she would kiss him, and say: 'Never you mind. I'll get you one that you can print a little newspaper on. Wouldn't that be fun?'

*   *   *   *   *   *

Ferdinand was roused by Angela's voice down in the parlor, singing, 'That Will Be Glory For Me,' to her own accompaniment on the melodeon. He was debating whether he should not go down and ask Aunt Martha for a piece of pie, now that he had slept through dinner-time. It was almost three.

Suddenly the music stopped abruptly. Angela was calling from the foot of the stairs.

'Ferdinand!'

'Ye-es.'

'You awake now?'

'Um-humm.'

'What are you doing?'

'Nothing.'

'Lonesome?'

'No — but I'm hungry.'

'Want me to bring you a piece of cake and a banana?'

'Well — if you want to.'

She came presently and sat down beside him on the bed, licking sticky fingers.

'Don't you want any?' asked Ferdinand, his mouth full.

'I just had some. Did you know that father and Aunt Martha have gone away for all afternoon?'

'No.... Let's go down and play croquet.'

'I'm so sorry you had such an unhappy birthday, Ferdinand.' Angela's voice was husky. 'I could have cried for you, this morning. Do you feel better now?' She put an arm around him and pushed him back on the pillow.

Ferdinand made a brave show of not being annoyed when Angela bent over him, burying her hot face in his neck, and blinding him with her tousled hair.

'Let me up, Angela. You're smothering me!' shouted Ferdinand. 'I don't feel like romping.'

'I'm not romping,' whispered Angela, trembling.

* * * * * *

Ten minutes later, Angela, with very red cheeks, went to the melodeon and continued where she had left off at the third verse of 'That Will Be Glory For Me,' hoping that Ferdinand's stubbornness meant he was too dumb to understand, or, having understood, would not unintentionally give her away.

The front doorbell rang loudly, and Angela, still scarlet and shaky, answered it. Mr. Trask had brought a telegram for Ferdinand. Whatever was Ferdinand doing with telegrams?

She rushed upstairs with it. He was standing at the window, drumming absently on the pane with his knuckles. He did not turn.

'Look what you got!' Angela hoped the message would be pleasant, at least diverting.

He clumsily opened the envelope and mystifiedly read the telegram several times before its meaning became quite clear. It was signed by the Winnetka Stock Farm.

WE HAVE BRUMMS WIRED PROPOSAL TO RESELL TO US PONY AND EQUIPMENT DELIVERED YOU TODAY STOP IF YOU DO NOT AGREE WIRE IMMEDIATELY COLLECT

'What is it?' Angela was bursting with curiosity.

Ferdinand crumpled the message in his fist, and shuffled past her toward the stairway. There he paused, his face working, his eyes brimming with angry tears.

'You're all a lot o' cheaters!' he screamed.

Angela stood in open-mouthed amazement.... So unlike Ferdinand to explode like that!

He clumped down the stairs, savagely shouting: 'I hate all of you! Do you hear me? I hate everybody in th' whole damn world!'

Angela brightened.

'He won't tell, then,' she reflected.

Ferdinand flung himself out of the house, banged the front gate, pulled his cap far down over his red nose, dug his fists deep into the pockets of his pants (cut down from a pair of his uncle's), and stamped sullenly up the road toward the railroad track, only three hundred yards away. The east-bound Erie Flyer was just due. It always stopped at Zanesdale for water.

Sometimes Ferdinand strolled down to the station and stood close beside the dripping water-tank when, at exactly three-thirty-six, the huge locomotive paused, gasping rhythmically, while the torrent poured into the capacious tender, the fireman on the coal-pile, holding the rope, calmly smoking his pipe, unmindful of his happy privilege.

Most of the fast trains thundered through Zanesdale with a terrifying racket. Ferdinand never failed to experience a surge of hot indignation over this arrogant contempt for his town. He knew it wasn't much of a town; had contempt for it himself; but it was annoying to have the utter insignificance of Zanesdale thrust upon him nine times a day.

He would not have time to run down to the station, now, even if he had been in a mood for running: besides, he didn't care to answer any questions that Mr. Trask might ask, so that he might be able to tell Mrs. Trask the sequel to the pony story which she would promptly explain to the town.

He climbed on top of the gate-post at the corner of Harsh's melon-patch — his favorite vantage when watch-

ing the long, black, proud Pullmans flick by, each adding
its own little 'Psst!' of disdain; and watched Number Nine
(he knew all the trains that way) slow to a screeching stop.
There was a long hiss of escaping air from the brakes; an
acrid smell of greasy, hot metal. The diner was directly in
front of him. Little tables with candles on them. A man
and a woman, with a black waiter hovering over them.
Too late for dinner, too early for supper: this must be
'tea.' People in stories were always having 'tea.' Ferdinand drew down the corners of his mouth and hated the
man and the woman, though he knew she was a pretty
woman. He hated the obsequious waiter, and mumbled,
audibly, 'Damn nigger!'

The train moved slowly on, so slowly that the locomotive was exasperated by the sluggishness of the heavy
Pullmans, and barked a staccato of short, angry demands
that it had better get to business, now, or we'd be late
again pulling into Washington. Ferdinand climbed down
from the post, made a detour around the rear of the
melon-patch, and entered the barn through the back door.
The pony looked around over its shoulder, stopped munching its mouthful of hay, and blew a long breath that made
its soft nostrils flutter.

He advanced slowly and laid a hand on the pony's flank
which twitched as if the light touch had tickled; moved
forward another step and took a wisp of tawny mane in
his fingers; was about to pat the friendly pet on the nose.

On sudden impulse he drew back and muttered, 'No —
I tell you — *No!*'

Retracing his steps through the back door, half-blinded
by tears, he stood for a long time gazing abstractedly into
the muddy water of the miasmic, green-scummed little
pond that belonged to Flook's Tile Factory; amblingly
circled the barn, and moved toward his little workbench
behind the woodhouse.

He took the new knife from his pocket, turned it over
several times, opened it, closed it with a sharp click; and,

deliberately drawing his long arm back to full torsion, he sighted carefully — his lower lip pinioned by a row of uncommonly straight teeth — and threw the knife all of forty yards with such velocity and precision that it landed with a mighty splash exactly where he had intended.

Ferdinand grinned. It was an ugly grin that did something to him on the inside — a brand-new sensation which defied his childish analysis, but seemed to be made up of such ingredients as, 'Damn them all!'...'I haven't a friend left in the world!'...'I've got to go it alone!'...'I _can_ go it alone!'...'I _will_ go it alone!'... '*You see if I don't!*... *Damn you all!*'

CHAPTER IV

FERDINAND arrived home at five, gayly whistling an improvised tune.

He was in unusually high spirits today; for Miss Carle, who had specialized in Creative English at Wellesley, and was hopeful of teaching it in a college, some day, had detained him again after school to discuss his latest composition as seriously as if they were equals in age and experience.

'But, Ferdinand,' she had cautioned, 'really, you're quite shockingly cynical, I'm afraid... for fifteen!'

He would have liked to leave the question of his age stand just that way, but when she added, 'You're not any older, are you?' he felt obliged to tell the truth.

'I'll be fourteen next May.'

'My word!' ejaculated Miss Carle. 'Owlish as Omar, when you ought to be out playing marbles.'

'I guess I grew pretty fast,' Ferdinand admitted, shyly.

'And pretty sour, too,' laughed Miss Carle. 'But you can write, young fellow! Just be a bit careful how you whirl that battle-axe! You might hurt somebody, and be sorry.'

It was evident, at home, that something important was afoot.

Aunt Martha had crimped her hair and was tidying up the house. Apparently all the major feats of putting to rights had been attended to, for she was now at the final stage of patting the sofa pillows and rearranging the trinkets on the mantel — the shepherdess he had carved, a year ago, the china cat that someone had given to Angela when she was five, the oval slab of polished stone that Uncle Miles had picked up on a vagabondish trip long ago in the Petrified Forest. A fire had been neatly laid in the grate, though it was only the second of October and unseasonably warm.

'Mr. and Mrs. Joel Day are coming to call, this evening,' explained Aunt Martha, impressively. 'Mind yuh don't leave yer things a-lyin' around.'

Angela, softly humming while she pressed the skirt of her blue dress on the ironing-board in the kitchen, broke off to say, as Ferdinand thrust a long slim hand into the cooky-jar, 'Mustn't scatter crumbs. The Days are to be here, tonight.'

Upstairs, Uncle Miles was found straightening books on the shelves in his study. Ferdinand paused in the doorway, half-minded to tell him that Miss Carle had encouraged him about his writing. He was bursting to tell somebody. On second thought, he decided that Uncle Miles might think him boastful.

A neat stack of opened letters lay on the corner of the desk, otherwise bare except for an engagement-pad which occupied a conspicuous position in the middle. The letters were making-believe they were the current mail of a busy man of affairs, the edge of an old telegram protruding slightly from midway of the deceitful pile.

Doubtless Uncle Miles meant to slip up here with Mr. Day for a half-hour's confidential chat about church business while Aunt Martha, in the parlor below, endeavored to infect Mrs. Day with a more passionate interest in the missionary box, the ultimate unpacking and distribution of which, Ferdinand grimly hoped, would put somebody in Paouting-fu to at least half the bother that the recruiting of its miscellaneous contents had already cost him.

He was seldom inquisitive about Uncle Miles's activities, but the engagement-pad caught his eye. He felt the makings of a grin at the corners of his mouth, and dealt with it severely.

A mere glance at tomorrow's crowded program should be sufficient to inform a sharp-eyed deacon that the new minister was not only industrious and popular, but was a person of orderly mind and much experience.

October 3

8–9 . . . . . Correspondence
9–10:45 . Study
11 . . . . . . Mercy Hospital (Mrs. Penfield)
12:15 . . . Luncheon YMCA Com. on Evangelism
2–4 . . . . . Pastoral calls on Brucker, Winona & Swift Sts.
4:30–6 . . Study
7:30 . . . . Midweek Service
8:40 . . . . Conference with S.S. Officers

'Don't disturb anything, Ferdinand,' remarked Uncle
Miles, importantly. 'Mr. Day is coming out, after supper...
and Mrs. Day... to make us a little visit.'

Ferdinand said he wouldn't, and retreated to his own
room at the end of the hall, grinning broadly.

There were a great many things about his transparent
Uncle Miles — affectations, pretensions, petty deceptions —
which, while they had shocked and distressed him at ten,
were only amusing, now. He had quite outgrown his earlier
illusions about absolute integrity as an indispensable to
anyone engaged in the spread of religion. His observations
had led him to suspect that there was as much duplicity
practiced in Uncle Miles's profession as in any other business, the main difference between sacred and secular callings
being that in the latter a man had at least a sporting chance
of getting something out of it worth the time and trouble.

Still — Ferdinand was obliged to admit — they had done
very well, as ministers' families went. The three years on
the rim of Fort Wayne had been good for them. Uncle Miles
— what with Angela's undeniably valuable coöperation —
had been very successful. The two of them had made themselves known soon after their arrival in the big town. Together they had put on noon meetings in the large railroad-
shops, where Uncle Miles had invited soot-smeared mechanics, munching their apple pie, to remember the faith of
their mothers — all of whom were presumed to be dead
and in glory — and Angela, assured of manner and easy to
look at, had sung mellow ballads in keeping with her father's

exhortations, accompanying herself on a portable organ which she played so effortlessly that many of the younger workmen wondered if she were actually pumping the thing with her own feet; and, having maneuvered their position to the satisfaction of their curiosity on this point, had remained steadfastly regarding the robust girl's well-turned ankles with an admiration she did not appear to resent.

After that, it had been easy to book engagements at Young People's social affairs in the down-town churches. At first Uncle Miles had imagined that his sentimental little talks, replete with touching anecdotes, were coming into demand; that Angela's contribution merely provided a unique embellishment to his addresses — a delusion he was gradually relieved of, however, as more and more invitations were extended to his gifted daughter alone. But, for all that, Uncle Miles had prospered beyond all reasonable expectations, and the call to the small church in Indianapolis had been no more appreciated than deserved.

They were still poor; not so poor as they had been, back in Zanesdale, but required to practice rigid economies. Aunt Martha, to whom frugality was a virtue, if not indeed an obsession, had succeeded in making poverty a noble estate.

For a long time they had been paying for a 'little piece of real estate' in Keokuk, Iowa. It had never occurred to Ferdinand to inquire what the 'little piece of real estate' consisted of, whether houses, lands, or business blocks. It had always been a 'little piece of real estate,' which, although involving much correspondence and many receipts of long envelopes from Keokuk, could not amount to very much on their wages, even though they skimped valiantly to make the payments on it.

Ferdinand made almost no demands upon the family purse, considering it no more than his share of the burden to wear the cheapest of clothes — though Aunt Martha didn't try to make them herself any more — and went about, uncomplainingly, with empty pockets. A stated allowance had never been thought of in their family. If Ferdinand wanted a five-cent pencil-tablet, he asked Uncle Miles for a nickel, please, to buy a pencil-tablet; and, to Uncle Miles's credit, the nickel was always forthcoming without argument or reluctance.

Angela had not yet achieved her ambition to appear as the head-liner in a revival. Uncle Miles, finding it quite impossible to leave his local duties for so long a time, and unwilling that Angela should attempt so responsible an undertaking by herself, had put her off; though he kept saying, when she pressed him, that they would surely do it, one of these days; or, if they couldn't, he would see what might be arranged for her 'next winter — perhaps.'

She had been growing almost rebelliously restless when the call to Indianapolis had eased the tension. She would be making new 'contacts' — Uncle Miles's redundant use of this word 'contact,' especially when he made a verb of it, always annoyed Ferdinand, who was unconsciously becoming something of a stylist — and doubtless 'opportunities would develop' if Angela would only bide her time; as indeed they had, for it had been barely a month now since their coming to Indianapolis, and Angela had already been pleasantly spoken of in the newspapers three times (and unpleasantly spoken to in the High School Principal's office twice for her bland nonchalance in respect to Cæsar's Gallic Wars).

It had not yet occurred to the Music Committee in Uncle Miles's church that Angela, who had quickly assumed the position of leading soprano in the choir, deserved a cash competence, for no such appropriations had ever been considered; but, on every hand — or at least almost every hand — one heard her appreciatively mentioned as having had much to do with the unprecedented attendance at church services.

Women declared at the Aid Society that they never had any trouble, now, getting their menfolks out of bed on Sunday mornings.

A few of the more conservative were for putting vestments on the choir, something they had never discussed before Angela joined it. One woman, convinced that the congregation, which was almost militantly non-conformist, would not consent to gowns on the choir, wondered — though it took a good deal of courage to say it, even in the privacy of a group of three — whether it might not be tactfully suggested to Mrs. Brumm that Angela was really a bigger girl than she thought; to which another woman, equally moved to candor, replied, 'No — we mustn't do that. It would do no good, anyway. Angela is just one of those people who, no matter how much they have on, always look as if they'd left something off.'

As for Ferdinand's attitude toward his uncle's bustling ministry, and the luxuriant Angela's aspirations, it stopped with merely wishing them well. Aunt Martha had long since discontinued her direct appeals to him to prepare himself vocationally to follow in his uncle's footsteps; and Uncle Miles, who had frequently besought the Lord, at family worship, to lead 'this lad into the ministry of the gospel' — mostly to please Aunt Martha, Ferdinand always thought — had lately omitted this supplication from his invoice of the family's wants.

Or course, there was no use pretending he had no interest in what went on at their church, for Uncle Miles's profession was singular in that neither he nor his household was ever for a moment free of it. The church was all they lived for. It was at once the hub and the rim, the corona and the periphera of their thoughts and conversation. Such friendships as they had, if not actually originating at the church, eventually brought up there — tentative, temporary, shallow-rooted friendships, for at any minute they might pack up and move elsewhere.

Three years had made structural changes in Ferdinand. They had spread some substantial and nicely distributed flesh on his gangling frame, the additional weight seeming to have given him more self-confidence. He was still rather

shy, but had almost outgrown his earlier tendency to a morbid self-dissatisfaction which, at ten, had made him painfully sensitive, touchy, and inclined to mope.

It had been a long time, now, since he had participated in
a family scene, contenting himself — when they glanced
apprehensively in his direction on occasions brimming with
the raw materials of argument — to draw a twisted smile,
which, although he had never seen it, he suspected of being
somewhat unpleasant. Situations that had once fetched out
of him a squeaky and savage indignation, popping off to the
ruination of a meal, and hurling him out of the room, and
tossing him onto his bed where he would lie for hours hating
all visible creation, including himself, were now handled
with an indifference so closely akin to contempt that the
family sometimes wished he had not tied down the safety-
valve.

Aunt Martha, particularly, viewed this change in Ferdinand with prayerful anxiety. Much as she had deplored the
lad's occasional releases of volcanic protest — mostly protests against the quite irksome and unquestionably silly
inhibitions which she herself laid upon him; for she insisted
that at ten he should carry himself like an experienced saint
of seventy, while she rigged him in babyish sailor-collars
and fussy girlish waists not worn by any child over five,
a manner of dress that promoted his misfortune in being
oversized to a farce so ludicrous that even he, murderously
angry as he was, sometimes laughed himself into wild
hysteria over his own appearance in the mirror, a storm
usually followed by a fit of rebellious weeping — he often
wondered if Aunt Martha did not secretly enjoy such
emotional hurricanes.

On several memorable occasions she had knelt, with
Ferdinand sourly crouched beside her (venomously despising them both), and prayed aloud — her wailing petitions
punctuated with convulsive sobs — that 'this wayward
orphan, whom Thou in Thine Infinite Wisdom, hast entrusted into our care and keeping, may be just brought
under the influence of Thy Blessed Spirit.'

All that was over, now. Aunt Martha had herself under much better control. Whether the benign rainbow that arched her had arrived to signal the biologic fact that she had graduated from her riproaring middle forties, or whether the promotion from a bucolic atmosphere of country-village piety into the relative sophistication of bigger towns and association with 'city folks' had pushed in a few of the shriller stops in her turbulent spirit, Ferdinand did not know.

Perhaps it was these early experiences of the utter break-down of emotional discipline that had produced in Ferdinand a mounting contempt for home theatricals. Unquestionably, these unbridled seizures of Aunt Martha's had been bad for him. They had made him despise any sentiment that threatened to evoke tears. He had wept himself out in early childhood.

At thirteen, plus, these deep lesions had healed, but not without leaving some impermeable scars on the lamina of young Ferdinand's soul at the very points of exposure most frequently bombarded in a home where prayer and piety, sentiment and emotion, were all in the day's work.

Adversions and appeals to Deity were, in Ferdinand's opinion, merely an unscrupulous and unsportsmanly method of having your own way in dealing with people who might be so weak-minded as to believe that you and God were at one as to the soundness of your cause. If you couldn't get what you wanted out of the other fellow by wheedle and whimper, purchase or threat, vituperation or violence, you bade him listen while you took it up with the Lord in prayer. You closed your eyes, and, in the lugubrious tone of one making funeral arrangements over the telephone, prosecuted your case while your helpless victim knelt beside you hotly wanting the courage to say, 'Either you're a fraud, or your God is a rascal!'

Ferdinand no longer took any stock whatever in prayer — either in the family worship kind of prayer that besought the Almighty to make you sweet-spirited and obedient to

His Holy Will, five minutes after you had stubbornly objected, at breakfast on Saturday, to spending the whole afternoon helping old Mullins clean out the church furnace, when you had been looking forward all week to a bit of carving on the fire-screen you meant to give Miss Carle on Christmas; or in the public kind of prayer that asked God to touch the generous hearts of this dear people (Gosh! how he loathed those smug antiques that stood in prim rows in Uncle Miles's prayers!)... and incline them to give sacrificially to some pet scheme they were being badgered into against their wishes.

He had been trying lately not to think about it at all; saying to himself that in any other environment than his the whole matter of religion in general and the activities of the church in particular would be giving him no concern.

Until recently, he had suffered frequent torments, as he watched his feverish disdain burning out to smoking cinders. Could it be that he had 'quenched the Spirit'? Uncle Miles was forever warning his flock against the cold apathy that meant one had committed the 'unpardonable sin.' These past few weeks, he had almost left off torturing himself with these morbid reflections. The 'unpardonable sin' was just so much more nonsense — all of a piece with everything else they ranted about and wept over and grudgingly subscribed to.... A lot o' bunk!... Tripe!

* * * * * *

Ferdinand tossed his books on the bed and clatteringly rummaged in the disordered lower drawer of his battered, second-hand, taffy-colored desk for a shoe-brush and the box of blacking. He, too, would be expected to help entertain these precious Days whose threat of a visit had set them all scouring and preening.

Poising one foot on the edge of the untidy drawer, Ferdinand grimacingly recruited a mouthful of lubricant and spat viciously into the noisomely pungent blacking-box. He, too, would be required to come down, with his hair roached high to show he had an intellectual forehead, and smirk for this rich and brittle Mr. Day, who, because his deceased father had organized Uncle Miles's church and paid for most of it, was in a position to make them all jump through the hoop — and like it.

He would have to sit there for an hour and a half, posing for an angel; just as if he gave a damn whether these wonderful Days liked him or not. He smeared the dauber side of the brush into the blacking, and anointed the toe of his shabby shoe.

Angela, of course, would sing for them in her most luscious manner. If the guests didn't ask her promptly, Aunt Martha would direct the conversation into that quarter. 'Yes — Angela has been a great help,' she would say, in her precise, company voice, 'what with her singin' 'n' all.'

'Won't you sing something for us now, dear?' — this Mrs. Day would beg, probably hoping she wouldn't. But you could count on Angela.... Well — so much the better. While that was going on, he wouldn't have to do anything.

Ferdinand banged and bumped and smeared the shoe-brush against the desk-drawer as he insured himself against being sent back to 'polish the heel as well as the toe' — meanwhile carrying on with his sour prognosis of the evening's entertainment.

Angela, having more than satisfied the customers with her recital, closing it with an extended rendition of 'Crossing the Bar,' would smile, fold the music, push in the organ-stops, and slowly revolve on the hair-cloth stool to receive the inevitable 'My! — ain't that grand?'

And then this Mrs. Day — a feathery, fussy old dame, no doubt — would turn to him.... Ferdinand raised his other foot to the ledge of the drawer and again paid his respects to the vile blacking-box.... Ducking her big-plumed head, coquettishly, and grinning as if she were peering under the hood of a perambulator, she would inquire, 'And what do you do, Master Ferdinand?'

That's what she would say, and the way she would say it.

He had never seen her, but he knew. He had seen Mr. Day. Mr. Day had met them at the train. Uncle Miles had known he would, for he had written promising to do so. And there he was, sure enough, standing on the platform where the day-coach passengers alighted. Mr. Day had known they would be riding in the day-coach, though he himself wouldn't, of course.

Ferdinand had had no difficulty picking him out of the crowd on the platform — a square man, with square shoulders, square hands, square feet, square head, square mouth. He was to be their boss, because he had lots of money. Mr. Day had shaken hands all 'round and led the way to a shiny new Cadillac. Ferdinand hadn't liked the back of Mr. Day's square head or his square knuckles on the steering-wheel, though he was bound to admit that Mr. Day inspired respect. Mr. Day owned them now, same as he owned his Cadillac. Uncle Miles sitting beside him, with his arm stretched along the top of the seat, as if he were getting ready to hug Mr. Day, was already saying, 'Yes, yes; to be sure, Brother Day: ab-so-*lute*-ly!'

Ferdinand transferred his suspenders to his Sunday pants and emptied his pockets on top of the desk.

'Perhaps you sing, too,' Mrs. Day would suggest, 'like your sister.' And then Aunt Martha would heave the long sigh that meant she was going to explain how Angela wasn't his sister, a story that Angela would interrupt presently to reply to Mrs. Day's query.

'Ferdinand whittles,' she would say, crossing swiftly to the mantel for the little shepherdess. And Mrs. Day would gurgle, 'You don't mean to tell me! Look, Mr. Day, at this perfectly ex*quis*ite piece of carving!' And Mr. Day, deliberately finishing the long sentence he was on, and steadfastly looking at Uncle Miles from under his square eyebrows — just to show he was the kind of a man who mustn't be interrupted — but reaching out his square hand to signify that he would be pleased to take up Mrs. Day's case as the next order of business, would presently pinch his glasses onto his square nose, owlishly inspect the shepherdess, and say, as he handed it back, 'Nicely done, I'm sure.'

Ferdinand was tumbling the contents of the top bureau-drawer, looking for a clean collar that had no frayed edges.

'He prints, too,' Aunt Martha would add, proudly, though she was forever chiding him for wasting his time with all that type-settin'. Before she and Angela were through with it, he would be sent upstairs for 'that meenoo and program' he had made for the Annual Canvass Dinner at Fort Wayne, last winter. And Mrs. Day would squint at it, and twist in her chair to get a better light on it, and borrow Mr. Day's glasses; and Mr. Day would suggest that Ferdinand might do a lot of the church printing, 'just for good practice.'... Gosh! — how he hated these hellish exhibitions!

* * * * * *

Ferdinand put his Harvey's Grammar face down on the desk and listened for the doorbell. It would soon ring, now, for he had heard the car-doors slam, opulently. It rang, sharply, as if Mr. Day were saying, 'Don't keep us waiting! I paid for most of this house, myself!'... and Uncle Miles was opening the door, his hearty 'Well — well!' meaning, 'I know you did, Brother Day, and I came running fast as ever I could — ab-so-*lute*-ly!'

They were all talking at once, now, and drifting through the hall into the parlor. Mr. Day was remarking dryly that the floors needed to be gone over, and Mrs. Day — who sounded quite elderly — was asking Aunt Martha, in a high key, how she was finding the house, anyway.

Presently, Angela came to the foot of the stairs and called him. He would have to go. He gave his hair a final scrub with the brush, scowled into the mirror, and started. Hopeful of slipping into the room so quietly they would hardly notice his arrival, Ferdinand made as little noise as possible on the way down.

Slowly negotiating the last few steps, he was able, by the

location of their voices, and a panoramic glimpse through
the wide doorway, to place their positions — Aunt Martha,
first; then Mrs. Day, a white-haired, little old lady, old
enough to be Mr. Day's mother (as indeed she was, he soon
discovered); then Mr. Day, on the brussels sofa, polishing
his glasses with a large silk handkerchief, Uncle Miles
sitting close beside him with a hand on Mr. Day's knee.

Another step located Angela, close to the melodeon, of
course, talking animatedly, and, for her, rather affectedly,
to some unidentified person not yet in the picture.

Ferdinand cautiously moved forward and brought gradually into view a slim, modishly shod foot and a generous
glimpse of the first silk stockings he had ever seen, a pair of
gracefully crossed, tailored knees, a shapely arm negligently
thrown back across the top of the chair — it was a dining-
room chair, put there for him, and she had evidently preferred it to the patent rocker which stood vacant — her fur
boa tossed back from her shoulder.

Nobody like that had ever been in their house before.
Ferdinand hadn't yet seen her face — it would require some
courage to do this next step — but he knew she did not
belong to their world, at all. Something in her posture told
him that.

'Come on in, Ferdinand,' called Angela, pleasantly, in the
tone of thirty addressing six, which made him know the
stylish stranger could not be very old, if Angela was playing
grown-up.

Summoning all his valor, Ferdinand stepped to the door
and found himself staring — open-mouthed, he feared —
at the most beautiful woman he had ever seen. She smiled,
a slowly widening smile, which seemed to mean they were
already friends of long standing, bending her head forward
and looking at him from under long black lashes, her lips
puckered a little, teasingly, as if to say, 'I know you don't
want to come in here and be bored; but — let's have it
over.'

Ferdinand's heart skipped a beat, and then made up for

it with a hard bump that put him quite out of breath and
made his voice unsteady when, reluctantly detained by
Aunt Martha's hand on his arm, he paused to speak to
Madame Day and Mr. Day, who obligingly made short
work of him to resume their briefly interrupted remarks.
All the previously inactive minerals in Ferdinand's blood
responded to the first potential magnet he had ever approached, his natural shyness giving way to a new sensation
of actually belonging to someone!

She did not rise or offer her hand when Angela said,
'This is Ferdinand, Mrs. Day.' People, when introduced,
always stood up and gravely shook hands. Eighty rose to
shake hands with eight. Mrs. Day merely tipped back her
pretty head, so he could see the fringe of glossy little black
curls under her big picture hat, and smiled, with red lips
parted.

He could not speak for an instant. The routine phrase,
'Pleased-t'-meetcha,' which he had been obliged to mumble
so often that it was all one word, would not come. It was
inappropriate. He swallowed, rather noisily, and said,
'I'm glad — I'm glad to — I'm very glad!'

'By Jove, boy,' she drawled, 'I really believe you *are!*'
She pointed to the vacant chair beside her. 'Do you always
say such delightfully nice things?'

Angela, hopeful of smoothing over his unsuccessful
attempt to manage the usual formula, explained maternally: 'Ferdinand is so shy, Mrs. Day. He always
hates being introduced.... You can sit in the rocker,
Ferdinand. Mrs. Day thought she would like this straight
chair better.'

'Yes,' said Ferdinand, still in a trance, 'she would.'

He sat down, and while wondering if it would be all
right for him to look her straight in the eyes again — wanting to, but afraid he would stare at her — he gazed interestedly at her hands, wishing she did not have gloves on.
She leisurely unbuttoned them and began slowly to take
them off, tugging at one finger-tip after another. He

glanced up, a bit abashed, and they both smiled, understandingly.

'I'm always wondering about hands, too,' she said,
lazily. 'Your sister has been telling me what interesting
things you do with yours; but I think I could have guessed
— now that I see them.'

Ferdinand instinctively spread them out, glad now that
he had taken pains with his nails.

'You make things, too,' he ventured. 'Maybe you
paint.'

'Rather badly. I've been having better luck, lately,
dabbling with wood-cuts. That's great fun!'

'I expect you have lots of carving-tools.'

'Too many! I keep experimenting with all these dif-
ferent-shaped chisels, and never use any one of them long
enough to——'

'Hard wood?' queried Ferdinand, professionally.

'Oh, dear, no; not yet! I've just begun it, you see.'

'I have tinkered with some little designs,' confessed
Ferdinand, modestly, 'but I don't know what they look
like.'

Angela, recovering from her amazement over the taciturn
Ferdinand's easy talk, put in, 'He hasn't a press, Mrs.
Day — nor hardly anything to work with.'

'Pine?' asked Mrs. Day, having briefly turned her head
to acknowledge Angela's comment.

'No — oak and walnut.'

Mrs. Day's finely modeled eyebrows lifted a little in
surprise.

'How would you like to come over, some day, and see
what I have been doing? Perhaps I might trade you a
reamer or two for some good advice.'

'I'd like to!' Ferdinand flushed with pleasure. 'But
I don't think I could tell you anything that you don't
know.'

'Saturday — maybe?'

'Yes — after dinner?'

'No — I'm to be out for dinner. Come about two.'

She belonged, Ferdinand realized, to a different world from his drab little island where the conversation never rose above the dull tittle-tattle of domestic drudgeries in homes like theirs, and the equally stupid prattle about rummage sales that were to finance a new cement sidewalk around the church and mend the plumbing in the basement. Hers was a world that had dinner at night instead of noon, an unself-conscious world that spoke correctly without stiffness, that moved with dignity but without embarrassment, a world that leisurely went out to the diner for 'tea.' The difference between her world and his swept over Ferdinand, not to his discontentment, but to his almost painful wistfulness. He felt that she had recognized him as eligible to citizenship in her world, and was glad.

'That's agreed, then. I'll expect you,' she said, rising, as Aunt Martha — still talking primly to Madame Day, and nervously smoothing her shapeless black skirt — moved toward them, apparently intending to draw Mrs. Day, whom for excellent reasons she was obviously shy of, into the adult section. 'Your father can tell you where we live,' concluded Mrs. Day, with another smile that sent Ferdinand's damaged heart racing.

Aunt Martha's curiosity spoke in her strained face. Aunt Martha's face was never under very good control. Bulletins announcing her every doubt, anxiety, hope, and fear were posted about her restless mouth and myopic eyes immediately upon arrival. At the moment, Ferdinand knew what was going on in her mind as certainly as if she shouted it. She was engaged in a struggle, attempting to be obsequiously courteous to Mrs. Day because it was incumbent on her to be deferential to Brother Day's Mrs. Day, while endeavoring to warn Ferdinand — with one fleeting glare of stern disapproval — that he was on no account to be permitted to come under the influence of this frivolous, worldly creature whom Brother Day — so steady and sensible about everything else — had had the misfortune to marry.

Conversation broke off, in the other corner of the room, in acknowledgment of Mrs. Day's arrival in their midst. Brother Day stiffly stood at attention, tapping his nose-glasses on his thumb-nail. Uncle Miles tardily scrambled to his feet, pulled down his vest, and said, 'Well — well!' just as if Mrs. Day had quite taken them by surprise, dropping in unexpectedly.

Madame Day snapped the massive silver latch of her black leather bag several times, and pursed her lips resignedly.

Aunt Martha proffered her chair and drew up another. They were all ready now, it appeared, for Mrs. Day to explain why she had intruded.

'Ferdinand has promised to come and see me,' she said, in a tone that hoped she was giving his parents pleasure —'to talk about wood-cuts.'

'Very good of you, Sister — er — Mrs. Day,' beamed Uncle Miles, in the voice he used when patronizingly commending a shy testimony offered at prayer-meeting.

Mr. Day elevated his chin, stroked the back of his bald head, gazed critically at the ceiling, and tapped his lean knee with his glasses. There was the suggestion of a frown creasing his forehead. Ferdinand wondered if the frown did not mean that Mrs. Day should first have consulted Mr. Day before making her proposal.

'Well' — said he, judicially —'perhaps the lad had better be encouraged to do something more useful than fiddling with wood-cuts.'

Aunt Martha, cannily reasoning that, while Brother Day might enjoy handing his wife a surly rebuff, he probably wouldn't thank anybody for being so impertinent as to applaud him, remarked: 'Ferdinand comes natural by his taste fer wood-carvin'. His grandpa's folks in th' old country was all wood-carvers. When he come t' this country, he changed the name to Miller because his family

name was hard fer folks t' say. Their name was Mueller
— M-u-e-l-l-e-r.'

'I wonder if they were related to the very famous family
of Muellers in Dresden. Do you know, Mrs. Brumm?'

Aunt Martha, hugging her angular elbows and rocking
gently, nodded with pride.

'My father was born in Dresden in the house of Frederick Mueller. He was the great-grandson of Hans Mueller.'

'Indeed!' exclaimed Mrs. Day. 'What a heritage!'

'Ye-es,' agreed Mr. Day. 'Very interesting.'

Angela had slipped over onto the chair recently vacated
by the charming Mrs. Day.

'Awfully odd, isn't she?' whispered Angela.

'Hunnh?'

Ferdinand was barely conscious of her comment, so intent was he on the developments in his own case, now under
discussion on the other side of the room.

'Odd!' repeated Angela, guardedly, behind her hand.

Ferdinand reluctantly detached his gaze from the object
of his adoration, and regarded Angela with an inquisitive
stare.

'How do you mean — odd?' he said, absently. 'I think
she's the most wonderful person I ever saw!'

CHAPTER V

'LOOK, Janet!' Ferdinand laid the limp proof on the imposing-stone, folded his smudged arms, and glanced over his shoulder for her approval. 'Rather good, wouldn't you say? How fortunate we could use one of those quaint, diamond-shaped colons on the very first page.'

'Perfect!' Janet Day hovered close, snuggling a hand affectionately under his elbow, her cheek pressed lightly against his broad shoulder. 'Old Thomas Caxton would be green with envy. Really, Dinny, you're marvelous!'

'It's you that's marvelous, Janet. I would never have known anything about this, but for you.'

For a moment she neither responded nor turned away; stood soberly staring at the first page of what was going to be General Bryce's annual Memorial Day greeting to the diminishing survivors of his brigade — a sixteen-page brochure done in two colors on hand-laid Italian vellum, the price no object, for the General was rich. It was the most pretentious thing they had attempted.

Janet had been very quiet and pensive today. Twice, as they had encountered each other, face to face, in the narrow quarters of the little printing-shop that cluttered the whole south bay of her attic studio — screened off to segregate its inevitable untidiness — Ferdinand had been made uneasy by the entreaty in her brown eyes. Janet wanted to ask him something, and didn't dare. Janet wanted to tell him something, but was afraid. Had he done something to grieve her? What could it have been? He had failed her somehow: in what? But no — it was rather as if she, herself, was on the defensive.

Her competent fingers tightened their warm grasp on his arm. Perhaps she was going to talk about it now.

'No,' she said, preoccupiedly, 'you would have done all this, anyway, sooner or later. However, I'm glad I have had a little part in it.... I want you always to think well of me, Dinny. You've been such a dear, and I'm so proud of you.'

Impulsively he lifted her hand to his lips, an act that surprised them both, a little. Ferdinand despised sentiment.

'What is it, Janet?' he asked, gently. 'Something bothering you?'

'Now you've ink on your nose, Dinny,' she laughed, a bit nervously, he thought. 'No — it's nothing. Just moody, because it's raining and dark. I didn't intend it should rain, today.'

'Well — if you're sure that's all. I was afraid you were unhappy. I didn't do anything, did I, Janet?'

Shaking off her dolorous mood, and facing him with a twisted little smile, Janet slipped her palms slowly upward on his well-muscled arms, grasped his ear-lobes in her slim fingers, made a gesture of chastising him, and murmured, 'Of course not, simpleton.'

He had called her 'Janet' from the first; ever since that enchanted Saturday, now more than three and a half years ago, when, shy and excited, he had followed the solemn butler over the deep-pile Oriental rugs from the impressive front entrance to the broad, winding stairs, and along a narrower corridor to narrower stairs leading into the huge attic room.

'Master Brumm, ma'am,' the man had said, leaving them.

Under a large north skylight, young Mrs. Day — who had not been absent from Ferdinand's thoughts, waking or sleeping, since the night he had met her — sat on a tall three-legged stool before a composing-case, distributing type, her high heels hooked on a rung. Her heavy black hair was braided in one long plait. She wore a short skirt, and a long, green, open-throated jacket with capacious pockets, the costume diminishing her age and urbanity until she was quite another person than the queenly Mrs. Day whose black voile nearly touched the floor, whose white lace yoke had brought up in a tight, ribbed collar that almost reached to her dainty ears, her slim height emphasized by the big black hat with the orange velvet tips, on the night she had made their house, and all the people in it, outmoded and shabby.

Except for the slow, half-teasing, puckery smile with which she turned to welcome him, this girlish Mrs. Day might have been someone else than the mysterious goddess who had been playing the deuce with his imagination and staling his appetite for dinner.

Slipping down from her high stool, she had thrust her hands deep into the pockets of her smock, her head tilted as if in critical judgment of a picture.

'You seem ever so much bigger, taller,' she said. 'How old are you?'

'It's this collar, I think,' Ferdinand had replied, soberly. 'Going on fourteen.... Aunt Martha would have me wear it.'

'Who's Aunt Martha? Does she live with you?'

'But you met Aunt Martha. Mrs. Brumm is not my mother.'

Mrs. Day's shapely arm was thrown up suddenly in a gesture of happy discovery emphasized by a vigorous snap of the fingers, her face alight.

'By Jove!' she shouted. 'So — that's the answer to the riddle!'

'My mother died when I was born,' explained Ferdinand.

'And your father — what became of him?'

Ferdinand was very sorry that the subject had arisen. He had come, eager and inquisitive, hoping to see Mrs. Day's wood-working equipment; and here we were, wasting precious time.

'He's living... out West... I never saw him.... You're putting the type back in their boxes; aren't you?' Ferdinand drew nearer the case. 'May I watch you do it?'

'Oh — we're going to talk about wood-cuts,' said Mrs. Day. 'But, first, sit down. Tell me some more about yourself.'

'There isn't much,' he replied, gloomily; but he took the big club chair she pointed to, and began to tell her what little he knew. Seated on a low ottoman at his feet, she listened intently, asking brief questions when he paused. There was, after all, a good deal of the story. It was a whole hour before Mrs. Day seemed satisfied, and they sat silently.

'I think you should have kept the pony,' she said, after a long pause. 'That must have hurt him, dreadfully.... And you never wrote to him?'

Ferdinand drew a long sigh, with a convulsive catch in the middle of it, and abstractedly twisted Mrs. Day's soggy little handkerchief into a slim rope. Her understanding sympathy and affection had loosed a long-pent flood of suppressed misery. He smiled, feebly.

'That's the first time anybody ever defended my father,' said Ferdinand. 'Why should I have written to him? He never wrote to me.'

Mrs. Day rose, and, walking slowly to the dormer window, stood looking down at the busy street.

'I'm guessing that there's some more of that story... that you never heard,' she said, impressively.

Then there had been some hot chocolate and cakes, and Ferdinand became quickly absorbed in Mrs. Day's explanation of the new printing-press which her good friend, Mr. Oscar Zimmerman, had lent her. Mr. Zimmerman had made quite a hobby of art-craft printing; had done some beautiful things; now he had tired of it; had sent her his entire equipment for use while he was abroad.

'He will be so interested in you, Ferdinand. I wrote him you were a Mueller descendant, and that I intended you should have a go at these things — wood-cuts, art printing, etchings.'

They became very well acquainted, that day. Ferdinand's name was too bulky and mature, and was abbreviated to 'Dinny,' which seemed to make him rather light-hearted, as if his name had weighted him.

'You may call me Janet, if you like,' she had suggested.

'If we're going to play together with these things, you'll
probably be teaching me, very soon, and I mustn't be much
older than my teacher, you see, or it might discourage
me.'

'I never knew anyone named Janet, before,' said Ferdinand. 'I'm glad.'

'Dinny, you say the most adorable things... and all unconsciously, too. That's the best part of it. You're developing into a young courtier; I can see that.'

* * * * * *

Ferdinand was also developing into a young liar, he
feared, after he had answered all of Aunt Martha's pressing
questions relative to that first visit with the problematical
Mrs. Day. Naturally disposed to be suspicious of well-
groomed femininity, Aunt Martha was troubled. Ferdinand
was required to reproduce the afternoon, item by item.
How was Mrs. Day dressed? Was Mr. Day at home?
Was Madame Day present? What did she have to say?
What all happened?

Ferdinand promoted himself, that evening, from the
mere happy estate of apprentice to a beautiful crafts-
woman. He achieved the dignity of a great story-teller.
Baron Münchausen would have been proud of him. Amazing himself by the increasing glibness of his tale, he invented
a conversation he had had with Mrs. Day that represented
her as most ardently concerned about the welfare of the
church, albeit she never attended, due to a slight heart
affection which made it dangerous for her to expose herself
to strong emotional appeals; garbed her in a somber dress,
laid a gray shawl about her shoulders, had the audacity to
put her hair up in curl-papers; located her workroom in the
busiest part of the great house; caused servants to stand
by her, handing her the things she needed in her work —
and wound up with an account of his hostess's admiration
for Aunt Martha and Uncle Miles and Angela.... Fearing
he had been extravagant in this, Ferdinand decided to risk

nothing further and excused himself on the pretense of having to study.

But Aunt Martha was never quite at ease over Ferdinand's two and three afternoons a week — and all day Saturdays — with Mrs. Day.

'I never did like the looks o' that woman,' she would say, anxiously, to Mr. Brumm. 'You wait!... We'll see!'

And when, at length, having waited, they saw, she muttered, grimly pleased that her forecast had been so prescient, 'Didn't I tell yuh? Didn't I warn yuh? Where were yer eyes?'

* * * * * *

Dinny carefully unwound the inky string from the type-form and went about the extraction of an upper-case H that seemed a bit defective.

'Rather rubbishy sentiment; wouldn't you say?' he called across to Janet, bent over a wood-cut with a big reading-glass in one hand and a slim reamer in the other, putting stripes in a wind-blown flag.

'Oh — I don't know,' she replied, as from a considerable distance. 'It's about what one would expect, isn't it, from a mellow old gentleman, trying to be lyrical about war; trying to remember and forget at the same time, like the proud but poor old lady in London who went out to sell papers, mumbling, "Times, tuppence! Times, tuppence! Lord, I hopes nobuddy 'ears me!"... And no one will actually read this, anyway, you know. They'll be saying, "What a *lovely* piece of printing! Whoever did it? And especially these bee-ootiful ornamental capitals, and this incomparable tail-piece! Just look at that *flag!*"... That's what they will be saying, Dinny.'

'That's rather cynical... for you, Janet,' laughed Dinny. 'I'm always the one that's scolded for being more concerned over the way things look than what they mean. You must be deteriorating.'

He ran the sticky, snapping, black brayer over the face

of his corrected galley, and began pounding another proof-page onto it with a plane.

'I think words get their definitions, not from the dictionary, but from the private sentiments of the people who use them,' continued Dinny, philosophically. 'Take the General's word "misunderstandings." That's what caused the war — "misunderstandings." Fact is, they all understood one another too well. People are forever calling their quarrels "misunderstandings." Nonsense! So long as they were misunderstanding, each one could give the other credit for a bit of ignorant honesty. But when they begin to understand each other, they call out the troops and distribute the gunpowder.'

'You amuse me, Dinny,' drawled Janet, intent on her occupation. 'You would never have thought about that, at all, if you hadn't been annoyed because "misunderstandings" is too long to look well in a line of twelve-point Caslon set to fourteen ems. It's just when they begin to inconvenience us that we find fault with words and have hot debates over them. We think up shorter synonyms that look better on whatever page we're making up, and then imagine we've discovered a new idea, or expressed a pleasanter thought. If "licentiousness" is too unwieldy, we change it to "liberty."'

'"Parsimoniousness" *is* easier to set, if you call it "thrift,"' agreed Dinny, willing to go on with the game, but a bit bewildered over Janet's choice of an illustration.

'It all depends upon who's talking,' she added, absently, 'and when. "Liberty" is a pretty word, isn't it?'

'I should think these old soldiers,' pursued Dinny, didactically, 'would never want to hear another word about war. It must give them the heebie-jeebies in the night. I saw a team of farm-horses run off with a mowing-machine, when I was a little boy. The man fell off the iron seat, and got tangled in the knives. The scared horses turned short when they came to a fence-corner and had their hind legs nearly chewed off, not having sense enough to stop. I see it yet, sometimes, when I'm slow going to sleep. It's the most reliable of all my pet horrors. Wouldn't you think these old veterans would be just as happy not to be reminded of screaming horses with eyes dangling on a string, dragging their insides after them in long muddy ropes; and neighbor boys with the white splintered ends of bones sticking through their bloody pant-legs, and sticky globs of warm brains——'

'I say! Dinny! Stop it! What a ghastly imagination!'

'I'm going to fetch it to market, one o' these days.'

'Going to be a butcher?'

'Going to write a book... called "Balderdash." Chapter one — patriotism; two — religion; three — I haven't quite decided on three yet, but it's to be something about the superstition that people with money have a right to play wheel-barrow with everybody who works for them or lives with them. Ever play wheel-barrow, Janet?'

'Yes, I think so. How do you play it?'

'Well — you get down on the floor, on your hands, and I pick you up by the feet and push, and you either have to walk on your hands or bump your nose.'

'Oh, yes — I've been playing that, all my life. Nice game!'

For a little while, Dinny rattled on with his sour diatribe against war, Janet remotely keeping track of his excursion.

It hadn't been quite true that she'd always been playing wheel-barrow. Father — God bless him — had been infinitely tender and considerate. How he had humored her every wish — hers and her mother's. Maybe that was why he could leave so little when he died; almost nothing, indeed, but extravagant tastes. She could have seen it through; but not her mother. Mr. Day had proposed such an easy solution. 'You'd be a fool, Janet,' her mother had said. 'It's a chance in a lifetime.' What a pity her mother had died, seeing the sacrifice had been made to please her.

'All this sweet hokum of the General's about "shot-and-shell,"' Denny was declaiming. 'He's singing hymns about the varnished shot-and-shell piled in pyramids at the foot of the Soldiers' Monument. If he really wants to give the old fellows a thrill, why doesn't he remind them of the slippery shot-and-shell — all ooky and slimy with ——'

'I heard you, Dinny, the first time!... Hand me that slide-rule, will you, dear?... But, you see, that's the way to keep patriotism alive.'

'Patriotism's tripe!'

'Yes, Dinny.... Come over here and see my flag. Is that any better?'

He bent his five-feet-eleven over her soft shoulder, leaning his weight against the table on an ink-smeared hand.

'Fine, Janet! Much improved!... Now you take my Uncle Elmer; not meaning that he was worth a hoot before he went to Cuba, but just supposing he was. Gets himself all hotted up about his patriotic duty when somebody pounds a drum; sobs into his beer; hep-heps to Havana in boots two sizes too small for his big feet; curries the Colonel's horse; comes home with dysentery from eating spoiled meat that the get-rich-packers unloaded on them; and... Janet — perhaps you might give the eagle's left wing just a bit more spread... and expects to spend the rest of his life lying about in the shade at the Soldiers' Home. Patriotism — rot!... Look out for those stars, Janet! You'll have a deuce of a time putting them back in, you know, once they're out!'

'I know, Dinny. By the way,' she laughed, 'that's what the General's little book is about; isn't it? He believed that. Once the stars were out, it would be hard to put them back in.'

'Rubbish! Sentiment!'

'Then why are we doing this, at all?'

'Because I'm earning money to go to college this fall.' Dinny turned back to his table and carefully peeled off a new proof.

'Speaking of college — has your uncle relented?'

'Him — relent? He's more convinced than ever. Says

he has already assured old Dean What's-His-Name that I'd come to Magnolia; says it would do him a terrible lot of damage in the conference, or whatever it is, if I went to a godless State University. Everything's godless that Uncle Miles doesn't happen to know about. Odd jumble of conflicting ideas in Uncle Miles's head. I'd give something for a picture of the inside of it. Long ago, he was out in Arizona and visited the Petrified Forest. Never gets done talking about it. Picked up a piece and brought it home. Fondles it, and says, in a stage whisper, "That's *a million years old*, my friend!"... But, on Sundays, it's only six thousand years old, so it won't antedate the sun, moon, and stars.'

'Don't be too hard on him, Dinny. He can't contradict Genesis, you know. His whole flock would stampede.'

'I'll bet Mr. Day wouldn't follow along in that stampede,' said Dinny, eager as usual to find something meritorious in Mr. Day, seeing Janet had to live with him — a sore trial, he suspected. Or, was Dinny championing the cause of Mr. Day because he feared that Janet was thinking too much about Mr. Zimmerman, who was at home again, and so frequently visited her?

'No,' replied Janet, gravely. 'Mr. Day wouldn't follow in that stampede. He never follows. He'd lead it.'

'But — you don't mean to tell me Mr. Day believes that old Jewish myth about the universe being created in six days!'

'On Sundays, when he's in church — yes.'

'And the yarn about Adam... and Eve made out of Adam's rib?'

'Oh, yes; he believes that, every day and no matter where he is — especially about the rib.'

'Meaning... you're a rib, Janet?' queried Dinny, laughing, but half-wishing he had not said it.

'One of the shorter ones, Dinny.'

'They're called "floating" ribs.'

'How do you mean — "floating"?... Loose?'

'Oh, no,' scoffed Dinny, pretending pride in his superior knowledge of physiology, 'they never get loose.'

'I should have known that much; shouldn't I?'

'You probably never thought about it before.'

'Don't be too sure about that, my son,' she said, in a tone that worried him a little. It wasn't like Janet to be so mysterious. He couldn't quite understand her, today. Even her immediate change of topic was not at all reassuring.

'So — I suppose you'll be going to Magnolia, then.'

'I'm in for it, all right. However, I am not particularly interested in science, so it doesn't matter much. The Lit. course at Magnolia is probably no thinner than in many a bigger school. Professors in English Comp. can't tell you how to write. If they knew how to do it, they'd be doing it; wouldn't they? All I want is a chance to do some reading, on my own hook, and plenty of time for scribbling. I can have that at Magnolia. They're much too hard up to enforce any discipline. I can go my own gait.'

'I'm going to miss you — terribly.' Janet left her work, and stood beside him. Her eyes were troubled.

'That's the only thing about it, Janet. I don't know how I'm to get along without you.'

She walked to the window and stood looking out.

'There isn't very much more I could do for you, Dinny; is there?'

'You're the only real friend I ever had, Janet.' He put down the brayer and joined her at the window. 'Sometimes, I've wondered if I wasn't leaning too heavily; monopolizing you.'

'It's been the other way about, dear,' said Janet, soberly. 'I've monopolized you. You haven't been interested in the girls of your class in school.'

'Pooh! They're nothing but silly little gigglers.'

'Maybe you wouldn't think so if you made any effort to know them.'

'You're all the girl I want, Janet,' said Dinny, lightly.

'That's just the trouble. It isn't good for you. I'm not

your girl; nor am I your sister, or your mother.' She faced about, and abruptly changed the subject. 'Oscar — Mr. Zimmerman — wants you to have the stuff he lent us; all the Caxton and Cheltenham and the rest of it, and the seven-by-nine press, and this fancy Caslon, too. He says you're to take it along to college with you. He hopes you will set up a little shop and make it pay your way. Rather nice of him; don't you think?'

'Very!' said Dinny, trying to sound grateful. 'But weren't you going to use it, any more?'

'No — not after you leave, Dinny.'

He wasn't quite sure whether he wanted to be under such obligation to Mr. Zimmerman. True, it would be of no consequence to the rich bachelor globe-trotter whether Dinny used the printing-equipment or not. Otherwise it would probably be idle in a storage warehouse. But he disliked accepting anything from Mr. Zimmerman. He was candidly jealous of Mr. Zimmerman, of his easy grace, his urbane manners, his charming personality, his casual allusions to the places he had seen — Singapore, Calcutta, Moscow — mentioning them in about the same tone Dinny might have used when speaking of Oak Grove or Zanesdale or Unger. He often wondered if Mr. Day were jealous, too; not that he cared, greatly. Perhaps Mr. Day's private feelings were modified, somewhat, by the fact that Mr. Zimmerman was one of the heaviest stockholders in the Day Wholesale Provision Company. Money made a lot of difference.

'Dinny' — Janet's voice was a bit uncertain — 'we're getting awfully crowded and cluttered in this room. Lately, I've been thinking we might move our printing-stuff to larger quarters. I looked at a room yesterday. It's in the Woolford Block on Superior Street ——'

Dinny remembered that Mr. Zimmerman owned the Woolford Block, and with difficulty suppressed a scowl.

'—— and I can get it for a song. Suppose you run in, next time you're down-town, and see what you think of it.'

She took up her purse from the table, and handed him a key.

'Number 306. Go in on Monday, after school, and look it over.'

Dinny was in no position to debate the matter. He nodded, and took the key. It was growing dark, though only five-thirty, and the rain was falling in torrents.

'Take my umbrella, dear.'

'Thanks, Janet. I'll telephone you, when I've seen the room.'

'Good-bye, dear.' She reached out her slim hand, and looked up, fleetingly, into his perplexed eyes. It was so unlike her to offer her hand. They never shook hands. Dinny took it, rather confusedly, and was at a loss what to say.

'I'm afraid you're dreadfully worried about something.' Dinny swallowed hard, and put his hands lightly on her shoulders.

''Bye, Dinny!' Impulsively she threw her arms tightly around his neck and kissed him on the lips; then, turning quickly away, walked toward the window, stood with both hands outspread on the broad sill, a mere silhouette in the gathering gloom.

That was the picture he retained of Janet for a dozen years.

With another long, anxious look, he reluctantly went out, and closed the door.

*   *   *   *   *   *

On Monday afternoon, he went to inspect the room in the Woolford Block; went without interest, and weighted by an unaccountable depression.

The room was not empty, as he had expected. All their printing-equipment was there, installed in orderly fashion, ready for work.

On the imposing-stone was a receipted bill for three months' rental. At the bottom of the paper, hurriedly written in pencil, were a few lines in Janet's tall, slim letters:

God keep you always, dear Dinny. Forgive me for going away. I'm not really bad, Dinny. It's just that I'm tired playing wheel-barrow.

He gazed woodenly at the message for a long time, with an aching throat and burning eyes. Then he tore it into small bits, savagely stuffed the scraps into his pocket, went out, locked the door, and clumped slowly down the stairs.... Janet was no better than the rest of them. They were all cheaters! Damn them!

CHAPTER VI

AFTER a wheezing ascent of four steep flights in the wake of his young employer and guide, the gruff expressman had unshouldered Ferdinand's small, old-fashioned trunk, with a groan of relief and reproach, and had ambled off down the bare, resounding dormitory hall grumblingly fingering the four dimes and seven nickels that totaled his exact charge.

Obedient to some atavism urging him to establish a claim to his new property without delay, Ferdinand laid his coat and collar on the sagging bed, and went through the preliminary gestures of making himself at home. The room was cramped, shabby, and incompletely furnished, but it was his, and the feeling of possession was pleasurable.

The convex lid of the antiquated trunk was thrown back against the dingy wall, and the welcome task of unpacking proceeded; his meager, outmoded wardrobe, a handful of books, a dozen cheap towels, and the case of carving-tools, over which there had been such a row, Aunt Martha's eloquent disapproval rending the Yuletide peace and reaching an impassioned climax in her unexecuted threat to carry the expensive gift back to that there high-'n'-mighty Mrs. Day with her own hands.

'With love to Dinny from Janet.'

It was the engraving on the silver plate inside the velvet-lined lid that had detonated Aunt Martha's tightly corked resentment against a mysterious (and probably questionable) friendship which had ripened without benefit of her sanction, and was increasingly fulfilling her dire prediction that the attachment would wean Ferdinand away from his 'humble home 'n' all that it stands fer.'

And what right had this Mrs. Day to be 'Janet' to a mere half-grown boy, inexperienced, unworldly, and calfishly infatuated? What kind o' 'love' was this, we'd like to know, that had the impudence to flaunt itself in the face

of his family? And since when had his name been changed
to 'Dinny'?... 'Dinny' — indeed!... '*Dinny!*' — well, we'd
see about that!

Ferdinand sat down on the edge of the weak-spined bed
with the silver-mounted box in his hands.

Queer — wasn't it? — how an inanimate thing, pieced
together of wood and screws and glue, silver and velvet
and steel, could take on a personality possessed of so many
sensitive, changing moods? One day you couldn't bear to
look at it for the worry and chagrin it had caused you.
Next day you loved it so tenderly it made your throat
thick. Another day you despised it for reminding you of
a tragic disenchantment that had all but killed you.

The box of carving-tools and his mother's little walnut
desk; living things, they were!

The desk!... One winter Sunday afternoon when he was
seven, in a promptly repented unveiling of cankered memories, Aunt Martha had told him the story of the desk;
just the bare, ugly, shameful facts about the storm of
jealousy it had provoked, a storm which Aunt Martha
deplored but partly justified.

'I always said yer grandpa never should 'a' done it.
He might 'a' knew it wouldn't set right with th' rest o' th'
family; not that I ever cared, myself. I had t' work too
hard, goodness knows, ever t' spend any time a-settin' at a
desk. But Julia was always his favorite. It broke his heart
when she died.'

'And grandpa died, too, that same night, Aunt Martha,
didn't he?'

Aunt Martha had nodded, shuddered, and laid another
stick on the fire.

The desk had come along when Aunt Martha had left
'th' old home,' her brothers and sisters pressing no claim
to a share in it. As a little lad, he saw it only when they
moved from one house to another; and not even then, for
it had remained thickly wrapped in the dusty burlap in
which it had been shipped to Unger.

Shrouded, it had lived in dark corners of attics, damp corners of cellars, a thing neither to be used nor thrown away. It was almost as if they carried his mother's corpse about with them.

When they had moved to Indianapolis, Ferdinand had asked for it. Consent was rather grudgingly given. He had one desk, hadn't he? However, Aunt Martha supposed he had a right to it, if he wanted to crowd his room with it. Sometimes he wished he had not insisted. He almost never used it, and when he did he felt depressed.

Perhaps he had better ask Uncle Miles to ship him the desk.... Dinny drew a wry smile. He could put the case of carving-tools in the drawer of the desk, and let them settle their problems between themselves. Now that he was in college, there would be plenty of other things to occupy his attention. New friends and fresh interests would lay his ghosts.

But, what about these new friends; these fresh interests?

The past three hours had been a disappointing surprise. 'College' was not quite as he had pictured it, a comradely, democratic, open-hearted aggregation of irresponsible youngsters, bent on getting acquainted with one another by the shortest routes.

At almost every station stop, en route from Indianapolis to Magnolia — so close to Cincinnati as to think of itself as a suburb — young people boarded the train. Doubtless they were going to college; perhaps to Magnolia. A few suitcases were adorned with pink and white stickers, pennant-shaped, cheering for the school. Already he was entertaining a growing sense of loyalty and pride.

For the most part, however, the pilgrims bound for Magnolia, if they greeted each other at all, seemed shy and restrained; a mere nod, 'Hello, Buster; back to the mill?' ... 'How 'r' yuh, Prichard; good summer?'

But this was the day-coach, and these the day-coachers. The distinction gradually dawned on Ferdinand. For some time he had been curious, when the train stopped in the larger towns, over festive sounds on the platform well to the rear. At Richmond, he strolled to the steps, and, leaning out, saw a score or more of well-dressed, high-spirited people, old and young, bidding good-bye to a handful of students, gathered at the entrance to a Pullman, the white-jacketed porter busy with their baggage.

He went back through his own car, and overheard their cryptic banter as they scrambled up the steps, the porter banging the vestibule doors behind them. These, too, were Magnolians — the real, traditional college students of song and story, larkish, noisy, devil-may-care. He wished he had committed the extravagance of riding in the Pullman. It would have made all the difference. Not quite, however, he reflected — not in these clothes.

A month afterward, burning with hot resentment against the discrimination that had bled his pride white, Ferdinand marveled that nearly four years of intimate association with a person so sophisticated as Janet Day had contributed almost nothing to his knowledge of that other world to whose citizenship he aspired.

Analyzing their relations, however, he saw that it was neither his fault nor hers that the friendship had done so little for him in this respect. Such community of interest as they had was based almost exclusively on their shop-work. Ferdinand had never taken a meal with her except the sandwiches, cakes and tea, casually enjoyed during a few minutes of recess from their occupation. Janet was always dressed in an inky, paint-daubed smock, her hair down her back; he was always in his working togs. They rarely talked of anything else than their immediate concerns. Janet had not given him a ticket to the world of smart people.

Alighting from the train, Ferdinand confronted a gay scene. A spirited crowd — modishly dressed, bareheaded, beautiful girls, and white-sweatered, flannel-trousered, handsome fellows — cheered and chaffed the recruits descending from the Pullmans; their classmates, no doubt;

old acquaintances: but no — fully half of them were obviously newcomers, like himself. Solicitously in tow of the old-timers, they were now being presented to the welcoming throng. A phalanx of motor-cars was drawn up along the platform, engines noisily churning and clamoring to be off, drivers' seats occupied by debonair greeters, sons and daughters of the other world, the world that rode in Pullmans and came to meet people who rode in Pullmans.

Ferdinand had not been expecting anyone to meet him, and therefore had no occasion to be disappointed; but he was overcome with a feeling of such loneliness as had never afflicted him before. He took up his battered old suitcase, made some inquiries of a policeman whose amused attention was grudgingly distracted from the real people's festivities, boarded a street-car, reached the campus — a gently undulating grove of oaks and elms, zigzagged with winding paths of white, hard-tramped gravel-ribbons that negligently wandered about from one main entrance to another of the dozen or more nondescript buildings of brick, of stone, of cement, of wood, in attempted imitation of every known school of architecture and ranging in age all the way from raw newness to pathetic dilapidation.

He had anticipated, without relish, the quiet chat he would probably have with Dean Sloke. He would be shown into Dean Sloke's office, when his turn came.

'Ah — so you are Ferdinand Brumm, the nephew of my esteemed friend, the Reverend Miles Brumm of Indianapolis, who has been a valuable supporter of Magnolia. We are glad to have you here, Mr. Brumm. Now what can we do for you to make you comfortable?'

Ferdinand was pointed to the Registrar's office. He saw that there was no necessity for seeking an interview with Dean Sloke. There was a long line of bewildered freshmen leaning an elbow against the long, tall counter. No one of them in any way resembled the urbane youths who had been so hilariously received at the station. Surely they had had time to arrive here, by now. Mailed advice had counseled freshmen to come to the Administration Building immediately upon arrival. Where were these others? But perhaps there was a special room for their accommodation. Maybe the freshmen who came to town in Pullman cars were handled in some distinctive manner, or at some other hour.

He took his place in the line, and, advantaged by his height, surveyed his neighbors. The girl in front of him was a nervous, home-made, little thing; the boy whose broad, square back obstructed her view of the distant goal had the black-tanned neck of a farmer. The criss-cross furrows on the neck announced that their bearer was older than the others by four or five years. He'd been ploughing deep and saving his pennies against the day when he might come to college.

Ferdinand was half-ashamed of himself over this critical invoice of his companions. Come to think of it — this was his own crowd, after all; wasn't it? By what right was he assuming a supercilious attitude, in his mind, toward these yokels?

At length he had reached the impressively business-like, barricaded throne of the Registrar and his self-consciously competent assistants. He answered a few crisp, inquisitorial queries, wrote his name on three or four blanks which were promptly and soundly smacked with a big rubber stamp, counted out forty-two dollars at an adjoining wicket for which he received another emphatic whack on his credentials, moved forward to 'Rooms,' paid another fee, earned another whack, took his key, picked up the old suitcase he had been pushing along with his foot, and milled through the crowd to the doorway. It moved back, a little, to make room.

Nobody had spoken to him except the perfunctory clerks, nor he to any; though there had been a few shy, bucolic grins accompanying the 'Beg your pardon' which went along with sundry unintentional jabs of elbows in the jostling line-up of rookies.

They were a very ordinary lot of people, he thought, on both sides of the counter. Those back of the counter were a bit more seasoned, had learned their tricks, had developed something of the arrogance so appropriately worn by petty officials peering through wickets and sourly handing dipped pens to the public for its signature; but there was no essential difference between the green clodhoppers on this side the barrier and the ripe clodhoppers on the other.

As he had stood there waiting, Ferdinand wondered if Magnolia wasn't trying to impress the new arrivals; trying to make-believe she was a big university. Where was this warm, home-y friendliness that bubbled on the comradely pages of the college catalogue? Was all this swanky, big-business-y, card-index-y, cash-register-y atmosphere, this frowning fussiness, this cool official insolence, this elaborate hocus-pocus of labeled wicket-windows and ostentatious thud of rubber stamps a lot o' bunk? His instinct told him the whole affair screamed of insincerity....'Just a friendly, home-y, little college' — hell!

* * * * * *

Ferdinand answered a vigorous rat-a-tat-tat of knuckles and admitted one who, promptly identifying himself as Orville Kling, junior, resident across the hall, candidate for the ministry, leader of the college band in need of new material, and Religious Editor of *The Blossom*, requested pay, in kind, at his first full stop, for his generous tender of a biographical sketch.

With less to tell about himself, Ferdinand made short work of his own story. Pressed for further disclosures, he admitted he had no idea what he would 'take up.' No — not the ministry; he was sure of that much.... Well — he had no taste for it, no fitness for it, and, to be frank, no interest in it. Kling thought this odd, considering Ferdinand's home environment.

'Hope you'll come down to the Y rooms, second floor,

tonight at seven,' suggested Kling. 'Just an informal little get-together of the fellows to meet the new Frosh; a sing-song, brief devotional service, some short prayers, a few snappy talks; all through by eight.'

'Thanks,' said Ferdinand, graciously, but without enthusiasm.

'That's the spirit,' approved Kling, anxious to exhilarate Ferdinand's wan interest. 'It makes all the difference, later, if you begin your college life right.'

Ferdinand nodded obligingly, and conceded that this must be true, but his acquiescence lacked fervor. Bent on saving a soul from anæmia, Kling rose to defend his moral precept. Hands deep in his coat pockets, and rhythmically elevating himself on his toes, he dealt seriously with Ferdinand's limp aspirations to make a right start.

'Yes, sir — it makes all the difference, you'll find. The whole four years depend on the first week's contacts. Down there on Sunnyside Avenue, the upper classmen are teaching the new fraternity pledges to smoke a pipe, scorn the barbs, and beat the profs.... Up here, we have different ideas. You'll start right, won't you, Brumm?'

'You mean — at a prayer-meeting?'

'Well — that kind of a beginning would make for safety; wouldn't it?' queried Kling, slightly accelerating the tempo of his adroit bouncing up and down on his toes.

Ferdinand grinned amiably, and walked to the window, leaning against it; long, rangy arms folded.

'I'm pretty well up on prayer-meetings, Mr. Kling. I've been raised on them. And — as for safety, I have all my credits in that, too.... I mean to be friendly, and I'd like to meet the fellows, and I appreciate your asking me, but ——'

Kling stopped his bouncing and drew a long face.

'But — you won't be there.'

'I don't think so.'

Kling smiled bravely, shook his head regretfully, seemed reluctant to leave. His eye wandered about the room.

'Play on anything?' he inquired, brightening.

'No — I'm not musical. Sorry.'

'Thought that might be a clarinet. We need another clarinet.'

'It's a case of carving-tools.'

'Carving-tools.... I never saw any. Mind if I look?'

Ferdinand's consent and the snap of the latch occurred simultaneously. Kling glanced up and smiled.

'They call you "Dinny," don't they?'

'Ye-es.'

'Rah, rah, rah — Dinny Brumm! That's what we'll be hearing next fall. You'll be going out for football, of course. They wouldn't let a big fellow like you escape.... Janet your sister?'

'Yes.... Is the athletic field close?'

Kling pointed north with his head, deeply interested in the shining tools.

''Most everybody's there now, watching the varsity warm up. Want to go over? I'm going.'

Ferdinand begged off with an excuse that he had a few errands in town.

'Well — so long, Dinny. See you later.'

* * * * * *

Supper was at five-thirty, the tenants of the dormitory preferring it early. Ferdinand was not hungry, nor was he keenly disposed to risk further interrogations about his plans for the evening. Waiting until the clangor of the second bell and the last clatter of descending feet had subsided, he put on the rather yellow and battered straw hat that Aunt Martha felt would do quite well enough, though he had entertained some doubts, walked quietly down stairs, down the slope, and turned to the left on Sunnyside Avenue. The broad verandas of the fraternity houses were filled with bareheaded students, some standing, some lounging in the big wicker chairs, some sitting on the railings swinging white-flanneled legs. Ferdinand was conscious of their amused attention, as he passed the Beta House — the last on the row, opposite which one took the street-car.

A merry voice sang out, accompanied by good-natured chuckles, and followed by a mature growl, 'Cut that out, Reddy! What th' hell!' —

'Hey, Reuben! How's the weather up there?'

Ferdinand scowled, flushed, and gave his full attention to the approaching street-car. He wondered if he wasn't going to hate Magnolia.

After supper, at a downtown restaurant, for which he had little relish, he went to the office of *The Morning Star*, and made his way to the Managing Editor's desk. He was a little more sure of himself in this environment, and presented his cause without nervousness.

'What experience have you had?' asked Mr. Brophy, tilting back in his chair, and scrutinizing Ferdinand not unpleasantly from under his green eye-shade.

'I've been doing amateur and semi-professional art-craft printing for some time. Since early June, I was on the display ads with *The Ledger*, Indianapolis.'

'How could you work evenings, and go to college?'

'I think I could manage, sir. No classes in the afternoon.'

'You'd have to be on from seven to ten-thirty, six nights a week... all but Saturday.'

'I could do that.'

'Take this out to the composing-room, and set it.'

Ferdinand nodded, took the ad-copy, and pushed his way through the metallic racket of linotypes to the row of cases in the corner. It was the first time he had felt at home in Magnolia. The smell of ink revived his spirits, straightened his broad shoulders. Mr. Brophy followed him along, and spoke laconically to the grizzled foreman who nodded without looking up or removing his pipe.

'You may begin tomorrow evening, if you like,' said Mr. Brophy, an hour later, glancing over Ferdinand's shoulder.

'Ninety cents an hour. Six nights; seven to ten-thirty. Time and a half for overtime. Pay on Mondays. Right?'

'Right!... Thank you, sir.'

After a while, the foreman strolled over.

'Pretty fair, for a dub,' he growled, fetching his *r*'s rolling up from far back under an Irish pharynx. 'Mr. Brophy says you'll be goin' to college, day-times. Sure it won't be too much for ye, me boy?'

Ferdinand lowered his half-filled stick, and warmed to the genial, ruddy-faced Timmy Fagan. No — he could do it, all right. Liked it. Besides — he needed the money. Couldn't stay here without some kind of a job.

'You're luckier 'n 'most, t' have a trade,' said Timmy. 'Most uv 'em has to wait table and wash dishes at th' frats.'

'I'd see myself doing that!'

'Well — somebody's got t' wait on th' rich boys 'n' girls, 'n' see that they have enough t' eat, when they come in from their tennis, all tired and hungry,' drawled Timmy, his eyes wrinkling with delight as he noticed the flexing of Ferdinand's jaw-muscles. 'But,' he added, 'I can see that you'd rather somebody else 'tended to it.... And — now that we're speakin' o' meals, maybe you'd like to come over and have a bite o' honest Irish hospitality on Sunday, say, after the eleven o'clock Mass which you won't be to, bein' a heathen. The missus'll be glad, and th' kids, too. You'll be lonely like, for a while.'

Only an ungrateful snob could refuse such an invitation, thought Ferdinand. He accepted gladly, promptly; but, a moment later, and all the way back to the campus, where the dormitory windows gleamed with a welcome he wished he might respond to with more warmth, he was uneasy over his promise to old Timmy. Timmy, God bless him, had him all wrong.... Right, of course, about thinking he would resent the necessity of a job to wait table for these precious young well-to-do's, but quite wrong in thinking that he wanted to hold himself in sour aloofness from them.

It was the world they lived in that he most wanted to explore! And how was he ever to invade that world if he approached it via Sunday dinners at the Timmy Fagans'? Perhaps he'd better trump up some excuse.... But Timmy was no fool. Timmy mustn't be hurt.

However — no use worrying about it. Nobody need know. The Fagans probably had no college connections, at all. The 'kids' would be freckled little Micks — a half-dozen, maybe, who would show him their toy aeroplane... and that would be the end of it. 'Such a nice time, Mrs. Fagan!... Thank you, Mr. Fagan.... Yes, indeed, Mr. Fagan, I'll be glad to!... Good-bye, little Fagans!'

* * * * * *

He couldn't help being so tall that his contemporaries presumed him able to get forecasts of the weather, but he could help looking like a Rube. Pursuant to that resolution, he went into town, the next day, strode up to the counter of the best clothing store, and possessed himself of a natty new suit of blue serge.

His immediate college bills had been paid, and there was more than a hundred dollars in his pocket — earned by himself, every cent of it! Why shouldn't he do what he liked with it? His wages were assured. They would amply cover his expenses, with a comfortable margin.

Ferdinand paid for the suit and spent the remaining forty-eight dollars of the hundred he had allotted to this adventure in a neighboring haberdashery. Uncle Miles, he knew, would have scowled and remarked that even friendly little colleges have a 'subversive' (pet word of his) influence on youth; and as for Aunt Martha, she would have had — if aware of his amazing profligacy — a fit.

* * * * * *

Up early on Friday, arrayed in all his new finery — the blue, double-breasted suit that squared his shoulders, the soft gray fedora set at a sporty angle on his freshly groomed head, russet shoes, smart fawn shirt, tie a shade darker matching the handkerchief that peeped from his breast pocket — Ferdinand found he still had half an hour to spare before his first encounter with the class in English Composition.

Yesterday there had been mere lesson-assignment sessions in Beginner's Greek with old Appleton who promised to be a hard taskmaster; Algebra under nervous and self-conscious young Peters who would be lenient (it was devoutly to be hoped); and Latin under the meek and obsequious little Harwood, commonly spoken of as The Bearded Lady.

He would bone in Greek not only because he really wanted to learn it but was afraid of Appleton — a sarcastic old savage. He would toddle along in Cicero, Latin being a cinch for him. And as for Algebra, it could go to the devil along with the inexperienced Peters who was clearly too frightened over his new responsibility to pay much attention to anybody else's dilemmas.

But English Composition was quite another matter. This was going to be a bread-and-butter affair. Ferdinand knew he would be writing, all his life; writing for a career, writing for wages. No fooling, here.

He could have wished that Professor Grover's sketch in the catalogue had hinted at a wider experience. A degree from some well-known university would have added luster to his biography.

That Professor Grover had not been much of a nomad was obvious. Never had he been taken up, in foreign parts, for vagrancy. He had stayed on home base and kept himself unspotted from the world.

Topping the list of courses offered by the English Department was an impressive and extended survey of the Grover equipment.

WILLIAM ERNST GROVER, A.B., A.M., PH.D., LITT.D.

So far; so good. But the rest of it indicated that Professor Grover's mileage was disturbingly low.

Educated Magnolia Public Schools; Magnolia Academy (grad. 1878, with high distinction); Magnolia College (A.B., 1882, *m.c.l.*, Class pres. and hist.; winner Rebecca Winters Dutton medal); Master of Arts (Magnolia College, 1885. Thesis: 'Prehistoric Mounds near Magnolia'); Ph.D. (Magnolia College, 1889. Thesis: 'Magnolia Under Doctor Swits'); Litt. D. (Magnolia College, 1896). Author: 'Magnolians Who Made Their Mark' (Magnolia College Press, 1899), 'Fifty Years of Magnolia' (Magnolia College Press, 1902), 'Forward, Magnolia!' (Magnolia Ptg. and Engv. Co., 1910).

Three cheers for good old Magnolia; eh, Professor Grover? Ferdinand would have grinned had he been less disturbed over the prospect.

The time came when he did grin; shouted with laughter; slapped his leg and yelled with delight. That was while engaged in composing the article on 'Rhododendron College,' midway of his junior year. He sold the article to *The Iconoclast*, receiving, two months later, in the same mail, a check for one hundred dollars from the editor in New York, and a crisp request for an early interview with President Braithwaite of Magnolia.

'It might have been more discreet,' said President Braithwaite, endeavoring to suppress a twinkle, 'had you gone to the fauna rather than the flora for a fictitious name. "Rhododendron" made it a bit obvious, you know.... This about the Pyncheon chickens — facetious enough but cruelly unkind!'

'I had had the chickens in mind for a long time, sir,' said Ferdinand, on that occasion. 'It simply had to be said.'

He did not say how long, but the fact was that this idea had first occurred to him on the morning early in his freshman year when, with a few minutes to spare before going down to his first class in English Composition, he had put aside *The House of the Seven Gables* which he had been reading, and had glanced at the college catalogue's sketch of Professor Grover.

Apropos of 'Rhododendron's' policy of recruiting her Faculty exclusively from the ranks of her own alumni, Ferdinand, the junior, wrote:

'Concerned as this institution is over the mental and moral improvement of the outer world, particularly such parts of it as must be reached by water, it occurs to some of us that Rhododendron College might well consider a philanthropy nearer home.

'Year after year, proud of her children, Alma Mater has refused to permit their acceptance of chairs in other schools.

'Yale, Harvard, Princeton, Columbia — does Rhododendron not owe it to these institutions, all of them doing good work and undeniably excellent in their way, to encourage their efforts not only by consenting that a few of our alumni may join their faculties, but by inviting some of their more distinguished sons to accept minor posts on our instructional staff?

'Not a Rhododendron alumnus on the faculty of any other college! Not a single professor at Rhododendron bearing a degree from any other school!

'Should it be said that our policy of intellectual inbreeding insures the integrity of our academic tribe, and guarantees against the debilitating invasion of alien blood, it may be replied that dangers lurk in the way of such aloofness.

'Witness, for example, the tragic plight of Hepzibah Pyncheon's poultry. Generation after generation, they had carried on, gloriously free of any exotic contamination, dourly scornful of the frivolous vulgarians in neighboring coops. And did not the fateful day arrive at length when these same Pyncheon chickens stalked about, spurless, combless, and without plumage; still proud, still grave, still haughty, but lacking the sense of humor necessary to the laying of an egg, to say nothing of the thermal dynamics required to hatch one?

'Featherless, eggless — but not crowless. Even when

they were too feeble to scratch, either for provender or
reasons of personal hygiene, they still raised their voices in
the old pæan of praise that they had been kept free of
foreign taints. They had the pip, yes; but, thank God,
they were not mongrels!'

* * * * * *

Discovering, to his dismay, that the new russet shoes
were much too snug, Ferdinand hurriedly divested himself
of the entire ensemble, resolved that he would wear none
of it until he could wear it all.

Professor Grover was kindly patronizing, playfully
paternal. The class would begin by submitting, on Tuesday, a fifteen-hundred-word theme on 'Early Impressions
of Magnolia.'

As the class straggled out, Ferdinand overheard a col-
loquy in the hall. The Pullmans were talking it over, as
they ambled toward the main doorway.

'Freddy says the old boy always asks for that, the first
day. He says if you dash off a lot o' rot about the great
honor and privilege, and all that sort o' bilge, you're solid
with him for keeps; says if you write that when you saw
the campus for the first time you just sat down on the grass
and cried out loud, you'll be a Phi Beta Kappa when
you're a senior.'

'Phi Beta Kappa! D'you mean they've got a ——?'

'Don't be a silly ass!... Phi Beta Kappa, my eye!'

* * * * * *

The elder of the two Fagan kids was a girl with the black-
est hair, the bluest eyes, the whitest skin, the evenest
teeth, and the most heady smile that Ferdinand had ever
seen done into one picture of glowing, high-school-girlish
vivacity. Patrick, Kitty's brother, was fifteen.

Timmy Fagan's elder kid was going to resemble her
mother, one day, as to amplitude of charms; you could see
that. At seventeen, however, this threat, that at forty-two

Kitty's physique would probably be redundant, evoked no pity.

The dinner was all that it had promised to be, and more; a gay meal, Ferdinand at his best, glad he had come.

It was over now. Young Pat had left for a ball game. Timmy's eyes began to swim in response to custom's demand for the Sunday afternoon nap. Mrs. Fagan's housewifely conscience had conveyed her to the kitchen, scorning the volunteered assistance of her attractive child.

They sat in the swing on the little side porch overlooking the trim, tiny garden. Ferdinand was actively in the market for the companionship Kitty was so ready to bestow. He had been quite desperately lonely, almost ill of loneliness.

'You haven't seen our beautiful park yet,' said Kitty. 'You'll like it, I think. It's very nice, and there's a big lagoon with boats. Lots of people go there, Sundays.'

They stood for a long time at her gate, laughing, bantering, occasionally lowering their voices to brief seriousness, on their return at five-thirty.

Ferdinand regretfully looked at his watch.

'Good-bye, Kitty,' he said. 'Next Sunday, then.'

'Okay, Dinny... 'Bye.'

There was a deliciously lilting circumflex accent over the ''Bye' that rang and sang in Dinny's ears, all evening, as he stood at the case and stuck large, boastful type certifying that Wemble's would be doing the city of Magnolia a good turn, tomorrow, with some unprecedented values in sheets and pillow-cases.

CHAPTER VII

'No use,' said the nurse, decisively. 'He won't see you.'

'He's got to,' growled Dinny.

'Oh, I don't know as he's got to,' countered Miss Lash, suddenly defiant. 'The police couldn't make him talk. What makes you think ——?'

'Sister' — Dinny drew an ominous frown — 'you go back to Mr. Peter Andrews and tell him *The Star* knows all about it, anyway ——'

'Thinks it does, maybe,' scoffed Miss Lash.

'Which comes to the same thing, so far as tomorrow morning's report of the accident is concerned, he'll find. I'm here to let him correct us on any of the minor details. It's ten o'clock, and we've no time to fritter.'

'You certainly have a lot of crust — for a kid.'

'You ought to know,' grinned Dinny, companionably. 'Just a kid yourself.' The accusation was ridiculous. Miss Lash was not seriously annoyed, however, and the little nose she made at him developed into a smile.

'I'll try him again,' she said, in the manner of a fellow conspirator.

Dinny was covering his first assignment as a reporter. Mr. Brophy had urged him to work full time through the Thanksgiving recess, the display ads being particularly heavy at this season.

'And if you have nothing better to amuse yourself with in the evenings,' added the editor, 'you may share Anderson's police beat with young Maloney. Anderson's off to see his Alabama relatives. You've been hankering to try your hand at reporting: here's your chance.'

Mr. Brophy had been prompt to make his promise good. The Thanksgiving vacation had begun only today at noon, a general hegira leaving the campus all but deserted. Happy to have a congenial occupation, Dinny worked on the ads all afternoon and early evening. At nine-thirty, Timmy Fagan called, 'Mr. Brophy wants ye.'

'You're just leaving for the Protestant Hospital, young feller' — Mr. Brophy tossed him a memorandum scribbled on a card — 'to interview an old man, mysteriously shot in the leg; has no police record, good citizen, but won't talk. Make him tell you.... Scatter along, now, and see what you're good for.'

'Mr. Andrews says you can come up,' announced Miss Lash, amiably. 'I told him he'd better get it off his chest; but don't pester him, will you? He's a fine old man, and wouldn't hurt a fly. I won't have him persecuted.'

'It seems he's told you,' deduced Dinny.

She raised her brows, smiled archly, and led the way, Dinny following with long, confident strides.

'Very sick?' he inquired, as they traversed the third-floor corridor. The pungent reek of antiseptics and spent ether were doing odd tricks with Dinny's unaccustomed nostrils, and the hoarse, unhuman moans of some patient groping out of anæsthesia shortened his steps. Miss Lash grinned.

'No — or you wouldn't be seeing him; superficial wound, no infection, he can go home in a day or two. But' — she paused at the door — 'I'll not have him hectored; understand? If he doesn't want to talk freely, that's that, and there's your hat. Promise?'

Mr. Andrews's gaunt old frame was so slight that the bed seemed unoccupied except for the benign face on the pillow. He shyly projected a thin, white hand from beneath the sheet, cleared his throat nervously, and drew a timid, embarrassed smile.

'Nurse thinks I may as well tell you,' he murmured, with a weary sigh. 'If I don't, you'll probably make it worse than it is, though it's none of the public's business, far as I can see.'

'The public,' sympathized Dinny, taking the chair Miss

Lash had pushed up for him, and sensing with satisfaction the revival of his self-confidence, 'is an old hen.... And the newspapers are impudent gossips.... And reporters are a pest.... But — such things being as they are — how *did* you get shot in the leg?'

'My next-door neighbor, out in Lambert Park, is Mr. Charles McCutcheon —— ' The old man sighed again, deeply, as he watched the name sprawling across the reporter's untidy wad of copy-paper; but, having burned his bridges, there was no retreat. '—— A longtime friend of mine. We both work for the Buckeye Implement Company. We have a croquet-ground together, a small garden, and in the winter we play chess.'

'He has been to see you, I presume,' encouraged Dinny.

'No — er — well, yes; but I had them say I was too sick. ... I'll be coming to that, in a minute.'

The weary old voice droned on, reminiscently. Charlie was a widower, you know; he, a bachelor; nobody else mattered; went down town in the morning on the same car, lunched together, pretty nearly inseparable.

''Bout two weeks ago, Charlie's daughter — the one that lives in Pinckney, and doesn't like me very well because I monopolize Charlie — gave him a St. Bernard pup to keep him company, a big-footed, empty-headed, destructive beast that tore up Charlie's house, all day — what time he wasn't tearing up mine — and howled like the devil all night. I could see that Charlie was worried, but he kept saying the dog would settle down and feel at home presently.

'And so, yesterday — wasn't it, nurse? — Charlie had gone down to Tiro to spend the night with William's folks; wedding anniversary, or something. You see, I hadn't slept for more 'n' a week. Guess I was kinda out o' my head. Charlie had him out in a kennel at the far end of the lot; but, Gosh! that hadn't helped any.... I had an old revolver that hadn't been fired off for ten years or so. Three o'clock, I was pretty desperate, and put on my pants 'n' went out there. Somehow the hammer got caught in my pocket ——'

'You could have made up a story, couldn't you?' inquired Dinny, solicitously.

'I'm not very good at that,' replied the old man. 'Besides — my leg hurt pretty bad. I managed to get in before it had bled very much, and 'phoned for the doctor. He brought me here — and that's all there is to it. You can print it, if you want to, and all the neighbors will despise me — and Charlie will never speak to me again.'

'What did you do with the gun?' asked Dinny.

'Threw the darned thing in the cistern.'

'Excellent! Now don't you worry any more,' soothed Dinny, patting the emaciated hand. 'We'll see you through it.'

Dinny caught a car and hurried back to *The Star*, eyes bright with inspiration, so eager to document his scheme for the easement of good old Andrews that it never occurred to him there might also be some inquisitiveness on the part of *The Daily Eagle* concerning this mystery. That night, Dinny recognized for the first time unmistakable signs of his talent as a potential novelist. He warmed to his task. It was an unusual story, and toward the last of it they were snatching unfinished sheets out of his typewriter and rushing them, page at a time, to the linotypist.

Next morning, December twenty-second, subscribers to both papers were amazed at the difference between the two accounts of this strange affair. According to *The Eagle's* report — a mere stick on page seven — Mr. Andrews had accidentally shot himself while endeavoring to pot his absent neighbor's noisy dog, a minor injury from which he was rapidly recovering.

The Morning Star — (first page, with a carry to three) — offered a long, dramatic story of Mr. Andrews's heroic silence about the shooting. In his delirium, however, the brave old fellow had muttered, 'Don't shoot again, lad... I haven't any money except what's there in my pocket-book.... You can look, if you like.... Take it — and hurry before somebody comes.... I won't tell on you, boy.... It would break her heart.'

From these broken fragments, *The Star* had adroitly built up a tale of romance and adventure impressive enough to stand in the museum alongside the mastodon — all lath and plaster and imagination, except the third dorsal vertebra and two molars. Chivalrous old Andrews! Brave old Andrews! Attacked in his little home by a marauder, he had recognized the wayward son of an old friend.

Nobody knew, nobody was likely ever to know — for Andrews seemed determined to keep his own counsel — what a wealth of romance lay undisclosed in the heart of this kindly old bachelor. Ambitious as she was to print all the news, *The Star* had quietly withdrawn from the bedside of this valiant knight, challenged to match his sportsmanship by declining to press the matter any farther.

That afternoon, industriously distributing big type, Dinny, out of the tail of his apprehensive eye, observed the approach of his boss, paper in hand. He redoubled his zealous interest in his occupation. Mr. Brophy was at his elbow now, but Dinny did not look up. It was a very busy day.

'My son,' said Mr. Brophy, reproachfully, '*The Eagle* will probably try for a goal from the field with your Andrews story, tomorrow morning. They'll make us look like a cageful of monkeys.'

'I've been thinking a little about that, too, sir,' admitted Dinny, confidentially, 'but, you see, the tale they tortured out of old Andrews, late last night, was concocted in sheer self-defense. He was resolved not to tell the straight story, so he made one up, on the spot, to satisfy their greedy curiosity. He would have done the same for me, if I had badgered him. Takes all the blame on himself! Risks the good opinion of his neighbors, risks his job at the shop, throws away the lifelong friendship of Mr. McCutcheon.... Shoot McCutcheon's pet? Nonsense! You wait until the people see the picture of saintly old Andrews, in bed at the hospital, near death's door, staring up out of those big, wistful ——'

'Hell! — they're going to discharge him this afternoon.'

'No, sir. I beg your pardon, sir. They had thought of it, but the nurse and I agreed it wouldn't do. I was out there and told them *The Star* would pay for all it cost to keep him a week, at least.'

'He won't stay. Even if he does, he'll talk.'

'No, sir. The nurse says his room is rapidly filling up with flowers and baskets of fruit. And Mr. Kellerman was there, making a fuss over him ——'

'You mean old man Kellerman?'

'Yes, sir — president of the Buckeye — he was there; and Norton of *The Eagle* tried to see him, but Andrews sent down word to him that they'd practically forced him to tell them the tale he'd made up. The nurse says he likes our version of the affair ever so much better, though he told Mr. Kellerman he didn't think it was very sporting of us to print what he said while he was unconscious.'

'Well — I'll be damned!'

'So will Doctor Cummings,' drawled Dinny, 'for he told me he would. And, as for that ——' He hesitated, grinning.

'So will you, I presume,' assisted Mr. Brophy.

'*The Cincinnati Democrat* was there, taking pictures, when I left.'

'Well,' said Mr. Brophy, 'it's your affair. Carry on with it. This is going to call for a lot of expert lying, so I'll let you manage the campaign. I've been in the newspaper game for twenty years, my boy, and you're the biggest liar I have ever known.'

'Thank you, sir,' said Dinny. 'D'you think maybe I'd better go out there again?'

'Yes,' replied Mr. Brophy. 'I think maybe you had; and if old Andrews weakens and tells the truth, you needn't ever come back.'

Timmy Fagan had silently joined the party, obviously enjoying himself.

'Timmy,' said Mr. Brophy, 'I'm going over to headquarters for a chat with Chief O'Brien. I'll be back in half an hour.'

'Yes, sir,' said Timmy, 'but it's all right, Mr. Brophy. I was over there at noon, and he's called 'em off the case. He sent you this long, black cheroot, sir, and said to tell you those greasy Republicans on *The Eagle* could whistle for any more dope on the Andrews shootin'.'

'You editing *The Star* now, Timmy?' asked Mr. Brophy, lighting the gift, dubiously.

'Well, sir' — Timmy lowered his voice, confidentially — 'we couldn't let th' boy down, sir, seeing it was his first offense. I told the chief he was a fine lad, and I'd seen him at Mass, last Sunday.'

'Nonsense, Timmy. Brumm's not a Catholic.'

Timmy smiled, omnisciently, and turned toward his stone table.

'My Kitty's attendin' t' that, sir.'

* * * * * *

Dinny Brumm's freshmanhood at Magnolia which, at the outset, had threatened to be drab and uneventful, was not altogether unsatisfactory.

Startled, after five days, by the realization that he was likely to become a lone wolf on a campus where everyone else had entered into budding friendships — his nightly employment, and his boarding at a restaurant in town having made it quite impossible for him to be sociable — Dinny resolved to mend matters by spending an hour, late afternoons, on the athletic field. He could at least relieve himself of the just accusation that he wanted no friends and preferred to go it alone.

At three o'clock on Wednesday, therefore, he had presented himself at the freshman wing of the 'training quarters' in the inadequate old gymnasium, where, without asking any questions or announcing his purpose, he was glee-fully welcomed by young Assistant Coach Roberts and the awkward assembly of prospective gridiron heroes, the tallest of whom he overtowered.

His whole time having been occupied by other more im-portant matters, Dinny had never taken any active interest in high-school football, but from the first moment of his ad-venture with the pigskin he seemed to have an instinctive feel for the game.

What came later to be referred to by sports writers as his 'reckless courage,' was in evidence that first day, possibly attributable to the fact that the savagery of hard tackling, on the open field, appealed to his mood. The utter futility of life had laid so low an estimate on the claims of personal safety that Dinny was indifferent to bruises or the hazard of broken bones.

When, at five, two teams were lined up by Coach Roberts, Dinny observed that the personnel of the combating squads could easily be identified even in their muddy, handed-down toggery. As usual, the real people were on one side, giving battle to the people who didn't matter much. The real people had naturally gravitated, some chemical affinity pulling them together. He found himself playing right tackle on the team that didn't matter much. The Pullman cars were to recognize the Day Coaches to the extent of us-ing them for experimental purposes — to try out their own strength, speed, and skill.

There was quite an accumulation of sentiment in Dinny's mind on that subject, and in the ensuing thirty minutes of play he expressed it so convincingly that, toward the end of the game — which attracted a vociferous crowd of specta-tors who found the battle of the 'frosh' more exciting than the experienced maneuvers of the varsity on the adjoining gridiron — there seemed to be a unanimity of consent, on the part of the opposition, when Dinny took the ball, that he might go down the field with it, undetained.

Perspiring, and secretly exultant, Dinny divested himself

of the tight-fitting old mole-skins that reeked with the acrid memories of many celebrated engagements, his team-mates and foes respectfully assisting. As he left the gymnasium, he found himself walking alongside Barney Vaughn, against whom he had played in the line. Barney was friendly, inquisitive. Where had Brumm been keeping himself?

'You must drop in and see me,' said Barney. 'I'm at the Custer Cottage, Sunnyside Avenue. That's where the Sig pledges live, you know.'

'No — I didn't know where they lived,' said Dinny. 'I don't even know what "Sig pledges" are,' he added. 'Red-headed ones, maybe?'

Barney ran his fingers through his untidy mop of burnished bronze, and laughed. Then he was serious.

'I'll bet somebody's been getting your goat, Brumm. You played like it. My Uncle! but you were a brute. Look at that elbow o' mine, will you?'

They overtook a couple of seniors, strolling back toward the campus — seniors of the Pullman car variety.

'Yeah,' one was drawling, 'the barbs were running circles around 'em. Who is this Brumm fellow, anyway? How-come we heard nothing about him? Hell of a scouting committee we've got, this year.'

'That's what comes of letting the Sophs attend to it,' replied the other. 'We'd better have Bristol look this bruiser up, and tow him into camp.'

Barney winked, companionably, at Dinny, as they passed the self-assured strollers.

'Stock going up, eh?' chaffed Barney, out of the side of his mouth. 'Couple o' my brethren, those ginks.'

'Why didn't you speak to them?'

'Frosh aren't supposed to: you knew that, didn't you?'

'Democratic little school, isn't it?'

At the foot of the slope, their ways separated. Barney urgently renewed his invitation. Dinny evasively mumbled excuses: no time to visit, nose to the grindstone. Thanks, all the same, old man. See you tomorrow.

* * * * * *

On Friday morning, as Dinny entered the rapidly filling classroom of Professor Grover, and looked about for a vacant chair, the long arm and beckoning fingers of Barney Vaughn summoned him to a seat in the back row, where he was received with friendly smiles. He realized at a glance that he was in a Pullman car.

Professor Grover, who did not have to eat a whole egg to determine whether it was bad — a quip he often repeated without bothering to enclose it in inverted commas — reported that the papers submitted on Tuesday were, in the main, satisfactory. They would be returned, with notations, to their makers, at the close of the hour. (On the back of the last page of his essay, in red ink, Dinny read, later, 'well conceived, meritorious for perspicacity, clarity, and force.')

However, pursued Professor Grover, deliberately, it was not to be supposed that all the papers were of equal value; and, for the benefit of those who hadn't quite caught the idea, he would ask that one of the more excellent themes be read at this time.

Experience had taught him — Professor Grover pulled a benevolent smile — that it was usually embarrassing to the author when called upon to read his own piece aloud to the class. He would therefore request — he adjusted his glasses and glanced down at the unfamiliar roster — he would therefore request Miss — er — Adams to read the paper he had chosen as among the best.

A bit flustered, Miss Adams detached herself from her immediate environment, rather self-consciously approached the sanctum with much nervous jingling of bracelets, bangles, and other light hardware, faced her audience rosily, and began to intone her unknown classmate's anthem of praise to Magnolia in a dulcet tone so cooingly mellifluous that covert grins were exchanged among the more sophisticated.

Barney Vaughn leaned toward Dinny, pressed the back of his hand against the side of his mouth, and whispered, unctuously, 'Gawd is love.'

Dinny grinned, feebly.

The tender passion of the impromptu score which Miss Adams was fervently attaching to the sticky sweetness of the libretto produced a strange effect upon the class. By the time she had turned the first page, the dullest dolt in the room had his open palm against his mouth, apparently engaged in a battle for air.

Professor Grover smiled, hopefully, as if promising that it would eventually come out all right, and moved slowly back and forth in his chair, his outspread hands rhythmically rubbing his knees. It was easy to see, however, that he was worried. He had only read into this piously grateful tribute to the college far enough to see that it was definitely committed to a loyalty of high degree. He hadn't noticed, at the moment, that it was quite so superlatively silly as it now appeared, set to the sloppily sentimental adagio affected by Miss Adams whose mark for the semester's work in English Composition he had now determined upon in terms of three flats.

Dinny's flair for satire was not an achievement, but a gift. He had not deliberately planned the early pages of his impressions of Magnolia with a view to disarming the reader in order, later, to smite him with a volley of ridicule.

About midway of page four, it became evident in the mounting flush and occasional hesitations of Miss Adams that even she, herself, infatuated as she was with her elocution, had begun to suspect the increasing digression of the text from the melody, and realized the enormity of the farce to which she was unwittingly contributing the ultimate touch that gave it perfection.

She was reading now the early impressions of the freshman as he watched the masterful manner in which the rubber stamp was affixed to impressive documents, the stony stare of experienced officials which heightened the newcomer's respect for a college of such magnitude that its most insignificant underlings felt the dignity and superiority of their honored trust, the crispness of their laconic 'Next window, please, for that.'

Barney inclined toward Dinny, at this juncture, and guardedly whispered, eyes intent upon the reader, 'Somebody's been pulling the old man's leg,' to which the awe-stricken Dinny added, absently, 'The paralyzed one.'

They were hearing now about the democracy of a friendly little college, the one place in the world where social caste was regarded with the scorn it properly deserved in the opinion of all people to whom the Almighty had vouchsafed even the bare elements of humor.

Dinny sighed, rubbed his red cheek, and reflected that his essay was quite too long. The class must be frightfully tired of it by this time. He glanced at Professor Grover and imagined that the roving eye flashed him a baleful threat of hard times. Pulling himself together and affecting nonchalance, he turned cautiously to Barney and remarked, lips barely moving:

'The old boy should have eaten one more spoonful of this egg before he served it.'

Barney thoughtfully dug deep in a trouser pocket and came up with a penny.

'This says you laid it,' gambled Barney.

'Vulgar display,' whispered Dinny, loftily.

Professor Grover was fussily rummaging through the pile of papers.

'Just a moment, Miss — er — Adams,' he broke in, huskily.

Miss — er — Adams lowered the paper and looked up for further orders.

'I think we have heard enough of this essay, now, to gather what must have been in the mind of the writer. It seemed only fair that any slight irritation or disappointment should be recognized. Happily, such sentiments are held by a very small minority. Magnolia does not assume responsibility for the irascibility of newcomers who expect immediate preferments.... We have here another paper, written in a better temper, which I shall ask Mr. Bristol to kindly read.... Thank you, Miss — er — Adams.'

'"To kindly read,"' observed Barney, 'shows the old thing to be human, anyway.'

Dinny wiped his brow, and nodded with the pensiveness of a convalescent consenting to a proffered pill; then rallied enough to reply, wanly:

'This must be a rough day on the sea.'

* * * * * *

During the first two months of Dinny's residence in Magnolia, Kitty Fagan frequently had occasion to come to *The Star*, early evenings, with important messages for her father, the delivery of which would be but the work of a moment.

Not wishing to appear ungracious toward Timmy's lonesome young friend, she would wave a hand, fingers twinkling; and Dinny, resolutely blind to the amused interest of a score distracted from their gainful occupations in the composing-room, would meet her halfway to his case and amblingly accompany her to the door where they would pause and chat amiably for a moment. He always worked half an hour overtime, on his own hook, to make sure he had not visited with Kitty at the expense of the company.

By the middle of November, Kitty's emergency messages for her father had all been delivered, and *The Star*, suddenly bereft of these pleasant interludes scheduled to be played about eight-thirty, twice a week, became mildly curious.

Bert Snyder, on machine No. 1, observing Dinny emerging from the coat-room at ten, sharp, one night, dressed for the street, re-lit his corn-cob pipe, tossed a hot slug bearing the cryptic phrase 'etaoin shrdlu' into the bubbling pot, and ventured his guess to Stub Harley, on No. 2, that Timmy had advised her not to come up any more. Stub thought it more likely that Mr. Brophy had set down on it. Pinky Gormer, assistant telegraph, hung a few smeary pages on each of their hooks, and bet there had been a quarrel.... But nobody knew and, after a little while, nobody cared.

On the fourth consecutive Sunday at the Fagans', Dinny realized that he was being gradually, unprotestingly assimilated. Noting that the living-room which gave directly on to the front porch was unoccupied, he did not rap on the screen-door, but opened it and made his way through to the kitchen.

'We heard you coming, Dinny,' said Mrs. Fagan, too intent on the beautifully browned chicken she was taking from the oven to give him better attention than a fleeting smile. 'I can't think what's come over that gate.'

'Where's the oil-can?' inquired Dinny. 'I'll touch it up.'

'I know,' said Kitty, putting down the bowl of whipping cream.

'Let him find it himself.... It's up on the sewing-machine, Dinny, in the back room.' Mrs. Fagan vigorously beat the potatoes. 'Don't look around in there. It hasn't been picked up.'

Timmy met him halfway up the stairs, and said it was too warm for a coat.

Kitty's attitude became proprietary.

'Dinny doesn't want that much sugar in his tea.... Dinny mustn't have another piece of pie, father. It's bad for his wind. If we're going to make the team, we'll have to go easy on the pie.... Dinny, we really must look after those poor fingers: that nasty acid. Can't they use something else on their dirty old type?'

On the fifth Sunday, Dinny met the four of them on the imposing front steps of Saint Vincent's at eleven o'clock. It was his first experience in a Catholic church. He knew next to nothing about that institution, and suspected that what little he did know was untrue. Of course, he took no stock in his own family's estimate of it, aware that their passionate prejudice had been slowly percolated through a filter of ignorance and contempt — a musty old filter clogged with nearly four centuries of gritty deposits precipitated from neighborhood brawls and border wars.

In the questionable judgment of Uncle Miles, whose proud boast it was that his feet had never crossed the threshold of 'Rome,' the Pope was 'the Anti-Christ.' Dinny had but a vague idea who 'the Anti-Christ' was, beyond his natural deduction that it was a cryptic epithet never employed in eulogy.

Aunt Martha maintained that practically all Catholic churches were secret arsenals, their subterranean grottoes stuffed with rifles and ammunition. She wagged her head ominously when she predicted the day of 'a great uprisin' that'll make th' rivers run red.' This was, on the face of it, mere drivel and nonsense. You could tell, because the rivers were to run red. Aunt Martha was always quite definitely off the rails when she talked in terms of red or any of the collateral hues. She always got excited, hysterical, and incoherent when she discoursed on Sin, which was scarlet, or Salvation, which was crimson.

As they mounted the church steps, pressed close on either side by pilgrims of all sorts, Dinny felt himself a member of the Fagan family. There was something tender and intimate in this new relationship. He would sit in the Fagan pew. He would belong to them, for an hour, in bonds of a common wistfulness. Not that he expected to get much out of it further than the satisfaction of sitting quietly with them. Doubtless he and Kitty would share a hymn-book. There would be a long, tiresome sermon, but they would not have to listen to it. Perhaps he would touch Kitty's fingers, when the clergyman inveighed against some sport or pleasure, and they would steal a pious glance at each other, tongue in cheek.

The instant they entered the dim, vasty nave, Dinny found himself quite alone. His Fagans had vanished, their places taken by four strangers who suddenly went about the business of dipping finger-tips in the huge marble shell, touching themselves with an adroitness that could not possibly have been achieved through experience, but must be accounted for by some instinct which Dinny knew he did not possess.

The supple grace of their genuflections set them apart from him and all his kind. The only movement he had ever seen, comparable to it for artless dexterity, was the sweep of a lithe tiger's breast against the bars as it reached the end of its brief journey and turned to pad softly but determinedly to the other corner of the cage.

He followed these people, dressed like the Fagans, half-way down the broad aisle, where, pausing, they dipped again, not by conscious effort, but as if each of them had been gripped by some current flowing from the wood of the pew-end, so that when their fingers touched it, they responded — galvanically.

Kitty glanced sideways and offered him a fragment of a smile — a mere, transparently thin cross-section of a smile — as she slipped swiftly from the seat to her knees beside Pat and her parents. Dinny lumberingly joined her on the bare narrow rail on which they knelt, ashamed of his awkwardness. Adjusting his joints with much difficulty, he distributed his weight so that his elbows on the top of the pew might ease the discomfort of his knees. When all this had been attended to, he glanced down at the profile of the rapt face beside him. The smart little white hat with the blue ribbon looked very much like Kitty's hat. The firm, round, white chin was amazingly like Kitty's lovely chin. The steady fingers, gently moving from one bead to another on her rosary, resembled Kitty's competent fingers. But Kitty had escaped. This girl beside Dinny was a foreigner. Kitty and Pat and good old Timmy and hospitable Mrs. Fagan had left him forlorn, chagrined, and lonely on the beach while they, diving with the skill and precision of graceful seals, had whisked away into their Sea.

Kneeling thus on the hard pebbled beach of that mysterious Sea in which the Fagans were so confidently at home, the sublimity of it all began to lay hold on Dinny Brumm. He realized now that something inside him had been calling, faintly but urgently, all his life, demanding exercise, sustenance, liberty; something aquatic that couldn't walk on the hard ground.

They were back in their seats now, but the mesmeric spell did not lift. They rose, they sat, they bowed, they crossed themselves with sure, deft strokes, Dinny trying to keep pace with them in the rising, and sitting, and kneeling, feeling himself a mere stumbling baby trudging with short, drunken steps in the wake of experienced track-sprinters.

Now the congregation hummed briefly with swiftly flowing, unintelligible fragments of liquid sentences, sentences prodded out of it by stately challenges addressed to the great white and gold and flickering altar by an ornately garbed figure. The celebrant was attended by small boys in vestments, who needed no telling what to do, boys who anticipated each impending phase of the ancient drama, boys whose very backs seemed to disdain such childish fripperies as marbles, tops, and kites, having forsaken all that was secular to pledge their life to all that was sacred.

Presently it occurred to Dinny that these strangers whose pew he shared might be as well pleased with their guest if he made no further ridiculous attempts to imitate them in their worship. The next time they sat, he resolved to remain seated.

He looked about. It was the first occasion on which the Gothic had ever spoken to him directly. The Gothic beckoned him to attempt a spiritual journey.

Dinny's eyes rested on the beautiful window nearest him, a multi-colored window crowded with brave events upheld and flanked by miniatures of enhaloed saints — enraptured saints bearing massive keys and open books, bearded saints leading submissive lions, beardless saints led by victorious lambs with a fore-foot sustaining a shouldered banner; crowns and crests, shields and swords, cups and censers, purple grapes and yellow wheat-sheaves, and hilltops tipped with spires.

His eyes traveled up until the window narrowed to a pointed arch that led the way to the base of a flying buttress. He gave himself willingly to its graceful curve, and followed along past innumerable sign-posts — all pointing up... Up... *Up!* — each arch, and tip, and spire daring him to leap to another... higher... Higher... *Higher!* — until visibility was lost in the shadows overhead.

Perhaps that was the way Religion really ought to be, thought Dinny. No wonder the Catholics had lasted so long without the necessity of change, reorganization, reappraisals. The old Church invited you to look up. That was all she asked. She made no promises that she could reveal the Ultimate. It was up to you... how far you could see. You looked up — and the Church carried you from one aspiring arch to another until you could go no farther, not because the arches ended, up there, but because your frail sight could no longer follow them into the Mystery whose depths they plumbed.

Meantime, the rhythmic tide of the venerable ritual came rolling, rumbling on in strong, confident waves — music out of a Past that was also a Future; music that took no account of infinitesimal weeks and months, but dealt with a thousand years as if it were only a day; music that never even glanced down to see whether you were following an ox-drawn plow or addressing parliament from a throne, much less noticed whether you rode in a Day Coach or a Pullman; spoken music, drifting from within the chancel, chanted music, drifting from the choir overhead.

For a period there was much made of a small jeweled case, set into the altar; hushed silences bounded by the silvery tinkle of a bell; deep, deep reverence between the silvery tinkle of the bell.

The sweetish-brownish aroma of incense hung in the air, invisible in the nave, though above the heads of the celebrants it drifted like a torn tapestry — a very old, brownish-gray tapestry. To Dinny's unaccustomed nostrils the elusive scent was an indissoluble combination of mingled appeals to the most spiritual of all the senses. He tried without success to analyze its weird effects upon his imagination. At first it seemed to possess a certain medicinal quality — faintly stimulative. No — it was not a stimulant, but an exultant, insisting upon the exultation produced by calm acceptance, confident repose.

There was something primitive about it, too; something woodsy, as if it exuded from the enshadowing trees beneath whose branches valiant men of old had knelt to worship — trees which the Gothic had preserved in stone.... Dinny wondered what strange magic the incense was conjuring in the trained, consecrated nostrils of the transported Fagans.

Aunt Martha had scorned the institution that tried to worship in a heathen language.

'Nothin' but gibberish!' declared Aunt Martha, who knew only her mother tongue, and that imperfectly.

Dinny did not find it so. In the mounting radicalism of eighteen plus disillusionment, he was ready to do bumptious battle with any detailed invoice of 'I believes,' hawked in the language of the clearing-house and the market-place. But there was a sudden tightening of the throat, a burning of the eyelids, when the sonorous phrases came welling forth from the dimly lit chancel:

Et in Jesum Christum... Dominum nostrum... qui conceptus est de Spiritu sancto... natus ex Maria Virgine...

You didn't have to believe it: you just knew it was true. His eyes groped into the vaulted roof. Up there, out there, beyond there — what? When you had it all explained for you in the patter of the machine-shop, the language of the garage, the department-store, the football field, you waved it away and muttered, 'Stuff and nonsense!' It was a different matter when sung to you in an otherwise unused tongue, through an aromatic veil of incense:

... carnis resurrectionem... vitam æternam!...

That was the glory, then, of this Catholic religion. It didn't ask to be understood, as Chemistry asks to be understood.

Perhaps that was the whole trouble with Uncle Miles's religion. It explained everything, succeeding only in making itself absurd. Its speculations were hard-and-fast facts to be weighed on the scales, poured into a test-tube, shaken over a flame.

Not much wonder, thought Dinny, this Catholicism had carried on.... Every so often, turbulent little sects had spewed themselves out through the heavy bronze doors of cathedrals to quarrel and dogmatize; obliged, when their fury was spent, to build cheap and ugly little imitations of the eternal thing from which they in their willfulness had fled.

Every new generation of the self-outcast had revised the imitation. Never were they done tinkering with it, reconditioning it, modernizing it, making it over 'to meet the new day.' And — meantime — while their most progressive engineers dug deep under the thing to install new heating, climbed high on the thing to equip it with a tighter roof, repainted it, relandscaped it — The Everlasting Church stood fast!... 'sanctum Ecclesiam Catholicam!'

That was the Sea!

All the time the inquisitive and heady were busily building their little dams, and draining their miasmic ponds, and changing the courses of their impotent, muddy, little creeks, the Sea had steadily throbbed to the tune of the stars without so much as a by-your-leave to any earthly powers. That Sea did not even pause to smile at the snarls and fist-shakings of the engineers. The Sea did not know they existed!... Dinny Brumm devoutly hoped he could learn to navigate that Sea. He went out of Saint Vincent's, into the October sunshine, tentatively committed to the great experiment.

'How did you like it?' asked Kitty, smiling a little, but wide-eyed with genuine concern.

'I really can't talk about it, Kitty,' he murmured.

She grasped his arm for a moment, and patted his sleeve lightly.

'"*Dominus vobiscum*," Dinny!' recited Kitty, gently, gratefully.

'What do I say now — anything?'

'You say, "*Et cum spiritu tuo*," Dinny.'

He repeated the words after her, adding, 'dear.'

* * * * * *

That afternoon — a golden-russet, burnt-sienna afternoon — they climbed the high hill overlooking the city park. The southerly slope of the hill was a cemetery. It was a full quarter-mile to the nearest white stones; a half-mile to the broad granite arch of the old-worldish gateway flanked on either side with clumps of cypress trees.

Dinny was reflective, eyes moody, lips pursed, as he reclined on an elbow, Kitty sitting cross-legged beside him, endeavoring to punctuate the long silences with sprightly talk.

'Wise old owl,' she pouted, 'come out of your trance.'

Their eyes turned toward the cemetery gate, far below. Some secret order in uniform was creeping along, led by a brass band, en route to bury a brother... Chopin's Funeral March... As the band passed under the broad stone arch and through the cypress trees, a whole half-dozen measures were completely obliterated. Kitty supplied the missing passage, keeping time with martial bobs of her bare black head, her pretty cheeks distended as if she blew the notes on the big, shining tuba that presently led the way out into the sun.

'Pumm, pum-te-pumm, pum-te-pum, te-pum, te-pum,' pummed Kitty, soberly.

The cortège was marching out into the glow, now, but the dirge was still in the gloom, candidly hopeless of anything to come of this dignified enterprise further than the wretched anti-climax of ropes and shovels and the bouncing of clods on a box.

Dinny lay outstretched on his back, gazing straight up, listening to the wisps of the despairing march which Kitty continued to accompany, softly. Now it was quite stilled again for an instant, while the band rounded the other side of a massive cliff. Presently there swept up the hill a great wave of hope. 'Nevertheless!' sang the dirge. *'Nevertheless — I tell you!'*

Kitty scrambled to her knees, facing Dinny, her eyes bright, dancing, her pretty teeth sparkling, keeping time with both hands, fingers outspread, chanting, happily:

'Tra-la — Tra-la — la-la-la-la — la — tra-la' . . .

'You actually believe that; don't you?'

'That it's going to come out all right? Sure! Of course! Don't you?'

'I think I do . . . when . . . when it's said in Latin.'

'I don't quite get you, Dinny.'

'Well,' he drawled, dreamily, 'I think the belief in ever-lasting life is silly . . . but *"vitam æternam"* is sound.'

'Funny boy,' laughed Kitty. 'Old owl!'

Then he told her almost everything he had thought about, that morning in church. On the way down the hill, she promised to ask Father Donovan for some little books he might read, though Dinny was not sure he wanted them.

'I'm contented,' he said. 'Besides — I would have trouble reading them. Latin's tedious . . . in large quantities.'

'Oh — but this will not be in Latin,' explained Kitty.

'Maybe we'd better leave well enough alone,' said Dinny, thoughtfully.

* * * * * *

Two disquieting books came into Dinny's hands, within three hours of each other, on the next Thursday night.

The first was lent by Father Donovan and delivered into the hands of Dinny, at his case, by Kitty Fagan — a book he opened at one A.M., in his room, and perused for a scant five minutes. Then he closed it with a snap. He had read the English — the modern, workaday English, under the

pitiless glare of electric light — the English explanation of
The Mysteries.

Here was the 'Profession of Faith' for converts:

'I., N. N., having before me the holy gospels, which I
touch with my hand and knowing that no one can be saved
without that faith which the Holy, Catholic, Apostolic
Roman Church holds, believes, and teaches, against which I
grieve that I have greatly erred ——'

Dinny ran his eye down the page:

'I believe in one only God in three divine Persons, distinct from, and equal to, each other — that is to say, the
Father, the Son, and the Holy Ghost.'

How often he had heard Uncle Miles tangle himself up in
the labyrinthian mazes of this incomprehensible 'three in
one' business — as if it mattered; as if anybody knew.

'I believe in the true, real and substantial presence of the
Body and Blood, together with the Soul and Divinity, of
our Lord Jesus Christ, in the most holy Sacrament of the
Eucharist.'

That's what the little jeweled case was about. The Lord
Jesus Christ was in there. They took Him out, and then
put Him back in again.... Uncle Miles had some queer
ideas, too; but ——

The rest of it Dinny merely glanced at.

'I believe in the seven Sacraments...

'I believe in Purgatory...

'I believe in the Primacy, not only of honor, but of jurisdiction, of the Roman Pontiff, successor of Saint Peter,
Prince of the Apostles...

'I believe in the veneration of the Saints and of their
images.'

'And' — the book was closing now, and in an instant it
would be shut with a sharp slap — 'I believe in everything
else that has been defined and declared by the sacred Can-
ons and the General Councils, and particularly by the
Council of Trent ——'

Dinny didn't know what the 'Council of Trent' was, but

it was with the 'Council of Trent' that his spiritual exploration terminated. It was seven years before he smelled incense again.

He undressed, and went to bed with the book Mr. Brophy
had lent him at midnight. Mr. Brophy had asked him along
to lunch, for on Thursday nights he always worked overtime, ads being heavy in the Friday morning edition of *The
Star*.

They went to Clancy's, which closed at eleven, in accordance with the law, and remained open until one to accommodate the Fourth Estate, certain other discreet, and Sergeant O'Shane, who paused at Mr. Brophy's table to exchange the customary:

'Annything new, Misther Brophy?'

'More fighting in Ireland, Sergeant; that's all.'

'And that's not news, Misther Brophy.'

'Dinny,' said Mr. Brophy, when Clancy, himself, had put
down on the bare table a plate of Swiss cheese, rye bread,
and two steins of beer, 'did you ever read Hardy's *Jude the
Obscure?*'

Dinny, his mouth full, shook his head.

'I'll lend it to you,' said Mr. Brophy, taking the book
from his pocket and pushing it across the table.

'Thanks,' mumbled Dinny. 'What's it about?'

Mr. Brophy made up a cheese sandwich, painstakingly.

'It's about a tremendously ambitious youngster who
wanted a college education, so he could be somebody, and
threw a wrench into the machine by marrying out of his
class.'

'And so he didn't get to be anybody?'

'He didn't even get a college education.'

'Why do you want me to read it, Mr. Brophy?'

Mr. Brophy shrugged a shoulder.

'It will do you good to get acquainted with Thomas
Hardy... vigorous style... sound workman.'

In bed, now, with the book, Dinny became absorbed in
the tribulations of Jude's boyhood — strikingly like his

own, in spots. He read until four, lowered the book, stared for a long time at the wall, sighed deeply, and turned out the light. It had been a long day. Dinny had grown much older, since sunrise.

CHAPTER VIII

MAGNOLIA students, unable to return to their homes, were welcome to the seven o'clock dinner at the President's house on Christmas.

That no bones were made about the purely philanthropic nature of this affair was blandly certified by the technique of recruiting its guests. The bulletin boards, a few days in advance, announced that if these stranded would make themselves known to the Y.M. and Y.W. secretaries, they would receive personal invitations.

It was easily to be deduced, from the character of the agencies thus serving as a clearing-house for this social function, that its guest-list would consist largely if not wholly of barbs; for, almost without exception, the fraternity and sorority element had no truck with the Y.M. or Y.W. beyond the dollar perfunctorily disgorged during the early October campaign for their maintenance. The Greeks were not, as a rule, religious.

Tradition held that these Yuletide festivities, however praiseworthy in their altruistic intent, lacked brilliance. Indeed, when a seasoned Magnolian — whether Greek or barbarian — was hard pressed for a simile adequate to bound some experience of boredom *in extremis*, he was apt to liken it to the Braithwaites' Christmas Party, even if he had never attended one himself and might have added but little to its incandescence if he had.

Dinny had missed the affair, a year ago, truthfully offering the excuse — though he could have invented one — that he was obliged to work at that hour.

Nothing was more remote from his intention than attendance at this year's Christmas conviviality in the big, square, dormer-windowed, brick house which dominated this end of Sunnyside Avenue, dignifiedly aloof from the long row of Greek chapter houses — for it was set in spacious grounds

— but obviously mothering them and sharing with them the same Strozzi lamp-posts in the broad green parking, four to the block, on either side, as if the Old Lady, upon installing hers, had said they might as well provide similarly for the children.

But it now turned out that Dinny was to be one of the guests at the annual barbarian spread.

Encountering President Braithwaite, whom he sincerely admired, Dinny impulsively pledged himself to attend the feast. They had met in the almost deserted hall of the Administration Building on the morning of the twenty-second. The college session had closed.

'Not going home, Brumm?'

'No, sir; not this time, sir.'

Dinny did not feel it necessary to add that he was done going home; never expected to go home again; had, in fact, no home to go to since the receipt of Angela's astounding letter, a month ago, easing her burdened soul of a confession that, while rummaging in her father's desk, she had discovered evidences of long-continued misappropriation of funds rightfully Dinny's — a defalcation in which Aunt Martha was a silent but culpable accomplice. Angela, deeply stirred in a revival staged by the celebrated 'Buster' Brown and the incomparable song-leader, 'Merry' Merriweather, had experienced 'the third work' — an altitudinous degree of sanctification involving the wholesale confession of sins, venial and mortal, in which salutary enterprise she had, after a manner of speaking, spilled the beans.

'The money,' wrote Angela, in an affected back-hand on reeking pink paper, 'must have stopped coming about two years ago.

'I think my father must have begun to be scared, about that time. Your father probably wanted to arrange to send you to college, though I couldn't find that letter in the package.

'The only one on that was dated more than two years

ago. It was written on a New York Central train. It said, " If it is true my son has no inclination to go to college and has a good job and bitterly resents any further help from me, there is nothing more to do."'

Savage with indignation, Dinny rapidly composed and destroyed a half-dozen letters — three to the rascally old Uncle Miles; two, slightly less ironical, to pious Aunt Martha; concluding with a real masterpiece of shocking sacrilege to the thrice-blest Angela. Having thus documented his sentiments in regard to the elementary decencies, and the mysterious ways of Providence in delegating the propagation of sweetness and light to ambassadors so nonchalant on the subject of common integrity, he screwed the cap back on his fountain-pen, and called it a day's work.

Presuming, correctly, that Angela's purgation demanded her having it out with Uncle Miles and Aunt Martha, Dinny thought he would wait until these unctuous defaulters had had time to concoct some ingenious explanation. But they, judging by their silence, were waiting for his offensive; so, communication was cut off. As Christmas neared, it occurred to him that, aside from the greeting cards he meant to mail to Mr. Brophy, old Peter Andrews, and the Fagans (whom he rarely visited now, Kitty having impatiently transferred her affections to young Mike Slattery, a handsome and promising department manager in the Crystal Laundry), he had no occasion for shopping. Dinny hoped Aunt Martha would not trouble herself to send him anything. But it would be quite like her to do so — a sappy book of preachments, perhaps, written, published, and peddled by the Reverend Bouncing Bilgewater, or some such moron.

'Then you will be coming to our Christmas dinner,' said the President, genially.

'Oh, yes, sir,' declared Dinny, with grateful enthusiasm, 'Thank you very much, Doctor Braithwaite.'

Almost from his first day, Dinny had found himself wondering how little Magnolia, so narrow and reactionary, had invited a man of President Braithwaite's broad sympathies and urbanity to direct her affairs. And how had Doctor Braithwaite ever persuaded himself to lead a cause so unpromising?

It was common knowledge on the campus — even the freshmen chattered it — that the President was in hot water, the conservatives furnishing the fuel. The President had been elected for his skill as a money-getter. But for that he would have been ousted long ago. But for that he would never have been called from the Financial Secretaryship of little Minton, in Wisconsin, a despairing toy college that he had rescued from the grave. Minton had called him to that job in the very nick of time to save him from a heresy trial at the instigation of his Conference. As a minister, he had been too modern, nobody but the young people following him.

'Everybody knows ——' Orville Kling, still Dinny's dormitory neighbor, and now President of the Y., had come over, last week, to borrow a pot of mucilage; for, as Religious Editor of *The Blossom*, he was always out of paste. 'Everybody knows,' declaimed Kling, fresh from a meeting of his cabinet, in which Doctor Braithwaite had been put in the pan, 'that he's an out-and-out higher critic!'

'Critic of what?' inquired Dinny, absently, intent on the trail of an irregular verb in his Greek lexicon, 'Critic of *what?*' he repeated, 'and higher than *who?*'

'You wait! ——'

Disdaining the persiflage, Kling slowly closed one eye and tipped his head far back, hinting at inside information he dared not reveal.

'You just wait until Braithwaite has finished this two-year drive for the Half-Million Endowment Fund. The Board will give him his walking papers!'

'Not very sporting, I should say,' observed Dinny.

Kling hooked a leg over the corner of Dinny's table, rested an elbow on his knee, and beat time to his oracle with an impressive forefinger.

'The conservation of Christian faith,' he intoned, 'is not a sporting proposition.'

'I had noticed that,' drawled Dinny, not very pleasantly.

'What I say is,' continued Kling, warming, 'if Braithwaite wants to make a dash for this so-called liberty of religious thought, let him do it — but not while he's on the payroll of an orthodox institution.'

'Like Martin Luther, for instance?' queried Dinny.

'That's quite a different matter,' growled Kling, pacing to the window and backing up defensively against the sill, 'Luther, as it happened, was right!'

'But the conservatives didn't think so,' amended Dinny, 'or did they? I'm not very well posted on that.'

'No — I don't suppose you are,' muttered Kling, meaningly, 'though you ought to be, considering your background.'

Dinny impetuously pushed back his chair, and was on the point of offering a sarcastic discrimination between 'back-ground' and 'back-fire,' but thought better of it, and turned again to his lexicon.

Kling strode heatedly toward the door.

'Here,' said Dinny, 'you've forgotten the mucilage.'

'Thanks,' said Kling, stiffly, 'I think I can find some.'

'Sure you can find your scissors?' teased Dinny, grinning.

'I suppose you think that's witty, son.' Kling had his hand on the knob.

'I think it's a scream, Brother Kling,' retorted Dinny, '*all of it!* — the Board of Directors, Christian faith, home background, the Y.M.C.A., *The Blossom's* Religious Column, and — and the paste-pot and the scissors! ——'

The door banged with a resounding wallop.

'——and you, too,' finished Dinny, addressing the infuriated footsteps in the hall. 'You're a scream, too!'

* * * * * *

At three, still uncomfortable over his promise to attend

the Christmas party, which was going to be dull with an exceeding great dullness, no matter how the Braithwaites might tear their hair to make it interesting, Dinny went skating in the park.

There was nothing he enjoyed so much. The day was perfect, air crisp, tonic, the sky turquoise, the sun bright.

He recognized no one on the pond, but it required no company to complete his satisfaction.

With long, lazy strokes, he traversed the quarter-mile longitudinal stretch of the steel-blue lagoon, delighting in the ease of a locomotion that always gave him the sensation of flying. There was a unique exhilaration in the ability to let oneself go; to lean back confidently on the promise of that strange centrifugal energy developed by 'the outer edge roll' — a confidence more exacting, and better rewarded, than the faith of the floating swimmer.

He glanced without much interest at the indifferent skaters as he swept past them. Most of them were huddled in small parties, hacking away with short, stumbling steps, what time they were not clawing at each other for support, or spilling themselves, or shrieking hysterically over the misfortunes of their neighbors, or fussing with their straps. Magnolia was a bit too far south to breed able ice-skaters.

Presently Dinny sighted a tall girl, apparently alone, who knew what she was there for. My word! — what a competent young eagle she was! He wheeled, and followed her at a respectful distance.

She was slender, but beautifully formed; exquisite from the top of the brown fur toque that matched her curly hair to the flashing blades of the high-laced skating-boots which intriguingly disclosed attractive segments of gleaming silk between them and the short brown skirt. Her gauntleted hands — long, strong hands — were outspread at the tops of her hips as if they signaled the measured strokes like a coxswain. She clasped them behind her back, now, as if they had nothing whatever to do with it.

The girl had leisurely slowed down, at the end of the pond, finishing the lap with a series of incomparable 'eights.'

Observing that she was quite absorbed in her own affairs, Dinny did not linger to join the admiring circle that collected rapidly to view her skillful maneuvers, but drifted negligently away toward the farther end of the lagoon. Turning, there, he noticed with satisfaction that she had detached herself from her little theater and was again on more extensive flights. He hoped she would come on. Pursuing a small orbit, in reverse, Dinny waited. His heart gave a hard bump as she swept closer. Her face was radiant with vitality — a patrician face, thought Dinny; a portrait face, finely modeled brows, sensitive nostrils, red lips curved like the bent bow of a medieval arbalest. Little curls peeped from under the fur toque, softening the lines of a gallant forehead.

She smiled, as one artist to another.

'Very good ice,' she said, casually, in a tone that made Dinny think, if she sang — and surely she did — it would be contralto.

'You skate beautifully,' said Dinny.

Her slightly raised brows and parted lips accepted the candid tribute.

'You should know,' she replied.

'But you didn't learn it in Magnolia,' Dinny hazarded, flushed a little by her bland compliment. He held out his hands, invitingly.

'Shall we?'

'Why not? I'd like to.'

She had hardly consented before they were beginning to drift, crossed hands clasped, into a long, indolent roll that inclined their tall, lithe forms so far off balance none but the expert could have trusted to it.

Their wake was a double row of graceful fern-fronds, laid down almost end to end on the glassy lagoon. At first the fronds were twenty feet long and sixteen inches apart. Then they lengthened to thirty feet and narrowed to thirteen inches, for Dinny had drawn her closer, and she had instantly responded.

They moved as one body, their rhythm perfect. Sometimes the long twin fronds seemed pointing directly toward a mighty collision with a group of wobbly-ankled gigglers; but, without signaling each other by so much as a pressure of the fingers, the welded pair of ice-artists would bend the arc of the fronds and sail past with the grace of a yacht acknowledging the sudden puff of a capricious breeze. Preferring to sense to the full the ecstasy of reckless swallows, they had not attempted conversation, but their thoughts had been active.

It had required no deduction on Joan's part to identify her overtowering companion as a Magnolia athlete, for there was a huge pink *M* on his white sweater. Dinny was still in the dark, his curiosity mounting.

'What's the letter about?' she asked, when they idled to the first stop at the eastern end of the pond where they had met.

'Football — but this is a lot more fun, don't you think?'

'Yes,' she laughed, 'but I never played football.... You must live here — or you would have started home.'

'No,' replied Dinny, 'do you?'

'Yes... Are you coming to our Christmas party?'

'I certainly am!' said Dinny, fervently. 'Whose party?'

'I'm Joan Braithwaite.'

'I should have known,' said Dinny. 'But you're always away. University of Wisconsin — isn't it?... I'm Ferdinand Brumm, Miss Braithwaite.'

'Oh!' Joan's pretty mouth rounded in happy surprise. 'So you're the lad that galloped the sixty yards with all Camford hanging on to you! I read about it.... You're "Dinny"!'

'Thanks!... But it was only the last three or four yards that they all got on.... Like to do it some more?'

'How many of them were there — actually?' laughed Joan, taking his proffered hands.

'I believe they had eleven on their team, that day,' said Dinny, thoughtfully. 'It may have been a few more. Camford is frightfully unscrupulous, you know.'

They chatted, amiably.

Yes — she loved Wisconsin, but her father was insisting on her coming to Magnolia, next year. Dinny expressed his sincere regrets.

'I mean, of course,' he amended, 'I'm sorry for *you*, having to leave your friends... and Magnolia will be quite a change, you know.... Not much doing here.'

'Oh, I won't mind — much,' said Joan; adding, after a considerable pause, 'The Gammas gave a nice party for me, last night — that's my sorority, you know.... By the way — where were *you?*'

'I'm a barb,' drawled Dinny.

'Oh... I didn't know.... Pardon me, won't you?' She endeavored to cover her confusion with a contrite little laugh as she added, 'I didn't know the — the non-fraternity men called *themselves* "barbs."... I thought they quite bitterly resented the word.'

'Why should they?' asked Dinny, dryly. 'We know that when the fraternity men call us "barbs," it's just a bit of friendly chaffing — same as when we call them "Greeks." We haven't the courage and vitality to be barbarians, and they don't know any Greek. Why — if their badges weren't of different shapes and colors, they'd never know when they met a brother.'

'Frightfully satirical, aren't you?' Joan's tone was crisp.

'It's the best thing I do,' boasted Dinny, in mock seriousness. 'I've been commended for it by Professor Grover, a couple of times. In fact, he gave me *E*, last semester, in Creative Composition. *E* stands for Excellent, doesn't it?'

'Oh, yes,' consented Joan, 'and it stands for some other things — when it's grading satire and sarcasm.'

The twin fronds on the ice behind them widened a little.

'What — for instance?' Dinny wanted to know.

'No matter,' said Joan, idly. 'Forget it.'

'But I quite insist. You had something you wanted to say.'

'I'm afraid it isn't very polite,' ventured Joan, 'but doesn't *E* stand for Enraged — and Embattled — and Embarrassed — and ——'

'And — what? ——'

'Envious.'

'You're quite frank,' said Dinny, after an instant of recovery.

'Well — you would have it, you know.... I told you I didn't like irony.'

'But — you like humor, don't you?... and if there's anything funnier than a bunch of college students taking on airs because they're "Greeks," I'm sure I don't know what it is. You'd think they would tumble all over themselves getting into old man Appleton's classes. We barbs have Homer all to ourselves. Oddly enough, old Appleton is a barb, himself!'

Joan disengaged her hands, a little before they reached the end of the pond. Her face showed disappointment.

'Does it make you happy,' she asked, soberly looking him straight in the eyes — 'to be... that way?'

'I've had very little occasion to be happy,' parried Dinny.

'You mean here?... at Magnolia?'

'I mean everywhere... and always,' said Dinny, suddenly sincere. 'If I were to tell you ——'

'Do you want to?' Joan's tone deepened, and her dark brown eyes searched his rugged face.

'No,' he answered, brusquely, adding, suddenly contrite, 'Thank you — all the same. I think I'd — I wouldn't mind telling you — if it weren't such a dull story.'

They simultaneously felt that their little visit was over. Joan glanced at her wrist-watch. Dinny squinted at the declining sun.

She reached out her hand.

'I'll be seeing you, then, on Christmas?' she said.

Dinny felt very lonely as she glided away. She was the most superb creature he had ever seen.

* * * * * *

President and Mrs. Braithwaite were warmly effusive as they welcomed him in the wide doorway of their spacious parlor.

Joan was standing a little to one side, within the room, talking animatedly with Barney Vaughn, who seemed in unusually high spirits. Dinny had forgotten that Barney, who had passed a dozen universities en route from Phoenix, Arizona, to Magnolia — to the never-flagging curiosity of all, unaware that his father was a Magnolian — might be a guest tonight.

He had not talked with Barney since last May. They had briefly informed each other about the weather, when they happened to pass on the street, unless they sighted each other early enough for one of them to cross over and avoid even this laconic exchange of cool civilities.

The constraint that stiffened their previously close friendship dated from Dinny's refusal to become a Sig.

The Sigs had not bidden him promptly. Within a week after his first appearance on the athletic field, the Delts had spent two hours with him, reciting the honored names of alumni (none of them Magnolians, as it happened) who had gone forth to hold aloft the good old banner, and the Pies had offered to share their refined salt, but he had politely declined. Barney had urged him to wait.

The Sigs were a good while getting around to it. His work at *The Star* kept him occupied, and made it difficult for him to be sociable. The preliminary overtures of the Sigs were made somewhat listless by the fact, which developed in casual conversation when Barney had him in as his luncheon guest, that he would be unable to conform to many of their regulations for the disciplining of 'the frosh.' The Custer Cottage was already crowded to capacity with their pledges.

The bid was not issued until early December, Dinny learning, later, through an outburst of confidence on the part of Barney, who had had it from Curly Sprague, a soph, that Spike Davis had held out for some time, threatening to blackball Dinny, if it came to a vote. Spike had been talked into consent on the night after the Thanksgiving game with Camford in which, as fullback, he had kicked the goal that tied the score and rent the sky. He was feeling very much at peace with all mankind, and a bit drunk; so he waived his objections, and agreed to Dinny's election.

Dinny was unsure whether he wanted to accept the belated invitation. He confided his dilemma to Mr. Brophy, one night.

'You'd better, I think,' counseled Mr. Brophy. 'Otherwise you're rated a barb, and that will be awkward for you, not only while you're in college, but — always.'

So — Dinny had accepted the little button symbolic of the tardy honor the Sigs conferred, and merged into the pack, to his considerable inconvenience, for the new relationship levied irksome requirements. He bolted his six-thirty dinner at 'th' House,' dashed for a street-car, and arrived at *The Star* usually ten minutes late, requiring double-measure overtime at his own expense. He never had time to eat a dessert, except on Saturday.

The fraternities initiated their freshmen during the first week of June. The Sigs did not initiate Dinny.

Each candidate, according to custom, was assigned a special test of his nerve, or an earnest of his eagerness to become a Greek. Barney was to stand in front of The Palace Theater, one night, from eight to eight-thirty, with a hand-organ and a monkey — a salutary lesson in humility, though he had been cuffed about almost enough to have cured him of any uppishness. Chuck Rawlins was to present, on the occasion of his initiation, a live sparrow, the Sigs offering no suggestions for its capture, but insisting that his approach to the classic shrine, minus a live sparrow, would be undesired. Porky Bennet was to attend the Pan-

Sorority tea, that afternoon, as Carmen, the Sigs volunteering to furnish the tambourine from their property closet.

Spike Davis was chairman of the committee on initiation. Most of the stunts had required no imagination on his part, having been bequeathed, through many generations of Hellenic forbears.

Dinny's special assignment had cost Spike several contemplative hours. Cocky young Brumm had taken his honors too lightly; had dodged too many disciplines on the ground of his employment in town. Furthermore — though this factor Spike would have denied with fists and fangs — Dinny had played exceptionally good football at fullback on the frosh team. The local sports writers had made no riddle of their belief and hope that next fall, when he was eligible, he would add luster to the varsity. Even Woods, reviewing the season in *The Cincinnati Times-Telegram* (recently popularized and circulation-boosted through its absorption by The Craig Syndicate), had remarked, of next year's prospects, 'Magnolia has an excellent chance at the Conference pennant, what with her strong line, and the long-legged Dinny Brumm, who will have reached the age of responsibility.'

All these things being as they were, Spike had something unique for Dinny to do as proof that he was worthy to wear a Sig pin.

'What's eatin' you, Spike?'... 'You can't have him do that!'... 'Snap out of it, old son. That's much too thick.' Thus did the seniors try to talk him out of it. But Spike held his ground. It was his show, wasn't it? He was running this affair, wasn't he? Brumm had it all coming to him, didn't he?

Dinny was to carry a football under his arm, to all his classes, for a week. It was to be the one monumental pigskin on which Jim Faucett, the frosh captain, had vaingloriously inked the scores of their games with other classes — most of which triumphs had been freely conceded to Dinny's fleetness and ruthlessness at fullback.

'I can't do that, Spike.' Dinny shook his head, determinedly.

'Very well,' said Spike, loftily. 'That's that, then! If you want to be a Sig, you know what you've got to do. Think it over.'

Barney Vaughn came to Dinny's room, that afternoon, troubled.

'Dinny — you've got to, you know,' pleaded Barney. 'They've talked to him, but he won't budge.'

Dinny sat toying with a paper-knife, his brows knitted in a brown study.

'He told me to find you.' Barney's voice trembled a little. 'And come back with an immediate reply.'

Dinny rose, presently, tossed the paper-knife on the desk with a clatter, thrust his hands deep into his trouser pockets.

'No, Barney; there isn't anybody at Magnolia who can give me such an order — and if there was anybody who could, it wouldn't be Spike Davis.'

'But ——' Barney was half-frantic. 'What am I to do? ... What shall I tell him?'

Dinny took the little button from his lapel, laid it in Barney's hand, and said, slowly, but without heat:

'You can give this to Spike, with my compliments, and tell him to go to hell.'

'Do you realize, Dinny, what this is going to do to our friendship — no matter how I feel about it, personally?'

'I'm afraid I do,' muttered Dinny. 'That's the worst part of it, of course.'

'Want to sleep over it?'

'No — that's final. I shan't change my mind.'

'Awfully sorry, Dinny.... Good-bye.'

* * * * * *

Mrs. Braithwaite, buxom, black-gowned, maternal, proceeded to adopt Dinny, who had been the last to arrive, engaging him in a conversation which she endeavored to pivot around himself, somewhat to his anxiety, for any discussion of his home and his people was distasteful.

Joan and Barney had moved away, joining the group clustered about Miss Gresley, whose parents were missionaries in India. She would rejoin them, after her graduation in June. Miss Gresley was always an object of interest, frequently appearing at missionary teas and church affairs in Hindu costume which became her more than the clothes she wore now.

Dinny wanted very much to speak to Joan; hoped she would presently welcome him. But dinner was announced at that moment. Tall, genial, handsome Doctor Braithwaite excused himself to find Miss Gresley, who, as the farthest away from home, was clearly eligible to sit at her host's right hand.

'I am going to take you with me, Mr. Brumm,' said Mrs. Braithwaite. Dinny offered his arm.

It was not until they were all standing with their hands on the tops of their chairs, waiting for whatever of ceremony was in order, that Dinny noticed the position of Joan at the right of Barney, who sat next to Miss Gresley. Their eyes met, briefly, and Joan accorded him a little nod of recognition.

The President suggested that they sing a verse of 'Holy Night,' after which they sat, fully three fourths of the score of shy guests immediately and concertedly helping themselves to a nervous sip of water, as if to say that they knew what *that* was for, anyway, whatever baffling dishes might challenge their social experience later.

'You met our Joan, didn't you, Mr. Brumm?' Mrs. Braithwaite had dipped a spoon into her fruit cocktail. 'She told me. So nice you could skate together. She quite enjoyed it. See — she's looking this way now ——'

Dinny glanced in Joan's direction, not quite sure whether the smile was for him or her mother. Barney, at the moment, was speaking to Miss Gresley.

'Of course you know Mr. Vaughn. You are classmates,

aren't you? Joan met him, last night, at the Gammas' reception. I'm so anxious for Joan to make some good friends, for she's coming to Magnolia, next year. Her sorority sisters were so kind to her, last night.'

'Yes — they would be, I should think,' assented Dinny, hopeful that the conversation might soon veer away from the reception. Apparently it occurred to his hostess, at that moment, that Hellenic activities might not be of interest to him.

'The Y.M. and Y.W. have just lovely parties, too,' she said, 'don't you think?'

'So I'm told,' replied Dinny, in a tone that evinced about as much personal knowledge as if she had remarked on the exceptionally large pineapple crop grown last season on the Island of Oahu.

'You're a naughty boy,' chided Mrs. Braithwaite, smiling. 'I don't believe you go to them, at all, and they're really very pleasant affairs.'

'I work nights, Mrs. Braithwaite,' explained Dinny; and, when she had inquired for particulars, he told her, their conversation broken, now and then, by her brief exchange of talk with Orville Kling — though he was mostly occupied with Miss Naylor, the Y.W. secretary — and Dinny's futile efforts to find some mutual interest with sallow, little Miss Upton. His eyes roved about the table, and when he reached Joan, they exchanged a steady look of inquiry, as if she still asked, 'Does it make you happy — to be — that way?'... and as if he countered, 'Why should you care?'

'But you have almost no social life at all, Mr. Brumm,' lamented Mrs. Braithwaite. 'What a pity you are tied up to such an exacting schedule.'

'It's no great matter, Mrs. Braithwaite.' Dinny lightly dismissed the dilemma with a slight shrug. 'I rather enjoy my work on *The Star*. And — as for society — well, I'm not eligible to it, you see. As a matter of fact' — he lowered his voice, confidentially — 'I came into this town in a day coach.'

Mrs. Braithwaite laughed a little, glanced about the table, fleetingly, and replied, 'But so did most of us, I fancy.'

'I dare say,' agreed Dinny; adding, 'You understand.' Again his eyes wandered toward Joan, who met him with a level gaze that continued to ask, 'Does it make you happy?——'

'I do understand,' said Mrs. Braithwaite, as if they were done with riddles, 'and I'm sorry, and something ought to be done about it — but I'm sure I don't know what.'

After dinner, Kling announced — bouncing up and down on his experienced toes — that, at the request of the President, they would sing a few songs. Miss Noble, invited to the grand piano, carefully put her handkerchief down on the ledge of the key-board, and accompanied 'On, Magnolia,' to Kling's encouraging direction, all joining with loyal enthusiasm. Then they sang 'America,' with unusual heartiness, for patriotism was in the air, and 'God Save the King,' as a second verse, for the 'neutrality' of early autumn had been buried under the falling leaves and the snow. Kling suggested 'The Marseillaise,' which they hummed, uncertainly, no one knowing the words very well.

Dinny was not quite sure which wing of the party he belonged to, after the dinner. Mrs. Braithwaite had signed him to remain by her, just a little to his discomfiture, for perhaps she was making an effort to pay him special attention, in atonement for the indifference of her sort toward the social redemption of day-coachers. But Dinny felt remote. On the other side of her, the President, Joan, and Barney represented the kindly condescending element that viewed the party as finely bred settlement workers look on at the games promoted for the uplift of slum brats.

In all fairness, Dinny reflected that he was supersensitive on this subject; told himself that what appeared to be conscious superiority on their part was nothing but an acknowledged inferiority of his own. But the situation was awkward, and he wished himself well out of it. He felt like an overgrown child, sitting with adults, at a children's party.

Kling, who appeared to be the spokesman for the guests, ventured upon a little speech of gratitude on behalf of them all. Pleased with the success of his remarks, he pulled out the tremolo stop, and, gradually increasing the tempo of his teetering up and down, jambed his stubby hands deeply into his coat pockets, achieving the posture and meter that presaged an early outburst of emotion.... Of course, none of us was forgetting, in the midst of our Christmas gayety, the bereavement and suffering of our hard-pressed neighbors beyond the sea, waging valiant warfare to protect civilization against the ruthless selfishness of The Hun.... Kling was roundly applauded.

'Terrible — isn't it?' Mrs. Braithwaite turned to Dinny, her brows knitted in painful reflection.

'You mean the war?'

'You're a bad boy,' said Mrs. Braithwaite, reproachfully.

Kling now suggested that they have a few words from the President, and sat down, smiling expectantly.

Doctor Braithwaite rose, rather soberly, thanked them for coming, invited them to drop in when they liked, through the lonely vacation days.... It was true, as Mr. Kling had indicated, that our happiness should be tempered with sympathy for the millions defending themselves in an unnecessary war. We would be justified in extending sympathy, also, to the millions who, through no fault of their own, were being pushed into a conflict, as aggressors, for which they had no personal inclination.

'The thing we want to avoid — or postpone as long as possible — is the attitude of hatred toward the Germans,' went on Doctor Braithwaite, deeply earnest. 'Germany has contributed too much to the enlightenment and beautification of the world to be dismissed, lightly, as an enemy of civilization.... These lurid tales of atrocities may, or may not, be true. I, for one, do not believe them!'

Dinny pounded his hands, the others tardily and rather doubtfully joining in the applause for politeness' sake.

'I see you agree with Doctor Braithwaite — about the war,' said his hostess, upon the conclusion of the President's brief address. 'It's not the popular thing, I'm afraid.'

'I'd agree with Doctor Braithwaite — no matter what he said!' declared Dinny, fervently. 'He's always right — and I know he's right about this.'

'Thank you, Dinny!' she said, softly, adding, 'You won't mind if I call you "Dinny"?... I'm afraid Mr. Braithwaite will find only a minority willing to share his views.'

'He doesn't need to care — a man like him!' declared Dinny, with assurance.

Mrs. Braithwaite shook her head, uneasily.

'People are growing more and more militant,' she said.

The party was breaking up, now. The Braithwaites attended to their duties as hosts. Joan was shaking hands with the girls, as they filed out and up the stairs to recover their coats. Barney had escaped. He and Dinny had not exchanged a dozen words.

'Going up the hill?' inquired Kling, breezily, still under the influence of his success as an impromptu speaker.

Dinny assented, without enthusiasm.

Joan moved toward him, her eyes troubled. Overriding the antagonism that had developed between them there was a curious intimacy in their attitude as he bent to listen to her swiftly spoken confidence. It was as if they had known and trusted each other for years.

'Don't say or do anything to encourage my father in his — his attempt at suicide!' pleaded Joan. 'He's dead wrong, and he's going to get into trouble! Don't lead any more applause that might make him think he has backing. Please!'

'How do you know he's wrong?' Dinny's gray-green eyes challenged her brown ones with a steady look.

'Indiscreet, then,' she compromised, impatiently. 'My

father —— ' Joan lowered her voice almost to a whisper. 'My father has quite enough problems on his hands, just now, without incurring any more. You like him, don't you?'

'More than any man I ever met!' said Dinny, with fervor.

'Well — so do I,' murmured Joan, 'and I'm not going to let him ruin himself if I can help it.'

Dinny offered his hand.

'Good-night — Miss Braithwaite.... Sorry my little gesture of loyalty to your father has distressed you.'

Joan's brown eyes fired, angrily.

'I don't like sarcasm,' she muttered, 'and I think you're perfectly hateful, Dinny Brumm!'

Dinny's hand was still extended. She seemed determined to ignore it. Her hot eyes winked rapidly as she faced the faint traces of a conciliatory smile — half-reproach, half-indulgence — on Dinny's lips.

Impetuously, she took his hand, for a fleeting instant, and turned away.

* * * * * *

'What did I tell you?' exhorted Kling, as they trudged up the slope toward the dormitory. 'The man's positively dangerous! You'll find' — Kling measured his syllables with a didactic hand — 'that when a man's religious faith breaks down, it isn't long until his patriotism isn't much good, either!'

'Looks like it's going to snow again,' observed Dinny, with exasperating unconcern.

'And *you* want to be careful, too, young fellow,' warned Kling, ominously.

'Meaning *what?*' growled Dinny, dangerously, with a savage clutch at Kling's sleeve that flung him almost off his feet.

Amazed at this unexpected onslaught, Kling was speechless for a moment, and then said, nervously, 'I'm not going to fight you, Dinny, if that's what you want.'

'Oh — so you are a pacifist, after all,' taunted Dinny. 'Well — you needn't fight, this time, if the idea of it alarms you, or violates your convictions; but' — he clutched Kling's overcoat collar in the strong grip of his long fingers — 'if I ever hear of you dishing out any more of your damned impudence about Doctor Braithwaite — ever again — in public or private — I'll beat hell out of you, whether you defend yourself or not! Have you got that, now, so you can remember it?'

He left Kling standing there on the path.

Without turning, he proceeded on up the hill, climbed to his room, slammed the door, disrobed, and wrote two letters, the second addressed to the Reverend Miles Brumm.

Dear Sir:

I have instructed the Speedway Moving and Storage Company of Indianapolis to call at your address for a small walnut desk of mine, formerly the property of my mother.

You will be good enough to let the moving people have the desk for immediate shipment to me, at my expense.

This, I think, will terminate our business and other relationships.

Any fear you may entertain relative to the possibility of an effort on my part to recover the money you stole from me, can be safely dismissed.

In view of the fact that my contempt for Mr. Alexander Craig is all of a piece with my contempt for you, I would not press the claim.

No reply to this letter is expected or desired.

Yours truly
FERDINAND BRUMM

CHAPTER IX

MAGNOLIA COLLEGE was considered good copy during the academic year of 1915-16.

It was a period when any recognition on the front page, crowded with heavy artillery, marine disasters, massacres of millions, and the multisonous clangor of a world on fire, required more racket than small church schools were accustomed to add to the cosmic din.

Even the Associated Press, sated with sensation, conceded, at the close of her second semester, that Magnolia — for sixty-three placid years an earnest little violet, staking her last shy petal on the nobility of diffidence — had done her bit in leaded black-face.

In the fall, Magnolia spectacularly won nine smashing victories on the gridiron with scores that dizzied her competitors, no one of whom got within ten yards of her goal-line. Egged on by sports writers, she tentatively booked an exhibition game with Harvard to be played the next September, an engagement which was canceled in the spring, Harvard having lost interest, Magnolia having lost Dinny Brumm.

On New Year's Eve, the Recitation Hall burned to the ground, unquestionably the work of an incendiary, public opinion agreeing that some ardent 'preparedness' fanatic had thus expressed his sentiments toward a college so spiritless as to permit an uncompromising pacifist to direct her destiny.

On March tenth, the most widely known member of the undergraduate body, whose long legs and reckless courage had been primarily responsible for Magnolia's brilliant achievements in football, was expelled for adorning the President of the college Y.M.C.A. with two black eyes and a split lip.

The prosecution, appealing to the increasingly popular

cause of patriotism, made large capital of the fact that the plaintiff had come by his injuries as a result of an impassioned address in behalf of his country's injured pride. The defendant's spirit of disloyalty was further evidenced by the recent appearance of his article in *The Iconoclast*, a discordant organ of protest, in which the author had heaped contumely upon his Alma Mater, and shown a disposition to bite the hand that fed him.

The defense endeavored to show that the attack on Mr. Kling's person was an honest, albeit overenthusiastic, reprisal for certain damaging remarks made in reference to Doctor Braithwaite. It further ventured to prove, politely as the circumstances permitted, that the statements of Mr. Brumm in *The Iconoclast* — though admittedly phrased in the pardonable superlatives of rampant youth — were unfortunately true.

The faculty jury, Professor Grover, chairman, was out only five minutes.

Had it been Kling who was being fired, the press might have passed over the matter with negligent observation. The expulsion of Dinny Brumm was quite another affair. *The Cincinnati Times-Telegram*, in particular, wanted to know all about it, and set forth Dinny's cause with so much unction that the Magnolia Board of Directors was deluged with letters and telegrams inquiring, in varying degrees of indignation, whether the college had lost her mind.

On March thirteenth, a student mass-meeting was held. The use of the college chapel — Magnolia's only adequate assembly hall — having been denied for this purpose, the auditorium of the City Building was secured. Unwittingly, the promoters of the event thus recruited not only the attendance of almost the entire student body (the Sigs refusing to participate), but augmented the audience by several hundreds of interested towns-people whose concern for Magnolia's welfare was largely based on her athletic activities.

Mightily cheered and heartened from the packed galleries, which included not only ardent football fans with nothing at stake beyond their own enjoyment, but anxious representatives of the Chamber of Commerce, the Better Business Association, and scores of influential resident alumni, the undergraduates, after an accelerating tempest of fervid oratory, voted as one man for the rescinding of the faculty's action and a prompt reinstatement of Dinny Brumm.

A few of the more audacious wanted a trailer affixed to the peremptory resolution, threatening a general strike in the event of refusal on the part of the faculty to conform to student opinion. This, however, was voted down, the Magnolians, as a whole, recovering their habitual prudence even in the tumult of revolution vociferously fanned by the town.

On March twentieth, after an all-night session of the faculty and the Board of Directors, Dinny Brumm was restored to his previous rating. A mild proviso was attached demanding that Mr. Brumm settle for Mr. Kling's personal repairs and the mending of sundry articles of furniture which had impeded the celebrated fullback in his task of chastising his neighbor — it having leaked out that Dinny had already made these reparations.

On March twenty-first, Dinny left Magnolia to accept the position offered him by wire from Mr. Steinberg, the Managing Editor of *The Cincinnati Times-Telegram*.

The Athletic Association, getting wind of Dinny's offer and acceptance, hastily organized plans to see him off with a procession led by the college band, but he had already gone when the committee rushed to his room to disclose the nature of the vindication they had arranged for him; was, in fact, sitting in Mr. Steinberg's office, listening to the latter's expectations of him, at the very moment when the committee was scouring Magnolia in quest of him.

The bone of contention having been thus providentially dragged from the arena, the Board of Directors again assembled to focus its attention upon the President and in-

quire diligently of itself whether, in view of all the controversy stirred by his pacifistic opinions, it might not be better to set him free to preach his unpopular gospel of non-
resistance on his own hook, undetained by any further obligations to the college.

The Board split squarely in two on this issue, the objec-
tors maintaining that a considerable number of important
'prospects' whose contributions to the Endowment Fund
would depend upon the retention of Doctor Braithwaite,
were awaiting the outcome of this affair with a concern that
might affect Magnolia to the tune of a hundred thousand
dollars, or so.

Notwithstanding this meeting was conducted *in camera*,
every member under pledge to give out no interviews, the
discussion, the decision, and the underlying cause thereof,
were good for a first-page column with a throw to three,
next morning, in the public prints.

On May nineteenth, President Braithwaite delivered the
address to the graduating class of the Theological Seminary,
in which he lost the support of the well-to-do conservatives
whose influence had previously fended off the attacks of the
swashbucklers.

Later, at the funeral, it was remarked on all sides that
Doctor Braithwaite was not quite himself while delivering
this 'unfortunate' speech. He should have been in bed; was
running a temperature of 101°.

At the hour, however, no alibis were offered, and the address was judged on its demerits. Doctor Braithwaite proceeded vigorously to reappraise the preacher's job for the
edification of the fledgling prophets.... We were entering
upon a Reformation of the Church comparable to that of
four centuries ago. The bulk of the old beliefs were irrelevant. The oncoming generation would be so disinterested
in them that it would never even glance in their direction.
The old credos were as dead as Queen Anne.... We had done
with musty metaphysics, at least for the epoch with which
we would have to do, and would concern ourselves so ex-

clusively with kinetic energies that speculative philosophy could safely retire to the sanctuary of the museum.... The only service any longer possible for the old theology would be rendered in the capacity of an ancient landmark from which explorers might plat the curve of Christian progress.

The Board went into conference, late that afternoon, and passed a resolution requesting Doctor Braithwaite's resignation. But he was too ill to be handed the document, next morning, for he had developed a grave pneumonia.

On the following Friday, he died. It was quite obvious that the minority who agreed with him would say he died a martyr. It was equally obvious that the majority, who had thrown him out, would refer to him as a sincere, misguided radical whose disaster was easily to be accounted for: he had broken loose from the old moorings. Let this be a lesson.

A few of the elderly invincibles muttered that it was a judgment of God. One bushy-haired apostle, large of lung and expansive of gesture (eight years later elected Sublime Cyclops of the Ku Klux Klan in that region), ventured to preach, the following Sunday, on 'Vengeance is Mine: I will repay, saith the Lord.' Hopeful of riding into public notice on the shoulders of a corpse, he sent his manuscript to *The Star*, which, on the indignant Mr. Brophy's orders, was printed exactly as written, inclusive of all the bad spelling, bad grammar, and bad temper which distinguished it as a flagrant example of passionate ignorance.

It was an eventful year at Magnolia College. Hitherto it had been her proud boast that in her quiet corner she had preserved the faith once delivered to the saints. Having bred no speedy hares, she had gone in for steady tortoises, promising that great merit occasionally accrued through a race won by the plodder whose brilliant competitors had gone to sleep, on the course, overcome by sheer boredom. The highest mark ever accorded the winner of a Rebecca Winters Dutton Medal had been scored by an essay entitled Obscure Martyrs.'

Little Magnolia, in the fierce glare of the spot-light, felt stark naked, and was ashamed.

* * * * * *

But if the college year was a succession of dramatic events so interesting to the public that Magnolia's carryings-on were fetched in, every morning, off forty thousand doorsteps, along with the milk — events in which Dinny Brumm continuously figured either as an active principal or an unwitting accomplice — the season was replete with unpublished episodes vastly more upsetting to this junior's peace of mind.

Having worked full time on *The Star* through the three months' vacation, Dinny's economically administered savings were augmented to the point where he felt safe in launching upon his junior year without a job.

With more leisure in prospect, he had accepted the associate editorship of *The Blossom*.

Had the barbs been able to move concertedly, they might easily have had their way in all the college elections relating to non-academic activities, for they outnumbered the Greeks three to one; but, lacking such unity, they were usually trounced by the sophisticated minority. This time, the Sigs and the Pies had failed to get together on a slate for *The Blossom* staff, each offering a favorite son. The sororities took sides, the Gammas, as usual, lining up with the Sigs, the Lambies throwing their vote to the Pies. The barbs elected their ticket.

Gates, the impecunious senior editor, less concerned about becoming famous as a journalist than for the commercial success of his paper (the staff receiving a modest rake-off, if the year's business justified a bonus), encouraged Dinny to assume unrestricted liberty on the editorial page.

Faithful to its innocuous name, *The Blossom* had ever been a frail and shrinking organism, a mere amplified bulletin of collegiate announcements and uncritical comments. Its platitudinous editorials roused no breeze. Such spoofing as it indulged in usually applied to budding romances on the campus, calfish persiflage worthy of a high-school 'annual.'

Grinning with satisfaction, Dinny milled the college paper into a giant cracker that went off, every Thursday afternoon, with a loud bang. After the first issue, *The Blossom* sold on the news-stands over in town, and was warmly discussed in the faculty meetings. Gates raised his advertising rates on unengaged space.

The Cincinnati Times-Telegram reproduced, in its Sunday supplement, *The Blossom's* first long editorial entitled, 'What Every Freshman Ought to Know.'

Satirically featuring the unsurpassed spirit of friendliness, democracy, and smug insularity of Magnolia College, which rejoiced in its self-containment and its ability to make of its student-body 'one happy little family,' the editorial proceeded to explain the fraternity system for the benefit of bewildered newcomers.

'Less than one fourth of our students,' continued the editorial, 'are domiciled in large, imposing residences on either side of two sacred blocks at the western end of Sunnyside Avenue. Here dwell the Greeks in dignified sequestration from the raucous shouts of the proletariat.

'On each massive front door there are secrets carved in classic Greek, and on each roof is a mortgage presumably printed in the baser argot of the contemporary banking-house.

'You are advised to ask no questions about these institutions or their tenants. If they recognize you as a Greek, they will tell you. In that case, their secrets will be entrusted to you, and you may be assured that they are secrets, and no mistake; for when a senior who knows no Greek confides a Greek secret to a freshman who knows no Greek, it is guaranteed to remain a mystery. You will also be encouraged to carry with you to your ancestral home a generous portion of the venerable mortgage and drape it a-straddle your father's chimney. If he is of a grateful mind, he will realize the honor thus brought to your tribe.

'If, unfortunately, you are not of the stuff instantly identifiable as Hellenic, make no struggle to simulate a virtue which cannot be achieved by personal effort. In almost any pawnshop in town you will see jeweled fraternity badges on exhibition. To purchase and wear one of these emblems would not improve your rating.

'Neither will it aid you, in this endeavor, to enroll in Greek courses with the hope of promoting your eligibility, for the tongue of Olympus is a native gift with our fraternity and sorority people, and you will rarely meet one of them in the inquisitive groups that cluster about the feet of Professor Appleton.

'Pass quickly through the Delphian groves, when you must needs venture upon Sunnyside Avenue, lest you be blasted by anathemas from some Corinthian portico.

'And when — as sometimes happens — you are snubbed and snooted by the Greeks, because you are a barb, if it so be that the gods have blest you with even the atrophied vestigial remains of any sense of humor, permit yourself the luxury of breaking forth with wild spasms of "inextinguishable laughter."

'If you are a co-ed barb, so much the worse for you. It ill becomes a girl to be a barbarian. You are not built for it. Submissively accept your unkindly fate. Defer to your more sophisticated sisters when you encounter them on the campus. Step off the path, and humbly address them in their own language. Many of them have never learned to speak English correctly, and it will be a pleasant courtesy if you salute them in Greek.

'While it may be superfluous, perhaps impertinent, to suggest a suitable amenity, *The Blossom* will cheerfully furnish upon request, a brief salutation to be employed on such occasions. We do not guarantee, however, to provide applicants with the English translation.'

* * * * * *

Of all the people who relished Dinny Brumm's sour diatribe, nobody more keenly enjoyed it than Professor Ernst Martin, for eighteen years master of Geology, Archæology, Anthropology, and sundry other brittles.

Professor Martin's odd gait, due to a club foot, and amazing tricks of facial expression, acquired through diligent dealing with a stammering tongue — (sometimes he hung on a dead center in the middle of a sentence, and whistled himself out of it, to the utter devastation of persons unacquainted with his slight disability) — amply explained why, at fifty-two, he was a dry old bachelor.

Long-time faculty wives could well remember when 'Ernie' had laid frank and futile siege to every good-looking girl within hobbling distance.

Convinced, at length, that he was at his best when in pursuit of inorganic objects of nature, Professor Martin had reluctantly renounced romance in so far as it related to himself, but he had never relaxed his interest in the heart attacks of other people. His library shelves were crammed with love stories, the more ardent of them re-read until he knew them by rote. He was a devotee of the movies, and at least twice a week followed the sinuous grace of his favorite stars with hungry eyes.

But nothing afforded him more pleasure than to observe the brief and covert exchange of wistful, exploring glances in his class-room. He had become so adept as a heart-diagnostician that he believed he could tell, almost the first day of a new semester, what pairings-off were likely to develop.

It was the shy ones who interested him most, the pairs who sat farthest apart, never entering or leaving the room together, until — one day — oh, joy! — the tortured stag would maneuver to the side of the flustered doe, as the herd filed out of the room, and Ernie's secret forecast had come true.

Sometimes he would mate a pair so sluggishly moving toward each other that he was exasperated beyond endurance. On one occasion, he had waited a whole year for signs of advancement on the part of two diffident young things, who were forever looking at each other, and, caught at it, would quickly busy themselves in some other quarter. Unable to be patient any longer, Ernie contrived an errand that would speed their affair.

His class in Anthropology was taken to 'the mounds,' near Pinckney. The gate was locked. He sent the timid pair to the owner's house, a half-mile away, over a narrow, rocky path, and through a tangle of uncleared forest, for the key. They were gone an hour, and when they returned, they were no longer on foot, but floating in a gossamer golden cloud. The stag's shoulder was white with powder, and the doe's ears were pink with embarrassment. But they had remembered to bring the key. It was a great occasion.

By far the most baffling problem that had yet engaged Ernie's attention was the annoying current case of Joan Braithwaite and Dinny Brumm who were now members of his junior section in Anthropology.

In Professor Martin's expert opinion, if ever two handsome thoroughbreds had been destined from all eternity to find each other — even if they had to meet halfway round the globe — these tall, proud, self-sufficient personalities were that privileged pair.

It was a small class, seventeen in all, accommodated by the first semi-circular row of chairs in the room whose walls were eventful with high glass cabinets stuffed with meteorites, stalactites, fossils, pottery, and plaster casts of extinct animals and approximate humanity of uncertain date.

'If my l-lectures bore you,' Ernie was accustomed to say, at the opening session of a class, 'there are p-plenty of interesting trinkets to look at, a c-ca-casual inspection of which would do you no dis-s-s-service.'

Joan had chosen the chair at the extreme end of the curved row, Dinny had taken the seat nearest the door. The intervening chairs were occupied by average examples of *homo sapiens* in its commonest variety, worthy and well-meaning young persons, no doubt, but clearly of a different biological category from the two who, at opposite ends of the row, were so definitely of a higher species of primate. The amusing, the infuriating thing about it was that neither of them seemed to know what anybody should have been able to observe at a glance.

There was that good-looking young cub, Barney Vaughn, for example. *He* knew it. Vaughn was pathetically infatuated with Joan. Anybody could see that. But Vaughn avoided Brumm. Once Ernie thought Vaughn had purposely snubbed Brumm in a brief clash of opinion in a class discussion.... Why did Vaughn have an aversion for Brumm? Obviously — Vaughn knew, by instinct, that Joan Braithwaite was Dinny Brumm's property!... Ernie was furious.

After a few sessions of this class, Professor Martin became increasingly excited over his secret discovery that the calm disinterest of Joan and Dinny was more calculated than a mere mutual indifference. There was something between these two. Their avoidance of each other was intentional. They were not strangers, but enemies.

At ease in his woolen dressing-gown, with his bad leg outstretched on a neighboring chair, Ernie read the editorial, that Thursday night, in *The Blossom*, and laughed aloud. It was Brumm, of course. None of the others would have risked it. None of the others could have done it, had he been as audacious as the devil. It was Brumm! My Uncle! — what a savage disposition the young beast had!... Then the corners of Ernie's mobile mouth drew down, and his thin brows met.... The surly piece was funny enough, God knew, but Dinny shouldn't have done it. Wasn't Joan Braithwaite the acknowledged queen of the whole sorority outfit? What did the chap mean by jumping up and down with his big feet on the soft white neck of Joan's exclusive social tribe?

For a full hour he sat tugging his lip, relighting his pipe, occasionally grinning, faun-like, sometimes shaking his head despairingly. At length he arose, limped to the grate, poked the fire, and muttered, grimly,

'D-a-a-a — dammit... I'll t-t — try it! It w-w-worked w-w-w — once!'

* * * * * *

On the following Wednesday afternoon, the class in Anthropology made the annual excursion to view the mounds.

It was a comforting late October day, hazy and lazy, blue and white on top, purple around the edges, brown underfoot. Blackbirds were noisily mobilizing for the southern expedition. Gray squirrels were working overtime storing their warehouses. Red-headed woodpeckers were drilling deep for drowsy hide-aways. The woods glowed with smouldering embers of summer, and the narrow black stream that had carved a rough toboggan through the limestone cliffs ran swift and cold.

The seventeen budding scientists, conducted by Professor Ernst Martin, were glad to be out in the country. At one they had met for the twelve-mile trip on a jerky, jangling, little accommodation train to Pinckney. The sexes had segregated in the dusty coach. Barney Vaughn, seated proprietarily beside Joan, made himself agreeable to the cluster of girls. Some of the men read newspapers, others stared out at the windows.

Dinny sauntered to the rear platform, where, watching the grass-grown ties and rusty rails squirm through the hills, he was presently joined by his preceptor, who nodded amiably and seemed, by the companionable twinkle in his sharp little eyes, to be threatening an intimacy. They stood for some time, swaying with the motion of the train, eyes intent on the reeling hills.

'B-Brumm,' shouted Professor Martin, against the racket, 'as a s-sour old barb, permit me to c-c-congratulate you. It was very c-c-clever.'

'Thanks.' Dinny grinned down into the bright, beady eyes. 'Great scenery, down this way, isn't it?'

'Especially at this season.... B-but it would have been even more c-c-clever if you hadn't done it.'

'Somebody had to,' defended Dinny, suddenly clutching the thin arm of his master as the train whip-cracked around a hairpin curve. 'It was long overdue.'

'T-too bad it had to be you,' shrilled Martin. 'Y-you might have c-c-capitalized your p-popularity.... N-n-no use baiting the d-d-damn frats.... And there are some m-m-mighty fine girls in the s-sororities.... T-t-take a g-girl like Mmmm-iss Braithwaite, for example. W-well w-worth c-c-cultivating, I should say. N-n-not mmm-any like her!'

'Plenty of nuts, this year,' observed Dinny, pointing to a clump of tall hickories, vanishing around the screeching bend.

'Y-y-yes... j-j-just what I was s-saying!... N-not all of 'em on t-trees!... I'm g-going back inside. T-too c-c-cool out here for me.'

Dinny turned, and regarded his professor with fresh interest.

'It's a rough road,' he said, smiling.

'I-i-it always was for m-me,' rejoined Martin, meaningly. 'B-but it ought to be easier f-for you.' One little eye winked, sardonically.

Dinny felt that something was expected of him, though if the fantastic little geologist thought a confidence was in order, he was going to be disappointed.

'You're fond of riddles; aren't you, Professor Martin?'

Martin chuckled, nodded vigorously, and shouted over his shoulder as he retreated:

'Y-y-yes — and I've s-solved a f-f-few!'

Now what did the uncanny little devil mean by that?... Something up his sleeve, no doubt.... Had women on his mind.... Unhealthy imagination.... Meddling matchmaker. ... Damn fool.

Arrived at the dingy wooden station in Pinckney, they straggled off toward the path that led a mile toward the grove of the Indian mounds, Martin hobbling ahead, cane-whisking at brittle milkweed pods, the girls single-file behind him, Barney Vaughn leading the male contingent, occasionally pressing solicitous attentions upon Joan as if she needed assistance on the rugged stone ledge of the ravine. Dinny brought up the tail of the procession, quite conscious — he had had one fleeting glance from her, as they entered the train — that he was in high disfavor with the only person in this party that mattered.

At length a path diverged from the ravine and ambled toward the left, through a seared meadow strewn with huge boulders. In groups, the expedition crossed leisurely toward the high-fenced grove. At a considerable distance, keen young eyes learned that the place of interest was somewhat lacking in hospitality.

NO TRESPASSING! THIS MEANS YOU!

'W-w-what's this?' exclaimed Professor Martin, indignantly, as they gathered in front of the padlocked gate. 'Mr. B-Bowers assured me it would be left open for us. I m-must g-g-go for the k-key. The sh-short way to his house is d-d-down the ravine. N-n-no — I shall deputize a c-c-couple of you to go. It w-would take me too long. W-we must not be delayed.'

With the critical air of making a momentous decision, he deliberately took a careful invoice of the company, obviously contemplating the appointment of an important committee. His little eyes shone. They devilishly rested, for an instant, on the expectant face of Barney, wistfully posing for an Eagle Boy Scout who had not yet had a chance, today, to do a good turn.

Dinny could hardly believe his ears. What had possessed the ugly little jackass to hurl them at each other's heads in this ruthless fashion? He glanced apprehensively at Joan, but she had quickly recovered. She smiled, graciously enough, left the group of girls, and joined him. Professor Martin had suggested that Mr. Bowers might be glad if the President's daughter and the varsity's best-known star were sent to ask the favor. If they had no objection, would they go and get the key?

'Martin's a nice little arranger,' said Dinny, when they were out of earshot.

'Yes,' returned Joan, frostily, 'charming idea.'

'You don't have to talk to me, you know,' explained Dinny, indifferently.

'That's good,' returned Joan, quickening her steps.

In sullen silence, they retraced to the ravine. Joan briskly led the way along the narrow ledge, bending forward the stiff branches of intruding shrubbery, and not caring what became of them.

'Perhaps you'd better let me go first,' called Dinny.

There was no reply. Joan hurried on.

'And look out for those loose stones!'

It happened, presently. Joan, with a startled exclamation, disappeared over the edge. She was attempting to rise from her knees in the shallow, rock-strewn stream, when Dinny reached her.

'Now you've gone and got yourself in a mess, haven't you?' scolded Dinny, reaching out both hands toward her. She ignored them, and tried to scramble to her feet.

'You needn't bother,' she protested, hotly. 'I don't want your help — a bit!'

'Yes, you do,' he drawled — 'and quite a lot of it. You've hurt yourself. Haven't you?'

She nodded, reluctantly, like a defeated child, and reached up for Dinny's hand.

'Help me over to that flat rock, won't you?... No — not that way!' Dinny was gathering her up in his arms. 'Take my hands, please. I can manage, if you steady me.'

Joan took one short step and unsuccessfully tried another, shook her head, held out her arms. Her lips were white. Dinny lifted her clear of the water and deposited her gently on the little limestone island.

'It's my knee.... It hurts dreadfully.' She was trying to keep her voice steady, but she was trembling.

'Think it's broken?' Dinny knelt beside her, anxiously. 'Can you bend it? Try.'

Her eyes were tightly closed, and her face was drawn. She began slowly unrolling her stocking.

'Rather I'd go away?' Dinny swallowed, nervously, and felt foolishly helpless.

Joan eased back on both elbows, dizzy with pain, too sick to inspect the purpling bruise. Dinny wet his handkerchief in the cold stream, and was about to lay it on her forehead. Anticipating, she took the handkerchief, and dabbed at her temples, clumsily.

'Does it — look broken?'

Dinny carefully examined the damaged knee, resolutely telling himself he was a cad if he failed to concentrate his attention on the immediate field of Joan's injury. It was not broken, he reassured her, but it was frightfully bruised. Perhaps the sharp pain would ease up, presently.

'But you mustn't stay here any longer,' he decided, promptly. 'I'll take you to this Bowers place, and we'll have a doctor.'

'You can't,' objected Joan. 'Better leave me here, and get some help.... Oh — what a beastly nuisance!'

Had anyone been watching, thought Dinny, the pair of them must have made an amusing spectacle as he waded downstream, carrying Joan — huntsman fashion — on his back, her head drooping forward over his right shoulder, her curls tickling his ear, her warm cheek close against his. His left arm circled under her knees, his left hand firmly clasped her right. With difficulty he repressed a grin, and wondered if she was too uncomfortable to realize the absurdity of it all.

For the first fifty yards, nothing was said, Dinny picking his steps, deliberately.

'Am I jolting it too much?' he inquired.

'I can stand it,' said Joan, 'if you can.... I'm sorry.... I was hateful.'

'You were going pretty fast,' reproved Dinny. 'It was rather reckless.'

'I was furious!' Joan's voice registered directly into his ear a justification of her imprudent speed. 'He had no business asking me to go... with you.'

'Well — why did you?' growled Dinny, sourly. 'I'm sure I made no bid for it. I was surprised when you came along.'

'Couldn't make a scene — could I?' demanded Joan.

'Of course you could.... I don't believe you're above making a scene.... I never knew a woman who didn't like a — like a chance to exhibit her resentments.'

Dinny plodded along for several steps, conscious that he was carrying an explosive, and wondering how long it would be until the detonation occurred.

'Yes,' mocked Joan, acidly, 'I expect it's a lot you know about women — as irresistible, and polite, and ——'

'You see that little bridge ahead?' interrupted Dinny. 'I'm going to put you down, if you can stand on one foot, and try to hoist you up.... Pardon me — you were saying ——'

'I was saying' — Joan bit her words into hot little shrapnel — 'that you're a beast... and I don't like you!'

'There's no reason why you should,' muttered Dinny.

Hostilities were briefly suspended during the process of mounting over the rocks to the foot-bridge. Joan independently made her way alone to the end of the railing, and looked wistfully in the direction of the stone house, a hundred yards away.

'Well — here we go again,' said Dinny, cheerfully, ready to resume his burden. 'It won't be far now.'

'I can't see why you wanted to write that mean thing,' complained Joan, after Dinny had lifted her to his back.

'Just for devilment.'

'Sure it wasn't for revenge?'

'No.'

'"No," it wasn't? — or "no," you're not sure?'

'I'm not sure it wasn't.'

There was a long silence. Dinny was almost to Mr. Bowers's little lawn, now.

'I wish you weren't... that way,' murmured Joan, in a tone of genuine regret.

'Why should *you* care?' drawled Dinny, with cool indifference.

He carefully lowered her to the porch steps, where she slumped down, spent with the fatigue and strain of their trying half-hour. Dinny stretched his arms at full length, drew a deep breath, readjusted his scarf, ran his long fingers through his damp hair.

Late that night, as he sleeplessly reviewed the afternoon, alternately glowing with the memory of Joan's physical warmth and chilled by her hostility, he wondered what he might have said in reply to her tardy rejoinder had the front door not opened, at that moment, with Mrs. Bowers hurrying out, all sympathy and concern.

'Why should *you* care?' Dinny heard himself saying, in a tone of sarcastic self-depreciation.

Joan had looked up, wide-eyed, lips parted, searching his face with the undisguised candor of a child inspecting a total stranger.

'I — don't — know,' she said, slowly, her lips trembling a little. Then she glanced toward the opening door. 'Thanks, Dinny, for helping me.'

Mrs. Bowers had rung down the curtain on this disturbing scene, murmuring solicitous little cries of motherly interest, and Dinny felt his immediate responsibility transferred to her competent hands. He waited until the telephone conversation assured the early arrival, by motor, of President Braithwaite and a physician.

The men were playing ball in the meadow, when Dinny returned with the key. The girls were seated in the shade. Martin was consumed with curiosity, the brief explanation failing to satisfy.

He endeavored to corral Dinny into a corner, later, on the train. When all hints and subtleties of inquiry had been adroitly parried, he threw delicacy aside and asked a direct question.

'D-d-did you have to c-c-carry her?'

Dinny's eyes narrowed as he stared absently into the questing little gray beads that flashed a hungry wish.

'Miss Braithwaite said she needed no assistance,' he replied, dryly.

Ernie gave it up then, mumbled something about the stuffiness of the atmosphere, and hobbled aimlessly out to the sooty back platform, where he hung on to the begrimed iron railing and gazed moodily into the gathering dusk.

'H-h-hell!' he muttered. 'D-d-damned ungrateful c-c-cub!'

* * * * * *

So few swans had fledged in the Magnolia duck-run that the approaching visit of Congressman Philemon Bascom, '98, resident of Washington and Dubuque, was an event demanding celebration.

The Honorable Mr. Bascom had consented to deliver the principal address at the formal opening of the new Science Building on the afternoon of March thirtieth.

That the reception in his honor, on the night previous, might be loyally backed by undergraduate interest, the faculty had appointed a student committee of five to cooperate with their elders and betters in making arrangements.

Wesley Tinker, President of the Hellenic Council, was to represent the fraternities. Dinny Brumm was easily the most conspicuous figure among the barbs. Sophia Wise, temporarily in the public eye as winner of the recent essay contest, would speak for the girls who knew no Greek secrets. Joan Braithwaite naturally epitomized the sorority element at its best. Orville Kling was asked to appear in behalf of the theological students.

At the committee meeting, held in the library at the President's Mansion, lent to Joan for the occasion, an hour and a half was spent, that first Thursday night of March, in a rubber-stampish approval of the 'tentative suggestions' sent from the faculty 'as a basis of discussion.'

Hopeful of enlivening the stupid and perfunctory chatter of obsequious acquiescence, Dinny ventured the opinion that a reception was no place for a long program of speeches. Would it not be sufficient for Doctor Braithwaite to welcome the honored guest, briefly, and let the guest say 'thanks.' Why all these amateurish student harangues. There would be plenty of oratory touched off next day, at the impressive dedication.

Kling, whom Dinny suspected was over-eager to represent the seminary on the reception program, promptly sustained the policy of offering the student body a chance to express itself.

'Speaking for the theologues,' he declared, determinedly, 'I think the faculty's wish in this matter should not be questioned.'

Unable to resist the temptation to tease, Dinny soberly remarked:

'One might imagine the theologues would be quite relieved if they were not pressed to participate.'

'How so, may I inquire?' demanded Kling, bristling.

'Well' — explained Dinny, with a nonchalant gesture — 'this reception impinges on the opening of the Science Building, doesn't it?'

Kling truculently protested that he didn't care to enter into any controversy, but could assure Mr. Brumm that the Church was heart-and-soul in sympathy with Science — 'of the right sort.'

Dinny wished, a moment later, that he had been content to let the matter rest there; but, resentfully remembering Kling's impudent attacks on Doctor Braithwaite's liberalizing beliefs, he decided to jab the harpoon a bit deeper.

'How do you mean — "the right sort of Science"? — the kind taught in Genesis, maybe?'

Kling's ears were red, and he folded and refolded his notepaper, angrily.

'I did not come here, sir, to debate theology with a — an atheist.'

'In that case,' said Dinny, conciliatorily, 'I withdraw my suggestion.... Let the theologues express themselves, by all means.... I would like to propose that Mr. Kling be asked to speak on "The Contribution of Orthodoxy to Scientific Research."'

'You're trying to be funny.... Aren't you?'

'Of course — *I* think it is funny. But I wasn't sure that *you* would. May I apologize for underrating your capacity for humor?'

Tinker, the chairman, rapped on the table with his knuckles.

'Now — if you two will hire a hall, sometime, the rest of us will be happy to attend. For the moment, you're both out of order, I think. Let us proceed with our business.'

The meeting adjourned, presently. As Dinny passed Joan, who stood in the doorway of the parlor, she whispered, 'Wait.'

When the others had gone, she returned to the parlor, where Dinny, standing by the table, was leafing a magazine.

'Dinny — I wish you wouldn't.'

'I'm sorry,' he said, contritely. 'But that chap's always needing a trimming... and never getting it... not properly.'

'Oh — I think I know why you feel that way.' Joan motioned toward the divan, and they sat. 'Mr. Kling has been very annoying in his attitude toward my father.... I think you like my father, don't you?'

'You know I do, Joan. I would do anything for him!'

'Then — don't try to fight his battles. I don't want this to sound ungrateful, Dinny, but it won't help my father for you to be on his side.... Because — well, you see, you're too often on the *wrong* side! And you are so dreadfully savage and sarcastic that you infuriate people!'

'Very well,' said Dinny, slowly, 'if you think it annoys your father... for me to be loyal to him, I'll not intrude again.'

Impulsively Joan laid her hand on his, and exclaimed, impatiently:

'Now — there you go!... That's just what I mean... that ironical... cruel —— ' Hot, angry tears welled in her eyes.

Dinny rose, glanced at his watch, smiled.

'We won't quarrel,' he said, indulgently.

Joan stood, facing him, eyes flashing.

'Yes, we will, Dinny Brumm! You've been perfectly hateful! I don't know what all's happened in your life to poison you so, but if you don't get rid of it — somehow — you'll be wretched forever!... And so will everybody else that's... that's interested in you... at all.'

Unable to think of an appropriate reply, and stirred to frank admiration of her militant pose, Dinny grinned, appreciatively.... Gad — she was a superb creature!

Joan turned away, utterly exasperated.

'I won't keep you!' she snapped, hotly. 'Good-night.... The maid will show you out.'

Dinny followed her toward the doorway.

'Joan,' he called, 'please — don't be angry.'

She hesitated, turned, waited.

'I didn't mean to hurt your feelings,' he said, gently.

He reached out both hands, and looked down repentantly into her reproachful eyes. She took his hands, and regarded him with an expression of pity.

'Why do you do it — Dinny?' she said, pleadingly.

'Because' — Dinny was serious, sincere, contrite — 'because I can't help it!... I was started — all wrong.... The world's full of — full of bunkum, and I can't help laughing at it.... I fancy I shall keep on laughing at it, until I die.... That's the way I'm made.... I'm sorry, sometimes, and wish I wasn't that way.... But — you mustn't trouble yourself about it.'

She loosed her hands, slowly, and stood looking down at the floor.

'Good-night, then,' she said, huskily, with a wan little smile.

'Good-night — Joan — dear.'

Very tenderly, Dinny drew her, unresisting, into his

arms. She laid a soft palm on his cheek, and looked up into his face.

'Oh, Dinny,' she whispered, 'please... please!'

He bent to kiss her. She shook her head, buried her face in his breast. Dinny gently touched her hair with his lips. His voice trembled a little when he spoke.

'I'll try, dear, to be good,' he said, sincerely.

'Honest?' Joan was smiling through her tears. She raised her head slowly, rather shyly, cheeks aflame.

'Honest!' promised Dinny, tightening his embrace.

Joan closed her eyes. The hand that was laid against his cheek moved slowly upward, caressed his hair, circled his neck.

Very gently, Dinny's lips sought hers. It was a chaste, comradely kiss that he offered her, symbolic of a resolution to cultivate a more amicable spirit. Only on such terms, he felt, would Joan permit this intimacy. Passionately in love with her, it was difficult to discipline that kiss.

To Dinny's amazement and exultation, Joan met the endearment in quite another attitude than that of a pleased reformer enheartening a penitent to keep his vows. At the touch of his lips, she responded as to an electrical contact, drew a long, convulsive breath that confessed the depth of her emotion, and the kiss she gave suffused him with an ecstasy he had never known.

They clung to each other for a full minute before Joan, her lips still on his, shook her head ever so slightly, and then, with a contented sigh, laid her cheek affectionately against his shoulder.

After he had gone to his room, that night, Dinny sat for a long time on the edge of his bed staring straight ahead, trying to reconstruct each separate instant of that exultant experience. Had any other girl than Joan Braithwaite consented to — much less joined him in — a kiss like that, he might have wondered a little about her.

But, because the girl was Joan, the warm, tingling memory of it carried a peculiar possessive, protective tenderness. His eyes were wet. Joan belonged to him! He walked to the window and looked out, down the hill, at the big house, loving it because it sheltered Joan.... Dear Joan!

* * * * * *

The next afternoon at the Athenian Literary Society, which Dinny rarely attended, believing it worth a fifty-cent fine to spare himself the irksomeness of sitting through a protracted session of parliamentary wind-bagging, Kling made a patriotic speech.

As an alumnus, he was there on invitation, and glad to be back in the spacious room, where, he averred, he had learned to speak on his feet.

His attacks on Doctor Braithwaite were ostensibly cryptic, at first, but as he warmed to his theme, the clumsy devices of indirect accusation were abandoned. It was an insolent address. Dinny hotly scowled through it, promising himself that Kling would have to pay for his surly impudence.

That night, he executed the threat he had held over Kling, so blind with indignation he gave no thought to consequences. What Joan might think of it did not occur to him.

Next day, the campus hummed with the story. Dinny called up Joan, but she was not at home.

On Monday, current copies of *The Iconoclast* were in circulation. Dinny had sold it many weeks earlier; had almost forgotten it. But Joan, without considering how much time must have elapsed between the composition and publication of this brutal effrontery, avoided him when they met in the hall; ignored him in the class-room.

He dropped her a note, attempting explanation, but was indiscreet enough to jest about the article as 'a hang-over' from his 'unredeemed estate.' The note, plus the spreading rumor that Dinny had made savage war on Kling, so distressed Joan that she was at a loss to know what to reply. While she debated, the faculty moved in the direction of punishment for Dinny. Her father's affairs were already sufficiently complicated. Any attempted reconciliation with Dinny, at this moment, might add to the President's problems. She waited.

Almost before she realized the swiftness with which Dinny's case had become a *cause célèbre*, he had left town. He telephoned to her. Mrs. Braithwaite answered.

'May I speak to Miss Braithwaite?'

'Who is speaking, please?'

'This is Dinny Brumm.'

'Miss Braithwaite is not in, Mr. Brumm.'

Her voice was not unkind, but Dinny interpreted.

Considering how much variegated disaster menaced Doctor Braithwaite, from all sides, it was obvious that the family was better off without any further traffic with Dinny. He appreciated the situation, and felt almost sympathetic with Joan's mother. She had done the right thing.

CHAPTER X

LOUNGING with athletic arms negligently disposed along the back of a slatted, sun-drenched iron seat in Central Park, overlooking undulous acres of verdant velvet, the prosperous young creator of the column capped 'Green Cheese' absently twirled an inventive pencil between thumb and finger-tips; but he was worried.

His deep-set, gray-green eyes, shaded by a brim-turned felt hat of the same color, were half-closed against the bright distractions, the tiny crow's-feet at their outer corners registering an habitual, detached amusement which he daily sent to market in forty newspapers.

On the broad gravel path immediately before him, perambulators that had cost thrice the price of Uncle Miles's jump-seat surrey leisurely trundled smug, superior kewpies whose interest in the narrow ribbons dependent from their lace bonnets seemed an earnest of future adroitness in the fingering of ticker-tape.

A hundred yards down the slope, kneeling around the lip of a gigantic concrete saucer, small scions of the well-to-do alternately righted unseaworthy sloops and wiped April noses on monogrammed coat-sleeves. Farther down and to the left of this mimic ocean, clumps of tourists, undistressed by the discomforts of their caged kin, idled from the monkey-house toward the bear-pits, pausing briefly to glance up through the untidy steel netting of the squawking, acrid aviary.

Sometimes — as today — the manufacturer of Green Cheese glumly wished he had chosen another vehicle for his syndicated satires than these fantastic 'conversations in the moon'; but they had proved immensely popular and profitable — even more so than his earlier, riskier series of 'Unfrosted Persimmons,' whose astringent quality had so unexpectedly piqued the public palate, jaded by a quadrennium of sentimental superlatives ranging all the way from lush and morbid pathos and the agony of hair-tearing despair to the loud and hysterical hallelujahs of Utopianism at its ultimate peak of drooling idiocy.

Still young in years but prematurely seasoned by cumulative disillusion, Dinny Brumm had been among the earliest to venture a bit of whimsical spoofing, indulgently phrased in the soothing 'Now, now; there, there; come, come,' of the psychiatrist making his afternoon rounds in a genteel madhouse. Dinny approached his increasing constituency gently, regarding them as convalescing victims of a pestilential neurosis superinduced by a long debauch under potent emotional stimulants.

At the outset, his covert fun-poking at the perfervid apostles of idealism who, watch in hand, galloped to catch trains that hurled them from platform to platform, where, daily and nightly, they beckoned and bellowed — saving the world for democracy, for civilization, for altruism, for our children and our children's children, for God the Father and Christ His Son — had been as shocking as a ribald joke told in a funeral address at the expense of the corpse.

But presently it began to appear that a considerable section of the public — weary unto death of the unconscionable nonsense brayed and bleated from ten thousand pulpits, lecture halls, luncheon clubs, women's clubs, open forums, and whithersoever the tribes of salvation-hucksters went up — found itself grinning over the audacities of a youthful cynic who, with no reputation to lose, offered comic relief in the midst of the wearisome epilogue following the final act of a tragedy that had spun itself out overlong.

Two years later, there was none so timid for whom it was not entirely safe and righteous to damn war and invent wry jokes to caricature the apostles and slogans of the noble cause that aspired to world-brotherhood and the Golden Age; but, at the hour, only the venturesome dared apply for such hazardous employment.

Dinny had promised himself the luxury of sweet revenge. Plenty of times he had staggered under the garbage
and scoured the latrines for failing to wear the right expression of empty-eyed awe when stiffening to salute the
self-conscious lieutenant who, only last winter... or was
it the year before? — no matter... used to mince, limp-
wristed, to the light of the department-store door, a bolt
of silk under his arm, trailed by the plumber's haughty
spouse, murmuring, meekly:

'It's a real mauve, madame, as you shall see — and
prettuh, very prettuh.'

But the lieutenants and the captains and the majors
were not permitted to come to bat every day in the column
of 'Unfrosted Persimmons.' The civilian orators had their
innings. Dinny was at his best when pitching them a fast
one.

The ubiquitous civilization-savers, to whom everybody
had listened spell-bound, in a desperate state of finger-
gnawing fright, as they luridly depicted the crash and
clatter of a blown-up world, were now become somewhat
of a nuisance. With the arrogance of Jonah they had
howled disaster into the ears of the populace until they,
themselves, were fallen afoul of a nasty psychosis unpleasantly akin to sadism.

The war was over that had been so great a Godsend to
the large of mouth and small of faith, but the frantic ink
and screech of the calamity-merchants was unabated....
Ethical journals of opinion wagged an ominous pen.
Prophetic fists pounded verbally inspired Bibles, and cited
Jeremiah the empty-umpth chapter beginning at the
orty-erth verse. Journeyman seers stamped the rostra of
village chautauquas pointing bamboo fish-poles at the
seething hot spots on the reconstructed map of Yurrup....
Could civilization survive?... Was not the whole social
order on the rocks?... What shall we do to be saved?
... (What's become of the treasurer who was supposed to
hand me my check?)... Let us humble ourselves before

God!... Socialize! Evangelize! Fraternize! Organize! Do your bit! Till it hurts! The ushers will now distribute the pledge-cards.

Dinny had a good time.

It pleased his whim, one day, to set the clock back to the closing hours of the fifteenth century. Indulgences were on sale at the tail of a cart.... Step up, terror-stricken, and bail your bloody brothers out of hell!... Yesterday, with valor shining in their eyes, they went forth to make the supreme sacrifice for you and yours... Christ leading on... who had come not to bring peace, but a sword.... Come, now, wipe out this stain... for war is crime, and soldiers are murderers — shame on them!

The more devastating of these ironical gas-bombs, charged from the corroded coils of Dinny Brumm's bitter laboratory, were thrown from the pages of the candidly caustic magazines of protest, the sour humor of the 'Unfrosted Persimmons' being somewhat less diabolical. 'Green Cheese' was even more gentle and conciliatory.

Dinny yawned, and resharpened his pencil. He was tiring of his product. However — one could endure a certain amount of drudgery and boredom over the daily output of Green Cheese, seeing its present market value was two hundred and fifty dollars a week, just as one had endured the tedium of plucking and hurling the Unfrosted Persimmons whose spontaneous acceptance at the hands of the disenchanted had liberated him from his nightly desk at *The Philadelphia Ledger*, and set him loose to live where and as he pleased.

He was not a conscious apostle of common-sense. Had anyone asked him if, in the spirit of a crusader, he were not aware of his mission to a public whose emotions had been scarified and cauterized by the lancets and blisters of the sensation-smiths and calamity-quacks until there wasn't another kick left in them, Dinny would have denied it with a scowl... 'Crusade?... Mission?... Me?... Hell!'

Nevertheless, he daily polished the mirror so that the

people might see themselves almost exactly as they were — a pitilessly honest glass it was, that neither convexed to them a reflection of cherubic amiability nor concaved them to misanthropy.

In these genially mocking 'Green Cheese' columns, synchronous in two scores of widely read papers, the Man in the Moon, ancient, wise, sated as Solomon, drowsily replied to the imbecilic queries and comments of Luna, the Lady of the Moon, an effervescent flapper.

A few experimental lines, raw material to be fabricated for today's output, had been scribbled on the bulky wad of paper reposing on Dinny's lanky knee.

'Lookit, Gramp!' pointed Luna, wetting a finger and setting a curl. 'Lookit what they got now!'

'More progress, I dare say.... Another epoch-making invention.... Civilization at the cross-roads... now marching on, eh?... Heads up... nothing to fear... *altus et altior*. ... What's this, Luna; an electric banana-peeler?'

'Don't be ridiculous, Gramp!... It's a new cigarette-lighter. They're all quite mad about it!'

'Out of matches?'

'Certainly not! — but this automatic lighter's so much more convenient.... It's a little metal lamp — all the way up to sixty dollars. You unscrew at the bottom and pour in a special kind of oil. When you want a light, all you have to do is snap a small iron wheel a few times with your thumb — it doesn't seem to hurt the thumb very much unless you have to do it too often — and it scratches a flint that quite frequently strikes an electric spark that sets off a little wick that's soaked in the oil, and ——'

'How do you mean — it's more convenient?'

'Don't be so grumpy, Gramp!... Aren't you interested in progress, at all?'

* * * * * *

Very shortly after Dinny Brumm, fresh from the pandemonium that was Magnolia, had walked into the office of Mr. Steinberg to inquire what *The Cincinnati Times-Telegram* expected him to do, interesting things began to happen.

The first month — he had been told to 'sub' for Clint Mitchell on 'police and fires' until he learned at least the points of the compass — was too routinish and uneventful for his liking; but presently life was galvanized by the enlivening hubbub stirred when it was announced there would be a visitation from Zandy Craig — *the* Craig, of the Craig Syndicate — first week of May.

The 'T-T' — employees of *The Times-Telegram* always abridged the name — was in a grand state of excitement. Everything was speeded up, soaped, scraped, scoured, scrubbed, sponged, shined. High efficiency prevailed.

Reporters put fresh ribbons on their machines (it was in the uncoddled days when reporters were still able to do that for themselves), cleared their desks, bought a new hat. The girls at the Want Ads counter stopped doing their nails in the presence of customers. Linotype operators tried valiantly to break themselves of the reprehensible habit of tossing pied slugs back into the pot. Windows were washed in the composing-room. The devil wore a clean shirt.

For Zandy Craig saw everything; eyes of a hawk and nose of a hound.... Last time he was here, the entire Circulation was fired in a body, every man-jack of them. Forty salaries were raised. *The Enterprise* was bought in and swallowed up. A new off-set press was installed. Four pages of funnies were added.... The very building had rocked on its bricks for six dizzy days. God only knew — certainly no one else, not even Mr. Steinberg — what might happen this time.... You just kept out of the way, and hoped for the best. If what you were doing satisfied Craig, all he wanted out of you was silence — and damn' little o' that!... So went the tribal chatter out of apprehensive mouth-corners.

It had not occurred to Dinny that the omnipotent

Zandy Craig could be of more intimate concern to him than as the Dread Jehovah of Journalism, his absentee boss. He was related to the great Craig as a blade of grass to a forty-acre meadow. The dim, far-away figure of the contemptible fugitive who had left in the lurch an unsophisticated, over-trustful, little school-teacher, had never been spoken of in his presence as 'Zandy' Craig. He did not even reflect upon the unlikelihood of his unknown parent's achievement of so great prominence. The name roused in him no curiosity, at all.

Everybody spruced up for the big dinner at the Barstow, with Zandy Craig as both host and guest, and all hands present, as was the custom, from the Managing Editor's office down to the coal-bins. The dinner was always an inspiration. Besides, Craig was not niggardly with the fare. You heard what was good for you, and what you'd — By God — better do if you wanted to work for *The T-T*, but you also ate the food of a gentleman, and plenty of it.

Dinny sat by Mitchell, whom he easily liked, far down the T-shaped table seated for six score. The common herd had been settled and was fussing with its spoons.

'You never saw him,' remarked Mitchell, offering a cigarette; 'quite strikin' personality.'

'No,' replied Dinny, furnishing a light. 'He would be, of course.'

'Straight as the scales — and hard as hell.'

A slight commotion at the door of the banquet-room signaled the arrival of the important guest and his retinue. Dinny followed with intent, inquisitive eyes the progress of the tall, dynamic, early-frosted figure, as he strode to the seat of honor, preceded by the Mayor and Mr. Steinberg, and trailed by Mr. Latimer, the City Editor, and Mr. Orton, of the Circulation Department. A genuine outburst of applause acknowledged Zandy Craig's advent. Chairs were pushed back and the company stood, still pounding its hands. Dinny joined in the clapping, through sheer animal reflex to the racket, hardly conscious of what he did.

The big man signed to his slaves with a downward push of the heel of his long, strong hand, and they sat. The orchestra was off at full gallop. A battery of white-jacketed waiters trooped in, with soup aloft, a buzz of conversation broke out, and the dinner was in high gear.

'Dinny,' oracularly observed Mitchell, who was short and chubby, 'it takes beef to make a big man. You've gotta be tall if you're ever goin' to look down on 'em.'

'Napoleon was rather — brief, wasn't he?' suggested Dinny, encouragingly.

'Not on a horse,' defended Mitchell. 'Napoleon never hollered at his tall grenadiers unless he was walkin' on four legs.'

'How about us getting a horse, Clint?'

'Us? Me — you mean. You're rangy enough. Tall as Craig, himself.... Damned if you don't look a little like him. Same eyes; sort o' navigator eyes — if you know what I mean.'

Dinny, leaning far forward to gaze down the long table, was only half-conscious of Mitchell's prattle. Tugging suddenly out of his mesmerism, he returned to Clint with an abstracted stare, apologizing for his inattention.

'Beg pardon, old man; you were saying something ———'

'Yeah,' drawled Clint, indifferently, 'you better come to, and munch your fodder.'

Handsome Bob Moore, Municipal Building and The Courts, leaned across Dinny to inquire: 'Know if he brought the angel along, this time, Clint?'

'Haven't heard. She's probably in school, some place.' Then, for Dinny's enlightenment, Mitchell added: 'Craig's got a girl, seventeen or eighteen, that left a trail o' destruction behind her, last July. Moore's never been the same man. They told him off to show her the finish of a dramatic lawsuit in Circuit Court — she'd never seen a trial — and he was so stampeded by her amazin' pulchritude that he forgot where they were goin' and took her to a ball-game. It was reported the old man asked her, that night, who won the case, and she said, "The Sox."... But, even at that, Bob had his pay raised, when he thought he'd be fired.'

Young Welland, Clubs and Theaters, nosed in from Mitchell's left.

'Yeah, she's here, all right. Saw her in the lobby with Mrs. Steinberg, Mrs. Forsythe, and some other swells. All dolled up to kill and cripple. Very easy to look at.... Guess they were going to a show.'

Dinny was having difficulty keeping his eyes away from the head of the table. It was a curious, unaccountable fascination. Never had he been so engrossed by a personality. He wished he could be close enough to hear Craig's voice as he turned from one to the other of his immediate companions, occasionally putting down his fork to make short, expressive gestures with both hands.

Successive courses came, and clattered away on sagging white shoulders. Coffee arrived, smoke curled upward, chairs diagonaled.... 'Pardon my back, old son.'... Legs crossed, comfortably. Eyes roved to the gavel-zone.

Steinberg hitched about, stroked his chin, rose slowly, pulled down his waistcoat, told an old yarn about Henry Watterson, teased the Mayor discreetly, waited for the polite chuckle, waved a John-Baptist hand toward Craig, and backed out of the picture.

Craig was on his feet quickly.... No stories, no felicitations, no preamble. He strode swiftly, confidently, to the end of the plank and dived off. Dinny never forgot that first sentence — crisp, curt, cold, impudent, kinetic, arresting! With bushy black brows contracted, and narrowing his gray-green eyes, Craig bit his opening sentence into five ragged chunks and spat it, growled it:

'The only chemicals — imperative to evolution — are water, blood, and ink — and the greatest of these —— is ink!'

Craig talked for an hour, his voice rarely rising from the

deep, searching, commanding, dynamic diapason of the dogmatic credo with which he began.

He was speaking to a hard-boiled, blasé crowd, not only fully aware of its thick hide, its cynicism, its fish-eyed challenge that dared any man to speed its heart, tighten its throat, or flush its temples; but unafraid of it. Dinny viewed him as a reckless lion-tamer, stalking arrogantly into the cage, blacksnake whip confidently flicking bristling manes into a corner.... Shades of Nietzsche — but Craig was hard!

Now he had eased up on the old brutes with the long, yellow fangs, and was growling at the cubs; trying to make lithe lions of them.... Dinny responded to the tug. Gad — but life seemed potential, the way Craig talked about it! In his hands, a driving, obsessing ambition seemed august! You wanted to thrust out impatient elbows, crackle your chrysalis, and take wing!

One life!... One chance!... One enchanted youthtime!... Make it pay!... Hurl into it!... Take the cash, and let the credit go!... Be something — quickly!... Let the dead bury the dead!

Dolts and dawdlers, pull up along the right curb and let the unscared strong go by. If you haven't the nerve to pass your sluggish leader, don't hog the middle of the road, but clear the way!... Live precariously! — and like it!... Be sportsmanly; gamble with Life; play for big stakes!... Choose now — whether to scoop or be scooped — all the way to the box that latches on the outside!... My God — but Craig was cruel!

And yet — and yet — Dinny Brumm was drawn to him with an uncanny yielding. Craig had the idea. Craig was a superman, made of superstuff. It was impossible to withstand the attraction of the man's kinetic energy. Dinny's pulse pounded with an admiration close to idolatry.

He shuffled along with short, impeded steps, thick in the ruck that jammed the exits, and cramped with a chunk of the pack into the noxious elevator. The passengers were silent, a bit constrained. Dinny wanted only to hurry to his room, twenty blocks away and up the hill, to beat out a few hot resolutions while they were still malleable with the glow of the Craig forge.

The lobby swarmed. The revolving, leather-lipped street-door spun — plop, plop, plop, plop — as the animals, in line, left for the kennels; the grizzled and mangy, the playful and cocky, the yawning and gamboling.... Dinny squared his shoulders.

Mitchell was calling from the rear, somewhere. Annoyed, but complacent, he left the line, sauntered back, inquired.

'Moore's met the Craigess, Dinny.... We're asked to watch her nibble a rarebit in the grill, and do her a little genuflection. Want to?'

'Sure... Thanks, Clint.'

The princess was already at court, and presiding uncommonly well. No need to have her identified as the daughter of Craig; it was on her face, in her eyes, in her hands. She was Craig — young Craig, drawn to about three-fifths scale. The Craig *savoir faire* pleasantly veneered what promised to be — when it matured — a ligneous substratum of will-to-power. She was not haughty, not arrogant, not vain; but consciously assured. Whatever-it-was-she-had seemed to be saying: 'It's mine: give it me: thanks.'

Nobody needed to guess which was the head of the round table, seated for six. All were standing, for the moment, surrounded by twice as many more, half of them collected by Mitchell, en route to the grill. In the polite bedlam of introductions and renewals of acquaintance, Dinny, with no responsibilities, stared appraisingly at the self-possessed blonde, frankly envying her birthright to a magnetic personality that dominated from her gray-green eyes and firm, red mouth, and pink palms.

'How do you do, Mr. Brumm?' She gripped his hand like a man, and gave him a steady, smiling look of honest welcome, same as she had done for young Fitzgibbon who had come along with *The Enterprise* since her last visit.

'It must be nice to come back,' said Dinny, 'and find everybody so happy to see you, Miss Craig.'

She had not released his hand. Her smile had vanished. Her eyes had contracted slightly, and shuttled from his brows to his chin, as if attempting to recover a long-forgotten acquaintance.

'You're new, too; aren't you?' she said. 'I'm sure I never met you.... Did I?' She shook her head, still searching his eyes. 'Funny,' she added, half to herself.

He made way for the others behind him. She released his hand slowly.

'Auntie Alison, Mr. Brumm would like to meet you. Mrs. Forsythe, Mr. Brumm.' Her eyes momentarily dropped to the hand he extended, and again swept inquisitively to his face, before she turned to listen to Mitchell's next presentation.

'My son — Mr. Victor Forsythe, Mr. Brumm,' murmured the tall, rather imperious lady in mourning.

'Mrs. Steinberg, this is Mr. Brumm,' reiterated Victor, whose sleek, black hair was extraordinarily long. The tip of a white handkerchief peeped from the sleeve of his dinner-coat.

Mitchell's recruits were insisting that the diners resume their seats, and most of them, waving good-nights with smiles, were drifting away. Dinny followed, laggard, ostensibly lingering a little for Mitchell and Moore, in the process of tearing themselves away from the girl who paid flattering attention over her white shoulders. Something she was saying now made them glance in his direction.

'Dinny!' beckoned Moore.

He obediently joined them, inquiry in his eyes.

'Miss Craig wants you,' explained Clint, adding, with pretended pique and as if the remark were *sotto voce*, lucky devil!'

'Mr. Brumm,' she asked, almost inquisitorily, 'did you ever work for any of my father's other papers?'

Dinny shook his head, regretfully.

'Should I have?'

She did not join in the chuckle with which his colleagues rewarded his naïve query.

'Do you mind telling me where all you have lived?' she persisted, as to a witness under cross-examination.

'Well — we'll leave you now,' interjected Mitchell, breezily, laying a propelling hand on Moore's shoulder. 'It would be like you, Dinny, to discover that you and Miss Craig had been schoolmates, or something.... This chap has more lives than a cat, Miss Craig.... Got fired from college for knockin' the steeple off the Y.M.C.A., and made 'em take him back and pay him for lost time.... Good-night!... See you some more, I hope.'

'Nowhere you're likely to have been,' said Dinny, when the clamor had subsided. 'Indiana — and Magnolia College.... We never met before, Miss Craig.... But' — recklessly — 'now that we have, let's pretend we're old friends.'

He had laid his hand on the back of her chair, and when she looked up with still serious eyes to reply, her warm, supple body glowed against his fingers.

'I have never seen the Rookwood Pottery,' she said. 'Would tomorrow be convenient?'

'About eleven, preferably. You work at night, don't you?' She was looking squarely into his eyes, sheltering her voice a little from her table companions.

'And luncheon?'

'Yes — I think so.'

She held out her hand, like a man, without coyness.

'Good-night — Miss Craig,' said Dinny, deferentially as became an obscure employee taking leave of the magnate's daughter.

'My name is Alison.' Her lips barely moved, as she spoke, making no effort to disguise the fact that their conversation was private. Slowly she disengaged her long strong hand, gave him another swift, serious scrutiny that circled his face and came to rest, for an instant, on his lips; and rejoined her company.

* * * * * *

Alison was amazingly direct. The bland candor with which she ignored all the age-old subtleties of her sex, proclaiming in every look, tone, and gesture that Dinny Brumm was hers, by priority claim, all but took his breath away.

It was not brazen, but transparently ingenuous. Dinny was neither amused nor annoyed. Her attitude was that of a willful child daring all-comers to dispossess her of a toy. She had lost no time defining her convictions, indifferent alike to their possible effect on Dinny or any who might discover them.

Even on that first morning, strolling beside an impressed executive, who, learning her identity, had volunteered to guide them through the celebrated pottery, she put herself to no bother of pretense that their interest in art accounted for their visit.

Mr. Dabney would reverently hold up an exquisite vase, turning it, slowly, kaleidoscopically, inviting her to luxuriate in its mellow, parti-colored translucence; but, with a nonchalance so unconcerned that Dinny was half sorry for the fine old pagan, Alison's eyes — briefly, abstractedly regarding the treasure — returned to search his face. She held tightly to his arm. Employees grinned, slyly; exchanged an appreciative wink.... Honeymooners... second day out... utterly dippy... at least, the bride was.

They lunched downtown at the Hofbrau, where Alison expressed no preferences when their fingers touched on the menu-card, and seemed unaware what she was eating. Dinny was surprised to find himself quite unembarrassed by this devotion. It was too genuine to provoke a smile.

When she talked of herself, it was of herself and Geneva, herself and Montreaux, herself and Paris, as if she hadn't had an existence prior to her school-days in Switzerland, begun at fifteen, a few months after her parents' separation. When she talked of Dinny, it was all in the future — hot burning fires of ambition for Dinny. She all but suffocated him with it.

The goal of success was leisure to live, write, and play in Europe. That's what Dinny must live for, look to, as the reward of genius multiplied by hard work. That's what she lived for, looked to — Europe! She implied they were both going there, one day. She did not say they were going on the same ship, but she described moonlit nights on the boat-deck in a dulcet tone and ecstatic mood whose implications were almost shockingly direct.

Whether Zandy Craig was so confident of his dynamic daughter's self-sufficiency or so infatuated with his own business affairs that he gave her no thought, Dinny Brumm could not divine. It was enough to know that Alison's society, for ten memorable days, was not only accessible to him at all hours but flatteringly urgent.

She casually disclosed that Mrs. Forsythe, who lived in New York, was visiting in Cincinnati, hopeful of interesting the well-to-do music-lovers of the city in the budding talent of young Victor, whom Alison catalogued, briefly, brutally, as 'a bit of a cad, too dumb to succeed, and too lazy to bluff'; though she spoke almost tenderly, for her, of Tommy, the eldest, and Grace, who were forever stepping aside to make way for the callow prodigy in whose thin, listless fingers their ambitious mother had placed a fiddle almost before he was able to stand alone.

Alison's disgust and distaste for Victor apparently had wrought somewhat of constraint between her and Mrs. Forsythe. In view of this circumstance, and also the exigent desire of her aunt to promote Victor among Cincinnati's art-patrons, perhaps it was natural that the girl should be independent of much restriction.

After three crowded days in Cincinnati, almost constantly tied up in business conferences, Craig had scurried to Louisville. If Alison had been mistress of her own fate before, she was now even more completely in charge of her time. That time was Dinny's.

At Alison's suggestion, they procured saddle-horses and rode all day in the hills. They ferried to Covington, and strolled in the country. She even had the audacity to call up Mr. Steinberg, late one afternoon, from some undesignated outpost, reporting that she had asked Mr. Brumm to entertain her for the evening, and he would not, therefore, appear at six, as was his custom; to which information Mr. Steinberg replied, dryly, that he hoped she would return him, eventually, to *The T-T*, unspoiled by the honor.

Mulling over the whole tragic affair, later, Dinny found a little comfort in the fact that he had made no effort to capitalize Alison's devotion to the discredit of either of them. Nor was it easy to maintain his attitude of chivalry in the face of her quite abandoned, ruthless, reckless disclosure of a fascination for him to which she had yielded utterly.

Every day tightened their intimacy. Often she hinted of a story she meant to tell him; he would be 'quite frightfully' interested in it, as a scribbler, she knew; a long story, it was; she would let him have it when there was time. Dinny did not press her for it. She had implied that the tale impinged somehow on her family affairs.

*　*　*　*　*　*

It was Saturday afternoon.... Craig had wired he was returning that night. Alison was to be packed and ready to leave with him for New York, next morning, at ten.

They had tied their horses at the edge of a grove; had sauntered to a favored rendezvous on the rocky lip of a glen; were promising each other more happy days when she returned with her father in the fall.

'I'm going to tell you that story, now, Dinny,' she said, snuggling close to him, and childishly tracing patterns on his lapel with a possessive finger.

'Do,' said Dinny. 'Don't leave anything out.'

They leaned comfortably back against the warm rock, his arm around her, and the story began; just a bit diffidently, at first, for the story was not hers, really, but her father's.

After ten minutes of Alison's calm narrative, paving the way for the most pleasant possible interpretation of her father's youthful tragedy by recalling many of his college experiences, the story abruptly shifted to another locale.

Dinny relaxed his affectionate hold, and fumbled awkwardly in his coat pockets for cigarettes and matches.

'You smoke too much, dear,' said Alison, rather petulantly, annoyed at the distraction. 'It isn't good for you. ... Your hands are trembling.... Look!' She gripped his fingers. He did not reply or smile, but obdurately lighted the cigarette.

'And then,' continued Alison, sinking back against the rock, with a little sigh of disappointment not to find his arm there, 'the most natural thing happened.... You know my father.... He's always been that way.... What he wants, he wants — that same day!'

Dinny sat with eyes half-closed, listening, smoking; lighted another cigarette off the hot end; averted his face, savagely ran his fingers upward through his hair.

Too disconcerted over his unaccountable mood to continue without some explanation, Alison broke off, presently, in the midst of a sentence, groped for his hand outspread on the rock between them, and asked, anxiously:

'What is it, Dinny?'

He did not turn to her or respond to the pressure of her fingers.

'Dinny!' she entreated, pressing her face against his shoulder, 'tell me, dear!... What did I do?... What's come over you?'

'I'm afraid' — he said, hoarsely, after some delay — 'I can't tell you.'

She sat for a moment half-stunned and silent; then, with

a little sob, she wrapped both arms tightly around his neck, and murmured, thickly: 'I can't bear it, Dinny. You must be good to me. You've made me love you. I'm mad about you!'

She raised her face, eyes closed, and offered him her parted lips.

Suddenly haggard, Dinny gripped both her hands and drew them down, holding them vise-like against his knee. He swallowed, convulsively, and when he spoke, his voice was hollow.

'You mustn't, Alison,' he muttered.

'Don't you love me — even a little, Dinny?' she pleaded, with brimming eyes.

'I mustn't!... We can't!' he whispered, staring into her face, the muscles of his cheeks twitching.

'Why?' she asked, inaudibly, her lips forming the query.

He drew her head tightly to him, with a gesture of protection, as if to shield her from a blow, and, after a long minute, measured out the words, dully, one at a time:

'You — are — my — sister.'

* * * * * *

Dinny never pretended this was the reason for his almost immediate decision to join the artillery unit mobilizing at Gettysburg, where the only artillery to be had, at that moment, was in the cemetery, slightly outmoded, as such things went.

Neither did he ever explain to himself — much less to others — that he had waived the exemption Craig had provided somehow for 'necessary members of editorial departments' (meaning everybody on the payroll) out of a sense of patriotic duty.

He wryly, profanely, squirmed into an ill-fitting, ludicrous suit of khaki solely to save his face, and because he was quite too fit a specimen of physical vitality to be at large in civilian clothes at a time when so many hundreds of thousands of inspired patriots were rushing about extolling 'the supreme sacrifice' as a noble privilege dangled before the enchanted eyes of 'our valiant boys.'

Most of this exultant talk was offered by prophets and soothsayers of forty-five and up, who, albeit unable to make such renunciation themselves, were obviously uplifted by the thought that they were not standing in the way or taking the place of some other brother, hungering and thirsting for such righteousness as might be had by blowing a Teuton's head off with a handful of blasting-powder.

Dinny's long, monotonous months in camp never benefited his native land by so much as a feather's weight; and, as for what he himself got out of it, either in discipline, experience, or stimulating friendships, the total result was exactly nil; unless his increasingly bitter cynicism, later capitalized to a monetary advantage, might be said to have fermented a little more through those hateful days.

Even with unpleasant memories as his chief stock in trade, memories fetched to market and savored by the similarly disillusioned, Dinny did not like to cogitate too much about his life at Gettysburg. The revulsion made him ill.

As for 'heroism,' the most heroic act anybody in that camp was expected to perform consisted of the valiant refusal to commit the half-dozen murders for which Justice clamored.

Uniforms played weird tricks on people who, in civies, must have been halfway decent. It seemed to make very little difference about a man's previous character or relation to society, once he had been required to perfect the debasing art of revolving himself stiffly on one heel, by some reflex to a growl that brought the flat of his hand smack against the brim of his cap, the only way he could square with his own soul, for this indignity, was to look promptly for somebody else, even more debased than he, who might be rank-badgered to do him a kow-tow.

Nobody ever saluted Dinny Brumm. Nobody would have saluted Dinny Brumm had he remained in the army until the Dawn of Everlasting Peace. He wasn't the type. According to the letter, he went through all the motions, which largely consisted in offering sustenance to the vanity of suddenly ordained Plattsburgers and surly non-coms; but Dinny's spirit — such as it was — refused to participate. His contempt glared in his eyes, against his will. It was chiseled in the deep lateral cleft between his lower lip and chin, quite beyond his control.

They nearly let him die, during the flu epidemic, for offering frank comments, when half-delirious, relative to the institution with which he was connected, and the important members of its personnel. Before he was able to pull his trousers on again, he had learned a disheartening thing or two about the only profession for which he retained the slightest degree of respect. Always had he venerated the medical profession. Now he had discovered, regretfully, that a few metal buttons, a squeaking new belt, and a pair of spurred boots would frequently play the same amount of hell with the Hippocratic oath that they so incomprehensibly wrought in the disordered minds of formerly gracious grocery clerks and collegiate sons of honest farmers. He saw many a competent, generous, integrity-loving physician degenerate into a pompous, puffy, arrogant ass.

Even the nurses went about, stiff-necked and consciously professional, mouthing the phrase, 'War is no tea-party!'

Dinny Brumm never went over the top, in France, at four A.M., but he spent six weeks in a military hospital, during the flu contagion, which called for almost as much patriotism, and lasted longer.

On the day he went back into civilian togs, he promised himself he would get even with eight anthropoids, to wit; one captain, one lieutenant, two sergeants, two doctors, one orderly, and a nurse. He expected to hunt them down, in their post-war haunts, and pummel them to a jelly — all but the nurse, who was to be enticed to some public place and spanked in the presence of a large, appreciative audience.

The determination to do these animals physical harm cooled, after a while, to an acidulous contempt which he occasionally tapped with a pen for the approval of demobilized thousands who, with ungodly glee, found in his devastating satires a vicarious vengeance.

Alison wrote to him almost every week while he was 'in the service.'

'I am not going to tell father,' she stated, in her first note. 'Poor man couldn't do anything about it, could he?... But, Dinny, darling, it is a frightful thing he's done to us.'

In sober truth, Dinny was incapable of viewing their tragedy with the same despair. Much as he admired Alison, their brief and unfortunate affair had not been of his own contriving. As for permanently linking his life with hers, he would as soon have married a hoisting-engine. Indeed, he had already begun to wonder, before discovery of their blood relationship, by what pleasant, painless process he might adroitly excuse himself from an impending attachment brimful of agony.

He replied to her letters at the rate of one to three, painstakingly shifting their mood, by a calculated katabasis of affection which, within three months or so, had — at least so far as he was concerned — placed their relations on an approximately normal and sound footing.

Angela wrote from the midst of a great revival in Hamilton that the Lord was blessing her labors in a miraculous way. It was not her first important revival, but the first in which she had starred. From now on, she expected to be at the head of her own company. Angela made no effort to disguise her natural gratification over the material features of her success. Dinny was pleased at this honest, albeit unintended, confession, and thought a little better of Angela. She didn't mind admitting that she was in the show business ... on behalf of The Lord, to be sure, but — well — the show business.

Joan Braithwaite was much in his thoughts. Upon the death of her father, he had written her a note. Her reply, some six weeks later (though he had promptly received a black-edged card from her mother, acknowledging his flowers), was post-marked New York. Whether she was there temporarily, or to stay, he did not know. That she expected no further correspondence was implied by the absence of a specific address. There was no one of whom he cared to inquire.

Mr. Steinberg occasionally wrote to him, as became the employer of a volunteer hero, and there was a letter from his father, shortly after he enlisted, commending him on the splendid thing that he had done. The letter was dictated, and signed in a feminine hand, doubtless the same hand that had done a score of them.

'Take this, Miss Rabbit, and make twenty originals for our enlisted employees. Miss Hare has the list of names.'

'Wish to see them, sir?'

'No — you can sign 'em.'

Dinny had chuckled while composing samples of conversation between his father and the stenographer, relative to the issue of Craig sentiments *in re* the war to end war, and save civilization.

The T-T confidently expected Dinny to come back and resume his place, wrote Mr. Steinberg, immediately after the Armistice; but there was to be no more of the family salt eaten; starve first!

With surprising ease, he found a place on *The Philadelphia Ledger*. And then, with no more effort, the bright idea came, the 'Unfrosted Persimmons' offered to be plucked, the mounting wave of prosperity rolled in, and Dinny was at liberty from clocks, bells, and whistles.

He resolved to live in New York. Why not? It was the mecca of journalism and such as do syndicated columns. He did not go there saying to himself that Joan might be accidentally encountered; but, every bus that passed him, as he strolled Fifth Avenue, was thoroughly raked with a questing eye, the roll was swiftly called in the subway-train, traffic-blocked taxis were peered into with undefended impudence, the peacock-alley of the hotel, stuffily scented, was daily, gravely, tallied off — for Joan.

Sometimes, though he was not given to worrying, naturally, Dinny found himself distressed over imagined predicaments in which she was posed in a tragic rôle. He was not quite able to reconstruct the face of a sad or beaten Joan; but, annoyingly often, he had a vision, at night, of lovely shoulders slumped in grief or pain, and the back of a curly head bowed in serious trouble.

It became a mild obsession. He had no use for telepathy, and the slightest hint of any mystical thought-conveyance was, in Dinny's opinion, the sign of a weak mind. But — he was looking for Joan, and the longer and farther he looked, the more deeply he felt that when he found her she would be vastly in need of help.

Dinny wished her well, but honestly wondered whether his anxiety might not be the product of an undefined hope that he could find Joan in a mood to accept his affection, even if at the price of some substantial favor of which she stood seriously in need. Indeed, he brooded so much over the matter that it became a definite fixation. Joan was in some kind of a scrape. Joan was hungry. Joan was walking the streets, looking for a cheap lodging-house. Joan was being imposed upon by some predatory rascal who controlled her rations.

He even tortured himself with fears of which he was ashamed. Joan was, he had discovered, possessed of a pretty active 'temperament.' Could she take care of herself if ruthlessly stampeded?

Today he was weary of the job that almost anyone might have envied him; wearied and worried.

He interlaced his long fingers behind his head, closed his eyes, and re-canvassed all the expedients he had contemplated for the recovery of his Joan.

Budding April in Central Park left him unstirred. Life was stale, flat, and unprofitable.

He began to toy with the idea of a vagabond trip through some foreign country.

CHAPTER XI

'HAD it ever occurred to you,' elaborated Dinny, as the speakeasy waiter made off with their luncheon order, 'that my gifted cousin Victor comes perilously near being an ass?'

Tommy Forsythe traced a brief design on Joe Lombroso's white tablecloth with the tip of his spoon, and grinned wryly. It was not the amiable smile that so readily curved Tommy's lips. The grin threatened a bit of irony.

'I've known that,' he said, slowly, 'for a long time; but — I hadn't supposed *you'd* ever find it out.'

'Thanks,' returned Dinny, dryly, not a little surprised at the satirical come-back. Tommy was always so direct, so honest, so transparently sincere.

'And may I inquire,' pursued Tommy, with an excellent imitation of his cousin's calculated ridicule, 'just when and how you contrived to make this belated discovery of my brother's asshood?... He arrived home only yesterday. You haven't seen him, have you?'

Dinny nodded, sipped his cocktail.

'Last night — down in the Village.... Tommy, he was just a little this side of unbearable.'

'"This side"? — looking from where?' Tommy's sour query rasped and crackled.

'Who's been feeding you raw meet, Pollyanna?... My God — I didn't know you had it in you!' Dinny stared at his cousin with honest amazement.

The Damon-and-Pythias comradeship of Dinny Brumm and Tom Forsythe, which was to rake fore and aft the whole gamut of emotion, from high delight to frantic misery, dated from the latter's receipt of a letter from Alison Craig, written from Seattle in June.

Reticence impulsively discarded, Tom's dynamic young cousin had told him everything, even to confessing an affec-

tion for Dinny out of all proportion to their blood relationship; declared she 'never expected to be the same woman
again'; urged her beloved Tommy to lose no further time in
hunting down this attractive collateral to their tribe.

Before sunset, that day, telephone communication had
been established between Tommy's office in the huge department store on Thirty-Fourth Street and Dinny's bohemian three-room suite in Greenwich Village, the shabby
equipment of which — save for his sturdy typewriter-table,
and his mother's little walnut desk — consisted of ill-related
rubbish that had passed from one impecunious artist's keep
to another's, each piece with a story to tell of battered ambitions, pitiful frugalities, and somewhat of despair.

They spent the evening together in Dinny's rooms; and
when, at midnight, they parted at his street-door, each felt
the other an old friend.

From the first, they were conscious of having little in
common, as to temperament and outlook, Dinny finding his
steady-going cousin amusingly naïve, boyishly enthusiastic
over the elementary simplicities, a 'typical case of arrested
adolescence,' though Tommy was nearly four years his
senior, and had been extraordinarily successful in business.

Tommy, encountering for the first time a determined
cynic, obviously proud of his versatile collection of disbe-
liefs, distrusts, and disenchantments, regarded his new acquaintance with fascinated interest. Dinny Brumm didn't
appear to belong to this world, at all. He had merely
dropped in, as a spectator. He stood on the side-lines, paper
and pencil in hand, watching the human race plod by, making ironical notes and grinning when it stumbled.

In general appearance, the two were strikingly alike; of
approximately the same height, weight, carriage, and pigments. They had the Craig eye, deep-set, searching, flanked
by innumerable, faintly traced crow's-feet. They shared
many an odd little trick of gesture and posture.

Alison's suggestion that Dinny's relation to their clan
should not be disclosed was approved by both of them. Tom

promptly took his handsome new acquaintance home with him, the next Sunday evening, to the Forsythe apartment in White Plains; was pleased to observe how easily his mother accepted him; was surprised at Victor's enthusiasm, for Victor rarely had any use for Tom's friends; was anxious over the eager Grace's frank display of admiration.

'Why — you two things actually *look* alike!' commented Grace, with the half-impudent candor she had learned at the feet of Victor. 'Aren't you afraid you'll quarrel?'

Victor — at that time temporarily home from Italy at the suggestion of his mother, who, as his *impresario*, thought it prudent to have the talented violinist back, occasionally, 'to conserve his contacts,' and give the papers a chance to stir his potential public to remembrance of his existence, progress, goings and comings — instantly attached himself to Dinny with a proprietary air that threatened to elbow Tommy out of the picture.

He couldn't contrive how his unimaginative old dray-horse of a brother, who knew everything about leather baggage and nothing about the creative arts, had captured the friendship of this sophisticate. He must see more of this Dinny Brumm. Brumm had the good sense to live in the Village, too, where everybody who was anybody in the field of the arts found freedom, stimulating companionship, encouragement, inspiration.

It had taken Dinny only ten minutes to discover that the Forsythe establishment operated exclusively to serve the high destiny of Victor.

Grace — dark, swarthy, shiny, with a button popped and loose hairpins — lived solely for the talented fiddler, fetching and carrying for him like an earnest retriever. Tom, nearing thirty, had apparently accepted it as his manifest destiny to devote the bulk of his salary to this lofty emprise.

Once, after three months of increasing intimacy had broken down all reserve, Dinny ventured an expression of his feelings on this matter. He and Tommy were dining together at The Astor. Victor had sailed, that morning, re-

turning to Ghili in Milan, bon-voyaged by a score of friends
from the general vicinity of Washington Square, the family,
and not quite enough inquisitive reporters to satisfy Mrs.
Forsythe.

'If I were you, Tommy, and Victor my brother, I'd request him to unstraddle himself from around my neck, and
try walking on his own feet.'

Tommy had been tardy with a reply; shook his head,
slowly.

'Victor,' he said at length, deliberately, 'was born without feet.... Victor's all soul.'

'But he eats!' persisted Dinny, indignantly.

'You don't understand. It's a long story. You see — my
mother — God bless 'er — managed to make quite an important personage of my father. She married him to make
him, and succeeded. She was so ambitious for his success
that for thirteen years she gave him twenty-four hours a
day; became just a bit obsessed, maybe.

'He died early — as you know — just as her hopes had
been fully justified, and the rewards were rolling in.... It
nearly finished her. I was only eleven, at the time, but her
condition was serious enough to worry me, dreadfully,
though just a kid. I'll not inflict you; but — she was in a
sanitarium for six months.

'Then — with the patience of a spider, she began all over.
With a kind of fierce determination, she set about building
Victor up for a career with a fiddle. Father had left prac-
tically nothing but the royalties on his phonograph records.
This income was pretty good, at first; large enough to war-
rant expensive foreign study for Victor.... Afterwards,
when the records of my father's voice began to slip — well
— I couldn't let my mother down; could I?

'Besides' — added Tommy, brightening — 'Victor might
put it over.... I sincerely hope so — for my mother's sake.'

* * * * * *

That had been in late September. It was November, now,
of the succeeding year.

Tommy Forsythe had just returned from a month in Mexico, full of interesting experiences, though not of the specific business errands that had taken him there. They rarely discussed Tommy's business. His phenomenal rise at Lacey's, from the shipping department up to the leather goods, and from successful salesman to assistant manager of the department, and from assistant to Department Chief, had been achieved in seven years; but Tommy did not often talk about it.

Dinny rather regretted now that he had spoken his thoughts about the asininity of the parasitical Victor. Tommy had enough to bear. It would have been more gracious to keep off it. However, the subject had been pushed into the open: it would have to be discussed.... The picture of last night's affair in the Village drifted unpleasantly across Dinny's memory.

He had been surprised to find Victor at the midnight arty-party in the untidy kitchen of The Red Bear. He had not known Victor was back. But, of course, he would lose no time coming to collect adulation from the art colony to which Dinny, at his fervent request, had earlier introduced him.

Victor — still boastfully giddy from eight nauseous days of hurdling home over a shrieking sea which, he was averring, had put the doctor to bed in his cap and boots, and shattered not only a thirty-year Atlantic storm-record and the captain's elbow, but all the *Vendome's* crockery (not — he languidly chortled — that the latter had been much missed after the first twelve hours out) — had come to The Red Bear in tow of Diane Wimberly, a lanky, pink-haired, lower-case poetess who needed a dickey and a thousand dollars' worth of dentistry.

Dinny had gone late to Felice's party. Once he had thought Felice quite interesting; but, in recent months, she had begun to weary him. In fact — the whole outfit, now that their novelty had worn off, lacked the originality and sparkle he had earlier imputed to the Villagers when, as a lonely stranger in New York, he was in need of quick and easy friends.

Last night's bizarre affair had palled on him. The thing had been carried on in murky gloom feebly tinctured with magenta by a sooty lantern suspended from a peg in one of the massive, ancient, weathered-oak rafters — made of half-inch pine, and installed the previous summer.

Victor — whose voice Dinny instantly recognized, even before his eyes had adjusted to the thick fog into which he groped — was seated in the dilapidated wheelbarrow intended for the 'fagots,' when there were any — The Red Bear, with reckless leanings toward Communism, pretended to be a Russian peasant's hovel — loathsomely detailing his recent discomforts at sea.

Dinny's tardy arrival had not interrupted the undulating flow of his cousin's obnoxious reminiscence, nor was the company much distracted from its wan interest in the nautical narrative.

Felice (Mamie) Manners (Johnson), the hostess, seated on the floor near the doorway, on an outspread newspaper, moved over a little to make room; and, pursing her scarlet mouth in apology for the humble offering, handed him, with her fingers, a large, pallid cream-puff which she ruefully extracted from the bottom of a brown-paper bag wherein the dessert course had been served.

Dinny gingerly surveyed the gift, in the manner of a fastidious dowager examining a freshly exhumed skull, to the considerable amusement of Felice, who, a little drunk was finding Victor tediously verbose, and wished to be playful.

Wanting Dinny to know that she shared his carnival attitude toward her party, Felice strangled the empty bag, put the neck of it to her blood-red mouth, and with many long, cheek-distending, eye-bugging exhalations, proceeded to the task of its inflation; or nearly so, the final blast proving abortive due to her sudden conviction that her employment was ridiculous enough to merit a shocking explosion of suppressed mirth.

Victor reproachfully glanced in the direction of the disorder, but calmly continued his monologue in a marcelled, affected baritone that inspired Dinny — a little drunk, also — to nudge Felice to attention while he feigned to take careful aim at the self-infatuated minstrel with the soggy token of her vanished hospitality.

'Dare you!' whispered Felice, cupping her mouth with her hand, but Dinny reprovingly shook his head, pretending shocked regret that she would entertain the thought of such an effrontery.... Then he had stretched out his long legs, and tried to listen.

Victor had finished with his disgusting *mal-de-mer* and was now in a messianic mood concerning the martyrdom of all true artists, and the tribulations of cat-gut and horse-tail artists in particular. Evidently somebody with a bit of money had recently stepped on Victor's slim, expressive fingers, for he was swishing about with a bare rapier that threatened to annihilate the well-to-do.

Dinny wondered if this were the formal opening of Victor's campaign to impress his friends that he had a good excuse for failure; wondered if Victor was frightened, now that he had finally caught up with his exceedingly bright future, and had it to demonstrate.

'Old Victor,' reflected Dinny, as he sat listening to the makings of an alibi — 'good old Victor knows time's up. He's either got to catch fish, or cut bait, or bail the boat.'

Abstractedly, Dinny had let his heavy eyes rove about the room while his blasé cousin deprecated the necessity for living in a world propelled by the almighty dollar.

He was acquainted with all but two — the youth with the black velvet jacket and negligent Windsor tie, and the thin girl beside the youth, a blue beret drawn down over one eye, and a limp, home-made cigarette dangling precariously from her lip.

The rest of them he knew quite well. Gregory, thirty-five and tuberculous, had confided freely. Gregory was writing an important novel; quite a bit daring, it was; might have to be privately printed. He had been at it now for upwards of three years. It was his first novel, though there had been a slim, mauve, deckle-edged (Gregory was ashamed of the deckle — but Aunt Agatha, of Phoenix, Arizona, who was financing it, quite insisted) volume of unpunctuated verse. Dinny had one of these, a presentation copy, autographed with a scrawl that beckoned the beneficiary to consult the title-page for verification of the little book's parentage.

Vivacious Anne Pelham, who, to better her credit at the expense of her artistic integrity, had confessed her degeneration to drawing for commercial purposes — though what or for whom she drew Dinny had never learned — caught his vagrant eye, smiled, twinkled friendly fingers. The salute would cost him five dollars, thought Dinny. Anne already owed him thirty, not that he cared: the poor little fellow was always hungry.

Sylvia (what the devil was her other name? — He had always thought of her as Carmichael) sang, or was going to ... in opera... once she got a chance. Squat and shaggy Carmichael, next her, did portraits — quite atrocious ones, Dinny thought, though it was out of his line — which Sylvia, who lived adjacent on the fourth floor of a cheap and dirty, gas-reeking, bug-infested tenement house, and shared the bow-legged painter's kitchen, bath, studio, and fatuous ambitions, considered masterpieces.

They had never struck Dinny Brumm quite this way before. He had sympathetically appraised them as a wistful tribe of aspirants to success in creating something interpretative of their thoughts. They had become suddenly ridiculous. There wasn't one of the dozen present, he reflected, who had ever done anything worth a second look. With the possible exception of the gloomy Victor, whose career was unpredictable, not a man or woman of the lot was likely ever to get to first base in the game whose lingo they prattled with such glib familiarity.

At long last, Victor's monotonous harangue was concluded. The audience untangled its legs, milled about the room, yawned toward the door. Felice led Dinny to the little group still clustered about the wheelbarrow.

Victor extended a limp, soft, slim hand.

"'Lo, Dinny.... So you're here....Who told you I was home?'

'Nobody... I didn't know you were back.'

Somehow — the raw impudence of the chap annoyed him. His egotism was insufferable.

'In fact,' drawled Dinny, 'we've ventured to have several little social affairs much like this, in your absence; just to keep our spirits up until you returned.... Hope you don't mind.'

No — Victor didn't mind. He smiled, indulgently, and said it was quite the proper thing to do, he was sure; and turned to luxuriate in the twitter of the new girl with the blue beret.

Dinny had slipped out, presently. The Village was beginning to bore him.

* * * * * *

Tommy impatiently shattered one of Joe Lombroso's crusty rolls with his fingers, a bit heated by Dinny's spoofing.

'Ordinarily,' replied Tommy, 'I don't permit myself to become disturbed over anyone else's damned foolishness besides my own; but, now you've invited it, I'd like to tell you something that will be good for your soul — if you still have one.'

'Attaboy, Tommy!' applauded Dinny, merrily. 'Skin 'em alive!'

Tommy drew a heavy frown that Dinny had never seen him wear before.

'This isn't going to be funny,' he muttered. 'After lunch, we're going over to your squalid hole in Daubville, where you're to listen to something I've got for you.... And here's hoping you won't get sore.'

Dinny threw back his head and laughed.

'I'd really like to see you on the war-path, Tommy.'

The subject was not resumed until, having climbed the dirty stairs, and tossing their hats on the littered table, Dinny, amused and expectant, lighted his pipe, and signed Tommy to 'turn it on.'

'As I understand it,' began Tommy, didactically, 'you are one of the most venomous — certainly the noisiest — of all the animals now in revolt against everything your betters have built up over a period of five thousand years, or so.

'You've distinguished yourself as a kicker, knocker, scorner, spoofer, and snarler. Your sour comments on faith, piety, and patriotism are worth a dollar a line.... And, incidentally, I bet you anything you care to put up that the time will come — not long from now — when you've repeated, over and over, all the smart and surly words you know — your stuff won't be worth ten cents a garbage-pailful.... Some of it's beginning to run a bit thin already, Dinny, if you don't mind my speaking of it. I just noticed in the last issue of *The Emancipates* that you used the word "moron" nine times. Better get yourself a new thesaurus. ... You're writing too much, anyhow, my son. Your rhetorical disbursements are so far ahead of your intellectual income that you'll be bankrupt, presently. However — that's your affair.

'You've been the great champion of sincerity. You've thumbed your nose at the hypocritical Bible-whackers, and the gavel-swingers, and the sword-toters. Everybody's an ass but you — and the Villagers; you — and your little hand-picked minority of freedom-fanatics.... Parsons and professors, doctors and lawyers, senators and judges, philanthropists and missionaries — you've had 'em on the grill in a dozen contemptible magazines. You've roasted 'em whole, brought 'em back in a stew, served 'em cold in a salad with sulphuric acid dressing.

'And yet — you'll live down here in this poisonous rat-hole, chumming with a bunch of third-rate, would-be artists, yodeling about liberty to express themselves!

'You rant about hypocrisy! Hypocrisy!... My God!... Can you imagine anything more utterly rotten with pretense than the rubbish that's written and daubed and sculped by these ——'

'Have a light, Tommy,' interrupted Dinny, offering a match, 'and don't yell so loud.... It's Sunday.'

'You wipe that smile off your face, and sit down! I'm not through yet. I mean to tell you some more, and if you don't like it you can go straight to ——'

'I know, Tommy, what you have in mind.... Proceed.... I'm liking it.'

'The new art! Bah! I've been supporting art since I was a youngster; missed college to become an art-patron; had the house littered with artists for years.... Ninety per cent of 'em too incompetent to hold a job, too lofty to earn a living, and too lazy to wash their ears.

'The new literature — realism! Tripe! A lot of dirty stories dignifiedly told by dirty-minded little shrimps, and solemnly discussed by pretenders who make-believe they are enduring the dirt so they can capture the beauty of the "style," when it's plain they're only enduring the "style" for the sake of the dirt.... Kidding themselves!

'Modernism — modernistic painting!... Cubist stuff!... Nobody can fool me, any more, about that.... This latest whelp of modernism is nothing but an idiot begotten of Gin and Geometry.

'And *you* — cramming the magazines full of high-browed sarcasm about the dull slaves of superstition!... chanting about freedom!... yowling about the unpardonable sin of stupidity! Haven't you any sense of humor, at all?... These birds have imposed on you, down here. They've made you believe they were artists — most of 'em clumsy dubs who couldn't draw an honest picture of a long-tailed rat.... Try it out, if you don't believe me. Ask one of these paupers to draw you a picture. Offer this Felice person a hundred dollars to draw — not paint — but *draw* a picture of those two hats on your table, and see what you'll get.... Hypocrisy — hell!'

'Tommy — I've an idea!... Just came to me.... I'm going to write a novel... about the Village.... It's marvellous! Wonder I never thought of it before.'

Tommy scowled, relighted his pipe, puffed moodily.

'What you'd far better do is to let up on mean and surly criticism for a while. There ought to be some kind of a mental laxative on sale for chaps like you. Why don't you treat the world as if you weren't too superior to live in it? Pity there isn't some neighboring planet for you scoffers to go to, once in a while, for a vacation.'

Dinny suddenly recalled himself from the absorbing reverie into which he had drifted. Tommy had been chiding him, pitilessly, and he had missed much of the latter part of it. He reproached himself for his wool-gathering at such a moment.

'You're quite outspoken, Tommy.... But — Boy! — you've given me a whopping inspiration... for the novel, you know. I mean to do it, without delay.... It will be a wow!'

There was no further withstanding the contagion of Dinny's enthusiasm; no use bristling against Dinny's conciliatory smile. Tommy capitulated with a sigh. The chap was incorrigible, utterly inaccessible to reproof.

'Let's go do something,' he said, restlessly, reaching for his hat.

'Young Vladimir Polovsky's talking at three in the Village theater,' suggested Dinny. 'Shall we hear him?'

'Rot!' exploded Tommy. 'Hell of a lot of amusement that would be! More dribble about Communism; eh?'

'It might improve your mind,' exhorted Dinny, paternally. 'I'll bet you never heard a real Communist talk?'

'Don't you believe I haven't. Just got done firing one — a female one — from the store.... Talk? That girl could talk down a Senate filibuster!'

'Yes,' Dinny wagged his head, knowingly, 'that's the answer of capital... big business... to any independent opinion offered by the slaves!... Poor girl airs her theories — and gets fired!'

Tommy chuckled, reminiscently.

'Well — this happened to be the answer of big business to a young slattern who refused to act on the broad hint that she'd be improved by a shampoo. Nobody at Lacey's cared a damn about Sophie's bad opinion of the capitalistic system. It was her revolt against soap.'

Dinny remained loftily skeptical, but willing to grin.

'Lacey's may have pretended that was the reason, but Sophie would probably have been given the sack, just the same. Sophie' — Dinny feigned a sympathetic tear — 'Sophie wanted to be a little candle of liberty — and you snuffed her out!'

Tommy shook his head, laughing.

'We sniffed her out.'

'You've a mean tongue, Tommy.... Suppose we go up to The Capitol and see Hollywood canonize some racketeer who's just come home with his pockets full of money to lift the mortgage off his widowed mother's cottage.... That's about your speed.'

* * * * * *

Dinny began work on his novel, that night. It was his first long story, and he meant to spread it on a huge canvas that would provide plenty of room for the minutiæ of detail.

He knew he could draw Victor — to the life — and meant to make him lead the ludicrous procession of enchanted bums across an elaborate stage set for Art passionate with Revolt.

He believed he would let Victor succeed, at least measurably, and return from time to time collecting laud, honor, and glory from his satellites. As an affected, arrogant ass, Victor would be hard to beat.

There would be room in the story for a bit of honest pathos, too, he thought. These people's ambitions would be vapid enough, and their pretensions no end silly; but there was nothing fictitious about their hunger and heart-break.

Dinny paused in his swift typing of the rough memorandum for the first chapter, and wondered if he would be able to do the *lento* movement, when he came to it. Hadn't he debarred himself from any such excursions into the 'human interest' zone of sincere yearning mixed with tears? He had so consistently mocked at everything savoring of the sentimental that he doubted his ability to write about the deep emotions without inviting a hilarious 'haw-haw' from his cynical constituency.

He settled back in his chair, long hands dangling inert over its arms, and gave himself to sober reflection on this dilemma.

His field had always seemed so pleasantly inexhaustible. Why — a man could keep on spoofing current movements forever! There was positively no limit to the materials at one's elbow. So long as there was an absurd human race, competing in silliness, there would be daily something new to grin at. The satirist's mine had barely been scratched.

Tonight, Dinny's ironically amusing profession seemed suddenly to have walled him in. His field of exploration was quite restricted, after all. Tommy Forsythe had given him an anxious moment, that afternoon, hinting that certain pet phrases of ridicule and contempt, which had served him well, were in danger of becoming tarnished ornaments.

Perhaps he had better stop using the words 'moron' and 'imbecile.' It was a fact that he had called them in to explode disparaging comment rather more frequently than he should.

For a long time he sat meditatively tugging at his left ear-lobe, absently fingering the key-board with the other hand.... Nonsense! He couldn't do a novel! He had had so much highly lucrative sport in ridiculing every phase of tender sentiment — the sickly slobber of penitence, the mawkish drool of the meddling doers-of-good, the exultant imbecility of idealism, the owlish asininity of philanthropic fuss-budgets and sniffling uplifters who loped about crying aloud over the plight of care-free people who desired only to be left alone — that he seriously doubted whether he dared risk a forthright invasion of 'heart issues.'

Viewed from a slightly different stance — Dinny, adroit in metaphor, was fond of considering his problems in the algebra of his craft — the section of the woods where he claimed the right to swing his axe was limited to a very small tract of the forest. It was his job to cut down, chop up, stew, and distill astringents, bitters, and lethals from henbane, hemlock, and wormwood — a sophisticated employment. He would only seem ridiculous tapping maple trees, or sawing down hollow sycamores for their wild honey.

Who would have thought that staid old Tommy would pip off like that?... Talked a little like Joan.... Tommy and Joan would have a good time together, if ever they met.... Dear Joan!

Slowly disrobing and easing himself into dressing-gown and slippers, Dinny recapitulated the strategic might-have-beens of his arrested romance with Joan; relived that passionate half-hour when he had sat, fists clenched, in his dormitory room at Magnolia, debating whether to punish the insufferable Kling.

Suppose he had cooled off, and decided to let Kling go unrebuked.... Suppose the piece in *The Iconoclast* had not appeared at that unlucky moment.... Suppose Doctor Braithwaite had been secure enough in his position for Joan to risk a response to his honest overtures of reconciliation.... He might have had Joan!

And then — what? Joan would have insisted on his living in a Fool's Paradise, no doubt. She would have coaxed and nagged him into a pretense of sharing her ingenuous optimism. He would have spent his life driving spiles into maples, and boiling the sap down to syrup and selling it to the fudge-makers. Ye gods — what a career!... Thirty-five or forty dollars a week, riding up and down elevators, interviewing candidates, magnates, and redeemers who would impressively keep him waiting in their outer offices while they sat hungrily watching the clock, lusting to let him in for a padful of their oracles.... No — it wouldn't have done. There would have been no 'Unfrosted Persimmons.' Joan would have seen to that. The 'Persimmons' would have been brought to market ripe — sticky — sicky sweet — rottenly soft.

And yet ——

Dinny sighed, turned on his bed-lamp, rolled in, and tried to read the current Lawrence; pretty clever dirt, that. ... Rather amusing — Tommy's appraisal of erotica. Tommy was more than half right, of course. Previous to the recent emancipation from superficial prudery, the male youths had climbed up into the haymow to exchange convictions on the ever-exciting subject, and the girls, in threesomes, their arms twined around each other, had taken a nice long walk, whispering with red cheeks.... Something unhealthily furtive about that, of course.

Now the talk was all out in the open.... Lecturers packed hotel convention-halls with rosy-faced, eager, wide-eyed customers who owed it to themselves to post up on psychology as it related to the old, old problem.... No longer was it necessary for the inquisitive youngster to hide his nasty little paper-backed shocker in a corner of the oats-bin.... The subject had been milled up into 'literature,' now.... There need be no further hypocrisy or furtiveness about this matter.... Dinny audibly expelled a contemptuous 'Pish!'... Old Tommy was dead right!

All these college boys and girls swarming into classes on 'Abnormal Psychology'... all these altruistic women elbowing into the Court of Domestic Relations... all these questors of culture, hunting for rhetorical gems in the new, breath-takingly frank, censor-baiting literature of libidinousness!... Same old story... same old furtiveness. But — while the earlier crop of curious youngsters had deceived their parents, the new outfit were deceiving themselves!

Dinny turned a few pages, and pushed the book off the bed onto the floor; snapped the light, closed his eyes, scowled.

And yet ——

Whatever Joan might have been able to do to him and his literary aspirations, it might have been worth the sacrifice.... Gad — what a thoroughbred!

Vivid pictures of her came, lingered, and made way for others even more luminous.... Joan — radiant, supple, agile, tantalizing, generously blending her splendid body with his, that first afternoon on the ice... Joan — demurely eyeing him, and denying it with an indignant toss of the head when he caught her, in silly little Ernie's fussy museum... Joan — warm across his shoulders, her cheek against his, scolding into his ear and hating him with all her might while she drove him nearly mad with her rampant vitality... Joan — gently chiding, tenderly wistful, in his arms!... Joan's kiss!

He must find Joan. Suddenly, the slumbering, half-hopeless, half-abandoned yearning for her almost suffocated him. Whatever it might cost — even to the ruinous price of degrading himself to the maple-sugar business — he must see Joan. They were made for each other. How often he had said 'Rot!' in comment on some such observation made in reference to a congenial pair. But, it wasn't rot. Joan was his — and he meant to have her.

Item by item, Dinny recovered her in every remembered posture, expression, mood, each delicious recollection confirming his decision to track her down and have it out with her.

He reinvoiced all the tentative projects that had occurred to him, earlier, for quests of the vanished Joan. This time he would see it through. He would pocket his prudence, and ask questions of people who might know.

A light suddenly broke. Dinny grinned, nodded, rose, went across to his mother's desk, and began to scribble. For a half-hour he wrote and tore and flung away. At length he was determined to be satisfied with his production, addressed an envelope to *The Times*, Want Ads, enclosed his copy and a five-dollar note.

Dressing hurriedly, he went downstairs, telling himself he was silly to be so precipitate, seeing there was nothing to be gained by posting his letter at two-thirty A.M., but eager to relieve his impatience, somehow.

Wide-awake, mentally turbulent, he walked all the way to The Battery, seeing nothing en route but a stuffy little coffee-shop where he stopped and gulped a cup of scalding brown stuff that had been stained by the original grounds described in the lease.

Now that he had made the adventure, Dinny wondered if he could wait until Tuesday. His ad would appear then. Joan would probably read it before the day was out.... And then what?

Time dragged very slowly, all Monday. It was impossible to concentrate. Dinny was thankful he was a few installments ahead of the game in the manufacture of his 'Green Cheese.'

At seven, Tuesday morning, he rushed over to The Brevoort, bought a *Times*, went in to breakfast, rummaged deep in the advertising pages, found the column of 'Female Help Wanted,' and searched for his request.... It looked a bit crazy.

> RESEARCH   SECRETARY — by   feature writer. Applicant must be at least casually interested in Indian mounds, preferably of southern Ohio: graduate small college, member sorority; native Wis.; 26, ht. 5:7¼; wt. 125; brown hair and eyes. Experienced ice skater preferred. Excellent salary. Reply in handwriting to Times X29008.

CHAPTER XII

His decision, a fortnight later, to see Angela in action was one of the most unaccountable caprices to which Dinny Brumm had ever yielded.

The sudden resolve to go to Dorchester, New York, and watch Angela heal the sick and cast out devils, was arrived at one Wednesday evening shortly after a casual little dinner with four neighbors at the Purple Pig.

Indeed, the first insistent bleat of desire to do this eccentric thing had whimpered from the depths of Dinny's mind during the dinner conversation when Felice Manners had moodily mooned over her early adventures with religion back in Gimmel, Illinois.

Felice, to judge from the blue circles under her heavy eyes, and the smeary elisions of her thick talk, had been steadily tippling all day. She was now making a muddy landing from her ascension into the upper ether of Bacchanalia.

On such occasions, Felice shamelessly turned her soul inside-out for the edification of whosoever happened to be within range of her appalling self-disclosures.

This time, a brief — and, to Dinny, unwelcome — conversation about Angela, now well on the way to becoming a national figure, had set Felice going about the ponderous piety of Grandfather Johnson's home in frowsy little Gimmel where, at nine, she had been dutifully taken in, after the death of her mother, and had remained until, at sixteen, she had fled unfunded and unpursued.

And while Felice rumbled heavily on, recovering fugitive scraps of a stormy girlhood that had creased the brow and whitened the whiskers of Grandfather Johnson — 'and Grandmothersh, too,' she had added, with an irresistible touch of realism — Dinny, possessed of memories not dissimilar, twirled his own reel back to weedy little Zanesdale.

Now and again, and at briefer intervals, Dinny had been aware of momentary surges — something very like nostalgia. Increasingly given to self-analysis, as life became more and more stale and unpromising, he found this the most singular of his mental phenomena.

It was quite natural, reflected Dinny, that a fortunate man who, in youth, had lived in a congenial home from which he had emerged, at length, reluctantly, would so cherish his memories that there would ever be a strong tug in that direction. It was easy to understand how, across a widening chasm of miles and years, such a man might so long for home and a recovery of its endearments that the yearning would obsess him.

But — as in his own case — for a man who, in youth, had fretted in his home, counting the days which must elapse until he could escape its intolerable irksomeness, eventually rushing out of it without one backward glance, asking nothing but to be spared the necessity of a return, these occasional tidal-waves of homesickness were inexplicable.

Dinny found himself wondering if it might not be true that the homing instinct is universal, omnipresent, inevitable; not very much conditioned by any individual's immediate reactions to his native environment while in it. Why, he even had fleeting seizures of desire to see frumpy old Aunt Martha!

Frequently he told himself that the next time he had an errand in Chicago, he would start a day early and drop off in Zanesdale; he would sit on the fence at the corner of Harsh's melon-patch, and watch the Erie 'fast-lines' whiz by.

These attacks did not last long, however, and when he had regained his sober senses, Dinny would accuse himself of a growing tendency toward weak-mindedness. It would be entirely consistent with his unhappy career, he thought, if, at about forty, he would have to be carted off to a funny-house.

He had rarely thought of Angela for several years. Lately

she was much on his mind. Angela was becoming famous — or notorious — the choice of an adjective depending on the mood of the reader who found her startling exploits, at the behest of Heaven, demanding larger space in the newspapers.

The first important tidings of her spectacular ministry had broken from Spottswood, Pennsylvania, where for six hectic weeks she had had that smoky mill-town by the ears.

The revival had begun in the custody of the biggest church in Spottswood; had rapidly outgrown its quarters and migrated to the city auditorium; and, because it was September, had swarmed to the County Fair Grounds where the Holy Ghost had obliged Angela with a recurrence of Pentecost.

Hundreds — screamed the big black headlines — had rushed about, babbling 'tongues' which sounded strangely even in the ears of a polyglot foundry-town composed of a little of everything all the way from Mesopotamia and the parts of Libya about Cyrene to the uttermost jungles of Siam and the suburbs of Babel.

Still other hundreds, unblest with tongues, had ecstatically rolled in the sacred sawdust, popping out of one trance into another. In the hilarious 'after meetings,' happy converts milled up and down the aisles, affectionately embracing their fellow-lunatics without regard to age, sex, or color.

After a short interval of recuperation, Angela was reported at Wrayville, Tennessee, from whence the news proceeded of a miraculous restoration of sight to an elderly woman, nine years blind. A local doctor had verified the miracle, though there had been some difficulty verifying the doctor, who, the Wrayville Medical Association insisted, was not an oculist, but a specialist in botts and glanders.

Presently Angela was again on the hook in twenty score of composing-rooms, this time at Stillman, Iowa, whither excursion trains from neighboring towns hurried with yearning cargoes of sick and afflicted.

'Thish Ashula Brumm' — Felice had thickly inquired,

that Wednesday evening, at the Purple Pig — 'sisher o' yoursh, Dinny?'

The Carmichaels, and the Strothers boy who played Sylvia's accompaniments, laughed.

'Do I strike you as having come from a family of deities?' countered Dinny, rather annoyed that the question had come up.

Felice nodded, thoughtfully.

'Sush ash you, Dinny, alwaysh come f'm holy hillsh.'

'Perhaps Dinny's a fallen angel,' suggested Sylvia.

'No — I mean 't,' persisted Felice, with an expansive gesture. 'If all th' atheish and agnoshish in thish rotten villish were honesh, nine out o' ten would shay... born pioush home.'

'Let's begin with you, then,' proposed Strothers, indulgently. 'You're an atheist, aren't you, Felice?'

'Ever' mornin',' went on Felice, woodenly, 'Grandfa'r took twenty-poun' Bible on hish lap, an' read long chapter f'm Deuteromony er Ebeneesher ——'

'No such book as Ebenezer,' corrected Dinny.

Felice grinned, cannily, over having scored a point.

'Uh-huh! — jushesh I sushpected, Dinny Brumm.... You were brought up on 't. You're f'm holy hillsh — jush like me.'

'Go on, Felice,' urged Carmichael. 'What did Grandfather do next?'

'Well — after he had read longesh chapter he could find, 'bout th' Amalekitesh an' th' Stalactitesh, all eight o' ush shwoop' faish-down into our chair cushionsh, an' tied an' untied an' retied th' yarn knotsh while our Heav'ly Fa'er wush thanked that He had shpared ush to shee th' light o' 'nother day... hell of a compliment f'r Heav'ly Fa'er... Heav'ly Fa'er hadn't murdered ush all in our bedsh.'

Aware, from previous experience, that Felice, at such moments, was very sensitive, Dinny had done his honest best to keep a straight face during this recital; but, having clamped down a bit too hard on his feelings, he now regretfully blew up with a loud report which sent Felice into a pitiable drizzle of maudlin tears.

Dinny had never been party to an event at once so tragic and so devastatingly ridiculous. Felice, barely intelligible, poured out a story that might have made the angels weep while they laughed. As a child, the lonesome little thing had gone out by herself into a far corner of the garden and looked bravely up into the blue, telling God she didn't believe a word of it, and hoping He'd please excuse poor old Grandfather Johnson, who didn't know any better, and meant all right.

'An' God ushe t' talk t' me... Nosshir, I mean 't!... He would jush grin, and shay, "Thash all ri', li'l' Felish. You run an' play!"'

Sylvia had taken Felice home when it was generally agreed she had talked enough, and was attracting too much attention.

Leaving the mussy little restaurant, Dinny had gone to his room somewhat depressed. Felice had stirred some quite vivid recollections of his own boyhood. There had been a time when he, too, had been acutely conscious of something — something winged, inside himself — looking up inquiringly, hopefully. Felice had apologized to God in behalf of Grandfather Johnson. Dinny remembered having had much the same feeling as a little boy. God had been maligned. God was their Father... and they had gone down on all fours, twice a day, grovelling like heathen.

But, strangely enough, Dinny wanted to see what was this peculiar energy that Angela had laid hold on. Angela might be no end a mountebank — probably was nothing less or else than that — but thousands were finding something at her hands. Surely she hadn't inherited anything from his smug and stupid Uncle Miles that would stampede city after city into orgies of repentance and hysterias of joy.

At ten-thirty, that night, he was in his berth, listening to the trucks pound the rail-ends as his train scampered up the right bank of the Hudson, and wondering what had possessed him to spend any time or money on such a silly adventure.

*   *   *   *   *   *

Thursday afternoons — Dinny learned at *The Dorchester Sun*, where he had been cordially welcomed when applying for a press ticket to the Angela Brumm Revival — were set aside for the healing of children.... Lucky, he thought... couldn't have struck a better day!

He lunched with Fred Channing, the editor, after having met a few of the boys at the office, where, as was inevitable, he had been chaffed about his gifted 'relative.'

Channing had slowly closed one eye, impressively, in the midst of the banter.

'You wait!... Some woman!... May be a quack and a faker — but, you take it from me — Angela's got a lot o' *It!*'

They went to the stage door of the big public auditorium at two-thirty. Literally hundreds of people stood about the entrances, hopeful of crowding in to secure standing-room after the ticket-holders had been accommodated. In tow of Channing, Dinny followed through a long concrete corridor, swarming with the surpliced choir, busy functionaries, reporters, parsons, and up the stairs to the large stage, set for three hundred.

The auditorium was packed to suffocation. A tense feeling seemed to pervade the place, as if some astounding event — some sickish tragedy, perhaps — were imminent. Dinny's eye swept the huge hall; raked the galleries into a vertiginous smear of wide-staring, open-mouthed, morbidly curious expectants. Then he analyzed the crowd — small sections of it — item by item; nervously thumbing their paper-backed hymn-books with mechanical fingers, gnawing their lips, apprehensively, as if they had come to a hanging.

The great choir filed in, confident and conscious of its importance, and stood, as in a tableau, until the celebrated

Maurice Manwaring, lithe, athletic, leonine of head, an extraordinarily handsome brute, strode on, raised both modishly white-flanneled arms, and with a commanding gesture that seemed to reach far forward and grab the first triumphant note out of their obedient open mouths, he summoned them to the great declaration that the affair was on, and Heaven was being called in to witness. The piece was Gounod's 'Unfold, Ye Portals.'

Dinny had not been so stirred to the depths — ever! He had come as a spectator; rather a cold-blooded spectator, too. Now he felt himself vigorously pushed into the crowd.

'Un — fo-o-o-o-l-l-ld!... *Unn — fo — o-o-o-ol-l-ld!*... *UNNN–FO–O–O–O–OL–L–LD!!* — YE POR–TALS EV–ER–LAAAST–ING!'

The great crowd couldn't resist the pull of it another minute; came up out of its seat in response to something gripping that reached out, and took hold, and lifted up. Dinny found himself on his feet, his heart pounding, his eyes smarting, his throat dry.

Angela came on, passing him so nearly he could have reached out a hand and touched her black velvet gown. She was an insuperably regal figure, exquisitely formed, incredibly beautiful, with the carriage of a goddess and the rapt eyes of a mystic. Except for the white silk stole which depended almost to her knees, she wore no ornament. Walking confidently to the center of the stage, she rested an expressive white hand on the pulpit and gazed over the multitude with a sort of inspired compassion. Dinny would have given his all for a faithful picture of what was actually going on, at that instant, in Angela's mind.... It was utterly impossible, preposterous, that this woman could stand there, before this yearning crowd, swept by the nerve-tingling influence of such music — and be calmly plotting a hoax!... Angela should have the benefit of every doubt. *Angela was not a fake!*

The anthem rose to a great *crescendo*. The multitude

sat. Angela stood. There was a heavy hush. She prayed. It was a quiet voice, but commanding. Angela maternally gathered up the three thousand in her soft, strong arms, and, having affectionately held them to her ample breast and wiped their tears and fears away, tenderly handed them over into the infinitely stronger arms of their Father.

It was not God's wish that any of these little ones should suffer, or face life unable to savor its sweetness.... Dinny remembered it was a 'Children's Healing Day,' and, glancing about, became aware of babies in arms, little cripples in arms, big-headed, empty-headed, pallid, grotesque *monsters* in arms. Never had he seen such a conglomeration of juvenile misfortune. They seemed suddenly to spring into existence. He had not noticed them before.

God did not want these little ones to suffer.... By faith, they would be healed.... God had promised.... It was enough. We could take Him at His word.

Spontaneously, the choir, as if unable to restrain its pent-up emotions, quietly hummed the old hymn-tune which Dinny recognized as 'My Faith Looks Up to Thee.'

Angela, face uplifted, blue eyes wide, enraptured, called upon her Father, these little ones' Father, to keep His word with her — with them — with us.... Then there began to come from the depths of the auditorium a surge, a sobbing surge of questing song, as if it was welling up out of hearts rather than throats. Dinny's eyes filled. He didn't sing; couldn't have sung; but he was conscious of being in and of that longing multitude whose honest faith — or whose desperate hope, at least — was reaching up.

Dinny never liked to remember, afterwards, the procession that came down the aisles, and up the stairs to the stage, bearing its pitiable freight to the Lamb of Calvary and His calmly confident representative.... Pale, twisted, little children... blind babies... hare-lipped... club-footed ... hunch-backed.

Angela laid her potent hands upon each of them, raised her eyes, murmured a prayer, and a motherly woman in white gently propelled them on, across the stage, to another stairway leading back into the auditorium.

At the foot of this stairway, a huddle of young women, also in white, were receiving the bewildered mothers with encouraging smiles, distributing gifts to the children — gay trinkets, oranges, little dolls for the girls, mechanical toys for the boys.

Dinny began to understand the reason for this quite dismaying anti-climax to Angela's wholesale conferment of God's grace. It was a shock-absorber to provide distraction of the hapless victims' minds from their disappointment in case the power of God was not immediately manifest. There was no question about Angela's excellent intent. Her faith looked up to the Lamb of Calvary. She sincerely hoped — more than hoped; expected — that the Lamb of Calvary would take pity on these wretched. But if, for some baffling reason unknown to Angela, the Lamb of Calvary let her down, there would still be dolls and oranges and toy automobiles, and a red, red rose for mother.

The long procession kept coming on. Dinny was seated where he could observe the faces of the mothers at the moment Angela was in the act of bearing their anxieties to the Throne. He winced as if witness to surgery performed without benefit of anæsthesia. The faces of the mothers seemed strangely alike, the tense, stiff, open lips showing tips of teeth in half-open mouths, as if expectant of sharp and sudden pain; as if Angela were a surgeon, and they had come to have her lance some deep, dangerous infection; waiting, now, for the plunge of the knife. The faces were all set in masks — masks through whose stiff vents, round, wide eyes, and open, straining mouths — the mothers were prepared to shout for joy or scream with despair.

Not often did the mothers immediately inspect their children, after the supplication. They dared not tarry to do that. The thing was to hurry on, as bidden. Dinny suspected the management did not encourage any loitering on the stage, any looking to see.

One mother's trembling hand ran swiftly down the thin leg of her six-year-old boy, and felt for the crooked little foot. The crooked little foot was still there, just as she knew it would be, her tightly pursing lips seemed to say. Perhaps her faith had not been very robust.

One young mother paused, momentarily blocking the traffic, while she lifted her blind baby shoulder high and gazed hungrily into the child's opaque eyes. All the sickening grief of a sickeningly grieving world spread across her face as she slowly turned her head and made a pitiful little sucking noise with her lips as if she had been stabbed. A compassionate hand was laid under her elbow, and she resumed her tramp to the stairs, consulting each step for safe footing as she descended from Calvary's Fountain to have pressed into her trembling fingers an amiable, smiling, wide-eyed, blue-eyed, china doll — the gift of the white-organdied angels, and the black-velveted Angela, and the blood-red Hands, nailed to a Tree. They also handed her a red rosebud. Dinny hoped the management had had the forethought to snip off the thorns.

A bit of unusual stir about Angela detached his gaze from the retreating figure of the blind baby's mother. A nine-year-old boy, with steel braces on his emaciated legs, was being gingerly put down from his father's arms, at Angela's command. She prayed — audibly, this time — in a tone of assurance, of gratitude, as if the boon she asked was already a *fait accompli*.

The silence was absolute, as Angela unbuckled the boy's braces. The clatter they made, as she cast them aside on the floor, had the effect of heavy chains dropped by a prisoner freed. She took the child by the hand, and bade him walk.

He walked! There was a sudden, concerted intake of breath in three thousand open mouths. The father of the boy, an embarrassed farmer, smiled self-consciously, smoothed his tawny mustache, and followed along. The mother stooped and picked up the braces. Angela darted a swift glance, noting the act. She betrayed a faint, fleeting trace of annoyance, but instantly regained her grateful smile, put the skinny little hand of the lad into the big red hand of his unstirred father, and quickly returned to her post beside the pulpit.

Dinny's quick intuition suggested that the little drama had gone bad. The boy's father was a dolt, and his mother was a woman of little faith. Doubtless both of them knew the boy could take a few faltering steps without his braces if someone held his hand. To the vast crowd, however, the miracle was genuine enough. Anyway — the crowd had come to see miracles, and was definitely on Angela's and the Lord's side.

The meeting was drawing to an abrupt close now. The choir had risen and was leading the congregation in praising God From Whom All Blessings Flow, with an unction that certified to the complete success of the demonstration of grace outpoured.

Angela, with face a bit drawn, evidencing that the neural strain of the hour had cost something, raised a graceful, pontifical hand, pronounced a brief benediction, and left the pulpit. As she passed Dinny, she glanced straight into his staring eyes, stopped, searched his face, and spoke:

'Ferdinand!'

Dinny extended his hand soberly, almost deferentially. Angela did not take it.

'Come to the hotel — the Savoy — at five.'

She did not pause for a reply to her command. When Dinny turned, somewhat disconcertedly, to observe what Channing might have made of this revealing episode, his friend had taken prompt advantage of the priestess's exit, and was rapidly escaping. Channing glanced back over his shoulder, drew a quick, non-committal smile, and pointed significantly in the direction of the stage door, as if indicating they would meet there.

He had vanished, however, when Dinny, thick in the exodus, reached the pavement.

* * * * * *

They did not call her 'Miss Brumm,' but 'Angela Brumm,' as if it were a four-syllable word accented on the ultimate.

When the girl at the Information Desk turned to the switchboard operator, relaying Dinny's request to see 'Miss Brumm,' she said:

'Mr. Ferdinand Brumm has an appointment with Angela Brumm.'

She did not say, 'Mr. *Ferdinand* Brumm has an appointment with *Angela* Brumm.' There was only one authentic Brumm, and that Brumm was Angela *Brumm.*

The bell-hop, whom he trailed to the elevator and over the padded carpet of the seventh floor, did not ring, but opened the door to the first room of what proved to be an extensive suite. This first was a very business-like reception office where Dinny stated his errand to a white-gowned secretary.

'Angela Brumm is expecting you, sir. Come with me, please.'

They passed through another room, equipped for secretarial purposes and occupied by three typists zealously tapping noiseless machines. The large sitting-room adjacent was brightly appointed, clearly the boudoir of a woman who knew how to surround herself with the indispensables of the well-to-do; everything in excellent taste, Dinny thought, as his conductress signed him to a rust-silk davenport, and retired.

Angela sauntered in presently, from the opposite door, her shimmering gold hair plaited down her back, dressed in a flowing négligée of unrelieved black silk, black silk stockings, black silk slippers. The high heels added a touch to her regal carriage. Dinny stood, wondering what manner of take-off this conversation might have, after a lapse of more than eight years. Would Angela begin with something conventional — 'unexpected pleasure' — and that sort of thing?

'People call you "Dinny," now; don't they?' she asked,

negligently, as she approached. 'I would have told you to
come at once, dear,' continued Angela, putting both hands
on his broad shoulders and lifting her face for the kiss which
speeded his heart a little — 'but I'm frightfully uncomfortable until I've had a bath and a mauling by my mas-
seuse.'

Dinny understood and expressed his amazement that
she could go through so much nerve-wrecking business,
daily, without breaking.

'But you're the picture of vitality,' he added, honest admiration in his eyes. They sat, at her inviting gesture, on
the luxurious davenport.

'Well?' — Angela glanced up brightly, smiling inquisitively — 'now you've seen it, what do you think?... Is
the Man in the Moon disgusted, or amused, or — amazed?'

'He hasn't quite made up his mind yet, Angela,' returned
Dinny, thoughtfully. 'He's always reserved, you know;
probably a bit over-cautious.... Maybe due to his age.'

Angela puckered her full, red lips into a playful tease.

'I presume Luna thought it a good show,' she ventured,
blue eyes widening roguishly.

'Luna leaps at conclusions, of course,' parried Dinny,
Angela's woman-of-the-world air and tone mystifying
him: he hoped he was keeping his surprise out of his voice.
'However' — weighing his words — 'instinct may be more
trustworthy, in such matters, than sheer intellect.... If you
don't mind leaving the Moon out of it, for a moment, I'll
admit I was never so uplifted, and — expectant, and ——'

'—— and shot down, tumbling, wings broken, scatter-
ing a trail of bloody feathers ——' prompted Angela, when
he paused, groping for the right word.... 'Am I right?'

Dinny soberly studied her face, somewhat perplexed by
her candor.

'Not quite,' he said, indecisively. 'Not shot down, exactly; a little more as if one had risen rapidly, dizzily, in
a balloon — and it had sprung a leak.... One had to come
down, then.'

'And it was a rough landing,' sympathized Angela. 'I knew by your face.'

'Quite!' admitted Dinny — 'but one still has the balloon. Whether it is beyond repair remains to be seen. I'm afraid I haven't had the courage to look.... Anyway — there's been no time. This sort of thing deserves some — some thinking over.'

She nodded, comprehendingly.

'You may find you've lost nothing by your cruise, Dinny. ... Judging from the things you've been writing — and I follow them closely, dear, laughing and crying, laughing at them and crying for you — it seems you haven't even known you *had* a balloon.... Perhaps it's been worth a trip to Dorchester, just to find that out.'

Which of his sardonic, satirical cronies, thought Dinny, would have had the effrontery to predict that, some day, he might sit in a confessional, unreservedly pouring his sincere wistfulness into the dainty pink ear of an itinerant woman evangelist and miracle-worker? His mood amazed him.

'Honestly, now, Dinny!' Angela had murmured, intertwining her fingers with his. 'Let yourself go — a bit.... It'll be good for you.'

'It has come — only twice' — said Dinny, dreamily — 'in about fifteen years — this strange, brief, uncanny tug; this afternoon, and another time, in a Catholic Church, when I was a freshman.... But — when I was a small boy, Angela, I frequently experienced big, suffocating waves of — of exultation. They never came in winter, as I recall, and never except when I was alone.'

Dinny reclined, staring at the ceiling, and reflected.

'Yes — go on,' said Angela, quietly, patting his hand.

'Only on summer afternoons, flat on my back, looking up into the blue and white, a gentle breeze stirring, bees humming, birds singing, squirrels scampering about — I used to get it, then — just a big wave of it, and it would be gone.... I didn't know what it was, and I can't describe

it now, but — I suppose brave old Walt came about as
nearly ——'

'Walt?' queried Angela.

'Whitman.'

'Oh — I never knew him that well,' confessed Angela.
'Somebody gave me a book of his poems. I've always meant
to ——'

Dinny glanced in the direction of a well-filled book-case.
Angela, following his eyes, rose, and crossed the room.

'Maybe you can find the place, Dinny, and read it to
me. I think I'd like to hear it,' she said, returning with the
book.

'It's pretty long,' warned Dinny, leafing rapidly. 'I'll
try to give you just an idea of it.... Of course' — he laid
the open book face-downward on his knee — 'I'm not meaning to say that I had precisely these thoughts when I was
a little chap, but the thoughts I had have never been put
into words more adequate to describe my feelings than
these.'

Angela impatiently took up the book, and confronted
him with it, nodding her head.

'Just a minute, Angela — and then I'll read some of it
for you.... I think I hated religion, from the start. As I try
to recover my boyish opinions, I think I always knew that
religion was a selfish, ignorant, hole-in-a-corner affair per-
petuated by small people.... God had instantly fallen out
with the world, soon as He'd made it. But He was glumly
allowing the Whole Thing to go on, despising It, deploring
It, enduring It, and wondering how long it would be yet
until all the people became Baptists; and the Baptists,
aware of His impatience, shouted back, "How long, O
Lord, how long?"... Previously — ages before the Baptists — God had wondered how He was going to put up
with everybody but the Jews, who seemed to have caught
His fancy.... I knew, by instinct, that all such stuff as that
was rubbish!... Adam! — and Adam's "fall"! — I think I
knew, even as a freckle-nosed, barefooted, little boy, that

it was nothing but a fairy-tale, and not a very pleasant one, at that. It didn't ring true.... And all that tiresome story of early Jewish magic left me cold. I hated it!

'But — sometimes — on summer days, a wave-like surge of — of gladness, of — of understanding, would sweep over me. I would suddenly *belong!* — if you get what I mean. The Whole Thing was all of a piece, and I was a part of it, and ——'

Dinny took up the book.

'Whitman says he had heard a great deal of talk about the beginning and the end; and he writes' —

There never was any more inception than there is now,
Nor any more youth or age than there is now,
And will never be any more perfection than there is now,
Nor any more heaven or hell than there is now.

In all people I see myself, none more and not one a barley-corn less,
And the good or bad I say of myself I say of them.

I know I am august.
I do not trouble my spirit to vindicate itself. or be understood.
I see that the elementary laws never apologize.

I think I could turn and live with animals, they're so placid and
    self-contain'd.
I stand and look at them long and long.
They do not sweat and whine about their condition,
They do not lie awake in the dark and weep for their sins,
They do not make me sick discussing their duty to God.

They show me their relations to me and I accept them,
They bring me tokens of myself...

I wonder where they get these tokens.
Did I pass that way huge times ago and negligently drop them?

Angela sat, with brooding eyes, venturing no comment, when Dinny paused.

'Just for a moment — today — I had one more strong, quick *tug* of that... whatever-it-is! Perhaps you know. Of course you know!'

'Exactly when — Dinny?' murmured Angela, scarcely above a whisper.

'Well — I'd like to say — it would be the most gracious thing to say — that I got it through something you said, or did; but that wouldn't be quite true.... It came while your choir was singing that opening anthem — the Gounod thing — "Unfold!"... Angela — did you ever catch a big, fighting trout? — I mean a huge, muscled, determined, *savage* trout?... No?... Well — you've been casting, for three hours; quite confidently, at first, having been told there's trout in the pool; rather impatiently and exasperatedly, after an hour; and then dully, unhopefully, mechanically, half-inclined to quit, scorning yourself for going to the bother ——'

'I'm following, Dinny,' prodded Angela. 'Do catch one!'

'And then — suddenly — there's a *strike!*... I don't mean there's a timid little nibble of some sluggish, grubby four-inch blue-gill.... I mean a swift reaching and grabbing and a *tug* that bends the rod to a horseshoe, and the reel goes "Zzzing"!'

'Great!' shouted Angela, eyes shining.

Dinny stilled her enthusiasm with an outspread palm.

'And then — the line falls limp — and whatever-it-was had given you that instant's exultant thrill — is gone!... But' — pursued Dinny, meditatively — 'just to know you're still capable of a fleeting exultation like that, even if it's only for an instant — well, as you say, it's worth a trip to Dorchester.'

'Can't you stay a few days, Dinny?' pleaded Angela.

'No — I'd probably not get it again. In fact, I'm quite sure.... The physical healing — you know.... It was — do you mind if I speak plainly, Angela?... It was the most shockingly cruel affair I ever saw.... My dear—*how can you?*'

Angela's voice trembled when she replied.

'Sometimes I help them,' she said, hoarsely. 'I — I thought I could at first. I was honest, Dinny.... And then — they just expected it, and insisted, and there'd been so much talk about it.... But, Dinny, sometimes I do help them... a little... Really!'

He shook his head, with a faint, incredulous smile.

'I didn't come here to rebuke you, Angela. You know your own business, and you handle it — *superbly!* God knows I've no right to offer you any counsel — but ——' He hesitated.

Angela gripped his hand in both of hers.

'Say it!' she commanded, soberly.

'Very well — I think you're making a cheap and grotesque thing out of a mystery that's too big for you — too big for anyone!... It's a great pity.'

Dinny rose, laid his long hands under Angela's elbows, looked her squarely in the eyes.

'I'm quite proud of you — all but *that*.'

'Must you go? Have dinner with me. I don't eat — much — but I'll watch you. Please?'

When she saw he was quite determined to leave, Angela gave him her hand, gave him her lips, smiled, pushed a bell. Dinny left without a further word.

* * * * * *

In the morning, he found among the many letters waiting in his box, another package — they came daily — from *The Times*. He opened them without interest, tossing them aside, half-read. Here was one addressed from Pine Hill, Wisconsin. Dinny's curiosity was stirred.

Dear Sir:

This is in reply to your recent advertisement for a 'Research Secretary.' I formerly worked in New York, and the clipping was sent me by a friend.

As to age and physical dimensions, I could qualify for your position, if it is still open.

I know almost nothing about Indian mounds, but am willing to learn from you.

Very respectfully
JOAN BRAITHWAITE

P.S. — I do need a job, Dinny, quite frightfully!

JOAN

CHAPTER XIII

IN THE pursuit of his singular trade, Dinny Brumm's requirement of a 'research secretary' was about as urgent as his professional need of a trap-drummer or a tea-taster.

At the moment of his frantically impetuous decision to advertise for news of Joan, it had not occurred to him that he might soon be put to the necessity of inventing an occupation for her.

As for the expense involved in taking on an employee, the prospect of assuming such a responsibility, with Joan as the incumbent, filled Dinny with proud delight. He had plenty of money. His residence in cheap bohemian quarters and his association with friends mostly of simple tastes and meager means, while not an intentional frugality, had made but small demands upon his mounting income.

He had preferred that manner of living. Had he possessed a fortune yielding a million a year, his sense of humor would have stood in the way of its distribution by any of the customary tactics employed by the gilded whose alleged exploits in quest of pleasure would, he believed, have bored him to an early and welcome grave.

With the exception of mild extravagances for books, theaters, and clothing — for while Dinny always dressed conservatively, he dressed well — his personal outlay was so trifling that for more than two years his disbursements per month had rarely exceeded his income per week; nor was that quite all of the story, for he had been very fortunate in his discreet speculations.

Tommy Forsythe, whose natural flair for prognosticating movements in the stock market had been capitalized to his own very considerable advantage, was generous with timely tips. Without making much more than an interesting avocation of his investments, at Tommy's canny suggestion, Dinny had been doubling his income. If, therefore, he should find himself disposed to take on a 'research' or any other kind of a secretary, it would be no inconvenience.

It was quite evident from the plaintiveness of her little distress-signal that Joan was in straitened circumstances. Dinny tried to imagine the glorious satisfaction he would experience at sight of the superb creature, exquisitely groomed, smartly gowned, happily independent, with pride in her eyes and money in her purse — himself responsible for her well-being.

For the first hour after his receipt of her letter, Dinny's entire attention had been devoted to the pleasant daydream of wrapping a probably half-starved Joan around an expensive collation of Vitamins A, B, and C, to the accompaniment of haunting melodies dispensed by the Hungarian orchestra at Dexter's. Joan, stifled and staled by who knew what drudgeries out in little Pine Hill, Wisconsin, should have a sunny, gayly equipped apartment, high up, somewhere on Riverside Drive, with a beautiful view. He would show her how a successful young syndicate writer thought his secretarial help ought to be treated. It would be great fun.

But when he tried to construct a tentative portrait of Joan's patrician face, in its response to a detailed statement of his happy plans for her comfort, he found himself dismayed. Joan would not fit into that picture. Joan would not consent to become his beneficiary, nor would she accept a penny more than such secretarial services were worth on the open market.... And, by the way, just what would be the nature of such services? Any flimsy subterfuge he might ingeniously invent would only invite Joan's indignation, once she discovered herself in a mere sinecure.

Only one tenable suggestion offered itself. Dinny, as an ardent student of Pepysian lore and the Restoration which he considered the most interesting period of English history had lately amused himself by tinkering with an idea for a magazine article to be entitled 'Pepys on Lord's Day.' His only reason for not proceeding to the first draft of it, a once, was explained by his own distaste for the considerable drudgery involved in digging out of the diary all of Samuel's chronicles in reference thereunto.

He could set Joan at that. Surely she need not suspect that such employment was mere make-believe. By Gad, he wanted that information. Dinny found himself becoming rather indignant in his imaginary debate with Joan, who had looked him squarely in the eye and accused him of giving her something to do that nobody in his proper senses would ever want done.... What do *you* know about what I want? Maybe I'll ask you to mole out some further data about other people's observance of the Sabbath. Maybe I'm going to write a book — two or three books — on this subject. Maybe I'll want to know how all the characters in Dickens, Scott, Thackeray, Hawthorne, and a lot more, entertained themselves on the Lord's Day.... That's what a research secretary is about! Funny you didn't know that!

By evening, Dinny felt himself prepared to answer Joan's letter. His manner of approach was friendly but dignifiedly business-like. He needed secretarial help, and it had occurred to him that Joan, if footloose and attracted by such employment, would admirably adapt herself to that position.

He didn't mind admitting — this sheet had to be torn up, several times, before it carried just the right degree of restraint — that it would give him more personal pleasure to be working with Joan than with anyone else of his entire acquaintance. (Joan mustn't be frightened off by hints that he hoped their association might be a bit closer than the business relationship contemplated.) ... And he was looking forward with keen anticipation to her arrival; and when might he expect her — for the Pepys matter would not stand much putting off — and might he hand her the enclosed draft to cover traveling expenses?

Eight days elapsed before there was a reply. Dinny's face fell when the money he had sent her dropped out of the letter.

She had not expected, she said, that Dinny would personally engineer a job for her on his own staff. She had written that she needed work, hoping that if Dinny happened to know of anything he would tell her. Her reply to the advertisement in *The Times* 'really couldn't be resisted.' It had so pointedly singled her out as its object.

You have kindly inquired what I have been doing. Shortly after father left us — we were quite out of funds, mother and I — it seemed best for me to apply for work. That was not so easy, for I had not been trained for any specific kind of employment.

Barney Vaughn's father — he was very kind to mother and me through all that dreadful time ——

Dinny scowled, wondering apprehensively what might be the nature of the obligation Barney's father felt he owed to Joan.

—— knew a man of influential position with Minch & Grimsby's in New York. I got my position that way; started as a saleswoman; was soon advanced to the Personnel Department. I liked that very much.

How I came to leave there is too long a story, but you will know it wasn't because I stole anything or slighted the work in which I was greatly interested. Is it sufficient to say that I walked out, late one afternoon, nose in air, on receipt of a significant hint that I might have a much larger income by assuming other tasks than I had bargained for? (Now please don't go plunging into Minch & Grimsby's waving a hard fist and offering to kill somebody.)

Mother was far from well. She had gone to live with Aunt Patty and Uncle Jim at Pine Hill, Wisconsin. Uncle Jim Bailey has a furniture store and is the town undertaker. He had wanted me to help him in the store.

So I came to Pine Hill. Mother continued to decline. She was never well after father's death. Three months ago, she passed away.

Since then, my life here has seemed almost unendurable. There is nothing to do that interests me. Uncle Jim and Aunt

Patty are very kind and want me to stay, but know that I am restless and consent to my going to New York.

'By Gad!' shouted Dinny. 'She's coming! She's coming!'

I'm returning the money. It was good of you to offer it. I have saved enough to pay my expenses. If you really think I can be of use to you as a member of your organization ——

'My organization,' chuckled Dinny, a bit worried. 'Wait till she sees it! What could I have said to make her think that?'

—— I'll do my level best. If it doesn't work out, maybe you can help me find something else.

I expect to leave here about the middle of next week. I shall call you up about ten o'clock Friday morning, and get my orders.

Gratefully

JOAN

* * * * * *

She did not expect to be met at the train, but he would surprise her. Deducing from the time-tables, Dinny hypothetically routed Joan to arrive at six-thirty on Thursday evening. Short of funds, she would not patronize an extra-fare train. Neither would she linger in Chicago. Six-thirty was the time.

Thursday was the longest day he had ever spent. In the forenoon he went up to The Roosevelt and reserved a room 'for a lady who is to be my guest for a couple of days, at least,' the clerk, recognizing Dinny's name, promising every attention and giving definite assurance that the bill would not be presented to Miss Braithwaite. Yes — and he would personally see to it that the flowers would be in her room when she arrived.

A few moments after six o'clock, Dinny was wandering about the huge concourse of the Grand Central, nervous as a cat. He tried to kill time by inspecting the various wares at the news-stand; bought an expensive box of chocolates and the latest *L'Illustration*. At the quarter-hour, he strolled toward the gate. As the minutes slimmed down to four, three, two, Dinny found his heart beating rapidly. The suspense was eating him up.

The straggling group of welcomers began lining up along the ropes. The gate was open now. The train was in. The vanguard of the day-coachers plodded up the incline, bumping their legs with their fat, frumpy luggage.

Here came Joan!... She was carrying her own bags. She looked weary. Now they had found each other's eyes, and her half-reproachful, half-pouting little smile seemed to be saying, 'You really shouldn't have gone to the trouble. I didn't expect it.'

Dinny reached for her baggage and passed it along to a red-cap. Joan put both her hands in his, as his welcoming gesture invited, and lifted her brown eyes inquiringly.

'How did you know?'

'Oh — I meet all the trains,' said Dinny. 'Sometimes people come to New York alone — and appreciate a little friendly greeting.'

'Taxi, sah?' inquired the red-cap.

'No,' snapped Dinny — 'The Roosevelt.'

'Yassah... At the desk, sah.'

'But — Dinny!' protested Joan, as she watched her bags bobbing away through the crowd, 'I can't afford to go to The Roosevelt — even for tonight.'

'We're going there for dinner.' Dinny took her arm, and signified by his manner that there was to be no debate about this.

'Oh, but I've had my — really, Dinny, I'm so mussed and the train was so dirty. All I want is to go some-place where I can clean up.' Joan halted, obdurately.

So — she had made this long journey in day-coaches, and was worn to a frazzle!

'Where had you thought of going?' demanded Dinny.

'Out to the place on Eighty-Sixth — where I lived before.'

'You come with me, and do as I say.... You're my employee, now, and this is an order.' Dinny tried to be very stern.

'I don't begin work until tomorrow.'

'Nevertheless... Let's have no nonsense. You're tired.'

Rather confused and reluctant, Joan demurely consented to be propelled through the throng in the brightly lighted station. Dinny paused at the desk, spoke to the room-clerk, and, turning to Joan, said, in a tone that expected her prompt compliance:

'Follow the boy... Give yourself plenty of time... If there's anything you want, ask for it... I've an errand. I'll meet you here in the lobby at eight.'

Joan shook her head.

'I don't want to, Dinny.' Her eyes were troubled.

'It would be quite embarrassing — if you didn't.'

She stood for a moment, debating, and then said, her voice lowered almost to a whisper — 'I can't pay for it... I'm sorry.'

Dinny looked her soberly in the eyes.

'Please do as I tell you!' he said, biting his words into a crisp command.

She drew a tired little smile, and followed the boy.

'Strike *one!*' said Dinny, triumphantly, to himself, as he watched her enter the elevator... 'The darling!'

* * * * * *

Joan's hour and a half had done wonders for her. When she came down, Dinny, who had been pacing about, rest-lessly, watching the clock and counting the minutes, quickly joined her, wondering if other people were not thinking him a lucky dog.

She was simply dressed in black crêpe, but carried herself with all the poise and confidence of a queen in ermine. Dinny's admiration shone in his face. He was recklessly ecstatic.

'Haven't you grown some more, Dinny?' she asked, taking up her napkin.

'I hope not... I wasn't exactly frail, before, if you recall.
... Remember the trip we took through the ravine, the time
Ernie sent us for a key?'

Joan smiled, nodded, flushed a little.

'I'm afraid I wasn't a very pleasant companion,' she said,
regretfully.

'You had good reason, Joan... I had been behaving very
badly. You'll find I've changed... Vastly improved —— '
Dinny broke off to order their dinner, consulting her wishes,
but making it evident that her negatives were not taken
seriously when she demurred against unnecessary items.

'What's the nature of this vast improvement, Dinny?'
queried Joan, when the waiter had retired. 'I've been reading your articles.'

'Have you?' Dinny's eyes sparkled, appreciatively.
'Then that means you like them!'

Joan pursed a doubtful smile.

'Not necessarily... One doesn't always have to like what
one reads... But — I'm an optimist, you know. I keep on
hoping you'll write something I'll like, sometime.'

'For instance?' — Dinny was too happy to be dashed by
her criticism — 'If you'll tell me what sort of thing you'd
enjoy, I'll make a special effort, dear.'

There was a considerable delay before Joan replied, and
when she lifted her eyes they did not immediately meet his
own.

'Dinny' — she said, as if announcing a resolution that
had required some debate, and might not be warmly received — 'let's start right... I've come here to work for you
... Please don't make it awkward for me. Or — I'll not be
able to do it, you know.'

'But you *are* my dear, Joan!... You needn't try to recip-
rocate, the least bit. I'm not expecting it. I'll not worry
you with it. You're to think of me as your employer, and
you can be assured of the sort of treatment that would be
desirable by an employee... But — you will be my dear
Joan... just the same!'

'Thank you, Dinny,' she replied, respectfully grateful. 'Now let's talk about something else... Where is your office? Do I come at nine? Are there other — help? How much of my work will be done in the library? I hardly know what you want me to do, you know.'

Neither did Dinny know. He suggested that they eat their dinner untroubled by dull care: plenty of time for that. Her hours would be of her own choosing. There was no office. There were no other secretaries. Joan was to make the researches for him, and report 'from time to time.'

'Once in the morning — and once in the afternoon, maybe?' guessed Joan, vaguely.

'Something like that — or once a week, anyhow,' agreed Dinny, indecisively — 'unless, of course, you were working on an assignment like this Pepys affair, which will probably take you a month, at the least.'

'Then I won't see you for a month — after you've told me exactly what you want?'

Dinny made a quick gesture of protest.

'See me! Of course! Every day! We'll be having dinner together, and there are at least a dozen good shows you'll have to see without delay.... You didn't think I would let you perish of loneliness, did you?... Shall we dance?'

Joan was thoughtful for an instant; bit her pretty lip, and reflected, seriously. Then, apparently coming to an impulsive decision, she nodded brightly, rose, and offered herself to his arms. Dinny held her very close, and whispered, 'You precious darling!'

She brushed his cheek lightly with her hair, and murmured, entreatingly, rather breathlessly:

'Oh, Dinny — please — let's don't — I mustn't.'

But her fingers tightened on his shoulder, and Dinny's happiness was almost more than he could bear.

'You *are* my darling... aren't you, Joan?'

She did not reply, but glanced up into Dinny's eyes, searching them soberly — and smiled.

* * * * * *

Dinny was aroused at eight from sleep, profound because belated, and felt a great wave of happiness breaking over him.

The messenger at his door handed in a letter bearing the device of the Roosevelt Hotel.

Dear Dinny:

I've been thinking things over. I don't see how I can work for you. Maybe you will help me find something else to do. Please don't try to dissuade me. I'll meet you in the hotel lobby at one, as we agreed. Would you like to take me to the Metropolitan Art Museum after luncheon? I'd love it. Thanks for everything.

JOAN

So — that was that. Joan insisted on having something else to do. Perhaps she was right. He would consult Tommy. He would tell Tommy all about it — everything! No — Joan wouldn't like that. He would approach Tommy as if the applicant for work were a casual acquaintance.

At ten, he had Tommy on the telephone. Would Tommy do him a favor? Very capable young woman, daughter of the late president of his little college in Ohio, was in town seeking employment. Yes — she had had good experience at Minch & Grimsby's. Did Tommy know of an opening anywhere?

'Might possibly place her here with us, if she's all you say,' replied Tommy, obligingly. 'Tell her to come in at once. I'll talk to her.'

Splendid! Dinny called Joan, who was in — and delighted. She would go over to Lacey's at once. Mr. Forsythe? Thanks!... Dinny should hear all about the interview when they met. Yes — at one. She'd be waiting. Thanks again, Dinny!

'Such a busy morning!' exclaimed Joan, breathlessly, when he joined her. 'I'm moving back to my old place on Eighty-Sixth, where I lived before. My trunk has gone out there already.'

'How did you make out with Tommy Forsythe?' queried
Dinny.

'Beautifully!' Joan was radiant. 'He was so friendly.
I'm to be in his department for a month, beginning Monday;
and then, after I've learned my way about, as he put it, I'm
to be given a chance in the Personnel... I'm so happy...
What all did you tell him, Dinny?'

He gave her a proud smile.

'Just that you were an acquaintance, daughter of my
college president, fine girl. I didn't add that you were an
adorable, lovely ——'

'Tut, tut!' cautioned Joan, softly.

'The taxi-driver won't tell — and, as for Tommy, he'll
discover it. Tommy's one of the best there is, Joan. I hope
you'll like him.'

She was sure she would. Tommy had treated her as an
old friend. She was going to like it at Lacey's.

'And so' — regretted Dinny, dolefully — 'you're not to
be my fair employee, after all. I'd quite counted on it, you
know.'

'Perhaps I can help you, anyway. I wouldn't mind digging out the story of what Sam Pepys did on Sundays. I
might do it, evenings... Any more work on the novel,
today?'

'Very little... No composition; just a few more rough
notes, and a short cross-section of conversation between
Cecil and Margery who've got themselves in no end of a
scrape.'

'You mean *you've* got them into a scrape,' accused Joan.
'You created them; didn't you?'

'It's a fairly accurate picture of real life, I think,' said
Dinny, defensively. 'Such things happen every day.'

They had arrived at a little French restaurant on Forty-
Fifth, a favorite of his, and were investigating — Joan with
curiosity — their variegated assortment of *hors d'œuvres*.
She had insisted on knowing something more about the
new story which Dinny had begun to tell her last night.

Throughout the luncheon he talked and she listened attentively, without more comment than little murmurs of encouragement and interest.

When, however, he had brought the narrative up to date with the stark outline of an episode considerably to the discredit of his principal characters, Joan frowned — a little flushed.

'It had never occurred to me before,' remarked Joan, when their taxi had reached Fifth Avenue and had turned north en route to The Metropolitan, 'what a heavy responsibility rests on the shoulders of a story-writer.'

'In what way, dear?... Let's have your theory.'

She hesitated, groping for adequate phrases.

'Perhaps I can't express it, but it's something like this: when a man builds a bridge, or a tower, or paints a picture, or composes a song, he really isn't a creator in the sense that a novelist is a creator.... You — for example — created Cecil and Margery, just as Jehovah created Adam and Eve ——'

Dinny laughed, teasingly.

'That Garden of Eden affair points no moral, Joan. That was just a story — about Adam and Eve.'

She nodded, victoriously.

'Exactly! — and so is this just a story — about Cecil and Margery. Who's ever going to estimate the wholesale damage done to human personality, through the ages, by that Eden tale?... No — I don't believe it, and I know you don't, but millions have believed it, and do believe, at this moment! Think of the centuries of unfair, unjust, belittling appraisals of God — all derived from some ancient shepherd-minstrel's fantastic story, told at an evening campfire on some desert oasis!'

'Bravo — Joan! Proceed! Gad! — that's good!'

'One of the best things you've done, Dinny, is to sneer and scowl at that old story, and its monstrous implications. Many times, in your ridicule of orthodoxy, you've pointed the finger of scorn at a crafty Jehovah who would bring an innocent pair of inquisitive people into the world, and immediately direct their attention to some experiment brimming with tragedy.... But aren't you doing the same thing to Cecil and Margery?'

'How absurd!' laughed Dinny.

'It's too serious to be absurd,' persisted Joan, soberly. 'Your new book will be on the stands in a few months. It will have a great sale among all the restless, scornful, idol-smashers in the land. They follow you as if you were a new messiah. You've never done a novel for them, and they'll grab at this one while it's still damp from the binders.'

'*Laus Deo!*' exclaimed Dinny, fervently. 'I hope you're right!'

'It's a very pretty picture you draw of Margery, innocently yearning for an expanded life. Little Glenville, Missouri, offers security, three meals a day, and a minimum of struggle; but Margery isn't quite satisfied with her easy Eden. She wants a larger life. Well — why, in Heaven's Name, don't you give it to her?'

The taxi drew up at the curb. They sauntered up the steps, momentarily diverted from their serious theme, traversed the spacious foyer, and continued through to the huge chamber of replicas and models of classic buildings.

'Let's sit here a moment, Dinny... I think I want to finish what I was saying... It's quite important — to me, at least.'

She laid her hand lightly on his arm, and swept his face with an entreating query.

'This Cecil — he was so discontented, too, in Sparrow, Minnesota; wanted to go places and do things. Why didn't you let him?'

'Didn't I?' protested Dinny.

'What makes it all seem so pitifully tragic,' Joan went on, unheeding, 'is just the fact that a hundred thousand young Cecils and Margerys, fretting and steaming in their little Glenvilles and Sparrows, are sure to identify themselves with this pair of revolutionists. Can't you think of some better destination for these people of yours, who are sure to be trailed by a nondescript army of admirers, than this degrading wallow you've planned for them?'

'Oh — it isn't quite that bad, Joan... Come now!'

'Dinny — you've a great chance! There isn't a priest or a preacher or a poet or a professor in the whole world who has the opportunity that you have.... You haven't gone in for sentiment. You haven't had any use for religion. You've been a fire-eating iconoclast. Every cynical young fellow, bent on freedom from the old frustrations, is hanging on your words. There isn't one single idealist, in the whole crew of modern apostles, able to command the attention of these discontented people — people like you and me.... Why don't you capitalize this peculiar grip you've got on the imagination of your — your Cave of Adullam, and show them the way out!... *What a chance!*'

'Nonsense, Joan!' scoffed Dinny, superiorly. 'What sort of a figure d'you think I'd cut? I'm not writing Rollo books. There'd be a laugh go up that you could hear to the poles! ... Besides — I'd rather draw honest pictures of life as it is, no matter how ugly, than to paint frescoes and friezes of the heavenly host. I'll leave that job to the parsons.'

Joan smiled a little, her expression reminding him of the gentle dejection she had shown, one eventful night, in her parlor at Magnolia. She snapped the latch of her bag, absently, a few times, and rose.

'Let's forget it — then,' she said, strolling over to the model of the Acropolis.

Dinny joined her, silently, and not a little troubled.

* * * * * *

He had not seen Joan for five days. She had begged off from engagements on the ground of fatigue. Her hours were long, her new work was exacting because unfamiliar, a great deal depended upon the record she might make for herself at Lacey's, especially through these probationary days. The excuse was valid, and Dinny had tried to be patient.

Tonight they had dined at Dexter's and were now en
route to a musical show at The Strand.

'Been seeing much of old Tommy?'

'Of course — every day.... We lunched together, yesterday.'

'I didn't know that was customary,' commented Dinny,
with a surprised little chuckle. 'You might as well have
worked for *me*.' He tried to make this sound like a pleas-
antry.

'Don't be silly. Tommy thinks I've the makings of a
buyer, and wanted to tell me a lot of things there's no time
for, when we're working. It was very interesting.'

Dinny pretended interest in the traffic-jam, ahead.

'That's quite reasonable. Tommy can do a great deal for
you, if he wants to — and evidently he does. You've got on
well with him.... Calling him "Tommy" now, eh?'

'He's just a big boy.' Joan's tone was maternal. 'It's
awfully easy to call him "Tommy," don't you think? It
was you got me into it.... Rather I'd not?'

'Why should I care?' Dinny's magnanimity was almost
militant. 'I just asked out of curiosity. I had hoped you
two would like each other.... Well — here we are, dear.'

The show was good; tuneful, colorful. Joan seemed to enjoy every minute of it. Gad — how vital she was! Dinny
tried to share her enthusiasm, but had to confess to himself
that the piece was dull and tedious. Annoying little dis-
sonances, rasping from deep inside him, shrilled the ensemble
until the clamorous yelp of it tore at his nerves. He was
glad when it was done, and inhaled the first tonic draft of
the outer air with reinvigorated spirits.

Joan was graciously remote, almost too interested in her
distractions to be giving much thought to the new phase of
their comradeship. Whether she was still sensing the slight
constraint which had slowed them up, on that afternoon at
The Metropolitan, or had some other reason for mentally
fending him off, Dinny could not make sure. They were on
the way to her quarters, now — she had insisted, because of

her work — and within another five minutes Dinny would be headed for home tormented by forebodings.

'Can't we take a little spin in the park before we put in?' suggested Dinny. 'It isn't late.'

'If you like.'

He spoke to the driver, who nodded, and slackened the speed.

'Life has become very important, darling, since you came.' Dinny's voice was tender. He reached for her hand.

'I'm glad I came, too, Dinny,' she responded, promptly. 'I never was so happy before... almost as happy as I'd like to be.'

'I wonder if I'm supposed to know what that means — about your — your wish to be happier.... Is it — anything I can do?'

Joan did not immediately reply.

'I — don't — know, dear,' she said, at length, doubtfully. 'I rather hoped you could, but — maybe not.'

He drew her to him.

'Joan, dear — we do belong to each other, you know.'

'Sometimes — I've thought that, too, Dinny.' There was a weary little sigh. 'But — you see — I have to live. I need air, light, sunshine! You don't seem to require it. Sometimes we really do belong — just for a moment... and then... well — we don't belong any more than — than rocks and petunias belong!'

'But, darling, we needn't try to be alike! That's the real beauty of a comradeship like ours. Neither has to sacrifice personality, opinions, or individuality of outlook.'

'No — we needn't try to be alike,' repeated Joan, thoughtfully, 'but it would be preferable if we belonged to the same kingdom of nature. I'm for the world! I like it! It warms me, and I respond to it.... You're at war with it, Dinny.'

'Oh, Joan, dear — can't you forget this silly little difference in our viewpoint.... I love you, darling.'

'I know,' murmured Joan, laying her cheek lightly against his shoulder.

'And you?' he whispered. 'You do care — don't you, Joan?'

'Yes — Dinny — I care.... I care so much that I simply couldn't bear to live that close to perfect happiness — and — and be robbed of it.'

'I'll try — very hard — Joan,' promised Dinny, sincerely.

'Do — please — Dinny!'

Joan's cheeks were wet with tears when he kissed her. He was stirred to an almost painful ecstasy by her response to that kiss.

For a long moment she clung to his lips; then, nestling her face against his arm, with a tremulous little sigh, she said, with passionate insistence:

'Don't fail me, Dinny.... You know — now — how much I love you.'

CHAPTER XIV

JOAN, who had been crying, was mechanically collecting the remains of their picnic; the mockingly gay paper plates, the paper cups, the half-emptied little bottles of olives, artichoke hearts, anchovies, the sandwiches, the deviled eggs, the chicken, the ingenious French pastries.

'Don't bother, Dinny,' she said, pensively, as he ventured to assist.

He put down the salad plate and made quite a task of lighting his pipe, uncomfortably wondering if Joan felt herself not only an object of compassion but of chagrin, too, as she sat, tousled and swollen-eyed, gathering up the pitifully absurd litter of the feast she had spread, an hour earlier, with such a bright, confident air, archly mystifying him with the delicacies she conjured from her wicker basket.

It was rather debasing to Joan, wasn't it, to sit here and owlishly watch her attend to these little drudgeries? Perhaps it was even more humiliating to her if he tried, awkwardly, to share them.

'Go take a stroll and smoke your pipe,' she suggested, divining his perplexity. 'I'm not very nice to look at, anyway.' She smiled, with a sort of childish contrition. 'I'm sure my nose is red... Awfully sorry, Dinny.'

'It was a crime for us to quarrel on a day like this,' growled Dinny. 'All my fault, Joan.'

She shook her head, preoccupiedly.

'I'll divide the honors with you... Run along, dear. I'd so much rather you did... And we won't talk about it again — ever!... Anyone would think we might have learned better — by now.'

'My God — yes! We're a couple o' fools!' Dinny unfolded his long legs and scrambled to his feet. 'I'll be back presently, then. You've the book... Think I'll saunter down and see the chap's sailboat.'

They had left shortly before eight, that June morning, bound for the country in Dinny's new sport roadster which he had bought with just such excursions in view. They had had the streets to themselves. Dinny had called the tubby old Hoboken ferry their private yacht.

Shady, lawn-clipped Montclair was still asleep when they rolled softly through. Except for an ambling group of little girls with long curls and short skirts, three of them walking backwards, obviously bound for Sunday School, and a slim, sedate lady of forty-plus, carrying a black parasol loftily over a high-perched black hat, who was being overtaken and passed by a square, craggy, determined man with a Bible, the residence streets were deserted.

Joan had furnished most of the talk, gayly offering an unpunctuated flow of light persiflage, undaunted by Dinny's silent and studious attention to the road, for he was still far from a competent driver. It was clear, though, that he had something on his mind besides his responsibility at the wheel.

Greenwood Lake, their objective, was all that Joan had hoped it might be when, last night, they had touched heads over the road-map in her little parlor.

The shiny blue car was parked in the grove, at eleven.

Suddenly shaking loose from his dourly reflective mood, Dinny made up for his taciturnity on the road by exhibiting a noisy hilarity as he unloaded their festival cargo and spread the new motor-rug on the grass, fifty yards from the lake-shore. But his impetuous jollity bubbled by artifice, thought Joan. It was not quite spontaneous... Perhaps he would tell her.

They were nearly finished with their luncheon when, Joan having come to a full stop in her narrative of recent events at Lacey's, Dinny, who had been fixedly staring at her face without hearing a word she said, suddenly blurted out:

'I've some news for you.'

Joan nodded, understandingly.

'I knew you had,' she said, playfully, but a little anxious.

'I'm not sure you will approve,' he warned, 'but I've accepted the editorship of *Hallelujah*... Begin in September.'

She recoiled as if he had struck her.

'Oh, Dinny — how could you — after what you'd promised? There isn't a magazine in the whole lot of them that's been so mean — and cynical — and fault-finding... It has hurt me when you even contributed to it. Now you're to operate it!... I'm sorry you told me.'

Dinny did not meet her eyes, but gazed glassily at the lake, scowling.

'Don't my feelings count, at all, dear?' persisted Joan, tenderly reproachful.

He recalled himself, then, as from a distance, and regarded her critically.

'I've never undertaken to discipline your thoughts, Joan,' said Dinny, crisply, 'and — I hope this isn't going to sound too surly — I dispute your right to regulate mine.'

'In other words — it isn't any of my business.'

Dinny leaned back on one elbow, toying with the fringes of the rug.

'I wouldn't have thought of using that phrase, Joan, but — is it?... You see' — Dinny's brows contracted as he felt for his words — 'it's very difficult to refashion another's mind, even if both the — the redeemer and the sinner are ——'

'I don't think that's very kind, Dinny... And I dislike being talked to that way,' interrupted Joan, her lips trembling.

'Well — putting the mere choice of words aside — you've honestly and lovingly wanted to make me over into something other than I am... And I have honestly and lovingly tried to accommodate you. But it's no good. It won't work. I can't do it. If our difference of taste were ——

Look here: if I hated golf, and you liked it, I would go with you and play it — just because it brought you pleasure. I'd learn to like it for that reason. But this is a different matter, dear. This is a problem of work and wages, bread and butter. I'm a journalist. That's my profession. I'm not omniscient, and I can't write about just anything and everything. My line is criticism. And when you ask me to leave off criticism, and go in for hymn-writing and sappy little twitters set to the score of "Buttercups and Daisies," you've asked too much!'

Joan, with mounting indignation, made an impatient little cry, but Dinny raised a hand, briefly, and went on doggedly:

'There's a whole battalion of sugary smilers, rocking and knitting and purring on the front porches of "Houses Built By the Side of the Road." I doubt if there's room in the journalism of loving-kindness for one more dulcet coo; and, if there were, I'm mighty sure I haven't the voice for it. I know you've set your heart on my doing it; and, because I wanted to please you, I've made some sincere experiments in that direction; bought a little volume of verse entitled "Just Folks," and tried to set my big feet in those dainty tracks, but it was hopeless, darling. I put on my starchy white pinafore, tied my little pink sunbonnet under my chin, and went skipping merrily down the road with a nice basket of pansies for rheumatic old Granny MacDoodle, but before I had gone very far I found myself grinning again. I can't help grinning, Joan. You'll either have to get used to that grin — or ——'

'Or — *what?*' queried Joan, soberly.

Dinny was tardy with his reply.

'I'm afraid the alternative is — up to you.'

'May I talk now?'

'Please do. It's your turn.'

'Well — I never asked you to scribble soft sentimentalities. I hate them, too. There's been too much of it. But there's a pretty wide gap between "Pollyanna" and *Halle-*

lujah. It's easy enough to understand why people crowd about the news-stands to buy *Hallelujah.* They've been fed up to the throat on the other thing.... But *Hallelujah* isn't the right answer to their demand for something more sturdy and sensible than mawkish slush.

'There are a few things that deserve better than to be ridiculed. I looked through the last issue of *Hallelujah* — because you asked me to. One article was a reprint of a little booklet some man had written for private circulation among his friends and neighbors. It was dedicated to the Kiwanis Club. He was its president in Littlegrass, or somewhere, Oklahoma. He and his wife had just returned from a six-weeks trip to Europe, and he wanted to tell his friends what they had seen. It was badly written, and full of childish comments; but the man hadn't prepared it for the smart young spoofers who read *Hallelujah.* It was intended for simple-hearted, inexperienced people who own the houses they live in, and pay their bills, and go to church on Sunday, and have only one wife.... And *Hallelujah* — that's always ranting about the bad manners of yokels who eat with their knives, and don't know whether Chekhov won the last Irish sweepstakes or swam the Channel or designed the dome for Saint Peter's — printed that friendly little booklet — mistakes and all — to fetch a chuckle from the really cultured people, the smart people who've been about, and know which spoon comes first — and who wrote "Ulysses."... I don't believe I could bear it to see your name at the top of the staff in a magazine so — so ——'

'Yes?'

'—— so self-consciously clever! So pompously superior! So insolently vulgar!... If that's the kind of company you find yourself at home with, Dinny Brumm, I'm sure you'd never be very happy with me!... You've said you aren't "omniscient," and mustn't be expected to write about everything. That's just where we disagree. You *do* think you're omniscient! *Hallelujah* is omniscient! There isn't anything that *Hallelujah* doesn't know, far better than anyone else. It cackles at theology for being dogmatic, and calls all the preachers idiots and all the creeds rubbish — and after it's through ridiculing them, the all-wise *Hallelujah* proceeds to be just as dogmatic and arbitrary as the people it reviles.... It's always poking fun at Jehovah.... You'd think, from the way it hands down sublime oracles about Art, the Drama, Music, Literature, that it expected the whole world to reserve its opinion about any art-form until *Hallelujah* had spoken.... After that, the wise would know just what it would be safe for them to think.... And now you're going to be the Solomon who supervises the schooling of the sophisticates.... No — Dinny! — I don't believe I could live comfortably quite that close to the summit of Olympus. I'm afraid the bright light would hurt my eyes. I'd always be at a terrible disadvantage!'

'Very well, then,' rasped Dinny, 'that's that — and now we know where we stand.... It would be tragic for us to go on with it.'

'I'm glad you see it, at last,' agreed Joan, in the same tone.

Dinny's lip curled, unpleasantly.

'By the way,' he drawled, dryly, 'speaking of sarcasm and ridicule, you're fairly good at it yourself. I may be bitter enough, but I'd never talk that way to anyone I loved. ... And I don't believe you could, either.'

Joan hung her head, and put both hands over her eyes, and wept like a little child.

'Oh, Dinny, forgive me,' she pleaded, brokenly. 'I didn't mean to hurt you.'

For an instant, he was moved to join her with assurances, but still smarting under the sharp raps, he delayed; and the longer he delayed the harder it was to conciliate.

Joan's little storm of emotion cleared. She wiped her eyes, and tried to smile. Dinny stole a quick glance, and solemnly looked away, heavy-eyed. With a long sigh, broken by little sobs, she began to gather up the fragments, Dinny watching her automatic movements dully. She was a typical picture, he thought, of Woman — instinctively carrying on with the tasks Nature had assigned to her, regardless of what tragedy might rake her heart.... No man would have done it. A man would stalk away — and let the damned dishes go to hell!

He pitied her, and his pity was tinctured with a trace of vicarious mortification. He could have wept, himself. He picked up the smeary little paper plate on which his salad had been served him, and was in the act of passing it across to her.

'Don't bother, Dinny,' she said, pensively.

He walked down to the shore where a tanned youth was untangling some new white ropes in his little sailboat, and was surprised at the steadiness and nonchalance of his own voice as he chatted, amiably, with the young stranger. Here he was — only three minutes and one hundred and fifty feet away from a disaster that had pulled his very house down about his ears — calmly puffing his pipe and inquiring whether the yacht's ropes were the same thing as sash-cord.

Did that mean, he asked himself, that his love for Joan was of less consequence to his happiness than he had thought? Or was his quick recovery due to the fact that he was taking the instinctive course of Man? Woman, anchored to dishes and brooms and beds and babies, always had had time to think — to grieve, to regret, to mope and grow morbid. Man, whacked over the head with a battle-axe, had had no chance to sit down and nurse his hurts. He must instantly be on the alert for another wallop from some other direction.... He and Joan were faithful to their respective atavistic responses to their mutual disaster. She was sitting there on the grass, crying softly, and telling herself her world had gone to smash. He was smoking his pipe, and talking to a stranger about different weights and weaves of rope.... But that didn't mean his little Paradise hadn't been hurled to Purgatory — same as Joan's.... Odd — reflected Dinny.... Elemental forces! — he had never felt their grip, or appraised their long reach, quite so discriminatingly before.

She joined him, after a little; sauntering down to the shore with all the evidences of her grief discarded. While he had been philosophizing over the easy resilience of the male — the quick, decisive rebound of the male who, no matter how strait the gate, how charged with punishment the scroll, would remain the master of his fate, the captain of his soul — the moody, brooding female had deftly repacked the hamper, stowed it in the car, combed her hair, adjusted her swanky little hat at a jaunty angle, powdered her nose, reshaped her lips, donned a smile, and had now slipped a hand through his arm as much as to say to the boy in the boat, 'I've tamed this Animal to drive single or double; rack, pace, trot, run — or what gait would you like to see him do?... I've been training him for fifty thousand years.... He doesn't know it, of course. The silly ass thinks he's the warden of the asylum instead of a patient.'

Dinny wasn't sure he liked to have his theories tossed about in this reckless fashion.

'I've been thinking,' he said, after they had driven a mile without much talk. 'I've had my nose to the grindstone for a good while — in my work, you know — and I believe a change of air would be good for me. I'm going abroad for a few weeks.'

'Splendid!' enthused Joan. 'I wish I could.'

He laid a hand gently on her arm.

'Very well — I'll take you.'

'No, Dinny — we've settled that!' Her voice was casual now.

'I'd be glad to, you know.'

'I believe you would — but it's quite impossible.'

The long silence that followed gave her words a chance to chisel their way quite deeply into her memory. She recalled them, with a start, one September evening, when, in response to a similar invitation as sincerely offered, she used them again, *verbatim*.

A swarthy gypsy girl, one afternoon, last summer, had padded softly back to the little office in Uncle Jim Bailey's dimly lighted, varnish-reeking furniture store, and, pausing before Joan's high desk, had said:

'Your fortune — for four bits?'

Joan had declined.

'Please — I'm hongry.'

The girl had slipped the half-dollar into a dirty, beaded purse attached to her belt, and reached for her client's hand.

'Make it short,' advised Joan. 'I'm busy.'

The girl had stooped over the extended palm, scrutinizing it intently, Joan, with equal interest, marveling at the black, straight, coarse hair on the bowed head, seeming to belong to a well-groomed horse rather than a young woman.

'You are going on a far jorney... on a beeg boat... with a tall man.'

'Is that all?' asked Joan, as the girl moved off, with the slinky gait of something born in the woods.

She paused, spread one brown hand high on her hip tossed her head arrogantly, and retorted, her white teeth gleaming in the twisted, half-envious smile:

'Ees that not enough?'

* * * * * *

According to Dinny's weekly letters, the cynical amuse-ment he had expressed in his first laconic, staccato, dash-sprinkled note, scribbled on his return from viewing the changing of the guard at Buckingham Palace, was giving way to an unexpected admiration for monarchy.

Joan needed never to have been in England to guess what might be Dinny's instant reaction to the ancient shrines and tombs of the departed great. He had a flair for making his-tory vital, and was extraordinarily well posted on the lives of British sovereigns.

As for the bronze and marble memorabilia of departed kings and queens, Dinny's interest was assured, and Joan confidently expected him to relay observations faithfully, interestingly reflecting the half-dreamy mood in which he would saunter through the gloom of the cathedrals.

She was quite unprepared, however, for his comments on contemporary pageantry.

'It will have to go, of course,' ruminated Dinny, in mid-July, writing from the Victoria Hotel in London. 'The general drift is toward republics, and the last of the kings have already been born. There will be no revolution, no choppings-off, no slow tanning of royal heads on iron-spiked towers. The British manage to express themselves with but few gestures. They are not a yelping, mobbish, excitable race. When the time comes, the king will be retired on half-pay and allowed to keep his horses, dogs, and grouse-gun.

'But it will be a great pity when "the captains and the kings depart"; especially the kings, though I presume you couldn't very well have kings without captains. They'll leave the stage together.

'I'm afraid I've become quite a tory, Joan. I have had time and opportunity for a lot of thinking about this. Humanity hasn't evolved out of the king phase. It's a wise, practical government. Republics sound promising enough in their constitutions, highfalutin slogans, apostrophies to "liberty," senatorial oratory, and patriotic verse, but it's no good in practice.

'I'm for the king! I'm for the divinely ordained king who can do no wrong, no matter what capers he cuts. America would be vastly better off topped by a real, honest-to-goodness king, with twenty million dollars' worth of diamonds in his hat, bells on his fingers and rings on his toes, than a harried, worried, temporary president whom any sleek-haired little squirt, paragraphing and cartooning for some impudent, wisecracking editor, can smear with his smartaleckisms.'

'Why — Dinny!' exclaimed Joan, happily, to his photograph on her table. 'Whatever's happened to you?'

'The whole king business is on the skids, no doubt; but it's a great misfortune. So's the Established Church close to the end of the last inning. Nobody on bases, two men out, and two strikes already called on a feeble bat.... But it's a pity. The thing's had a sort of majestic dignity. It's never been in a suppliant attitude, panhandling the brethren and sisters for sixpences to pay the parson's coal-bill. It has been guaranteed by The State, okayed by The Crown. It's been lofty, confident, time-worthy!

'Maybe it hasn't been quite so fussily, busily, frantically energetic, and maybe the rank and file of the people have accepted it rather perfunctorily — about the way they accepted breathing and the circulation of their blood — but it has stood there calmly certifying to an Eternal Fact (or at least an Everlasting Wish). It will be voluntarily supported, pretty soon, I suppose. And that will be the end of its greatness.... Oh — it will still go through the motions; but its dignity will have departed.

'That's what ails the nine score different sects in the States. No dignity; because voluntarily financed by people whose Sunday dime has given them the right to dictate its policies. Even they — especially they — who presume to manage the thing have no respect for it. How could they? Don't I know? Didn't I grow up in it?

'Wormy, shiny-elbowed, little Jonas B. Pring, lifetime errand-boy and cuspidorian for some fusty old firm of lawyers, snubbed by his betters, henpecked at home, hectored by bill-collectors, a measly little nobody, contemptuously snooted by his own dog — he's quite a tremendous fellow at The First Church of Christ.... Only place in the whole world where Jonas can let himself go, and be somebody.... Gets up at the annual business meeting and tells the thirty-six women, nine old men, and four little girls, that the Reverend Blubb is no executive and had best be asked to move along.... And on what meat hath this our nasty, contemptible, little Jonas fed? How came he so important?

'Jonas was a subscriber. For fifty cents a week, Jonas had bought the right to swagger up and down the aisles, distributing hymn-books, himself yelping the tune at the top of his lungs. At the small cost of twenty-six dollars annually, Jonas B. Pring, who everywhere else was dodging sharp elbows, shoe-tips, snarls, and skillets, could fold his important arms high over his inflated chest, tuck in his forceful chin, draw a sagacious frown, and tell 'em all where to get off at when the Lord's business was under discussion at The First Church of Christ.'

Odd, reflected Joan, Dinny's concern about the Church of England. The only comment she'd ever heard him make about the Anglicans was a sour remark to the effect that their chief job was 'to apologize for the Reformation.'

She did not commend him for his slightly altered attitude toward 'institutions,' fearing her approval, however casually phrased, might sound I-told-you-so-ish; evaded discussion of his new ideas; filled her letters with current news, and doings at Lacey's.

There was a great deal in her letters about Tommy, inevitable because her busy life was now bounded by Lacey's, and Tommy was Lacey's so far as Joan was concerned.

She wrote much too much about Tommy without realizing what conclusions Dinny might come to. Tommy's luggage department had been augmented by a line of motor-rugs and other whim-whams relating to cars. Tommy had had a raise. Tommy had been to Chicago, but was back now.

Tommy's brother Victor hadn't been at all pleased with the reception he had received on his Western tour, and was thinking of giving up the fiddle and studying voice. Someone had told him he could sing. Tommy had said he wasn't sure yet whom the joke was on, but suspected it might be on himself.

Tommy had a new eight-cylinder car, very pretty and very easy riding.

After she had mailed her longest and last letter, the second week of August, and recalled what an inordinate amount of Tommy had found its way into her chronicle of current activities, Joan heartily wished she could have it back for revision. However, Dinny would understand. Besides, he liked Tommy; didn't he?

But it was an unfortunate letter to be her last to Dinny, seeing he was so far away, and alone. Joan had expected to write at least once more.

Then the September issue of *Hallelujah* appeared. She bought it hoping to find nothing in it about Dinny's accession to its tripod. The announcement was there — on page one. *Hallelujah* stated, with a swagger, that, from henceforth and until further notice, the increasing success of the magazine was assured, and gave the reason that had all but broken her heart.

Leafing with distaste and disgust through the condescendingly superior titles, Joan presently came upon Dinny at his worst in a venomous attack on a certain great newspaper syndicate.

It was capped 'Greck.'

Soon after her coming to New York, Dinny, in a mellow moment, had confided his story to Joan. It was not told to solicit her sympathy, or to interpret his maladjustment to the normal ways of viewing human relationships; but, with the whole picture of Dinny's frustrated, disillusioned, and embittered childhood, she had tried to understand the savagery of his cynicism.

Sympathetic as she was, however, toward his disaffection in regard to his father, there was no excuse, she thought, for this unconscionable onslaught.

It seemed that some prominent editorial writer in the employ of 'The Greck Syndicate' had caustically criticized *Hallelujah* on much the same grounds as she herself had based her disastrous comments on the magazine in discussing it at Greenwood Lake.

The Craig Syndicate, as everybody knew, had in its

employ, at the top, a considerable number of keen, clever, high-powered Jews. They were forever playing to the prejudices of the vast, unintegrated, dissatisfied, general riff-raff.

Hallelujah was in the same business, of course, but bidding for the interest of a different clientèle. *Hallelujah* and the Craig Syndicate were as nearly alike as identical twins, except for this: *Hallelujah* appealed to the prejudices and dissatisfactions of some fifty thousand self-confessed intelligentsia; the Craig Syndicate appealed to about the same invoice of aversions possessed by ten millions of illiterati.... How natural that they should hate each other!

Some editorial writer for 'Greck'— Joan presumed it must have been the chief incendiary, Enoch Birnbaum — momentarily forgetting, according to Dinny, that he had been divinely ordained to minister unto the feeble-minded, had remarked of *Hallelujah* that it suffered of 'grandiose paranoia in the penultimate phase of that malady, with paresis indicated as the unhappy sequela.'

Dinny, breathing out slaughter, had assumed championship of the besieged *Hallelujah*. Joan, who knew him as well as or better than he knew himself, could easily picture with what lip-smacking, demoniacal glee he had hauled up the drawbridge, dropped the portcullis, and heated the oil he meant to pour down upon the haughty head of 'Greck.'

She did not read it all. Undeniably clever, fantastically cruel, Dinny's indictment of 'Greck' described him in terms of Moses; Moses the law-giver, Moses the sea-cleaver, Moses the manna-man, Moses the medicine-man.

'Greck,' assisted by all Israel, and trailed by millions of uncircumcised, untutored, and largely unwashed hicks and yokels, was headed for the Promised Land. True, he hadn't got any farther than the wilderness, but Jehovah would doubtless look after His People, as was His pleasant custom.

The last paragraph — the one that gave Joan a sickish feeling as if she had witnessed parricide — was a masterpiece of brutality.

'If the great Greek ever made a mistake, he does not recall it. This, too, was a Mosaic gift — forgetfulness. In his youth, Moses ran away and hid himself after having killed a young neighbor; but if he ever remembered, or was regretful, the Good Book — which almost never omits anything resembling contrition — fails to document his misgivings. It is said that Moses' victim was a young man. Had he killed a young girl, he would of course have forgotten the incident utterly, and remembered it against himself no more.'

Joan tossed the nasty thing into the waste-basket and washed her hands.

* * * * * *

Tommy Forsythe was sailing tomorrow for Lisbon on the *Vulcania*. It was a business trip. He would go to Italy, also, returning to New York in late November.

Joan had lunched with him at Dexter's. He had seemed distraught, probably due to his anxiety that all the last-minute duties should have attention. He had little to say, Joan furnishing most of the talk.

At six, he bade her good-bye as she left the store. It was a casual farewell; a brief handclasp, a bit of banter.

At eight-thirty he called her on the telephone. Might he see her for a moment about something rather important? ... Would she object to a short drive?... He would call in ten minutes.

They headed for Central Park. Tommy was nervous and moody. Joan's curiosity mounted.

'What's on your mind, Tommy?... Anything I can do?' He was a long time finding words.

'Joan' — the car slowed down to five miles an hour — 'I'm to be away quite a while. There's something I'd like to know before I leave. I have become very fond of you, as you can't help knowing.... Are you engaged to Dinny Brumm?'

She shook her head.

'Then I've a right to tell you that I ——'

'No, Tommy, please don't!'

'Will you think about me sometimes, Joan?'

'You know I will, Tommy. You've been such a dear friend. And I hope you're going to have a wonderful trip.'

'I wish you were going along.... I'd take you if you'd go, dear.'

'I believe you would — but it's quite impossible.'

There was a long silence.

'Joan — tell me this much. Are you in love with Dinny?'

'Must I say?'

'No — you needn't say. I understand.'

Joan patted his arm gratefully.

'Tommy — you are a dear.'

He drove her home then, as he had promised, and soberly said good-bye again at her door. Joan felt very much depressed. Early in the evening one of the girls where she lived had suggested their going to a movie. She should have gone. It was too bad — about Tommy. She had known he liked her, but she hadn't been prepared for this.

Now she could not work for Tommy any more. She would have to leave Lacey's. It was rough sledding... for a girl... in business; difficult to retain the proper balance. If you were up-stage and untouchable in your attitude toward your employer, you had no chance of promotion. If you were friendly, he made love to you.

Old Mr. Abercrombie, of Denver, with business at Lacey's in July, had spent an hour with Tommy. Evidently something pleasant had been said to Mr. Abercrombie about her, for when Tommy introduced him, he said:

'If you're ever tired of New York, and want to live in a

really good town, where the air is pure and the wages are right, wire me.'

'Maybe I'll do that, Mr. Abercrombie,' she had said, accepting it as a gracious little courtesy.

Then Mr. Abercrombie had met several others of the department, and was about to leave, but had returned to her, saying, seriously:

'I meant that, Miss Braithwaite.... We would like to have you at Abercrombie's.... Here's my card.'

By midnight, Joan had dismantled her room of everything that belonged to her, and was ready to be off, pending instructions. She called a taxi at midnight and went to the nearest Western Union branch on Broadway. After dispatching the night-letter to Denver, she returned to her room and slept — badly.

At ten-thirty, next morning, there was a wire telling her to come at once. The telegram expressed delight. Joan was cheered.

'Where shall we send your mail, Miss Braithwaite?' asked the mystified Mrs. Higgins.

Joan hesitated, and impetuously resolved upon a bit of bridge-burning.

'I'm not looking for any,' she said.

'Are you going far?' inquired Mrs. Higgins.

'Very — and I shall not be back for a long time.'

The train left at noon. Joan, feeling like a fugitive, was glad when it was in motion. Once through the tunnel and out into the sunshine, she had a pleasant sensation of freedom from an accumulation of perplexities. She dallied long over her lunch. They had passed Poughkeepsie before she had finished.

* * * * * *

The *Berengaria* docked at ten on Friday. Dinny, who had never asked himself whether he felt at home in New York, was glad to be back. England had done his mind a few small services. The passionate impatience with which he had viewed nearly all the traditional reliances — now that they were outgrown, outworn, and anachronistic in a new, mechanized era — had tempered considerably.

There was an assuring solidarity in the massive gray stones of England, poise in the recumbent, armored effigies that lay in single-file through the vaulted transepts of her quiet cathedrals, peace in her tranquil greensward.

On the homeward voyage, with much time for thinking, Dinny had determined upon certain changes in his manner of living. He would take life a little more comfortably, for one thing. He would live less feverishly, as became a balanced mind. The thought of returning to his shabby little suite in the Village was distasteful. He would move uptown, equip his bachelor apartment with a few solid comforts, and make a less hectic and hurried thing of his life.

Now that he was actually home again — his light baggage had been quickly inspected by customs — he was eager to carry out his resolution. He would proceed to it without delay. Joan would be happy to see him well out of the Village and its associations. How pleased she would be when he told her!... He had quite abandoned his novel. Joan would be gratified.

The rooms were shabbier than ever. The few pieces of furniture that were his should be sent out for redressing. His mother's walnut desk had had no attention ever, for all that it had been knocked about from pillar to post for a quarter-century. Its legs were scratched and scored and its body bore many scars. He must not trust its rehabilitation to any but an expert in such matters.

Why not get going on it at once? He called up Becker's, who dealt in antiques, and inquired for Mr. Becker himself; explained who he was, what he had, what he wanted. The elderly Becker, with an errand in the vicinity of Washington Square, said he would run in and have a look at the desk himself.

Dinny was sorting over his books when old Becker arrived, having found it important to occupy his mind with such diversion as was to be had. He knew Joan did not like to be called to the telephone during business hours. It would be a long day.

Old Becker was a thin, wiry, little man with a gray beard and pale blue myopic eyes that peered at you in an absurdly childish fashion.

'Lofely!' murmured Becker, caressing the rich wood with an appreciative palm.

'My grandfather made it a long time ago for my mother, when she was a young girl,' explained Dinny. 'The old fellow was quite handy with tools, I've been told; though, of course, the value of the desk is largely sentimental.'

Becker drew down the lid, almost reverently.

'Handy mit tools!' he muttered, ironically. 'Handy mit tools? Mein Gott! A greadt ardtist! Und you say — handy mit tools; hein?'

He peered inside the desk.

'Vas iss dat?... Mueller?... Mueller!' His pale little eyes searched Dinny. He poured out a torrent of queries. Where did this grandfather live? Was that his name — Mueller? Indiana? Gott in Himmel — no!... Where had he lived before that?

Dinny said his grandfather had migrated from Dresden as a youngster.

'Ah — so!' Becker wagged his head and tugged at his straggling whiskers. 'Der Muellers made no desks... but your grandvadder Mueller — he made a desk for his childt.... It iss very lofely!'

So — Aunt Martha's occasional vague, proud references to the glory that was Mueller, back in 'th' old country,' had some substantial basis of fact. He had always thought the story an exaggeration — one of Aunt Martha's pipe-dreams.

Old Becker was grinning mysteriously, and Dinny regarded him inquisitively.

'Leedle secret, too; hein?' He significantly tapped the

exquisitely crafted little pilaster between the center pigeon-holes with an understanding thumb.

'I'm afraid I don't understand,' said Dinny, stooping to inspect the pilaster critically. 'Secret?'

Becker's expression was a study. He had stumbled upon two secrets — a secret drawer — a mystified owner.

'What makes you think so?' inquired Dinny.

The old man was slow with his reply; looked Dinny up and down, searchingly, as if wanting to satisfy himself that his client was really entitled to know what an owner of such a treasure should have known. Apparently assured on that point, he explained that the central pigeon-holes were an inch wider apart than any of the others. Back of the ornamented pilaster there was a narrow drawer.

Dinny was on the point of suggesting that they experiment, but on second thought decided to make the exploration alone. He quickly came to terms with Becker about the expense, and the old man left, saying: 'Ve vill treadt it vell.... Mein Gott!... a *Mueller!*'

With the point of his knife-blade, Dinny endeavored to loosen the pilaster and start the alleged secret drawer. The little pilaster was unbudgable. Doubtless something else had to be pushed, pulled, moved, before the drawer would open. He inquired of every nook and cranny for a suspicious knob, button, or unexplained gadget. The desk remained calmly innocent of any duplicity. He would have to fall back on old Becker, after all.

Tommy Forsythe would hardly have gone out to luncheon by now. He wondered if they might not go together. Perhaps he might find Tommy free to do so. He called Lacey's and connected with Tommy's department.

No — Mr. Forsythe was not in. Mr. Forsythe was out of town. Who was this — please? Oh — Mr. Brumm. Mr. Forsythe sailed for Europe on Wednesday. Yes — Wednesday noon.

Dinny decided to risk asking for Joan, so long as he had the connection.

'May I speak to Miss Braithwaite?'

There was quite a little pause.

'Miss Braithwaite isn't with us, any more, Mr. Brumm.'

'You mean she's not with Lacey's? Since when? Where's she gone?' Dinny tossed his prudence aside, and fired his questions as if he'd the right to ask them.

'She's not been here since Tuesday — closing time. We do not know where she is.'

'That's strange!'

'Yes, sir... Is that all, Mr. Brumm?'

Dinny's hands trembled as he hunted for the telephone number of Mrs. Higgins. His voice was unsteady when he asked his questions.

No — Miss Braithwaite wasn't there any more.... Yes, she had taken all her things and left shortly before noon on Wednesday.... No — she hadn't said.... No — they positively did not know!... And who was this, talking?

Dinny slammed the receiver back on the hook, and sat for a long time, lost in moody thought, wondering if it were really so. He brought both long hands down with a despairing slap on his knees, rose with a sigh, caught up his hat, went downstairs, and strolled down the street, hands deep in pockets, his mind in a tumult. He had lost Joan!... Damn Tommy Forsythe!... Damn Greenwich Village!... Damn *Hallelujah!*... To hell with Everything!

CHAPTER XV

A RAGGED, rumpled, yellowed scrap of paper, solidly printed on both sides in nonpareil, fluttered to the floor.

Dinny picked it up and held it between his fingers while he unfolded the bulky letter from which it had fallen. The fragment could wait. He laid it on the desk.

It had taken him an hour, that night, to open the narrow little drawer faced with the miniature Corinthian pilaster.

In the afternoon he had dragged the desk to the window and painstakingly inspected every square inch of its surface. Nothing had come of it. At nine he had laid aside his coat, emptied the desk of its meager contents — for he almost never used it — and set about his task determined to see it through.

The long, shallow drawer below the lid which, when let down, was the writing-table, he removed. This operation promised little, for the drawer was a full fifteen inches below the pilaster and clearly unrelated, but he had done everything else and had now arrived at the phase of his exploration where the incredibilities were being examined.

Taking up this skillfully mortised drawer in his hands, Dinny scrutinized it, inch by inch. In the center of the back panel there was a notch in the top, half an inch deep and three-eighths of an inch wide. It excited his curiosity. Perhaps there was some small projection in the depths of the desk, at the rear of the aperture from which this drawer had come, something articulating with the unobtrusive little notch.

Aware of his inability to thrust a well-muscled forearm into this shallow drawer-space, he inserted a walking-stick and probed about with the tip of it until he found a small, squared, wooden tongue. He pushed up on it gently. It instantly responded with a sharp metallic click that seemed to come from higher up in the region of the pigeon-holes.

The quick, decisive tap, unquestionably the release of a spring, startled him; for, upon having reached the path of discovery, Dinny's nerves had keyed to the sensitiveness of fiddle-strings.

Lowering the hinged writing-table, which he had been supporting on his arm, he glanced toward the little pilaster. It was protruding about three inches. Attached to it was a narrow upright drawer. He drew it farther out. It contained a thick letter which all but filled its limited space.

With rapidly beating heart, Dinny held it closer to the desk-lamp, for the writing on the sealed envelope was faded almost to illegibility, and read the words written in a sprawling feminine hand: 'Confidential — To my child — from Julia Miller Craig.'

The letters were so large, and growing larger as the end of the sagging line was reached, that there had been no room on it for the 'Craig,' which was written below 'Miller,' almost as if it were an afterthought.

Dinny drew up a chair to the desk, sat down, and, with a strange sensation of having stepped into the presence of a disembodied spirit, he carefully opened the brittle old envelope with his paper-knife. A ragged, crumpled fragment of paper fell out. He picked it up from the floor without regarding it closely. Doubtless the letter would explain.

It was not easy to read even the first page on which his girl-mother had clearly spent the best of her waning energy. This fact she recognized at the outset. She was writing in bed; she was very ill; she would do her best. She was burning up with fever, and things were all 'out of drawing.'

'God!' muttered Dinny.

She had seemed rather remote — a mere sacred symbol — until he came upon that little phrase.

Why — that was exactly the way he would have said it, himself! He and this girl, nearly ten years his junior, were not only of the same flesh and blood; they were mentally, temperamentally kin!

For the first time in Dinny's life, his mother assumed

definite reality. She came alive in this letter — in this single phrase — and spoke as clearly as if she were at his side. He had a curious feeling that he was not alone. He drew a quick breath, and slowly turned his head, glancing up over his left shoulder. Then, pulling himself together, resolutely, he returned to the letter. A wave of tenderness swept over Dinny; something other than a feeling of filial reverence; rather the sense of desire to lend her his strength, as if she were a young sister in dire need of his protection.

Things were all 'out of drawing' because she was so hot and weak. Yesterday she had been quite excitable from the fever, and had wandered a little. She would speak of that, later, if her strength held out, she said —

I'm not out of my head now. In fact — my wits seem to be speeded up by the fever. Everything's so much brighter and louder. Father is working, out in his shop, and when he lays his chisel down on the bench, I can hear it drop, both ends of it, the wooden end and the iron part. Each leaf on the maple — I see the tree through the window — is twins, after I have looked awhile. One of the twins is blue, the other yellow. At first, when I look out, each leaf is green. After I have looked hard, for a minute, the leaves are twins, like I said, one blue, one yellow. Then my eyes hurt, and I stop looking. At noon I heard the cracked school-bell over at Hinebaugh's. That's four miles. You can't hear it this far. That's how sick I am, and that's how this kind of sickness sharpens you till you're sharper than you want to be, and it hurts. You don't hear things with your ears, when you're this way, but with your eyes. Every tiny noise is big, and pounds in your eyes, deep behind them.

So, if I say anything queer, you will know why, if you're old enough. But I'm not crazy, and I know what I'm doing. I hope you believe this, for I'm going to tell you something very important before I am through, if I can still hold my head up that long. It's pretty dizzy.

'God!' muttered Dinny, half-sick.

If I only knew how to talk to you, dear, it would be easier. I can't quite place you. You're not a baby. I know that. I'm never going to have a baby. One minute, you seem a boy about fourteen that looks ever so much like Zandy, and next minute you're a girl about my age, and look a little like me. I expect they will put me by mother, near the fence, close to where Zandy first told me. There will be some comfort in that — at least there is now.

Dinny's eyes were smarting; his throat ached.... 'God! — what a cruel thing for the dear little chap to endure!' He read on.

The Dresden part of it was difficult to interpret. It demanded hours of study, later, and the utmost concentration, for Dinny to disentangle the crashed and telescoped detail of the jumbled memories. The narrative resembled nothing so much as a cycloned house, with the refrigerator upside-down on top of the piano, and a large, ragged chunk of identifiable dining-room plastering — wall-paper holding it together — in the kitchen-sink alongside a gift copy of Maeterlinck's *The Life of the Bee* and an old wreath of immortelles. The stuff was all there, but out of normal juxtaposition, by no means easily put to rights.

But for the fact that Dinny had already been given reasons for respectful credence in the Mueller tradition, his mother's confused reference to Dresden would have been too fantastic. The things he most wanted to know about that were absent. The superficial detail was highly elaborated; the garden, the garden-wall, hollyhocks, the door in the wall and the wrought-iron hinges on the door, the grassy-banked river, the boats, and a punt with a red-and-blue canopy — but almost nothing about the life of the place.... The cushion on the window-seat in father's room was of rose velvet, but there was not a word about father's reason for running away from home to America or what had become of the people left behind.... There were lily-pads on the pool in the garden and goldfish under them.

The part about his own father was in keeping with the lyrical quality of the Dresden story — a girlishly romantic reminiscence of tender things said and done. Dinny felt, at this point, that the letter had drifted slightly away from the original intention of confiding to a child, and had taken on the style of a personal journal quite too private for any other eyes than the writer's. He was reluctant to read certain parts of it.

Dinny found it very difficult to reverse the career of the spread-eagle, dictatorial, dominant Zandy Craig, of the Craig Syndicate, and return him to the bewildered, gentle, downy fledgling that had been the 'dear, dear Zandy' of his mother's memoirs.... He would have given ten thousand dollars for the unpublished manuscript of 'Greck.'

Perhaps he had misjudged his father. After all, Zandy — Dinny found himself thinking of this man as 'Zandy' — had been but a youngster when it happened. If he had had it to do over again, five years later, he might have shown up better. There was no doubt Julia — Dinny was thinking of her as 'Julia' now — loved him, trusted him. Surely that was worth something. You could mark that up to Zandy's credit.

But — all the same — By God! — Craig had killed her! You had that to remember, too.... Well — we could think that over — later.

Dinny turned to the next page, and continued. The writing was even less legible now. What with the cloudiness of the composition, and the almost indecipherable script, his mother's attempt at a discussion of an apparently bizarre theory she had arrived at, in her disheveled mental condition, was not a thing to be read with full understanding.

The curious metaphysics she seemed trying to express, phrased in whatever naïve terms a country school-teacher might catch up hastily in the exigency of her fatigue and fever, was still further enshadowed by the increasing uncertainty of the nervous pen. The faded letters were so ill-formed that a given character might be *h*, *n*, *u*, *r*, or *v*, with the adjacent vowel offering you your pick of *a*, *e*, or *o*.

* * * * * *

It was nearly three o'clock before Dinny had reached the reference to the little scrap of crumpled paper which, in the stress of translating the letter, he had all but forgotten. He took it up, and read it now, but it seemed strangely irrelevant to the matters his mother was treating with such a valiant struggle to make herself understood.

Dinny went back a few paragraphs, and re-read. Julia had written this at mighty cost. She deserved his best efforts to interpret it.

Long before this trouble came to me... don't feel badly, child, it wasn't your fault... I had been frightfully bitter about lots of things. I was lonesome, and didn't belong in this house. I had never been taught anything worth knowing. I didn't even know how to eat. If it hadn't been for the books I read about the habits and little courtesies of refined people, I would have known no more about how to do at the table than old Florrie.

I got so I hated the sight of them. Father, poor old darling, I loved him with my pity, but that was about all. The girls — Martha never was a girl — were so silly and coarse and ignorant that I despised them with all my heart, hating myself for feeling better than they were. For I was not naturally conceited. I am shy and bashful, really. But I was always ashamed that I was related to Susan and Greta.

I hated Martha. I got so I hated everything she said and did. Since I've been sick — up to yesterday... I'll tell you soon about that, dear... I couldn't bear even to have her touch me. The sound of her voice, down in the kitchen, made me want to get up and shout that she was nothing but a sour old simpleton, even when I couldn't hear a word of what she was saying — nothing but the nasty noise.

I hated the boys. I think I had always hated them. They were dirty, inside and out. They were exactly the same as the rest of the loafers that sat along the porch at Baber's store, and got all quiet when you came, and, after you had passed, there would be a rough rumble of a dirty voice, and then they would all spit and laugh a dirty laugh. If you're a girl, maybe you'll know what I mean, though I hope not much. If you're a boy, and you ever laugh just like that, I hope there'll be no chance for me to hear it wherever I'm going to. I'd rather die like a dog, and stay dead forever, than endure such shame.

I don't know what's going to become of you, child, but I do hope you'll never have reason to hate things and people the way I have.

Then — when this trouble came, and lately when it's seemed pretty doubtful — I got to hating the whole world until I was just as sick from that as this other trouble. It was just like a poison that was eating me, burning me on the inside. My hate hurt clear up in my throat. I hope you'll never know what that kind of hate feels like.

'God! — don't I know?' muttered Dinny. 'You poor little thing!'

Well — yesterday a queer thing happened. Part of it was awful, and I hope you won't think less of me. Martha came and wanted to read the Bible to me, and I wouldn't let her. She put it under my pillow then, and went away. I was so angry at her and it that I tore it up. Maybe you'll be shocked. It was too bad, and I'm sorry. But I tore it up because it was full of what Martha called 'precious promises' — and look what had happened to *me!* This was God's Book, and He had been mean to me. So I tore up His Book. I'm ashamed to tell you this, but it gave me a kind of terrible pleasure to do it — a kind of hot joy that I used to think the Devil had when I was a little girl and believed there was a Devil.... You don't believe there's a Devil, do you, child? I'm thinking of you as a little girl, now, about the size I was when they used to frighten us at revival meetings. I hope you're not living with ignorant people who believe in hell and devils. Surely you've a right to a little better raising than that. I couldn't bear it if I knew you were that poor and degraded.

I quit tearing at the Bible only when my hands were so tired I couldn't move a finger. Pretty soon I fell asleep. Father found the awful mess I had made and cleaned it up before anyone else saw. But there was a little piece left. The next time I was alone I read what it said, and it seemed so different, maybe because it was all there was left.

It seemed to be intended for me. Maybe it won't mean just the same thing to you, because you're not all full of poison and hate and mean feelings toward almost everybody and everything, the way I was. At least I hope you're not, for it's dreadful and worse than any sickness. It really *is* a sickness!

This little piece that I read wasn't like religion at all. I hated religion. You did something wrong, and had to go crawling on your hands and knees to be forgiven for it. You had to cry and beg and whine like a dog. But this wasn't like that. It wasn't anything to sniffle about the way they have to do in church when they are sorry for hating people who have wronged them. I always despised whiners. They said in church that God wanted you to whine, for He liked to hear sniffles from scared people. So I despised Him for that. He wasn't my sort.

Dinny put down the letter, rubbed his tired eyes, and shook his head. His mother's reminiscences were his own. Again he felt that strange kinship between himself and this unhappy girl who had given him birth. Her blood coursed through his veins. Her queries were his. His criticisms were hers. It was in the blood-stream! His temperament was a biologic inevitability. You grew figs on fig-trees. You grew thorns on thistles. Didn't you? Well — there you are, then! Nothing to be done about it! Is there?

Julia had despised whiners. God liked whiners. 'The sacrifices of God are a broken spirit.' God liked broken spirits; liked to hear 'em wail; liked to see 'em wring their hands, and pour ashes on themselves. That had been his own chief objection to the whole structure of traditional theology. He wanted to be a man. He wanted to stand upright and face the sun. God wanted him to grovel like a cowed animal. Dinny knew now how he'd come by his passionate aversion to such self-abasing, personality-destroying, soul-defiling ignorance! He wanted to reach across the Border and clasp the hand of this fearless, unfettered spirit. He was proud of his Julia. His eyes were wet with emotion.

This little piece of religion that I had left, lying under my hand as if it was meant for me, doesn't whine at all. It doesn't ask you to whimper for mercy.

It's just a business proposition same as if you owed a thousand dollars to Mr. Smith, and ten other people owed you a hundred dollars apiece, and Mr. Smith said, 'Pay me that thousand dollars,' and you said, 'I can't — with all these people owing me.'

And Mr. Smith said, 'I don't need the money so much, but I like you and want to be friends with you, and as long as you are owing me you'll be keeping away from me for fear I'll ask you for it and make you ashamed. And it won't do any good for me to tell you just to keep the money and forget it, because that would make you ashamed, too, and you would always feel in debt. So — I'll make you a proposition. If you will cancel all the debts of these people who owe you, and are afraid to face you, so that they can afford to cancel the debts of the people who owe them, I'll call it square with you. Then we can all be good neighbors again, and nobody will be afraid of anyone else, or shy, or ashamed.'

This all sounds so much more sensible to me, dear, than the way they talk about it at the meetings. It's just as if God wanted us to do business with Him about these things that have kept us strangers.

Maybe this will sound silly to you, but I closed my eyes and said, down inside myself where there seemed a little spot that brightened up, 'Please forget that I tore up Your Book, and help me to forget it too, for it makes me very sorry to remember.' And God said, speaking from down inside of me, just as plainly as anything I ever heard, 'Will you forgive your father for drinking up the opportunities you might have had, and Susan for refusing ever to come into your room on account of the desk, and the boys for being rude, and Martha for not wanting you to have any fun?'

And I said, 'Yes — I will.'

And then He said, 'Will you forget everything they ever did that has made you disappointed and sorry — just as I'm going to forget everything you've done to disappoint and sadden Me?'

And I said, 'Yes — I will.'

Of course I can't expect you to understand the strange feeling that came over me, but it wasn't like anything else that ever happened. Please don't think I'm telling you something I dreamed. I was quite wide awake. The queer thing that happened was just as if some wonderful doctor who knew how to cure any disease instantly had given me a powerful medicine that cleared out all the poison! I felt all *clean* and *new!* ... Then I found myself smiling, and I laughed. And — this was because I am so weak, I suppose — I cried a good deal; but not for being unhappy or afraid or ashamed. Maybe I can't explain this very well, but I felt proud, just as if I had been promoted or had won a great prize, or had discovered I was a princess or something!

It's awfully hard to try to make this sound the way it actually was. For I don't know whether I'm talking to a little girl with a doll in her hand, or a big boy old enough to go to college, but this thing that I've got is a sort of *power!*

That's the best I can do to explain it. When you get it, you'll know. I want you to have it, for there's no other feeling like it. I believe that if I could get well, now, I could do almost anything!

It's great to be able to talk to God, now, any time you want to, and say anything you like, and know that you're fast friends. It would be wonderful to get well, and see Zandy again; but if I don't, I'll see God exactly as He is; and I'm not afraid.

I thought about it nearly all night — and kept talking to Him, and He would answer me. Please don't think I'm out of my head. I'm awfully tired. That's what makes the writing so bad. And I said I was dreadfully sorry I had misunderstood Him so, and he said, 'Well — Hiram and Elmer misunderstand *you*. They think you consider yourself too nice to have anything to do with them. And Susan and Greta think the same thing, that you're above talking to them about their little troubles.'

This morning Susan came to the door and looked at me. She seemed so shy and scared, as if she had never seen me before, and I motioned to her to come in, and she sat down on the little chair by the bed. And it was just about as easy as it had been, last night, when God and I made up. I just reached out my hand and rubbed my fingers over Susan's face, softly. It was the first time I'd intentionally touched her for years, and we almost never had anything to say to each other, not for years and years. And Susan slipped down on her knees by the bed, and put her arms around me, and we both cried, but I was happy and I loved Susan for the first time in my life.... Dear Child — the poison is all out of me now. Of course, I'm too sick of the other trouble to get well — but it doesn't really matter. I'm happy. I love the boys, too, and I'm going to let them know. And poor father — he does feel so badly about everything.

Dinny put down the letter, and paced the room, unable to endure another line of it. Of course, poor Julia was laboring under intense emotion, terrific neural strain. A great deal of her experience could be charged to an hallucination easily explained. Naturally, the whole family would be wrought up. Susan would have been a beast to remain cold and aloof under the pitiful little tender of affection. Nobody was normal at the time.... But — God! — suppose such relief and release were real! Suppose that for the mere act of unloading one's memory of all the bitter hatreds and cankered grudges, one might feel free to lift one's eyes and smile into the face of God — as dear Julia had — and be cleared of all the 'poison!'

Suddenly there came a definite surge of such painful wistfulness to lay hold upon some strength beyond his own as had never possessed him — not even for the instant when Angela's choir, bursting forth with an exultant 'Unfold! Unfold!! Unfold!!!' had tugged at his soul — not even in that brief, boyish quest of The Mystery when he had sat in church with the Timmy Fagans.

In those fleeting experiences Dinny had glimpsed the possibility, resident in him, for rapture and radiance. For these ecstatic instants, the Light had broken through, certifying to two facts: there was a Light, and he possessed the spiritual retina to see it. The shutter clicked — and for that one little split-second the Light poured in; but, afterwards, the darkness settled again.

Maybe Julia had found the way to a permanent possession of that spiritual illumination which, rarely, he had sensed with a brief ecstasy that stirred him to the depths, and promptly left him cold.

If Julia had found it, and in such high degree that she was undaunted even by the impending tragedy that stared into her girlish face, might he hope to capture that strange magic

for himself? Why not? They were the same sort of people;
weren't they? Julia and he were kin. Her queries were his
queries. They had shared much the same dilemmas of frustration, disillusion, disappointment. They had shared the
same hot hate of a world that had consistently let them
down.... Julia had never 'belonged,' but, at last, *she had
'belonged'*!

* * * * * *

Slumping down in his chair, taut with the emotional tension of the past half-dozen hours, Dinny covered his face
with his outspread hands, and muttered, half aloud:

'I'll give it a trial!... God! — I wonder if I'm losing my
mind.... I'm going to make the experiment, and see what
comes of it.'

He reached for the crumpled scrap of paper, and sat staring at the well-remembered words which he had heard Uncle
Miles read, monotonously, scores of times, words now highly
charged with energy. He felt himself studying a formula in
Physics. Again Dinny returned to his mood of deep
meditation.

God! — suppose the thing were real!... But, if it was
real, why didn't more people know about it? If there was
anything to it, surely the religious would have practiced it.
A man who possessed this dynamic joy that Julia had found
— why, you could spot him at a thousand yards by the
light in his eyes!

That was the appalling obstacle in the way of Dinny's
confident belief in the reality of the mysterious 'lifting
power' that had caught Julia up, and held her, in an hour of
crisis.

Would she have discovered it, at all, had she been well,
mentally sound, physically fit? According to her own documented testimony, she was upset to the point of having to
plead with her child for belief in her sanity. Was she any
too sure of it, herself?

Sane people had no capacity for permanently possessing

this uncanny spiritual strength. They had brief experiences of ecstasy. He had had them. Doubtless everyone, according to his temperament, had felt these occasional tugs from Otherwhere. Perhaps every inquisitive person nourished the vague dream of making lasting connections with this strange energy of exultation. That's what the religious were out after. They wanted to 'fix' their idealisms on the highly sensitized plate, and make them permanent... But — with what success?

Dinny found himself recalling instance after instance, in the little churches he had known as a growing boy, when the activities of a congregation of alleged Christians seemed actually to interfere with the personal peace of the individuals thus brought together. Not only did their religion fail to illumine them: it quite definitely got in the way of their self-confessed aspirations.

He remembered his own grinning, as a lad, over the celebrated rumpus that had rent Uncle Miles's little church at Zanesdale. Mrs. Bilger wanted the Sunday School chairs for the Eastern Star banquet on the same night that Lida Kronk had promised them to the Modern Woodmen of which her Claude was the Chief Axe-Swinger, or whatever it was. And before they had done with the acute phase of the battle, not only was the whole congregation lined up in two hostile camps, but the town itself was involved. Uncle Miles had raced frantically back and forth across No Man's Land, pleading for arbitration, meanwhile being himself potted from both sides. Even as a small boy in short pants, Dinny had considered the affair a howling farce.

Now — in the light of what Julia said she had found, Dinny knew that the vulgar and noisy controversy over the church chairs hadn't been funny, at all. The whole matter had been tragic beyond the telling. Was it not just such small-minded jealousies and stupid little exhibitions of egotism brazenly flaunted by persons conspicuous in the business affairs of country and village churches that had made the general public laugh the whole institution to scorn?

Surely, thought Dinny, he had done his bit toward making such *gaucheries* ridiculous. Conventional religion, in the custody of the typical church of his own acquaintance, was not merely banal, farcical, impotent. By Gad — that sort of thing was definitely blocking our evolution! It was shutting off even such fugitive glimpses of the Light as a man might find for himself if left to his own devices as an untaught pagan!

Of course, reflected Dinny, here and there, even in the stifling antagonisms forever on display in Uncle Miles's little churches, a rare spirit contrived somehow to grow.

There flashed across his mental screen the picture of 'old man' Houk. They never referred to him in any other way: 'old man' Houk, who kept the light hardware and notion store near their church on the edge of Fort Wayne. There was a peculiar light in the old fellow's eyes. There was the quality of thermo-dynamics in his smile. How good God was to him, 'old man' Houk was always saying in that gentle voice of his. How 'blest' he had been. And sometimes the people laughed a bit when they talked about 'old man' Houk's gratitude, for if ever anybody had his nose to the grindstone with nothing tangible to show for it, Houk won the prize. The two girls had married early, one bringing a worthless husband home to live; the other had abandoned hers, returning with three small children. As for the boy, he was no end lazy, impudent, and always in trouble. But 'old man' Houk had something!... However — he may not have been quite all there. Even Uncle Miles had said that the old chap had a loose screw.

Now the question arose, in Dinny's mind; was 'old man' Houk a bit unhooked mentally, or had he managed to 'lay hold' on the energy that Julia had found? Were these occasional mystics inspired or demented?

Pursuing his recollections of Uncle Miles's ugly little churches that seemed bent on nothing but trivial expedients to pay their insignificant bills, in the course of which silly endeavors — rummage sales, ice-cream socials, and shock-

ingly dull home-talent plays — they generally stirred up
fresh rows, Dinny's honesty forced him to concede that you
really couldn't expect much fineness to develop in the weedy
Zanesdales and Ungers, where there was nothing to think
about but one's treadmill and the callosities worn thick and
hard by one's ill-fitting harness. It wasn't quite fair to judge
religion, as an institution, by what one observed of it in
Zanesdale.

But then — there was Magnolia! Magnolia had been the
mecca for a religious cult whose constituency in that zone
numbered well into six figures, a cult that regarded its
neighbors with sour pity. Had not smug and pious little
Magnolia excoriated and discharged the only Christ-like
personality on her staff — the only man in the whole outfit
who had had the valor to stand up and say that the Master
he followed was an uncompromising apostle of peace?

Dinny remembered how they all used to laugh over the
perennial feud between the factions that backed Professor
Strickler, who taught Hebrew, and Professor Munger, who
taught Homiletics, each of whom had been trying for years
to discredit the other in the opinion of the parsons over a
region five hundred miles in diameter.

But here, again, fairness demanded that Dinny take account of all the facts in the case. Magnolia, after all, was
but a little tea-pot. You couldn't appraise religion at large
by the disgusting envies that stood out awkwardly, like
sore thumbs, interfering with everything the college and
seminary aspired to do.

Who were Professors Strickler and Munger — for all
their unctuous mouthings and frock-coated pomposities —
but grown-up farmer lads, innocent of any experience whatsoever in an outer world of urbanity and culture? Dinny
knew their story. Having graduated from the seminary,
they had been fortunate enough to marry the daughters of
well-to-do lay members of the Board. After a few years of
inconspicuous paddling about in the mud and dust of small-
town parishes, their fathers-in-law had engineered them

into seminary chairs (rocking-chairs), where, between venomous thrusts at one another, they had taught the young fry what they ought to know about the Old Testament in the original, and the theory of preaching the gospel of peace and salvation. Admittedly, that was pretty bad; but you mustn't judge all institutionalized religion by the performances of fat and furtive little Stricklers or lean and malicious Mungers.

No — to be decently fair, you had to look at The Thing higher up. But what results did you get from such investigation? What spirit had actuated the organization of the greater sects in Christendom? What ghost had haunted the passionate conclaves in which reformations, reappraisals, and re-evaluations had taken wing? Surely not the Holy Ghost! Which one of them had walked out of a Mother Church because it wanted a better chance to believe and exemplify the theory of whole-hearted forgiveness, tolerance, sympathy, and 'second-mile-ish-ness,' which had constituted the vary solar plexus of the Galilean gospel? Stand 'em up in a long row and demand their reply to this question, and see what you get: 'Do you believe in the celestial commerce whereby you, yourselves, come into the possession of permanent power and radiance, in exact proportion to your ability to condone and explain and forget other people's "trespasses"?'

And yet — here stood this Ancient Thing.... By Gad — everything else in the world, by comparison of age, reeked of fresh paint, green lumber, hot rivets, and perspiration. It had outlived every other institution on earth, despite the fact that its early death had been forecast by the wiseacres of each generation for nearly two millennia. A new day had come. The arm-wavers were saying that more had happened in the past twenty years than in the preceding five thousand. Radical changes were tearing down yesterday's customs, mores, laws, dogmas. Religion was on its last legs. But was it? Not so you could notice it. The Thing had as much vitality as ever.

What, actually, did it stand for? You had to explain its enduring life somehow, didn't you? Had it arrived at this apparent guarantee of perpetuity by virtue of its high achievement in promoting the world's peace? — Nonsense. It had been a notorious fighter.... Had it offered notable service in encouraging scientific progress? — Ha! ha! Now you tell one!... Had Rome shown much inclination to walk a second mile? Had Calvinism presented the other cheek? Had Wesleyanism handed over its cloak when sued for its coat? Had the Anglicans agreed quickly with their adversaries, 'whilst in the way with them?'... Hosts of them were unquestionably excellent people, the majority wanting to improve themselves; occasional individuals, in all the cults and sects, contriving to 'lay hold'; but, considered as institutions — considered as An Institution — exactly what did it stand for? How, in the face of all the dismaying facts, had it earned its evident immortality?

It had always done a bit of philanthropy, yes; but so had the 'unredeemed,' for that matter. Its sporadic efforts at charity were always being outranked in volume and administrative acumen by secular agencies. It had always pretended to educate, but was without caste in the opinion of high-powered schools. Sometimes the parsons made a great to-do about the imposing array of North American Universities, all of which had been founded by preachers, and backed by churches. Even so, at the beginning; but such of these institutions as had actually won high recognition had long since lost their original religious affiliation.

In short — what was religion good for? What did the Ancient Thing stand for? What made it last? Dinny thought he knew. Organized religion stood for the people's *yearning!* It was a costly monument to the people's *wistfulness!* All the people, considered as individuals, felt occasional little clicks of the camera shutter: the Light poured in on them for an instant: they kept hoping to make these fleeting surges of ineffable luminosity permanent, good for all weathers!

But, in the face of this testimony of religion — intolerant, irascible, pig-headed, hair-triggered — was it really worth the effort for a person so materialistic, so critical, so unsentimental as himself, to hope that he might find the spiritual dynamics which had come to the rescue of his disappointed and embittered girl-mother?

Dinny looked at his watch. It was four o'clock. He had exhausted the last tag-end of his mental resources. Any further thought about these matters, in his present condition of fatigue, would be merely exasperating. He threw off his clothes, snapped out the light, and slept.

*   *   *   *   *   *

Street noises roused him at nine from a deep sleep, and he sat up dully trying to remember where he had left off. There was an odd sensation that the day promised to be eventful, though in what manner Dinny had no definite idea. The best he could make of it was a nervous tension of expectancy, anticipation, novelty, somewhat as he had felt when he awoke on the day he had sailed to England, and on the day Joan was to arrive. Something was going to happen.

Tuning himself up with a cold shower and ten minutes of vigorous calisthenics, he dressed carefully and walked over to The Brevoort for breakfast. There were several important things he had planned yesterday to do today. He must go up to the *Hallelujah* office for a bit of conference, for one thing.

On his homeward voyage, Dinny had looked forward to this new position with interest; hardly with pleasure, for it had been difficult to feel quite satisfied over it while haunted with the memory of the hurt look in Joan's eyes. And even now that she had run away, and didn't belong to him any more, and was probably pacing the deck of the *Vulcania*, at this very moment, fondly arm in arm with Tommy Forsythe, Dinny still sensed a feeling of unrest and dissatisfaction over the whole *Hallelujah* business, heartily wishing he had never gone in for it. Perhaps tomorrow would be soon enough to report there.

He had planned also to go uptown and look at a few bachelor apartments somewhere in the west eighties, but there was really no hurry about it.

Well — then — what *was* the important thing he had on his mind? — this something that had to be done without delay.

Dinny never wearied of analyzing his own mental processes. He had learned that it was no longer considered scientific to speak of one's 'subconscious mind.' The new Psychology said there wasn't any such thing. 'Subconscious mind' was as obsolete as 'Soul.'

But you could call it what you liked, or refuse to call it at all; the fact remained that two distinct mental processes could be carrying on at the same time in one individual's head. Dinny often marveled at this queer phenomenon. Here he was, this morning, rumpling his hair with his fingers and trying to remember just what it was that so urgently demanded his attention, and, all the time he was wondering, his subconscious mind — which was mere nonsense, of course; for he didn't have a subconscious mind, there being no such organ now recognized by science — was quite certain that he would return promptly to his room and attempt an experiment based on Julia's letter.

While he was drinking his second cup of coffee, Dinny rather reluctantly admitted to his subconscious mind — which he didn't have — that such had been his intention from the moment he had wakened, an hour ago, and that if it would just have the decent courtesy to wait until he had finished his breakfast, he would do as he had planned to do, anyhow, without benefit of such counsel. In these occasional interior conferences, Dinny's subconscious mind always seemed much older and more mature than the rest of him, which he was inclined to resent. There was something a bit too paternal and hortatory and all-wise in the advice offered from that quarter.

This morning, the distinct identity of his two minds seemed more clearly defined than ever in his experience. Perhaps he had been thinking about that one matter, bringing both his conscious and subconscious minds to bear on it, until they had temporarily lost their capacity for integration, like the green leaves on Julia's maple tree that she had stared into twins — one blue, one yellow. It was almost as if he, himself, were facing a battle with a very mature and omniscient ghost who, normally benign and approximately acquiescent, had suddenly decided to say 'Yes — you will!... And I'll see to it that you do!'

Dinny was determined, however, not to give in too promptly. On his way back to his rooms he decided not to take another look at the gripping letter until he had done at least one 'Green Cheese' essay. He always tried to keep about three weeks ahead of the release date, and was now four days behind his schedule, due to indolence on shipboard.

Taking every advantage of current and seasonal topics, Dinny's theme for this morning's composition would relate somehow to the national observance of Columbus Day. He had scribbled a few rough notes, yesterday; nothing of value, however. All he had was:

'Lookit, Gramp!... They got the flags out again!... Some festival or other.'

'That doesn't mean anything, Luna. The Ku Klux have terrified them into buying flags. They're flying almost every day now. Hadn't you noticed?'

'Yes — but the Knights of Columbus have run one up on their buildings.'

'Humph! — it must be something else, then. What happened on October twelfth, Luna? You wouldn't be likely to know, would you?'

Dinny typed this much, and, thrusting his hands deep in his coat pockets, appraised it with a critical eye. What was the good of it? Many people would grin, no doubt. Some of them would be sore. All of them would again be made aware of the widening rift between the 'One Hundred Per Cent Americans' and the field, embracing other pigments, other creeds, other nativities, than the increasing organization of sheeted patriots who had bought their right to hate their neighbors for Ten Dollars and the price of a white cotton disguise.

He drew the paper out of the machine, and crumpled it in his fist. Why not try to do the thing constructively once. Surely the readers of his 'Green Cheese' column would forgive him a wee digression from his habitual spoofing, scoffing cynicism. They might even enjoy just a tough of sincerity; not too sentimental, of course: that would spoil everything.

Why not try it? It would be in line with the experiment he hoped he was going to make, wouldn't it?

Dinny inserted a fresh page into the typewriter, and wrote the opening phrase which always distinguished his feature article.

'Lookit, Gramp!'

And then he sat for full five minutes, absently toying with the keys, utterly unable to proceed.

But — I can't do anything like this, reflected Dinny. If there's any substantial fact in what Julia says, there are a few things you have to do first before you can take an affirmative position. You've got to 'un-bitter' yourself.

He grinned, rather foolishly.

'Very well, Mr. Smith,' he soliloquized, half aloud, 'we'll say I've owed you a lot of money; and Zandy Craig, and gloomy old Aunt Martha, and the Reverend Miles Brumm, and Spike Davis, and Major Clemens, M.D., and Barney Vaughn, and Orville Kling, and — and Tommy Forsythe — owe me. And you're prepared to call it square, and sweeten me up, if I stop despising these other people.... All right, sir, I'll take you up!' Dinny made a sweeping gesture of dismissal to the imaginary company of his enemies.

'I'll forgive the outfit at one swoop. Or, if you'd rather, I'll forgive 'em one at a time. Here they go. I'll forgive Uncle Miles, first — the damned old embezzler.'

Suddenly the sardonic grin left Dinny's face, and a wave of self-disgust swept him. What a cad! — to let his chronic cynicism defile a situation that had been brought about by a farewell message from the dear girl who had died to give him his life!

There would be no more of this vulgar sacrilege, he could promise himself that much. He would give up all attempts to do the impossible thing, of course. It was not for people of his type. He had carried his load of aversions too long. It had grown fast to him. But, at least, he could honor Julia's faith by refusing to make a travesty of it!

That much settled, then, Dinny lighted his pipe, and drew up to his machine, quite confident that he had shaken off this strange temporary psychosis that had been playing the devil with his thoughts. The page wasn't quite straight, and he made himself a great deal of bother adjusting it. The machine needed a drop of oil, and it took quite a while to find it. The ventilation in the room wasn't very good, and he opened both windows. Having sat down again, ready now to go at his task in earnest, he felt a draft and got up to close one window partly. His coat cramped him, and he took it off.

And then — from far in the depths of himself, where his subconscious mind might have been, had he had one — there welled up a solid, substantial, mature thought, as definite as if it were actually phrased in a spoken command: 'You may as well proceed with the thing you are going to do. You're wasting your time. You've lost your knack at Green Cheese. There'll never be any more; not from you. You've gone into this liberty-quest too far to back up! Admit you're beaten — and see what you can make of the other thing.'

Dinny rose, with a sigh, went to his mother's desk, and sat for a half-hour with his elbows on the writing-table, his head in his hands.

Rousing, at length, with an air of determination, he went to the telephone, called a familiar number, and was almost startled by what he found himself saying.

'*Hallelujah?*... Mr. Brumm speaking.... Is Johnny Keaton there?... Please.... Johnny?... Dinny Brumm.... Very good. How are you?... I'd rather expected to be in, today, but I've just had word that I'm required to make a business trip West. May be all of a couple o' weeks. Wish you'd carry on without any coöperation from me until you hear from me.... That's fine.... And Johnny — how would you like to do my Green Cheese stuff for a while. You can, you know. Better than I.... If you like it, and can get away with it so everybody's satisfied, it'll be a nice thing for you. I'm tired of it. And I may have to do quite a little traveling for a few weeks. Might even have to go to Europe. You take over all the editorial responsibility up there until you see me again.... No — this is something sudden; more or less personal business; emergency stuff.... Thanks, Johnny. I'll write you more in detail.... Yes — tonight; if I can get a reservation. Just now learned that I had to go.... Goodbye.'

Dinny turned to his clothes-closet, reached to a high shelf and threw down the bags he had put away yesterday.

'There may be nothing in it,' he muttered, as he began peeling his clothes off their hangers and tossing them onto the bed, 'but I'm going to give it an honest work-out.... God! — if the thing should be true!'

CHAPTER XVI

'I'm a-goin' out that way myself soon as this here gol-darned loafer changes my oil,' volunteered the middle-aged farmer, who had taken his foot off the hub and sidled up to help answer the query about transportation to Oak Grove. 'Yuh c'n come along, if yuh don't object t' ridin' with a hawg.'

'Bet you'd raise hell if anybody else called yuh thet, Jase,' drawled a voice that apparently belonged to the pair of legs protruding from beneath the truck's engine.

Jase spat, nonchalantly, grinned, and rubbed a stubbly chin; then winked companionably.

'If yuh ever wants t' take one o' them slow movin' pitchers,' he advised, elaborating a confidential air, 'yuh can't do better 'n t' come t' Larwill. These here fellers in Lije Hinebaugh's garage has been a-practicin' till they's purty good.'

'Thanks for the offer of a lift. I'm wanting to go out and see my Uncle Miles Brumm. That's my name, too — Brumm.'

The obliging farmer left off his bantering attitude, stared hard from under his shaggy brows, and rubbed his palm on his blue denim pant-leg before presenting it.

'Yer Julia's boy, mebby?'

'Yes. Did you know her?'

'Reckon I did. My name's Schrofe. We was neighbors like. She taught our school fer a winter — er a part of it. You ain't never been out here afore?'

'Once,' said Dinny, shoving his bags out of the way, as the legs began to wriggle out from under the engine, followed by a large pan of spent oil. 'I was about seven. Aunt Greta was being married. We were here only for a day. How long have my Uncle Miles and Aunt Martha lived up here? I'm afraid I had almost lost track of them, for a while.'

'Well — it's about two years, come Christmas. I've owned th' little place fer quite a spell. Angela writ a-askin' could her folks come back 'n' live there. 'Pears like th' ol' man 'd had a stroke, er somethin'.'

'How's he now?'

'Oh — he gits about.'

'And Aunt Martha?'

'She's well as common. Makes a little garden, 'n' that. Chickens, 'n' that... Yuh ain't seen 'em lately?'

Dinny shook his head, waiving the opportunity to explain.

'Guess we c'n go now,' said Jase, pulling out a fat roll of soiled money. 'Here's yer filthy lucre, Lije. I'll be gol-darned if that ain't what it is. Time a dollar bill's made a dozen trips t' one these here little garages ——'

'We don't have no trouble a-gettin' people t' take 'em,' drawled Lije. 'Better have an understandin' with this feller, Mr. Brumm, afore yuh start north, er he'll charge yuh th' price of his dang truck fer th' ride.'

'Any time I'd take a dime offen Julia Miller's boy ——' said Jase, soberly. 'Climb in, won't yuh, and we'll go down t' th' express office fer that Berkshire shoat. Bought 'er last week over at th' fair in Wayne. Wasn't fixed t' take 'er home with me. Had th' family along — pap 'n' th' girls. Ain't got none o' my own. I'm a old batch.'

They were rattling down the dusty street toward the railroad station, Jason waving a hand to the hicks idling in front of the implement store.

'I s'pose yer married, this good while, eh?' he shouted.

'No,' replied Dinny, adding, 'The only girl I wanted wouldn't have me.'

Jason made a careful job of backing the truck up to the station platform, turned off his engine, and climbed down.

'Same as me,' he said, grinning mysteriously. 'The gal was yer maw.'

There was a little surge of resentment in Dinny's mind over the impudence of this untutored old yokel. He didn't like the idea of Julia's having been admired to this extent by a person so far beneath her. What right did this fellow have to cherish the memory of Julia?

The rough wooden crate scraped into the truck with a screech accompanied by the pig's shrill squeal of alarm. Jason climbed up, started the rackety engine, which added to the pig's consternation, and they rumbled through the village, and out upon the highway, driving at a snail's pace.

'This damn pig cost four hundred and twenty-five dollars,' explained Jason, ''n' she's got t' be handled with care. I spect yer quite anxious fer t' git up there, too, seein' it's been so long since yuh heared from 'em.'

'I hadn't supposed pigs were so expensive,' commented Dinny, hoping to distract attention from his obvious lack of knowledge about his relatives. 'How much is pork worth now?' He tried to make the query sound as if he had at least a passing interest in such matters.

Jason guffawed loudly.

'Well — pork ain't a-bringin' much, just now; but this here shoat ain't pork, 'n' when she has pigs, 'bout a year f'm now, they ain't a-goin' t' be pork, neither. I got a Berkshire boar over t' our place that I'd like fer t' show yuh. By Golly — nobody's ever called that feller pork. Say — if yuh was t' slit that there big boy's belly up intuh bacon, I guess it 'd cost yuh 'bout fifty dollars a slice. It's easy fer t' see yuh ain't no farmer.'

Dinny listened with a pretense of interest, but conscious of an uncomfortable irritation over the fact that his Julia, once upon a time, had been the object of this crude old chap's attentions. Somehow it pushed Julia farther away from him, even if she had been unaware of this devotion. This pig-fancier had unwittingly thrust his rough, unrefined bulk between him and the idealistic image of his mother.

'I've saw pieces o' yourn in th' papers,' Jason went on, grinning broadly. 'Seen 'em in *Th' Tribune*, when I've went t' Chicago. Our papers 'round here don't seem t' take t' 'em like. I brung a couple o' 'em home once f'm Chicago, 'n' I thought pap 'd laugh hisself t' death. Pap says, "Gol-darned if that ol' feller in th' moon ain't about right." I mind one time yuh writ a piece 'bout them flossy automobiles a-splashin' mud on people 'long th' sidewalk when there wasn't nothin' in th' car but a poodle dog a-ridin' by hisself in th' back seat. Yuh oughta heared pap holler 'n' laugh. He likes 't when yuh git 't on 'em, 'specially th' tony folks. Pap's always a-braggin' 'bout yuh, 'cause yer Julia's boy, 'n' he set such store by her. He says, "Gol-darned if Julia's boy ain't a sharp feller that they's got t' leave alone, fer he's got a mean tongue, 'n' enough pizen in him t' start a bran' new hell."'

'Was that what he said — "poison"?'

'Yeah... 'Course pap was only a-foolin'. He likes yer pieces. Pap didn't mean 't harmful. It was just a joke, 'n' that.'

'It's no joke with me, Mr. Schrofe.' Dinny was surprised to find himself saying this. He had blurted it out, impulsively. Now he would have to explain, best he could. 'Your father's quite right. And he meant what he said as a friendly joke. I know that. But — there's been too much poison in me, and it's not good for me. I don't mind telling you that I'm taking a little treatment for it.'

'Pills — 'n' that?' inquired Jason, interestedly.

'The equivalent of pills — yes. I'm going to look up a few of the people I've had occasion to despise, and see if I can't come to terms with them. Perhaps that will do the trick. Just confidentially — I haven't seen my uncle and aunt for many years; not since I started away to college.'

'Forgot 'em — mebby?'

No — Dinny hadn't exactly forgotten them. It was not easy to explain, but he had gone away to school, and then the war had come along, and then he had gone East, and always his time and mind had been occupied.

'Yeah — I reckon,' agreed Jason, indulgently. 'But I bet there's more to 't than that. We always thought Preacher Brumm was a kind o' slippery ol' cuss. Mebby he done somethin'. As fer Martha, she prob'ly wouldn't a-done nothin', a-bein' what she is, so pious 'n' that.'

'I thought it would be good for me to see them again.'

'Yeah — that's proper — 'n' let bygones be bygones, eh?'

'Exactly.'

'Well — that's proper like, if yuh can do 't. Pap's always a-sayin', "Fergive 'n' fergit, 'n' like th' ol' Indian says, 'Always remember!'"'

Dinny indulged in the first hearty, spontaneous laugh he had had for several days.

'That's the only brand of forgiveness I've ever carried in stock, I'm afraid.'

'Well — there's only just one feller in th' world I ain't never a-goin t' feel right about, I guess. They's lots o' people what I don't care fer, not special, but this here feller I hate. I ain't never got over 't. Long time ago, come winter, 'n' nothin' much t' do, nights, but set 'n' think, I used fer t' do a little plannin' how I c'd go out West where he lived, 'n' stick a knife in him.'

'I don't suppose I could guess his name,' ventured Dinny, half-suspecting Jason would not be averse to a confidential chat on the subject.

'Reckon yuh could. That's th' feller, all right. He prob'ly never done nothin' fer t' help yuh. Gol-darned selfish brute! By Golly — I'd like t' kill him!'

'It's been a sore spot with me, too, Mr. Schrofe, though I think it's only fair to say that he made an honest effort to show an interest in me. I suppose it was my own fault that his generosity was unrewarded. I didn't care to take anything from him. However ——'

'By Golly — I honor yuh fer 't. So'll pap.' Jason idled the truck to a stop on the grassy roadside, and pointed across the highway to a barbed-wire gate fronting the dense woods. 'Mebby yuh'd like t' see th' ol' path. Let's git out, 'n' I'll show yuh.'

They ambled across the road, and Jason hooked an elbow over the top rail of the gate.

'Julia used fer t' leave th' road, right here, 'n' take that there path through th' timber, when she was a-teachin' th' Schrofe school. It used fer t' b'long t' ol' Squire Craig, damned ol' hawg.' Jason drew a bunch of keys from his pocket and unlocked the gate.

'Apparently it belongs to you now,' observed Dinny, as they entered the woods.

'Yeah — I bought 't. Didn't rightly have no use fer 't, er nothin', but ol' Craig was purty hard up afore he died, 'n' was willin' t' sell.'

Jason stooped and picked up a dead branch that had fallen across the almost obliterated trail.

'Right along here she come, ev'ry day.'

Dinny felt sobered in the chilly shade. Hardly conscious of his act, he removed his hat. His resentment over Jason's attitude toward Julia was quite gone now.

'Yeah — yer Julia's boy, all right,' muttered Jason, candidly studying Dinny's face. 'That there little point where yer hair sort o' grows down like, right in th' middle.'

'You have asked me several personal questions today, Mr. Schrofe,' said Dinny, seating himself by Jason on a fallen log beside the grassy path. 'Would you object to my asking you one?'

Jason's eyes crinkled with understanding.

'Yeah — I guess that's the reason I bought 't. That's what yuh was a-goin' t' ask, eh? I kep' 't secret from pap fer awhile. But when he found out I'd bought 't, he said, "Glad yuh done 't, Jase. No use fer ev'ry Tom, Dick, 'n' Harry to be a-trampin' through them woods."'

Dinny impulsively laid a hand on Jason's knee.

'Julia would have appreciated it, I know,' he said, a bit unsteadily. There recurred to him certain fragments of adroitly crafted ridicule he had hurled at the insensitiveness and general stupidity of the hicks and yokels who composed so large a percentage of America's population. What could you expect, he had often queried, of people who never went anywhere, never saw anything, never read anything? What did a ballot amount to in their hands? What did they know about the type of government that speeds the spread of culture?

Here was a hick, sitting beside him on this log. He talked like a hick, dressed like a hick, and was on the way back from a hick town with a pig in a crate. The hick was just now in the act of rummaging in his overall pockets, with clumsy fingers. His big brown thumb had a purplish-black discoloration at the root of the nail. Now he was bringing up in one hand a huge jack-knife and in the other a soggy plug of chewing tobacco. Typical hick! Cow-companion! Pig-comrade!... But he had bought a twenty-acre tract of second-growth timber that he didn't need or want, because there was the faint trail of a path through it that a neighbor girl had traveled on the way to her school, more than a quarter-century ago... Ignorant hicks! Country full of them! And what could you expect — Dinny had often inquired, superiorly, in the smart journals of sophistication — of a civilization so loaded down with dull dolts who spent their lives wading about through the ooze of the barnyard?

'Want a chew?' inquired Jason, hospitably.

'I've never been quite brave enough to do that,' grinned Dinny. 'I'll smoke a cigarette. Would you like one?' He tendered his gold-lined, monogrammed, silver case.

Jason chuckled quietly and shook his head.

The unexplained chuckle was just a bit disquieting. Dinny had long been of the opinion that yokels possessed no sense of humor, at all. Evidently this one had what passed for that, though it was odd what things amused him.

'I want to tell you a secret,' said Dinny.

For ten minutes, he reviewed the peculiar circumstances which had concealed Julia's letter from him, until now.

Jason's eyes interestedly followed Dinny's long, slim, well-kept hands as they brought out the leather wallet containing the precious legacy. He took the letter, rather timidly, and turned it over and over in his calloused palms, before handing it back.

'I'm going to read you some of it — all of it, if you wish. I believe Julia would want me to.'

'I'd like fer t' hear 't,' replied Jason, huskily. 'That is,' he added, admonishingly, 'if yuh don't think she'd mind — my knowin'. We was never close like, yuh unnerstand. It wasn't her, yuh unnerstand. It was just me. Julia never knowed, not proper like, 'bout my feelin's 'n' that.'

Dinny nodded, comprehendingly... Hicks and yokels couldn't be taught good taste, he had said, in the ultra-refined pages of *Hallelujah*. All these silly attempts to add anything to their culture were wasted time. You only made them restless, self-conscious, and ridiculous. They didn't have the *savoir-faire!*

'I know Julia would want you to share this secret, Mr. Schrofe,' reiterated Dinny, impressively. 'Some of it I found just a bit difficult to understand — but you're the kind of a person to see through it... Much more clearly,' he added, 'than I.'

* * * * * *

An hour had passed. They had been dimly conscious of dinner-bells. Through the latter part of Dinny's reading, Jason had made no further effort to conceal his emotion, trumpeting into his voluminous red bandanna with an abandon of restraint. It was as if Julia's tragedy had occurred only yesterday.

'I s'pose there must 'a' been somethin' to 't, like she says,' he remarked, thickly, as Dinny folded the letter. 'She c'd forgive 'em all, and get th' power like, 'n' that. But Julia wasn't just ordinary folks. You 'n' me, we couldn't. 'Tain't in us. Leastwise — 'tain't in me. D'yuh think yuh c'd do 't?'

'I don't know,' said Dinny, soberly. 'That's what I'm trying to find out.'

The wrinkles around Jason's eyes deepened as he candidly studied Dinny's face.

'Not meanin' any offense,' he ventured, 'but I sure w'd never 'a' picked yuh fer th' part. Yuh don't 'pear t' be th' kind o' feller that c'd make a go of 't.' He rubbed his knee and grinned, broadly, hinting that a new idea had struck him amusingly. 'Say — if yuh do get this here big power t' be free 'n' happy like, yuh'll sure have a hell of a time writin' them sassy pieces, won't yuh?'

Dinny stared, amazed at the old chap's quick deduction.

'You've touched a mighty live wire. I'll tell you something about that. It's a queer story.'

'No — I don't think that's s' gol-darned queer,' decided Jason, after Dinny had spent some time explaining how, since finding Julia's letter, he had been unable to get himself into the mood for composition of 'sassy pieces.'... 'Yer handlin' dynamite, by Golly! Julia said 't was a sort o' power, 'n' yuh c'd always count on what she spoke. She's put this stuff in yer hands, 'n' told yuh how t' shoot 't off. Gol-darned if yuh hadn't better do 't th' way she says.'

'You're joking. It's serious with me. I've ruined myself for my work. I've lost a taste for the only thing I know how to do.'

'Like hell I'm a-jokin'!' protested Jason. 'It's just like I said. Julia has handed yuh some high explosive! Yuh c'n either blow stumps with 't, 'n' clear yer ground so yuh c'n raise somethin' — er yuh c'n leave 't a-lyin' around, and take th' risk o' a-blowin' yer brains out... Ain't there nothin' else yuh c'n do b'sides make snoots at people in the papers 'n' that?'

This last was too much for Dinny, and he laughed, Jason joining, apparently well pleased that he had lifted his young friend from his gloomy mood.

'I learned to handle a chisel, a little, when I was a lad,'

said Dinny, reminiscently. 'I think I could make a living.'

''Pears like th' more sensible thing t' do is t' carry on, now yuh've started out t' experiment with Julia's idear. Mebby, if yuh git that there power, what she talks about, yuh c'n write anything yer a-mind t'.'

'I'm afraid I've a long way to go.'

'I know I couldn't do 't. That there one feller'd always be in th' road. I'd fergive 'n' that — but I wouldn't stop a-thinkin'. What he done t' our little white stone, what pap 'n' me put up — I'd never fergit that, not in a thousand years.'

'What was that?' asked Dinny, sympathetically.

Jason busied himself for some time, breaking a handful of dead twigs into little pieces of equal length.

''Twouldn't do yuh no good t' know 't. Yuh got a big job afore yuh, anyways. 'Twouldn't help yuh none — yer knowin'.'

'Very well — if you'd rather not tell me.'

'Julia's name really was Mueller, after all,' soliloquized Jason. 'We thought they'd made a mistake on th' big stone what he had made fer her. But this here letter looks as if he was right. We always thought 'twas Miller... Well — sh'll we go now?'

Jason had leaned forward to turn the ignition key, after they had boarded the truck, but, apparently impressed with a fresh idea, straightened to offer a further comment on Dinny's problem.

'Just now come t' me — somethin' mebby yuh hadn't thought about much. If yuh did grab on t' this here power o' Julia's t' be steady 'n' happy like, 'n' begun a-writin' afterwards, yuh c'd write about that! By Golly — I bet lots o' folks 'd read 't. Gol-darned if they wouldn't eat th' paper 'twas writ on, a-thinkin' 'twas medicine. 'Course — if yuh'd been a parson, always a-snifflin' 'bout fergiveness, 'n' that, 'n' a-gettin' paid fer bein' friendly with God like, that'd be differ'nt. Th' people'd all say, "Aw — hell!" — 'n' turn over t' th' funnies... But if ever a feller like yerself took t' a-writin' that he'd rech up 'n' got some power f'm on high what had cleaned out all his pizen 'n' made him happy 'n' that, fer keeps, by Golly, there'd be a million folks a-wantin' th' recipe fer 't!'

Jason felt satisfied with this long speech, finishing it with vigorous nods of his head and convincing smacks of his brown fist on the steering-wheel. He drove the truck back onto the road, and began making up for lost time without concern for the comfort of the indulged shoat. Dinny was thinking. The old fellow might be a hick, but he possessed extraordinary native sense.

In a few minutes, they had turned to the right, and were nearing the little white Baptist Church. Jason pointed it out, as they approached, but did not slacken speed, nor did he turn his head as they passed it and the quiet cemetery that lay to the rear. Dinny suspected that the treasured path through the woods had come to be the hallowed ground in Jason's opinion, rather than the grave where, apparently, some misunderstanding about a monument had seriously embittered him.

'Not very fer now,' he shouted. 'Just b'yond that there little holler. Yuh c'n see th' chimbly. There's yer Aunt Martha, a-pickin' up them winter pears... Well — I'll set yuh down. Wish yuh c'd come over 'n' see pap, whilst yer here. I c'd come 'n' fetch yuh.'

'I think I would like to,' said Dinny, gratefully. 'Could you come over in the morning? I want to see your father.'

Aunt Martha was shading her eyes with both hands, her inquisitive grimace distorting her face into an expression of naïve perplexity. The vanished years spun like a top. Dinny felt eight, as he lifted his bags down, and started toward the house. Uncle Miles, shaggy, seedy, and minus the short burnsides of yesterday, appeared in the doorway. He had drawn the well-remembered, benevolently patronizing smile.

'Well, well, well!' boomed Uncle Miles.

*   *   *   *   *   *

'Would yuh care fer another piece, Ferdinand?' Aunt Martha was saying primly.

'By all means, Ferdinand,' heartily seconded Uncle Miles, taking up Dinny's purple-stained pie-plate. 'Absolutely!'

It had been amazing to Dinny with what ease and dispatch he had fitted back into the environment he thought he had outgrown.

Aunt Martha was a little grayer, and laid her thin hand on the backs of the familiar chairs as she moved about. There were nice new teeth, but she still shielded with the corner of her lip the area where once there had been a missing right upper canine. One of Uncle Miles's legs was not quite so up and coming as the other. The shoulders sagged, the least bit, making the shiny black coat a size too large. Otherwise, they were the same people; mellower, perhaps; a little more subdued.

Dinny had feared a painful constraint. As he had neared the house, bags in hand, his heart had pounded. For the moment he would have given much to efface himself from this awkward reunion. But there had been no dilemma. Uncle Miles was as openly cordial as if he were welcoming home a son in whom he had invested his all. Aunt Martha murmured little tendernesses as she nervously clutched at his sleeves.

He had lied effortlessly when they inquired whether he had had his dinner, and responded with enthusiasm when they wanted to show him 'th' place.' He was shown the chicken-coops, the barn, the little shop that had been his grandfather's. Dinny lingered there for a time. It was long since it had been in use, but it smelt of good, sound wood in process of fabrication, as if fuddled old Ferd had just stepped out of it.

They did not hint to know why Dinny had come. So far as he could observe, they were not craftily concealing that query. He was not asked where all he had been, or what he had been doing. They made no comments on his success. The fact that he had withdrawn to another world with which they were totally unacquainted, and now belonged to it as he had never for one moment belonged to them, gave them no apparent sensation of diffidence.

Uncle Miles rigged two cane fishing-poles, later in the afternoon, and invited Dinny to go with him down the hill to the little stream where they caught a few small perch and talked freely about Angela, of whose celebrated exploits her father was gratefully proud.

At supper, served shortly after five, to Dinny's high satisfaction, Aunt Martha accounted for the scattered family whose ghosts vaguely hovered about the well-worn door-steps, the old-fashioned thumb-latches, the paths to the shop, the pump, the barn. Poor Susan, of course, was dead. Ferdinand knew that, didn't he? Yes — she had worked fer the Squire Craigs, and died there. Greta was still out in Californy. They had an orange farm and three fine boys. Yes — Greta wrote, about twice a year. No — she had never came back. It was purty fer. Elmer was still down at Lafayette in 'th' Home.' Hiram was up in 'th' Thumb,' a-workin' at a sawmill... Dinny followed the Miller saga, at a distance, interested mostly in the fact that these people and their affairs were as remote as if Aunt Martha had reported on the goings and comings of a family in Zanzibar.

He waived his proffered right to a second helping of huckleberry pie, and, having easily gained the floor in the process of graciously declining their hospitable entreaties, Dinny ventured, without preamble, to account for his unexpected visit.

He had become convinced, he said, that his life was not being very well lived. The phrase struck him oddly, once he had uttered it. Doubtless it had been shaped by this environment. It was the way Uncle Miles might have said it, had he been in a mood of confession. Life had lately seemed to lack fulfillment, he said. He had felt a desire to make peace with the few people whose relations to him had been a source of 'disquiet' to himself — and doubtless to them also. He paused.

'So yuh've been 'n' got converted, Ferdinand,' murmured Aunt Martha, sanctimoniously. 'Bless th' Lord fer that!' She lifted the corner of her white apron, and, raising her spectacles, wiped her eyes. 'Miles,' she said, brokenly, 'our prayers has been answered. Our wandering boy has at last saw th' light. Praise t' His Blessed Name!'

'Abso*lute*ly!' ejaculated Uncle Miles, smiling approvingly, and hitching his chair back to cross his legs. 'And your aunt and I are very glad you came. How long can you stay, Ferdinand? Hope you won't have to hurry away. There'll be lots to talk about, now you're here after such a long time.'

'Thanks, Uncle Miles,' returned Dinny, in a brief aside. 'As I was saying, it has recently distressed me that I had permitted certain misunderstandings to ——'

'That's all right, Ferdinand,' broke in Uncle Miles, 'and there's nothing to forgive. You're as welcome as — as the flowers in May.'

Aunt Martha was crying now, noisily. A sudden wave of distaste for the whole adventure flooded Dinny's spirits. His old repugnance claimed him. He might have known there would be just such a calamitous scene. It had been his hope that there might be a calm, conciliatory talk. The tension would be eased. But clearly it was hopeless. Uncle Miles wished only to dodge the issue that had hurled them apart, offering an effusive and blustery hospitality as an alternative to the air-clearing discussion which the situation so urgently called for. Uncle Miles was extravagant with his tender of huckleberry pie, but winced at the thought of an honest invoice of their disaffection. It was somewhat like Angela's gift of an orange and a doll to the baby whose eyes she could not open. Aunt Martha, as usual, had taken refuge behind a tear-drenched apron.

'I shall be leaving, in about an hour,' said Dinny, calmly, 'and it would please me greatly if we three could have a quiet talk.'

Aunt Martha left off sobbing, wiped her eyes, and listened. Uncle Miles broke out with vigorous protests. Dinny raised a hand, insistingly, and the old man subsided, rather crestfallen.

'I don't mean to make a long story of it,' pursued Dinny, 'but something has happened to make me quite seriously anxious to be on the very best of friendly terms with everyone. You have wondered, Aunt Martha, if I had been converted. Probably not — in the way you mean. I don't feel any more religious than before. It's only that I have discovered myself to be thoroughly poisoned with aversions, disgusts, and bitter memories, which are making a sorry mess of my life. I want now to rise above all that, if I can.'

'But that's conversion, Ferdinand!' exclaimed Aunt Martha, fervently. 'It's th' workin' of th' Spirit! Blessed be His Holy Name!'

Uncle Miles nodded, sagaciously, and his lips formed the large word that denoted unqualified endorsement.

'And so — I'm here to ask you to forgive me, my dears, for putting myself completely out of your lives. I would like also to be forgiven for all the hot, hateful thoughts I have had in regard to you both — especially toward you, Uncle Miles, and for the bitter contempt that has swept through me whenever I thought of you. I'm asking for your pardon. I want to be at liberty. I'm weary of carrying that load.'

Aunt Martha was crying softly. Uncle Miles's face impulsively brightened, wreathed with an absolving smile. He cleared his throat, and stretching out a hand, patted Dinny assuringly on his coat-sleeve. Dinny took the old hand in his, and, observing that Uncle Miles was in the very act of booming out a volley of gallant 'abso*lute*lys,' leaned far forward, stared questioningly into his uncle's eyes, and slowly, meaningly, shook his head.

'No, Uncle Miles — not that! It's your turn to talk — but not that! Say what you're thinking! You'll feel much better afterwards — I can promise you!'

The old fellow slowly withdrew his hand, and with the back of it rubbed his forehead, beaded with perspiration. Then he swallowed hard and essayed a grisly yawn. Dinny had once seen a man die who, after the exhalation of his last breath, had yawned just that way — a yawn with no breath either coming or going.

They waited — and Uncle Miles spoke, hollowly.

'Well — it was like this, Ferdinand. At first, you were only a baby, and had no use for the money. Our salary was too little to live on, comfortably. What came in for you was a great help — a great help. Your income was larger than mine — than ours. I suppose I must have had a worldly pride, and dreaded to see the time come when you would be better off than the rest of us.' He hesitated, rubbing his eyes with his knuckles.

'I can understand that perfectly, Uncle Miles,' declared Dinny. 'It must have been a very real problem.'

'Well — then I saw how you felt toward your father, and knew you would never accept any help from him. That's when I should have ——'

Dinny nodded, comprehendingly.

'It was a great temptation, I am sure, Uncle Miles.'

'Yer Uncle Miles kept a-sayin', when he went into that Holstein cattle business, out in Ioway — and lost ev'ry cent to that rascally, thieving ——' Aunt Martha's voice was growing shrill.

'Yes — I had the thought that perhaps I could invest your money so you could ——' Uncle Miles groped for the right word.

'Don't spoil it, Uncle Miles,' admonished Dinny, hardly above a whisper. 'It's a great sensation, let me tell you! I hope you can have it! You'll find it's worth it, sir!' Dinny's voice had risen to his exultant words. Aunt Martha murmured, 'Bless th' Lord!'

'No!' shouted Uncle Miles, in a tone that explained how much effort that one agonized little bark cost him. 'The fact was — I wanted to put away something. I wasn't

saving it for you... Now — you know all about it!... God
— help me!' The brave old head sank, lower and lower,
there came a sort of inhuman guttural cry from his tight
throat.

Aunt Martha rose, with a little whimper of alarm, and
put her arm around him, pressing her cheek hard against
his.

'Miles — my *dear!* Yuh done it — at last! Bless th'
Lord! Bless th' Lord!... Oh, Ferdinand, you've been sent
f'm God to help your poor uncle — 'n' me.'

Dinny was deeply moved. He did not attempt to analyze his strange sensations, but, eclipsing the surge of
sympathy for these repentant, broken-hearted old people,
there rose in him a consciousness of an almost uncanny
vitality — the 'will-to-power' consciousness, as nearly as
he could define it at the moment. He felt suddenly matured! It was as if his permanent mind — what he was
always thinking of as his 'sub-conscious mind' in spite of
anything the new Psychology might say — had not only
ceased complaining at the decisions and intentions of his
'conscious mind,' but had actually taken charge of the
whole enterprise! He knew now what Julia meant, though
he had fresh reasons for understanding her lack of words
to explain her strange sensation. She had called it a
power! Well — that's what it was. It would sound trite
and sentimental if he attempted to elucidate. But — what
he had come by was not a sentiment — any more than the
roar of the turbines beneath Niagara is a sentiment. Julia
was right! *This was a kind of power!* God only knew what
all you could do with it — but here it was!... Power!

Uncle Miles rose, his old face twisted in a pathetically
tearful smile, and offered Dinny his hand, Aunt Martha
still hugging his arm.

'Seems like we ought to have a word of prayer,' suggested
Aunt Martha, when they had passed through the doorway
to the little sitting-room.

'We've just had that, Aunt Martha,' said Dinny —

'the real kind. Now — suppose we sit down and talk a little more about this. Did I understand you to say that some man, out in Iowa, had defrauded you of — of that money?'

They told him the story in relays, Uncle Miles becoming so excited over the rank injustice they had suffered that Aunt Martha tried to calm him.

'Yer uncle gets almost sick, sometimes, a-thinkin' and a-talkin' about it. I do wish he could ferget it.'

'That's why I asked,' said Dinny. 'Uncle Miles — whatever became of that fellow? Do you know?'

'The last I heard,' growled Uncle Miles, 'he was back on a rented farm not far from Unger, where I first met the dirty skunk. He broke up, out there, as he deserved.'

'Broke up — did he? Perhaps he did not intend to cheat you. Probably he was a poor business man. Chances are he's burning up his insides hating the people who took his property away from him. Knowing what I do now, Uncle Miles, if I were you I'd write him a friendly letter — you and he were once good friends, weren't you? — and ask him to come up here, this fall, and spend a Sunday. Tell him you and Aunt Martha have a big, fat hen that ought to be stewed. Noodles, too, and huckleberry pie.... Treat yourself to a thrill! Set yourself free!'

'Ferdinand,' said Aunt Martha, smiling pensively, 'it sure does sound queer — yer a-talkin' like this — when yuh look so worldly like 'n' all.'

'It doesn't sound a bit queerer than it feels, I can assure you, Aunt Martha.'

'You'll stay the night with us now, won't you, Ferdinand?' entreated Uncle Miles.

* * * * * *

Old Abner was leaning on both elbows, his boot on an inverted three-gallon tin swill-pail, gazing down into one of the pig-pens. He turned his head as Jason and Dinny approached. His jaw sagged, and chopped up and down, nervously, as he stared. The worn tabs of his ancient coon-skin cap lopped his ears. Had Dinny seen a faithful photograph of him, a week ago, he would have identified the subject as the patriarch and original founder of The Hicks.

He came slowly to meet them, rubbing his gnarled hand on his short, stuffy, leather coat. There was no introduction.

'Take off yer hat,' requested Abner. 'Jase says yuh've got that funny little point o' hair, like her'n.'

Dinny obliged.

'Powerful funny 'bout that, Jase,' drawled the old man, pointing a crooked forefinger at Dinny's head, as if in-specting an animal. 'Her pap had that there, same as her, same as him. The old feller always had his cap on, mostly, 'n' I never rightly noticed 't until he was a-layin' on th' coolin' board, next mornin' after he hung hisself. Gol-darned if he didn't have 't, too! Danged if he didn't look like a 'ristocrat, a-layin' there!... Well — come in t' th' house, son, 'n' be welcome.'

'I never knew before that my grandfather had taken his own life.' Dinny became aware that many mysterious silences and evasions of Aunt Martha's had now been ex-plained.

'Well — it won't hurt yuh none t' know 't. Yuh c'n be proud o' your grand-pap, son. Gol-darned if 'twasn't purty fine 'n' brave o' th' old codger. I sure never'd a-thought he had 't in him. Ev'rybody was a-moonin' around, that night, a-feelin' scared like, 'n' kind o' shamed fer the Millers. Gol-darned if I wasn't proud o' th' old cuss!'

'You have some unusual ideas on the subject of — sui-cide, Mr. Schrofe.'

'Well — o' course — I wouldn't 'xac'ly recommend 't t' nobody, but, all th' same, if I'd knowed yer grand-pap had 't in him, I'd 'a' had a lot more respect fer him whilst he lived.'

They drew up their chairs before the grate — stiff, prim, narrow rocking-chairs that had a tendency to creep about on the worn rag carpet — and spent two hours talking about Julia's monument.

Old Abner's bitterness about Craig's shocking discourtesy in having their little stone cast aside had obviously become an obsession. Once he had launched upon the painful topic, there was no distracting him.

'Guess we'll have t' start now,' admonished Jason, consulting his big nickel-cased watch. 'I'm a-drivin' him over t' Wayne, pap, to ketch a train fer Cincinnati.'

''Pears like I done all th' talkin',' regretted Abner. 'Lot o' things I wanted t' ask yuh, too. Seems like when I get a-goin' 'bout that there feller, I can't stop.'

'Yes,' said Dinny, 'it's too bad. I'm sorry. I am on my way to see him, and I mean to ask him about it. I don't believe he ever knew the particulars. It must have been a terrible mistake. Would you be glad if you found out it was a mistake, and that he was not really to blame?'

The old fellow slowly nodded his head.

'Gol-darned if I wouldn't give ev'ry one o' them Berkshires, out there in them pens, t' hear that feller say he hadn't knowed, 'n' was sorry 'n' that!'

'Like hell yuh would, pap! Half o' them hawgs b'longs t' me!' Jason, vastly pleased with his joke, gave the old man an affectionate whack between the shoulders.

'All fun aside, Mr. Schrofe,' said Dinny, seriously, taking his hand, 'I hope to find out that my father never meant to do you generous people this harm. I believe it would hurt Julia, terribly, if she had known about the misery it's caused you.'

As they sauntered toward the sedan, standing by the old hitching-rack, Jason said, 'Would yuh mind if I told pap?'

'About the letter?'

'Yeah — th' letter 'n' that.'

'I believe Julia would want him to know about it, don't you?'

'Yeah — I'll tell him.'

CHAPTER XVII

ALTHOUGH aware of the curious phenomenon of familiar streets narrowing, during one's extended absence, to about three fourths their previous width, and tall buildings shrinking to a mere travesty of their former stateliness, Dinny Brumm was unprepared for the shock when, at midnight, he followed his bags from the taxi to the desk at The Barstow.

Even allowing for the fact that when he had first timidly ventured through its spacious, shriekingly ornate lobby, as an untraveled youth, The Barstow was vain-gloriously, self-consciously new, it seemed impossible to believe that a few years could have so tarnished its gilt and frayed its cushions.

The once impressive gargoyles still reared on their hind claws to support massive old-worldish lamps, but the awe-inspiring challenge of their 'How dare you, worm?' that had darted from their shocked, staring eyes, was now replaced by a simpering, apologetic servility. Their orbs were dull, their flanks were lean, their talons had straightened out as if to ward off a slap.

The desk, formerly to be approached hat in hand and with regret that one had not brought a joss-stick, had had its stinger pulled, too, its smile resembling the conciliatory smirk of the urgent driver upon invitation to pull up at the curb and state his name and address for the augmentation of certain statistics in process of assembly at Police Headquarters.

And yet, barring the normal wear and tear of a half dozen prosperous years, The Barstow, Dinny knew, had not altered appreciably. The change was all in himself.

But whatever of modified outlook had been gradually coming to pass in his mind, due to the liberating experiences of the years, to the tarnishment of earlier glosses and glitters, and the reduction of once astounding dimensions, it was nothing compared to the uncanny magic that had suddenly recreated him into something so different from the self whose habitual deductions and reactions had been stabilized — so utterly different that he found it difficult to recognize his attitudes and opinions as his own. His habitual responses were inactive, as if he had been smitten with an amnesia.

Yesterday's experience of complete reconciliation with Uncle Miles and Aunt Martha had performed some queer tricks on Dinny's mind. He had not been surprised at the sound of his own words soliciting pardon for the bitter animosity he had nourished in regard to them. That was what he had gone there to do, and he had meant to see it through, hoping for no further results than the satisfaction of getting it off his chest. Down inside himself, whatever he might say to Uncle Miles, there would unquestionably remain the private opinion that the pompously pious old fellow was a piker.

All that Dinny would have to show for his strange adventure in the voluntary enterprise of crow-eating would be a sense of having made an honest experiment with Julia's theory for the purgation of poison. He did not expect that his estimate of Uncle Miles would be in any way reappraised.

But when he had finished with them, last night, he had not only told Uncle Miles that he fully forgave the wrong he had done; he really had forgiven the old man and was in a mood of sympathy for him. Uncle Miles had faced an odd predicament as custodian of a child's annuity exceeding his own salary. Dinny could understand how his uncle had postponed doing the thing that required to be done, saying to himself, 'Next year I must tell him,' but always fearful of the consequences. What indeed would become of a small boy, living in a frugal home, were he suddenly handed an allowance in excess of the family's total income? Uncle Miles had drifted into an unhappy perplexity, but not because he had the instincts of a thief. And Aunt Martha had consented to it, ruefully, no doubt, believing that Uncle Miles knew best.

Once upon a time Dinny had felt that if ever the occasion arose when he could back the old weasel into a corner and force him to confess himself an unmitigated fraud the sensation of seeing his despised pomposity shrivel and peel off like snake-skin would be worth all the mental torture he had suffered.

Uncle Miles had crumpled to a degree surpassing the most extravagant hopes Dinny had sourly cherished, but there was no diabolical pleasure afforded by it; Dinny had shared the old man's sorrow with an understanding that seemed to enhance the value of his own personality. He began to appreciate what Julia had written concerning her altered estimate of herself, after sincerely making peace with Susan. She had felt 'promoted.' It was as if she 'had won a prize.' It was as if she had discovered herself to be 'a princess.'

Throughout today Dinny had reviewed last night's strange experience in Julia's room where he had slept.

At ten, Aunt Martha had lighted the way up the steep, narrow, uncarpeted stairs, piloting him with a reeking kerosene lamp.

'Almost nothin's been changed in here since it was her'n,' said Aunt Martha, turning down the patchwork quilt. 'Hiram had a sale cried when him 'n' Lucy moved to Michigan, but Jase Schrofe, who had previous bought the house, bid in these here things o' Julia's and had 'em left where they was. Exceptin' fer the desk, it's the same.' Aunt Martha patted the pillows. 'Yes,' she sighed, reminiscently, 'dear Julia died in this here old bed.'

So it was here that Julia had summoned her slimming strength to write the letter that was 'promoting' Dinny to something of the lofty dignity that she had won 'like a prize.'

Ordinarily, he thought, it would not be much of a recommendation for a bed to say of it, five minutes before one climbed in, that someone of far-reaching posthumous influence had died in it, in a lugubrious tone hinting that the departed spirit might be within earshot; but if Julia's ghost haunted the room, so much the better, thought Dinny.

He was a long time going to sleep, and even when, from sheer fatigue produced by the emotional strain of the day, he drifted into semi-consciousness, there was a strange sense that Julia was coming along into his dreams.

There never had been a photograph of her except a cheap little tintype of a group of girls taken at the county fair. The cheeks had been tinted to an unhealthy flush, and the mouth had been drawn into a prim little pucker. It was unfair to Julia, of course, as even Aunt Martha admitted to whom beauty was but skin deep.

In his half-somnolent state, Dinny conjured a portrait of Julia, the radiant. It was a satisfyingly clear picture, and, as he half-consciously brought it alive and put it through a variety of moods, he felt he was recovering his girl-mother.

The dream, if it was a dream, was not altogether pleasant, however. Julia seemed to proceed into an attitude of entreaty as if he had done something to make her very unhappy. And when, at length, sitting opposite him on the grass, her feet folded under her short skirt, she began pensively gathering up the little paper cups and plates, her eyes downcast and swollen with crying, Dinny roused with a painful recurrence of the one tragic mistake that could not be mended.

He had made peace with Uncle Miles to their complete mutual satisfaction. And tomorrow he would have an interview with his father who, he had learned by wire before leaving New York, was in Cincinnati for a week on one of his periodical inspection visits; doubtless that interview would lift the burden of misgiving he had carried in respect to Zandy Craig. He had it in mind to stop at Magnolia, also, and attempt to revise his opinions of that institution, in the light of his new flair for sympathetic understanding.

But there was nothing to be done in the case of Joan. She had made it quite impossible for him to repair the damage he had done to an affection which, instead of relaxing its grip, seemed to be mounting!

He tossed about for an hour, worrying over the utter hopelessness of his longing for Joan. Conceding that their romance was a closed incident, what might still be done to insure her happiness? For, surely, Joan could not feel satisfied with the manner in which she had left him without a word when she had decided — quite impulsively, he presumed — to run away with Tommy. What a dismal honeymoon for Joan! And for Tommy, too, who couldn't be expected to be pleased with himself.

If they weren't on the other side of the Atlantic, reflected Dinny, he would go to them with his comradely congratulations and the assurance that he not only bore them no ill-will but sincerely wished them great and lasting joy. It would be worth almost any length of journey to replace, in his memory, a contented and joyful Joan for the torturing image of her tear-stained face as she collected the pitiful little remains of their picnic luncheon. It would be a quite dreadful thing to have that picture of Joan's dejection and disappointment increasingly menacing his peace.

His decision to mend matters with Joan in so far as might be achieved through a friendly interview with her and Tommy involved a long series of imaginary circumstances in which they were brought together now at a little dinner he would give for them at Dexter's, now at their own table in an apartment somewhere up town. But — by Gad! — why wait? Lacey's had said Tommy was to be in Europe until early November, hadn't they? Why shouldn't he slip over there, directly, and give the poor things a chance to enjoy their honeymoon, undistressed by the remorse which Joan would inevitably feel? By Gad! — he would do it! As soon as he had finished with his father, and the intended visit to Magnolia, he would sail. He would make his relations to Tommy and Joan so pleasant for them and him that they could expect to be comrades forever! That would take but a day. Then he would go to London for the winter, and try to write. He had no notion what he would be writing, but there was a sensation of desire. That was good: he had quite lost it.

It was a great idea! He would sail next week. That would solve the problem. He couldn't have Joan back, but he could do his utmost to make her happy. Dinny had gone to sleep constructing scenes and dialogue for the little play that was to dispose of the paper dishes.

* * * * * *

At ten, next morning, Dinny telephoned up to the suite which Zandy Craig occupied on the ninth floor, requesting an interview.

A male secretary informed him that Mr. Craig's day was entirely engaged. If Mr. Brumm wished to confide the nature of his business to Mr. Craig's assistant, Mr. Effelbaum, an appointment could be arranged.

Dinny sensibly refused to be irritated over this slight delay. It was consistent with good business that Zandy Craig should not be open to the importunities of any bore or beggar who happened to drift in. He said he would be glad to see Mr. Effelbaum and explain his errand. The time was set for eleven. That was excellent. Mr. Effelbaum would quickly clear the way for him. Perhaps he and his father might lunch together.

With keen anticipation, and not a little nervous excitement, Dinny dressed carefully, and, at eleven sharp, took the elevator to the ninth floor, where he was shown into the suite, the secretary taking him immediately into the presence of the bright-eyed, urbane, little Jew who served as the last barricade between his exalted master and the public.

'So you would see Mr. Greck?' began Mr. Effelbaum, tapping his desk lightly with a long steel paper-knife.

Even making due allowance for Mr. Effelbaum's Hebraic handling of gutturals, there was something rather ominous in the manner of his pronunciation of 'Greck.'

'Mr. Craig is my father,' replied Dinny, suddenly re-solved to make his story short and come to the point with-out circumlocution.

'Mr. Greck has no son,' said Mr. Effelbaum, stiffly.

Instantly Dinny understood. Effelbaum, resentful of the 'Greck' article in *Hallelujah*, was treating himself to a helping of revenge.

However, Effelbaum was acting according to his best knowledge, no doubt. He was honest in his belief that Zandy Craig had no son. Dinny was a mere impostor, so far as Effelbaum's information went.

'Perhaps you had better ask him. He is in, I presume?' Dinny was patient, respectful.

'There is no needt I should inquire, Mr. Brumm.'

Dinny reached in his pocket for a card, scribbled a line on it, and handed it across the desk.

'Would you mind giving this to Mr. Craig?'

Effelbaum read the brief message and returned the card with a crooked smile.

'Mr. Greck will nodt see you, sir. You may tell me whadt you want.'

Dinny flushed uncomfortably, and leaned forward with an elbow on the mahogany desk.

'Is he in?' Dinny's tone hinted at an impatience that was rapidly getting out of hand.

Effelbaum, savoring the situation, grinned sardonically and nodded.

'Budt not to you — Mr. Brumm.'

Impetuously, Dinny rose, and observing that Effelbaum's hand was moving toward the row of ivory buttons on the left corner of the desk, quickly grasped him by the wrist.

'You may think you're doing your duty,' he growled, 'but this time you're exceeding it. I came here to see my father, and I mean to! Understand? Which of us takes that card in — you or I?'

To Dinny's surprise, Effelbaum glanced up with a taunting distortion of lip, and laughed.

'You take idt in to Mr. "*Greck!*"' He wagged his head in the direction of the adjacent door and shrugged a shoulder, self-absolvingly. 'I haf triedt to spare you a bainful moment. You are determinedt to haf it... Go — and haf idt!'

Dinny released his grip on the unresisting hand and searched Effelbaum's sneer with eyes suddenly nonplussed.

'Do you mean to infer that my father has given instructions I am not to be admitted?'

Effelbaum's brows, lips, shoulders and palms raised, concertedly, in a gesture that wished himself well out of the awkward *contretemps*.

'Mr. "Greck" toldt me he had no son. If you can convinze him to the contrary, I shall nodt detain you.' He rose, opened the door, and bowed Dinny in, with an elaborate gesture.

'Mr. "*Greck*" — Mr. Brumm.'

The stenographer at Zandy Craig's elbow rose and retired. Craig pushed in the slide on which her notebook had rested, leaned back in his opulent swivel-chair, folded his arms, and regarded his intrusive caller from under lowered brows.

'You may sit down, if you like,' he said, coolly, dashing Dinny's intention to offer his hand. 'I assume you are my son. In fact — now that I see you, I know you are. There is a certain likeness. And you have something of the facial lines of your mother.'

Dinny smiled, half-heartedly, wondering, as his father paused, whether it was time for him to speak.

'May I inquire why you came, and how I may serve you?' continued Craig, steadily.

'I came to ask your pardon.' Dinny's voice was sincerely contrite.

The big man slowly raised both long arms, clasped his hands behind his leonine gray head in a pose that Dinny recognized as a natural posture of his own when in a quandary, and closed his eyes.

'I am sorry I have waited so long,' added Dinny.

'Yes — I'm afraid you waited... too long!' Craig looked squarely at the tardy prodigal, his expression severe.

Dinny nodded.

'I never thought I wanted to see you, sir, until lately. Something quite important has altered my opinion. I would like to tell you about it.'

'That can wait,' said Craig, folding his arms on the desk. 'I'll talk first, if you're agreed. I've probably thought more about this matter than you have; and, anyway, I'm your father. It's my right to speak first, is it not?'

Dinny smiled approval.

'When you were a lad, young fellow, I made many efforts to show you that I meant to do everything I could for you, in face of the circumstances that kept us apart. I could not hold it against you when you resisted my attempts to ——'

'I did not understand, sir. I had been led to think that ——'

Craig signed that he did not wish to be interrupted.

'Yes — I know, or can surmise, what you were led to think. Your Aunt Martha would have seen to that. And as for your parson uncle, I dislike to think of him. But — to continue — I did indulge the hope that once you were away from that atmosphere, it might please you to reflect that you had a father who had tried to do what is customarily thought of as the right thing.

'After Mr. Brumm had informed me you had a job and were on your own, I still waited. Sometimes I hoped that you would be moved to write me at least a note of appreciation. I disliked to think that I had bred a child who, in his later teens, had not managed to develop as much common courtesy as would have seemed to demand some sort of response.'

Dinny's chagrin and remorse were painful. He lowered his eyes, and nodded, slowly.

'Through that period when you would have been going

to college like a gentleman, and backed by the full support of your father, I happened to be heavily worried by a variety of cares, by no means the least of which — though I'm damned if I know just why I'm telling you this, for you have no right to my confidence — was my wife's separation from me. She had found me incompatible, though I was very fond of her. My duties required a great deal of my time. I was much away from home. We drifted apart. She left me.

'My daughter Alison was shortly sent abroad to school. Had you come to me, in those days, informing me that you had been an ass and an ingrate, I should have attempted to dissuade you of that estimate of yourself, I think, just from sheer loneliness and a natural wish for a reconstruction of my family ties.

'Eventually, Alison comes home, and accidentally encounters you here, though I was not informed of that until much later. Why she did not tell me, at once, I do not know, though I have surmised, and if that unfortunate accidental meeting brought either of you any unhappiness — and I rather suspect, from chance remarks of Alison's, that it did — I am sorry. She did not tell me until the appearance of your assault on me in that damned dirty little rag which, I am told, you are now editing.'

Craig's voice had risen, indignantly, with the last few words. His eyes were full of pain and his big fists clenched. He pushed back his chair, and rose, thrusting his long hands deeply into his trouser pockets.

'That day,' he shouted, savagely, 'whatever desire I still had for a sight of you — my son — was utterly abandoned. God knows which one of your ancestors you may resemble, but you're not like your charming mother, and I have the self-esteem to think you're not like me!'

Craig had flung the chair back against the wall, and was pacing up and down behind the desk, biting his words into hot bits.

'If you had come here shabby and broke, I would instruct

my secretary to draw you a check. That would be for the relief of my own mind. You do not appear to be in want. You are well dressed and apparently have had your breakfast. I presume your position as the editor of a filthy magazine devoted to sophisticated blackmail and parlor socialism puts you beyond the necessity of my alms.... So — there is nothing you are likely to want that I can give you. As for this belated request for pardon, suppose we don't go into that, at all. I am not a sentimental person, either by instinct or practice. Neither are you, if I have correctly interpreted your temperament as reflected in your writing. Whatever made you come here, I don't know — and I don't care to know! If you have any remorse, run along with it! If I have any regret, it's my own business.... Now — I think that's all, and if you're sure you are in need of nothing but my pardon, may I ask you to excuse me. This is a busy day, and, as you know, this interview was unsolicited by me.... Mr. Effelbaum will show you out.'

He pushed a button, and Effelbaum appeared as if he had been waiting, hand on knob, for his cue.

This sudden move of his father's had been so unexpected, so ruthlessly conclusive, that Dinny was at a loss to know what, if anything, to do.

The door was wide open, Effelbaum was in the room waiting, Craig had readjusted his gold nose-glasses and was busying himself with the papers on his desk. Dinny had been definitely dismissed, and nothing remained for him to do but leave. He felt himself chastised like a half-grown boy. This man was his father, in very truth. Dinny's complete breakdown of self-possession was obviously an automatic response demanded by filial instinct suddenly recognizing the paternal authority of this man who, a stranger, had now loomed large as the sire.

For a moment only Dinny hesitated, took one step forward, was on the point of entreating for a chance to be heard. His father did not look up. Effelbaum fiddled with his watch-guard. Dinny turned slowly away. At the doorway he paused.

'I am very sorry, sir,' he said, respectfully.

There was no reply. Effelbaum was at Craig's elbow, receiving a handful of opened letters. The trim stenographer was waiting for the retiring caller to make his exit. Dinny's interview with his father seemed to be over.

* * * * * *

Magnolia was only fifty minutes away, but in those fifty minutes Dinny carefully examined his own mind in respect to the adventure on which he had launched, a few days earlier, and was delighted to discover that the unfortunate meeting with his father had not dashed his interest and belief in the thing he had set out to do.

A week ago his mind would have been tempestuous with bitter hate and stormy schemes for reprisal. He could easily picture the nature of his burning thoughts as he rehearsed, item by item, the progressive phases of his defenseless humiliation in his father's office. No! — By God! There wasn't a man alive who could put Dinny Brumm into such a debasing predicament and expect to get away with it unscratched! Least of all the man who had been responsible for so much of his mental torture, all through the years! Craig should have his pay with usury! Damn him! *Damn him!*

Dinny was surprised, this afternoon, at his mood; not surprised so much over his attitude of sympathetic understanding for Zandy Craig who had waited and hoped for some manner of response from his disaffected son — waited until the wound had healed and left an impermeable scar. The thing that amazed Dinny was the nature of this new serenity. It was not a mere hand-folding inertia. He tried vainly to define it in a phrase, and could arrive at nothing more adequate than 'dynamic peace.'

As he sat looking out at the window of the club car which served as a hub for the revolving wooded hills, faintly tipped with early autumn tints, Dinny's mental state was a novelty to himself. Whatever description his mood deserved, it was certainly not apathy. There was something vital, vibrant, kinetic in it. Jason Schrofe had not been far afield when he thought of this peculiar energy as 'dynamite.'

Always Dinny had entertained varying degrees of contempt for the unworkable theory of non-resistance. Sometimes he grinned when he saw the word in print. What sort of people were advocates of non-resistance? Strong men — likely to make some constructive contribution of skill or genius? Not at all. The non-resisters had had their frail, other-cheeking, boot-licking program of life handed to them at birth. It was less a sublimity of soul than a feebleness of body.

As for organized warfare, that was quite another matter. That was a mass-madness inspired by predatory bankers and swashbucklers, diabolically unconcerned about the cost of their greed and pomposity to the drafted and driven who were herded into the tragic hoax by the stimulating rattle of brave drums, stampeded into indifference to the likelihood of their being ushered out of it to the depressing tune of scalpels and saws and forceps tinkling metallically on glass-topped, rubber-castored tables. That was, indeed, another matter!

But non-resistance, attemptedly practiced by an individual, was sheer cowardice. How idiotic — for a churchful of people to stand up, of a Sunday morning, and bellow their lungs out for a theory that none but the sick, crippled, and undersized actually believed in to the point of practical demonstration.

How deliciously absurd — when some hollow-cheeked, hollow-chested, dreamy-eyed, five-foot-four, one hundred and nineteen pound Christian boosted himself up at prayer-meeting to declare, in a thin, piping squeak, that, as for him, he believed in non-resistance.

The only sane answer to that, offered by the people who really had the world's work to do, was a laughing 'By Gad — you'd *better!*'

'But,' shrills the altruistic little fellow, 'this is my honest conviction! I sincerely believe that it's more sensible never to fight back!'

'Doubtless,' grins the ham-handed six-footer. 'You would! You're a wise little man. You just keep on thinking that, if you know what's good for you!'

Invoicing his own feelings, today, Dinny marveled that the hymns and liturgies and homilies of Christianity had taken so little account of the fact that non-resistance, far from being a state of supine lethargy, was a dynamic of high potentiality.

Why didn't the Church leave off singing, 'I am Jesus' little lamb,' and recognize the very substantial and demonstrable power of *the spirit in action!* Dinny had never felt so alive, so alert, so energized in all his life. His compliant understanding of his father's rudeness and refusal to conciliate was accompanied by a rising tide of personal poise and power. Perhaps this serenity was at least approximately denoted by the ancient phrase — 'the peace that surpasseth understanding.'... By Gad — it was a fact!

For a moment there was a flash of belief, as if he had discovered a universal cure-all for every possible anxiety, that the potent sentence printed on Julia's salvaged scrap of scripture was possessed of magical properties. But, of course, even this formula for power was conditioned somewhat by circumstances. He could forgive Joan for running away from him without a word of regret or explanation. Doubtless he deserved it. She had given him his chance. By what right could he expect her to live interminably on the hope that he might wear himself out with hateful cynicism, and, having eventually burned up all his carbon, ask her to take charge of the ashes! The girl had her life to live; hadn't she?... Oh, yes — all that was plain as a pikestaff; but the fact remained that no length of his love, no depth of his understanding, no dynamic of forgiveness could restore Joan to him. Some mistakes were irrevocable! ... He could forgive — had forgiven — his father for

the savage rebuff, but that would not give him back his
father.

* * * * * *

Magnolia was a mere pocket-edition. The clangor of the
gong with which the motorman cleared the track, as the
Sunnyside Avenue car demanded her right of way at the
corner of Main and Broad — busiest spot in town — was
surely redundant, seeing how little traffic she coped with.
All activity on the streets had been slowed down to the
tempo of Zanesdale and Unger.

Dinny watched the familiar shops amble by, smiling
unconsciously at their decrepitude. Had the town built
nothing new? Yes — here was an important replacement;
a full half block of glossy yellow brick six stories high! The
car had stopped on the red, and there was ample time to
read the names of the businesses that occupied the imposing new building. Some of the names he recognized. There
was Hunter the Hatter which he had always considered
a choice bit of alliteration, often wondering whether Hunter's selection of a vocation had been influenced thereby.
Some of the names were unfamiliar. The whole transparent
corner of the ground floor was occupied with swagger
motor-cars — 'Spencer Davis, Manager.'

Was it possible that this was 'Spike'? That was his
name — Spencer. It would be interesting to see what
manner of man Spike had evolved to. Dinny impulsively
strode to the rear platform as the car started forward, and
swung himself off. He had all but forgotten Spike. Once
upon a time, he had hated him with all his might, but in
recent years nothing had been left of it but a dulled, dis-
passionate aversion.

The place was empty except for the display cars, a workman with a chamois-skin, and a neat girl with an adroit
nail-file who was advertised as ready to furnish 'Information,' in case — as appeared unlikely — anyone should
desire it.

'Yes, Mr. Davis is in,' replied the girl, indifferently, as if the fact could scarcely be expected to interest anybody. 'Through there,' she added, pointing over her shoulder with the nail-file, and resuming her occupation.

It was Spike; no question about that. There was a symmetrical bald spot on his crown about the size of a tonsure, but it would hardly have been mistaken for that if the picture of it had included the ears which, viewed from the rear — he was bent over a desk telephone — were built rather for enduring combats than confessions.

Dinny waited, just inside the door, for Spike to finish and greet him. Becoming aware that the conversation was embarrassingly private, for Spike was in an attitude of frantic supplication, he quietly backed out, but in that moment he had accidentally heard enough to inform him that his erstwhile opponent was in difficulty.

'Yeah — but see here, Mr. Amberly, I simply can't do it today! Maybe I can by Monday or Tuesday, if I can make some collections. Give a fellow a break, can't you? Yeah — I know it's a sight draft, but I can't raise seventeen-fifty this afternoon, and that's all there is to it!... Hell! It's impossible!'

The receiver had banged back on the hook, and Spike, considerably shaken and distraught, was moving toward the open door. Dinny was occupied with reading a large bulletin pasted on the glazed partition setting forth the merits of a new oiling system that had just made over the whole motor industry into something theatrically other than it had been. Spike looked his age — plus.

'Do you remember me?' asked Dinny.

Spike stared hard for a moment; then grinned as amiably as his perturbation would permit, and nodded, extending his hand.

'Y-e-a-h!' he marveled, as the light slowly filtered through. 'Dinny Brumm! I'll be damned! What are you doin' here?'

'A little business trip, Spike, and' — a sudden impulse

prompted Dinny to rush on into an unintended remark —
'I have decided to buy a car here and drive back to New
York. Thought you might be willing to talk it over with
me.'

'That's what we're here for, old-timer,' rejoiced Spike,
noisily. 'About what are you looking for, Dinny? You're
turning something in, I suppose.'

'No — I disposed of my car some time ago when I was
to be out of the country for a while.'

'That's good — and unusual.'

They stepped out into the show-room, where Spike, who
knew his business, proceeded without delay to an energetic
sales-talk, utterly oblivious of their earlier antagonism and
the marked changes wrought upon each of them by the
intervening years.

Dinny was only a half-hour making up his mind to purchase the dark blue coupé with the gray whipcord uphol-
stery. It was, he said, about what he wanted.

'How soon can it be ready for the road, Spike?'

'It's ready now!'

'How about plates?'

'I'll get 'em for you. You can take it along with the
demonstration tags; they'll be all right for today.'

They returned to the office desk and sat down.

'The usual terms — over ten months?' Spike straightened the carbon in his order-book and prepared to write.

'No — I'm going to pay cash for it.' Dinny produced his
check-book, and unscrewed the top from his pen. 'Seventeen hundred and fifty — right?'

'Yeah — that's right,' repeated Spike, with a combination gasp and sigh that struck Dinny as one of the most
startling expressions of surprise and relief he had ever
heard.

'There you are,' said Dinny.

Spike fanned his shoulder with the unblotted check, and
laughed nervously.

'By God, Dinny, you don't know it, but you've damn'

near saved my life. I don't mind telling you that if I hadn't sold you this car — right now — for cash — I likely would have lost my agency!'

'Glad I happened in, then, at the opportune moment.' Dinny tried to make the comment sound casual.

Of a sudden, Spike's face grew serious and he gnawed his lip, reflectively.

'Just when did you come in, Dinny?' he asked.

'Two-forty — from Cincinnati.'

'Yeah... No — I mean, how long had you been here when I found you outside the door?'

'Only a moment... It's quite all right, Spike. I can use the car. I had expected to buy one, sooner or later.'

'Well — it's pretty damn' decent of you — I'll say,' muttered Spike, in a tone of mingled gratitude and contrition.

'You would have done the same thing, doubtless, if you had accidentally stumbled in on me and found me in a jam.'

'I doubt it!' confessed Spike, brusquely. 'What's come over you, Dinny? You sure weren't that sort of a chap when we were in school, and' — he chuckled, dryly — 'nobody would think you were a Fairy Godmother, to read your ——'

'It's all happened just lately, Spike. Like to hear about it?'

'Yeah — if it isn't private. I sure would... Wait till I tell that boy to put on a new spare. The one she's carrying has had couple o' hundred miles about town.'

It was not an easy task to confide the secret to Spike. He was quite unprepared for such thinking, and he had important matters on his mind. He had first to talk to Mr. Amberly. Dinny could not help being amused at the vast alteration of tone with which he informed Mr. Amberly, crisply, that he would be over presently to take up 'that little matter' in full. It called to mind the story about the rabbit that found the whiskey.

'Well — I'm damned if I ever thought you'd get religion,' observed Spike, after listening, rather absently, for some minutes. 'You're the last man in the world.'

'I don't think it is that,' said Dinny. 'I've discovered that it's impossible for a man to be healthy and up on his toes with his system poisoned by old grudges. I suppose it's like arthritis. The poison's all through you, though the focal infection may be in one place and the pain in another.'

'Yeah — I see. You've got an infected back tooth, and a pain in your shoulder. Is that what you mean?'

'Precisely! You've an old grudge against your uncle, and — and take it out on your girl.'

'Married — Dinny?'

Dinny shook his head without looking up.

'You must have had a grudge against your uncle. Have you fixed it up?'

'Yes — but I waited too long.'

'Lost the girl, eh?'

'Quite definitely.' Dinny rose, and they went out to the curb where the new car was parked.

'I suppose you'll be driving over to the college,' wondered Spike. 'Lot o' changes over there since you ——'

'Since I was fired,' assisted Dinny, smiling.

'Yeah — I wouldn't blame you if you never wanted to see it again. They sure did give you a rotten deal.'

'I thought that, too, until just lately.'

'By God! — I believe you're in earnest! Do you honestly think that it would make a fellow more efficient in his business if he made friends with all the people he despised, and everybody that had got his goat, and not given him a break?'

'Well — if he went into it for the sole purpose of selling more cars — that's what you mean, don't you? — I doubt it very much. But if he made an honest stab at it, with the hope of cleaning out his poison and promoting himself to a higher class of animal, his increased efficiency would inevitably follow, don't you think?'

'It sure sounds sort o' moonshiny. God! — I'd feel silly going into old man Kennerly's place, for instance, to ask him to be friends. Couldn't, if I wanted to, now,' added Spike, with apparent relief that a good excuse had occurred to him, 'The old double-crosser's laid up at home, I understand, with some kind of a heart attack. Damned if I knew he had one!'

Dinny smiled broadly.

'Maybe he's poisoned. Why don't you go and help the doctor pull the old bird through?'

'How would that help *old Kennerly* get rid of his poison, if I went to see him with the idea of getting rid of *mine?*'

Dinny shook his head, admitting his perplexity.

'Funny thing about that,' he said, thoughtfully. 'It's true, though: this stuff's contagious, Spike.... You know' — he went on, after a momentary reflection — 'I didn't come here today to do anything for *your* poison. I'm trying to be free of *mine.* If you go to old Kennerly to be free of *yours,* I dare say that before you're done with it, Kennerly will have unloaded *his.* Might save his life! Or — if it didn't, he might at least be able to die like a gentleman.'

Spike stood staring.

'My God! — Dinny! Do you believe there's anything in this?'

Dinny took Spike's coat lapel lightly between thumb and fingers, looking him steadily in the eyes.

'Yes — and *so do you!*'

He opened the car door, and climbed in. The engine responded smoothly to the starter.

'You remember the way, don't you?' called Spike.

'Yes... But I'm not going out there, just now. How's the road down to Pinckney?'

'Perfect! And pretty, too. Remember the cliffs and mounds, down there?'

Dinny nodded, let in the clutch, rolled slowly down the familiar street. In his present state of mind, he wondered if he was really competent to drive. His hands were trembling.

Old Jason was right. This stuff — whatever it might be — was like dynamite. You had to handle it with care... Sentimental moonshine? My God! The stuff acted like radium! It didn't go off with a bang — but you had to look out! There was no question but it would destroy a man who trifled with it! He decided he would think twice before he told anyone else. A conviction was taking form in his mind that hadn't occurred to Dinny before. An energy as potent as this mustn't be trusted in the hands of people without definite instructions concerning its nature. He must find out a little more about it before he passed it on any further. Canny old Jason had seen the dangers at a glance. *Anybody who tried to use this dynamic for his own material advantage would almost unquestionably burn his fingers!*

* * * * * *

'Yes — poor old Clancy had to give up the battle,' drawled Mr. Brophy, pushing the mustard-pot across the table. 'The beer was no good, any more, and cost too much, and, anyway, the old chap had a certain self-respect; didn't care to be associated with the young crop of bootleggers. So — he closed up.'

'If they could have had Clancys dispensing beer, all over the country, perhaps we would never have come to this pass,' observed Dinny. 'But the thing had got out of bounds, most places. The Clancys were in the minority.'

'But there were enough Clancys to justify a bit of steady thinking on that subject before the whole liquor industry was turned loose to be operated by pick-pockets and safe-crackers!... Well — it's too late to be owling over that tragedy. It's done; we're in for it!... Let's talk about *you!* What brings you here?'

Dinny had strolled into *The Star* office at midnight, finding Mr. Brophy taking his coat off the peg preparatory to going out for lunch. After a warm welcome, or as warm as was to be expected of the unexcitable editor, who was not given much to hysteria, Dinny went back into the composing-room and renewed old acquaintance with the four or five who remained. Old Timmy Fagan had died.

'Shall we go over and see Clancy?' asked Dinny, when they were out on the street.

'No — that's a speakeasy now,' growled Brophy. 'I don't like the people who run it. They'd sell you a stroke of paralysis for a dollar. We'll drop in here at Ketolphus's place. You like Greeks, I recall.'

'I came out this way on several errands,' said Dinny, replying to Mr. Brophy's inquiry. 'I'm on a sort of peace commission.'

'Didn't suppose you went in for that kind of thing, Dinny.'

'No — it has been rather out of my line.'

Brophy grinned.

'Out of your line!... You've been a young hell-cat! Whoever sent you out with the impression that you were a cooing dove? You've been a storm-center so far back as I can recall... Well — let's hear all about it.'

It would be interesting to try it out on Mr. Brophy. The chances of his accepting it, to his damage, were as nothing is related to everything. Dinny, somewhat obscure and hesitant with the preliminaries — for his auditor's impassive face held out no promise of sympathetic comprehension — reported quite fully on his strange legacy and his recent experiences in so far as he could without violating confidences.

Brophy had smoked, stolidly, and listened.

'My son,' he said, gravely, when the narrative had reached the point of highest ecstasy for Dinny, and highest density for the white-haired Brophy, 'you've been working too hard. It's a natural penalty for philosophizing. You've made it your job, for years, to find out how much is the matter with the world. You never tried to treat it for its diseases; you just diagnosed, and shook your head, and telephoned for the undertaker. Now you've tired of that and are looking for some kind of a patent medicine. I think you're crazy as hell, and ought to be in a sanitarium.'

Dinny laughed, heartily, and tapped the end of another cigarette on the table.

'I never felt so well in my life, Mr. Brophy.'

'Any lunatic will tell you that. You'd better have a nice, long talk with a reputable psychiatrist. What do you suppose Beaton and those other chaps on *Hallelujah* would think if they knew you were cruising about in this state of mind? Why — you talk like this what's her name... My God!... she's no relation of yours, is she?'

Dinny's attempt to defend himself and his theory was not very satisfactory, chiefly for lack of time. Brophy had pressing work to do before *The Star* was put to bed, and made no disguise of his urgent necessity to be off.

When they parted, he was not only cordial but rather disconcertingly solicitous. Dinny must have a bit of rest. It was clear he had been working too hard, and had let things get on his nerves.

Back in his room at the hotel, Dinny suffered a moment's reflection that people victimized by psychoses are usually unaware of their misfortune. However, Spike Davis didn't think him crazy... or did he? His father didn't think him crazy, or he would hardly have thrown him out so indifferently. Old Jason didn't think him crazy. By Gad — he was never so sane in his life! Of course Brophy couldn't see it. Suppose Brophy had come to *him*, a month ago, with a similar story: what would he have thought of *Brophy?*

*   *   *   *   *   *

It was an exquisite chapel, the gift of Mr. Joel Day in memory of his mother. Expense had not been considered. It was a work of art.

Recalling the general stampede of the old days when the ten-fifty bell summoned all Magnolians to compulsory prayers in the barn-like, taffy-colored assembly-hall, Dinny was amazed at the apparent reverence with which the students filed into the beautiful Gothic structure, dimly lit by mellow tints sifted through windows of unquestionable æsthetic value. He was struck by the fact that the current crop of Magnolia students was vastly superior in appearance and bearing to the hicks of his own collegiate generation; then promptly decided that the change was probably within himself. His appreciation of almost everything was on the rise; why not his respect for Magnolia? There was a rightful place for the little college, after all. His long-time disdain of it had been unjust.

But, even allowing for his own alteration of outlook, Magnolia had broadened. There were candles on the altar, and when the college choir appeared in the stalls it was appropriately vested. The organ, concealed behind chaste grillwork, was playing *Ein Feste Burg* with skillfully conceived variations. It was a good place to be. All the old feeling of antagonism toward everything that was Magnolia had vanished. She had suddenly become Alma Mater.

A tall chaplain in academic robes had followed the choir into the chancel, approaching the lectern where he stood for a moment with bowed head. Even in the uncertain light, Dinny recognized him at once. Doubtless Kling was a professor in the Seminary now; a commanding figure, obviously deserving of the confidence they had in him. After the service, Dinny would seek him out, and the old constraint would be lifted.

The *a cappella* choir sang, very impressively, one of Tschaikowsky's haunting anthems. With dignity and feeling, Kling began to read the last chapter of Ecclesiastes.

It was as if Dinny listened to the majestic thing for the first time. Often he had made some ribald joke that played on 'the grasshopper' who, perhaps through overindulgence, had become a 'burden.' That this ancient confession of a cynic was great literature had never occurred to him. What a superficial, heady fool he had been! What insufferable impudence! Speaking of hicks and yokels, who but an ignoramus could have been guilty of impertinences so raw?

Here was an incomparable pen-portrait of the penalties of such sophistication as had all but quenched the springs of Dinny's life. In this drab picture, the shutters had been closed, the garden had dried up, the porters at the gate sat dully oblivious of the world's activity. In the adjacent mill, the sound of the grinding was low. Things were so quiet that the voice of a bird startled one. The great palace was all but dead.

Once upon a time, fountains had played, flowers had bloomed, the spacious corridors had been flooded with music. The whole institution had throbbed with vitality. The joy of life had been drawn up from the inner spring of the luminous spirit as if by a silver cord attached to a golden bowl.

But the magic elixir had not been valued for what it was worth. The silver cord had slipped through unheeding fingers and *the golden bowl had been broken!* It was necessary now to go outside one's own gates and seek the fountain for one's water-of-life, using the communal pitcher that served other unfortunates who had broken their golden bowls. One day *that pitcher was found broken beside the fountain!* There was nothing left, now, but to go to the public cistern and stand waiting one's turn; and finally there came a day when *the wheel was found broken at the cistern!*

It was at that exact moment in Orville Kling's sonorous reading of this ancient cynic's lament — as Dinny often confessed, later — that the inspiration suddenly came which produced his monumental story, *Thirst* — a book so gripping that it was carried to the farthest corners of the literate earth; laughed over, wept over, prayed over by hundreds of thousands who, though hosts of them may have broken their golden bowls, or had been so unfortunate as to have found the pitcher broken at the fountain, resolved they would see to it that the wheel was not broken at the cistern!

When Kling had finished his reading, and closed the Book, he prayed. Every head was bowed; Dinny's, too. He found himself simple-heartedly grateful for the mental guidance of the man for whom he had long nourished a sullen hatred. There was a benediction while they sat in reverence; then, after a moment's absolute silence, the congregation stirred, rose, and quietly departed. But Dinny was too deeply moved to lift his head. A feeling of great exultation swept the strings of his soul. There had been laid on him a commission. He had been appointed an apostle to them whose gardens were wilting, whose silver cords were slipping, whose golden bowls were in danger of breaking.

The organ had returned to its versatile adventures with the courageous score of 'A Mighty Fortress is Our God.' Dinny's eyes were suffused with a rush of hot tears. His heart was pounding. His consciousness of his new responsibility was almost more than he could bear.

'Lookit, Gramp!... at *Dinny Brumm!*'

'What's the matter... Did he upset his vinegar jug?'

'No!... Lookit!... *Lookit!*'

CHAPTER XVIII

It was not an ideal evening for a stroll. The air was damp and uncomfortably chilly. Apparently it had been raining very hard, a little earlier, for the wet leaves on the sidewalks were laid in semi-circular festoons as if swept there at the turn of a tide, and the gutters were filled with tight-packed, soggy piles of them.

But Dinny wanted to move about under his own power. The rough voyage had been tedious, and the trip from Cherbourg had tried his patience, for now that he was nearing his journey's end he was eager to have done with it and proceed to the singular errand that had brought him so far.

It was too late to locate Tommy and Joan tonight. To-morrow, pursuant to the advice he had secured from Lacey's, he would endeavor to connect with Tommy through their Paris office. If lucky, he might have the contemplated visit with the honeymooners before the day was out. Next morning he would run up to Calais, and so to London, where he had already engaged a room at the Victoria.

Descending the steps of the Continental, Dinny sauntered up and down the arcaded block, strolled over to the Place Vendôme and back again to Rue de Rivoli, wondering how he might amuse himself for the remainder of the evening.

On impulse he took a taxi and drove across the river. On Raspail, a little below Saint-Germain, he decided to get out and walk. After ten minutes of aimless rambling, he sighted a café that seemed more active than any he had seen.

Pleasurably recognizing its name, for he had often heard of 'The Dome' and its popularity with Americans, he turned in among the little iron-legged tables that cluttered the sidewalk, found one unoccupied, ordered a glass of sauterne to ensure his welcome, and leisurely took stock of the amiable crowd, most of whom were youthful, many of whom were reminiscent of the Greenwich Village habitués, and all of whom — with one single exception in sight — appeared to be in a more or less festive mood.

The unaccompanied woman who sat facing him, a little distance away, took no interest in her neighbors. She did not appear to be in acute trouble, but was downcast, meditatively toying with a half-empty glass of something that looked like cognac. Hers was not a problem of poverty, for she was the best-dressed person there. She could have pawned the silver mesh handbag on her table for enough to put her up at the Ritz for a few days, and the price of her black fur coat would have kept her in good comfort for six months.

In a moment their eyes met briefly, and, because hers were unmistakably American eyes and full of loneliness, Dinny was faintly conscious that his face must have reacted a bit to his recognition of the fact that they were fellow-countrymen. If she noticed the fleeting smile in his eyes, she made no response to it, abstractedly returning to her pensive fingering of the glass.

Dinny found it difficult to detach himself from her, and studied her face with interest. In her depression, she looked forty. Later, when she smiled, five years vanished magically. She was a lady — with a story; no doubt of that. But it was not necessarily a sordid or discreditable story, for though her face was sad, it was not hard and it was not ashamed.

She glanced up now, smiled faintly as their eyes momentarily met again, drained her glass casually, and drew the collar of her fur coat more snugly about her neck. Doubtless she was on the point of leaving now, and Dinny was half-glad. Her dejection was dampening his own spirits, already low enough, for, as the distance lessened between him and the courage-testing event that had invited him to Paris, the more sensitive he became to his irreparable loss. He had moments when he wondered whether he would be able to go through with it.

Rising slowly, she took up her expensive bag from the table, and, with eyes regarding him inquisitively, came over to Dinny, paused, laid a black-gloved hand on the back of the vacant chair. He rose instantly, and invited her to sit down. She did so, with entire self-possession, folding her arms on the table.

'Were you surprised, Dinny, when you found my note?'

'Janet! — my dear!'

He reached out both hands to hers.

'You didn't recognize me,' she said, ruefully. 'I must have changed more than I had thought.'

'But it has been so long, dear, and of course I wasn't expecting to see you, and — you've bobbed your hair, haven't you? It's quite becoming, Janet.'

'No — I've changed. I know that, Dinny. The game I've been playing alters one.'

'How does it compare with — wheel-barrow?'

'Less exciting. Much slower than chess; and if you win, there's no prize.'

'It wears the players out, you mean?'

She nodded, with just a faint recovery of the Janet look of quick understanding.

'Exactly. The players are worn out, and it's after midnight, and finally one of them makes the last move, which both had seen coming for an hour, and — the game's over. The guest yawns and goes, and the drowsy host calls in the cat and puts out the milk-bottle. And that's all. Not very stimulating, would you say?'

'Where is he now, Janet? Want to talk about it?'

'As for wanting to — no. But I'll tell you. We separated more than a year ago. Oscar returned to the States for a while. He is in Florence now; or was, the last I heard from him.'

'Who won the game?'

She shrugged slightly and dismissed the query with a lazy little flick of her fingers.

'I believe I made the last move, but by that time we were

both too indifferent to care, or to remember — certainly not with any pride of victory, or ——'

'Humiliation of defeat,' assisted Dinny, comprehendingly.

'I'm not so sure there wasn't some humiliation,' confessed Janet, after a pause, 'even for the winner — if I won.'

'The money part — maybe?' Dinny wondered.

Janet nodded.

'Why do you ask? The story will surely bore you, and it makes me unhappy to remember.'

'Sometimes it helps a little to talk things over, dear.'

'Well — I fancy you know that Mr. Day divorced me, as of course he should. Along with word of that came notification that he had made over a great many valuable securities to me. I declined them, through our attorneys, but Mr. Day's decision remained unchanged. You may recall that Mr. Day's temperament was not to be described as — as vacillating, or volatile.'

Janet's drawling understatement left so very much unsaid that Dinny laughed, appreciatively. She had not changed, after all.

'The dividends kept coming along,' continued Janet, in an even tone, 'and I used them, reluctantly at first.... And then, when Oscar and I parted — it was mostly my fault, for I think I was the one who remarked that we both knew we were weary of each other — he gave me his blessing and three thousand shares of T. and T.'

'You're well provided for, dear.'

'Oh, yes — I have almost everything anyone would want except self-respect, and I've been doing without that for so long I hardly miss it.' She had tried to make this last sound dryly cynical, and ended it with a twisted little smile.

'Janet,' said Dinny, soberly, 'you've broken your golden bowl!'

She lowered her eyes, and nodded; then glanced up, inquiringly.

'What's this — about a golden bowl, Dinny?'

'It was attached to a silver cord,' he explained cryptically. 'And whenever you wanted happiness, you drew it up from the spring. I'm afraid you've let the silver cord slip through your hands.'

'Is that what that means — "Or ever the silver cord be loosed, and the golden bowl be broken"? I never knew.' She laughed, quietly. 'Since when did you go in for such philosophy, Dinny? I've read enough of your hellish satires to know that you're not in the golden-bowl business.'

'I'd like to tell you all about it, Janet. You say you've changed. I wonder that you recognized me! It's quite a long story.'

She pushed back her chair.

'Suppose we go over to the Crillon — I live there — and sit in the lounge. And you can begin at the beginning, and tell me everything.... But you won't scold me; will you, dear?'

*   *   *   *   *   *

Dinny's heart was beating furiously, and his mouth was dry, as he paced nervously to and fro near the little elevator. The shaft of it, rising from the lobby, was a mere skeleton of ornamental wrought-iron curlycues, and one could see the descending occupants long before they arrived on the ground floor.

At any moment now, Tommy would be coming down, and Joan, too, more than likely, for it was nearly ten and she would undoubtedly be up and dressed for the day.

They would greet him with a brave show of cordiality, trying hard to cover their mystification with a rapid fire of questions. 'Why — of all things! — Dinny Brumm!'... 'How lovely to see you here!'... 'Where are you stopping? When did you come? How nice of you to look us up! But underneath all the friendly racket, how much of constraint would there be?

It had not been difficult to locate them. At nine-thirty, Dinny had telephoned Lacey's office. Yes — Mr. Forsythe was in town, stopping at the Regina. Perhaps he had not left yet; might catch him there. It was only a step over from the Continental.

'Down in two minutes, old chap!' Tommy had answered, on the house telephone. 'Powerfully glad you're here! Delightful surprise!'

Was it, really? Dinny wished he could be more certain of that.

The little elevator had again slipped slowly upward through the gold ceiling. And now — a few frantic weeks of waiting having elapsed — it was coming down, bringing Tommy's long legs, broad shoulders, expectant smile. Dinny was steadied and comforted, a little, by the smile.

'This is certainly a great treat, Dinny!' Tommy gave him a comradely thump on the shoulder, and beamed.

'I'm on my way to London,' explained Dinny, hastily, as if his train were waiting. 'It occurred to me I'd like to have a glimpse of you and Joan — for old sake's sake ——'

'Joan?' echoed Tommy, happily. 'Is she here, too?'

'My God — Tommy! You don't mean to tell me ——'

Tommy stared, uncomprehendingly, for a moment, and then grinned.

'You didn't think we were here together, did you? The last I saw of Joan was the night before I sailed in September.'

They were standing near a little gilt and scarlet divan; and Dinny, whose knees were shaky, sat down, Tommy joining him, much amused by his sudden collapse.

'The fact is,' resumed Tommy, 'Joan has been much on my mind, these past few weeks. She vanished, the same day I left. She did not show up at the store, next morning. They made inquiries without results.'

'Had anything happened,' inquired Dinny, huskily, 'to account for it? Do you suppose some harm has come to her?'

'I'll tell you all I know,' said Tommy, soberly, after a

moment's delay. 'I suppose you've a right to all the information there is.'

* * * * * *

'Her Uncle Jim ought to know where she is!' shouted Dinny, excitedly. 'Perhaps she's there! She went to him once before when she was in trouble. I'll cable!'

'I'll go along. You're not fit to be at large, Dinny. You'll get yourself run over. Buck up now! You look like a ghost. We'll find her. Uncle Jim will know — if you can get it out of him.'

* * * * * *

He knew that Janet and Tommy were amusing themselves at his expense, as the boat-train started. Tommy had said something funny to her, and nodded toward him, as he waved from the window of his compartment. She had laughed, gayly. Had anyone ever heard of so good a joke? A round trip from New York to Paris for information about his girl! — information he might have had for ninety cents if he had queried Uncle Jim in the first place.

The three of them had lunched together, Dinny well satisfied over the prompt congeniality of Janet and Tommy, whose amiable chatter left him without much responsibility for the talk. He had never been in such a state of utter rout, mentally. Uncle Jim's cable had not arrived until nearly four. After that there had been a great panic about getting Dinny aboard the first ship. The Olympic was due to call at Cherbourg at eleven. He could just make it.

The train was increasing its strides now. Dinny's hands trembled as he took the cablegram from his pocket. Bless old Uncle Jim! He had come through without a moment's delay. The message was brief, but illuminating.

ABERCROMBIES DENVER

Tommy had fortunately been able to fill in the details. He remembered Mr. Abercrombie's call at Lacey's, and his unusual interest in Joan.

It was a long trip to Cherbourg, and the Olympic was exasperatingly slow getting herself persuaded to draw up the anchor and amble on toward the west. Dinny wondered, as he stood at the rail, whether it would help things along if he volunteered assistance.... What? Another big netful of mail-bags? What did so many people have to write about that was so important?

* * * * * *

There was a telegram from Janet at the purser's office when he called to arrange for his passage.

TOMMY TELLS ME MUCH TO DO FOR SHOP GIRLS IN NEW YORK STOP PERHAPS CAN USE MONEY MENDING BROKEN BOWLS PITCHERS CISTERN WHEELS STOP THANK YOU DEAR FOR COMING STOP KISS JOAN FOR ME STOP TOMMY ADJACENT SAYS ME TOO STOP LUCKY DEVIL

* * * * * *

Every day en route Dinny composed radiograms to Joan by the dozen, informing her he was on the way and hurrying as fast as possible. None of them was sent. He couldn't explain, by radio, that he was ready now to keep his promises, several times broken, nor dare he risk frightening her away from Denver with the announcement that he was about to press his claim.

The Olympic might have been an old square-rigged threemaster from the way she wallowed and plodded as if it was of no concern to her whether she ever reached New York or not; but one morning, after ages and ages, she nosed her way into her berth, and at two Dinny was on the train, composing speeches for Joan... The *darling!*

* * * * * *

He had firmly decided, after much debate, that he would not attempt to see Joan at the store. He would call on Mr.

Abercrombie, briefly explain his mission, and Mr. Abercrombie would give him Joan's street address. From what Tommy had said about the fine old fellow, that seemed quite reasonable.

The train arrived shortly after three, and Dinny went directly to the big store. Mr. Abercrombie listened with interest.

'We should be very sorry to lose Miss Braithwaite,' he said. 'But I'm afraid I couldn't stop you, even if I tried. So — find her, my boy, and good luck to you.'

He sent a message to her house from the Blackstone, asking her to give him a ring at the earliest moment, and waited in a state of near-lunacy. Six-twenty! — twenty-five! — thirty! Joan should be at home by this time. He sat near the telephone, ready to leap to it.

At seven, unable to endure another minute of this torture, he called her house. The voice replied cheerfully, 'Hold the line, please,' and a little later said sympathetically, 'Sorry — but Miss Braithwaite is out.'

He sat for a long time with the telephone in his hands, wondering what next to do. His hopes were tumbling to pieces.

At eight, he resolved that nothing was to be gained by moping in his room, and was putting on his coat to go down when a letter was delivered by messenger. He opened it, in a panic of apprehension.

Dear Dinny:

You and I have caused each other a great deal of misery. And nothing could be easier for us to do than keep on making ourselves and each other utterly wretched until one of us died or ran away.

I'm not going to pretend that I'm happy, but I'm busy, and I like my work. It cost a good deal to decide that it was better for us never to see each other any more. But, having made that decision, I know it is to your best interest, and mine, that I stick to it. You know I would love to see you; but, Dinny, I can't go through it again!

> Please don't try to persuade me. Here is once when I'm
> certain that I know what's best for us.
>
> Ever yours
>
> JOAN

After a half-hour of suffering, Dinny resolved to play the
last card in his hand.

He went to the desk, and wrote:

> Dearest Joan:
>
> I'm not asking you to renew friendship with the Dinny
> Brumm of the Green Cheese and *Hallelujah*. It may be
> hard for you to believe, but I'm definitely done with all that.
> I am just learning to walk. I need you as never before, and I
> love you desperately.
>
> You will find enclosed a letter that I found secreted in an
> old desk that was the property of my mother. Please read it,
> dear. I have made the experiment that Julia recommended to
> me. And it has worked!
>
> Do let me see you, if only for a moment, tomorrow!
>
> Loving you dearly
>
> DINNY

Having dispatched the letter to Joan's address, he went
down and walked the streets for an hour. He remembered
that he had had no dinner, but was not hungry enough to
care. Returning at length to his room, he went to bed, and,
utterly exhausted with the long strain, drifted off into a
troubled sleep.

How long the telephone had been ringing he could only
guess. The insistent demand had been punctuating a series
of dreams in which he was being entreated, urged, bela-
bored, to respond to some desperate situation. Half-awake,
he groped for the instrument, noting, as he turned on the
light, that it was half-past five.

'Dinny!' Joan's voice was very low, and broken.

'Yes, darling.'

'Dinny — I'm afraid I can't wait till morning.'

'Come on down here, then... I'll meet you in the lobby.'

'Would that be too dreadful?... What would people think?'

'Hang the people!... Oh, Joan!... My dear!'

There was a considerable pause.

'Very well... I'll come... Half an hour... Good-bye.'

Dinny found himself laughing aloud, half-hysterically, as he dressed. He bet his last dollar nothing like this had ever happened before. His fingers were clumsy as he wrestled with his collar. Joan was coming! He glanced out of the window. There was a faint dawn-glow.

The lobby of the hotel was deserted except for a sleepy clerk at the desk, and two old fellows with damp mops scrubbing the tiled floor.

Dinny stood just inside the revolving door, and waited.

A taxi drew up. He rushed out to meet it, opened the door, stepped in.

After a while the taxi-driver closed the door with a bang, but whatever hint it was intended to convey had been too subtle for his passengers.

Five minutes later, he opened the door again, and said:

'I'm goin' across here for a cup of coffee and a doughnut. And if the cop gives me a ticket for parkin', I'll expect you to pay for it!'

* * * * * *

There was a very simple little wedding that afternoon at five. Joan had made no objection to its immediacy. She was beside herself with happiness, and whatever Dinny wanted to do, no matter how impetuously arrived at, was acceptable.

At breakfast, Dinny said:

'What would we be waiting for, I'd like to know, if we waited another day?'

'That's so,' agreed Joan. 'It would be silly, wouldn't it?'

'This afternoon, then?'

She nodded, enthusiastically.

'And go away — directly afterwards.'

'As you like, dear.'

'Far off... somewhere on a ship... around the world, maybe. That's a great thought, Joan. We'll go 'round the world... Want to? We can, you know.'

'I'd love to, Dinny.'

'Why are you smiling?'

'I'm happy.'

'No — it was something more than happy. Tell me.'

'I was just remembering,' said Joan, 'what a gypsy girl told me, a few months ago. I was soon to go on a long "jorney" with a tall man on a "beeg" ship.'

'By Gad, Joan, I was afraid you had!... We'll take the first train out, after we're married. Right?'

'Yes — we couldn't go any sooner than that.'

'To San Francisco... and sail! Agreed?'

'Let's!'

*   *   *   *   *   *

The lobby of the Saint Francis was astir with dinner guests arriving for a banquet when Dinny and Joan came down from the room they had occupied for an hour. It was a newspaper affair, they learned. Zandy Craig was meeting the entire *Enquirer* outfit and a score of prominent citizens.

'There's Alison, darling,' exclaimed Dinny, as a half-dozen modishly gowned women stepped out of the adjoining elevator. 'We must speak to her.'

She turned as if she had overheard her name spoken, and joined them with a little ejaculation of happy surprise.

'Dinny!... You don't mean to tell me you've managed to persuade this lovely ——'

'Joan, please meet my sister.' Dinny was ecstatic.

'I would give anything for a couple of minutes with you, Alison,' murmured Joan. 'But you're going to the dinner, and I mustn't detain you.'

'No — I'm not. Father couldn't be bothered with mere women at his parties. Do you want to tell me something that won't keep another minute?'

'We're sailing in the morning. I may not have another chance.' Joan seemed much disappointed.

Alison searched her eyes with an inquisitive glance, and fleetingly regarded Dinny with a similar inspection.

'Very well. I'll talk to you now. We'll step over into the lounge.... Will you wait for me, a few minutes, Mrs. Baumgarten? I'll not be long.'

They disappeared, Joan's hand tucked under Alison's arm. Dinny was very proud of them. They were thoroughbreds!

Ten minutes later, when they rejoined him, they were smiling as if the interview had been mutually pleasant. Alison collected her party and hurried away.

'Big secret, Joan?' queried Dinny, consumed by curiosity.

'Don't try to make me tell you, dear; not yet.'

'I'll wait, but don't keep me at it too long!'

* * * * * *

Returning from the theater, which they had found rather tame, for it had concerned itself with the tribulations of a pair who were put to tremendous bother and expense to find each other after a long misunderstanding, they went to their room and were bending over an array of cruise literature, outspread on the table, when the telephone rang.

'It's for me,' said Joan, taking up the instrument... 'Yes, Alison... That's wonderful!... Now?... Nine-sixty-seven?... I'll be up in two minutes!' She put down the telephone on the table, and smiled into Dinny's eyes. 'I've an engagement, dear, for a little talk with — can you guess?'

'That's marvelous, Joan. Hope you'll not be disappointed.'

'May I take Julia's letter along?'

'I don't know who has a better right to it.'

* * * * * *

Joan had been gone for more than an hour. Dinny had

tried to pass the time by studying the itinerary of the long journey on which they were about to embark.

Utterly unable to command his thoughts or concentrate his attention on the gaudy promises of the illustrated prospectus, he sat staring at the wall, wondering how Joan was making out with her strange adventure. It would be quite a monstrous pity if anything had happened to distress her. She had been barely touching the ground with her toes. Never had he seen anyone so radiant!

There was a peremptory summons from the telephone. Joan's voice sounded as if she had been deeply stirred.

'Come up here, dear, please... Room nine hundred and sixty-seven; I'll wait here for you.'

Joan and Alison met him at the elevator, when he arrived. They had both been crying recently, he thought. They parted as he came toward them and, turning, each took an arm. He waited for them to speak, but they had nothing to say as they piloted him down the long corridor.

At the door they stopped, and released him.

Dinny looked inquiringly from one to the other.

Alison turned the knob, pushed the door open a little way, patted Dinny affectionately on the arm, and stepped aside.

'He is waiting for you, Dinny,' she said, softly.

Joan put her arm about his neck, and, standing on tip-toe, whispered, brokenly:

'Be very tender, dear.'

THE END